NAPOLEON III
AND EUGÉNIE

By the same author

NICHOLAS RIDLEY
THOMAS CRANMER
JOHN KNOX
LORD PALMERSTON
GARIBALDI
THE ROUNDHEADS

JASPER RIDLEY

NAPOLEON III
AND
EUGÉNIE

WITHDRAWN

CONSTABLE
LONDON

First published in Great Britain 1979
by Constable and Company Ltd
10 Orange Street London WC2H 7EG
copyright © 1979 by Jasper Ridley

Set in Monotype Baskerville 11pt
Printed in Great Britain by The Anchor Press Ltd
and bound by Wm Brendon & Son Ltd
both of Tiptree, Essex

British Library cataloguing in publication data

Ridley, Jasper
Napoleon III and Eugénie
1 Napoleon III, *Emperor of the French*
2 Eugénie, *Empress, consort of Napoleon III, Emperor of the French*
3 France – Kings and rulers – Biography
4 France – Empresses – Biography
1 Title
944.07′092′2   DC280

ISBN 0 09 461380 x

To my wife
VERA

CONTENTS

ILLUSTRATIONS

ILLUSTRATIONS

The Prince Imperial on his eighteenth birthday, 16 March 1874
(*Mansell Collection*) *facing page* 559

Eugénie, about 1880 (*Mansell Collection*) 590

(Left to right) Piétri, Antonia d'Attainville, Eugénie and Primoli
at Farnborough Hill about 1912 (*courtesy Mrs Veronica Burnett*) 591

Eugénie and her relatives at the Liria Palace in Madrid a few
days before her death in July 1920 (*courtesy the late Mrs Rowena
Paice*) 591

FOREWORD

THIS is not a history of the Second Empire, but a biography of Louis Napoleon and a biography of Eugénie. Some political events, like the power struggle in France under the Second Republic, the campaign in Mexico, and the revolutionary movements in Paris in 1869 and 1870, are examined in some depth to show the significance of Louis Napoleon's and Eugénie's reaction to them; but others of great political and economic importance – the industrialization of France under the Second Empire, the commercial treaty with Britain of 1860, and the army reorganization before the Franco-Prussian War – are ignored. It is only the lives of two people, husband and wife, which link, in my story, the events which occurred at Gavarnie in 1807, in Madrid in 1843, in Paris in 1851, in Zululand in 1879, and at Farnborough in 1920.

The first biographies of Napoleon III were written by his supporters in Paris during his campaign for election as President of the Republic in 1848. By 1850 Wikoff's biography had been published in Dublin, and De Puy's in the United States followed in 1852. Throughout the Second Empire the laudatory articles in the French press were countered by the libellous brochures of the Republican refugees in England and other countries which were secretly circulated by the underground resistance movement in France.

The fall of the Second Empire led to a spate of violently hostile books in France. Larousse's *Grand Dictionnaire Universel du XIXe Siècle* did not spare Napoleon III. The 'Grand Larousse' had begun appearing under the Second Empire. When the volume containing the letter B was published in 1867, the article on 'Bonaparte' began by stating that Bonaparte was 'the greatest, the most glorious, the most brilliant name in history, not excepting the name Napoleon', and then devoted 108 columns to the career of Napoleon I up to his accession as Emperor in 1804, leaving the rest of his life to be treated in due course under the entry 'Napoleon'. But by the time the volume with the letter N appeared in 1874, the Second Empire had fallen. Napoleon I's exploits from Austerlitz to his death at St Helena were dealt with in only 15 columns, and Napoleon III was violently denounced in language more appropriate to a political tract than to an encyclopaedia.[1]

In 1874, the year after Napoleon III's death, his English friend Blanchard Jerrold published the first volume of his biography; the fourth and last volume was published in 1882. Considering that this was an official biography written by a friend with documents supplied by the Emperor's widow, Eugénie, it is remarkably objective. Jerrold must surely be unique among English Victorian official biographers in writing about his hero, frankly and bluntly: 'He kept a mistress.'[2]

By the 1890s, many people were publishing their reminiscences of Napoleon III and the court of the Second Empire. It is difficult to assess the reliability of these works. Many of the writers were in a position to have first-hand knowledge of the facts; but some of them lent their name to hack-writers who wrote scandalous gossip, and all of them wrote with the benefit of hindsight. Some of these books are fabrications, like the *Mémorial de Chislehurst* by the fictitious 'Baron d'Ambès', who was said to be a high-ranking intimate friend of Napoleon III writing under a pseudonym, but who can be proved, by internal evidence, never to have existed. The memoirs of Englishmen who knew Napoleon III in England are nearly as unreliable. Those who wrote before 1870 describe how, when they met Prince Louis Bonaparte in London in the 1830s and 1840s, they intuitively felt that he was a man of genius who would achieve his seemingly impossible dream of becoming Emperor of the French. Those who wrote after 1870 stated that as soon as they met him they discerned the fatal weakness of character which led him to disaster. On the other hand, the daily reports in *The Times* during the twenty-two years of the Second Republic and the Second Empire are enormously valuable. It was the work of reporters like the *Times* correspondent in Paris, O'Meagher, which made Palmerston and other statesmen say that modern journalism had made espionage unnecessary.

Simpson, writing nearly fifty years after Napoleon III's death, had much less excuse than Jerrold for hagiography; but his book is much less objective than Jerrold's. Simpson's first volume, dealing with Louis Napoleon's career up to his election as President of the Republic in 1848, was published in 1909; it is a useful book marred only by minor errors. The second volume, covering the years from 1849 to 1856, did not appear until 1923 – three years after Eugénie's death. It is much less satisfactory. In his specious justification of all Napoleon III's acts, Simpson sometimes almost distorts the facts and misleads by selective quotations, and he is as hostile to Eugénie as he is sympathetic to Louis Napoleon. He never completed his work by carrying the story beyond 1856, although he lived for fifty years after the publication of his second volume. This was apparently because he was discouraged by the hostile review of his second volume by Philip Guedalla, who criticized it – for the wrong reasons – in *The Times Literary Supplement*.[3]

Of the modern works, the most useful is Adrien Dansette's *Histoire du Second Empire* (Paris, 1961–76); the first volume, *Louis Napoléon à la conquête du pouvoir*, adds important information to Thirria's exhaustive study, *Napoléon III avant l'Empire* (Paris, 1895). Dansette is the only historian who has been granted permission to use Prince Napoleon's archives; but it did not enable him to discover a great deal of new material. André Castelot's two-volume biography, published in Paris in 1973–4, in the main follows Dansette and other published sources, though Castelot found some new material about Mexico in the Royal Belgian archives. Among modern English works there is T. A. B. Corley's *Democratic Despot* in 1961 and W. H. C. Smith's excellent short biography, *Napoleon III*, in 1972.

Biographies of Eugénie began appearing just before the end of the nineteenth century, when old people in Madrid still remembered her as a young girl and told the biographers all the malicious gossip which had been circulating at the time of her marriage to Napoleon III. Many books about her were published during the last twenty years of her life and in the months which followed her death in 1920. Some of them were written by people like Filon, Primoli, Barthez, Mademoiselle de Larminat, Madame Carette, Lucien Daudet, Paléologue and Isabel Vesey, who knew her well at various times during her life. More recently her great-nephew and close friend, James, the seventeenth Duke of Alba, the Spanish Ambassador in London, delivered a lecture at Barcelona University in 1947 which contains much first-hand information.[4] Alba thought that Sencourt's book (London, 1931) was the best biography of Eugénie; but since Alba's death Suzanne Desternes's and Henriette Chandet's biography has been published in Paris and Harold Kurtz's in London, both of them in 1964. Kurtz's charming book has been deservedly popular, though his zeal for his heroine's reputation sometimes led him to suppress and distort the facts. Nancy Nichols Barker's *The Distaff Side: The Empress Eugénie and the Foreign Policy of the Second Empire* (University of Texas, 1967) is based on extensive research into the manuscript sources and is a work of great interest; but I do not agree with her conclusions.

I wish to express my gratitude for the help and kindness which I have received from so many quarters while writing this book.

Her Majesty the Queen graciously permitted me to work in the Royal Archives at Windsor and to make use of the information in the documents there. These include Queen Victoria's Journal, the correspondence between Eugénie and Queen Victoria, the letters from the

British ambassadors in Paris, the documents relating to the death of the Prince Imperial, and Nassau Senior's Journal of his yearly visits to Paris between 1848 and 1863. Only parts of the Journal were published by Senior's daughter, and the original diary not only includes a considerable amount of additional information, but also revealed, for Prince Albert's benefit, the identity of Senior's informants, among them Drouyn de Lhuys, who were referred to in the published book only by deliberately misleading initials.

Her Royal Highness the Princess of Baviera y de Borbón graciously gave me information which Her Royal Highness had received from her father and mother, Fernando, Count of Mora, and Solange de Lesseps, and from other members of the Empress's family.

Her Grace the Duchess of Alba kindly permitted me to work in the archives of the Liria Palace in Madrid and to make use of the information there. These include Eugénie's letters as a child to her father and those which she wrote in later life to her sister, her mother, her nephews and nieces and their children. Most of the more interesting letters were published in their original French and Spanish by the seventeenth Duke of Alba in *Lettres Familières de l'Impératrice Eugénie* (Paris, 1935); but there is a great deal of unpublished material relating both to the Montijo family and to state affairs in France.

Mrs Veronica Burnett kindly permitted me to see the papers of her aunt, Miss Isabel Vesey, who was the Empress's companion during the last fourteen years of Eugénie's life. These include not only the typescript which Miss Vesey wrote about her memories of the Empress (part of which was published in *The Times* in October 1920) but also Miss Vesey's diary and her letters to her mother, her aunt and her sisters in the years 1906–20. Some of these documents were used by Harold Kurtz, but Mrs Burnett was kind enough to permit me to see others which Miss Vesey did not show to Kurtz. I am also grateful to Mrs Burnett for telling me her personal recollections, as a child, of the Empress, and to both Mr and Mrs Burnett for their repeated hospitality to me while I was working on these manuscripts at Bethesden.

I am grateful to the Benedictine community of St Michael's Abbey at Farnborough, Hampshire, for permission to read and make use of the manuscripts in the Abbey and for their hospitality to me while I was working there;

to Dr John Attenborough, Mrs Bryan Butler, Mrs R. L. Butler, Mr B. Coxwell, the Syndics of the Fitzwilliam Museum, Miss Alice Oreman, Miss Jill Quaife, and Mrs Phyllida Ovenden for permission to read and use manuscript material in their possession;

to Mrs Burnett, the Syndics of the Fitzwilliam Museum, Mr J. A. Hollins, Brigadier W. J. Jervois, Mrs Rowena Paice, and the Royal

Aircraft Establishment in Farnborough, Hampshire, for permission to publish for the first time portraits, drawings and photographs in their possession;

to Mrs Rowena Paice for telling me her recollections of Eugénie, dating from the time when she taught the Empress's Spanish nephews and nieces to play hockey at Farnborough Hill in about 1910;

to Mrs Anne Chamberlin for telling me about her childhood reminiscences of the Empress, and to her and Mr Chamberlin for their hospitality to me at Rodbourne;

to all the other people who knew Eugénie and told me their personal memories of her – Mrs Florence Barber, Major J. A. F. Barthorp, Lord Clark, Mrs Ruby Crotty, Dom Austen Delaney, Mrs Goode-Crook, Mr Arthur Hall, Mrs Kathleen Harris, Brigadier W. J. Jervois, Mrs Adela Mason, Sister Dorothy Mostyn, and Mrs Sheila Redmond;

to Mrs Jean Cadell for help, involving a great deal of work, in connection with the translation and appreciation of Spanish documents and publications;

to Mrs Penelope Chilton, Miss Sibylla Jane Flower, Mrs Lucille Iremonger, Mrs Agathe Lewin, and Mrs Barbara Murphy, for their considerable help with my research; to Mr Herbert Rees, for his advice at the typescript stage; and to my wife Vera for her patience and skill in deciphering the handwriting of Queen Victoria's royal German relatives;

to Mr Ivor Guest, for drawing my attention to the invaluable collection of letters, notes and other documents which he assembled in 1946–50 when he was writing his book *Napoleon III in England* and which he deposited in the Central Library in Bromley;

to Dr Michael Smith, for his advice on the medical aspects of Eugénie's attempted suicide and Napoleon III's illness and death;

to Mr Marcel Pressburg, for his advice and help with the illustrations and with research;

to those persons who provided me with personal information from family and other sources about Napoleon III and Eugénie – Mr Robert Adams, Mrs Josephine Birchenough, Miss Claire and Miss Margaret Blount, Mrs Helen Dove, Mrs Marjorie Edwards, Mr James Forsyth, Mrs Fowke, Mr Heilyn and Miss Alouette Isambard-Owen, Mrs Lois Johnston, Mrs B. A. Jones, Mrs Yvonne Jones, Mrs Louis Kentner, Mrs Yehudi Menuhin, Mrs Marjorie Osbourn, Mrs Lilian Peach, Mrs H. C. Rafferty, Mr E. E. Stott, Lieutenant-Colonel Patrick Turnbull, Miss Margaret T. Traill, and Mr Ainsworth Wates;

to the Sisters of Christian Education at Farnborough Hill, who permitted me to see the house where the Empress had lived and gave me every assistance with my work;

to Mr J. A. Irons, the Secretary of Camden Place Ltd, who allowed me to see Camden Place at Chislehurst and to read and make use of the correspondence and notes in his possession;

to the Countess of Longford, for telling me that there was information about Napoleon III and Eugénie in Wilfrid Scawen Blunt's secret memoirs and for making no objection to my reading and making use of this unpublished material at a time when she had sole right of access to these memoirs which she was using for her own book on Wilfrid Scawen Blunt;

to Mr and Mrs Jim and Nuccia Foulkes for their hospitality at Saint-Germain-en-Laye while I was researching in Paris and for taking me to Malmaison, and to Mr and Mrs Harry Pollak for their hospitality at Netstal and for taking me to Arenenberg and Gottlieben;

to Señor D. J. M. Hernández Andrés of the Alba Archives in the Liria Palace, and the staff of the Biblioteca del Ateneo, the Biblioteca Heremetica Municipal, and the Biblioteca Nacional in Madrid; to the staff of the Bibliothèque Nationale in Paris; to Miss E. M. Plincke, the Local History Librarian at the Central Library in Bromley; to Dom David Placid Higham, O.S.B., and Mr Ernest Weal of the *Souvenir Napoléonien*, the librarians at St Michael's Abbey in Farnborough, Hampshire; to Mr Paul Woudhuysen of the Fitzwilliam Museum in Cambridge; to the staff of the Inner Temple Library in London; to the staff of the London Library for their repeated assistance; to Mr James Ritchie and the staff of the National Library of Scotland; to the staff of the Public Record Office at Kew; to Sir Robin Mackworth-Young, Miss Jane Langton, Miss Elizabeth Cuthbert, and the staff of the Royal Archives at Windsor Castle for their kindness, courtesy, efficiency and readiness to place their expert knowledge at the disposal of researchers; to the staff of the Victoria and Albert Museum; and to Mr David Gallup and the staff of Yale University Library.

My work on this book has been seriously impeded by the misguided decision of the British Library to transfer to microfilm all foreign newspapers published between 1850 and 1950; but I nevertheless extend my thanks to the staff of the British Library in Bloomsbury and the British Newspaper Library in Colindale.

I am grateful to everyone else who helped me by providing information, by helping me with research, by lending me books, and by giving me any other assistance – Mr Will Allan, the staff at Arenenberg, Mrs M. F. B. Atherton, Mr James Anderson, Miss L. F. Anderson, Mrs Alex-Barr, Mrs Barbara Baker, Mrs E. M. Barron, Miss Elizabeth Bateman, Dr R. H. Beck; Mr G. R. Sanderson, Mr P. A. Harrison and Señorita Ana Maria Calvo of the British Council in Madrid; the staff of the British Council in Paris; Mr J. Bodsell, Miss Renee Bos, Mr P. F.

Boswell of the Grand Hotel, Brighton, Mrs Margaret Brody, Miss Julia Brown, Mr A. D. Burnett of Durham University Library, Mr I. Cantlé, Mrs Joyce Cartlidge, the staff at the Palace of Compiègne, Miss Margaret Crosland, Mrs G. Crowther, Mr E. G. Deavin, Mrs E. Delaney, Mr L. T. Denson, Mr W. M. Dwyer, Miss Mabel Fish, Mr Robin Fletcher, Mrs Diana Fox, Mrs J. H. Gwalter, the Earl Haig, Mrs Monica Hamlyn, Mr P. H. Hoare, Miss Ann Hoffman, Mr T. Herbert Jones, Mr D. Klean of the North London Franco-British Group, Mr W. Kuhnberg, Air Commodore C. R. Lousada, Mr Edward McDougal, the staff at Malmaison, Mrs Moyra Nellist, Mr C. O'Connell, Miss P. O'Connor, Mr C. O. R. Phillips, Mrs Ingrid Price, Miss Josephine Pullein-Thompson, Mrs D. Rowe, Dr J. C. H. Shaw, Mr P. Sherlock, Mr W. H. C. Smith, Mr A. H. Spring, Mr Andrew A. Stock, Mr Valentine Swain, Mr J. J. Szostak-Farmer, Mr G. Tallack, Miss Tesartey, Miss Norah Titley, the Rev. H. Ward, and Captain A. V. S. Yates.

JASPER RIDLEY
West Hoathly, Sussex
17 April 1979

PART I

PRINCE LOUIS BONAPARTE

CHAPTER 1

KING LOUIS AND QUEEN HORTENSE

O N 20 April 1808 the Queen of Holland gave birth to a son. The Queen was not a princess of the House of Orange, and her baby was not born in Holland. She was Hortense de Beauharnais, wife of Louis Bonaparte and both stepdaughter and sister-in-law of the Emperor Napoleon. Her son, Louis Napoleon, was born in Paris and during his life spent only a few days on Dutch soil. After living for many years in Germany, Switzerland and England, he became Napoleon III, Emperor of the French, and then returned to England to die in exile at Chislehurst.

He married Eugenia del Montijo, a Spanish countess who was born in Spain twelve years after Wellington won the Peninsular War and died there sixteen years before Franco began the Civil War of 1936. She lived for eighteen years at the Tuileries as Empress of the French, and for fifty years as an ex-empress in exile in England at Chislehurst and Farnborough.

Napoleon III's four grandparents – Carlo Buonaparte, Letizia Ramolino, Alexandre, Vicomte de Beauharnais, and Marie Rose Joséphine Tascher de la Pagerie – came from very different backgrounds in Corsica, Paris and Martinique. None of them, in their youth and at the time of their marriages, could have considered it as remotely possible that they or their descendants would ever occupy a throne.

The Buonapartes originally came from Tuscany, but settled in Corsica in the sixteenth century at the time of the final conquest of the island by Genoa.[1] Carlo Buonaparte was born in Ajaccio in 1746, and became the leading local solicitor. During his childhood the Corsicans rose in revolt, expelled the Genoese, and proclaimed their independence. But Genoa sold Corsica to the King of France – as they had nothing to sell except an empty title and an island in revolt the French got it cheap – and Corsica was conquered by France in 1769. Carlo Buonaparte, after playing a prominent part in the struggle against the French, made his peace with the victors and built up a thriving legal practice in Paris and Versailles as well as in Ajaccio.

Carlo Buonaparte had married Letizia Ramolino in 1764; he was

3

eighteen, and she was fourteen. It was a good match for Buonaparte, as Letizia's father had been an army officer and Inspector of Roads and Bridges under the Genoese. The Ramolino family had lived in Corsica for several centuries. Some said that they had been there since the days of the Carthaginians two thousand years before, which led the French historian Jacques Bainville to put forward the far-fetched but delightful theory that Letizia was descended from Hannibal, and that Hannibal's military genius, after lying dormant in the family for seventy generations, was inherited by her son, Napoleon.[2] But it seems more likely that the Ramolinos came to Corsica from Lombardy during the Middle Ages.

Letizia's father died when she was very young, and her mother remarried. This second husband was a Swiss named Fesch. Their son became a priest in Corsica, and when he was aged thirty-nine his nephew Napoleon forced the Pope to make him a cardinal.

Soon after her marriage, Letizia Buonaparte gave birth to a son, who died within a few days. Her second son also died at birth. A third son, named Joseph, was born in January 1768, and survived. On 15 August 1769, at the age of nineteen, she gave birth to another son, who was baptized Napoleon. It was he, and he alone, who was responsible for the family's future glory, and for the fact that thirty years after his death his nephew ascended the throne of France as the Emperor Napoleon III. At the beginning of the twentieth century his immensely wealthy niece, Princess Mathilde, holding semi-royal court in her Paris mansion, said to Marcel Proust and her other guests: 'If it weren't for him, I'd be selling oranges in the streets of Ajaccio',[3] though in fact she would probably have been a reasonably prosperous solicitor's wife.

Letizia's third surviving son, Lucien, was born in May 1775, and her first daughter, Elisa, in January 1777. Louis, the father of Napoleon III, was born on 2 September 1778. He was followed by Pauline in October 1780, Caroline in March 1782, and the youngest child, Jerome, in November 1784. Three months later, Carlo Buonaparte died of cancer at the age of thirty-eight. Shortly before his death he arranged for his son Napoleon to enter the military academy at Brienne, and in due course Louis was also sent to a military academy to be trained as an officer.

The Beauharnais family had been gentlemen of the Orléanais at least since the fifteenth century, but it was through service in the royal navy that they rose to a higher position in society in the reign of Louis XV. François de Beauharnais became a naval officer and was so successful in his career that at the outbreak of the Seven Years War in 1756, when he was aged forty-two, he was made an admiral and appointed Commander-in-Chief and Governor of the French territories in the West Indies. At the end of the war he was created Marquis de

La Ferté Beauharnais. While he was stationed in Martinique he became friendly with the Sieur Tascher de la Pagerie, one of the wealthiest planters in the island. The Tascher family had also been gentlemen of the Orléanais, and thirty years earlier had emigrated to Martinique. Tascher's sister became the Admiral's mistress, and after living with him for nearly forty years she married him when he was eighty-two and she was fifty-seven.[4] The Admiral and Tascher arranged a marriage between Tascher's daughter Josephine and the Admiral's second son by his first marriage, Alexandre, Vicomte de Beauharnais. When Josephine was sixteen she sailed for France and married Alexandre in December 1779.

Alexandre de Beauharnais was one of those aristocrats who had read Voltaire and Rousseau and adopted the ideas of the young men of the Enlightenment. He had watched with enthusiasm the American Revolution and longed for the overthrow of absolutism and aristocratic privilege in France. Josephine was in sympathy with her husband's ideas, but was too self-centred and frivolous to worry very much about political injustice. She was temperamentally ill-suited to be the partner of the earnest idealist Alexandre.

Their first child, a boy named Eugène, was born in September 1781. Two years later, on 10 April 1783, they had a daughter, Hortense, who became the mother of Napoleon III. But by this time their marriage was already breaking up. Josephine enjoyed the gay social life of Paris, which Alexandre despised. She was often seen in the company of other men, and was said to have lovers. She separated from Alexandre, and in the summer of 1788 took Hortense to Martinique.

When the French Revolution broke out, Alexandre de Beauharnais became one of the leaders of the revolutionary party. He was elected President of the National Assembly, and supported the establishment of the Republic and the trial of the King. In 1792 the Prussian and Austrian armies invaded France with the intention of crushing the revolution. Alexandre Beauharnais – he had abandoned the 'de' and his title of viscount – was made a general and appointed to command the Army of the Rhine which was fighting the invaders.

The effect of the revolution was soon felt both in Corsica and in Martinique, and brought danger and adventure into the lives of two children, Louis Bonaparte and Hortense de Beauharnais. The Corsican nationalists had at first welcomed the French Revolution, but in the summer of 1793 they rose in revolt against the extremists in Paris and, with the help of the British navy, drove out the French. Napoleon Bonaparte had joined the minority of Corsicans who supported the French revolutionary government. He was placed in command of the small French garrison at the port of Bastia, but his force was too weak

5

to enable him to hold his position, and he could do nothing except organize the evacuation to France. His mother was in Ajaccio with her five youngest children. Leaving Caroline and Jerome, who were aged eleven and eight, in the care of their grandmother, Madame Ramolino, Letizia Buonaparte set out with her half-brother Fesch, with Elisa aged sixteen, Louis aged fourteen and Pauline aged twelve, to walk the sixty miles to Bastia, travelling by night to avoid interception by the nationalist forces who might have lynched them if they had caught them. They eventually joined Napoleon in Bastia and sailed with him and his troops to France, while the mob looted their house in Ajaccio, but did not harm Caroline or Jerome.[5] Louis was very conscious that his life had been saved by his wonderful elder brother, Napoleon.

When Napoleon was appointed to command the revolutionary army operating against the Royalists and the British at Toulon, Louis joined him there. Louis was slow, quiet and unambitious, but conscientious, loyal, and by no means stupid. He developed an intense admiration for Napoleon, his senior by nine years, and Napoleon loved him and took good care of him. Louis went with Napoleon on his Italian campaign in 1794. At Saorgio, where the French encountered an Austrian force, Louis insisted, to Napoleon's great annoyance, on standing in front of Napoleon to shield him from the bullets.[6]

The news of the revolution in France led to social unrest in Martinique. The majority of the population were black slaves, many of whom had been subjected to horrible cruelties by the planters, though others, like the household slaves of the Vicomtesse de Beauharnais, were treated with kindness and were devoted to their masters and mistresses. Suddenly, one night in September 1790, Josephine was told that an army of rebellious slaves was marching on Fort-Royal, killing, raping and burning, and that her only chance of saving her life was to take ship at once for France. She went on board with Hortense early next morning. When the slave army entered Fort-Royal a few hours later, Josephine's ship had already put out to sea, but was still in sight of the harbour. The slaves signalled to the ship to return to port, and when the captain refused to do so, they opened fire with the cannon in the harbour; but the ship was out of range, and after being nearly wrecked off the coast of Morocco, she docked safely at Toulon.[7] Josephine did not resume cohabitation with her husband.

In 1793 a struggle for power broke out between the two revolutionary groups, the Jacobins and the Girondins. The Jacobins were victorious, and arrested and guillotined the Girondin leaders. The government in Paris was taken over by the Committee of Public Safety, which was dominated by Robespierre. Alexandre Beauharnais supported the Girondins, and resigned his command in the army. In March

1794 he was arrested as a traitor to the Republic and imprisoned in the prison of Les Carmes in Paris. Within six weeks Josephine, who was living with the children at Croissy near Versailles, was denounced under the Law of the Suspects to the local revolutionary committee of the Tuileries district, who received an anonymous letter stating that 'the former Vicomtesse de Beauharnais' was a traitor. The Committee of Public Safety thereupon ordered the arrest of 'the Citizeness Beauharnais, wife of the former general',[8] and she was taken to Les Carmes, but held in a different wing from Alexandre. Eugène and Hortense, who were aged twelve and eleven, were entrusted to the care of Mademoiselle de Lannoy, a middle-class young lady who claimed to be connected with the aristocracy and had been compelled to earn her living as a governess. She regarded the revolution and its low-born supporters with an intense hatred and contempt. She moved with the children to cheap accommodation in the Rue Saint-Dominique in Paris.[9]

The period which became known as the Reign of Terror had begun. In eight weeks 1350 people were guillotined. But Eugène and Hortense were healthy, lively children, and though they were made deeply conscious by Mademoiselle de Lannoy of the terrible injustice which was being inflicted on their parents, they made the best of the situation and spent some happy days during the Reign of Terror. They did not object when the local revolutionary committee ordered that the children of all aristocrats were to be taught a menial trade, and that Eugène was to learn to be a joiner and Hortense a seamstress; and they enjoyed the banquets which, by order of the Convention and to the disgust of Mademoiselle de Lannoy, were held in every street in Paris, at which all the residents in the street were forced to fraternize at dinners around tables set up in the open air during the summer of 1794. Eugène and Hortense liked the rowdy atmosphere at the banquets and chuckled with delight when the indignant Mademoiselle de Lannoy was kissed by an uncouth working man.[10]

On 23 July 1794–5 Thermidor, Year II, in the new revolutionary calendar – Alexandre Beauharnais was guillotined, having been earlier that day convicted before the revolutionary tribunal of being a traitor to the Republic. He died loyal to the revolution which had destroyed him. In his last letter to Josephine he declared that he was innocent of all the charges against him and was loyal to the revolution, and asked her to work in due course for his posthumous rehabilitation; but he told her to wait for some years before doing this, because if he were rehabilitated too soon, this would discredit the revolution, by showing that the revolutionary government was executing innocent people. 'During revolutionary storms', he wrote, 'a great people fighting to pulverize its chains must adopt an attitude of justifiable mistrust, and has more to fear from allowing a guilty man to escape than from striking down an innocent one.'[11]

Three days after the execution of Alexandre Beauharnais, Robespierre rose in the Convention and announced that he had a list of the names of men in the highest positions in the government who were traitors to the Republic, and that he would reveal the names at a session of the Convention next day. His colleagues on the Committee of Public Safety feared that their names might be on Robespierre's list, and they got together and decided to destroy him. When he rose to speak in the Convention next day, he was shouted down, and within twenty-four hours he and his supporters had been arrested, condemned by the revolutionary tribunal, and guillotined. The men of the Committee of Public Safety who had overthrown him on 9 Thermidor became known as the 'men of Thermidor', and although they had hitherto been as ruthless as Robespierre himself in executing counter-revolutionaries of all descriptions, they now rapidly put an end to the Reign of Terror and released nearly all the inmates of the prisons. They acted four days too late to save Alexandre Beauharnais, but Josephine, who would almost certainly have been guillotined if Robespierre had lasted for another few weeks, was released from Les Carmes.

Napoleon Bonaparte was under a cloud for a time after July 1794 because of his association with Robespierre's government; but the men of Thermidor decided to use his services, and in October 1795 he saved their government by suppressing a royalist revolt in Paris. Their leader, Barras, introduced him to Josephine Beauharnais.[12] He fell in love with her at once, and on 9 March 1796 he married her before leaving Paris to command the army that was fighting the Austrians in northern Italy.

Louis Bonaparte served with Napoleon in Italy. He particularly distinguished himself at Arcola. On one occasion during the fierce three-day battle Napoleon's horse bolted and carried him into a marsh. Louis, ever-watchful over his great brother, galloped to the rescue and with one or two assistants managed to drag Napoleon from the marsh and thus save his life. Two years later, when he was still only nineteen, Louis served under Napoleon in Egypt.[13]

On 9 November 1799 – 18 Brumaire in the revolutionary calendar – Napoleon carried through his *coup d'état*, dispersing the Council of Five Hundred, overthrowing the government of the Directory, and making himself ruler of France with the title of First Consul. His action was approved by the French people in a referendum held under universal suffrage, in which 99.95 per cent of the voters voted Yes. Louis Bonaparte had become the brother, and Josephine's daughter Hortense had become the stepdaughter, of the dictator of France.

Hortense de Beauharnais – the prefix 'de' was beginning to reappear in France – had been educated, since Thermidor, at a fashionable school for young ladies at Saint-Germain. In 1800 she was seventeen, and her mother and stepfather were considering the question of her marriage. She fell mildly in love with several young officers, but Napoleon thought that none of them would be a suitable match for Hortense, and saw to it that they were posted to their regiments where they could no longer meet her. Napoleon and Josephine had been unable to have children, which worried Napoleon, who, even before he made himself Emperor, was thinking of founding a hereditary dynasty. They planned for Hortense to marry Louis Bonaparte, hoping that Louis and Hortense would provide a male Bonaparte heir. Hortense was not in love with Louis, and he was in love with her cousin, Émilie de Beauharnais, who had married the Comte de Lavalette and in 1815 heroically arranged her husband's escape from prison on the eve of his execution.[14]

Hortense was an unsuitable wife for a dull and devoted husband. She was attractive, very intelligent, and cultured. She was intensely self-centred; the opening sentence of her memoirs – 'My life has been so brilliant and so full of misfortunes that the world has been forced to take notice of it'[15] – is very revealing of her character. She was a gifted pianist, and composed the music of many popular romantic songs, which were known as her *romances*, on such themes as gallant medieval knights bidding farewell to their ladies on castle ramparts. Her 'La sentinelle' was sung by the French soldiers during the Peninsular War; and her most famous song, 'Partant pour la Syrie', became the favourite song of the troops during the Wagram campaign,[16] and when her son became Emperor was the unofficial French national anthem during the Second Empire. She enjoyed admiration of all kinds – the esteem of famous writers for her literary appreciation, the friendship of women inferior to herself in rank and intellect, the obsequious respect which, as etiquette demanded, was paid to the royal rank which she acquired, and the admiration of men who found her sexually attractive. She only fell seriously in love once in her life, and was not a woman of strong sexual desires.

She was easily put out by minor discomforts, such as the lack of amenities at a wayside inn, and became very irked if crossed in any way. She did not hesitate to use her acquaintances and friends for her own advantage, and could put an end to friendships, even those of long standing, abruptly and callously, when she felt that her friends could no longer be of use to her. But she was generous, both in her public charities and to her servants and to those friends who took her fancy, especially, in later years, to charming young English gentlemen. The members of her household were devoted to her, and few men or women could resist her charm. As a wife she was certainly difficult. She was married to a husband whom she did not love and who would have tried any woman's patience, and she made no effort to help him in his difficulties and would not compromise an inch. Her only real loyalty was to her family – to her brother Eugène, with whom she had shared those traumatic childhood experiences, to her mother Josephine, and afterwards to her two sons, Napoleon Louis and Louis Napoleon.[17]

Her feelings for her stepfather Napoleon were more complex. She was not blind to his faults, at least in her later years, but she admired and feared him for his political achievement and dominating personality. Like many other French men and women who had been born under the old régime and survived the Reign of Terror, she venerated Napoleon as the man who had restored law and order in France and had raised French prestige abroad, while retaining all the benefits which the revolution had won for the people and the middle classes.[18] She believed that Napoleon was the middle way between the dreadful alternatives of a return to the archaic injustices and inequalities of the Bourbons or the anarchy and horrors of Jacobin rule. In due course she passed on these ideas to her son. For seventy years large numbers of Frenchmen, at most times a majority, held the same view, and believed that if France was to avoid being subjected either to aristocratic arrogance or to the guillotine, it must be governed by a dictator who was a member of the Bonaparte family.

Hortense, believing that only Napoleon could save France, was prepared to tolerate not only his political dictatorship but also the petty tyranny which he exercised over his family and over her. The gossipmongers in the *salons*, noticing Napoleon's affection for her and domination over her, spread the rumour that she was his mistress;[19] but it is unlikely that a woman like Hortense would have adopted this submissive attitude towards any man who had made love to her.

At the time when Napoleon and Josephine were arranging the marriage of Louis and Hortense, Louis was developing a skin disease. The gossipmongers said that it was syphilis and had made him sterile, but his physicians stated that he was suffering from rheumatism and the effect of a fall from his horse. Whatever the cause, he acquired a scrofulous hand and forearm which Hortense found repulsive.[20] She never loved her husband, and soon came to despise him for his weaknesses. Louis, on the other hand, periodically fell in love with Hortense, but it was a jealous love, and alternated with feelings of hate towards her. One major cause of the breakdown of the marriage was Louis's extreme suspiciousness, which was a product of his lack of confidence and led him from time to time to accuse Hortense of infidelity on the strength of some unfounded rumour, or more often without any reason at all.[21]

Louis and Hortense were married in Paris on 4 January 1802. Nine months later their first child was born, a son who was christened Charles Napoleon. His birth was hailed in the entourage as providing the heir whom Napoleon and Josephine could not produce; Hortense's maids referred to the baby as 'our Dauphin', and earned a sharp rebuke from Hortense and Louis.[22] In the summer of 1804 Hortense was pregnant again. Napoleon had just had himself proclaimed Emperor, and the new imperial constitution had been approved by a referendum. The constitution laid down that Napoleon was to be Emperor of the French, and that two of his brothers, Joseph and Louis, were to hold the title of French Princes. His other two brothers, Lucien and Jerome, were not made Princes because they had married wives of whom Napoleon disapproved. If Napoleon died without issue, he was to be succeeded by any of his nephews whom he had adopted as his children after they reached the age of eighteen, and, in default of such adoption, by Joseph and his heirs, and then by Louis and his heirs. Hortense's children were therefore third in line for the imperial throne after Joseph and Louis. Lucien and Jerome and their children were excluded.[23]

Hortense's second son was born on 11 October 1804, and given the names of Napoleon Louis. He was christened in the following March by the Pope himself, who had come to Paris for Napoleon's coronation. The gossipmongers said that the Emperor was the father of both Hortense's sons. The story reached Louis's ears, and he accused Hortense of infidelity. Matrimonial relations became very strained. Hortense made frequent visits with Josephine to the fashionable watering-places of Aix-la-Chapelle, Plombières and Aix-les-Bains, which was then known as Aix-en-Savoie, while Louis stayed in Paris. She spent more and more time with her mother and less and less with her husband.

In the summer of 1805 Napoleon prepared to invade England. He assembled his Grand Army in the neighbourhood of Boulogne and set up his headquarters there. Louis was undergoing a health cure for his skin complaint at Saint-Amand, and as Josephine was taking the waters at Aix-la-Chapelle, Hortense went with Napoleon to the Channel coast, acting as hostess at the receptions at Boulogne and Montreuil, and standing at his side as he watched the manoeuvres and the great practice embarkation which the soldiers, at the time, thought was the beginning of the real invasion of England.[24]

In the autumn Napoleon suddenly abandoned his projected invasion of England and marched his Grand Army unexpectedly against the Austrians in Bavaria. On 2 December, the first anniversary of the coronation, he defeated the Austrian and Russian armies at Austerlitz in Moravia. Five days after the battle, at his army headquarters, he issued a decree setting up a school at Écouen to provide free education for the sons and daughters of all his soldiers who had fallen at Austerlitz. He appointed Hortense as 'Princesse Protectrice' of the school. The school was later opened to the orphans of soldiers who had died on other battlefields. Hortense took her duties as Patroness very seriously. She often visited Écouen, and supervised the administration of the school.[25]

Soon after Austerlitz, the Emperor began his consultations about a project which he had formed for the government of Holland. In 1794–5 the French revolutionary armies overran the Austrian Netherlands (the modern state of Belgium) and Holland, which since the sixteenth century had been ruled by the Princes of Orange as Stadholders. Belgium was annexed to France, but Holland became an independent republic after the Prince of Orange had escaped to England. The republic came under the domination of its leading statesman, Count Schimmelpenninck; but as the other Dutch politicians became jealous of Schimmelpenninck, Napoleon proposed to them that the republic should be converted into a kingdom with Louis Bonaparte as its king.

Napoleon's Foreign Minister, Talleyrand, conducted the negotiations with the Dutch, who knew that they were in no position to resist Napoleon but haggled for a long time over the financial and commercial terms of the treaty. In the spring of 1806 the Dutch envoys came to Paris, and after another four months of bargaining the treaty was signed. Napoleon had overlooked one minor detail: he had forgotten to tell Louis that he was to be King of Holland. Josephine had told Hortense, but Hortense had said nothing to Louis, no doubt because she assumed that he knew already. The first that Louis heard of it was when one of the Dutch delegates happened to mention it to him shortly before the ceremony at which they solemnly offered him the crown.[26]

Louis and Hortense arrived at The Hague in the middle of June 1806; but after a month they went to Wiesbaden and Aix-la-Chapelle, where Louis was treated for his skin disease. When Louis returned to his kingdom in September, Hortense stayed at Aix-la-Chapelle. At the end of the month she returned to Holland for a week, and then left for Germany with Louis, who joined his Dutch troops in Napoleon's campaign against Prussia, while Hortense stayed at Mainz with Josephine. Despite several adverse comments in the Dutch press about her absence, she did not return to The Hague until 29 January 1807. She had her compatriots' dread of those cold, foggy countries which the French call by the grim term 'the North', and the fact that, to her, Holland was 'le Nord' was a good enough reason not to go there; but another reason was her growing dislike of her husband.[27]

When at last she reached The Hague, she picked quarrels with Louis on every pretext; and when he, in his typically solemn and pompous way, and in a well-meant attempt to settle their differences by a compromise, drew up a written document containing the conditions which they should mutually observe in their life together, she refused to accept the document or make any concession.[28]

At the beginning of May 1807 their eldest son, the four-year-old Prince Charles Napoleon, fell ill with croup. Within three days, on 5 May, he died. Both parents knelt at his bedside, heartbroken, as he passed away, and their grief brought for the first time a reconciliation between them. Louis cancelled his official engagements and went with Hortense to the quiet of the palace of Laeken across the French frontier in Belgium. But their reconciliation did not last long. In her grief Hortense turned, as usual, to her mother rather than to her husband, and after a few days went to Josephine's house at Malmaison near Paris, while Louis returned to Holland. She was still completely cast down by her child's death, though she received a peremptory order from Napoleon to cease mourning for him to this excessive extent: a short period of grief was proper, he told her, but if she were to prolong it he would regard it as an affront to himself. She bowed to his great wisdom and, leaving her son Napoleon Louis with Josephine, went to the Pyrenees for a rest cure at Cauterets. She travelled incognito, with only a small retinue, but her presence there immediately became known, especially as she drew attention to herself by the lavish tips which she gave to the porters and guides. She found herself being received with due formality by fussy and pompous mayors who tried her patience, but she treated them all with her usual charm, and made herself very popular in the district.[29]

Louis's reconciliation with Hortense had made him fall in love with her again. He determined to seize a favourable opportunity, and as soon as possible he left Holland and joined her at Cauterets. In the days after Charles's death, at The Hague and Laeken, Louis had realized that Hortense was in no mood for love-making, and he made no sexual demands upon her; but at Cauterets he tried to persuade her to grant him his marital rights. She shrank from him, and refused. In later years both Louis and Hortense, on different occasions, stated that they had had no sexual relations at Cauterets.[30]

After spending a fortnight there, Louis left to take the waters at Ussat in the Ariège district, and Hortense left on a tour of the Pyrenees. For the first time since Charles's death two months before, she was almost gay, and rode and walked long distances through the mountains with a speed and energy which surprised the guides, who were charmed by her informal and light-hearted manner. On 25 July she visited the waterfall at Gavarnie, high up in the Pyrenees, and was stranded there overnight, sleeping at a small wayside inn.[31] This visit to Gavarnie has attracted a great deal of attention on the part of historians, as it took place nine months, almost to the day, before the birth of Napoleon III. It has often been suggested that at the inn at Gavarnie, or somewhere else during her travels in the Pyrenees, she went to bed with some man who was Napoleon III's true father.

It is not surprising that when Louis Napoleon was President and Emperor of France, his enemies spread the rumour that he was not King Louis's son. As he owed his popularity with his supporters and his advent to the imperial throne entirely to the fact that he was thought to be the nephew of the great Napoleon, he would have been completely discredited if it could have been proved that he was not a Bonaparte; and the state of relations between Louis and Hortense at the time of his birth gave good scope for this insinuation. But gossip of this kind is usually wrong. For some reason it selected the Dutch Admiral Verhuell as Louis Napoleon's father; but apart from the fact that there is no evidence at all that Verhuell was ever anything more than a casual acquaintance of Hortense, there is no doubt that he was in Holland throughout the summer of 1807 and did not go to the Pyrenees when Hortense was there, though his brother did. Another suspect is Élie Decazes, the future Duc Decazes and Prime Minister, who was attached to Louis Bonaparte's household as his legal adviser. He visited Hortense at Cauterets in the summer of 1807. There were rumours at the time that he was her lover, and possibly the father of Louis Napoleon; but, according to Hortense, she was irritated by his advances, and repulsed him. Several other men have been suggested as the father.[32] The strongest case can perhaps be made out for Hortense's Chancellor, Villeneuve, who stayed with Hortense and her party in the inn at Gavarnie, and a week before, at Cauterets, had hurried the other gentlemen off to bed so as to have the opportunity of being alone that night with Hortense.[33]

Louis was still in the south of France, and Hortense travelled to Toulouse and met him there on 11 August.* Both Hortense and Louis afterwards declared that he made love to her at Toulouse, and that, unlike at Cauterets, she granted him his wish. They travelled together

*All authorities give 12 August as the date, which is the day given by Louis in his reproachful letters to Hortense of 23 November 1809 and 14 September 1816 (Turquan, *La reine Hortense*, II.131; Duboscq, *Louis Bonaparte en Hollande*, p. 229). But *Le Moniteur* of 22 August 1807 reported that Hortense left Cauterets on 10 August, arrived at Toulouse on 11 August, and spent 12 August visiting various public places in the town with Louis before leaving Toulouse with him on 13 August; and Louis, in his letter to Napoleon of 9 August 1807 (Rocquain, *Napoléon Ier et le Roi Louis*, p. 123), wrote that he was expecting Hortense to arrive in Toulouse on 'Tuesday', i.e. 11 August. Could it be that Louis, two years later, remembered the date wrongly, thus unconsciously making the case against Hortense, and against Louis Napoleon's legitimacy, look blacker by twenty-four hours than it really was?

from Toulouse to Paris, and had sexual relations on several occasions during this journey. After reaching Saint-Cloud on 27 August, Louis returned to Holland at the end of September, and Hortense remained in Paris.[34] They did not meet again until after the birth of Napoleon III in Paris on 20 April 1808 – just over eight months after Louis and Hortense had met at Toulouse.

In 1816, after Louis had finally decided to end his matrimonial relations with Hortense, he wrote her a reproachful letter in which he stated that during the whole of their married life there had only been three short periods, totalling three months in all, when they had had sexual relations – in the first weeks after their marriage in January 1802, in January 1804 when Napoleon Louis was conceived, and at Toulouse and on the journey to Paris in August 1807.[35] Why did Hortense, after refusing for more than three years to go to bed with her husband, suddenly agree to do so at Toulouse on 11 August 1807? One possible explanation is that, having had sexual relations with a man in the inn at Gavarnie on the night of 25 July, she realized that she might be pregnant – modern methods of contraception were not available in 1807 – and therefore hastened to Toulouse and into Louis's bed so that it would be impossible for anyone to prove that her baby was illegitimate. But most of the historians who have carefully examined the question have decided to give Hortense the benefit of the doubt and accept the legitimacy of her son. All that can be said with certainty is that it is very unlikely that it will ever be possible to prove whether Louis Bonaparte was, or was not, the father of Napoleon III.

CHAPTER 2

THE PRINCE OF HOLLAND

WHEN the government at The Hague heard that the Queen was pregnant, they expressed a hope that she would return to Holland for her confinement; but though Louis urged Hortense to come, she refused, and decided to have the baby in Louis's house in the Rue Cerutti (today the Rue Lafitte) in Paris.[1] Her stand was as usual upheld by Josephine and Napoleon. She believed that she would have better doctors in Paris, and this was the worst psychological moment to expect her to endure the horrors of 'the North'. In any case, Napoleon was determined that the child should be born in Paris, for he regarded her baby, if he were to be a boy, not as a Prince of Holland but as a possible heir to the French imperial throne. He himself was still child-less and King Joseph only had daughters; if Hortense had a son, he would be fourth in succession after Joseph, Louis, and Louis's eldest surviving son, under the provisions of the Constitutional Law of 1804.

Three weeks before the child arrived, Napoleon left Paris for Bayonne to meet the King of Spain, and he stayed there for four months, bullying the King into abdicating the Spanish throne in favour of Joseph Bonaparte. King Louis was at Utrecht, preparing to make a state entry into Amsterdam. He had decided that the capital of Holland should no longer be at The Hague, where the Princes of Orange had lived among the old aristocracy and the court bureaucracy, but in the commercial centre of the kingdom, among the middle-class merchants of Amsterdam. He would live in the old town hall in the Dam square, which was now for the first time converted into the royal palace which it is today.[2]

Before leaving Paris, Napoleon had given instructions to the Arch-Chancellor of the Empire, Cambacérès, to supervise the birth of Hortense's baby with full solemnity. Hortense, who had been told not to expect the child for at least another week, went to a party at the house of Napoleon's sister, Caroline Murat, on the evening of 19 April. Cambacérès was also at the party, and as he was feeling ill he told Hortense that he would retire to bed, since he obviously would not be called out that night to witness the birth of her baby. But Hortense suddenly developed labour pains and hurried home from the party, and Cambacérès was sent for. He had been bled by his doctors, but arrived, swathed in bandages, at the Rue Cerutti in time to witness the birth of a prince at 1 a.m. on Wednesday 20 April 1808. At 5 a.m. Hortense's Chancellor, Villeneuve, and Louis's Chamberlain, Count Bylandt, left Paris, Villeneuve heading for Bayonne and Bylandt for Amsterdam, to carry the news to Napoleon and Louis.[3]

When Napoleon heard about the birth from Villeneuve, his first reaction was anger that Hortense's Chancellor had arrived with the news before the messenger carrying the official notification from his own Arch-Chancellor, Cambacérès; but he soon forgot his irritation in his joy at the event. He had massed his army on the Spanish frontier in order to overawe the King of Spain, and he ordered a salvo of guns to be fired in salute by every regiment along the whole frontier.[4]

King Louis, who entered his new capital in state, escorted by marching troops and amid cheering crowds, on the afternoon of 21 April, heard the news of the birth of his son on the following morning. Later in the day, while the drums beat and the church bells rang, a court official read out a proclamation, outside the palace in the Dam square, which stated that the King wished the people of his new capital to be the first to know about the birth of the Prince. In the evening messengers left Amsterdam to carry the news to the provinces, and the city, already *en fête* in honour of the King's state entry, was illuminated to celebrate the Queen's delivery.[5]

While Napoleon and Louis were celebrating, Hortense was in despair. She had hoped that the baby would be a girl this time, and though she soon reconciled herself to it being a boy – for political, as opposed to personal, reasons she was pleased that it was – she was frightened because he was so delicate. He had to be placed in a basin of wine, and later wrapped in cotton wool, to keep him alive. Hortense was sure that both she and the baby would be dead within twenty-four hours. Unkind people said that Hortense made up this story in order to confirm her assertions that the baby was premature, and that he could therefore be King Louis's son; but she continued to worry about him, and he was still weak when he was several months old. She dismissed his nurse, and replaced her with a new nurse, Madame Bure, whom she herself had found in a small village. The baby grew stronger in Madame Bure's care, and by 22 August was well enough to be vaccinated with no ill effects.[6] Madame Bure's own baby, who shared his mother's milk with Louis Napoleon, grew up to become a great friend and loyal supporter of his foster-brother, who appointed him to be Treasurer of the Household under the Second Empire.

Neither Louis nor Hortense knew what their son's name was to be, as this was a matter to be decided by Napoleon, and he was too busy at Bayonne to deal with it. The Code Napoleon had enacted that the birth of every child in France must be registered, along with the child's names, within three days of the birth; but an imperial decree suspended the operation of this law in the case of the King of Holland's son, and for six weeks the baby had no name except 'the Prince of Holland'. Then on 2 June Cambacérès and other officers of state called at the Rue Cerutti and informed Hortense that the Emperor had ordered that the Prince should be named Charles Louis Napoleon. His christening was postponed until such time as Napoleon ordered it. [7]

King Louis's initial response to the news of his son's birth had been to rejoice in private as well as in public, but within a month he had realized that the baby was born only eight months and eight days after the earliest date on which he could have procreated it. His old suspicions were aroused, and he told his closest friends that he was sure that he was not the child's father. His relations with Hortense had deteriorated sadly since the previous summer, and were made worse by his political differences with Napoleon.

One of Napoleon's weaknesses as a statesman was his tendency to underrate the people with whom he had to deal, and he had not realized that there was much more to Louis than appeared at first sight. During the Italian campaign ten years before, Napoleon had praised Louis for his abilities; but recently – was it since friction had arisen between Louis and Hortense? – he found fault with everything Louis did. [8]

When Louis became King of Holland he made up his mind to serve his subjects to the best of his ability. He wanted to convince the Dutch, by good government and by gaining their good will, that the political, military and above all the commercial interests of Holland were best served by a close alliance with France. On the first occasion when he addressed the Dutch Parliament he declared: 'From the moment I set foot on the soil of the kingdom, I became a Dutchman.' [9] This inevitably led to conflict with Napoleon, who regarded Louis as an agent whom he had appointed to bleed Holland white in the interests of France. [10]

In November 1806 Napoleon issued his famous Berlin Decree imposing an embargo on all trade with Britain throughout his empire and in all occupied territories. Holland, as a trading nation, was particularly hard hit, and many Dutchmen carried on a surreptitious trade with England. Though Louis had misgivings about the Berlin Decree, he loyally applied it in Holland, but he insisted that it should be enforced by Dutch officials and not by the French army, and he protested to Napoleon when French officers arrested Dutchmen. There was in fact less smuggling in Holland than in most other parts of occupied Europe, and less than in France itself; but Napoleon blamed Louis for the smuggling in Holland. He forced Louis to cede the port of Flushing to France and in exchange gave Holland some territory in Germany which no Dutchman wished to have.[11]

In March 1808 Napoleon tried to make it up with Louis, and at the same time put an end to his pro-Dutch policy, by offering to make Louis King of Spain; their brother King Joseph of Naples would then replace Louis as King of Holland, and Murat would become King of Naples. Louis refused the offer; he was just getting to know Holland, and did not think that kings should be switched around like ambassadors. So Joseph was made King of Spain and Murat King of Naples. Louis wrote privately to Joseph and expressed his misgivings about the whole Spanish involvement, which he shrewdly believed might eventually lead to disaster.[12]

Louis had for many years had a lingering suspicion that Napoleon was Hortense's lover, and he now believed that Napoleon was encouraging Hortense to stay apart from him. He was even more distressed about his separation from his elder son, Napoleon Louis. The boy, now aged three, was a great favourite of his father's, and in the spring and summer of 1808 Louis wrote repeatedly to Hortense, asking her to send him to Holland. Hortense either evaded his requests by promising to send Napoleon Louis at a later date, or did not reply to his letters. He appealed to Napoleon, but received no answer. He wrote to his mother Letizia, who bore the official title of 'Madame Mère'. She was the only member of the Bonaparte family who took his side in his disputes with Hortense; but she could do nothing to help him.[13]

On 23 August 1808, Louis wrote a piteous appeal to Hortense, begging her to send Napoleon Louis to him:

I have spent the winter without him; I am alone, absolutely alone. . . . Do you dare, Madame, does your conscience permit you to refuse to send a son to his father? Have you not got his brother with you, and in any case are you not in Paris, surrounded by your friends, by your family, with none of my sufferings and my painful occupations?[14]

Three weeks later the Dutch Ambassador in Paris was abruptly informed that, in view of the failure of the Dutch government to enforce the Berlin Decree against British goods, Napoleon was placing an embargo on all trade between the French Empire and Holland. This was a crippling blow to Dutch trade, which could not afford to lose the only market still open to it. Louis was forced to capitulate, and to agree, as a condition for the lifting of the embargo, that French officials should be stationed in Holland with power to arrest and execute Dutchmen who infringed the Berlin Decree. All this time Napoleon Louis remained in Paris. In March 1809 Napoleon, without informing Louis in advance, created Napoleon Louis Grand Duke of the Duchy of Berg in Germany, and at the same time, under the provision of the Law of the Imperial Family, appointed Hortense to be the boy's guardian.[15]

In December 1809 Louis went to Paris to discuss his differences with Napoleon. He stayed at his mother's house, refusing to live at his own house with Hortense. A week after he arrived, he was summoned to a family council at which Napoleon announced that he had decided to divorce Josephine because of her inability to give birth to an heir.[16] The divorce did not end the friendship between Napoleon and Josephine, nor his regard for Hortense or for Eugène, whom he had appointed Viceroy of Italy and who was a prominent general in his army. Four months later Napoleon married Marie Louise, the daughter of the Emperor of Austria.

During his stay in Paris, Louis was mercilessly bullied by Napoleon in stormy interviews and in acrimonious letters addressed to him at Madame Mère's house. 'Monsieur my brother,' wrote Napoleon on 21 December,

> I hoped that, having been brought up at my side, you would have had such an attachment to France as the nation has a right to expect from its children. . . . I hoped that, in placing a prince of my own family on the throne of Holland, I had found a medium of reconciling the interests of the two states and of uniting them in one common cause, in a common hatred of England. . . . But my expectations were frustrated, and Your Majesty, on ascending the throne of Holland, forgot that you were French, and even bent all the powers of your reason, and tortured the delicacy of your conscience, to persuade yourself that you were Dutch. All the Dutch who leaned towards France have been neglected and persecuted; those who have served England have been promoted.

He ended by warning Louis that he would not tolerate resistance from the Dutch: 'At the first affront offered to my flag, I will cause the first officer who shall dare to insult my eagle to be seized by force and hung up at the yard-arm.'[17]

Napoleon demanded that four provinces of South Brabant, which had been Dutch since the sixteenth century, should be ceded to France, offering in return to give Holland some more territory in Germany. At first, Louis firmly refused; but he soon discovered that he was being held as a virtual prisoner in Paris; guards were placed in front of his door, and followed him wherever he went. After four months' resistance, he agreed to sign the treaty, and received his reward for his submission. Not only was he allowed to return to Holland, but Hortense and Napoleon Louis went with him.[18]

It was the first time for nearly three years that Hortense had been in Holland, and she remained there for less than six weeks. She disliked the old town hall in Amsterdam even more than the Palace of the Wood near The Hague. She found the new palace dark and eerie, and at the beginning of June 1810 she left to take the waters at Plombières; but Napoleon Louis stayed behind with his father. Three weeks later, Napoleon, on the pretext that a Dutchman had insulted the French Ambassador's coachman, ordered the French army to occupy the whole of Holland.[19]

Louis, feeling that he could no longer be of use to his subjects, abdicated in favour of Napoleon Louis and, failing him, of his younger son Louis Napoleon. He appointed Hortense as Regent, and during her absence from the kingdom her powers were to be exercised by a Council of Regency composed of Dutchmen. After saying good-bye to his beloved son – he had too much respect for the laws of the Empire to remove him from the Emperor's jurisdiction – he went to Teplitz in Bohemia, in the Emperor of Austria's territories.[20]

Napoleon immediately annulled Louis's abdication and annexed Holland to the French Empire. He sent an official to bring Napoleon Louis to Saint-Cloud, where he received him at a public ceremony and addressed words to him which were reported in the official newspaper, *Le Moniteur*:

'Come, my son, I will be your father. The conduct of your father grieves my heart; only his illness can account for it. When you are grown up, you will repay his debt and your own. Never forget that in whatever position my policy and the interests of my empire may place you, your first duty is to me, your second duty is to France; all your other duties, even those towards the peoples whom I may confide to your care, come after these.'[21]

Napoleon III, in later times, interpreted the clash between his uncle, the great Emperor, and his father in a manner that was not discreditable to either of them. He believed that Napoleon had acted throughout in the interests of France; Louis, finding that the interests of his Dutch subjects conflicted with his duty as a Frenchman, abdicated his throne because he put duty before power or wealth.

Napoleon sent messengers to Louis at Teplitz, ordering him to return to France and offering him an annual pension. Louis refused to return and refused the pension. Napoleon then settled all Louis's property in France, and a large annuity, on Hortense and the two children, as a result of which Hortense obtained an income of three million francs a year, with an additional 500,000 francs a year for Napoleon Louis and 250,000 francs for Louis Napoleon. By an imperial decree, she was given a household consisting of sixteen officials, including one count, two countesses, two barons and one baroness. She was to remain a French Princess, but was to be referred to as 'Queen Hortense' instead of 'the Queen of Holland'. The children were no longer to be known as Princes of Holland; Napoleon Louis was 'the Duke of Berg', and his younger brother 'Prince Louis Napoleon'.[22]

Louis Napoleon was two years and three months when this change in his status took place. His position was further affected by the news that the Empress Marie Louise was pregnant, for both Joseph and Louis's children would be displaced from the imperial succession if she gave birth to a son. His down-grading was shown by his baptism ceremony. The Emperor at last ordered it to take place at Fontainebleau on 4 November 1810. Twenty-three other children were baptized at the same time, all of them being the sons of Napoleon's highest councillors – the Prince de Neuchâtel, the Duc de Montebello, the Duc de Bassano, and other dukes and counts. The children were baptized by Cardinal Fesch; Napoleon and Marie Louise, who were both present, were their godparents. Louis Napoleon was placed first of all the children in order of precedence, but the fact that he was included together with the sons of even the highest noblemen showed a relative fall in his status since the public celebration of his birth two-and-a-half years earlier.[23] A far more important ceremony took place in the following June, when the son of Napoleon and Marie Louise, who had been safely delivered on 20 March 1811, was christened with great pomp in Notre-Dame. He was named Napoleon, and given the title 'King of Rome'.

Louis Napoleon was brought up in the constant company of his brother Napoleon Louis, who was three-and-a-half years older than he; they were taken everywhere together, and were only separated for the few weeks in the spring of 1810 when Hortense took Napoleon Louis with her to Amsterdam and Louis Napoleon remained in Paris. The boys lived in their mother's household in the Rue Cerutti, in the large mansion which Louis had bought when he was created a French Prince on the establishment of the Empire, as his previous residence was too small; it had been given to Hortense when he fled to Teplitz. It was too dark and gloomy for Hortense's taste. The real or imaginary state of her health made it necessary for her to spend several hours every day in bed, and she was annoyed that her bedroom did not face south and get the midday sunshine. She asked the Emperor to pull down the house and rebuild it to suit her fancy; but he playfully pulled her ear – a favourite habit of his – and told her that this would have to wait until after the war.[24]

The children spent just as much time at her house in the country at Saint-Leu, some thirty miles north of Paris. Louis had purchased this early eighteenth-century mansion and had modernized it, and like the rest of his property it was given to Hortense in 1810. It was surrounded by a large park of nearly two hundred acres and about fifty miles of forest land. Some twelve miles away through the forest was the College of Écouen, the largest of the schools for the orphans of fallen soldiers of which Hortense was Patroness, and she often took the children on her inspections of the school. When they were at the Rue Cerutti, the boys were often taken to spend the afternoon with their grandmother, the Empress Josephine, at her house at Malmaison, about seven miles west of Paris. They saw their uncle the Emperor quite frequently when he was in Paris.[25]

In after years, Napoleon III wrote down a few fragmentary notes of what was perhaps intended to be an autobiography, and described some of his most vivid memories of his early childhood. He remembered his christening in the presence of Napoleon and Marie Louise when he was two years six months old. He remembered walking and playing in the garden at Malmaison with Josephine, and being permitted to suck the sugar cane which grew there. He remembered a magnificent guardsman on sentry duty at Malmaison who sprang to attention and presented arms with mock solemnity at the command of the little boy, and whom the admiring child rewarded by giving him a biscuit to eat; and he remembered the way in which Napoleon, when they were small children, would pick him and his brother up by their heads with his two hands and lift them on to the table, to the great distress of Hortense, who had been told by her doctor that it was a very dangerous practice.[26]

Hortense appointed Madame de Boubers to be the chief governess of the Princes, with Madame de Boucheporn and Madame de Mailly-Couronnel (formerly Mademoiselle de Mornay) as the under-governesses; but Louis Napoleon remained in the charge of his nanny, Madame Bure, who was constantly with him. She was utterly devoted to him, and he to her. The lively and lovable little brunette was universally popular. One day, when she took Louis Napoleon to see the Emperor at the Tuileries, Napoleon said: 'This little fellow has got a pretty nanny.' Madame Bure never wearied of telling this story.[27]

Hortense carefully supervised her children's upbringing. She usually spent the morning with them, when she refused to see visitors, and permitted them to be present while she dressed and had her hair done before going out in the evening, after which the boys, carrying her gloves and shawl, would escort her to her carriage as she left for an evening party or a reception at court.[28]

Despite all her regal airs and her enjoyment of high society and expensive living, Hortense retained many of the democratic sentiments of her father and the progressive circles of 1789. Like all the Bonapartist supporters, she believed that the Napoleonic monarchy and aristocracy, unlike the Bourbon monarchy and the aristocracy of the *ancien régime*, were based on a close link with the common people.[29] The members of the imperial family observed a formal etiquette; even brothers and sisters, and husbands and wives, addressed each other, in letters and conversation, as 'Your Majesty' and in the third person. But Hortense wished her children to have some experience, in their youth, of a more ordinary way of life. She forbade their governesses and servants to address the boys as 'Your Royal Highness', and told them to call Napoleon Louis 'Napoleon', and Louis Napoleon 'Louis', as she did herself.[30] In Louis Napoleon's case, his efforts to pronounce his name Louis, when he was learning to talk, made the name sound like 'Oui-oui', and he thereby acquired the nickname 'Monsieur Oui-oui' in the family and the household.

Hortense brought up the children to be aware of the sufferings of the poor, to appreciate their own good fortune in being born into a very wealthy and highly-placed family, and to be conscious of their duty to relieve the lot of their less fortunate fellow-beings by charitable gifts and otherwise. She taught them to be even more conscious of the sufferings and heroism of the soldiers who were fighting in Spain, Germany and Russia for the glory of their Emperor and of France.[31]

One day, when Louis Napoleon was aged four, he encountered a child chimney-sweep in the Cerutti mansion. He was frightened by the child's dirty face, and cried out in terror about 'the little black man'. Madame de Boubers took him on her knee and told him that he should pity, not fear, the poor orphan child who was forced by poverty to live the hard life of a chimney-sweep. Louis Napoleon was deeply affected by what his governess said. A few months later, the chimney-sweep boy was cleaning the chimneys in the middle of the night when by mistake he came down in the bedroom where the two Princes were sleeping. Louis Napoleon woke up, and saw the boy. He managed, with some difficulty, to climb out of his cot, and, going to the desk where his money was kept, handed it all to the little chimney-sweep.[32]

Hortense, partly for reasons of health and partly for pleasure, spent several weeks each year at Aix-la-Chapelle, Aix-les-Bains and Plombières. Sometimes she took the children with her, but more often sent them to stay with Josephine at Malmaison. The children went with her in the summer of 1809 to Plombières, where she fell seriously in love, probably for the only time in her life. The lover was the Comte de Flahault. His mother, the Comtesse de Flahault, was the novelist Madame de Souza; his father was almost certainly her lover, Talleyrand. Flahault's official father, the Comte de Flahault, was guillotined as an aristocrat in 1793, but he himself joined the revolutionary army and by 1809 was a colonel aged twenty-four, two years younger than Hortense. She had been interested in him for some time. He had first seen her at an official ball at the Tuileries, when he had admired her dancing and had applauded her with hand-clapping and shouts of approval, and she had sent him a haughty message that she considered that his behaviour had been presumptuous. They later became acquainted and he declared his love for her, though she, according to her own story, gave him no encouragement.

She first became his mistress at Plombières in 1809, and in the spring of 1811 learned that she was pregnant by him. As it was nearly a year since her husband had gone into exile at Teplitz, this was very embarrassing for her. She went into hiding in a little house in Paris and gave birth to a son there in October 1811. She persuaded a Prussian officer and his Creole wife to pretend that they were the parents of the baby, who was put into the charge of his grandmother, Madame de Souza.

One of the most important duties of Napoleon's secret police was to spy on the members of the imperial family, and they discovered about Hortense's love affair and the birth of the child. A full report of the affair was duly sent to Napoleon, but as usual he was more indulgent to Hortense than he would have been to any other member of his family who had become involved in such a predicament. The details about the birth of the baby and the names of its parents were falsified in the records at the local council offices, at the orders, and under the supervision, of the secret police, and as soon as she had recovered from the effects of her confinement Hortense resumed her position in society. The whole matter was effectively hushed up, though rumours circulated. The baby grew up to become the Duc de Morny and to play a very prominent political role in the reign of his half-brother, Napoleon III.[33]

Paris was exceptionally gay and carefree during the carnival of 1812. Napoleon had never been more powerful, though the war was not going well in Spain. The people sang the popular song:

> Bientôt plus de guerre,
> Tous les rois sont morts,
> Il n'y a que l'Angleterre
> Qui résiste encore.[34]

In June the Emperor led his army into Russia, and by September he was in Moscow. Hortense found Paris unbearable, because all the men seemed to be in Russia.[35] Throughout November and December the newspapers, publishing communiqués from the Emperor's headquarters written two or three weeks earlier, reported that the army was coming home from Moscow in triumph in a winter which was turning out to be exceptionally mild. Just before Christmas it was known that the weather on the Russian plains had suddenly turned very cold, that the army had suffered heavy losses, and that the Emperor had met with a great military disaster. Almost at the same time Napoleon himself arrived in Paris, having left the command of the remnants of the Grand Army in Russia to Murat and Eugène de Beauharnais. Although he assembled another army for next year's campaign, a mood of despondency spread in Paris, and the superstitious noted that the new year began on a Friday and included the unlucky number, thirteen, in the date 1813.[36]

Napoleon had ordered that the annual New Year's Day celebration should be particularly festive this year. Hortense, after attending a state reception at the Tuileries in the morning, took the children in the afternoon to Malmaison to wish Josephine a happy new year. They returned to Paris, where Hortense was due to attend a dinner party at the Tuileries in the evening. As her hairdresser, the famous Charbonier, fixed her hair for the dinner party, the children as usual played around. Louis Napoleon, aged four, stood under the long, ash-blonde hair which hung down his mother's back as Charbonier combed it out. She urged Charbonier to hurry, for she feared that the Emperor would scold her if she were late for the dinner. Charbonier insisted that he must do the job well, for otherwise the Emperor might make some comment about her unsatisfactory coiffure, and his reputation as a hairdresser would be ruined. Hortense's new lady-in-waiting, Mademoiselle Cochelet, realized that the chief concern of both the Queen and the hairdresser was to avoid displeasing the Emperor.[37]

The campaign of 1813, after an encouraging start, ended disastrously for Napoleon, when his armies were defeated by the Allies at Leipzig in October; but the year passed happily for Napoleon Louis and Louis Napoleon in the Rue Cerutti, at Saint-Leu, and at Malmaison. In May the Empress Marie Louise, whom Napoleon had appointed Regent during his absence with the army, visited Hortense at Saint-Leu. In the evening an entertainment was provided for her, a performance by the comedian Brunet and his company. The children were allowed to stay up to watch the show. Napoleon Louis enjoyed it greatly, but Louis Napoleon fell asleep.[38]

In May Hortense went as usual to Aix-les-Bains, where she had the terrible experience of seeing her intimate friend Madame de Broc, the sister-in-law of Marshal Ney, slip and fall into a waterfall and lose her life. The children had stayed with Josephine at Malmaison. When Hortense returned to Saint-Leu, she stayed there only a few days and then set off at the beginning of September for another holiday at Dieppe.[39] This time she took the children with her. They were accompanied by her ladies and by a new member of the household, the Abbé Bertrand, who had recently been appointed tutor to Napoleon Louis. As Louis Napoleon grew older, the Abbé acted as tutor to the younger as well as the elder boy. Bertrand was a charming, and rather lazy, elderly man, who spent more time paying compliments to Hortense's young ladies, and in making witty conversation, than in giving lessons to the boys.

Hortense had rented a little mansion outside Dieppe, near the sea. They stayed here for a fortnight, visiting the eleventh-century Norman castle at Arques and the site of Henri IV's famous victory in 1589, and walking in the town of Dieppe, where Hortense spoke to the people and introduced her two sons to them. Arrangements had been made for her to bathe in the sea in one of the new bathing-machines which had been in use in England before the turn of the century but had only recently been introduced into France. She put on a woollen chocolate-coloured bathing dress, tightly fastened at the neck and stretching down to the ankles, an ugly garment which could not look elegant even when worn by Queen Hortense. Clad in this costume, she walked along the sea-front, surrounded by gaping crowds who were held back by the police as she entered the bathing-machine. She was then carried into the sea by two sailors who dipped the machine, with the Queen inside it, into the water, repeating the operation several times. The sailors were so clumsy that Hortense stopped her sea-bathes after three days.

When the time came to return to Saint-Leu, they left Dieppe at 11 p.m. and travelled by night, as Hortense did not wish to make arrangements for a night's lodging on the road. Earlier that day, Hortense's ladies had noticed a sailing ship waiting out at sea some miles from the coast. They decided to tease and frighten old Abbé Bertrand by pretending that Hortense was leaving in the middle of the night because she had been warned that it was an English ship which had been sent to kidnap her and her sons and take them as hostages to England. The Abbé took this very seriously, and became increasingly anxious as the ladies, in mock alarm, kept urging the coachman to drive faster through the night as the English were chasing them. They travelled so fast that they reached Saint-Leu, nearly a hundred miles from Dieppe, by the evening of the next day.[40]

When they returned to Paris in the autumn, they were confronted with a grim situation. Wellington's troops had crossed the Spanish frontier and were fighting on French territory, and the Russian, Prussian and Austrian armies were preparing to invade eastern France. To the bewilderment of the people of Paris, their soldiers were now fighting, not to conquer foreign nations a thousand miles away, but to defend the soil of the motherland as they had done in 1792. The Emperor was in Paris encouraging morale and raising new armies to drive out the invader. Hortense had her private cause for worry. On 1 January 1814 her husband unexpectedly arrived in Paris. He had heard, at Graz, of the disasters that had everywhere befallen Napoleon's armies. When the Dutch, like the other nations of occupied Europe, rose in revolt against the French garrisons, he offered to go to Holland to attempt to placate the people; but as both Napoleon and the Prince of Orange made it clear that they would not tolerate his intervention, he decided to return to Paris to support his country and his brother in the hour of danger. He was given a lukewarm reception by Napoleon, but was allowed to stay.[41]

In the face of all these troubles, it was poor consolation for Hortense to find that the Emperor had authorized the structural alterations that she desired at the Cerutti mansion, and that she now had a bedroom facing the sun. She wondered how long it would be before the room was ransacked by Cossack soldiers.[42]

CHAPTER 3

THE RESTORATION
AND THE HUNDRED DAYS

O N 25 January 1814 Napoleon left Paris, and for two months waged one of his most brilliant campaigns, winning several victories over greatly superior forces. The people of Paris waited for news in a mood of patriotic exultation. Hortense was determined to make her sons realize that a grim struggle for survival was being waged on the soil of France, and she stopped the dessert which they normally ate for their dinner in order to give them a sense of having contributed to the sacrifices which were being made on all sides to save France.[1]

On the night of 28 March, Hortense was awakened by her maid with the news that the Allied armies were at the gates of Paris. They had slipped past Napoleon's armies and were demanding the surrender of the city. Napoleon sent messages from his camp that he was marching to relieve Paris, but panic spread in the capital. The Empress-Regent Marie Louise and the courtiers and government officials prepared to flee from Paris. Hortense's first instinct was to remain, but everyone was urging her to leave.

A further complication was the attitude of Louis Bonaparte; during his stay in Paris, he had fallen in love with Hortense again, as he did from time to time. His state of health, which had progressively worsened in the last few years, prevented him from riding on horseback, so he had planned to travel with Marie Louise in her carriage, and urged Hortense to come with them to Rambouillet; but as Hortense refused to come, he stayed behind when the Empress left on the morning of 29 March, telling Hortense that he would not leave without her and Napoleon Louis. He posted a servant outside the Cerutti mansion to report to him on Hortense's movements, and asked her whether he could travel with her in her carriage now that Marie Louise had left. But Hortense was much more eager to escape from her husband than from the Russians and Prussians. 'It seemed to me that he had waited for this moment to recapture his prey',[2] she wrote.

All day on 29 March Hortense waited with the children in the Rue Cerutti, resisting the pressure to leave. But in the evening she received word from Count Regnault de St Jean d'Angély, one of the Secretaries of State, that she must go at once, as the Allies had begun to occupy the heights of Montmartre and would soon be bombarding the city. She put the children in her carriage and left for the west, with her ladies following in two other carriages, and reached Glatigny, near Versailles. The village was packed with refugees from Paris, but Hortense found lodgings for the night, and put the children to bed. More refugees were arriving every hour, and the wildest rumours were spreading among them. Just as dawn was breaking, Hortense received a message from the Military Governor of Versailles, telling her to leave Glatigny immediately, as he was evacuating Versailles and expected the enemy to occupy the area within a few hours. She woke the children and they left for Rambouillet, where they arrived on the evening of the 30th. There Hortense met her brother-in-law, King Jerome of Westphalia, who told her in confidence that Paris had surrendered and that the Allied troops had entered the city earlier that day.

Hortense's chief aim at Rambouillet was to avoid meeting her husband, who was there with the Empress Marie Louise. This she succeeded in doing, though she received a furious letter from him in which he upbraided her for leaving Paris without him. In the middle of the night she was awakened by a panic-stricken servant with the news that the Cossacks were coming. The whole village was in a state of panic, with everyone hastening to their carriages. Marie Louise and King Louis took the southern road to Chartres and Blois; Hortense decided to go in the opposite direction, to Josephine's house at Navarre near Évreux, fifty-five miles north-west of Paris. She and her party set off at once for the north-west, changing their route from time to time to avoid meeting the Cossacks. As they were passing through the Forest of Rambouillet they saw a Cossack horseman, but he was alone and made no effort to interfere with them. They reached the château of Louye that night and arrived at Navarre next morning, where Josephine welcomed them. It was 1 April.[3] On that day, Napoleon abdicated at Fontainebleau, bade farewell to his Old Guard, and surrendered to the Allies.

The Empire was overthrown; France was conquered and occupied by the foreign invader; the Bourbons had returned, with Louis XVIII as King; Napoleon was made King of Elba, and prohibited from leaving his kingdom. At Navarre, Hortense tried to explain to the children what had happened. Napoleon Louis was nine, and Louis Napoleon was three weeks short of his sixth birthday. She told them that they were no longer imperial princes, but were ordinary citizens with a very uncertain future, and that this was perhaps the best thing that could have happened to them, though they would need to exercise great patience in adversity. She thought of returning to Josephine's estate in Martinique,[4] where she would be a long way from her husband; but for the moment she was safe from him in France, as he had gone to Lausanne after leaving Marie Louise at Blois.

The Allied governments, and especially the Emperor Alexander I of Russia, had decided to promote a peace of conciliation. A week after the fall of Paris, Hortense received a letter at Navarre from Prince Leopold of Saxe-Coburg, who later married Princess Charlotte of England, and still later became the first King of the Belgians and the 'uncle Leopold' of Queen Victoria's letters. He was now serving on Tsar Alexander's staff. He informed Hortense of the Tsar's esteem for her:

> He has instructed me to express to Your Majesty and also to your August Mother the desire that he has to make your acquaintance, that he would have come to Navarre if it had not been so far away, and suggests that Malmaison would be a more agreeable place for him to meet Your Majesty and Your Majesty's children.[5]

Josephine and Hortense agreed that Josephine should meet the Tsar and try to cultivate his most useful friendship; but Hortense herself refused to meet him, either, as she stated, because she did not wish to be friendly with the conqueror of her country,[6] or, as her critics have suggested, because she was deliberately hoping to excite the Tsar, by her coquetry, into pursuing her.

Josephine, Hortense and the children returned to the neighbourhood of Paris, Josephine going to Malmaison and Hortense and the children to Rambouillet. On the afternoon of 16 April, Hortense took the children to visit Josephine at Malmaison. They found the courtyard of the house full of Cossack horsemen, and learned that the Tsar was there. Josephine introduced her daughter and grandsons to him, but Hortense was aloof. 'A cold reserve was the only attitude which I could adopt in the presence of the conqueror of my country', she wrote in later years. Josephine firmly took the children by the hand and led them round the garden, leaving the Tsar alone with Hortense. He told her how much he deplored the recent war, and offered to help her and her sons in any way that he could. By the time that Josephine and the children returned from their stroll, Hortense had thawed only a little, but the Tsar was deeply attracted to her.[7]

The French Royalists, who resented the leniency shown by Louis XVIII's government and the generous financial settlement in favour of the Bonapartes in the Treaty of Fontainebleau, did not fail to notice the friendship that appeared to be developing between the Tsar and Josephine and Hortense. The gossipmongers began talking about Alexander and Hortense. On 14 May a requiem mass was held in

Notre-Dame for the martyred King and Queen, Louis XVI and Marie Antoinette. The Tsar was the only one of the Allied sovereigns and dignitaries in Paris who did not attend the ceremony; he spent the day at Saint-Leu with Hortense, Josephine, Eugène de Beauharnais and Madame Ney. A week later, the Tsar took Hortense and the children to see the *machine de Marly*, the hydraulic engine at Marly which since 1684 had pumped water to Versailles and was to continue in operation until 1962. Hortense held Napoleon Louis's hand and the Tsar and Eugène held Louis Napoleon's. The Tsar's clothes became caught up in the machine, and he might have been killed if Hortense had not quickly pulled him away.[8]

Other Allied leaders followed the Tsar's example and called on Josephine. On 23 May the King of Prussia and his sons came to Malmaison, where they met Hortense and the children as well as Josephine. Prince William of Prussia was aged seventeen, and was serving in his first campaign with the Prussian army; he now for the first time met the six-year-old Louis Napoleon, who was to become his prisoner fifty-six years later at the Battle of Sedan. Next day the Tsar's younger brothers, the Grand Duke Nicholas – the future Tsar Nicholas I – and the Grand Duke Michael, visited Malmaison. Louis Napoleon asked whether he should address the Tsar and the King of Prussia as 'uncle', for until now every emperor and king that he had met had been one of his uncles; but he was told to address them as 'Sire'. They on their part addressed him as 'Monseigneur' and 'Your Imperial Highness', which surprised him, as all the members of the household called him 'Louis'.[9]

When Josephine went to Saint-Leu to meet the Tsar on 14 May, she caught a chill. It grew rapidly worse, and she died at Malmaison on 29 May. Napoleon Louis and Louis Napoleon were taken to her bedside to say their last farewell to the grandmother whom they had so dearly loved. The Tsar hastened to Malmaison, and was in the house with Hortense and Eugène when Josephine died. He had by now become sufficiently intimate with Hortense to tell her about his matrimonial difficulties with the Tsaritsa. He also became very friendly with Eugène.[10]

But the time had come when the Tsar had to leave France and go on a state visit to London. After completing all his engagements in Paris, he left for England thirty-six hours earlier than he had planned in order to spend a day at Saint-Leu, where he arrived with a small escort very late in the evening, and went without ceremony to the bedroom that had been prepared for him. After spending a second night at Saint-Leu, he left for England, from where he wrote several intimate letters to Hortense.[11]

Before leaving Paris he had made it plain to Louis XVIII that he would not tolerate any failure by the French government to implement the Treaty of Fontainebleau in Hortense's favour. Many of the Bourbon officials were very reluctant to do this, but eventually the treaty was carried out, after Wellington had paid a courtesy call on Hortense and had intervened with the French government on her behalf. Hortense received 400,000 francs a year for herself and her children, and the title of Duchesse de Saint-Leu which Louis XVIII conferred on her, though she lost her queenly rank. Apart from her annuity under the treaty, she had inherited seven million francs under Josephine's will, which left her with a balance of over four million francs even when Josephine's many debts had been paid.[12] Louis Bonaparte, who since his abdication as King of Holland called himself the Comte de Saint-Leu, was annoyed that Hortense had been created Duchesse de Saint-Leu, especially as the newspapers sometimes made fun of him over the discrepancy between his title and hers.

The children spent a happy year in 1814, but Louis Napoleon had one painful experience. He developed toothache, and a dentist came to the Cerutti mansion and extracted the tooth. The six-year-old boy was very brave throughout the operation, which was of course performed without any anaesthetic; but two days later he developed a haemorrhage from the gum. The aperture was filled with amadou to stop the bleeding, and he was put to bed. In the middle of the night Hortense awoke from a nightmare in which she saw him bleeding to death. She hastened to his room and found Madame Bure and the two children fast asleep, with Louis Napoleon lying in a pool of blood gushing from his mouth. Hortense sat at his side all night with her finger in the wound to stop the flow, and was convinced that but for her nightmare he would have bled to death.[13]

King Louis had been deeply hurt by her behaviour at the time of the fall of Paris; he had forgiven her for all her unkindness in the past and had stayed in Paris, risking capture by the enemy, in order to save her, only to find that she had rejected his offer of help and had preferred to fall into the hands of the Cossacks rather than escape with him. In the summer of 1814 he published a statement in a Lausanne newspaper declaring that he was bringing proceedings for a separation against her in the French courts; and he wrote to her demanding that she send Napoleon Louis to him, though he would allow her to keep Louis Napoleon. Hortense was absolutely determined not to hand over Napoleon Louis; apart from her other reasons for wishing to keep him, she knew that he and Louis Napoleon were so close to each other that both children would be very unhappy if they were separated. Louis began proceedings in the French courts to obtain the custody of Napoleon Louis.[14]

Hortense was advised by her lawyers that it was pointless for her to contest the action, because French family law gave complete control of the children to the father; but she was determined to fight. The only card which she could play was the anti-Bonaparte prejudice of the Bourbon government, and despite all her own background and her admiration for Napoleon she played it ruthlessly. She wrote to her influential friends in the government, and asked for and obtained a private interview with King Louis XVIII, in the hope that they would interfere with the ordinary judicial process by ordering the judges to find in her favour against Louis. She pointed out that if Louis Bonaparte was given the custody of Napoleon Louis, the boy, who under her recent grant from Louis XVIII was the heir to the French dukedom of Saint-Leu, would have to live abroad with a cosmopolitan father who bore the name of Bonaparte and was the brother of the hated usurper, Napoleon. When they spoke to her about the principle of paternal authority, which was enshrined in French law, she said that ordinary law must give way to the overriding interests of the state, and that the principle of paternal authority would be disregarded if Napoleon brought an action in the courts demanding that the King of Rome, who was living with his mother Marie Louise in Vienna, should be sent to him in Elba. But she received a formal communication from the Chancellor stating that the King had decided that it was impossible for him to interfere with the ordinary process of law.[15]

The trial of the action opened in the Paris Assize Court on 7 January 1815. It attracted great attention in Paris, and was widely reported in the press. Both parties were represented by the most eminent advocates at the Paris bar. Maître Bonnet, who appeared for Hortense, was a dramatic and brilliant orator who specialized in making emotional appeals to juries; Maître Tripier, Louis's counsel, was a profound and subtle lawyer, who presented his arguments dispassionately with cool, unemotional logic. Maître Bonnet made a strong attack on all the Bonapartes, and a passionate appeal for the rights of a mother against the archaic laws which considered only those of the father; Maître Tripier countered the effect of Bonnet's eloquence by a slow and lucid speech in reply, in which he showed that there was nothing in the law which could override a father's power over his children as laid down in Section 560 of the French Civil Code.

The advocates concluded their arguments on 10 February, and the court reserved judgment. Maître Bonnet's speech had been so brilliant that many people thought that, despite everything, Hortense would win; but on 8 March the court gave judgment in Louis's favour, and ruled that Napoleon Louis must be sent to him within three months. Seven days earlier, Napoleon had landed in the south of France, and by 8 March he was advancing on Paris and the first report of his return from Elba had appeared in the Paris newspapers.[16]

Napoleon's return to France for the Hundred Days was the most formative event in the youth of Louis Napoleon. The events of March 1815 convinced him that a Bonaparte had only to land in France with a handful of men and the whole nation would rally to him, and that only foreign armies of intervention could impose any other ruler upon the French people.

On 6 March, Hortense was returning from a walk when she met Lord Kinnaird, an English acquaintance of hers, who was out riding. He told her that he had just heard that Napoleon had landed at Cannes. He warned her that there might be an outburst of anti-Bonapartist feeling among the Royalists, and that she and the children might be in danger. She arranged to send the children to stay with the mother of a friend of her lady-in-waiting, Mademoiselle Cochelet, at a little house in the country near Paris, and they went there the same evening. As soon as it was dark, Mademoiselle Cochelet told the boys that Hortense was sending them away to a place of safety because they might otherwise be in danger, that they had no reason to worry about their mother's safety and would see her again soon, and that they must not utter a sound during their journey. She took them, accompanied by Madame Bure, through the garden of the Cerutti mansion and out into the street through the back gate. They walked through the dark streets for a considerable distance to a place where Hortense's manservant was waiting for them in a cab; it had been thought safer not to bring the cab to the garden gate in case it was seen and followed by Royalists, who would thus discover the children's hiding place. They arrived safely at their destination in the country. Napoleon Louis and Louis Napoleon greatly enjoyed their nocturnal walk and the drive in the cab, though they had kept absolutely quiet in conformity with Mademoiselle Cochelet's orders and with the spirit of the adventure.[17]

Hortense herself stayed on in the Cerutti mansion for another five days, but on 11 March she moved to the house of a mulatto woman, whom she had known in Martinique, in the Rue Duphot in Paris. She feared for her safety because rumours were circulating that she had been responsible for Napoleon's return from Elba.[18] By this time she had heard that her husband had won the lawsuit, but she was too excited by the news of Napoleon's landing to worry about the court's decision, and she was sure that she could persuade Napoleon to set it aside if he returned as Emperor.

When Napoleon landed at Golfe-Juan he issued a proclamation in which he declared: 'The eagle . . . will fly from steeple to steeple until it reaches the towers of Notre-Dame.' The royal troops who were sent against him went over to his side, and on the afternoon of 19 March Louis XVIII fled from Paris and took refuge in Dutch territory in Ghent. Hortense, from the window of the house in the Rue Duphot, watched the local Royalists remove the white ribbons from their button-holes, and by next day the streets around the Tuileries were crowded with excited people awaiting the arrival of the Emperor. He eventually drove up in his carriage at 9 p.m. As soon as she heard the news, Hortense drove to the Tuileries to greet him; but he received her very coldly, and accused her of having collaborated with the Bourbons. After a time he suddenly asked her why she had not brought the children with her, and she promised to bring them next day. She had already sent Mademoiselle Cochelet to fetch them. Mademoiselle Cochelet found them playing in the little garden of the middle-class house in the country. They had spent a very happy fortnight there, away from Abbé Bertrand and their lessons, and enjoying a greater freedom than they had known among the under-governesses and servants in the Cerutti mansion, though for security reasons they had not been allowed to go for walks outside the garden.[19]

Hortense took them to the Tuileries on the morning of 21 March. Napoleon was as cool to her as he had been on the previous evening, but he greeted the boys very warmly, and embraced them with great affection. The crowds were still surrounding the palace, cheering the Emperor and calling for him to appear at the window. Napoleon took Napoleon Louis and Louis Napoleon by the hand, and went to the open casement-window, where they were greeted with tremendous enthusiasm by the people. Hortense, who had been left behind in the room, pushed her way to the front and joined them at the window.*[20]

In the afternoon, Napoleon reviewed the army in the Place du Carrousel near the Tuileries, where his old soldiers had been waiting to greet him since 3 a.m. Napoleon Louis and Louis Napoleon asked Hortense to be allowed to see the parade, and watched the cheering and marching troops with great delight.[21]

Napoleon soon forgave Hortense, and on 12 April he came to lunch at Malmaison. By this time he was hastily preparing an army to resist the Allied invasion. Already before he reached Paris, the Allied statesmen at the Congress of Vienna had issued their famous declaration of 15 March: 'The Powers ... declare that Napoleon Bonaparte has placed himself outside civil and social relations, and that, as the enemy and disturber of the peace of the World, he has delivered himself to public punishment.' Napoleon sent messages to the Allied governments

*This, I believe, is what happened, though Hortense, in her memoirs, tries to make out that she was pushed to the front against her will by the pressure of the other people in the room.

offering peace and friendship, but none of them replied or were willing to receive his letters. He also announced his intention of reigning in France as a liberal and constitutional Emperor, and promised the people a completely different type of government from the dictatorship which he had established during his previous reign. He issued decrees establishing the freedom of the press, and went several times to the Faubourg Saint-Antoine, where the revolutionary artisans demanded arms in order to fight, under his leadership, to prevent the re-enslavement of France by the Bourbons.[22]

Eugène de Beauharnais was in Vienna in attendance on Tsar Alexander, with whom he had been on very friendly terms ever since their meetings at Saint-Leu in the previous year. Immediately after Napoleon reached Paris, Hortense wrote to both Eugène and the Tsar and told them that the French people were tired of war and would never permit Napoleon to resume it, but that the whole nation had enthusiastically welcomed his return because the people wished to be ruled by him and not by the Bourbons. She received an anonymous reply from the Tsar, which he communicated to her indirectly through Louise Cochelet. 'Neither peace, nor truce, no more reconciliation with this man; all Europe says the same. Apart from this man, anything you like; no preference for anyone; as soon as he is set aside, no war.' Some Liberals urged Napoleon to resign to save France; but Hortense thought that if he were to retire, this would merely mean that liberal and pacifist France would have to face the Allied invasion without the only man whom the people would follow and whose military genius could give them a chance of victory. The Allied statesmen in Vienna wished to arrest Eugène and imprison him in a fortress in Bohemia; but the Tsar intervened on his behalf, and he was allowed to remain at liberty after he had given his word of honour to stay neutral in the coming war.[23]

Napoleon Louis and Louis Napoleon spent the summer of the Hundred Days at the Cerutti mansion. They were often taken in a carriage to the Bois de Boulogne, where they walked and played in the wood. One morning they were walking there with Hortense, the Duchesse de Bassano and Mademoiselle Cochelet, when they noticed five sinister-looking individuals lurking in the wood and showing an unhealthy interest in the little Princes. The children were hastily put in the carriage and driven back to the Cerutti mansion. Napoleon had wrongly interpreted the outlawry proclamation of the Allied statesmen as an incitement to assassinate him, and Hortense and her household feared that the men in the Bois de Boulogne had been sent to murder or kidnap his nephews. After this the boys were not allowed to go to the Bois de Boulogne, but took their daily exercise and play in the gardens of the Tuileries or in the Champs-Élysées.[24]

Marie Louise and her son, the King of Rome, remained in Vienna during the Hundred Days, and the people thought that Napoleon, deprived of the company of his own son, was lavishing his parental affection on Hortense's children, and giving them the place which would normally have been filled by the King of Rome. After his reconciliation with Hortense in April, she and the boys were invited to take their place on state occasions and at the military parades which were repeatedly held to whip up the enthusiasm of the people of Paris. The boys were present with Hortense at the great ceremony in the Champ-de-Mars on 1 June, when the Emperor took an oath to uphold the new liberal constitution which he had granted, and the people pledged their loyalty to him and their determination to resist the attempts of foreign tyrants to impose Bourbon despotism upon them at the point of the bayonet.[25]

Napoleon decided to forestall his enemies' preparations for an invasion of France by destroying their armies in Belgium. On Sunday 11 June he invited Hortense, Napoleon Louis and Louis Napoleon to attend one of those private family lunches at the Tuileries which he had always held on the day before his departure to join his armies at the start of a new campaign. He was very gay, and discussed literature during the lunch. In the evening he received his ministers, and at his instructions Hortense brought the children to say good-bye to him. The story that the seven-year-old Louis Napoleon begged the Emperor not to go on his campaign because he had a premonition that some terrible disaster would befall him is certainly untrue. Apart from its improbability, it is not mentioned by either Hortense or Louise Cochelet in their memoirs, or by any writer before Persigny, the most unscrupulous of all Bonapartist propagandists, first published it in 1840.

Hortense and the children stayed with Napoleon until quite late in the evening. A few hours after they had gone he left Paris at 4 a.m. and joined his army at Avesnes.[26] On 14 June he led them into Belgium after issuing his Order of the Day:

Soldiers! Today is the anniversary of Marengo and Friedland, which twice decided the fate of Europe. Then, as after Austerlitz, as after Wagram, we were too generous. We believed in the protestations and the oaths of the princes whom we allowed to remain on the throne. Today . . . they have begun the most unjust aggression. Let us go to meet them![27]

This was already the beginning of the new Napoleonic myth, of Napoleon as the over-generous conqueror and the victim of unjust aggression in 1815, which was to become firmly planted in the mind of Louis Napoleon.

CHAPTER 4

THE ROAD TO EXILE

A WEEK after the farewell party at the Tuileries, on the afternoon of Sunday 18 June 1815, the people of Paris heard the roar of cannon. It was the guns of the Invalides firing a salute to the Emperor's victory over the Prussians at Ligny two days before, the news of which had just reached Paris. At the same hour the guns were firing on the battlefield of Waterloo. Next day, as the shattered remnants of the French army staggered back across the frontier into France, the Paris newspapers carried the reports of the victory at Ligny on 16 June.

Hortense had invited some friends to the Cerutti mansion on the afternoon of Tuesday 20 June to hear Benjamin Constant read his autobiographical novel, *Adolphe*, which was not published until later in the year. As the tragic climax of the novel was reached, most of those present, including Constant himself, were in tears. During the reading Hortense was informed that the Duc de Rovigo, the head of the secret police, had arrived and wished to speak to her immediately. He told her that there were unconfirmed rumours that the Emperor had suffered a disastrous defeat in Belgium. Hortense returned to Constant and her guests and gave no indication, either by word or gesture, of what had occurred. When they left her they had no idea that she had received bad news which, if true, meant utter ruin for her. That evening General Sébastiani called on her and confirmed the full extent of the defeat at Waterloo.[1]

Napoleon reached Paris on the morning of 21 June, when the press published the news of the defeat. Next day he abdicated. The Chambers proclaimed his son, the King of Rome, as Napoleon II. Napoleon asked Hortense if he could come to stay with her for a few days at Malmaison, a house which had happy associations for him from the days that he had spent there with Josephine. Hortense's friends urged her to refuse, warning her that she would fatally compromise herself, and perhaps risk assassination by Royalists, if she identified herself now with the fallen Emperor; but in one of the few completely disinterested actions of her life, she refused to abandon Napoleon at such a time. She sent the children to stay with a woman who owned a hosiery shop in the

39

Boulevard Montmartre, and went herself to Malmaison to receive Napoleon.

He arrived on 25 June and stayed there for four days. He knew that resistance was hopeless, but could not decide what to do. The Allied armies had entered France and were advancing on Paris, refusing to recognize Napoleon II and closely followed by King Louis XVIII and his entourage; rumours reached Malmaison that they had bypassed Paris and would arrive any hour at Malmaison. Eventually Napoleon decided to go to America. He told Hortense to follow him as soon as possible with her children, so that they could all live together in the United States; but though she urged him to go at once to an Atlantic port and sail as soon as possible, he could not bring himself to leave Malmaison.

At last, on 29 June, he decided to go, but asked first to see the children once again to say good-bye to them. Hortense was not happy about this; she feared that if she sent a carriage to bring the children from the Boulevard Montmartre to Malmaison and to take them back again to the Boulevard Montmartre, this would attract attention and might lead to their hiding place being discovered by Royalists. But she could not refuse Napoleon's last request. The boys were brought to Malmaison and taken back that same afternoon after spending a short time with Napoleon, without anyone noticing the coming and going of the carriage to the humble shop in the Boulevard Montmartre.

Napoleon left at 5 p.m. on 29 June and made his way to Rochefort. On 8 July he took ship, hoping to reach the United States, but was intercepted by the British warship *Bellerophon*, to whom he surrendered. He and the Bonapartist propagandists later alleged that he had surrendered on a promise of safe-conduct which was shamefully violated by the British government, but in fact Captain Maitland of the *Bellerophon* refused to give him any guarantees when he offered to surrender. He was taken to Plymouth, and after a few weeks set sail for St Helena. At Malmaison, after he had left, Hortense wandered round the house, looking for the last time at the art treasures which she knew would soon be confiscated by the Allied authorities or destroyed by the Cossack soldiers. Then she returned to the Cerutti mansion, leaving the boys in the Boulevard Montmartre.[2]

On 3 July the Allied armies entered Paris and King Louis XVIII arrived five days later. Hortense was warned by her friends that she was in danger, because it had been widely reported that Napoleon had stayed with her at Malmaison. One day, as she walked in her garden, a band of Royalist irregulars – the famous Chouans of the Vendée – drove past the house. They saw and recognized her, made threatening gestures, and shouted abuse. After this she decided to go into hiding, and moved to a little house in the Rue Taitbout at the end of the garden of the Cerutti mansion. As this seemed to be a safe hiding place, she brought the children there from the Boulevard Montmartre. But on 10 July the Austrian Field-Marshal Prince von Schwarzenberg commandeered the Cerutti mansion and established his headquarters on the ground floor. Hortense thought that with the Austrian Commander-in-Chief and his staff in the house, she would be safe there from French Royalist partisans, and with Schwarzenberg's consent she returned to the Cerutti mansion and lived in rooms on the first floor. She kept the children in hiding in the little house in the Rue Taitbout.[3]

Tsar Alexander had entered Paris with the Allied armies. Hortense was determined not to make any approach to him, but she expected that he would approach her. The Tsar made no move. She heard from mutual acquaintances that he was angry that she had supported Napoleon during the Hundred Days after she had accepted his friendship in 1814 and the pension and title from Louis XVIII. He was also annoyed because he had been told – untruly, according to Hortense – that she had boasted, in a letter to a friend, that she could twist him round her little finger any time she chose. He decided not to be fooled a second time. When Napoleon's mistress, the Polish Countess Marie Walewska, interceded with him on behalf of Madame Mère, who was complaining of vexations from the occupying authorities, he replied: 'Why should I bother any more about that family? Look at Queen Hortense. I protected her in 1814. Well, she is the cause of all the troubles which have befallen France.'[4]

A few days after she had returned to the Cerutti mansion, Hortense saw the Tsar ride into the courtyard with an escort of Cossack cavalry. He had come to pay a courtesy call on Prince von Schwarzenberg. She expected him to come up to the first floor to visit her after he had finished his talk with Schwarzenberg, but he left the Cerutti mansion without making any attempt to see her. Although she told her ladies that she would have refused to see him if he had asked leave to call on her, she had hoped that he would try to approach her, and she was both saddened and alarmed at his failure to do so. A few days later the Paris newspaper *L'Indépendant*, no doubt as a result of the Tsar's visit to the Cerutti mansion, reported that he had met Hortense and Madame Mère. On 21 July *Le Moniteur* published a statement, officially authorized by the Tsar, denying the report, as 'His Majesty the Emperor Alexander has not granted to any of the persons named the honour of being admitted to his presence.' Hortense interpreted this as a public notice to all concerned that the Tsar would not intervene to protect her.[5]

She wrote to Alexander, returning all his letters, and saying that if he no longer desired her friendship she would consider their relationship to be terminated. He replied with a cold and formal letter in which he stated that her conduct during the Hundred Days had been unpardonable. But he continued his friendship with Eugène, and when, some time afterwards, he met Louise Cochelet, with whom he had become quite intimate in 1814, she felt that he was now less bitter about Hortense, though he had been too deeply hurt by her conduct to be willing to resume their former relationship. He helped Hortense and Eugène by buying, and returning to their former owners, some of the *objets d'art* at Malmaison which Napoleon had seized as war booty and given to Josephine, so that Hortense and Eugène received the money for these *objets d'art*, which would otherwise have been confiscated.[6]

Hortense's chief anxiety was for her children, and she made plans to get them safely out of France. Her friend Gabriel Delessert had a Swiss manservant, and she obtained a passport in the name of this servant for himself and his wife and two children. Her plan was that her own manservant and Madame Bure should travel to Switzerland with Napoleon Louis and Louis Napoleon, passing themselves off as the Swiss servant and his wife and children. But on the morning of 17 July she received an order from General Baron von Müffling, the Prussian commander who had been appointed Military Governor of Paris by the Allies, requiring her to leave Paris within two hours, and offering to provide a military escort to convey her to the frontier, as the authorities had heard that French Royalists intended to attack her. It was widely believed that she was planning to leave France with all her valuable jewellery and vast sums of money in cash; robbers, as well as Royalists, were said to be lying in wait for her carriage on the road from Paris to the frontier.

Hortense sent her major-domo to General Müffling's headquarters to say that it was absolutely impossible for her to be ready to leave in two hours. The General agreed to extend the time, but insisted that she must leave before nightfall on that day. Hortense began feverish preparations for her departure. But what should she do about the children? General Müffling had given her passports for the children, but she could not decide whether it would be safer for them to travel with her in her carriage, which might be attacked by Royalists or bandits but would be under the protection of an Allied military escort, or, as she had originally planned, for them to go with her manservant and Madame Bure on the false Swiss passport. In the end she decided to take them with her, and they were hastily fetched from the house in the Rue Taitbout. Hortense left Paris at 9 p.m. on 17 July, with the two boys, Madame Bure, and a lady and a gentleman of her household.[7] They were escorted by a small detachment of Austrian cavalry under the command of Captain von Woyna, a twenty-year-old officer who later became a Field-Marshal and an Ambassador. They travelled in three carriages, with Hortense and the children in the first, Woyna and Hortense's gentleman in the second, Madame Bure and Hortense's lady-in-waiting in the third, and the troopers riding at their side.

They stayed the night at Bercy, which at that time was outside Paris, thus complying with the order to leave Paris the same day. After three days' travelling, on the evening of 20 July, they reached Dijon, which had been occupied by the Austrian army on the previous day. This was fortunate for Hortense, for hardly had they arrived at the inn at Dijon when it was surrounded by a crowd of French Royalists demonstrating against her. A band of Royalist partisans forced their way into the inn, led by a very young lad with a sword which was much too big for him and clattered on the ground at his side. He announced that he had come to arrest Hortense. Woyna told him that she was under the protection of the Allied army of occupation, and invoked the help of the commander of the Austrian troops in Dijon. The partisans told the Austrian commander that Woyna was a Bonapartist impersonating an Austrian officer, but fortunately the commander turned out to be a personal friend of Woyna. As the partisans had made it clear that they intended to prevent Hortense from leaving next morning, Woyna persuaded the general commanding the French troops in the area to call a military parade for the hour of departure, which all the partisan units were ordered to attend. The young partisan leader disobeyed the order and turned up again at the inn, but as all his followers were attending the parade, he could do nothing but glower in anger as Hortense and the children came down from their bedroom, closely surrounded by the Austrian troopers, and drove off with Woyna and their escort towards the frontier. By the evening they had reached the Hôtel d'Angleterre in the village of Le Sècheron on the northern outskirts of Geneva, in Swiss territory.[8]

The journey had been a bitter experience for Hortense. Like all Bonapartists, she had believed that the whole French nation was loyal to Napoleon and united against the foreigner, and had indignantly declared that she had no need to be protected from Frenchmen by foreign soldiers. The events at Dijon had shown clearly that this was untrue, and she felt compelled, despite her prejudices, to thank Woyna for his protection and for the courtesy which he had shown her throughout the journey.[9]

When he left her at Le Sècheron and returned to Paris, she soon discovered how much she still needed the help of the Allied military authorities. The pro-French Radical government of Switzerland had been overthrown after Austrian troops occupied the country in 1813, and the old constitution of the Helvetic Confederation, which gave almost sovereign powers to the cantons, was restored. The Conservative governments of the cantons had no sympathy for Bonapartists. On 28 July 1815 the French Ambassador* to Switzerland wrote to the President of the Swiss Diet asking the Swiss to refuse permission to live in Switzerland 'to any of those individuals who participated in the infamous revolution which has recently taken place in France', and the President of the Diet promised to ask all the governments of the cantons to refuse asylum to the Bonapartists.[10]

A few days earlier, Madame Mère and Cardinal Fesch had arrived in Geneva, but they were promptly ordered to leave the territory of the canton. Before going on to Italy they visited Hortense and her children at Le Sècheron. In this time of adversity Madame Mère forgave Hortense all her unkindness to King Louis, and warmly thanked her for having given hospitality to Napoleon at Malmaison after Waterloo. At Le Sècheron, Hortense learned for the first time the tragic news of Napoleon's capture by the English. The report in the Paris newspaper, the *Journal de Paris*, stated that on the English ship *Bellerophon*, Bonaparte had ended the journey which had begun at Elba with the connivance of 'Madame Hortense'.[11]

She also heard of the decree issued by Louis XVIII on 24 July, ordering that nineteen prominent Bonapartists, including Marshal Ney and Hortense's friend La Bédoyère, should be put on trial for treason if they were apprehended. The decree provided that all persons expelled from France were to be given one year in which to sell their property in France, after which it would be confiscated by the state. But Hortense could not even try to forestall confiscation by selling the Cerutti mansion and the house and estate at Saint-Leu, because her husband claimed these properties which Napoleon had taken from him and given to Hortense in 1810. In September 1815 Louis sold both the properties. The house at Saint-Leu, which was resold four years later to the Bourbon Prince de Condé, was pulled down after Condé hanged himself in 1830; the Cerutti mansion passed into the ownership of the Rothschilds, who lived there throughout the Second Empire, and was demolished in 1899.[12]

Hortense had not been more than a few days at Le Sècheron when the government of the canton of Geneva ordered her to leave. She had hoped that she would be allowed to live on the estate at Prégny which she had inherited from Josephine, but as Prégny was also in the canton

---

*At this time the title of 'ambassador' was given only to the diplomatic representatives of the Great Powers in one another's countries; the heads of all other diplomatic missions, including all the diplomatic representatives of the United States, were called 'ministers'. They were often, however, informally referred to as 'ambassadors', and this term is used throughout this book in order to avoid confusion.

of Geneva she was not permitted to go there. She therefore moved to Aix-les-Bains in Savoy, where she rented a rather gloomy and ugly house. She was joined there by Mademoiselle Cochelet, the Abbé Bertrand, and other members of her household.

The Congress of Vienna had restored the province of Savoy to the King of Sardinia – the ruler of Piedmont, who had held Savoy until 1792 as the descendant of the ancient Dukes of Savoy – and the Piedmontese army had begun to take over the territory from the Austrians. The Piedmontese Military Governor was very hostile to Hortense. At first she was not permitted to leave her house unless accompanied by a Piedmontese officer; but the Austrian military authorities again came to her help, and ordered the Piedmontese to allow her freedom of movement provided that she stayed in Aix.

Hortense heard nothing but bad news at Aix – the arrest of Marshal Ney, the execution of La Bédoyère, and the lynching of Marshal Brune by a Royalist mob in Provence; and she suffered a heavy blow when her lover, Flahault, visited her and told her that he was about to marry a Scottish girl, Lord Keith's daughter Margaret Elphinstone, with whom he had fallen deeply in love. But the children settled in happily at Aix. They made friends with two or three little boys living near them, and played at soldiers in the courtyard of Hortense's house, with Napoleon Louis, who at the age of ten was the eldest of them, acting the part of the general with a tin sword, Louis Napoleon carrying out his orders with a wooden sword, and the smallest of their friends beating on Louis Napoleon's toy drum. The neighbours watched their play, and talked about it; the story was repeated with exaggerations; and a report reached the Piedmontese military authorities that a band of Bonapartist partisans was undergoing military training at Hortense's house.

At the end of August, Hortense was visited at Aix-les-Bains by two gentlemen of her husband's household. Louis Bonaparte had remained in Rome during the Hundred Days, and had assured the Pope of his loyalty to the Allied cause. Now that Louis XVIII's authority was restored in France, he called on Hortense to comply with the decree of the Paris court which had given him custody of Napoleon Louis, and asked her to hand the boy over to the gentlemen of his household. Hortense realized that she could not oppose him in the present circumstances, and in view of the uncertainty and dangers which confronted her she felt that she could not honestly deny that Napoleon Louis might be better off with his father. After prevaricating for a month she sadly let him go, and he left for Italy at the beginning of October. The separation was as painful to Louis Napoleon as it was to Hortense. He had always been delicate, and he now fell ill with an attack of jaundice. Hortense believed that this was caused by his grief at his separation from his brother.[13]

Meanwhile the Allied governments had issued a declaration on 27 August stating that they had decided 'that the places of residence of the members of Bonaparte's family must be subject to restrictions, because their places of residence cannot fail to concern the maintenance of public order'. They added that they would permit Louis Bonaparte to live in the Papal States and Hortense in Switzerland, where she would be under the surveillance of the British, Austrian, Russian, Prussian and French ambassadors.[14]

On 21 October the Allied governments authorized Hortense and Louis Napoleon to live in the canton of Saint-Gall; but the Genevan authorities refused to give her a transit visa to pass through their canton on her way to Saint-Gall. Hortense did not wish to live in Saint-Gall, where she had no friends, and she wrote to Woyna in Paris asking him to use his influence to obtain permission for her to go to Constance in the Grand Duchy of Baden; the Grand Duke of Baden had married Hortense's cousin and friend, Stéphanie de Beauharnais. At the end of November, Woyna obtained permission for Hortense and Louis Napoleon to live in Constance. About the same time she heard from the Federal Swiss authorities that the canton of Saint-Gall had not yet decided whether to grant her application to live in the canton, but that if she wished to go to Constance they would grant her a transit visa for her to travel through the cantons of Geneva, Vaud, Berne, Aargau and Thurgau. She left Aix-les-Bains on 28 November with Louis Napoleon and the members of her household.[15]

It was an eventful journey. The weather had turned very cold, and snow lay on the ground. After crossing the border into the canton of Geneva, Hortense, not wishing to spend the night at an uncomfortable inn, went to her property of Prégny and slept there. At 4 a.m. the house was surrounded by Swiss police, who angrily told her that the terms of her visa did not permit her to go to Prégny. The authorities were particularly nervous because Metternich was paying an official visit to Geneva, but Hortense and her party were eventually allowed to continue on their journey. They stayed a night at Lausanne and another at Payerne, and then entered the canton of Freiburg, although they had not obtained a transit visa for Freiburg. They had reached Morat and had only a few miles to go before leaving the canton when they were stopped by the police and informed that they had entered Freiburg illegally. The police refused to allow them to proceed, and to Hortense's indignation forced her to remain for two days at the local inn at Morat, which was uncomfortable and cold. Then they were allowed to go on, and at last reached Constance on the evening of 7 December.[16]

CHAPTER 5

MONSIEUR LE BAS

ON arriving at Constance, Hortense and Louis Napoleon and their retinue took uncomfortable rooms at the Hôtel de l'Aigle. A few days after their arrival the Chamberlain of the Grand Duke of Baden called on Hortense and informed her that the Grand Duke regretted that he was unable to permit her to stay in his territories, because the Great Powers had forbidden him to grant asylum to any Bonaparte. Hortense said that she was too tired and ill to travel for the time being, and begged to be allowed to stay until she received permission to live in the canton of Saint-Gall. The government of Baden relented, and she remained in Constance for seventeen months.

After a few weeks in the discomfort of the Hôtel de l'Aigle, Hortense rented a house in the suburb of Petershausen in Constance early in the new year. When the spring came, she found a charming spot overlooking Lake Constance which delighted her. She wished to buy it and build a house there which she could make her permanent home. But the government of Baden refused to permit her to buy land in Baden, and reminded her that she would not be allowed to remain permanently in the Grand Duchy.

They could get French newspapers in Constance, but the news was depressing. Almost as soon as they arrived they heard of the execution of Marshal Ney, and next month of the statute of 12 January 1816 which permanently banished all members of the Bonaparte family from France, prohibiting them from entering the kingdom on pain of death. She also heard from her husband. Louis, who had become a very devout Catholic and was high in favour at the court of Rome, had fallen in love with the daughter of a high Papal official. As he wished to marry her, he began divorce proceedings aganst Hortense on one of the grounds recognized by the Catholic Church as justifying a dissolution of a marriage – that he had been forced to marry Hortense against his will, under duress. He contacted Hortense at Constance, but she told him that she would oppose a divorce; either, as she claimed, in order to safeguard the position of her children or out of a desire to spite Louis. In any case, Louis's argument about the duress was ridiculous, and he abandoned his action;

he could get no evidence to support it, and it was strongly disapproved of by his prospective father-in-law and the officials in Rome.[1]

With all her troubles, Hortense was fortunate in one respect: she was immensely rich. This was to have an important influence on the lives of her family for the next hundred years. Neither Hortense in Constance in 1816, Louis Napoleon in London twenty-three years later, or his widow Eugénie at Farnborough at the beginning of the twentieth century, were ever short of money. They were able not only to live in luxury, with a large household, but also to finance Bonapartist newspapers in France and buy uniforms and firearms for Bonapartist filibustering expeditions. Even after Hortense had lost her pension from Louis XVIII, and the Cerutti mansion and Saint-Leu, she still had Josephine's fortune of nearly 4 million francs, much of which consisted of property outside France, chiefly in Italy. Her income was about 70,000 francs a year – £275,000 tax free at today's prices. She also had many pieces of valuable jewellery which Napoleon had given her, and from time to time she would sell a diamond or other heirloom when she needed money urgently. Both she and Louis Napoleon sometimes complained of being in financial difficulties and made strict economies, but this was never anything worse than a temporary shortage of cash, and they were always able to borrow money on the security of their assets.

Like other people who had been brought up to believe in Liberty, Equality and Fraternity, Hortense was more conscious than earlier generations of the extreme inequalities of wealth in early nineteenth-century society. She had taught Louis Napoleon to be conscious of it when he was a little prince in Paris, and she continued to implant it in him in exile at Constance. She encouraged him to mix with people of lower rank, and at Constance, as at Aix-les-Bains, he played with the neighbours' children. One day, escaping from his aged and lazy tutor the Abbé Bertrand, he went out walking by himself. In the street he met two boys begging for alms. As he had no money in his pocket, he gave the boys his jacket and his shoes, and returned home barefoot and in his shirt-sleeves.

In June 1816 Hortense took Louis Napoleon to visit his uncle Eugène at his château at Starnberg near Munich. Eugène had married in Napoleon's time the daughter of the King of Bavaria, who had then been Napoleon's ally but had joined the Allies in 1813. Eugène was now living at the court of his father-in-law, with the title of Duke of Leuchtenberg and Prince of Eichstädt; he was still in favour with Tsar Alexander. Louis Napoleon played with Eugène's children, one of whom later became Queen of Sweden, another King Consort of Portugal, and a third Empress of Brazil. At Starnberg they were surprised and delighted to meet an unexpected guest – the Comte de Lavalette. He was a devoted Bonapartist, and was one of the officers in Louis XVIII's army who joined Napoleon during the Hundred Days. He had been sentenced to death, but escaped from prison a few days before the date fixed for his execution when his wife visited him and remained behind in his cell while he walked out disguised in her clothes. He was later smuggled out of France by the British general, Sir Robert Wilson, who had Radical sympathies and served a short prison sentence for his part in the escape. The Allied governments were searching all over Europe for Lavalette, but he was hiding in a cottage in the grounds of Eugène's house at Starnberg. Lavalette played with Louis Napoleon, who adored him, but the boy was not let into the secret of his identity until several years afterwards.

In September 1816 Hortense's cousin Stéphanie, the Grand Duchess of Baden, decided to visit Hortense at Constance. The French Ambassador to Baden learned about the intended visit, and not only protested strongly to the Grand Duke's government, but renewed his demand that Hortense and Louis Napoleon should be expelled from the Grand Duchy. The Grand Duke regretfully told Hortense that she would have to leave as soon as possible, though she had still not been granted permission by the government of Saint-Gall to live in the canton. Hortense had meanwhile received a very courteous letter from Metternich, informing her that she would be welcome in Austria, and suggesting that if she enjoyed living on Lake Constance she should move to the Austrian town of Bregenz at the eastern end of the lake, where she would be treated with the respect to which she was entitled. Hortense did not fall into the trap: she realized that Metternich wished to hold her and Louis Napoleon in Austria in the honourable and disguised captivity in which he already held Napoleon's son, the former King of Rome, now the Duke of Reichstadt. It was the policy of the Allied powers to make it impossible for the Bonapartes to live in the smaller European states in order to force them to accept the hospitality of the Great Powers. Hortense replied with a tactful and non-committal answer.

She was playing for time. In the summer of 1816 she and Louise Cochelet had been for a short holiday in Switzerland, leaving Louis Napoleon with the Abbé Bertrand and the household at Constance. During her visit she had seen a small romantic castle at Arenenberg in Thurgau which had greatly attracted her. It stood on the south shore of the inner lake on the western side of Lake Constance, with splendid views over the lake of the surrounding woods, of a number of near-by villages, churches and other castles, and of the Isle of Reichenau. She wished to buy Arenenberg, though she realized that she would have to enlarge and modernize the house. The Liberals who controlled the government of Thurgau were prepared to allow her to live in the canton, and in February 1817 she purchased Arenenberg, having taken the precaution of inserting a clause in the contract which stipulated that the purchase should be rescinded if the Great Powers refused to permit her to live in Thurgau.

But Hortense did not wish to spend all her time in a place as remote as Arenenberg. She therefore asked Eugène to use his influence to obtain permission for her to purchase another residence in Bavaria. She wrote to Tsar Alexander, and although she received only a cold and non-committal answer from his Foreign Minister, Capo d'Istria,[2] the Tsar used his influence in her favour, and her request was granted. She realized that it would be undesirable for her to live in Munich with the court, so she bought a house at Augsburg.

On 6 May 1817 Hortense, Louis Napoleon and the household left Constance and moved to Augsburg. Soon afterwards the repairs and improvements at Arenenberg were completed, and Hortense moved in.[3] The Great Powers offered no objection to her living there, though the British Ambassador to Switzerland, the young Stratford Canning, reported to Castlereagh that it was an undesirable place for her to live in, as it would be very difficult for a secret agent to keep the house under observation without being seen himself.[4] Hortense and Louis Napoleon usually lived at Augsburg during the winter and spent the summer at Arenenberg.

Louis Bonaparte now made another overture to Hortense. In October 1817 he sent Napoleon Louis to stay with her for two months at Augsburg, and asked her to bring Louis Napoleon to see him. Hortense agreed, and in the summer of 1818 took Louis Napoleon to Leghorn, and Louis brought Napoleon Louis there. At Leghorn, Louis fell in love with Hortense again. He persuaded the two boys to go on their knees to her and beg her to return to him so that they could all live together. Hortense was disgusted that Louis could use the children for this purpose, especially just after he had begun divorce proceedings against her. She was determined to give him nothing that he wanted, neither her love nor a divorce, and she and Louis Napoleon resumed their separate lives apart from Louis and Napoleon Louis.[5]

At Augsburg and Arenenberg, Louis Napoleon continued his studies with the Abbé Bertrand. These did not advance very far. The abbé spent his time discussing literature and politics with Hortense, flirting with her ladies and being teased by them, and engaging in a long and learned correspondence with eminent European scholars, and studying his favourite subject of French medieval heraldry; but he did not concentrate on the boring task of teaching Louis Napoleon French grammar, Latin and arithmetic.[6] Everyone agreed that Louis Napoleon was a charming and very lovable child, and had real abilities, though he could not equal his precocious and brilliant elder brother. Hortense herself taught him drawing and dancing, spending a few hours every day, and nearly all day Saturday, with him. He showed a real aptitude for drawing, and would fill in any spare moment sketching some real or imaginary object, usually a romantic subject like a soldier or an eagle. He was handicapped by a delicate constitution, but he engaged in outdoor activities such as riding and swimming, and became a strong swimmer. He seemed to be lazy and to lack mental concentration. This was perhaps because the Abbé Bertrand was not a good teacher; Louis Napoleon was so bored with the Abbé's lessons that he used to wish that he was a bird and could fly out of the window and escape.[7]

By the autumn of 1819, when Louis Napoleon was aged eleven, Hortense became conscious that he was not making enough progress with Bertrand; and though she had no intention of turning the Abbé out of her household, she looked for a more energetic tutor for Louis Napoleon. A young man of twenty-five named Philippe Le Bas was recommended to her. He was the son of a Parisian artisan who had been a member of the Committee of Public Safety during the Reign of Terror and a supporter of Robespierre. Philippe Le Bas was five weeks old in July 1794 when Robespierre was guillotined and his father committed suicide in prison to avoid the same fate. Madame Le Bas and her baby were promptly arrested and imprisoned for four months in the Conciergerie. They were released in the middle of the cold and hungry winter of 1794–5 to find themselves victimized and penniless, and Madame Le Bas was forced to work as one of the washerwomen of the Seine to earn enough to buy a little food for her baby. He was lucky to survive, and grew up devoted to the memory of his father and of Robespierre, and with a hatred for the men of Thermidor, the middle classes and the rich. As a boy he joined the navy, but transferred to the army and took part in the campaigns of 1813 and 1814. He had recently married a young wife, but had been further embittered by the death of their new-born child. In 1819 he was trying to earn a modest living as a tutor.[8]

As a republican and Jacobin, he did not approve of the Bonapartes, but preferred them to the Bourbons,[9] and had no objection to taking employment with Hortense. Indeed, he welcomed the opportunity to inculcate republican principles into a young Bonaparte, and to impose a frugal and Spartan way of life on a pampered little prince. He was resolved to teach Louis Napoleon that 'a virtuous and educated man is superior to a titled valet who has no merit except his ignorance and his name'.[10] The chief drawback to the job was that Hortense insisted that her son's tutor should be a single man, or, if he was married, that his wife should not live with him in the household, for she did not wish him to be distracted from his duties. Le Bas could not afford to turn down a well-paid job, and had no alternative but to agree to a temporary separation from his wife.[11]

He took up his duties as Louis Napoleon's tutor in June 1820. Soon after he arrived at Arenenberg, Hortense had a long talk with him, and asked him all about himself. When he told her about his young wife and the loss of their child, she was so touched that she offered to relax her rule against wives, and invited Madame Le Bas to come and live near Arenenberg. When she arrived, Hortense was particularly charming to her, and arranged for her to stay in a little house near by, while Le Bas lived alone with Louis Napoleon in two rooms in an annexe to Hortense's house. After December 1821, Hortense allowed Le Bas and his wife to live together in her house at Augsburg.[12]

Le Bas was shocked at the indolence and backwardness of Louis Napoleon. After six weeks he was in despair. The boy was aged twelve, but was at the stage of development of a normal child of seven. He could not spell French properly; he knew hardly any Latin grammar; his arithmetic was dreadful; it had taken him half an hour to explain to Le Bas what a verb was, for he had the greatest difficulty in explaining even those things which he did understand. Yet Le Bas felt that he was not really unintelligent, and that he could be saved by strict discipline and very hard work. Louis Napoleon was in the habit of getting up at 7 a.m., 8 a.m. or even 9 a.m.; but Le Bas made him get up at 6 a.m., walk in the mountains till 7 a.m., and do three hours of grammar and Latin before breakfast at 10.30. At 11.30 work was resumed with lessons in arithmetic, German and Greek. From 3 to 4 p.m. his manservant took him swimming, which was followed by a history or geography lesson from 4 to 6 p.m. After dinner at six, which was followed by a walk, an hour was spent from 8 to 9 recapitulating the lessons of the day, and at 9 p.m. the boy was sent to bed.

After the indulgent régime of the Abbé Bertrand, Louis Napoleon found that his daily schedule of nine-and-a-half hours' lessons was a strain, and he became nervous and agitated. Monsieur Le Bas believed that this was due to the physical exertions of his riding, swimming and dancing, and suppressed all these recreations; in future his only exercise was to be walks with Monsieur Le Bas, during which he would be taught botany and astronomy, so as not to waste time which could be spent in learning. When the autumn came, and they moved from Arenenberg to Augsburg, Le Bas, who believed that the boy was still backward, increased the working hours; in winter Louis Napoleon was to rise at 6.30 a.m., and from then until he went to bed at 9 p.m. he was to spend one hour at meals, two hours at play and exercise, and the remaining eleven-and-a-half hours at his lessons. He became very nervous, and had nightmares nearly every night, often being awake for two or three hours during the night. Le Bas decided not to punish him for this, because he thought that he could not help it, but he showed no indulgence to the weakness. The Abbé Bertrand had allowed Louis Napoleon to have a candle burning all night, as he was afraid of the dark; Monsieur Le Bas, who was perhaps conscious that many children in the slums of the Faubourg St Antoine had to sleep in the dark because their parents could not afford candles, refused to permit Louis Napoleon to have the candle. After a few days the boy no longer screamed with terror for half the night.

Le Bas's stern methods produced beneficial results in a few months, and Hortense was very pleased with Louis Napoleon's progress. She allowed Le Bas a free hand, but insisted that every evening, before Louis Napoleon went to bed, he should spend an hour with her and her ladies in the drawing-room. Le Bas did not approve of this, but was powerless to prevent it. All the rest of the day he and Louis Napoleon were completely isolated and alone together, but this one hour which they spent in the drawing-room seemed to Le Bas to be not only a waste of time but also positively dangerous, for it taught the boy to engage in idle conversation.

Le Bas suggested to Hortense that Louis Napoleon should be sent to school at the well-known *Gymnasium* in Augsburg, where he would meet other boys and be subjected to the spur of their competition. Hortense agreed, and Louis Napoleon began attending the *Gymnasium* in April 1821. It was hard for him to have to do his lessons in German instead of in his native French, but Le Bas believed that he could overcome this handicap. In view of the language difficulty Le Bas was reasonably satisfied when, in his first term at the school, Louis Napoleon came fifty-fourth out of the ninety-four pupils in his class in a test which involved writing a composition in German, translating a passage from German into Latin, and solving a problem in arithmetic. In his second test he was fiftieth in the class, but by the time of the third test in June 1821 he had risen to twenty-fourth. Le Bas congratulated himself on having 'won this victory over maternal affection'.[13]

Hortense and all the household were delighted, and the Abbé Bertrand wrote from Arenenberg to congratulate Le Bas. 'You say, comrade, that Monsieur Oui-oui has jumped from being fifty-something to twenty-fourth. Well, what a triumph for you republican curs! We old Ultras are not capable of achieving such prodigious feats.'[14] In February 1822 Louis Napoleon came fourth out of sixty-six in his class, though all the other boys were Germans taking the test in their native language.

Louis Napoleon was aged thirteen in the summer of 1821 when he heard of Napoleon's death. Napoleon died at St Helena on 5 May, but it took two months for the news to reach Europe. The Abbé Bertrand, who had accompanied Hortense on a journey to Baden, wrote from there on 14 July to tell Le Bas that he was to break the news to Louis Napoleon. After performing this duty, Le Bas gave his pupil three days' holiday from his lessons in order to give him time to recover from the shock.[15] On 24 July, Louis Napoleon wrote to Hortense:

> When I do wrong, if I think of that *great man*, I seem to feel his shade within me telling me to be worthy of the name of Napoleon. . . . If my usual gaiety sometimes returns, this does not mean that my heart is not sad and that I have not an everlasting hatred for the English.[16]

As Louis Napoleon continued to make good progress and to learn algebra, the Aeneid and the Odyssey, Monsieur Le Bas became increasingly pleased with him, though he still commented on his lack of concentration and his weakness in mathematics. One of his worries was that Louis Bonaparte expected Louis Napoleon to visit him in Italy from time to time. Le Bas felt that this would mean a long break in the boy's studies, and as Hortense was very ready to uphold Le Bas's objections to the visit, Louis Napoleon did not go to see his father. But in September 1823 Louis visited Arenenberg with Napoleon Louis, and persuaded Hortense to allow him to take Louis Napoleon, with Le Bas in attendance, to spend a short holiday with him and Napoleon Louis at Marienbad in Bohemia. Le Bas's encounter with Louis Bonaparte at Arenenberg and Marienbad confirmed his worst fears. He took a strong dislike to Louis, with his indolence and his changeable moods, and was distressed to see that Louis Napoleon did virtually no work at all at Marienbad, because his father was continually offering him enjoyable but unprofitable distractions.[17]

Le Bas was equally perturbed when, beginning with the winter of 1823–4, Hortense insisted on taking Louis Napoleon with her to Italy and spending six months of each year, from November to May, in Rome and on the road between there and Arenenberg. Le Bas went with them, and was treated as a favoured member of the household. He was introduced to several Bonaparte and other Princes and Princesses; but he was worried because Louis Napoleon's studies suffered badly. Louis Napoleon went to bed late, went out riding every day at noon, returned exhausted three hours later, yawned at his studies till 5 p.m., and spent the rest of the day at his father's; and he did virtually no lessons at all on the long journeys between Arenenberg and Rome.[18] On several occasions Le Bas complained, in his letters to his family, that 'a solid education cannot be given on the great highways'.[19]

Louis Napoleon was just sixteen when they returned from Italy to Arenenberg in May 1824. Between Rimini and Bologna they crossed the stream which was probably the Rubicon that Julius Caesar crossed when he marched on Rome to make himself dictator. In a dry May there was barely a trickle of water, but Louis Napoleon was very excited to see the Rubicon; he got out of the carriage and filled a bottle with water from the stream.[20] Twenty-seven years later, when he planned his *coup d'état* of December 1851, he gave it the code name 'Rubicon'.

Le Bas stayed with Louis Napoleon for seven years until his pupil was aged nineteen. He had become genuinely fond of Louis Napoleon, and was touched by the sincere friendship that the young Prince felt for him and his wife. But the older the boy grew, the more disillusioned Le Bas became. For the first three years of his tutorship, Hortense had given him a free hand, and had approved of his efforts to educate her son by discipline and hard work; but after Louis Napoleon reached the age of fifteen, Hortense thought that other things than study should play a part in his life, and encouraged him to ride, hunt and attend balls and parties with young men and women of his own age in high society in Rome and Florence. Le Bas became conscious once again of the vices of princes and aristocrats as he became less and less able to control the destinies of his pupil. He felt ill at ease at Arenenberg at the big house parties with Casimir Delavigne and the Grand Duchess Stéphanie of Baden, though she had once written him a charming letter.[21] He complained of 'the comedies, the shows, the parties on the water, in carriages, and everything that it is possible to invent in order to waste time', and told his stepfather, the old Jacobin: 'I never feel so lonely as when I am in high society.'[22] Louis Napoleon, on his side, became more and more irked at Le Bas's attempts to impose restrictions on him, and became aware of Le Bas's resentment of royal and aristocratic privilege. He said that Le Bas could not bear always having to take the third best helping of chicken.[23]

In September 1827, when they were at Arenenberg, Hortense suddenly dismissed Le Bas, telling him that his services would no longer be required after 1 October. Though she thanked him for all that he had done in the past seven years, he deeply resented the manner of his dismissal, and felt that he should have been given more than three weeks' notice, and paid until 1 January. He wrote her a bitter letter of protest, but then decided not to send it. He returned to Paris and, finding that he had no academic qualifications, enrolled as a student at the university at the age of thirty-four, and after obtaining his degree was in due course appointed to important academic posts as a professor of Greek and of ancient history.[24]

He remained a republican and Jacobin sympathizer all his life, and opposed Louis Napoleon's election as President of the Republic in 1848, his *coup d'état* in 1851, and his assumption of the imperial title in 1852. During Louis Napoleon's presidency, Le Bas had occasion to write to Falloux, the Minister of Public Instruction, and did not hide his opinions: 'I am a republican, Monsieur le Ministre, a republican by birth, and I have never ceased to be so, not even when I was tutor to Charles Louis Napoleon Bonaparte.'[25]

He met Louis Napoleon only once again after leaving Arenenberg in October 1827. On New Year's Day 1859, as President of the Institut de France, it was his duty to present the delegations of the five national Academies to the Emperor Napoleon III. Neither the former tutor nor the former pupil gave any sign of recognizing the other. Some people said that the Emperor wished to invite Le Bas to the Tuileries to have a friendly talk with him about old times, and was prevented by the Empress, who disapproved of Le Bas's republican politics; but this is probably a typical Radical anti-Eugénie story.[26]

When Le Bas died in May 1860, his funeral oration was given by the President of the Académie des Inscriptions et Belles-Lettres. The speaker referred at length to Le Bas's years of public service to education, but did not mention his connection with the Emperor.[27]

CHAPTER 6

REVOLUTION IN THE ROMAGNA

THE winters that Louis Napoleon spent in Italy were a very for-mative influence in his life. They brought him into contact not only with many members of the Bonaparte family, but also with English tourists and Italian revolutionaries who perhaps had their share of responsibility for the pro-British and pro-Italian policy of France during the Second Empire.

Italy had become the meeting-place of the Bonapartes. Louis Napoleon's father, King Louis (now the Comte de Saint-Leu), had houses in Florence and Rome; his uncle Lucien (now Prince of Canino) lived in Rome, as did Madame Mère and Cardinal Fesch. The Cardinal, like the Comte de Saint-Leu, had become a staunch supporter of the old régime and Papal power, and played his part at the Papal court and in the College of Cardinals as an orthodox Papist, if not an Ultra-montane reactionary. Louis Napoleon's aunt, Caroline Murat, the former Queen of Naples, lived at Trieste, but often came to Italy. His other two aunts, Elisa and Pauline, were dead by 1825, but he sometimes met their husbands, the Corsican Félix Bacciochi and Prince Camillo Borghese. His uncle Jerome, King of Westphalia (now the Prince de Montfort), lived in Baden, but like Hortense usually spent the winter in Rome.

Louis Napoleon occasionally met the black sheep of the family, Jerome's first wife, Elizabeth Patterson of Baltimore, whose marriage to Jerome had been annulled by Napoleon and by his subservient Pope. As long as Napoleon was Emperor of the French, Elizabeth Patterson had agreed to stay in the United States and to keep her mouth shut in return for a pension which he paid her, but after 1815 she frequently came to Europe, especially to Italy, and took part in the life of European high society which she greatly enjoyed, styling herself 'Madame Bonaparte' and shocking people at dinners and parties by the coarse-ness of her language and by her gossip about the love affairs and im-potence of leading figures in society.[1]

The only absent members of the family were Napoleon II, the former King of Rome, now Duke of Reichstadt, whom Metternich did

57

not permit to leave Austria, and King Joseph (now Comte de Survilliers). He had gone to the United States in 1815 and lived at his house near Bordentown in New Jersey.

Madame Mère, who was nearing eighty, lived alone with her servants in the Palazzo Rinuccini at the corner of the Corso and the Piazza Venezia in Rome. She never left the house, and as she was nearly blind she could no longer knit, sew or read. She depended on the services of her long-suffering companion, Mademoiselle Rose Mellini, who had lived there with her since 1816; they hardly ever saw anyone outside the household, except the members of the Bonaparte family who came to talk to Madame Mère, or to read to her, when they were in Rome. Letizia lived entirely in the past, talking with animation about the days when she had escaped with her children from the nationalists in Corsica in 1793, and about the glories of her son Napoleon, for whom she had interceded so movingly and so unsuccessfully with the Allied governments when he was a prisoner on St Helena.[2]

Of the younger generation of Bonapartes, Napoleon Louis had married his cousin Charlotte, King Joseph's daughter. He was showing every sign of fulfilling his early promise. He had opened a paper factory at Serravezza, near Spezia, designing all the machines himself, and had developed a great interest in aeronautics and revolutionary politics. Men had been flying in balloons for nearly fifty years, but Napoleon Louis was experimenting with projects for mechanical flight through the air by means of revolving propellers. He had also invented a new method of producing steel, as well as writing a history of Florence.[3] Lucien's son, Carlo Bonaparte of Canino, had become a zoologist, and like Napoleon Louis, King Jerome's son Prince Jerome, and Lucien's younger son Pierre, was connected with Radical revolutionary groups in Italy. Jerome's other two children by his second marriage, Princess Mathilde and Prince Napoleon, were younger, being born in 1820 and 1822.

Louis Napoleon met a number of young Englishmen in Italy. He had been brought up to hate the English as the chief enemy of France and as the persecutors of the fallen Emperor at St Helena. Napoleon had certainly not been ill-treated at St Helena; but he had been involved in friction with the Governor, Sir Hudson Lowe, who had received orders from the British government not to recognize his title of Emperor and to refer to him as 'General Bonaparte'. This was deeply resented by Napoleon. The books published by Napoleon's attendants at St Helena gave the impression that the Emperor had been bullied, insulted and half-starved by Hudson Lowe, though the daily allowance of twelve bottles of wine, 75 lb of beef or mutton, 30 lb of cheese, 32 lb of bread, 225 lb of butter, and thirty-four eggs, plus nine hams per month,[4] for Napoleon and his retinue seems to fall a long way short of a starvation diet.

There had always been a Radical minority in Britain, and a handful of members of the House of Lords and the House of Commons, who sympathized with the French Revolution and with Napoleon, and opposed the war which Britain was waging against France. Pro-French feeling among the Whigs increased after Waterloo with the removal of the danger from France and the growth of feelings of magnanimity to the defeated enemy and of opposition to the Tory government's support for the reactionary policy of their allies in the Holy Alliance. This sympathy for Napoleon was particularly strong among those English noblemen and intellectuals who visited Italy in the years after 1815, when it became fashionable either to reside there permanently or to spend the winter in Rome, Florence or Venice. Many of them were eager to pay their respects to Queen Hortense, and she and Louis Napoleon often met them at dinners, balls and receptions. Hortense liked these young Englishmen with their charming manners, their fluent French, and their guilty conscience about Napoleon at St Helena and Castlereagh's foreign policy, and Louis Napoleon did not allow his theoretical hatred of England to interfere with his personal friendships for these English visitors to Italy.

He became particularly friendly with one of them, Lord Fitzharris, the Earl of Malmesbury's son. Fitzharris was introduced to Hortense by the Countess Guiccioli, who had been Byron's mistress. He was very sympathetic to the Bonapartes, although his family had always played a leading part in Tory politics. His old friendship with Louis Napoleon was useful, though it was also occasionally embarrassing, when Louis Napoleon was Emperor of the French and Fitzharris, as the third Earl of Malmesbury, was British Foreign Secretary in the 1850s. It was at this time that Louis Napoleon first became friendly with Count d'Orsay, whose father had been one of Napoleon's generals. D'Orsay, after serving as an officer in the army of Louis XVIII, had established himself as a leader of fashion in London, where he lived with his mistress, the Countess of Blessington, when they were not travelling together in Italy. Another of Louis Napoleon's friends in Rome was Edward Blount, an adventurous young gentleman from a Roman Catholic family in Worcestershire, who had been given an appointment at the British Consulate in Rome. He met Louis Napoleon during the winter of 1830–1, and often went riding with him in the Borghese Gardens.

Malmesbury and Blount have described in their memoirs their impressions of Louis Napoleon in Italy, when he was aged twenty-one and twenty-two. He was handsome in the romantic way which was so much admired at the time. He did not look strong or robust, but his pallid face, which was emphasized by his dark hair and moustache, and his slim figure gave him an attractively delicate appearance. He dressed expensively and stylishly. Unlike his voluble and extrovert elder brother, he was taciturn, reserved and even shy; but the young ladies who fell in love at first sight with the gallant Napoleon Louis were intrigued, and a little baffled, by the dark, mysterious Louis Napoleon. When Louis Napoleon mounted a horse, he was transformed; the melancholy, frail young man became a dashing and reckless cavalier, galloping down the cobbled streets of Rome, scattering the pedestrians and vaulting over every obstacle in his horse's path.[5]

It was an era of revolutionary youth, of the younger generation in revolt against their parents on a scale which was not to be seen again until the latter half of the twentieth century. In 1815 the *ancien régime* appeared to have triumphed over Napoleon and the revolutionary Liberalism to which he had turned for support during the Hundred Days. In France, the Bourbons had been restored, in Spain the Inquisition, and in Rome the rule of the Papal hierarchy, which had suppressed the popular education, vaccination and street lighting which had been introduced by Eugène de Beauharnais as Napoleon's Viceroy, and reimposed torture and the discriminatory laws against the Jews. In the Netherlands and Prussia, two rigid and intolerant Protestant autocrats, like the Anglican Tory government in Britain, persecuted Roman Catholics and Radical atheists with the tacit approval of the Pope, who likewise refused to condemn the suppression of Polish freedom and the ill-treatment of the Catholic Poles by the Christian Orthodox Tsar of Russia. The younger generation revolted against the autocrats. Throughout Europe, particularly in Italy, the young men wore their hair long, grew beards and smoked cigars as a gesture of protest, and disrupted classes at high schools and universities. The authorities closed the schools and universities, expelled the unruly students, and ordered the police, when they met young men in the street wearing long hair and beards, to march them off to the barber's and have them forcibly cropped and shaved.

But a more sinister form of resistance developed in the secret society of the Carbonari, the first of the modern revolutionary 'underground' organizations. The Carbonari built up the type of illegal organization which was adopted in later years by their imitators, from Mazzini's Young Italy to the resistance movements during the Second World War and by terrorist groups in recent years. Each group was composed of only a handful of members, so that any member who was interrogated and tortured, and any police agent who had infiltrated the movement, would be unable to reveal the names of more than a few of his comrades. Only one member of each group had links with a regional committee, but through these links the central leadership maintained a rigid discipline over all the groups and members, which it enforced if necessary by the assassination of traitors, informers and dissidents.[6]

Though the Carbonari were strongest in Italy, they were an international organization with branches in Spain and France. They arranged for French and Italian members to travel to Spain to fight for the Liberals during the revolutionary upheaval of 1820–3. They even had a few contacts in Britain. In January 1831 the Paris police informed the British Ambassador, Lord Granville, that four French and Italian revolutionaries had come to London to meet their English supporters and were staying at the King's Arms Tavern in Compton Street, Soho.[7]

By 1830 rumours were circulating that Napoleon Louis and Louis Napoleon were members of the Carbonari, and historians ever since have been arguing about the truth of these rumours. In view of the secrecy of the Carbonari organization, it is not surprising that it is impossible to prove whether or not they were members. The Carbonari relied on the sympathy and help of supporters, and of those who today would be called 'fellow-travellers', and it is not very important whether Napoleon Louis and Louis Napoleon were actually members of the Carbonari, or only fellow-travellers. Many years later, at Chislehurst, when he had no reason for concealing the truth, Louis Napoleon told a friend that he had never been a member of the Carbonari; and in 1908 his widow Eugénie repeated this in a letter sent through an intermediary to the Italian historian, Luzio. Perhaps Napoleon Louis, who lived permanently in Italy, was a member, while Louis Napoleon, who spent half the year in Switzerland, was only a fellow-traveller.[8]

In 1821 the Carbonari, who had many supporters among the aristocracy and the younger army officers, organized a successful revolution in Piedmont and Naples; but Metternich sent the Austrian army in Lombardy to crush them, and the leaders of the risings were incarcerated for many years in the Austrian dungeons in the Spielberg fortress in Moravia. A few months earlier a revolution had broken out in Spain, and had forced King Ferdinand VII to grant a Liberal constitution, with freedom of the press and universal manhood suffrage. In 1823 the powers of the Holy Alliance authorized King Louis XVIII's government to send the French army across the Pyrenees to overthrow the Liberal régime in Spain, and though the French commanders promised an amnesty to the revolutionaries, King Ferdinand violated its terms, and the Liberal leaders were executed or sentenced to long terms of imprisonment.

The revolutions in Italy and Spain had been suppressed while Louis Napoleon was still a child, but the Greek War of Independence against Turkey was still continuing after seven years of struggle when he reached the age of twenty. Byron had lost his life fighting in Greece, and so had Lucien Bonaparte's son Paul; and Louis Napoleon was one of a number of young idealists who were eager to fight for Greek freedom. In May 1828 Russia, having declared war on Turkey, invaded the Turkish provinces of Moldavia and Walachia – the modern Romania – in support of the Greeks, and in January 1829 Louis Napoleon, who was with Hortense in Rome, wrote to his father in Florence asking his permission to join the Russian army in Romania. Hortense, after some hesitation, had approved of the idea, because she thought that she could arrange for Louis Napoleon to be on the Tsar's General Staff.

Not surprisingly, the cautious Louis was more opposed to the scheme than Hortense. He replied that he could well understand that Louis Napoleon was eager to help the Russians drive the Turkish barbarians from Europe and to win military glory in war; but war was a very terrible thing, and no one had any excuse for taking part in it except for the interests of his own country and the defence of its soil. Louis Napoleon followed his father's advice and did not volunteer. He was perhaps not altogether sorry to have an excuse to remain with his mother at Arenenberg and to enjoy the gaieties of social life in Rome.[9]

But he was determined to put on a military uniform and perform some kind of military service. He applied for admission to the military academy at Thun, which had recently been opened by the Swiss government for the training of officers for the Federal army. The government of the Confederation had doubts about accepting him; he was not a Swiss citizen, and to have a Bonaparte serving in the Swiss army might displease the Great Powers, and above all Charles X's government in France. But after a considerable delay his request was granted, and he joined the college at Thun in June 1830. The commanding officer at the college was Colonel Dufour, who had fought in Napoleon's army, and later, as General Dufour, was to lead the Federal and Liberal forces to victory in the Swiss Civil War of 1847.

The cadets at Thun were put through a course of hard training, but Louis Napoleon survived it and showed that, both physically and mentally, he was tougher than he looked and than his mother and friends gave him credit for. He rose at 5.45 every morning, marched thirty miles and more a day with a pack on his back, up and down the mountains surrounding Lake Thun, and slept in the open air on the edge of the glaciers.[10] He had been less than a month at Thun when he heard the news that delighted the Bonapartes and shook all Europe – the outbreak of the revolution of 1830 in France.

On 27 July the people of Paris rose and fought for three days on the barricades. The army went over to their side, and King Charles X abdicated and fled to England. When the news reached Thun, everyone in the college was pleased, and Louis Napoleon was exhilarated. 'We are very quiet in our little corner while further afield people are fighting for our dearest interests', he wrote to Hortense. 'At this very moment the Tricolore is flying in France. Happy those who first succeeded in restoring it to its old glamour!'[11]

Many Republicans and Bonapartists had taken part in the rising in Paris, but the benefit of the victory went to Charles X's cousin, Louis Philippe, Duke of Orleans. He had been connected with the opposition parties under the Bourbon monarchy, and he now became King. Joseph Bonaparte issued a protest on behalf of the Duke of Reichstadt, who was living under Metternich's eye in Vienna and was not free to act, in which he denounced Louis Philippe's usurpation of the throne which of right belonged to the Emperor Napoleon II; but the revolution in Paris was everywhere accepted as a sign that Liberalism was once again on the march. It took several years for the absolutist sovereigns of Europe to realize that Louis Philippe was not a dangerous revolutionary, and for the Liberals in other countries to discover that they could not look for aid to France, the country of the revolution.[12] The Bonapartes had hoped that they would now be able to return to France, but on 11 September 1830 Louis Philippe's Parliament passed an Act renewing the Law of 12 January 1816 under which all members of the Bonaparte family were banished from France on pain of death.

The July revolution in Paris had immediate repercussions throughout Europe. Within a month, revolution had broken out in Brussels, the Dutch garrisons were expelled, and in due course the Great Powers recognized the independence of Belgium, with Prince Leopold of Saxe-Coburg reigning as a constitutional King. In November the Poles in Warsaw rose in revolt against the Tsar, and it took the Russian armies nine months to reconquer the country and once again enslave Poland. The spirit of revolution spread throughout northern Italy and in the Papal States.

In October 1830 Louis Napoleon, having been granted indefinite leave from the military college at Thun, left Arenenberg with Hortense, her new lady-in-waiting Mademoiselle Valérie Masuyer, and other members of her household, to spend the winter as usual in Florence and Rome. They took the new road through the Tirol to Bolzano and Trent, and on to Venice. As they crossed the battlefields of Napoleon's campaign of 1796–7 Louis Napoleon gave his mother's ladies a detailed description of the marches, manoeuvres and battles in which the Emperor had engaged so triumphantly thirty-four years before. On 23 October they reached Venice, and Louis Napoleon, seizing the oar of a gondola, rowed them to their hotel near the Rialto bridge. During their stay in Venice he walked down to the harbour and saw a French ship, which had docked there, flying the new French flag, the Tricolore. He was delighted to see the Tricolore, and spoke to the sailors.[13]

Hortense and Louis Napoleon continued their journey and, crossing the frontier from Austrian territory into the Papal States, arrived in Bologna, where they were invited to dinner by Prince Bacciochi, the widower of Elisa Bonaparte. Elisa's son Félix, who was aged fifteen, had strong Radical sympathies, which were not approved of by his German tutor. During dinner at Bacciochi's, Louis Napoleon, having discovered the conservative and anti-Italian prejudices of the tutor, delighted his cousin Félix and enraged the tutor by singing revolutionary Italian songs.[14]

After dinner they were taken to Bacciochi's box at the opera to see Rossini's *La Donna del Lago*, which was based on Sir Walter Scott's popular poem, 'The Lady of the Lake'. Although it was usual, in Italian theatres, to put out the lights in the auditorium during the performance, the opera house at Bologna left them full on, and Hortense, who had dressed in her best evening *toilette*, attracted great attention as she sat in the box with Louis Napoleon, young Félix Bacciochi and Valérie Masuyer. The leading male part was played by the very popular tenor, Rubini; but the part of the leading lady, which was usually sung by Rubini's French wife, Adèle Chomel, had at the last moment been given to a less well known soprano who was popularly believed to be the mistress of Cardinal Benvenuti, the Papal Legate and Governor of Bologna. This had angered the opera-going public; they thought that the casting was a flagrant example of the favouritism and immorality which prevailed among the hierarchy in the Papal States.

The management was expecting trouble, and in the hope of averting a demonstration had posted notices announcing that no encores would be demanded or sung. Rubini's first entrance was greeted with tremendous enthusiasm, and his first aria with a demand for an encore. He thereupon sang the forbidden encore, to the applause of the audience. When the leading lady appeared, she was booed and hissed before she had sung a note, and there were calls for Adèle Chomel. The noise got worse during the second act, with every song of Rubini's being encored, and whenever the leading lady sang her voice was drowned by the clamour. On two occasions the curtain was lowered, and once the performance was suspended for an hour while the demonstrations continued. Eventually the manager announced that the performance would be abandoned and the theatre cleared. During the demonstrations, Louis Napoleon and Félix rose in their box and joined in as ostentatiously as possible, calling 'encore' for Rubini and booing the leading lady in full view of every member of the audience in the lighted auditorium. Hortense was annoyed; she told the young men that it was disgraceful for her son and nephew to behave in such a manner in public. They said that there was no other way in which they could make their protest against Papal tyranny.[15]

On 1 November they reached Florence and met Napoleon Louis, who was enthusiastic about the revolution in France and the chances of a rising to liberate Italy from Austrian, Papal and ducal despotism. The older members of the Bonaparte family were alarmed at the attitude of the young men. King Louis and Cardinal Fesch did not wish their sons and nephews to do anything to discredit them with the Pope and the Great Powers; Louis, with his cautious and worrying disposition, was particularly anxious, both because of his anxiety for his beloved Napoleon Louis and for the sake of his own reputation. Madame Mère disapproved for different reasons; she could not understand why nearly all her grandchildren were supporting the revolution in France and Italy when the only thing that ought to concern them was that the King of Rome should succeed to his rightful place as Emperor of the French.*[16]

Hortense was much more sympathetic to her sons' political attitude than were any other of the older Bonapartes, but she did not share the young men's optimism. She told them that she had been taught the realities of international power politics by the great Napoleon, that she had no doubt that if revolution broke out in Italy the Austrians would again intervene to crush it, and that the fact that La Fayette and other leading figures in Paris were making speeches in support of Italian freedom did not mean that the French government would take active measures to prevent the Austrians from sending troops into the Duchies and the Papal States. Nor did she have the republican enthusiasm of Napoleon Louis and Louis Napoleon. Her experiences of 1794 and the Eighteenth Brumaire had convinced her that the cause of progress and Liberalism could be victorious only under the leadership of a dictator.[17]

As usual they met several of their Bonaparte relations in Florence. Lucien Bonaparte and his wife Alexandrine, the divorcee whom he had married to Napoleon's disgust, came with their son Louis Lucien and Alexandrine's daughter by her first marriage to Monsieur Jouberthon. Mademoiselle Anna Jouberthon had married Prince Hercolani at an early age and was a widow by the time she was twenty; in 1830, at thirty-two, she was one of the most beautiful women in Florence, with her perfect figure and her jet-black hair and eyes and her long dark lashes. Louis Napoleon fell in love with her at first sight, but he was too shy to approach this majestic beauty, who was ten years older than he,

*Although the obvious meaning of this passage in Valérie Masuyer's memoirs is that it was Hortense, not Madame Mère, who held these opinions, there is no doubt that Valérie Masuyer was referring to Madame Mère.

and, having bought a small gift for her, he timidly asked his sister-in-law Charlotte to present it to her, which Charlotte refused to do. He met Princess Hercolani again on the following evening, when she came to a party at Hortense's and recited part of a drama in verse written by her stepfather Lucien. Louis Napoleon was overcome by the combination of Princess Hercolani's beauty and Lucien's Liberal sentiments. He gazed at Anna in admiration during her recital, and burst into applause when she reached the line 'La femme d'un tyran ne doit pas être mère'. Afterwards Princess Hercolani persuaded Louis Napoleon to sing a song for them – a remarkable feat, for though Louis Napoleon was always willing to play the piano at a party, he usually refused to sing.[18]

On 15 November, Hortense and Louis Napoleon and their retinue left Florence for Rome. Hearing that Louis Bonaparte was staying at Viterbo on his journey from Rome to Florence, Louis Napoleon left his fellow-travellers and rode to Viterbo to see his father. Hortense was not eager to meet Louis, but Louis brought Louis Napoleon to rejoin her on the road at Montefiascone; the two carriages stopped for a moment wheel to wheel, and husband and wife exchanged a few words while Louis Napoleon changed carriages. When Louis Napoleon and Hortense reached Rome they took up residence, not as in former years at the Villa Paolina but in an apartment in the Palazzo Ruspoli on the Corso at the corner of the Via della Fontanella Borghese.[19]

They found Rome in a state of political unrest. There was talk of plots, of the Carbonari, of police spies, and of the imminence of revolution. The uncertainty was made worse by the death of Pope Pius VIII on 1 December, after a pontificate of only twenty months, and by the election of his successor. It took the Conclave sixty-four days to choose the very reactionary Cardinal Cappellari as Pope Gregory XVI against the opposition of the more Liberal Cardinals, including Cardinal Fesch. Hortense was worried; she noticed that Louis Napoleon often left the Palazzo Ruspoli without telling her where he was going, and she strongly suspected that he was attending secret meetings with revolutionaries and members of the Carbonari.[20]

At the beginning of December the Governor of Rome, Cardinal Capelletti, visited Cardinal Fesch and asked him to persuade Louis Napoleon to leave Rome immediately, because he was in contact with revolutionaries. Fesch repudiated the suggestion that Louis Napoleon was in touch with the Carbonari, and refused to advise him to leave Rome, which he thought would be tantamount to an admission of guilt. A few days later, fifty policemen arrived at the Palazzo Ruspoli, and their captain explained that he had orders to escort Louis Napoleon forthwith to the frontier of the Papal States and deport him. Louis Napoleon hastily packed a few belongings, and before leaving with the policemen had time to tell Hortense that that morning he had smuggled into the house a Roman revolutionary who was in hiding from the authorities, and that the man was concealed in his rooms. Without a moment's hesitation, Hortense promised to continue hiding the revolutionary in the Palazzo. Fortunately the police did not search the house before leaving with Louis Napoleon.

They left Louis Napoleon on the Tuscan frontier, and he made his way to his father's house in Florence. King Louis, like Cardinal Fesch and all the Bonaparte family, was indignant at the deportation order, and at another deportation order which was served on Jerome Napoleon, the sixteen-year-old son of King Jerome. They succeeded in obtaining the withdrawal of the deportation order against Jerome Napoleon, and urged Hortense to protest against the order against Louis Napoleon. Hortense, who alone of them realized that the Papal government had good reasons for making the order, was pleased that Louis Napoleon was being sent away from his dangerous contacts in Rome.[21]

The Carbonari planned a revolution throughout Italy to end what they called 'Austrian domination of the peninsula', and to force the Italian rulers to grant a Liberal constitution and political freedom, and to unite their independent sovereign states in a loose-knit Italian Confederation under the presidency of the Pope. The government of Louis Philippe had proclaimed its adherence to a policy of non-intervention in Italy, and the Italian revolutionaries hoped that the fear of war with France would deter the Austrians from intervening.[22] The revolutionaries believed that all that was needed was to find a prominent figure to lead the revolution. A wealthy young merchant of Modena, Ciro Menotti, who was a member of the Carbonari, tried to persuade the Duke of Modena to become the leader. The Duke was not only a Habsburg related to the Emperor of Austria, but was also one of the most brutal and repressive of the Italian rulers; but Menotti hoped that he might be persuaded to lead the revolution out of personal ambition, and the Duke encouraged his hopes. As Menotti knew that Napoleon Louis was a supporter of the Carbonari, he wished to make use of the name of Bonaparte by persuading Napoleon Louis to take the post of second-in-command of the revolutionary forces under the Duke of Modena.

It must have been in the last days of January 1831 that Menotti's brother and four other Italian revolutionaries, one of whom was the young Count Orsi, met Napoleon Louis and Louis Napoleon in Florence and discussed with them detailed plans for an insurrection in Modena, the Romagna and in the city of Rome. According to Orsi, who many years later wrote an account of this meeting which is certainly inaccurate in some details, Louis Napoleon said very little during the discussion, which was dominated by Napoleon Louis. On this occasion, as during their childhood days, Louis Napoleon acknowledged the leadership of his elder brother. Menotti's brother assured the two Bonaparte princes that the rising was about to begin under the Duke of Modena's leadership.[23]

On 3 February the Duke of Modena arrested Menotti on a charge of high treason, for he realized that any attempt at revolution would fail, and he wished to curry favour with the Austrians. Two days later, the people of Modena rose spontaneously in revolt. The Duke fled to Mantua in Austrian territory, taking Menotti with him as a prisoner in chains. After the Austrians had suppressed the revolt, the Duke returned to Modena and hanged Menotti there. Menotti was revered as a martyr by the Italian revolutionaries, including Garibaldi, who named his eldest son Menotti when the child was born in Brazil in 1840.

On 4 February the people of Bologna rose and established a provisional revolutionary government of the Papal States; on the 6th the rising spread to Ferrara, on the 8th to Ancona, on the 14th to Perugia and on the 16th to Pesaro. On 12 February there was a riot in Rome, but it was suppressed after the Papal guards had opened fire and killed several of the demonstrators. On 17 February the Austrian troops in Lombardy crossed the frontier and entered the Papal States to restore the Pope's authority. As Hortense had predicted, the French government took no action.

Hortense realized at once that her sons would wish to join the revolutionaries, and she hurried to Florence to dissuade them from doing so. She arrived too late. She found her husband in a state of great agitation, because Napoleon Louis and Louis Napoleon had left Florence a few days earlier. They had written a letter to Hortense, expressing their regret for having acted without consulting her and Louis, and for any trouble or anxiety which they might have caused them, but explaining that their duty required them to fight in the revolutionary army. Louis asked Hortense to go to the revolutionary headquarters and bring them back, but she dismissed the idea as absurd. Pierre Bonaparte of Canino, Lucien's fifteen-year-old son, had also decided to join the revolutionaries. His mother Alexandrine asked the government of Tuscany to arrest him and keep him in custody until the revolution was over, and he was imprisoned in Leghorn for six months. A minister in the Tuscan government suggested to Hortense that she should write to her sons telling them that she was ill and wished to see them at a place on the Tuscan frontier, so that the Tuscan police could seize them when they came and hold them safe in prison until after the revolution. Hortense indignantly rejected this proposal.[24]

The revolutionaries, who had been joined by more than 6000

volunteers, divided their forces into two parts. Some 4000 men were stationed in the north to resist the Austrian invasion; they were commanded by Colonel Armandi, a former officer in Napoleon's army, who after 1815 had been employed as a land agent by both Jerome Bonaparte and Hortense, and for some years by Louis Bonaparte as Napoleon Louis's tutor. A force of 2400, under the command of General Sercognani, advanced in the south against the Papal forces, and threatened Rome.

Napoleon Louis and Louis Napoleon, after leaving Florence on 20 February, joined Sercognani's forces at Spoleto, where they were warmly welcomed and each was given the command of a unit. They advanced with Sercognani's troops to Terni, some fifty miles north of Rome. Here the two brothers separated; Napoleon Louis led a raid into the Sabine Mountains to the south-east of Terni, while Louis Napoleon moved forward on the direct route to Rome and reached Otricoli, less than forty miles from Rome, which was the nearest that any of the revolutionary detachments had come to the city. Here they encountered some Papal troops, with whom they fought a skirmish in which Louis Napoleon was involved in hand-to-hand fighting.

At San Lorenzino he had a narrow escape. His men had engaged some Papal troops, who had retreated, leaving a few wounded men lying on the ground. As Louis Napoleon rode up, one of the wounded Papal soldiers fired a shot at him, but missed. Louis Napoleon drew his pistol and advanced on the man, but when he reached him he said that he would spare his life. As Louis Napoleon turned his back and began to ride away, the Papal soldier made a second attempt to kill him by snatching up the carbine of another wounded Papalist and aiming at Louis Napoleon; but Louis Napoleon's sergeant-major rushed forward and killed the man with his sabre before he had time to fire.

The prospect of the two young Bonapartes leading a revolutionary army against the Pope in the Eternal City caused great alarm to King Louis, King Jerome and Cardinal Fesch, and to Napoleon Louis's wife, Charlotte, who believed that Louis Napoleon had led her husband astray, although the other members of the family assumed that it was the elder brother who had subverted the younger. King Jerome obtained permission from the Pope to send an officer of his household, Baron von Stölting, through the lines to the revolutionary headquarters at Terni with a letter to the two Princes ordering them to leave the rebel army. Napoleon Louis's only reply was to give Stölting a letter for the Pope in which he demanded that the Pope should immediately grant a Liberal constitution and freedom of the press if he wished to prevent the revolutionary army from marching on Rome. But the revolutionaries did not advance on Rome. Sercognani favoured an immediate attack, but

Armandi and the other revolutionary generals thought that it would be folly for an army of 2400 men to try to capture a city of 160,000 inhabitants, many of whom were devoted to the Pope and opposed to the revolutionary cause.

Cardinal Fesch and King Jerome, with King Louis's consent, wrote to the revolutionary Provisional Government in Bologna, asking them to release Napoleon Louis and Louis Napoleon from their service; and Louis asked Armandi to send them back to Florence. Armandi wished to please his former employer, King Louis; and he was also anxious about the international repercussions which might result from the presence of the two Princes in the revolutionary army. The French and Austrian diplomats in Rome and Florence had hastened to report it to their governments, and Armandi feared that Louis Philippe would be deterred from giving military or other aid to the revolutionaries if he thought that they were fighting for the Bonapartist cause. He therefore asked Sercognani to relieve the two young Bonapartes from their commands and to send them to him at Ancona. When they arrived, he told them to go to Bologna and wait there till arrangements could be made to send them back to their parents.

Napoleon Louis and Louis Napoleon were angry and disillusioned that their youthful revolutionary idealism had been frustrated by parental influence and international diplomacy. At Bologna, ignoring Armandi's instructions, they persuaded the revolutionary Provisional Government to appoint Napoleon Louis as a major and Louis Napoleon as a captain in the local militia which was being organized to fight the advancing Austrians; but Armandi heard about this, and the Provisional Government revoked the appointments after Armandi had convinced them that this was necessary to avoid offending Louis Philippe. Napoleon Louis and Louis Napoleon then asked permission to serve in the revolutionary army as common soldiers under false names, but the Provisional Government would not agree to this. In a passionate outburst, Napoleon Louis offered to surrender to the Austrians and go into lifelong captivity in Austria if this was the only way in which he could help the revolutionary cause.

By this time the revolutionary resistance was almost at an end, as the Austrian army was rapidly overrunning the country. Armandi prepared to make a last stand north of Ancona while the Provisional Government tried to obtain the best possible terms. The Austrians had meanwhile offered an amnesty to all the revolutionaries who laid down their arms with the exception of a few named leaders. The rumour spread in diplomatic circles in Florence and Rome that Napoleon Louis and Louis Napoleon had been excepted from the amnesty, though in fact their names did not appear among the thirty-eight leaders who were excepted in the final proclamation issued by the Papal government. Napoleon Louis and Louis Napoleon decided to go to Ancona; if they were not allowed to take part in the last battle against the Austrians, they would try to make their way to Poland to fight for the Polish revolutionaries against the invading Russians.[25]

They left Bologna on 6 March, and on the evening of the 10th reached Forli and took lodgings at the Albergo del Capello. Next morning Napoleon Louis fell ill with what was first diagnosed as being merely a heavy cold, but he was too feverish and weak to be able to travel and spent the day in bed. The other members of their party went on to join Armandi's army, but Louis Napoleon stayed with his brother in the inn at Forli. As Napoleon Louis grew worse, Louis Napoleon called the local doctor, who prescribed various medicines and treatment, but could not diagnose the disease. Louis Napoleon was constantly at the bedside, looking after his brother and reading the newspapers aloud to him. On 15 March the doctor at last diagnosed measles, but said that it was now too late to treat it, and that the case was hopeless. Napoleon Louis died at 3 p.m. on 17 March. If he had lived, he, and not Louis Napoleon, might twenty years later have become Napoleon III and perhaps a more determined and successful ruler of the Second Empire.

Next day an inquest was held on the body by the doctor and the local officials at Forli, and measles was certified as the cause of death; but already it was being rumoured throughout Italy that Napoleon Louis had been murdered by one of his revolutionary colleagues, Count Orsini, on the orders of the Carbonari. This story acquired an added interest after 1858, when Orsini's son was executed for throwing a bomb at Napoleon III in Paris, and the mystery of the death of Napoleon Louis has continued to be a matter of controversy.

According to the story, a fortnight before his death, Napoleon Louis received orders, at Terni, from the leaders of the Carbonari to lead his soldiers in an attack on Rome. He refused because he did not wish to endanger or embarrass his father, Cardinal Fesch, or his other pro-Papal relatives. The Carbonari thereupon decided that Napoleon Louis must be put to death for his disobedience. They sent Orsini to carry out the sentence. Orsini and a few of his Carbonari colleagues caught up with Napoleon Louis at Forli, and on the evening of their arrival held a 'trial' in the dining-room of the inn, and sentenced Napoleon Louis to death, after which Orsini stabbed him with a dagger. Two alternative explanations are put forward to account for the delay between Napoleon Louis's arrival at Forli on 10 March and his death on the 17th, which is difficult to explain if the measles story is untrue. One theory is that he was killed on the evening of his arrival at Forli,

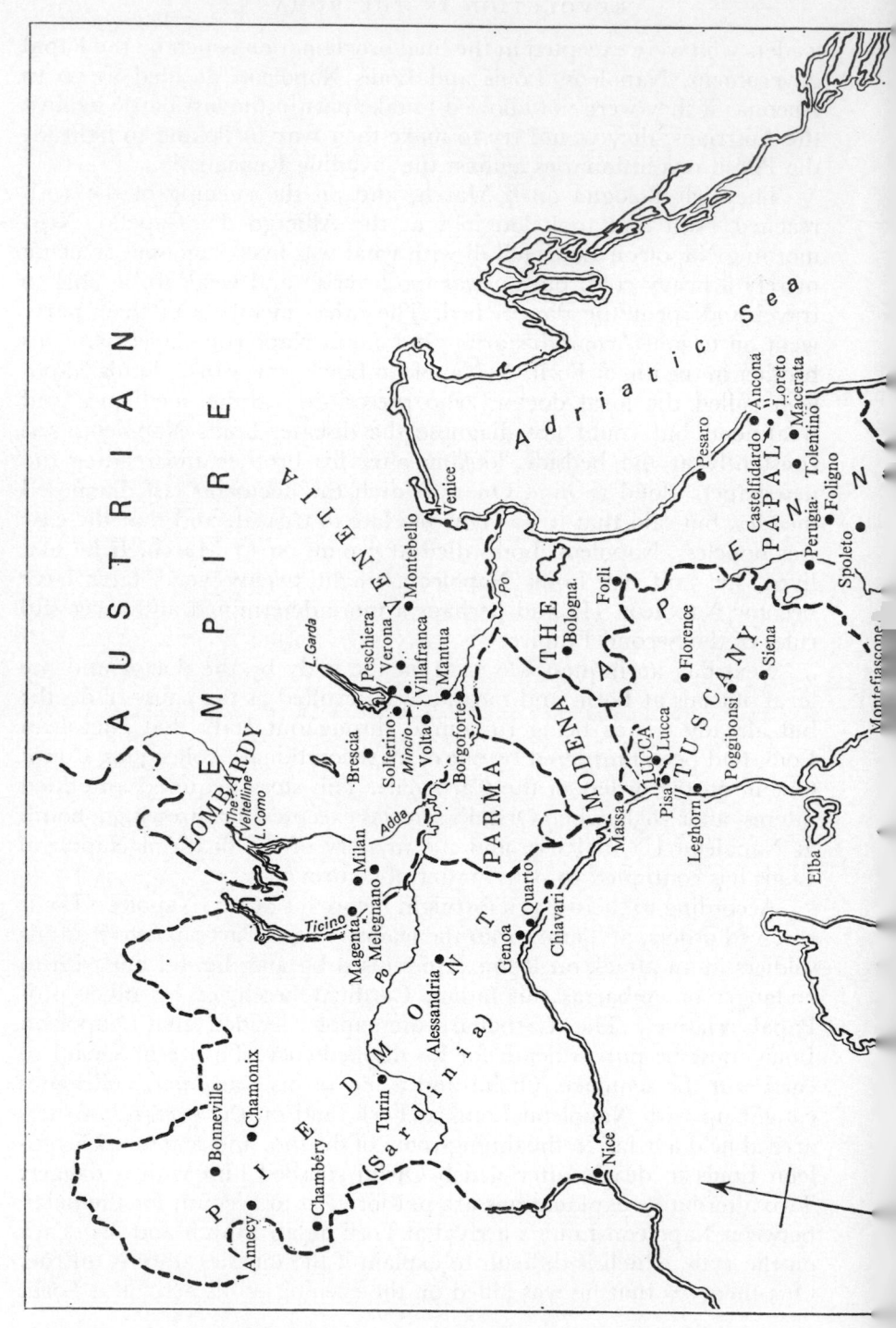

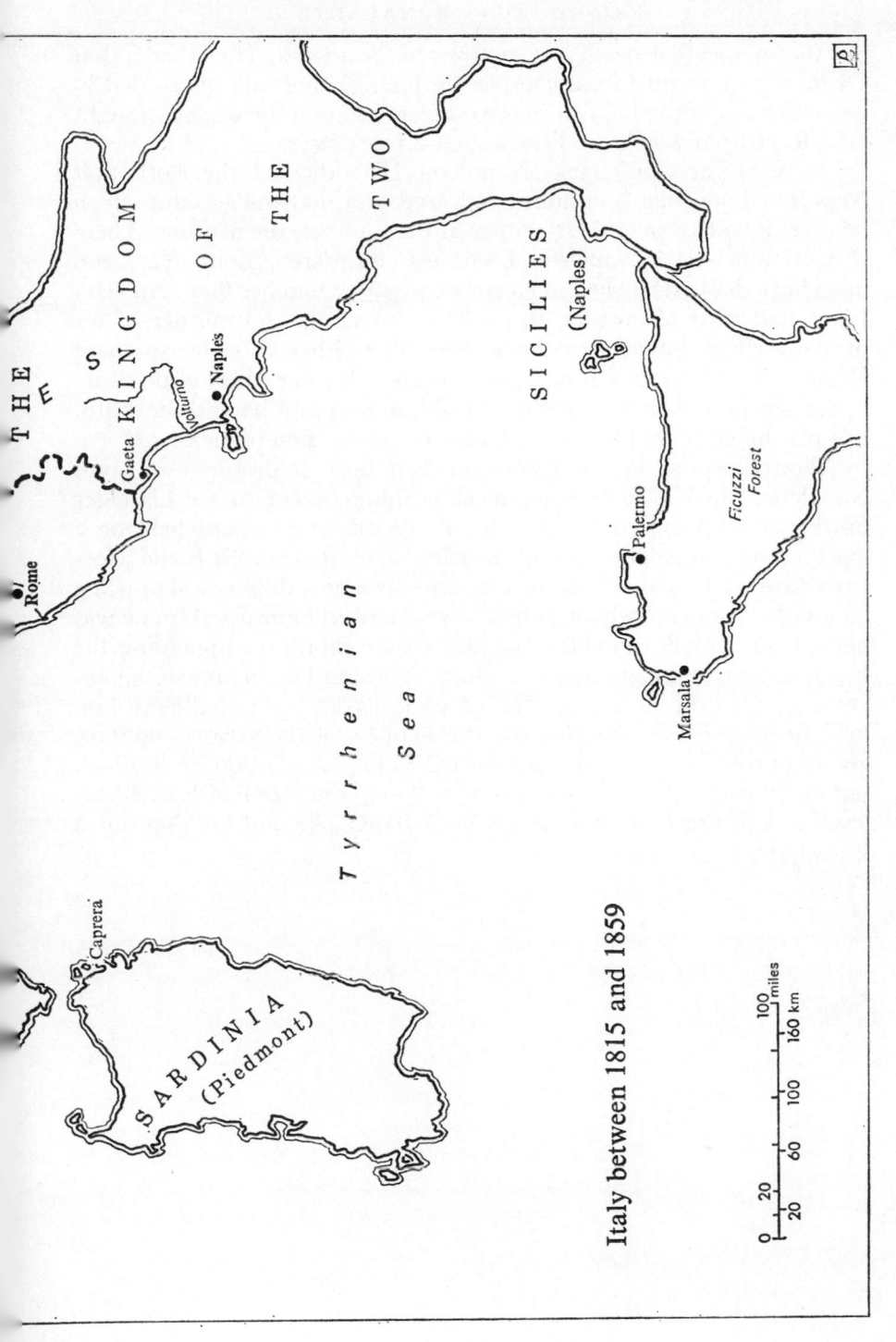

Italy between 1815 and 1859

but that news of his death was suppressed for a week. The other is that Orsini was prevented from completing his task and only succeeded in wounding Napoleon Louis with the dagger, and that the wound brought on a fever from which the Prince died a week later.

In 1872, at Chislehurst, Napoleon III ridiculed the story that Napoleon Louis had been murdered, and said that the account which he himself had given to their mother at the time was the true one. There is no doubt that if Napoleon Louis was murdered, Louis Napoleon must have deliberately lied to Hortense when he told her that Napoleon Louis had died of measles, in order to cover up the murder of his brother. He is supposed to have done this either in order to spare Hortense's feelings, or out of loyalty to his fellow-members of the Carbonari, or from fear of what they would do to him if he told the truth. But it is much more likely that Napoleon Louis died of measles.[26]

The enterprise in the Romagna had been a disaster for Louis Napoleon. He had achieved almost nothing except to see his elder brother and mentor die, not a hero's death on the battlefield or a martyr's on the gallows, but of measles. According to his friend Hortense Cornu, he changed in one day and became a different man when he lost the brother to whom he had always looked for leadership; he was henceforth acutely conscious that the responsibility for upholding the Bonapartist cause had passed to him.[27] He also lost his revolutionary enthusiasm in the Romagna. The revolutionaries had not allowed him to fight for them because he was the nephew of the greatest military genius of modern times. He had wished to be a revolutionary Radical, but everyone had thought of him as a Bonaparte. He had learned his lesson; in future he would always be a Bonaparte and nothing but a Bonaparte.

CHAPTER 7

FROM ANCONA TO TUNBRIDGE WELLS

WHEN Hortense heard of the defeat of the revolution and the advance of the Austrian armies, she set out to find her sons, determined to use her experience, her rank, her money, her contacts and her woman's wiles to help them as far as possible. She asked her friend George Hamilton Seymour, the British Consul in Florence, to give her a false British passport for herself and her two sons.[1] Seymour agreed to do so – in those days passports did not contain a photograph or any description of the holder's appearance – but he warned her that he would have to report what he had done to the British government. Hortense replied that she had no fears on this count, as 'Lord Holland and Lord Grey, the former members of the Opposition who nobly defended the prisoner of St Helena, will not be the ones to blame you for saving the lives of his nephews'.[2]

She left Florence on 12 March armed with two passports which she could use whenever necessary – one for herself, as Duchesse de Saint-Leu, and two servants, and the false British one in the name of Mrs Hamilton and her two sons. On 19 March, near Foligno, she received a message from Louis Napoleon telling her that Napoleon Louis was very ill at Forli, and urging her to come to his bedside as soon as possible. Next day she met Louis Napoleon at Pesaro, and he told her about Napoleon Louis's death. He had left Forli as soon as his brother died and hurried to meet her, without waiting for the funeral in the cathedral at Forli on 21 March. The Austrian armies entered Forli on 24 March.[3]

Hortense's only object now was to save her last surviving son. They went to Ancona, where Eugène de Beauharnais's family owned a mansion. Ancona was crowded with the defeated revolutionaries who were hoping to find a ship in which they could escape to British territory in Corfu before the Austrians arrived. Hortense was reluctant to use this escape route, because she feared that the Austrian navy would be patrolling the coast to catch escaping revolutionaries; and to make matters worse, on the day that they reached Ancona, Louis Napoleon fell ill with measles, which he had caught from Napoleon Louis. Hortense therefore decided to hide Louis Napoleon in the Beauharnais mansion at Ancona until he had recovered from his measles, and then take the most unexpected course and go with him to England by way of France, using the British passport which Seymour had given her. No one would expect them to go to France, because the Law of 11 September 1830 forbade the Bonapartes to set foot in France on pain of death; but she was sure that Louis Philippe and his government would neither wish nor dare to execute a Bonaparte under this law.[4]

She put Louis Napoleon's belongings on a ship as ostentatiously as possible, and told everybody that he had sailed to Corfu. She even arranged for Louis Napoleon to write a letter to his father, ostensibly from Corfu, stating that he had safely arrived there. Louis afterwards complained bitterly that she had not taken him into her confidence, but she knew that he was sometimes indiscreet, and she thought that the fewer people who knew the truth about Louis Napoleon's whereabouts, the safer he would be.[5]

The Austrian advance-guard entered Ancona on 29 March, and immediately requisitioned the Beauharnais mansion as the headquarters of their commander, General Baron von Geppert. Hortense said that she would gladly place the house at their disposal, but asked to be allowed to continue living for a short while in a few rooms in the house. At first her request was refused; but she discovered that Colonel Woyna, who had escorted her out of France in 1815, was with the Austrian army in Ancona, and she asked him for help. She was allowed to stay with her ladies and servants in some rooms on the first floor, to which she could only gain access by going through a room in which Austrian soldiers were accommodated. She hid Louis Napoleon in a room which was separated by only a thin wall and a locked door from the room which General Geppert used as his office. She warned Louis Napoleon never to speak above a whisper, to cough as quietly as possible, and to make no noise as he lay on his bed in a feverish state. He was cared for by an Italian doctor whom Hortense had taken into her confidence. She pretended to the Austrians that she herself was ill, in order to give the doctor an excuse to call every day.

Hortense told General Geppert, who visited her, that she intended to go to London as soon as she had recovered from her illness, and asked Geppert for documents which would facilitate her passage through the Austrian lines. He gave them to her, and he and all his officers treated her with the greatest consideration. She wished that they had not been quite so kind, as it almost gave her a guilty conscience about deceiving them.

After eight days the doctor said that Louis Napoleon was fit to travel. Hortense made her preparations to leave on Easter Sunday, 3 April, and told the Austrians that she would be going out very early that morning in order to attend Mass at the monastery of Loreto, some twelve miles south-east of Ancona. As she had originally intended that Napoleon Louis should travel with them, she had obtained a passport for herself and two manservants, and the British one for 'Mrs Hamilton' and her two sons. She now offered to take with her, in Napoleon Louis's place, a young Italian, the Marquis Zappi, who had fought in the revolutionary army and was hiding from the Austrians in Ancona. Zappi slipped into the Beauharnais mansion on the Saturday evening.

Hortense and her party rose at 4 a.m. on the Sunday, and Louis Napoleon and Zappi dressed in footman's livery. They walked quietly through the ante-room occupied by the Austrians, stepping over the soldiers, who were all asleep. They passed the sentries at the gates of the mansion, and set off in two carriages. Valérie Masuyer and Hortense's servant, Charles Thélin, travelled with them. Louis Napoleon and Zappi, in their footman's livery, sat outside with the coachmen on the boxes of the two carriages.[6]

They went to Loreto, where they stopped for a brief moment and attended Mass; Hortense had been a pious Catholic ever since her experience of revolutionary atheism in 1794, and was becoming increasingly devout as she grew older.[7] Then they drove on in a south-westerly direction across Italy before veering north and heading for the French frontier. At Macerata a revolutionary supporter recognized Louis Napoleon, but did not mention this to anyone. A less friendly passer-by recognized him at Tolentino, and informed an Austrian officer; but the officer, who was lazy and happy-go-lucky, did not believe the informer and took no action. After passing through Foligno and Perugia they crossed the frontier between the Papal States and Tuscany. The Tuscan immigration officials had received orders from their government not to allow Louis Napoleon to enter Tuscany; but it was 2.30 a.m. when Hortense's party arrived at the frontier post, and the officials let them through after Hortense's courier had sworn that Louis Napoleon was not with them. They went on to Siena, Poggibonsi and Pisa. Just before they reached Pisa, they stopped for an hour at dawn at a wayside inn, where Louis Napoleon and Zappi removed their footman's livery and put on gentleman's clothes, while the coachman changed into English coachman's livery. Henceforth they would travel on their false British passports as Mrs Hamilton and her sons, leading the authorities to believe that Hortense and her footmen, who had last been seen at Poggibonsi, had sailed from Leghorn to Malta.

After passing through Pisa they entered the Grand Duchy of Lucca on 8 April, five days after leaving Ancona. They had discovered after leaving Siena that Zappi had got measles, so they left him behind at Lucca to recuperate and went on in one of the carriages towards

Massa, in the Duke of Modena's territories, leaving the second carriage with Zappi at Lucca. They had an embarrassing moment at a stopping-place on the road to Massa when they met an English traveller. Seeing their coachman in an English livery, the Englishman began addressing 'Mrs Hamilton' and her son as fellow-countrymen. Hortense could not speak English, and though Louis Napoleon was reasonably fluent in the language, his French accent gave him away at once. The Englishman politely excused himself, saying to Louis Napoleon: 'I am sorry, I thought you were English people.'[8] Fortunately, when they reached Genoa, the British Consul visa'ed their British passport without asking to meet them.

At Genoa they were in the kingdom of Piedmont, and went on towards the French frontier with Zappi, who had recovered from his measles and had rejoined them in the second carriage. As they approached Chiavari, Louis Napoleon and Zappi, who were following in the second carriage a few miles behind Hortense, noticed a pretty girl at the roadside, and gave chase in a manner of which Valérie Masuyer did not approve:

> They stopped the carriage at a bend in the road; I saw them pursue a woman and disappear with her behind a rock, no doubt in order to force their kisses on her and to pester her. This new exploit, taken together with the things they say and their delight in the stories of Boccaccio, shows me very clearly what their attitude is.[9]

After leaving Nice, which had been taken from France and returned to Piedmont in 1814, they crossed the French frontier on the River Var on 14 April, and for the first time for sixteen years Louis Napoleon and Hortense set foot in France.[10] Louis Napoleon was delighted to be in France again, though he complained that the French girls were less attractive than he had expected. They took the road to Paris, and on 16 April reached Montélimar, where Louis Napoleon drafted a letter to King Louis Philippe, appealing for permission to return to France and to serve in the French army:

> I could console myself for not being in my native country while Liberty summoned me to her standard in an unhappy land; but now courage has had to yield to numbers, and I have been obliged to flee from Italy.

France was the only country in Europe

> where I shall not be judged guilty of a crime for having embraced the sacred cause of a people's independence; but a cruel law banishes me from her soil.

Hortense de Beauharnais about the time of her marriage, by Gérard

Louis Bonaparte, by F. J. Kinsoen

His only ambition was to return to France,

> happy if I could one day die fighting for my country. France and Your Majesty could rely on my oath and on my gratitude.[11]

Hortense was deeply moved by Louis Napoleon's letter, but she persuaded him not to send it to the King; she wished to play her difficult hand in her own way. On 18 April they reached Lyons. Here Zappi took Valérie Masuyer aside and told her that before they left Ancona he had heard that Napoleon Louis had not died of measles, but had been either stabbed or shot by the Carbonari in the inn at Forli, after Count Orsini had denounced him as a traitor for his refusal to march on Rome. Valérie was horrified at the news, but agreed not to reveal the secret to Hortense or Louis Napoleon.[12]

At Fontainebleau they joined the tourists who were being shown round the palace. Hortense took the precaution of wearing a veil in case any of the old servants at the palace recognized her, and she pointed out to Louis Napoleon, in a whisper, the font in the chapel where he had been baptized by Cardinal Fesch in 1810. On Saturday 23 April, they entered Paris and took a suite of rooms at the Hôtel de Hollande in the Rue de la Paix. From their window they could see the column in the Place Vendôme.[13] Napoleon had erected a statue of himself in the garb of a Roman hero, with toga and laurel-wreath, on the top of the column. The statue had been removed in 1814 and melted down for the brass to be used for a new equestrian statue of the first Bourbon king, Henri IV. Louis Philippe had now ordered that a new statue of Napoleon should be placed on the Colonne Vendôme, showing the Emperor in his military greatcoat and three-cornered hat, but it had not yet been erected.

Hortense told Valérie Masuyer to wrote to the King's A.D.C. informing him that if he came to the Hôtel de Hollande and asked for Mrs Hamilton, she would give him a message from Queen Hortense. When he arrived, he was very surprised to see Hortense and to hear that Louis Napoleon was in Paris with her. Next day the Prime Minister, Casimir Périer, visited Hortense at the hotel, and on the evening of 26 April she was secretly taken to the Palais Royal where she met the King and Queen in their private apartments. Louis Philippe told her that he hoped that it would soon be possible to repeal the law which banished the Bonapartes from France, but that as long as the law was in force it would be very embarrassing if it became known that she and Louis Napoleon had been in France and had met the King and the Prime Minister, and he begged her to keep it a strict secret. She told him that they were only passing through France on their way to England, and he promised her that they would be granted a transit visa through France when they returned from England to Switzerland later in the summer.

She had intended leaving Paris for England immediately, but suddenly Louis Napoleon fell ill again, with a temperature and a sore throat. Hortense asked the management of the hotel to fetch a doctor for him. They told 'Mrs Hamilton' that there were English doctors in Paris who could be summoned, but she explained that though she was English by marriage she was French by birth, and would prefer to have a French doctor. The doctor diagnosed that Louis Napoleon was suffering from a recurrence of measles; he bled him, and ordered complete rest. But the government was becoming anxious about their residence in Paris. The fifth of May was approaching, the tenth anniversary of Napoleon's death, and the authorities had been warned to expect Bonapartist demonstrations in the Place Vendôme on that day. Hortense explained that Louis Napoleon was too ill to move. The King sent his A.D.C. to visit Louis Napoleon and make sure that the illness was genuine, and pressed Hortense to hasten their departure.

The government were very agitated to find, on 4 May, that the Bonapartes were still there, within a stone's throw of the Place Vendôme, and sent word to Hortense that they must leave immediately unless the doctor certified that the move would endanger Louis Napoleon's life. She asked the doctor's opinion, pretending that she had urgent business in England in order to explain why she wished to leave so hurriedly. He told her that, though it would be better if Louis Napoleon could rest for a few more days before travelling, it would be safe for him to go.

They were still there on 5 May, when Hortense, from the hotel window, watched the crowds gathering in the Place Vendôme and placing flowers at the foot of the column. Many of the flowers were in the shape of a crown. The rumour spread among the crowd that Prince Louis Napoleon was in Paris and was there, in disguise, among the crowds in the Place Vendôme. The police did not interfere with the crowds, but during the night they removed those flowers which were in the shape of a crown, and next day there were clashes between the police and Bonapartist demonstrators in the square.

Hortense and Louis Napoleon, having said good-bye to Zappi, left Paris with Valérie Masuyer and Charles Thélin at 3 p.m. on 6 May. They reached Calais four days later, and sailed in the British ship, the *Royal George*, to Dover. Louis Napoleon survived the journey better than Hortense, who was violently sick in the ship, as the crossing was very rough and lasted many hours. They were forced to leave their carriage, which had been fastened to the deck, and take refuge in the cabins below.[14]

In the spring of 1831, Britain was in the midst of the political struggle which led to the passing of the Great Reform Bill in the following year. The general election in May was fought on the issue of the bill and the extension of the Parliamentary franchise, and political passions ran very high. Hortense and Louis Napoleon had carefully followed British politics for many years, and regarded the more Radical sections of the Whigs as pro-French and pro-Bonapartist. They spent their first night in England at Canterbury in a hotel immediately opposite the committee rooms of Hodges and Rider, the Liberal candidates, and they were delighted when they heard, a few days later, that Hodges and Rider had been returned for Kent and that Lord Grey had won the general election with an increased majority in the House of Commons.

Hortense and Louis Napoleon took rooms in London at Fenton's Hotel, but after a few days they rented a house at 30 George Street, where Louis Napoleon rapidly recovered from his illness under the care of the eminent physician, Dr Henry Holland. During their three-month stay in England they were warmly welcomed in Whig society, to which they were introduced by Louis Napoleon's cousin, Lady Dudley Stuart, the daughter of Lucien Bonaparte. Lord and Lady Holland, who had made themselves notorious during the war by their pro-French sympathies, gave several receptions and dinners for them at Holland House. They met Lord Grey, Lord Brougham, and other members of the government; General Sir Robert Wilson, whom they admired for saving Lavalette; and Lady George Seymour, whose son, George Seymour, had given Hortense the false British passport on which they had travelled from Italy. At that period of bitter political controversy there was not much social friendship between the Whig and Tory families, and Hortense and Louis Napoleon did not meet Wellington and Londonderry and the Opposition leaders; but they met the Tory Lord Mahon, and Hortense became quite intimate with Lady Tankerville, who was French by birth, the daughter of Louis XVI's courtier, the Duc de Gramont. They paid several visits to the Duchess of St Albans, the famous Harriet Mellon, at her house in Hampstead. She was the illegitimate daughter of an Irish shopgirl, but through her beauty and personality she had become first a successful actress, then the wife and widow of Thomas Coutts the banker, and finally a duchess. Hortense hoped to sell her the diamond necklace that Josephine had worn at her coronation, but the Duchess was too shrewd and level-headed to pay Hortense's price.

The Duchess of Bedford, whom they met in London, invited them to Woburn at short notice, and hurried down to Bedfordshire in the middle of the night to prepare the house for their reception. Hortense and Louis Napoleon arrived there next day, after a journey which

Valérie Masuyer called 'the fastest in the world';[15] their carriage had covered the forty-two miles from London in three-and-a-half hours. They admired Woburn, being impressed by the size and grandeur of the house and gardens, and by the heating system, by which a hundred stoves kept the house at an even temperature throughout the winter at a cost of 50,000 francs (£2500) a year. The Duchess showed them 'her village, her school, her hospital', and Hortense reflected on the opportunities to do good which were conferred by great wealth. 'The aristocracy would perhaps be loved, and its privileges forgiven', she wrote, 'if it were always so protective.'[16] They passed the time on the journey back to London by reading Victor Hugo's historical novel *Notre Dame de Paris* (*The Hunchback of Notre Dame*), which had been published earlier in the year, and Paul de Kock's *La Maison Blanche*. Louis Napoleon was bored by both novels, but was much more interested in Victor Hugo's recent poem, 'A la Colonne', a salute to the Colonne Vendôme and to Napoleon.

They were impressed, not only by the size and splendour of Woburn, which they would have expected to find only in the palace of an Emperor or Prince, but also by the houses of the gentry and the middle classes. The country house of about twenty rooms, surrounded by fifty or a hundred acres of gardens or woodland, which they came across so frequently on the roads in south-east England, seemed to them to symbolize the prosperity and social status of the middle classes in England. They liked the relaxed informality of English social life, and the fact that the lower classes were neither subservient nor hostile to the aristocracy; the excellent pavements and street lighting in London, the well-kept state of the public parks, and the fact that everyone went in carriages and omnibuses instead of walking, gave them an impression of general prosperity. 'Where are the poor?' wrote Hortense. 'There are many of them, I am told, but to judge from the people's clothes and houses one could doubt this.'[17]

Their attitude is a little surprising, in view of the events that were taking place in England in 1831. It was the year in which Tommy Hepburn led the miners of Durham and Northumberland to win a twelve-hour day for young persons under eighteen, when the Assize Courts in Hampshire and Wiltshire were sentencing agricultural rioters to death or transportation, and when the letters and diaries of the English upper and middle classes are full of references to the stoning of aristocrats' carriages by hostile mobs and the rudeness shown by the lower classes to their superiors. But Hortense and Louis Napoleon did not become aware of the poverty and discontent in the industrial and agricultural districts, and England seemed to them to be largely free of the class hatred which existed on the Continent.

They were pleasantly surprised that the English people were so friendly to them and to France. Apart from the welcome that they received in Whig high society, Louis Napoleon found that when people in the shops and streets discovered who he was, they would shake him warmly by the hand and assure him that the English no longer bore any ill-will towards the French. Plays about Napoleon were running at three London theatres – Astley's, the Surrey, and Drury Lane – and Louis Napoleon went to Covent Garden to see a series of tableaux of scenes from the Emperor's life.

The presence of Hortense and Louis Napoleon in London was reported in the French and British press. The Conference of the Great Powers to settle the future of Belgium was meeting in London, and had decided to offer the throne of Belgium to Prince Leopold of Saxe-Coburg. The rumour spread that Hortense had come to London in order to obtain the crown of Belgium for Louis Napoleon. Louis Napoleon wrote to the Paris newspaper, Le Temps, contradicting the rumour.[18] When Hortense met Prince Leopold at a party, he laughingly said to her that he hoped she had not come to England to deprive him of his kingdom.

Hortense had kept her promise to Louis Philippe not to reveal the fact that she had passed through France. She had even gone to the lengths of telling her acquaintances in London that she and Louis Napoleon had landed at Portsmouth, not Dover, pretending that they had sailed there direct from Malta; but it became known that they had travelled through Paris and had met the King and Casimir Périer. The French government was attacked in the Chamber for having connived at this violation of the law, but Périer won a vote of confidence after an emotional speech in which he said that if necessary he would ask for an Act of Indemnity to exempt him from the penalties which he had incurred by helping an unhappy mother to smuggle her sick son to safety.[19]

All this encouraged the Bonapartist supporters in Paris. The most prominent of these was the mysterious Count Lennox, an American citizen of Scottish descent who had achieved some fame as an aeronaut and had settled in Paris, where he embraced the cause of Bonapartism from a mixture of romantic idealism and unscrupulous adventurism. Hortense was not happy when Lennox's wife and other Bonapartist agents arrived in London and urged Louis Napoleon to send Lennox money to finance Bonapartist newspapers in France and to enter into secret contact with illegal revolutionary groups in Paris who were planning to overthrow Louis Philippe's régime. She believed that Louis Napoleon was inexperienced and rash, and was liable to be drawn into disastrous adventures which would be fatal to his cause, especially if the conspirators took advantage of his weakness for beautiful women. When he went to the St James's Theatre, where plays in French were regularly performed, a voluptuous beauty in another box made eyes at him, and next day sent him a note inviting him to meet her in Hyde Park. Hortense thought that the woman was at best an unscrupulous adventuress, and at worst an emissary of Lennox. Hortense was worried that Louis Napoleon went out so often without telling her where he was going. Once when she was in her carriage on her way to visit Lady Holland in Kensington, she saw Louis Napoleon walking in Kensington Gardens, and discovered that he was on his way to Madame Lennox's house.

Hortense could not return to Arenenberg until she received the French transit visa which Louis Philippe had promised her, for she knew that she would not be allowed to travel through Belgium as long as the political uncertainties continued there. While she was waiting for the visa, she took Louis Napoleon to Tunbridge Wells, where she could not only take the waters but also keep her son away from Lennox's agents. They stayed first at the Kentish Hotel, and then rented a house in the town and spent a fortnight there in July, meeting the Duke of Richmond's daughter, Lady Louisa Tighe, whom Valérie Masuyer called 'la reine de Townbridge',[20] and the local gentry and the other visitors who were taking the waters. They went for walks to the High Rocks a mile to the south of the town. Louis Napoleon enjoyed his stay, as Tunbridge Wells was full of very pretty girls, all of whom seemed to speak excellent French.

He fell in love with one of them, Miss Sarah Godfrey, sufficiently seriously to lament the fact that it was impossible for Napoleon's nephew to marry an Englishwoman. Miss Godfrey, who had been brought up in Ireland, was intelligent, spoke fluent French and Italian, and played the piano very nicely. She sang English songs for Louis Napoleon, and he sang Neapolitan songs for her and told her the story of Madame Cottin's novel, *Malvina*, about a man of sixty and a young girl who fell in love and killed themselves when they could not marry. He grew his moustache long, and curled it, in order to impress Miss Godfrey, but as she did not like it, he cut off the curls and reverted to a short moustache. At one of Hortense's parties he paid too much attention to other young ladies for Miss Godfrey's liking; she turned her back on him and refused to speak to him. But by the end of the party they were sitting together on the sofa, exchanging loving words and looks.

Hortense was quite happy about Louis Napoleon's flirtation with Sarah Godfrey. She was much more anxious when he went to London, ostensibly to see the dentist, and she discovered that he had visited Lennox's agents to discuss the publication of a Bonapartist proclamation which he had drafted.[21]

As soon as they received their French visas, they paid farewell visits to the Whig hostesses in London, and left England on 7 August. At Boulogne, Hortense showed Louis Napoleon the places where she had acted as hostess for the Emperor during the preparations for the invasion of England in 1805. They passed close to Saint-Leu, but Hortense would not go to the house; at Malmaison, the mansion was not open to the public, and they did not try to enter. Hortense had intended to spend a few days in Paris, but changed her mind after Louis Napoleon had said that if demonstrations took place while they were there, and the authorities sabred the people, he would join the people in the streets and fight on their side.

They were in Sens on 15 August, the anniversary of Napoleon's birthday. It was a perfect summer day, and they mixed with the crowds in the streets, and heard the people say how much better things had been in the days of the Emperor. They reached Arenenberg before the end of August, more than ten months after they had left it on their annual visit to Italy in October 1830.[22]

CHAPTER 8

PRINCESS MATHILDE

WHILE Hortense and Louis Napoleon were travelling from London to Arenenberg, the Radicals throughout Europe were watching in anger and agony the death-struggle of the Polish revolutionaries, who for nine months had held out against the Russian armies. The Polish resistance had aroused great enthusiasm in France; the windows of the Russian embassy had been broken by angry crowds. But Palmerston, the British Foreign Secretary, who wished to prevent a European war, had dissuaded the government of Louis Philippe from intervening to help the Poles; and when Warsaw fell to the Russians the French Foreign Minister, Sébastiani, caused the greatest resentment in France by his statement: 'Order reigns in Warsaw.'

Louis Napoleon wrote letters to the newspapers supporting Poland and condemning Louis Philippe's government for their failure to intervene; and as soon as he arrived at Arenenberg he received a letter from a Polish revolutionary in Paris inviting him to lead an expedition to help the Poles. He was to come to Paris in disguise and meet a band of Poles, who would go with him to Le Havre, where they would embark in a vessel and sail to Lithuania, attack the Russian fortresses, make a deep raid into the country, and relieve the pressure on the Poles in Warsaw. Louis Napoleon turned down the proposal. The scheme seemed to him to have no chance of success, and in any case he was less eager to risk his life for revolutionary causes since his experience in Italy. He had learned that it was impossible for a Bonaparte to be an altruistic revolutionary soldier, and had decided to devote himself to achieving his personal and family ambitions in a country where his name would be an asset and not a liability.[1]

The failure of Louis Philippe's government to give effective aid to the Polish and Italian revolutionaries, and the increasing conservatism of its policy at home, drove the French Republicans into opposition to the Orleanist régime, which was also threatened by the Bourbon Legitimists and the Bonapartists. Unlike the Legitimists before 1830, who had vilified Napoleon as a usurper, the Orleanists glorified him as a national hero; but they considered that his military glory was a thing of the past, and that the Frenchman of the 1830s wanted peace and prosperity. Louis Philippe relied on the support of the middle-class business man who wanted to make money. The government propagandists hailed the King as the 'happy medium' between despotism and revolution; but the term was turned into one of ridicule by the Republicans and Bonapartists, who invariably referred to Louis Philippe as 'the Happy Medium' ('le Juste-Milieu').

The régime allowed free elections on a limited franchise, and freedom of speech and of the press, but restricted these freedoms by a half-hearted and pettifogging tyranny. Republican journalists were often arrested and prosecuted for sedition. From time to time the Republican opposition erupted in street-fighting, the most serious incident being the battle on the barricades on 5 June 1832, which was afterwards immortalized by Victor Hugo in *Les Misérables*.

The government also arrested and prosecuted the Legitimist supporters of Charles X's daughter-in-law, the Duchesse de Berry, and Lennox's Bonapartist agents; on one occasion, when the police arrested a Polish refugee, they found a cipher-key written in Louis Napoleon's handwriting. Trade unions were suppressed and strikers were arrested; in Lyons, the silk-weavers' strike led to prolonged street-fighting between the strikers and the army. Petty restrictions were placed on the distribution of pamphlets; working-class educational centres were suppressed; and the police closed the churches of priests who denounced, in their sermons, the oppression of the poor. The Saint-Simonian Socialists, who had no political ambitions but wore outlandish clothes, lived in hippy communes, and advocated and practised free love, were imprisoned and banished from France; and the Polish and Italian refugees in France were subjected to travel restrictions and harassment. Plays were suppressed if the authorities considered that they had a dangerous tendency to ridicule the Establishment, like Victor Hugo's *Le Roi s'amuse*; and the indefatigable chief of the Paris police, Monsieur Gisquet, even thought it his duty to reveal the past peccadilloes of apparently respectable young women to the sons of wealthy families whom they were about to marry. Monsieur Gisquet's proudest achievement was to have invented the system by which anyone staying the night in a hotel or lodging-house was required to fill in a form giving his name, address, occupation and date of birth.[2]

Soon after Louis Napoleon returned to Arenenberg, he published *Rêveries politiques*, the first of a series of pamphlets and books in which he formulated his political doctrines. He advocated a combination of Radicalism and Bonapartism. He had learned from his mother and the Bonapartists of her generation to regard Napoleon as the only alternative to both the injustices of the *ancien régime* and the horrors of the

87

guillotine, and he developed this idea to take into account the new phenomena of Louis Philippe and Socialism. Ever since his early childhood he had been brought up to be aware of the sufferings of the poor, and he became far more sympathetic to the ideas of the Socialists than were the bourgeois supporters of Louis Philippe. When the army clashed with the artisans of Lyons during the silk-weavers' strike, he left Arenenberg and hurried to Geneva to be available if he were called upon to head the revolutionary forces in Lyons; but no call came, and he returned to Arenenberg after the rising had been suppressed.[3]

In his *Rêveries politiques*, Louis Napoleon wrote that Europe was in the throes of the struggle between tyranny and liberty, between reactionary and progressive forces. The worst enemy of Liberty was not the tyrant who suppressed it, sabre in hand, but 'weak governments who, under the mask of Liberty ... are unjust to the weak, and humble before the strong' – a clear reference to the government of Louis Philippe. The Republic had stood for equality and liberty; the Empire for patriotism, glory and honour; the Restoration of 1815 for the re-establishment of ancient privilege and arbitrary government; and Louis Philippe's régime for fear, selfishness and cowardice. He stated that he believed that the only salvation for France was to unite the two popular causes of Napoleon II and the Republic:

> The son of the great man is the only representative of the greatest glory, as the Republic was of the greatest liberty. With the name of Napoleon, no one will fear the return of the Terror; with the name of the Republic, no one will fear the return of absolutism.

Frenchmen must be fair to the memory of the great Napoleon; if one day the peoples were free, they would owe this to him, who had carried civilization from the Tagus to the Vistula. 'Do not reproach him for his dictatorship; it led us to freedom.' In the pamphlet, Louis Napoleon called for the establishment of a régime in France where there would 'no longer be an aristocracy of birth or an aristocracy of wealth, but only one of merit'.[4]

In April 1832 the authorities of Thurgau invited Louis Napoleon to become a naturalized citizen of the canton. He accepted, realizing perhaps that it might be an advantage to him at some future time to be a Swiss citizen. He made it clear, in accepting, that he was not renouncing his French nationality, declaring that 'as a Frenchman and a Bonaparte' he was proud to become the citizen of a free country.[5]

He wrote both as a Frenchman and as a Swiss in the book that he published in Paris in July 1833, *Considérations politiques et militaires sur la Suisse*. The name of the author was given as 'Napoleon Louis C.

Bonaparte, son of Louis Bonaparte, ex-King of Holland'. Since the death of his elder brother Napoleon Louis, Louis Napoleon had styled himself and signed his letters 'Napoleon Louis Bonaparte', but he was still referred to by his acquaintances and in the press as 'Prince Louis Napoleon', or more often as 'Prince Louis Bonaparte'.

In the book, Louis Napoleon supported the demands of the Swiss Radicals for a strong central government. The Great Powers in 1815 had restored the old Swiss constitution, which had existed before the French invasion of 1798, under which the cantons were virtually independent states united only for purposes of foreign policy and defence. The Federal Diet had no executive government administration, its affairs being administered in turn by each of the three cantons – Berne, Zürich and Lucerne – in which the Diet sat, in rotation, for a year at a time. This system was favoured by the Swiss Conservatives; but the Radicals wished to substitute a much stronger central government, such as had existed in Switzerland during Napoleon's domination, and which could suppress the trade restrictions imposed by the governments of the cantons and the antiquated laws which, in some of the Catholic cantons, provided for judicial torture and other barbaric practices. This dispute was to lead to the civil war of 1847, to the triumph of the Radicals under General Dufour, and to the establishment of the modern federal government of Switzerland.

Louis Napoleon criticized particularly the existing system under which the armed forces were controlled by officials of the cantons. A force such as this could not defend the country of William Tell; but the Swiss could rely on assistance from the old soldiers of Napoleon, who in France had reddened the scaffolds of the Restoration with their blood, in Greece had helped the slaves to win back their independence, and in Italy and Poland had led the fight for national freedom. 'What part of Europe can we pass through without finding traces of French glory? If you cross a bridge its name reminds you that our battalions once carried it at the point of the bayonet.' If liberty were threatened in Switzerland, Napoleon's soldiers 'would be the first to fly to defend the frontiers'.

But he urged, in his book, that the federal system which he supported in Switzerland should not be adopted in France. He criticized those French Liberals who were now as eager to adopt the American political system as they had formerly been to imitate the British, and he pointed out that circumstances in France were very different from those existing in either Britain or the United States. France was not an island protected by the sea, like Britain. There were 32 million Frenchmen living in a territory of 20,000 square leagues (153,000 square miles), whereas in the United States a population of ten million inhabited an area of

280,000 square leagues (2,139,000 square miles).* The citizens of the United States devoted all their energies to commerce and agriculture; they had no impoverished industrial populations; and they did not, like France, have political parties 'who, forgetting that they are sons of the same country, bitterly hate each other and are continually making the government totter'. Above all, they were not surrounded by powerful neighbours 'who make their frontiers bristle with bayonets as soon as the word Liberty resounds in their ears'.

Why did Frenchmen look back with admiration at such cruel rulers as Louis XI and Richelieu? Because they had united the nation and created a strong centralized government. Yet no one could now tolerate the government of despotic rulers of this type. There must be new institutions erected by 'the people, the only source of everything that is great and generous'.[6]

Louis Napoleon took the opportunity, in *Considérations politiques et militaires sur la Suisse*, to pay a warm tribute to his father and to refer to the embarrassing subject of Louis's conflict with Napoleon in 1810. He wrote that his father, unable to reconcile the interests of his Dutch subjects with those of France, preferred to lose his kingdom rather than go against either his conscience or his brother. 'There are few examples in history of such disinterestedness and loyalty.' King Louis did not appreciate the tribute. He wrote to Louis Napoleon that he considered these compliments to be an insult, because they denigrated his brother and dishonoured the Bonaparte family. Louis himself had written a book in which, unlike Louis Napoleon, he criticized Napoleon for his policy towards Holland; but he was not going to approve of criticism from 'a young man aged twenty-four'. Louis Napoleon learned the lesson. When he became Emperor and authorized the publication of Napoleon's letters, he suppressed the correspondence between his uncle and his father which revealed the rift between them during Louis's reign in Holland.[7]

Louis Napoleon had rejoined the military college at Thun when he returned to Switzerland in 1831, and he continued to serve there under Dufour during the next four years; but he was often on leave at Arenenberg, impressing the neighbours, the people of the district, and the guests at the castle by his slim, handsome figure, which was displayed to advantage in his tight-fitting Swiss officer's uniform and high shako, by his slightly condescending affability, and by his prowess on horseback as he rode in the countryside and hunted in the forests. Once, when riding along a road and meeting a peasant woman leading a calf on a rope, he made his horse jump over the calf. On another occasion he

*This was of course before the incorporation into the United States of Texas, California and the rest of the territory which was afterwards acquired from Mexico.

was able to save a woman and her two children in a carriage when their lives were in danger from runaway horses; he galloped after the horses and stopped them in full career, to the applause of the on-lookers.[8]

He increased his popularity in some quarters, and aroused dis-approving comment in others, by his amorous escapades. His sexual instincts had developed early. At the age of twelve he fell in love with a little girl in the neighbourhood, and wrote out her name in cress-seeds in a flower-bed, and he deeply resented it when Le Bas, who had just been appointed his tutor, angrily raked out the name with a pickaxe. As a schoolboy at the *Gymnasium* at Augsburg, he was often seen looking out of the classroom window at the girls passing in the street, when he ought to have been concentrating on his lessons. At fourteen, he leaped fully dressed into the Neckar when his cousin Marie, the daughter of the Grand Duke of Baden, threw a flower into the river and dared him to retrieve it for her, as a medieval knight would have done for his lady. A year later he fell romantically in love with a girl he saw sitting at a window, and although he did not speak to her and never saw her again, he told Valérie Masuyer in London in 1831 that he had not forgotten the girl at the window and would remember her all his life.

Now in Switzerland, in his middle twenties, he flirted with women of every class – with the daughters of his mother's friends who visited Arenenberg, with the wives of the gentry and tradesmen of Constance, and with the servant-girls in the local inns, reciting to them passages from the romantic novels and poems of La Motte Fouqué, Walter Scott and his favourite author, Schiller, serenading them by moonlight, and doing all that was expected from a lover of the 1830s. The neighbours told stories of a pretty barmaid at the near-by inn at Ermatingen whom Louis Napoleon on one occasion helped with the washing-up while singing passionate love-songs to her. Valérie Masuyer, who, though an attractive-looking girl, was still unmarried at thirty-five and died an old maid many years later, was fond of him, but wrote in her diary that she had rejected him when he tried to make love to her, and disapproved of his constant flirtations with other women and of his fickleness as a lover.[9]

There is good reason to believe that he had an illegitimate child by a local girl, to whom he sent money many years later when he was Emperor of the French;[10] but many of the stories about his love affairs are almost certainly either wholly untrue or grossly exaggerated. The most scandalous comes to us at sixth hand from Valérie Masuyer; she was told it by Hortense's elderly lady-in-waiting, Mademoiselle Elisa de Perrigny, who strongly disapproved of Louis Napoleon and his flirtations. Elisa had heard it from Frau von Graimberg, who had it from

Frau von Zeppelin, who had it from her cousin. The girl involved was the daughter of Baroness de Reding, who was the governess and companion of Jerome Bonaparte's daughter, Princess Mathilde, and was often a guest at Arenenberg.

On one occasion, after the Baroness and her daughter had been staying at Arenenberg, Mademoiselle de Reding left on a visit to Italy escorted by her cousin, Monsieur Hanz. Louis Napoleon rode after them and caught up with them at the inn at Rorschach where they stayed the first night. They were very surprised to see him, but had no objection when he joined them at dinner, during which he paid lavish compliments to Mademoiselle de Reding. In the middle of the night, he burst into her room, fell sobbing at her feet, and begged her to grant his desires. When she threatened to call for help, he told her that he had bribed the servants at the inn and that no one would come to her assistance. Although Mademoiselle de Reding had the reputation of being an excitable girl, she kept her head on this occasion, and succeeded, quietly but firmly, in getting rid of him. Next day she complained to her cousin, who said that if he had known about Louis Napoleon's intrusion he would have given him a sound thrashing. If there is any truth at all in this story, Mademoiselle de Reding and her family soon forgave Louis Napoleon, because she and her mother continued to be regular visitors to Arenenberg.[11]

Hortense adopted a very tolerant attitude to Louis Napoleon's love affairs, but she became a little anxious about his association with a widow from Mauritius, Madame Saunier, who owned a castle in the neighbourhood. Hortense feared that she was trying to trap Louis Napoleon into marrying her, though, according to Louis Napoleon's friend, Charles Henri Bac, Madame Saunier refused Louis Napoleon's secret proposal of marriage, pointing out that their difference in rank made this impossible. It was partly to get Louis Napoleon away from Madame Saunier that Hortense encouraged him to go on a visit to England with his Italian revolutionary friend, the young Count Arese.[12] It gave him an opportunity to meet his uncle Joseph Bonaparte, the former King of Naples and Spain, now calling himself Comte de Survilliers, who had left the United States for the first time since 1815 and had arrived in London.

In July 1832 the Duke of Reichstadt died of consumption in Vienna at the age of twenty-one. In his will, he bequeathed his father's sword to Louis Napoleon, though Alexandre Dumas told Hortense that it would be rather a heavy sword for an officer in the Swiss army to carry.[13] The death of the Duke of Reichstadt, in Bonapartist eyes, made Joseph Bonaparte the Emperor of the French, as he was next in the line of succession laid down in the Act of the Senate and approved by the

French people at the referendum in 1804 – an Act which the Bonapartists considered to be still in force, as it had been repealed only by an illegal government imposed upon the nation by foreign armies of occupation. Unfortunately for the Bonapartists, Joseph Bonaparte had no desire to become Emperor of the French, and as his only ambition was to be allowed to return to France and live there in peace and anonymity under the government of King Louis Philippe, he refused to have anything to do with his supporters in France who were trying to overthrow the Orleanist régime and place him on the imperial throne. Like his brothers Louis and Jerome, he had become a conservative in his old age, and had disapproved of Louis Napoleon's connection with the Italian revolutionaries.

Louis Napoleon and Arese left Arenenberg at the beginning of November 1832 and travelled to England through Belgium, where they spent a day at Waterloo, wandering all over the battlefield and searching out particularly the farm of La Belle Alliance, which had been Napoleon's headquarters during the battle.[14] Before crossing the Channel, Louis Napoleon secretly slipped across the French frontier and visited La Fayette at his country house near Calais. The old hero of the American War of Independence and the French Revolution of 1789 was now aged seventy-five, but had recently returned to active political life after the Revolution of 1830 and had become the leader of the campaign to force the French government to intervene in defence of Poland. He had made himself very unpopular with the Bonapartists by the part he had played in forcing Napoleon to abdicate after Waterloo; but Louis Napoleon declared that he would not hold this against him, as it was necessary for all patriots to unite. 'No one will ever say of me', he said, 'what the Emperor used to say about the Bourbons, that during their long exile they had learned nothing and had forgotten nothing.'[15]

When Louis Napoleon arrived in London, he called on Joseph Bonaparte at his house at 23 Park Crescent on the south side of Regent's Park. Their relations were strained from the first. Joseph thought that Louis Napoleon was a young Radical hothead who had compromised the whole family by his revolutionary adventures; Louis Napoleon thought that Joseph was a tired and jaded old man who was proving unworthy of his destiny and was failing in his duty to his loyal supporters. Despite his misgivings, Louis Napoleon treated Joseph with the deference due to the Emperor of the French, and he was deeply hurt when Joseph failed to welcome him warmly as a nephew and treated him with a cool reserve. He received a much more cordial welcome from the Whig hostesses in London society, where he aroused great interest both as a forlorn and romantic exile and as an aloof but attractive young man. At a party given by Henry Webster, Lady Holland's son by her first marriage, he coolly administered a snub to Talleyrand, who as Louis Philippe's ambassador in London had pointedly ignored his presence. Seeing Talleyrand talking to Lady Tankerville, he walked up to her and greeted her in their native French right under Talleyrand's nose without saying a word to Talleyrand.[16]

Louis Napoleon was eager to see the industrial Midlands and North of England; the political influence of these areas had at last been recognized with the passing of the Reform Bill. He visited Birmingham and Lancashire, and in March 1833 travelled for the first time in his life by railway, going from Manchester to Liverpool only two-and-a-half years after the opening of the line and eight years after the first passenger train in the world had run on the Stockton–Darlington line. In a letter to his friend Narcisse Vieillard, who had been tutor to his brother Napoleon Louis, he gave a detailed description of the structure and appearance of a railway train. It had five or six carriages linked together with metal chains; the carriages were not unlike those of a horse-drawn public coach, with seats for eighteen passengers in each carriage. The train took only one hour and twenty minutes to cover the thirty-six miles from Manchester to Liverpool, and was therefore travelling at an average speed of twenty-seven miles per hour. He wrote to Hortense that the train

> starts off at an ever-increasing speed, then all objects flash by at an incredible pace; houses, trees, fences and everything else disappear before you can really see them . . . half-way along the track you meet another vehicle which passes quite close to you at the speed of lightning.[17]

During the English winter, he fell ill, as he had done in Italy and in Paris in 1831, and as he was to do often in later life. Louis Napoleon was blessed with the two great advantages of family connections and great wealth, but he was cursed from his youth with ill-health and with a basic lack of robustness which he could not overcome by vigorous exercise, a temperate diet and high spirits.[18] His health let him down in several crises of his life, and worst of all, fatally, in 1870. As he lay ill in London, he tried again to read Victor Hugo's *Hunchback of Notre Dame*, but enjoyed it no more than he had at the first attempt. He found that it made his fever worse, not better.[19]

He returned to Switzerland in May 1833 and took up his former life at Thun and Arenenberg. In June 1834 he published his *Manuel d'artillerie à l'usage des officiers d'artillerie de la République helvétique*. It was a military textbook, written in a clear and lucid style. Although one of his objects in writing it was no doubt to gain further publicity, it revealed another aspect of his character – his bent for painstaking scholarship, which thirty years later made him spend many months, at the height of his imperial power, writing a learned biography of Julius Caesar. His *Manual of Artillery* was very well received by the military experts, and the authorities of the canton of Berne promoted him to the rank of Captain of Artillery in the Berne militia. As he rode away in his captain's uniform after the promotion ceremony, his comrades and men shouted 'Vive Napoléon!'[20]

He was now twenty-six, and his mother thought that it was time that he married, especially in view of his susceptibilities for pretty women and the danger that he might be trapped into marriage by some adventuress. Hortense was determined that his bride should be his equal in rank, and that she should bring him a good dowry; but any marriage with a princess of a reigning European house would have been viewed with suspicion by the Great Powers, and prospective fathers-in-law were reluctant to provide the high dowry which Hortense demanded. There was the further difficulty of persuading Louis Bonaparte to agree to any match which Hortense favoured, or of her accepting any that he proposed.

In the autumn of 1835 reports appeared in several European newspapers that Louis Napoleon was being considered as a husband for Queen Maria da Gloria of Portugal, the young widow of Eugène de Beauharnais's son, Auguste, Duke of Leuchtenberg. Maria had returned as Queen of Portugal after winning the civil war against her uncle, King Miguel, with the help of the Liberals and Radicals. The Portuguese government's plan to marry her to Louis Philippe's son had been foiled by Palmerston, who eventually arranged for her to marry Prince Ferdinand of Saxe-Coburg-Gotha. Louis Napoleon was never in the running, and he issued a statement denying that he aspired to the hand of this 'young, virtuous and lovely Queen'. He added that, though he had admired the struggle of the Liberal forces of Queen Maria in the Portuguese civil war, his interest lay in France, not in Portugal:

> Convinced that the great name I bear will not always condemn me to exile in the eyes of my fellow-countrymen, because it recalls to them fifteen years of glory, I wait quietly in a free and hospitable country until the people recall to France those who were banished from their native land by twelve hundred thousand foreigners.[21]

Hortense was in fact planning to marry him to a distant cousin, the daughter of Arrighi de Casanova, who was Madame Mère's cousin and had been created Duke of Padua by Napoleon. Casanova, who was very rich, offered a dowry of 600,000 livres.* Hortense asked for a million livres, but eventually agreed to accept 600,000 livres on

*About £25,000 in 1835, or at least £1,500,000 in terms of 1979 prices.

condition that it was paid into a Swiss bank. Louis Napoleon, who had never met Mademoiselle de Padua, was not enthusiastic about marrying her, but he wrote to his father to ask him for his advice as to whether he should make a formal proposal for her hand. Louis would not agree, giving as his reason that he did not approve of marriage between cousins, and to Hortense's annoyance the marriage negotiations were broken off.[22]

Louis Napoleon had meanwhile fallen in love again – more seriously, perhaps, than ever before – with Louise de Crenay, the adopted daughter of the Marquis de Crenay, who lived in a castle near Arenenberg. As she firmly refused to become his mistress, he wanted to marry her; but Hortense did not consider her to be of sufficiently high rank to be a bride for Louis Napoleon, even if Louise had been prepared to accept him, which was by no means certain. Louise's resistance increased Louis Napoleon's ardour, and he continued to show her every attention on the many occasions when the Crenays visited Arenenberg.[23]

But his closest and most lasting friendship with a woman was of a different kind. From his earliest childhood he had been brought up with Hortense Lacroix, the daughter of one of his mother's maid-servants. The ladies-in-waiting considered Madame Lacroix to be socially far beneath them; but Queen Hortense encouraged Louis Napoleon to play with her little girl, who was just one year younger than he. They told each other their children's secrets, and gave each other moral support. The friendship continued after they grew up and Hortense Lacroix married and became Madame Cornu. They corresponded frequently, Louis Napoleon telling her his innermost thoughts, and receiving encouragement from her. Their relationship was the more intimate and permanent because there had never been anything sexual in it. 'The feeling that I have for you', he wrote to her, 'is worth more than love; it is more lasting. It is worth more than friendship; it is more tender.'[24]

He remained very close to his mother, spending much time with her, and often embracing her; and he resented it when she encouraged any gentleman of her household to become too intimate.[25] His widow Eugénie said in 1912 that he always showed 'an extraordinary veneration' for his mother, and added: 'I do not know if she deserved it to such an extent.'[26] He enjoyed his days with Hortense at Arenenberg. The enlargements which she had made to the castle after she bought it in 1817 included adding an annexe which she put at Louis Napoleon's disposal. He lived here with a friend of his own age, Charles Henri Bac, who was an illegitimate son of King Jerome Bonaparte. Louis Napoleon spent much of his time writing his books and studying in a sparsely furnished room which they called 'the map room', because of all the books and documents, including maps and charts, which lay about on the tables. He slept in a simple military bed with sheets and blankets in the French style, unlike the continental quilts used by the Swiss and the other residents at Arenenberg.

Bac liked Louis Napoleon, but even in the intimacy of their living quarters he found him reserved and uncommunicative. He was often disturbed by Louis Napoleon's sleeplessness, and noticed that at night he showed a nervousness which he managed to conceal during the day. The young Prince, who could perform such fearless equestrian feats, and was so daring with women, would sometimes wake in the middle of the night in great agitation and insist on searching the house because he believed that burglars were lurking there or that he was threatened by some unknown danger.[27]

Hortense entertained many visitors at Arenenberg – her cousin the Grand Duchess of Baden, members of the Bonaparte family, neighbours like the British General Lindsay and his Creole wife, and distinguished French writers. Alexandre Dumas, Delphine Gay, Madame Récamier and Chateaubriand came to Arenenberg. The fact that Chateaubriand had always been an upholder of the *ancien régime* and the Restoration of 1815 did not prevent Louis Napoleon from admiring him as a writer and thinker. 'How lucky the Bourbons are to have a genius like yours to uphold them', he wrote to Chateaubriand in May 1832 after reading a pamphlet of his in defence of the Legitimist monarchy. When Chateaubriand visited Arenenberg three months later, he was charmed by Hortense and impressed by Louis Napoleon.[28]

The distinguished guests were eager to visit the famous Queen Hortense and her son, and Hortense always proved to be a delightful hostess, from the moment of their arrival, when, with almost childish delight, she showed them round the castle and the grounds of which she was so proud, pointing out the beautiful views over Lake Constance and the forest of Ermatingen. At dinner she put them all at their ease. When King Jerome Bonaparte and his wife gave dinner parties they were served before their guests; but the only royal privilege which Hortense claimed was to have a finger bowl laid ceremoniously before her by a servant. Later in the evening she would play the piano and sing her *romances*, Louis Napoleon would pay compliments to the beautiful women, and both of them would engage in sparkling and erudite conversation on political and cultural topics.[29]

In November 1835 King Jerome, who now styled himself Prince de Montfort, visited Arenenberg with his children – Prince Jerome aged twenty-one, Princess Mathilde aged fifteen, and the thirteen-year-old Prince Napoleon Joseph, who was known in the family by the pet-name of 'Plom-Plom' because he had been a round, fat baby.[30] In later years, the name passed into general use by journalists and the public at large, who spelt it 'Plon-Plon'. The Montforts stayed for a few weeks on their way to Italy, and came again in the spring, when they stayed for nearly two months in April and May 1836.

Princess Mathilde, though six weeks short of her sixteenth birthday, was already a skilled coquette, and she set out to fascinate her cousin Louis Napoleon with a determination which shocked some of the older ladies of Hortense's household. Valérie Masuyer, who was more tolerant than the other ladies towards Mathilde, noted that on the evening of their arrival King Jerome scolded Mathilde for wearing a dress which was too *décolleté*. 'He was right,' wrote Valérie;

> there was too much nudity. But everything that she displayed was so pretty that it was a joy to look at. The Prince was quite overcome, and devoured her with his eyes. With him, the flesh is weak. In the morning he had been serious, cold, unimpressed, and in the evening the pretty shoulders revived him and he was most inspired.[31]

Though Mathilde attracted Louis Napoleon from the very first evening, he did not immediately fall sufficiently seriously in love with her to forget his other lady friends, and on several evenings during the stay of the Montfort family he went off by himself to Constance to visit the handsome Frau von Zeppelin, the wife of the Mayor, or the pretty girls at the local inns. On these occasions, Mathilde sulked. Valérie Masuyer noted that when Louis Napoleon was out for the evening, Mathilde 'was parsimonious with her pretty shoulders', and did not waste them on the other members of the household. But on the following evening, when Louis Napoleon was there again, the shoulders 'reappeared in all their glory'.[32] Elisa de Perrigny strongly disapproved of Mathilde, with her flirtatiousness, her teasing nature, her habit of suddenly bursting out in loud, mocking laughter. Elisa thought that Mathilde was too young, too carefree and too selfish for the reserved, pensive Louis Napoleon, who was twelve years older than she; but Louis Napoleon became increasingly fascinated by the gay young coquette, and Hortense approved. For the first time, Louis Napoleon seemed to be on the point of falling in love with a girl whom he might properly marry.

The four young princes and princesses – Louis Napoleon, Jerome, Mathilde and the precocious thirteen-year-old Plom-Plom – enjoyed themselves at Arenenberg in April and May 1836 in a light-hearted and inconsiderate manner which often annoyed their elders. They did things together and ignored the rest of the household. They whispered to each other and burst out laughing – were they laughing at Elisa and the other ladies? Once they sat down to dinner and started eating without waiting for Elisa and Valérie. When a party from Arenenberg went across to the Isle of Reichenau in Lake Constance to see the famous monastery which had stood there for more than a thousand years, they played a trick on Elisa, leaving her stranded alone on the island, where she was insulted and stoned by some young peasant boys and had some difficulty in finding a boatman to row her back to Arenenberg. When she arrived home she complained to Hortense and to King Jerome, and wept copiously. Mathilde and both her brothers laughed; but when Valérie told Louis Napoleon that a gallant prince should protect his mother's elderly ladies from insult, and not expose them to it, he went out of his way to be courteous and considerate to her during the next few days.

By the middle of May, when the Montforts had been a month at Arenenberg, Louis Napoleon was spending all his evenings at home. When Hortense and the household went on excursions for the day, he normally refused to go in the carriage with them, and insisted on riding on his Andalusian mare Cora alongside the carriage, or riding ahead. Now he chose always to travel in the carriage with Mathilde. They spent much time holding hands and gazing romantically at each other. It was a period at which romantic love was idealized in novels and in operas, and young lovers imitated the behaviour of the heroes and heroines of fiction. Mathilde gave up eating at meals, and sat at the table gazing at Louis Napoleon, the very picture of a heroine pining away for love. Elisa told the other ladies that Mathilde stole secretly to the pantry between meals and stuffed herself with cakes.

The Montforts left Arenenberg a week before Mathilde's sixteenth birthday on 27 May. On the evening before their departure, Hortense gave a special birthday dinner-party for Mathilde; she dressed her in one of her own dresses in the style of the First Empire of thirty years before – a long clinging dress of white satin which won universal praise. Louis Napoleon hired a group of singers who rowed up in a boat to the end of the castle garden and serenaded Mathilde during the evening. Next day the Montforts left for Italy, after a tearful farewell, with Mathilde sobbing dramatically and Louis Napoleon sad and silent, an utterly disconsolate lover. Hortense immediately began tactful negotiations with King Jerome about marriage and a dowry.[33]

Louis Napoleon did not remain disconsolate for long. At the end of June, five weeks after Mathilde left Arenenberg, he spent the evening with his arm around the waist of Louise de Crenay, who was visiting the castle. Hortense's ladies, remembering Louise and Madame Saunier, had been shocked when they heard Louis Napoleon say to Mathilde that he had never been seriously in love before. They were even more shocked now to see him embracing Louise.[34]

But, unknown to any of the other members of the household at Arenenberg – unknown even to Hortense – Louis Napoleon was in contact with another group of friends during the spring and summer of 1836. He was planning a military *coup d'état* in France.

CHAPTER 9

FROM STRASBURG TO NEW YORK

IN 1835 Louis Napoleon met the man who was to have the greatest influence on his life. Jean Gilbert Victor Fialin was a ruthless and unscrupulous adventurer, but he was utterly loyal to Louis Napoleon and to Bonapartism. He was prepared to go to any length in order to further the Bonapartist cause.

He was born in the same year as Louis Napoleon, and was brought up from the age of seven in the France of Louis XVIII. In 1825, when he was seventeen, he enlisted in the army of Charles X, and by 1830 had reached the rank of sergeant in the cavalry. He was one of many soldiers who refused to fire on the people and went over to the revolutionaries during the revolution of July; but his Republican sympathies aroused the suspicions of Louis Philippe's government, and he was discharged from the army. He then became a journalist and a Bonapartist, and founded Bonapartist newspapers in Paris. It was at this time that he began calling himself 'Comte de Persigny', a family title which had lain dormant for several centuries. When he visited Arenenberg in the summer of 1835 he immediately became a friend of Louis Napoleon. Each of them was attracted by the other's energy, daring and adventurism; they decided to risk all and to sink or swim together.

In the summer of 1836, Louis Napoleon and Persigny planned a revolution in France. Others in the plot included Major Denis Parquin, who had married Hortense's former lady-in-waiting Louise Cochelet and lived in a house near Arenenberg, and the well-known singer Eléonore Gordon. She was the daughter of an officer in Napoleon's Guard and the widow of an English officer. She was twenty-eight when she met Louis Napoleon in the summer of 1836. She was attracted by his dark reserve and charm, but there was no truth in the current rumour that she was his mistress.

The conspirators' plan was to win the support of the garrison at Strasburg, to seize the town, proclaim the Empire, and call on the people of France, and above all the army, to rise and overthrow the government of Louis Philippe. Louis Napoleon always denied that he wished to make himself Emperor;[1] he intended to march on Paris and establish a provisional government which would invite the people to decide, at a referendum held under universal manhood suffrage, whether they wished to be ruled by Joseph Bonaparte, Emperor of the French under the Act of the Senate of 1804. Strasburg was a good place to choose for the *coup*. As it was on the frontier, it was easy for the plotters to make contact with their supporters in Strasburg from the territory of the Grand Duchy of Baden across the bridge over the Rhine; and two of the officers of the garrison, Colonel Vaudrey and Lieutenant Laity, had joined the conspirators. Vaudrey and Parquin, who were aged fifty, were veterans of Napoleon's armies; all the others were under thirty years of age. Parquin had always been an enthusiastic Bonapartist, but Vaudrey apparently only joined the plot on condition that Eléonore Gordon went to bed with him.[2]

Louis Napoleon had hoped to gain the support of General Voirol, the General Officer Commanding the Strasburg garrison, and his aide-de-camp Colonel de Franqueville, who had married Valérie Masuyer's sister. He also wrote to General Exelmans; the General was a hero in Bonapartist eyes because he had defeated a Prussian force in a skirmish near Versailles on 2 July 1815, the day before the surrender of the French armies, thus enabling them to claim that France had won the last battle of the war. Voirol, Franqueville and Exelmans all refused to join the plot; but they seemed to be not unsympathetic. In August, Louis Napoleon secretly visited Strasburg and met a number of officers of the garrison, all of whom were friendly, though they refused to give definite promises of support.

The army, like the French people as a whole, was vacillating between Louis Philippe and Bonapartism. They were disgusted by the timid foreign policy of Louis Philippe's ministers, who had been outwitted by Palmerston in Belgium, Italy, Portugal and Spain; but the Orleanist régime was safe, and gave the middle classes the opportunity of making money. Louis Napoleon hoped that decisive action would bring the waverers to his side. He remembered the Hundred Days, when a man bearing the name of Napoleon Bonaparte had appeared on the furthest frontiers of France and the whole nation had risen and driven the King from Paris without a drop of French blood being spilt. If he went to Strasburg, once again the eagle would fly from steeple to steeple until it reached Notre-Dame.

On 25 October 1836 Louis Napoleon left Arenenberg, telling Hortense that he was going on a hunting expedition in Germany.[3] He met his fellow-plotters at Freiburg in the Grand Duchy of Baden, and late in the afternoon of the 28th crossed the Rhine bridge and entered Strasburg, just as the city gates were closing for the night. They went, as arranged, to a small house at 24 Rue de la Fontaine, where all the conspirators met: there were fifteen of them, including Louis Napoleon, Persigny, Parquin, Vautrey, Laity and Eléonore Gordon. They spent next day discussing their plan of campaign. The *coup* had originally been fixed for the early morning of the 31st, but it was decided to bring the time forward by twenty-four hours in order to forestall any possibility of betrayal.

Louis Napoleon sat up all the night of 29–30 October, too nervous to sleep. He wrote out the draft of his proclamations to the army, to the people of Alsace, and to the people of France:

I present myself to you with the Will of the Emperor Napoleon in one hand and the sword of Austerlitz in the other. In Rome, when the people saw Caesar's bloodstained corpse, they overthrew their hypocritical oppressors. Frenchmen, Napoleon is greater than Caesar; he is the emblem of the civilization of the nineteenth century. ... Men of 1789, men of 20 March 1815, men of 1830, arise![4]

He then wrote two letters to Hortense, one telling her that the *coup* had been successful, and the other saying that it had failed. By next day he would know which letter to send to Arenenberg.*[5]

At 4.30 a.m. on 30 October all the conspirators except Eléonore Gordon left the house in the Rue de la Fontaine. It had just stopped snowing, and a light fall of snow covered the ground. Some of them went to the houses of General Voirol and the Chief of Police, while others occupied the printing works and the telegraph office. Louis Napoleon went with Vaudrey to the Austerlitz Barracks at the south side of the city, where the 4th Artillery Regiment, which Vaudrey commanded, was stationed. Louis Napoleon was dressed in a colonel's uniform, such as Napoleon had always worn, with the Legion of Honour on his breast; as a Prince of the imperial family, he had been entitled to wear it from his birth. Vaudrey wore a general's uniform, having just been promoted to this rank by Louis Napoleon.

At 6 a.m. Vaudrey aroused his officers and men, introduced Louis Napoleon to them, and called on them to join him in overthrowing the government of Louis Philippe. The 4th Artillery was the regiment in which the great Napoleon had first served as a young lieutenant, and the Austerlitz Barracks resounded with shouts of 'Vive l'Empereur!' as the whole regiment followed its commanding officer and joined Louis Napoleon, who set off at the head of nearly a thousand men of the 4th Artillery to march to the city centre. The civilian population cheered them as they passed, crying 'Long live the Emperor!' and 'Long live Liberty!' Some Bonapartists shouted 'Long live Napoleon III!'

*After Louis Napoleon was arrested, the wrong letter was at first sent to Arenenberg, and for a few hours Hortense thought that the *coup* had succeeded.

The Republicans among the onlookers made a counter-demonstration, shouting equally prophetically 'Long live the President of the Republic!' as Louis Napoleon passed.[6]

If Louis Napoleon had been an experienced organizer of military *coups*, he would have gone at once to the barracks of the 3rd Artillery Regiment. If the 3rd Artillery had come over with its 150 guns, he would have controlled the town, and the other military units would not have opposed him. But Louis Napoleon had rejected this proposal when it had been put to him; he did not wish to terrorize the garrison and people of Strasburg into submitting to him, but to win their support by persuasion.[7] He therefore went to General Voirol's house, where the General had been detained by Parquin and other conspirators, and tried to persuade Voirol to join him. As Voirol refused, Louis Napoleon placed him under arrest and marched at the head of the men of the 4th Artillery to the Finckmatt Barracks, where the 46th Infantry Regiment was stationed.

Here he made another tactical error. Instead of leading his thousand followers into the Finckmatt Barracks and thus impressing on the men of the 46th that the *coup* was succeeding, he entered the barracks alone with a few of his leading supporters, and tried to harangue the officers and men of the 46th, calling on them to join him. But just as he was beginning to speak, the commanding officer of the regiment, Lieutenant-Colonel Taillandier, called out that Louis Napoleon was an impostor; and another officer shouted that he was not Prince Louis Bonaparte, but was Colonel Vaudrey's nephew masquerading as the Prince. This swung over the waverers, and the whole regiment shouted 'Vive le Roi!' Taillandier then ordered one of his officers to arrest Louis Napoleon and those who were with him; Louis Napoleon, who was determined that no French blood should be spilt, surrendered without resistance. By 8.30 a.m., the *coup* was over, two-and-a-half hours after it had started.[8]

Thirty-eight years earlier, a telegraph line had been installed between Paris and Strasburg. It operated by means of semaphore stations, where wooden arm-signals, like railway signal posts, were used to send messages in cipher from one telegraph station to the next, the stations being in sight of each other, a few miles apart, all the way from Strasburg to Paris. The result was that whereas it took two days for news to travel to Paris from Calais, news from Strasburg arrived in the capital in a few hours. This very useful method of communication was the pride of French industry until the development of the electric telegraph after 1843.[9]

At 8.30 a.m. on 30 October, General Voirol sent the following message by telegraph to the Minister of War in Paris: 'This morning, at about six o'clock, Louis Napoleon, the son of the Duchesse de St Leu, who was acting in league with Colonel of Artillery Vaudrey, went through the streets of Strasburg with a party of —'[10] At this point the message broke off. The winter had set in early in Eastern France, and the countryside was covered with freezing fog which made it impossible for the operators at the telegraph stations to see the signals flashed from the previous station. Consequently the incomplete telegraph message did not reach Paris for nearly thirty-six hours. As soon as the Minister of War received it on the evening of 31 October, he informed the King and the other ministers, and the Cabinet was hastily summoned to meet at the Tuileries. Louis Philippe and his government waited all night in great anxiety for further news from Strasburg, and it was not until 6 a.m. on 1 November that Franqueville, angry and anxious about his sister-in-law's connection with the Bonapartes at Arenenberg, arrived in Paris with Voirol's official dispatch.[11] This informed the Minister of War that the 'criminal attempt of young Louis Napoleon Bonaparte' to subvert the loyalty of the troops at Strasburg 'had failed, thanks to the noble and courageous conduct of our soldiers'.[12]

The authorities at Strasburg detained in custody only eight of the Bonapartist leaders, including Louis Napoleon, Parquin, Laity, Vaudrey and Eléonore Gordon, who had been found and arrested at the house in the Rue de la Fontaine. Persigny succeeded in escaping, and reached Arenenberg. The prisoners were transferred to the local jail, where Louis Napoleon was given a comfortable room with a servant to wait on him. In accordance with the usual French criminal procedure, the local *juge d'instruction* began a lengthy interrogation of the prisoners. Both Louis Napoleon and Vaudrey accepted full responsibility for the *coup*, and untruthfully said that none of their companions had had any previous knowledge of their plans before the morning of 30 October.[13]

The press, both in France and abroad, was almost unanimous in interpreting the events at Strasburg as a proof of the stability of the Orleanist régime, and in condemning and ridiculing Louis Napoleon. The official Paris newspaper, *Le Moniteur Universel*, called for the stern punishment of the rebels, while insisting that due forms of law must be followed in dealing with them. The local Strasburg journal, the *Journal du Haut et Bas Rhin*, wrote that the events of 30 October had shown that 'in France today, people want a calm, pacific and guaranteed liberty', not the rule of the despot's sabre, or the reactionary rule of the Restoration, or the savage and ridiculous rule of the Republic. *The Times* strongly condemned Louis Napoleon's 'senseless wickedness', and though it described his attempted *coup* as 'contemptible' and 'ridiculous', it took it sufficiently seriously to warn the French nation that the Great

Powers would never permit a Bonaparte to reign in France. In Germany, the *Frankfurter Journal* quoted the words of Metternich, 'Bonapartism without Bonaparte is an absurdity', and added: 'Sensible people understand this; an ambitious young man did not.' It called Louis Napoleon 'a young fool, without genius, without talent, without fame'.[14]

Delphine Gay thought that Bonapartism was finished. Napoleon's son, the Duke of Reichstadt, had been 'l'Aiglon', the young eagle, in Bonapartist eyes; but Delphine Gay did not believe that Louis Napoleon, as the Emperor's nephew, could succeed the Duke of Reichstadt in this role. 'An eagle, alas! has *aiglons*, but not collaterals', she wrote.[15]

But Louis Napoleon was undismayed and unrepentant. 'What do I care', he wrote to Hortense, 'for the cries of the mob, who will call me mad because I have failed, and who would have exaggerated my merits if I had succeeded!'[16]

The government of Louis Philippe was determined to make themselves more ridiculous than Louis Napoleon. On 13 November they announced that the King had decided not to take any further proceedings against Louis Napoleon, but to place him in a French warship and deport him to the United States; the other seven prisoners arrested with him would be tried for high treason. This announcement was strongly criticized in the press. The government supporters denounced the decision not to prosecute Louis Napoleon as an act of unpardonable weakness; the Republicans regarded it as an example of favouritism caused by Hortense's intrigues with Louis Philippe; the Bonapartists said that it was because the authorities did not dare to put the popular Prince on trial before a French jury, and considered it as a pernicious attempt to divide Louis Napoleon from his followers. The government spokesmen tried half-heartedly to praise it as an example of the King's magnanimity which was justified because Louis Napoleon, unlike the officers who had followed him, had never been a subject of Louis Philippe; but the general public thought that it was very unfair to prosecute the followers and allow the ringleader to go free.[17]

After Louis Napoleon had been imprisoned for twelve days at Strasburg, he was taken to Paris in a post-chaise during the night of 9–10 November, and detained for two days at police headquarters in Paris. When the Prefect of Police, Delessert, told him that he was to be deported to the United States, he protested against the order, saying that it would prevent him from giving evidence on behalf of his followers at their trial; but Delessert said that as they had released and exiled the Duchesse de Berry after her attempted Legitimist *coup* in 1832, they could do no less for him. He was then taken, again by night, to Lorient, where he arrived at 2 a.m. on 15 November. He was due to sail that morning in the warship *Andromède*, but rough seas and contrary winds prevented this, and he was held in Fort Saint-Louis until the *Andromède* sailed on 21 November.[18] As he went on board, the local Sub-Prefect handed him 15,000 francs to cover his expenses in the United States. It was not, as has often been stated, a gift from Louis Philippe, but part of the 200,000 francs which had been taken from him by the authorities at Strasburg at the time of his arrest. The Sub-Prefect wished him well and said that he hoped that he would one day return to France as a peaceful citizen. 'I shall not be able to return', replied Louis Napoleon, 'as long as the lion of Waterloo is standing guard on the frontier.'[19]

As soon as Hortense heard about the events at Strasburg, she hurried to Paris to see Louis Philippe in an effort to save her son. When she reached Viry she was stopped by the authorities, who informed her that Louis Napoleon was to be deported to the United States, and she returned to Arenenberg. She was pleased that he had been treated so leniently, but was anxious for his safety on the sea as she read in the newspapers about the gales in the Atlantic.[20]

At the end of January she was comforted by an item in the newspapers which reported that he had arrived safely in Philadelphia; but it was a false report.[21] The *Andromède* had encountered very rough seas after leaving Lorient, and had been forced to shelter off the north-west coast of Spain. She then sailed west through calm weather. But the captain had been given sealed orders, with instructions not to open them until he passed the 32°W. line of longitude.* When he reached this point in mid-Atlantic, he discovered that the orders required him to sail, not to New York, but to Rio de Janeiro, and he changed course for the south. Louis Napoleon was treated with great kindness and courtesy by the captain and the ship's officers throughout the voyage. The captain gave up his cabin to him, and the officers came to wish him a happy new year on New Year's Day. But he was disappointed that he was unable to catch a distant glimpse of St Helena as they crossed the South Atlantic.

They reached Rio de Janeiro on 10 January, at the height of the South American summer. The captain of the *Andromède*, in compliance with his sealed orders, anchored for a month in the harbour at Rio, but did not allow Louis Napoleon to leave the ship. Louis Napoleon had a splendid view of the magnificent harbour and Sugar Loaf Mountain, of the streets of the great city teeming with Negro slaves going about

*Louis Napoleon, in his letter to King Joseph of 22 April 1837 (Jerrold, I. 471), Persigny (*Relations de l'entreprise du Prince Napoléon-Louis*, 3rd edition (1837), p. 47), and Laity (*Relation historique des Événements du 30 Octobre 1836*, p. 72) all say 32° of latitude; but 32° W. of longitude (measured from Paris) must be meant, because if the captain of the *Andromède* believed, until he opened the sealed orders, that he was to sail to New York, he would not have gone as far south as 32° N.

their work, of the white houses, the fountains and the elaborate system of street lighting which was in advance of most of the cities of Europe; and as he still enjoyed drawing, he sketched the scene.

At the beginning of February the captain of the *Andromède*, following the last paragraph of his instructions, sailed from Rio de Janeiro for the United States. After a two-months journey they reached Norfolk in Virginia, where Louis Napoleon was put ashore on 30 March 1837, having spent 135 days on board the *Andromède*.[22]

There can have been only one reason why the government of Louis Philippe went to such lengths to send Louis Napoleon to the United States by a roundabout route of 10,000 miles and a journey lasting more than four months: they wished him to be *incomunicado* during the trial of his followers. The trial began on 6 January at Strasburg before the Assize Court of the department of the Bas-Rhin. Despite the bitterly cold weather, large crowds were queuing for seats in the spectators' gallery at 7 a.m., two hours before the trial began. The defendants disclosed in detail all their correspondence and secret meetings with Louis Napoleon in the months before 30 October, and justified their conduct by invoking the memory and glory of the great Napoleon; but the strongest argument of the defence lawyers was the absence of Louis Napoleon. Before he went on board the *Andromède* at Lorient, Louis Napoleon had written a letter to Parquin's brother, who was a barrister and appeared for the defence at the trial. 'Yes, we are all guilty, but I am the most guilty', wrote Louis Napoleon.[23] Maître Parquin and his colleague Maître Barrot stressed this again and again at the trial. 'What entitles us to ask for an acquittal for all the accused', said Maître Parquin, 'is the removal of Prince Louis.' 'There is one firmly established principle in our society', said Maître Barrot; 'it is equal justice for all.'[24]

The speeches for the defence were emotional appeals to the sentiments of the jury, with Maître Parquin ending his peroration with a special appeal for his brother. He told the jury that when he next saw his dear old mother of eighty-two, she would ask him: 'Parquin, what have you done with your brother?' He would reply: 'Ah, my good, venerable mother, dry your tears; a jury of Alsace will return your son to you.'[25]

On the twelfth day of the trial, the jury retired to consider their verdict, amid shouts from the spectators of 'Acquit! Acquit!', and threats to clear the court by the infuriated Judge. The jury were out for only twenty-two minutes before returning a verdict of Not Guilty in favour of all the defendants. The verdict was enthusiastically acclaimed by the Opposition newspapers. The government press and spokesman commented drily that they had too great a respect for the rule of law established by the July monarchy to make any comment on the verdict.[26]

Louis Napoleon's father and uncles – King Louis, King Joseph and King Jerome – strongly condemned his mad escapade at Strasburg. They were being blamed for it in some quarters: *The Times* warned the Bonapartes that although 'playing at kings and queens and princes is a pastime harmless enough within the precincts of a private dwelling', the game must not be played elsewhere, and advised the older Bonapartes to stop their children engaging in 'such mischievous follies as have outraged public decency in Rome, and more recently in Strasburg'.[27] Only Hortense was sympathetic. She thought that Louis Napoleon had been rash and foolish, but she loved her son, and despite all her wealth, her royal etiquette and her diamonds, she still retained something of her father's respect for revolutionary activity. King Jerome made it clear that, in view of what had happened, there was no question now of a marriage between Louis Napoleon and Mathilde. Louis Napoleon had realized this without needing to be told. Three weeks after leaving Lorient, when on board the *Andromède* in mid-Atlantic, he wrote that he had always had a presentiment that he would lose Mathilde.[28]

After landing at Norfolk, Virginia, he spent three days being entertained on shore by the officers of the *Andromède*, with whom he had formed a real friendship during their twenty weeks together. He then took the steamboat to Baltimore and Philadelphia, and from there went by steamboat and railroad to New York. On his journey from Baltimore to Philadelphia he passed Joseph Bonaparte's country house on the New Jersey shore of the River Delaware – an impressive villa in the Italian style at Point Breeze, just outside Bordentown on the road to Trenton, surrounded by several miles of woods and ornamental lakes, with panoramic views of the plains of Pennsylvania across the Delaware; but Joseph was in London, and did not return to Point Breeze for another eighteen months.* Like all the European visitors to the United States at this period, Louis Napoleon was greatly impressed by the steamboats used for passenger transport on the rivers; they were fast and luxurious, having several compartments reserved for women, and supplied excellent food and refreshments.[29]

New York was a busy and rapidly growing city, which was already attracting a sufficient number of foreign immigrants to more than double its population every twenty years. People aged over sixty had seen the population rise from 10,000 in 1780 to 300,000 in 1837. Louis Napoleon stayed at the Washington Hotel on Broadway. Twenty-eight

---

*Louis Napoleon, in his 'Quelques mots sur Joseph-Napoléon Bonaparte' (*Œuvres de Napoleon III*, II.449), wrote that Joseph returned to the United States in 1837; but Joseph's physician, Dr A. B. Granville, points out in his *Autobiography* (II.315) that this is an error, as Granville saw King Joseph in London nearly every day between January 1837 and the end of July 1838.

years later, a young French Radical, Georges Clemenceau, stayed there soon after his release from the prisons of Napoleon III, and was given the same room which his Emperor had occupied in 1837.[30]

In New York, Louis Napoleon found letters waiting for him from Hortense and his family and friends, including a kind message from his father which he greatly appreciated. 'All my women cousins have written me charming letters, except Mathilde',[31] he wrote to King Louis. He wrote to his mother that, in view of Mathilde's attitude, he would never agree to marry her. Mathilde afterwards said that she had wanted to write to him, but had been forbidden to do so; but she gave no indication of being heartbroken at the breach with Louis Napoleon. She did not even write a letter of sympathy to Hortense, but enjoyed herself at parties and balls that winter, though George Ticknor thought that he detected a touch of sadness in her face when he met her in May 1837.[32]

The most hostile member of the family was King Joseph, who wrote an indignant letter from London to Louis Napoleon in New York. In his respectful but frigid reply, Louis Napoleon wrote that if he had triumphed at Strasburg – 'and we were very near it' – and had reached Paris and seized power, it would have been a noble action of Joseph's to have repudiated him; but he resented the fact that, having failed, after risking his life for the family cause, 'I find on the part of my family only contempt and disdain'.[33] His father, of course, blamed Hortense for the Strasburg adventure.[34]

Louis Napoleon was a great success in New York society. Twenty-six days before he landed at Norfolk, the formidable Andrew Jackson had ended his second term as President of the United States, and had been succeeded in the White House by Van Buren. This had coincided with a financial crisis which led to panic selling on the Stock Exchange and the repudiation of their debts by several state governments. But though Louis Napoleon's friends in New York apologized to him for the fact that the splendour and gaiety of New York social life had been affected by the loss of confidence, he received many social invitations. His hosts and their guests seemed to be equally fascinated by his title of Prince and by his romantic failure as a Pretender; but the strangers who met him in the street were most interested in his moustache, for though moustaches were beginning to be worn by fashionable young men in Europe, they were so disapproved of in the United States that Louis Napoleon thought it was almost dangerous to have one.[35]

He was entertained by General Scott, by the leading families in New York, and by eminent authors like Washington Irving and Fitz-Greene Halleck. Irving invited him to the house which he had just

Philippe Le Bas

Princess Mathilde, about 1840

Drawing of Louis Napoleon, by d'Orsay, 1839

acquired near Tarrytown on a promontory overlooking the Hudson River, some thirty miles north of New York. It was a turreted building in the Dutch style, and Irving had embellished it with ivy brought from Sir Walter Scott's house at Abbotsford; at this time he called the house 'The Roost', but later changed its name to 'Sunnyside'. A few years earlier, Irving had lived for a while at Granada in Spain, where he had become friendly with Maria Manuela, Countess of Montijo, and her six-year-old daughter Eugenia. In later years he was pleased to think that he had known both the Emperor Napoleon III and the Empress Eugénie before they had first met each other.[36]

In after years, when Louis Napoleon had become Emperor, he was accused in the American press of having led a dissipated life in New York. His defenders denied this, and said that the critics had confused Louis Napoleon with his cousin Pierre Bonaparte of Canino, who also visited New York later in 1837. In view of the way in which Louis Napoleon had pursued women of every class in Switzerland, it is very likely that he met some of the less respectable ladies of New York; and the Reverend C. S. Stewart, who met him in New York and afterwards defended his reputation against the American critics, admitted that, like Dickens and other distinguished foreigners, he 'may have carried his observations . . . to scenes in which I would not have accompanied him'.[37] But there is no reason to believe that he led a life of great debauchery.

One of his respectable women friends was Mrs Roosevelt, the daughter of General Van Ness. She had lived in Spain when her father was United States Ambassador to Madrid, and like Washington Irving she had known Eugenia del Montijo as a child. Mrs Roosevelt invited Louis Napoleon to meet Fenimore Cooper and other authors at her house. Like the people who knew Louis Napoleon in Europe, Mrs Roosevelt and her guests were intrigued and fascinated by his cool reserve and quiet, silent charm.

His friend from Arenenberg and London, Count Arese, happened to be in New York at this time, and Louis Napoleon took Arese with him to the parties and dinners. They visited Washington together and went to Niagara, where they crossed the river and stood for a moment on Canadian soil.[38] They planned a much more extensive tour through Pennsylvania and Ohio to Missouri, then north-west to Montana, and back to New York by Chicago and through Canada.[39] But at the beginning of June, Louis Napoleon received a letter from Hortense, telling him that she was about to have a serious operation which might be fatal. The doctors had diagnosed cancer. She ended her letter: 'Come! Come!'[40]

Louis Napoleon abandoned his plan to go to the West with Arese, who made the tour by himself, and prepared to return to Europe immediately. Before leaving, he wrote to President Van Buren, apologizing for leaving the United States without calling at the White House. The letter was written in the language of one head of state to another, and when it was published in the press it was treated as a typical example of Louis Napoleon's impudence.[41]

After being held up for four days by contrary winds, he sailed from New York on 12 June in the packet-ship *George Washington*, bound for Liverpool.[42] He told Hortense that his fellow-passengers were a doctor from Boston and a New York business man with their families, 'two ladies who seem to me to have arrived from the moon, two very good English actors', an English army officer, two Swiss, a priest, 'an Italian sculptor who carves in marble at Washington the great deeds of American history', a gentleman with whom he played chess, 'and the rest – freight'; but he and this random selection of people were as happy together as if they had been old friends.[43] One of the 'English actors' was the Irish comedian, Tyrone Power, who was returning home after a successful tour in the United States. He fell ill during the voyage, and Louis Napoleon read aloud to him in his cabin.[44] Four years later, Power was drowned on another Atlantic crossing.

The voyage to Liverpool took only twenty-eight days, and Louis Napoleon reached London on 10 July. He immediately applied to the French, Belgian and Prussian governments for a transit visa to cross their territories on the way to Arenenberg, but they refused to grant it. He eventually obtained a passport from the Swiss Consulate in London in the name of Robinson, a United States citizen whom he knew. Fearing that he was being trailed by agents of the French embassy, he left London on the evening of 30 July and stayed the night at a hotel in Richmond – this was quite a common practice for wealthy Londoners – and next day returned secretly to London and took a public omnibus to Gravesend, where he embarked on the *Batavia*. He was in fact being watched by the Metropolitan Police who had been ordered by the Home Secretary, Lord John Russell, to send secret reports of his movements to the French embassy. They told the embassy that they had lost all trace of him after he arrived in Richmond, but that they thought he had sailed for the Continent.[45]

He sailed to Rotterdam, and for the first time in his life set foot in the country where his father had reigned as King at the time of his birth. From there he travelled through the Rhineland and Baden and reached Arenenberg on the evening of 4 August. Hortense had not had her operation, because her doctors thought that it would be too risky, and she was sinking slowly. She and Louis Napoleon had two months together before she died on 5 October, at the age of fifty-four. The last days were painful, but the ordeal ended at last, with the ladies and officers of her household in great distress, and Louis Napoleon sobbing on his knees at her bedside, as was considered proper on the Continent in 1837.[46]

CHAPTER 10

FROM SWITZERLAND TO LONDON

As soon as Hortense's funeral at Ermatingen was over, Louis Napoleon dismissed her ladies and most of the household staff, after giving them gifts in addition to the generous legacies which they received under her will.[1] He left a skeleton staff in residence at Arenenberg, and in January 1838 moved to Gottlieben, five miles from Arenenberg at the junction of the inner lake of Lake Constance with the greater lake. It was a ruined medieval castle where Pope John XXII had stayed during the Council of Constance in 1414; more recently the grounds had been a public park, and there was a ramshackle abandoned building in the garden which had been used as a café. Hortense had bought the property from King Jerome. The castle was in a very dilapidated state, and there was a risk of the roof falling in; but Louis Napoleon lived happily on the third floor, the only habitable part of the castle, with his Strasburg colleague, Laity.[2]

He was not allowed to live there in peace for long. Louis Philippe's government was alarmed at his presence in Switzerland. They spread the story, often repeated in later years and always denied by Louis Napoleon, that when he was deported to the United States after the Strasburg *coup* he had given his word of honour that he would not return to Europe.[3] On the day after he moved to Gottlieben, the French government suggested informally to the Swiss Diet that he be expelled from Switzerland, as his presence there constituted a danger to the internal security of France and was a violation of the undertaking given by the Swiss government in 1815 not to grant asylum to French Bonapartist refugees. The government of the Confederation replied, as usual, that Louis Napoleon's residence in Thurgau was a matter for the canton to decide. The French government, though dissatisfied with this reply, took no further action for the time being; and soon afterwards Louis Napoleon left Gottlieben and moved back to Arenenberg.[4]

In June 1838 Laity, who had returned to Paris, published a book on which he and Louis Napoleon had worked together at Gottlieben, though Laity alone was named as the author. His *Relation historique des Événements du 30 Octobre 1836* gave the Bonapartist version of the

Strasburg events, glorifying Louis Napoleon and the *coup* and giving a distinctly misleading impression of the strength of the Bonapartists and how near they had been to success. The French government, in which Napoleon's former Minister of Justice, the Comte Molé, was Prime Minister and Foreign Minister, decided that though they had been unable to punish Laity for taking part in an abortive revolution, they could at least punish him for writing about it. He was prosecuted for sedition on the grounds that his book glorified, and therefore incited, revolution;[5] but this time he was not tried before a judge and jury, but by the Upper House of Parliament, the Chamber of Peers.

The Peers convicted Laity, sentenced him to five years' imprisonment and a fine of 10,000 francs, and ordered that after his release from prison he was to be placed under police supervision for the rest of his life. The prosecution and sentence were strongly criticized in the Opposition press, and were unpopular throughout the country. It was not only Bonapartist sympathizers who condemned this belated and spiteful victimizing of Laity as a scapegoat for the conspirators of 30 October 1836, and the government's decision to try him before the Chamber of Peers instead of a jury was especially criticized.

On 1 August, Molé sent a note to the Federal government of Switzerland. It was presented by the French Ambassador, the Duc de Montebello, Marshal Lannes's son, who had been one of the children christened at Fontainebleau in 1810 at the same time as Louis Napoleon. The note stated that the French government was surprised that after Louis Napoleon's criminal enterprise at Strasburg the Swiss government should allow him to use Arenenberg as a centre of new conspiracies; and they demanded his immediate expulsion from Switzerland. The French government realized that Louis Napoleon was a naturalized citizen of Thurgau, but they claimed that he always spoke as a Frenchman in his seditious appeals to the French people, and had only assumed Swiss nationality as a shield when he was in trouble. The Swiss Diet, after a heated debate in which the delegates of fifteen of the eighteen cantons supported Louis Napoleon and attacked the French demand, appointed a committee of seven of their members to consult with the authorities in Thurgau as to what should be done.[6]

Molé was not prepared to wait for these consultations. On 14 August he sent what was virtually an ultimatum to the Diet. He told Montebello to apply for his passports if the Diet did not expel Louis Napoleon from Switzerland; and Montebello was to make it clear to the President of the Diet 'that France, strong in her right and the justice of her demand, will resort to all the means which she possesses to obtain from Switzerland a satisfaction which no consideration can ever cause her to forgo.'[7] Molé was trying to reassert French prestige in international affairs by bullying small nations; having picked a quarrel with Mexico on a trivial pretext, he hoped to gain glory by going to war with Mexico and Switzerland at the same time. The government press in France became very bellicose, and with great publicity 25,000 troops were sent from Lyons to the frontier near Geneva, army officers' leave was stopped, and two battalions entered the demilitarized zone of Gex. Austria, Prussia and Russia gave France full diplomatic support, and the Grand Duke of Baden prohibited Louis Napoleon and any inhabitant of the Arenenberg district from going to Constance in the Grand Duchy.[8] These menaces and military preparations enraged the Swiss Liberals, who declared that the Swiss people would defend their liberty against the foreign invader, as their ancestors had done at Morgarten, Sempach and Morat in the fourteenth and fifteenth centuries.

Louis Napoleon wrote to the Grand Council of Thurgau, denying that he was plotting at Arenenberg against the French government, declaring that as a Swiss citizen he wished only to live quietly in Thurgau, and thanking his fellow-citizens for their defence of his rights and of the national freedom. Five years later, he told a friend that he had wished to be expelled from Switzerland in order to win a martyr's halo, and that he had urged Laity to publish his book in order to provoke Louis Philippe into demanding his expulsion. This was perhaps being wise after the event, but he was undoubtedly delighted at the international publicity which he was receiving as a result of the French government's action. All over Europe people were disgusted at the spectacle of four Great Powers uniting to bully a brave little country into expelling one young man from the home where he had lived for twenty years, and where his beloved mother had so recently died. When Louis Napoleon's letter was read out in the Grand Council of Thurgau on 22 August, he received the unanimous support of the councillors.[9]

The Diet's committee of seven, by a majority of four to three, advised that Louis Napoleon should be allowed to remain in Thurgau on condition that he renounced his French nationality and gave an undertaking never in the future to interest himself in affairs in France. This put Louis Napoleon in a very embarrassing position; but the committee's recommendation was attacked by the Radicals on the committee, in the Diet and in the country, and did not satisfy the French government. When the Diet decided to consult all the cantonal governments about their views on the committee's recommendation, and adjourned for a month, war seemed inevitable. The British diplomats in France and Switzerland told the Foreign Secretary, Lord Palmerston, that Molé was not bluffing, that a French invasion was imminent, and that Austria would support France by blockading Switzerland.

Palmerston, who knew that he could not help the Swiss and was anxious that the incident should not weaken the Franco-British alliance, offered to mediate and to persuade the Swiss to expel Louis Napoleon, provided that a face-saving formula could be found.[10]

On 22 September, Louis Napoleon wrote again to the President of the government of Thurgau. After thanking the people of Switzerland, and particularly those of Thurgau, for their support, he offered to leave Switzerland in order to spare the country the horrors of war and a French invasion.

In leaving voluntarily today the only country in Europe in which I have found support and protection, in going far away from those places which for so many reasons had become dear to me, I hope I will prove to the Swiss people that I was worthy of the marks of esteem and affection which they have bestowed on me.

He expressed the hope that it would one day be possible for him to return to Switzerland.[11]

Montebello was immediately informed of the contents of the letter, but it did not appease the French government. On 25 September, General Aymar, the commander of the French troops on the Swiss frontier, declared in a well-publicized message to his soldiers: 'Soon our turbulent neighbours will realize, perhaps too late, that instead of their declamations and insults they would have done better to have satisfied the just demands of France.'[12] When the Swiss Diet informed the French government that they rejected the French right to demand the expulsion of Louis Napoleon, but that owing to the fact that he was leaving voluntarily this was no longer a matter of practical importance, Molé reacted by angrily demanding that the Diet should formally expel him and that he should be compelled to leave Switzerland on the day and by the route prescribed by the Diet at the suggestion of the French government. This further inflamed public opinion in Switzerland, and in the first days of October war again seemed inevitable. But Molé eventually agreed to take no further action provided that Louis Napoleon left the country forthwith. Both sides could, and did, claim victory in the encounter.[13]

Louis Napoleon's decision to leave Switzerland voluntarily won him great sympathy both in France and abroad. In England even *The Times*, which had always disliked him and throughout the crisis had consistently refused to support the Swiss, now condemned the attempt by France 'to bully and crush a State presumed to be of inferior military power'. In France, the Opposition press condemned the government's handling of the matter. *Le National* pointed out that Louis Napoleon would be nearer to France in Brighton or Jersey than in Thurgau. The *Courrier Français* said that hitherto there had only been one Pretender in France, the Bourbon Legitimist Duc de Bordeaux, but that henceforth, thanks to the stupidity of Molé's government, there would be two; and *L'Europe Industrielle*, coining a happy phrase which was often to be quoted in future years, wrote that Louis Napoleon 'is no longer a Swiss citizen; he is Napoleon III'.[14]

At this juncture Metternich, repeating his tactic of 1816, offered Louis Napoleon an honourable asylum in Austria; but Louis Napoleon had no desire to become a second Duke of Reichstadt, and refused. He had decided to live in England, and was promptly given a passport to get there by the British Consul. He left Arenenberg on 14 October. The local people came in strength to say farewell, lining the road from Arenenberg to Constance, where the whole town turned out to cheer him; the streets were full of people, with women waving from every window. He travelled through Germany, attracting great attention, and received an ovation from the crowds in Mannheim and Düsseldorf. He reached Rotterdam, and paid a hurried visit to The Hague, where he spent a few hours looking round his father's old capital before sailing for England.[15] He reached Fenton's Hotel in London on 25 October.[16]

He was warmly welcomed in London. Apart from renewing his acquaintance with the Whig families – the Bedfords and the Hollands were as hospitable as ever – he now met Tories, for British politics were no longer as bitter as they had been in 1831 and 1832, and as time went by the Bonaparte family became acceptable in Tory circles. The Duke of Wellington expressed a wish to meet him, and there was a brief exchange of courtesies between them at the Duchess of Cannizzaro's party. He became much more intimate with another leading Tory, the Marquess of Londonderry, Castlereagh's half-brother, who was hated almost as much by British and European Radicals as he was by the miners in his Durham coalfields whose strikes he crushed so mercilessly. Despite their political differences, Louis Napoleon became very friendly with Londonderry, who was an intelligent man and had acquired a wide knowledge of Europe through his military and diplomatic service. He renewed his friendship with Lord Fitzharris, the Earl of Malmesbury's son, whom he had known in Italy before 1830 and who was now a rising Tory M.P. There was hardly anyone in London society at the time who could not truthfully say, when they wrote their memoirs in later years, that they had met the Emperor Napoleon III in London after his arrival from Switzerland in 1838.[17]

In London, as in New York, he became friendly with the leading literary figures. He met Bulwer Lytton and Benjamin Disraeli, who was a great friend of his friends Count d'Orsay and Lady Blessington. He also met Charles Dickens at Lady Blessington's. On one occasion he and Persigny were invited to a breakfast party at Bulwer Lytton's house, Craven Cottage, at Fulham. They arrived late to find no one there except Mr and Mrs Disraeli, who had also arrived late; Bulwer Lytton had taken his other guests on a cruise on the river. Louis Napoleon hired a rowing boat and, taking the oars, rowed the Disraelis to meet Lytton's party on the river. At first he made good progress, but lost control in the swell of a passing steamship, and their rowing boat was forced on to a mud bank in mid-stream, from which they were eventually rescued by the boatman from whom they had hired the boat. Mrs Disraeli, who was famous for her tactlessness, berated Louis Napoleon for his carelessness: 'You should not undertake things which you cannot accomplish. You are always, sir, too adventurous.' Disraeli was amazed at the perfect good humour with which Louis Napoleon took the scolding.[18]

His expulsion from Switzerland had made him a hero to the general public, as well as a favourite in society. When he visited the Tower of London and Woolwich Arsenal, the guard turned out to present arms. At the Bank of England he was shown round by the Governor and entertained to breakfast by the directors. When he went to watch the Lord Mayor's show a fortnight after his arrival in London, the Lord Mayor, who saw him standing at a window as the procession passed, saluted him. A few carping critics sneered at him, and even questioned his right to call himself a prince; but his friends pointed out that his title had been recognized by the Great Powers in the Treaty of Fontainebleau of 1814.[19]

He had no difficulty in gaining admission to Almack's, the most select club in London, from which the aspiring middle classes were rigidly excluded; though Lady Jersey, one of the capricious Lady Patronesses who governed the club, disliked him and refused to invite him to her house. He joined several other fashionable clubs. The reception given in his honour by the Duke and Duchess of Somerset at Wimbledon was one of the best attended and most widely reported events of the season.[20]

He tended to overdress a little by English standards. Sir William Fraser, who saw him riding in Rotten Row, described his dress as just the opposite of 'studied negligé'; he always wore dark colours, his trousers were strapped down, and his frockcoat was buttoned up. The playwright and antiquary, James Planché, the first time they met, recognized him before they were introduced, because he thought that Louis Napoleon was the only man in England who would venture to wear so large a diamond eagle and ruby thunderbolt on the clasp that fastened his black satin kerchief to his evening dress.[21]

Charles Greville, who dined with Louis Napoleon, Lord Durham, Alfred de Vigny, Bulwer Lytton and others at Lady Blessington's in February 1839, described him as 'a short, thickish, vulgar-looking man, without the slightest resemblance to his imperial uncle, or any intelligence in his countenance'.[22] But Greville was usually a censorious critic.

The French government was annoyed at Louis Napoleon's reception in England, and, encouraged by their diplomatic success against the Swiss, requested the British government not to permit him to live in London, but to order him to reside at some house in the country and to remain there. No demand could have created a worse impression in Britain, and the Prime Minister, Lord Melbourne, sharply refused the French request, informing the French Ambassador that the British government had no power under English law to prescribe a person's place of residence. So Louis Napoleon, after living for a short while in Waterloo Place, rented a house from Lord Cardigan at Carlton Terrace, where he lived for a year. In December 1839 he moved to Carlton Gardens, taking a lease of Number 1 from the Earl of Ripon.[23]

Both residences were on the fringe of that small area, bounded by Pall Mall, St James's Street, Piccadilly and the Haymarket, which the author and socialite Theodore Hook called 'the only real world'.[24] Louis Napoleon lived there with a household of seventeen stalwart supporters, including some, like Persigny and Parquin, who had been with him at Strasburg, and Hortense's old servant Charles Thélin and the coachman Fritz who had escaped with them from Ancona in 1831. Thélin had promised Hortense, on her deathbed, that he would always stay with Louis Napoleon. His promise, and his faithful service, became part of the Bonapartist legend.

Persigny took charge of Bonapartist propaganda. In 1840 he published his *Lettres de Londres*, in which he told the story of Louis Napoleon's life, including the fictitious tale of his farewell and warning to the Emperor before Waterloo. Persigny also stage-managed Louis Napoleon's public appearances in London. He arranged for him to drive around London with eagles painted on his carriage. When Louis Napoleon went to the opera at Covent Garden, Persigny and another officer in uniform stood at attention behind his seat in his box throughout the performance.[25]

In *Lettres de Londres*, Persigny, after praising the Spartan simplicity of Louis Napoleon's life as a child and as a young man in the annexe at Arenenberg, described his daily routine in Carlton Gardens. He wrote that Louis Napoleon rose at 6 a.m. and worked in his study till noon, when he ate his first meal of the day, which only took him ten minutes.

He then read the newspapers till 2 p.m., when he received visitors. At 4 p.m. he went out if he had any business to transact, and went riding in the park at 5 p.m. before his dinner at 7 p.m., and 'usually he finds time to work again for some hours in the course of the evening'.[26]

There were some who believed, and wrote, that Persigny had omitted certain items from this time-table, and had failed to mention not only Louis Napoleon's round of social engagements but also the hours which he spent in gambling dens, in drinking orgies, and in the company of *demi-mondaines* and harlots. It may safely be assumed that the stories about his debaucheries in London were greatly exaggerated, but there is no doubt that he owned Arab racehorses, betted at race-meetings, played cards for high stakes in London clubs, made love to beautiful women, and was on very friendly terms with characters like d'Orsay and Lady Blessington who were considered to be not quite respectable.

He often went to the theatre, seeing Charles Kean as Hamlet at the Haymarket and patronizing the St James's Theatre, where French plays were regularly performed in the original French. It was the year in which London raved over the dancing of Marie Taglioni in *La Sylphide* and *La Bayadère*. Taglioni was aged thirty-five in 1839; she had been married for seven years to the French Comte de Voisins, and divided her time between Paris and London. She was not considered to be beautiful off stage, but according to a report in two hostile French newspapers, Louis Napoleon wished to have her as his mistress, and on one occasion, when they were both watching a French play at the St James's Theatre, he sent her a note stating that Prince Louis Bonaparte would like to have dinner with her *tête à tête*. She sent a haughty reply that if Monsieur Bonaparte cared to call at her box, she could spare him a few moments. He made no further attempt to approach her.[27]

He made frequent visits to the provinces. He went several times to Brighton, which for the first decade of Queen Victoria's reign still remained a fashionable centre patronized by the royal family. He stayed in Leamington, another fashionable spa, dined with Lord Warwick in Warwick Castle, hunted in the district, and toured the industrial towns of the Midlands. He attracted great attention in Birmingham, which had been famous as a Radical stronghold ever since the riots which had preceded the Reform Bill of 1832; when he went to the theatre the whole audience rose to their feet to applaud him. He again visited Manchester and Liverpool and the industrial towns of Lancashire, staying in Southport and at Bryn Hall, near Wigan, and hunting with the local gentry.[28]

He became friendly with Henry Rowles, a successful builder who had made his fortune when he obtained the contract to rebuild Drury

Lane Theatre after the fire of 1809 and became the director of the Globe Fire Insurance Company. In 1839 Rowles lived in Stratton Street in London; by a strange coincidence, he had formerly lived at Camden Place, the house at Chislehurst in Kent where Louis Napoleon himself was to live and die more than thirty years later. Less than two years after Rowles met Louis Napoleon, he committed suicide; but during the short period of their friendship Louis Napoleon on several occasions visited Rowles and his beautiful Spanish wife, and he became intimate with Rowles's daughter, Emily.* There were rumours of an engagement, but Emily Rowles was only sixteen, and in due course married the Italian Marquis Campana. She continued her friendship with Louis Napoleon and lent him money when he was in serious financial difficulties as President of France in 1851. He repaid her by gifts and annuities to a far higher value and by intervening with the Papal government when her husband was convicted of embezzlement in 1858. As a result of his intercession, Campana's sentence of twenty years' hard labour was commuted to banishment from the Papal States.[29]

He was naturally invited to take part in the Eglinton Tournament. It was a period when the middle classes as well as the aristocracy built turreted gothic ruins in their gardens and enjoyed fancy-dress balls; and when the Earl of Eglinton announced his intention of holding a medieval tournament on his estates in Ayrshire at the end of August 1839, the press gave the widest advance publicity to the tournament. Leading members of the aristocracy were invited to attend, clad in medieval armour, as knights, accompanied by their squires and pages, to joust with lances on horseback and compete for the prize of a laurel crown presented by the Queen of Beauty, Lady Seymour, who was one of the famous Sheridan sisters.

Before they could take part in the tournament, the knights had to learn to joust, and during June and July Louis Napoleon, like many other competitors, practised the old forgotten art on Tuesdays and Saturdays at the Eyre Arms Tavern in St John's Wood, on the road to Golders Green, watched by society ladies and journalists, and on the final Saturday by 2690 spectators. Then, at the end of August, he set out for Ayrshire, accompanied by Persigny, who was to act as his squire. They went by train on the nine-and-a-half hours' journey from London to Liverpool, where they caught the overnight steamship to Ardrossan, arriving at dawn less than twenty-four hours after leaving Euston.[30]

*Sir William Fraser's statement (in his *Napoleon III*, p. 217) that Louis Napoleon told him at Camden Place in 1872 that he had often visited Rowles 'here', must be one of Fraser's not infrequent errors. Rowles had lived there at the time of Emily's birth in 1823, but the Martin family were in residence at Camden Place from 1835 to 1862.

This was the fastest way to travel from London to Ayrshire at the time.

On the morning of Wednesday 28 August the crowds flocked to Eglinton Castle, near Irvine, to see the first day of the tournament, but the event was spoiled by heavy rain. It rained again next day, so the tournament continued indoors, in the ballroom, on a floor covered with fleur-de-lis, where the combatants fought on foot with staves. Louis Napoleon became involved in a combat with Lord Eglinton's half-brother, Charles Lamb, who attacked him so violently with his staff that the organizers became alarmed and intervened. On the Friday the weather was fine at last, and there was a good joust in the open air; but on Saturday it rained again, and the tournament was called off.

Louis Napoleon appeared at the tournament wearing a polished steel cuirass, trimmed with crimson satin, and a visored helmet with a high plume of white feathers. For the fancy-dress dinner on the Friday evening he changed into a suit of dark green velvet, with crimson satin sleeves, flesh-silk hose, a sword, and a cap of crimson velvet with a yellow feather. The great banquet was held in a specially built pavilion 175 feet long and 45 feet wide, where the knights and their squires and ladies dined sumptuously at three tables which extended for the whole length of the pavilion. Louis Napoleon, as the Visiting Knight, sat at the centre of the table of honour with Lady Seymour the Queen of Beauty, Lord Londonderry the King of the Tournament and Lady Londonderry, Lord Eglinton the Lord of the Tournament, and the Duke and Duchess of Montrose.[31]

Despite the rain, the tournament had delighted the local residents and many readers of the national newspapers; but it gave rise to some sour and mocking comments from the industrious middle-class Liberals of Lancashire and from the Chartists and trade unionists, to whom it seemed a supreme example of the antiquated outlook and extravagance of the aristocracy, for it had cost £40,000. There were also some sarcastic comments in France about Louis Napoleon's participation in the tournament; his enemies suggested that mock medieval heroics was a suitable recreation for the ridiculous hero of the Strasburg fiasco. Persigny and the Bonapartist propagandists explained that the tournament was simply a harmless piece of fun, but Louis Napoleon's participation in it did him no good politically.[32]

In March 1840 he became involved in an incident which might have had far more embarrassing consequences. A French adventurer, Comte Léon, who was the illegitimate son of Napoleon and one of Caroline Murat's ladies, came to London, having recently been released from imprisonment for debt in France. He wrote an insolent letter to Louis

Napoleon, beginning 'My dearest cousin', in which he demanded an interview. He had already unsuccessfully approached Joseph and Jerome Bonaparte, who were staying in London at the time; and Louis Napoleon, like his uncles, refused to meet him, as he was convinced that Léon was an agent in the pay of Louis Philippe's police. Léon thereupon challenged him to a duel. Louis Napoleon, as the challenged party, had choice of weapons, and chose swords, having shown an aptitude for fencing ever since he had been taught to fence at Arenenberg. He selected Parquin and d'Orsay as his seconds, and they arranged a meeting on Wimbledon Common, where duels often took place.

Duelling was beginning to go out in England, though it was to remain in fashion in France and Europe for another hundred years. Although it was barely a decade since the Prime Minister of the day, the Duke of Wellington, had fought a duel, serious efforts were now being made to suppress duelling by the government and the courts. Two years before, a man had been sentenced to death for taking part in a duel in which a combatant was killed, and, six months after Louis Napoleon's duel with Léon, Lord Cardigan was unsuccessfully prosecuted before the House of Lords for wounding his opponent in a duel on Wimbledon Common.

Louis Napoleon and Léon and their seconds met on the common at 7 a.m. on 3 March, but became involved in prolonged bickering over the procedure which was to be followed in the duel. Léon refused to fight with swords, and though Louis Napoleon thereupon agreed to pistols, Léon raised further difficulties. While they were arguing the police arrived, arrested them all, and took them to Bow Street Police Station, where they were charged with unlawful assembly. When they appeared before the Metropolitan Magistrate at Bow Street, they all pleaded guilty to the charge, and were let off with a caution, being bound over to keep the peace. Louis Napoleon was sure that Léon was in the pay of the French embassy, that he had picked a quarrel with him and challenged him to the duel in order to get him into trouble, and that he had warned the police in advance that the duel would take place and had deliberately delayed the start of the duel until the police arrived.[33]

During his stay in London, Louis Napoleon wrote another book, *Des Idées napoléoniennes*,[34] which was published in France in the summer of 1839. It aroused more interest than any of his earlier publications. Bulwer Lytton, to whom Louis Napoleon presented an autographed copy, commented that it was 'the book of a very able mind; with few ideas, but those ideas bold, large and reducible to vigorous actions'. Louis Napoleon's friend and biographer, Blanchard Jerrold, admitted 'that to the English eye there is a tawdry tinsel look' about the book, but thought that it must be remembered that it was written 'not for the contemplation of the statesman in his closet, but to catch the uncultivated mass and the half-educated middle-class'.[35]

The central ideas of *Des Idées napoléoniennes* were summarized by Louis Napoleon in a short article, 'L'Idée napoléonienne', which he wrote early in 1840.[36] Once or twice in a millennium history produces a great leader who transforms society and shapes it for several centuries. Only by following such a leader, and by adhering to his principles after his death, can a nation attain its salvation. For centuries the peoples of the Jordan had followed the law of Moses; the empire established by Mahomet still survived in the Orient; the policy of Julius Caesar preserved Roman unity for six hundred years; and the feudal and religious system established by Charlemagne governed Europe for eight centuries. But the men of 1840 had known, in their lifetime, a leader who combined all the qualities and greatness of Moses, Mahomet, Caesar and Charlemagne rolled into one. 'Shall we seek anywhere except in his precepts a political example and synthesis?'

He argued that where freedom and tyranny were concerned, there was a contradiction between appearance and reality. When the dictatorship of Napoleon was overthrown, many people regarded this as a triumph for Liberal institutions; but the fall of Napoleon brought the victory of reaction and the *ancien régime*, whereas the absolute rule of Napoleon had alone safeguarded the gains of the French Revolution and prevented the destruction of its Liberal doctrines by the united monarchs of Europe. The men who admired the oligarchic English system were called Liberals; those who supported the 'guardianship and democratic power of the plebeian hero' were stigmatized as partisans of absolutism. Napoleon was the executor of the revolution. He had saved the revolution by removing its excesses; he had centralized government administration and spread education. He had longed for peace, offering peace after every victory; but 'all our wars came from England', who wished to restore aristocratic rule in France, because she did not realize that the feudal aristocracy of France was not the enlightened aristocracy of England.

History had been carried forward by a few great men, each greater than the last; it had advanced from Alexander to Caesar, from Caesar to Constantine, from Constantine to Charlemagne, from Charlemagne to Napoleon. At the present time, only two governments were fulfilling their historic duty; these were the governments of the two giants at the opposite ends of the world – the United States and Russia. In the United States the government hardly intervened at all and allowed its citizens to initiate by their own instincts the great drive to the West; in Russia the imperial dynasty alone, during the last century and a half, had dragged a people out of barbarism at the command of a single auto-crat. But the France of Henri IV, of Louis XIV, of Carnot and of Napoleon had lost its sense of destiny, and did not even pay pensions to the disabled ex-servicemen of Waterloo.

What was needed was the Napoleonic idea. The Orleanist régime of Louis Philippe had failed to improve the conditions of the poor or to reduce taxes. But the Napoleonic idea was based

> on principles of eternal justice. . . . It replaces the hereditary system of the old aristocracies by a hierarchical system which, while it ensures equality, rewards merit and guarantees order. It finds an element of strength and stability in democracy because it disciplines democracy. . . . It follows neither the unsure steps of a party nor the passions of the mob.

It regarded Frenchmen as brothers who needed to be reconciled, and the various nations of Europe as members of one great family. It did not seek to overturn society, but to reorganize it. 'The Napoleonic idea is therefore by its nature an idea of peace, not of war; an idea of order and reconstruction, not of upheaval.' It appealed to reason, not to force; but if driven too far by persecution, it would once more take up its helmet and lance.[37]

By this nebulous but stirring programme, Louis Napoleon hoped in 1840 to incite the French people to overthrow Louis Philippe and restore the Bonaparte dynasty. It won him considerable support. On the one hand, it impressed even his uncle King Joseph, who became friendly with him in London at this time; on the other, it gained him the sympathy of many Socialists. The French Communist leader Étienne Cabet visited him in London and had several talks with him in 1839; and when in the same year Barbès led an unsuccessful Socialist rising in Paris, Louis Napoleon was accused, wrongly, of having been in touch with the rebels.[38]

But very few of his friends and supporters believed that he would ever return to France. The people who met the reserved young man at dinner parties in London did not take him seriously when he broke his long periods of silence to tell them, quietly but confidently, of some project that he would carry out 'when I am Emperor'.[39]

CHAPTER 11

BOULOGNE

LOUIS NAPOLEON and Persigny were taken in by their own propaganda. They had claimed that they had nearly succeeded at Strasburg in 1836, and had failed only through extraordinary bad luck; from this it followed that they might very well succeed next time. They had an urgent reason for trying again in the summer of 1840: the corpse of Napoleon was about to be returned from St Helena to France.

Napoleon had asked, in his will, that he should be buried in France. When the British government were asked by the Bonapartists in 1821 to return the body to France, they replied that they would consider the request sympathetically when it was supported by the French government; but the ministers of Louis XVIII had of course opposed it. The British government's stand made it more difficult for them to refuse when Louis Philippe's government formally asked them, in the spring of 1840, to return the body. At this time, relations between Britain and France were more strained than they had been for many years, owing to their taking different sides in the struggle between the Sultan of Turkey and Mehemet Ali, the Viceroy of Egypt; but Palmerston thought that Napoleon's corpse would be a placatory gift from Britain to France at a time when Britain was thwarting the French on more important matters.

Louis Philippe sent his son, the Prince de Joinville, in a French warship to St Helena to fetch the body, and prepared to take part in a great state ceremony when the corpse was laid to rest in the Invalides in Paris. Louis Napoleon and his followers were not happy about this development. There were some people at the time, like Metternich – and many more afterwards with hindsight – who thought that Louis Philippe made a great error in encouraging the Napoleonic cult, because the more the French people admired Napoleon, the more they would want his nephew to be their ruler. But the Bonapartists in 1840 were not so confident of this; they would in many ways have preferred a Legitimist Bourbon government which vilified the great Napoleon rather than an Orleanist one which glorified him, which contrasted his greatness with the pettiness of his nephew's antics at Strasburg, and which taught the French people that they could combine the adoration of Napoleon with the rule of Louis Philippe.

Louis Napoleon decided to forestall the coming of the corpse and to make sure that a Bonaparte was in power in Paris ready to receive it when it arrived. He planned another *coup* on the Strasburg model, but this time it was to be at Boulogne. Once again he entered into secret communication with officers of the garrison, and once again obtained promises of support from one of them, who was confident that he could bring over the local regiments to Louis Napoleon's side. Again he planned to seize a military base at the entrance to the country, to lead the troops who joined him to Paris, to proclaim a Provisional Government, and to hold a referendum to decide whether the people of France wished to be ruled by their Emperor, Joseph Bonaparte, who as usual knew nothing about his nephew's plan.

Louis Napoleon selected about sixty men to go with him on the expedition to Boulogne. They included Persigny, Parquin, and his old friend from Arenenberg, Dr Conneau. Some were his household servants, others were French Bonapartists, and there were a few foreign sympathizers, chiefly Italians and Poles. The most eminent member of the expedition was General Montholon, who had been with Napoleon at St Helena and was shortly to publish his *History of the Captivity of Napoleon at St Helena*, in which he described the sufferings of the imprisoned Emperor even more movingly than Las Cases had done. Only a handful of the sixty knew their destination or the precise object of the expedition. Most of them assembled secretly at a large house near Gravesend which belonged to a mysterious lady, known sometimes as Mrs Mary Edwards and sometimes as the Countess d'Espel, who, according to *The Times* and other newspapers, was Louis Napoleon's mistress.[1]

Louis Napoleon chartered a ship, the *Edinburgh Castle*,* for the ostensible purpose of taking a party of sixty tourists on a pleasure cruise to Hamburg. In order to avoid attracting attention by embarking so large a number of travellers in one body, they divided into three parties: some of them were to embark in London, some at Gravesend, and some at Ramsgate. From Ramsgate they would sail to Boulogne, where they would land at dawn on 5 August, when their contact, Lieutenant Aladenize, would be expecting them, and the commanding officer at Boulogne, Captain Col-Puygellier, who was known to be absolutely loyal to Louis Philippe, would be absent on leave for a day's shooting.

*The name of the ship is given, in the French police reports, at the trial, and in the press, sometimes as the *Edinburgh Castle* and sometimes as the *City of Edinburgh*. The ship's captain, in his statement to the French authorities, called it the *Edinburgh Castle*.

The French Minister of the Interior, Rémusat, had at least one spy in Louis Napoleon's household,* and knew that Louis Napoleon was planning some action before Napoleon's corpse reached France. Louis Napoleon himself made no great effort to keep his intentions secret; two days before he sailed for Boulogne, he invited his fellow-guests at Lady Blessington's dinner-table to dine with him at the Tuileries on the same day next year. But Rémusat received conflicting reports as to where Louis Napoleon would strike. One agent's report said that he would land in Belgium and march on Lille; another, that he planned to seize the Emperor's corpse at sea on its journey from St Helena.[2] According to Captain Hay of the Metropolitan Police, who collaborated with the French authorities in spying on Louis Napoleon in London, the full details of Louis Napoleon's plan were discovered by a young gentleman in the pay of the French government who became friendly with Mrs Edwards on her journey from London to Paris and stole her documents at Calais.[3]

On the morning of 4 August – a fine summer day – Count Orsi, who had been with Louis Napoleon in the revolutionary forces in the Romagna in 1831, loaded on to the *Edinburgh Castle* at London Bridge a carriage, nine horses, and many crates labelled 'Hamburg', containing sixty rifles, ammunition, sixty uniforms of the French 42nd Regiment at Boulogne, printed copies of Louis Napoleon's proclamations to the French army and people, and £20,000 in gold and British banknotes. From London Bridge the ship sailed to Greenwich and Blackwall, picking up members of the expedition at each landing-stage, and then proceeded to Gravesend, where Louis Napoleon and more of the party were due to come aboard at 3 p.m. But Louis Napoleon failed to arrive at the appointed time. He had noticed that his house in Carlton Gardens was being watched by a group of men whom he suspected of being agents of the French government, and he had delayed his departure for Gravesend while he dodged around London to try to throw them off the scent. Orsi was worried that the ship seemed to be attracting a certain amount of attention at Gravesend, both from Customs officials who came alongside and asked about the freight to Hamburg, and from holiday-makers in the Clifton Hotel, who watched them through their opera glasses. The Customs officer expressed surprise that they were not taking any women with them on their trip to Hamburg. Orsi told him that they would be picking up the women at Ramsgate, and the officer agreed that Ramsgate was the place for girls.

While they were waiting impatiently at Gravesend for Louis Napoleon to arrive, Parquin went ashore to buy some cigars, and saw a boy

*The tentative suggestion, put forward by Dansette (I.170–4), that General Montholon was the spy who informed Rémusat, appears rather far-fetched.

near the quayside feeding a tame vulture. As the vulture looked very like an eagle, Parquin thought that it would be a good mascot for them to take on the expedition to Boulogne, and he bought the bird for £1 and took it on board.

At last, at about 8 p.m., Louis Napoleon arrived at Gravesend, and the ship went on to Ramsgate, where the last of the party came aboard. But by now it was 1 a.m., and in view of the state of the tides it would be impossible to reach Boulogne by 4 a.m. They would have to postpone the expedition for twenty-four hours, which was very unfortunate, as it would mean that the landing could not take place on a day when Captain Col-Puygellier was away on leave. Louis Napoleon called a meeting in his cabin of twelve of his leading assistants to discuss what was to be done. Three of them advised him to call off the whole project and return to London; the other nine urged him to go through with it after twenty-four hours' delay, to try to win the support of the garrisons at Boulogne, and if they failed to do this, to march to St Omer, where the troops were said to be sympathetic. Louis Napoleon was determined to go ahead, for he believed that they could not return to London and disembark without running the risk that the Customs officers would find the arms and ammunition on board, and that the plot would be discovered, with disastrous consequences for them, both in Britain and in France.

Next morning the weather was as perfect as on the previous day. In order to avoid the risk of a visit and an inspection by the Customs authorities at Ramsgate and of attracting too much attention from the holiday crowds on the beach, Orsi ordered the captain of the *Edinburgh Castle* to go for a day's cruise along the Channel coast to Rye, pretending that they were being joined by another party at Rye who would sail with them to Hamburg. After waiting for some hours at Rye, he told the captain that as the other party had not come, they would go to Hamburg without them, and they returned to the South Foreland, from where they sailed about midnight, ostensibly for Hamburg.

As soon as they were out at sea, Louis Napoleon informed the captain that they were not going to Hamburg on a pleasure-cruise, but to Boulogne in order to make a revolution in France. The angry captain was forced to comply with Louis Napoleon's instructions to sail to the French coast and anchor off Wimereux, where they arrived at 3 a.m. on 6 August. All the party had by now been informed of the object of the expedition, and had dressed in the uniforms of the 42nd Regiment.[4] They went ashore in relays in their only boat, landing some three miles north of Boulogne. They were challenged by a coastguard patrol, but said that they were soldiers of the 42nd Regiment coming from Dunkirk to join the garrison at Boulogne. They marched on towards the town, passed through the gates, and entered the barracks of the 42nd Regiment, giving the password, which had been revealed to them by Lieutenant Aladenize.

Some of them went through the streets distributing the proclamations, signed 'Napoleon', which were addressed to the army, to the people of Boulogne and the Pas-de-Calais, and to the French nation. 'Soldiers! France was made to command, and she obeys', wrote Louis Napoleon, telling the army that he was now bringing back to them the eagles of Arcola, Austerlitz and Jena. He denounced the traitors who had degraded France by 'ten years of lies, usurpation and ignominy'; told the 'town of Boulogne, which Napoleon loved so much,' that its inhabitants would be the first link in the chain that would reunite all civilized peoples; promised that his advent to power would not mean war, as he was coming to offer peace to the world; reminded the farmers, the artisans and the business men, of the oppression, high taxes, and other disadvantages which they suffered under Louis Philippe; and invoked the spirit of Napoleon, who was watching them from the top of the Column of the Grand Army which had been erected just outside Boulogne, and was demanding that when his corpse returned to France it should not be soiled by impure and hypocritical homage.[5]

Louis Napoleon himself with other members of his party entered the barracks of the 42nd Regiment, where they encountered Captain Col-Puygellier. General Montholon addressed him: 'Here is Prince Louis Napoleon; follow us, Captain!' But Captain Col-Puygellier replied: 'Prince Louis or not, I do not know you', and, using a familiar Orleanist argument, said that it was absurd of Louis Napoleon to base his claim on his hereditary descent from Napoleon, who had overthrown the hereditary principle. He ordered Louis Napoleon to leave the barracks at once. A great clamour erupted, the Bonapartists denouncing Col-Puygellier and he denouncing them. In the excitement, Louis Napoleon fired his pistol in the air, and the bullet ricocheted and wounded one of the soldiers of the garrison. The other soldiers then prepared to fire on the Bonapartists, who withdrew, with Louis Napoleon protesting that his pistol had gone off by accident and that he was determined not to shed French blood.

Meanwhile the middle-class volunteers of the National Guard of Boulogne, seeing the proclamations which were being distributed in the streets and hearing the shouts of 'Vive l'Empereur!', turned out in strength, shouting 'Vive le Roi!', determined to fight for Louis Philippe. Louis Napoleon and his followers withdrew from the town and marched to the Column of the Grand Army; he had decided to stand here and fight to the death. His supporters, realizing that all was lost, advised an immediate retreat to the ship, not knowing that the *Edinburgh Castle* had been boarded by the French patrols, and that its bewildered captain and crew were prisoners in the hands of the harbour authorities. At first Louis Napoleon refused to go; he clung to the iron railings of the Column, and said he would die here. But his companions dragged him away, and, finding a boat on the shore, they embarked and made for the ship.

As they were moving off, the National Guard arrived on the shore and opened fire on them. The boat capsized, and Louis Napoleon and Persigny were thrown into the sea. The National Guard continued firing at the men swimming in the water. Two men were killed and several were wounded, but the National Guards and the coastguards dragged Louis Napoleon and the others out of the water and took them prisoner. Only one of the company escaped.[6]

They were marched to the prison at Boulogne, and handed over to the examining magistrate. The captain and crew of the *Edinburgh Castle*, having persuaded the authorities that they knew nothing about the plot and had been forced against their will to take the rebels to Boulogne, were released after a few days and allowed to return to England in their ship. On the night of 8 August, Louis Napoleon was taken to the castle of Ham near Saint-Quentin in order to prevent him from having any communication with the other prisoners, who remained at Boulogne; and four days later he was transferred to Paris and imprisoned in the Conciergerie.

The French government newspapers denounced the Boulogne *coup* as a wicked act of rebellion by the ungrateful Louis Napoleon, to whom the King had shown mercy in 1837. They also ridiculed him, contrasting his playboy character and his pitiable failure with the triumphs of the great Napoleon, whose body was about to be returned to France, thanks to the diplomatic influence of King Louis Philippe. They were particularly sarcastic about the 'eagle' which was found on the *Edinburgh Castle*, and which had remained chained to the deck of the ship instead of flying from steeple to steeple until it reached Notre-Dame. They accused Louis Napoleon of being an English agent, a lie well calculated to discredit him in the eyes of Napoleon's old soldiers and admirers. Three weeks before Louis Napoleon landed at Boulogne, Palmerston had signed the Treaty of London, by which Britain repudiated her alliance with France and joined with Austria, Russia and Prussia to crush Mehemet Ali in Syria and destroy French influence in the Middle East. This had led to an outburst of anti-British fury in France and to the stoning of the carriage of the British Ambassador's daughter. At such a time, when war between Britain and France seemed very near, Louis Napoleon's expedition had sailed from English ports, carrying arms made in England and £20,000 in English gold and banknotes.

The French press stated, quite untruthfully, that he had had a long interview with Lord Melbourne a few days before he sailed.[7]

The government announced that Louis Napoleon and fifty-two other prisoners were to be charged with high treason and brought to trial, not before a judge and jury but before the Chamber of Peers. If guilty, they were liable to the death penalty, although no one had in fact been executed for a political offence since 1822. The preliminary investigation, which ordinarily in criminal cases was conducted by the Procureur du Roi, was entrusted to a special commission of seven members of the Chamber of Peers, presided over by the Chancellor of the realm, Baron Pasquier, and including the Duc Decazes, who had once been suspected by some gossipmongers of being Queen Hortense's lover and Louis Napoleon's father. Louis Napoleon said very little during his preliminary examination, but claimed sole responsibility for the attempted *coup*, and said that none of his followers had known in advance about his plan.

The trial before the Chamber of Peers began on 28 September. The Chancellor presided, and 166 other peers sat with him to hear the case, among them such former Bonapartist stalwarts as Marshal Oudinot and General Exelmans, though 206 of the peers failed to attend. The trial lasted six days. The defendants were allowed to speak freely and to address the court in person, as well as being represented by counsel, and were liable to be examined by the counsel for the prosecution in accordance with the usual French criminal procedure.

Louis Napoleon's counsel, Maître Berryer, represented him throughout the trial and addressed the court on his behalf, but Louis Napoleon himself made a personal statement to the court on the first day:

For the first time in my life, I am at last permitted to raise my voice in France and to speak freely to Frenchmen. Despite the guards who surround me, despite the charges that I have just heard read out, as I stand here within the walls of the Senate, so full of memories of my early childhood ... I cannot believe that I have to justify myself here and that you can be my judges.

He pointed out that the people of France had never voted to rescind the referendum result of 1804, and that Joseph Bonaparte was the only lawful ruler of France:

One final word, gentlemen; I stand before you representing a principle, a cause, a defeat: the principle is the sovereignty of the people; the cause is the Empire; the defeat, Waterloo. You have acknowledged the principle; you have served the cause; you wish to avenge the defeat.[8]

He did not see how they could condemn him. He then attempted to challenge the jurisdiction of the court to try him, but was, for the first time, interrupted by the Chancellor and not allowed to proceed. During his examination by the Chancellor, he answered courteously but very briefly and sometimes inaudibly, giving the impression that he was not interested in the proceedings.

On 6 October the Chamber of Peers returned verdicts of Guilty on all charges against all except four of the less important defendants, who were acquitted for lack of evidence. No death sentences were passed. Louis Napoleon was sentenced to imprisonment for life in a fortress in France; Aladenize to be deported to a penal settlement in the colonies; Montholon, Parquin, Persigny and Lombard to twenty years' imprisonment; and the rest to shorter terms of imprisonment, Orsi and Conneau each receiving five years.[9]

Next day Louis Napoleon was taken to Ham, and at midnight on 7 October 1840 entered the castle where he was to serve his sentence. On 15 October, Napoleon's corpse was exhumed from his coffin at St Helena and handed to the Prince de Joinville. It arrived at Cherbourg on 30 November, and on 15 December was laid to rest in the Invalides, in the presence of the King and a vast crowd of people.[10] The glory of the Napoleonic triumph went to Louis Philippe; and Louis Napoleon could only write a message to Napoleon's ghost from his prison at Ham:

Sire, you come back to your capital, and the people crowd to salute your return; but I, from the depths of my prison, can see nothing except a glimpse of the sunlight that illuminates your funeral. . . . From your sumptuous cortège, despising the homage of some people, you have cast a momentary glance at my dark dwelling and, remembering the caresses which you lavished on me in my childhood, you said to me: 'You are suffering for me, friend, I am pleased with you.'[11]

PART II

EUGENIA DEL MONTIJO

CHAPTER 12

CHILDHOOD IN SPAIN AND PARIS

ON the morning of 5 May 1826, the town of Granada in southern Spain was shaken by an earthquake. Doña Maria Manuela, the wife of Don Cipriano de Guzmán y Palafox y Portocarrero, Count of Teba, was in labour with her second child. Because of the danger in falling houses, she was carried into the garden of her house at Number 12, Calle de Gracia, and laid in a tent, where her daughter Maria Eugenia Ignacia Augustina was born.[1]

The fifth of May was a date of strange significance for the Bonaparte family. On 5 May 1789, the States-General met at Versailles and inaugurated a new historical era by beginning the French Revolution, which made possible the rise of Napoleon and his relations. On 5 May 1807, Charles Napoleon, the eldest son of King Louis Bonaparte and Hortense, died at The Hague at the age of four; had he lived, he, and not his younger brother Louis Napoleon, would have been the heir to the Bonaparte throne in 1852. On 5 May 1818, a middle-class German Jewish woman in Trier gave birth to a son, Karl Marx, who wrote a famous denunciation of Louis Napoleon and whose First International played an important part in the final disruption of the Second Empire. On 5 May 1821, Napoleon died at St Helena, making the date one of the most sacred in the Bonapartist calendar. On 5 May 1826, the Empress Eugénie was born in a tent in the garden of the house in Granada. On 5 May 1860, Garibaldi and the Thousand sailed from Quarto on the expedition to liberate Sicily which led to Napoleon III's first great diplomatic setback. On 5 May 1862, at Guadalupe Hill near Puebla, the Mexican Radicals inflicted a humiliating defeat on the French army – an event which may be regarded, in retrospect, as the beginning of the end of the Second Empire.*

Eugénie's father, Don Cipriano, was the younger brother of Don

---

*In view of the fact that Napoleon I throughout his lifetime was frequently compared to Oliver Cromwell, and named the 'Cromwell of France', it is curious that Cromwell should have been born on a day which, according to our modern calendar (already then in force in France and elsewhere) was 5 May 1599, though in England, where the old style calendar still prevailed, the date was 25 April.

Eugenio, Count of Montijo. Cipriano was the heir to the Montijo title if Eugenio, who was a widower, died childless. During Eugenio's lifetime, Cipriano was known as the Count of Teba, one of the family's many other titles. The Counts of Montijo were Grandees of Spain – a title which, by the nineteenth century, conferred only honour and certain peculiar privileges, like the right to wear a hat in the King's presence.

But the heir to the title, Don Cipriano, Count of Teba, was a Radical who believed in Liberty, Equality and Fraternity. He was born in 1786 and grew up under the influence of the French Revolution, when Spain was ruled by the 'unholy Trinity' – King Charles IV, his wife Queen Maria Luisa of Parma, and her lover, Godoy. The Trinity tried to preserve the *ancien régime* in Spain while allying themselves with revolutionary France in their attempt to recover the old Spanish colonies which Britain had taken from them during the previous hundred and fifty years; but instead of regaining Jamaica and Gibraltar, Spain lost the whole of her enormous empire in South and Central America, and by 1821 held nothing in the American hemisphere except Cuba and a few small territories. This loss of the empire affected many Spaniards, and still distressed Eugénie at the beginning of the twentieth century.[2]

The young Count of Teba, despite his detestation of Godoy's oppressive régime, could serve in the navy with a clear conscience because Spain was fighting on the side of Napoleon and revolutionary progress against the kings of Europe. At the age of nineteen he went into action for the first time when the united French and Spanish fleets met the British navy off Cape Trafalgar on 21 October 1805. It was a savage battle. After Nelson fell, the British seamen fought with a revengeful fury, and the snipers tried to pick off every enemy officer who was in an exposed position on deck.[3] One of the snipers hit Don Cipriano, inflicting a wound in his arm and shoulder from which he never fully recovered.

When Napoleon, in 1808, forced Charles IV to abdicate and made Joseph Bonaparte King of Spain, nearly the whole Spanish nation rose against the French. The Radicals joined with the Conservatives against the hated invader, and their guerrilla units gave valuable help to Wellington's army. The Spaniards killed and tortured their French prisoners, and the French retaliated with wholesale executions of guerrillas and hostages. The Count of Montijo played a leading part in the national resistance, but his brother Cipriano was one of a small minority of Spaniards who supported the French, believing that Napoleon, despite his dictatorship and the overbearing way in which he exploited the subject peoples, was the only leader who could defeat the old régime in Europe. Cipriano applauded when Joseph Bonaparte's government abolished the Spanish Inquisition and aristocratic privileges, including the title of grandee. He himself renounced the title of Count of Teba, and served in the French army under the name of Colonel Portocarrero. He was wounded in the leg in action against the British army; but his most serious wound was the result of an accident behind the front line, when a gun that was being tested in the arsenal at Seville exploded and caused him to lose the sight of his right eye. For the rest of his life he wore a black patch to cover the socket.

When Wellington drove the French out of Spain and invaded France, Cipriano retreated with the French army, and in March 1814 took part in the last defence of Paris. On 29 March, while Queen Hortense was hastily leaving Paris with Louis Napoleon, Cipriano was commanding the French battery on the heights of Montmartre which fired the last shots of the war at the advancing Allies. After the war he returned to Spain. As an officer in the French army he was protected by the surrender terms from criminal proceedings for high treason or other judicial punishment; but he was unable to take any part in political or public life, and was a social outcast. He had the melancholy satisfaction of seeing that he had been right to believe that the defeat of Napoleon would inevitably entail the triumph of the old régime. King Ferdinand VII abrogated the democratic Constitution of 1812 which had been proclaimed during the war by the Radical leaders of the guerrilla movement, and restored the aristocratic privileges, the title of grandee, and the Inquisition. The Count of Montijo was high in favour with the King; his brother Colonel Portocarrero, though he resumed his title of Count of Teba, did not change his opinions, and went into retirement in disgrace at the age of twenty-nine.[4]

Two years later, he had the consolation of marrying a fascinating wife, Maria Manuela Kirkpatrick. Her father, William Kirkpatrick, was born in Scotland, the seventh of nineteen children of William Kirkpatrick of Cowheath, near Dumfries, a small landowner who was in very serious financial difficulties. Like several of his brothers, William Kirkpatrick the younger emigrated – not, as was so often stated in later years, because of his Jacobite sympathies, but in the hope of retrieving the family fortune. He set up in business as a fruit and wine merchant at Malaga. He rapidly prospered, converted to Roman Catholicism, and became a leading figure in the social life of Malaga. He sympathized with the American and French revolutions, and was appointed United States Consul in Malaga by President George Washington. He married Françoise de Grivégnée, the daughter of a Belgian baron who, like Kirkpatrick, was in business as a wine-merchant in Malaga. Their daughter Maria Manuela was born there in 1794.[5]

Kirkpatrick sent Maria Manuela to complete her education in

Paris. She was nineteen when she attracted attention there during the social season of 1813, and first met Colonel Portocarrero, who had come to Paris on leave from the front line in Spain. He met her again when he visited Malaga in 1817, and married her after obtaining the royal consent, which was necessary in the case of the marriage of a Spanish nobleman. When Eugénie became Empress of the French, the British press were interested in her Scottish descent, and wrote that King Ferdinand VII only consented to Cipriano's marriage to Maria Manuela because Kirkpatrick produced a bogus pedigree showing his descent from the legendary third-century Irish hero, Fingal; but in fact the Spanish College of Arms were satisfied with a family tree which had been drawn up in 1791 for one of William Kirkpatrick's brothers and which traced his line to a Kirkpatrick who was created Baron of Closeburn in 1232, through the famous Kirkpatrick who assassinated the Red Comyn for Robert Bruce.[6] The Spanish College of Arms were perhaps unaware that in thirteenth-century Scotland a baron was a local squire, not a nobleman.

In 1820 a Liberal revolution broke out in Spain, and Ferdinand VII was forced to proclaim the Constitution of 1812 and appoint a Liberal government. Teba strongly supported the revolutionaries and offered his services to the Liberal authorities at Granada. After three years of disorder in Spain, the governments of the Holy Alliance authorized the French government to invade Spain and suppress the revolution. Ferdinand VII was restored as an absolute monarch, and though the revolutionaries had surrendered to the French army on the promise of amnesty, Ferdinand violated the agreement. The revolutionary leader, Riego, and other Radicals were shot, and many Liberals were imprisoned. Teba was arrested, but was allowed to live with his wife under house arrest, at first in the remote town of Santiago de Compostela in north-west Spain, and later in Granada. He was living there when Maria Manuela gave birth to her first child, a daughter, Francisca, known as 'Paca' in the family, on 29 January 1825, and to her second child, Eugenia, fifteen months later.*[7]

In his isolation, Teba turned more and more to his family for happiness, and they did not let him down, though it was hard for Maria Manuela. Despite her pro-Bonapartist background, she did not take

*Kurtz, in *The Empress Eugénie* (p. 10), states that Cipriano was confined for eighteen months at Santiago de Compostela, and that Paca was born in her grandfather's house at Malaga; but Maria Manuela told her counsel, Grandperret, at the time of her libel action in 1876 (Alba Archives, Montijo c. 43–3) (see pp. 595–6, below) that she lived with Cipriano at Granada from 1823 to 1826 and that Cipriano was present at the birth of both the daughters. Llanos y Torriglia, in *Maria Manuela Kirkpatrick Condesa del Montijo* (p. 27), states that the authorities granted Cipriano permission to live in Granada on 28 December 1823.

kindly to the prospect of suffering social ostracism and enforced residence in Granada for her husband's devotion to the cause. She longed for the gaiety of social life in Madrid or Paris, and as Cipriano was unable to leave Granada she went off by herself. It was widely reported that she had lovers. Count Horace de Viel Castel wrote in his diary that his brother was one of them; but her friend Prosper Mérimée, who was generally assumed to be her lover and usually liked to boast of his conquests, told Stendhal that she had never been his mistress. She liked to make people believe that she was unfaithful to her husband. When Napoleon III, at the time of his marriage to Eugénie, asked her about the rumour that Eugénie was the daughter of Lord Clarendon, the British Ambassador in Madrid, she made her famous reply: 'The dates don't fit'.*[8]

Maria Manuela's flippancy, and the fact that circumstances caused her to live for long periods apart from Cipriano, gave rise to the rumour that she was on very bad terms with him; but there is no evidence of this. She seems to have been sincerely fond of Cipriano. She certainly stood by him loyally in dangerous times. She was right to think that she could help him by being seen in society and becoming friendly with influential supporters of the government, and she believed that she was responsible for saving his life after the counter-revolution of 1823.[9]

She had always tried to remain on good terms with her brother-in-law, Don Eugenio, Count of Montijo, in the hope that he would use his influence at court to obtain the release of Teba from house arrest at Granada; for this reason she had called her second daughter Eugenia after him. But she was alarmed when Montijo, at a fairly advanced age, married a prostitute who had been his cousin's mistress. Fortunately there seemed to be no prospect of the prostitute-countess giving him an heir who would oust Cipriano from the Montijo title, because Eugenio had been paralysed by a stroke and was confined to a bath-chair; but soon after the marriage it was announced that the Countess of Montijo was expecting a child at Ariza House, the family mansion in the Plazuela del Angel in Madrid.

The birth of an heir to a Spanish nobleman was a ceremonial occasion, at which every member of the family was entitled to be present; but Teba could not insist on exercising his right when he was unable to leave Granada by order of the government. Maria Manuela took the matter in hand. She travelled to Valencia, where Ferdinand

*Villiers, in his biography of Clarendon (*A Vanished Victorian*, pp. 80, 98, 259) states that Clarendon met Maria Manuela in Paris some years before 1832; but he is wrong in believing that Maria Manuela was not living in Madrid during the early years of Clarendon's residence there as ambassador.

VII was in residence, and persuaded him to authorize her to attend the Countess of Montijo's confinement as Teba's representative. When she arrived at Ariza House she found a male baby who had been brought there from an orphanage. She had no doubt that the Countess had intended to pass off the baby as her own child; but in view of Maria Manuela's arrival she abandoned her scheme, announced that she had been mistaken in thinking that she was pregnant, and stated that she had adopted the orphan as an act of charity. This may even have been true, for the baby from the orphanage continued to live in the Montijo mansion during Eugenio's lifetime. Maria Manuela kept him in the household after Eugenio's death, brought him up as a friend of the family, and bought him a commission in the Army Engineers. According to Eugénie, he became a competent but undistinguished army officer.*[10]

In 1829 Ferdinand VII married his fourth wife, Princess Maria Cristina of Naples. Under her influence he adopted a slightly more liberal policy, and released many of the Liberals from prison. In 1830, after seven years under house arrest, Teba was released and allowed to travel where he would. He and his family were often in Madrid, but kept their house in Granada. Although Cipriano was still unpopular in Spanish society, he was happy with his family. His relations with Eugénie were particularly close. He taught her to ride at an early age, and then went on long riding excursions with her – the sad but not embittered Bonapartist officer who was still only in his forties, with the black patch over his eye which he had worn since the Peninsular War, and the little girl of five or six, who had inherited his auburn hair and clear blue eyes. They rode all day across the countryside and up the mountain passes of southern Spain, talking to the peasants and visiting the gipsy encampments, where Eugenia, fascinated, watched the dancers, jugglers and fortune-tellers. On these happy outings she heard, too, about the principles of the French Revolution, and the glorious deeds of Napoleon and the tragedy of St Helena.[11]

Her delight in this outdoor life, in riding, and in her father's tales of his military adventures, made her wish that she was a boy. There is a tradition in her family that when she was very young she believed that if a girl fell downstairs she would be changed into a boy, and she threw herself down the great staircase in Ariza House hoping to achieve this transformation.[12]

Eugenia was perhaps less close to her mother than to her father. She was not on bad terms with Maria Manuela, but she became

*This is the story as told by Eugénie more than seventy years later in a letter to her niece in 1902, though her biographers have usually adopted a more dramatic and improbable version of the incident.

increasingly irritated, as she grew older, at her mother's insistence on managing everything. Maria Manuela introduced Eugénie to literary circles with which Cipriano had no connection, though it was thanks to a chance encounter with Cipriano that Prosper Mérimée first met Maria Manuela and Eugénie. Maria Manuela liked the company of writers, and they found her attractive and intelligent. George Ticknor, who met Maria Manuela in Spain in 1818, just before he returned to the United States to take up his appointment as Professor of French and Spanish Literature at Harvard, wrote that she was not only 'young and beautiful' but also 'the most cultivated and the most interesting woman in Spain'; and Mérimée said that she combined the solid virtues of a woman of the North with the charm and informality of an Andalusian girl.[13] Distinguished authors not only liked Maria Manuela, but also enjoyed talking to her two intelligent daughters. Before Eugénie was six, she had met Washington Irving and Mérimée.

Washington Irving had been living in Europe for fourteen years when he took up his residence in Granada in 1829. He had become internationally famous through his creation of the character of Rip van Winkle, and had already spent some years in Spain working on his biography of Christopher Columbus. He came to Granada to write a history of the conquest of Granada and sketches on the Alhambra. He loved Granada. It was an era in which a traveller from New York, after taking nearly two months to reach Andalusia, found himself in a country where very few of the inhabitants had ever left their native village and where the costumes of the peasants were different from those of their neighbours in the next valley. At Granada, Irving spent many hours wandering around the Alhambra and was introduced to Maria Manuela by his friend the Duke of Gor, a Spanish nobleman who was interested in literature. Irving often told stories to the six-year-old Paca and the five-year-old Eugenia.[14]

Prosper Mérimée first came to Spain in 1830, when he travelled through the whole country and was fascinated by the sun, the colour, the romance, the music, the lust and the cruelty of Spain, and by a way of life which was so different from what was to be found elsewhere in nineteenth-century Europe. He met Maria Manuela in Madrid and began a lifelong friendship with her. It was during this first visit that she told him about a young gallant of Malaga who had recently fallen madly in love with a prostitute and had killed her in a fit of jealous rage. Mérimée was intrigued by the story. Fifteen years later, after several other visits to Spain, he published his story 'Carmen' in the *Revue des Deux Mondes*. The novel became an international best-seller, though its fame was afterwards almost eclipsed by the opera which Bizet made from it. Mérimée wrote to Maria Manuela that it was she who had given him the idea for the novel by her story of the lover of Malaga, but that he had changed the prostitute into a gipsy because he had recently been studying the customs of Spanish gipsies.[15]

In September 1833 Ferdinand VII died. His brother, Don Carlos, would have succeeded to the throne under the old law of Spain; but shortly before his death Ferdinand had been persuaded by Queen Maria Cristina to repeal the Salic law which prevented females from inheriting the crown. Their daughter Isabel, who was aged three, became Queen, with her mother as Regent. Don Carlos immediately proclaimed himself King, raised an army in the north, and started a civil war which lasted for nearly six years. It was the first of a series of particularly ferocious civil wars which were to be fought in Spain during the next hundred years. The Carlists were supported by the most reactionary elements in the army and the Church, by large sections of the peasantry, by the Basque separatists, and internationally by Tsar Nicholas I, Metternich, and the Holy Alliance; the Isabelinos relied on the support of the professional military leaders, the Liberal middle class, the artisans in the towns, the revolutionary Radicals, and of Palmerston and King Louis Philippe. Revolutionary mobs murdered priests and Carlist supporters, and the Carlists carried out wholesale massacres of Radicals. Cipriano, with his Radical sympathies, enthusiastically supported the Isabelino cause and became a member of the Senate.

In July 1834 Don Eugenio died, and Cipriano succeeded him as Count of Montijo. A death in the family of a Spanish aristocrat was marked by lugubrious mourning ceremonies. The house was darkened, and all the family assembled in a room where they sat in complete darkness while one by one the adult members of the family spoke in solemn tones about the virtues of the deceased and the sorrow which his death had caused. Then they walked in procession to another room where the coffin had been placed; the coffin was opened, and each member of the family leant over it in turn to gaze for the last time at the dead relation. The children always took part in these ceremonies; but Eugenia, who was a highly imaginative child, was distressed and frightened. She was nevertheless required on several occasions to participate in these last farewells to deceased relatives. But once, as they entered the room to view the corpse, she was so terrified that she ran to the window and tried to throw herself out in order to escape. She was pulled back, and consoled, and was excused from attendance on such occasions in future.[16]

July 1834 was a disturbing time for the eight-year-old Eugenia. The great cholera epidemic had reached Spain, after spreading westwards from Russia and causing thousands of deaths and much panic in France and Britain. It led to an outburst of fury against the priests and monks, who were bitterly hated by the Radicals and were suspected, with some justification, of being secret agents of the Carlists in Isabelino territory. The rumour spread that the monks had caused the cholera by poisoning the wells. On 17 July, the day after the Count of Montijo died, a mob attacked the church of San Sebastian in the Plazuela del Angel, just across the little square from Ariza House. Eugenia was warned not to go to the window, but the temptation to do the forbidden thing proved too strong for her, and from the window she saw a monk being stabbed to death by the mob in the square. All her life she remembered the dreadful sight of many hands repeatedly stabbing the monk with their knives and the blood gushing forth.[17]

Cipriano and Maria Manuela decided that Spain was not a suitable place for Paca and Eugenia, and next day Maria Manuela set off with the children for Toulouse. Cipriano, as a senator, felt bound to remain in Madrid. When Maria Manuela and the children reached Barcelona, they were forbidden to proceed, because the local authorities had imposed quarantine regulations which prohibited the entry of any travellers from Madrid. But Maria Manuela had become friendly on the journey with a popular bullfighter who was travelling to Barcelona to take part in a fight there. He was Francisco Sevilla, the most famous *picador* of his time; his colleagues said of him that if he had horns, no bullfighter would dare to face him in the ring. The quarantine authorities were prepared to make an exception for Sevilla, because they feared that there would be a riot if he were not allowed to take part in the bullfight; and as he refused to enter Barcelona unless Maria Manuela and her daughters were also allowed to go on, they were permitted to proceed to Perpignan on the French frontier. This was the beginning of a friendship between Maria Manuela and Sevilla. He often visited her at her country house at Carabanchel outside Madrid, and died there at an early age in 1841 of cancer of the liver, after surviving all the hazards of the bullring.[18]

Perpignan was crowded with Spaniards, most of whom, like Maria Manuela, were travelling from Madrid to Toulouse. Maria Manuela, Paca and Eugénie took lodgings in the Rue Espinasse in Toulouse and then went on to Paris. Soon after they arrived, Maria Manuela returned to Spain, leaving Paca and Eugénie in the care of the nuns of the Convent of the Sacré Cœur in the Rue de Varenne in the Faubourg Saint-Germain, the most fashionable quarter of Paris. It was a school for young ladies of the best families, and very Catholic.[19]

This was a new experience for Eugénie. Napoleon had encouraged the Catholic religious revival in France which followed the Jacobin atheism and deism of the Reign of Terror, because he thought that a soldier who believed in God and an after-life was more willing to risk his life on the battlefield, and that a Catholic education encouraged women to be submissive to their husbands. But Bonapartists were more often nominal Catholics than pious ones, and Cipriano del Montijo was no exception. When Eugénie became Empress, she was accused by the Radicals of representing the extreme Catholic Ultramontane influence at Napoleon III's court, and this was often attributed to her Spanish background; but Eugénie did not inherit Catholic zeal from her Spanish Bonapartist father. Her Scottish-Belgian mother, who was a much better Catholic than Cipriano, encouraged her religion to some extent; but if Eugénie, who became more religious than either of them, owed her Catholicism to any external influence, it was the nuns of the Sacré Cœur in Paris who were responsible. Her religion, though deep, was in fact more spiritual than dogmatic or Ultramontane, and sprang from her own emotional and highly imaginative character. Religion was a great consolation to her, especially after she had experienced a succession of personal tragedies during her long life.

In July 1835 Cipriano and Maria Manuela joined the children in Paris, where they lived together happily but not ostentatiously. Don Eugenio's death had made the new Count of Montijo a very wealthy man; but Cipriano, the revolutionary and Bonapartist soldier, did not succumb to the temptations of a life of luxury or allow his daughters to do so. He himself had always preferred a simple life, though he smoked excellent cigars; and he insisted that Paca and Eugenia should have a rigorous and Spartan upbringing. They were made to wear the same linen garments in summer and winter, were not allowed to carry umbrellas when they walked in the rain, and were discouraged as much as possible from going in their mother's carriage, being expected to walk or ride everywhere.[20]

In the autumn Cipriano returned to Spain to perform his parliamentary duties. Maria Manuela and the children remained in Paris and took a house at 37 Rue de la Ville l'Évêque. Eugénie was very unhappy to be separated from her father; and Maria Manuela, though she enjoyed Parisian social life under Louis Philippe, was anxious about Cipriano. She told Mérimée that she feared that Cipriano would be hanged if the Carlists won the civil war, as she would not be able to save his life a second time from Spanish political vengeance.[21]

Paca and Eugénie continued to reside as boarders at the convent of the Sacré Cœur, where, on 25 March 1837, when Paca was twelve and Eugénie nearly eleven, they made their first communion. But at Cipriano's insistence they went for physical training to the Gymnase Normal, Civil et Orthosomatique, a very progressive co-educational school under the management of a Spanish Bonapartist colonel who had served in Napoleon's armies and had learned modern teaching methods at the Pestalozzi Institute in Madrid. They also had an English governess, Miss Cole.[22]

Paca would probably have settled down well in the convent, as she was an adaptable and contented child, though she could be naughty and uppish; but Eugénie was difficult and highly-strung, and did not like school life, either at the Pestalozzi school or at the convent. She was embarrassed by her red hair. She had been unhappy about the hair already in Spain, where she was first teased about it by a cousin, though she was comforted a little when Cipriano engaged a gardener whose hair was even redder than her own. The teasing about the red hair got worse at school in France, and continued to be an embarrassment to her until she became Empress of the French, when she found that the colour of her hair was called 'auburn', not 'red', and that society ladies were dyeing their hair 'auburn' in imitation of her.[23]

She was too lively to submit easily to discipline. She found it unbearable to keep quiet at meals in the presence of adults, and to speak only when she was spoken to. The urge to speak was so strong that if she found no one to talk to, she would take her child's chair into a corner and there hold long conversations with herself.[24]

She was saddened by her separation from her father, to whom she wrote very often, after drawing pencil lines, with the help of a ruler, on the notepaper to guide her childish hand.[25] They were affectionate letters, and showed a surprising interest in politics for a child of ten. On 2 January 1837 she wrote to him, lamenting that they had not been together at Christmas, and telling him that

> it is impossible to live in Paris, they want to kill the King all the time, the other day the gas exploded and broke many window panes and we were told that it was because some men had set it on fire. The funniest thing was that the soldiers came with their weapons, thinking that it was a revolution. Dear Daddy, we are very sad at the moment because we are so far from our country. You tell us to read Napoleon and learn his history, it made me cry a lot; particularly when Sir Hudson Lowe refuses to give the letter to the governor, wasn't it very cruel of him, doesn't he deserve to be well punished? Mummy has bought us Robinson Crusoe and Swiss Robinson. Daddy, how I want to kiss you and how glad I will be on the day when I am with you and see the end of the Pyrenees.[26]

Three months later, she wrote again to her father: 'I cannot wait any longer without seeing you, why did I come into the world except to be with my father and my mummy? What then is the arm which separates us? It is war. O war, when wilt thou have finished thy career?'[27]

In May 1837 Maria Manuela took Paca and Eugénie to England,[28] and sent the children to a school for well-bred girls at Clifton near Bristol. It was there that they heard the news of the death of William IV and the accession of Queen Victoria on 20 June. They stayed at the school for less than two months. Eugénie hated the school, but became friendly with a little Indian Princess, who was equally unhappy and was homesick for India. Eugénie was fascinated by her schoolfriend's tales of the wonders of the East, and they decided to run away from the school to the port of Bristol and stow away in a ship bound for India. They tried to persuade Paca to come, but Paca was too cautious and refused to go with them. They slipped away on one of the school walks, and found their way to the harbour at Bristol. They went on board a ship bound for India without anyone stopping them, and sat down on deck waiting for the ship to sail; but before she weighed anchor their schoolmistress arrived and took them back to the school.[29]

Maria Manuela, Paca and Eugénie returned to Paris in August,[30] and the children resumed their education at the Convent of the Sacré Cœur and at the Pestalozzi Gymnase. They also had the benefit of another English governess, Miss Flower, who had come over from England with them. She was a timid and rather slow-witted girl, and she allowed Paca to bully her.[31] 'Poor Miss Flower',[32] Eugénie would often say in later years when she talked about her governess and her childhood days; but Miss Flower gained in confidence as she grew older, and stayed in Maria Manuela's service for more than forty years. Eugénie learned to speak fluent English with a slight foreign accent.[33] She already spoke perfect French, and usually spoke and wrote in French to her parents, signing her name in the French style, 'Eugénie Palafox'.

One of Miss Flower's most difficult tasks was to get Eugénie up in the morning. When Miss Flower woke her at seven, she would not get out of bed, but turned over to face the wall, repeatedly holding up the five fingers of her hand as she tried to coax the governess into allowing her five more minutes in bed, and then another five minutes.[34]

Soon after they returned to Paris, they met Cipriano, who had been granted permission by the Queen Regent to go to France to take the waters for his health. He took a house at 24 Rue d'Angoulême, where he lived with Maria Manuela, and with the children during the school holidays.* This time he stayed for four months in Paris, where he met

---

*Kurtz (p. 17), observing no doubt that Eugénie wrote a letter at this time to her father addressed to 24 Rue d'Angoulême, deduced that he and Maria Manuela were living at separate addresses in Paris, and thought that this was evidence of their strained matrimonial relationship. But as we know from Mérimée's letters (C.G., II.127) that Maria Manuela was living at 24 Rue d'Angoulême, Eugénie's letter to Cipriano was obviously written during term time from the convent school.

some French army officers to discuss the military aid which France was giving to the Isabelinos.[35] It was a happy time for Eugénie, and she was sad when he had to return to Spain in January 1838. On the evening of his departure she visited the house in Paris of her cousin, the Duke of Alba, and a few days later wrote to Cipriano: 'I looked at the clock all the time. When it struck seven I knew that this was the hour of your departure.'* She never saw him again.

In Paris, the children had the benefit of the best cultural education. Maria Manuela took them to the theatre to see Rachel in *Horace*, though the play was not generally considered to be suitable for children. Paca and Eugénie were enraptured by Rachel. Maria Manuela spent much time with Mérimée, who was as delighted with Paca and Eugénie as he had been in Madrid. But Eugénie, at the age of eleven and twelve, had an even more devoted admirer. Stendhal was introduced to Maria Manuela in Paris by Mérimée, and though he enjoyed the company of Maria Manuela and Paca, he was utterly captivated by Eugénie.[36] Monsieur Beyle – Eugénie always called him by his real name – had served in Napoleon's army, including the campaign in Russia, and when he began writing in 1814 his unsuccessful works included a short, unfinished biography of Napoleon. His first successful book, *Le Rouge et le Noir*, was published in 1830, and when he first met Paca and Eugénie in the autumn of 1837 he was working on *La Chartreuse de Parme*. He told the children stories about Napoleon which increased their Bona-partist zeal.

Stendhal visited Maria Manuela regularly every Thursday, partly for the pleasure of discussing literature with her, but chiefly in order to see Eugénie, with whom he had almost fallen in love. He could not get her out of his mind. On 24 March 1838 he wrote to his friend Dr Fiore, whom he had met at the Countess of Montijo's: 'I often think of you and of the two twelve-year-old Spaniards.'[37] Later in the year, when he was correcting the proofs of *La Chartreuse de Parme*, he had the whimsical idea of inserting coded messages in Spanish to Paca and Eugénie in the footnotes of the book. On 15 December 1838 he was working on Chapter 3 – the chapter describing Fabrizio's adventures at the battle of Waterloo – and inserted a footnote at the end of the chapter: 'Para v. P. y E. 15 x 38'. Only two of his readers knew that it

*Kurtz (p. 17) quotes from this letter, which he saw in the Alba Archives in Madrid, where I was unable to find it. He dates it April 1837; but most of Eugénie's other childhood letters are undated, the date being added in nearly every case in a later hand. There is no doubt that Cipriano left Paris in January 1838. Maria Manuela gave the dates of his stay in Paris as October 1838 to January 1839 in her statement to her lawyer in her libel action in 1876 (Alba Archives, Montijo c. 43–3); but Mérimée's letters (*C.G.*, II.139–40) and other facts show that she meant to give the dates as October 1837 to January 1838.

meant: 'For you, Paca and Eugénie, 15 December 1838';*[38] but the footnote duly appeared in print, and stayed in all the editions of *La Chartreuse de Parme* until it was deleted by the editors of twentieth-century reprints.

Eugénie seems to have been happier now, though there were no further visits from her father, to whom she still wrote regularly, sending him for his birthday a pair of slippers which she and Paca had made. Her school report from the Gymnase in October 1838, when she was twelve and a half, was encouraging. Her height was 4 ft 5 in. ('*4 pieds, 5 pouces, 8 lignes*'), though she weighed only 35 kilos (5 stone 6½ lb). Her temperament was 'optimistic', but 'nervous'; her health, good; her complexion, pink and white; her eyes, blue; her hair, red. She had a great liking for physical exercises – a point to which the Pestalozzi institutions attached great importance. Her character was 'good, generous, active, firm'.[39]

This generosity of character, which was to last all her life, expressed itself at an early age in a deep compassion and indignation at injustice. She was probably only twelve when she was walking with Paca on the boulevards in Paris and saw a pauper's corpse being taken for burial to the Père-Lachaise cemetery without a single relative or mourner following the hearse. Eugénie was shocked. She and Paca followed the corpse and stood by the graveside during the short funeral service, so that the unknown pauper should not die quite unmourned and without prayer.[40]

In February 1839 Maria Manuela received news that her husband was dangerously ill in Madrid. She hurried to him at once, but did not take the children with her, because she did not wish them to risk the journey in the cold weather. She told Miss Flower to bring them when the weather improved in the spring. Paca and Eugénie, who did not realize that their father was seriously ill, had a carefree time during their last weeks in Paris. Paca took charge, and treated Miss Flower so outrageously that Mérimée felt obliged to intervene. He gave Paca a severe scolding, with very beneficial results.[41]

Paca and Eugénie left Paris with Miss Flower on 17 March in fine weather which appeared to be settled. They did not know that Cipriano had died two days before. When they reached Oloron they were held up by bad weather which prevented them from crossing the Pyrenees. Eugénie wrote from Oloron on 23 March to both Mérimée and Stendhal. Her departure from Paris had saddened Stendhal. He was writing his biography of Rossini, and wrote in the margin of his manuscript: '17 mars 1839, cour des Messageries. Depart. of Eouké' (departure of

*The 'x' refers not to October, the tenth month, but to the Latin 'decem', i.e. to December. The practice of writing the date in numerals had not been adopted in 1838.

Eugénie). A few days later he inserted another footnote to baffle the readers of Chapter 26 of *La Chartreuse de Parme*: 'P. y E. in Olo' (Paca and Eugénie in Oloron).[42]

The children heard the news of their father's death when they reached Madrid. It was the first of several tragedies in Eugénie's life. She was nearly thirteen.

CHAPTER 13

'AN INFURIATING GIRL'

MARIA MANUELA and the children did not return to Paris. The civil war was in its last stages, and there was no longer any danger of Madrid being disturbed by the Carlists, who eighteen months before had been within sight of the city. In September 1839 Don Carlos fled to France, and the Carlist resistance ended after General Maroto had been bribed to surrender his army to the Isabelinos. Eugénie wrote to Stendhal that bribing Maroto to desert was 'not nice', and many Isabelino supporters agreed with her; but they were glad that the war was over and that they had won, however shamefully.[1]

In later years, Eugénie told Paléologue that although she had closely followed Spanish politics in the 1840s, she was not interested in the party political struggles for power, only in great issues affecting the national honour and interest.[2] But she had little else to observe during her adolescence in Spain except the most sordid and complicated intrigues for power between the parties. As soon as the war was over, General Espartero, the most successful of the Isabelino generals, placed himself at the head of the Radical party and in September 1840 overthrew Maria Cristina's government and proclaimed himself Regent in her place. Maria Manuela and the children were at Carabanchel when Espartero made his *coup d'état*, and took care not to venture into the city while the crisis continued. Mérimée, who was staying with them at Carabanchel, went to Madrid every day to witness the events with a mixture of disgust and amusement, and then returned to Carabanchel to have dinner, as he put it, with six women, the eldest of whom (Maria Manuela) was thirty-six.[3]

Mérimée was not the only visitor who was charmed by Maria Manuela's house, the Casa de Miranda, at Upper Carabanchel. The property had belonged to her husband's family since 1469; but it was in the wealthier and more cultivated eighteenth century that Eugénie's great-grandfather erected a modern mansion there and surrounded it with gardens, shrubberies, ornamental lakes and waterfalls in 1746. Maria Manuela, who was a great garden-lover, embellished the grounds with new and rare plants and trees which she obtained from Paris with the help of Mérimée, who described it as the only place in the district which was luscious in summer. It was a delightful oasis on the south-western outskirts of Madrid across the River Manzanares, with splendid views of the Somosierra and Guadarrama mountains. Many other aristocratic families had country houses in the neighbourhood, and the Queen Mother's palace at Vista Alegre was less than four miles away. Upper Carabanchel was still unspoilt, but Lower Carabanchel, nearer Madrid, was becoming urbanized, and factories were springing up there. The road to Madrid was usually crowded with travellers, who were hampered by the bad road surface and by the branches of the overhanging trees. Despite repeated protests to the authorities, nothing was done to repair the road until Maria Manuela persuaded the other local landowners to club together and carry out the repairs at their own expense.[4]

Eugénie spent the greater part of every summer at Carabanchel, but lived for the rest of the year in the Montijo town house, the Casa Ariza, in the Plazuela del Angel – today the Plaza del Angel – in the centre of Madrid. The house stood on the north-east side of the little square, at the corner with the Plaza Santa Ana, on the site now occupied by the Simeón bank and department store and the Hotel Victoria. But Eugénie preferred Carabanchel; of all the family, it was she who most appreciated the Casa de Miranda.

In August 1842 the Countess of Montijo announced the engagement of her daughter Paca to Jacobo Stuart y Ventimiglia, eighth Duke of Berwick and fifteenth Duke of Alba,[5] a Grandee of Spain, and one of the richest men in Europe. His house, the Liria Palace in Madrid, was, according to Washington Irving, the most splendid in Spain after the royal palace. Alba was a quiet and rather shy young man of twenty-one, four years older than Paca and five years older than Eugénie. He was their cousin and a childhood friend of both girls. Eugénie took the news of the engagement very badly, because she was herself in love with Alba.

Maria Manuela was determined to arrange a magnificent wedding. She announced that it would take place in the spring, and made preparations to go to Paris to buy Paca's wedding dress and trousseau.[6] But as the spring of 1843 drew near, the wedding was postponed until the autumn, because Maria Manuela had not been able to complete the lavish arrangements in time. Was there perhaps another reason for the postponement? Could it have been due to Eugénie's opposition to the marriage, to some doubt in Alba's mind as to which of the girls he wanted to marry, or, more likely, to Paca's reluctance to distress Eugénie by marrying the man whom both of them loved?

Instead of the wedding, Maria Manuela gave a splendid Carnival ball in February 1843, at which all the people taking part wore fancy dress, except Maria Manuela herself and a few elderly Duchesses. It was the sensation of the season, and was reported at length in the Madrid newspaper *El Heraldo*. Maria Manuela went to great lengths to obtain exciting dresses from Paris for the younger members of her family: Paca was dressed as a Cracow girl, Eugénie in Scottish Highland costume, and their cousin Carlotta Kirkpatrick in Italian dress.[7]

One of the guests at the ball was Jerome Bonaparte's son, Prince Napoleon (Plon-Plon). He was aged twenty-one. His sister, Princess Mathilde, after breaking off her relations with Louis Napoleon, had married the very wealthy Russian Prince Demidov, who treated her so badly, insulting her and striking her in public, that Tsar Nicholas eventually ordered him to live apart from her and to pay her a handsome allowance. Demidov had at least enabled her, as a Russian princess, to live in Paris, which no other Bonaparte was permitted to do, and she was trying to use her influence at the court of Louis Philippe to obtain permission for her father and brother to return to France. The French and European press gave great publicity to Prince Napoleon's visit to Madrid, and wrote that he had gone there in the hopes of arranging a marriage between himself and Queen Isabel, though she was only twelve.[8]

After Eugénie became Empress of the French, her relations with Prince Napoleon were very bad. He was the leader of the Radical and pro-Italian faction at Napoleon III's court, and Eugénie championed the cause of the Pope and the Catholic Church. His enmity grew, and after the death of Napoleon III it led to a split in the Bonapartist ranks which finally destroyed the last remaining hope of a Bonapartist revival in France. Not surprisingly, the gossipmongers, journalists and biographers suggested that Prince Napoleon's hatred for Eugénie was the hatred of a rejected admirer for the proud beauty who had scorned him, and stories were published of how he had unsuccessfully made love to her when they first met in Spain. It is very likely that Prince Napoleon, who was as lascivious as his cousin Louis Napoleon, was attracted by Eugénie in Madrid in 1843, when he was twenty-one and she was seventeen; but when, in her old age, she talked very freely to Paléologue about her relations with Prince Napoleon, she attributed his hatred of her to the fact that by giving birth to the Prince Imperial she had ousted him from the succession to the imperial throne; and she said nothing to Paléologue to suggest that he had ever been in love with her.*[9]

*Kurtz (p. 23) translates the passage in Mérimée's letter of 24 February 1843 to Maria Manuela, 'Dites-moi quelle espèce d'homme est le Bonaparte qui vient faire le Don Juan chez vous', as 'Tell me, what sort of a man is the Bonaparte who has come to play Don Juan in your house', and, like Llanos y Torriglia (p. 130), thinks that it

The preparations went ahead for Paca's wedding to Alba in the autumn of 1843. On 17 May,* Eugénie wrote a dramatic letter to Alba. 'My very dear cousin', she began, writing in French and addressing him as 'tu',

> You will find it very strange that I am writing you a letter like this one, but there is an end to everything in this world, and my end is very near. . . . I do not wish to excuse my behaviour, but still, when people are nice to me I will do everything they want me to do. But when I am treated like an ass and beaten in front of everybody, this is more than I can bear. My blood boils and I do not know what I am doing. . . . I love and hate to extremes, and I do not know if it is better to have my love or my hate; I am a mixture of terrible passions. . . . I fight against them, but I am losing the fight and at last my life will end miserably, lost in a mass of passions, virtues and follies. You will say that I am romantic and naughty, but you are good and will forgive a poor girl who has lost all those who loved her, and who is regarded with indifference by everybody, even by her mother, her sister, and – dare I say it? – by the man she loves best, for whom she would have begged for alms and would even have consented to her own dishonour; you know who this man is. Please don't say that I am mad, have pity on me; you don't know what it means to love someone and to be despised by him. But God . . . will give me the courage to end my life peacefully deep in a sad cloister and no one will ever know whether or not I have existed.

After wishing him and Paca every happiness in their married life, and urging them to show equal affection to all their children – 'Never lose the friendship of one by showing more affection to the other' – she ended: 'I will finish my life far from the world and its affections. . . . My decision is taken, for my heart is broken.'[10]

This letter, written a fortnight after Eugénie's seventeenth birthday, has been interpreted as a suicide note, and there are passages in it which show that she was thinking of imminent death, although her forecast that she would end her life 'peacefully deep in a sad cloister and no one

---

refers to Prince Napoleon's attempt to seduce Eugénie. But undoubtedly by 'chez vous' Mérimée, writing from Paris to Maria Manuela in Madrid, meant only 'in Madrid', and was referring to the press reports that Prince Napoleon had gone there to woo the Queen. This is clear from the passage in the letter in which Mérimée says that the marriage between the Queen and Prince Napoleon will not take place, because it is Sir Robert Peel, the British Prime Minister, who will be buying the trousseau for this bride.

*The letter is dated 'Wednesday evening, 16 May 1843'. As 16 May was a Tuesday, the letter was probably written on Wednesday 17 May.

will ever know whether or not I have existed' is certainly not a threat of immediate suicide. Within less than a month after Eugénie wrote the letter, Maria Manuela had left for Paris to buy Paca's trousseau, taking Paca and Eugénie with her. Mérimée, meeting them for the first time for nearly three years, wrote on 24 June that all three were in sparkling health. They stayed in Paris for three-and-a-half months, and returned to Madrid in October, taking with them forty-eight pairs of shoes for Paca and a large number of dresses. The wedding was due to take place in November.[11]

But the wedding was again postponed, for reasons which baffled Mérimée, though he was one of Maria Manuela's most intimate friends. On 4 November he wrote to Maria Manuela expressing his surprise that she had not written to him about the wedding. On the 11th he wrote again, asking when Paca would be Duchess of Alba; and in his letter of the 18th he playfully wrote that Alba might wither away if Maria Manuela made him wait until December. She made him wait longer than this; it was not until January that the invitations were sent out for the wedding on 14 February. 'So you have at last taken pity on the poor Duke's sighs', wrote Mérimée to Maria Manuela on 2 February.[12]

It is certainly possible that the second postponement of the wedding was due to a suicide attempt by Eugénie. Although every attempt was made to keep it dark – Maria Manuela did not tell even Mérimée – rumours were soon circulating in Madrid that Eugénie had tried to commit suicide because Paca was to marry Alba. Alba's grandson, the seventeenth Duke, who knew Eugénie very well in her later years, believed the story that she broke off the heads of phosphorus matches and drank them dissolved in milk.[13] The white phosphorus heads of the matches used in 1843, which had been invented some ten years earlier, were well-known to be very poisonous, and Eugénie had doubtless been warned about them from her early childhood.

The wedding of Alba and Paca took place on 14 February 1844 in the private chapel at the Ariza mansion, where the ceremony was performed by the Archbishop of Toledo, and was followed by a sumptuous feast. Washington Irving, who had returned to Spain in 1842 as United States ambassador and had renewed his friendship with Maria Manuela and her daughters, was unable to attend the wedding because of ill-health. He wrote to his nieces that Paca's wedding presents were worth 120,000 dollars, that some of her handkerchiefs were valued at 200 dollars each, and that her trousseau was said to have cost 600,000 francs. 'The young Duchess is thought to be one of the happiest and best-dressed young ladies in the whole world', he wrote; 'she is already quite hated in the *beau monde*.'[14] But she was not hated by her sister. Despite all the agony and despair to which Eugénie had been reduced by Paca's marriage, she never allowed this to turn her against Paca. From this time onwards she was closer than ever to her, and remained on excellent terms with Alba. In due course she became very intimate with Paca's children and grandchildren.

With Paca so splendidly and happily married, Maria Manuela's next aim was to find a husband for Eugénie; but this proved to be difficult. Eugénie was eighteen in May 1844, and was strikingly beautiful with her red hair and blue eyes, her fair skin and perfect figure with a very slim waist. She was surrounded by admirers; but, reacting from her unhappy love for Alba, she was determined not to become emotionally involved with any of them. She flirted and coquetted with them all, but refused all offers of marriage, and became famous as a cold and heartless beauty who would not grant the slightest favours to her suitors.

She had every opportunity to meet eligible young men, as her mother moved in the highest society. During the winter season, from the middle of November to Shrove Tuesday, Maria Manuela entertained at Ariza House every Sunday evening, leaving the other days of the week to other society hostesses. Three times a year she gave a magnificent ball – on the day of Eugénie's patron saint, St Eugenio of Toledo (15 November), on Paca's birthday (29 January) and on Carnival Sunday. On these occasions Ariza House was a blaze of lights, for Maria Manuela had installed gaslight in 1845; she was one of the first householders in Madrid to do so. The balls were attended by most of the higher aristocracy, by members of the government, by foreign diplomats, and by rather sycophantic journalists who invariably wrote in their newspapers that the occasion had eclipsed in splendour all the Countess of Montijo's previous entertainments.[15] It was a world in which Maria Manuela felt very much at home, for morals in Madrid were very lax for married, though not for unmarried, women. 'Whenever one asks at the Opera, or at Court, or indeed anywhere,' wrote Lord Canning to Malmesbury, 'who such and such a lady is, the answer is always in the same form: she is the wife of D—, the daughter of C—, and Mr So-and-So is her lover.'[16]

Maria Manuela did not like Espartero's Radical government, with its high taxation and forced loans levied on the owners of large mansions in Madrid; but she tried to keep on good terms with Espartero, and often invited his officers to her balls.[17] In July 1843, while Maria Manuela, Paca and Eugénie were in Paris buying Paca's trousseau, Espartero was overthrown by a *coup d'état* carried out by Ramon Narvaez, another Isabelino general who had distinguished himself in the civil war against the Carlists. The Queen Mother returned from

France, and, to the joy of Maria Manuela and all the landowning and wealthy classes, a government of Conservatives and moderate Liberals was established.

It did not last long. In May 1844 Narvaez made himself dictator, suppressed the freedom of the press, and had over two hundred Radicals shot and many more imprisoned. He declared that the Spanish nation was an ass that had to be driven and disciplined with the stick. When he was urged to forgive his enemies, he replied that he had no enemies: they were all dead.[18]

Narvaez – short and stout, with his sleek black hair and bushy blonde moustache, his impeccable dress and his coarse barrack-room language and low-class Andalusian accent – had a certain personal charm, and Maria Manuela became very friendly with him. She became one of the most prominent ladies at the court. Her daughter Eugenia went with her to the balls and garden parties at the royal palaces in Madrid and at Buena Vista and at the Queen Mother's at Vista Alegre, as well as attending Maria Manuela's balls and receptions. At first, unlike her sister Paca, she did not attract much attention among the beautiful señoras and señoritas of the Gor, Santa Cruz and Zamora families who also attended these functions; but after she reached the age of twenty, she made a great impression, and was usually singled out for praise by the newspaper gossip-columnists as one of the most beautiful girls at the ball. She was painted by Federico de Madrazo, the most fashionable portrait-painter in Madrid, in an elegant dress, and by Édouard Odier in smuggler's costume on horseback.[19]

Eugénie loved dressing up, and enjoyed the fancy dress-balls which her mother gave. They had become popular in society in many countries, but the Countess of Montijo was the pioneer who introduced them into Spain. By 1846 Queen Isabel had become enthusiastic about them, and she gave a ball at the palace at which all the guests were directed to wear fancy dress. All of them did so, except Narvaez and two other ministers, who insisted on wearing uniform. After this, the other generals also came in uniform, and the Queen was forced to say that either fancy dress, uniform, or conventional evening dress should be worn. The result was that nearly all the women, but only a small proportion of the men, wore fancy dress. They came dressed as Mary Queen of Scots, as Queen Elizabeth of England, as courtiers of the time of Louis XIV or of Charles III of Spain, in the peasant costumes of Andalusia or Calabria, or as Jewesses or gipsies. Eugénie was a great sensation, at a series of fancy-dress balls, as a Jewess, a Sicilian girl, and a Greek woman.[20]

She enjoyed the amateur theatricals at Carabanchel, where Maria Manuela built a little theatre and put on plays and operas in which her society friends took part. Eugénie had loved the theatre ever since she had seen Rachel in *Horace* as a child in Paris. As a young woman in Madrid, she participated in the thriving theatrical life of the capital. At the Circo, the Teatro del Palacio, and the Teatro del Principe, Barbara and Teodora Lamadrid, Julian Romea, and Romea's wife Matilde Diez, whom the Paris press had called 'the Rachel of the Peninsula', acted throughout the season in classical and contemporary Spanish plays and in translations of Shakespeare, of Molière, and of the latest Paris successes of Victor Hugo and lesser French playwrights; Señora Guy-Stephan danced in *Giselle*, *Ondine*, and *La Esmeralda*; and a standard repertory company sang regularly in the latest operas of Verdi, Donizetti, Rossini and Bellini.[21] Romea was a friend of Maria Manuela and Eugénie, and sometimes acted with the amateurs in the productions at Carabanchel.

Eugénie appreciated opera less than the theatre. In later life her lack of musical ability and interest was a well-known joke in her circle; she was supposed to be unable to sing a note, and in her later years at Farnborough Hill it was said that she could not distinguish between 'God Save the King' and 'Partant pour la Syrie'.[22] This lack of musical ear was probably exaggerated. Eugénie liked gipsy music and the rhythm of the traditional Spanish dances; but Maria Manuela was a gifted musician with a great love of opera, and Eugénie's failure to emulate her mother probably gave rise to the idea, which was firmly impressed on her from her childhood days, that she had no ear for music.

Eugénie was always fond of telling stories against herself. In later years she told her secretary Augustin Filon that when Bellini's *Norma* was performed at Carabanchel, she was only given a walking-on part, as she could neither act nor sing, and that she so bungled her entry with the baby that she ran off the stage and was never asked to take part in theatricals again. 'So now you know all about my career as an actress!', she told Filon.[23] This was far from the truth. Even if the dramatic critic of *El Heraldo* was being insincere when he praised her performance as Clotilda, and if we accept the more plausible version of this story which Eugénie told to her friend, Count Primoli, her appearance in *Norma* in September 1844 was certainly not the last occasion on which she took part in the productions at Carabanchel, though Maria Manuela did not again make the mistake of giving her a singing part.[24] She often acted the leading lady in the performances there. She may not have been a great dramatic actress, but she delighted the audiences when she played the part of the flirtatious heroine in light comedies.

Maria Manuela was a friend of the very popular playwright and librettist, Ventura de la Vega, and on several occasions he produced amateur performances of his plays in her theatre. In 1845 he produced his most successful comedy *El Hombre de Mundo* at Carabanchel, a few months before its first performance on the professional stage in Madrid. Eugénie acted the part of Clara, the model wife who remains faithful to her husband despite the succession of unfortunate coincidences and misunderstandings which lead her wrongly to believe that he has reverted to the lecherous life which he led as a bachelor. Paca played the second woman's part of Emilia; the Duke of Alba was the cynical servant, Ramón; and Ventura de la Vega himself acted opposite Eugénie in the part of the reformed husband, Luis. In the same year Eugénie was praised for her performance in the comedy *Bandera Negra* in Alba's private theatre in the Liria Palace.[25]

She loved horses and dogs – the great watchdogs at Carabanchel who barked so ferociously in the night if anyone approached the house, and her own lapdog and her large Newfoundland dog who was devoted to her and had to be shut out of the bathing pool when she went swimming, to prevent him from jumping in to save her life. Riding was her favourite pastime. As a child she had ridden through the countryside with her father; now she caused comment by riding alone. At Carabanchel the country folk stared in admiration as she rode out at full gallop with her red hair hanging down her back on her way to the mountains or to visit a gipsy encampment where, according to the stories told in later years, the fortune-tellers prophesied that she would marry an Emperor or rule over a kingdom. She drove her barouche with her frisky ponies so recklessly that she and her escort were sometimes thrown into the ditch; but Mérimée thought that most young men would be delighted to lie in a ditch with Eugénie.[26]

She went out to dinner with actors and actresses, and was said to have ridden bareback through the streets of Madrid, smoking a cigar or a cigarette. In later years she disliked smoking, and only occasionally accepted a cigarette when she thought it would be discourteous to refuse; but it is more than likely that she smoked at this time, though no conventional aristocratic lady smoked. Eugénie had been brought up among smokers at Ariza House and Carabanchel. Mérimée told his English friend Sutton Sharpe that if he visited Maria Manuela he would have the unique experience of being able to smoke in the house of a duchess.*[27]

Eugénie loved the bullfights which had both horrified and fascinated her friend Mérimée by their cruelty and glamour. At this time the great Montes was the undisputed champion of the bullring, but two other *matadors* – Cuchares and José Redondo, who was known as El Chichanero – were friendly rivals for second place. These leading bullfighters

*Maria Manuela was Duchess of Peñaranda as well as Countess of Montijo.

had acquired perfect manners and social self-confidence, and were received in the mansions of the aristocracy and even at the royal palace. Eugénie became very friendly with El Chichanero. The gossipmongers said that she was his mistress, but it is much more likely that she teased him and kept him at arm's length.[28]

She turned up at the bullfights unconventionally dressed in scarlet boots, with a dagger in her belt, and carrying a whip instead of a fan; and her provocative behaviour to the bullfighters was frowned on in certain quarters.[29] On other occasions, too, her dress aroused unfavourable comment. When she went to Toledo in June 1848 with Paca, Alba, and her cousin Pepe, Marquis of Alcañices, she and Paca dressed up as smugglers in Calabrian hats, riding through the streets and even visiting the cathedral in this costume.[30]

One year, at Easter, Eugénie and one of her girl-friends attended the famous Festival of Flowers in Seville. They put on gipsy costume, and set up a tent at the fair, where they flirted with the men and danced gipsy dances, to the delight of the visitors to the fair. The Spaniards probably recognized them for what they were, but two young English gentlemen watched in admiration, believing that they were seeing two genuine Spanish gipsy girls; they praised the girls' skill and physical attractions in their presence, in English, assuming that the girls would not understand what they said. One of the Englishmen wished to give the girls some money; the other was not sure that this would be the right thing to do. After they had discussed this for a little while, Eugénie said to them in her fluent English: 'Perhaps you would like to know who we are', and introduced herself and her companion. The Englishmen promptly fell in love with them.[31]

Eugénie made a deep impression on a young diplomat in the Spanish Foreign Office, Juan Valera, who had not yet pubished his first novel but already had the psychological perception and the gift of style which were to make him one of the leading Spanish writers of the nineteenth century. He wrote to his mother in January 1847 that he had been introduced to the Countess of Montijo and had been invited to a ball held on 15 November in honour of the beautiful Eugénie's patron saint. He described Eugénie as

an infuriating girl who, with childish playfulness, shrieks, makes a noise, and gets up to all the naughtiness of a six-year-old child. At the same time she is quite the most fashionable* young lady of this town and court, and she is so short-tempered and bossy, so fond of physical exercise and the flattery of good-looking gentlemen, and, in short, is so adorably badly brought up, that one can be virtually

*The word 'fashionable' is in English in Valera's original Spanish.

certain that her future husband will be a martyr to this heavenly, aristocratic, and above all wealthy, creature.[32]

But there were many young gentlemen who were desperately eager to undergo the martyrdom of being Eugénie's husband. One of them was the young Duke of Osuna, the premier nobleman in Spain – Alba was the second. Osuna had come to her rescue at the Queen Mother's garden party at Vista Alegre in April 1845, when some of the guests went boating on the lake, and the gondola carrying Eugénie, Maria Manuela and Señorita de Zamora overturned. They escaped with nothing worse than a ducking, but had to return at once to Madrid in Osuna's carriage to get a change of clothes. Apart from Osuna, several Spanish noblemen were in love with Eugénie. Prince Albert de Broglie, who was the Second Secretary at the French legation in Madrid, was another admirer.[33]

In the autumn of 1846, Louis Philippe and Guizot scored one of their few diplomatic triumphs over Palmerston and arranged the marriage of Queen Isabel to her cousin Francisco Duke of Cadiz, and of her sister the Infanta to Louis Philippe's son, the Duc de Montpensier. The weddings were followed by a succession of splendid balls and receptions at the royal palace, which were attended by Montpensier's brother the Duc d'Aumale and many distinguished guests from France. Johann Strauss the father, who was visiting Madrid, was a guest at one of the balls, and two days later was asked to conduct the band at a ball at the French embassy at which the Queen and King Consort, Aumale, Montpensier and the Infanta, and nearly all the court and nobility, including Maria Manuela, Paca and Eugénie, danced with zest in the rigadoons, polkas and waltzes which Strauss conducted with tremendous *élan*. Alexandre Dumas *père* and Alexandre Dumas *fils* were present. The elder Dumas was at the height of his fame, having published his *Three Musketeers* and *The Count of Monte-Cristo* two years before; the younger Dumas, who was only twenty-two, did not become well-known until his novel *La Dame aux camélias* appeared in 1848. Both father and son were delighted with Eugénie, and the younger Dumas fell seriously in love with her.[34]

Ferdinand Huddleston, of Sawston Hall in Cambridgeshire, proposed to Eugénie after he had met her when he visited Spain in the summer of 1846. Apart from being a pleasant gentleman and a moderately wealthy landowner, Huddleston had the advantage of being a Roman Catholic, coming from a famous family which had rendered great services to the Catholic cause in the days of Mary Tudor and Charles II. But Eugénie refused him. Her reply showed that, despite her liking for gipsy encampments and her unconventional dress and habits, she could decline a proposal of marriage with all the tact and consideration which was expected of a well-bred young lady of the period:

As a *friend* I shall always be happy to see you.* You tell me that I am undecided, and you would wait for me to make up my mind. But I feel too much friendship for you to raise hopes which I could never fulfil. At the risk of losing your friendship I prefer to act loyally towards you. I hope nevertheless to see you here again, if not at present, then later on. You know that you will always find in me a friend.[35]

She also refused her cousin José de Xifre, with whom she had been very friendly ever since they were small children in Paris. She persuaded José to give up gambling, realizing that he was rapidly losing his family fortune at the gaming tables, and he then took to the less expensive pastime of chain-smoking cigars. Eugénie was very fond of this young man with his long nose and his pensive and melancholy manner, but she would not marry him, which made him more melancholy than ever.[36]

No one was more put out by Eugénie's reluctance to marry than Prosper Mérimée. When he wrote to Maria Manuela about Eugénie, he adopted an attitude which was a mixture of a kind old uncle and an experienced gallant and man of the world. After Paca's wedding he was sure that Eugénie would be 'inclined to allow herself to be swept away' by Paca's example. But Eugénie did nothing of the kind, and three months later Mérimée was reflecting sadly on her cruelty to her admirers. 'There is a great depth of cruelty in all women', he wrote to Maria Manuela; 'when they feel that they are loved, they treat you like niggers.' In the autumn his hopes rose, only to be dashed again. 'I thought that Eugénie was on the point of pronouncing the fatal "Yes" ', he wrote on 30 November 1844; 'I dread for E. these second lieutenants of the Hussars who have not got a penny but have beautiful moustaches and a brilliant uniform.' But penniless subalterns were as unsuccessful as wealthy noblemen in their pursuit of her, and by February 1846 Mérimée was reduced to writing: 'What a pity that Eugénie is not a boy!'[37]

Eugénie was still unmarried in June 1847, when she was just twenty-one. Mérimée told Maria Manuela that the Italian opera singer, Madame Pisaroni, had driven one lover to suicide and another mad, and thought that this proved that it was always ugly women with whom men fall passionately in love. 'This explains why your Eugénie,

*Eugénie wrote this sentence in English. The rest of her letter was written in French.

who is so beautiful, has not yet found her perfect man.' But in September he was surprised and relieved to hear that José de Xifre had found her 'very amiable, and what is even better, very reasonable and not feather-brained as her enemies say'.[38]

She was as enthusiastic a Bonapartist as ever, making snide remarks about Louis Philippe in her letters. 'I am not at all surprised', she wrote to Mérimée, 'that the Father of the People goes incognito in the streets to find out what is happening, like the Sultan of the Indies in the *Thousand and One Nights*. No doubt he is tired of etiquette, which is not surprising, as he is not used to it.' In December 1840 she wrote to Stendhal to express her delight at the return of Napoleon's corpse to France. Some years later, when she and Maria Manuela and Paca were on holiday in the Pyrenees, they attended a concert at which Eléonore Gordon sang. They were eager to meet her, because they had read of her part in Louis Napoleon's Strasburg *coup* in 1836 and of her acquittal at the trial which followed. Madame Gordon had recently visited Louis Napoleon in his prison at Ham, and offered to arrange for Maria Manuela and Eugénie to visit him there. They eagerly accepted her offer, but did not go to Ham, because Maria Manuela was recalled to Madrid on important business.[39]

Like many other Bonapartists in the 1840s, including Louis Napoleon himself, Eugénie was interested in Socialism. She read the books of Fourier, the French Socialist philosopher who had published his *Théorie des quatre mouvements* in 1808 and *Le Nouveau Monde industriel* in 1830. Fourier combined his somewhat far-fetched philosophical theories with a caustic wit. In his books, after a devastating analysis of the inefficiency and waste involved in economic competition, and the contradiction between the theory and practice of Liberal *philosophes* and economists, he proposed that society should be divided into agricultural communes with 1600 people in each commune. In these communes, everyone would be free to choose the kind of work that he preferred to do; and the fact that the young child usually enjoys wallowing in dirt until he is discouraged from doing so by his elders convinced Fourier that there would be no lack of volunteers to do the dirty jobs once the social odium attached to them was removed. Fourier thought that it would be possible and desirable to preserve a certain degree of family life within the commune, but he believed that marriage as an institution was primarily designed to subjugate the woman to the man, and that the marriage laws were an example of his central thesis, that the source of human misery was the restrictions placed by law on the freedom and natural instincts of the individual.

Fourier died in 1837, but his followers continued to propagate his doctrines, and by 1843 had established a daily paper, *La Démocratie pacifique*, in Paris. Their theories were calculated to make a favourable impression on the aristocratic and middle-class youth in the first half of the nineteenth century, who were conscious, as no previous generation had been, of the injustices of economic inequality, and did not believe, like their parents, that these injustices were designed by God for the benefit or punishment of the human race. It is not surprising that so imaginative and unorthodox a girl as Eugénie read Fourier enthusiastically, and was a convinced Fouricrist at the age of sixteen;[40] nor is it surprising that the Countess of Montijo thought that it was an unsuitable occupation for her beautiful young daughter whom she was trying to marry off to an eligible Spanish aristocrat, especially as Eugénie disconcerted her many admirers by asking them what they thought of Fourierism.[41]

Eugénie had ceased to be a Socialist by the time she was twenty-five. According to Count Primoli, this was because of a painful incident which soured her political idealism. Her friend and teacher, the French Socialist Chiffrey, inherited from his uncle a plantation in Cuba with the slaves of the estate. Eugénie urged Chiffrey to free the slaves immediately, which he did. The slaves thereupon left the estate, and, having no means of subsistence, formed themselves into bands of robbers and terrorized the district. The authorities in Cuba blamed Chiffrey for the robberies, because he had emancipated the slaves. Chiffrey then appealed to the former slaves to return to his plantation and work for him as free, paid labourers; but they, thinking that this was a trick to re-enslave them, set fire to his plantation, which ruined him financially. In Madrid, Eugénie's elders did not fail to point out the disastrous results of her attempt to do good by urging Chiffrey to free his slaves.[42]

Whatever her own political inclinations may have been, Eugénie's connection with Narvaez was the first of many occasions when she became labelled through association as a supporter of Conservative reaction. As Narvaez was a great personal friend of her mother's, she saw a great deal of him. He was not seriously in love with her, but he paid her lavish compliments and praised her beauty to Maria Manuela.[43] He adopted a tolerant attitude about her Socialism, which he did not take seriously; in any case, in many countries at this time autocratic Conservative rulers were on much better terms with Socialist thinkers than they were with the Liberal democrats who were trying to assassinate them and to overthrow their governments by revolutionary violence.

Eugénie's generous and emotional nature made it possible for her to be on friendly terms with Narvaez while instinctively revolting against his brutal political methods. When she came on a platoon of his soldiers in a street in Madrid who were on the point of carrying out a summary execution of Radical revolutionaries, she told them to halt the execution until she had found Narvaez and persuaded him to pardon the prisoners; but as she rode off she heard the volley as the men were shot. Once she gave refuge to a terrorist who had just carried out a political murder, hiding him in Ariza House and smuggling him out of Madrid. Her former governess, the English Miss Flower, was shocked at this defiance of the law; but Eugénie told Miss Flower that in Spain it was unthinkable to surrender a political terrorist to the police.[44]

Sometimes she quarrelled with Narvaez, refusing to submit to his bullying. She was talking, at a ball, to one of his young A.D.C.s when Narvaez joined them. The A.D.C. prepared to withdraw at once and leave Eugénie to Narvaez, but Eugénie asked him to stay. Narvaez angrily ordered the embarrassed A.D.C. to go away, whereupon Eugénie said that she needed some fresh air and followed the A.D.C. into the garden, refusing Narvaez's offer of his arm and telling him that she would not trouble so important a person as he, but would ask his A.D.C. to escort her. Another story, which is better substantiated than many others, was that on one occasion she angered Narvaez by arguing with him about politics, and Narvaez declared that a woman was not entitled to express a political point of view because women could not face cold steel. Eugénie promptly snatched his dagger and plunged it into her arm to show him that she did not fear steel. Primoli told an even more surprising story of how one evening, at a party at Caraban-chel, Eugénie angered Maria Manuela so much by expressing Liberal political views that Maria Manuela tried to strike her. Eugénie dodged the blow, ran to the top of the stairs, climbed over the banisters, and, clinging to the newel, threatened to let go and fall to her death if Maria Manuela approached her.[45]

By 1846 Narvaez had aroused the fears of the Queen Mother and most other influential persons in Spain, and they united against him. He was ousted from office, and though he returned to power in October 1847 it was only as the result of an alliance with the Marquis of Mira-flores. Miraflores had been a friend of Cipriano del Montijo, but he had always been hostile to Maria Manuela, and had wrongly accused her during the civil war of being a Carlist agent. When Narvaez resumed office, he appointed Maria Manuela to the very influential position of Camerara Mayor, the chief of the Queen's ladies-in-waiting. The *Times* correspondent in Madrid was baffled as to the political significance of this appointment; he wrote that the Countess of Montijo, who was famous for her balls and parties, had been on very friendly terms with every government that had held power in Spain, and he had no idea on which side she would use her influence, as Camerara Mayor, over the Queen.[46] It is not surprising that he was puzzled about Maria Manuela's politics, because although she was so close to Narvaez and the pro-French faction, she had formerly been an intimate friend, and possibly the mistress, of Lord Clarendon when he was British Ambassador in Madrid; and she was on friendly terms with Clarendon's successor, Henry Bulwer, who was Narvaez's bitter enemy and was eventually expelled from Spain for intriguing with the Radical revolutionaries against the dictator. In fact, Maria Manuela's friendship with the leaders of all the parties, which did her no good politically, was the result of her liking for friendly social intercourse and her lack of interest in politics.

On becoming Camerara Mayor, Maria Manuela appointed Paca to be one of the Queen's ladies-in-waiting, and took the occasion to exercise her right to transfer some of her titles to Eugénie. On 21 October 1847 the Queen granted Doña Maria Eugenia de Guzmán y Porto-carrero the right to bear her father's titles of Count of Teba, Count of Baños, Count of Mora, Count of Ablitas, Count of Santa Cruz de la Sierra, Marquis of Ardales, Marquis of Osera, Marquis of Moya and Viscount of La Calzada, both the Baños and the Mora titles carrying with them the rank of Grandee. She was known and addressed as Countess of Teba, the most senior of these titles. While her mother was Camerara Mayor, Eugénie spent much time at court, and on 15 November the Queen and King attended the ball which Maria Manuela gave for Eugénie at Ariza House, the King dancing the first riga-doon with Eugénie.[47]

But Maria Manuela did not hold the post of Camerara Mayor for long. Narvaez had been forced, as part of his bargain with Miraflores, to appoint Miraflores as Master of the Queen's Household. Miraflores immediately countered Maria Manuela's appointment by ordering that his friend the Marchioness of Santa Cruz, who had been dismissed from her post as Camerara Mayor six months before because she was hated by the Queen and the Queen Mother, should take precedence over the Camerara Mayor. Maria Manuela was indignant, and threatened to resign unless the precedence of the Marchioness of Santa Cruz was revoked; but Miraflores threatened to resign if this were done. After eight weeks of wrangling, Narvaez gave in to Miraflores and told Maria Manuela that she must agree to take second place to the Marchioness of Santa Cruz; but Maria Manuela refused, and resigned as Camerara Mayor.[48]

On 16 December she wrote to the Queen and explained that she had accepted the post out of loyalty at a time when she would have preferred to devote all her energies to 'the care and education of my younger daughter at the most critical period of her youth'. If it had been merely a question of precedence between the most worthy Marchioness of Santa Cruz and her who now has the honour to write to Your Majesty, I would not have hesitated for a moment to give way to one who has rendered so many distinguished services to Your Majesty and who has for so many reasons my most profound consideration and respect;

but as the question was one between an ex-Camerara and the present Camerara, it involved the dignity of the office.[49]

The Queen regretfully accepted Maria Manuela's resignation. Her period of office had been a disturbed one during which a popular singer had been discovered in the Queen's bedroom in the middle of the night, and one of the Queen's chaplains had been arrested on a charge of murdering a woman servant in the palace.[50]

During the summer months, Eugénie was often away from Madrid, staying either at Carabanchel or further off. In August 1847 she went with Paca and Alba for a holiday to Biarritz. It was her first visit to the little fishing village just across the French border from Spain, and she was enchanted by it. She swam in the Atlantic; she clambered into the caves on the shore which could only be reached at low tide, and where, according to the local legend, a pair of lovers had once been cut off and drowned; and she persuaded the fishermen to take her out in their boats when she had been warned that it was too dangerous to go because of the rough seas.[51] When she was Empress of the French she spent as much time as possible in Biarritz, and destroyed the quiet, solitary beauty of the village she had loved by making it, through her presence there, a fashionable seaside resort.

Not all her holidays were as peaceful as her days in Biarritz. One very hot July – Eugénie could not remember which year it was when she told Primoli about it in 1877 – she went with Paca and Alba and a party of their friends to the Alba estates near Seville for the hunting. Spain was continually troubled, during Narvaez's years of power, by both Carlist and Radical uprisings and guerrilla actions, and a well-known bandit chief with vaguely Carlist sympathies was active in the district where Eugénie and her friends were staying. One night, when they were staying at Romanilla Castle, they were awakened at 2 a.m. and told that the bandit chief and his men were planning to attack the castle and kidnap them, in order to hold these young ladies and gentlemen of prominent society families until a ransom was paid. Eugénie and her friends hastily dressed and rode off into the forest.

They travelled for several days in a great semicircle towards the Portuguese frontier and the north-west. The weather was very hot and dry, and they lived and slept quite happily in the open air. Eugénie and her girl-friends had heard stories about the bandit chief's gallantry towards beautiful women, and were perhaps half-hoping that they might be captured by him; but one day a faithful old servant of the Montijo household who was with them promised Paca and Eugénie that if the bandits caught them he would shoot them both rather than allow them to fall alive into the bandits' hands. Paca and Eugénie were horrified, and after this were much more alarmed at the prospect of the bandits catching up with them. But they eventually reached Burgos without suffering either death or dishonour, none the worse for their experiences except that Eugénie's face was temporarily disfigured by a rash which she had caught from lying on the moss in the forest.

A few years later the bandit chief was caught and hanged. Eugénie afterwards said that she wished that he had not been captured until after she became Empress of the French, when she could have used her position to intercede on his behalf with the Spanish government and to persuade them to spare his life.[52]

But when would Eugénie marry? She had refused Osuna, Xifre and Huddleston. She seems to have been more than a little in love with Pepe, Marquis of Alcañices, the Duke of Sesto's heir. There had been rumours of an engagement between them ever since they had played the leading parts in Alfred de Musset's *Caprice* at Carabanchel; but although they were close friends, Alcañices never proposed to her, apparently because he was put off by her unconventional habits and her dominating personality.[53]

But another story casts Pepe Alcañices in a much more discreditable role, and makes him, and not the fifteenth Duke of Alba, the reason for Eugénie's attempted suicide. The story of the suicide attempt is one of the best known of all the stories told about her youth in Spain. It was told and retold by the gossipmongers under the Second Empire and after 1870. They were fascinated by Eugénie's cold beauty; they thought that her frigidity explained why the Emperor had so many mistresses, and why, despite her husband's infidelity, no one ever succeeded in seducing the Empress herself. What had made the lovely Eugénie so averse to men? It could only have been an unhappy love affair in her youth, and the story took root of the one great love affair in Eugénie's life, which had caused her to attempt suicide and to resolve never again to fall in love.

The story was widely circulated at the time of her marriage to Napoleon III, and was published during her lifetime in biographies of her by the Norwegian writer Clara Tschudi in 1899, by Jane Stoddart in 1906, and in Princess Caroline Murat's memoirs in 1910.* Eugénie never made any public comment on the truth or falsehood of these

*Princess Murat wrote her memoirs shortly before her death in 1902. They were published posthumously in 1910.

stories; she told her friends that it was impossible for her to correct the errors in the books written about her because nearly every statement in them was wrong. The most suspect thing about the suicide story is that while all the writers were agreed that Eugénie had only loved once in her life, they could not agree on the identity of this lover who had driven her to attempt suicide. Some said that it was the Duke of Alba, others that it was Alcañices. A more recent biographer, Harold Kurtz, put forward the new idea of two unhappy love affairs, one with Alba and a later one with Alcañices, while connecting the suicide attempt with Alcañices. [54]

The most detailed version of the Alcañices story was told by Dame Ethel Smyth in her book, *Streaks of Life*, which was published a few months after Eugénie's death in 1920. Ethel Smyth had often visited Eugénie at Farnborough Hill during the previous thirty-seven years. Eugénie liked her, but on one occasion warned her friends, with a smile, not to believe all the stories that Ethel Smyth told about her. According to Ethel Smyth, Eugénie fell in love with the 'Duc de S—', who is obviously Pepe Alcañices, afterwards Duke of Sesto. He wrote her passionate love-letters, and made her believe that he reciprocated her love; but then she discovered that he was in fact in love with her married sister Paca, and had pretended to be in love with Eugénie in order to have an opportunity to seduce Paca. In her despair Eugénie took poison. Her action was discovered, and an antidote was prepared, but she refused to take it. Alcañices was then brought to her bedside in the hope that he would persuade her to take the antidote; but he merely whispered to her: 'Where are my letters?' His callousness brought Eugénie to her senses, and she swallowed the antidote. [55]

A slightly different version of this story had been published in 1862 by the French Republican refugees in Berlin in a scandalous book, *Les femmes galantes des Napoléons*. It included a pornographic and obviously fictitious description of Alcañices and Paca committing adultery in a garden in Spain, though in the printed text the most obscene passages were replaced by tantalizing asterisks. [56]

Ethel Smyth wrote that this story was 'well known in the inner circle' and was told to her by one of Eugénie's relations who was her intimate friend and to whom Eugénie had told the story. It was accepted by Kurtz, who dated it as occurring in the summer of 1848 without giving any reason for thinking so. But there are several reasons for rejecting the story, and the seventeenth Duke of Alba did not believe it. He was sure that Eugénie had attempted suicide – by taking the phosphorus match-heads – because of her love for his grandfather at the time of Paca's marriage, not five years later because of Alcañices. [57]

It is unlikely that the truth about the suicide attempt will ever be known. Eugénie and the family would naturally have gone to great lengths to hush it up, and the historian's task is made no easier by the destruction of so many archives and contemporary newspapers during the upheavals in Spain in the last 130 years. But the greatest weight must be attached to the statement of Eugénie's great-nephew, the seventeenth Duke of Alba, in his lecture at Barcelona University in 1947.[58] Whatever may be thought of Alba's politics, he was a very conscientious historian, and one of Eugénie's most intimate friends during her old age; and if he categorically stated that Eugénie tried to commit suicide by swallowing match-heads, she had probably said something to convince him that the story was true. There are therefore good grounds for believing that she tried to kill herself because of Alba when she was seventeen in 1843; but it is very unlikely that the gay coquette of twenty-two would have done such a thing because of Alcañices in 1848.

As often happens, the gossipmongers were so busy inventing fictitious stories about Eugénie that they missed one of the best stories which is almost certainly true. The story of the robber under the bed is better substantiated than most; it was published in the memoirs of the Spanish polo champion, the Marquis of Villavieja, a close friend of the seventeenth Duke of Alba, who heard it from Eugénie herself at Farnborough Hill.*

One evening – it must have been between 1844 and 1852 – she was staying in a large castle in the country somewhere in Spain. She had attended a ball in the castle, and retired well after midnight with her maid to her bedroom in an isolated turret at the end of long passages and staircases. As she sat at her dressing-table combing out her hair, she saw, in her mirror, that there was a man hiding under the bed. She told her maid that she had left her fan in the ballroom, and wrote out a note which she asked her to give to the servant in the ballroom, saying that the note directed the servant to give her the fan; but in fact she had written that there was a man hiding under the bed. The maid departed with the note, leaving Eugénie alone with the man; and Eugénie, knowing that help was on the way, proceeded to torment him with the courage and cruelty of a *picador* in the bullring. She sat on the bed softly humming a tune, slowly removed one stocking, and then dangled her bare leg down the side of the bed, pushing it gently backwards until it just touched the man's face. She repeated the process with the other leg.

Soon afterwards the castle servants arrived, and dragged the man out from underneath the bed. He was a notorious robber, but he told

*According to Mrs Burnett, Eugénie also told this story, in her old age, to her companion Isabel Vesey.

them that he had broken into the castle, not in order to rob, but to get a glimpse of the beautiful Countess of Teba, who was said to be staying in the castle. He knelt before Eugénie and begged her to grant him one favour before he was taken to prison. He said that he had been driven nearly mad by her tiny feet when she had dangled them before his face, and he asked to be allowed to kiss them. She extended each foot to him in turn and he kissed them passionately. As he was taken away, he said to her: 'Good-bye, Señorita. I am proud to think that both you and I are Spaniards.'[58]

PART III

CITIZEN LOUIS NAPOLEON BONAPARTE

CHAPTER 14

THE 'UNIVERSITY' OF HAM

THE castle of Ham, where Louis Napoleon had been condemned to live for the rest of his life, had undergone only minor structural alterations since it was built in 1460 by the Constable of France, St Pol, who was for many years the all-powerful minister of King Louis XI until Louis cut off his head. It had two great towers, an inner and outer courtyard, and ramparts. The government of Louis Philippe kept a garrison of four hundred soldiers there to guard Louis Napoleon and two of his colleagues in the Boulogne adventure – General Montholon and Dr Conneau – who, at his request, had been allowed to share his imprisonment. He also had the company of his devoted servant, Charles Thélin, who was not a prisoner but was allowed to spend all day in the castle, waiting on his master, and to come and go from the prison into the town as he wished.[1]

Ham is in the plain of Picardy near Saint-Quentin, some eighty miles from Paris, a hundred miles from the coast, and sixty miles from the Belgian frontier. The Bonapartist propagandists, who wished to emphasize the sufferings of Louis Napoleon at Ham, wrote a great deal about its bleak surroundings and dismal climate; the district is often damp, cold and foggy in winter. But the sentence of imprisonment in a fortress, to which Louis Napoleon had been condemned, was the most honourable and lenient form of imprisonment known under French law. The conditions in which he lived at Ham were very pleasant in comparison not only with the dungeons and concentration camps for political prisoners in earlier and later times, but also with those suffered in 1840 by Italian revolutionaries in the Austrian prisons, by Chartists and Irish nationalists in the penitentiaries in Britain or the penal settlements in Tasmania, and by trade unionists and strikers and ordinary non-political criminals in the prisons and hulks in France. The Radicals and Republicans complained about the difference between the conditions of Louis Napoleon's captivity and those of Louis Philippe's Socialist and Republican prisoners; but according to Count Orsi, who was imprisoned with Persigny and several of the other Boulogne prisoners at the fortress of Doullens in conditions which were only marginally worse than those of Louis Napoleon at Ham, they themselves had no privileges which were denied to the Republican prisoners in Doullens.[2]

Louis Napoleon was allowed to have all the books and writing materials that he wanted, and he spent his time studying, reading and writing. He afterwards used to say that he was educated at the University of Ham.[3] He was permitted to write and receive letters after they had been censored by the Commandant of the prison. When his friends in Britain and America wrote to him in English, there was a delay before he received the letter, because as neither the Commandant nor any other official at Ham could speak English, the letters were sent to Paris to be censored. He was allowed to receive visitors with the consent of the Minister of the Interior, who sometimes made difficulties in the case of active Bonapartists who had themselves served a term of imprisonment. When the American theatrical agent, Henry Wikoff, visited Louis Napoleon at Ham, he had to wait for several weeks in Paris, being fobbed off by courteous but evasive officials, before he received the permit to see Louis Napoleon and stay with him for four hours; but even Orsi, after his release from the five years' imprisonment to which he was sentenced for his part in the Boulogne expedition, was eventually granted permission to visit Louis Napoleon at Ham. Many of his old friends from Arenenberg – Madame de Crenay, Madame Salvage, Vieillard, and of course Hortense Cornu – visited him several times.[4]

The Commandant allowed one visitor to come without official permission from the ministry in Paris. This was his laundress, Eléonore Veugeot-Camus, a pretty, local girl known as Alexandrine by the people at Ham. Louis Napoleon was given every facility to see her and seduce her, which he did. She was his mistress for several years at Ham, and the Commandant, who knew very well what was going on, pretended not to notice. He could no longer keep up the pretence in the autumn of 1842, when Alexandrine became pregnant. He told Louis Napoleon that she would have to be sent away for her confinement in order to avoid a scandal; but though Louis Napoleon promised to arrange this, Alexandrine was still there at the beginning of December, when the Commandant felt obliged to write to the Ministry of War about her. Louis Napoleon was sad to see her go, and he was very kind to her, as he always was to his pregnant mistresses. He arranged for her to have the baby with the Cornus in Paris, though Hortense Cornu did not like Alexandrine and thought that she was only interested in Louis Napoleon's money. When Louis Napoleon discovered that Alexandrine was a little overawed by Hortense Cornu, he wrote to Hortense and asked her to be very kind to Alexandrine; and when Alexandrine gave birth to his son Eugène, he wrote to ask Hortense to send him a sketch of the mother and child.

Alexandrine returned to Ham after the birth of the baby and resumed her relations with Louis Napoleon. Two years later, she was pregnant again, and Louis Napoleon again arranged for Hortense Cornu to take care of her. This time she went to Batignolles-Monceaux, where her second child by Louis Napoleon, Louis, was born in March 1845. When the boys were grown up, and Louis Napoleon was Emperor, he created both of them Counts just in time before the fall of the Second Empire in 1870.[5]

Louis Napoleon's living quarters consisted of two very small rooms and one larger room at the top of two flights of narrow, winding stairs of the old castle. He slept in one of the small rooms; the other, which he used as a study, had hardly any furniture except a small table with a desk lamp, three or four wooden chairs, and a clock on the mantelpiece. It was piled high with books on shelves and boards which Louis Napoleon himself had built to house the books. There were two very small windows high up in the wall, covered by heavy iron bars. The larger room was used as a dining room, where General Montholon and Dr Conneau joined him every day for lunch and dinner.[6]

Louis Napoleon's only genuine cause of complaint, apart from the climate at Ham, was the bad state of repair of his living quarters. In all the rooms there were holes in the ceilings, the wallpaper was peeling, and the brick floors were broken and damp; and the staircase was in a dangerous condition. But the government refused to spend money on repairs, and though they offered to carry out the work at Louis Napoleon's expense, he would not agree to this, saying that he was not responsible for the upkeep of French prisons. Eventually, after he had developed rheumatism and the doctors had certified that the damp and dilapidated state of the fortress was endangering his health, the Commandant was authorized to spend 600 francs on the repairs and was able to carry out the most urgent work.[7]

Louis Napoleon was determined to present to the world the image of a persecuted Prince, and wrote letters to the government protesting against the conditions of his imprisonment, more with a view to their publication in the Bonapartist press than in the hope of improving the conditions. The castle of Ham, including the rooms in which he was imprisoned, had been used ten years earlier as a prison for the Prince de Polignac and the other ministers of Charles X after the Revolution of 1830. Louis Napoleon was incensed that the government had allocated 10 francs a day for the food and drink of Polignac and each of his colleagues, whereas they had given him an allowance of only 7 francs a day for food and wine, which was 5s. 10d. in terms of English money at the time, and about £20 at today's prices.[8]

On 22 May 1841 Louis Napoleon wrote a protest to the Minister of the Interior. Ever since the time of Napoleon I, Bonapartism had presented a double-face of a popular revolutionary movement, under a leader elected by the votes of the people, and of a royal family acutely conscious of its privileges. It is therefore not surprising that while Louis Napoleon wrote books at Ham advocating Socialist measures, he also demanded preferential treatment on account of his royal blood.

> The government which has recognized the legitimacy of the head of my family is bound to recognize me as a prince, and to treat me as such . . . its conduct will be inconsistent and dastardly if it treats me, who am the son of a King, the nephew of an Emperor, and allied to all the sovereigns of Europe, as an ordinary prisoner. . . . The sovereignty of the people made my uncle an Emperor, my father a King and me a French Prince by birth. . . . If for the first time in my life I boast of the accident of my birth, it is because pride suits a man in my position.

The ministers of Charles X had been better treated at Ham; 'and yet these ministers were not born on the steps of a throne', and 'they were not the representatives of a cause which is an object of veneration in France'. He signed his protest with the signature which he always used at this time, 'Napoleon Louis Bonaparte'.[9]

Whatever he might say in these propaganda protests, the friends who visited him thought that he was surprisingly resigned to his fate. He spent most of the day working at his books, but every morning after breakfast he went for a walk on the ramparts. On these walks, apart from the fact that there were sentries posted at every point, he was followed by a plain-clothes policeman who made sure that none of the soldiers of the garrison disobeyed the government's orders that they were not to speak to him or salute him. He was given permission to make a little flower garden in one corner of the ramparts, for he had been fond of flowers ever since he had loved his mother's flower garden at Arenenberg. Every afternoon the Commandant visited him, having orders to do so at least once a day to make sure that he had not escaped. The Commandant usually came again in the evening to make a fourth at whist with Louis Napoleon, Montholon and Conneau.[10]

For a man used to physical exercise, like Louis Napoleon, the walks on the ramparts were not enough, and he asked permission to ride on horseback in the courtyard of the castle. After some hesitation the authorities agreed to this, and he was allowed to ride round and round the courtyard for half an hour in the afternoon under the close scrutiny of a strong body of the garrison, who were posted at every exit. He found their presence irksome, and became bored with riding in such a restricted space, and after he had had a nasty fall from his horse he gave up riding in 1842 and contented himself with walking along the ramparts several times a day.[11]

He decided to learn chemistry. He set up a laboratory in one of his rooms with the help of a local chemist, Monsieur Acar, and studied the principles of electro-magnetism. False modesty was never one of Louis Napoleon's faults, and after studying the subject for a few months he wrote a treatise on the future of electro-magnetism which he sent to Dominique François Arago, the secretary of the Academy of Sciences. He received a polite acknowledgement, and the thesis was accepted for study by the Academy.[12]

He then returned to the more familiar fields of history and politics, and planned to write a biography of Charlemagne. He had always admired Charlemagne as Napoleon's predecessor, who had created a social system which had brought order and progress to Europe for a thousand years. The librarians of the National Library and other public libraries in France made special arrangements to send him the books that he needed, but as his opportunities for research were obviously limited, he asked Madame Cornu and other friends to help him with the research. He even wrote to the famous Swiss historian, Sismondi, although Sismondi had written in 1838 in support of the French government's demand for his expulsion from Switzerland. Sismondi wrote him a courteous and helpful letter in reply.[13]

But Louis Napoleon found it too difficult to do the research in these circumstances, and abandoned the Charlemagne project. Instead, he wrote another book about artillery – a long and learned study of the development of cannon from the fourteenth century to the end of Louis XIII's reign. He also regularly wrote articles for two provincial Radical newspapers, *Le Progrès du Pas-de-Calais* and *Le Guetteur de Saint-Quentin*. The authorities did not object to his writing these articles, which he submitted to the prison censorship in the ordinary way, although the articles strongly criticized the government's policy.[14]

In May 1841 he published his *Fragments Historiques 1688 et 1830*. Many commentators had compared the English Revolution of 1688 and the French Revolution of 1830; after the ferocious revolutions of Cromwell and Robespierre and the Restorations of Charles II and Louis XVIII there had come the tolerant revolutions of 1688 and 1830 and the compromise régimes of William III and Louis Philippe. But Louis Napoleon barely mentioned 1830 in his book, which was a shrewd and scholarly analysis of the policies of Charles I, Charles II, James II and

William III. He drew the conclusion that William, though intellectually less gifted than the Stuarts, had triumphed because, unlike them, he expressed the will of the English people. Louis Napoleon noted in passing that the English, after willingly submitting to the despotism of Queen Elizabeth, had revolted against the milder despotism of Charles I, and he drew the conclusion: 'A government can often violate with impunity legality and even liberty; but if it does not place itself openly at the head of the great interests of civilization, it will have only an ephemeral duration.'[15]

A year later, in the autumn of 1842, he published a pamphlet on the controversial sugar-beet question. In the eighteenth century, France had imported sugar from her West Indian colonies, but during the Napoleonic Wars, when the British blockade interrupted the trade, Napoleon encouraged the cultivation of beet-sugar in France. It prospered, and continued after the war, and was now a serious competitor to the colonial sugar-planters. The planters also faced another problem. Slavery had been abolished by the Jacobins in 1794; but Napoleon had restored it in the French colonies, where it was still in force, though it had been abolished in the British Empire in 1834. Napoleon had banned the slave trade in France when he was playing for Liberal support during the Hundred Days, and the government of Louis XVIII had reluctantly adhered to the ban; but the trade of supplying Negro slaves from Africa to the French West Indian colonies was still illegally carried on from Nantes on quite a large scale. The Great Powers at the Congress of Vienna had entrusted Britain with the task of suppressing the international slave trade, and to achieve this, Palmerston bullied or cajoled foreign governments into signing treaties with Britain giving both parties to the treaty the mutual right to stop and search each other's vessels on the high seas to see if slaves were being carried on board – a face-saving formula which meant in practice that the British navy could board any foreign ship and release the slaves.

The French colonial sugar-planters were not seriously worried by the activities of the anti-slavery societies in France, which had no political influence comparable to that of the Abolitionists in Britain; but they were angry when Louis Philippe's government at last agreed in 1841 to sign a treaty with Britain providing for the mutual right of search, which seriously threatened the illegal activities of the Nantes slave-traders, and by restricting the replenishment of the stock of slaves, threatened the continuation of slavery itself in the French West Indies. They therefore felt particularly vulnerable to the competition of sugar-beet in France. They formed one of those political pressure-groups which played such an influential role in France under Louis

Philippe, and put pressure on the government to restrict the production of beet-sugar. This was naturally resisted by the organizations of the sugar-beet growers.

Louis Napoleon, after arranging for Hortense Cornu and his other friends to do the necessary research and to supply him with the statistics that he required, wrote a pamphlet in support of the sugar-beet industry.[16] He argued that it had been created by the great Napoleon, not only in order to deal with the wartime emergency, but also because the Emperor's visionary genius saw the long-term benefits of an industry which could provide cheap sugar for the French working class. Having thus backed the sugar-beet industry, Louis Napoleon conciliated the colonial planters by opposing the abolition of slavery, and by criticizing Louis Philippe's government for submitting to British dictation over the right of search.

Louis Napoleon's family had always been consistent supporters of Negro slavery. Napoleon had despised the abolitionists of the French Revolution as sentimental do-gooders, and had sent an army to San Domingo in an unsuccessful attempt to reconquer the colony in order to restore slavery; and Josephine's Tascher relations in Martinique still owned slaves. Louis Napoleon was influenced in favour of slavery by his ideas of authoritarian and paternalistic government, and by his recollections of the faithful coloured house-slaves who had followed Josephine to France and had been so well treated by her; and although, when he became Emperor, he did not restore slavery, which was finally abolished by the Republican government in 1848, his sympathy with the slave-owners was one of the factors which influenced him in favour of the South in the American Civil War.

Like Charles Kingsley and Thomas Carlyle in Britain, Louis Napoleon thought that the underpaid and overworked white factory-worker in Britain and France was much more oppressed and deserved far more sympathy than the lazy Negro slave in the West Indies; but, with that brutal frankness which has always been more marked in French than in British political controversy, he justified the retention of slavery, in his pamphlet on the sugar-beet question, merely on grounds of French self-interest. To abolish slavery would be tantamount to abolishing the French colonial sugar industry; it would end cheap sugar for the poor in France, and would be placing the interests of 90,000 Negro slaves before those of 100,000 free labourers in France. If France were to follow the British example and compensate the slave-owners for abolition, this would be taxing the Frenchman for the benefit of the colonists; but 'the colonies were established for the benefit of metropolitan France, not metropolitan France for the benefit of the colonies'.[17]

He returned to this question in an article on the treatment of Negroes and the right of search in the *Progrès du Pas-de-Calais* of 4 February 1843.[18] He attacked those humanitarians who were 'insensible to the misery of the French proletarian, to the destitution of the worker living under their own roof, but as soon as some iniquities are committed in our antipodes, Oh! then their passions are aroused!' He pointed out, quite truthfully, that the attempts of the British navy to suppress the slave trade had greatly worsened the conditions of the Negroes in the slave-ships, who were packed in more tightly than before and were sometimes thrown into the sea by the slave-traders so that the slaves were not found on board when the ship was captured by British warships. He claimed that the English were using the suppression of the slave trade as a pretext for revenging themselves on France.

The French Socialists, trade unionists and working class, unlike the West Indian slaves, were becoming a force to be reckoned with in French politics, and while Louis Napoleon was a prisoner at Ham he wrote a number of publications designed to win their support. In his articles in the *Progrès du Pas-de-Calais* he protested against the sufferings of the poor, and he expounded his opinions more fully in a pamphlet, *Extinction du Paupérisme*, which he wrote in the spring of 1844. In it he championed 'the right to work', which had been proclaimed by Socialist and Radical writers but had been condemned by the orthodox economists as a disastrous and dangerous doctrine which would wreck the national economy by interfering with the laws of supply and demand and destroying the reserve of unemployment which provided cheap labour for the employer. He proposed that legislation should be enacted setting up associations of working men which would have the power to acquire, by compulsory purchase, the 9 million hectares of wasteland in France. The state would lend the money to these associations to enable them to pay the landowners the current market rent of the land, and the associations would be required to repay the money to the state in four annual payments. The unemployed workers of the towns would be given employment on the land as agricultural labourers and would be provided with their keep and a reasonable wage and the opportunity to enjoy a healthy outdoor life, until they could again find work in industry; and the associations would raise the money to pay the workers, and to repay the loan to the state, by selling their agricultural products. If critics objected that the cost of establishing the associations would be a burden on the taxpayer, Louis Napoleon pointed out that this would cost the state about 300 million francs, as compared with 300 million francs spent annually on military expenditure, 120 million francs in building new prisons, 300 million francs for the fortifications of Paris, a milliard in compensation to the émigrés who had fled from the Revolution of 1789, and two milliards as a war indemnity to the Allies under the peace treaty of 1815.[19]

The ideas which Louis Napoleon put forward were not original, as they closely followed the proposals made by Hippolyte Mansion in a book published in 1829. But *Extinction du Paupérisme* delighted the Socialists, who for the first time had found a national figure, the leader of a powerful political faction, who was prepared to take their ideas seriously, instead of dismissing them as silly and utopian. The Socialist leader, Louis Blanc, visited Louis Napoleon at Ham, and was allowed to spend three days in discussions with him. George Sand also visited him. Both of them told him that they agreed with what he had written in *Extinction du Paupérisme*, but that they could not reconcile this with his Bonapartism, which stood for inequality and royal privilege and the subjection of the people to the will of an imperial autocrat. George Sand wrote that she was distressed that some of her Socialist friends thought that Louis Napoleon was their most dangerous enemy, because he had put forward an attractive Socialist policy which might mislead the workers into supporting him. Louis Napoleon replied to their criticism with his usual argument: if they were living in a perfect, peaceful world he would be a Republican, but as the popular cause was menaced by the armies of foreign despots, they needed an imperial dictator like Napoleon to lead them and save them.[20]

But he was prepared to conciliate the Republicans and the Socialists on their most sensitive point – Napoleon's *coup d'état* of the Eighteenth Brumaire in 1799. For the Republicans, Napoleon's unforgivable sin was his overthrow of the Republic by this unconstitutional *coup* which led to the establishment of the Consulate as a first step to the Empire. In August 1843 Louis Napoleon wrote from Ham to the editor of a book to which the poet Lamartine, who sat as a Liberal in the Chamber of Deputies, had contributed a critical article on Napoleon and the Eighteenth Brumaire. In his letter, Louis Napoleon criticized Lamartine for failing to shed a tear over 'the sight of our eagles falling at Waterloo and of our plebeian Emperor dying at St Helena'; but he excused, rather than justified, the Eighteenth Brumaire. 'I do not defend the principle of the revolution of 18 Brumaire, nor the brutal manner in which it was carried out. An insurrection against an established power may be a necessity, but never an example to be elevated to a principle.'[21] Did he remember these words in December 1851?

During his years at Ham, Louis Napoleon became involved in the projects to build a Nicaraguan canal to link the Atlantic and Pacific oceans. The advantages of such a canal were obvious to travellers and traders who, if they wished to go from New York to California, had the choice of travelling 3000 miles overland through dangerous territory by horse or covered wagon, going by sea on the 10,000-mile journey around Cape Horn, which took more than six months in each direction by sailing ship, or suffering the inconvenience of hauling luggage or commercial products across the thirty-five miles of the isthmus of Panama. This was the shortest distance between the two oceans; but the rocky soil made it impossible to cut a canal across the isthmus of Panama until, after the invention of more modern machinery, this became a practical possibility fifty years later. A more hopeful alternative was to build the canal across Nicaragua, where the distance was 156 miles, but where for most of this distance the route would lie through the Lake of Nicaragua and the river San Juan, so that only 29 miles of canal would need to be built.

The government of Nicaragua, which had become an independent sovereign state in 1839, were eager to interest European capitalists in the project, and hoped to form a syndicate to raise the money with Louis Napoleon as chairman; they thought that the name of a Prince, even an imprisoned Prince, would impress investors. In 1842 they tentatively suggested to the French government that Louis Napoleon might be released from prison on condition that he gave his word of honour to go to Nicaragua and stay there. But Louis Napoleon was determined not to put himself for a second time in a position where he could be accused of having obtained his release from prison by a false promise to stay in America, and he told the Nicaraguan representatives that he would refuse to accept any amnesty offered on this condition.

In the summer of 1844 the Nicaraguan government sent Señor de Castellon on a diplomatic mission to Paris to urge the French government to give financial and diplomatic support for the building of the canal. The Prime Minister, Guizot, refused to become involved in a project which might bring France into conflict with both Britain and the United States, but offered no objection when Castellon asked permission to visit Louis Napoleon at Ham. Castellon told Louis Napoleon that a Belgian company was about to be formed, that they all hoped that he would become the president of the company, and that it was proposed to name the canal the 'Canale Napoleone de Nicaragua'.[22]

It was typical of Louis Napoleon's enthusiasm and self-confidence that instead of merely accepting the nominal chairmanship of the company, he immediately arranged for Hortense Cornu to send him books and to undertake the research into the subject, and soon produced a pamphlet in which he vigorously urged the building of a canal, and the advantages of the Nicaraguan route over the alternative suggestions of a canal across the isthmus of Panama or any of the other possible routes. Writing in his usual flamboyant style, he referred to the historic fame of such great trade centres as Tyre, Carthage, Constantinople, Venice, Genoa, Amsterdam, Liverpool and London. Just as Constantinople was the centre of the old world, so Masaya in Nicaragua would be the centre of the new:

> Even better than Constantinople, the State of Nicaragua can become the required route for the great commerce of the world, for it would be, for the United States, the shortest route to China and the East Indies, and for England and the rest of Europe to New Holland, Polynesia and the whole of the western coast of America. The State of Nicaragua seems therefore destined to attain an extraordinary degree of prosperity and grandeur.[23]

But alas! Nicaragua was about to experience twenty years of civil war.

CHAPTER 15

ESCAPE

I<small>N</small> July 1844 Joseph Bonaparte died. Under the provisions of the Act of the Senate confirmed by the referendum of 1804, his brother King Louis was now Emperor of the French and Louis Napoleon was heir apparent. Louis Bonaparte was only sixty-six, but had been in poor health ever since his youth, and by the autumn of 1845 it was known that he was slowly dying.

On Christmas Day Louis Napoleon wrote to the Minister of the Interior asking to be released from prison so that he could visit his dying father, and giving his word of honour to return to captivity after the visit. He followed this three weeks later with a personal appeal to Louis Philippe; but despite the protests of several deputies in the Chamber, the King and the government refused his petition.[1] He then decided to try to escape.

This was obviously going to be very difficult, with sixty guards always on duty, many sentries posted on the walls, and two guards stationed day and night at the foot of the stairs leading up to his apartments. But in the spring of 1846 the Commandant informed him that the repairs to the structure of the castle, long overdue, would shortly be carried out, and that building workers would soon be arriving to do the work. It occurred to Louis Napoleon that, if he could disguise himself as one of the workmen, it might be possible to walk out of the prison, though this would involve passing the two guards at the foot of the stairs and a third guard at the entrance to the block, the sentries in the courtyard, the officer of the guard at the guardroom, and the sentry at the main gate of the castle, as well as the windows of the Commandant's lodgings. He confided his plan to his servant Charles Thélin and to Dr Conneau, whose five-year prison sentence had expired in October 1845 but who had been allowed to remain voluntarily at Ham, at his own expense, as a companion to Louis Napoleon. But he did not tell General Montholon, because he did not wish the old hero to be implicated in an escape attempt for which he might be punished.

He lulled the Commandant and the jailers into a state of complacency by a simple trick. Thélin arranged for Bonapartist supporters in Paris to write letters to Louis Napoleon, which would of course be read by the censor at Ham, telling him that they had inside information which led them to believe that he would soon be released under a general amnesty which was to be granted before the forthcoming elections. If he was expecting to be freed very shortly under an amnesty, he would obviously have less motive to try to escape and would be foolish to risk spoiling his chances of an amnesty by an unsuccessful escape attempt. Thélin also obtained a false passport for him, so that he could cross the frontier into Belgium.

The workmen arrived at the castle in the middle of May, and Louis Napoleon, Conneau and Thélin made their detailed plans for the escape. They noticed that when the workmen arrived at 5 a.m. they were carefully scrutinized and their passes checked, and that the same process was repeated even more carefully, in the presence of the Commandant, when they left the castle in the afternoon after finishing their day's work. But quite often a workman would walk out of the castle during working hours to collect some equipment from a dump which the builders had set up outside the castle, and on these occasions his pass was not inspected, unless one particular sentry was on duty. This soldier, alone of all his colleagues, insisted on zealously inspecting the pass of every man who went in and out.

At all normal times there were two guards on duty at the foot of Louis Napoleon's staircase; but on some days in the week one of them went to fetch the morning newspapers for the garrison at about 6 a.m. During this time, for about a quarter of an hour, there was only one sentry at the foot of the stairs. Louis Napoleon, Conneau and Thélin decided to make the escape attempt during this quarter of an hour on one of the days when the newspapers were fetched and when the over-zealous sentry was not on duty. This plan also had the advantage that it would be safer to pass the Commandant's house at 6 a.m., as he did not get up until later.

The plan was for Thélin, who was free to leave the castle when he wished, to stroll out of Louis Napoleon's quarters with the Prince's dog Ham, followed closely by Louis Napoleon who, having shaved off his moustache and whiskers, would be disguised in workman's clothes, with a false wig. It was hoped that Thélin, by playing with the dog and chatting to the sentries, would distract their attention from Louis Napoleon, and could intervene if any of the guards, or another workman, began to talk to him. If they succeeded in getting out of the castle, Thélin would go off to fetch a cab which he would hire without a driver, and pick up Louis Napoleon as soon as possible on the road to Saint-Quentin. Louis Napoleon had never been in the town of Ham except when he was brought to the castle from Boulogne during the night, taken to Paris for his trial, and brought back, after his sentence, at midnight, nearly six years earlier; but he carefully studied and memorized a map of Ham, having learned map-reading during his service as an officer in the Swiss army at Thun. He and Thélin would drive to Saint-Quentin and hire a post-chaise there with a driver to take them to Valenciennes, where they would catch the train for Brussels and cross into Belgium. Meanwhile, in the castle at Ham, Dr Conneau would pretend that Louis Napoleon was ill in bed and unable to see anyone, and thus prevent the guards from discovering the escape for as long as possible. There was no telegraph line to Ham, and the nearest railway station was at Valenciennes, so once Louis Napoleon was in the carriage on the way to Valenciennes, he could only be caught by a rider or carriage from Ham travelling faster than he, unless by bad luck he happened to meet someone who recognized him on the journey.

Louis Napoleon needed, for the escape, a suit of workman's clothes identical with those worn by the painters or the joiners who were working at the castle. It did not seem to matter whether he wore a painter's or a joiner's clothes, so Thélin arranged for Louis Napoleon's foster-brother, Bure,[2] to obtain the clothes of a joiner. These included a pair of wooden clogs large enough to make it possible for Louis Napoleon to wear some very high-heeled boots inside them without the boots being seen. This would make him appear to be some three or four inches taller than he really was.

The time for the escape was fixed for 6 a.m. on Saturday 23 May, which was one of the days when the newspapers were fetched and the officious sentry would not be on duty. But on the previous evening the Commandant informed Louis Napoleon that some English visitors would be coming to see him on the Saturday afternoon. Louis Napoleon had invited them some months before, but it was only now that they had obtained the necessary permission in Paris. If he escaped on the Saturday morning, his absence was certain to be discovered in the afternoon when the visitors arrived, whereas he had hoped that Conneau would be able to prevent the escape from being known for longer than this. He therefore decided to postpone the escape until another day when the newspapers would be fetched and the zealous sentry would be off duty. Louis Napoleon duly received his English visitors; but after they had gone, Thélin discovered, to his consternation, that the builders had almost finished their work and might not be coming next week.

This would mean the ruin of their whole plan; but Thélin kept his head. He asked the builders if they would do one more job and erect some extra bookcases for him. This would ensure that the workmen would come on Monday, which would probably be the last day on which the escape would be possible. They would have to risk it on Monday, although this was not a day on which the newspapers were fetched.

After an anxious Sunday, they were awake and ready on the morning of Monday 25 May 1846. At five o'clock the workmen arrived at the castle; Conneau and Thélin watched them from behind the curtains of the windows of their rooms, removing their shoes so that the guards should not hear them at the window and guess what they were doing. But now everything seemed to go wrong. They had taken careful note of the duty rota of the sentries, but on that morning the rota was changed and the zealous sentry was on duty at the foot of the stairs at 5 a.m. They knew that it would be madness to make the attempt while he was on duty, but he would be there until 7 a.m., and by that time there would be more guards in the courtyard, and soon the Commandant would be stirring in his house and might be looking out of the window which Louis Napoleon would have to pass. It also happened that none of the workmen who came into the castle that morning were joiners, so that none of them were wearing joiner's overalls like those which Louis Napoleon had obtained; and as it was a warm day, none of the workmen were wearing clogs. Louis Napoleon had no alternative but to risk wearing the joiner's overalls, and though he considered dispensing with the clogs, he decided against it as it was better to have the misleading extra height by wearing the boots inside the clogs.

He put on the joiner's clothes and clogs over his own clothes. In his pocket he carried two of his most cherished souvenirs – a letter from his mother, and one from the great Napoleon. He hesitated about taking them, fearing that if he were searched at the frontier they would be discovered and his identity revealed; but sentiment, and a superstitious belief that they were omens of good luck, were stronger than reason. He also put a dagger in his pocket, for he had decided that he would not allow them to recapture him alive; he would not face the ridicule if the escape attempt should turn out to be another fiasco.[3]

He sat and waited for the officious sentry to go off duty. He had made all the preparations for the escape except for shaving off his moustache and whiskers; once this had been done, there could be no going back, as the escape plot would be discovered if it were known that he had shaved. Then at 6 a.m., unexpectedly, the officious sentry was replaced an hour earlier than the usual change-over time. The moment had come to risk everything.

Thélin hastily shaved off Louis Napoleon's moustache and whiskers, and as soon as he had finished, Conneau invited the workmen to enter his room for refreshment. At 6.45 a.m., Thélin walked out with Louis

Napoleon's dog. Louis Napoleon followed him, carrying one of the makeshift bookshelves in his study, in order to look like a workman carrying a plank and to hide his face from the sentries. He carried the plank on his right shoulder, knowing that the sentries would be on his right. He had a white clay pipe in his mouth. The two warders at the foot of the stairs looked at him, but merely stepped aside to avoid being hit by the plank, and he walked slowly on past the sentries in the courtyard. But he was not used to walking with a pipe in his mouth – it was something that a gentleman did not do – and as he passed the first sentry he dropped his pipe. Coolly and slowly he bent down and picked it up, standing within a few feet of the sentry and still keeping the plank in a position where it obscured the sentry's view of his face. As he walked through the courtyard he met several workmen and soldiers, but they did not speak to him. He passed quite close to the officer commanding the guard, who was reading a letter, and he walked past the sentry at the gate who hardly looked at him.

He had passed the last sentry; but as he was crossing the draw-bridge, still within earshot of the sentry, he met two more workmen entering the castle. They seemed surprised to see him, and called out to him as they approached. They were passing to his left, so before he reached them he stopped and put down the plank, pausing for a moment as if he were resting, and then transferred the plank to his left shoulder, placing it between himself and the oncoming workmen. As he passed them, he heard one of them say to the other: 'Why, it's Bertou!' He crossed the drawbridge and walked on into the town. Many things had gone wrong, but he had been lucky.

His experience of map-reading stood him in good stead. He found the way without difficulty to the Saint-Quentin road, and walked for two miles, still carrying the plank, till Thélin overtook him in the cab. He threw the plank into the ditch and entered the cab. It occurred to them that people in the town who knew Thélin might wonder why he was driving in a cab with a building worker; so they decided that Louis Napoleon should pretend to be the driver of a hired vehicle. He sat in the driver's seat and drove the carriage, which he had not forgotten how to do after six years in prison. As soon as they were out of the town he took off his workman's clothes and clogs and wore the gentleman's costume and boots which he had on underneath; but he kept on his wig.

They covered the fifteen miles to Saint-Quentin in good time, and there Thélin made arrangements to hire a post-chaise with a driver to take them on to Valenciennes. Louis Napoleon, in order to minimize the risk of being recognized, walked through the town along the Cambrai road, where Thélin was to pick him up in the post-chaise.

He waited impatiently, but Thélin did not come. A man came along in another carriage, and Louis Napoleon asked him if he had seen a post-chaise that he was expecting. The man said that he had not. Louis Napoleon afterwards discovered that he had been speaking to the Public Prosecutor of Saint-Quentin.

After what seemed an interminable time, Thélin arrived with the post-chaise and driver; but though it seemed to Louis Napoleon that hours had passed since he had left his prison, it was only 9 a.m. They had a few anxious moments when they passed some gendarmes, but the gendarmes went off along the Péronne road. The post-chaise travelled fast and reached Valenciennes at 2.15 p.m. Here they had to pass the frontier control. Thélin showed his false passport, and no one asked to see Louis Napoleon's.

The train to Brussels was due to leave Valenciennes at 4 p.m., so they had an hour and three-quarters to wait. Louis Napoleon was tempted to hire a cab and drive across the frontier into Belgium; but they thought that this might arouse suspicion, because since the recent building of the railway, no one travelled across the frontier by carriage. They therefore waited for an agonizing hour and three-quarters at the station, only nine miles from safety, but fearing that Louis Napoleon might be recaptured at the last moment; though unless his escape had been discovered immediately, it was very unlikely that he could now be caught. Suddenly a man came up to Thélin and greeted him by name. It was a gendarme from the town of Ham, in civilian clothes; he was off duty. He paid no attention to Louis Napoleon, but he asked Thélin what he was doing in Valenciennes, and whether Prince Louis Bonaparte was in good health. Thélin said that he was no longer in the Prince's service, but had taken a job with the Northern Railway at Valenciennes.

The gendarme went away, and Louis Napoleon and Thélin, in mounting anxiety, waited for the train. Thélin could not prevent himself from constantly looking back at the road along which they had come from Cambrai, to see if they were being followed; but he need not have worried. The escape had still not been discovered at Ham. When the Commandant paid his usual afternoon visit to Louis Napoleon, Conneau told him that he was ill in bed, and the Commandant went away, saying that he hoped that the Prince would be well enough to play whist as usual that evening. When he came again in the evening, Conneau said that Louis Napoleon was still too ill to see him; but this time the Commandant insisted on seeing him, and discovered that he was not there. Even then he did not send anyone out to search for Louis Napoleon, but sent messengers to carry a report to Paris and Amiens, and awaited further orders. Conneau was afterwards put on trial and sentenced to three months' imprisonment for helping Louis Napoleon to escape.[4]

At 4 p.m. the train arrived at Valenciennes on time, and half an hour later Louis Napoleon was in Belgium. He was not yet absolutely safe, because the government of King Leopold, who had married Louis Philippe's daughter, was on friendly terms with the French government, and had an extradition treaty with France which covered political offences. So Louis Napoleon and Thélin spent only a few hours in Brussels, and then went on to Ostend, where they took ship for England. They arrived in London in the early evening of Wednesday 27 May, and went straight to the Brunswick Hotel in Jermyn Street.[5] As they were entering the hotel Lord Malmesbury happened to pass by, on his way to dinner with the Duke of Beaufort at Hamilton House. He was surprised to see Louis Napoleon, whom he had known intimately in Rome and London and had recently visited at Ham. Louis Napoleon told him about his escape; no one in London had heard the news, and the French Embassy had not yet been informed.·

Malmesbury went on to Hamilton House, where at dinner he sat opposite the Comte de Noailles, who was an attaché at the French Embassy. As they were sitting down to dinner, Malmesbury said to Noailles: 'Have you seen him?' 'Who?' asked Noailles. 'Louis Napoleon', said Malmesbury; 'he is in London, having just escaped.' Malmesbury noted in his diary: 'De Noailles dropped the lady who was on his arm and made but one jump out of the room. . . . I never saw a man look more frightened.' Malmesbury had told the best dinner-table story of the season.[6]

CHAPTER 16

LONDON AGAIN

O N the day after he arrived in London, Louis Napoleon wrote to the French Ambassador informing him that he had escaped only in order to visit his dying father, and that he had no intention of taking part in politics or of disturbing the tranquillity of Europe. He gave similar assurances in letters which he wrote to the Prime Minister and the Foreign Secretary, Sir Robert Peel and Lord Aberdeen. He immediately made arrangements to visit his father in Florence, but was unable to reach him. Both the Belgian and Austrian governments refused his application for a transit visa, and the Belgian government announced that if he set foot in Belgium he would be extradited to France as an escaped convict. In any case, the Grand Duke of Tuscany refused to permit him to enter his territory. Louis Napoleon and King Louis could therefore only exchange affectionate letters during the two months that remained before King Louis died on 25 July 1846.[1] In Bonapartist eyes, Louis Napoleon was now Emperor of the French.

The time had long since passed when Louis Bonaparte suspected that Louis Napoleon was not his son, or mistrusted him on account of his political adventurism. In the last years, King Louis had shown him every possible sign of parental affection, and in his will he left him the bulk of his property in Italy. This legacy came at a useful time for Louis Napoleon, who, during his imprisonment at Ham and in the years after his escape to London, was for the first and last time in his life in some financial difficulty, partly because of his extravagant way of living, partly because of his generosity to his supporters – he bought Conneau a medical practice in London when Conneau came to England after his release from prison – and partly because of the expenses which he had incurred in financing the Boulogne expedition. During his imprisonment he sold both Arenenberg and Gottlieben for substantially less than Hortense had paid for them; and he sold many valuable souvenirs of Napoleon – antiques which Napoleon had brought back from Egypt, and the draft of his first abdication – as well as a wash-basin which had belonged to Louis XIV. In December 1845, while he was at Ham, he signed what was termed a 'treaty' with the exiled

Duke Charles of Brunswick, who had been driven from his Duchy in 1831 because of his Republican sympathies. In this treaty, which was negotiated by Orsi and the English Radical M.P., Thomas Duncombe, Brunswick agreed to lend Louis Napoleon £6000 and both parties agreed to help each other to gain power in France and Brunswick. Louis Napoleon afterwards repudiated the treaty when Brunswick refused to lend him more money in 1848, and he broke off relations with the Duke.[2]

A week after Louis Napoleon reached England, the ambassadors in London of the leading powers held a meeting at which they agreed not to have any intercourse with him. This may have caused minor complications for the London hostesses, but it did not prevent Louis Napoleon from being received in society and resuming his contacts with his old friends. Before the end of May he was dining at a house on the river,* and as he looked out once again at the Thames he found it difficult to believe that a week before he had been in the castle at Ham. He met d'Orsay and Lady Blessington, Disraeli and Dickens. He joined several fashionable London clubs – the Army and Navy Club, the Junior United Services Club, and the Athenaeum; but Comte de Jarnac, First Secretary at the French Embassy, succeeded in black-balling him when he applied for admission to the Coventry Club.[3]

In the summer of 1846 he went to Bath and called on Walter Savage Landor. 'Yesterday I had a visit from Prince Louis Bonaparte', wrote Landor at the end of August, 'I told him, in the course of our interview, that he had escaped two great curses – a prison and a throne. He smiled at this, but made no remark.'[4] At Bath he insisted on occupying the best and most expensive suite at Pulteney's Hotel, but graciously gave it up to the Marchioness of Anglesey, whose husband had lost a leg at Waterloo; he told Lady Anglesey that it was a privilege to be able to render a service to the wife of so distinguished a soldier. Hortense Cornu and her husband joined him at Bath for a short holiday in the hot and sunny September of 1846. He enjoyed the country round Bath. He was still fond of drawing, and sketched the ruins of Farleigh Hungerford Castle.[5]

In October he went from Bath to Brighton, arriving in time to meet the full force of the equinoctial gales. This did not prevent him from taking a walk every day along the front from his hotel, the Bedford, which overlooked the sea. He saw Charles Mathews and Madame

*Jerrold (II.357) states that this house where Louis Napoleon dined was Bulwer Lytton's house at Craven Cottage in Fulham, and this has been followed by all the authorities; but Lytton's new biographer, Miss Sibylla Jane Flower, has pointed out to me that Lytton had left Craven Cottage in 1845, and that Sir Ralph Howard was living there in May 1846.

Vestris in their season at the Theatre Royal, and often rode along the South Downs; it was much better riding country than the courtyard of the prison at Ham. He said that he realized for the first time what freedom meant when he was cantering over the Sussex Downs.[6]

He returned to London in November, and in January 1847 moved from the Brunswick Hotel to a house at 3 King Street, St James's, which he rented for £300 per annum. From here he could stroll down the road in the evenings to play whist at Lord Eglinton's in St James's Square. He also visited Eglinton at Eglinton Castle, where he had not been since the tournament of 1839, and went to other places in Scotland – Loch Lomond, Loch Katrine and the Trossachs, and Dumbarton Castle, which fascinated him – and apparently paid a short visit to Ulster. He stayed at Brodick Castle in the Isle of Arran with the Marquis of Douglas, who had married Louis Napoleon's cousin Marie, the daughter of Stéphanie de Beauharnais, Grand Duchess of Baden. He visited the Londonderrys at Wynyard Park in Durham, and Samuel Cartwright, who had been the Prince Regent's dentist, at Nizels near Sevenoaks.[7] He formed a very favourable opinion of English country life, admiring the local nobility and gentry for their friendly attitude to the villagers, and enjoying the dinners and break-fasts which they provided for their guests.[8]

It is not surprising that he should have resumed his pursuit of pretty women, for Alexandrine Veugeot at Ham had not been a fully satis-factory substitute for the pleasures of the chase of society beauties. At thirty-eight he was not yet married, and whenever he was seen paying any attention to an eligible girl there were rumours of an engagement. It was said that he was going to marry Miss Angela Burdett-Coutts, who was staying at the Bedford Hotel in Brighton when he was there. The daughter of Sir John Kirkland, the bluff squire and churchwarden of Patching in Sussex, was also named by the gossipmongers as a possible bride for him.[9] So was Miss Georgiana Damer, the daughter of Colonel Damer of Came House in Dorchester and the grand-daughter of the Earl of Dorchester. Damer, a veteran of Waterloo, was eager to extend his hospitality to Boney's nephew; but it was as a witness, not as the bridegroom, that Louis Napoleon attended Miss Damer's wedding in Dorchester when she married Viscount Ebrington in March 1847.

He travelled to Dorchester from London by the fastest available way, taking the train on the newly opened Great Western line to Tiverton, and going back to Dorchester, fifty miles to the south-east, by carriage along the country lanes. During his stay at Came House, he sat up till 2 or 3 a.m. smoking cigarettes and talking politics with Lord Alvanley, one of Wellington's generals. He told Alvanley what he would do when he was Emperor. His host, Colonel Damer, thought that he was very 'gentlemanlike' and had 'a thousand good and agreeable qualities', but told Alvanley that 'on the subject of politics, my dear Alvanley, he is as mad as a hatter'.[10] The editorial staff of *The Times* took a different view when the journalist Forbes Campbell brought Louis Napoleon to the *Times* office one night and showed him round while next day's edition was being prepared. One of Campbell's colleagues said that he had found that Louis Napoleon talked very seriously about politics, and was not, as they had been informed, 'a frivolous man of pleasure'.[11]

The outstanding social event of the hot summer of 1847 was a brilliant season on the London stage. It was organized by a charming and enterprising Jew, Benjamin Levy, who had taken the name of Lumley and abandoned a career as a Parliamentary reporter in order to become the most successful theatrical impresario of his time. In 1847 he had London society raving over the Swedish opera singer, Jenny Lind. Marie Taglioni, dancing for the last time at the age of forty-three, returned to Her Majesty's Theatre with three of her leading rivals – Carlotta Grisi, Fanny Cerito and Carolina Rosati; and Rachel, Virginie Déjazet and Rose Chéri took part in a repertory season of French drama at the St James's Theatre.[12]

It was also the year of the great famine in Ireland, when, for the first time in history, the conscience of the English aristocracy and middle classes was shocked that thousands of the Irish poor were dying of hunger. Officialdom condemned any state intervention or public assistance as a violation of sound economic principles; but private charity was considered permissible, and the proceeds of several theatrical performances were given for the relief of distress in Ireland. In May 1847 Louis Napoleon was one of many leading figures in society who were present at the St James's Theatre when Queen Victoria and Prince Albert attended an amateur performance in which various aristocratic ladies and gentlemen acted an English translation by Lord Ellesmere of Victor Hugo's *Hernani*.[13]

Louis Napoleon attended regularly at Her Majesty's Theatre during the summer of 1847, taking out a subscription, like many other fashionable gentlemen, which entitled him to attend all the performances at the theatre except on special gala nights. He saw Jenny Lind in *La Sonnambula, La Figlia del Reggimento, Norma, Ernani, I Masnadieri*, as Susanna in Mozart's *Nozze di Figaro*, and in an Italian translation of Meyerbeer's *Robert le Diable*. Her performance as Alice in *Robert le Diable*, according to the critic in *The Times*, was 'a complete personation of feminine goodness'; the audience were moved to tears when she clung to the crucifix as she warded off the lascivious Bertram.[14]

Louis Napoleon attended at least twenty of her thirty-four performances.*[15] Queen Victoria and Prince Albert were nearly as assiduous in their attendance, coming eighteen times; and the Duke of Wellington, who, despite his increasing deafness, was still fond of music, attended nineteen performances. Both Wellington and Louis Napoleon were at Her Majesty's on 17 July, when Taglioni, Grisi, Cerito and Rosati ran on to the stage hand in hand to dance their famous *pas de quatre* of 1845, and the whole audience rose to their feet to applaud them.[16] Louis Napoleon went to the French plays at the St James's, where Rachel was almost competing with Jenny Lind for the attention of the dramatic critics and the connoisseurs by her performances in Corneille's *Horace*, in Racine's *Britannicus*, in Voltaire's *Tancrède*, as Mary, Queen of Scots, in Le Brun's French version of Schiller's *Maria Stuart*, and, playing comedy for a change, as a delightful Célimène in Molière's *Le Misanthrope*.[17]

He became friendly with Lumley, who at the end of the season at Her Majesty's invited him to a garden party which he gave at his house in Fulham for his opera singers and ballet-dancers. Louis Napoleon met Jenny Lind at the party, and was one of the dancers in a quadrille with Taglioni, Grisi and Cerito.[18] He and Taglioni bore each other no ill-will for their conduct on the occasion of their previous meeting eight years before. She thought him very charming, but he made no further attempt to seduce her.

He may have made love to the very beautiful Rose Chéri during her season in Scribe's comedies at the St James's in April 1847, for she allowed him to visit her alone in her lodgings. He was unsuccessful with another French actress, Eugénie Doche, who two years after he met her in 1846 was the first Marguerite Gautier in *La Dame aux Camélias*. She refused to become his mistress, and chose instead the Earl of Pembroke, who abandoned her a few months later.[19]

Louis Napoleon compensated for his failure with Eugénie Doche by his success with the fascinating Rachel. Élisa Félix, the daughter of a wandering Jewish pedlar, born in a wayside inn in Switzerland and brought up in the gutters of Paris, had gone on the French stage under the name of Rachel and had become the most famous actress in Europe and the mistress of several prominent gentlemen. Her lovers included Alfred de Musset and Count Walewski, the illegitimate son of Napoleon and the Polish Countess Marie Walewska, who was now a top-ranking diplomat in Louis Philippe's service. Although she specialized in acting the parts of majestic and tragic heroines, in

*Jenny Lind appeared thirty-four times in opera, and in addition sang once at a concert. On six occasions the list of those attending the performances was not published in the press.

private life she was vivacious and gay, and very proud of her back-ground and of her Jewish race – 'moi toute juive', she would boast. She became Louis Napoleon's mistress in the summer of 1846, after he had seen her in her greatest role in *Phèdre* at the St James's. Her love affairs were as notorious as the outbreaks of fury to which she some-times subjected her unsuccessful and discarded lovers. She was sup-posed to have said that she could not remember the time when she was a virgin; but Louis Napoleon was sufficiently infatuated with her to write to his friend Vieillard, when Rachel returned to Paris after her London season in 1846, asking him to watch over this 'young and in-experienced girl, threatened with many dangers and beset by in-numerable temptations'.[20]

In the autumn of 1846 Louis Napoleon was visited in Bath by his cousin 'Plon-Plon',[21] who, since the death of Louis Napoleon's brother Napoleon Louis, could without confusion be referred to as 'Prince Napoleon'. They had not met since the days when Plon-Plon was fourteen, when he was at Arenenberg with Mathilde in 1836. They became very intimate, and despite the ill-feeling which later arose between Prince Napoleon and Eugénie, Louis Napoleon himself remained on friendly terms with Prince Napoleon for many years. Prince Napoleon was an enthusiastic Radical, which was the chief reason – though not the only one – why he was unpopular with Eugénie and with so many of his acquaintances.

In December 1846 Henry Wikoff came to England and called on Louis Napoleon, whom he had visited at Ham. He met Prince Napo-leon at 3 King Street, and became involved in a somewhat heated argument with him when Prince Napoleon attacked Wikoff, as an American, for the continued existence of slavery in the United States. Wikoff noticed that Louis Napoleon adopted what Wikoff considered to be a much more balanced and less Radical attitude about politics than his cousin did.[22]

In August 1847, Rachel finished her season at the St James's with a performance of Alfieri's *Virginie*,[23] in which she played the part of the plebeian girl in ancient Rome who prefers death to dishonour at the hands of the lustful decemvir, Appius. Immediately afterwards, she went on tour, acting in Birmingham and Edinburgh; and Louis Napoleon and Prince Napoleon went with her. They took the train from London to Birmingham, the three of them travelling together in a reserved first-class compartment. On the journey, Louis Napoleon fell asleep. After a while he awoke and, opening his eyes, saw Prince Napoleon and Rachel making love on the seat opposite him. He quickly closed his eyes, pretending to be asleep and not to have seen them; but next day he took the train back to London without a word of explanation, leaving them to entertain each other in Birmingham. He did not allow the incident to interfere with his friendship with either Prince Napoleon or Rachel. In later years he told this story to Eugénie, and she told her secretary Augustin Filon, who published it in his book *Recollections of the Empress Eugénie.** But we should perhaps remember that Eugénie had not liked Prince Napoleon, and that she was always capable of improving a good story.[24]

Louis Napolcon formed a more lasting and important attachment than his liaison with Rachel. There are conflicting stories of where he first met the woman who is remembered in history as 'Miss Howard', though she was more often called 'Mrs Howard' by her contemporaries. Elizabeth Ann Haryet was born in 1823 in Brighton, where her grandfather owned the Castle Hotel and her father was a shoemaker. By the time she was twenty-four, in the summer of 1847, she had been a riding instructress in Cambridge, had been the mistress of the jockey Jem Mason, who won the first Grand National in 1839, and had lived in style in a large house in St John's Wood as the mistress of Major Martyn of the Life Guards; but it is unlikely that she had ever been a common prostitute on a beat in Tottenham Court Road, as spiteful people said. Major Martyn had introduced her into the semi-respectable fringe of society which was dominated by Louis Napoleon's friends, Count d'Orsay and Lady Blessington. According to one story, Miss Howard first saw Louis Napoleon, and fell in love with him, when she went with the crowds to watch him and his fellow-competitors practising for the Eglinton Tournament at the Eyre Arms Tavern in St John's Wood. Another story is that she ran into him in the fog outside the Theatre Royal in the Haymarket in London during the winter of 1846–7, that he escorted her home, that she gave him a tip, thinking that he was a policeman, and that he called on her next day, identified himself, and told her that he would keep the coin which she had given him for the rest of his life as a souvenir of her. It is more likely that Lady Blessington introduced them at Gore House.

Miss Howard was very unhappy at this time, as Major Martyn, with whom she was very much in love, had deserted her. She was immediately pursued by several peers and gentlemen who were eager to take the major's place; but she chose Louis Napoleon. Among those whose advances she rejected was A. W. Kinglake, the barrister, traveller and author. Kinglake could not understand how Miss Howard could prefer Louis Napoleon to himself. He afterwards became an M.P., and both in the House of Commons and in his history of the Crimean

*Filon says that the incident occurred when Rachel was touring in 'the North of England'; but Birmingham and Edinburgh were the only two towns that she visited in her provincial tour in August 1847.

War he strongly criticized Napoleon III's policy. It has been suggested that he did this out of jealous spite because Louis Napoleon had beaten him in their contest for Miss Howard's love; but this does a great injustice to Kinglake, who was by no means the only Englishman to denounce Napoleon III at that time.

Louis Napoleon installed Miss Howard in a house at 9 Berkeley Street, which was not far from his own house in King Street, St James's. She was devoted to him, and very useful to him. Despite her humble origins she was very rich, having inherited a large legacy; and she placed her money, as well as her services, at the disposal of Louis Napoleon and the Bonapartist cause, and thus helped to relieve his financial difficulties.[25]

These difficulties led him into an unpleasant situation in the summer of 1847. He instructed his business agent to try to arrange for him to obtain a loan. A few days later he was visited by a man named Charles Pollard, who offered to lend him £2000 – £800 in cash and a cheque for £1200 – if Louis Napoleon would sign two bills of exchange, made payable to bearer, for £1000 each. Louis Napoleon made inquiries about Pollard, and after discovering that he was a member of Crockford's Club agreed to the transaction. When Pollard called again, Louis Napoleon signed the bills of exchange and handed them back to Pollard after Pollard had promised to bring the cash and the cheque next day. But Pollard did not do so, and when Louis Napoleon and Orsi called on him at his house in Essex Street, Strand, Mrs Pollard said that her husband was not at home, though in fact he was watching them through the curtains of the front room. A few days later, Louis Napoleon received a letter from Pollard in Birmingham, saying that he was unable to raise the £2000. Louis Napoleon immediately informed the police, and Pollard was arrested and charged with larceny.

D'Orsay knew the successful barrister, Serjeant Ballantine, and he took Louis Napoleon to see him in his chambers. To Louis Napoleon's astonishment, Ballantine told him that Pollard would be acquitted. He explained that Pollard had not been guilty of larceny, because when Louis Napoleon gave him the bills of exchange he had intended to transfer the ownership of the bills to Pollard. The subtle distinction between larceny and obtaining by false pretences enabled many criminals at this time to obtain verdicts of Not Guilty on the grounds that they had been charged with the wrong offence.

Louis Napoleon would not accept that this could be the law. 'I could not convince the Prince, who seemed quite unable to grasp the idea that the law of this country was not regulated by the Code Napoleon', wrote Ballantine many years afterwards. He added that the interview left him with an unfavourable view of Louis Napoleon's intellect, and suggested that his inability to understand realities was responsible not only for the fiascos of Strasburg and Boulogne, but also for the disasters of his future career; but Ballantine was perhaps viewing Louis Napoleon with the advantage of hindsight when he published his memoirs in 1882.

Ballantine refused to take the brief or to accept a fee from d'Orsay; but Louis Napoleon bore him no ill-will, and in later years, when he was Emperor and saw him at the races in the Bois de Boulogne, he asked for Ballantine to be presented to him and gave him a seat in the imperial box.

Pollard was defended by Mr Henry Hawkins, a young barrister who afterwards became one of the greatest criminal judges of the nineteenth century. Despite Hawkins's arguments, the magistrate insisted on sending the case for trial at the Central Criminal Court, and refused to grant bail. The case was tried at the Old Bailey before Mr Baron Alderson and a jury on 9 July 1847.

Louis Napoleon gave his evidence coolly and well, as he had done in the Police Court; but then Mr Humfrey, who led Hawkins for the defence, rose to cross-examine. 'I have only one question to ask His Highness', said Humfrey. 'When the bills were produced, did the prisoner take them away with his consent?' Louis Napoleon agreed that he had consented, expecting that Pollard would bring the money on the following day. Humfrey then submitted that there was no case to answer, because, as Louis Napoleon had intended to part with the bills when he handed them to Pollard, no larceny was committed. The judge directed the jury to return a verdict of Not Guilty: 'There is no doubt that it was a most dishonest transaction, but it did not constitute the offence with which the prisoner was charged, and I regret that I must direct the jury to return a verdict of acquittal.' Louis Napoleon had at least the satisfaction of knowing that the publicity which the prosecution had received was a warning to the public to be on their guard against Pollard in future.[26]

He was rewarded for his courtesy to Lady Anglesey at Bath with an invitation to spend Christmas in 1847 at the Angleseys' country home at Beaudesert in Staffordshire. The old hero of Waterloo, who had just been made a Field-Marshal, was a charming host. Among the guests at Beaudesert was a fascinating and unconventional girl of twenty-two, Louisa de Horsey, who was a great favourite of Lord Anglesey. There was something about her which appealed to elderly generals, for she afterwards married Lord Cardigan, the monster-hero of the Charge of the Light Brigade; and she lived well into the twentieth century as the Spanish Countess of Lancastre Saldanha. Miss de Horsey found Louis Napoleon very charming, 'always courtesy itself', and she enjoyed her stay at Beaudesert, 'although', as she wrote many years later, 'we did not smoke cigarettes, lose money at Bridge, or scour the country in motor cars'. Instead, there were walks, and piano-playing and singing in the evenings. Louis Napoleon used to ask her to sing Schubert's 'Adieu' to him every evening; she thought that it recalled for him some happy memory of the past. The beautiful Countess of Desart was one of the guests at Beaudesert. When someone asked Louis Napoleon how he liked the house, he replied, turning to Lady Desart: 'J'aime beaucoup Beaudesert, mais encore plus la belle Desart.'[27]

He was still at Beaudesert on New Year's Day 1848. Even if he had been as over-confident as he was in the days of his attempts at Strasburg and Boulogne, he could not have believed it possible that before the end of the new year he would be in Paris as the ruler of France.

1848

ON 12 January 1848, the people of Palermo began the 'year of revolutions' with a rising which spread to the whole of Sicily and drove out the government of the Bourbon King of Naples. On 22 February, thousands of demonstrators came out in Paris to protest against the banning of a public banquet which the Opposition parties had planned to hold. On the night of the 23rd, barricades went up all over Paris, and the troops and National Guard joined the revolutionaries. On 24 February, Louis Philippe abdicated, and after hiding for a week on the Channel coast crossed to England and found safety and a night's lodging at the Bridge Hotel in Newhaven.

The leading part in the revolution which had overthrown Louis Philippe had been played by the artisans under Socialist leadership. They demanded a 'democratic and social republic'. To the Conservatives and moderate Liberals a political party which called itself 'Social-Democratic' and raised the slogan 'La république démocratique et sociale' seemed to menace the very existence of the social order and property itself. The incident at the Hôtel de Ville on 25 February, when the Social-Democrats demanded that the red flag should replace the Tricolore as the national flag and Lamartine resisted the demand, made a deep impression, and gave to the scarlet banners of the Socialists, and to the words 'the red flag', a frightening significance for the middle classes which it still retains to some extent a hundred and thirty years later.

Thiers and the leaders of the Orleanist Opposition – the politicians who had opposed Guizot's Conservative government but had supported King Louis Philippe and the Orleanist régime – were brushed aside, and power passed into the hands of a coalition of the Moderate Republicans Lamartine, Marrast and General Cavaignac, the revolutionary Radical Ledru-Rollin, and the Socialists Louis Blanc and Albert, the first working man to be a member of a French government. They declared themselves to be the Provisional Government of the Republic, introduced universal manhood suffrage, abolished slavery in the colonies and the death penalty for political offences, proclaimed

the 'right to work', and set up National Workshops where any unemployed man who wished to do so could enrol and be paid two francs
a day for working on some public works in Paris. The National Workshops, which were introduced at the insistence of Louis Blanc, were
based on the theories of Fourier. The Socialist Caussidière entered the
police headquarters and appointed himself Chief of the Paris Police.

News of the events in Paris reached London almost immediately
over the electric telegraph, which had been installed between Paris
and Calais and between Dover and London a few years before; but no
details were available, as the revolutionaries had torn up the railway
line along stretches of the Northern Railway, and no letters or newspapers from Paris had reached London. Shortly before midnight on
Saturday 26 February, Louis Napoleon decided to leave for Paris at
dawn, and at 6.30 on the Sunday morning he left King Street and with
Orsi and Thélin caught the train from Charing Cross to Dover. He had
a false British passport and pretended to be an Englishman, because he
was not at all sure whether he might not find, when he reached France,
that Louis Philippe and his ministers were back in power, or that they
had been succeeded by some Legitimist or Republican government
which was as hostile as the Orleanists to a Bonapartist pretender.

At Dover they caught the steamer to Calais. It was a beautiful day,
and as the sea was calm nearly all the passengers were on deck; but
Louis Napoleon remained below in his cabin, where there would be
less chance of his being seen and recognized by one of the other passengers. At Calais the immigration officer asked him whether he was an
Englishman, and he said that he was. At 11.30 a.m. he left Calais with
Orsi and Thélin on the Paris train, which was running despite rumours
to the contrary, and reached Amiens at 2.30 p.m., where they had to
change trains.

At 4 p.m. they boarded the train for Paris, but their departure was
held up by the arrival of a crowd of Republicans who had been released
from prison at Doullens. They stormed into the station at Amiens,
some of them still wearing their prison clothes, shouting Republican
slogans and singing the Republican songs of '93 – the 'Ça Ira', the
'Carmagnole', the 'Chant du Départ', and the 'Marseillaise'. They
insisted on travelling to Paris free of charge, and tried to board the train
without tickets. Orsi recognized one of them as Lieutenant Aladenize,
the only one of the Boulogne plotters, apart from Louis Napoleon, who
had received a sentence of life imprisonment. Leaving Louis Napoleon
in the compartment, he got out of the train to talk to Aladenize, and
persuaded him not to tell his comrades that Louis Napoleon was on the
train, as he wished his identity to be kept secret. The eager young
Prince of the Romagna days, of Strasburg and Boulogne, might have

thrown caution to the winds and greeted his faithful follower who had received a sentence of life imprisonment for his sake; but the more calculating forty-year-old politician realized the dangers that he might incur if his presence in France became prematurely known.

The Republicans were still arguing with the station-master about the need for tickets when the train pulled out of the station. At Creil, thirty miles from Paris, they were told that the train could go no further because of the destruction of the railway line. They spent the night in the train. Seven hundred miles to the south, Eugenia del Montijo was dancing the night through at her mother's Carnival ball at Ariza House, dressed as a Sicilian peasant girl. Queen Isabel had promised to attend, and had chosen her fancy dress, but decided not to come when she heard the news of the revolution in Paris, as she was worried about the safety of her sister, the Duchesse de Montpensier.[1]

Next morning Louis Napoleon, Orsi and Thélin found a cab which took them to Paris. When they reached the city barrier they found a ten-foot-high barricade which had been erected during the revolution five days before. Like every other passer-by, they were ordered by the National Guard to remove one stone each from the barricade, which had to be demolished. Louis Napoleon and his companions did as they were directed without demur, but they asked the cab-driver to take them through the side streets where they would not pass any more barricades which they would have to help dismantle. The driver, after laughing at them for being three good bourgeois, found a way to their hotel which avoided the barricades.

As soon as they had arrived at the Hôtel des Princes in the Rue Richelieu, Louis Napoleon made contact with the Bonapartists in Paris. They advised him to make his presence known at once. He wrote immediately to the Provisional Government:

> Gentlemen, the people of Paris having destroyed by their heroism the last traces of the foreign invasions, I hasten back from exile to place myself under the flag of the Republic which has just been proclaimed. Without any other ambition than that of serving my country, I announce my arrival to the Provisional Government.[2]

During the day the Bonapartists made it widely known that he was staying at the Hôtel des Princes. They placarded the city with pictures of him under the one-word caption: 'Lui!' In the evening a large crowd gathered in front of the hotel; but Louis Napoleon did not appear at the window.

Next day, on 29 February, several Deputies and politicians of various parties called at the hotel and spoke with him; but in the course of the morning General Montholon, whom Louis Napoleon had last seen in their prison at Ham, arrived with a letter from the Provisional Government. Montholon was a tactful choice for an embarrassing mission. In their letter, the Provisional Government asked Louis Napoleon to leave France immediately in order to avoid exacerbating a dangerous situation.

Louis Napoleon called a meeting of his supporters to decide what to do. Some of them advised him to comply with the Provisional Government's request and announce that he was withdrawing temporarily from France in order to avoid any risk of endangering internal peace by his presence; but Persigny, who had just been released from prison and was as adventurous as ever, urged him to refuse to go, and thus force the Provisional Government to take the responsibility for deporting him.

After hearing the advice of his counsellors, Louis Napoleon reached his own decision, quickly and irrevocably. He wrote to the Provisional Government, stating that although it was a bitter disappointment to him to find that after thirty-three years of exile he was still unable to live in his native land, he would give the best possible proof of his patriotism by leaving France at once rather than run any risk of endangering the safety of the Republic.[3] He stayed one more day in Paris and left on 2 March, reaching Folkestone next morning. He was back in England five days after he had left it, eight days after the abdication of Louis Philippe, and a few hours before the former King and Queen of the French landed at Newhaven.[4]

On 17 March the artisans of Paris streamed out of the National Workshops and the slums of the Faubourg Saint-Antoine and demonstrated in the streets, waving the red flag and demanding the overthrow of the Provisional Government and the establishment of the Democratic and Social Republic. Their representative in the Provisional Government, Louis Blanc, persuaded them to go home peacefully and to allow the Provisional Government to remain in power for the time being. Blanc was bitterly denounced for this by many of his followers, who felt that he had betrayed the revolution. For Karl Marx, who based his whole theory of revolution on the experiences of France in 1848, and for twentieth-century Marxists, Louis Blanc became the prototype of the Social-Democrat leader who, because of his folly, cowardice or treachery, persuades his followers not to seize power at the crest of the revolutionary wave, with the result that the bourgeoisie raise their heads once again, and a reaction sets in which destroys the revolution and the cowardly Social-Democrat leaders as well.

The demonstration of 17 March alarmed the French middle classes. They had objected from the beginning to the National Workshops on the grounds that for the state to pay unemployed workmen for doing useless unproductive work was a violation of sound economic principles as well as being a burden on the taxpayer. Now they had another reason to object: the workmen in the National Workshops seemed to be always available to take part in street demonstrations at the call of Socialist agitators.

These Socialist agitators, under the leadership of Barbès, Raspail and Blanqui, were concentrating their attacks against Lamartine and the bourgeois Republicans in the Provisional Government; but they had considerable sympathy for Louis Napoleon, because they had heard that he had Socialist leanings and had written a book advocating the establishment of some form of National Workshops. His image as a Socialist sympathizer was helped to some extent by the activities of his cousin, Carlo Bonaparte, Prince of Canino, Lucien's son, the well-known ornithologist. During the last few months Carlo Bonaparte had become one of the most extreme leaders of the Radical revolutionary movement in Tuscany and throughout Italy, and his activities helped to foster the belief that the younger generation of Bonaparte Princes were Communists. When the workers in Paris marched through the streets under the red flag, there were always shouts of 'Vive Napoléon!' as well as of 'Vive Barbès!'

The revolution spread quickly across Europe. In the course of one week in March, autocratic governments were overthrown in Vienna and Berlin, and the Austrian troops were expelled from Milan. In England the Chartist leaders called for a monster demonstration to assemble on 10 April at Kennington, from where the demonstrators would march on the Houses of Parliament and force the government to grant universal manhood suffrage and the other demands of the People's Charter.

The government took the Chartist threat very seriously. The old Duke of Wellington was placed in command of 10,000 soldiers and 170,000 special constables, who blocked the Chartist demonstrators' road from Kennington Common to Parliament Square and were stationed at all important points in London. The special constables had a great moral effect on aristocratic and middle-class England. The conscript armies and the centralized *gendarmerie* of the Continent had given way before the forces of revolution; but England would resist them, without abandoning her traditional system, by swearing-in able-bodied men of property and their tradesmen and servants as special constables to defend the Queen and the law during the emergency. Louis Napoleon was sworn-in as a special constable for two months at Marlborough Street Police Court by the Metropolitan Magistrate, and then went happily to the opera at Her Majesty's

Theatre, like other leading figures in society, including Wellington himself, as a gesture of calm confidence.[5]

At all the important points in London the constables assembled on the fateful morning of Monday 10 April. Louis Napoleon was on duty in Trafalgar Square, and also, perhaps, on London Bridge.[6] The Chartist leaders called off their proposed march on Westminster when confronted with Wellington's forces, and the Establishment celebrated the triumph of the British way of life over foreign revolutionary doctrines. But in France the fear of the Red Republic was spreading among the middle classes as taxes and prices rose and the workers came out of the National Workshops into the streets with increasing frequency. In the fashionable *salons* and the middle-class drawing-rooms in France the stories circulated about how the workmen in the National Workshops were paid one week for laying down paving-stones and in the following week were paid for removing them; of how Louis Blanc and Ledru-Rollin and their subordinates in the provinces were paying themselves large salaries and perks from the public funds; and how the housemaid of one of their friends had given her mistress notice because her husband had been appointed to be the Prefect of a department. On all sides there was a feeling that the existing state of affairs could not last. What would take its place – the Red Republic? a return to the Orleanist régime with Louis Philippe's son, the Prince de Joinville, as King? or the Legitimist descendant of Charles X, who called himself King Henri V? Hardly anyone suggested that there was another possibility – a Bonaparte Emperor.[7]

On 23 April, elections for a National Constituent Assembly were held by secret ballot under universal manhood suffrage, which had not been introduced in any other country in Europe. Over 9 million electors were entitled to vote, as compared with a total electorate of 250,000 under Louis Philippe. The Bonapartists urged Louis Napoleon to offer himself as a candidate. He was wise enough to refuse, knowing that if he only received a handful of votes it would be a serious setback to his political hopes in the future. But Prince Napoleon, Prince Pierre Bonaparte of Canino, and Prince Lucien Murat, the son of the former King of Naples, stood as Bonapartist candidates. The people flocked to the town halls to exercise their new right to vote; 84 per cent of the electorate voted – a higher proportion than would vote in any future election in France during the nineteenth century.[8] The results were surprising. Lamartine and the Moderate Republicans won a clear majority with 500 of the 880 seats in the Assembly; Ledru-Rollin's Radicals and the Socialists won under 100 seats; Thiers and the Orleanist Opposition won just under 200 seats; and the Legitimists won 100 seats. Prince Napoleon, Pierre Bonaparte and Lucien Murat were all elected. The voting showed that France as a whole was more Conservative than Paris.

In the middle of May, news reached Paris that a minor disturbance had broken out in Prussian Poland and had been brutally suppressed. The fate of Poland always aroused great sympathy in France, especially among the large group of Polish refugees who had escaped to France after the defeat of the Polish revolution in 1831 and who had been subjected to continual harassment by the police under Louis Philippe's régime. This powerful pro-Polish feeling helped Louis Napoleon's cause. The Bonapartists reminded the people how, in the glorious days of the Empire, France had not pursued a cowardly foreign policy, but had sent her soldiers marching across Europe to liberate Poland and Italy from their foreign oppressors.

The Polish refugees, the Radicals and the Socialists called a protest demonstration in Paris on 15 May to demand French military intervention in support of Poland. The demonstrators broke into the National Assembly, manhandled some of the deputies, and proclaimed that the Assembly was dissolved. As usual, the demonstrators had shouted 'Vive Barbès!' and 'Vive Napoléon!' The middle classes preferred them to cry 'Vive Napoléon!' rather than 'Vive Barbès!'

The Provisional Government regarded the demonstration of 15 May as a challenge to the Republic and its elected representatives. Louis Blanc, Raspail and Barbès were held responsible for it, though in fact they had tried to restrain the demonstrators. Louis Blanc was forced to resign from the government, and there was talk of arresting him. Raspail and Barbès were imprisoned at Vincennes.

Under the complicated election law, twenty-three vacant seats in the National Assembly had to be filled by elections at the beginning of June. In view of the successes of Prince Napoleon, Pierre Bonaparte and Lucien Murat at the elections in April, the Bonapartists nominated Louis Napoleon as a candidate in Paris, Charente-Inférieure, Yonne, Eure, Sarthe and Corsica. His election campaign was directed from offices in the Rue d'Hauteville and the Passage des Panoramas in Paris, where his old followers were constantly to be found – Vaudrey, Aladenize, Laity, Conneau, Eléonore Gordon, and above all the director of operations, Persigny.[9] They were short of money, and, with their candidate absent abroad, held no public meetings and relied entirely on billposting the constituencies with placards, at a total cost of 400 francs.

The campaign was primarily designed to win the support of patriotic Frenchmen and Socialist workmen. The electors were told that a vote for Louis Napoleon would be a protest against the treaties of 1814 and 1815 and against the foreigners who had persecuted the Bonapartes.

By electing him, the workers would show their gratitude to him for having thought about them when he was a prisoner at Ham, where he wrote his book on pauperism. An appeal written by Laity, but signed 'An old Republican of '92, a soldier of Zürich and Waterloo, a worker who fought on the barricades of February', called on the Parisians to vote for 'Napoleon Louis Bonaparte, child of Paris', the 'soldier of Italian independence in 1831', who at Strasburg and Boulogne had proclaimed the sovereignty of the people, and had paid with seven (*sic!*) years' imprisonment for having preceded in 1840 the heroic population of Paris in 1848. The Bonapartists assured the voters that Louis Napoleon was 'one of the noblest children of France', and that although his moustache and his little imperial beard made his facial appearance somewhat different from that of his uncle Napoleon, 'the Napoleonic type' was faithfully reproduced in his features. He had always led a simple and frugal life and was a superb horseman, having once saved the lives of a mother and her two children when two runaway horses were hurtling their carriage towards a precipice overlooking Lake Constance.[10]

The results of the election in Paris on 4 June showed no clear political pattern, but it was a success for Louis Napoleon. There were exactly 200 candidates for the 11 vacant seats. The Socialist Caussidière headed the poll with 146,716 votes; Goudchaux, the Moderate Republican banker who was Minister of Finance in the Provisional Government, was third with 106,982; Thiers, fifth with 97,546; Victor Hugo, who at this time supported the Moderate Republicans, seventh with 86,726; and Louis Napoleon came eighth with 84,431 votes. Proudhon, the Socialist theoretician, was last of the successful candidates with 74,118. Louis Napoleon was also elected in the Yonne, in Charente-Inférieure, and in Corsica, where he received 35,903 out of a total of 38,197 votes cast. He was defeated in Eure and Sarthe.[11]

His election caused alarm among the Conservatives and the Moderate Republicans. The former Catholic rebel priest, Lamennais, who had become an agnostic and a Radical, wrote in *Le Peuple Constituant* that 'the name of Louis Bonaparte is a flag of conspiracy', and condemned 'this young man whom England has sent us'. The *Journal de La Rochelle* reported that during the election in Charente-Inférieure thousands of peasants had gone to the polling stations shouting 'Vive Napoléon!', and in the same district, at Saintes, they had worn notices in their hats inscribed 'Louis Napoleon! Long live the Emperor! Down with the Republic!' In the very different economic and political atmosphere of the metallurgical town of Charleville in the department of the Ardennes – one of the few areas in France where workers were employed in factories, as opposed to small workshops* – the streets were billposted during the night with placards which called on the people to take arms and fight under the leadership of Louis Napoleon against the oppressors of the people, and ended: 'Long live the Emperor!'[12]

Neither Louis Napoleon nor Persigny and his agents in France were responsible for these indiscreet utterances; but they led to an immediate anti-Bonapartist backlash. The legality of Louis Napoleon's election was promptly challenged in the Assembly in view of the fact that the law of banishment against the Bonapartes was still in force, and on 12 June a debate took place as to whether he should be allowed to take his seat. The government took the view that he was not eligible, and in an attempt to prejudge the issue Ledru-Rollin, as Minister of the Interior, ordered that he was to be arrested if he set foot in France.

The Bonapartists replied by placarding the walls of Paris with the text of the letter which Louis Napoleon had written to the electors of Paris, in which he thanked them for electing him and declared: 'Let us rally round the altars of the country under the flag of the Republic!' In the next few days seven new Bonapartist newspapers appeared in Paris. One of them, *Le Napoléon Républicain*, was directed especially at the Socialists; two were designed for the army and ex-servicemen, *Le Petit Caporal* and *La Rédingote Grise*. Bonapartists demonstrated in the streets, shouting out their slogans: 'Vive Napoléon!' 'Vive le Prince Louis!', and ' 'Poléon, nous l'aurons!' Barrel-organs churned out Bonapartist songs, 'Napoléon, rentre dans ta patrie!', 'Napoléon, sois bon républicain!'[13]

In the debate in the Assembly on 12 June, the Socialists moved a vote of censure on the government for having ordered the arrest of Louis Napoleon. Louis Blanc and Proudhon spoke in his defence. So did Jules Favre, who was a supporter of the Provisional Government; as a lawyer, he could not see how it was possible to admit Prince Napoleon and Pierre Bonaparte and exclude Louis Napoleon. The government brought its strongest spokesmen into action, with Lamartine, Ledru-Rollin and General Cavaignac, the Minister of War, denouncing Louis Napoleon as a danger to the Republic.

The debates in the Assembly during the next five days demonstrated not only the unreliability of a Parliament of democratically elected politicians in times of revolutionary fervour, but also the unscrupulousness of the Moderate Republicans. The mood of the deputies changed from hour to hour as one orator followed another. Lamartine

*In 1847, less than 10 per cent of workmen employed in industry in the Paris area worked in establishments where more than ten persons were employed (Price, *The French Second Republic*, p. 7).

tried to frighten them by stories of Bonapartist plots against the Republic, and of a regiment at Troyes who had cried 'Vive l'Empereur!' While he was speaking the Bonapartists and Socialists were demonstrating outside the Parliament building in the courtyard of the Palais Bourbon, demanding that Louis Napoleon be allowed to take his seat. Lamartine's speech seemed to be falling flat when someone rushed in and handed him a note as he stood at the rostrum. He read it, and informed the deputies that he had just been told that Bonapartists had opened fire on the troops and National Guards who were protecting the Assembly and had wounded three of them: 'It is the first drop of blood that has stained the eternally pure and glorious revolution of 24 February.' The story was a lie; no shots had been fired and no one had been wounded. But the indignant deputies shouted down the Bonapartists and the Socialists, and gave the government a vote of confidence for their action in ordering the arrest of Louis Napoleon if he came to France.

But Lamartine and his colleagues slipped up; they did not immediately demand a vote on the question whether Louis Napoleon should be allowed to take his seat in the Assembly. Next morning Persigny, Laity and many of the Bonapartist demonstrators were arrested; but by the time the session of the Assembly was resumed in the afternoon the deputies had discovered that Lamartine had lied on the previous day. They swung the other way, and amid great excitement voted by a large majority to allow Louis Napoleon to take his seat in their midst, only twenty-four hours after they had endorsed the government's decision to order his arrest.

The government and the Moderate Republicans made a final effort to exclude Louis Napoleon, and resorted to even more disreputable tactics than Lamartine had adopted on 12 June. On 14 June they spread the rumour in the press and in the lobbies that the Bonapartists were preparing to carry out a *coup d'état* in the course of the next few days. On the same day Louis Napoleon in London wrote a letter to the President of the Assembly, Sénard, which he hoped would finally convince the deputies of his lack of personal ambition and his devotion to the Republican régime; but unfortunately it contained some phrases which created a very unfavourable impression when they were read out in the Assembly on 15 June. He wrote that he had been on the point of leaving London to take up his duties as a deputy in Paris, but had not done so when he heard of the groundless anxiety which his election had caused. He had not sought the honour of being a representative of the people, and still less did he desire power; but 'if the people entrusted me with duties, I would know how to perform them. . . . My name is a symbol of order, of nationality, of glory, and

I would be greatly distressed to see it used to increase the troubles and the rifts of our country. To avoid such a misfortune I would rather stay in exile. I am ready to undergo all sacrifices for the welfare of France.'[14]

Cavaignac declared that the letter proved that Louis Napoleon was a danger to the Republic, because nowhere in the letter had he used the word 'republic'. Amid increasing hysteria, the Bonapartists and Socialists demanded that Sénard should read out Louis Napoleon's message of thanks to the electors of Paris which he had enclosed in his letter to Sénard, and in which he had written: 'Let us rally round the altars of the country under the flag of the Republic'; but Cavaignac and his Republican colleagues in the Assembly shouted down the demand for the reading of the message to the electorate. The Moderate Republican, Duprat, moved that it should be suppressed; and Jules Favre, who two days before had spoken in Louis Napoleon's favour, moved that his letter of 14 June should be referred to the Minister of Justice to consider whether criminal proceedings should be brought in respect of it.

Again Louis Napoleon was saved by an adjournment, which was agreed after some deputies had demanded an immediate vote. On the evening of 15 June, at the very moment when this debate was taking place in the Assembly, he wrote another letter from London to the President of the Assembly, in which he stated that, in view of the friction which his election had caused, he was regretfully resigning his seat.[15] The fear of a Bonapartist *coup* which had been expressed in the Paris newspapers of 14 June had been prominently reported in *The Times* on the morning of the 15th, and Louis Napoleon was shrewd enough to appreciate the danger and the need to act with the greatest possible speed. He handed his letter of resignation to his friend Briffault in King Street, St James's, at 8.30 p.m. on 15 June in time for Briffault to catch the boat train to Dover. Briffault crossed on the night steamer to Boulogne, where he arrived at 1 a.m. After an infuriating wait of two-and-a-half hours the train for Paris left Boulogne at 3.30 a.m. and reached the Gare du Nord at 10.45 a.m.; and Briffault placed the letter in Sénard's hands an hour and a half before the session of the Assembly was resumed at 2 p.m.[16] When Sénard read it out in the Assembly, it appeased the indignation of the deputies, and no action was taken against Louis Napoleon.*[17]

*The story told by Aristide Ferrière, of how he was sent by the Bonapartists in Paris at great speed to London to tell Louis Napoleon about the debate in the Assembly on 15 June, and how Louis Napoleon thereupon immediately sent Briffault to Paris with his letter of resignation, has been accepted by many of Louis Napoleon's biographers, but cannot be true because of the time factor. Nor is there any need, or

The efforts of the Republican government to exclude Louis Napoleon had only strengthened the loyalty of his supporters, and many other people were beginning to consider him as a possible alternative to the chaos which was engulfing France. Countess Guiccioli, now the Marquise de Boissy, wrote to Lady Blessington on 20 June:

> I can assure you that Prince Louis's party is very strong, and it would be much stronger if the honest folk who desire order everywhere were not a little suspicious of him, seeing him supported by the party that is called the *Red Republic*, and even by the Communists. But in any case his party is very strong, and in the provinces and particularly in the rural districts the name of Bonaparte and the Empire exercises an immense prestige. . . . People suggest a President, and already Prince Louis is named. If he can save this poor France under any name, he will be welcome.[18]

Dissatisfaction with the government was growing everywhere. 'Today is the anniversary of Waterloo', wrote Mérimée on 18 June; 'were we as low as this thirty-three years ago?'[19]

On 21 June the government issued an order directing that all men between the ages of seventeen and twenty-five were to be ejected from the National Workshops and conscripted into the army, while the older workers were to be sent from the Workshops to work in the marshes of the Sologne, where the climate was said to be unhealthy. Next day the workmen in the Workshops decided to resist. By the morning of 23 June the barricades were going up in many parts of Paris.

Lamartine and his colleagues in the government called on General Cavaignac to suppress the revolt. Although Cavaignac had been a regular army officer under Louis Philippe, he had always been a sincere Republican; his father had been a prominent revolutionary in 1793, and his brother had been imprisoned as a leading Republican in 1834. He waited for reinforcements from outside Paris, and then attacked the rebels with 50,000 men of the regular army, the National Guard from the middle-class districts of Paris and from the provinces, and the Garde Républicaine, which was largely composed of the Radical followers of Ledru-Rollin. After three days' street-fighting, Cavaignac had cleared all Paris of the rebels except the Faubourg Saint-Antoine, where the workmen, sheltering behind an enormous barricade which sealed off the whole district, and with the active support of all the local inhabitants, held out for another twenty-four

---

reason, to believe that Louis Napoleon paid a secret visit to Paris in June 1848, as there is nothing in his letter to Sénard of 15 June to indicate that when he wrote it he knew about the debate in the Assembly on the evening of that day.

hours before Cavaignac stormed the barricade. By 26 June he could issue his order of the day: 'Order has triumphed over anarchy. Long live the Republic!'[20] He had lost more officers in the four days' fighting than had fallen in any of Napoleon's battles. On the day after the fighting stopped, the great gutter in the Rue Saint-Antoine still ran with blood.[21]

No one has been able to discover who were the leaders of the rebels during the June Days, and it seems that it was a spontaneous rising which was not instigated by any political organization. It was certainly not led by the Bonapartists. The *Times* correspondent reported that everybody had suddenly forgotten about Louis Napoleon, with the government forces crying 'Vive la République!' and the rebels 'Vive la République démocratique et sociale!' On the first day of the fighting, when the barricades went up, a revolutionary on the barricade at the Porte Saint-Denis had harangued his followers: 'If we are to fight, let it be in the name of the democratic republic, and not in that of a pretender.'[22] But the Moderate Republicans were convinced that Louis Napoleon and the Bonapartists had instigated and led the June revolt.

Louis Napoleon spent the evening of 21 June, when the Socialist workmen of Paris were assembling and launching the call for insurrection, at a ball in London given by the Marchioness of Ailesbury.[23] Among the guests was another Frenchman, the Comte Alexis de Vallon. He had a low opinion of Louis Napoleon. Two days later he wrote to Mérimée:

Alas! It suffices to see this common and notorious little gentleman to realize how vain are all the hopes that are placed in him. His stature is hardly suitable for the part that he is expected to play. Imagine a little man of four-and-a-half feet, ugly and vulgar, with large moustaches and the eyes of a pig! So much for his appearance. As for his morals, he lives openly, to the great scandal of English prudery, with a fifteenth-rate actress, very beautiful admittedly, named Miss Howard; this behaviour, which has slowly closed the doors of London high society to him, casts him out and pushes him into the world of low-class actors. People here strongly suspect that if fate should elevate him to some high position in France, he would lean on the Socialist Communist Party, perhaps even on the Red Republicans.

Vallon added that when he scrutinized Louis Napoleon at Lady Ailesbury's ball, 'I said to myself that it would only be necessary for this little pretender to run around the boulevard for an hour in his dark suit and his white cravat for his prestige to be lost for ever.'[24] Vallon was wrong on nearly every point.

The June Days left a great legacy of hatred. The Republican newspapers published stories of dreadful atrocities committed by the rebels during the fighting, of how secret Socialist sympathizers among the nurses in the hospitals tore off the bandages from the wounded government soldiers, and of Socialist women who had cut off the heads of wounded soldiers with kitchen knives and had gleefully washed their hands in the blood of their dead enemies. None of these stories was substantiated by the Committee of Inquiry which investigated the origin and course of the rising; nor did the investigators succeed in eliciting a statement from any of the participants that they had been paid to take part in the insurrection with Louis Napoleon's gold. This did not prevent Marrast, the Moderate Republican Mayor of Paris, from issuing a statement that the Bonapartists had purchased the arms which the rebels had used on the barricades, although for several weeks before the uprising the Republican press had been complaining that the men in the National Workshops were buying ammunition for their muskets with the wages which they received from the Workshops. In fact, most of them had acquired their weapons as members of the National Guard in the working-class districts of Paris.[25]

On 25 June the Assembly, following the practice of the ancient Romans when the republic was in danger, appointed Cavaignac to be Dictator and proclaimed the state of siege. Only the Socialist deputies opposed these resolutions in the Assembly; Prince Napoleon, Pierre Bonaparte and the other Bonapartist deputies kept silent in all the debates about the insurrection. Cavaignac's first act on taking office as Dictator was to suppress eleven newspapers, including Le Napoléon Républicain as well as the Socialist journals. His victory was followed by summary executions of the defeated workmen. Marrast, going out to congratulate Cavaignac's troops on their victory, arrived at the Rue Geoffroy Langevin just after the commander there had ordered sixty of the rebel prisoners to be summarily shot. The commander told Marrast not to worry, as he was sure that not more than five or six of the sixty were wholly innocent of any crime. Those of the rebels who survived the summary executions were held in terrible conditions in the barges on the Seine and in various prisons until they could be tried by court martial and sentenced to transportation to the penal settlements in the overseas territories. By the end of June, 15,000 were in prison, including some Bonapartist supporters.[26]

On 7 July the Assembly voted to extend the state of siege indefinitely, and Cavaignac's government, which consisted entirely of Moderate Republicans, placed drastic restrictions on the press and on political organizations. Newspapers were required to deposit a large sum of money as security for good behaviour, thus effectively preventing anyone who was not rich from publishing a newspaper. All the Bonapartist newspapers which had been launched at the beginning of June had ceased to appear by the end of the month, except *Le Petit Caporal*. It was made a criminal offence to attack the Republic, the Assembly, or 'the principle of property and the rights of the family'. Restrictions were placed on meetings of clubs, those revolutionary organizations which had played so important a part in 1789, 1830, and since February 1848. No club was allowed to meet in private; no women or males under twenty-one were to be allowed to attend meetings of a club, although hitherto women had played an active part in them; and the members of the clubs were not permitted to discuss any resolution which was against public order or which challenged 'the sacred rights of the family and of property'.[27]

The National Workshops were closed down completely. The statute fixing a maximum ten-hour day for factory workers, which had been enacted a week after the February revolution, was repealed, though the government reluctantly accepted an amendment fixing a maximum twelve-hour working day. At Cavaignac's request the Assembly suspended the Parliamentary immunity of Louis Blanc and Caussidière so that they could be prosecuted for their part in the demonstration of 15 May. They escaped to England. As soon as Louis Blanc arrived in London he received a visit from Louis Napoleon, who expressed his sympathy with Louis Blanc and with the French Socialists.[28]

Cavaignac was pitiless in the role of a modern Cato, the stern Republican who spared neither himself nor others in the service of the Republic. The defeated Socialists regarded him as a monster, and for Marxists his name is still today a byword for infamous cruelty. He was also disliked by many of his subordinate officers and by other people who had personal dealings with him, because of his rigidity, tactlessness and rudeness, and his refusal to temper Republican severity with any trace of human weakness. But he was for the moment the hero of the hour for the wealthy and middle classes, and for the Moderate Republican deputies who were the majority in the National Assembly.

Political observers believed in July 1848 that Louis Napoleon had suffered a serious setback through being associated in the public mind with the rebels of June. But as he lived his life in London society, and admired Jenny Lind in *La Sonnambula*,[29] his faith in his destiny was as strong as ever.* When a woman friend found him sitting on Brighton

*The entertaining story of Louis Napoleon's encounter in the summer of 1848 with the Irish journalist John Sherer – told at third hand by Peter Rayleigh in his *History of Ye Antient Society of Cogers* (pp. 137–44) – has been accepted by many of Louis

pier and commiserated with him on his political inactivity, he told her, if we may believe a story from a somewhat doubtful source,[30] that he had bet Princess Mathilde that he would be Emperor within four years. Most other observers believed that Cavaignac had stolen the part that Louis Napoleon had hoped to play of the strong man who would save France from anarchy; but Louis Napoleon told Lumley: 'That man is clearing the way for me.'[31]

At the end of August, Cavaignac eventually gave way to pressure in the National Assembly and ordered that by-elections should be held for eleven vacant seats in the Assembly, three of them being in Paris. Louis Napoleon allowed his name to be put forward as one of the candidates in Paris. The Moderate Republicans nominated three candidates for the three vacant seats, and the Socialists also put forward three candidates, one of them being Raspail, who was in prison at Vincennes. The Orleanists nominated the banker Achille Fould and Marshal Bugeaud, the old hero of the war in Algeria; and Émile de Girardin stood as an independent. The three Moderate Republicans, as supporters of Cavaignac, were strong favourites; but the result, which was declared on 21 September, was sensational. Louis Napoleon was top of the poll with 110,752 votes; Fould was second with 78,891; and Raspail third with 66,963. When the result was announced at the Hôtel de Ville, the National Guards sang the old Bonapartist song, 'Veillons au salut de l'empire', and the crowds cried 'Vive Napoléon! Vive l'Empereur!' But on the Bourse the funds fell by $1\frac{1}{4}$ per cent.[32]

As soon as the news reached London, Louis Napoleon hurriedly packed his bags and left King Street for Paris. When his landlord entered the premises next morning he found that the bed had not been made, and that the water had not been let out of Louis Napoleon's marble bath.[33]

Napoleon's biographers, but must sadly be rejected as an invention. The story tells how Sherer met Louis Napoleon at a debate in the Cogers Society in Bride Lane, and went home with him to Louis Napoleon's lodgings in a disused tobacconist's shop near Leicester Square; and how Louis Napoleon, fearing that their conversation would be overheard by his landlady's daughter, took Sherer to Berry's wineshop in St James's Street, where he asked Sherer to draft an appeal to insurrection, pretending that it was for use in Ireland, but really intending to distribute it in France. Sherer wrote several proclamations, and Louis Napoleon paid him £1 for them. In fact, Louis Napoleon did not live in lodgings near Leicester Square; he was not planning an insurrection in France in 1848; he would not have been so foolish as to pretend that he wished to foment insurrection in Ireland; and he did not need to pay an Irish journalist to draft his proclamations for him. The only germ of truth in the story is that Louis Napoleon undoubtedly frequented Berry's wineshop, where his weight was regularly recorded on Berry's scales; and he may perhaps have taken Sherer there once for a drink. Nor is there any truth in Sherer's story that Louis Napoleon's journey to Paris in 1848 was paid for by Palmerston.

CHAPTER 18

THE TENTH OF DECEMBER

O N 24 September 1848, Louis Napoleon arrived in Paris and took up residence at the Hôtel du Rhin in the Place Vendôme. The rumour spread through Paris that he was about to be arrested and that the government had ordered the troops to fire on any demonstrators who assembled to protest; but Cavaignac announced that while any disorders would be sternly repressed, he would not prevent Citizen Louis Napoleon Bonaparte, representative of the people, from taking his seat in the National Assembly. On 26 September, Louis Napoleon went to the temporary building which had been erected to house the Assembly in the courtyard of the Palais Bourbon, and took the oath as a deputy. He then made a short speech, in which he declared his loyalty to the Republic. It was received with silent hostility by the majority of the deputies.[1]

Louis Napoleon had none of the qualities which in the ordinary way were necessary for political success in the National Constituent Assembly of the Second French Republic. In that excitable and emotional body, where issues were decided not by party discipline and intrigue in the lobbies but by oratory on the floor of the chamber, the deputies were swayed from hour to hour by the speaker who could catch the President's eye at the right moment and sweep his fellow-deputies off their feet by the skilful use of the resonant voice, the histrionic gesture and the well-timed lie. Such tactics were repulsive and psychologically impossible for Louis Napoleon, and he was a complete failure in the Assembly. But it was not Parliamentary oratorical skill which impressed the people of France; it was the name 'Napoleon Bonaparte'.

Two days after Louis Napoleon arrived in Paris, he received a visit from Ledru-Rollin's friend, the Radical deputy Joly, and the Socialist leaders Proudhon and Schmelz. Proudhon had some qualms about going, but was reassured when Joly reminded him that Louis Blanc had met Louis Napoleon in London three weeks earlier. Louis Napoleon was charming; he criticized Cavaignac and the continuation of the state of siege, and told Proudhon that he did not believe the slanders that were being spread about the Socialists. But Proudhon was suspicious, and wrote in his diary:

26 September. Visited Louis Bonaparte. The man seems to be well-meaning – head and heart chivalrous; more obsessed with his uncle's glory than with any strong ambition; otherwise, moderate abilities. I doubt very much, once he is closely scrutinized and well-known, whether he will make much headway. Mem.: To mistrust him. Every pretender is in the habit of courting the party leaders.[2]

When Louis Napoleon took his seat in the Assembly, the deputies were engaged in framing the Constitution of the Republic, discussing a draft which had been submitted to them by a committee of eighteen members of the Assembly. After long discussion, the Assembly adopted a Constitution under which the head of state, the President of the Republic, was to be elected for four years and not to be eligible for re-election for a second term. He was to have a salary of 600,000 francs a year. He was to choose his ministers, who were declared to be 'responsible' to the Assembly without it being made clear whether or not they were expected to resign if defeated on a vote of confidence in the Assembly. He was to be commander-in-chief of the armed forces, but was not to take personal command of any military force. He was to have a right to veto the legislation passed by the Assembly, but could only exercise the veto with the consent of a Council of State elected by the Assembly. In case of misconduct he could be impeached before a special Constitutional Court appointed by the Cour de Cassation, the supreme court of appeal; this Constitutional Court could remove him from office. He was to submit to the Assembly a list of three names from whom the Assembly were to elect a Vice-President of the Republic who would exercise the presidential powers if the President died or was removed or was unfit to act. The Assembly was to consist of a single chamber of paid deputies elected by universal manhood suffrage for a term of three years; it could not be dissolved at an earlier date by the President. The Constitution could be changed by a three-fourths majority in the Assembly, but only in the last year of an Assembly's life.

But how was the President of the Republic to be elected? Republican logic insisted that it should be by a direct vote of the people by universal manhood suffrage; but after Louis Napoleon's electoral victory in September, there was a real possibility that if the President were elected by popular vote, Louis Napoleon might defeat the Republican hero, Cavaignac, especially as the total number of votes cast had fallen sharply in the by-elections in June and September as compared with the high proportion in the first elections in April. With a low poll and a large number of candidates, Louis Napoleon might get more votes than any other single candidate. Various proposals were put forward in the committee drafting the Constitution, and at the full meetings of the Assembly, to defeat Louis Napoleon. Marrast proposed in the committee that, though the President should be elected by popular vote, the electors' choice should be limited to choosing one of five candidates nominated by the Assembly. The committee rejected this suggestion, but they accepted a proposal that, if no candidate in the presidential election obtained an absolute majority over all the other candidates and at least two million votes, the election of the President should be transferred to the National Assembly. An amendment to increase this minimum from two million to three million votes was defeated on the grounds that this would mean in practice that no candidate could ever be elected by popular vote.[3]

On 5 October the Assembly debated a motion proposing that the President should be chosen by the Assembly itself and not by popular vote. This would have ensured that Cavaignac would be elected by the votes of his 500 Moderate Republican supporters in the Assembly; but Lamartine exerted all his eloquence to defeat the motion. His appeal was prompted not only by his devotion to the democratic principle of manhood suffrage, but also by the hope that he himself, and not Cavaignac, would be elected President if the issue was decided by a popular vote. He had been the hero of the revolution in February, but had lost his influence over the deputies, who held him responsible, by his weakness, for the June insurrection, when he had called in Cavaignac to get France out of the mess in which he had landed her. He did not realize that his stock had fallen just as sharply in the country as it had in the Assembly. But many of the deputies, despite their low opinion of him, were swayed by his appeal to principle, and the motion that the Assembly should elect the President was defeated by 602 votes against 211.[4]

On 9 October, the Radical deputy Antony Thouvet, an extreme left-wing member of Ledru-Rollin's group, proposed that no member of a family which had once reigned in France should be eligible to stand for President. There was great interest in the Chamber when Louis Napoleon, who had not addressed the Assembly since he took the oath a fortnight before, made his way to the rostrum. His speech was a complete failure. He made a very short statement, in halting tones with one or two long pauses, in which he said that he did not rise to oppose the motion but only to declare that he was a loyal citizen of the Republic, not a pretender to a throne. Then, to everyone's surprise and to the consternation of his supporters, he left the rostrum and resumed his seat. Thouvet rose and stated, amid general laughter, that in view of the speech which they had just heard he would withdraw his motion, as it was clear that there was no possibility that Louis Napoleon could ever constitute a danger to the Republic or win any election. Louis Napoleon sat motionless in his place as the mocking laughter spread through the Chamber. Thiers said to a colleague that Louis Napoleon was obviously a cretin.[5]

Next day the press wrote in the same vein. *Le National*, the chief organ of the Moderate Republicans, ridiculed Louis Napoleon's 'laborious address', and made the allegation, which was often repeated in later years, that he had spoken with a foreign accent. 'We are forced to translate,' they wrote, 'as it was not exactly in French that he expressed himself.'*[6] The talk went around the corridors of the Assembly and the dinner tables in Parisian society that Louis Napoleon was just a joke; but the *Times* correspondent thought that they were laughing to hide their anxiety, and that it was almost certain that Louis Napoleon would be elected President by a popular vote. 'In the Assembly', wrote *The Times*, 'Louis Bonaparte would probably not obtain thirty votes for the Presidency – in the country he may have millions.'[7]

On 25 October, the Radical deputy Clement Thomas attacked Louis Napoleon in the Assembly as a pretender who threatened the Republic. When Prince Napoleon rose to defend his cousin, there were ironical shouts of 'Not you!', 'Louis!', 'The other one!' Louis Napoleon felt obliged to go to the rostrum next day. He made a very short statement, saying that although he had been criticized for not speaking more frequently in the Assembly, there were other ways of serving the Republic than by making speeches, and that he did not intend to address the Assembly unless he had something important to say. He then announced, very briefly, that he would be standing as a candidate in the forthcoming presidential elections.[8]

The date of the election was fixed for Sunday and Monday, 10 and 11 December, after a motion to postpone it until May had been defeated; but on 3 November Thouvet made a last attempt to prevent Louis Napoleon's election when he again brought forward his motion to exclude members of the Bonaparte family. Cavaignac himself spoke against it, saying that he would have supported it six months ago, but that it was no longer possible to exclude Louis Napoleon; and the

---

*The story that Louis Napoleon could not speak French properly because he had been educated at a school in Germany was often repeated in later years; it was even said that he could not pronounce the name 'Eugénie' properly, and called his wife 'Oogenie' – an absurd story, as no German has any difficulty in pronouncing the word 'Eugénie' in the French manner, the German sound 'ö' being the same as the French 'eu'.

proposal was heavily defeated. Next day the Constitution was adopted in the Assembly by 739 votes against 30, with only Ledru-Rollin and the Radicals voting against it.[9]

Five candidates stood in the presidential election – Louis Napoleon, Cavaignac, Lamartine, Ledru-Rollin and Raspail, who was still in prison in Vincennes awaiting trial for his part in the demonstration of 15 May. Few observers believed that Lamartine would take many votes from Cavaignac. Ledru-Rollin, after supporting the government during the June insurrection, had turned against Cavaignac, indignant at the Dictator's ruthless punishment of the rebels and at the suppression of freedom under the state of siege. In November he founded a new party, named 'the Mountain' after the party of Danton and Robespierre of 1793, and put forward the slogan: 'The Democratic and Social Republic'. But the Socialists had not forgiven him for his attitude during the June Days; Raspail condemned him as a 'last-minute Socialist' and refused to collaborate with him in any way.[10]

Two important right-wing parties did not put up a candidate, because neither the Legitimists nor the Orleanists were willing to identify themselves with the Republic by contesting the presidency. The Legitimist pretender, Henri V, was in exile, and in their leader's absence the Legitimists had become a party of extreme right-wing Catholics, fighting to uphold the liberties and privileges of the Catholic Church in education and other fields. The Orleanists had formed a new political party, the Party of Order. They had reluctantly accepted the Republic, though they much preferred a constitutional monarchy; and they had unsuccessfully opposed the creation of a Democratic Republic with universal suffrage.

The dominating figure in the Party of Order was Louis Adolphe Thiers. He was born in Marseilles in 1797, the son of a locksmith of moderate means – not, as he made out, of a wealthy cloth-merchant who had been ruined by the Revolution. Thiers became first a barrister and then a successful journalist, and achieved fame before he was thirty by writing a *History of the Revolution*, which he later followed with his *History of the Consulate and Empire*. He entered the Chamber of Deputies after the Revolution of 1830 and became Foreign Minister and Prime Minister under Louis Philippe. He was only five feet in height, and very short-sighted, but his ungainly appearance, which was a target for the wits and cartoonists, helped to make him a well-known public figure. His sarcastic wit won him a reputation in the Chamber of Deputies, but made him many enemies. Although he was in many ways a shrewd politician, his extreme conceit sometimes led him to make serious political blunders, and caused him to misjudge the situation in the autumn of 1848.

Thiers feared and hated 'the mob' and revolutionary Radicals, and he was very alarmed at the menace of Ledru-Rollin. He was also very suspicious of Cavaignac. He had approved of Cavaignac's action against the Socialists in June, but he did not trust him to show equal determination against Ledru-Rollin and the revolutionary Radicals; he said that if you were to unbutton Cavaignac, you would find him Red underneath. On the other hand, he had nothing but contempt for Louis Napoleon and was convinced that he could manage 'the cretin'. He consulted with his colleagues on the possibility of supporting Louis Napoleon against Cavaignac in the presidential election. Later he was to claim that his friend Molé – who as Louis Philippe's Prime Minister had demanded the expulsion of Louis Napoleon from Switzerland in 1838 – had persuaded him against his better judgement to support Louis Napoleon in the presidential election; but Thiers himself was convinced in the autumn of 1848 that the cretin Louis Napoleon was less dangerous than Cavaignac the concealed Red. He believed that he could handle Louis Napoleon, and told a friend: 'We will give him women and we will lead him.'[11]

As soon as it was finally decided that the President was to be elected by popular vote, Louis Napoleon was the favourite to win. His electoral triumph in September had converted him overnight from a despised outsider to the almost certain victor in the presidential election, and the funds on the Bourse fell steadily at the prospect of his victory. The business men were disturbed by Louis Napoleon's flirtation with the Socialists, and also feared that, if he were elected, Ledru-Rollin's Radicals would immediately launch an insurrection.[12] It was important to Louis Napoleon to reassure the middle classes, and there was no better way of doing this than by gaining the support of Thiers and the Party of Order. Twenty years later, Persigny described the political strategy which Louis Napoleon had adopted in 1848. First he would win the support of the masses, including the Socialists and the revolutionary workers; next, he would gain the support of the Conservative bourgeoisie by persuading them that he could control the masses and could be relied upon to protect law, order and property. If he failed to win the support of the bourgeoisie, he would lead the masses in an attack on them and bully them into obedience.[13]

The supporters of Louis Napoleon, Cavaignac and Ledru-Rollin all held a number of public meetings in Paris. Ledru-Rollin spoke at several Radical banquets, under the close supervision of the police, and at a great demonstration of 100,000 supporters in the Champs-Élysées; but neither Louis Napoleon, with his lack of oratorical talent, nor Cavaignac, with his Olympian aloofness as ruler of France, wished to address large public rallies. The Bonapartists held four large public

meetings in the Paris area, one of which was broken up by the Socialists; but Louis Napoleon himself did not appear at any of these
meetings. Nor did Cavaignac attend the only large rally held by his
supporters at the Manège Fitte in the Chaussée d'Antin, which was a
quiet and sober affair compared with the enthusiasm shown by the
Bonapartists at the Salle Valentine.[14]

The campaign was also conducted through the press, and by
placards billposted in the streets. Louis Napoleon engaged in a good
deal of canvassing, being taken by Persigny and his other prominent
supporters to ride through Paris on horseback, to greet the crowds in
the streets and the soldiers in the barracks. This ability to fraternize
with the people cannot have come easily to Louis Napoleon, who still
preserved his usual silent reserve in society. When Victor Hugo dined
with him at an Orleanist dinner-party at Madame Odilon Barrot's at
the height of the presidential election campaign, he noted that Louis
Napoleon 'ate little, spoke little, laughed little', although it was a very
gay party. At the dinner table, Louis Napoleon sat next to Rémusat,
who as Minister of the Interior had set agents to spy on him in London
at the time of the Boulogne expedition.[15]

Both Émile de Girardin, who detested Cavaignac, and Victor Hugo
promised Louis Napoleon their support. Victor Hugo told him that he
had been a candidate for the presidency ever since Austerlitz – a distinct
exaggeration, since the battle had been fought two-and-a-half years
before Louis Napoleon's birth.[16]

Louis Napoleon periodically attended meetings of his active
supporters and canvassers in order to encourage them by his presence.
A reporter from *Le National* managed to get into one of these meetings,
and wrote a sarcastic account of it in the paper: 'When he appears
among his friends he sends on ahead a *chasseur* in grand livery, who
announces his entry with the solemn words: "The Prince!" At once the
ladies rise, and form a double line from the door to the chimney. The
Prince, one hand behind his back and the other in his waistcoat, in
imitation of his uncle, advances, distributing salutations and smiles to
his court.'[17]

The highlight of his campaign was the daily demonstration outside
his hotel in the Place Vendôme, at 1 p.m., when he drove out from the
Hôtel du Rhin to go to the National Assembly, which remained in
session throughout the election campaign. The crowds grew larger as
the campaign progressed, and by the end of November there were
nearly 4000 people outside the hotel every day; they included men and
women of all classes, but most were from the lower class. Ferrière, who
met many of them during the election campaign, wrote that they were
ex-servicemen who had fought in Africa, discharged domestic servants

with Legitimist sympathies, unemployed artisans, small shopkeepers on the verge of bankruptcy, and discontented Radicals who were attracted by what they believed was Louis Napoleon's Socialism. They cheered Louis Napoleon and sang the Bonapartist song 'Nous l'aurons, nous l'aurons, Louis Napoléon!' to the tune of the popular song, 'Les Lampions'. Occasionally someone in the crowd shouted 'Vive Ledru-Rollin! Vive la République démocratique et sociale!'; but a man who cried out 'Down with the pretenders!' was manhandled by Louis Napoleon's supporters, egged on by indignant Bonapartist women. When Louis Napoleon drove out in his carriage with the Bonapartist deputy Larabit, the crowds were so thick that the horses could not reach the Rue Castiglione and had to go round the Colonne Vendôme and gain access to the street on the other side of the square. Louis Napoleon bowed gracefully to the crowd and drove off amid wild cheering.[18]

On Sunday 12 November, the Constitution was solemnly proclaimed at a public ceremony on the Place de la Concorde at which the Archbishop of Paris celebrated Mass and the army and National Guard paraded in front of Cavaignac, who officiated as the head of the government. Although there was a heavy fall of snow during the proceedings, the soldiers and the crowd cheered Cavaignac, and in the next few days the political commentators thought that his chances of success in the election had slightly increased. The funds rose a little on the Bourse. The Bonapartists complained that the officers had promised the soldiers a double ration of rum if they cried 'Vive Cavaignac!' during the parade.[19]

Louis Napoleon's supporters considered that they were fighting the election at a disadvantage. Cavaignac was supported by 190 newspapers throughout France, Louis Napoleon by 103, and Ledru-Rollin by 48; and Cavaignac did not hesitate to use the advantage which he held as head of the government. The civil servants and government employees were in many cases given to understand, by their superiors, that they were expected to vote for Cavaignac. The official army newspaper, the *Moniteur de l'Armée*, supported Cavaignac, and the Minister of War ordered army officers to ensure that copies of the paper were widely distributed throughout the camps and barracks.[20]

The two main candidates, Cavaignac and Louis Napoleon, were both subjected to violent personal attacks in the hostile press. The Socialist and Radical newspapers, and Émile de Girardin in *La Presse*, taking advantage of the ending of the state of siege on 19 October, attacked 'butcher Cavaignac', 'Cavaignac, Prince of the Blood'. The supporters of Cavaignac and Ledru-Rollin attacked Louis Napoleon as a pretender to the imperial throne, a 'Lilliputian Caesar,' a playboy,

226

the laughing-stock of Strasburg and Boulogne. They reminded the Catholics and the Conservatives that Louis Napoleon had once advocated Socialist measures, and that his cousin Carlo Bonaparte was one of the leaders of the Red revolutionaries in Italy. They reminded the Socialists and Radicals that Louis Napoleon had lived in high society in England, had squandered money on the Eglinton tournament, and had enrolled as a special constable against the Chartists. They reminded all the electors that he had lived nearly all his life abroad. The *Moniteur de l'Armée*, writing for the soldiers and ex-servicemen, the group to which Louis Napoleon specially hoped to appeal as a Bonaparte, contrasted the glorious achievements of General Cavaignac in the French army in North Africa and in the bloody street-fighting in Paris with the military record of Citizen Bonaparte, captain in the Swiss army and special constable in England, whose only active service had been to fire one pistol-shot by mistake at Boulogne and to brandish a truncheon at democratic demonstrators in London.[21]

The attitude of the Party of Order was vital for Louis Napoleon. Thiers first approached Cavaignac and offered him the support of the Party of Order on conditions – if he would maintain, as a permanent measure, the legislation restricting the freedom of the clubs; would keep an army of 50,000 men in Paris, ready to suppress any attempt at insurrection; and would refuse to support the revolutionary Radicals in Germany and Italy. Cavaignac as usual adopted a somewhat haughty tone towards the Orleanists; he stated that while he intended to pursue the course of action which Thiers suggested, he would not give any electoral pledge as to what his government would do.[22]

Unlike Cavaignac, Louis Napoleon was very eager to win the support of the Party of Order. He visited Thiers three times at the party's headquarters in the Rue de Poitiers, and not only offered to give the pledges which Thiers had demanded from Cavaignac, but also promised, if elected President, to appoint a government composed of a majority of ministers from the Party of Order. Thiers was far from satisfied. When Louis Napoleon showed him the draft of his election manifesto, he rejected it as unacceptable to the Party of Order; he complained to his friends that the manifesto contained too much Socialism and bad French, and he lectured Louis Napoleon at length on the art of politics. He wrote out a new draft for Louis Napoleon to adopt, and gave him advice about his dress and personal appearance, urging him not to wear uniforms or too stylish clothes if he were elected President, and to shave off his moustache and his little imperial beard. Louis Napoleon listened quietly and meekly to Thiers's strictures, and Thiers told his friends that Louis Napoleon was unbelievably weak and stupid.[23] But in his usual quiet, obstinate way, Louis Napoleon did not budge. He did not shave off his moustache and beard, and he did not adopt Thiers's manifesto.

Instead, on 28 November – only twelve days before polling day – he published an election manifesto which was much shorter than Thiers's draft, and which did not please the Party of Order. It offered something to all classes and parties. If elected, he would seek to reduce taxation; he would increase the pay of the officers and men of the armed services; he would build homes for elderly workers. It was necessary 'to lessen, not to increase' the burden of compulsory military service – a statement designed above all for the peasants, who resented conscription because it interfered with work on the farm. He promised to protect religion and the family by ensuring freedom of worship and of religious education; he promised to protect private property, which was the necessary foundation of civil liberty. He would enact 'industrial laws', not in order to 'ruin the rich to the profit of the poor', but to 'base the well-being of everyone on the prosperity of all'. He threw out hints, but made no definite promises, on the controversial subject of an amnesty for the imprisoned rebels of the June Days, which was being demanded by Ledru-Rollin and strenuously resisted by both Cavaignac and Thiers: 'I, who have known exile and captivity, pray fervently for the coming of the day when the country can without danger end all proscriptions and erase the last traces of our civil disorders.' He declared that he did not dream of empire or war, and promised that at the end of his four-year term of office he would hand over a peaceful France to his successor.[24]

A fortnight before the election an unfortunate complication arose for Louis Napoleon. In Rome, Pope Pius IX had begun his pontificate determined to modify the reactionary repressive policy of his predecessor Gregory XVI and to grant his subjects in the Papal States some kind of constitutional and representative government; but this was not enough to satisfy the revolutionary Radicals in Rome. On 15 November, the Pope's moderate Conservative Prime Minister, Count Rossi, was stabbed to death by a revolutionary as he entered the Capitol, and a few days later the people stormed the Papal palace and lynched a priest who was said to have fired on the mob. On the night of 24 November the Pope escaped from Rome and took refuge at Gaeta in the King of Naples' territory. From there he issued an appeal to all the Catholic states of Europe to come to his rescue, restore him to authority, and suppress the revolution in Rome. One of the leaders of the revolution was Carlo Bonaparte, who had come to Rome after playing a prominent part in overthrowing the government of the Grand Duke of Tuscany in Florence.

On 28 November, Cavaignac announced in the Assembly that in

response to the Pope's appeal he was sending a naval squadron to Civitavecchia and holding 3500 troops at Toulon and Marseilles in readiness to intervene to protect the Holy Father. Cavaignac was not a particularly zealous Catholic, but he was eager to suppress the revolutionaries in Rome, who were being denounced in the press throughout Europe, even in Britain, as 'Red Republicans', 'Socialists' and 'Anarchists'. His action was applauded by the Legitimists and other Catholic groups in France, especially by the Comte de Montalembert, one of the leaders of the Party of Order. Montalembert had begun his political life as a Catholic rebel against the tyranny of Gregory XVI, but he had moved from Liberal Catholicism, not, like his brother-in-arms Lamennais, to Radical agnosticism, but to his own brand of reactionary Catholic orthodoxy. Ledru-Rollin and the Radicals strongly denounced Cavaignac's threat of intervention in Rome as a shameful attack on the freedom of the Roman people and a violation of the newly adopted Constitution of the French Republic, which stipulated that France would never suppress the liberty of foreign nations.

This put Louis Napoleon in a predicament. With his cousin Carlo leading the revolution in Rome and his principal opponent for the presidency offering himself as the Papal champion, it would be difficult for him to avoid offending either the Socialist and Radical, or the Conservative and Catholic, electors. Nor could he entirely forget the old sympathies which he had felt for Italian Liberalism in the days when he and his brother had fought in the ranks of the Roman revolutionaries against Papal rule. He took no part in the debate in the Assembly on the expedition to Civitavecchia, but when the Assembly voted by 480 votes against 63 to support Cavaignac's policy of intervention, he abstained from voting.

His friends and allies, and the political commentators, considered that he had committed a blunder. Although he had begun his election campaign as a favourite of the Socialists and Radicals, he was now relying much more on the support of the Party of Order and on the votes of the mass of the Catholic peasants. The Moderate Republicans hastened to inform the electorate that he was Carlo Bonaparte's cousin and that he had not voted in favour of the expedition to save the Pope.[25] On 2 December, Louis Napoleon wrote a short letter to *Le Constitutionnel*, which was published in the paper on 4 December, less than a week before polling day:

Sir, Having heard that there have been comments about my abstention from voting on the expedition to Civita Vecchia, I think it my duty to declare that while I am determined to support all measures which are likely to guarantee effectively the liberty and the authority of the Sovereign Pontiff, I could not by my vote approve of a military demonstration which seemed to me to be dangerous even for the sacred interests which it was designed to protect and of a nature likely to compromise the peace of Europe. I am, Sir, etc., Louis Napoleon Bonaparte.

He also wrote to the Papal Nuncio in France and told him that he had disapproved of Carlo Bonaparte's activities for a long time.[26]

Some commentators believed that his letter in *Le Constitutionnel*, by offending both the Catholics and the Socialists, had made matters worse; but perhaps the complication caused by the events in Rome came too late in the campaign to influence it. At all events, it did not alienate the Catholic and Conservative leaders. On 3 December, Thiers wrote a letter which was published in the *Echo Rochelais* of La Rochelle, in which he declared that the Party of Order was not wholly satisfied with any of the candidates, but nevertheless called on its supporters to vote for Louis Napoleon as the lesser evil. Marshal Bugeaud, who before becoming a Marshal of Louis Philippe had been a subaltern under Napoleon, also wrote a letter to the press in support of Louis Napoleon. So did General Changarnier, who sat in the Assembly as a Legitimist deputy, and his colleague General Oudinot, whom Cavaignac had just appointed Commander-in-Chief of the projected expedition to Civitavecchia. A hundred and fifty leaders of the Catholic Legitimists called on their followers to vote for Louis Napoleon.[27]

But the prophets were now foretelling that Cavaignac was cutting down Louis Napoleon's lead in the final stages of the race. Louis Napoleon's campaign seemed to be petering out. His supporters held their last public meeting in Paris on 29 November, eleven days before polling day. This was said to be because they had run out of money, for they had not been able to run this election on the cheap, relying only on billposting, as they had done in the by-elections for the Assembly in June. Cavaignac's supporters took comfort from the fact that even if Louis Napoleon got the largest number of votes, he would not obtain an absolute majority over all the other candidates or the minimum number of 2 million votes, with the result that the decision would be referred to the Assembly, where Cavaignac would be certain to win. While officially they were claiming that Cavaignac would top the poll, they leaked their canvass figures to the press; the total number of voters would be 3,600,000, and even if Louis Napoleon managed to obtain more than half this number, he would certainly fall short of 2 million, which meant victory for Cavaignac in the Assembly. At this news, prices rose on the Bourse; but a spokesman for Louis Napoleon claimed that 6 million electors would vote, and that 4 million of them would vote for Louis Napoleon. Many business men sent their agents orders to buy if Cavaignac won, but to cancel the orders if Louis Napoleon won.[28]

In cold, damp weather polling began on Sunday 10 December, and continued on the Monday. There was no disorder as the electors went in large numbers to the polling stations at the town halls, taking the candidates' polling cards from the party workers at the doors. The journalists wondered whether there was any significance in the fact that Cavaignac's polling cards, with his picture on them, littered the wet and dirty streets of Paris, where they were trampled underfoot by the passers-by; and they wondered what was happening in the country, where the peasants, who had no political party and no newspapers to voice their feelings, were numerous enough to win the election for any candidate for whom they voted in strength, even if he had no other support.[29]

The first results were known by 12 December, and the final figures a few days later. They exceeded the Bonapartists' most optimistic forecasts. Louis Napoleon received 5,434,226 votes; Cavaignac 1,448,107; Ledru-Rollin 370,119; Raspail 36,329; Lamartine 17,910. General Changarnier, who had not offered himself as a candidate and had supported Louis Napoleon, received 4790 votes, and 12,600 were cast for a multitude of other candidates.[30]

Louis Napoleon had received about 75 per cent of the votes cast, and over 60 per cent of the total electorate had voted for him. He had an absolute majority in 62 of the 85 departments of France, and came top of the poll in all except four, winning every *arrondissement* in Paris as well as the rural areas, where the peasants had voted for him in great strength. Only in the departments of Finistère and Morbihan in Brittany, and the Bouches-du-Rhône and Var in Provence, had he been defeated; in these traditional Legitimist strongholds the electors, defying the advice of the Legitimist leaders, had voted for Cavaignac. Thirty-three years after Waterloo, twelve years after Strasburg, eight years after Boulogne, a Bonaparte was the head of state in France.

PART IV

THE PRINCE-PRESIDENT

CHAPTER 19

THE ÉLYSÉE

As soon as he knew that he had been elected President, Louis Napoleon invited Thiers to be his Prime Minister. Thiers refused; he was too good an Orleanist to wish to take office under the Republic, and preferred to be the power behind the scenes. At Thiers's suggestion, Louis Napoleon chose Thiers's colleague in the Party of Order, Odilon Barrot, as Prime Minister;[1] Barrot's brother Ferdinand was a Bonapartist who had been chief counsel for the defence at the trial in 1837 of Louis Napoleon's followers after the Strasburg *coup*. Most of the Cabinet were politicians of the Party of Order; but Louis Napoleon went even further to the Right in appointing the Legitimist Comte de Falloux as Minister of Education. This appointment infuriated the Radicals, because Falloux had played the leading part in the Catholic campaign to secure control of education, and was denounced as a Jesuit by the Left. Louis Napoleon appointed another Legitimist, General Changarnier, as Chief of the National Guard in Paris, where he would have the duty of crushing any insurrection which might be started by Ledru-Rollin's defeated Radicals.

On 20 December, Louis Napoleon was inaugurated as President of the Republic. He appeared in the National Assembly dressed in the simple black suit, with the Legion of Honour, that he had worn at his trial in 1840. Marrast, as President of the Assembly, announced that Citizen Charles Louis Napoleon Bonaparte, born in Paris, was qualified to be, and had been duly elected, President of the Republic. Louis Napoleon took the oath of loyalty to the Constitution and made a short speech, stressing his loyalty to the Republic, and paying tribute to Cavaignac's services while head of the government. On leaving the rostrum he went up to Cavaignac and shook his hand before walking out of the Chamber with Odilon Barrot and Changarnier and a group of leading deputies of the Party of Order. Cavaignac had been taken by surprise by Louis Napoleon's gesture of reconciliation. When Louis Napoleon offered him his hand, he did not rise from his seat and only half-extended his hand, so that Louis Napoleon only shook one or two of his fingers. Some observers reported that he had refused to shake hands with Louis Napoleon; but Cavaignac, regretting his hesitation, called at the Élysée Palace that afternoon and left his card.[2] Louis Napoleon had taken up his residence at the Élysée, although there had been rumours that he would move into the Tuileries, the royal palace where the Bourbon Kings, Napoleon and Louis Philippe had lived.

Louis Napoleon did not appoint any of his Bonapartist supporters as members of the Cabinet, but they filled the offices of his presidential household at the Élysée. He had Persigny, Laity, Vaudrey, Fleury and Edgar Ney, the son of Napoleon's Marshal, among his A.D.C.s and equerries. Mocquard, who had been a close friend of his mother – the scandalmongers said that he was Hortense's lover – was his political secretary; and his distant cousin Count Félix Bacciochi, a relative of Elisa Bonaparte's husband, was his social secretary.

He completely forgave King Jerome and Princess Mathilde for their behaviour after the Strasburg *coup*. He appointed Jerome to be Governor of the Invalides, and chose Mathilde to act as his hostess at all the receptions and balls at the Élysée. According to Mathilde, he asked her to marry him soon after he became President of the Republic, but she refused him. It is surprising that so obstinate and proud a man as Louis Napoleon could have proposed a second time to the girl who had jilted him in 1837 and whom he had sworn he would never marry; and it is even more surprising that he should have been prepared to compromise himself in the eyes of his followers and of the Church hierarchy by marrying the divorced wife of a Russian nobleman. But everyone who met Mathilde at this time agreed that, at thirty, she was very handsome; and Louis Napoleon showed on other occasions that he was prepared to act rashly when a beautiful woman whom he desired refused to become his mistress.

Louis Napoleon now made the acquaintance of his half-brother, the Comte de Morny, the illegitimate son of Queen Hortense and the Comte de Flahault. According to Émile Ollivier and other writers, Louis Napoleon knew nothing of Morny's existence during Hortense's lifetime, although her ladies often gossiped about her love-affair with Flahault and her illegitimate baby. He first learned the truth when one of Hortense's ladies handed him a letter from Hortense to Morny after Hortense's death, and he burst into tears at this revelation of his venerated mother's infidelity.[3] Morny, although officially the son of a Prussian officer and his Creole wife, was pushed to the front by his father Flahault, who was a peer of France under Louis Philippe; and after distinguished military service in North Africa he was created a Count with the title of Comte de Morny. He became a business man, speculating in beet-sugar, and made a fortune with the help of his mistress, the Comtesse Le Hon, the wife of the Belgian Ambassador in Paris.

He was a loyal supporter of Louis Philippe until the February revolution, but during the presidential election of 1848 he supported Louis Napoleon. The half-brothers met for the first time, and became friends. There was occasional friction when Morny tried to boast of his relationship with Louis Napoleon; but after Fleury had warned him not to do this, he accepted the role of the President's confidential adviser, and became second only to Persigny in influence.[4] Persigny and Morny were always urging Louis Napoleon to adopt a daring policy, and to overcome his scruples about resorting to illegality and trickery.

At the Cabinet meetings the President of the Republic, without any of his Bonapartist supporters, sat alone among the Orleanists and Falloux, listening to the ministers' speeches and saying nothing; but there were signs that he might prove to be more difficult than Thiers had expected. At the first Cabinet meeting on 23 December, when the majority of the ministers proposed that the troops at Marseilles and Toulon should be sent to Civitavecchia, he refused to agree to any armed intervention in the Papal States. He was in favour of granting an amnesty to the June rebels, and when the Cabinet unanimously rejected the suggestion he used his prerogative of pardon to order the release of sixty-three women who were being held without trial in the Saint-Lazare prison in Paris for their part in the June Days.[5] 'It was with the utmost difficulty', said Thiers to Nassau Senior, 'that we could prevent his granting indiscriminate amnesties to the most ferocious' of the Socialist rebels.[6]

He became involved in an altercation with the Minister of the Interior, Malleville, within a week of taking office. He asked to see the confidential documents of the Ministry of the Interior of 1836 and 1840 dealing with his attempted *coups* at Strasburg and Boulogne – perhaps in order to discover the identity of the government's spy in his household in London. Malleville said that it would be constitutionally improper for him to see these papers of a previous administration; and when Louis Napoleon insisted on seeing them, Malleville resigned. The Cabinet backed Malleville unanimously. Louis Napoleon climbed down, admitted that he had been wrong to ask to see the papers, and requested Malleville to withdraw his resignation.[7] Malleville insisted on resigning, but Louis Napoleon appointed Faucher, another member of the Party of Order, to succeed him, and Thiers and the ministers were satisfied that there would be no further trouble from the President.

The President did not follow Thiers's advice to dress in sombre civilian clothes; he usually wore the uniform of a general of the National Guard. Thiers and the Conservatives did not like this, but they were pleased that he was becoming so popular with Parisians of all classes, because his personal popularity made things much easier for the government of the Party of Order. Louis Napoleon had made a very favourable impression at his inauguration parade on 24 December, when he reviewed the troops and the National Guard in his National Guard uniform on a spirited stallion that he had brought with him from England, in the presence of King Jerome, Princess Mathilde, and a great crowd of spectators. He appeared in public on horseback whenever possible, because then his short legs and rather ungainly walk were not noticed, and his equestrian skill was much in evidence.[8]

Nor did it do him any harm with the majority of Frenchmen when it became generally known that he had brought the lovely Miss Howard with him from England and had established her discreetly in a house in the Rue du Cirque near the Élysée Palace. People said that the President could not be the cretin that Thiers and the politicians thought him to be if he had succeeded in acquiring such a beautiful horse and such a beautiful mistress in England.[9] Miss Howard was only twenty-six, but she had travelled far from her father's cobbler's shop in Brighton; after Jem Mason the jockey in the stables at Cambridge and Major Martyn of the Guards in St John's Wood, she now had the President of France within a stone's throw of the Élysée.

Thiers had said that he would give the President women, and lead him. The President had found the women for himself, and spent more time with them than in dealing with affairs of state. This suited Thiers very well. His colleague Lanjuinais, who was Minister of Agriculture in Odilon Barrot's government for five months in 1849, afterwards told the English economist, Nassau Senior, that Louis Napoleon was very lazy, and disliked the drudgery of government and reading dispatches. He rose at 10 a.m., and spent two hours dressing and having breakfast before working for an hour on the state papers. At 1 or 1.30 p.m. he would preside at a Cabinet meeting which normally finished at about 3 p.m., and then went out, driving in an open carriage to the Rond Point des Champs-Élysées. Here he would meet Miss Howard, who had come in another carriage from her house in the Rue du Cirque, and the two of them would spend about two hours riding in the Bois de Boulogne. They often dropped in, after their ride, to have a glass of rum at the pavilion café in the Bois, before riding back to the Rond Point and returning to their homes in their carriages. Louis Napoleon then had dinner, and did no more work that day; if he was not attending some reception, he would spend the evening at Miss Howard's house, or at a private supper party with some other lady.[10]

These accounts of the President's daily routine, given by the unenthusiastic Lanjuinais and the hostile Victor Hugo, entirely omit the many occasions when Louis Napoleon had important political

Miss Howard in 1850

Hortense Cornu

General Cavaignac in 1857

Morny in 1858

Persigny

Marshal de Saint-Arnaud

discussions with ambassadors, generals and politicians, and do not tell the full story of his daily activities; but undoubtedly he thought that his chief duty was not to work in his study but to be seen in public and to make social contacts. He did not possess the ability of Louis XIV and Frederick the Great to give concentrated attention to dispatches and detailed work of government.

The Socialists who had voted for Louis Napoleon, against the advice of their leaders, had placed in power a President who appeared to be completely in the pocket of the Conservatives. Faucher ordered the police to harass the Socialist and Radical clubs and the banquets which were held in the working-class districts of Paris for men and women paying 1 fr. 25 c. – about half the daily wage of the lowest-paid worker. The diners toasted the Democratic and Social Republic, the imprisoned Barbès and Raspail, and Mazzini and the revolutionaries in Rome; they listened to speeches from their leaders, from fraternal delegates from Radical and Socialist organizations in Germany, and from women speakers who demanded sex equality and the right of women to vote and sit in the National Assembly. The police usually came to the banquets and demanded admission under the powers granted to them by the Assembly in July 1848; when the organizers refused to admit them, the police forced their way in, and the organizers immediately abandoned the banquet.[11]

But while the government was preparing an onslaught on the Radicals and Socialists, Louis Napoleon entered into secret contacts with them. Thiers afterwards said that he carried on negotiations with them behind his government's back during the whole of his term as President.[12] The go-between was the Swiss Radical, James Fazy, who had been a friend of Louis Napoleon when they were both young men in Switzerland and since then had led a successful revolution in Geneva and established a Radical government in the canton. In January 1849, Louis Napoleon asked Fazy to invite two hundred leading Radicals and Socialists, including their deputies in the Assembly, to meet him in the Élysée. Only thirty of them came, and they showed no inclination to respond to his advances.[13] He was in fact offering them an agreement under which they were to keep quiet and acquiesce in the rule of a Conservative government, in return for his protection against persecution and a possible alliance with them against the Conservatives at some time in the future. But they were not prepared to collaborate in any way with him.

He also came into conflict with the Moderate Republican majority in the National Assembly. In the Constitution which they had drafted, the deputies had provided for the election of a new Legislative Assembly; but they were now reluctant to dissolve themselves and fix a date for the election to be held, and rejected a proposal of the Party of Order that the Assembly should be dissolved on 19 March 1849.

The government struck on 24 January. On that day the police suppressed three Radical clubs in Paris, and Changarnier issued an order disbanding thirteen regiments of the Garde Mobile – a force composed largely of small shopkeepers and artisans who had fought valiantly against the Socialists during the June Days, but most of whom were Radicals in politics and followers of Ledru-Rollin. A delegation of four officers of the Garde Mobile called on Changarnier to protest against his order. One of them was Lieutenant Aladenize, Louis Napoleon's comrade at Boulogne. When Changarnier refused to withdraw the order, Aladenize threatened him with an insurrection of the Garde Mobile, and Changarnier immediately arrested him. A larger delegation from the Garde Mobile then went to the Élysée to protest to Louis Napoleon. He was coolly courteous, but firmly refused to overrule Changarnier's order.[14]

On Saturday 27 January, Ledru-Rollin moved the impeachment of Faucher and Changarnier in the Assembly. The Assembly defeated the motion, but also defeated a government bill for the suppression of all clubs. On the same day, Proudhon published a strong attack on Louis Napoleon in his paper Le Peuple:

> Louis Bonaparte has raised the question of the dissolution of the Assembly; next Monday the Assembly will raise the question of the dismissal of the President. . . . On Monday a decisive battle will be joined between the Revolution and the Counter-Revolution, between the Revolution represented by the National Assembly and the Counter-Revolution represented by Louis Bonaparte.[15]

That evening, Changarnier called at the Élysée and urged Louis Napoleon to permit him to send troops to dissolve the Assembly by force on Monday 29 January. Louis Napoleon invited Thiers, Molé and the Duc de Broglie, all three of them former ministers of Louis Philippe, to be present at his talk with Changarnier. Thiers urged him not to dissolve the Assembly by force, but to allow the deputies to 'go on screaming' for the time being. Louis Napoleon listened in silence to their arguments, and then decided, to Changarnier's disgust, not to dissolve the Assembly; but he authorized him to make a massive military demonstration on the Monday. As Changarnier left the meeting he spoke to Thiers contemptuously of the President, using obscene army language.[16]

On 29 January the people of Paris heard the rappel sounding to summon the National Guard; they had last heard it during the June

Days. Fifty thousand troops were on the streets; they lined the boulevards, sealing off the entrances to the boulevards from the side streets, though the shops on the boulevards remained open. It was a bitterly cold day, and the officers marched the men of their units round and round the trees in the boulevards to keep them warm.[17] Early in the afternoon it began to rain, but thousands of people were on the streets to see what was happening. The troops surrounded the Assembly building at the Palais Bourbon. The Radical deputies inside denounced this as an attempt to overawe the Assembly; but the deputies, debating within the ring of soldiers, passed the second reading of the bill to dissolve the Assembly by 416 votes to 405.

The official newspaper, *Le Moniteur*, published a government statement on the morning of 29 January, explaining that the troops were on the streets of Paris because the government had received information that the Garde Mobile was planning a Radical revolution. *Le Moniteur* also stated that at a Cabinet meeting that morning, the President had assured the government that they had his full support for their action in calling out the troops. 'The issue is clearly set forth this time', wrote the Conservative newspaper *Le Corsaire*; 'it is between the guillotine and society.'[18]

At 2 p.m. on 29 January, Louis Napoleon rode out of the Élysée, escorted by only a handful of officers, and visited the town halls in various parts of Paris. He rode through the Place de la Concorde, the Boulevard de la Madeleine, the Boulevard des Capucines, the Rue de la Paix, the Place Vendôme and the Rue de Rivoli. He was surrounded by enormous crowds, cheering him and shouting 'Vive le Président!' and 'Vive Napoléon!' The well-dressed ladies and gentlemen watching from the balconies of their houses in the fashionable quarters were particularly enthusiastic.[19]

Four days later, he reviewed the troops on the Champ-de-Mars, congratulated them on their conduct in the hour of danger, and awarded crosses of the Legion of Honour to several selected officers and men. He noticed that one sergeant who was due to receive the decoration was absent, and was told that it was because the sergeant had gone to see his dying mother. The President sent his equerry to the sergeant's house with orders to bestow the Legion of Honour on the sergeant at his mother's bedside, so that she could see the cross on her son's breast before she died. The press, reminding its readers of the President's devotion to his own mother, Queen Hortense, reported that his orders were duly carried out and that the dying woman recovered her health when she saw her son wearing the Legion of Honour.[20]

On 16 February the President held the first of a fortnightly series of Friday evening balls at the Élysée. It was a splendid affair – a more glamorous social occasion than any held since the February revolution or even under Louis Philippe. It was announced that though the President would dearly have wished to invite all his supporters in France, the accommodation was limited and only those persons who had received invitations would be admitted. There was great competition to obtain invitation cards, which went mostly to the élite of the old aristocracy, to distinguished foreign visitors in Paris, to high-ranking military and civilian officers, and to the diplomatic corps.[21]

The three thousand guests who attended the ball given by the Prefect of the Seine at the Hôtel de Ville on the following Monday were drawn from a wider and slightly lower stratum of society. To their surprise and delight, Louis Napoleon turned up at 11 p.m., escorting Princess Mathilde. The band greeted him with his mother's tune, 'Partant pour la Syrie'. The ball at the Hôtel de Ville was the talk of the town next day. The guests told their friends that the President was there – not Marrast, the President of the Assembly, but Louis Napoleon Bonaparte, the President of the French Republic! One of the guests, on leaving the ball, had picked up a cab at the door of the Hôtel de Ville, and was asked by the cab-driver to tell him about the President. 'Talk about him!' said the driver; 'he is a gay fellow; you see, my good bourgeois, I love him, how I love him! Those little men of the Provisional Government – what a difference!'[22]

The Bourse had long since forgotten its fear of Louis Napoleon's victory in the presidential election. When he arrived there one day at lunch time, unannounced and almost unaccompanied, and chatted informally with the stockbrokers, they were so delighted that the funds rose sharply during the hour that he was on the premises.[23]

The government prosecuted Proudhon for seditious libel for his article against the President in *Le Peuple* of 27 January, and sent Barbès, Raspail, and the other prisoners at Vincennes for trial at Bourges for having plotted an insurrection on 15 May 1848. Most of the defendants were sentenced to transportation – Barbès and Albert for life, Blanqui for ten years, and Raspail for six years. Louis Blanc and Caussidière, who were safe in England, were tried and convicted in their absence. Socialists were still being arrested and sentenced to long terms of transportation for their part in the June Days, and Socialists and Radicals for making speeches and writing articles against the President and the government; and the Assembly rejected the amnesty for the June rebels.

In February the trial began by court martial in Paris of the murderers of General Brea and his A.D.C. Captain Mangin, who had been shot by the rebels in the June Days when they went to the barricades under a flag of truce to persuade the rebels to stop fighting. The case had aroused great indignation among the middle classes; but the February revolution had abolished the death penalty for political offences, and the Socialists and Radicals – and Louis Napoleon before the presidential election – had demanded the complete abolition of capital punishment. Proudhon and the other Socialist editors denounced the trials and claimed that the killing of Brea and Mangin had been political offences. On 7 February the court martial convicted eight of the defendants of the murders, and sentenced five of them to death and three to life imprisonment with hard labour.

Louis Napoleon was petitioned to commute the death sentences. He took over a month to decide. It was rumoured that he wished to commute all the sentences, but that the Cabinet opposed it, as did the Council of State whom he was bound by the Constitution to consult over the exercise of his prerogative of pardon. The case of Nourry, the youngest of the men, aroused particular controversy; he was only nineteen, but had behaved with great defiance at his trial, at which he proudly boasted of having been chiefly responsible for killing Brea and firing the first shot. Eventually Louis Napoleon commuted the death sentences on two of the five, but decided that three of them must die, including young Nourry. The execution was fixed for Wednesday 14 March, but Louis Napoleon insisted that it should not be carried out on that day, as he was giving a ball at the Élysée in the evening, and he felt that it would be unsuitable to hold a ball on the same day as an execution. It was therefore arranged that the murderers should be guillotined – in public, as the law required – on the following Friday, 16 March, at dawn, when few people would be about in the streets and the chances of demonstrations would be less. The area of the execution, near the Barrière de Fontainebleau, was full of troops, but the executioner overslept and the execution had to be put off for twenty-four hours. During this time fresh efforts were made to win a reprieve for Nourry, and in his case Louis Napoleon commuted the death sentence, after he had been told that Nourry had become very penitent at the eleventh hour. The other two were guillotined at dawn on the Saturday.[24]

The ball on the Wednesday had been a particularly splendid affair. It was held in two great galleries at the Élysée Palace, the one 120 feet long by 40 feet wide, and the other 90 feet by 30 feet. The rooms were decorated in yellow and crimson damask; rich candelabra hung from the high ceiling, and lamps were attached to every column, creating the atmosphere of an Oriental bazaar. Over two thousand guests were present. By 10 p.m. the line of carriages stretched from the Élysée to the Boulevard de la Madeleine, and those guests who thought it smart to arrive late found that it took them an hour and a half to get to the door, which they did not reach till 1 a.m. Every general in the army was there except Cavaignac, and the guests included the old Princesse de la Moskowa, Marshal Ney's widow. The President had also invited eight young privates from the Polytechnic and the École Militaire, whose simple uniforms contrasted with the superb embroidery on the splendid uniforms of the generals. There was a hitch in the catering arrangements, and the guests had to wait a long time for their supper; but Louis Napoleon turned this to good account. He went out several times to the terraces and apologized for the delay to the guests, who were charmed by his casual informality as he told them: 'Unfortunately it is not yet ready; we shall have to wait a little longer.' It was served at last at 11.30 p.m., the President leading Madame Faucher in to supper. He withdrew at 1 o'clock, explaining that he had to deal with important affairs of state; but the dancing did not end till 5 a.m.[25]

Proudhon, in his paper on 19 March, attacked both the ball and the execution of Brea's murderers: 'The week began with a brilliant entertainment at M. Louis Bonaparte's, and ended with the restoration of the political scaffold.' The President had consented to the execution of

two men, guilty indeed, but guilty of a purely political crime. Frightful precedent! Now all parties are absolved in advance from every act of reprisal which it pleases them to commit, and the instrument of blood is placed at the service of all factious passions. . . . While the knife operates and the blood runs, M. L. Bonaparte dances,

and entertains his guests with money wrung from the meagre wages of the people. Proudhon went on to describe how Louis Napoleon had been flirting with a beautiful Duchess at the ball when he was called away for an interview with the Archbishop of Paris, who had come to plead unsuccessfully with tears in his eyes for the life of Brea's murderers.[26]

Another charge of seditious libel was brought against Proudhon for publishing this article. He disappeared. It was easy to go to the Gare du Nord, take the train to Brussels, and cross to England before the Franco-Belgian extradition treaty could be invoked. Louis Blanc and Caussidière had taken this route in August 1848. Delescluze, the Socialist editor of *La Révolution Démocratique et Sociale*, made the journey in April 1849, when he was charged with seditious libel; but Proudhon was hiding in France. Both Proudhon and Delescluze were sentenced in their absence to three years' imprisonment.

But the balls and receptions continued, attracting the highest circles of society to the Élysée. 'Fêtes, concerts, banquets and balls', wrote *The Times*, 'are becoming so numerous, are given on so large a scale, and attract such crowds, as to almost require the daily labours of a minister for that department alone.'[27] The aristocrats who intrigued to get tickets for the parties at the Élysée were very conscious that the President was also a Prince. Neither they nor the old Bonapartists, for whom Louis Napoleon had always been 'the Prince', could bring themselves to refer to him now as 'the President', and while he was always referred to in official documents, and by the politicians, by his proper title of 'President of the Republic', in society and at the Élysée he was called 'the Prince-President' and addressed as 'His Highness' and 'Monseigneur'.

One feature of the receptions and balls was the number of distinguished foreigners present. Apart from the diplomatic corps there were Russian, Austrian and German Princes and Dukes, but above all there were guests from England. One could always hear a good deal of English spoken at the balls at the Élysée, for the Prince-President had not forgotten his old friends in London society. Lord and Lady Londonderry, Lord Malmesbury, and Miss Angela Burdett-Coutts attended receptions in the spring and summer of 1849. D'Orsay was received at the Élysée, despite the fact that he was not considered to be quite respectable and had fled to Paris to escape his creditors. But Louis Napoleon saw no reason why he should invite Lady Jersey, who had never invited him to her parties when she was the leading hostess in London and he was living there in exile. Eventually the Duke of Cambridge, Queen Victoria's cousin, told Louis Napoleon that his failure to invite Lady Jersey had been commented upon, and especially asked the Prince-President to invite her as a favour to himself. Louis Napoleon then sent her an invitation to a reception. She had not, after all, blocked his admission to Almack's in 1831, when she ruled the club as one of its seven Lady Patronesses.[28]

Louis Napoleon did more for his old friend Benjamin Lumley than merely to invite him to receptions at the Élysée. Jenny Lind had established Lumley's reputation as the most successful impresario in Europe, but she had not been able to save him from the financial ruin in which his expensive productions had involved him. By 1849 he was on the verge of bankruptcy. He shut down his London enterprises and went to Paris, where Louis Napoleon, hearing of his plight, appointed him to a salaried position as manager of the Italian opera. Louis Napoleon also extended his patronage to Rachel, whom he had completely forgiven for her escapade with Prince Napoleon. With Lumley at the Italian opera, Rachel at the Comédie Française, the Rothschilds attending regularly as guests at the Élysée, and the Foulds as Louis Napoleon's bankers, people began to say that the President was in the pocket of the Jews, though violent anti-semitism did not arise in France until thirty years later.[29]

Naturally Maria Manuela, Countess of Montijo, with her old Bonapartist sympathies and her flair for getting to the top of the social tree, procured an invitation to an Élysée ball for herself and her daughter Eugénie when they came to Paris in March 1849. They arrived after the end of the winter season in Madrid – a season which had been interrupted when news arrived of the revolution in Rome and the Pope's flight to Gaeta; Queen Isabel had proclaimed a period of mourning and prayer for the Pope, and the Countess of Montijo cancelled her weekly receptions. Maria Manuela's friend the Duke of Sotomayor, the Spanish Ambassador and the doyen of the diplomatic corps in Paris, arranged for her and Eugénie to receive invitations to a dinner at the Foreign Office given by the Foreign Minister, Drouyn de Lhuys, and Mérimée obtained for them an invitation to Princess Mathilde's, and in due course to the Élysée.[30] Maria Manuela enjoyed society everywhere, especially in Paris; but the beautiful Countess of Teba, now nearly twenty-three, was lonely in Paris, and enjoyed nothing there except the theatres. She longed for the trees in the Avenida de la Reina in Madrid, the gardens of Carabanchel, her sister Paca, and the freedom of the mountains and forests of Spain.

She did not wish to go to Princess Mathilde's party. Just before she dressed for it, she wrote to Paca:

I have to go with Mother to Princess Mathilde's, where there will be nobody I know, nobody at all. I am really frightened that I shall begin to cry, which is what I want to do more than anything else. I am going to put on my blue dress, the last dress that I wore in Madrid. Fortunately I shall be able to spend the time thinking of you and of Madrid, because I don't suppose anyone will talk to me.

She finished the letter when she got back from the party: 'My fore-boding was right, nobody, absolutely nobody spoke to me. I have two claims to be treated thus, as an unmarried girl and as a foreigner. . . . I think I shall avoid going in society whenever I can.'[31]

The reception at the Élysée went a little better, but was hardly a success for Eugénie. Here she and Maria Manuela were presented to the Prince-President. This pleased Eugénie, because her Bonapartist background and sympathies had led her to admire Louis Napoleon, and she had been delighted at his victory in the presidential election. When she was presented, she immediately addressed him, with her usual frankness and disregard for formal etiquette, and told him how pleased she was to meet him, because she had heard about him from a lady who was one of his devoted partisans. He asked who the lady was, and she told him it was Madame Gordon. He seemed a little put out, and passed on to speak to other guests, leaving Eugénie with the feeling that she had made a *faux pas*.[32] Perhaps it was imagination on her part, or perhaps Louis Napoleon felt that he should not appear to react too warmly to the mention of Eléonore Gordon's name in view of the fact that it had once been falsely reported that she was his mistress.

But Louis Napoleon, like many of the other gentlemen who saw Eugénie at parties and thought it was improper to accost an unmarried young lady, had noticed that she was very beautiful. A few weeks later, Maria Manuela and Eugénie received an invitation from Louis Napoleon's social secretary, Bacciochi, to dine with the Prince-President at his house at Saint-Cloud on the south-western outskirts of Paris. Eugénie dressed herself in her best evening *toilette*, expecting that it would be at least a semi-formal dinner party with a large number of guests; but when she and Maria Manuela reached Saint-Cloud, they were taken to a little house called Combleval in the park between Saint-Cloud and Villeneuve, and discovered that it was a private supper for four – the Prince-President, Bacciochi, and themselves. The presence of Maria Manuela and Bacciochi made it perfectly respectable, but Eugénie felt sure that Louis Napoleon wished to make love to her and had asked them to the private supper party as a preliminary step.

It was a warm spring evening, and Louis Napoleon suggested that they should stroll in the park. He offered his arm to Eugénie, while Bacciochi hung back to escort Maria Manuela. Eugénie politely declined the Prince-President's offer of his arm, and told him that as her mother was present, the honour of being escorted by him belonged to her. Louis Napoleon, equally courteously, agreed with her, and walked in the park with Maria Manuela, while Eugénie followed behind on Bacciochi's arm.[33] The Prince-President's conduct was impeccable; but he did not invite the Countess of Teba to a second private supper party.

CHAPTER 20

RESCUING THE POPE

FOR the last three hundred years the French had periodically fought the Austrians in Northern Italy. When Napoleon led the French revolutionary armies to victory at Lodi and Arcola in his campaign of 1796, he established the tradition of France as the country of the Revolution whose liberating armies would defeat the forces of tyranny which oppressed the Italian people; and no one had complained louder than Louis Napoleon and the Bonapartists of Louis Philippe's failure to go to the help of the Italian revolutionaries in 1831. Lamartine and Cavaignac had likewise done nothing to help the armies of King Charles Albert of Piedmont and the Italian Liberals in their war against Austria in the spring and summer of 1848.

In March 1849 Charles Albert, under the pressure of the Piedmontese Radicals, repudiated the armistice of August 1848 and began hostilities against Austria. Field-Marshal Radetzky defeated him at Novara and crushed the Piedmontese army in a campaign which lasted only five days. In France, Ledru-Rollin and the Radicals, who were demanding that France should refrain from intervention against the revolutionaries in Rome, urged the French government to go to the assistance of the Italian patriots and intervene against Austria in Piedmont; but Louis Napoleon sent a confidential agent on a diplomatic mission to Vienna. He refused to intervene either in Piedmont or in Rome; it was said in Paris that he had resisted pressure for intervention in Rome from his Cabinet, and had declared: 'No intervention, but God help anyone who touches France!'[1]

On 23 March, a few hours after his defeat at Novara, Charles Albert abdicated, and next day his son Victor Emanuel, the new King, went to Radetzky's headquarters to sue for peace. The Austrians did not demand any territorial cessions, but imposed a very heavy war indemnity of nearly £10 million and urged King Victor Emanuel to abolish the Liberal constitution in Piedmont. The British Foreign Secretary, Lord Palmerston, then put diplomatic pressure on Austria to grant Piedmont more lenient terms, and Louis Napoleon, who on 29 March had an interview with the Austrian envoy, Baron Hübner, did likewise. In the end, Austria abandoned her demand for the abolition of the Piedmontese Constitution and agreed to reduce the indemnity to £3 million. The Moderate Republican, as well as the Radical, press in France accused the government of betraying Piedmont through their refusal to intervene; but Louis Napoleon and his ministers claimed that they had succeeded, by diplomatic negotiations, in gaining very reasonable terms for Victor Emanuel.

On 16 April Odilon Barrot announced in the Assembly that the troops at Marseilles and Toulon would sail to Civitavecchia and occupy the Papal States, in order to protect the dignity and preserve the legitimate influence of France in Italy. The Austrians were on the point of invading the Papal States from the north in response to the Pope's appeal for help; the Neapolitans were marching in from the south; and Narvaez had sent a small token Spanish force and naval squadron to fight for the Pope. Odilon Barrot explained that France could not stand idly by and see the triumph of either Red revolution or savage Austrian counter-revolution in the Papal States, and that the French would go to Rome in friendship to protect the Roman people from the Austrians. The Radical and Socialist deputies strongly opposed his motion, but his arguments won over the majority of the Moderate Republicans, and the credits which the government demanded were voted by 395 votes to 283.[2]

General Oudinot and his 9000 soldiers reached Civitavecchia on 26 April. Mazzini, who had been invited to head the revolutionary Republican government in Rome, was eager to avoid hostilities with Republican France. He informed Oudinot that if the French troops came to protect the Roman people against Austria they would be welcomed as friends, but insisted that they be stationed outside Rome. Oudinot, while not admitting that he had come to overthrow the Roman Republic and restore the Pope, insisted on entering Rome and refused to recognize Mazzini's government. Mazzini therefore decided to resist, and confided the defence of Rome to Giuseppe Garibaldi, who, after a decade of brilliant generalship in South America and a fortnight's guerrilla campaign against the Austrians in 1848, had arrived in Rome with his volunteers.

As the French army marched from Civitavecchia to Rome, they found that the walls of the houses in the villages which they passed had been placarded with posters in French quoting from the provision in the new French Constitution which declared that France would never threaten the liberty of any foreign nation. The Roman force under Garibaldi was waiting for them in the gardens of the villas on the western outskirts of Rome; it consisted of revolutionary artisans and students from all over Italy, of Polish revolutionary refugees, and of

Socialist and Radical volunteers from Germany and from France itself. Oudinot was certain that he would encounter no resistance, because he thought that Italians were cowards. When Garibaldi opened fire with his cannon, Oudinot thought that it was the guns in Rome firing a salvo to announce that it was 12 noon; only when men fell dead at his side did he realize that the Romans would fight. Garibaldi's 4000 volunteers charged Oudinot's 9000 troops and routed them. Oudinot retreated to Pola leaving nearly 400 prisoners-of-war in Garibaldi's hands.

The prisoners were subjected to intensive propaganda in Rome, and were finally sent back to Oudinot's camp with a gift of 50,000 cigars, much impressed with the kindness of the Roman people and the justice of their cause. The wounded prisoners were treated with great consideration by the Roman Republican nurses in the medical corps organized by Princess Belgioioso, who had been a friend of Louis Napoleon in Rome before 1831. Her opponents called her 'the Communist Semiramis', and she and her nurses were violently denounced by the French Catholic writers for attempting to seduce the French soldiers from their duty.[3]

In Paris, the official government press published completely untrue communiqués from Oudinot and reports from Rome, and started a practice which in due course won for the official newspaper *Le Moniteur* the nickname of 'le menteur'. On 3 May the Conservative newspaper *La Patrie* wrote: 'A report was current this afternoon that the French expeditionary column had had an engagement with the Roman troops. This report has no foundation. Our troops have entered Rome without impediment. It is thought that Mazzini and the leaders of the government have left the city.' On 7 May the non-party paper *L'Estafette* denied a rumour that Oudinot had received a setback in his attempt to enter Rome, but next day virtually admitted that the story was true; and by now this was generally known in Paris, though the government press continued to publish reassuring communiqués from Oudinot which made no reference to the battle of 30 April. On 9 May the *Times* correspondent in Paris reported that the French troops had entered Rome. On the same day *Le Siècle*, for the first time, admitted the defeat of 30 April but gave an absolutely untrue version of the facts: it reported that the Roman authorities had surrendered the keys of the city to Oudinot, but that after a few French troops had entered, the Romans treacherously shut the gate, and Garibaldi's bands massacred the French who were inside. Four days later, the press published Oudinot's order of the day of 8 May, which stated that only thirty French soldiers, all of them wounded, had been taken prisoner by the Romans.[4]

By now the truth was known in Paris from the foreign press and private letters from Italy, and it was a heavy blow to French pride.

The government was severely criticized, and not only by the Radicals, in the Assembly on 7 May; and the general feeling in Paris was one of shame and indignation. It was particularly embarrassing for the government, for though the Constituent Assembly was still in session, a general election for the new Legislative Assembly was in progress. The disaster outside the walls of Rome might destroy their hopes of securing the return of a large majority of deputies of the Party of Order to the new Assembly.

But the President of the Republic remained calm and confident. On the day after the debate in the Assembly on the defeat at Rome, Louis Napoleon wrote a letter to Oudinot, which was published in the press on 9 May. He told him that he had been deeply distressed to hear of the 'unforeseen resistance' which he had encountered before the walls of Rome. He had hoped that the Romans would have eagerly welcomed an army which came on a 'benevolent and disinterested mission'; but

> our soldiers have been received as enemies. Our military honour is at stake. I shall not allow it to suffer the slightest injury. You will not lack reinforcements. Tell your soldiers that I appreciate their valour, that I share their hardships, and that they can always count on my support and my gratitude.[5]

The Socialist and Radical press denounced the President's letter. The Fouricrist newspaper *La Démocratie Pacifique* – which was no longer read by Eugénie, Countess of Teba – said that a government of Jesuits had sent French soldiers to oppose, not to assist, a people fighting for their national freedom. Proudhon's paper *Le Peuple* wrote that 'Louis Bonaparte ... stabbed the Revolution with Oudinot's sabre'. The police seized from the newsvendors all copies of *La Démocratie Pacifique* and *Le Peuple*. But the ordinary non-political Frenchman was impressed by the President's support for the troops under fire.[6]

The results of the general election on 13 May showed a polarization of French politics, a victory for the Right and an advance for the Left. The Moderate Republicans, 500 strong in the old Assembly, fell to 80 in the new; Lamartine, Marrast and other leaders lost their seats. The Party of Order increased their seats from 200 to 450, and had an absolute majority in the Assembly. The Radicals and Socialists, who this time had united in a joint list of candidates, increased their seats from 80 to over 200,[7] despite the fact that their meetings had been broken up by the police and their newspapers and posters seized and torn down by the authorities. In Paris, where Lucien Murat topped the poll, Ledru-Rollin was a close second; and Boichot, a sergeant-major who had been arrested on Changarnier's orders when he announced that he was standing as a Socialist candidate, was elected fourth. Marshal Bugeaud and Thiers were defeated in Paris, though Thiers was elected for Le Havre.

The government sent an envoy to Rome to try to reach a peaceful settlement with Mazzini. The envoy was Ferdinand de Lesseps, a career diplomat whose mother, Catherine de Grivégnée, was the aunt of Maria Manuela, Countess of Montijo. After serving in Cairo and the Middle East, he had been Consul in Malaga and Barcelona, Consul-General in Spain, and ultimately Ambassador in Madrid, where he had become a close friend of Maria Manuela and Eugénie. He went to Rome very prejudiced against Mazzini, but found that Mazzini was eager to reach a friendly agreement with France, and he signed an armistice with him. Oudinot, whose sympathies were strongly Legitimist, disapproved of the armistice; he was determined to restore the Pope's authority, and he wished to retrieve his military reputation by winning a victory which would avenge the humiliation of 30 April. He was supported in Paris by Montalembert and the Catholic pressure-groups, who called for a crusade to restore the Pope to power. France, the first country in Western Europe to turn Christian under King Clovis in 496, was 'the eldest daughter of the Church'; what more fitting than that the Holy Father should now be rescued by his eldest daughter?[8]

On 31 May, Lesseps and Mazzini reached an agreement with a formula which, while avoiding anything which could imply recognition of the Roman Republic by France, allowed French troops to remain on Roman soil outside Rome, the Pope to return in safety to the Vatican, and the democratically elected Assembly of the Roman Republic and Mazzini's government to continue in office. But Oudinot repudiated the agreement, and showed Lesseps dispatches recalling him to Paris. When Lesseps reached Paris he found that he was publicly branded as a weakling, if not a traitor, who had been duped by Mazzini and had disobeyed his instructions from the French government. He published a well-documented defence of his actions, which showed that he had acted in absolute good faith and well within the scope of his instructions; but he was ignominiously dismissed from the diplomatic service, the scapegoat for the double-dealing policy which the government had pursued while they awaited the results of the general election in France.[9]

On 1 June, Oudinot informed the Roman authorities that he was ending the armistice immediately; but he added that he would not attack 'the place' until 4 June.[10] On the night of 2 June his troops occupied the vital strategic strongpoint of the Villa Corsini outside the walls of Rome, from where his cannon could bombard the city; the Roman defenders, believing that the armistice was still in force, were unprepared for the attack. When Oudinot was accused of breaking the truce, he replied that when he had promised not to attack 'the place' until 4 June, he meant, by 'the place', the city itself and not the Villa Corsini outside the walls. Garibaldi, realizing that he must regain the Villa Corsini at all costs, attacked it for seventeen hours from dawn till dusk on Sunday 3 June; again and again his young volunteers, few of whom were aged over thirty, charged with the bayonet up the garden path of the Villa Corsini, under the murderous musket fire of Oudinot's troops stationed at the windows of the villa at the hilltop. At the end of the day Garibaldi had lost 1000 of his men, one-sixth of all his force, and Oudinot still held the Villa Corsini. Neither the Italian, nor the French and European, Radicals would ever forgive Louis Napoleon for the deaths of those thousand young revolutionary idealists on 3 June 1849.

In Paris the defeatism, and the distrust of the government press, were so strong after the lying reports of the battle of 30 April that when the news of the fighting for the Villa Corsini came through, it was widely believed that the French had suffered a second disastrous defeat. When the truth was known, the Radical deputies violently attacked the government in the Assembly, while the political world awaited the President's message to the Assembly on the state of the nation, which he was required under the Constitution to deliver at the beginning of a new Parliamentary session. After being twice postponed, it was delivered on 7 June. Louis Napoleon drafted it without consulting the Cabinet, and when it was published there were passages in it which were criticized by three of the ministers.[11]

In the message, the President told the Assembly that he had performed his electoral pledges:

> to defend society, so audaciously attacked; to strengthen a good, great, honest Republic; to protect the family, religion, property; to instigate all possible improvements and economies; to protect the press against arbitrary conduct and licence; to reduce the abuses of centralization; to remove the traces of civil disorder; finally, to adopt a policy abroad which is neither arrogant nor weak.

After condemning the Russian invasion of Hungary, where the Tsar was helping the Emperor of Austria to suppress the Hungarian nationalist revolution, he justified French policy in Italy. France could never have permitted Austria to annex Piedmont and destroy that friendly buffer state on her south-eastern frontier; but his diplomacy had prevented this, and had forced Austria to grant Piedmont reasonable terms. He said that the revolution in Rome had shocked both Catholics and Liberals throughout Europe; Pius IX, ever since he became Pope, had worked to grant his subjects a Liberal constitution, but his efforts had been destroyed by the violence of a revolutionary minority. In this situation, the French government had three possible courses of action; they could have intervened on the side of the Roman Republic, thereby placing themselves in opposition to every other Catholic state in Europe; they could have washed their hands of the whole affair, and allowed Austria to overrun the Papal States and restore the Pope, destroying French influence in Italy and all hopes of Liberalism in Rome; or they could have adopted the course which was in fact pursued, and intervened in Rome to restore law and order and a Liberal Pope, and to protect the Romans from the Austrians. The Roman people, understanding this, would have allowed the friendly French forces to enter Rome in peace if Garibaldi and his band had not arrived there three days earlier, seized control of the city, and made an unprovoked attack on the French soldiers.[12]

Mazzini appealed to Ledru-Rollin and the Mountain, in the name of international Radical solidarity, to come to the aid of their Roman brothers and stop the French attack. Ledru-Rollin denounced the renewal of the fighting at Rome as a violation of the Constitution of the French Republic, and moved the impeachment of Louis Napoleon in the Assembly. When the motion was defeated, Ledru-Rollin accused the majority of the Assembly of being accomplices of the President in his violation of the Constitution, and invoked Article 110 of the Constitution, which provided that in the last resort it was the duty of the people of France to defend the Constitution. On 11 June he appealed to the people, from the rostrum of the Assembly, to defend the Constitution, 'with arms if necessary', by removing from office the President, his ministers, and the majority of the National Assembly, and next day he called on the National Guard to assemble in the Place du Château d'Eau and march on the Assembly; but he expressly directed them to come on the march without their arms.[13]

Louis Napoleon entrusted Changarnier with the duty of maintaining order in Paris, and treated the Radical move to overthrow the government by passive demonstration as an attempt at insurrection. On the morning of 13 June, 14,000 Radicals – 4000 of them wearing the uniform of the National Guard – marched from the Place du Château d'Eau towards the Élysée Palace and the Assembly. Changarnier's cavalry and riflemen were waiting for them at the corner of the Rue de Rivoli, and as the demonstrators passed, they were charged by the cavalry, who split them up and chased them in all directions. Some of the demonstrators hastily built three barricades in the Boulevard des Italiens with the chairs from the cafés and restaurants on the pavements, reinforced by two or three carriages parked in the boulevard; but the cavalry knocked over these flimsy barricades at the first charge, and pursued the demonstrators along the Rue Royale and the Boulevard Montmartre and through the Faubourg du Temple, while the proprietors and waiters of the cafés ran out to reclaim the chairs from the demolished barricades.

At 3 p.m. Changarnier rode out from the Élysée to survey the scene, and was received with great enthusiasm by the troops and National Guard and by well-dressed ladies and gentlemen. Louis Napoleon had wished to go out into the streets himself, but was dissuaded by Changarnier and Odilon Barrot, and remained in the Élysée, which, like other key points, was heavily guarded by detachments of the 70,000 troops who had been brought into Paris. It was not until 5 p.m., two hours after Changarnier, when the demonstrators had long since disappeared, that Louis Napoleon, with Changarnier at his side and an escort of cavalry, rode from the Élysée along the boulevards to the Place de la Bastille and through the Faubourg Saint-Antoine, returning to the Élysée by the Rue de Rivoli. He was loudly cheered, but not as loudly as Changarnier had been when he first appeared in the streets at 3 o'clock.[14]

On the evening of 13 June, the President issued a proclamation to the people. He told them that the attempted insurrection and the repeated disturbances prevented him and the government from going ahead with their plans for improving the economic conditions of the people. 'The time has come for good men to feel reassured and for wicked men to tremble. . . . The cause that I defend is your cause, your family's cause, your property's cause, the cause of the poor and of the rich, the cause of all civilization.'[15] That same evening, at Louis Napoleon's request, the Assembly proclaimed the state of siege in Paris and gave power to the Prefects to extend it to any city of France which was likewise threatened by an armed insurrection. There were demonstrations in various towns in France, and street-fighting in Lyons, where the army used cannon to bombard Radicals and Socialists who were holding out in the houses in the working-class districts; several people were killed and over a thousand arrested. Ledru-Rollin and many of his leading supporters fled to England.

The President's action was welcomed in all the newspapers that were allowed to appear; the Radical and Socialist journals had been seized on 13 June and suppressed. The government intensified the repression against the Radicals and Socialists. A new press law made it a criminal offence to insult the President, to spread subversive ideas among the armed forces, or to invite the public, in a newspaper, to subscribe money for the payment of a fine imposed on a defendant by a court of law. During the summer and autumn the newspapers reported nearly every day the arrest and conviction of Socialists and Radicals. Men were sentenced to imprisonment for shouting 'Long live the Democratic and Social Republic!', and for distributing copies of Leroy's song 'The Ball and the Guillotine', which referred to Louis Napoleon's ball at the Élysée and the execution of Brea's murderers. A man was imprisoned for uttering insulting words about Louis Napoleon in a café, and a Radical mayor for wearing a phrygian red cap in the town hall. Three soldiers were arrested merely for saying that they were Socialists. The 'trees of liberty' – poles surmounted by the red cap – which had been erected in many public places by Socialist and Radical local authorities, were cut down by order of the government; but when some working men of Saint-Antoine nailed to the remaining base of the 'tree' a document containing a protest against cutting down the tree, they were arrested for damaging a public monument, on the grounds that the truncated pole was still a public monument.[16]

The *Times* correspondent thought that barbers would be doing a good trade, as so many people were cutting their hair shorter and shaving off their beards so as not to be taken for Socialists. He wrote that a long black beard, a dirty face and a rusty black frock 'were the acknowledged insignia of pure Socialism', but that now clean linen and brushed frock-coats were becoming respectable, and 'whites, greens, blacks, blues – all colours in the rainbow – are popular, but not red'.[17]

At the gates of Rome, Oudinot relentlessly pressed on with his operations, assisted by the commander of his artillery, General Vaillant, who with the aid of a number of new-type cannons bombarded the Roman defences and the civilian population almost continuously day and night. On 30 June, after some very bloody hand-to-hand fighting, Garibaldi informed the Roman Constituent Assembly that further resistance in the city was no longer possible. Mazzini escaped to England; Garibaldi, with his wife Anita at his side, led 4000 volunteers on a night march out of Rome to begin a journey which culminated in heroic tragedy at Magnavacca; and the Romans surrendered to Oudinot, whose troops entered Rome on 3 July. In the north, the Austrians had invaded the Papal States and occupied Bologna, but Oudinot warned them, in firm and almost threatening language, not to come any nearer to Rome.[18] The revolutionary régimes had been overthrown in Berlin, Vienna and Budapest, and only Venice still held out. Here the Liberal revolutionary, Daniele Manin, had proclaimed a republic, and was still defending the city against the Austrian army and navy which were besieging and attacking Venice by land and sea.

One of Manin's leading officers in Venice was General Armandi, who had kept an unwelcome protective watch over Louis Napoleon and his brother when they were serving under his command during the revolution in the Papal States in 1831. He now wrote to Louis Napoleon, congratulating him on his election as President of the French Republic and asking him to help Venice. Louis Napoleon replied with a friendly letter of sympathy, but offered no practical assistance.[19] The help that the Venetians needed was the presence of a French squadron in the Adriatic to threaten or engage the Austrian fleet attacking Venice; but this would have meant incurring a serious risk of France being involved in a major European war in which Russia would have supported Austria against France, and Britain, though sympathizing with France and with Italian liberation, would have remained neutral. Some of Louis Napoleon's other old friends, like Vieillard, wrote to him expressing their disquiet at events in Italy. On 4 June he replied to Vieillard: 'We have to finish this wretched Roman affair by cannon shot. I deplore it; but what can I do? I also weep for Venice.'[20] Venice finally surrendered to the Austrians in October 1849.

The President was extending his contacts with the people, and increasing his popularity every time he appeared in public. The hot summer of 1849 led to a cholera epidemic in Paris. Louis Napoleon visited the hospitals in Paris and comforted the cholera victims; this impressed the people who were used to seeing kings and aristocrats leave the city during a cholera epidemic and take refuge in their country châteaux. When Louis Napoleon heard that some government officials had abandoned their posts and left their districts because of the cholera, he dismissed them from office.[21]

There had been a great spate of railway construction in the previous decade. This made it possible for the President to pay lightning visits to places some distance from Paris and to visit several towns and villages in one day, which would have been impossible ten years earlier.* In the summer of 1849 he went to many towns in Central and Northern France, often in order to officiate at the opening of a new stretch of railway line. He took the opportunity of making speeches on questions of national policy and on themes particularly suited to the place where he was speaking. At Chartres, where St Bernard had preached the Second Crusade in 1146 and Henri IV had been crowned during the Wars of Religion in 1594, he spoke about the moral grandeur of a crusade for the Catholic faith and of the greatness of Henri IV, who,

*On Saturday 28 April 1849, he left Paris by train at 5 a.m. for a visit to Champagne, reviewed the National Guard at Morel, Ornes, Romilly, Montereau and Troyes, where he attended a banquet, and returned to the Élysée at 8.30 the same evening.

as the founder of the Bourbon dynasty, was a cult-object to the Legitimists. He praised Henri IV for reconciling Catholics and Protestants in France after thirty years of savage civil war. At Amiens, where the peace treaty with England had been signed in 1802, he spoke of his peaceful intentions in international affairs in a speech which made a very favourable impression in Britain.

He went on from Amiens to Ham with Dr Conneau and Persigny and some of his other old Bonapartist friends. He attended an official banquet in the town and inspected the castle where he had been imprisoned. He found his old rooms in the prison occupied by the Arab chief Bou-Maza, who had been captured when fighting against the French in Algeria. Louis Napoleon ordered him to be set free. [22]

In July and early August he visited Angers, Nantes, Blois, Rennes, Le Havre – where 50,000 people came out to see him – and Rouen. He was cheered by great crowds as he travelled by steamship down the Loire and the Seine and by rail and road through Legitimist Brittany and Conservative Normandy. The people sometimes shouted 'Vive la République!' and 'Vive le Président!', but much more often 'Vive Napoléon!' and 'Vive l'Empereur!' Those who went too far were reprimanded. The Sub-Prefect at Rambouillet, who in his speech of welcome described Louis Napoleon's train as 'the carriage that carries Caesar and his fortune', was dismissed from his office by the Minister of the Interior, Dufaure. At Rouen, Louis Napoleon would not permit an old soldier to kneel to him; he told him that a soldier should kneel only to God or to fire at the enemy. The mayors, the clergy, and the chairmen of the Chambers of Commerce were as enthusiastic as the crowds; in their speeches they acclaimed Louis Napoleon as the man who had saved France from anarchy and had restored the Holy Father to the Eternal City. At Blois, the Bishop hailed him as the Elect of Providence. [23]

There was a slight difficulty at Tours, because Miss Howard had accompanied the Prince-President. The crowds would not have minded if they had known that the beautiful Englishwoman in his entourage was his mistress; but as she was seen walking arm in arm with Bacciochi, the word went around that she was Princess Bacciochi. At Tours, the officials who were responsible for the accommodation sent Miss Howard to stay the night at the house of Monsieur André, a higher civil servant in the Ministry of Finance. Monsieur André was away on holiday in the Pyrenees, but he was angry when he discovered that the lady who had stayed in his house was not Princess Bacciochi but the President's mistress. He wrote an indignant letter to Odilon Barrot. 'Have we returned to the period when the mistresses of Kings paraded their scandals through the towns of France?' he asked the Prime

Minister. Odilon Barrot gave the letter to his Bonapartist brother Ferdinand, who showed it to Louis Napoleon.

The Prince-President wrote to Odilon Barrot strongly defending Miss Howard and condemning Monsieur André's hypocrisy:

> How many women a hundred times less pure, a hundred times less devoted, a hundred times less forgivable than the lady who stayed at Monsieur André's would have been received with all possible honours by this Monsieur André if they had had a husband behind whose name they could have hidden their guilty love affairs?

He suggested that the puritanical Monsieur André should remember that true religion was not intolerant, and that Christ had challenged the adulteress's accusers to cast the first stone at her. He thought that, as his position had hitherto prevented him from marrying, and as he had no parent or childhood friends in France who could provide him, amid the cares of government, with the sweetness of family life, he might well be forgiven for a love which harmed no one and which he did not seek to publicize.[24]

The French Catholic Bishops, priests and propagandists did not think of Louis Napoleon as Miss Howard's lover but as the Pope's saviour. They were jubilant over the victory at Rome; they boasted that the eldest daughter of the Church had crushed the revolutionary hydra. Oudinot immediately dissolved the Roman Constituent Assembly which had been elected by universal suffrage, suppressed the Republican newspapers, and tore down all Republican emblems in the streets. His soldiers became involved in incidents with the civilian population, cuffing impertinent youths in the streets, closing down cafés where the waiters refused to serve them, and in a few cases shooting terrorists who had murdered French soldiers; but they behaved better than the Austrians in the north, and were not violently disliked by the conquered inhabitants. In Milan, the women spat at the Austrian soldiers; in Rome, they made eyes at the French.[25]

The Pope did not hurry to return to Rome. Instead, he sent three cardinals to suppress all traces of Liberalism there. The assassination of Rossi and the revolution of November 1848 had convinced him that his Liberal policy had been a mistake; his pronouncements and the repressive policy of the cardinals made it clear that he would henceforth be as despotic as Gregory XVI, and that Louis Napoleon's soldiers had succeeded in riveting an arbitrary tyranny on the people of Rome and the Papal States. Louis Napoleon was displeased. He had always believed that Bonapartism and the Napoleonic idea meant a Liberal middle way between privilege and the guillotine, between the old autocracies and Red revolution. He did not wish to become, like the Tsar of Russia, the gendarme of Europe, restoring tyrants to their thrones; but this was precisely what he had done in Rome. He was also angry that after Oudinot had been at such pains to ensure that Rome should be liberated by French troops alone, with the Austrians, the Neapolitans and the Spaniards kept firmly at a distance, the three cardinals made no express reference to France in their thanksgiving proclamation, but merely thanked all the Catholic states of Europe for having launched a crusade on the Pope's behalf.

On 7 August, Louis Napoleon, as a sign of his displeasure, ordered Oudinot to return to France, though the French army of occupation remained in Rome. On 18 August he wrote to his A.D.C., Edgar Ney, whom he had sent on a mission to the French headquarters in Rome. In his letter he urged the Pope to grant a general amnesty, establish a civil service of laymen instead of clergy, introduce the Code Napoleon, and appoint a 'Liberal government'. He wrote that he had been personally wounded by the failure of the three cardinals to refer to the achievements and sacrifices of the French army, for 'any insult to our flag or our uniform goes straight to my heart', and declared:

The French Republic did not send an army to Rome to smother Italian freedom. When our armies went all around Europe, they left everywhere, as evidence of their passage, the destruction of feudal abuses and the germs of liberty. It shall not be said that in 1849 a French army acted in a different way and with other results.[26]

Louis Napoleon had not consulted his ministers before writing this letter to Ney. When he read it out to them at a Cabinet meeting, Falloux protested vigorously, and insisted that it should not be published. After some hesitation the Cabinet supported him, and Louis Napoleon agreed to suppress the letter; but it was leaked to the foreign press, and was widely discussed in Paris. The Cabinet then decided to publish it in Le Moniteur on 7 September, nearly three weeks after it was written, and Falloux resigned from the government in protest.[27]

The Catholic press in France immediately launched a campaign of criticism of the President. The Legitimist paper L'Univers wrote that the expedition to Rome had placed Louis Napoleon 'first among the most energetic and most intelligent defenders of the social order. . . . By restoring the Pope, Monsieur Bonaparte maintained the keystone of the European edifice and opened for himself an immense future of glory. He closes that future today.'[28]

The rift became worse after Pius IX issued his motu proprio on 18 September, in which he completely disregarded the wishes expressed by Louis Napoleon in his letter to Ney. The Pope promised to consider the establishment of some local government bodies, but made it clear that he did not intend to grant a Constitution or to have a Liberal government; and he referred to the 'valiant armies of the Catholic powers' without making any explicit mention of France.[29]

When the Assembly resumed its sittings on 1 October after the summer recess, the deputies of the Party of Order, as well as the Legitimists, criticized Louis Napoleon's letter to Ney. Montalembert declared that for France to seek to impose conditions on the Pope as to how he governed his subjects would be to raise the flag of France against the cross and the tiara, and to act like Garibaldi, not like Charlemagne; and though the Foreign Minister, Tocqueville, denied that the Cabinet had disapproved of the letter, no member of the Cabinet defended it in the Assembly. Louis Napoleon wrote a letter to Odilon Barrot, justifying his attitude towards the Pope, which he asked the Prime Minister to read out in the Assembly. Odilon Barrot refused to do so; but the contents of the letter were published in the press, and the deep differences of opinion between the President and the Cabinet became public knowledge.[30]

For the first time since the presidential election, the Paris press was almost solidly against the President; the Legitimist and Party of Order newspapers attacked him not only for his letter to Ney but also for his triumphal tour in the provinces and the ominous cries of 'Vive Napoléon!' and 'Vive l'Empereur!' A further cause for alarm was the formation in September of a new political organization, the Society of 10 December, so called in honour of the day of Louis Napoleon's election to the presidency. The chairman of the society was Carlier, the Chief of the Paris Police, and its leadership included many old Bonapartists, some of whom held positions in the President's entourage at the Élysée – Persigny, Edgar Ney, Briffault, Laity – as well as Ferdinand Barrot, General Montholon, and General Exelmans, who in 1840 had sat as one of Louis Napoleon's judges in the Chamber of Peers. There were rumours of a Bonapartist *coup d'état*. Meanwhile the Prince-President continued to meet the people. In October he not only reviewed the troops at a great military parade at Satory near Versailles, but also visited the workshops in the Faubourg Saint-Antoine, where he talked to the workmen.[31]

Suddenly, on 31 October 1849, he dismissed the government. In a Message to the Assembly he announced that he had demanded the ministers' resignation because it was essential, in order to defeat the forces of anarchy at home and to sustain French honour abroad, that the government should work together with the President, the elect of the people, and be prepared to accept his leadership. He declared that 'a whole system triumphed on 10 December, because the name of Napoleon is a complete programme in itself. It means, at home, order, authority, religion, and the welfare of the people; and national dignity abroad.'[32]

He did not appoint a Prime Minister to replace Odilon Barrot. General d'Hautpoul, who had never played an active part in politics, became Minister of War; La Hitte, the former A.D.C. of Charles X's brother-in-law, the Duc d'Angoulême, was Foreign Minister; Ferdinand Barrot, Minister of the Interior; and the Orleanist Jewish banker, Achille Fould, Minister of Finance. After ten months Louis Napoleon had not only broken free of the tutelage of Thiers but had also defied the principle of responsible government as it had existed under Louis Philippe and hitherto under the Second Republic – that the head of state should choose his ministers from the political leaders who had the support of a majority of the deputies in the National Assembly.

Nearly all the press attacked the President's action. Those Socialist and Radical newspapers which had managed to survive, despite the press laws and police harassment, were as critical as the Legitimist and Orleanist press. But *Le Constitutionnel* – which, with *Le Dix Décembre*, was the only Paris paper to support Louis Napoleon – was convinced that he had the support of the French people, if not of the French press. It claimed that whereas Louis XIV had said, 'L'état c'est moi', 'today the enormous majority of Frenchmen say: "Le Président de la République, c'est nous." '[33]

CHAPTER 21

CRUSHING THE REDS

THE Prince-President seemed to be set for a head-on clash with the Assembly. On 4 November, four days after he had dismissed the Odilon Barrot ministry, he received an enthusiastic welcome from both the troops and the spectators when he attended the cavalry manoeuvres at Versailles. Encouraged by the support of the nation, he ordered the Minister of the Interior to dismiss many of the Prefects – the civil servants who represented the central government in the eighty-five departments of France – replacing those who had been appointed by the Party of Order with Bonapartist supporters.[1] The rumour spread through Paris that Louis Napoleon would carry out a *coup d'état* on 10 December, the anniversary of his election as President. The *Times* correspondent was a little sceptical about this, as his informant was

> one of those who see a deep political meaning in the most ordinary acts of the domestic life of Louis Napoleon – who detects a leaning to the Reds should he at his dinner table trifle with the claw of a lobster – who discovers a leaning to Legitimacy if he ask for white sauce, and who swears to a downright Imperial tendency if his thirsty and impatient lip bathe itself in a glass of Chambertin, the favourite wine of the Emperor Napoleon.[2]

There was no *coup d'état* on 10 December. At the anniversary banquet at the Hôtel de Ville, the President of the Assembly – Dupin, of the Party of Order – proposed Louis Napoleon's health, and Louis Napoleon proposed the toast 'The National Assembly'. But the stories continued to circulate. One of the most popular was that Rachel, when invited to tour Russia and see the Tsar's Empire, had replied that if she wanted to see what an empire was like she would wait to see it in Paris.[3]

In the Assembly, Louis Napoleon's friends – who were beginning to be called 'the Party of the Élysée' – voted with the Radicals and Socialists and the Moderate Republicans to defeat by four votes the Education Bill introduced by Louis Napoleon's former Minister of

Education, Falloux, which would have placed education in the hands of the Catholic Church. The Left was in favour of free universal state education, which had been embodied in the Constitution of 1848. Thiers opposed free public education, not only because it was a waste of public money, but also because free education was 'a Communist principle'; a boy who had been educated would not wish to serve behind the plough. The Catholic spokesmen rejected this view, and emphasized that a religious education was essential to counteract the spread of Socialism. 'Who defends order and property in the country-side?' asked Montalembert.

Is it the teacher? No, it is the parish priest. . . . In France there are two opposing armies. Each one has thirty to forty thousand men. They are the army of the teachers and the army of the parish priests. . . . We must counter the demoralizing anarchical army of the teachers with the army of the clergy.[4]

On 8 November 1849, Falloux's bill was defeated by 303 votes to 299.

Louis Napoleon, in the face of strong opposition from the Party of Order, took steps to grant an amnesty to the Socialist rebels of June 1848. He was a kind-hearted man, and genuinely wished to exercise his prerogative of mercy whenever possible; but he was not averse to having his mercy well publicized. On 28 October 1849, when he was returning from a military parade and from watching a steeplechase at Saint-Germain-en-Laye, a shabbily dressed working-class woman flung herself at his carriage as he was entering the gates of the Élysée. She was seized by the guards, but Louis Napoleon ordered them to bring her to him, and he spoke to her from his carriage. She told him that her son, one of the rebels of June 1848, was a prisoner in the fortress at Belle-Île, and she begged Louis Napoleon to show him mercy. Louis Napoleon granted her wish, and wrote immediately to Victor Foucher, the Attorney-General, ordering that he be set free. As the happy mother turned away, she said to the onlookers: 'I was sure that the President of the Republic would have pity on my tears and would restore my child to me.'[5]

There were 1200 other prisoners from the June Days in Belle-Île, and on 11 November – a Sunday – Louis Napoleon called a meeting of the Cabinet at 11 p.m. and told his ministers that he had decided to release all of them. The ministers said that some of the June prisoners were dangerous criminals with a long list of convictions, and that it would be very unwise to release them. The President then agreed to review each individual case on its merits, and sat up all night with the Cabinet, Foucher, and the Chief of the Paris Police, Carlier, examining the 1200 cases. As a result, he pardoned 711 of them, but the other 500 remained in prison.[6]

The prisoners who remained at Belle-Île rioted, and one of them was killed by the guards. The authorities seized the Socialist newspaper *La Réforme* which published the prisoners' accounts of the riot, and the editor was sentenced to three months' imprisonment. The Conservatives blamed Louis Napoleon for having precipitated the trouble by pardoning the 700 detainees,[7] and their deputies in the Assembly passed a bill authorizing the government to transport the detainees to penal settlements in Algeria, having rejected Mayotte Island, near Madagascar, and Cayenne as too unhealthy and harsh. Lamartine, in an unsuccessful attempt to persuade the Assembly to insert a provision in the bill which would allow the detainees' families to accompany them, urged the deputies to remember the sufferings which Napoleon had undergone at St Helena. 'That is blasphemy', shouted General Regnault de St Jean d'Angely. 'Yes,' said General Husson; 'to compare Napoleon with such miscreants is blasphemy. Nobody can be compared with Napoleon.'[8]

At the very time when Louis Napoleon was releasing seven hundred of the rebels of June 1848, the High Court at Versailles was trying Ledru-Rollin and his colleagues, some of whom were present and others absent, for instigating a rebellion in June 1849. They were convicted and sentenced to long terms of transportation. The Assembly then expelled 31 Socialist and Radical Deputies who had been convicted at Versailles, and by-elections for the 31 vacant seats were held in March 1850. Three of the vacancies were in Paris. The Socialists and Radicals and the left wing of the Moderate Republicans formed a united front, and nominated De Flotte, Vidal and Carnot as their candidates. De Flotte had been born the Vicomte de Flotte, and had served as an officer in the navy, but he became a Socialist and fought with the rebels in June 1848. After being imprisoned without trial for eighteen months he was pardoned by Louis Napoleon. He was later to lose his life fighting for Garibaldi in Calabria in 1860. Vidal had been a close colleague of Louis Blanc in 1848. Carnot was a Moderate Republican, who had been Minister of Education in Lamartine's Provisional Government after the February revolution, but had lost his seat in the Assembly at the election of May 1849. He was a leading opponent of Falloux's education bill. They were opposed by three Conservatives, one of whom was General La Hitte, the Foreign Minister. As a minister, La Hitte was entitled to speak in the Assembly, but he now sought election to it as a deputy.

The police persecution of Socialists and Radicals was relaxed a little during the by-election campaign. The Socialists held a number of public meetings in Paris without interference, though they were impeded by the new press law and by the fact that their electoral organization, the *Solidarité Républicaine*, was illegal. In some cases their known supporters in the army and the civil service were prevented from voting by their officers or intimidated by their superiors. But they won the three Paris seats on 10 and 11 March. Carnot headed the poll with 132,797 votes; Vidal received 128,439, and De Flotte, with 126,982, just beat the highest of the Conservative candidates, who obtained 125,643 votes. The Mountain altogether held 21 of their 31 seats. The Left acclaimed it as a great victory, a prelude to their triumph in the general election in two years' time. '10 March was a revolution', wrote Marx in the *Neue Rheinische Zeitung*.[9]

This was a distinct exaggeration. All the by-elections had taken place in seats already held by the Mountain, and did not therefore indicate any change of opinion in the Conservative constituencies; and the Mountain had actually lost ten of their 31 seats. But in view of the circumstances, and the pressure which had been applied against them, they were justified in claiming a victory, and their enemies accepted it as a defeat. On the Bourse, the funds immediately fell by 3 per cent. The police reported that the mood among the wealthy classes at Versailles was one of utter panic when the result of the Paris by-election was announced. The *Courrier de Marseille* stated that Paris had 'flung down the gauntlet to civilization'. The commercial travellers of Arras who were on the road to Paris turned back and cancelled their orders when they heard the news.[10]

But the Prince-President remained calm. His newspaper, *Le Napoléon*, which had started publication two months earlier – many people thought that he himself wrote some of the articles in the paper[11] – stated that there was no need for panic:

> The barbarians are at our gates; but . . . they shall not enter either by stratagem or by force. We have behind our ramparts an immense population who, despite a few traitors, will always prevent the triumph of an enemy whose sole object is pillage.[12]

The Paris by-election result threw Louis Napoleon once more into the arms of the Conservatives. On the evening of the official declaration of the poll, he invited Thiers, Molé, the Duc de Broglie, Montalembert and two other leaders of the Party of Order to a conference at the Élysée.[13] In the Assembly, the Party of the Élysée abandoned their opposition to Falloux's Education Bill, which passed into law on 15 March. It provided for a system of public and private education. The public sector was placed under the joint control of the State and the

Church, who were to agree on the syllabus; and in the localities the teachers were to be appointed by, and remain under the control of, the local mayor and parish priest. No one could become a teacher unless he was either a university graduate or a priest, in which case he needed no academic qualifications. In the private sector, anyone would be entitled to open a school, and the state would exercise no supervision over it except to ensure that the buildings complied with health regulations and that no Socialist or seditious doctrines were taught there. In practice, this favoured a Catholic education, since the Catholic Church was the only organization wealthy enough to run private schools on a large scale. This remained the educational system in France throughout the Second Empire.[14]

The Conservatives consoled themselves by believing that the election result in Paris had been a freak by-election reaction and that Paris was not really Socialist. They soon had an opportunity to test their theory. In the elections in March, Vidal had been elected in Alsace as well as in Paris, and as he chose to sit for Alsace there had to be another by-election in Paris in April. The Mountain nominated the famous novelist Eugène Sue. He had been a prominent figure in society under Louis Philippe, but had recently become a Socialist, and now wrote novels, in his luxurious mansion on the banks of the Loire, about life in the underworld and the sufferings of the poor. The Conservative press denounced Sue as a hypocrite and a pornographer. *The Times* described his latest book, *Les Mystères du Peuple*, as 'an epitome of all the falsehoods, the calumnies, the blasphemies which have in turn assailed religion, the principles of authority and of respect for law and order'.[15]

A number of prominent Conservative politicians entered the contest to secure the nomination as Sue's opponent; but a fortnight before polling day they all withdrew in favour of a candidate who was thought to have a great popular appeal. Leclerc, who had fought at Waterloo, ran a small paper-manufacturing business in the Rue Saint-Joseph. He had never had any political ambitions, but had become a national hero during the June Days in 1848. When his eldest son was killed fighting under Cavaignac, he and his second son, a lad of 17, had volunteered to take the dead son's place, and had fought on until the Socialist rebels had been finally defeated.

His candidature was supported by 300 Deputies of all the anti-Socialist and anti-Radical parties, including Cavaignac himself, 'as a protest against the principle of insurrection, immorality and contempt for religion which some were attempting to force on the citizens of Paris in the person of a Socialist candidate'.[16] His supporters fought a much more active campaign than had La Hitte and the government

267

candidates in March. Paris was covered with placards calling on the electors to vote for Leclerc, 'that living protest of order against anarchy'.[17] His commanding officer during the June Days spoke at one of his election rallies, and told the cheering audience how Leclerc had come up to him at the barricades and had said: 'Captain, here is my second child, who has come to avenge his brother and defend the cause of order and society.'[18]

The police did not allow the Socialist canvassers the liberty which they had granted them in March. On three occasions when the Socialists arrived to hold their election meetings in the Salle Valentine and other halls which they had booked, they found that the police had ordered the proprietors not to allow them to enter, and the meetings could not be held. The police raided the kiosks on the boulevards and removed all the Socialist and Radical newspapers and any other newspapers which urged the electors to vote for Sue. They ordered the café proprietors not to permit Socialist newspapers to be sold or read in their cafés, and when a Socialist lawyer went to a café to protest that the police action was illegal, he was beaten up by Conservative supporters. The police tore down Sue's election placards from the walls in the streets. They arrested a number of Socialist canvassers, and a few days before polling day rounded up and deported from Paris a large number of vagrants who would probaby have voted for Sue.[19]

To the surprise and alarm of the middle classes, Sue was elected by 127,812 votes against 119,726 for Leclerc. 'The ballot has decided against us', wrote Le Constitutionnel; 'Paris persists in declaring for the most notorious disorder that can be conceived.' 'The Reds are again victorious', wrote Changarnier's L'Assemblée Nationale, and foretold that as a result there would be an exodus of visitors from Paris and that the value of property would fall by one-fifth.[20]

The Conservatives decided that the only remedy was to take away the right to vote from the Socialist and Radical workers of France and especially from those of Paris. This was not easy, as universal suffrage was laid down in the Constitution. Thiers urged the Assembly to disregard the Constitution, to disenfranchise the 'vile multitude' who had always throughout history supported tyranny against freedom, and to impose a property qualification such as had existed under Louis Philippe and still existed in Britain;[21] but the majority of his Conservative colleagues preferred the indirect approach. The electoral law of 1848 stipulated that an elector must have resided for six months in his electoral district before being entitled to vote. A bill was now introduced to extend this period from six months to three years. This would have the effect of disenfranchising those workers who in periods of unemployment wandered from one part of France to another. The Socialists were particularly indignant at the provision in the bill that the three years' residence must be proved either by evidence of payment of direct taxes – which would apply only to the wealthier classes – or by a certificate issued by the voter's employer.

Universal suffrage had been for twenty years one of Louis Napoleon's most sacred principles. He had always based the Bonapartist claim to the imperial throne on the referendum held in 1804 under universal suffrage, and since his election to the presidency he had often stressed that universal suffrage was the source of his authority. When the proposal to restrict the franchise was put forward, his first reaction was to oppose it; then, when the Conservative politicians pointed out that the Mountain would probably win a majority in the Assembly at the next general election if it was held under universal suffrage, he agreed not to oppose the bill, but suggested that it should be introduced by the Deputies of the Party of Order and not by the government. This would have suited him excellently; the Socialist and Radical menace would have been destroyed, and the Party of Order would have been blamed for taking away the people's right to vote. But Thiers was not prepared to allow Louis Napoleon to play this game, and insisted that if the electoral reform bill was to go through it must be introduced by the Minister of the Interior as a government bill.[22] In the end a compromise was reached; the Assembly elected a committee of seventeen, composed of the leading Deputies of the Party of Order, to draft the bill, and it was then introduced by the Minister of the Interior.

The bill aroused the strongest political passions in the Assembly and in the country. Conservative municipal councils and local Chambers of Commerce passed resolutions supporting it, and the Socialists organized petitions and street demonstrations against it.[23] In the Assembly, the bill was opposed by many Moderate Republicans as well as by the deputies of the Mountain. Victor Hugo declared that the moral right of insurrection, which had been removed by universal suffrage, would be restored by the bill. Some prominent friends of Louis Napoleon voted against the bill, including Prince Napoleon, Pierre Bonaparte, General Montholon, and Edgar Ney, as well as Cavaignac, Lamartine and General Lamoricière; but it passed the Assembly on 31 May by 433 votes to 241.[24]

The effect of the electoral law of 31 May 1850 was to reduce the total electorate from 9,618,057 to 6,809,281.* The great majority of the three million who were disenfranchised were Radical and Socialist voters;

*Before the bill became law, under 'universal suffrage', less than 27 per cent of the total inhabitants of France had the vote. The law of 31 May 1850 reduced the proportion to 19 per cent. In Britain in 1850, 7 per cent of the population had the vote. The proportion in Britain in 1979 is 73 per cent.

in Paris, where the Red successes had so alarmed the government, the electorate was reduced by 144,000, and 61 per cent of the electors lost the right to vote. In Lille, the electorate fell from 15,068 to 4524; in Amiens, from 16,875 to 5505; and in Nantes, from 25,000 to 7460.[25]

Louis Napoleon's friends believed that he had done himself great harm by agreeing to the law of 31 May, not only because it had made him unpopular with the lower classes, but also because he had disenfranchised electors who would have voted for him in a future presidential election. King Jerome told him that Molé and Thiers had been right to call him a cretin. Louis Napoleon replied: 'Wait and see.'[26] Hortense Cornu asked him how he, the child of universal suffrage, could support a restricted suffrage. He said to her: 'You don't understand anything. I am destroying the Assembly.' 'But you are destroying yourself with them', she said. 'Not at all', said Louis Napoleon; 'when the Assembly are hanging over the precipice, I shall cut the rope.'[27]

For the moment, he seemed to be as popular as ever. At the height of the bitter controversy over the electoral reform bill, he continued to ride through the streets of Paris, sometimes in state, accompanied by an escort of cavalry, but often with only one or two attendants, as he visited some public building or private workshop, or rode in the Champs-Élysées and the Bois de Boulogne with Miss Howard. On 11 May he gave a dinner at the Élysée to the seventeen commissioners who had drafted the electoral bill; it was reported in the press, and everywhere interpreted as a public gesture of his support for the bill. But the next evening he alarmed his household and the police by attending a benefit performance for an old actor at the popular Gaieté theatre in the Boulevard du Temple which was frequented by a working-class audience of a Socialist arrondissement. The workmen in their blouses showed no sign of hostility to the Prince-President in his box, and when some of them, in their usual way, stamped their feet in protest at the long delay between the acts, other members of the audience asked them to desist, on this occasion, out of respect for the President.[28]

In June he went to Saint-Quentin to open the railway. Napoleon had gone there in 1802 for the opening of the canal. In his speech, Louis Napoleon told the people that he would repeat what Napoleon had said to them forty-eight years before: 'Stop worrying; the storms have passed away. I will ensure the triumph of the great truths of our revolution; but I will repress, with equal force, new errors and old prejudices.' He added that they must always accept what was good in the revolution and reject what was evil in it. He distributed prizes to the workmen who had accumulated the largest deposits in the savings bank at Saint-Quentin. 'My sincerest and most devoted friends', he told them, 'are not to be found in palaces; they are in cottages. They

Napoleon III, by Maguès

Eugénie, by Winterhalter

are not in rooms with gilded ceilings, but in workshops and in the fields.'[29] Before leaving Saint-Quentin he had distributed nearly 20,000 francs in gifts to the workmen and the patients in the hospitals. At La Fère, he gave 500 francs to a workman who had tried to commit suicide because his wife and four children were starving.[30]

Occasionally, both in Paris and in the provinces, he encountered a hostile Socialist demonstration. The Socialists, often wearing red cravats, ran beside his carriage shouting 'Vive la République!' This was something that they could shout without being arrested, for those who ventured to shout 'Vive la République démocratique et sociale!' or 'Vive la Sociale!' ran the risk not only of being assaulted and kicked by Louis Napoleon's supporters in the crowd, but also of being arrested and sentenced to several months, or even years, in prison.[31]

But the Socialists' zeal and readiness for martyrdom was unlimited. Workmen dressed in the traditional working-class *blouse* – and middle-class intellectuals wearing the *blouse* over expensive underclothes – continued to risk arrest by shouting 'Vive la Sociale!' and after they had been arrested made things as hard as possible for themselves by refusing to obey prison regulations and organizing demonstrations and riots in the jails. Their aims were disclosed in the semi-literate documents which the police found when they raided their houses and meeting-places – universal manhood suffrage; free state education for all children; unemployment, sickness and retirement benefits for workmen and their families; freedom to form trade unions and to strike; a restoration of the ten-hour working day which had been granted after the February revolution and later repealed by the Conservatives; the abolition of usury; free credit for the working man; and public ownership of land. Their methods were violent; bred in the traditions of 1793 and embittered by their recent sufferings, they demanded death for the aristocrats and cried 'Vive la Guillotine!' at the same time as they denounced capital punishment. They affronted public opinion, denounced religion, defied their parents, insulted priests, and sometimes attacked policemen.[32]

In the spring of 1850 the drive against the Socialists and Radicals was intensified. Acting through the Prefects, Louis Napoleon removed from office 421 mayors and 183 deputy-mayors who were suspected of Socialist or Radical leanings. He dissolved the National Guard in 153 towns and communes where the local units were under left-wing control. The civil service and the judicial tribunals were purged of Reds. Politically unreliable schoolteachers and university professors, including the famous historian Michelet, were dismissed; and a schoolmaster near Paris was sentenced to three years' imprisonment and a fine of 300 francs and loss of voting rights for five years for corrupting the morals of the children in his charge by teaching them Socialist doctrines.[33]

The police carried out house-to-house raids in working-class districts, searching for arms and Socialist propaganda material.[34] At the house of a tailor in Lyons they found 20,000 Socialist leaflets. In the army, where the military authorities were very apprehensive of Socialist influence among the soldiers, haphazard searches were made of soldiers' knapsacks which sometimes unearthed Socialist leaflets or incriminating letters. The police approached private employers, particularly the railway companies, and asked them to dismiss Socialists and Radicals, or to deny them promotion. In Lyons, where the state of siege had been proclaimed after the rising of June 1849, General Castellane, knowing that the funerals of old Socialist stalwarts were often made the occasion for a Socialist demonstration and for anti-religious speeches at the graveside, made it a criminal offence for more than 300 persons to attend the funeral of a Socialist.[35]

Two Radicals in a village in Provence were sentenced respectively to four and three months' imprisonment for making a toy guillotine for the amusement of the children at the local carnival. Socialist theatres were raided, and the Paris police banned the performance of *L'enfant de Paris*, a play about a Socialist urchin who died on the barricades, and of *Rome*, which glorified Rossi's murder and the Roman Republic of 1849. People were arrested for singing Socialist songs – 'Le cri du peuple', 'Le bal et la guillotine', and Pierre Dupont's song

> Mettons au bout de nos fusils
> Falloux, Faucher, Barrot, Passy,
> Les Changarnier, les Radetzky,
> Les oppresseurs de tous pays.*

The 'Marseillaise' was regarded as seditious. The official reports refer to the singing of '*La Marseillaise* and other Socialist and seditious songs' and persons who were heard singing it were often arrested.[36]

Strikes and trade unions had been illegal in France ever since Napoleon banned them in 1805; but friendly societies of workmen had been permitted, to which the workmen contributed money and which provided them with funds when they were sick or unemployed. In the summer of 1850 the Prefects and the police dissolved friendly societies and seized their funds in many areas on the grounds that they were a cover for Socialist activities. At the end of June, the police arrested 27 workmen who were attending a secret meeting of a new organization, the General Association of Industrial Solidarity, though many other

*The song was sung in several slightly differing versions.

members escaped because the organizers had stationed a woman at the door who was to give a warning, by opening her umbrella, of the approach of the police.[37]

A number of illegal strikes were launched by quarry workers, restaurant cooks and calico-printers for an increase in wages, against reduction of wages, and for the ten-hour working day. The police arrested the strike-leaders, and broke the strikes, at Laon, Beauvais, Châteaudun and in the new iron works at Le Creusot, whose founder, Eugène Schneider, joined Louis Napoleon's government in January 1851. In August 1850 Carlier, the Chief of the Paris Police, dissolved the Association for Mutual Relief which had been formed among the Paris calico-printers and had organized the strikes. Their funds, which were confiscated, amounted to 50,000 francs. The police arrested Socialists and Radicals who secretly collected money for the relief of the schoolteachers who had been dismissed from their employment for political reasons; and the courts invalidated a bequest in a will whereby the testator left 220,000 francs for the purchase of a home for workers who had suffered imprisonment or victimization on account of their Socialist opinions.[38]

The Assembly followed up the electoral law of 31 May with a new press law, which made it illegal to publish an unsigned article in a newspaper, gave powers to the authorities to ban the importation of foreign newspapers, abolished trial by jury in prosecutions for offences against the press law, placed a stamp duty on all newspapers, and doubled the sum to be deposited by newspaper proprietors as surety for good behaviour, raising it to 24,000 francs in the case of the Paris press. Another law made it illegal to hold a meeting during an election campaign which, although the ostensible object was to secure the election of a candidate, was in fact an excuse for propagating seditious doctrines.[39]

The press law was vigorously enforced. Hardly any Socialist, Radical or even Moderate Republican newspaper escaped a prosecuction at some time or other, and occasionally Legitimist papers were also seized and their editors brought before the courts. The most usual reason for seizure and prosecution was for publishing an article which attacked or ridiculed Louis Napoleon; but there were also many cases where the newspapers had denigrated religion or encouraged class hatred. Proudhon was prosecuted for an article in *La Voix du Peuple* in which he accused the army authorities of responsibility for the deaths of 220 soldiers who were drowned when a suspension bridge across the Maine at Angers collapsed as they were crossing it. The Socialist paper, *Le Vote Universel*, was fined 6000 francs and its editor imprisoned for six months for publishing an article, 'Social Contrasts in the Nineteenth

Century', which was signed by the Socialist Deputy, Gillaud, but which many people believed had been written by George Sand. It contrasted the happy childhood of the children of wealthy parents who played in the Tuileries Gardens with the life of the children of the poor in slums and caves.[40]

Victor Hugo's son, Charles Hugo, was imprisoned for publishing an article in *L'Événement* in which he denounced capital punishment and the execution of a man at Mâcon who had murdered two gendarmes and whom Louis Napoleon had refused to reprieve. The editor of *La Feuille du Village* received three months for accusing an employer in Loiret of sending a servant to his death down a well with a callous disregard for his safety. Contributors and editors were sentenced for drawings and cartoons as well as for articles. The author and publisher of a lithograph entitled 'The Republican Trinity', showing Jesus Christ, Robespierre and Barbès, received prison sentences of six and two months; and the humorous magazine *Charivari* was prosecuted for a cartoon showing Louis Napoleon's ministers shooting at a target named 'The Constitution' and Louis Napoleon offering a prize for the minister who came closest to hitting the target.[41]

Sometimes writers and editors were punished under the press laws on a mere technicality. The editor of *La République* was imprisoned for printing a second edition of the paper without paying an additional sum as surety money. In the village of Borée in Lorraine, a Socialist local councillor, who was almost illiterate, asked a friend to draft a letter for him to the local newspaper, *Le Patriote de la Meuse*, and another friend suggested a few alterations to the draft. The letter was published, signed by the councillor's name. The police, claiming that the friends who drafted and amended the letter, not the councillor, were the true authors of the letter, prosecuted the three of them and the editor of the newspaper for publishing an article without giving the author's name. They were acquitted by the local tribunal, but the government appealed to the Court of Appeal in Nancy, who sentenced them all to six months' imprisonment and to the joint payment of a fine of 1000 francs and costs. As a result, *Le Patriote de la Meuse* had to cease publication.[42]

This persecution of the Left angered several of Louis Napoleon's oldest friends. Émile de Girardin published in *La Presse* some of the Liberal sentiments which Louis Napoleon had expressed at the period when he visited him at Arenenberg, and wrote that he hoped that he would not be prosecuted for publishing the Prince-President's statements.[43] Vieillard and Hortense Cornu became increasingly worried: but Hortense successfully used her influence in favour of several revolutionary Radicals who had fallen foul of the police. She persuaded Louis Napoleon to annul the order for the expulsion from France of

Cernuschi and other Italian revolutionaries who had fought against the French at Rome. 'My dear Hortense,' he wrote to her, 'I will do what you wish for your protégés. But Cernuschi is said to be very dangerous.'

This did not disarm her criticism of his government, and he was hurt by it. He told her that the police did not indulge in unnecessary persecutions, but that he could not be expected to tolerate the plots of Mazzini's agents against every government in Europe. When she reminded him of his own revolutionary past, he wrote that he remembered without blushing that he had once been a conspirator and a prisoner, but thought that the governments at that time had been fully justified in fighting him and imprisoning him.[44]

In the midst of these domestic troubles, Louis Napoleon was able to win some unexpected triumphs in foreign policy. By September 1849 the Russian and Austrian troops had crushed the Hungarian revolution. The defeated revolutionary army, which included a large contingent of Polish refugees, retreated across the Turkish frontier. Austria and Russia demanded that their rebellious Hungarian and Polish subjects should be handed over to them for punishment; but the British Ambassador in Constantinople, Sir Stratford Canning, persuaded Turkey to refuse the Austrian and Russian demands, and when Austria and Russia threatened Turkey, Britain and France sent their fleets to the Dardanelles and warned both Powers that they would go to war in defence of Turkey. Austria and Russia accepted the position. The incident made Palmerston the hero of the European Radicals; and Louis Napoleon's part in supporting Britain enabled him to claim that he had won a diplomatic victory for French prestige and the cause of freedom.[45]

On the way home from the Dardanelles, the British navy called at Athens to settle Palmerston's differences with the Greek government. Palmerston had espoused the cause of 'Don Pacifico', a Portuguese Jew who had lived for many years in Greece but who qualified as a British subject because he had been born in Gibraltar. When Pacifico's house was attacked by a mob in an anti-semitic Easter riot at Salonika, Palmerston demanded compensation for Pacifico – not only £8500 for the damage to the house and the fear to which he and his family had been exposed, but also an additional £27,000 because of the destruction in the house of title deeds and documents which, according to Pacifico, would have enabled him to win a lawsuit for £27,000 in the Portuguese courts.

As the Greek government persisted in their refusal to meet these claims, Palmerston ordered the British navy to blockade the Piraeus, with disastrous results for Greek trade. Russia, who had political and religious links with Greece, protested strongly. Louis Napoleon offered to mediate. Palmerston wished to refuse his offer, but the Prime Minister, Lord John Russell, compelled him to suspend the blockade and accept the French mediation. The French Ambassador in Athens, Baron Gros, set about attempting to mediate between the Greek Foreign Minister and the British Ambassador, Mr Wyse, who had married Louis Napoleon's cousin Letizia, the sister of Carlo Bonaparte of Canino. Negotiations were simultaneously carried on in London between Palmerston, the French ambassador Drouyn de Lhuys, and the Greek ambassador.

Drouyn de Lhuys in London and Gros in Athens decided that the British attitude was unreasonable, and suggested a compromise. Under pressure from Lord John Russell, Palmerston reluctantly agreed with Drouyn de Lhuys and the Greek ambassador in London that the Greek government should pay Pacifico £8500 compensation for the damage to his house and that the claim for the £27,000 for the loss of the documents should be referred to impartial arbitrators. But Wyse in Athens refused all compromise, and without consulting Gros re-imposed the blockade and demanded full satisfaction of all Pacifico's claim. A few hours before the blockade was due to begin, Gros heard from Drouyn de Lhuys about the agreement that had been reached in London, and he asked Wyse to postpone the re-imposition of the blockade; but Wyse refused, and before Palmerston's letter informing Wyse of the London agreement had reached Athens – some suspected that Palmerston had deliberately delayed sending the letter – the Greek government had submitted and paid over £32,000 to Wyse in satisfaction of Pacifico's claim. Palmerston then informed the French government that in view of this development Britain no longer considered itself bound by the agreement reached with the Greeks through the French mediation in London.

Louis Napoleon took a high line. He protested that Palmerston's action was an insult to France, and, conscious that he had the moral support of Russia, Austria and every state in Europe, he withdrew Drouyn de Lhuys from London as a protest. It was dangerous to confront Palmerston in international affairs, as he had nearly always had the best of his encounters with foreign statesmen. Perhaps for this reason, Louis Napoleon took the precaution of letting it be known that he had not been present at the Cabinet meeting at which the decision was taken to withdraw the Ambassador in London; the meeting had been held while he was visiting Fontainebleau.[46] But Lord John Russell and the Cabinet compelled Palmerston to give way, to agree to set aside the agreement reached between Wyse and the Greeks in Athens, and to refer Pacifico's claim for compensation for loss of the documents to arbitrators, as had been agreed through Drouyn de Lhuys's mediation in London. The arbitrators eventually decided that Pacifico was entitled, under this head, not to £27,000 but to £150.[47]

There was great jubilation among the Conservatives in Paris when La Hitte informed the Assembly that the dispute with Britain had been satisfactorily settled, and that Drouyn de Lhuys would be returning to London because the British government had acceded to all the French demands. In London it was thought that Palmerston would be forced to resign; but he scored the greatest triumph of his career with his 'Civis Romanus sum' speech in the House of Commons, where a vote of confidence in his policy was carried, and he rose to the highest peak of his popularity in Britain. He was perfectly happy that people in Paris should believe that Louis Napoleon had defeated him as long as the House of Commons and the British public believed that it was he who had won, and that he had vindicated British honour and the rights of a British subject. Palmerston always respected opponents who stood up to him, and from this time onwards he respected Louis Napoleon. In future years he was even ready to compromise his position with his Radical supporters for the sake of Louis Napoleon's friendship.

Later in the year Louis Napoleon was able to win a further success in connection with Schleswig-Holstein. The Duchies of Schleswig and Holstein were ruled by the King of Denmark in his personal capacity as hereditary Duke; but the Liberal and nationalist passions aroused in Germany by the revolution of 1848 led to a movement among the German population of Holstein to overthrow the King of Denmark's government and incorporate the Duchy in the German Confederation. The Liberal government of Prussia took the leadership of the German movement to liberate Schleswig-Holstein. The Great Powers intervened, and forced Prussia and Denmark to agree to an armistice while the very complicated problem was discussed at a Conference of the Great Powers in London. The autocratic empires of Russia and Austria supported Denmark and its King's hereditary right. The British government, who were influenced by the pro-German feelings of Queen Victoria and Prince Albert, were neutral. Liberal opinion throughout Europe was pro-German.

Louis Napoleon became President of the French Republic in the midst of the Schleswig-Holstein crisis. In November 1849 he sent Persigny to Berlin, and it was believed in diplomatic circles that he was offering Prussia an alliance against Austria and Russia over Schleswig-Holstein. The Conservatives became alarmed that the Prussian government would invite the French troops to cross the Rhine and launch a revolutionary war, in the traditional Napoleonic style, to liberate Schleswig-Holstein. But Prussia refused the French offers, and

Louis Napoleon changed sides. At the London Conference, Drouyn de Lhuys supported the Russian and Austrian position, and Denmark against Prussia.

In October 1850, Prussian troops invaded Schleswig-Holstein. Austria threatened to declare war against Prussia, and Russia gave Austria full diplomatic support, while Palmerston tried to mediate. In France the government press condemned Prussia for endangering European peace, and though Louis Napoleon declared that France would not intervene militarily in Germany, he called up the army reservists and sent 75,000 troops to the frontier along the Rhine. Once again the British government became alarmed that French troops would cross the Rhine, this time as Prussia's enemy, not her friend, and destroy the balance of power in Central Europe. But Prussia gave way under the Austrian threat of war, and withdrew her troops from Schleswig-Holstein – a retreat which was welcomed by the Prussian Conservative Opposition, including Bismarck. Louis Napoleon, without really doing much to influence the result, was able to claim that his action in sending troops to the frontier had preserved the peace of Europe.[48]

CHAPTER 22

CHICKEN AND CHAMPAGNE

B Y the summer of 1850 Louis Napoleon was nearly half-way through his term of office, which was to end in May 1852.* The Constitution stipulated that no President could be re-elected for a second term; but the Constitution could be changed by a three-fourths majority of the Assembly in the last year of the Assembly's life, which in the case of the present Assembly would begin in May 1851. In preparation for this, the Bonapartists began a campaign in the summer of 1850 for a revision of the Constitution to allow the President to stand for a second term. Louis Napoleon himself said nothing about revision, but some of his remarks in his speeches, about what he would do for France if he were given the time to do it, were interpreted as hints that he hoped for a second term.

A key factor in the situation was the head of the army and National Guard in the Paris area, the fifty-seven-year-old General Nicolas Changarnier. His suppression of the Radical demonstration in Paris on 13 June 1849 had made him the hero of the middle classes, who acclaimed him as 'the broom of the boulevards'; it was confidently predicted at fashionable dinner parties that 'the broom of the boulevards of the 13th would sweep up all Europe'[1] and finally eliminate the menace of Communism and Red Republicanism. In politics Changarnier was considered to be a Legitimist, but he was also very popular with the Party of Order. He usually voted with them in the Assembly, where he sat as a deputy, and supported their policy in the newspaper which he owned, *L'Assemblée Nationale*.

His relations with Louis Napoleon were problematical. Ostensibly they were the best of friends. Changarnier, who lived at his headquarters in the Tuileries, spent much of his time with the Prince-President at the Élysée; they were often seen riding together in the President's carriage on public occasions, and Changarnier sometimes accompanied Louis Napoleon on his tours of the provinces. Louis

*The Constitution laid down that future Presidents should hold office for four years, but as the presidential elections were to be held every fourth year in May, Louis Napoleon's term was to last only three years and five months.

279

Napoleon gave Changarnier the Grand Cross of the Legion of Honour, and praised him as the defender of society against the Anarchists.

But anyone who moved in government circles knew that things were very different beneath the surface. In private conversation, Changarnier did not hide his contempt for the Prince-President. When Louis Napoleon rejected his proposal to dissolve the Constituent Assembly by force in January 1849, he told Thiers that Louis Napoleon was a fool.[2] He made another outspoken remark at the end of May 1850. He attended a Cabinet meeting to discuss what measures should be taken to guard against Radical and Socialist demonstrations when the Law of 31 May, disenfranchising the three million electors, came into force. In the middle of the meeting Louis Napoleon went to fetch a map of Paris, and while he was out of the room Changarnier said to the others: 'I hope, gentlemen, that if we fight, it will not be for this Thomas Diafoirus.* I will go to the rostrum and ask for power to be given to the most worthy man.' Changarnier's remarks were reported to Louis Napoleon.[3]

In the summer of 1850 Louis Napoleon invited a number of army officers and N.C.O.s to a series of military dinner parties in the garden of the Tuileries. About twenty guests sat at each table, with officers and N.C.O.s sitting together without differentiation of rank. At the dinner on 7 August, Louis Napoleon invited an N.C.O. to sit on his left. Changarnier thought that this was 'Socialism of the most dangerous kind'.[4]

In August, with the Assembly in recess, Louis Napoleon made another tour of the provinces. This time he went further afield than in 1849, and ventured into more dangerous areas, visiting districts in eastern and south-eastern France where Red Republicanism and Socialism were strong. Despite the warnings of his advisers, he insisted on visiting the Socialist stronghold of Lyons. He arrived on 15 August – Napoleon's birthday – by steamer from Mâcon, and, mounting a white horse, rode to the town hall; he was received with great applause from the crowds who had assembled at the landing stage and in the streets. Although the authorities had decided that it would be unwise for him to enter the Red district of Croix-Rousse, he walked in Croix-Rousse with only a small escort, and granted the petition of a woman who accosted him in the street and asked him to release her husband, who was serving a five-year prison sentence for Socialist activities. The local council of the Lyons suburb of Guillotière, on which the Socialists held 33 of the 36 seats, refused to vote money for his reception; but the proprietors of the famous Winter Garden in Guillotière invited him to

*The name of the ignorant mountebank doctor in Molière's play, *Le Malade Imaginaire.*

attend a banquet in the Winter Garden for 2000 working-class diners from the district, who greeted him warmly as he sat at the high table on the bandstand among the palm trees and fountains.[5]

In his speeches at Lyons he stressed the popular origins of Bonapartism and its role as the alternative to both privilege and disorder. 'Mr Mayor,' he said at a banquet at the town hall, with the Cardinal Archbishop sitting at his right hand, 'I am the representative, not of a party, but of the two great national manifestations which in 1804 as in 1848 wished to save, by means of order, the great principles of the French Revolution.' On the eve of his departure, he spoke at another banquet. 'It would be presumptuous of me to say to you, as the Emperor did: "People of Lyons, I love you." But you will, I hope, allow me to say, from the depths of my heart: "People of Lyons, I beg you to love me." ' 'Yes, yes, we love you!' replied the audience.[6]

At Besançon arrangements had been made for him to spend a short time in the evening at a popular dance-hall in the Place de la Halle before going on to a gala performance at the theatre. The authorities heard that the Socialists and Radicals were planning to assassinate him in the Place de la Halle, but this did not prevent him from going there. As he crossed the Place de la Halle on his way to the dance hall with General Castellane, the Commander-in-Chief in south-eastern France, he was surrounded by a crowd of young Socialists who separated him from his bodyguard, jostled him, and tried to force him to shout 'Vive la République!', as the police fought with the demonstrators and General Castellane drew his sword. Louis Napoleon succeeded in reaching the dance-hall, and was welcomed by the working-class dancers inside. He stayed there for only ten minutes and then left for the theatre, again running the gauntlet of the Socialist demonstrators outside in the Place de la Halle. The middle-class audience in the theatre gave him a great reception, and a man wearing a red cravat who shouted 'Long live the Red Republic!' was immediately arrested. *Le Moniteur*, reporting the incident at the Place de la Halle, stated that the trouble had been caused, not by the loyal French population of Besançon, but by the immigrant Swiss watchmakers who had imported Socialism into the French Jura.[7]

Louis Napoleon went on to Alsace and Lorraine, where thousands of peasants came into the towns to see him, and stood for hours in the rain with the local townspeople waiting for him to arrive. At Strasburg he decorated two old soldiers, of whom one had lost an arm in the Pyrenees in 1813 and the other had helped to build a bridge of boats across the Beresina during the retreat from Moscow. He attended a banquet in the spacious dining-room of the Hôtel de Paris in Strasburg, which was said to be the largest dining-room in France, and in his speech thanked the people of Alsace for their support 'in the struggle between utopian schemes and useful reforms'. He told them that a few months of Socialist propaganda by 'foreign emissaries' in Alsace 'could not convert a people deeply imbued with the solid virtues of the soldier and the ploughman into a people hostile to religion, order and property'.[8]

At Metz he encountered a hostile demonstration from some members of the National Guard and from Socialist youths with red cravats, and there was an incident at the theatre in Nancy, where an aggressive individual forced himself on Louis Napoleon and demanded rudely that he shake hands with him. 'I do not shake hands with everybody when I do not know them', said Louis Napoleon, and the man was kicked out of the theatre by the angry bourgeois in the audience, while the ladies cheered the Prince-President and threw bouquets at his box. But two days later, Louis Napoleon willingly shook hands with an old veteran who claimed to be the oldest soldier in France and had served in every campaign from 1792 to 1815, when the old man politely asked the Prince-President for permission to shake his hand. Louis Napoleon also shook hands with many workmen in the chalkpits at Dieuze, where he lunched with the management and the workmen, and enjoyed himself greatly, though he got wet through in the rain.[9]

He followed his voyage in the East with a visit to the north-west, attending a naval review at Cherbourg and being received enthusiastically in Brittany and Normandy. His speeches were suitably adapted to the Legitimist and Conservative politics of the district; at Évreux, he replied to the Bishop's eulogy by stating that 'religion and the family are, with authority and order, the bases of all lasting society'.[10] On his return to Paris, he was met at the station in the Rue du Havre – later named the Gare Saint-Lazare – at half-past eleven at night by a large crowd of his supporters of the Society of 10 December, shouting 'Vive Napoléon!' and 'Vive l'Empereur!' Some Radicals and Socialists in the crowd shouted 'Vive la République!' and were attacked by the Bonapartists. They complained that the police had done nothing to protect them or to arrest their assailants, and pointed out that the Prefect of the Paris Police, Carlier, was also the President of the Society of 10 December. The Republican and Conservative press took up the matter, and the Permanent Committee of the National Assembly, which remained in session when the Assembly was in recess, asked the Minister of the Interior to investigate the activities of the Society of 10 December.[11]

The Republicans were becoming increasingly alarmed. When Louis Napoleon reviewed the cadets of the Military Academy at Saint-Cyr, the Commandant of the school, General Alexandre, called on the cadets 'to repeat with me the cry that thrilled France forty years ago, *Vive Napoléon!*'[12] The Republicans did not like the cry 'Vive Napoléon!', and still less did they like 'Vive l'Empereur!', which was sometimes heard on the President's tours. The Bonapartist press ridiculed the idea that to cry 'Vive l'Empereur!' was a threat to the Constitution; how could it be seditious to cheer the great Napoleon, whose reign as Emperor had been so glorious for France?

At the end of September and the beginning of October, a fortnight of military manoeuvres was held on the plain of Satory near Versailles. Louis Napoleon attended, escorted by Changarnier and by the Minister of War, General d'Hautpoul; he was loudly cheered, especially by the cavalry, who greeted him with shouts of 'Vive l'Empereur!' He ordered that all the officers, N.C.O.s and men were to be provided every day with a picnic lunch at his expense; there was champagne for the officers and N.C.O.s, wine for the privates, and chicken and cigars for everyone. The food and drink were laid out on the grass in hampers, with a meal for twelve men in each hamper; each officer and N.C.O. received a quarter of a chicken and half a bottle of champagne.[13]

This hospitality aroused caustic comments from the Republicans and the Party of Order, who regarded it as an attempt by Louis Napoleon to buy the support of the soldiers and to convert the army into a praetorian guard. The Legitimist paper, *Le Corsaire*, reminded its readers that the great Napoleon had once said to his soldiers: 'Grenadiers! Have I ever failed you when I promised you victory?', but that today one would say: 'Grenadiers! Have I ever failed you when I promised you a blow-out?' – and champagne, truffled chicken and Havana cigars? The copies of *Le Corsaire* were seized by the police, and the writer of the article and the editor were prosecuted for insulting the President of the Republic. The writer was sentenced to a year's imprisonment and the editor to six months', and they were jointly fined 2000 francs.[14]

On the last day of the manoeuvres, a colonel asked General Neumayer, who was Changarnier's second-in-command, what the troops ought to shout when the President arrived to review them. Neumayer told him that it was a contravention of military discipline for troops on parade to make any kind of political demonstration or to shout anything, and that when the President arrived they should receive him in silence. A few days later, the Minister of War removed Neumayer from his command in Paris and appointed him to what was technically a superior command at Rennes. This angered Changarnier and the Party of Order, and precipitated a political crisis. The matter was raised in the Assembly, and the deputies demanded an explanation from the Minister of War. Changarnier told Carlier, whom he knew was the President of the Society of 10 December and an admirer of Louis Napoleon, that he was only awaiting orders from the Assembly to send Louis Napoleon to the prison at Vincennes. Carlier repeated the remark to Louis Napoleon, which was perhaps what Changarnier intended.[15]

Louis Napoleon's first reaction was to give way in face of the mounting opposition. Instead of following the advice which Persigny and d'Hautpoul gave him to dismiss Changarnier from the command of the army in Paris, he dismissed d'Hautpoul from the War Office and appointed him Commander-in-Chief of the army in Algeria. He replaced him as Minister of War by General Schramm, a colourless figure who was overawed by Changarnier; and when Changarnier, on 2 November, issued an order of the day forbidding the army to engage in any political demonstrations or to shout any slogans when on parade, Louis Napoleon accepted this without a protest.[16]

In his presidential message to the Assembly on 12 November, he was conciliatory, and clearly implied that he was not seeking a second term of office. 'What preoccupies me above all, you may be sure, is not who will govern France in 1852, but how to use the time at my disposal in such a way that the transition of power, whatever form it takes, is made without agitation and without troubles.'[17] Meanwhile the press had published a story that twenty-six members of the Society of 10 December were involved in a plot to murder Changarnier and the President of the Assembly, Dupin. Louis Napoleon thereupon dissolved the Society, although subsequent investigations by a committee of the Assembly showed that the story about the plot was a complete fabrication.[18]

But Louis Napoleon was pursuing his usual tactic of making every possible concession to his enemies immediately before destroying them. He had had friendly talks with the deputies of the Mountain in January 1849 before launching the attack against them; and now, in November and December 1850, he invited Changarnier to the Élysée, told him that he regarded him highly, and offered him his friendship. Changarnier was unresponsive, and Louis Napoleon prepared to adopt a tougher policy in the new year.[19]

On 2 January, Changarnier issued another order of the day, instructing the army not to obey any orders which they might receive from any civilian authority, but only those of their military officers. Next day Louis Napoleon informed the Cabinet that he had decided to dismiss Changarnier from his command. The Minister of War, Schramm, refused to countersign the order dismissing Changarnier, so Louis Napoleon accepted Schramm's resignation.[20] Early next morning he sent his A.D.C., Major Fleury, to Changarnier with a letter informing him of his dismissal. Fleury handed the letter to Changarnier, who was having breakfast in bed. Changarnier read it, and said to Fleury: 'Your Prince rewards me for my services in a strange way.'[21]

There were strong protests in the press and the National Assembly against Changarnier's dismissal, and renewed rumours of a *coup d'état*. The Assembly sent a deputation consisting of its most prominent deputies, including Dupin, Thiers, Molé, Broglie, Odilon Barrot and Montalembert, to Louis Napoleon to ask him to rescind the order. They told him that Changarnier's order to the army not to obey any civilian authority was directed against revolutionary agitators, not against the President of the Republic or the Minister of War. Louis Napoleon replied that he could not be expected to retain in command of the army in Paris a general who had said that he was ready to imprison him at Vincennes.[22]

In the Assembly, the deputies of the Party of Order moved a vote of censure on the government, which was carried by 417 votes to 278.[23] The government resigned next day, but it made no difference, as Louis Napoleon formed another government composed partly of Orleanist politicians and partly of civil servants. Changarnier's threats had turned out to be empty bluster; the President whom he despised had removed him from office, and no one had been able to prevent it. The Austrian Ambassador in Paris, Hübner, noted in his diary that the dismissal of Changarnier had left the general public unaffected: 'The *salons* are getting excited. The streets remain quiet.'[24]

But the Assembly could make things difficult for the President; he needed money and a revision of the Constitution, and the Assembly could refuse to give him either. He was in financial difficulties. His annual salary of 600,000 francs provided under the Constitution was not enough to pay for all his entertaining and his charitable gifts. In March 1849 he persuaded the Assembly to vote him another 600,000 francs a year for his expenses. In June 1850, immediately after he had pleased the deputies of the Party of Order by consenting to the Electoral Law of 31 May, he asked the Assembly for another 2,400,000 francs, and succeeded with difficulty in persuading them to give him 2,160,000 francs. His requests for money aroused considerable opposition; Napoleon, when he was First Consul, had been satisfied with an annual allowance of 500,000 francs, and the President of the United States in 1850 managed with 125,000 francs (25,000 dollars) a year.

In February 1851 Louis Napoleon asked the Assembly for another 1,800,000 francs. Montalembert, who favoured a *rapprochement* with Louis Napoleon, spoke in favour of granting the request; but his colleagues of the Party of Order were not prepared to vote money for the President to spend in bribing the N.C.O.s of the Paris garrison with champagne picnics, and the motion to grant the money was defeated. Louis Napoleon tried to borrow money from his banker, Achille Fould's brother; but despite Achille Fould's efforts the bank refused. He obtained a loan from the Baring Brothers' bank in London, and from Narvaez, who spent several months in Paris in the summer of 1851, appearing with old King Jerome Bonaparte at Louis Napoleon's side at several military reviews. Narvaez agreed to lend him 500,000 francs in five annual instalments. Miss Howard lent him 800,000 francs, and Emily Rowles, now the Marchesa Campana, lent him 33,000 francs. He economized; he sold some of his horses and cut down on the receptions and balls at the Élysée, but not on the champagne for the army N.C.O.s.[25]

There was a feeling on all sides that the country was moving towards a terrible crisis, which would confront it in the following year, 1852, when the presidential election was to take place. The Socialists and Radicals launched the slogan: 'Universal suffrage by consent or by force in 1852'; if universal suffrage had not been restored, they would all march to the polling stations and insist on voting whether their names were on the electoral register or not. They believed that 1852 would see the dawn of the Socialist millennium. In the working-class cafés they toasted 'To 1852', and scrawled the date on walls. The idea spread from the working classes to the middle classes. In conversations and letters the middle classes spoke and wrote anxiously about 1852 and the unknown Socialist horrors that it would bring; Comte Horace de Viel Castel, who had strong Legitimist sympathies but was an intimate friend of Princess Mathilde, wrote in his diary on 23 June 1851 that everybody was saying, 'Goodness knows where we shall be this time next year', and were waiting for 1852 like the people in the tenth century had waited for the year 1000, thinking that it would bring the end of the world.[26]

Some believed that the horrors of 1852 could only be averted by a military dictatorship. Viel Castel's friend Romieu, a former Prefect of the Dordogne, put forward this view in two best-selling books which he published in 1850 and 1851 – *The Era of Caesar* and *The Red Spectre of 1852*. He warned the middle classes that they faced the imminent peril of a new *jacquerie* which the Reds had planned for 1852; there would be hideous massacres, worse than anything that had occurred in 1358. The bourgeoisie, who had misgoverned France since the deplorable revolution of 1789, would be unable to deal with the situation; only the army could save society, with cannon, 'even if it has to be brought from Russia'. Soon the leader would emerge – 'Who is he? Can we guess?' – who would suppress anarchy and regenerate society 'in rivers of blood' by establishing 'the most absolute dictatorship'.[27] Romieu would undoubtedly have preferred it if the leader had been

Changarnier, but he was prepared to accept Louis Napoleon as a substitute, despite the fact that Louis Napoleon proclaimed himself to be the heir of the ideas of 1789.

Louis Napoleon believed that he knew how to avert the danger. He wanted an amendment of the Constitution which would enable him to stand for re-election, and the restoration of universal suffrage, for he was sure that the masses would vote for him and not for the Socialists. But the Assembly would not restore universal suffrage, would not amend the Constitution, and would not vote him money, although the signatures on the petitions for revision, the resolutions of the councils of the departments, and above all the cheers of the people whenever he showed himself in public, convinced him that the great majority of Frenchmen wished him to continue as President. The only way in which he could prevent the Assembly from thwarting the will of the people was to destroy the Assembly and the Constitution by an un-constitutional use of force – the much-talked-of *coup d'état*.

He discussed the question of a *coup d'état* with a very small circle of friends. Even such ardent Bonapartists in his entourage as Laity and Edgar Ney were not let into the secret, which was confined to Louis Napoleon, his private secretary Mocquard, Persigny, Morny, Carlier, the Minister of Justice Rouher, and General Magnan, who had been in secret communication with Louis Napoleon at the time of the Boulogne expedition, though this had not been discovered. Magnan was now appointed to succeed Changarnier as commander of the troops in Paris. A *coup d'état* would require the support of the army. Louis Napoleon believed that the officers and N.C.O.s, and the great majority of the rank and file, were devoted to him; but Magnan was the only general whom he could trust to order the troops into action, perhaps in the face of a call to them from Changarnier to defend the Assembly and the Constitution against a *coup d'état*. He needed to find another general who would support a *coup d'état*.

In the spring of 1851 he believed that he had found this general. Fleury told him about an officer under whom he had served in North Africa – Brigadier-General Leroy de Saint-Arnaud.[28] Saint-Arnaud had been just too young to fight for Napoleon, but had enlisted as a private soldier in Louis XVIII's army. He served in the ranks for ten years without gaining promotion; he was too tempestuous and un-disciplined. He then left the army, and engaged in unsuccessful busi-ness speculation. After the Revolution of 1830 he rejoined the army as an officer, served with distinction in the force that suppressed the Duchesse de Berry's Legitimist revolt in the Vendée, and was appointed to be a colonel on Marshal Bugeaud's staff in Paris; but he ran into debt and became involved in so many notorious love-affairs that he was packed off in disgrace to the Foreign Legion in North Africa, where he distinguished himself by his reckless courage and by his ruthlessness in suppressing the revolts of the Arab tribesmen. He was posted to Paris in the last days of Louis Philippe's reign, and in February 1848 watched in impotent disgust when the troops went over to the mob and the King refused to order the army to shoot down the revolutionaries.

Soon afterwards he returned to Algeria, where he became increasingly alarmed, as he read the newspapers and letters from France, at the degeneration of the country and the Red menace of 1852. He was placed in charge of the Socialists and Radicals who were deported to Algeria after June 1849, and found that they were 'a mixture of artisans and instruments of disorder; journalists, poets, Masons, teachers, painters and escaped convicts ... all Socialists, all Reds'.[29] He had more faith in Changarnier than in Louis Napoleon, whom he mistrusted because of his failure at Strasburg and Boulogne; but he was prepared to follow any dictator who would save France from 'the social republic and Communism'. He thought that God had abandoned France, but believed that he could save the situation in Algeria:[30]

We have our habitual criminals disguised as Reds, but we are strong. I will have twenty shot at Constantine, as many at Bône and at Philippeville, and we shall be at peace. I will not hesitate for a second. I guarantee that my province shall not be invaded by the Reds.[31]

In April 1851 Louis Napoleon sent Fleury to Algeria with a letter for Saint-Arnaud, in which he complimented him on his military achievements and stated that he knew that he could rely on his patriotism. But Saint-Arnaud had two disadvantages as a leader of a military *coup*: he was only a Brigadier-General, and he was virtually unknown to the general public in France. A happy chance gave Louis Napoleon the opportunity to remedy these shortcomings. In May an Arab tribe revolted in the province of Little Kabylia. Louis Napoleon appointed Saint-Arnaud to command the army that was sent to suppress the revolt, and arranged for the Paris newspapers to report the campaign at length. Saint-Arnaud crushed the revolt in thirty-seven days, and by the end of June had become a well-known public figure. Louis Napoleon promoted him to the rank of Major-General and appointed him to a high command in the army near Paris.[32]

Of the seven plotters – Louis Napoleon, Mocquard, Persigny, Morny, Magnan, Rouher and Carlier – Persigny and Morny were the most eager to carry out a *coup d'état*, and Louis Napoleon was the most reluctant. Before authorizing it, the Prince-President decided to make a further effort to persuade or coerce the Assembly into voting for the revision of the Constitution. On 31 May 1851, three days after the Assembly began the last year of its term, a motion was tabled by 221 deputies calling for the amendment of the Constitution to permit the President of the Republic to stand for a second term. The Bonapartists intensified their campaign in the country. They obtained 1,356,000 signatures to their petitions in favour of revision, and the support of the departmental councils in 80 of the 85 departments.[33]

On 1 June, Louis Napoleon went to Dijon to open a new section of the Paris–Lyons–Mediterranean railway between Tonnerre and Dijon. He was enthusiastically cheered all along the railway line; 30,000 people turned out to see him at the station at Tonnerre. In Dijon the women were even more enthusiastic than the men, and threw flowers from their windows as he passed.[34] In a speech at Dijon, he criticized the National Assembly. He said that during the last three years he had always been supported by the Assembly whenever he had taken repressive measures against disorder, but whenever he had tried to improve the condition of the population the Assembly had been uncooperative. 'From one end of France to the other, petitions are being signed for the revision of the Constitution. I confidently await the manifestation of the country's will and the decision of the Assembly.'[35]

Once again, everyone talked about a *coup d'état*; but Changarnier, speaking in the Assembly, reassured the deputies and the nation. He promised them that the army would never support a *coup d'état*; the French soldier would always obey his officer, the officer would obey his general, and no general would order the army to overthrow the Assembly or the Constitution. 'Delegates of France,' he concluded, 'debate in peace!'[36] His words thrilled the deputies and the supporters of the Party of Order, and for a few months – but for a few months only – his peroration, 'Mandataires de la France, délibérez en paix!', was considered to be one of the great utterances of French history.

For six weeks the country waited while the Assembly discussed the revision of the Constitution. The proposal to allow Louis Napoleon to stand for re-election was supported by several prominent Conservatives, including Falloux and Oudinot, as well as by the Party of the Élysée; but it was opposed by Changarnier, Thiers, Lamartine and Victor Hugo, and by the Socialists and Radicals. On 14 July, Victor Hugo went to the rostrum. 'What!', he said, 'because we have had Napoleon the Great, must we have Napoleon the Little?' The Party of the Élysée interrupted him with shouts of protest.[37]

The vote on the motion to allow the second term took place on 19 July. It was carried by 446 votes against 278, but as this was 97 short of the three-fourths majority the motion was lost. When the result was announced, the deputies of the Mountain and the Moderate Republicans rose to their feet and shouted 'Vive la République!' They believed that the Republic and the Constitution had been saved. But on 7 August, Louis Napoleon, reviewing a military parade on the Champ-de-Mars, was greeted with cheers and shouts of 'Vive Napoléon! Vive l'Empereur! We chose him, we'll keep him!' On 10 August, the Assembly adjourned for the summer recess. On 15 August, Major-General Saint-Arnaud arrived in Paris from Algeria.[38]

CHAPTER 23

OPERATION RUBICON

O N 20 August, five days after he reached Paris, Saint-Arnaud was invited to a meeting at Saint-Cloud with Louis Napoleon, Mocquard, Morny, Persigny, Rouher, Carlier and Magnan. Louis Napoleon asked him if he would support a *coup d'état*, and he agreed. The date for the *coup* was fixed for 17 September. But a few days later, at Saint-Arnaud's insistence, the date was postponed. He pointed out that on 17 September, with the Assembly in recess, the deputies would be in their constituencies, where they might organize armed resistance to the *coup*; it would be much better to wait until the Assembly was in session, when his troops could surround the Palais Bourbon and arrest all the Opposition deputies at one swoop.[1] Louis Napoleon agreed to postpone the *coup* until after the deputies returned on 4 November, though he would have liked to have acted sooner as his money was fast running out.

Speculation about a possible *coup d'état* continued, not only in France but also in political and financial circles throughout Europe. When Faucher went to London in September he found that everyone there assumed that the *coup d'état* was about to take place. The Liberal Brussels newspaper, *L'Indépendance Belge*, published a surprisingly accurate account of the preparations for the *coup*.[2] But Louis Napoleon's friend, Louis de La Guéronnière, published a comforting story in *Le Pays*. He revealed that in 1834 Queen Hortense had consulted a Negress in Rome, who was a clairvoyante, about Louis Napoleon's future. The clairvoyante had told her that 'a great nation will choose him for its leader'. 'You mean he will be Emperor?' asked the delighted Hortense. 'He will never be an Emperor', replied the clairvoyante.[3] This did not reassure the deputies of the Party of Order.

At the last moment Carlier lost his nerve. He was afraid that the *coup d'état* would fail, and was perturbed to find that Persigny's and Morny's plans involved the wholesale illegal arrest of all the prominent Opposition deputies and leaders, for which Carlier, as Prefect of the Paris police, would be responsible. Louis Napoleon too had been worried when the plan for the arrests was put forward. But Saint-Arnaud agreed with Morny and Persigny that this was an essential precaution in order to avoid civil war.[4]

At the end of October, Louis Napoleon dismissed Carlier and replaced him by a man whom he considered eminently suitable for the job. This was Maupas, the Sub-Prefect at Toulouse, who had been involved in a scandal a few months earlier. Maupas had suggested to his chief, the Prefect of the Haute-Garonne, that incriminating evidence should be planted in the homes of a number of prominent Socialists and Radicals in Toulouse so that they could be arrested and prosecuted for sedition. The Prefect was shocked, and reported Maupas to the Minister of the Interior, and an inquiry into the case was pending. Maupas would be an efficient and obedient tool in carrying out the *coup d'état* if his misconduct in Toulouse was hushed up.[5]

On 14 October, Louis Napoleon presided at a Cabinet meeting at Saint-Cloud. He himself and Rouher were the only persons present who knew about the preparations for the *coup d'état*. He told the ministers that when the Assembly reassembled on 4 November he would ask the deputies to repeal the Electoral Law of 31 May 1850 and restore universal suffrage. This proposal was anathema not only to the deputies of the Party of Order, but also to Faucher and other members of the Cabinet, who thereupon resigned from the government. Louis Napoleon appointed a new government composed of non-political civil servants whose names were unknown to the general public, except for Saint-Arnaud, who was Minister of War. The new government was denounced in all the newspapers except the Bonapartist press, and aroused new fears of a *coup d'état*;[6] but Lamartine, well-meaning but fatuous as usual, wrote: 'A *coup d'état*? We reply by shrugging our shoulders, as we have done for three years. . . . We believe neither in madness, nor in crime, nor in an impossibility.'[7]

But Louis Napoleon believed, as he told Maupas, that unless action was taken to stop the drift towards 1852, civil war would be inevitable:

This wretched country will be delivered up to anarchy; we shall see the return of the horrors of '93. Only my name is strong enough to reassure the country, to carry the army with us. . . . I will dive in first, but for God's sake follow me, and the country will be saved.[8]

He had convinced himself and millions of Frenchmen of this. *Le Constitutionnel* wrote that only Louis Napoleon could defeat Socialism; only the Emperor's nephew could save the churches and the châteaux from destruction by the savages.[9]

He knew that he could rely on the support of the army, the business men, and the non-political masses of the people. On 9 November, General Magnan brought a hundred officers to the Élysée, where they pledged their loyalty to the Prince-President. Louis Napoleon said that if he were ever compelled to appeal to them for help,

> you know that I would ask you to do nothing incompatible with the rights granted to me by the Constitution, with military honour or with the interests of our country. . . . I would not act like the governments which preceded me, and I would not say to you: 'March; I will follow you.' But I would say: 'I am marching, follow me!'[10].

A fortnight later he received an ovation from three thousand business men and their wives at the Cirque National in the Champs-Élysées when he presented medals to those French manufacturers who had won prizes at the Great International Exhibition in London earlier in the year. He said that their achievement had been especially praiseworthy because they had made their products at a time 'when fiendish ideas were incessantly driving the workers to destroy the sources of industry itself, when insanity parading under the cloak of philanthropy was turning men's minds away from regular occupations into utopian speculations'. He ended by assuring them that they could continue to manufacture new products without anxiety. 'Have no fear for the future. Tranquillity will be maintained, whatever may happen.'[11]

As for the ordinary Frenchman, the non-political lower middle-class and proletarian man in the street, the foreign journalists in Paris were agreed that he was not worried by rumours of a *coup d'état*; in so far as he thought about it, he felt that if a *coup d'état* meant a change, it was to be welcomed. He distrusted all politicians, and admired Louis Napoleon. When Louis Napoleon opened the new building at Les Halles in Paris, where for several centuries the street-vendors had held an open-air market, the 'dames de la Halle', who were now for the first time provided with a building where they could erect their stalls on rainy days, applauded the Prince-President. One of the prettiest of them asked him if they could visit him at the Élysée some time. He invited them to come at ten o'clock next morning. He had apparently expected a delegation of about a dozen women, but when three hundred of them arrived he had enough champagne for them all, and for fifty of the workmen who had worked on the new building at Les Halles, who had also been invited. Louis Napoleon talked and drank with them, kissed the prettiest girls, and gave gifts of money to the workmen. They cheered him and cried 'Vive Napoléon!'[12]

When the new session of the Assembly opened on 4 November, the Prince-President's message was greeted with shouts of protest from the deputies of the Party of Order. The opening passages were to their liking: 'A vast demagogic conspiracy is being organized in France and in Europe. . . . They have made a rendezvous in 1852 not to build, but to destroy.' But he then proceeded to assert that by restoring universal suffrage the Assembly would make it possible for the people to destroy anarchy. He did not deny that he had approved of the Electoral Law of 31 May 1850, but only as an emergency measure designed to defeat the forces of subversion; like other emergency measures, it should be repealed now that it had served its purpose.[13]

He had played his cards well. His proposal to repeal the Electoral Law of 31 May 1850 had the desired effect of setting the Party of Order and the Mountain at each other's throats. When the vote on the proposal was taken on 15 November, the Mountain joined with the Party of the Élysée to support the motion, which was lost by only six votes, being defeated by 353 to 347.[14]

The Party of Order became seriously alarmed when Saint-Arnaud, on becoming Minister of War, sent a circular to the generals in the Paris district, telling them that the duty of the army was to obey the orders which he sent them as Minister of War, without questioning their legality. The deputies remembered that their Moderate Republican predecessors in the Constituent Assembly of May 1848 had included in the Constitution Article 33, which provided that if the safety of the Assembly were threatened, the President of the Assembly could call on the army to protect it, and that this power could be delegated to 'quaestors' elected by the Assembly. The deputies of the Party of Order now proposed that three quaestors should be elected for this purpose. The motion came up for debate on 17 November. Louis Napoleon decided that if the motion were passed, he would carry out the *coup d'état* immediately, before the quaestors had time to act.[15]

Magnan secretly assembled two hundred cavalrymen at the barracks at the Quai d'Orsay, where they would be ready to march to the Palais Bourbon and arrest the deputies as soon as he gave the order. He then went to the Palais Bourbon on 17 November with Morny and Saint-Arnaud and waited for the result of the debate. Louis Napoleon had told them to give the order for the dispersal of the Assembly and the arrest of the Opposition deputies the moment that the motion to appoint the quaestors was passed. But Louis Napoleon's manoeuvres had succeeded better than he had expected – too well, in fact, for his present plans. To everyone's surprise, the Mountain voted with the Party of the Élysée against the motion to appoint the quaestors, and since many members of the Party of Order hesitated to take a step which they feared might lead to civil war, the motion was defeated by 408 votes to 300.[16] Saint-Arnaud and Magnan were temporarily nonplussed. Instead of giving the order for the *coup d'état*, they went to the Élysée to tell Louis Napoleon the result of the vote. Louis Napoleon too was taken by surprise. Then he said: 'It is perhaps better this way', and countermanded the order for the *coup d'état*.[17]

During the next fortnight he made a last attempt to reach an agreement with the Assembly by which they would support the revision of the Constitution; but the Party of Order would not agree to any proposal for revision.[18] He then decided to go ahead with the *coup d'état*. He chose 2 December as the day – the anniversary of Napoleon's coronation in 1804 and of his victory at Austerlitz in 1805.

He held a ball at the Élysée Palace on the evening of 1 December. He was charming and relaxed. Only Caroline Norton, who was at the ball with the Marquis of Douglas, thought that he looked a little flushed; and Douglas said that if he did not know the Prince-President so well, he would think that he had had one more glass of wine than usual.[19] No one guessed that the *coup d'état*, which had so often been expected during the past two years, was about to take place at last.

Persigny, Saint-Arnaud, Maupas and Mocquard were at the ball. Morny had gone to the theatre in order to mislead the public into thinking that all was quiet in the political world. After staying until the end of the performance, he went to the Élysée and slipped quietly into Louis Napoleon's study, where a secret meeting had been arranged for 10.30 p.m. He was the first to arrive, but soon afterwards Louis Napoleon left his guests at the ball and joined Morny in the study. Persigny came a few minutes later, then Mocquard, then Maupas, and last of all Saint-Arnaud. The six men discussed the final preparations for the *coup d'état*. Louis Napoleon had labelled the file which contained the plans for the *coup d'état* with the code word 'Rubicon'. The time had come for Louis Napoleon to imitate his hero Julius Caesar and cross the Rubicon.

The discussion lasted only a few minutes, as the plans had already been worked out and no last-minute changes were thought to be necessary. The meeting was over by 11 p.m. As it ended, Morny said: 'We all of us realize, of course, that we may forfeit our skins over this.' Mocquard cheerfully replied that he did not care what happened to his skin, as it was already so old and worn. Louis Napoleon said that he was confident of success, because he was sure of his destiny and was wearing his mother's lucky ring. They left the study, and Louis Napoleon retired to bed.[20]

A few hours later, Maupas's police went to the houses of seventy-six persons and arrested them in their beds. Fourteen of the prisoners were deputies; they included Thiers and four generals – Cavaignac, Changarnier, Bedeau and Lamoricière. The others were well-known

Radical and Socialist leaders. They were all taken to the prison in the Rue Mazas. At the same time the police occupied all printing works in Paris, and ordered the printers to print copies of Louis Napoleon's proclamation to the people, which were posted up in the streets before daybreak. The police occupied the belfries, to prevent the tocsin from being rung to summon the people into the streets, and the headquarters of the National Guard, where they commandeered the drums which were used to sound the *rappel* which called out the National Guard at the outbreak of an insurrection. Large numbers of troops were stationed in the Place de la Concorde, the Champs-Élysées, the Tuileries Gardens, on the bridges, and on the *quais* on both banks of the river. Other troops surrounded the Palais Bourbon. At 7 a.m. Morny took possession of the Ministry of the Interior and proceeded to direct operations from there.

All over Paris the people read the Prince-President's 'Appeal to the People' as they went out to work in the early morning of 2 December: 'The present situation cannot continue. . . . The Assembly . . . is attempting to seize the power which I hold directly from the people. . . . I have dissolved it and I have appointed the people to judge between the Assembly and me.' The proclamation declared that the President had acted to save the country from the perfidious enemies who were plotting to destroy it. He was therefore inviting the people to vote, at a referendum, for or against a new constitution under which France would be governed by a Head of State elected by the people for ten years, with ministers responsible only to the Head of State, with a Council of State of the most distinguished Frenchmen who would prepare laws for submission to a legislature elected by universal suffrage, and with a second chamber of eminent men who would safeguard the liberties of the nation. If the people wished to have weak government, whether monarchical or republican, they should vote No in the referendum.

> If you believe that the cause of which my name is the symbol – that is to say, of France regenerated by the Revolution of '89 and organized by the Emperor – is still your cause, proclaim this by granting the powers which I demand of you. Then France and Europe will be saved from anarchy.[21]

The deputies coming to the Palais Bourbon were told by the army officers that the National Assembly was dissolved, and after making formal protests they went away. Three hundred of them searched for a building where they could meet, and eventually found one in the town hall of the tenth *arrondissement*. Here they passed a resolution deposing

Louis Napoleon as President, proclaiming that the executive power was vested in the Assembly, and ordering Magnan to place the armed forces under the command of Oudinot. Soon afterwards the soldiers arrived and arrested all the three hundred deputies, including Oudinot. They were imprisoned at Mazas, Saint-Valérien and Vincennes.[22]

The Constitutional Court, which had the power to depose the President for misdemeanour, met at the Courts of Justice to consider a complaint against Louis Napoleon. The army occupied the building and ordered the Court to disperse. The judges met in the evening at the house of the President of the Court, and gave judgment that Louis Napoleon was guilty of high treason and was no longer President of the Republic. They decided to take no steps to enforce their judgment, as there was nothing they could do.

The resistance to the *coup d'état* came not from the Conservatives of the Party of Order against whom Louis Napoleon had made the *coup*, but from his old enemies the revolutionary Radicals of the Mountain. On the morning of 2 December, the last number of *Le National* ever to appear contained an article by Léopold Duras, written on the previous day, which discussed the attitude to be adopted by the Republicans in the conflict between the Party of Order and Louis Napoleon. Duras wrote that the Republicans had two enemies, the Right and the Élysée. 'Of these two adversaries, which should we fear most? In our opinion, there is no doubt that the most to be feared is the stronger; and the stronger, beyond comparison, is the Élysée', which, unlike the Party of Order, had the means available to make a *coup d'état*.[23] In December 1851, as in December 1848, Louis Napoleon had begun a struggle against the Right, but had been driven by circumstances to rely on the support of the Right against the Left.

On the afternoon of 3 December a number of Radical deputies issued an appeal to the people of Paris, which was signed by Victor Hugo as President of a Provisional Government, calling on the people to rise in defence of the Constitution against Louis Napoleon, who had been deposed as a traitor by the Constitutional Court and was attempting to destroy the Republic. But the workers of Saint-Antoine refused to fight for men who had shot them down as rebels during the June Days. When the Radical deputy Baudin urged them to fight in defence of the Republic and build barricades, they replied that they would not fight to defend his salary as a deputy of 25 francs a day. 'You will see how a man is prepared to die for 25 francs a day',[24] he is said to have answered, and he was one of the few people killed in the clashes with the troops on the barricades in the Faubourg Saint-Antoine on 3 December.

In the other traditionally revolutionary districts of Paris – the

Faubourg Saint-Denis and the Faubourg Saint-Martin – there was a greater response to the Radicals' appeal, and the barricades went up on the afternoon of 3 December; but the journalists thought that there were more middle-class intellectuals than workers engaged in building and manning them.[25] Louis Napoleon proclaimed the state of siege in Paris, and proclamations were posted up in the streets announcing that anyone found carrying arms or helping to build a barricade would be immediately shot.

Louis Napoleon did not send the police or the troops to dismantle the barricades on 3 December. In July 1830 and in February 1848 the revolutionaries had triumphed by building barricades, disappearing when the troops demolished them, and rebuilding them as soon as the troops had passed on, thus exhausting and demoralizing the soldiers who capitulated after three days of this kind of street-fighting. Cavaignac in the June Days, and Windischgrätz in Vienna in October 1848, had defeated the rebels by adopting what had become the accepted counter-insurrectionary tactic, withdrawing from the revolutionary districts, allowing the revolutionaries to build and fortify their barricades, and then, counter-attacking in strength, demolishing the barricades with artillery and sending in the infantry to exterminate the rebels. Morny proposed that this tactic should now be adopted. Maupas thought that the revolutionaries manning the barricades were too few to make it necessary to adopt the slower and bloodier methods of Cavaignac and Windischgrätz; but Louis Napoleon supported Morny, and the army, after evacuating the centre of Paris on 3 December, marched against the barricades on the following day.[26]

In his proclamation, Louis Napoleon had urged all law-abiding people to stay at home and not impede the soldiers by coming out into the streets to see what was happening; but in the afternoon of 4 December the boulevards were full of middle-class onlookers, especially women and children. They did not realize that the centre of Paris was about to become a battleground, because the shops and theatres had re-opened after the first excitement on the morning of 2 December. The fashionable Café Cardinal at the corner of the Boulevard des Italiens and the Rue Richelieu was crowded as usual, as was the Café Anglais in the Boulevard des Italiens a few hundred yards away. During the course of the morning a large force of soldiers had moved into the boulevards, demolishing barricades but encountering no resistance. An English officer on holiday in Paris, Captain Jesse of Ingatestone in Essex, stood with his wife on the balcony of his apartment in the Boulevard Montmartre, watching the soldiers and noticing with disapproval that the cavalry officers were smoking cigars as they sat on their horses – 'not a very soldierlike' custom, he thought; British army officers did not smoke in public until after they had learned the habit from their French allies in the Crimean War.

Suddenly a shot was fired – no one was ever able to discover by whom – and in a moment the soldiers were breaking down the doors of the houses, firing indiscriminately at the onlookers in the streets, and turning their cannon on one of the houses in the Boulevard des Italiens and demolishing it completely because they thought that the shot had been fired from there. They broke into the music shop of Monsieur Brandus above the Café Cardinal and arrested him and his family and the terrified people who had fled upstairs from the café when the firing started. They shot Brandus's old servant Louis dead, but took the others unharmed to the Passage de l'Opéra, where they held them 'penned up like beasts of burden' for several hours before releasing them. An apothecary who was just coming out of his shop was shot and killed, as was a well-known local doctor who was going on his rounds and a landscape-painter who was painting a street scene from his balcony; but Captain and Mrs Jesse saved their lives by rushing in from their balcony and lying on the floor of their bedroom while the windows of of the room and the mirrors on the walls were shattered by musket fire from the troops in the street.[27]

The troops ransacked the Café Anglais, smashing nearly all the tables and chairs, before passing on up the Boulevard Montmartre towards the Porte Saint-Denis in their search for the revolutionaries against whom they were supposed to be fighting. The firing on the Boulevard des Italiens and the Boulevard Montmartre did not stop until General Canrobert, the brigade commander, arrived on the scene, and, unlike his subordinate officers, succeeded in bringing the troops under control.

Louis Napoleon's English friend, Captain Gronow, who was in Paris and welcomed the *coup d'état*, could understand why the soldiers on the boulevards had panicked and fired at the bystanders. He knew the resentment felt by the army against the people of Paris ever since the revolution of February 1848, and remembered the occasion when a soldier had been killed by a sniper shooting from the third-floor window of a house while the soldiers were looking at a girl who was standing on the balcony on the fourth floor. Gronow, finding himself on 4 December in a crowd who were taunting the soldiers, hastily departed before the shooting started.[28]

The Austrian Ambassador, Hübner, encountered some revolutionaries near the Porte Saint-Denis. He put on a fake English accent when he talked to them, thinking that revolutionaries would be more sympathetic to an Englishman than to any other foreigner. They let him go on to his club, the select Union Club in the Rue de Gramont.

Soon after he arrived the club windows were broken by a volley from the soldiers in the street, who burst into the club and threatened to arrest all the club members as snipers. Old General Ornano, who was in the club, succeeded with great difficulty in convincing the soldiers who he was, and he eventually persuaded them not to arrest him and his fellow members.[29]

By the evening of 4 December the revolt had been crushed in Paris.[30] According to the official figures – and future historical research has confirmed them – about 400 civilians were killed, many of them during the indiscriminate firing on the boulevards. The army lost 27 killed. The proportion of soldiers' and civilian deaths contrasted strongly with the 170 civilians and 130 soldiers killed during the street-fighting in Paris in 1832 and the 3000 civilians and 1600 soldiers killed during the June Days.[31]

Louis Napoleon had ridden out along the boulevards with his officers on 2 December, as he had done on 29 January and 13 June 1849; but he stayed in the Élysée all day on 4 December, while his troops shot down the bystanders during the quarter of an hour's panic on the Boulevard des Italiens and the Boulevard Montmartre. That quarter of an hour did great harm to his reputation. At the time, only a small fraction of the French people blamed him for the regrettable incident, but in future years it was remembered and held against him. Many who might have forgiven him for 2 December could not forgive him for 4 December.

The Paris artisans did not rise against the *coup d'état* at the behest of the Radical leaders; but the peasants, who in 1848 had been the keenest of Louis Napoleon's supporters, did so in Central, Southern and South-Eastern France, though the North and North-West remained quiet. For a week between 4 and 10 December, in Yonne and Nièvre, in Hérault, in the Var and the Basses-Alpes, bands of peasants, usually under the leadership of middle-class Radical lawyers and school-teachers, sometimes three or four thousand strong, marched through the countryside or occupied the local towns, in some cases killing hated policemen, and very occasionally a priest. The revolts were suppressed without difficulty by the army; but they confirmed the worst fears of the wealthy classes of a *jacquerie* and the Red peril of 1852. The wildest rumours circulated; Viel Castel, in Paris, heard and believed the story that at Clamecy, in Nièvre, the Socialists had forced thirty-eight of the prettiest girls to wait upon them at table naked, and had then selected men suffering from syphilis to rape the girls in the market square, after first tying the local priests to posts and forcing them to watch.[32]

On 3 December Louis Napoleon ordered that the voting in the

referendum should take place on 21 and 22 December on the question: 'The French people wish to maintain the authority of Louis Napoleon Bonaparte and delegate to him the necessary powers to establish a constitution on the basis laid down in his proclamation.' He ordered that every man over twenty-one should be entitled to vote, but voting was no longer to be by secret ballot. Each voter was to sign his name on either the Yes or the No register. He also ordered that all civil servants should be required to sign a written declaration that they approved of the *coup d'état* and would vote Yes in the referendum. But next day – the day of the street-fighting in Paris – King Jerome persuaded Louis Napoleon to vary the order about the referendum and to provide for voting by secret ballot. Louis Napoleon also withdrew the circular requiring the civil servants to sign a declaration of support.[33]

The Opposition had no opportunity, during the short election campaign, to try to persuade the electors to vote No. Morny had suppressed their newspapers, and had issued a decree forbidding any newspaper to be published without a licence from the government; and all public meetings were banned under the state of siege. On the other hand, government officials urged the electors to vote Yes; in some districts, the police warned opponents of the government that a note would be kept in the police files of the name of everyone who did not vote.[34] But these measures were unnecessary, because the great majority of the nation supported Louis Napoleon and the *coup d'état*, and even those Conservatives who disapproved of the overthrow of the Assembly preferred Louis Napoleon to the Reds. The Legitimists advised their supporters to abstain; but the Catholic clergy not connected with their party in the main supported Louis Napoleon. Cardinal Gousset declared that the hand of God was visible in the *coup d'état*, and many parish priests told their congregations to vote Yes in the referendum.

La Guéronnière, in *Le Pays*, wrote that he did not welcome the *coup d'état*, but that the voters had no choice but to vote Yes, since Louis Napoleon had saved France from 'the terrible settling day of 1852'. They would say Yes 'because, patriotically, we cannot say No. It will be a vote of necessity. Louis Napoleon Bonaparte is necessary today.' The only alternative to Louis Napoleon Bonaparte would be 'the government of terrorism and communism'. In *La Patrie*, Amédée de Cesena wrote that 1852 would have brought 'the confiscation of property, forced contributions levied on the rich . . . the massacre of landowners and owners of capital, the destruction of palaces and châteaux', closed churches, and 'the annihilation of civilization'. But '1852 is dead'; this was 'the immense result of the courageous and patriotic resolve of 2 December'.[35]

Montalembert wrote to the Catholic newspaper *L'Univers*, urging the electors to vote Yes.

The act of 2 December has routed all the revolutionaries, all the Socialists, all the bandits of France and Europe. . . . To vote against Louis Napoleon is to support the Socialist revolution. . . . It would be calling in the dictatorship of the Reds to replace the dictatorship of a Prince who for three years has been rendering incomparable services to the cause of order and Catholicism.[36]

Montalembert's more reactionary fellow-Catholic, the Ultramontane Louis Veuillot, who heard the news of the *coup d'état* 'seventy leagues from Paris in a district gangrenous with Socialism', also wrote to *L'Univers*: 'We must support the government. Its cause is that of the social order.'[37]

On the other hand, many Socialist artisans supported Louis Napoleon. The *Times* correspondent described their attitude: 'Up to the present moment, some say, each time we have made a revolution, at the cost of our blood and our industry, it is always the *bourgeoisie* who have profited by it.' But Louis Napoleon

began by attacking the *bourgeoisie*, and for us that is satisfactory. . . . Louis Napoleon is a Socialist. . . . He imprisoned Cavaignac, Lamoricière, Changarnier, who mowed us down with grape in June 1848; he has driven from France M. Thiers, who termed us the *vile multitude*; he has destroyed the power of men who took from us the universal suffrage given us by the Revolution of February.[38]

The less political sections of the working class also supported the *coup d'état*. Louis Napoleon's loyal admirers, the 'dames de la Halle', came again to the Élysée to present him with new bouquets and to assure him that the working classes appreciated 'his courageous initiative'.[39]

It took nine days to count the votes in the referendum, and the final figures were not announced until 31 December. The Yes votes were given as 7,439,216 and the No votes as 646,737, with 36,880 spoilt papers. The Opposition in exile, and many foreign newspapers, challenged the accuracy of the figures, and were particularly sceptical about the returns in the villages where every elector on the register was said to have voted Yes. But the voting returns were all preserved in the government archives, and this has enabled future historians to discover that, though in some cases the results were falsified, this made no essential difference to the results. In some districts the No vote was substantial. Paris voted Yes by only 132,000 votes against 80,000 Noes.

In some of the Legitimist departments in Brittany and Provence there were many abstentions, the Yes vote reaching less than fifty per cent of the total electorate. Only one electoral district in all France had a majority of No votes – the Protestant and Republican district of Vernoux in the department of Ardèche in the South, where the No majority was 1023 against 724.[40]

Where the officials gave untrue returns, it was not always because of a desire to please the government; sometimes it was to appease the indignation of the local inhabitants who would not believe that anyone in the district would vote against Louis Napoleon. When the returning officer at Nogent-sur-Seine announced that only one elector had voted No, an angry crowd demanded that he tell them the name of the single miscreant, so that they could lynch him at once.[41] George Sand wrote to Mazzini that though the government had used terror, the people would have voted Yes just the same if no terror had been used.[42]

When Louis Napoleon heard the result of the referendum, he declared that more than seven million votes had absolved him from an act which he had committed only in order to save France, and perhaps Europe, from years of misery and disorder. He ordered that a *Te Deum* for the success of the *coup d'état* and the referendum should be held in every cathedral and church in France on New Year's Day. He himself attended the service in Notre-Dame. Paris was covered with a thick fog as he left the Élysée and drove through the streets, which were lined with troops all the way to Notre-Dame. Great banners hung from the posts along the route with the initials 'L.N.' in gold braid; outside the cathedral, the great doorway was decorated with flags and flowers surrounded by the figure '7,000,000'. In contrast with the murky gloom in the streets, the interior of Notre-Dame was a blaze of light from nearly a thousand candles hanging from the roof, and was lavishly decorated with rich cloths and ornaments. A choir of five hundred sang the *Te Deum* which Lesueur had composed for the victory of Austerlitz. It was followed by the lighter and less suitable *Sanctus* of Adolphe Adam, who had achieved great success with his music for the ballet *Giselle*, but whose compositions were inappropriate for so solemn an occasion. Some thought that Berlioz should have been asked to compose something for the ceremony, but this would have displeased the traditionalists.[43]

After the *Te Deum*, Louis Napoleon did not return to the Élysée; he drove to the Tuileries, the palace of the Kings of France and of Napoleon, which was to be his principal residence in future.[44] The new year, 1852, was to bring not Red revolution but the Second Empire.

CHAPTER 24

'THE EMPIRE MEANS PEACE'

Louis Napoleon, elected President of the Republic for ten years, had been given power by the referendum to promulgate any constitution which he fancied along the lines which he had laid down in general terms in his proclamation of 2 December. He immediately appointed a commission of eminent jurists and ordered them to draft a constitution within ten days. Meanwhile he ordered the removal of the words 'Liberty, Equality, Fraternity' from the national emblem and from public buildings, on the grounds that they reawakened painful memories and divided the nation. Instead, the imperial eagle was to be superimposed on the Tricolore.[1]

The commission drafting the Constitution did not complete their labours within ten days, so Louis Napoleon gave them another twenty-four hours, and he had the draft by 12 January. Within a week he had promulgated it by presidential decree.[2] The executive government was vested in the President of the Republic, elected for ten years, who was responsible for his actions only to the people of France, whom he could, if it so pleased him, invite from time to time to vote Yes or No at a referendum on any question which he submitted to them. The ministers were to be appointed and dismissed by the President, and were to be responsible to him alone. The legislature was to consist of three chambers – the Council of State, the Legislative Body, and the Senate. The members of the Council of State were to be higher civil servants nominated by the President and removable by him at will. The Legislative Body was to be elected for a term of six years by universal manhood suffrage of every Frenchman over twenty-one who had resided in the constituency for six months; it was to be a smaller body than the late National Assembly, having one deputy for every 35,000 electors, which meant a total of 261 deputies. The Senate was to consist of all the Cardinals, Marshals of France, and Admirals *ex officio*, and anyone else nominated for life by the President of the Republic.

The duty of the Legislative Body was limited to approving or rejecting proposed legislation submitted to it by the Council of State, which it must either accept or reject *in toto*, and could not amend. It could not initiate legislation itself, or discuss any matter not submitted to it by the Council of State; it could not ask the ministers to appear before it; its President was to be appointed by the President of the Republic; it was not to sit for more than three months in any year. Its sessions were open to the public, but it was to be a criminal offence to report the proceedings in a newspaper or to quote any extract from speeches made there, except for the official summary of the proceedings which was to be drawn up by the President of the Legislative Body. The duty of the Senate was to examine the constitutional validity of the legislation which had passed the Legislative Body, and to veto as unconstitutional any measure which violated religion, morality, the family or private property. The meetings of the Senate, like those of the Council of State, were to be held in secret, and it was to be an offence to report any of the proceedings. Neither the deputies nor the senators were to be paid any salary or expenses, but the President of the Republic was entitled to order that a salary of up to 30,000 francs per annum should be paid to any deputy or senator who he thought had deserved it.[3]

As the country prepared for the election of the Legislative Body, nearly 27,000 political prisoners were being held in custody without trial on suspicion of having participated in the armed resistance to the *coup d'état* in Provence, Languedoc and the Massif Central. Some had been caught red-handed fighting or marching in revolutionary bands; but many had been rounded up, before they had time to act, in preventive arrests by the police. Morny had told the police to arrest those who, in their opinion, were 'leaders of Socialism', or who, either before or since 2 December, had 'encouraged the people to engage in disorders, to despise authority, and to feel hatred and envy towards the wealthier classes'.[4]

Louis Napoleon was not happy about the position. On 8 January, he ordered Morny to appoint commissions to investigate the cases of the detainees and to decide their fate as soon as possible. As the magistrates, the police and the army had all been responsible for the arrests, the commissions consisted in every district of three officials – one from the Ministry of Justice, one from the Ministry of the Interior, and one from the Ministry of War – and were popularly known as the Mixed Commissions. They did not see the detainees, or hear any witnesses either for or against them, but decided their fate solely on reports submitted by the authorities who had arrested them, and after considering representations from other persons who were influential enough to gain access to the commissioners. They worked quickly, and by the end of February had sent 886 of the detainees for trial by military or civil courts, where a few were sentenced to death and duly executed. They condemned 239 to be deported without trial to the penal settlements of Cayenne in French Guiana, and 9530 to Algeria; nearly half of these were to be detained there in a fort or camp, but the other 5000 were free to live anywhere they wished in Algeria; 2804 were to be detained somewhere in France, and 1545 were to be banished from France or from their local district. The brief notes which the commissioners made on the dossiers of the prisoners whom they condemned show the factors which influenced them: 'Trouble-maker', 'Criminal record', 'Socialist opinions'. But they released nearly 12,000 of the detainees unconditionally, and another 5000 subject to police supervision.

Louis Napoleon's natural kindliness made him as eager as ever to exercise his prerogative of pardon in any case which was brought to his personal attention. On 9 January he released Thiers, Changarnier, Lamoricière, Cavaignac, and most of the three hundred deputies of the National Assembly who had been imprisoned for just over a month. Eighteen of them, including Thiers, Changarnier, Lamoricière, Émile de Girardin and Edgar Quinet, were temporarily banished from France, as were Victor Hugo and sixty-three other deputies who had fled abroad, on the grounds that their presence in France was likely to foment civil war. Five deputies of the Mountain were to be deported to Cayenne. George Sand went to see Louis Napoleon to intercede for the five deputies condemned to Cayenne and for seventy lesser-known persons who had been sentenced to transportation. Louis Napoleon immediately pardoned three of the five deputies and all the other seventy for whom George Sand had interceded. Of the remaining two deputies sentenced to Cayenne, one escaped; the other one, Miot, was transported not to Cayenne but to Algeria.

This did not help the other ten thousand sentenced to transportation or imprisonment who did not know George Sand; but at the end of March, Louis Napoleon appointed three commissioners to inquire into their cases and to grant a pardon to those who deserved it. Colonel Espinasse, who dealt with the detainees in Languedoc, pardoned only 300 of the 4000 remaining prisoners in his area; he told Louis Napoleon that the Mixed Commissions had been too lenient and that the pardons which Louis Napoleon himself had granted had had a very bad effect. General Canrobert, who dealt with the cases in the Massif Central, pardoned 779 out of 4655. In the south-east, where the revolts in the Basses-Alpes, Var and Vaucluse had been the most formidable, Monsieur Quentin-Bauchart pardoned 3441, nearly all the detainees who had not already been released. Louis Napoleon told Quentin-Bauchart that he was the only one of the three commissioners who had acted in the way that he had hoped they would act.[5]

But on 22 January, Louis Napoleon, on Persigny's advice, took a step which angered the Conservatives and large sections of the middle classes far more than the detention or release of Radicals and Socialists. He prohibited all the members of Louis Philippe's family from owning any property in France, and required them to sell their property within a year, on pain of confiscation. This forced sale was exactly the same as that which the government of Louis XVIII had imposed on the Bonaparte family in 1816 and which Louis Philippe's government had decreed against the family of Charles X in 1832. Louis Napoleon justified it on the grounds that it was necessary to prevent the Orleans family from using the income from their property in France to finance political propaganda against him; but his critics at home and abroad denounced it as an act of spite against the family of the King who had treated him so leniently after his Strasburg adventure in 1836. The saying went around the Parisian salons that it was 'le premier vol de l'aigle' – a pun attributed by some to Dupin and by others to Madame Drouyn de Lhuys. Montalembert withdrew his support from the government, and four of Louis Napoleon's closest collaborators – Rouher, Fould, Magne and Morny himself – resigned from the Cabinet. Louis Napoleon appointed Persigny to succeed Morny as Minister of the Interior.[6]

Persigny issued regulations for the general election to the new Legislative Body. There were to be single-member constituencies instead of the system of lists in each department which had been adopted since the February revolution. If no candidate obtained an absolute majority at the first ballot, a second ballot was to be held in which the candidate securing the highest number of votes would be elected by a simple majority – a system which has been used in French elections ever since. Persigny banned all public meetings, and ordered the Prefects to suppress any newspaper, and to prevent the circulation of any leaflet, which called on the electors to vote for anyone except the official government candidate.[7] He ordered them to use all their efforts to secure the election of the government candidates, and told them that the electors would not be able 'to complete the popular victory of 20 December' without guidance from them. 'As it is obviously the wish of the people to complete what they have begun, they must be taught to discern who are the friends and who are the enemies of the government they have just created.' The Prefects were to display public placards giving the names of the candidates 'whom the government of Louis Napoleon considers are best suited to help their work of reconstruction'.[8]

The government candidates were elected in 253 of the 261 constituencies. In two constituencies, Persigny allowed some prominent local man with no political interests to be elected as an Independent, just for show. Despite all that the Prefects could do, Cavaignac and

Carnot were elected in two Paris constituencies, although they had not agreed to stand; a Socialist was elected in Lyons after slips of paper bearing his name had been illegally pushed under doors in the working-class districts during the night before polling day; and three Legitimists were elected in Brittany. Cavaignac, Carnot and the Socialist from Lyons refused to take the oath required by the new Constitution – 'I swear to obey the Constitution and to be loyal to the President of the Republic'. They forfeited their seats, and the defeated government candidates were declared to have been elected in these constituencies. The Legitimists from Brittany and the two Independents were prepared to take the oath, leaving the government with 256 of the 261 seats in the Legislative Body.[9]

In France, no criticism of Louis Napoleon was permitted. In the first days after the *coup d'état*, only the *Journal des Débats*, *La Patrie* and *Le Constitutionnel* had continued ordinary publication, with *La Patrie* and *Le Constitutionnel* strongly supporting the *coup*. *Le Siècle*, *Le Pays* and *L'Assemblée Nationale* appeared only to publish a statement informing their readers that in the existing circumstances they refused to make any comment about public affairs. After about a week they resumed as normal newspapers, *Le Pays* urging the voters to vote Yes in the referendum, and *L'Assemblée Nationale* and *Le Siècle* keeping silence on the subject. Before the end of December, *L'Assemblée Nationale* was praising the army for saving society from the 'vandals of the social order'. The satirical paper *Le Charivari*, which had often got into trouble because of its biting political sarcasm, announced on 10 December that it would henceforth make no reference to politics.[10]

On 17 February 1852 Louis Napoleon promulgated the famous decree on the press[11] which was repeatedly invoked, and strongly criticized by foreign Liberals, during the next eighteen years. It provided that when any writer or editor had been convicted in a court of law of any criminal offence in connection with a newspaper article, the court could order that the newspaper should cease publication. A newspaper could also be suppressed by the Minister of the Interior, without judicial proceedings, for the third offence after the Minister had sent to the newspaper two official warnings, specifying passages in articles published in the paper which, in the Minister's opinion, were insulting to Louis Napoleon or harmful to public order or good morals. A newspaper was entitled to appeal against a suppression order to the Council of State, but this body of appointed civil servants nearly always upheld the Minister's decision. Hundreds of warnings were issued every year to the national and provincial press, but the number of newspapers suppressed was comparatively small.

The French refugees abroad published newspapers and pamphlets attacking Louis Napoleon and smuggled them into France. Louis Blanc and the Socialist and Radical exiles in London immediately issued a manifesto on 3 December 1851, in which they stated that 'Louis Bonaparte has just crowded into a few hours more crimes than it would have been thought possible to include in the life of a man'.[12] They were joined early in 1852 by Victor Hugo, who evaded arrest in Paris after 2 December and escaped into Belgium. He settled in Jersey, and in 1852 published in London his book *Napoléon le Petit*.

It was a vicious personal and political attack on Louis Napoleon –

a man of middle height, cold, pale, slow, who looks as if he were not quite awake . . . with no resemblance to the Emperor . . . supported on the Stock Exchange by Fould the Jew and in the Church by Montalembert the Catholic; esteemed by women who want to become prostitutes and by men who want to become Prefects.

Victor Hugo accused Louis Napoleon not only – fairly enough – of violating his oath to uphold the Constitution, expelling deputies, arresting democrats, and dissolving the Constitutional Court, but also, without a shred of evidence, of having deliberately ordered the shooting of the onlookers on the boulevards on 4 December in order to terrorize the people of Paris. In what was obviously a completely fictitious account, he described how Louis Napoleon spent all day on 4 December in his study on the ground floor of the Élysée, leaning with his elbows on a table and his feet on the fire-dogs, having given orders that no one except his A.D.C., General Roguet, was to be allowed to enter. Roguet came in from time to time and told Louis Napoleon about the hostile demonstrations against him on the boulevards, of the shouts of 'Down with the dictator!' But every time Louis Napoleon replied with the same four words: 'Qu'on exécute mes ordres' ('Carry out my orders') – the orders being to fire on the people. Louis Napoleon

massacred the Parisians, treated Paris like a place taken by assault, sacked a district of Paris, violated the second Eternal City, murdered civilization in its sanctuary, shot down old men, children and women. . . . What Wellington had forbidden his half-naked mountaineers to do, what Schwarzenberg had forbidden to his Croats, what Blücher had not permitted to his Landwehr, what Platov had not dared to do with his Cossacks, you have done with French soldiers, you miserable wretch!

Victor Hugo tried, unfairly but with some effect, to belittle Louis Napoleon in comparison with the great Napoleon. In reply to those who compared Louis Napoleon's 2 December with Napoleon's 18 Brumaire, Victor Hugo wrote that Napoleon had made the *coup d'état* of 18 Brumaire because he wished to make Europe a vassal and dominate the continent by his power, but that Louis Napoleon made the *coup d'état* of 2 December because he 'wants to have horses and girls, to be called Monseigneur and to live well'.[13] Hugo continued his attack in his poem 'L'Expiation', which alone of all his polemics against Louis Napoleon has survived in French literature because of its description of the retreat from Moscow and of Waterloo. It describes how the great Napoleon is forced to expiate the sin of his *coup d'état* of 18 Brumaire not merely by suffering the disasters of 1812 and 1815 and his humiliations at the hands of Sir Hudson Lowe at St Helena, but also by the shame of seeing his name and place usurped by Louis Napoleon.[14]

Napoléon le Petit was of course banned in France, but circulated there illegally, as did a scandalous anonymous publication, *Les Deux Cours et les Nuits de St-Cloud*, which contained libellous revelations about the Bonapartes' private life – how Madame Mère had kept a brothel in Marseilles, how Napoleon I had poisoned his pregnant mistress and committed incest with his sisters, and how the bastard Louis Napoleon, whom it called 'Louis Verhuel-Bonaparte', only pardoned Radicals who were sentenced to deportation if their wives went to bed with him. In October 1852 two men were sentenced to one year's imprisonment and a fine of 500 francs for distributing *Napoléon le Petit* and *Les Deux Cours et les Nuits de St-Cloud* in Paris, on the grounds that the books were 'insulting to the Prince-President and contrary to public morals'; but two other men and one woman, who were charged with the same offence, were acquitted.[15]

Despite the violence of the anti-Socialist propaganda which Louis Napoleon's spokesmen, especially Morny, put out in the first weeks after the *coup d'état*, the two Socialist authors who wrote the most important books about the *coup d'état*, Proudhon and Marx, were less hostile, or at least less unfair, to Louis Napoleon than were Victor Hugo and the Radicals. Proudhon, who was recognized by a police informer and arrested in Paris after he had been tried in his absence for his article against Louis Napoleon in March 1849, was serving a three-year prison sentence, but had been allowed out on leave on 2 December 1851 to visit his sick wife. He met Victor Hugo in the street and tried unsuccessfully to dissuade him from calling for armed resistance to the *coup d'état*, because he believed that a rising would have no chance of success. On 28 December he had an interview with Morny, and told him that he believed that Louis Napoleon had a great opportunity to introduce Socialist measures now that he had become dictator. 'There

is not a human being in the hulks who is more unclean and depraved'
than Louis Napoleon, he wrote,

> but he can inaugurate social reform by his decrees. . . . I will sub-
> tract from his wrongs against democracy to the extent of his services
> rendered; I will forgive him his *coup d'état* and will give him the
> credit for having made Socialism a certainty and a reality.

Proudhon's book *The Social Revolution as shown by the Coup d'État of
2 December* was actually published legally in France, with the government's licence, in August 1852, and in September Proudhon was
informed that if he stood as a candidate at a by-election for the Legislative Body he would not be opposed by a government candidate; but
before the end of the year he had become disillusioned with Louis
Napoleon.[16]

Proudhon supported the *coup d'état* because he hated the Conservatives of the Party of Order and was delighted to see Louis Napoleon
turn the tables on them. Marx, to some extent, adopted the same attitude, though he never supported Louis Napoleon. In his *Eighteenth
Brumaire of Louis Bonaparte* he denounced Louis Napoleon and the *coup
d'état*, but could not prevent himself from chuckling at the fate of
Thiers, Cavaignac, and the Radicals, who had supported the shooting
down of the Socialists during the June Days:

> The bourgeoisie kept France breathless with alarm by talking about
> the menace of Red anarchy; on 4 December Bonaparte gave it a
> taste of the future it had prophesied when he had the most respect-
> able bourgeois of the Boulevard Montmartre and the Boulevard des
> Italiens shot while they sat at their windows. . . . The bourgeoisie
> glorified the sword; now it is to be ruled by the sword. It destroyed
> the revolutionary press; now its own press has been destroyed. It
> subjected public meetings to police supervision; now its own drawing
> rooms are under police supervision. . . . It had transported the
> workers without trial; now the bourgeois are transported without
> trial.

Marx's book was not only greatly superior, as a polemic, to Victor
Hugo's, but his analysis of Louis Napoleon's régime was more perceptive
than that of most of his contemporaries. While Conservatives all over
Europe were praising Louis Napoleon for saving society from Socialism,
and Guizot was declaring that his *coup d'état* was 'the complete and
definite triumph of Socialism', Marx thought that Louis Napoleon,
with the help of what he called the 'lumpenproletariat', had set up a

government independent of all classes which exercised a dictatorship over all classes, ruled by 'an adventurer from foreign parts, raised to power by a drunken soldiery bought with brandy and sausages'. Marx's reference to the 'lumpenproletariat' shows that he realized that large sections of the working class supported Louis Napoleon, even though he refused to call these Bonapartist workers by the honoured name of 'proletarians'.[17]

One criticism affected Louis Napoleon more deeply than those of Marx or Victor Hugo. Hortense Cornu broke off relations with him. When Princess Mathilde visited her a few days after the *coup d'état*, Hortense passionately denounced him as a traitor to the Republic who had shed the blood of the people and deserved to fall by the hand of an assassin. She almost threw Mathilde out, and told her to repeat to Louis Napoleon all that she had said about him. When Mathilde did so, Louis Napoleon sadly commented that he hoped that Hortense would not play the Charlotte Corday with him. But Hortense merely sent back a bracelet which Mathilde had once given her.[18] Vieillard too was critical of the *coup d'état*, but Louis Napoleon appointed him to be a member of the newly established Senate.

Everyone expected that Louis Napoleon's next step, following the *coup d'état*, would be to proclaim himself Emperor, even after he denied having any such intention in his speech opening the new Chambers on 29 March 1852.[19] Lord Malmesbury had no doubt of it. 'I have known him personally for many years', he wrote to Sir George Hamilton Seymour, who was now Ambassador in St Petersburg, on 29 March,

> and I can answer for the most remarkable feature in his character being an obstinacy of intention, which, as it is maintained on all subjects with an unruffled temper, is held to the last against all opposition. All projects once formed and matured in his head remain there perfectly uncommunicated in detail, but their practical attempts or fulfilment will be a mere question of time. To be Emperor has been his *marotte* since he was twenty years old.[20]

Persigny strongly urged him to become Emperor. As early as the autumn of 1849, Persigny had said that, having made Louis Napoleon a deputy in spite of himself and President of the Republic in spite of himself, he would yet make him Emperor in spite of himself.[21] But the proclamation of the Second Empire might cause international complications with the Great Powers, who applauded Louis Napoleon's actions against the Socialists and Radicals, but were still parties to the Treaty of Vienna of 1815, and associated a Bonapartist empire in France with Napoleonic attempts to conquer Europe. This did not worry Persigny, who told the Foreign Minister, Turgot: 'The Empire will be set up either with or against Europe.'[22]

Foreign reaction to the *coup d'état* had on the whole been favourable. Whatever the Socialist workers in France might think, it was seen by foreign political observers as a victory for Conservatism over Socialism and anarchy. In Austria, where the young Emperor Franz Joseph and his Chancellor Prince von Schwarzenberg had suppressed the revolutionary Liberals and re-established a government as autocratic as Metternich's, the official government newspaper, the *Oesterreichische Correspondenz*, declared that anyone who restored law and order and crushed anarchy in France deserved the gratitude of all Europe. The Viennese Conservative newspaper, *Wiener Lloyd*, and the *Wiener Zeitung* also welcomed the *coup d'état*, though the more moderate *Ost-Deutsche Post* was non-committal. In Prussia, where the Conservatives had returned to power, the government and Conservative press supported Louis Napoleon and the Liberal Opposition newspapers condemned him.[23]

The Liberal *Allgemeine Zeitung* of Augsburg, writing in a Germany which had not yet been disciplined by Bismarck, saw Louis Napoleon's triumph as proof that the French as a nation were always ready to submit to authority:

> Every gendarme, every sentry, every bus conductor seeks opportunities for making his authority seen or felt. Command, obey; obey, command. If there is anyone who can give France her orders, she stands in rank and file before him and shoulders arms. . . . Before a resolute man, who they think is able to command, the French will bend.[24]

In Spain, the Conservative newspaper *El Heraldo* declared that Louis Napoleon, by the *coup d'état*, had defeated the plans of Mazzini, Ledru-Rollin and the revolutionaries of Italy and Germany to carry through the international European revolution in 1852.[25] Even the Tsar, though he would have preferred to see a Legitimist Bourbon King in France, congratulated Louis Napoleon on having saved France from the 'perverse projects of the enemies of the social order'.[26]

The *coup d'état* was condemned in the free press of Britain and Belgium. *The Times*, which had become a Conservative paper, was as hostile as the Radical *Daily News*. The Radical *Morning Advertiser*, after first supporting the *coup d'état* and rejoicing that Thiers had been arrested and had received his just deserts, turned round when it discovered that Louis Napoleon was supported by Montalembert and all the European reactionaries.[27] *The Times* printed a long account from

313

Captain Jesse of his experiences during the shooting on the boulevards on 4 December, and a letter from an anonymous correspondent in Paris who stated that his maidservant's husband, an N.C.O. in the French army, had been forced to participate in the execution in the Champ-de-Mars of 156 revolutionaries who had been captured on the barricades. This story, which was believed and spread by the French Radicals and by Victor Hugo in his *Histoire d'un Crime*, was untrue. Some of the revolutionaries manning the barricades were shot by the soldiers when the barricades were captured, but there were no cold-blooded executions next day in the Champ-de-Mars.[28]

Many British Conservatives who admired Thiers and the Party of Order thought that the *coup d'état* was unforgivable, and the fact that the Catholic Bishops and priests in France had welcomed it made matters worse in the eyes of English Protestants. The indignant editorials in *The Times* culminated in an outburst on 27 December, describing how 'black flocks of Jesuits and priests of every shade already swarm' over France 'and raise their insolent song of triumph', as the country, having first been 'laid prostrate by her generals from Algiers' was then 'cast into spiritual bondage by the emissaries of Rome'.[29]

But the attitude of the British Establishment towards the *coup d'état* was divided. The Ambassador in Paris, Lord Normanby, condemned it, as did Lord Aberdeen, the former Conservative Foreign Secretary, whom Lord Derby thought was instigating the campaign of *The Times* against Louis Napoleon; and Derby himself, though much more sympathetic than Aberdeen to Louis Napoleon, wrote to Malmesbury: 'Your friend in Paris is going an alarming pace.'[30] Queen Victoria, taking her cue as usual from her uncle King Leopold, was uncertain and neutral. But Louis Napoleon had his supporters in Britain. *The Morning Post*, the *Globe* and the *Evening Standard* justified or excused the *coup d'état*. The Duke of Wellington had expressed the opinion in the summer of 1851 that 'France needs a Napoleon'. The ultra-Tory Lord Londonderry, who had liked Louis Napoleon personally even in the days when he was thought to be a Socialist, now wholeheartedly approved of the Prince-President for crushing the Reds. After the failure of the Strasburg *coup* in 1836, Louis Napoleon had written to his mother that many of those who were now condemning and mocking him would have applauded him if he had succeeded, and this was shown to be true in December 1851. Charles Greville, who had despised Louis Napoleon when he met him at Lady Blessington's in 1839, now admired him merely because he had been successful. 'The success of Louis Napoleon's *Coup d'État* has been complete', he wrote in his diary on 14 December, 'and his audacity and unscrupulousness marvellous.' He added that London society was far less hostile to Louis Napoleon than the British press.[31]

More surprising, at least to the Radicals, was Palmerston's attitude. The Foreign Secretary was at this time the hero of the Radicals; but in complete opposition to his Radical admirers, he supported the *coup d'état*. On 3 December he wrote to Normanby in Paris that as the Assembly had refused to amend the ridiculous Constitution of 1848, 'I do not wonder that the President determined to get rid of them as obstacles to all rational arrangement', and he added: 'If indeed, as we suppose, they meant to strike a sudden blow at him, he was quite right on that ground also to knock them down first.'[32] Palmerston congratulated the French Ambassador in London, Walewski, on the success of the *coup d'état*; but as this was contrary to government policy, Lord John Russell dismissed him from the Foreign Office.

The dismissal of Palmerston was a clear warning to Louis Napoleon of British hostility towards him, which distressed him both for personal and political reasons. At the end of January 1852 he invited nearly fifty prominent British visitors to Paris to dine with him at the Élysée, which he still used, as well as the Tuileries, for receptions. *The Times* got to hear of it, and reported that several English peers and peeresses, as well as an M.P., had been among the guests who had disgraced themselves by accepting Louis Napoleon's hospitality, though all respectable Frenchmen 'shunned the scandals of the Élysée'. Mr Alexander Baillie Cochrane, M.P., promptly wrote to *The Times* to say that he was not the M.P. in question; and when one of the guests wrote to *The Times* to state that it would have been discourteous for them to have refused the Prince-President's invitation, the writer of the *Times* article replied that no decent Englishman would consider it discourteous to refuse an invitation 'from a perjurer, traitor, butcher and robber'. *The Times* even brought in Miss Howard, and expressed the hope that these shameless English aristocrats would at least have the decency not to take their wives and daughters to visit her.[33]

Louis Napoleon issued a decree empowering the police to seize foreign newspapers imported into France. The power was not exercised against the English newspapers, though the Paris correspondents of the *Daily News*, the *Morning Chronicle* and *The Morning Advertiser* were summoned to the Ministry of the Interior and warned that their newspapers would be confiscated if they did not moderate their attacks on Louis Napoleon. The government were much more concerned about the Belgian newspapers, which were in French, and the authorities confiscated issues of the Brussels Liberal newspaper *L'Indépendance Belge* as well as all the Radical Belgian newspapers and those published in Belgium by the French refugees.[34]

Louis Napoleon was sufficiently annoyed at the attacks on him in the foreign press to instigate a prosecution in the Belgian courts in March 1852 against the Comte d'Haussonville, the Duc de Broglie's son-in-law, who had attacked him in his newspaper in Belgium; but the jury acquitted him. D'Haussonville was nevertheless expelled from Belgium, and went to England. Louis Napoleon put strong diplomatic pressure on the Swiss government to expel the French refugees in Switzerland, just as Louis Philippe's government had demanded his own expulsion from Thurgau in 1838. Many of the refugees left Switzerland for England; others remained, though the Swiss authorities periodically required them to leave Geneva and the frontier districts and move to the interior, and to moderate the vehemence of their attacks on Louis Napoleon in their newspapers.[35]

In England, Louis Napoleon handled the matter more tactfully, telling Lord Hertford, Lord Adolphus FitzClarence and his other guests at the Élysée that the unbridled attacks on him in the British press were endangering friendly relations between Britain and France.[36] On 3 February a number of Conservative peers, including their leader Lord Derby, raised the matter in the House of Lords and urged the press to moderate their criticism. This inspired not only a further series of indignant editorials in *The Times*, but also a poem from Alfred Tennyson. In 'The Third of February 1852', Tennyson denounced the peers who had argued

> That England's honest censure went too far;
> That our free press should cease to brawl,
> Not sting the fiery Frenchman into war.

He stated that he would 'not spare the tyrant one hard word', and asked:

> Shall we fear *him*? . . .
> I say, we *never* feared! and as for these,
> We broke them on the land, we drove them on the seas.[37]

A few weeks after the debate in the House of Lords, the Conservatives returned to power with Lord Derby as Prime Minister and Louis Napoleon's old friend Lord Malmesbury as Foreign Secretary. Louis Napoleon hoped that this would lead to an improvement in his relations with Britain; but in view of the mood of British public opinion Malmesbury had to be very careful not to appear to be too friendly to Louis Napoleon. Six days after his appointment as Foreign Secretary, the *Times* editorial stated that, though he might have entertained Louis

Napoleon in the New Forest and visited him in his prison at Ham, 'we can hardly conceive a more bitter accusation against the English nobleman and minister than that after the occurrences of the last three months he could still rank M. Louis Napoleon among his personal friends'.[38] Malmesbury was determined that no one could accuse him of sacrificing the interests of British foreign policy for the sake of an old personal friendship.

Louis Napoleon's chief ally abroad was, surprisingly, the Austrian Chancellor Prince von Schwarzenberg, the successor and disciple of Napoleon's great enemy, Metternich. Schwarzenberg knew that Louis Napoleon wished to become Emperor of the French, and he worked to persuade his allies the Tsar of Russia and the King of Prussia not to oppose the creation of a second Bonapartist empire in France, though the prevention of this had been the aim of Russian, Prussian and Austrian policy for the past thirty-seven years. Schwarzenberg had no difficulty in persuading Russia and Prussia that Louis Napoleon should be supported as a bulwark against Socialism, but he found it harder to make them realize that their support should go so far as to acquiesce in the creation of the Second Empire. Unfortunately for Louis Napoleon, Schwarzenberg died suddenly at the age of fifty-two in April 1852; but Tsar Nicholas, after trying unsuccessfully to persuade Lord Derby's government to join him in an anti-French alliance, resigned himself to accepting without protest the establishment of the Second Empire.[39]

In August, the Austrian General Haynau visited Paris. He was especially hated by all European Liberals for his executions of revolutionaries and flogging of women in Lombardy and Hungary, and he had barely escaped with his life from the fury of the draymen at Barclay and Perkins's brewery in London and of the people in the streets of Brussels. But Louis Napoleon's police saw to it that there were no similar incidents when Haynau went to the opera in Paris.[40]

Persigny had already begun to work up a campaign in France in favour of the Empire when Louis Napoleon left Paris on 14 September 1852 for the longest tour which he had yet made as President of the Republic. Petitions asking him to take the title of Emperor had been flowing in during the summer, and now, as he passed through Bourges, Nevers, Moulins and Saint-Étienne, he was met by shouts of 'Long live the Emperor! Long live the saviour of France!'[41] On 19 September he reached Lyons, where next day he unveiled a statue of Napoleon. In his speech, he said that Napoleon had 'killed the old régime by re-establishing all that was good in it', and had 'killed the revolutionary spirit by causing the benefits of the revolution to triumph everywhere'. He said that all along his route from Paris he had been met with cries of

'Vive l'Empereur!', but that prudence and patriotism required France to consider carefully before proceeding to unnecessary changes. 'It is still difficult for me to know under what name I can render the greatest services. If the modest title of President could facilitate the mission confided to me . . . I should not, from personal interest, wish to exchange that title for the title of Emperor.' When Persigny, in Paris, read Louis Napoleon's speech, he thought that it went too far in discouraging the movement in favour of the Empire, and he ordered the newspapers not to print a report of the speech.[42]

Louis Napoleon went on to Marseilles, where the police discovered a plot to assassinate him by means of a bomb; the opponents of the régime – and the new British Ambassador, Lord Cowley – believed that the assassination plot had been invented by the authorities in order to win popular sympathy for Louis Napoleon.[43] The Prince-President went from Marseilles through Languedoc to Toulouse and from there to Bordeaux, being everywhere received with great enthusiasm by crowds shouting 'Vive l'Empereur!' and 'Vive Napoléon III!'[44]

On 9 October he spoke at a banquet in Bordeaux:

It seems that France desires a return to the Empire. But there is one anxiety to which I must refer. . . . Some people say, The Empire means war. But I say, The Empire means peace. It means peace because France desires it, and when France is satisfied, the world is peaceful.

He declared that France needed peace to cultivate her waste lands, to build roads, ports, canals and railways, to develop North Africa, and to provide new and quicker means of communication with the American continent. These were the conquests which France would undertake if the Empire were restored.[45]

His speech was reported all over Europe, and interpreted as an acceptance of the imperial crown. As he travelled back to Paris through Angoulême and Tours, the enthusiasm was greater than ever. After calling at the château of Amboise to order the release of the Arab nationalist leader, Abd-el-Kader, who was imprisoned there, he reached the Gare d'Orléans in Paris on 16 October to find the city decorated with hundreds of triumphal arches and banners inscribed 'Vive l'Empereur! Vive Napoléon III!' Dressed in his Lieutenant-General's uniform, he rode through enormous crowds, alone, hat in hand, fifteen yards ahead of his escort, being received with tremendous enthusiasm, as the bands played 'Partant pour la Syrie'. The weather was perfect, and all along the route the people waved from their open windows. They had been instructed by the local authorities to open their windows; in the very few cases where the windows were closed, the police entered the houses and ordered the occupants to open them. At the entrance to the Tuileries, Louis Napoleon found an arch bearing the words: 'To Napoleon III, Emperor, Saviour of modern civilization, Protector of the sciences, the arts, agriculture, industry and commerce. From the grateful workers'.[46]

A few days later, he attended a gala performance at the Théâtre Français in the Rue Richelieu, where Rachel, walking up to his box, recited Arsène Houssaye's ode to Louis Napoleon, expressing the eagerness of all Frenchmen to serve the peaceful eagles:

> L'empire c'est la paix!. . .
> O Prince, . . .
> Et pour suivre avec toi tes aigles pacifiques,
> Les Français, tu l'as dit, seront tous tes soldats.

There was a gala performance at the Opera a few days later, where Abd-el-Kader, entering Louis Napoleon's box, kissed his hand and tried to kneel to him, but was prevented by Louis Napoleon.[47]

On 6 November, the Senate passed an Act to establish the Empire, with Louis Napoleon as the Emperor Napoleon III. He was to be succeeded at his death by his legitimate heir; if he had none, he could appoint any descendant of Napoleon I as his adopted heir, and fix the order of succession in the imperial family; no member of the imperial family could marry without his consent. In all other respects the Constitution which had been promulgated earlier in the year was to remain in force. Only one of the eighty-seven Senators present voted against the Act; this was Louis Napoleon's old friend, Vieillard. Louis Napoleon immediately wrote to Vieillard, assuring him of his continued friendship and inviting him to breakfast.[48]

The Act was submitted to the people of France at a referendum on 21 and 22 November. There were 7,864,189 Yes votes, 253,145 No votes, and 63,326 spoilt papers. The result of the referendum was officially announced on the evening of 1 December. Next morning, at a ceremony at Saint-Cloud, on the anniversary of Napoleon I's coronation, of Austerlitz, and of his own *coup d'état*, Louis Napoleon signed – with the signature 'Napoleon' – the decree establishing the Second Empire.[49]

CHAPTER 25

MADEMOISELLE DE MONTIJO

EUGÉNIE had not enjoyed the Paris social season of 1849. She felt lonely in Paris,[1] and the rather embarrassing private supper party with the Prince-President in the park at Saint-Cloud had done nothing to improve the situation. The French did not even call her by her right name. As the unmarried daughter of the Countess of Montijo, they addressed her, not as 'the Countess of Teba', but in the French fashion as 'Mademoiselle de Montijo', converting the correct 'del Montijo' into 'de Montijo', and pronouncing 'Montijo' in a way that no Spaniard would recognize.

She was bored and unhappy, and did not wish to marry any of the noblemen who were in love with her. The Duke of Osuna was particularly persistent. He came to Paris in pursuit of Eugénie. She saw a great deal of him, and allowed him to escort her in public, with suitable chaperons. This was noticed by the Paris correspondent of *La Época*, a new Madrid newspaper which had first appeared on 1 April 1849. It was destined to become one of the most respected journals in Spain, and to continue publication uninterruptedly until it perished amid the chaos of civil war in July 1936; but as a newcomer in the field in 1849, it had to make its way by adopting slightly more daring tactics than its established rivals. It therefore ran a story in June about the attentions which Osuna was paying to Eugénie in Paris, and reported that a public announcement of their engagement was imminent.[2]

The hot summer of 1849 brought an outbreak of cholera in Paris. Louis Napoleon visited the cholera hospitals and ordered all government officials to remain at their posts; but the leisured classes followed the time-honoured practice of hastily departing from the infected districts. In the middle of June, Maria Manuela, Eugénie and Osuna left Paris for Brussels. *La Época* duly reported that Osuna was escorting Eugénie in Brussels, and that their engagement would shortly be announced.[3]

A week later, *La Época* reported the tragic death of the beautiful young Countess of Teba, struck down in the flower of her youth. On 6 July a memorial service was held in the church of San Sebastian just opposite Ariza House in the little Plazuela del Angel, with the

Archbishop of Toledo officiating and most of the aristocracy of Madrid in attendance. Neither *La Época* nor any other Spanish newspaper ever published a retraction of the report, or gave any explanation as to why it had been published. Perhaps the rumours which had circulated in Madrid some years before about Eugénie's suicide attempt had something to do with the false report, though no one has ever suggested that Eugénie tried to commit suicide in Brussels in 1849.[4]

Mérimée thought that it was her rejected suitors who would shortly be committing suicide. Apart from Osuna, the French artist Édouard Odier, who had painted her on horseback in her smuggler's costume, had fallen in love with her and was courting her in Brussels. Like the robber in Spain, he was fascinated by her tiny feet, and begged her to let him have one of her slippers to treasure. Mérimée, quoting Corneille, called her an 'aimable inhumaine', and asked Maria Manuela how many young Belgians' deaths Eugénie had on her conscience.[5]

From Brussels Eugénie went on to Spa with Osuna and other friends and in November 1849 returned to Madrid with Maria Manuela in time for the winter season.[6] In the spring of 1850 she went to Seville, and wandered around the gardens of the Alcázar by moonlight. She was thrilled and pleasurably frightened, and imagined that she had seen the ghosts of King Pedro the Cruel and his mistress Maria Padilla. 'We have to admit', she wrote to Paca, 'that it is a great pity that these handsome Moors were driven out of the country. It must be said that the Christians came only to destroy, as they always do.'[7]

During the summer, Maria Manuela organized a series of plays and parties at Carabanchel. Most of the Cabinet ministers and the diplomatic corps in Madrid attended, as well as Eugénie's aristocratic cousins and other members of high society. After watching scenes from Ventura de la Vega's comedies acted in Maria Manuela's theatre, the guests spent the rest of the night dancing and enjoying an excellent buffet supper in the beautiful garden of the Casa de Miranda, which was lit by Chinese lanterns swaying gently in the warm breeze. They were, as usual, delighted by Eugénie's performances in the plays. She made a great hit in Ventura de la Vega's translation of Scribe's *Le Domino Noir*, which he named, adapting the title of Calderon's classic, *La Segunda Dama Duende*. As the heroine who has disguised herself as the Aragonese maidservant Inesilla, Eugénie had not only to flirt with the men but also do a dance with castanets to Auber's music. She was such a success that she appeared in her Inesilla costume at the Queen's fancy-dress ball in the following winter.[8]

Slowly, nineteenth-century progress was beginning to appear in Spain. In 1848 the first railway was opened, and rich parvenus were rearing their heads in Madrid society. One of them, Señor Santamarca, gave a fancy-dress ball on Carnival Sunday in 1851 at his palatial residence in Madrid's great boulevard, the Calle de Alcala, on the same night as Maria Manuela's fancy-dress ball in Ariza House, though Maria Manuela and her aristocratic friends were always careful to ensure that their dances did not clash. 'In the palace in the Plazuela del Angel', wrote *La Época*, 'all the old aristocracy were assembled; in the Calle de Alcala, all the modern aristocracy were to be seen.' Twenty-two Duchesses, Marchionesses and Countesses attended Maria Manuela's ball, among whom, 'it is unnecessary to say, the Duchess of Alba and the Countess of Teba shone as the most elegant and the most beautiful'. Señor Santamarca had only one Countess, but his lovely wife glittered with diamonds and his buffet supper was lavish. Santamarca could do better still, because two days later he gave another fancy-dress ball at which his guests included two Princesses and nine Marchionesses.[9] He was, in fact, the type of parvenu who would soon be found at the court of the Emperor Napoleon III and the Empress Eugénie in Paris.

In the spring of 1851, people all over Europe were talking about the Great International Exhibition which was to open in London on 1 May, and the 'crystal palace' which was being built in Hyde Park for the occasion. The enterprising firm of Saavedra organized an excursion from Madrid to London and back in thirty-two days – two-and-a-half days from Madrid to Bayonne, another two-and-a-half days from Bayonne to Paris, eight days in Paris, from Paris to London via Calais and Dover in fourteen hours with only one-and-a-half hours at sea, and ten days in London, with visits to the Tower, Hampton Court and Windsor as well as the Exhibition, before starting on the eight-day journey home to Madrid.[10] Maria Manuela and Eugénie made their own arrangements, but followed the same route, and arrived in London in April to see the Exhibition. They obtained an invitation to a ball at Buckingham Palace, but they were not presented to Queen Victoria.[11]

Narvaez, who spent most of the year in Paris in close contact with Louis Napoleon, also went to London for the Exhibition, and took Maria Manuela and Eugénie to one of Lady Palmerston's famous Saturday evening parties. These parties were afterwards associated in people's memories with Palmerston's residence at Cambridge House in Piccadilly, but in 1851 he was still living in Carlton Gardens. He made a point of inviting his political opponents, especially foreign statesmen with whom he had crossed swords: Thiers, Guizot, Metternich, and Mehemet Ali's son Ibrahim had all attended Lady Palmerston's parties. It was even more generous of Palmerston to invite Narvaez, as Narvaez had worsted him in their clash over Bulwer's expulsion from

Spain and had been acclaimed in Spain and by Conservatives all over Europe as the man who had defied and defeated the Radical English bully.

Lord Malmesbury went to the Palmerstons' on 21 June, and wrote in his diary:

> Went to Lady Palmerston's party, where I saw Narvaez and the Spanish beauty, Mademoiselle Montijo. Narvaez, an ugly little fat man, with a vile expression of countenance; Mademoiselle Montijo very handsome, auburn hair, beautiful skin and figure. Her grandmother was English or Irish, a Miss Kirkpatrick, which may account for her lovely complexion.[12]

He did not realize that Miss Kirkpatrick was the Countess of Montijo, who was also present at the party, and that Eugénie had inherited her colouring from her Spanish father.

Maria Manuela and Eugénie spent a few days with Ferdinand Huddleston at Sawston Hall in Cambridgeshire before going to Wiesbaden and returning to Paris in the autumn. Eugénie, who had probably heard from Narvaez about Louis Napoleon's financial difficulties in these weeks before the *coup d'état*, wrote to Bacciochi, offering to lend the Prince-President money if the *coup d'état*, which was so widely expected, proved unsuccessful. Bacciochi did not bother to show her letter to Louis Napoleon until some time afterwards; Louis Napoleon had other things to think about in the autumn of 1851. Although the press, in later years, alleged that Maria Manuela had spent 2 December with Louis Napoleon at the Élysée advising him about the *coup d'état*, in fact she and Eugénie left Paris on 5 November and reached Madrid on 30 November.[13]

Eugénie enjoyed what was to be her last winter season in Madrid. According to a Belgian diplomat who did not like her, and at the time of her marriage wrote a malicious report about her which eventually reached Queen Victoria, she spent the Carnival of 1852 flirting simultaneously with Alcañices and a bullfighter from Seville whom she had never met before. One morning she hastened to Alcañices's house and, entering his room unescorted, asked him to rescue her from the attentions of the bullfighter. Next day she told Queen Isabel that she had been seen going alone to Alcañices's house and begged the Queen to force Alcañices to marry her to save her reputation. But it is difficult to believe the diplomat's story, or to accept his account of how Maria Manuela tried to pester the unwilling Osuna into marrying Eugénie.[14]

At Easter Eugénie shocked conventional Spanish society for the last time when she appeared at a bullfight in the old Plaza de Toros in

Madrid wearing a pink moiré dress adorned with black plush, a black silk bodice, and shoulder-pieces and stripes in pink plush. Three other young ladies in her party – Paca, the Duchess of Medinaceli, and General Alvarez's widow – wore equally outrageous clothes. In May, Maria Manuela and Eugénie left Madrid for the French health resort of Les Eaux-Bonnes in the Pyrenees. When Eugénie next returned to Spain it was as Empress of the French.[15]

At Les Eaux-Bonnes, like everywhere else in France, people were discussing two great matters: when would the Prince-President assume the title of Emperor? and whom would he marry? It was generally believed that the two questions were closely connected. Louis Napoleon was aged forty-four, and seemed to be happy with Miss Howard; but if he became Emperor, he would obviously wish to have a son to succeed him. At his age, he could not afford to waste any time in producing an heir. He was therefore expected simultaneously to proclaim himself Emperor and to look for a bride among the royal families of Europe.

It was no doubt with a marriage in view that he ended his affair with Miss Howard. As always, he treated his old mistress very generously. He repaid her, many times over, the money that she had lent him during the critical months before the *coup d'état*, and after he became Emperor he created her Comtesse de Beauregard. But she bitterly resented his conduct and the fact that he never visited her again during the remaining thirteen years of her life, though she was living at Beauregard near Paris. She refused to withdraw into a discreet solitude, and made a point of taking a box at the opera, as near as possible to the imperial box, whenever the Emperor attended a gala performance.[16] If her object was to embarrass him, she succeeded; but she had no really justifiable grievance against him, except the grievance of any woman when her lover ends an affair.

Whom would Louis Napoleon marry? He could not expect to get a Habsburg or a Romanov Princess; but he was thought to be interested in Princess Carola av Vasa of the exiled Swedish royal house who had been replaced by the Bernadottes. Carola, who was nearly nineteen, was the grand-daughter of Louis Napoleon's cousin Stéphanie de Beauharnais, the Dowager Grand Duchess of Baden. In July, Louis Napoleon, who was visiting Alsace, crossed the frontier into Baden and stayed the night at Stéphanie de Beauharnais's palace.[17] It was the first time since he became President in 1848 that he had left French soil, and the international press assumed that he had gone to Baden because Grand Duchess Stéphanie was trying to arrange his marriage to Princess Vasa; but according to Princess Augusta of Prussia, the future German Empress, who was staying at Baden at the time, Stéphanie had not invited him and had no idea that he was coming until he arrived. The visit had been planned by her daughter Marie, the Marchioness of Douglas,[18] who had been a close friend of Louis Napoleon since they were children, and was suspected by many people, including Princess Mathilde, of being his mistress.[19]

Lady Douglas was very eager that Louis Napoleon should marry her niece Princess Vasa, and Carola herself and her mother were also enthusiastic about the match. The rumour spread among the anxious members of the German royal families that Carola had become a Catholic in order to marry Louis Napoleon, and that she had sent him a message: 'I have fought to become a Catholic, I have fought for you.'[20] But a few months afterwards the Princess's father, who was an officer in the Austrian army, announced her engagement to Prince Albert of Saxony. Louis Napoleon's enemies chuckled with delight, declared that Princess Vasa had rejected him, and interpreted it as a snub administered to him by the Austrian government, although her father always claimed that he alone was responsible for the decision – a decision which he did not regret in 1872, when Louis Napoleon was an exile at Chislehurst and Carola was about to become Queen of Saxony.[21]

After his failure with Princess Vasa, Louis Napoleon instructed his Foreign Minister, Drouyn de Lhuys, to open negotiations for a marriage with Princess Adelaide of Hohenlohe-Langenburg. Princess Adelaide was the daughter of a petty German Prince, but had at least the advantage of being Queen Victoria's niece, as her mother was the daughter of the Duchess of Kent by her first marriage to the Prince of Leiningen.

Maria Manuela and Eugénie travelled from Les Eaux-Bonnes to Paris in September, and took an apartment in the Place Vendôme. They were in Paris on 16 October to see the Prince-President's entry into the city on his arrival from Bordeaux among the cheering crowds and the triumphal arches saluting 'Napoleon III'.[22] On 6 November the Senate passed the Act creating the Empire subject to the consent of the people in the referendum to be held on 21 and 22 November. While waiting for the referendum, the Prince-President held a hunting-party at Fontainebleau from 11 to 14 November. Maria Manuela and Eugénie were among a large number of people who were invited to stay at Fontainebleau. The other guests included Drouyn de Lhuys, Saint-Arnaud and other Cabinet ministers and their wives, and the British Ambassador, Lord Cowley, who was the son, by her first marriage, of Lady Anglesey, whom Louis Napoleon had known at Bath and Beaudesert.

The Prince-President's visit to Fontainebleau, ten days before the referendum, aroused even more interest than usual; but the authorities were apprehensive for his safety, and took extraordinary precautions to keep the public and even the press at a safe distance from him. It was announced that he would hunt in the Forest of Fontainebleau on Sunday 14 November; but the hundreds of people from the neighbouring districts who came to watch on the Sunday found that the hunt had been held on the previous day. When Louis Napoleon and his guests rode off to the hunt on the Saturday, the road from the palace to the forest was lined the whole way by gendarmes. Plain-clothes policemen swarmed all round the district, and the hordes of beaters in the forest were more concerned to catch trespassing journalists and sightseers than to rouse the deer.[23]

Within the security cordon, the Countess of Teba showed her equestrian skill. It was something that she shared with the Prince-President. The hunting was not very good, but Eugénie led the field all the way and was first in at the kill.[24] Suddenly and impulsively, Louis Napoleon fell in love with her – not in the rational way that he had loved Princess Mathilde and Miss Howard, but as madly and overwhelmingly as he had fallen in love with Madame Saunier, Mademoiselle de Reding and Louise de Crenay at Arenenberg.

A week after Maria Manuela and Eugénie returned from Fontainebleau to the Place Vendôme, Louis Napoleon ordered his Master of the Horse, Colonel Fleury, to present Eugénie with a horse in recognition of her riding skill at the hunt. He also invited her to the ball which he held at Saint-Cloud on 21 November, the evening of the first day of the voting in the referendum. The Austrian Ambassador, Baron Hübner, noticed 'the young and beautiful Mlle de Montijo, much singled out by the President'.[25]

Louis Napoleon, who became the Emperor Napoleon III on 2 December, decided to spend the first Christmas of his reign at Compiègne, in the large palace where the Kings of France and Napoleon I had often resided and entertained their hunting-parties. He left Paris for Compiègne on 18 December, travelling by train in a private coach with the Rothschilds, whom he had invited to stay at Compiègne. He had also invited the Countess of Montijo and the Countess of Teba. In all, he had 101 guests at Compiègne, but everybody noticed that he had eyes for only one of them. None of the guests had any doubt that he was infatuated with Eugénie.[26]

At first the other guests naturally assumed, and said, that he had found an opportunity to seduce Eugénie at Compiègne. Then the truth dawned on them that Eugénie would not agree to be his mistress. The cynical courtiers and gossipmongers could offer only one explanation for this: Eugénie was a scheming adventuress who wanted to become Empress; incited and briefed by her mother, she was refusing to yield to the Emperor's desires unless he married her. The story spread that she had told him that the road to her bed went past the altar.[27] It is very unlikely that she ever said this to him, but both he and his advisers knew it; and though all the versions of the conversations between Louis Napoleon and Eugénie at Compiègne, which the diplomats heard from allegedly reliable sources and passed on to their governments, were probably pure invention, their analysis of the situation was fundamentally correct: Louis Napoleon, realizing that he could not have Eugénie as his mistress, was intending to have her as his wife.

Eugénie was not passionately in love with Louis Napoleon as he was with her; but she was touched by his devotion, and by the romantic chivalry with which he had always treated women whom he loved, ever since, at the age of fourteen, he had leaped fully clothed into the Neckar to retrieve a flower which his pretty little Beauharnais cousin – now Lady Douglas – had thrown in to test his love. 'He is a man', wrote Eugénie to Paca,

of an irresistible strength of will without being obstinate, capable of both great and tiny sacrifices. He would go and look for a flower in the woods on a winter's night, tearing himself away from the fire to go out into the wet in order to satisfy the caprice of a woman he loved. Next day, he risked his crown rather than forgo sharing it with me. He never thinks of the cost. He always stakes his future on one card, that is why he always wins.[28]

Nor would Eugénie have been human if she had not been affected by the possibility of becoming Empress of the French. This meant something, even to a Grandee of Spain who was not swept off her feet at the prospect of being Duchess of Osuna. But Eugénie knew that it was wrong to marry for rank instead of for love; she was conscious that, if the Emperor married her, it might cause him political embarrassments; and she was still a little in love with Pepe Alcañices, though he had never proposed to her. She sent a telegram to Alcañices, telling him that the Emperor had asked her to marry him. He replied with a letter of congratulation. Eugénie then realized that Alcañices was not in love with her, and decided to marry the Emperor. Her telegram to Alcañices was intercepted by the secret police, who were indignant that she should claim that the Emperor had proposed to her; but when they showed the telegram to the Emperor, he told them that Eugénie's statement was true.*[29]

The Foreign Minister, Drouyn de Lhuys, was the first of Louis

*In later years, Eugénie told this story to the seventeenth Duke of Alba, who was present when she and Alcañices discussed their ancient love affair in the Liria Palace in Madrid.

Napoleon's entourage to be seriously alarmed. Soon after the hunting-party at Fontainebleau, he spoke frankly to the Prince-President and told him that it would be politically very unwise for him to marry Mademoiselle de Montijo; marriage with a foreign royal princess was essential to consolidate the régime at home and abroad. Louis Napoleon said that he knew this, and that he had no intention of marrying Eugénie. As late as the beginning of December he did not realize the extent of his infatuation for her; and with his consent Drouyn de Lhuys sent an official request for Princess Adelaide's hand to the Prince of Hohenlohe-Langenburg. On 13 December – nine days after the proclamation of the Empire and five days before Louis Napoleon left for Compiègne – the French Ambassador in London, Walewski, officially informed the British Foreign Secretary, Lord Malmesbury, that the Emperor wished to marry Princess Adelaide. The Princess was spending Christmas with her grandmother and Queen Victoria at Windsor, and Walewski thought it proper to ask the consent of the Queen as well as of the bride's father.[30]

The problem occupied the Queen and the royal family, and the British Cabinet, over Christmas. The objection was not so much that the Bonapartes were parvenu royalty, but that so many Queens of France in the last sixty years had ended their lives in exile, if not on the scaffold. There was also the religious objection that Princess Adelaide would have to become a Roman Catholic if she married the Emperor. Queen Victoria was afraid to mention the proposal to Adelaide; she feared that the poor girl would be dazzled by it. Malmesbury thought that the Queen was not entirely hostile to the proposed match; but the Prince of Hohenlohe-Langenburg wrote to Prince Albert that he dis-approved of it on the grounds of Louis Napoleon's religion and morals.[31]

Walewski was determined to bring off the marriage, and left for Paris, intending to go on to Langenburg to use his personal solicitations with the Prince. When he reached Paris on 31 December, Lord Cowley got hold of him before he saw the Emperor or any member of the government. Cowley told him that the Emperor intended to marry Mademoiselle de Montijo. Walewski was flabbergasted; but when he met the Emperor later in the day, the truth of Cowley's story was immediately confirmed. As he entered the Emperor's study, Louis Napoleon seized his hands enthusiastically and said: 'Mon cher, je suis pris!', and told him that he was firmly resolved to marry Eugénie. Walewski reminded him that he had formally asked the Prince of Hohenlohe-Langenburg for Princess Adelaide's hand, that he had not yet received the Prince's answer, and that it would be politically impossible to jilt Queen Victoria's niece. Louis Napoleon very reluc-tantly agreed to wait for the reply from Langenburg. His torment lasted only twenty-four hours. The reply arrived on 1 January; to the Emperor's delight it was a refusal, on the grounds that Princess Adelaide was too young and did not feel worthy of the high position which the Emperor was offering her. Louis Napoleon thereupon decided that nothing would prevent him from marrying Eugénie.[32]

Scandalous stories about Eugénie were circulating at court – that Maria Manuela's husband, the Count of Montijo, had died three years before Eugénie was born, and that she was therefore illegitimate; that she was Lord Clarendon's daughter; that she had led a wild, unconventional and immoral life in Spain; that she wore a red wig because she had lost all her hair when she swallowed oxalic acid in an attempt at suicide because Alcañices was in love with her sister and not with her.[33] Lord Cowley heard 'that she had poisoned herself because her sister's husband would not consent to be her lover' and that she had an illegitimate child.[34] The gossip was still confined to court and official circles; not a word about it had appeared in the press. In November the Spanish newspapers had published a small item stating that the Countess of Montijo and her daughter the Countess of Teba had been the Prince-President's guests at Fontainebleau, and next month an equally discreet entry mentioned that they had had the honour of being the Emperor's guests at Compiègne. No French or other foreign newspaper mentioned their names.[35]

Some of the ladies at court openly showed their resentment against Eugénie. At the reception at the Tuileries on New Year's Day, Madame Fortoul, the wife of the Minister of Education, complained in a loud voice that Eugénie was entering the supper room ahead of her. Eugénie immediately drew back and invited Madame Fortoul to pass first through the door; but she could not conceal her distress, and the Emperor noticed it and asked her the reason for it. When she told him that she had been insulted and would not stay at court to be insulted a second time, he promised her that soon no one would dare to insult her.[36]

Persigny opposed the marriage; it spoilt all his plans for a dynastic alliance. Saint-Arnaud told the Emperor that the army would be strongly against it. Drouyn de Lhuys threatened to resign as Foreign Minister. Louis Napoleon replied that he hoped Drouyn would continue in office, and coolly told both him and Saint-Arnaud that he would take careful note of their advice; but everyone who knew him realized that he had irrevocably made up his mind. Prince Napoleon, who had heard the stories about Eugénie when he was in Madrid, expressed the general feeling of the Emperor's entourage when he said: 'One does not *marry* Mademoiselle de Montijo.'[37] But Viel Castel accepted the situation quite happily. He wrote in his diary: 'People talk of Mademoiselle de Montijo's chances of becoming Empress of the French. Why not? We live in an extraordinary century. Nothing surprises me any more.'[38]

Hübner, though he repeated all the gossip about Eugénie in his dispatches to Vienna, had formed quite a favourable opinion of her. He found her 'very attractive', and thought that although she was 'capricious' and 'eccentric', she had 'a force of will and a physical courage which one rarely encounters, even among women of the people'. She had 'an inflammable heart, a heart which has already had romantic experiences, though of a distinctly innocent kind'.[39] Cowley was more hostile. He admitted that he never saw 'anything more decorous than every thing that took place at Fontainebleau and Compiègne', but nevertheless believed that, in that 'society of adventurers, the great one of all has been beat by an adventuress'. He was shocked at the way in which people talked about their future Empress:

Things have been repeated to me, which the Emperor has sd. of her, and others which have been sd. to him, which it wd. be impossible to commit to paper. In fact she has played her game with him so well, that he can get her in no other way but marriage, and it is to gratify his passions that he marries her. People are already speculating on their divorce.[40]

On 12 January the Emperor gave a ball at the Tuileries. When the guests went in to supper, Baron Rothschild led in Eugénie and his son led in Maria Manuela. They took them to places at a table occupied by the wives of members of the government, where the Rothschilds bowed and left them. Madame Drouyn de Lhuys, who was sitting there, told Eugénie that the table was reserved for ministers' wives. As Eugénie and her mother moved away, looking for other seats, the Emperor saw them. He walked up to them and led them to the table reserved for members of the imperial family, where he sat down next to Eugénie. Hübner was delighted at the snub administered to Madame Drouyn de Lhuys, and at the malicious smiles of her colleagues at her discomfiture. 'One can say', he wrote in his diary, 'that the marriage was announced at that ball.'*[41]

On 15 January the Emperor wrote a formal letter to the Countess of Montijo:

*Filon's account, *Recollections of the Empress Eugénie* (pp. 23–24), of this incident, and of Louis Napoleon's wooing of Eugénie, though told to him by Eugénie herself, is almost certainly wrong in some points of detail.

Madame la Comtesse, for a long time I have loved Mademoiselle your daughter and have wished to make her my wife. I have therefore come today to ask you for her hand, because no one is more capable than she of making me happy or more worthy to wear a crown.[42]

The letter was solemnly delivered at Maria Manuela's residence in the Place Vendôme by Achille Fould, Minister of State for the Imperial Household. On the same day Eugénie wrote to Paca: 'My dear and good sister, I want to be the first to tell you about my marriage to the Emperor. He has been so noble, so generous to me.'[43]

The Emperor summoned the Senate, the Council of State and the Legislative Body to meet at the Tuileries on 22 January to hear a message relating to his marriage. The foreign press thereupon published the full story about Eugénie, and on 18 January the people of Paris for the first time heard of the existence of the lady who would be their Empress in less than a fortnight. Next day the Stock Exchange panicked about the marriage; the funds fell by $2\frac{1}{2}$ per cent, railway shares by 15 per cent, and those of the Crédit Mobilier by 20 per cent. The stories which had been circulating at court now spread among all layers of society. The *Times* correspondent was shocked that the worst slanderers of Eugénie were members of her own sex.[44] 'One circumstance I find has been made much of', he wrote: 'it is that the Countess of Téba has been occasionally addressed by some of her male acquaintances by her Christian name of Eugénie.' He explained that this was considered to be perfectly proper in Spain, where a friend of a family, even though not related to them, was entitled to address members of the family of both sexes by their Christian names, either with or without the addition of 'Don' or 'Doña';[45] but it was difficult to convince the average middle-class Frenchman or Englishman in 1853 that if Eugénie allowed men to whom she was not related to address her by her Christian name, this did not necessarily mean that she was an immoral woman.

The Spanish press was delighted that, for the first time since Louis XIV, a French sovereign was to marry a Spanish wife.[46] The British newspapers were sympathetic; only *The Morning Advertiser* attacked the marriage.[47] *The Times*, which had recently stated that Louis Napoleon was 'worse than Commodus, Philip and Domitian', now for the first time since the *coup d'état* approved of something that he had done. They wrote that the reaction of public opinion to the marriage had been 'rather favourable than otherwise' in Britain, 'questionable in the French provinces, decidedly unfavourable in Paris, and unwelcome to the greater part of Europe'.[48] Lord John Russell, who had just replaced Malmesbury as Foreign Secretary, wrote to Cowley that the marriage 'is a very false step. A marriage with a well-behaved young French-woman would, I think, have been very politic, but to put this "intri-gante" on the throne is a lowering of the Imperial dignity with a vengeance!'[49] It would have seemed strange to the Ajaccio solicitor, Carlo Buonaparte, who had died within living memory, that the world should think that his grandson was demeaning himself by marrying a Grandee of Spain.

Other foreign commentators were worried about the impulsive and obstinate way in which Louis Napoleon had decided to marry Eugénie and had adhered to his decision in the face of contrary advice from his ministers. 'Family, Friends, Ministers – nothing has availed', wrote Cowley in a private letter to Lord John Russell. 'Alas! poor human nature. Here is this man, with France prostrate at his feet, and all Europe afraid of him, unable to withstand the blandishments of an arrant coquette, and ready to risk everything for her fair Eyes.'[50] 'A man aged forty-five,' wrote Hübner, 'who decides, to satisfy a caprice, to marry for love, especially when that man is an Emperor, and to transform his flame into an Empress, at the risk of forfeiting public opinion in the country and abroad – such a man . . . is bound to arouse apprehensions.'[51] If Louis Napoleon could be so headstrong about marriage, might he not be equally headstrong on issues involving peace or war?

On 22 January the Emperor addressed the Chambers and informed them that he would marry Eugénie. He said that he hoped that France, whose revolutions had isolated her for some time, would be re-united in friendship with the old monarchies; but the foreign Princesses who, during the last seventy years, had married French rulers, had not been fortunate. On the other hand, the non-royal Josephine had been loved by the French people.

> When, facing the old Europe, a man is carried by the force of a new principle to the height of the old dynasties, it is not by making his coat-of-arms look older and by trying at all costs to introduce himself into the family of Kings, that he wins acceptance,

but

> by frankly taking up before Europe the position of a parvenu – a glorious title when it is obtained through the free vote of a great people.

He told them that Eugénie was of high birth. She was French in heart and by education, and her father had shed his blood for the

French Empire; but 'she has, as a Spaniard, the advantage of not having in France a family to whom it might be necessary to give honours and dignities'. She would be 'the ornament of the throne', and would support it in the hour of danger; she was a pious Catholic; and she would revive the virtues of the Empress Josephine. He had preferred a woman whom he loved and respected to an unknown woman who would bring him an alliance which might be useful or might be dangerous.

Soon, when I go to Notre-Dame, I will present the Empress to the people and to the army. The confidence that they have in me assures me of their sympathy for her whom I have chosen; and you, gentlemen, when you get to know her, you will agree that once again I have been inspired by Providence.[52]

The speech was badly received by the foreign diplomats, who did not like Louis Napoleon's proud reference to himself as a parvenu Emperor. Queen Victoria thought that it was 'in bad taste'.[53] At home, Viel Castel was not the only Frenchman who was amused at the reference to the virtues of Josephine, whose love affairs had been notorious.[54] But the speech, which was distributed by the government in every parish in the country, was popular with many of the lower classes. The Spanish Ambassador, the Marquis of Valdegamas, saw it as evidence that France was no longer ruled by the middle classes, as it had been under Louis Philippe, but by a 'crowned dictator' relying on the support of the masses.[55]

On the day of the speech, Eugénie moved into the Élysée – Louis Napoleon was at the Tuileries – and during the next week received widely publicized visits from the Archbishop of Paris, King Jerome and Prince Napoleon. Once she went shopping on the boulevards and in the Rue Vivienne, and was followed by large crowds. As the court gossip continued to circulate in the streets, Persigny announced that he had ordered the police to arrest and prosecute anyone who spread scandalous stories about Eugénie. Some men were arrested for doing this in the Rue du Bac on 27 January. The opponents of the régime said that a new crime had been created in France – the crime, not of lèse-majesté, but of lèse-Montijo.[56]

Eugénie herself was happy and excited, but overawed by her sense of responsibility. She wrote nearly every day to Paca from the Élysée, and told her of her anxiety 'on the eve of mounting one of the greatest thrones of Europe'. The most serious and dutiful aspect of her character now came to the fore.

I am saying goodbye to my family, to my country, to devote myself exclusively to the man who has loved me to the point of raising me to his throne. I love him, which is a great guarantee of our happiness; he is noble-hearted and devoted; you have to know him intimately in his private life to realize how highly you ought to esteem him. . . . I am still appalled by the responsibility which will rest on me, but I will fulfil my destiny. I am trembling from fear, not of assassination, but of appearing to be of less importance in history than Blanche of Castile or Anne of Austria.

But she hoped that two things would sustain her – 'the faith that I have in God and the immense desire which I have to help those unfortunate classes who have nothing, not even work'. Her faith in Louis Napoleon was unbounded. 'I have suffered a great deal in my life, and had almost lost all hope of happiness; well, now I believe in him!'[57]

The Paris city council decided to give Eugénie, as a wedding present, a necklace worth 600,000 francs. The Radicals were indignant that the taxes of the people should be spent on a present for Eugénie, who was already rich, especially as the city council decided, on the same day, to spend only 300,000 francs in relieving the distress of the destitute. Eugénie refused the gift, and asked the city council to give the 600,000 francs to the Paris poor. Her action was widely reported in the international press, and created a very good impression.[58] She even received a tribute in the book *Le Gouvernement du Deux Décembre* which the exiled Socialist deputy, Schoelcher, published in London and circulated illegally in France. 'We are bound to say', he wrote, 'that her letter of refusal was simple, dignified, honourable, in fact such as one could hardly expect from a woman capable of marrying the hideous author of 2 December.'[59]

Among the many wedding presents which Louis Napoleon and Eugénie received from the local authorities and individuals all over France, there was one which greatly pleased him. It was a simple present sent to Eugénie from Hortense Cornu. Louis Napoleon wrote her a personal letter of thanks in the warmest terms, and offered to help her at any time in any way he could. But Hortense Cornu had not forgiven him for the *coup d'état*, the shootings on the boulevards, and the arrests of Socialists and Radicals. She had sent the present – addressed to Eugénie, not to him – out of a sense of gratitude for his gifts to her in the past; but she did not reply to his letter, and did not write to him again for seven years.[60]

Louis Napoleon had first fixed the wedding for 10 February, but in view of the opposition and comment that had been aroused it was decided to hold it as soon as possible. The new date was Sunday

30 January. The workmen preparing the decorations and structures at Notre-Dame worked throughout the night by torchlight to get everything ready in time; but it was too short notice to make it possible for Paca and Alba to come from Madrid.[61]

In the evening of 29 January, Louis Napoleon and Eugénie were married at a civil ceremony in the Tuileries in the presence of the court and the diplomatic corps. Louis Napoleon was very buoyant, but Eugénie was nervous and pale as she sat for three-quarters of an hour on a throne while a succession of ministers and diplomats and their wives bowed and curtsied to her.[62] Next morning she wrote to Paca, two hours before she was due to leave for Notre-Dame. She told her that since the previous evening people were addressing her as 'Your Majesty', and that when they did so, she felt as if she were taking part in a play. She reminded Paca of a play that they had performed in Paca's theatre in the Liria Palace in Madrid. 'When I acted the part of the Empress, I did not know that I would be acting it in real life.'[63]

The authorities were afraid that there would be an assassination attempt during the journey to and from Notre-Dame. Eugénie was worried about the journey, and promised to send Paca a telegram as soon as they had arrived safely back at the Tuileries after the ceremony.[64] But no unpleasant incident marred the procession when Louis Napoleon and Eugénie, in a carriage drawn by eight horses, went by the Rue d'Arcole and the Quai du Louvre to Notre-Dame, the streets being lined all the way with soldiers. Five Cardinals were present in the cathedral, and all the Marshals of France and the diplomatic corps. Thirty thousand people were said to have applied for tickets, but there were seats for only 2800 of them and for sixty officers of every rank of the army in Paris. Louis Napoleon in General's uniform, and Eugénie in a dress of white velvet *épinglé*, with a diamond crown on her head, entered the cathedral through the great door to the strains of the march from Meyerbeer's *Le Prophète*, preceded by all the great officers of state, and walked hand in hand up the aisle to the altar, where they were married by the Archbishop of Paris. They returned safely to the Tuileries, and appeared on the balcony. Some observers reported that Eugénie was loudly cheered by the crowds; others thought that the enthusiasm was markedly less than it had been a year before at the *Te Deum* after the *coup d'état*. In the evening, Paris was illuminated.[65]

It was a day of triumph – not for Eugénie, oppressed by her sense of responsibility, but for Louis Napoleon, who had forced his ministers and courtiers and the powers of Europe, against their will, to accept the woman whom he loved as Empress. He had obtained the imperial throne and a beautiful bride to share it with him. Many of his critics thought that there was only one more thing he wanted – a war.

PART V

THE EMPEROR AND EMPRESS OF THE FRENCH

CHAPTER 26

TROUBLES AND SCANDALS

THE Emperor and Empress of the French were an impressive couple. A week after their marriage, on Sunday 6 February 1853, they reviewed the troops at Versailles. They rode, side by side, along the line, he in his usual Lieutenant-General's uniform, she, not riding bareback smoking a cigarette, but side-saddle in an elegant riding habit, and looking very beautiful. The troops and the spectators broke out with the cry which was so often to be heard in France in the next eighteen years: 'Vive l'Empereur! Vive l'Impératrice!'[1]

But the marriage seemed to bring Louis Napoleon ill-luck; everything seemed suddenly to go wrong in 1853. It had long been expected that the Emperor would celebrate his marriage by granting an amnesty to the political detainees in Algeria and Cayenne, and on the day after the wedding *Le Moniteur* announced that 3000 of the rebels of December 1851 would be freed; but this did not satisfy the Liberal critics abroad, who were dissatisfied that 4000 of the detainees were still held in custody when they had committed no crime except to resist an illegal *coup d'état* against the Constitution of the Republic. On the other hand, many Conservatives strongly condemned the amnesty as an act of unpardonable weakness by Louis Napoleon. The viciously reactionary Bonapartist, Viel Castel, thought that the country was again in imminent danger of being taken over by the Reds, who had infiltrated their agents 'everywhere' – into the editorial staff of *Le Moniteur* and into the police.[2]

Almost immediately after the amnesty there were new political arrests. In February seventeen people were arrested for making slanderous statements about the Empress; in June, three hundred Socialists were rounded up and accused of being implicated in a plot to assassinate the Emperor. The police intensified their drive against 'secret societies', by which was meant any illegal underground political organization, including trade unions. Under a decree which Louis Napoleon had issued a few days after the *coup d'état*, any person who was convicted in the courts of belonging to a secret society could be 'transported as a measure of general security to a penitentiary colony at

339

Cayenne or in Algeria' by order of the Minister of the Interior* for a term of not less than five or more than ten years. The usual practice was for the Minister to wait until the convicted man had served the prison sentence imposed by the court, and then to order him to be detained for another ten years in a detention camp in Cayenne, either on the mainland or on Devil's Island.[3]

The most formidable of the secret societies was the revolutionary Radical organization, *La Marianne*, which had branches in working-class districts in towns and villages all over France, especially in the areas of the Massif Central which had been the centre of the armed resistance to the *coup d'état* in December 1851. The branches were linked by travelling emissaries with the revolutionary leaders in London. But the revolutionary organizations, as usual, were quarrelling among themselves, and by 1856 another revolutionary Republican secret society, *Le Père de Famille*, was fighting *La Marianne* for control of the underground resistance movement.[4]

The leaders of the exiles in England, especially Félix Pyat and Victor Hugo, periodically issued the most violent manifestos denouncing Napoleon III. Victor Hugo called on all Republicans in France to boycott the rigged elections and plebiscites: 'faced with M. Bonaparte and his government, the citizen worthy of the name needs to do one thing only: to load his gun and await the hour.'[5]

In October 1853 Louis Napoleon's police scored a great success: they caught Delescluze, who had come secretly from London to organize the revolutionary underground in France. He was put on trial for forming a secret society, and sentenced to five years' imprisonment, which he served in Belle-Île. At the end of his term he was sent to Devil's Island.[6]

Occasionally there was an opportunity for a disguised form of public protest. In March 1853 Madame Raspail, the wife of the imprisoned Socialist leader, died at Doullens, where she had been given every facility for visiting her husband during his imprisonment. Five thousand people assembled in Paris when her funeral cortège set out for the Père-Lachaise cemetery; by the time it reached the cemetery, a crowd of 20,000 was following the coffin. Everybody knew that this was a Socialist demonstration. Maupas, the Minister of Police, instructed the Prefect of the Seine that such demonstrations at funerals must not be permitted in future. The police should combine security with respect for the dead by not allowing anyone except members of the family to

*These powers were transferred to the Ministry of Police which Louis Napoleon established in January 1852, with Maupas as Minister. In June 1853 the Ministry of Police was abolished, and its powers were again vested in the Ministry of the Interior.

enter the churchyard during a funeral, or any speeches to be made at the graveside.[7]

With the press censored and all opposition to the régime suppressed, criticism took the form of hostile jokes and malicious gossip against the Emperor and his leading ministers in cafés and in the streets. The critics called the Emperor by the nickname 'Badinguet'. It was the name used by Paris workmen to describe a worthless loafer and shirker.[8] An untrue story circulated that Badinguet was the name of the building worker at Ham in whose clothes Louis Napoleon had escaped from prison, and that this was the origin of the Emperor's nickname. This led a building worker named Pinguet to claim that he was nicknamed Badinguet by his workmates at Ham and that it was he who had helped Louis Napoleon to escape by giving him his working clothes. Pinguet used this story as an excuse to write begging letters to Eugénie in England in 1878 while he was serving a prison sentence for setting fire to his house in order to claim the insurance money.[9]

In 1853 'Badinguet' was the most dangerous word that anyone in France could utter. It almost automatically brought a prison sentence. In April some Legitimists received sentences ranging from one to six months for using the disrespectful term.[10] It was much safer to refer to the Emperor as 'Celui-ci'; in the privacy of their houses, Legitimists, Orleanists and Liberals talked freely to their English guest, Nassau Senior, about the political blunders which 'This man' was committing.

As Napoleon III was Badinguet, Eugénie was Badinguette, and immediately after the imperial wedding a poem, 'La Badinguette', was secretly circulating. It was said to have been written by a working man whose gifts as a poet had not been previously revealed. He fixed the poem surreptitiously to the gate of the Tuileries, but was caught in the act and sent for many years to a penal settlement in Cayenne. The police visited the printers of Paris and asked them to discover whether any of their employees had secretly printed the poem on their premises, and warned the printers that they would be held responsible if their printing-presses were used for this purpose.[11]

In the poem, Louis Napoleon meets Eugénie, is attracted by her, and asks King Jerome whether he thinks that she is worth six francs for a night in bed. Jerome replies that she is worth twelve francs a night, because of her rarity value as a red-haired Andalusian girl; but Eugénie proudly tells them that a Montijo will never sell her honour for six francs, but only for the crown of France.

Amis du pouvoir,
Voulez-vous savoir
Comment Badinguette,

D'un coup de Baguette,
Devint par hasard
Madame César? . . .
Elle avait eu pour pères
A ce qu'on dit
Tous les célibataires
De Madrid!
Et puis sur sa naissance on jase
A gogo;
On l'appelle par antiphrase
Montijo.
Quand la Badinguette débarque
A Paris,
Bonaparte, qui la remarque,
S'en éprit.
Ah vrai, dit-il, et sur mon âme!
Soyons francs:
Oncle Jérôme? Cette femme
Vaut six francs!
Non, dit Jérôme, elle vaut douze!
Savez-vous?
Qu'on n'a jamais vu d'Andalouse
Au poil roux. . . .
Viva Dios! s'écria la belle,
Caroco!
Sachez, Monsieur, que je m'appelle
Montijo!
Quand on a cinq ou six cents pères
Andaloux,
On vaut bien un Robert-Macaire
Comme vous.
Ne croyez pas que je me donne
Pour six francs.
Non, non! il me faut la couronne
Ou pas plan. . . .
Adieu, rire, amour, champagne,
Bal Musard.
La voilà, la chaste compagne
De César.
On dit, que la belle regrette
Quelques fois
Ses noces et sa cigarette
D'autrefois;

Que l'Espagnole trop fière
Pour plier,
De son mouton, sut bientôt faire
Un belier.[12]

After the wedding in Notre-Dame, people said that 'Notre-Dame de Paris' had become 'Notre-Dame-de-Lorette'[13] – the district of Paris where kept women and expensive prostitutes lived. They repeated an even more outrageous and libellous verse about the Empress:

Montijo, plus belle que sage,
De l'Empereur comble les vœux,
Ce soir, s'il trouve un pucelage,
C'est que la belle en avait deux.[14]

Even Mérimée commented that whereas Louis Napoleon had become Emperor by election, Eugénie had become Empress by erection.[15]

King Leopold of the Belgians had made it his business to find out all the scandal about Eugénie. He read, and forwarded to Queen Victoria, the letters written to the Foreign Minister in Brussels by Baron de Beijens, of the Belgian embassy in Madrid. King Leopold thought that as Beijens had married Señorita de Santa Cruz he was well-informed about Eugénie, not realizing perhaps how biased any reports from the Santa Cruz family were likely to be.[16] He also questioned the Infanta Isabel – who he admitted was 'not very good-natured' – when she visited him in Brussels in January 1853. She told him 'most positively strange things' about Eugénie 'that would keep any one in his senses from marrying such a Lady'; Eugénie was in the habit of wearing the Andalusian Maja dress 'which exposes the whole person to view', and of spending the night out in the open air near Madrid with parties of young men 'where the chief fun was the sleeping arrangements'. She had also worn the Maja dress when she visited Spa in 1849, where she 'was quite alone with a party of young men'. King Leopold passed on the information to Queen Victoria, and commented: '*She* is then to be your chère soeur! how odd.'[17]

He was still collecting gossip about Eugénie in April 1853, when he received a deputation from Spa. 'I slyly asked them some questions about the Empress Eugenie. They said that she was there in 1849 without her mother with the Duke of Osuna and some other gentlemen.'[18] Eugénie's position among European royalty was not well established. If Queen Victoria or the Tsaritsa of Russia had visited Spa, King Leopold would not have encouraged a deputation of the local citizens to spread scandalous gossip about these royal personages.

Prince Albert did not approve of Louis Napoleon's marriage. He had heard that Eugénie was beautiful and vivacious, but thought that these qualities made her more suitable as a partner at a ball than as a companion for life.[19] He told King Leopold that her way of life was as shocking as her mother's, and that 'she is said to be British on her father's as well as on her mother's side', because 'Lord Clarendon is supposed to be her father'.[20]

But Queen Victoria took a different attitude from the beginning. She might have been influenced by her two closest mentors, Prince Albert and King Leopold, if she had not received a favourable report about Eugénie from her Lady of the Bedchamber, the Marchioness of Ely, who had met Eugénie during her visit to England in 1851 and afterwards became her lifelong friend. When the news of Louis Napoleon's forthcoming marriage was announced on 20 January 1853, the Queen noted in her diary that 'the great news of the day' was that 'the Emp^r Napoleon is going to marry a beautiful young Spanish lady, Mlle. de Montijo by name. . . . Lady Ely knows Mlle de Montijo quite well'.[21] She replied firmly to King Leopold's stream of criticism of Eugénie. 'Mlle. Montijo is now the *Empress Eugénie*', she wrote on 1 February,

> It seems that her appearance & demeanour have produced a most favourable impression. What you have heard of her wild goings on – is I believe to a certain extent true at the same time without pretending to defend her or even to know much I dont believe the *scandales* circulated are true. Some such excellent people have known her so well that I hardly think that can be true.[22]

In French society, it became fashionable to criticize the Empress. In later years, Eugénie said that whatever she did was wrong: if she wore expensive dresses, and a new one every day, people said that she was extravagant; if she did not do this, they criticized her for failing to support the Lyons silk industry. She was condemned for adhering too strictly to formal etiquette, and for being too informal – sometimes by the same critics and at the same time. The diplomats thought it pretentious and absurd that when they came with their wives to a ball at the Tuileries, they went first through a room where Louis Napoleon and Eugénie were standing on a dais while the line of diplomats and their wives bowed and curtsied as they passed; at other courts, the guests just walked straight into the ballroom and merely bowed and curtsied when the sovereign entered. But many of the diplomats disapproved when the Empress played charades and other games with the young men and women at court with whom she was most intimate. The Grand Duchess Stéphanie of Baden was very shocked to see Eugénie dress up as one of the Muses and join her ladies in acting the first syllable of the word 'musard' in a charade at Fontainebleau in November 1853; and Viel Castel was disgusted when Princess Mathilde told him that the Empress had made the First Chamberlain of the Empire, the Comte de Tascher, gobble like a turkey and do other parlour tricks in order to amuse Mathilde.[23]

Queen Cristina, the Spanish Queen Mother, had no criticism to make of Eugénie. 'She has taken up her position very well,' she said, 'neither too high nor too low.'[24]

Eugénie quickly disposed of one of the strongest objections which her critics had voiced before her marriage. They had believed that the Countess of Montijo had schemed for Eugénie to marry the Emperor so that she, as the Empress's mother, could be the power behind the throne in France. But Louis Napoleon, Eugénie and Maria Manuela all agreed that it would be better if Maria Manuela returned to Spain, and she left Paris for Madrid six weeks after the wedding. From time to time she came to France for a holiday, visiting Eugénie in Paris and at Biarritz. Paca and Alba also visited Eugénie, staying at Alba's house in Paris; but they, like Maria Manuela, remained very much in the background, and refused to occupy the places of honour near the Emperor and Empress at court functions.[25] Eugénie continued to write regularly to Paca. Ever since they had been children she had written to Paca in French. Now for the first time she wrote either the whole or part of her letters to her in Spanish, though within a few years she had reverted to her habit of writing in French.[26]

Within a few weeks of her marriage, the Empress was touched by a scandal.[27] Louis Napoleon's cousin Elisa Napoleone, the daughter of Napoleon I's sister Elisa and Prince Félix Bacciochi, had married the Corsican Count Camerata. After Louis Napoleon came to power, Countess Camerata came to France with her son, the young Count Napoleone Camerata. Louis Napoleon granted her the title of Princess, and she lived in a beautiful country mansion in Brittany. Her son stayed in Paris and gambled on the Bourse, incurring heavy losses. In March 1853 he shot himself because he was unable to pay his debts. It was rumoured that he had asked the Emperor to pay them, but that the Emperor, who had paid up for him on several previous occasions, refused to rescue him again.

But there were also other rumours. It was said that Camerata had fallen madly in love with the Empress. At a ball at the Tuileries he danced with her, and took the opportunity to declare his love. The indignant Eugénie immediately complained to the Emperor, who sent an A.D.C. to escort Camerata to his carriage. Camerata went home and shot himself.

A few days after Camerata's death, a young actress of the Théâtre des Variétés, Mademoiselle Marthe, who had been one of Camerata's mistresses, was found dead in her room, having been asphyxiated by the fumes of two gas stoves. New rumours spread. It was said that Camerata had not committed suicide; that he had been Eugénie's lover before her marriage, and held compromising love letters which she had written him; that the Emperor had sent a member of the secret police – a Corsican named Zambo – to recover the letters, and that Zambo had shot Camerata dead in a struggle. Zambo had been unable to find the letters in Camerata's apartment, and the secret police thereupon suspected that Camerata had given them to Mademoiselle Marthe. They arrested Marthe, and took her to police headquarters in the Rue de Jérusalem, where she was tortured to force her to reveal where the letters were. She died under the torture, so the secret police carried her body back to her rooms and made it look as if her death had been caused by asphyxiation from the gas stoves. 'Thus did the monster of the Tuileries avenge on an innocent actress the infidelities of his Messalina',[28] wrote the Republicans in exile.

The story-tellers said that Zambo, being a Corsican, feared that Camerata's Corsican relatives would take revenge under the Corsican law of vendetta. Both the Corsican Chief of the Paris Police, Piétri, and the Corsican Emperor himself, understood his fears, and Zambo was given leave of absence and advised to go to London. A few months later, his unidentified body, covered with knife-wounds, was washed up from the Thames, to provide another unsolved murder for the Metropolitan Police.

Compared to the Camerata slander, the story of Eugénie and the conscientious sentry was relatively harmless, though it was used to show that the Empress was still the heartless termagant that she had been in Spain. Seeing a sentry standing rigidly at attention, and being assured by his colonel that nothing would make him move an inch, she determined to put his endurance and discipline to the test. She went up to him when no one else was present, and, standing so close that she almost touched him, mocked and reviled him. When this failed to produce any reaction, she slapped his face; but he continued to stand stiffly to attention. Next day she sent him some money in appreciation of his devotion to duty; but he returned the money with a message that it was a sufficient reward to have felt the hand of his beautiful Empress on his cheek when she struck him.[29]

At least one rumour about Eugénie was true. By March 1853 it was known that she was pregnant; but the first official announcement of it came on 1 May, when *Le Moniteur* published the short statement: 'Her Majesty the Empress, who was two months pregnant and has been indisposed for some days, had a miscarriage yesterday, Friday evening, the 29th. The health of Her Majesty is otherwise as satisfactory as possible.' Hübner wrote that the miscarriage had been caused by her having unwisely taken a hot bath. The refugees said that Eugénie, knowing that she was carrying Camerata's child, had had the baby kicked to death in her womb in order to destroy the proof of her dishonour, and had announced that she had had a miscarriage.[30]

The Emperor's enemies were delighted at the news of the miscarriage. Hübner was pained to see the callous pleasure shown in Parisian society at the Empress's misfortune. Clarendon was afraid that she might never be able to have a baby; but the Emperor took the disappointment calmly, saying that there was plenty of time for them to have children in the future.[31]

She was sufficiently recovered to attend a ball at the Tuileries in honour of the Duke of Genoa, the brother of King Victor Emanuel of Piedmont, at the end of May. Both Mérimée and Hübner thought that she looked very beautiful at the ball, and Mérimée wrote to Maria Manuela that 'the Empress' – he no longer referred to her as 'Eugénie' – was in 'high spirits', using the English expression in his letter.[32] Hübner noticed that she had changed after six months of married life. On 30 July he wrote:

She is no longer the young bride, the improvised sovereign, whose timidity added to her natural features; she is the mistress of the house, who feels her position and asserts it by her manners, by her gestures, by the orders that she gives to her ladies, by the glance – a little disdainful, a little blasé, but scrutinizing – with which she scans the hall, where nothing escapes her.[33]

She needed her self-confidence in the gloomy summer of 1853. The weather was cold and wet – the first of a series of bad summers in the 1850s which followed the long hot summers of the 1840s. The harvest failed, and food prices rose steeply. On the Bourse, confidence was shaken, not only by the bad harvest, but also by the fear of war, as the international crisis developed which culminated at the end of the year in the Crimean War. There was no panic selling, but the general sluggishness had a dampening effect on trade.

There was disappointment too about the coronation. One of the great events in Bonapartist history was the coronation of Napoleon I at Notre-Dame on 2 December 1804, when, in the presence of the Pope, he placed the crown on his own head. Since then there had been a traditional coronation at Rheims of the Bourbon King Charles X in 1825, though Louis XVIII and the 'Citizen King' Louis Philippe had

347

dispensed with the ceremony. What could now be more fitting than that Napoleon III and Eugénie should be crowned in Notre-Dame by the grateful Pope, who could be sure that the pious Emperor who had rescued him from Mazzini would not humiliate him at the ceremony as Napoleon I had humiliated his predecessor? By March the press was reporting that the coronation would take place on 10 May, that the workmen were already preparing the cathedral for the occasion, and that the Pope would shortly arrive in Paris; but he did not come, and the rumour spread that the coronation would take place, not on 10 May, but on Napoleon I's birthday, 15 August.

Pius IX, who depended for his security on the presence of the French troops in Rome, was particularly eager to show that he was not under French domination. He still resented Louis Napoleon's letter to Ney in 1849; he was displeased at his failure to abolish civil marriages in France, and to repeal other objectionable features of the Code Napoleon; and he was alarmed at the friendly relations between France and Cavour's government in Piedmont. He therefore made difficulties about crowning the Emperor in Notre-Dame. As a Legitimist coronation by the Archbishop of Rheims would have violated the Bonapartist tradition, the coronation was postponed until the Pope could be persuaded to come to Notre-Dame; but after a year or two, it was too late for a coronation, and Napoleon III was never crowned.[34]

By the summer of 1853 Louis Napoleon was proceeding with his plans for clearing away the old, narrow and unhealthy streets of Paris and rebuilding the city with great wide boulevards and impressive buildings worthy of the greatest capital city in the world. The project had the support of the health authorities and of the Ministry of War, who believed that if the narrow streets were replaced by wide boulevards it would lessen the spread of cholera and would make it more difficult for revolutionaries to build barricades; but the greatest impulse for the rebuilding programme came from the Emperor himself, who wished to build a beautiful and impressive Paris which would for ever be associated with his name.

The duty of supervising the work fell to the Prefect of the Department of the Seine, in which Paris was situated. The Prefect, Beyer, was lukewarm about the plan, and thought that it would be too expensive; so Louis Napoleon dismissed him, and appointed Haussmann, the Prefect of the Gironde, to succeed him. Unlike many Prefects, who were often unsuccessful politicians, Haussmann was a career civil servant. He had entered the service under Casimir Périer's government in the reign of Louis Philippe, and he had recently shown energy and efficiency in suppressing the Reds in his Department.

On 29 June 1853 Haussmann went to Saint-Cloud to take the oath of office on his appointment. As soon as the ceremony was over, Louis Napoleon produced a map of Paris on which he had drawn blue, red, yellow and green lines to mark the new boulevards which he wished to build. Haussmann responded to his enthusiasm. During his years as Prefect, he found that though the Emperor did not ordinarily interfere in the administration of the Department of the Seine, he personally directed every detail of the rebuilding of Paris. A rebuilding committee of notable persons was appointed, with Haussmann as chairman, but the other members of the committee were not active, and the work was in fact carried out by Haussmann and the Emperor.[35]

The work was carried on energetically for the next ten years; after this, it slowed down, but further rebuilding was being planned and carried out until shortly before the fall of the Second Empire. Great boulevards were built to a width of forty-five feet, in some cases to sixty feet.[36] Improvements were also made in the Bois de Boulogne; the sandy wasteland and the overgrown thickets, which were a favourite place for suicides and duels, were levelled and cleaned up and converted into laid-out paths, lawns and lakes.

In the course of time, the Paris that Napoleon III and Haussmann built came to be admired and loved, first by foreign visitors, then by Frenchmen from the provinces, and finally even by the Parisians; but in the early stages the rebuilding programme aroused bitter opposition. Nothing else that Louis Napoleon did, until he lost the war of 1870, made him so unpopular; and Baron Haussmann became the most hated man in France. The conservatives and traditionalists objected to the destruction of the familiar Paris that they knew. They complained that 'our old, medieval, picturesque town is to be turned into a St Petersburg, with long broad streets of pseudo-classical and pseudo-Gothic architecture, full of wind and dirt, taking the place of all that was historical in Paris'.[37]

The historians were saddened by the disappearance of the little streets around the Châtelet and the Hôtel de Ville and on the Île de la Cité, which had survived almost unchanged for six-and-a-half centuries since the time of Philippe Auguste; by the demolition of the house in which Admiral Coligny had been killed by the Guises during the Massacre of St Bartholomew; by the elimination of the narrow, winding Rue de la Ferronnerie, where Ravaillac had assassinated Henri IV. Shopkeepers were angry when their shops were pulled down; as it was impossible to buy another shop in central Paris, they had to set up in business in poorer areas in the suburbs. The occupants of the demolished dwelling-houses did not like being turned out of their homes and forced to look for other accommodation. It was far less common in Paris than in London for occupants to own whole houses in the fashionable

349

districts; but those who did, valued them highly. Guizot was furious when he heard that the line of a new boulevard had been drawn right through the splendid house in the Rue de la Ville l'Évêque which he had recently purchased. He complained that Paris, amid the débris of the demolition work, looked like a town under bombardment; and he told Nassau Senior that sometimes, when there was a change of plan, a house was pulled down only a few months after it had been built.[38]

The demolition and rebuilding programme provided work for the working classes; but because of this, thousands of workmen came to Paris from the provinces in search of work, and soon there were more applicants than jobs, and wages fell. The housing shortage became acute. By May 1853 fifty thousand dwellings had been demolished, and with the ejected occupants, and the labour force that had come to Paris from the provinces, all competing for accommodation, rents rose to double what they had been a few years previously.[39]

The householders and shopkeepers whose property was taken were offered compensation, but they complained that it was inadequate. Impartial juries were then set up to assess the compensation in cases of dispute. They usually awarded a sum about half-way between what Haussmann offered and what the property-owner claimed. When this became known, the property-owners demanded the most exaggerated sums and Haussmann offered absurdly low compensation. Occasionally, someone received very high compensation, much more than the price which he had given for the land a few months earlier. Then people asked whom he had bribed and who was his wife's lover.[40]

The resentment was partly caused by the local government system in Paris. In every town in France except Paris and Lyons there was an elected mayor and town council who governed the town in either a friendly or an unfriendly partnership with the Prefect of the department – the representative of the central government; but after the *coup d'état* of December 1851 the Socialist city council of Lyons was abolished and the administration entrusted to the Prefect of the Rhône department. In 1855 the system at Lyons was extended to Paris; the office of mayor and the city council were abolished, and the whole government of the city placed in the hands of the Prefect of the Seine. This was because Paris, as the capital of France, was said to be in a unique position; as the eyes of the world were on Paris, it was necessary that the national government should be responsible for everything that went on there. The loss of the right to local self-government was the price which Parisians had to pay for the great privileges which they enjoyed by living in the capital.[41]

There was also great resentment against Haussmann personally.

Like all civil servants under the Second Empire, he was subservient and sycophantic to the Emperor, but overbearing to his inferiors and to the public. He gave extravagant parties at the Hôtel de Ville to the Emperor and Empress; and whenever a foreign sovereign or a member of a royal family came to France on a state or official visit, one item in the programme was always a banquet and reception at the Hôtel de Ville, where the royal visitor and some three thousand other guests were lavishly entertained by Haussmann at the expense of the Paris ratepayers, who had not elected him and had no control whatever over his actions and expenditure. Jokes were made about his boorish manners, and about the dreadful *faux pas* committed by his wife, who had once had a mental breakdown and was savagely ridiculed as being insane.[42] The *Times* correspondent wrote about 'Baron Haussmann, Emperor – no – Prefect of the Seine';[43] and after the international exhibitions and the negotiations about the building of the Suez Canal had brought Turkish and Egyptian Pashas to Paris and had accustomed Parisians to Oriental titles, Haussmann was nicknamed 'Haussmann Pasha'.[44]

The opponents of the régime made the best use they could of the resentment over the rebuilding programme. They said that Louis Napoleon feared a popular revolt in Paris, and was determined to destroy the narrow streets where barricades could be built and to provide a system of great thoroughfares along which troops could be rushed into the heart of Paris from the barracks of Versailles in the west and Vincennes in the east. They pointed out that the generals had been invited to attend a Cabinet meeting at which the rebuilding programme was discussed and had been asked to submit their views on the construction of the boulevards. Then in 1858 Haussmann, hoping to disarm the criticism of the rebuilding project, stated in his annual report to the Council of the Department that it was a necessary safeguard against revolution and the building of barricades.[45]

The government press also stressed the health aspect, and the sharp fall in the number of cholera cases since the tightly packed houses had been demolished between the Tuileries and the Louvre and replaced by broad airy streets, with gardens and well-spaced residences;[46] but the strategic side was more dramatic, and after the fall of the Second Empire it became an accepted myth that this was the only reason why Napoleon III rebuilt Paris. It was in fact never more than a subsidiary motive; the Emperor never thought that wide boulevards were a complete answer to barricade-building, for the most formidable barricade of all time – the barricade in the Faubourg Saint-Antoine in June 1848 – had been built, not in a narrow street, but in a corner of the great Place de la Bastille. A much more effective anti-barricade

351

measure was the macadamizing of the streets, laying asphalt in place of the paving stones which were used to build barricades.[47]

At the beginning of June 1853, the Emperor and Empress went to the Hippodrome to see an ascent by the famous balloonist Letour, and on 5 July they attended a performance at the Opéra-Comique in the Boulevard des Italiens. While the crowds outside the theatre were waiting to see them arrive, a plain-clothes policeman spotted a man in the crowd whom he recognized as an Italian revolutionary. The police swooped and arrested the man and about seventy other people who happened to be standing near him. Most of them were released, without apologies, after spending a few unpleasant hours in the police station; but sixteen of the arrested men turned out to be Italian revolutionaries who were carrying daggers. They admitted that they had intended to assassinate the Emperor as he watched the balloonist at the Hippodrome, and that, having been unable to do so, they had hoped to succeed when he went to the Opéra-Comique.[48]

Eugénie refused to be upset by the incident, or by the other terrorist attempts against the sovereigns of Europe. 'The police are there to discover plots', she said at a dinner party at Saint-Cloud in September. 'There are no measures or remedies that one can take against fanatics like these latest regicides in Madrid and Vienna. So here's to a little luck!'[49]

Almost the only happy event in which the Emperor and Empress took part during the year was the National Holiday on 15 August. The idea of holding an annual *Fête Nationale* began in France in the reign of Louis Philippe, when it was celebrated on 27 July, the anniversary of the outbreak of the revolution of 1830. Under the Second Republic it was changed to 24 February, the anniversary of Louis Philippe's abdication during the revolution of 1848. Soon after the *coup d'état* of 2 December, Louis Napoleon abolished the *Fête Nationale* of 24 February, which henceforth was celebrated only in the prisons and the penal settlements in Algeria and Cayenne, where the prisoners demonstrated and clashed with the guards on the anniversary every year. Instead of 24 February, Napoleon I's birthday, 15 August, was fixed as the National Day. Some Liberals suggested that it should be held on 14 July, the anniversary of the taking of the Bastille in 1789, which could be celebrated by everyone except the Legitimists; but their suggestion was not adopted until after the fall of the Second Empire and the advent of the Third Republic.

The festivities of 15 August were preceded by a military parade on the 14th, when the Emperor rode into Paris from Saint-Cloud at the head of his troops, dressed as usual in his General's uniform and riding alone – a target for assassins – some thirty yards ahead of his escort.

Eugénie watched the parade from her carriage with Princess Mathilde in the Champs-Élysées. It was a glorious sunny day, one of the few in the summer of 1853, and during the next sixteen years the weather was nearly always fine for the *Fête Nationale*.

The 15th was a general holiday. All day and in the evening, thoussands of people strolled slowly along the Champs-Élysées and ˌthe Grands-Boulevards. After dark, Paris was illuminated by a million lamps and globes. There were 12,000 lights fixed to the Arc de Triomphe at the Étoile; 5000 to an enormous globe and eagle emanating from the fountain at the Rond Point des Champs-Élysées; 40,000 in the Place de la Concorde, 48,000 in the Tuileries Gardens, and 343,000 on the lamp-posts between the Concorde and the Étoile. The city was decorated with large banners bearing the letter N. The day's festivities cost a total of 700,000 francs.[50]

But the fear of war continued to affect the Bourse, and food prices continued to rise as the effects of the bad harvest were increasingly felt.[51] This was a challenge to the government and a test of the economic principles of the Second Empire. Liberal *laissez-faire* economic theory prescribed that no price control or other government interference should disturb the natural operation of the law of supply and demand. The Whig government in Britain had strictly adhered to this rule during the Irish famine of 1847, when they had refused to ban the export of corn from Ireland, had sent troops to guard the corn convoys on their way to the ports from the infuriated and starving people, and had refused to give public relief to the destitute except in the workhouses under the harsh conditions laid down by the Poor Law. Louis Napoleon, who still believed in the Socialist principles of his youth, despite his war against the Reds, acted differently. He imposed a temporary price control, fixing a maximum price at which bread could be sold in Paris, though he refused to apply any of the thoroughgoing proposals for state administration of shops and distribution which the Socialist theoreticians suggested; and he abolished the price control as soon as the worst shortages were over.[52] He repeatedly refused to abolish the time-honoured *octroi* system by which a local tax was levied on produce entering Paris.[53]

He also launched in May 1853 a large-scale scheme for the building of model workers' dwellings, with water and washing facilities in every room, which would be let to the working classes at low rents. The private landlords complained that this would lower the level of rents of living accommodation; according to the *Times* correspondent, some of the strongest objections came from former Socialists who had abandoned politics in the face of police persecution and had gone into the business of letting rooms to working-class families.[54] Liberal

353

politicians and economists condemned the whole project on principle, as did Changarnier's paper, *L'Assemblée Nationale*, which continued to publish veiled criticism of Louis Napoleon's government, though Changarnier himself was still a refugee in Belgium. 'We cannot express our opinion to the extent that the project deserves', wrote *L'Assemblée Nationale*. 'We only say that it is very serious, both in itself and in the tendencies which are shown in it.'[55]

But the Emperor continued with his plans for rehousing the lower classes, and for providing relief in times of distress. He set up a system of free distribution of food to the poor in Paris and other cities, whenever there was a food shortage in the winter months, throughout the years of the Second Empire, and saw to it that the press announced that, though part of the cost was contributed by the state, another part was paid for from the Emperor's personal allowance.[56] In November 1853 he ordered the Director of Public Assistance in Paris to organize a system by which doctors would visit the poor in their homes and give them free medical treatment there, in order to relieve the overcrowding in the hospitals.[57] The Socialistic authoritarian paternalism of Louis Napoleon's régime, together with the Roman Catholic traditions of almsgiving and charity, ensured a better treatment of the poor in France under the Second Empire than in the free Liberal Britain of the period.[58]

Louis Napoleon also had his own unique way of dealing with the high price of food during the shortage of 1853. He asked the directors of the railway companies, as a special favour to himself, to carry food-stuffs on the railways at a nominal freight during the food shortage, although this would involve carrying them at a loss. The directors were quite unable to resist the request, and were rewarded with an invitation to a *château* near Dieppe, where Louis Napoleon had taken Eugénie for a three-weeks holiday – a belated honeymoon – in August and September.[59] Personal charm played an important part in Louis Napoleon's style of government.

CHAPTER 27

THE DRIFT TO WAR

WHEN Walewski called on Malmesbury at the Foreign Office on 13 December 1852 to tell him that Louis Napoleon wished to ask for the hand in marriage of Princess Adelaide of Hohenlohe-Langenburg, Malmesbury also raised with Walewski the question of the disputes between the Roman Catholic and Orthodox Christians in Palestine, which had been worrying the British government for more than a year.[1] These quarrels began the chain of events which led to the Crimean War.

For many years the Kings of France had considered themselves to be the protectors of the interests of the Christians in the Ottoman Empire, and this right had been recognized by the Turkish government in 1740. More recently the Tsar of Russia had exercised a much more effective protection over the Sultan's Christian subjects under the terms of the treaties which he had imposed on the defeated Turks after the wars of 1768–74 and 1828–9. He extended this protection, not only to the Christian inhabitants of the principalities of Walachia and Moldavia – the modern state of Romania – but also to all Christians, including the foreign pilgrims, in the Holy Land. His policy was to favour the Orthodox Christians against the Roman Catholics. He claimed that the Orthodox Christians were entitled to privileged treatment because they had been living in Palestine, in friendship with their Muslim neighbours, since the seventh century, whereas the Roman Catholics had only come as invading Crusaders at the end of the eleventh century; and now, in 1852, three out of every four of the 7000 Arab Christian inhabitants of Palestine were Orthodox, as were all except eighty of the 10,000 Christian pilgrims who went there every year.[2]

In 1851, as President of the French Republic, Louis Napoleon took up with the Turkish government the cause of the Roman Catholics in Palestine and demanded that they should have equal treatment with the Orthodox Christians. Palmerston tried in vain to dissuade Louis Napoleon from doing this, as it could only create difficulties for Britain's ally, Turkey, and might lead to serious trouble in the Levant; he was sure that Louis Napoleon's motive was to gain the political support of the Catholic Church in France. The points at issue were the rights of the two Christian Communions in the Church of the Holy Sepulchre in Jerusalem, the Church of the Nativity in Bethlehem, and the other Holy Places in Palestine. On what days in the year, and at what hours of the day, were the Orthodox and Roman Catholic services in these churches to be held? Who was to have the right to carry out repairs to the cupola of the Church of the Holy Sepulchre? Were the inscriptions to be written in Greek or Latin? Was the figure of Christ, on the crucifixes in the Holy Places, to show His legs crossed in the fashion of the Roman Church or uncrossed in the style of the Orthodox Church? Above all, were the Roman Catholics to have a key to the great door of the Church of the Nativity, or only to enter at fixed times after the Orthodox priests had unlocked the door for them?

The French and Russian Ambassadors in Constantinople exerted pressure and counter-pressure in these matters on the Turkish government; and the Turks, who had no interest either way in the quarrel, found themselves in danger of being crushed between the two Christian powers. In the autumn of 1852 the French Ambassador succeeded in bullying the Turkish Foreign Minister, Fuad Effendi, into granting most of the French demands. The Tsar replied by mobilizing an army corps and stationing it in southern Russia near the Turkish frontier.[3]

Louis Napoleon had not originally intended to quarrel with Russia. He was impressed by the prospective power of the vast Russian Empire;[4] like other commentators on international affairs of the mid-nineteenth century, he believed that by the twentieth century the world would be dominated by the two super-powers, Russia and the United States of America.* He was also very conscious that although Napoleon I had repeatedly won battles and wars in Germany, Austria and northern Italy, he had been defeated by the British and by the Russians and had come to grief in Spain. So, while Louis Napoleon was always prepared to contemplate the possibility of a war with Prussia or Austria on the Rhine or in Lombardy, he was anxious to avoid war with England and Russia; and, despite the repeated accusations of his critics to the contrary, he always adhered strictly to a policy of non-intervention in the civil wars and troubles in Spain.[6]

When Louis Napoleon, in the summer of 1852, was preparing to take the title of Emperor, he was particularly eager to win Russian approval for this step. Knowing that Schwarzenberg was finding it difficult to

---

*The prophets, like those in other epochs, underestimated the time factor in future historical development. The editor of Le Constitutionnel, Amédée de Cesena, believed in 1858 that Russia and the United States would be the only great powers in the world by the year 1900.[5]

persuade the Tsar to recognize the Second Empire, Louis Napoleon raised the matter directly in talks with the Russian government.[7] Apart from official diplomatic channels, he had private links with the Russian statesmen, because the daughter of the Russian Prime Minister and Foreign Minister, Count Nesselrode, was the wife of Baron von Seebach, the Saxon Ambassador in Paris; and Princess Mathilde had preserved the contacts at the Court of St Petersburg which she had made when she lived there as Prince Demidov's wife. Louis Napoleon discovered that though the Tsar strongly approved of his *coup d'état* and his suppression of the Reds in France, the rigid adherence to principle, which on several occasions brought Nicholas I into difficulties, would not allow him to accept Louis Napoleon as hereditary Emperor of France.[8] The Tsar would welcome him as a President and Dictator for life, and was even willing to accord him the title of Emperor, provided that it was for Louis Napoleon's lifetime only, and was not the foundation of a new hereditary imperial dynasty; because Nicholas believed that hereditary dynasties could be established only by God.

Louis Napoleon therefore decided to make himself Emperor without Russian approval, especially as neither the Austrian nor the British government had any objection to the establishment of a hereditary Bonaparte dynasty in France. Malmesbury made difficulties only about the title 'Napoleon III'. Britain was prepared to accept Louis Napoleon as the Emperor Napoleon II, but thought that 'Napoleon III' implied that he claimed the throne by hereditary succession from Napoleon I after the Duke of Reichstadt, whom the Allies had never recognized as Napoleon II. It also implied that he denied the validity of the acts of the Bourbon Kings after 1815 and of the Treaty of Vienna which the Bourbons had signed. Louis Napoleon pointed out to the British government that he based his claim to the imperial throne solely on the Act of the Senate and referendum of November 1852, and that if he were claiming to reign by hereditary succession he would have called himself Napoleon V; because, as it was an accepted tradition that every Bonapartist Emperor took the name of Napoleon, Joseph Bonaparte would have been the Emperor Napoleon III and Louis Bonaparte Napoleon IV.[9]

The British statesmen did not realize the importance to Louis Napoleon of taking the title 'Napoleon III'. They believed the journalists' story that the title 'Napoleon III' had been adopted by accident – that during Louis Napoleon's provincial tour in the autumn of 1852, Persigny had written to the Prefects to display banners with the slogan 'Vive Napoléon!!!', and that the Prefect of Bourges had mistaken the three exclamation marks for the numeral 'III'.[10] In fact, 'Napoleon III' was the only possible title for Louis Napoleon. 'Napoleon II' was impossible, in view of the Bonapartists' emotive association of the name with the Duke of Reichstadt; and 'Louis Napoleon I' would have meant a breach of the rule that a Bonaparte Emperor took the name Napoleon. Malmesbury eventually saw the strength of Louis Napoleon's arguments, remembering that William of Orange had been called 'King William III of England', despite the fact that he did not claim to reign by hereditary descent from William Rufus; and Britain and Austria persuaded the reluctant Tsar of Russia to accept the numeral 'III' as well as a hereditary Second Empire.[11]

But on one matter the Tsar stood firm. He refused to address Louis Napoleon as 'my brother'; he insisted on beginning the letter of recognition 'Mon cher ami', not 'Monsieur mon frère'. The French Foreign Office told the Russian Ambassador, Kisselev, that the Emperor would refuse to accept a letter from the Tsar which began 'Mon cher ami'. The Austrian and Prussian governments proposed to Russia that their letters of recognition, and the Russian letter, should be presented simultaneously by the three Ambassadors in Paris, in order to show the unity of the three Northern Powers; but the form of address was a stumbling-block. Austria and Prussia refused to accept the Russian proposal that their three letters should all begin 'Mon cher ami', but agreed to delay presenting their letters until Kisselev had received further instructions from St Petersburg – a process which took at least a fortnight. The instructions that Kisselev received were that the Tsar stood absolutely firm in refusing to write 'Monsieur mon frère' to Napoleon III. Eventually Russia, Prussia, Austria and France reached a compromise solution; the Austrian, Prussian and Russian letters were to be presented simultaneously to the Emperor, with the Austrian and Prussian letters beginning 'Monsieur mon frère' and the Russian letter 'Mon cher ami'.[12] Louis Napoleon made a joke of the whole business; he said that he preferred to be addressed as 'Mon cher ami', because a man chose his friends but could not choose who was to be his brother.[13]

Queen Victoria made no difficulty about addressing Louis Napoleon as 'brother'. 'With us he has become mon frère,' wrote Prince Albert, 'but he must not become frère Cain.'[14]

There is certainly no truth in the story, which became widely accepted a few years later, that Louis Napoleon went to war with Russia in the Crimea in revenge for the Tsar's refusal to address him as 'Monsieur mon frère'; but Louis Napoleon had other incentives to go to war. The military tradition of French Bonapartism was very strong, and Louis Napoleon's enemies were trying to denigrate his peaceful foreign policy. Victor Hugo had repeatedly stressed his theme that the great Napoleon's *coup d'etat* of 18 Brumaire was almost, if not quite, excusable because of the military glory which resulted from it, but that Louis Napoleon's *coup d'etat* of 2 December was contemptible as well as wicked, because Louis Napoleon had not followed it up with an attempt to conquer Europe. In March 1850, when the press was still relatively free in France, Hugo's paper *L'Événement* had printed, side by side, a list of the twelve glorious deeds of Napoleon and the twelve glorious deeds of Louis Napoleon. Against Napoleon's Arcola, the Pyramids, the crossing of the Alps, Austerlitz, Jena, Madrid and Moscow, they set Louis Napoleon's arrival at the Élysée, the military demonstration of 29 January 1849, his inspection of the cholera hospitals and of the troops at Amiens, and his visits to Ham, Elbeuf and Rouen. 'It is very fine to be called Napoleon,' wrote *Le National* in June 1851, 'especially when one is the greatest captain of his century and the victor of Marengo and Austerlitz. . . . But where are your Marengos and Austerlitzes?'[15]

Louis Napoleon did not intend to allow his opponents to goad him into going to war; he meant what he said when he declared that 'the Empire means peace'. But he did not find it easy to convince the British government and public of this. It was an article of faith for English Liberals that a foreign dictator, who relies on a powerful army to maintain his power at home, must necessarily, sooner or later, become an aggressor in international affairs; and the traditional British fear of Napoleonic ambitions was still strong. When Louis Napoleon, in 1852, put diplomatic pressure on the Belgian government to muzzle and expel the French refugees, the British press believed that he was picking a quarrel with Belgium in order to have an excuse for invading the country and annexing it to France, as the French revolutionary government had done in 1794. They also feared a French attack on the Rhine.[16]

Nesselrode had other fears. In December 1852 he believed that Louis Napoleon would not go to war in Western Europe, where he would have to fight against a coalition of the Great Powers, but would incite Turkey into provoking Russia into a war in which Russia, not France, would be fighting alone against a powerful coalition. It was true that Russia's great superiority in man-power would enable her to win the war and to capture Constantinople, and that the Turkish Empire would collapse; but as Russia could not permanently occupy the whole of the Turkish territories, Louis Napoleon would be able to seize Tunisia, Egypt, and the western parts of the fallen empire, and either retain them or use them as a bargaining counter at the peace conference.[17] The most striking mistake in Nesselrode's analysis was his assumption that Russia would win the war.

In February 1853 the Tsar sent General Prince Menshikov on a mission to Constantinople. Menshikov demanded, and obtained, the dismissal of Fuad Effendi, the Foreign Minister who had made the agreement with France granting the privileges to the Roman Catholics. The Grand Vizier, who resented Menshikov's attitude, asked Britain and France for assistance. The British Ambassador, Sir Stratford Canning, who had always been regarded as the most anti-Russian of British diplomats, was in England for consultations; and as the new French Ambassador had not yet arrived, both Britain and France were represented in Constantinople by their Chargés d'Affaires, Colonel Rose and Benedetti. The Ambassador in Constantinople had been given power by the British government to summon the fleet from Malta to the Dardanelles in times of crisis – a power which had necessarily to be delegated to the Ambassador because, until a few years previously, it had taken a month for news to travel from Constantinople, though by 1853, thanks to the development of the electric telegraph, it now took only ten days. Rose proposed to Benedetti that they should jointly summon the British and French fleets to the Dardanelles in reply to Menshikov's demands. Benedetti was not prepared to take the responsibility, but informed the French Foreign Office that a very grave situation had arisen; Rose summoned the British fleet from Malta.

When the news reached London and Paris, the British and French roles were reversed; it was now the British who hesitated. In the Cabinet in London, Aberdeen carried the day against his Home Secretary, Palmerston, and ordered the fleet to return to Malta and not to go to the Dardanelles; but Louis Napoleon, with one of his sudden personal decisions, seized the initiative. He ordered the French fleet at Toulon to sail without the British to the Levant, but only as far as Salamis. Cowley was incensed; it was Britain, not France, that should be the protector of Turkey against Russia.[18]

In 1863 Kinglake, in his book *The Invasion of the Crimea*, placed a large share of the responsibility for the war on Louis Napoleon; and Aberdeen's son, Lord Stanmore, in his biography of his father in 1893, went further, claiming that Louis Napoleon deliberately schemed to bring about a war between Britain and Russia, and succeeded despite the efforts of those two peace-loving statesmen, Tsar Nicholas and Aberdeen.[19] This is a grotesque exaggeration. Louis Napoleon never intended his original championing of the cause of the Roman Catholics in Palestine to lead to war; and even if his action in sending the fleet to Salamis is regarded as a provocation instead of as a salutary warning to the Tsar, his diplomacy during the next six months shows that he was eager to preserve peace.

When Sir Stratford Canning returned to Constantinople – he had been created Lord Stratford de Redcliffe during his stay in England –

he set about trying to find a compromise in the Franco-Russian dispute about the Holy Places. He produced a plan which, subject to a few face-saving provisions, in effect restored the former privileged position of the Orthodox Church and revoked the concessions granted four months earlier to the Roman Catholics. Louis Napoleon accepted Stratford's proposals, and as the Russian government also accepted them, the quarrel about the Holy Places was settled in Russia's favour. But the Tsar felt that, in view of the earlier French challenge, something more than this was required; he demanded that the Turkish government should recognize him as the protector of all the Christians in the Ottoman Empire, and presented an ultimatum to Turkey: unless the Russian claim for a protectorate over the Christians was accepted within three days, Russian troops would cross the Turkish frontier and enter Walachia. Nesselrode warned the Tsar that such a step would mean war; but Nicholas was sure that Britain would not go to war and that France would not fight alone.

Stratford persuaded the Turks to refuse the ultimatum, and Menshikov left Constantinople on 19 May; but Russian troops did not invade the Danubian principalities. While the Tsar hesitated under Nesselrode's pressure, Stratford urged the British and French governments to send their fleets to the Dardanelles. This time Palmerston prevailed over Aberdeen in the British Cabinet, and Britain and France acted together. The British fleet sailed from Malta and reached Besika Bay, at the mouth of the Dardanelles, on 13 June; the French fleet arrived from Salamis next day. They did not enter the Dardanelles, which in peacetime would have been a violation of the Straits Convention of 1841; but the Tsar saw it as a provocation which made it impossible for him to appear to yield to a threat, and on 2 July 35,000 Russian troops crossed the Pruth and entered Walachia.

If Turkey, Britain and France had immediately declared war in reply to this invasion of Turkish territory, it might have been easier to persuade both their contemporaries and future historians that Russia was the aggressor in the Crimean War. But there were peculiar factors which made the Russian action fall short of a full invasion of Turkey. The principalities, which had a large measure of autonomy and a Christian population, were strongly pro-Russian, and Turkey had granted Russia extensive legal rights there under the Treaty of Adrianople of 1829. During the disorders of 1848, the principalities had been occupied by Russian troops with Turkish consent and the acquiescence of Britain and France. On that occasion, Russia had withdrawn her troops in due course; and on this occasion too the Tsar declared that he had no intention of remaining permanently in Walachia or of going to war with Turkey. So Louis Napoleon merely proposed to Britain that the British and French fleets should sail through the Dardanelles and the Sea of Marmora and enter the Bosporus, as a gesture of support for Turkey. The British government thought that this would be premature and a violation of the Straits Convention of 1841. They persuaded Louis Napoleon to keep the fleet at Besika and to accept an Austrian invitation to attend a Four-Power Conference in Vienna with Austria and Russia in an attempt to reach a peaceful solution.

During the negotiations in Vienna, Louis Napoleon was as eager as Aberdeen to reach a peaceful solution. As Russia refused to withdraw from the principalities unless Turkey gave a satisfactory reply to Menshikov's ultimatum, Aberdeen and Louis Napoleon, and even Palmerston, tried to find a formula which would satisfy Russia without compromising Turkish independence. It was in the Foreign Office in Paris that the 'Vienna Note' was drafted, under which Turkey in effect recognized Russia's claim to be the protector of the Christians. Russia accepted the Vienna Note, and agreed to withdraw their troops from the principalities if Turkey accepted it and the British and French fleets were withdrawn from the Dardanelles. But Turkey, who had not been represented at the Vienna Conference, refused to accept the Vienna Note, and suggested a number of verbal amendments which seemed to have no great significance. At that moment, a secret memorandum of the Russian Foreign Office was published in the Prussian press which showed how it would be possible for Russia to interpret the Vienna Note in a manner which gave Russia a far greater degree of control over the internal affairs of Turkey than Britain and France had intended.[20] This, in the eyes of the Western governments and press, justified the Turkish amendments to the Vienna Note; but the Tsar declared that he would not agree to any amendments to the Note which Britain and France had accepted in Vienna.

In September the Turks, without consulting Britain and France, sent an ultimatum to Russia to evacuate the principalities within twenty days. The Tsar replied by refusing to evacuate the principalities, but stated that if the Turks declared war, the Russian armed forces would confine themselves to purely defensive operations and would not attack the Turks. On 1 October the Turks crossed the Danube and attacked the Russians in the principalities. The Russians demanded that Britain and France should persuade their Turkish ally to cease military operations and to accept a peaceful settlement on the terms of the Vienna Note. Britain and France would not do so; instead, a few days before the Turkish army attacked the Russians, the British government at last agreed to Louis Napoleon's proposal that their fleets should sail from Besika through the Dardanelles and the Sea of Marmora and enter the Bosporus. Russia denounced this as a violation of the Convention of 1841. The British and French press applauded – and greatly exaggerated – the reports of Turkish successes against the Russians in Walachia; and in November Louis Napoleon invited the Turkish Ambassador to Fontainebleau for the hunting, and showed him great attention.[21]

On 30 November the Russian fleet attacked the Turkish ships which were at anchor in the port of Sinope in Asia Minor on the southern shore of the Black Sea, and sank nearly the whole fleet with great loss of life. There was an outburst of fury in Britain, and to a much lesser extent in France; it was seen as an unprovoked attack by the Russians, as the 'massacre of Sinope'. This completely ignored the fact that Turkey had gone to war with Russia two months earlier and had attacked the Russian land forces in the principalities; but the Russian attack at Sinope, hundreds of miles from the scene of the fighting in Walachia, was in breach of their undertaking not to resort to offensive action against the Turks, and the indignation was greater because the British and French fleets in the Bosporus had been unable to intervene.

In Britain, war was now regarded as inevitable; but in Paris, Louis Napoleon took no action, and a week after the news of Sinope reached Paris, he announced that a great International Exhibition, which would equal and indeed surpass the London Exhibition of 1851, would open in Paris in sixteen months' time on 1 May 1855. The British government and Cowley, who a few months earlier had thought that he was trying to provoke a war, now feared that he was weakening and was planning to make a deal with Russia behind the backs of the British and the Turks. At a ball at Princess Mathilde's on New Year's Day Eugénie opened the ball with the Russian Ambassador, Kisselev, and she was particularly attentive to him throughout the evening. The other diplomats attached a sinister political significance to Eugénie's last act of courtesy to a future enemy; and there were rumours that Mathilde and her Russian friends in Paris were acting as go-between in secret negotiations between France and Russia.[22] But on 4 January 1854 the French and British fleets in the Bosporus entered the Black Sea with orders to prevent any hostile movements of the Russian navy against the Turks.

On 29 January Napoleon III wrote a personal letter to the Tsar in a final effort to prevent war. He sent an advance copy of the letter to Queen Victoria and invited her to sign it and send it as a joint appeal to Nicholas. The British government were annoyed at the Emperor's démarche. They felt that, as a constitutional sovereign, Queen Victoria could not write a personal letter on a political matter to the Tsar, but that all negotiations must be conducted by her ministers. This was politely explained to Louis Napoleon, who sent the letter in his own name alone, with the result that the credit for the initiative went to him, and put Britain in second place among the Allies.[23]

The letter was a skilful piece of propaganda. Though very friendly in tone, it argued that Russia was entirely to blame for the dangerous situation which had been reached, because the Russian occupation of the principalities 'suddenly transferred matters from the realm of discussion to that of action'. Britain and France had nevertheless persuaded Turkey not to treat the occupation of Walachia as an act of war; but when it appeared that an agreement had been reached at Vienna, the Russian government, by its interpretation of the agreement in its memorandum, had made it impossible for France to put pressure on Turkey to accept the agreement without amendments. The attack on the Turkish fleet at Sinope, while the British and French fleets were in the Bosporus with their 3000 guns, was a challenge to France and Britain and a violation of the Russian pledge not to engage in offensive operations. But it was still not too late to avert war, and Louis Napoleon proposed to Nicholas that he should withdraw the Russian troops from the principalities, while the British and French fleets would withdraw from the Black Sea. He was confident that the Tsar would agree to this proposal, because 'Your Majesty has given so many proofs of your solicitude for the peace of Europe and has contributed so powerfully by your beneficial influence to the struggle against the spirit of disorder'.[24]

Cowley saw the letter as another sign that Louis Napoleon was weakening in his resolve to stand by the Turks. The British press criticized the letter as an act of appeasement, and noticed with some disquiet that on 16 February Louis Napoleon went with Eugénie to the Opéra-Comique to see Meyerbeer's opera *L'Étoile du Nord*, since Scribe's libretto told the story of how the hero of the opera, Peter the Great, defeated Charles XII and the Swedish invaders of Russia at Poltava in 1709.[25] But in fact, Louis Napoleon's proposal in his letter to the Tsar was one which it was almost impossible for the Tsar to accept. For Russia to withdraw from the principalities after her troops had been attacked there by the Turkish army would have been an unacceptable humiliation; and any chance of Russia accepting the proposal was lost when Louis Napoleon's letter was published in *Le Moniteur* before he had received the Tsar's reply.[26]

In his answer, Nicholas, addressing his 'cher ami' more in sorrow than in anger, said that he was defending the privileges of the Christians in the Turkish Empire which had been won by Russian blood. Britain and France were responsible for the situation, for the Turks would never have ventured to attack the Russians in the principalities without British and French connivance. He had sent his troops into Walachia because the British and French fleets had approached the Dardanelles, 'and besides this, long before this time, when England hesitated to assume a hostile attitude, Your Majesty took the initiative in sending your fleet as far as Salamis'. As for Louis Napoleon's proposal for a withdrawal on both sides, Nicholas stuck to the position which he had adopted ever since the previous August: he would withdraw from the principalities only if the Turks accepted the agreement which had been reached in Vienna; as Britain and France had been parties to this agreement, Russia would not agree to any other. 'Whatever Your Majesty may decide, threats will not induce me to recede. My confidence is in God and in my right; and Russia, as I can guarantee, will prove herself to be in 1854 what she was in 1812.'[27]

Louis Napoleon used less conciliatory language about Russia and the Tsar when he addressed the Chambers on 2 March:

We have seen, indeed, in the East, in the midst of profound peace, a sovereign suddenly demand further advantages from his weaker neighbour, and because he did not obtain them he invaded two of his provinces. This alone was enough to call to arms those who are disgusted by iniquity. But we have other reasons for supporting Turkey. France has as great an interest as England – perhaps a greater interest – to ensure that the influence of Russia does not permanently extend to Constantinople; because to reign at Constantinople means to reign over the Mediterranean; and I think that none of you, gentlemen, will say that only England has vital interests in this sea, which washes three hundred leagues of our shores. . . . Why are we going to Constantinople? We are going there with England to defend the Sultan's cause, and no less to protect the rights of the Christians; we are going there to defend the freedom of the seas and our rightful influence in the Mediterranean.[28]

The Tsar's proclamation told the Russian people: 'England and France have sided with the enemy of Christianity against Russia, fighting for the Orthodox faith. But Russia will not betray her holy mission.'[29] No war in history took longer to begin, but the ultimatum finally expired and war was declared on 28 March 1854.

CHAPTER 28

THE ENGLISH ALLY

NAPOLEON III was as conscious as the Tsar of what had occurred in 1812. He had no intention of sending an army on a disastrous march deep into the heart of Russia. He would cripple Russia by striking at her perimeters – at Kronstadt, and perhaps St Petersburg, in the Baltic, and at Sevastopol in the Black Sea – while the Turks engaged the Russian armies in the principalities and in Asia Minor, and a British Naval force from Hong Kong attacked Vladivostok in the Far East. This last project never materialized. As for the Russian armies in the principalities – the cause of the war – the Russians withdrew almost as soon as war was declared in order to retain the good will of Austria, whose gratitude for Russian help in Hungary in 1849 was modified by her fear of Russian expansion in the Balkans. By agreement with Russia, the Austrian armies occupied the principalities; but Austria remained neutral in the war.

It was obvious that if the war were prolonged, the bulk of the fighting men would have to be provided by France. Despite the victories which the Turks claimed to have won over the Russians in the principalities, Louis Napoleon and his advisers knew that the Turkish army was no match for the Russians in a full-scale war. Britain intended to fight the war in her traditional way – by sending a small and very efficient army of volunteer paupers under aristocratic officers, by hiring foreign mercenaries to supplement her own forces, by using her incomparable navy to assist the land army, and by encouraging and financing allies to attack her enemy. France, with her system of selective conscription, could immediately call up 500,000 men, though any conscript who was rich enough to do so was allowed to pay another man to take his place[1] – a system which was criticized by Radicals and perfectionists, but was accepted on grounds of expediency in France, as it was in other countries, like Italy and the United States. By the end of May 1854, 25,000 French and 15,000 British soldiers had reached Constantinople. Louis Napoleon appointed Saint-Arnaud to be Commander-in-Chief of the French forces in Turkey.

At Easter, Major-General the Duke of Cambridge, Queen Victoria's cousin, arrived in Paris with Lord Raglan, who had been appointed to command the British forces in Turkey. They were on their way to Constantinople, and had talks with Louis Napoleon and the French generals on the grand strategy of the campaign. It was decided to strike simultaneously at Sevastopol and Kronstadt. While Saint-Arnaud and the expeditionary force sailed from Toulon to Constantinople, 70,000 men were assembled in camp near Boulogne, ready to sail to the Baltic with their British colleagues at an opportune moment. Cowley tried to persuade the Emperor to have the camp in some place other than Boulogne, which he thought would remind the people of Britain of Napoleon I's camp at Boulogne for the invasion of England in 1805. But Louis Napoleon insisted on selecting Boulogne as the site for the camp, precisely because of its Napoleonic associations. The British press turned it to good account, contrasting the assembly of the hostile Grand Army in 1805 and the camp at Boulogne in 1854, where the French soldiers were waiting to sail with their British comrades against the common enemy.[2]

The press in both France and Britain emphasized the unity of their two nations, but old hatreds had not entirely disappeared. When the Emperor took Cambridge and Raglan to the Opera during their visit to Paris in April, they were greeted by the audience with shouts of 'Vivent les Anglais! Vive l'Empereur!' But as Raglan rode through the streets, with his loose sleeve hanging at his side, one man shouted: 'We tore that arm off him at Waterloo!'[3]

The usual lavish entertainment was provided for the British generals during their stay in Paris, including a state ball on the evening of Easter Monday. For some reason it was impossible to hold the ball at the Tuileries, so it was decided to have it at the Élysée; but the Élysée was being repaired and redecorated, and was not in a fit state for a ball. At 7 p.m. on Good Friday, Eugénie asked Lacroix, the architect in charge of the repairs at the Élysée – he was the brother of Hortense Cornu – to get the Élysée ready for the ball by the evening of Easter Monday. Lacroix told her that there were 3000 cubic yards of stone in the courtyard of the Élysée, that there was no staircase, that the walls consisted of wet stone and mortar, that nothing was ready except the roof, and that it would be quite impossible to get it ready in time. 'I am sure that nothing is impossible for you', said Eugénie; and so, though Louis Napoleon said that it was just a woman's caprice, Lacroix promised to do his best.

The workmen had gone home for the Easter holiday, but 400 of them were sent for and offered 20 francs for twelve hours' work, plus free food and brandy in their wine, if they stayed at work till the job was finished. The work continued non-stop for eighty-two hours; they worked all night by the light of seven hundred lamps and of torches carried by thirty men. In this time they built three kitchens and a new ballroom, 90 feet long by 35 feet wide and 30 feet high. Unfortunately the Archbishop of Paris had sent a pastoral letter to his clergy, which was read out in Notre-Dame and in all the Paris churches on Easter Sunday, in which he condemned those people who violated the Sabbath by forcing their servants to work on Sundays, especially on Easter Sunday; and all over Paris there were adverse comments about the work in progress at the Élysée. The people particularly resented the fact that these exertions and this expense were for the entertainment of an English Prince; they said that God had been sacrificed to the *entente cordiale*. But Lacroix and his men worked incessantly, encouraged by the Empress, who from time to time came and praised their efforts, and rewarded them with her smiles. On the Monday morning the Emperor arrived and saw that the 3000 cubic yards of stone were still lying in the courtyard and that there was no staircase; but Lacroix said that the work would be finished, and the building ready for the ball, by the evening; and it was.[4]

In the middle of July, Louis Napoleon and Eugénie went for a holiday to Biarritz. Eugénie had loved Biarritz when she went there in 1847, and the Emperor decided to build a house for her there, on the edge of the sea, where she could go for a holiday every year. The house was named the Villa Eugénie – a rather misleading name for the large mansion, with its complex of servants' cottages and guardrooms and its private chapel in the grounds. The building work was in progress in the summer of 1854, and proceeded under the close supervision of the Emperor, who stayed with the Empress in the northern part of the town while the villa was being built.[5]

It was a happy holiday, in lovely weather, with Maria Manuela and Paca coming from Spain. Eugénie went for drives along the seashore in a little carriage which she drove herself, with only one of her ladies in attendance, and bathed in the sea every day. They visited the neighbouring villages, where they attended Mass, and the Emperor talked to the peasants about the local crops; and as usual they gave freely to charities. They went to the mountain village of Cambo and tasted the water at the sulphurous springs. They admired the scenery in the mountains and had picnics, with Eugénie sitting on a wayside bench and the Emperor on the grass at her feet. Walking with Laity, who had been made Prefect of the Gironde, Louis Napoleon came across a rowing boat moored to the bank of the River Nive; he rowed Laity across the river and back again. He and Eugénie went for day excursions on the yacht *Australie*, crossing the bay and cruising along the Spanish coast and up the River Bidassoa, and landing at Irun, where the Emperor reviewed the local Spanish militia.[6]

Everyone expected that they would return to Paris in time for the National Day on 15 August; but shortly before the 15th it was announced that they would be prolonging their stay in Biarritz and would not attend the celebrations in Paris. This caused great dissatisfaction, and a renewal of anti-Eugénie talk: people said that the pleasure-loving Empress was luring the Emperor away from his public duties. On 15 August he and Eugénie went from Biarritz to the neighbouring town of Bayonne and attended the National Day celebrations there. He told the Mayor that his presence in Bayonne on the National Day showed the stability of the régime; he was not one of those rulers who did not dare to leave their capital in case a revolution broke out in their absence.[7]

On 27 August he at last left Biarritz, leaving Eugénie there with Maria Manuela, and after meeting King Leopold of the Belgians at Calais he went to the camp at Boulogne and took part in large-scale and well-publicized manoeuvres. They involved 70,000 soldiers and took place in a triangular area about 25 miles wide and 35 miles long between Ambleteuse, Montreuil and Saint-Omer. The participants were divided into two armies, the one commanded by General Schramm attacking Boulogne from Calais, and the other, under the Emperor himself, defending Boulogne. Not surprisingly, the umpire decided that the Emperor's army was victorious.[8]

Prince Albert came from England to see the manoeuvres and to cement the Anglo-French alliance by spending four days as the Emperor's guest. Apart from the Prince and his entourage, 15,000 English tourists also came to Boulogne as sightseers, as did 2000 French visitors from Paris who came on special cheap excursion trains, and crowded the decorated and illuminated streets of Boulogne on the warm September days and nights. There were banners with inscriptions and lamps arranged in the form of eagles and the letters V.N.A., standing for Victoria, Napoleon and Albert, though some of the people thought they stood for 'Vive notre amitié'. Everyone seemed to enjoy themselves, and the press reported that the French girls loved the Englishmen and the Frenchmen loved the English girls. At the Pavilion Hotel, which was henceforth renamed the Imperial Pavilion Hotel, Louis Napoleon and Prince Albert spent a businesslike four days, with no ladies present and no evening banquets, but going to bed early and rising at 6 a.m. to ride together in the Emperor's carriage to the camp at Helfaut or Marquise for the beginning of the day's manoeuvres at 7 a.m.; but there were some excellent breakfasts and lunches at the Emperor's headquarters. Prince Albert spent part of the time with the Emperor and part with General Schramm, and said that he was very impressed with the efficiency of both the armies.[9]

In a memorandum which he wrote a few days after the visit, Prince Albert recorded his impressions of the Emperor. He noted that Louis Napoleon was on very familiar terms with the gentlemen of his entourage, although they seemed afraid of him. 'The tone was rather the *ton de garnison*, with a good deal of smoking; the Emperor smoking cigarettes, and not being able to understand my not joining in it.' Prince Albert paid Louis Napoleon the compliment of saying that he not only spoke French with a German accent, but was thoroughly German in his character and mental processes, having had the benefit of a systematic German education. In their very frank political discussions, Prince Albert thought it necessary to warn the Emperor not to violate sound economic theory by imposing price controls in times of food shortage. Louis Napoleon told him that if he had not fixed a maximum price of bread during the shortage, there would have been a revolution. Prince Albert thought that this was a shocking state of affairs.[10]

During his stay in Boulogne, Louis Napoleon communicated every day by telegraph with Eugénie in Biarritz, and his secretary informed the press of the wonderful achievement of French technology which had made it possible for a message to travel from Biarritz to Boulogne – from one extremity of France to the other – in one-and-a-half hours. On 16 September the Emperor left Boulogne and went to Bordeaux to meet Eugénie and bring her to the camp. This necessitated the postponement of a new series of manoeuvres which had been fixed to take place at Boulogne, with the Emperor commanding one of the armies; and the soldiers in the camp grumbled, and complained because the Emperor had deserted his post in wartime for the sake of his wife.[11]

But all the criticism disappeared when Eugénie arrived at Boulogne, beautiful and gay. She was acclaimed by the citizens in the streets and by the soldiers at the camp. One day, when she was driving out to Courtreaux in the early morning to see the manoeuvres, she passed a soldier who was walking there by himself, having become separated from his unit. She offered him a lift in her carriage, and he travelled beside the coachman on the box. The *Times* correspondent was most impressed, and wrote that no one could conceive of Queen Victoria doing such a thing.[12]

In the middle of September an army of 58,000 men – 25,000 French, 25,000 British and 8000 Turks – sailed from Varna across the Black Sea and disembarked in the Crimea. They advanced on Sevastopol, and on 20 September defeated the Russians at the battle of the Alma. Saint-Arnaud was in the saddle all day during the battle, and gave no sign of ill-health; but nine days later he died of a heart attack which had long been expected by his intimate friends but astounded and shocked the public. If the Allies had immediately assaulted Sevastopol, the town would probably have fallen; but they delayed for three weeks, during which time the defenders put the city into a strong state of defence. Canrobert took over the command of the French army in the Crimea.

On 30 September news reached Paris from Vienna that Sevastopol had surrendered, and by next day the report had reached London. The French and British governments and press received the news with some scepticism, but on 2 October the Turkish embassies in London and Paris confirmed that the news was true. It reached Boulogne while Louis Napoleon and Eugénie were at the manoeuvres on 30 September. They reviewed the troops side by side in front of the Napoleon Column outside Boulogne, he on his English horse 'Phillips' – he had bought it from Mr Phillips of Knightsbridge – and she on an Andalusian grey that Paca had given her as a wedding present, and dressed in a black riding habit with a Spanish hat and white plume. They rode slowly down the hill at walking pace, going along the lines and talking to the soldiers amid the shouts of 'Vive l'Empereur!' and 'Vive l'Impératrice!'[13] Louis Napoleon addressed the troops and told them about the fall of Sevastopol: 'At the moment I speak I have little doubt that the flags of the Allied armies are waving on the walls of Sebastopol.'[14]

By 5 October it was known that the report was untrue. There was anger in Britain and France, but the origin of the report could not be traced further back than Vienna. It was thought that the Russians had started the rumour in order to cause the demoralization which followed the initial celebrations.[15] In the Crimea, the armies settled down to a long siege, and to a winter of cold and disease.

By going to war, Louis Napoleon had retrieved his popularity from the low point to which it had fallen in 1853. There was an overwhelming response to the government's appeal to the public to subscribe to the war loan. While the Ultramontane Catholic newspaper *L'Univers* supported the war for the Roman Catholic Church against Orthodox Russia,[16] Louis Napoleon almost achieved the impossible task of winning the support of the Radicals and Socialists, because Tsar Nicholas I was the only man in Europe whom they hated even more than they hated Napoleon III. Mazzini was irreconcilable, and denounced the Anglo-French war effort and the entry of Piedmont into the war on their side. Victor Hugo, Ledru-Rollin and the French refugees in England took the same line; and Kossuth, who had been banned by Louis Napoleon from entering France, toured Britain, calling at monster-meetings for the Allies to abandon their attempts to woo neutral Austria, and to convert the war into a revolutionary war of all the oppressed nationalities of Europe against Russian and Austrian despotism. But Garibaldi and Marx enthusiastically supported the Allies in the Crimea.[17]

In France, Barbès, who was serving in Belle-Île the life sentence imposed on him in 1849 for his revolutionary activities, wrote to Louis Napoleon on 18 September 1854:

> If you are a chauvinist . . . I am still more chauvinist than you, for I long for the victories of Frenchmen. Yes, yes, let them thrash the Cossacks well, and it will be so much gained for the cause of civiliza-tion and the world. Like you, I could have wished that we had no war; but since the sword has been drawn, it must not be sheathed without glory.

On 3 October Louis Napoleon wrote to the Minister of the Interior and ordered him to release Barbès at once. 'A prisoner who, in spite of long sufferings, retains such patriotic sentiments cannot under my reign remain in prison. Release him immediately, without conditions.'[18]

Barbès refused to accept the pardon, and for two days would not leave his prison cell. When he was taken to Paris and set free, he wrote to *Le Moniteur*, stating that the *coup d'état* of 2 December would always be an irremovable barrier between Louis Napoleon and himself; he would remain in Paris for forty-eight hours to give the government the opportunity to re-arrest him, and would then go into exile. The government, in one of its isolated fits of generosity and tolerance, allowed Barbès's letter to be published in *Le Moniteur*[19] – perhaps because they wished to strengthen his position among the Radicals and Socialists against that of the refugees who opposed the war.

The strongest opposition to the war came from a small group of extreme right-wing Legitimists, who had always regarded Russia as the champion of autocracy and order in Europe, and England – especially Palmerston – as the secret instigator behind every revolution. They could not openly oppose the war, but encouraged anti-British feeling by spreading suspicion of British motives in the Levant, by denigrating the British war effort, and by suggesting that Britain was using French soldiers as cannon-fodder to maintain her sinister anti-French influence in Constantinople. The secret police concentrated less on spying on the cafés and *bistros* in working-class areas, and more on collecting reports of what was said in aristocratic drawing-rooms and clubs. Any open criticism was impossible, and even jokes were risky.[20] When the popular comedian, Grassot, had to wait a long time to be served in a Paris restaurant, he made the pun: 'Mais c'est ici comme à Sébastopol, on ne peut rien prendre.'[21] He was arrested, and held for a few days in prison. The philosopher Jules Simon, who had been a Moderate Republican deputy in the National Assembly in 1848, was visited on one occasion by the police and questioned about an anti-government remark which he had made at a private party in his own house; but they let him off with a warning.[22]

CHAPTER 29

QUEEN VICTORIA

THE war had suddenly made Louis Napoleon very popular in England. When a foreign dictator suppresses the freedom of the press and imprisons his political opponents without trial, the only way in which he can win the temporary forgiveness of the British Establishment is by becoming their ally in wartime. *The Times* abandoned its virulent campaign against Louis Napoleon, and praised him lavishly, lauding the efficiency of the French army and the Emperor's wise policy of alliance with England and his loyalty in the struggle against the common enemy. When Mérimée went to England in July 1854 he found dreadful pictures of Louis Napoleon and Eugénie displayed all over London, and heard barrel-organs in every street playing the 'Marseillaise', which the English imagined was the French national anthem. The organ-grinders had no idea that they would have been arrested for playing the tune in Paris.[1]

For the first time, Louis Napoleon's complaints about the activities of the French refugees in Britain were sympathetically received by the British government and press. They warned and denounced the refugees in Jersey who published incendiary pamphlets against him.[2]

The *Times* war correspondent in the Crimea, William Howard Russell, exposed in his articles the incompetence of the British commanders at Sevastopol, and the terrible conditions in the field hospitals and in the base hospital at Scutari. He reported that the French wounded were much better cared for than the English, thanks to the efforts of the Sisters of Mercy who had come from France to work in the hospitals at Scutari. British patriotism and Protestantism were mortified, and Florence Nightingale and her nurses went out to remedy the position. No French newspaper published articles by French war correspondents denigrating the French generals or organization in the Crimea, and public opinion in Britain began to admire French efficiency and Napoleon III.[3]

In February 1855, Louis Napoleon decided to go to the Crimea and assume personal command of his army at Sevastopol. This decision worried his ministers. It was obviously desirable for an Emperor

374

named Napoleon to lead his armies to brilliant victories in the field; but what if there were no brilliant victories after the Emperor arrived in the Crimea? What would happen to the régime if he lost his life there? And what might his enemies in France do during his absence abroad?[4] Even the great Napoleon had been confronted with an abortive insurrection in Paris during his absence in Russia in 1812, at a time when his régime was much better consolidated than was Napoleon III's in 1855.

The British government did their best to encourage this opposition to the Emperor's going to the Crimea, for it was obvious that if he went there he would completely overshadow the British generals.[5] Their worst fears were realized when Louis Napoleon on 26 February wrote to Palmerston, who had become Prime Minister three weeks before, and asked him to place the British army in the Crimea under his command in all but name. He told Palmerston that he had decided to go to the Crimea

> because in my view it is the only way of quickly ending an expedition which otherwise would bring inevitable disaster to both England and France. I do not, of course, pretend to know more about war than the distinguished generals who are already in the Levant, but I am deeply convinced that I alone can establish in the Crimea, with your help, that unity of view and action which is indispensable for success and which can only be secured by the presence of someone sufficiently highly placed to take upon himself the responsibility of a supreme resolve on which the safety of the army depends.

He therefore asked Palmerston to grant him, when he went to the Crimea,

> not the direct command of the English army, but the power, after communicating my plans to Field-Marshal Raglan, to compel him to follow them even though he should not agree with them. For after all, I must really tell you sincerely that if the 20,000 English encamped before Sebastopol, thanks to their bravery, count as 50,000 men in the eyes of the French army, on the other hand Lord Raglan, by his delays, his uncertainties, and his resistance to all decisive combinations, is a permanent obstacle to every serious enterprise.

He then reminded Palmerston that when the intended reinforcements reached the Crimea, the Allied forces there would amount to 149,000 men, of whom 102,000 would be French, as compared with 20,000 British, 15,000 Piedmontese and 12,000 Turks.[6]

The British government kept the Emperor's letter a closely guarded secret, for they realized the resentment which it would arouse among many sections of the British public; and Kinglake and Louis Napoleon's other critics never found out about it. The Cabinet sent Clarendon, the Foreign Secretary, to meet Louis Napoleon at Boulogne, to persuade him not to go to the Crimea, and to tell him that the British people and the British army would resent it if the British forces in the Crimea were placed under the command of a French Commander-in-Chief. The opposition from his ministers and from his ally caused Louis Napoleon to hesitate about going to the Crimea; but his adventurous wife was strongly in favour of his going, and she worried him a little by her insistence that she should go too. In March the press announced that the Emperor would go to the Crimea, and would probably sail before the end of the month; but the opponents of the project continued to urge him not to go.[7]

He agreed not to leave for the Crimea until after he had paid a state visit to Queen Victoria, and the British government made preparations to give him a great reception, hoping to take the opportunity, during his visit, to persuade him to abandon altogether his journey to the Crimea. *The Times* welcomed him enthusiastically:

In this Emperor Louis Napoleon, we see first the friend and ally. . . . We see the man who has restored order, prosperity, and power to his country in the course of two or three years. . . . We see the man who does what we, with our boasted self-government, our Parliament and all the apparatus of a free constitution, cannot do, whether in the conduct of his armies abroad, or in the execution of great and beneficial works at home.[8]

A reader of *The Morning Post* wrote to the paper suggesting that the Marble Arch be renamed the 'Arch of Napoleon', as the 'beautiful figures of Fame' on the arch 'never will spread their laurels over a more deserving ally than Napoleon III'.[9]

Against this powerful chorus, Victor Hugo and the French refugees in London and Jersey could barely make themselves heard in England. Victor Hugo published his *Letter to Louis Bonaparte* a few days before the Emperor arrived. 'Do not come', he urged him, and went on to ask:

What blow are you planning against English freedom? Will you come full of promises as you came to France in 1848? Will you swear to the English alliance with your hand on your heart in the same way that you placed it there when you swore loyalty to the Republic?[10]

The English Radicals distributed a leaflet, *England's Disgrace*, protesting because

Louis Napoleon, The Murderer, the oath-breaker, the destroyer of the French and Italian Republics, who bribed the soldiers to massacre peaceful citizens on the Boulevards, exiled the best men of France, and paved the way to Power with the Dead Bodies of honest and inoffensive Men, Women, and Children, is coming to England.[11]

Less violent, but more widespread, anti-French prejudice was expressed in a broadsheet song:

The Emperor and Empress are coming so keen
To England, to visit our sweet little Queen. . . .
Thro' the West-end of London so nicely they'll prance,
With all the fine ladies of England and France,
Such wonderful things they are going to do,
Clear the road and get out of the way, parle veaux [*parlez-vous*]. . . .
The Emperor of France and his lady so gay,
Are coming to England – get out of the way. . . .
There'll be baked frogs, & fried frogs, & frogs in a stew,
And all the young ladies shall sing parle veaux![12]

On 16 April, Louis Napoleon sailed from Calais with Eugénie in the warship *Pélican*.[13] The weather was fine on the French coast, but they ran into fog in mid-Channel, and Queen Victoria was sure that it was only because they had an English pilot on board that they managed to land safely at Dover. Prince Albert was waiting to welcome them at the quayside, where a military band greeted them with 'Partant pour la Syrie'. After lunching at the Lord Warden Hotel, they travelled by special train to London. They were cheered by great crowds all along the railway line – by well-dressed ladies and gentlemen on the platform at Tonbridge Station, by the Addiscombe cadets at Croydon, and by parties of schoolchildren and agricultural labourers in their smocks in the fields, who waved to them as they passed through Kent.

They arrived at the Bricklayers' Arms Station in London and travelled in an open barouche with Prince Albert, almost at walking pace, with an escort of the household troops, by the Kent Road, Westminster Bridge, Whitehall, Charing Cross – where a band outside the Admiralty played 'Partant pour la Syrie' – along Pall Mall, St James's and Piccadilly, through Hyde Park, and by Victoria Gate and Eastbourne Terrace to Paddington Station, where another special train waited to take them to Queen Victoria at Windsor. As the imperial carriage and its escort passed up St James's Street, Louis Napoleon pointed with his arm down King Street to his right; and the crowds, realizing that he was showing Eugénie the house where he had lived from 1846 to 1848, broke into even louder cheers. But the Londoners' greatest enthusiasm was for Eugénie, elegant and beautiful in her tartan dress, grey cloak and straw bonnet. To their delight, she waved back at all the ladies who waved their handkerchiefs at her from the pavements and the windows of the houses.

The crowds in the London streets delayed the journey to Paddington, and at Windsor the privileged few who had been admitted to the station to greet the Emperor and Empress on their arrival had to wait for three hours before the train came in. Queen Victoria welcomed them at the Castle, where she had personally gone to great trouble to supervise the furnishing of their rooms. They slept in magnificent beds decorated with the initials N and E; the Emperor's bed was the one in which Tsar Nicholas had slept when he visited England in 1844.

Queen Victoria had to some extent shared her subjects' fears of the ultimate intentions of a Bonaparte Emperor – '*our* new *bon* Frère',[14] as she referred to him in a letter to King Leopold; and she strongly disapproved of Louis Napoleon's action in virtually confiscating the property of the Orleans family in France. But during their stay at Windsor, she was completely captivated by the Emperor and Empress. Louis Napoleon subjected her to all his personal charm. She wrote in her diary that 'the Emperor is so very quiet, his voice is low and soft, and *il ne fait pas de phrases*'. He was 'so modest' and 'good-humoured and amusing'. She was delighted when he told her that he had seen and admired her on the first occasion when she prorogued Parliament after her accession in 1837. He was 'very kind to the Children, and kissed and petted Arthur', her five-year-old son; and he wrote suitable German verses in the Autograph Book of the thirteen-year-old Prince of Wales. As for 'the dear sweet Empress', the Queen was delighted with her, and 'Albert admired her toilette extremely'. The Queen told the Emperor that she realized that Eugénie 'naturally . . . felt the "gène" of her position, from not having been brought up for it'; but Eugénie was soon at her ease with the Queen, who wrote that she 'talked away to me with Spanish liveliness'.[15]

During their two days and three nights at Windsor, there was a ceremony at which the Queen made the Emperor a Knight of the Garter; a state banquet, with the band playing 'Partant pour la Syrie'; and a ball in the Waterloo Gallery, at which the Emperor danced with the Queen, and the Empress with Prince Albert, in a quadrille. Afterwards the Emperor danced a waltz with the Queen's fourteen-year-old daughter Victoria, the Princess Royal, the Queen noting that 'Vicky behaved extremely well, making beautiful curtseys and was much praised by the Emperor and Empress, about whom she raves'. It struck the Queen as very strange 'to think of a granddaughter of George III dancing with the nephew of our great enemy, the Emperor Napoleon, now my most firm ally, *in* the *Waterloo Gallery*'. She thought that Eugénie's behaviour at the ball was 'the most perfect thing I ever saw – so gentle, graceful and kind, and so modest and retiring'.[16]

There were also political talks, and discussions on grand strategy, at Windsor, with Palmerston and Clarendon. At Louis Napoleon's insistence, and to the Queen's delight, Prince Albert took part in the talks, and the Emperor praised the Prince's understanding of the problems which confronted them. There was general agreement about the war and foreign policy, but not about the Emperor's intention of going to the Crimea; neither the Queen nor her ministers were successful in their strenuous efforts to persuade him not to go.[17] The Empress told the Queen that he must go. 'You have to surprise the French', said Eugénie, 'and not let them have the last word. This is what the Emperor has always done.'[18]

On 19 April the Emperor and Empress and the Queen and Prince Albert travelled to London together and went to Buckingham Palace. Louis Napoleon and Eugénie then went without their royal hosts to a banquet at the Guildhall. A hundred thousand people came out to see them pass down the Mall and past the Admiralty, where again a military band played 'Partant pour la Syrie'. The only untoward incident occurred near the Mansion House, where a captain of the household troops who were escorting the Emperor saw a man who persisted in running beside the imperial carriage with his hand on the door. The captain knocked off the man's hat with his sword and kicked him out of the way. The man was the chief of the detachment of the French secret police who were guarding the Emperor during his visit to England.

The luncheon room at the Guildhall was hung with portraits of Napoleon I, King Joseph and Queen Hortense – 'This is kind indeed', said Eugénie – and the guests sat on chairs marked N and E. During the six-course lunch, the Emperor ate sparingly, but Eugénie consumed a hearty meal with relish. Afterwards there were speeches from the Lord Mayor and Louis Napoleon, stressing Anglo-French unity.

In the evening Louis Napoleon and Eugénie went with Queen Victoria and Prince Albert to a gala performance at the Italian Opera in Covent Garden. The opera chosen was Beethoven's *Fidelio*, which some people thought was an unsuitable choice for the occasion because of its depressing, and even subversive, subject-matter. It had been announced that the royal and imperial couples would arrive after the first act because of their other important engagements; and their arrival, in the first interval, was greeted with applause from the audience, and with the playing of 'Partant pour la Syrie', followed by 'God Save the Queen', with a new verse which had been specially written for the occasion:

> Emperor and Empress,
> O Lord, be pleased to bless;
> Look on this scene.
> And may we ever find,
> With bonds of peace entwin'd,
> England and France combined.
> God save the Queen![19]

At the end of the performance, the orchestra played 'God Save the Queen', again with the 'Emperor and Empress' verse, and then 'Partant pour la Syrie'; the anthems had been arranged in this order so that the first and last notes that the Emperor and Empress heard on entering and leaving the opera house would be 'Partant pour la Syrie'. The press and the public wrote and talked at great length about Eugénie, who attracted far more attention than either the Queen or the Emperor.

Disraeli was one of the few Englishmen who did not admire Eugénie. He disliked her 'perpetual smile or simper' and her 'Chinese eyes', and thought that her behaviour was 'too natural for a sovereign'. He was shocked to hear that at Windsor she had sat on the edge of a table and had spent most of the time playing with the royal children.[20]

Louis Napoleon and Eugénie returned to France on 21 April. A week later, at 5 p.m. on Saturday 28 April, they went for a drive in the Bois de Boulogne. When they reached the Bois, Eugénie went on in her carriage while Louis Napoleon and his A.D.C., Edgar Ney, rode off for a canter towards the height of the Château des Fleurs. As Eugénie's equerry was away ill, Louis Napoleon sent his own equerry, Colonel Valabrègue, to escort her. She told Valabrègue to return to the Emperor, as he was more in need of protection than she was. As Valabrègue rode back to Louis Napoleon he heard a shot, and arrived in time to see policemen struggling with a man who had fired a pistol at Louis Napoleon at the corner of the Avenue Beaujeu and the Rue Balzac. He missed completely, and as he was preparing to fire a second time, a Corsican policeman leaped on him and wounded him with a dagger. Louis Napoleon called out to Ney and the police not to kill the assailant and to save him from the fury of the passers-by, who wanted to lynch him. He then rode slowly over to meet Eugénie.

He had not suffered even a minor wound. When Hübner called at the Tuileries an hour later to offer his condolences, Eugénie was in a state of great distress, but Louis Napoleon was quite unruffled. The Emperor told the Senators who brought him a message of sympathy from the Senate that he was not afraid of assassination, because 'there are beings who are the instruments of the decrees of Providence; until I have fulfilled my mission I shall be in no danger'. The Emperor and Empress had planned to go to the Opéra-Comique that evening, and they went as arranged, and received a tremendous ovation from the crowds on the boulevards.[21]

Messages of sympathy and indignation reached the Emperor from all over France. *The Times* wrote that it would have been a disaster for France, for the Anglo-French alliance, and for all Europe if Napoleon III had been killed. Queen Victoria was horrified. 'It shocked me *the more*', she wrote to King Leopold, 'as we had *watched over* him with such anxiety while he was with us.'[22]

The would-be assassin was an Italian revolutionary, Pianori, who had fought under Garibaldi in the defence of Rome in 1849 and had sworn to kill Louis Napoleon because he had overthrown the Roman Republic. He was tried for the crime of parricide. The trial was over in three hours, as he had no defence, and he was sentenced to suffer the death penalty prescribed by law. Only a few symbolic humiliations remained of the barbarous tortures which had accompanied the execution of a parricide under the old law of the Bourbons; but anyone sentenced for an attempt on the life of the sovereign was still made to walk barefoot to the scaffold and to stand there with a black cloth over his head while a recital of his crime was read out. Pianori awaited his fate with complete resignation and calm. Knowing that he had failed in his mission, in great pain from the dagger-wound which had been inflicted on him at the time of his arrest, and confined, like all other criminals awaiting execution, day and night in a strait-jacket in order to prevent him from committing suicide, he denied that he had any accomplices among the refugees in England, and asked only one favour – that the £100 found on him should be returned to his wife and two young children in England, so that they could have money to buy food for a few more months. He was guillotined on 15 May. He cried 'Vive la République!' as the knife fell.[23]

The Emperor had never been more popular in France; but if the Emperor was popular, the war was not. There was none of the aggressive enthusiasm to fight the Russians to a finish which was found in Britain – perhaps because there was conscription in France. Tsar Nicholas had died in March 1855, and was succeeded by his more Liberal and pacific son, Alexander II. The new Tsar was eager to make peace if he could obtain honourable terms, and the British government began to fear that Napoleon III would be too eager to grant them to him. They noticed that not only Princess Mathilde and Frau von Seebach, but also a personal representative of the Emperor attended a memorial service for Tsar Nicholas in the Russian church in Paris. Was this merely a case of the courtesy between sovereigns which always survived during wars in the mid-nineteenth century? Or was it something more?[24] In April, Drouyn de Lhuys and Lord John Russell went to Vienna to meet the Russian delegates to discuss peace terms. They reached an agreement with the Russians, but both the British and the French governments repudiated the terms as too lenient, and Russell and Drouyn resigned their portfolios.

The prospect of peace negotiations was one of the reasons which made Louis Napoleon decide, soon after his return from London, to postpone indefinitely his visit to the Crimea; he had to remain in Paris to take personal charge of the negotiations. Pianori's assassination attempt also played its part, for it brought home to the Emperor the dangers to which the régime would be exposed if he lost his life in the Crimea. In the last resort, it was Eugénie's attitude which decided him, although she was eager that he should go. The ministers, who were alarmed at the prospect that King Jerome and Prince Napoleon should be left in control in Paris, persuaded the Emperor that, if he went to the Crimea, it was essential that the Empress be left in charge at home; and as Eugénie was determined to go with him, he decided not to go.[25]

The Emperor's plans for holding the International Exhibition in Paris went ahead, and despite difficulties and delays it was officially opened by Louis Napoleon, only fifteen days late, on 15 May 1855[26] – the day of Pianori's execution. The world could witness the magnificent achievement of France and its ruler in organizing an international exhibition in wartime. Neither the war nor the cold weather prevented the success of the Exhibition, though it was a wet and unusually cold summer; across the Channel, in Sussex, the ponds froze in the middle of June.

The Exhibition was held in two great buildings – the industrial side in the Palais de l'Industrie in the Champs-Élysées, and the artistic side in the Palais des Beaux Arts a little distance away in the Avenue Montaigne. The press proudly announced that the Exhibition covered an area of 115,000 square yards, had 20,839 exhibitors, and cost 11 million francs, as compared with the area of 71,000 square yards, the 13,937 exhibitors, and the cost of $7\frac{1}{2}$ million francs of the London Exhibition of 1851; but the 5,162,330 people who visited the Exhibition before it closed on 15 November fell short of the 6,039,195 visitors to the London Exhibition.[27] There were exhibitors from Britain, Austria, Prussia, Bavaria, the Kingdom of Naples, the Papal States, the United

States, Peru, from more than twenty states in all, including Russia, whose traders were given a safe-conduct to visit Paris for the occasion; and Russian officer prisoners-of-war in France were allowed to go to Paris to see it after giving their word of honour to return to their prison camps. Paris swarmed with Germans and Spaniards, but especially with Englishmen and Englishwomen, who strolled along the boulevards, visited the *cafés chantants*, and went to the Théâtre Italien to see the Italian actress, Adelaide Ristori, who was threatening to eclipse Rachel, in Alfieri's play *Myrrha*, which had been banned by the Lord Chamberlain in London; and notices, 'English is spoken', were displayed in many restaurants and shops.[28]

In June, Eugénie hoped that she might be pregnant, and at the end of the month she went to the watering spa of Les Eaux-Bonnes in the Pyrenees. She did this on the advice of her close friend, Mrs Gould, the wife of an Irish merchant who had made a fortune importing port wine from Portugal into Britain. Mrs Gould had no great interest in politics, but was accused by the Radical propagandists of being a nefarious power behind the throne in France; nor were either she or her husband Jews, though her friendship with Eugénie was often cited as another example of Jewish influence at the Emperor's court. Like Eugénie, Mrs Gould had had a miscarriage in the spring of 1853, but was again pregnant, and had been advised by her doctors to take the waters at Les Eaux-Bonnes in order to increase the chances of a safe delivery; and she passed on the advice to Eugénie.[29]

At the end of July, Eugénie met Louis Napoleon in Biarritz, but their annual holiday there was shorter than usual,[30] because they had to return to Paris in the middle of August for the state visit of Queen Victoria. Eugénie was in splendid spirits. A few days before Queen Victoria arrived, she and Louis Napoleon held an informal supper party for a few friends at their cottage at Villeneuve l'Étang in the park at Saint-Cloud. During supper, Eugénie asked Louis Napoleon what was the password for the guard that evening. He said that it was a military secret, and refused to tell her. She was determined to find out. She slipped away from the guests and went out into the park, where she found a sentry on duty. She began flirting with him, hoping that it was too dark for him to recognize her, and tried to get him to tell her the password. He would not do so, and told her sharply to go away and leave him alone. After a while, he suddenly recognized her; he presented arms, and said: 'Yes, I think you are the Empress, but I will not tell you the password.' She had to return to the Emperor and the guests and tell them about her defeat. Perhaps she made up the whole story.[31]

On 18 August, Queen Victoria arrived with Prince Albert and their two eldest children, the Princess Royal and the Prince of Wales.[32] It was the first time since the reign of Edward II that a reigning English sovereign had paid a state visit to Paris, though Henry V and Henry VI had gone there as conquerors in the fifteenth century, and Charles II and James II as refugees in the seventeenth century.

The Emperor travelled all the way to Boulogne to meet the English royal family. When they drove through the streets of the town from the harbour to the railway station, he himself rode beside their carriage among the soldiers of their escort, riding next to the carriage on the right with Marshal Vaillant, the Minister of War, on the left. The train was delayed at Abbeville by a speech of welcome from the mayor and at Amiens by a presentation of flowers to the Queen by the children; but the train travelled so fast that, even with these delays, it took only four-and-a-half hours from Boulogne to the Gare du Nord in Paris. From there it was shunted along the newly built *ceinture* to the Terminus de Strasbourg – today the Gare de l'Est – from where the Emperor and Queen, with Prince Albert and the royal children, drove along the new Boulevard de Strasbourg and by the Grands Boulevards, the Rue Royale and the Champs-Élysées, through the Bois de Boulogne to Saint-Cloud, where Eugénie welcomed them. They were loudly cheered on their journey through Paris by a crowd that was estimated at 800,000, despite the fatigue of many of the onlookers who had been waiting in the streets for five or six hours in a very hot sun. A hundred thousand troops lined the streets, and the cannon of the Invalides fired a twenty-one-gun salute for the Queen, followed immediately by a hundred-and-one-gun salute for the Emperor. The streets were decorated with banners greeting the Queen and all the members of her family who were with her, and also paying a tribute to English ale – 'Vive l'Empereur, Vive l'Impératrice, Vive la Reine Victoria, Vive le Prince Albert, Vivent les petits Princes et les petites Princesses, Vive l'Alliance Anglaise, Vive le vin de l'Ale'.[33]

During their nine days in Paris, the Queen and Prince Albert visited the Exhibition and Napoleon's tomb at the Invalides, as well as the palace at Saint-Germain-en-Laye where James II of England had lived and died in exile; and there were the usual banquets and balls. Louis Napoleon renewed his attentions to Queen Victoria – in Clarendon's words, 'making love to her';[34] but he did so in a manner which did not offend either her strict moral principles or her devotion to her husband. The Queen did not, however, meet with a favourable response when she tried tactfully to intercede with him on behalf of the Orleans family and their property.[35] The Prince of Wales greatly enjoyed himself, especially when Louis Napoleon drove him around Paris in a carriage, with the Emperor taking the reins himself. He said to the Emperor: 'I wish I were your son.'[36]

The Emperor gave a great ball for the Queen and Prince Albert at Versailles. The Queen wrote in her diary that when they were waiting to enter the ballroom, 'the Empress met us at the top of the staircase, looking like a fairy-queen or nymph'. Eugénie was wearing a white dress trimmed with branches of grass and diamonds, and with diamonds round her waist and in her hair. When she appeared, the Emperor said: 'How beautiful you are!'[37]

Clarendon, who went with the Queen to Paris, had talks with the Emperor and his ministers about the war and the peace terms. The Allied armies were still bogged down in front of Sevastopol; but in May, Louis Napoleon had sent General Pélissier to the Crimea with orders to launch an offensive which would force the Russians to accept the Allied peace terms. On 18 June the armies of Britain and France, the former enemies, had celebrated Waterloo Day by a joint attack on Sevastopol; but the attack had been repulsed with 6000 French and 600 British casualties. Clarendon took the opportunity, while he was in Paris, to visit his old friend the Countess of Montijo, who was on a visit to her daughter. He was somewhat taken aback at the levity with which she told him that many people thought that he was Eugénie's father.[38]

The Queen and Prince Albert returned to England on 27 August. As they drove off from Saint-Cloud on their way to the station in the morning, a crowd gathered to cheer them. The Emperor, who was sitting in the carriage beside the Queen, noticed a rifleman of the Imperial Guard with one leg hobbling up on his crutches and trying unsuccessfully to make his way through the crowd. Louis Napoleon stopped the carriage, and, leaving the Queen, got out and walked up to the cripple. He spoke to him, and the man told him that he had lost the leg at Sevastopol. Louis Napoleon thereupon awarded him the Legion of Honour, and, removing the Cross of the Order from his own general's uniform, pinned it on the soldier's breast.[39]

Louis Napoleon travelled with his royal guests to Boulogne, where they arrived at 5 p.m. In an exhausting six hours before their yacht sailed, he took them to see a military review on the sands, drove with them to the camp at Honvault to see a new rocket tested, went on to another camp at Ambleteuse, and entertained them at a banquet at the Imperial Pavilion Hotel. He then went with them on their yacht as they sailed away, before bidding them good-bye and climbing down the ladder into his own barge which had travelled alongside.[40] Four days later he wrote to the Queen:

Although I have experienced a justifiable feeling of pride in having acted for a short time as host to the Queen of such a powerful

Empire, I am also happy to remember the woman who was so kind and gracious, the man who was so distinguished, and the children who were so charming.[41]

On 8 September the British launched an attack on the Redan fort at Sevastopol, and simultaneously the French attacked the Malakhov fort. The British were repulsed, but the French captured the Malakhov, and Sevastopol capitulated two days later. 'The capture of the Malakoff', wrote Pélissier to Louis Napoleon, has 'compelled the enemy to fly before our eagles.'[42] Paris was illuminated to celebrate the victory, and in their delight the people almost ignored another attempt on the Emperor's life; on the day on which the Malakhov was stormed, a lunatic fired a pistol at Louis Napoleon and Eugénie as they were entering the Italian Opera House, but no one was hurt.[43]

On 29 December the Imperial Guard returned in triumph from Sevastopol to Paris. The Emperor met them at the Place de la Bastille and led them through the streets to the Place Vendôme. The people cheered and cheered, and threw flowers before the Emperor's horse.[44]

For the British, the defeat at the Redan soured the victory at Sevastopol; for Louis Napoleon, the triumph was complete, and strengthened his hand in the peace negotiations. Backed by French public opinion, he was working for an early peace and the building of a post-war friendship with Tsar Alexander's more Liberal Russia.[45] The British government and public were eager to continue the war, but this was difficult after the Redan and the Malakhov; and Palmerston, who had hoped to force the Russians to cede the Crimea to Turkey, reluctantly agreed to waive this demand, provided that he obtained his most important objective – a peace treaty which forbade Russia to maintain a fleet of warships in the Black Sea. The Allies' terms also required Russia to cede part of Bessarabia to Turkey.

The Russian delegates at Vienna held out for some time against these demands, but eventually agreed when Austria, in an attempt to climb on the victorious bandwagon, threatened to enter the war on the Allied side. After the preliminary terms had been agreed in Vienna, the final treaty was left to be settled at the Peace Congress. There could be no argument about where the Congress was to be held,[46] and it opened in Paris on 25 February 1856. The powers were represented at the Congress by their Foreign Ministers, with the French Foreign Minister, Walewski, presiding; but Louis Napoleon himself played an active part in the negotiations behind the scenes, using all his efforts to persuade Clarendon to accept more moderate terms. Palmerston, in London, tried to strengthen Clarendon's stand; but a majority in the British Cabinet opposed Palmerston's intransigence, and Louis

Napoleon, unlike Palmerston, was in Paris and had all the advantages. Louis Napoleon, on the one hand, urged the British to make more concessions, and on the other assured the Russians that he had wrung the final offer from the British, and that this was Russia's last chance to obtain a relatively mild peace.

He finally carried the day by a masterstroke. He told Clarendon that public opinion in France had always favoured the idea of a revolutionary war to liberate the oppressed nationalities of Europe, especially the Poles. He said that although the French were weary of the war, the one way of persuading them to continue with it would be to pursue the Radical policy of Kossuth and to transform the war against Russia into a revolutionary war against Russia and Austria. This was the last thing that Palmerston wanted; he had been alarmed at the prospect ever since the beginning of the war. He abandoned his opposition to the proposed peace terms, satisfied that he had obtained the demilitarization of the Russian Black Sea fleet.[47]

It was known that the Empress was in her ninth month. Which would come first – the proclamation of the peace or the birth of the child who, if a boy, would be the heir to the throne? As the final settlement of the last details of the peace terms continued to be delayed, Eugénie began her labour at five o'clock in the morning on 15 March. Maria Manuela, who had come to Paris for the confinement, was with her. The Empress was in labour for more than twenty-two hours, but at 3.15 a.m. on 16 March she gave birth to a son. At dawn the cannon of the Invalides fired a salute. Twenty-one shots were to be fired for a girl, and a hundred and one for a boy; and as the Parisians heard the twenty-second shot, they knew that the Emperor had an heir.[48]

The Emperor celebrated the birth of the Prince Imperial by granting an amnesty to all the political detainees in Algeria and Cayenne, and a permission to return to France to all the exiles, if they were prepared to give their word of honour 'to submit loyally to the government which the nation has chosen'. Many of them refused to do so; but after this last amnesty, only 306 of the 11,000 deported rebels of June 1848, and only 1058 of the 11,201 deported after the *coup d'état*, were still in Algeria and Cayenne. The Emperor and Empress announced that they would be sponsors of all legitimate children who were born on 16 March 1856, the same day as the Prince Imperial. Mrs Gould's visit to Les Eaux-Bonnes was as successful as the Empress's, and she too gave birth to a son. The Emperor and Empress attended the christening and were godparents to the Gould boy, to whom they gave a magnificent pendant as a christening present.*[49]

*The pendant is today in the possession of the Gould baby's great-granddaughter. Mrs Yehudi Menuhin.

The congratulations poured in from foreign sovereigns and from the Emperor's loyal subjects, expressing their devotion to him and to the Prince Imperial and to the Prince's 'august mother'.[50] The Emperor was unable to grant permission to all the well-wishers who asked to be allowed to see the Prince Imperial; but he made an exception for his old friends the 'dames de la Halle'. When a number of them called at the Tuileries with bouquets two days after the Prince's birth, he took them himself to the Empress's apartments and showed them the baby.[51]

The Times, expressing the joy of the British people, pointed out the strange fact that not since Louis XIV became King on the death of his father Louis XIII in 1643 had a French sovereign been succeeded by his son. *The Times* thought that if the Prince Imperial succeeded to the throne when Napoleon III died, this would be the final proof of the Emperor's success. In the Crimea, where the armistice had been extended, the Russian artillery fired a salute all along the front in honour of the Prince Imperial's birth. The peace treaty was finally signed on 30 March, and the state of war with Russia was ended. Paris was illuminated and decorated with flags, including a few Russian flags.[52]

The Prince Imperial was named Napoléon Eugène Louis Jean Joseph, and christened at a ceremony in Notre-Dame on 14 June 1856. Among the gifts which he received was a golden rose from his godfather the Pope. Paris was illuminated to celebrate the christening. The great firework display was started by the Emperor himself, who fired a rocket from the terrace of the Ministry of Marine as the signal for the evening celebrations to begin.[53]

Just before Louis Napoleon and his party left for the Ministry of Marine, Persigny arrived at the Tuileries to congratulate him. Louis Napoleon invited him to come to the Ministry of Marine with them; but Persigny excused himself, as he was not wearing evening dress. The Emperor said that as he and Persigny were about the same build, Persigny could wear one of his evening coats. When Persigny put on the coat, he noticed that the Emperor's Cross of the Legion of Honour was fixed to the left side of the coat, as worn by the holders of the Grand Cross of the Legion of Honour, the highest of the five ranks of the Order. Persigny was a Grand Officer of the Legion of Honour – the second highest rank – and as Grand Officers wore the cross on their right breast, he asked the Emperor to wait while he transferred the cross from the left to the right side of the coat. 'Don't worry about that', said Louis Napoleon; 'wear it as it is.' Next day *Le Moniteur* announced that Persigny had been awarded the Grand Cross of the Legion of Honour.[54]

CHAPTER 30

THE HIGH NOON OF THE EMPIRE

THE Congress of Paris had, for all practical purposes, destroyed the work of the Congress of Vienna. Louis Napoleon had once again made France unquestionably the greatest power in Europe; and his beautiful Empress had perpetuated the Bonaparte dynasty by giving him a son. He was strong enough to surmount the temporary difficulties caused by the third bad summer in four years. The heavy rains in 1856 not only ruined the harvest and again sent up the price of bread, but caused some disastrous floods in the Rhône and Loire valleys. Louis Napoleon gave state relief to the stricken farmers, and made charitable gifts from his personal revenues to the sufferers in the districts which he visited;[1] 'I feel honour bound to ensure', he declared, 'that in France the rivers, like the Revolution, will return to their beds and not emerge from them again.'[2]

The Lord Mayor of London issued an appeal for funds to relieve the distress which the floods had caused to England's ally;[3] but the alliance was showing signs of strain. Disagreements arose between Britain and Russia on the detailed interpretation of the peace treaty, especially with regard to the exact line of the new frontier in Bessarabia. Palmerston adopted a threatening attitude to the Russian Ambassador in London, and even talked about renewing the war; but the French Foreign Office supported the Russian position in most of the disputes. A more serious difficulty arose about the principalities of Walachia and Moldavia. Under the peace treaty, they had both been granted virtual autonomy while remaining under the nominal sovereignty of the Sultan – a concession granted by Turkey and Britain to Christian sentiment and to the Liberal principle of nationality espoused by Napoleon III. Britain and France disagreed as to whether Walachia and Moldavia should be united in one principality or remain as two separate states. If they were united, they would obviously be stronger, and could more easily assert their independence from Turkey; so Russia wished them to be united, and Britain and Austria wished them to remain divided.

Louis Napoleon, against the advice of his Foreign Minister, Walewski, and his Ambassador in Constantinople, Thouvenel, was in favour of the unity of Walachia and Moldavia. He handled the situation skilfully. As Palmerston refused to give way, Louis Napoleon eventually agreed to the British demand that Walachia and Moldavia should be two separate states, each of them governed by a Prince elected by the local Assemblies. The Assemblies of both Walachia and Moldavia then elected Prince Alexander Cuza to be their Prince, and as Prince of the two principalities he ruled in effect over a united Romanian nation. The British government and press believed that Louis Napoleon had tricked them.

Louis Napoleon claimed the credit for creating Romania, though he was embarrassed, and always protested, at the anti-Jewish pogroms which periodically occurred at Jassy in Moldavia. In 1866, Cuza was overthrown by a military *coup*, and Prince Charles of Hohenzollern, a distant cousin of the King of Prussia, was chosen as Prince of Romania, with the strong support of Napoleon III. He never forgot that he owed his throne to France, and showed his gratitude by remaining strictly neutral during the Franco-Prussian War in 1870.[4]

Louis Napoleon scored another diplomatic success in solving the Neuchâtel crisis. Neuchâtel, which for four hundred years had been in close alliance with the Swiss cantons, was a family possession of the King of Prussia; but in 1815 it had become a member of the Swiss Confederation, while remaining under its hereditary ruler, as the only Swiss canton which was not a republic. This anomaly, which was possible as long as the cantons were almost independent sovereign states, could not survive the establishment of the new Radical Federal constitution in Switzerland after the civil war of 1847; and during the revolutionary upheavals of 1848, the King of Prussia's government was overthrown in Neuchâtel and a republic established there.

The King of Prussia seemed to acquiesce in the situation; but his hand was forced in 1856 when some of his supporters in Neuchâtel made an unsuccessful insurrection in an attempt to restore his authority there. They were arrested and charged with high treason by the Federal Swiss authorities. The Prussian government protested and demanded the release of the prisoners. The Swiss offered to release them as an act of Federal authority if the King of Prussia acknowledged their sovereignty over Neuchâtel and renounced his claims; but Prussia refused the bargain, and threatened war with Switzerland if the prisoners were not released unconditionally, the South German states having agreed to allow Prussian troops to march through their territory to attack the Swiss. Both Prussia and Switzerland asked France to support them. Louis Napoleon proposed a compromise which would save the King of Prussia's face: the Swiss were to release the prisoners unconditionally, after which the King of Prussia would voluntarily renounce his claims over Neuchâtel.

The Swiss at first refused to agree, but they sent an envoy to Paris to negotiate. He was Louis Napoleon's old commanding officer at Thun, General Dufour, who had become a national hero in Switzerland after he had won the civil war of 1847 for the Federal government in a fortnight. Louis Napoleon warned Dufour, courteously but firmly, that if the Swiss refused to accept his compromise plan, he would not support them against a foreign invasion either now or on any future occasion. The prisoners were released and crossed the frontier into France in January 1857; and the strong criticism of Louis Napoleon's action by the pro-Swiss Liberals throughout Europe died away after the King of Prussia, four months later, renounced his claims to Neuchâtel, retaining only the right to call himself Prince of Neuchâtel among his other titles as an empty honour.[5]

The life of Louis Napoleon's court had never been more brilliant than in the year after the Congress of Paris and the birth of the Prince Imperial, with the Empress, a radiant young mother, in her prime at the age of thirty. There was a succession of receptions and balls, with lavish decorations and lighting displays, and the Empress on every occasion wearing a new dress which always aroused widespread comment. She shocked many people by introducing at court the fancy-dress balls which she had so enjoyed at Ariza House and Carabanchel, and by wearing gipsy costume and other fancy-dress costumes herself. When she was not wearing fancy dress, she wore the enormous hooped skirts of the crinoline,[6] which had seemed as bizarre as any fancy dress when she first introduced it in 1855, and which had so surprised the English on her state visit with Louis Napoleon to London and Windsor.

Today, people who knew the Empress when they were young mention the extreme formality and rigid etiquette which prevailed in her household at Farnborough Hill; but if Eugénie's manners in 1912 seem formal by the standards of 1979, they were shockingly informal in 1856 by the standards of 1810. Napoleon I and Josephine, like Louis Bonaparte and Queen Hortense, always addressed each other, even in private, as 'Your Majesty'; but when Louis Napoleon and Eugénie were alone, he called her 'Eugénie' and she called him 'Louis'. She sometimes referred to him as 'Louis' in the presence of third persons, but this was obviously a slip, because in her letters, even to Paca, she always wrote about 'the Emperor'. She insisted on giving him precedence in public. When she went driving with him, he always sat in the seat of honour on the right-hand side of the carriage, though ordinarily when a husband and wife, or any lady and gentleman, rode together in a carriage, the lady sat on the right.[7]

Hübner thought that one of her nicest characteristics was her attitude to her old friends whom she had known before she was Empress – in the days 'when I lived in society,[8] as she usually expressed it. She treated them exactly as she had done before, though of course they felt unable to behave towards the Empress as they had towards the young Countess of Teba. When Mérimée, who at Eugénie's insistence had agreed to become a member of the Senate, went to the official reception for the Senators at the Tuileries on New Year's Day 1854, he came out of the hall where the Emperor had received him and found himself alone in a passage. Suddenly he heard a little laugh behind him, and turned to see the Empress, who greeted him as an old friend. 'She looked *extraordinarily* beautiful', he wrote to her mother.[9]

Sometimes her carefree and lively temperament caused her to slip up. In May 1854, Hübner was talking to her and the Emperor at a ball at the Tuileries, and he reminded her that it was almost exactly a year since he had told the Emperor in that very room of the marriage of the Archduchess Marie Henriette of Austria to the Duc de Brabant, the future King Leopold II of the Belgians. 'Yes', said Eugénie, 'it was here that the Emperor said to you: "If you marry Belgium, I will marry Switzerland" ', and she turned to Louis Napoleon and asked him if he remembered. Louis Napoleon was annoyed; in May 1853 his relations with Austria had been strained, and he had threatened Austria with an alliance with Radical Switzerland; in May 1854 he was wooing Austria, hoping to bring her into the Crimean War. He said drily to Hübner: 'It is true, but since then we have formed new ties.'[10]

Louis Napoleon was still eager to persuade Austria to join the Allies against Russia in February 1855 when the Austrian government sent General Count Crenneville to Paris for military talks with the French government. After spending half an hour with the Emperor, Crenneville was taken by Hübner to pay a courtesy call on the Empress. Eugénie was charming, but as the conversation lagged she dismissed Crenneville after five minutes. This was a dreadful *faux pas*; protocol demanded that she should speak for longer than this to the Austrian general. Crenneville was offended, and Hübner was worried about the effect on Austria's relations with France and Britain. He mentioned the matter next day to Eugénie at a ball at the Tuileries. She blushed and apologized, and said that she had been rather frightened of the formidable General Crenneville. Hübner accepted the explanation, as he realized that Crenneville looked like a bogy-man; but he wrote in his diary: 'This charming woman has not yet learned her job. It seems to be a difficult job to learn unless one has started having lessons as a baby.'[11]

Louis Napoleon and Eugénie spent less than half the year at the

Tuileries. They were there from about the beginning of December to May, but in May every year they moved to Saint-Cloud, which was their main residence throughout the summer, though they periodically spent a week or a few days at Fontainebleau. In 1856 the Emperor began the practice, which he continued every year, of going without Eugénie to take the waters for three weeks in July at Plombières, or sometimes at Vichy.[12] His doctors had advised him that it would be good for his rheumatism, and afterwards for the stone in the bladder from which, unknown to the public, he began to suffer in 1861.

The Emperor's annual visit was a great occasion in the life of Plombières, which was decorated with flags and illuminated to celebrate his presence. He and his entourage took over the first floor of the Grand Hotel, but other guests continued to stay on other floors in the hotel, and the Emperor often spoke to them, and to the members of the public whom he met on his daily visits to the baths to take the waters, on his frequent walks along the Promenade des Dames and elsewhere in the town and in the neighbouring fields and woods, and on drives in his carriage further afield to the villages of the district, when he often took the reins himself. In the evenings there were plays performed by the Théâtre Français or other companies who had come to Plombières for the occasion. Sometimes the Emperor attended a ball given for the local army regiment or for the citizens of Plombières, or Vichy, and danced with the wife of an N.C.O. or with a pretty peasant girl who had come into the town to go to the dance. As always, he distributed gifts of money in the town, and promised government aid to local industries.

He was repeatedly accosted in the street by place-seekers, by people with a grievance presenting petitions, by old soldiers wearing the St Helena Medal* – which he issued in 1857 to all survivors who had served in the army or navy between 1792 and 1815 – and by children. Once a little girl of five came up to him when he was walking in Plombières with his A.D.C. 'Which of you is the Emperor, Monsieur?' she asked. 'It is I, my child', replied Louis Napoleon. 'Well then,' she said, handing him a rose for the Prince Imperial, 'here is a rose for the little Emperor who is in Paris.'

In 1857 the Emperor established a great military camp near Châlons-sur-Marne, and in future years spent the last fortnight of August in the camp.[14] It covered an area of about 140 square kilometres between the River Suippe and the River Vesle, incorporating the villages of Mourmelon-le-Grand and Mourmelon-le-Petit; there were huts and tents for 40,000 men, with allotment gardens, canteens,

*The medal bore a portrait of Napoleon I and the inscription: 'Campaigns of 1792 to 1815. To his companions in glory, his last thoughts. 5 May 1821'.[13]

cafés and theatres which provided comforts and entertainments on a scale quite unknown in other military camps and barracks of the period. The Emperor's headquarters was on the brow of a hill on the old Roman road from Rheims to Bar-le-Duc which ran through the middle of the camp; it was a wooden hut with three rooms – the Emperor's bedroom, a dining-room and a drawing-room. The headquarters of General Regnault de St Jean d'Angely, who was in command of the camp, was about half a mile away.

The camp was about twelve miles from the town of Châlons, and when it was first opened there was no convenient transport from the town. The Emperor therefore ordered that a railway should be built from Châlons to the camp. He gave the order on 7 July 1857; work began on 12 July and the line was finished by 15 September. The work was carried out by the Chemins-de-Fer de l'Est, who had negotiated for the purchase of the land and had built the 25 kilometres of track in ten weeks. It was a great achievement which delighted the Emperor; but the peasants who owned the land, appreciating the situation, asked a very high price for it, and the 2400 workmen had to be paid at overtime rates. It therefore became a very expensive project for the railway company, and as there was very little traffic on the line during the nine months of the year when the camp was closed, the company had no possibility of recouping its losses. The shareholders grumbled under their breath; it was they who had to bear the loss, and the directors who received the thanks and the decorations from the Emperor.[15]

The Emperor's visit was always the occasion for a display of great enthusiasm by the soldiers, whose tents and barracks were decorated with slogans: 'Vive l'Empereur', 'Vive l'Impératrice', 'Vive le Prince Impérial'. He watched the manoeuvres and the experiments with new rockets, cannon and small-arms, and attended the performances of *Les Saltimbanques* and other popular entertainments at the camp theatre. One feature of camp life was the open-air Mass on Sundays, attended by the Emperor and some 20,000 soldiers, and celebrated by the Archbishop of Châlons or some other high dignitary of the Church at an altar erected in front of the Emperor's headquarters.

Louis Napoleon entertained distinguished foreign generals, including the Duke of Cambridge and the Prince of Baden, at Châlons Camp. Eugénie only visited the camp on four occasions.[16] The little Prince Imperial was a more frequent visitor. His name had been inscribed on the roll of the grenadiers of the Guard when he was eight months old, and he had been issued with the little red book which all privates had to carry.[17] The baby's honorary membership of the armed forces was widely publicized. When he was aged four, in August 1860, the Emperor took him to the camp, with his nursemaids but without the Empress, and showed him off repeatedly to the soldiers. He walked hand in hand with the Emperor along the line, and played with Marshal MacMahon's small children.

After 1857, the Emperor's annual visit to Châlons Camp caused him to postpone until September his holiday in Biarritz. Eugénie was happiest when she was in Biarritz.[18] The Villa Eugénie was the only one of the imperial residences where she could live an almost private life, and where etiquette was very largely relaxed. She enjoyed the visits to Bayonne, to the villages, and to The Refuge founded by the Abbé Castiac at Biarritz for reformed prostitutes, the walks in the mountains and the sea-trips across the bay and the day excursions into Spain, where she and the Emperor were sometimes entertained to lunch by the mayors of the towns that they visited. In Biarritz, as in Paris, she gave her usual parties on Mondays – *les lundis de l'Impératrice* – but notorious ladies of the *demi-monde*, like Wilfrid Scawen Blunt's mistress, 'Skittles' Walters, who were not on the guest list at the Tuileries, Fontainebleau or Compiègne, were invited with their lovers to the parties at Biarritz.

Eugénie was fascinated by the fury of the seas at Biarritz, where she once saw a metal bar lashed into the shape of a corkscrew by the force of the waves.[19] She would walk along the sands with the Emperor, and sit on the beach while the Prince Imperial played with the other children there, some of whom were sometimes invited to play with him at the Villa Eugénie. When Wilfrid Scawen Blunt visited Biarritz in 1863 he saw her going out in a boat every day with four handsome young Basque men, with whom she went swimming in the sea out of sight of the shore; but with or without the young men, she had always enjoyed swimming. The Emperor, who had been a strong swimmer in his youth,[20] still sometimes went swimming, and in June 1864 was nearly drowned when swimming at Fontainebleau.[21] Apart from shooting, his favourite sport was skating. When the lake in the Bois de Boulogne froze in winter, he usually joined the skaters on the lake, and sometimes, like other husbands, pushed his wife in her sleigh around the lake, or performed this service for some pretty woman who had attracted his attention at the lakeside.[22]

In August 1856 Louis Napoleon and Eugénie went to Biarritz as usual, although there had been some anxiety in the imperial entourage as to whether the air at Biarritz would be healthy for the infant Prince Imperial. The baby's physician, Dr Barthez, went with them on the first of several visits to Biarritz with the imperial family. He was charmed by the Emperor's friendliness and casual informality. When Louis Napoleon walked up to him in the garden of the Villa Eugénie, Barthez took his cigar out of his mouth and held it discreetly behind his back; but Louis Napoleon told him to go on smoking, and lit his own cigarette from the cigar.

Barthez found the Empress more disconcerting and more fascinating. She was gay, temperamental, and sometimes unreasonable. He was perturbed when she insisted on having lunch in wet shoes and duly caught a cold; and when he tried to stop her from going on a sea-trip because it would make her cold worse, she made 'a gesture that little gutter-boys are familiar with',[23] and playfully slapped his face. She both administered and received harder slaps in the boisterous parlour-games which they played in the evenings at the Villa Eugénie, where Barthez and all the men, including the Emperor, were sometimes chased around the room and over chairs and tables by the Empress and her ladies, who were hitting them with napkins. Once, at Saint-Cloud, Eugénie asked Barthez into her dressing-room while she was changing for dinner. She made him sit down very close to her as she sat at her dressing-table. He was driven almost mad by the proximity of her beautiful bare shoulders, by her perfume and her pink and white skin, and he had to look at the ceiling to prevent his voice from trembling when he spoke to her; but it was only many years later, when he was an older and wiser man and she was an ageing refugee, that he dared to think that she had been deliberately trying to torment him.[24]

At the beginning of October every year, Louis Napoleon and Eugénie returned from Biarritz to Saint-Cloud, but usually left after a week or two for Compiègne, where they stayed until they returned to the Tuileries in December. The life at Compiègne was more formal than at Biarritz. There was room for over a hundred guests at Compiègne, but usually there were about seventy in residence at the same time. They were invited to stay for a week, and five sets of guests came in turn during the five or six weeks of the Emperor's annual residence at Compiègne. It was a mark of special favour to be asked to stay for more than a week and to come again later in the month with a new house-party. Eugénie herself selected the guests. This was a complicated task, for she had to be sure not to invite anyone who would be unable or unwilling to accept, and not to offend anyone by asking another guest who was inferior in status to stay for longer or to come more often. The guests had to be allotted rooms in accordance with their rank, and with an eye to preventing anyone else from taking offence. Apart from members of the imperial family, all the most prominent people in public life were invited to Compiègne – politicians, generals, diplomats, writers and artists, and distinguished foreign statesmen, to say nothing of royal princes from the greater or lesser European houses who were visiting France in the autumn.[25]

There were stag-hunts and shooting in the forest at Compiègne on several days in the week, and the *curée* by torchlight, when the hounds devoured their share of the stag in the courtyard of the palace at ten o'clock on the November evening, before a crowd of the local inhabitants. For the hunt, the guests were required to wear a special hunting uniform which was prescribed in every detail – for the gentlemen, green coats with silk stockings coming over the knee, as in the time of Louis XIV.[26] Only Palmerston, when he came in 1858, failed to wear the proper costume; he appeared in his red English hunting coat, with no cloak to keep off the rain, explaining that 'rien ne perce un habit rouge'.[27] Sometimes there were excursions through the forest in *chars-à-bancs* to the castle of Pierrefonds. Mérimée was disconcerted to find that they were taken on these rides in open *chars-à-bancs* in a temperature of 7°C. of frost.[28]

In the evenings, after the banquets, there were often theatrical performances in the private theatre of the palace, either by the Théâtre Français or by some other company. Sometimes the guests themselves organized some amateur production.

There was some dissatisfaction in Paris that the Emperor spent so much time away from the capital,[29] especially at times of internal difficulties or of international crises, and there were whispered complaints that Eugénie was encouraging him to lead a life of pleasure and to neglect his public duties. Some of the complaints came from people who had not yet realized how much the railways had facilitated modern travel. At Compiègne, the Emperor was within a two-hour train journey from Paris; his ministers could come to Compiègne for a Cabinet meeting and return to Paris the same day, and he himself could travel up to Paris in two hours if his presence there were needed.

After British and French foreign policy had come into conflict over Romania, *The Times*, in the autumn of 1856, began to snipe again at Louis Napoleon, and exaggerated these complaints about the Emperor's absence. The *Times* correspondent also criticized the hospitality at Compiègne. He wrote that only the members of the imperial family and the most distinguished of the guests were given the luxurious state apartments; all the other guests slept in rooms which were unworthy of a second-class hotel, and the servants' quarters in the palace were dirty and disgraceful. But he admitted that everyone was given excellent food.[30]

The Times and the other English newspapers reverted to all their former criticism of Louis Napoleon during the French general election in the summer of 1857,[31] when the French people voted, by universal suffrage, to elect a new Legislative Body to replace the Legislative Body whose five-year term had expired. As in the general election of February 1852, the government used the administrative machine to secure the election of the official government candidates, refused permission to the Opposition candidates to form electoral organizations, and made it almost impossible for the Opposition to publish election propaganda, the courts having ruled that a polling card was a 'book' for the purposes of the laws restricting unauthorized publications. The Prefects, both publicly and privately, urged the people in their Departments to show their gratitude to the Emperor and his government by voting for the official candidates, and to remember that they could not expect the government to help them by financial grants to the district, by encouragement of local industries, or by bringing the railway to the area, if the electors voted for Opposition candidates. Several mayors who stood against the official candidates were dismissed from office by the Prefects.

In Paris, a number of prominent Liberals came together and nominated Carnot, Cavaignac, Émile Ollivier and other Opposition candidates; and Montalembert stood against the official candidate in the Doubs. The great majority of the press, including the Catholic Ultramontane paper *L'Univers*, urged the electors to vote for the government. The Liberal newspaper *Le Siècle* urged them to vote for the Opposition candidates, and received three official warnings in the course of the election campaign from Billault, who had replaced Persigny as Minister of the Interior. Billault informed *Le Siècle* that 'the government of the Emperor, founded upon the sovereignty of the people and on the principles of 1789, henceforth the immutable foundations of French society, can no longer allow the ideas of order and progress which it represents, and the electoral body which approves them, to be libelled'.[32]

Montalembert was defeated in the Doubs, after the Prefect had made particularly strenuous efforts to secure the return of the government candidate; but Carnot, Cavaignac and Émile Ollivier were elected in Paris, where the total government vote was only 110,000 against 96,000 for the Opposition. The government did much better in the country as a whole, obtaining 5,201,101 votes against 571,859 votes for the Opposition, while nearly $3\frac{1}{2}$ million of the $9\frac{1}{2}$ million voters abstained; but Louis Napoleon privately told Fould that he felt personally humiliated by the size of the Opposition vote, especially in Paris, and by the number of abstentions.[33]

In commenting on the results, *L'Assemblée Nationale* said that the elections could not be regarded as a free expression of public opinion, because in the rural parishes the people 'voted under administrative influences, and these influences should be taken into account when anyone tries to set the eagerness and fidelity of the rural electors against the opposition and the abstentions which were noticeable in the

The ball for Lord Raglan and the Duke of Cambridge at the Élysée, April 1854, reproduced from the *Illustrated London News*

Prince Napoleon

towns'.[34] Billault thereupon suppressed *L'Assemblée Nationale* for two months and sent the police to seize the next day's issue of the paper as it was going to press, as 'the government cannot permit libels to be published with impunity about the 5 million voters who in every part of the territory, both in town and country, gave it their loyal support'.[35]

On 28 June – the day on which polling took place in the second ballot in the general election – the government announced that three Italians named Tibaldi, Bartolotti and Grilli had been arrested in Paris for attempting to assassinate the Emperor. The official statement said that the men had been arrested more than a month earlier, but that the news had been kept secret until after the election so that no one could accuse the government of using the story for its electoral advantage. The three men had in fact tried to attack the Emperor in April while he was visiting his mistress, the Countess of Castiglione, and had been foiled by the Emperor's coachman, who had fought them off with his whip and had driven the Emperor away to safety; but there had often before been rumours of assassination attempts, and this latest story was denied by officials, and by well-informed courtiers like Mérimée, whenever they were questioned about it by their acquaintances in private. In fact, Tibaldi, Bartolotti and Grilli had been under observation by the police for some time, and the Emperor had been informed that they were planning to assassinate him; but he had willingly exposed himself to the danger – on his nightly visits to his mistress and on other occasions – in order to tempt them into making an attempt which would give the police the opportunity to arrest them. Eventually they were arrested at their lodgings in Paris, where the police found daggers and letters from Mazzini.

The press declared that the objective of the three men was the establishment of the Red Republic, which they knew would follow automatically if they succeeded in killing the Emperor; and the government claimed to have evidence that Mazzini and Ledru-Rollin in London had paid money to the three Italians to assassinate the Emperor. This was vigorously denied by Mazzini and Ledru-Rollin; but when Tibaldi, Bartolotti and Grilli were put on trial in Paris at the beginning of August, both Mazzini and Ledru-Rollin and two other refugees in London were jointly charged in their absence with being participants in the assassination attempt.

Bartolotti pleaded guilty, and said that Mazzini, whom he had met in London, had paid him money on condition that he murdered the Emperor. Grilli, who also pleaded guilty, confirmed Bartolotti's story; and a tailor, who was brought to the court from prison, where he was serving a four-year sentence for being a member of a secret society, gave evidence that in London in 1853 Ledru-Rollin had given him £500 which he was to pass on to a man whom Ledru-Rollin had hired to assassinate the Emperor. Tibaldi pleaded not guilty, and refused to make any statement about his contacts in London. All seven defendants were found guilty of parricide. Bartolotti and Grilli were given fifteen years' imprisonment and Tibaldi imprisonment for life; Mazzini and Ledru-Rollin were sentenced to deportation in their absence. The opponents of the régime thought that the trial was a crude frame-up, in which the arrested men had been promised relatively lenient sentences if they incriminated Mazzini and Ledru-Rollin.[36]

The elections and the trial led to a renewed campaign against Louis Napoleon in the British press, which also attacked the French system of passports. No one could enter France without a passport, which had to be visa'ed by a French Consul abroad or by the immigration authorities at the French ports; and a French subject in France could not travel, either abroad or within the country, without an external or internal passport. To obtain a passport, he had to produce two witnesses who would vouch for his being a respectable person and not a vagabond, and pay two francs for an internal passport and ten francs for an external one. This seemed to Englishmen to be not only wrong in principle as an infringement of the rights of the individual, but also irksome to British business men and tourists in France.[37]

The inconvenience of the French passport system was shown in the experiences of Monsieur Gustave Albitte, who had once been the French Consul in Ostend but had lived in retirement for many years in England in a middle-class residence at The Cedars in Woking. In August 1857 he went for a holiday to France, travelling on his old French passport; but when he wished to return to England, he was told that he would require a new passport for this. He went to the town hall in Versailles accompanied by two friends whom he found with some difficulty, as most of his acquaintances in the district had gone away to some spa for their summer holiday. After these two 'témoins patentés' had certified that he was not a vagabond, he was told by the official at the town hall that he would be issued with a passport in another office at the Préfecture, but that first he must go to a third office, that of the Précepteur des Contributions in the Avenue de Saint-Cloud, and there pay ten francs for the passport. He at once went there, but found that the office closed at 2 p.m. and would be closed next day, as it was only open three days a week.

On the third day he went again to the Précepteur's office and paid his ten francs, and then went with the receipt to the Préfecture, where he arrived at noon. He was told to return at 4 p.m., as the secretary never signed passports before 4 p.m., with the result that M. Albitte missed the boat train. It was therefore only on the fourth day that he was able to return to the free soil of England and the comforts of The Cedars, from where he wrote a letter to *The Times*, pointing out that if he had wished to return to England in a hurry to visit a dying relative, he would have been prevented from doing so by the petty tyranny of the bureaucracy of the Second Empire.[38]

CHAPTER 31

EUGÉNIE AND 'PLON-PLON'

IN 1856 Louis Napoleon and Eugénie were still a happily married couple, but his original passion for her had cooled, and he had reverted to his habit of pursuing other women. Everyone with connections at court gossiped in secret about his love affairs. He himself once said that whereas other men, in their relations with women, attacked, he defended himself as best he could against women's advances and sometimes surrendered[1] – a remark which he obviously did not intend to be taken as seriously as some of his biographers have done. The story went around that one lady at court had said: 'If I were cruel to the Emperor my husband would never forgive me.'[2]

After the birth of the Prince Imperial, Eugénie's doctors warned her not to have another child, and it seems likely that she made difficulties about having sexual relations with her husband after 1856. Some people believed that it was after this that Louis Napoleon began to be unfaithful to her; others thought that he had started immediately after the wedding.[3] But he himself told Princess Mathilde that he had been faithful to Eugénie for six months; after this, he felt that he needed his 'little distractions', but always returned with pleasure to Eugénie.[4] At Biarritz in September 1856, Dr Barthez, noticing the way in which the Emperor looked at the Empress and fondled her, had no doubt that he was lusting for her.[5]

Louis Napoleon's love affair with the Countess of Castiglione, which began when Eugénie was pregnant with the Prince Imperial, was wrongly thought to have profound political and diplomatic significance. Virginia di Castiglione was a recently married bride of eighteen, and was thought by her acquaintances to be the most beautiful girl in Europe, when she became the mistress of her sovereign, King Victor Emanuel of Piedmont; and she was still two months short of her nineteenth birthday when her cousin Cavour took both her and her husband with him to Paris in the hope that she would become the Emperor's mistress and would persuade Louis Napoleon to pursue a pro-Italian policy at the Peace Congress. She first met Louis Napoleon on the staircase of Prince Napoleon's house at the Palais Royal in Paris on the night of 26 January 1856; she arrived there for a party at midnight, just as the Emperor was leaving. He spoke to her, and said, in a tone of regret, that she was arriving rather late for the party.* Three days later, she went with Castiglione to a ball at the Tuileries. The Emperor spoke to her for a long time, and she noticed that everyone was looking at them.[6]

Cavour's hopes rose. He wrote to her on 20 February: 'Succeed, cousin, by any means you like, but succeed.'[7] Five days later, he informed Cibrario, whom he had left in charge of the Foreign Office in Turin: 'I have enrolled in the diplomatic service the very beautiful Countess X.X.X., whom I have invited to flirt with the Emperor, and to seduce him if she gets the chance.'[8] She succeeded in doing this without any difficulty.

Her husband happily accepted the situation. When he and she dined at Princess Mathilde's, he said at least twenty times: 'I am a model husband; I never hear or see anything.'[9]

At the end of June 1857 the Emperor, for the second year in succession, went to Plombières to take the waters, leaving Eugénie at Saint-Cloud, as he had done in 1856. After he had spent a fortnight there, Eugénie suddenly announced that she was going to join the Emperor at Plombières. Her unexpected decision upset the officials at Plombières, who had great difficulty in finding accommodation at short notice for her and her retinue. Rumours spread among the courtiers, the foreign journalists and the public that she was going to Plombières in a fit of jealous spite because she suspected that the Emperor was amusing himself there with the Countess of Castiglione, who was not, in fact, at Plombières. Louis Napoleon went to Épinal to meet Eugénie at the station, but arrived late, and met her on the road, riding towards him on horseback; and they rode into Plombières together amid the cheers of the people. After four days Eugénie returned to Paris, leaving Louis Napoleon to spend another fortnight without her at Plombières.[10] She never again went to Plombières, and she never went to Vichy with Louis Napoleon, though he spent July in either Plombières or Vichy in eight out of the next eleven years, and on one occasion took the Prince Imperial with him to Vichy.

By July 1857, Louis Napoleon was on the point of ending his affair with the Countess of Castiglione and of beginning one with the Comtesse Marianne de Walewska, the Florentine wife of his Foreign Minister,

*The well-known story, which was circulating in Paris soon afterwards, that the Emperor said: 'You are arriving too late', and that she gaily replied: 'Sire, you are leaving too early', is probably an invention. She wrote in her diary: 'Went at midnight to the ball at Prince Gerome's. Met the Emperor on the stairs; he said I was arriving rather late.'

Walewski. When the court went to Compiègne in October 1857 he made love to her on the train. The imperial railway carriage was divided into two compartments; Louis Napoleon was alone in one of them with Marianne de Walewska, while Eugénie, Walewski, Princess Mathilde and the other privileged travellers were in the other compartment. The jogging of the train caused the door between the two compartments to open, and Princess Mathilde saw 'my very dear cousin sitting astride on Marianne's knees, kissing her on the mouth and thrusting his hand down her bosom'.[11]

Whatever may have been the reason for Eugénie's unexpected journey to Plombières, she usually adopted a tolerant attitude towards her husband's love affairs. Her sound common sense, her lack of sentimentality, and perhaps the fact that she had never been really deeply in love with him, made her accept philosophically the fact that it was impossible to prevent Louis Napoleon from pursuing women or to stop women from offering themselves to him.[12] She knew that her deep and lasting friendship with Louis Napoleon would survive his passing infatuations. She sometimes made caustic remarks about the extent of the Countess of Castiglione's *décolletage*,[13] and put her foot down when a mistress behaved too brazenly; but if they were as charming and circumspect as Marianne de Walewska – whose exposure on the train to Compiègne was a rare lapse – the Empress could be as friendly towards them as she was in later years to Dr Hugenschmidt, who was thought to be the Emperor's illegitimate son by la Castiglione. 'Marianne', wrote Viel Castel, 'is a real little *rouée* who, while going to bed with the Emperor, has managed to become a friend of the Empress.'[14]

The Countess of Castiglione was not interested in politics, and was probably the least intellectual and intelligent of all Louis Napoleon's mistresses. Not for the last time, Cavour's Machiavellian schemes failed completely, and she did not exert the slightest influence over the Emperor's policy at the Congress of Paris. But la Castiglione has been wrongly credited, both by her contemporaries and by posterity, with having brought off a great diplomatic *coup*, for there were other factors which were driving Napoleon III into an alliance with Piedmont. In so far as personal influence played a part, Count Arese, Louis Napoleon's old friend of Arenenberg and New York, was more effective than the Countess of Castiglione. When Arese wrote to congratulate Louis Napoleon on his escape from Pianori's assassination attempt, he received a very friendly reply: 'Although I do not often write to you, I often speak about you to the Empress, who wants to meet you.'[15] Arese accepted the Emperor's invitation, and arrived in Paris in November 1855, where he acted as an unofficial political agent for Cavour.[16]

Louis Napoleon's old friends, like Hortense Cornu, knew that for many years he had dreamed that he would one day come at the head of an army to liberate Italy;[17] but there was a powerful obstacle which prevented him from pursuing a pro-Italian policy. The revolution of 1848 had led to a great Catholic revival in France; Conservatives who were disillusioned with the discredited and divided Legitimists and Orleanists turned to the Church as their salvation from Socialist atheism. Louis Napoleon was now their hero. Having rescued the Pope in 1849 and crushed the Reds, he continued to please the Church hierarchy by his measures for enforcing morality. The Prefects were given powers, which they often exercised, to forbid young people to frequent taverns; though the opponents of the régime believed that this was intended, not to protect the youth from alcoholism, but to prevent them from attending places which were often the centres of revolutionary political discussions.[18]

There was a vigorous drive against pornographic literature, and pamphlets which vilified or ridiculed the Church.[19] A play based on Victor Hugo's *Hunchback of Notre Dame* was banned because the villain was a priest.[20] In January 1857 Flaubert was prosecuted for publishing *Madame Bovary*.[21] The prosecution did not accept his lawyer's plea that it was a moral novel because the adulterous Emma Bovary comes to grief at the end; on the contrary, said the Imperial Prosecutor, the author had presented adultery as an enjoyable pastime. The Prosecutor also objected because Emma repents between her bouts of adultery, which suggested that the beneficial effect of repentance was short-lived; because her deathbed thoughts are worldly and carnal; and because a subsidiary character in the book is said to have been Marie Antoinette's lover, which was a libel on the martyred Queen. But the court acquitted Flaubert, though the judgment stated that the novel 'deserved severe censure' because it did not 'inspire disgust with vice'.[22]

The Catholic Ultramontanes were indignant at Flaubert's acquittal, and *L'Univers* condemned the verdict of the court. Partly because of this, the government launched another prosecution, a few months later, against Baudelaire for publishing his book of poems, *Les Fleurs du Mal*; they claimed that six of the poems*, which contained sensual descriptions of feminine beauty and love-making, were immoral. It was rumoured that the Cabinet had been divided about the prosecution, with the Jew Fould opposing it, and Billault and Abbatucci pressing for it, and that the Empress opposed the prosecution. Baudelaire was convicted, but got off with a fine of 300 francs.[23] He wrote a letter to Eugénie asking for clemency, and the fine was reduced to 50 francs.[24]

*'Lesbos'; 'Femmes damnées'; 'Le Léthé'; 'A celle qui est trop gaie'; 'Les bijoux'; 'Les Métamorphoses du Vampire'.

In December 1854 the Pope proclaimed the dogma of the Immaculate Conception, thus ending a debate which had continued for several centuries within the Catholic Church by ruling that the Virgin Mary had been born free from original sin. It reflected the increased veneration of the Virgin which had taken place in the Church, particularly in France. After the fall of Sevastopol, Louis Napoleon ordered that some of the captured Russian guns should be used in the construction of a colossal statue of the Virgin which was erected on the rock of Comeille in the department of Puy-de-Dôme, and he contributed 12,000 francs towards the cost of the project.[25]

The promulgation of the doctrine of the Immaculate Conception irritated not only the Protestants in Britain and elsewhere, but also many of the more Liberal Catholics. It so angered an unstable young priest, Verger, who had been suspended for his criticism of the doctrine, that he decided to murder the Archbishop of Paris as a protest, and on Sunday 4 January 1857 he stabbed the Archbishop as he was leading a procession to the Church of St Geneviève on the saint's holy day. Although many people believed that Verger was insane, he was condemned to death, and in view of the public indignation there could be no question of a reprieve. After being dragged, screaming and struggling, to the place of execution, he died calmly, shouting 'Long live Jesus Christ! Long live the Emperor!' The Catholics declared that his crime was the inevitable consequence of his Liberal and heretical opinions and his defiance of the authority of the Church.[26]

The Catholic Church in France was determined to use all its efforts to preserve the temporal power of the Pope from the attacks upon it by Italian revolutionaries. The Catholic spokesmen believed that the spiritual power of the Pope and the Church would be fatally weakened if the Pope were deprived of his temporal possessions: in this sinful world, he needed a temporal power-base if he were to maintain his prestige among the other temporal rulers; he must be the 'Sovereign Pontiff'. As his aims were spiritual, not temporal, he had no army beyond the minimum force required for police duties in his states; he relied for his defence against foreign invasion and internal revolution on the assistance of the Catholic states of Christendom. France, under Louis Napoleon's leadership, had nobly fulfilled this duty in 1849, and the Pope was grateful; but in saving the Pope, France had done no more than her Christian duty, and was not entitled to demand any national advantage in return or to dictate to the Pope how he should govern his states.

This French Catholic opinion was strong enough to ensure that Louis Napoleon maintained a garrison of 16,000 French troops in Rome for fifteen years but exercised almost no moderating influence on the government of the Papal States. Louis Napoleon had expressed his disapproval of Pius IX's policy in his letter to Ney in August 1849, but Pius paid no attention. When Jewish children were removed from their parents to be educated as Catholics in convents in Rome, Louis Napoleon's government and press protested; but the Jews were unable to free their children from the convents.[27] Louis Napoleon's aim had always been to pursue the middle way between Conservative tyranny and the guillotine of the Reds; in practice he had become an instrument of Conservative tyranny, and he did not like it.

Ideologically, he had a great deal of sympathy for the government of Piedmont, the only constitutional and Liberal government in Italy. Victor Emanuel and Cavour did in fact pursue the middle way between Papal despotism and Mazzinian revolution; although practising Catholics, they destroyed the political power of the Church in Piedmont and threw the Mazzinians into prison. To the Conservatives of Europe – to the Pope, the Tsar, the Emperor of Austria, and the French Catholic Ultramontanes – Victor Emanuel and Cavour were 'the Revolution'; to Mazzini, they were enemies of freedom who had betrayed the cause of Italian liberation by using Italian patriots to conquer Italy for the royal house of Savoy. But Louis Napoleon encouraged Victor Emanuel and Cavour to pursue the middle course which he himself was unable to pursue.

By 1854, Cavour was sure that he could achieve his aim – an Italy liberated and united under the leadership of a Liberal Piedmont – only by an alliance with Napoleon III. For this reason, he brought Piedmont into the Crimean War on the side of Britain and France, believing that if Piedmontese blood was shed on the Chernaya and before Sevastopol, Piedmont would gain territory from Austria in Northern Italy at the Peace Congress. Unfortunately for Cavour, Austria not only remained neutral, but forced Russia to accept the Allied peace terms by threatening to intervene on the Allied side; so Napoleon III gave Piedmont nothing at the Peace Congress except the right to sit at the table with the Great Powers. Cavour, though disappointed, thought that this was worth quite a lot.

In November 1855 Victor Emanuel and Cavour visited Paris. Both the King and his Prime Minister had been excommunicated for their anti-Papal policy, but Louis Napoleon and Eugénie nevertheless received them, and several of the French bishops took part in the festivities during the visit. Victor Emanuel made an unfavourable impression on Eugénie. When he met a lady at the Tuileries, he announced at the top of his voice that he had been to bed with her in Turin; and he asked Eugénie whether it was true, as he had been told, that in France the women ballet-dancers did not wear under-pants, because if so 'it will be absolute Heaven for me'. Eugénie had been known to laugh at a coarse joke when Louis Napoleon reacted with silent disapproval; she sometimes even made risky jokes herself. But Victor Emanuel's behaviour displeased her, and she decided that she did not like him.[28]

Although Eugénie afterwards became a strong opponent of Pied-montese policy and a champion of the temporal power of the Pope, she was not a reactionary Ultramontane like Veuillot, and her political position was probably in some respects more liberal than Montalembert's. She strongly opposed religious persecution. She greatly admired Alba's sixteenth-century ancestor, the third Duke of Alba, who was generally regarded as a cruel persecutor of the Protestants in the Netherlands; she obtained from her brother-in-law the correspondence between Alba and Philip II, and asked Mérimée to translate it and publish it in order to vindicate Alba's reputation. But her attitude was prompted by family loyalty and her pride in Spain, not by Catholic bigotry. She always criticized any case of injustice or intolerance against Protestants in Spain or in other Catholic countries. Some of her closest friends were Protestants, and she never made any attempt to convert them to Roman Catholicism; and she was equally opposed to anti-semitism. But she was a very religious woman, and the spiritual side of Catholicism meant a great deal to her.[29]

Eugénie's strong religious principles were the cause of the new political and personal image which she acquired. At the time of her marriage she was seen as the reckless girl who had run headlong into countless love affairs in Spain; but after the birth of the Prince Imperial not even her enemies suggested that she was unfaithful to the Emperor. Their new picture of her was of a cold, hard woman,[30] with a strong element of cruelty in her character. None of her close acquaintances saw her in this light. Her sense of discipline sometimes interfered with the pleasures of her ladies and servants. She did not permit any of her ladies to go out alone or to receive any visitors except their relations;[31] and she stopped the servant girls from hanging around the entrance hall of the palace on the evening of a state ball and flirting with the gentlemen as they arrived.[32] But the members of her household loved her, and she loved them. On one occasion she was so distressed when a maidservant died that she would not eat.[33]

Her refusal to take a lover, even after she knew that Louis Napoleon had several mistresses, was due to her principles, and also perhaps to a lack of enjoyment of the sexual act, but not to a natural coldness or hardness of character. Her secretary, Filon, stated that she was very tolerant to men who tried to make love to her. On one occasion a gentleman of the court who had become infatuated with her took the opportunity, while he was lighting her to her room at bedtime, to throw himself on his knees before her, with the candlestick in his hand, and make a passionate declaration of love. The Empress was not in the least offended. On another occasion she heard that the police had arrested a young student who had never met her but had fallen in love with her, and who was caught trying to break into the garden of the Tuileries hoping to accost her as she walked on the terrace. She was most interested and sympathetic, and repeatedly asked what had become of the young man.[34] According to Prince Napoleon, she once told him that the reason why she was so attached to her religion was to prevent herself from having love affairs, because 'to love, that is the only good thing'. Prince Napoleon told Ollivier that, though he was sure that she had never had a lover, he had seen her being kissed by a man at a ball.[35]

She had always been interested in politics,[36] and was pleased when Louis Napoleon insisted that she should be present at the Cabinet meetings, at which he regularly presided. She was invited to express her opinions at these meetings. It was widely believed, and reported in the foreign press, that she always supported right-wing and authoritarian policies in the Cabinet, and this was usually true. Within a few months of her marriage, Hübner was noting that the views which she was expressing on Spanish politics were so authoritarian that she must have got them from Narvaez.[37] Her remarks to Queen Victoria at Windsor in 1855 about the need for the Emperor always to have the last word over the French nation shows an undemocratic attitude; and on the same occasion she boasted to the Queen of the efficiency of the French police in infiltrating a secret agent into the Italian revolutionary group which had planned to assassinate the Emperor at the Opéra-Comique.[38] Eugénie's hard-headed realism and female common sense, and her lack of a philosophical or theoretical approach to politics, made her instinctively prefer authoritarianism – a kind and benevolent authoritarianism – to democracy.

She regretted the weakening of aristocratic privilege. In the spring of 1854 she wrote to Paca, who was about to go on a visit to Cadiz: 'I hope you will make them pay to you at Cadiz the honours due to a Grandee; not that these are important in themselves, but because they are still a faint remnant of the powers which we are losing every day and which we must regain.'[39] A few months later, she wrote to Paca's husband, Alba, to warn him against the French Radical refugees in Spain who were in contact with Ledru-Rollin, but told him that she hoped that the refugees would be tempted to take some action, so that they could be dealt with by 'those expeditious methods which are so common in Spain and which they well deserve, for they are capable of doing the greatest possible harm'. She added that she wished that Spain had a ruler like Louis Napoleon to deal with the situation:

A man like him, that is what you need. They say no man appears great to his valet, which applies even more to his wife; well, as for me, I admire him more every day, and I wish you another man who is as capable, if it were possible to find one.'[40]

She strongly approved of the Emperor's suppression of the freedom of the press. In December 1857, when she complained to Paca of the attempts of the French refugees to publish libels about her in the British and Belgian newspapers, she wrote approvingly that 'here, freedom of the press no longer exists'.[41]

She showed great interest – her critics called it a cult – in Marie Antoinette, buying mementoes of the unhappy Queen. The Republicans thereupon began to compare her to Marie Antoinette, the foreign wife of an autocratic despot who was her husband's evil genius, always urging him to pursue a hard, reactionary line. Eugénie herself was well aware of the similarity in their positions. She often compared herself to Marie Antoinette and said that she was sure that she would one day be guillotined by revolutionaries.[42] She was very conscious of the danger of revolution, and feared that political concessions to the opponents of the régime would encourage revolution.

She helped her enemies to portray her as a hard and cruel woman by her love of bullfighting and her eagerness to introduce bullfighting into France from Spain. The great wave of humanitarian feeling which spread through France under the Second Empire started a movement against cruelty to animals.[43] Madame de Ségur's book, *Mémoires d'un Âne*, which told the story of the cruel treatment inflicted on the donkey, Cadichon, was published in 1860 and appealed to a public which two years later was deeply stirred by a novel against cruelty to human beings that angered the conservative members of the Establishment, Victor Hugo's *Les Misérables*.[44] In April 1861 the Royal Society for the Prevention of Cruelty to Animals in London sent Samuel Gurney, M.P., General Sir Scott Lillie and two other members of the Society to Paris to protest to the Emperor about the horrible cruelties which were being practised on horses by vivisectionists at the veterinary schools at Alfort and Lyons. They had an interview at the Tuileries with Louis Napoleon, who expressed great sympathy and immediately ordered that all experiments at Alfort should be stopped until an inquiry was held into the truth or falsity of the R.S.P.C.A.'s allegations.[45]

There was therefore considerable opposition on humanitarian grounds to the Empress's attempts to introduce bullfighting into

France. Eugénie took Louis Napoleon to see a number of bullfights in Bayonne when they were at Biarritz, and at Christmas 1863 she brought some famous Spanish *picadors*, as well as some Spanish boars and cows, to take part in a great boar and cow fight at the Trianon at Versailles, at which Eugénie and her ladies pricked the cows with lances to goad them into fighting. The boars and cows broke loose and charged the ladies, who fled in panic, with only the Empress remaining calm. Many Frenchmen disapproved of this cow fight, and of the fact that it had cost 180,000 francs.[46] Eugénie was a kind-hearted, not a cruel, woman; but, like the equally kind-hearted Louis Napoleon – who often bagged two hundred game in a good day's shoot[47] – and like the fox-hunting members of the English R.S.P.C.A., her kindness to animals was qualified by her attachment to her national sport.

This love of bullfighting gave the French Radical exiles the opportunity, in their publications in London and Berlin, to paint a grotesque picture of Eugénie as a sadistic pervert. They described how Eugénie at bullfights in Spain – wearing a short skirt to show off her legs to the bullfighters – 'screamed with joy . . . pranced with enthusiasm and shrieked with pleasure' when she saw a bull lying bleeding in the arena or tearing out a bullfighter's belly with its horns. She 'yawns and sleeps' at the Théâtre Français, and would gladly forgo all the dramas of Shakespeare and Hugo for the joy of seeing a real dagger produce a real corpse in the bullring.[48] When one of the bullfighters falls writhing on the ground,

> you should see the lovely Eugénie, whose enthusiasm then turns into a paroxysm, become more and more passionate. Standing on her seat, waving her handkerchief, clapping her hands, her two blue eyes . . . shine with a strange light; her breast heaves . . . her mouth contracts . . . all her being shivers and palpitates with happiness

until, exhausted by her excitement, 'she resumes her seat swooning with pleasure'.[49]

This was certainly crude and lying propaganda; but Eugénie loved bullfighting and hunting, and many years later told her companion, Isabel Vesey, that she enjoyed the excitement of the kill, as well as the music of the horns, in hunting the stag. Dr Barthez saw the other side of her character when she prevented her guests at Biarritz from treading on insects, and insisted that they tenderly lift up the insects and carry them to a place of safety.[50] Once when she was walking near Biarritz she met a shepherd boy taking a lamb to slaughter. The lamb caught her fancy, and she bought it in order to save its life, telling the boy to take the money and find another lamb for slaughter. 'And this is the woman', wrote Dr Barthez, 'who watches with enthusiasm when a sword is plunged into a bull, to say nothing of the preliminary torments inflicted upon him.'[51]

Another of Eugénie's hobbies was used against her by her opponents, this time to show her up as a silly and superstitious woman. Both she and Louis Napoleon were fascinated by table-turning, which soon after their marriage became the current vogue in France. It was officially condemned as a superstition by the Catholic Church, but this did not prevent the Emperor and Empress from repeatedly taking part in table-turning at the Tuileries, Saint-Cloud and Biarritz. They were very impressed by the famous Scottish medium, Daniel Dunglas Home, who came to Paris in 1857 after a sensational success in the United States and elsewhere, and often performed at court. There were differing opinions about Home's achievements and good faith. The Chief of the Paris Police, Piétri, was impressed when he asked Home's table how many revolutionaries had been arrested that morning in a very secret police operation in Paris, and received the correct answer. Mérimée reacted less favourably when he went to Home's séance at the Prince de Beauvau's. The table was asked what a man must do to be saved, and the reply was written in pencil under the table: 'Il faut être bon catholiche.' Mérimée thought that a spirit from the next world ought to have learned there how to spell 'catholique' correctly.[52]

Some of the courtiers, who believed that Home was an unscrupulous charlatan, were shocked that the Emperor and Empress were taken in by him; but many serious European scholars believed in Home. Louis Napoleon refused to commit himself definitely either for or against Home, but said that Home had achieved some remarkable results;[53] and Eugénie was perhaps less carried away by Home than people thought.

On one occasion she was deeply moved when Home apparently succeeded in making it possible for her to receive messages from her dead father, to whom she had been so deeply attached, and to feel her father's hand under the table; but at other times she was prepared to joke about table-turning. Once, when the Minister of State, Fould, was about to set out on a visit to London, she urged him to take part in a table-turning session in order to see whether he received a message foretelling that he would marry Angela Burdett-Coutts, the English heiress, whom every adventurer was supposed to want to marry.[54] It is significant that in later years, when Eugénie had been profoundly affected by the death of the Prince Imperial, she made no attempt to get in touch with her dead son by table-turning, either because she no longer believed in it, as she had done in her younger days, or because the Prince Imperial's death was too sensitive a subject for an experiment.

The Emperor's cousin, Prince Napoleon, took the opposite attitude to Eugénie on every question, always adopting a Liberal policy against the Empress's Catholic and Conservative one. Prince Napoleon was a consistent and sincere Radical, though hardly any of the Radicals believed it; George Sand, with whom he had a long and intimate correspondence, was the only Radical or Socialist who was willing to believe in the good faith of a Bonaparte Prince. His relations with Eugénie were very bad, for their political differences developed into a strong personal antagonism, though as late as May 1858 Hortense Cornu, who was no longer in a position to speak authoritatively about Louis Napoleon's entourage, had heard that the Empress liked Prince Napoleon 'very much'.[55] Prince Napoleon's secretary Charles Edmond, and Eugénie's secretary Filon, believed that he was secretly in love with her, and that he hated her because he could not have her. Eugénie herself believed that he hated her because, by giving birth to the Prince Imperial, she destroyed the possibility that Louis Napoleon would adopt him as his heir to the imperial throne, which he might well have done if she had not had a son.[56] Princess Bacciochi told Eugénie's confessor, the Abbé Bauer, that Eugénie hated Prince Napoleon because, when he was present as a witness at the birth of the Prince Imperial, she overheard him say that she had ugly legs; but Prince Napoleon denied the truth of this story.[57]

As Prince Napoleon was rude and tactless, and Eugénie was charming and tactful, he behaved much worse towards her than she did towards him, with the result that she could usually make it appear, in their quarrels, that he had been in the wrong; but Louis Napoleon had always liked him, and, despite everything, remained his friend. According to one story which was widely believed – though it was almost certainly untrue – the Emperor did not dare to oppose Prince Napoleon, because the Prince was in possession of a document written by Louis Bonaparte which proved that Louis Napoleon was not his son.[58]

Louis Napoleon had reason to be grateful to Prince Napoleon. In the summer of 1848 there had been a movement among the Bonapartists in Paris to choose Prince Napoleon as their leader and as their candidate for the presidency of the Republic instead of Louis Napoleon. Prince Napoleon was in Paris, and was a deputy in the National Assembly, while Louis Napoleon was absent in London. Prince Napoleon, in his physical appearance, looked remarkably like his uncle, the great Emperor, whom Louis Napoleon did not resemble in the least; and he had not made a fool of himself by engaging in adventures like

Louis Napoleon's fiascos at Strasburg and Boulogne. But Prince Napoleon had firmly refused to usurp Louis Napoleon's place.

After Louis Napoleon became President, Prince Napoleon disapproved of his policy of giving power to the Party of Order, and founded a newspaper, *La Liberté*, which became the mouthpiece of left-wing Bonapartism. He voted in the Assembly against the Law of 31 May 1850 which abolished universal suffrage, and in December 1851 he let it be known that he opposed the *coup d'état*; but under the Constitution of the Empire he became a French Prince, with a seat for life in the Senate. The Conservatives, knowing Louis Napoleon's affection for him, feared that the Emperor would make him his heir; but Louis Napoleon made no move, and the birth of the Prince Imperial removed this possibility.[59]

At the outbreak of the Crimean War, Prince Napoleon asked the Emperor to appoint him Commander-in-Chief of the expeditionary force in Turkey. The Emperor refused, and gave the supreme command to Saint-Arnaud; but he gave Prince Napoleon the rank of general, and appointed him Commander of the Reserves. On arriving at Constantinople, Prince Napoleon made a *faux pas* – perhaps an excusable one – when he proposed the Sultan's health at a banquet at the French embassy. He proposed a toast to 'the illustrious Sultan whom we have come to defend'. The Turks were offended, because the Sultan was 'august', not 'illustrious', and 'defend' was a term used by a man who protects his inferior – his wife or his dog. Prince Napoleon should have referred to 'the august Sultan whom we have come to support'. But if the Sultan shared the resentment of his officials he disguised it, and invited Prince Napoleon to a banquet at his palace at which Prince Napoleon referred to the Sultan in the correct form.[60]

Prince Napoleon sailed to the Crimea with the army, and at the battle of the Alma was in the saddle all day at Saint-Arnaud's side. The press in France described how both of them had been under fire, and how an officer standing close to Prince Napoleon had been wounded. The Emperor awarded Prince Napoleon the Military Medal for his courage at the Alma; but soon afterwards Prince Napoleon left the Crimea and returned to Constantinople. The press reported that he had fallen ill with dysentery, and had been granted sick leave; but the officers and soldiers in the Crimea spread the rumour that he was a coward who feared lead bullets, and changed his nickname of 'Plon-Plon' to 'Craint-Plon'. This reputation for cowardice was another black mark against him in the eyes of the army and of his political opponents.[61]

On 21 November 1854, *The Times* published an article about his departure from the Crimea and the criticism of him which was circulating in the army. The authorities seized *The Times* from the kiosks on the boulevards and in the post office. This was the first time that the powers to confiscate a foreign newspaper had been exercised against *The Times*; it had been allowed to appear with its vicious attacks on Louis Napoleon every day during the months after the *coup d'état*, because Louis Napoleon did not wish to antagonize the British Establishment by suppressing it. He could have given no greater proof of his friendship for Prince Napoleon than that he should now, for the first time, ban *The Times*.[62]

In January 1855, Prince Napoleon returned to Paris; the press reported that he had been forced to leave the army because he was suffering from a pain in his spine. Before the war, Louis Napoleon had appointed him chairman of the organizing committee of the Paris Exhibition, and he took up his duties after his return from the Levant. The press reported on the efficiency with which he performed them, and as chairman of the committee he officiated at the opening and at the other public ceremonies connected with the Exhibition.[63]

Although the *Times* correspondent's scent for news had led him to publish his story about Prince Napoleon's unpopularity in the army, he and his paper were sympathetic to Prince Napoleon, whose Radical sympathies made him pro-British and anti-Russian.[64] After the war, he opposed the Emperor's policy of seeking friendship with the Tsar, and this led to another incident. In April 1857 the Tsar's brother, the Grand Duke Constantine, paid an official visit to France. One of Prince Napoleon's regular duties was to meet visiting foreign Princes at the railway terminal, and as Grand Duke Constantine was coming by sea to Toulon, it was arranged that Prince Napoleon should meet him on the quayside. At the last moment, Prince Napoleon refused to go to Toulon, and only the Prefect of the department was there to receive the Grand Duke. Prince Napoleon did meet Grand Duke Constantine at the Gare de Lyon when the train arrived in Paris; but he promptly went off to Berlin, and stayed there until after the Grand Duke had left Paris. This was everywhere interpreted as a gesture of protest against the Emperor's friendship with the arch-enemy of revolution, the Tsar.[65]

The Grand Duke's visit was not a great success, for this blonde young man lacked the social graces. At Fontainebleau he was placed next to Eugénie at dinner, but seeing one of his officers on the opposite side of the table, he spent a long time talking to the officer in Russian, a language which the Empress did not understand. Eugénie, on her side, was as tactless as she could sometimes be. She asked Grand Duke Constantine whether it was true, as the rumour said, that his uncle Tsar Alexander I had been assassinated. The Grand Duke was not at all put out; he said that his uncle had not been assassinated, but that a plot to assassinate him was only foiled because he died a natural death first.[66]

As usual, Eugénie was reproached for being both too formal and too relaxed, too haughty and too familiar, during the Grand Duke's visit. The inhabitants of Fontainebleau were annoyed when she ordered the park gates to be closed to stop them from seeing the firework display for the Grand Duke; and there were complaints of her undue insistence on etiquette at a ball at the Tuileries, where she sat in the centre of a semicircle of chairs, and no one was permitted to approach the semicircle unless he was invited by her Chamberlain to sit and talk with the Empress, although there was complete informality everywhere else in the ballroom, with the Emperor walking around and casually talking to everyone whom he met. But her critics were shocked by her informality at a garden-party for Grand Duke Constantine at Villeneuve l'Étang on a glorious summer day early in May. She and her ladies stood on the top of a little mound while the Emperor and the gentlemen tried to climb up the mound on all fours and catch a glimpse of the ladies' legs, with the Empress and the ladies repulsing them by throwing nosegays at them and striking them with their parasols. Hübner was glad that his daughters had refused to take part in the game.[67]

Despite the opposition of Prince Napoleon – and, what was much more important, despite the opposition of the British government – Louis Napoleon decided to arrange a personal meeting with Tsar Alexander II. From the time when the idea of the meeting first became known, it was the subject of constant talk and speculation among diplomats and journalists, and it was finally fixed to take place at the end of September 1857 at Stuttgart, where the King of Württemberg offered to act as host to the two Emperors. Louis Napoleon thought that it would be tactful to visit his British ally before meeting their former enemy at Stuttgart, and he asked Queen Victoria if he might visit her when she was on holiday at Osborne in the Isle of Wight. She agreed, though she warned him that 'our dear Osborne is not a Palace, but a simple country-house which is comfortable but with very small rooms'.[68]

On the evening of 5 August the Emperor and Empress sailed from Le Havre in the imperial yacht *La Reine Hortense*, and at seven o'clock next morning landed at the Queen's private wharf at Osborne. Malmesbury noted in his diary that he had never seen such extensive security precautions; the British navy joined with the British and French police to guard the Emperor, and kept up a patrol at Spithead throughout his visit, stopping any unauthorized ship from landing on the coast near Osborne. The visit was most successful, although it rained nearly all the time during the four days. The Emperor wore civilian dress to emphasize that it was a private visit, and it was chiefly devoted to political discussions with Prince Albert and the Queen's ministers; but Louis Napoleon and Eugénie had time to go with the Queen and Prince to Ryde and to Carisbrooke Castle, and they went to Mass in Newport on the Sunday. One evening there was a ball at Osborne, at which Eugénie fulfilled her ambition of dancing a Sir Roger de Coverley. Queen Victoria thought that she danced it very well, and was as delighted with her as she had been at their two previous meetings. Eugénie as usual used her charm and personal friendships in her husband's interests and in line with the needs of his policy; she told the Queen that she regretted that it was necessary for him to meet the Tsar.[69]

Louis Napoleon again exerted all his personal charm on the Queen. He told her that he was 'moved with admiration at the sight of all the virtues displayed by the royal family of England',[70] and felt better educated and more endowed with the power to do good through having come into contact with Prince Albert's widespread knowledge and elevated judgement, and that her seven children were 'les plus charmants enfants they had ever seen'.[71]

The Emperor's talks with Palmerston and Clarendon at Osborne about Walachia and Moldavia went so smoothly that both the French and the British Foreign Offices believed that the other side had given way on all points; the French hailed the Osborne visit as a diplomatic triumph for the Emperor, and the English as a victory for Palmerston. Louis Napoleon gave way on his demand for the unification of the principalities, being rightly confident that he could achieve this aim indirectly by getting Cuza elected as Prince of both Moldavia and Walachia.[72]

On their return from Osborne, Louis Napoleon and Eugénie went to Biarritz for their annual holiday before meeting the Tsar at Stuttgart. In September the Tsar arrived at Darmstadt in Hesse with his wife the Tsaritsa, who was the Grand Duke of Hesse's sister; but soon afterwards it was announced that the Tsaritsa was ill, and that her health prevented her from going on to Stuttgart with the Tsar. The rumour spread that it was a diplomatic illness, and that the Tsaritsa refused to meet Eugénie because she regarded her as an upstart adventuress. The press then reported that, in view of the Tsaritsa's absence, the Empress would not go with the Emperor to Stuttgart, and she remained at Biarritz, to the great disappointment of the people of Stuttgart, who had been very much looking forward to seeing her. When Louis Napoleon reached Stuttgart on 25 September, he discovered that the Tsar had arrived there the previous day with the

Tsaritsa, who had suddenly recovered from her illness. The Queen of Greece, the Queen of the Netherlands, and Prince Leopold of Bavaria were also on a visit to the King of Württemberg in Stuttgart; and the Crown Prince of Württemberg and his wife the Grand Duchess Olga, who was the Tsar's sister, were there too. So the Stuttgart meeting turned out to be a gathering of European imperial and royal families –without Eugénie.[73]

Louis Napoleon was not the man to allow the Tsar and Tsaritsa to put him at a disadvantage, and he was completely at his ease in the embarrassing situation. In the eyes of the people of Stuttgart and of the foreign journalists in the city, he eclipsed the Tsar. He strolled along the streets of Stuttgart escorted by only one A.D.C. and talked to the passers-by, although the Tsar did nothing so vulgar. When the King of Württemberg took his guests to the annual fair at Cannstatt on the Neckar, Louis Napoleon, who like the Tsar and the Princes arrived on horseback, attracted all the attention; and everyone in Stuttgart was saying that the Tsaritsa had refused to meet Eugénie because she knew that Eugénie was much more beautiful than she was.

Louis Napoleon and Alexander had only a short political discussion at Stuttgart; but Louis Napoleon spent longer with the Russian Foreign Minister, Gorchakov, who also had political talks with Walewski. The Tsar offered to sign a treaty of alliance with Louis Napoleon; but Louis Napoleon refused. He was playing a subtle diplomatic game, and playing it with great skill. He was seeking to isolate Austria diplomatically so as to be able to compel her, if necessary by war, to liberate Northern Italy. He wished to detach Russia from Austria without alarming Britain and thus fathering an Anglo-Austrian alliance.[74] He therefore strengthened his friendship with Russia at Stuttgart, but stopped short of a formal alliance. As a result, it was generally believed that the Stuttgart meeting had been much less successful than the interview fifty years before between Napoleon and Alexander I at Tilsit. This was what Louis Napoleon wanted people to think.

On the last evening of the three-day meeting at Stuttgart, there was a gala performance at the opera house of Balfe's *The Bohemian Girl*. Louis Napoleon sat in the royal box with the Queen of the Netherlands on his right and the Tsaritsa on his left. The Queen of Greece was on the Tsaritsa's left, and the Tsar sat between her and the Queen of Württemberg. There were so many royal personages present that there was no room for them all in the front row of the royal box. The King of Württemberg courteously sat behind his guests in the second row of the box, while the Crown Prince of Württemberg, with Grand Duchess Olga, Grand Duchess Helena and Prince Leopold of Bavaria, sat in the next box, and the King of Württemberg's two daughters – Princess Frederick of Prussia and the Countess of Neipperg – sat in another box. The Tsar and Tsaritsa left after the first act because they were very tired, but Louis Napoleon and the rest of the royal party stayed till the end. The *Times* correspondent reported that the Emperor looked much more relaxed and happy after the Tsar and Tsaritsa had gone; but *The Times* and the British government were eagerly watching and hoping for signs of a rift between France and Russia.

The Tsar and Tsaritsa left Stuttgart next morning, but Louis Napoleon stayed for one more day, and delighted the people by going again to the opera to see Weber's *Der Freischütz*, explaining that it was so long since he had had the pleasure of hearing an opera in German.

After leaving Stuttgart, Alexander met Franz Joseph at Weimar. The diplomats and journalists believed that the Weimar meeting was a setback for Napoleon III. But Louis Napoleon did not worry; he was sure that, after the Crimean War, Russia would prefer the friendship of France, the magnanimous victor, to that of Austria, the treacherous ally.

It was essential for Louis Napoleon's policy to maintain good relations with Britain; but public opinion in both Britain and France made this difficult. When news of the rebels' successes in the Indian Mutiny reached London and Paris in October 1857, Louis Napoleon made a gesture of sympathy with Britain by offering to allow British reinforcements for India to travel through France and embark at Toulon in order to shorten the time taken for their six weeks' journey to Bombay.[75] But Palmerston declined the offer, and greatly resented what he interpreted as an attempt by Louis Napoleon to make the world believe that Britain could not suppress the mutiny without his help. With more reason, the British were alarmed at the large-scale naval building programme on which Louis Napoleon embarked in 1857, though the French pointed out that even when the programme was completed, Britain would still have naval superiority over France.[76]

By September news had reached London of the atrocities committed by the Sepoy mutineers against British women and children at Cawnpore and elsewhere, and the British press were publishing editorials demanding vengeance on the whole Indian people and letters from British officers serving in India boasting of how they had hanged and burned wholesale in Indian villages and massacred unarmed civilians at the capture of Delhi. This was too good an opportunity for the French press to miss. For years they had been lectured by *The Times* and other English newspapers on the cruelties of the French in Algeria and the wickedness of Louis Napoleon's despotism in France; and they now gave great publicity to the decree of the Governor-General of India suppressing all native-language newspapers, and to the most hysterical of the demands for hangings and floggings that were published in *The Times*, *The Morning Post* and the *Bombay Times*. The French Catholics, remembering the outcry in the British press a few months earlier when the government of Naples executed thirty-five revolutionaries, said that the British objected to executions and atrocities only when the victims were Reds. They also pointed out that the British government was insisting that the King of Nepal surrender the Sepoy rebels who had escaped to his territories. Why, then, did they refuse to extradite Mazzini and Ledru-Rollin and the other 'Socialists' who had planned to murder the Emperor?[77]

The French attitude aroused great resentment in Britain, where *The Times* asserted – quite untruthfully – that the French press had not reported or condemned the Sepoy atrocities which had provoked the British reprisals.[78] In November, Palmerston, at the Lord Mayor's banquet at the Guildhall, made a pugnacious speech about Britain's ability to win a war against a hostile power, which everyone interpreted as being a reference to France. But the anti-British feeling in France was held in check by the Emperor's well-known eagerness to maintain the Anglo-French alliance. The journalists hesitated to denounce British atrocities too violently in case they received warnings, or were suspended or suppressed, under the press laws.

Austria had far more reason than Britain to be alarmed at Louis Napoleon's policy, and Hübner knew it. He was not invited to Compiègne in the autumn of 1857, and commented wrily that Louis XIV would never have allowed diplomatic differences to lead him to commit an act of discourtesy.[79] He noticed that Louis Napoleon seemed to be avoiding him at receptions and balls. Eugénie, on the other hand, spoke her mind with her usual frankness: 'Austria is not loyal; she works against us everywhere',[80] she complained to Hübner when he presented three Austrian officers to her. The diplomats were always puzzled by Eugénie's outbursts about international affairs. Was it merely a case of spontaneous indignation on her part? Or had she been carefully briefed by Napoleon III to commit a calculated indiscretion?

On 1 January 1858, Hübner went to the New Year's Day reception of the diplomatic corps at the Tuileries. The Emperor shook hands only with the British and Russian Ambassadors; 'he said some polite words to me, but nothing more.'[81] Next day, there was the usual reception given by the Empress to the diplomats and their ladies. Hübner attended, and wrote in his diary: 'The atmosphere of the court is certainly anti-Austrian.'[82]

CHAPTER 32

ORSINI'S BOMBS

ON 14 January 1858 the Emperor and Empress went to the opera house in the little Rue Lepelletier off the Boulevard des Italiens to attend a special performance for the benefit of the opera singer Massol, who was retiring after a successful career. The programme was a combination of drama, opera and ballet which had been selected in order to give the famous performers taking part the opportunity of appearing in their greatest roles: Adelaide Ristori played a scene from Schiller's *Maria Stuart*, Carolina Rosati danced in *Le bal masqué de Gustave* – a ballet of the assassination of King Gustavus III of Sweden – and Massol himself sang in Rossini's *Guillaume Tell* and in Auber's *La Muette de Portici*, an opera about the revolution in Naples in 1745.[1] It was pure coincidence that every item in the programme dealt either with regicide or with a popular revolt against a despot.

Eugénie was suffering from a cough, for an epidemic of 'flu and colds had spread in Paris as the mild weather succeeded the cold fog of New Year's Day;[2] but she felt well enough to accompany the Emperor to the performance.

As the crowd in the Rue Lepelletier was waiting to see the Emperor and Empress arrive, at about 8.10 p.m., a policeman on duty recognized an Italian revolutionary named Pieri, who was standing in the crowd. Pieri was immediately arrested and taken to a room in the opera house for questioning. Two minutes after they reached the room, they heard the sound of an explosion in the street outside, and Pieri cried out: 'Do what you like with me; I am content, the blow is struck.'[3]

The Emperor and Empress drove up to the opera house surrounded by an escort of cavalry. As their carriage was drawing up at the main entrance, a bomb was thrown. It killed and wounded some of the horses and bystanders, and a fragment of the bomb broke the gas pipes on the front of the opera house and put out all the gaslight in the street, which was plunged into darkness. The noise of the bomb, the screams of the wounded, and the sudden darkness caused the horses of the cavalry to panic and plunge forward alongside the imperial carriage. This saved the lives of Louis Napoleon and Eugénie, for at that moment two more bombs were thrown, and the horses and their riders caught the main force of the explosion which would otherwise have struck the carriage. As it was, two of the horses of the Emperor's carriage were killed, and the carriage was battered by the bomb splinters. Two of the splinters pierced the Emperor's hat, and his nose was slightly cut by a piece of broken glass from the shattered carriage windows. Eugénie's cheek was slightly grazed by the flying glass and a tiny splinter entered her left eye. The Emperor's A.D.C., General Roguet, who was sitting in the front of the carriage, was wounded in the back of the neck by a bomb fragment, and blood from the wound spattered Eugénie's white evening dress. The three bombs killed eight people and wounded 156 – some of them soldiers and policemen of the Emperor's escort, and others civilian bystanders, including a citizen of the United States who was visiting Paris and a little French girl of twelve who was badly wounded in the leg. Some of the victims were blinded.

Louis Napoleon and Eugénie got out of the carriage, and stood, perfectly calm, among the screams of the wounded people and horses and the panic of the police and the public. Eugénie called to the officials to look after the wounded and not to worry about her and the Emperor – 'It is our business to be shot at' – and she noticed that a workman in the crowd took advantage of the confusion to kiss her on the shoulder.[4] Louis Napoleon showed himself to the people at the door of the opera house and wished to stay and comfort the wounded; but Eugénie, thinking that a fourth bomb might still be thrown, said to him 'Don't be silly!'[5] and dragged him into the opera house. They received a great ovation from the audience in the theatre, and from the crowds in the boulevards when they returned to the Tuileries at midnight after the end of the performance. The cheers reached a climax when the Empress, beautiful and elegant in her evening *toilette* and apparently quite composed and fearless, lowered the carriage window, stretched out her arm, and waved with her handkerchief to the people.

The assassination attempt had been made by a group of four Italian revolutionaries, of whom Pieri was one. The other three escaped after throwing their bombs, but were all arrested soon afterwards. One of them was the famous revolutionary leader Count Felice Orsini, the son of the man who was popularly supposed to have murdered Louis Napoleon's brother Napoleon Louis at Forli in 1831. Felice Orsini had been Mazzini's Governor of Ancona under the Roman Republic of 1849, and had afterwards been captured by the Austrians and imprisoned in the notorious prison fortress at Mantua. In 1854 he escaped and took refuge in England, where he wrote a best-selling book, *Austrian Dungeons in Italy*. The other two conspirators, Rudio and Gomez, were less eminent revolutionaries.[6]

The police discovered that Orsini and his three colleagues had left London at the end of November and had travelled to Paris through Brussels on a British passport issued to Orsini for himself and his three servants in the name of Thomas Allsop. The French police then asked the British police to help them, and they discovered that the bombs thrown in the Rue Lepelletier were made in Birmingham on the order of a Mr Allsop. The J.P.s in the village of Nutfield in Surrey issued a warrant for the arrest of Mr Allsop; but he had disappeared.

All over Europe the journalists asked: who was the mysterious Mr Allsop? This was no mystery to the members of the small intellectual circle to which Mr Allsop belonged. He was an elderly English gentleman of leisure who in his youth in the 1820s had been a friend of Samuel Taylor Coleridge, about whom he sometimes lectured to exclusive gatherings of poets. In 1849 he surprised his friends by going off to California to join the Gold Rush, but he returned to England a few years later and settled at Riverside in Kent, from where he moved to Nutfield in the spring of 1857. His political opinions were vaguely Radical. He became friendly with Dr Simon Bernard, a Radical French physician who came to London as a refugee after Louis Napoleon's *coup d'état*. On 1 January 1857 Allsop sent a letter of New Year's greetings to Bernard. 'My dear doctor,' he wrote,

> the abominable miscreant of 2 December seems to have reached his culminating point. . . . If I was in California now I would at once double the amount offered by Landor to the man who should perform an act of justice upon that most wretched caitiff. . . . He must be killed, and with him the system which he somehow seems necessary to keep up. . . . Be kind enough to assure Orsini of my warmest sympathy.[7]

The police, knowing that Bernard often met Orsini and other refugees at the Café Suisse in Tichborne Street, searched Bernard's rooms in Bark Street, Bayswater, and found Allsop's letter.[8] The Home Secretary offered a reward for information about Allsop, and ordered the arrest of Bernard on a charge of being an accessory to the murder of the people killed in the Rue Lepelletier by Orsini's bombs.

There was an outburst of anti-British feeling in France when it was known that the bomb-throwers of the Rue Lepelletier, like Pianori and Tibaldi, had come from England. When Hübner went to the Tuileries on the day after the incident to convey his sympathy to the Emperor, he found Louis Napoleon's social secretary, Bacciochi, denouncing the English for sheltering Mazzinian assassins.[9] Eugénie, as usual, shared the popular indignation, and as usual expressed herself forcibly. One evening at a reception at the Tuileries, the fiery General Espinasse, forgetting that the Empress was present, used a coarse expression to describe the English. Then, realizing that she had heard him, he apologized profusely. 'Go on,' said Eugénie enthusiastically, 'say it again! The English are just that!'[10]

But Louis Napoleon did nothing to encourage anti-British feeling. When he opened the session of the Chambers on 18 January he went out of his way to refer to his successful visit to Osborne and his friendly relations with Britain; and a week later he and Eugénie attended a ball at the British embassy to celebrate the marriage of Queen Victoria's daughter Victoria, the Princess Royal, to the nephew of the King of Prussia. He cheerfully told Lord Cowley, the Ambassador, that if he saw about twenty strangers at the ball, they would be members of the secret police who had come as his bodyguard.[11]

He was unable to resist the pressure from his ministers to introduce new repressive measures. Within a week of the bombs Billault, the Minister of the Interior, had persuaded him to suppress one Legitimist and one Republican newspaper, and on 1 February Billault produced the draft of the law which was unofficially known as the Law of the Suspects, which duly passed the Chambers. Apart from creating new offences and increasing penalties for the unauthorized manufacture of explosives and for seditious propaganda, it gave power to the Minister of the Interior to deport to Algeria or Cayenne any person who had been arrested or banished for taking part in the June Days of 1848 or in the resistance to the *coup d'état* of December 1851, if the Minister believed that this was advisable in the interests of public security. This meant that a respectable Conservative like Thiers, who had returned to Paris and was living there in political retirement, as well as many Socialists and Radicals who had been deported in 1848 or 1851, and amnestied, could be sent to Cayenne even though they had played no part in political life for ten years.[12]

Billault, having drafted the new law, was dismissed from office, as the scapegoat for the failure in security which had made the bomb outrage possible.[13] He was succeeded by General Espinasse, who was hated by the Radicals and Socialists for his conduct as military governor of Rome in 1849 and for his support of the *coup d'état* of 2 December. Espinasse immediately began to use his powers under the Law of the Suspects. He sent instructions to the Prefects to arrest a given number of trouble-makers in their departments, a higher quota being fixed for those departments which were famous as centres of Republican resistance. The Prefects then looked around for suitable people to deport in order to complete their quota.

Nassau Senior heard about the quota system from a high official of the Ministry of the Interior with whom he dined at Drouyn de Lhuys's house. The official said that the object of the arrests was not to imprison dangerous revolutionaries, but to terrify the population. Mérimée told Senior that the Minister's directive had been misunderstood: Espinasse had merely ordered the Prefects not to exceed a certain number of arrests; it was a maximum, not a quota. But the Prefects interpreted the figure as being a quota; and in all the Opposition houses where Senior dined and breakfasted – from Tocqueville, Jules Simon, and Hortense Cornu – he heard stories of innocent men, who had supported the Radicals or Socialists in 1848 but had long since abandoned politics, being seized, sometimes as a result of mistaken identity, and sent to die in Cayenne or at Lambessa in Algeria.[14]

The Prefect of Loire-Inférieure ordered the arrest of a foreman in the dockyard at Nantes who had been denounced as a Red by a former employee whom he had dismissed for stealing. When the foreman's employer raised the matter with the Minister, Espinasse said that unfortunately it was too late to stop it now, as the foreman was already at Le Havre waiting to sail for Cayenne. 'We do not retrace our steps,' said Espinasse; 'the matter is closed; he will have to go.'[15] But at Auxerre, the Prefect was persuaded to release a doctor who had been sent to Algeria by mistake for his brother, and to look for another victim to fill the quota. As usual, the best chance for a deportee was to have his case brought to the Emperor's personal attention. Hortense Cornu said that Louis Napoleon's sensibility was in the eye. 'He is deeply affected by any distress that he actually sees. He is indifferent to any that is not brought before him in detail.'[16]

In all, about five hundred Socialists and Radicals were arrested and deported, though rumour placed the figure very much higher. A hundred were deported from Paris and twenty from the Nièvre, which, as the centre of the Red resistance in December 1851, had the largest quota outside Paris. In some departments the quota was only four.[17] Among those arrested was an old Radical of the Vendée, Dr Benjamin Clemenceau, whose son Georges Clemenceau was aged sixteen. Young Georges whispered to his father 'I will avenge you' when the old man was taken away from the family home; but like most of the suspects, he was soon released.[18]

Delescluze had only a fortnight of his three-year prison term still to run when Orsini threw the bombs. Three days before he was due to be released from his prison in Corsica he was told that at the expiry of his sentence he would be deported to Cayenne under an order signed by the Minister of the Interior. The treatment which he received during the next eighteen months varied greatly, and depended on the whims of the individual officials with whom he came into contact. He was sent from

Ajaccio to Marseilles, where he was taken in handcuffs through the streets and insulted by the police before being sent to Toulon. In the notorious *bagnes* of Toulon, the Governor placed his own room at his disposal and treated him with every courtesy. He was starved and brutally ill-treated by the captain and officers of the two ships that took him from Toulon to Bordeaux and from Bordeaux to Brest, where he was transferred to a third ship and treated with kindness by the captain and officers who took him from Brest to Cayenne. In Cayenne he was imprisoned both on the mainland and on Devil's Island, where his only complaint was that he had to queue a long time for his daily food ration.[19]

The authorities believed that the assassination of the Emperor on 14 January had been intended to be the signal for revolutionary uprisings throughout France. The official propaganda therefore emphasized that even if the attempt on the Emperor's life had been successful, the army would have rallied to the support of the infant Prince Imperial and his heroic mother, whose coolness and courage on 14 January had so greatly impressed the people. The Chambers hastily passed a law appointing Eugénie as Regent for the baby in the event of the Emperor's death, and *Le Moniteur* published the text of many messages of loyalty from army regiments, from the judges, and from public bodies. Those from the army proclaimed their devotion to the Empress, to whom they would rally if, like a second Maria Theresia of Austria, she appealed to them to protect her and her infant son; they would encircle the cradle of the Prince Imperial with their bayonets, would ensure that the dynasty of the Napoleons would reign for ever in France, and would cry: 'Napoleon III is dead! Long live Napoleon IV!'[20]

Some of the messages reflected, at least by implication, the national feeling with regard to England. The 82nd Infantry Regiment stated that

the wild beasts which periodically leave foreign soil to flood the streets of your capital with blood, fill us with disgust; and if Your Majesty needs soldiers to reach these men even in their lairs, we humbly pray you to select the 82nd Regiment as part of the vanguard of this army.

The 2nd Brigade of the 1st Infantry Division at Lyons stated that 'it is not enough for the army to form a rampart around its sovereign; it is ready to shed its blood anywhere in order to reach and destroy the artisans of regicide'.[21] The 1st Regiment of Engineers asked if 'your faithful army is destined to remain for ever, with arms in hand, as peaceful spectators of these frightful plots which are periodically launched from abroad to bring desolation into our country'.[22] The 22nd Infantry Regiment thought 'it is impossible to consider as friends those governments which are capable of giving asylum to these bandits'.[23]

The first reaction of the British press to the bombs had been to express their horror of terrorism, their admiration for Eugénie's courage, and their esteem for Napoleon III.[24] But public opinion in Britain reacted against the Law of the Suspects, the anti-British mood in France, and the messages from the army regiments in *Le Moniteur*. The statements about destroying the wild beasts in their lairs were quoted in full in the British press, which did not point out that only five out of a total of 157 messages published in *Le Moniteur* could by any stretch of the imagination be construed as referring to Britain.

Walewski sent notes to the governments of Britain, Belgium and Switzerland, asking them to expel the French and Italian Red refugees on their territory who were plotting the assassination of the Emperor of the French. The Belgians as usual were the most compliant; they immediately suppressed three Socialist newspapers and expelled some of the refugees. The Swiss promised to introduce legislation to give the Federal government greater powers to expel aliens from the cantons. In Britain, Palmerston's government introduced the Conspiracy to Murder Bill to deal with residents in Britain who attempted to murder foreign sovereigns, though many lawyers believed that the English common law already gave the courts the necessary powers to deal with this crime.

The bill aroused great opposition in Britain. The Radicals organized a press campaign against it, and held a demonstration in Hyde Park. Some demonstrators marched to the French embassy in Albert Gate intending to burn an effigy of Napoleon III in front of the embassy windows, but they were dispersed by the police.[25] The Conservative Opposition at first supported the bill, but on the second reading in the House of Commons Disraeli could not resist the temptation to play party politics. He led the Conservative M.P.s into the division lobby in support of the Radicals who opposed the bill, which was defeated by a majority of 19. Palmerston resigned. The Conservatives took office with Lord Derby as Prime Minister, Disraeli as Chancellor of the Exchequer, and Malmesbury as Foreign Secretary.

The trial of Orsini, Rudio, Pieri and Gomez opened in the Paris Assize Court on 25 February. Popular opinion was violently against them; in the aristocratic and middle-class drawing-rooms, the ladies were saying that legislation should be introduced to allow Orsini to be tortured before execution. He was defended at his trial by Jules

Favre, who had been a Radical deputy in the National Assembly in 1848, and after the *coup d'état* had retired from politics and practised at the bar. Orsini told Favre that he knew he would be convicted and executed, but hoped to have the opportunity of making a statement in court explaining his motives for wishing to assassinate the Emperor. Favre, who often appeared for the defence at the trial of Reds, knew that the Judge would be on the alert to stop him from using the trial to make political propaganda. He was sure that the Judge would prevent Orsini's statement from being read in court; but he also knew that there was one man in supreme authority in France whose sympathy for Italian nationalism and whose natural generosity might cause him to overrule the Judge. Favre suggested to Orsini that he should draft his statement in the form of a letter to the Emperor.

Orsini at first refused, but ultimately agreed. He wrote to Louis Napoleon, stating that he had nothing against him personally or against the people of France, and had once looked to France to rescue Italy from Austrian oppression; but after Louis Napoleon destroyed the Roman Republic, he decided that he was the chief enemy of Italian and European freedom, and must be removed if freedom was to flourish. He did not now ask the Emperor for a pardon, as he knew that his life was forfeit for his crime; instead, he asked him to reverse his Italian policy and to liberate Italy from Austria, as his great predecessor Napoleon had done.

The problem was how to ensure that the Emperor read Orsini's letter, because Favre knew that the government officials and the imperial secretariat were adept at preventing letters and petitions from reaching Louis Napoleon, especially in cases where they thought that he would be likely to grant the writer's request.* But Favre contacted the Chief of the Paris Police, Piétri, who on several occasions visited Orsini in prison to interrogate him. The Corsican Piétri had pro-Italian sympathies, and he personally delivered Orsini's letter to Louis Napoleon. The Emperor was moved by the letter, just as he had been by the letter that Barbès wrote to him during the Crimean War. He made a few minor alterations in Orsini's letter and sent a message by Piétri to Favre, telling him that he could inform the Judge at the trial that he had the Emperor's permission to read out the letter in court.[26]

When the trial opened, and the hated Orsini appeared in the dock

---

*The Liberal economist, Wolowski, meeting Louis Napoleon at a reception about this time, discovered that Louis Napoleon had never received a letter that he had written to him some months before. One petitioner was so convinced that Louis Napoleon had never read the petitions sent to him that he walked around the streets near the Bourse with a paper stuck in his hat containing the words 'The Emperor does not know'. For this he was arrested and sentenced to a term of imprisonment.[27]

with his three colleagues, he made a very favourable impression, especially among the fashionable ladies who a few days earlier had been saying that he ought to be tortured. He was a strikingly handsome man of forty, with the manners of a perfect gentleman and a cool and courageous bearing; and by the second day of the trial the ladies had fallen in love with him. Favre asked permission to read out in court the letter that Orsini had written to the Emperor, and announced that he had the Emperor's permission to do this. The Judge could not, of course, refuse, and the letter was not only read out in court but was published in *Le Moniteur* and the other Paris newspapers in their very full reports of the day's proceedings in court.[28]

Hübner protested to Walewski against the publication of the letter in *Le Moniteur*, which he claimed was an unfriendly act towards Austria. Walewski expressed his regret, and ordered a secret investigation to discover who had slipped up and allowed the letter to reach the Emperor. When he discovered that it was Piétri, he was furious but powerless. The letter was published, from *Le Moniteur*, in the foreign press, and very prominently in the Turin newspapers.[29]

The four defendants were all found guilty, and sentenced to death; but Orsini's letter and his conduct at the trial won him so much sympathy that there was a strong movement, especially among society women, in favour of a reprieve. Eugénie, who on 21 January had written to Paca that the capture of 'these wretches' proved that 'it was the will of Providence that the crime should not remain unpunished',[30] now used all her influence with Louis Napoleon in favour of a reprieve. It was only with great difficulty that she was prevented from visiting Orsini in the condemned cell. Louis Napoleon too wished to commute the sentence on Orsini, but his ministers strongly opposed this, and said that it would be regarded as an act of weakness. They also pointed out the anomaly of pardoning Orsini, whose bombs had killed eight people, whereas Pianori had been executed for an attempt on the Emperor's life, although he had not killed or even wounded anyone at all. This argument had no effect on Eugénie; she said that Orsini was a patriot, and an idealist, not a vulgar murderer like Pianori, and that although there had been other victims of the bombs of 14 January, she and the Emperor, as Orsini's prime target, were entitled to pardon him if they wished.*[31]

Louis Napoleon informed the Cabinet that he had decided to commute the death sentence on all the four defendants. The ministers protested, and threatened to resign. Fould reminded the Emperor that

*For Eugénie's kindness to Orsini's wife and children at the time of the execution, see the letter of Signora Emestina Spadoni (Orsini's daughter) to Luzio, 20 July 1913 (Luzio, *Felice Orsini*, pp. 314–15n.).

French blood had been shed in the Rue Lepelletier. This argument seemed to shake the Emperor. The Archbishop of Paris was consulted, and he suggested, as a compromise, that two of the guilty men should be pardoned, but that Orsini and one of the others should die. The Emperor then commuted the sentence on Rudio and Gomez to imprisonment for life, but agreed to the execution of Orsini and Pieri.[32]

The ministers were determined that Orsini should be executed before 16 March, which was the Prince Imperial's birthday, for they feared that the Emperor would go back on his decision and use the birthday as a pretext for pardoning Orsini and Pieri.[33] The two men were guillotined in a snowstorm at dawn on 13 March. Their last words were 'Long live Italy! Long live France!'[34]

The defeat of the Conspiracy to Murder Bill and the fall of Palmerston's government had further soured Anglo-French relations; but both Louis Napoleon, and Derby and Malmesbury, were eager to play down the anti-British and anti-French feeling in their respective countries. Derby's government therefore decided to go ahead with the prosecution of Dr Simon Bernard. If Bernard could be convicted under the existing common law of England, this would prove that the Conspiracy to Murder Bill was unnecessary.[35]

Bernard came before the magistrate at Bow Street on 23 February and was committed for trial at the Central Criminal Court on a charge of being an accessory to a murder committed in the Rue Lepelletier in Paris on 14 January. His counsel applied for bail on the grounds that Bernard, although a foreigner, was a gentleman by station; but the magistrate said that he would refuse bail on a murder charge even to an English gentleman, and Bernard was held in custody until his trial began at the Old Bailey before the aged Lord Campbell, the Lord Chief Justice, and a jury on 12 April 1858.[36]

Bernard was defended by Mr Edwin James, Q.C., M.P., who, after starting life as an actor, became a successful criminal defence advocate, and had recently caused a political sensation by unexpectedly winning a Parliamentary by-election at Marylebone as a Radical candidate. He decided to appeal to the English insular prejudices of the jury. When two low-ranking Paris policemen were called by the prosecution to give what was expected to be formal evidence that a man had been killed as a result of the bomb explosions in the Rue Lepelletier on 14 January, Mr James asked each of them, in cross-examination, whether he was the chief of the French Emperor's secret police. The chief witness for the prosecution was Mrs Rudio, a very pretty nineteen-year-old English girl from Nottingham who worked in a lace factory there before she married Rudio. She gave evidence that she had been present when Bernard and Rudio discussed how to assassinate Napoleon

Marianne de Walewska

Countess of Castiglione in 1860

Napoleon III and the Prince
Imperial, in 1859

Cartoon of Napoleon III
walking on the beach at
Biarritz in 1863, by Wilfrid
Scawen Blunt

III. Edwin James handled her very gently, but pointed out that whereas Orsini and Pieri had been guillotined, Rudio's death sentence had been commuted; that she had been taken from Nottingham to Paris at the French government's expense and allowed to visit her husband in prison on several occasions; and that she was now staying at the Bedford Hotel in London with detectives of the French secret police who refused to allow anyone to have access to her.

Mr James was less gentle with Detective-Sergeant Rogers of the Metropolitan Police who had attended private Radical meetings in plain clothes and had taken shorthand notes of the speeches made there, including speeches in which Bernard had attacked the Emperor of the French in violent language. Mr James denounced Rogers the spy – 'I will not hesitate to call him so in an English court' – and wondered whether Rogers's next assignment would be to go down to the House of Commons and report what he heard there to his superiors.

On 16 April, James made his final address to the jury. He told them that he would not attempt to explain the intricacies of French politics, because 'thank God we cannot appreciate such a state of things in this country, living as we do under the undisturbed sway of a sovereign whom all loved and revered'. He said that he deplored the killing of people in the streets of Paris on 14 January 1858, but deplored even more the killing of hundreds of people in the streets of Paris on 4 December 1851, 'when a drunken French soldiery were let loose upon an unresisting mass of men, women and children'.

At last he reached his peroration. He asked the jury to do their duty as English jurymen and to give a verdict which would not only do justice to Bernard but would be a proper answer to the man who had bullied the British government into bringing this prosecution.

Tell him that the verdicts of English juries are founded on the eternal and immutable principles of justice. Tell him that, panoplied in that armour, no threat of armament or invasion can awe you. Tell him that, though 600,000 French bayonets glittered before you, though the roar of French cannon thundered in your ears, you will return a verdict which your own breasts and consciences will sanctify and approve, careless whether that verdict pleases or displeases a foreign despot, or secures or shakes and destroys for ever the throne which a tyrant has built upon the ruins of the liberty of a once free and mighty people.

Next day Lord Campbell, in his summing up, told the jury to disregard all the irrelevant things that Mr James had said about French politics and to consider only the evidence; but after retiring for half an hour they returned a verdict of Not Guilty. It was greeted with an outburst of applause in the court; people rose to their feet and cheered, society ladies waved their handkerchiefs at Bernard, and the jurymen crowded round the dock to shake his hand. There was another demonstration in the street outside the Old Bailey when both he and Edwin James were carried shoulder high by their supporters.[37]

The case made Edwin James a public hero. Three years later, it was discovered that he had been engaging in improper financial transactions. He was disbarred and adjudicated bankrupt, and became an actor on the New York stage.

The French press was more restrained than might have been expected in its comments on the Bernard case. *La Patrie*, writing more in sorrow than in anger, said that the verdict and the scenes outside the Old Bailey were disgraceful, but that the Emperor had expressed the wish that they should refrain from criticism of England, as it was more important to preserve friendly relations with their wartime ally than to express the indignation felt by every Frenchman. Eugénie wrote to Lord Cowley protesting against the verdict. She said that she was not vindictive, and had interceded for Orsini, but that to make a hero of an assassin like Bernard was unforgivable.[38]

The whole British Establishment, from Queen Victoria downwards, condemned the acquittal of Bernard.[39] Mérimée was able to confirm this when he came to London to see Panizzi in April 1858. Mérimée had been appointed Curator of the Bibliothèque Impériale – today the Bibliothèque Nationale – and Panizzi, the Librarian of the British Museum, who was compiling the Catalogue of Books, was very pleased to give Mérimée the benefit of his experience. Mérimée found not only collaboration in academic circles, but also great indignation among his English friends that the 'jury of drapers' had acquitted Bernard.[40]

While Mérimée was in London he was approached by 'a very pretty woman' – she was Lady Tennent, the wife of the Irish politician – who offered to sell him some original letters written by Napoleon I to Josephine from Italy soon after their marriage; in one of them, Napoleon wrote that he wished he was in Josephine's bedroom watching her undress instead of being with the army in Italy. Mérimée thought it essential to buy these letters in order to suppress them, for it would be dreadful if it were known that Napoleon, in his hour of glory in Italy, had been thinking of his wife undressing in her bedroom; but as Lady Tennent asked £40 each for the letters, he thought he ought to refer the decision to the Emperor in Paris. Louis Napoleon refused to agree to the purchase, saying that he doubted the authenticity of the letters. Mérimée was sure that they were genuine, but could understand that the Emperor refused to buy them at a price which was so exorbitant as to savour of blackmail.[41]

Louis Napoleon hoped to improve relations with Britain by recalling Persigny from the London embassy, where he had become unpopular with Malmesbury and the Conservative government, who suspected that he was passing on diplomatic secrets to his friend Palmerston.[42] The new ambassador was Marshal Pélissier, the conqueror of Sevastopol, who in honour of his victory had been created Duc de Malakoff. In 1858, at the age of sixty-three, he unexpectedly married a twenty-five-year-old Spanish girl who was a protégée and a distant relative of the Countess of Montijo. He lacked the social graces, and many stories were told about his outrageous behaviour. Once when he was the Emperor's guest at Compiègne, he was taken by the Emperor and Empress in their carriage on a drive through the forest to Pierrefonds, when suddenly, so the story went, he asked the coachman to stop the carriage, and, climbing out, relieved himself by the roadside in full view of the Empress and her ladies. The Emperor was so angry that he ordered the coachman to drive on, leaving Pélissier behind.[43]

When Pélissier reached London, he committed further gaucheries. He was supposed to have told Queen Victoria and Prince Albert a coarse joke, which the Queen did not understand but the Prince did. On one occasion, he said in the hearing of his guests at the dinner table that he hoped that he and his wife would have a baby next year. When he was invited to stay at a country house, he arrived without a valet, and carrying his own bag.[44] But his appointment was very popular in England. He was cheered when he showed himself in the streets of London, because the people remembered him as the hero of the Crimea;[45] and despite all the stories to the contrary, he made a favourable impression on Queen Victoria. She found 'the little Marshal' clever and agreeable, 'as simple & naif as a child – making the most amusing Remarks', and 'not at all so very fat but broad & stout & very little'.[46]

CAVOUR AND CHERBOURG

WHEN Thiers heard about the enactment of the 'Law of the
Suspects' and the new wave of deportations which followed
the bombs of 14 January, he commented that though terrorists do not
succeed in assassinating sovereigns, they can make them commit
blunders.[1] But Orsini's assassination attempt not only provoked Louis
Napoleon into pursuing unpopular repressive policies; it also made it
possible for his enemies to spread the most unjustified of all their
slanders – that he adopted a pro-Italian policy and went to war in 1859
because he feared that otherwise he would be assassinated. The story
was widely believed in France, and was spread abroad by the two
ambassadors in Paris, Hübner and Cowley, who were most hostile to
Louis Napoleon's policy. It was said that Louis Napoleon in his youth
had been a member of the Carbonari; that Orsini's bombs made him
realize that the Carbonari had resolved to put him to death because he
had betrayed the organization; and that he therefore agreed to carry
out the policy which the Carbonari required, as the only way of saving
his life.[2] This absurd story is contradicted by the many examples of
Louis Napoleon's personal courage; it overlooks the fact that the
Carbonari had ceased to exist for many years before 1858, and that the
Mazzinian and other Italian terrorists would have had no interest in
punishing its defectors; it does not explain why Orsini's bombs influenced Louis Napoleon in this way when the daggers of Pianori and
Tibaldi had failed to do so; nor does it account for the foreign policy
which Louis Napoleon had been pursuing for more than a year before
14 January 1858.

The bomb-throwing of the Rue Lepelletier was in fact a setback for
Louis Napoleon's policy of forming an anti-Austrian alliance with
Piedmont. It had never been more difficult than in the first weeks after
14 January to persuade the French people to go to war to liberate
Italy, for the first effect of the bombs was to arouse a feeling of hatred
in France, not only for Mazzinian terrorists but for all Italians; and it
caused a temporary estrangement between France and Piedmont.
On 20 January, Walewski sent a note to Turin demanding in peremptory tones that the government of Piedmont suppress the Mazzinian

newspapers and take firmer action against the Piedmontese revolutionaries; and Louis Napoleon, in a personal letter to Victor Emanuel, asked him to suppress Mazzini's newspaper, *L'Italia del Popolo*, which he thought ought to be called 'l'Italia del diavolo'.[3] Victor Emanuel and Cavour, who were already harassing the Mazzinians by all means which the law of Piedmont allowed, were reluctant to interfere with the law of the freedom of the press. 'I can shoot Mazzini if I catch him,' wrote Cavour, 'and bombard Genoa if it stirs, but if I brutally lay hands on the press law I lose my prestige.'[4] The King and Cavour were annoyed by the tone of Walewski's demand, and sent a defiant answer. After some weeks of tension, Louis Napoleon accepted the position, and told the Piedmontese envoy that he admired Victor Emanuel for having the courage to resist him.

As soon as the initial anger against Italians had evaporated, Louis Napoleon resumed his preparations for an alliance with Piedmont. He pursued the negotiations secretly, behind the back of his own Foreign Minister. In March he sent Dr Conneau to Turin on what was ostensibly a private visit, but with secret instructions to propose to Victor Emanuel and Cavour that France and Piedmont should go to war with Austria in order to drive Austria out of Northern Italy and to acquire Lombardy and Venetia for Piedmont. For the first, but not for the last, time he used Eugénie as an agent in his secret diplomacy; in May she was dropping hints to the Piedmontese ambassador, Nigra, that Italy should be divided into three states – Northern Italy, Central Italy and Naples.[5] Louis Napoleon also proposed that Prince Napoleon should marry Victor Emanuel's daughter, Princess Marie Clotilde. Victor Emanuel and Cavour welcomed the idea of a war against Austria, but considered it necessary to discuss the matter with Louis Napoleon himself; and Louis Napoleon, without informing Walewski, arranged a secret meeting with Cavour at Plombières where he again went to take the waters in July 1858.

On 11 July, Cavour left Turin for a holiday with his friends the Comte and Comtesse de la Rive at their château near Geneva, where he made his presence known by attending a shooting match at the local rifle club; but on 18 July he secretly went to Strasburg and took the train to Plombières, travelling incognito on a passport in a false name and sitting as unobtrusively as possible in the corner of a first-class carriage immersed in the first volume of Buckle's *History of Civilization in England*.[6] He arrived in Plombières in the early evening of 19 July, and at eleven o'clock next morning* visited Louis Napoleon at the

*There is no doubt that Cavour stayed two nights in Plombières, and spent the intervening day in talks with Louis Napoleon; but there is a surprising conflict of reliable evidence as to whether these talks took place on 20 or 21 July; cf. Cavour to

Grand Hotel and spent four hours with him. While they were talking, the Emperor's secretary brought him a telegram from Walewski in Paris, informing the Emperor that Cavour had entered France incognito at Strasburg.[7]

Four days later, Cavour wrote a report to Victor Emanuel of his talk with Louis Napoleon. It is quite clear from this report that Louis Napoleon had a much clearer grasp than Cavour of the realities of the situation and that he, and not Cavour, was the architect of the Franco-Piedmontese alliance and the war of 1859. He told Cavour that he was prepared to go to war against Austria in alliance with Piedmont and was confident that they could win a quick victory in Northern Italy provided that the conflict did not develop into a general European war. The neutrality of Russia, Britain and Prussia was an essential prerequisite of Louis Napoleon's policy. He had received a promise of neutrality from Russia. Britain was traditionally Austria's ally against France, and would certainly be suspicious of a French attack on Austria; but sympathy with the cause of Italian freedom was so strong in Britain that it would be politically almost impossible for a British government to enter the war on Austria's side. There remained the problem of Prussia, who was Austria's colleague in the German Confederation; but Louis Napoleon believed that Austro-Prussian rivalries would ensure that Prussia would remain neutral and would not cause a diversion by attacking France on the Rhine.

Louis Napoleon told Cavour that in order to ensure British and Prussian neutrality it was important to find a plausible pretext for war. Cavour suggested that Austria's refusal to renew the commercial treaty with Piedmont would give Piedmont an excuse for declaring war. Louis Napoleon rejected this preposterous suggestion, and said that a failure to renew a commercial treaty would nowhere be accepted as a justification for war. Cavour then proposed that the presence of Austrian troops in the Romagna in the Papal States should be given as the reason for war. Louis Napoleon dismissed this idea as well, because Piedmont had tolerated their presence there for many years, and France could not complain of this when Louis Napoleon himself maintained troops in Rome. He suggested that Piedmontese agents should incite a revolution at Massa in the Duke of Modena's territories,

---

Villamarina, 21 July 1858 (Chiala, *Lettere di Cavour*, II.321); Napoleon III to Victor Emanuel, 20 July 1858 (*Cavour-Nigra*, I.103); *L'Indépendance Belge*, 23 July 1858; *The Times*, 26 July 1858; Hübner, II.201 (who states that Walewski told him that the Emperor's meeting with Cavour took place on 'Tuesday', i.e. 20 July). Although 21 July has been generally accepted as the date, 20 July seems a little more likely; but the point is of no real importance.

in the hope of provoking an Austrian ultimatum to Piedmont which Piedmont could reject and thus cause Austria to declare war.

They then discussed the peace treaty which they would impose on defeated Austria. The Austrian provinces of Lombardy and Venetia, the duchies of Modena, Parma and Lucca, and the Papal provinces of the Romagna and the Marches should be transferred to Piedmont, which would become the kingdom of Northern Italy; the Papal province of Umbria and the Grand Duchy of Tuscany should form the kingdom of Central Italy, with the Duchess of Parma appointed as Queen; Rome and the surrounding territory, known as the Patrimony of St Peter, would be retained by the Pope; and the kingdom of Naples, which Louis Napoleon hoped would one day be given to his cousin Murat, would for the time being remain under the hated King Ferdinand as the fourth independent state of the Italian peninsula.

Louis Napoleon proposed that, in return for French assistance, Piedmont should cede the province of Savoy and the town of Nice to France, because the French people would expect France to derive some national advantage from the war, and he would not be able to justify himself in the eyes of his subjects if he asked them to shed their blood altruistically for the advantage of Italy alone. Cavour saw the strength of this argument, and agreed to the cession of Savoy; but he objected to ceding Nice, which was not a French-speaking district like Savoy, but an Italian town. Louis Napoleon agreed to defer a decision about Nice.

They ended their talk at 3 p.m., but the Emperor asked Cavour to return at 4 p.m., when the two men went for a drive alone together in the Emperor's carriage, with the Emperor taking the reins, and escorted by only one horseman who rode a little way behind. They drove for three hours through the woods of the Vosges, and discussed the Emperor's proposal for the marriage of Prince Napoleon and Princess Clotilde. Cavour explained as tactfully as possible that Victor Emanuel was not eager for his daughter to marry Prince Napoleon, who at thirty-six was twice Marie Clotilde's age and was known to have several mistresses – though no more than Victor Emanuel himself. Louis Napoleon spoke up strongly in his cousin's favour; he admitted that Prince Napoleon was sometimes indiscreet and tactless, but insisted that he was a good fellow at heart.

They returned to Plombières and separated after Louis Napoleon had given Cavour a letter for Victor Emanuel and had shaken him warmly by the hand. Next morning Cavour took the train for Baden.

Cavour had been spotted in Plombières. A few days later Hübner in Paris was attending the Conference on the Danubian principalities at the Foreign Office. He was just about to enter the Conference chamber when he was told of a report in *L'Indépendance Belge* that Cavour was having secret talks with Napoleon III at Plombières. Villamarina, the Piedmontese delegate to the Conference, said that there was no truth in the story; but Walewski's obvious embarrassment at the news convinced Hübner that the report must be true. Within a day or two the press in every country in Europe had reported Cavour's presence in Plombières.[8]

It was not uncommon for foreign statesmen who happened to be in the vicinity to pay courtesy visits to Napoleon III during his annual holiday at Plombières or Vichy, and if Cavour had done this without any attempt at secrecy he might not have stirred up the diplomatic excitement and speculation that took place at the end of July and the beginning of August 1858. The Piedmontese newspapers were the best informed and most indiscreet; several of them reported that Napoleon III and Cavour had reached a secret understanding at Plombières to make war on Austria in the following spring.[9]

After the secrecy of Plombières came the great publicity of Cherbourg, where Louis Napoleon and Eugénie arrived on 3 August for the quadruple purpose of inaugurating the new Paris–Cherbourg railway line, opening a deep-water dock, unveiling a statue of Napoleon I – who first thought of making Cherbourg an important port – and meeting Queen Victoria in an attempt to improve Anglo-French relations.[10] Cherbourg was crowded out with visitors. It had a resident population of 20,000, but 60,000 visitors arrived there in the first days of August, most of them coming from Paris, where there were queues of over 700 people at the Préfecture for the internal passports which they needed to allow them to travel to Cherbourg. As there was no room for them in the hotels at Cherbourg, the Chemins-de-Fer de l'Ouest erected temporary accommodation for them near the railway station and provided them with a theatre where the best actors from Paris, including Eugénie Doche, Hyacinthe and Grassot, took part in performances in aid of the local charities. The building of the single-track railway had been a great engineering feat, for it crossed seventy bridges over rivers and streams and passed under 310 road viaducts. The work had been largely carried out by British engineers, several of whom were awarded the Legion of Honour by the Emperor on this happy occasion.

For the opening of the great dock by the Emperor, the authorities had erected an elaborate series of promenades from which the public could look down at the dock. The peasants held out their little children most precariously to enable them to see the concrete basin of the dock nearly twenty-five metres below; but there were no fatal accidents.

Louis Napoleon and Eugénie received a great welcome from the people of Cherbourg. Eleven thousand medallions of the Emperor's head were sold on the quayside for five francs apiece in one day. The weather was glorious throughout the four days of the festivities. The only mishap occurred at the opening of the dock: the Emperor pressed the appropriate button, but only a trickle of water ran into the empty basin instead of the impressive onrush which had been intended. There was another slip-up of which the public knew nothing. When the Emperor's Chamberlain, Chaumont-Quitry, brought Walewski for an audience with the Emperor in his hotel at Cherbourg, Chaumont-Quitry opened the door of the Emperor's room and he and Walewski saw Louis Napoleon kissing Madame de Walewska. But Walewski as usual managed not to see anything.[11]

Queen Victoria came from England with Prince Albert and the Prince of Wales, as did the Duke of Cambridge, Admiral Lord Lyons, Malmesbury, Disraeli, thirty M.P.s and 140 private English yachts. The Queen's arrival was greeted with a salute from the three thousand guns of the great fortress of Fort Roule and the warships; and every movement that either the Queen or the Emperor made was accompanied by salvoes which shook the yachts in the harbour, including those at quite a distance from the shore. The Emperor and the Queen entertained each other at banquets on their yachts, and there were happy speeches from the Emperor and the Prince Consort on Anglo-French friendship.[12] At first, Louis Napoleon was a little colder and more reserved than he had been at his previous meetings with Queen Victoria – 'rather "boutonné" ' was the Queen's expression – but there was no change in Eugénie's attitude; she was 'so amiable, so clever, & agreeable'. Afterwards the Emperor thawed, and spoke frankly to the Queen about the strained relations between Britain and France.[13] Both his attitude and Eugénie's were probably the result of careful calculation on his part.

The Emperor took the Queen and Prince to see Fort Roule, and after driving up the steep climb to the summit of the fort, the Emperor and Empress, and the Queen and Prince, and their escorts of admirals and A.D.C.s walked down from the fort to a banquet at the town hall, a distance of over a mile – for both Queen Victoria and Napoleon III, like most of their contemporaries, enjoyed walking. As they passed between the lines of troops and onlookers, the people shouted 'Vive l'Empereur!' 'If you wish to please the Emperor, cry "Vive la Reine!" ', said Louis Napoleon.[14]

But at lower levels it was not so easy to maintain Anglo-French friendship.[15] The correspondent of *The Times* in Cherbourg wrote slightingly about the street decorations and the hundreds of golden eagles on the lamp-posts; he thought they were inferior to the decorations at a very ordinary English fair. As for Fort Roule, he wrote that

'Cherbourg protects the Emperor against all the world, and La Roule protects the Emperor against Cherbourg. Not a dog could bark or a cat mew in Cherbourg against his imperial master while a gunner was left in Fort Roule.' But he duly noted, as the French hoped he would, that Fort Roule was impregnable from the sea.[16]

From Cherbourg, Louis Napoleon and Eugénie set out on a tour through Brittany. Louis Napoleon had visited Brittany when he was President of the Republic, but it was the first time that a reigning French sovereign had set foot in the province since Henri IV went there at the head of his army during the Wars of Religion in 1598. Louis Napoleon received a great welcome from the people, and Eugénie delighted everyone by her beauty and elegance and the informal affability with which she accepted the bouquets which the children presented to her in the towns through which they passed.[17]

But the visit to Brittany led to another unhappy Anglo-French incident. *The Morning Post* sent a reporter, Mr William Bernard MacCabe, to report the Emperor's tour. He wrote in enthusiastic terms about the people's welcome to Louis Napoleon and Eugénie;[18] but although he was issued with a passport at the French Consulate in London, he forgot to get it visa'ed when he landed at Cherbourg. When he was travelling through a village on the road from Rennes to Lorient, he was asked to produce it by the village policeman. The policeman caught sight of the name 'Bernard', and at once accused MacCabe of being the infamous conspirator Simon Bernard who had plotted to assassinate the Emperor. He hired a cab and, with another policeman, took MacCabe to police headquarters in Lorient, where MacCabe was questioned and locked up for the night in the cells. Next day he was told that instructions had been received from Paris to release him, but not until he had paid 25 francs for the cost of the cab which brought him to Lorient, plus a surcharge of 16 francs for carrying the two policemen as additional passengers. MacCabe described the incident in *The Morning Post*, and *The Times* protested against this flagrant example of French despotism. MacCabe also wrote to the Emperor and asked for redress. He received in due course a reply from Mocquard informing him that he had only himself to blame because he had not had his passport visa'ed at Cherbourg; the police could not be blamed for holding him until further inquiries had been made, because 'your word alone, however honourable when you are known', could not be expected to satisfy the police who did not know him. The Emperor could therefore give him no compensation beyond expressing regret for the inconvenience which he had suffered.[19]

Almost everything that happened in France somehow became a new cause of Franco-British friction. In February 1858 the fourteen-year-old Bernadette Soubirous saw a vision of her 'lady' in a grotto at Lourdes. At first the local authorities of both Church and State disbelieved her story; but her case was championed by the well-known Ultramontane journalist, Louis Veuillot, in *L'Univers*. When the Minister of Education and Religion, and the Prefect of the Hautes-Pyrénées, issued an order forbidding all access to Bernadette's grotto with its healing water, Veuillot was one of many who defied the law and went to the grotto; and so did the Prince Imperial's governess, Madame Bruat, the widow of Admiral Bruat, who had commanded the fleet in the Crimea. When Louis Napoleon was at Biarritz in September 1858, the Archbishop of Auch persuaded him to rescind the Minister's order and to authorize the opening of the grotto; and he ordered Fould – who was hated as a Jew by the Catholic Ultramontanes – to go to Lourdes to make sure that the Prefect had reopened the grotto.[20]

In France, the argument eventually ended with the vindication of Bernadette; but the British press, with *The Times* in the lead, launched a violent attack on 'the White Lady of Lourdes' as a blasphemous lie propagated by Veuillot, who had recently stated that all the disasters of the nineteenth century would have been prevented if Luther had been burned as a heretic three hundred years before. Bernadette unconsciously played her part in presenting the Second Empire to the British public as a dark realm of Papist ignorance, superstition and tyranny.[21]

The British press launched another attack on Napoleon III when some French sailors on the merchant ship the *Regina Coeli* off the west coast of Africa were killed by a band of African Negroes on board the ship. The Negroes escaped to the Spanish colony of Sierra Leone, and as the Spanish authorities granted them asylum, the French government demanded compensation from Spain for the deaths of the sailors. The Negroes were being taken to the new colony of Senegal which the French were establishing on the west coast of Africa under a scheme by which Negroes in the Spanish and Portuguese colonies were persuaded to sign five-year contracts of employment and were taken on French ships to Senegal. The British press accused Louis Napoleon of re-establishing the slave trade under another name; and in a debate in the House of Lords, Earl Grey praised the Negroes who had killed the French sailors on the *Regina Coeli* as heroes who were fighting for their freedom against the slave-traders.[22] The French press indignantly denounced the British attitude. *Le Constitutionnel* suggested that the British philanthropists would be better employed in bewailing the atrocities committed by their own troops in suppressing the Indian Mutiny rather than in protesting about conditions in the French colonies, where 'no one has shot, hanged, or tied to the mouths of cannons thousands of prisoners without any form of trial', or handed over towns 'to all the passions of the soldiery, that is to say, to pillage, rape and murder'.[23]

In September 1858 the Portuguese navy seized a French ship, the *Charles et Georges*, which was bringing a cargo of Negroes from Mozambique to Senegal. The Portuguese judge ruled that the *Charles et Georges* was slave-trading, and the ship was taken to Lisbon as prize. Louis Napoleon denounced the seizure of the *Charles et Georges* as an act of piracy, and demanded her release with an apology and compensation; and when the Portuguese government refused, he sent the French fleet to Lisbon and threatened to blockade the port unless he obtained full satisfaction for this insult to the French flag. He rejected the Portuguese proposal to refer the dispute to the mediation of a third power, and Portugal gave in and complied with all the French demands. Public opinion in Britain was incensed, and Derby's government was criticized for allowing Louis Napoleon to bully Britain's ally Portugal.[24] As soon as the Portuguese had yielded, Louis Napoleon announced that as it had been suggested that the Negroes brought to Senegal were being taken there against their will, he had ordered the project to be suspended until the allegations had been investigated; and it was quietly abandoned.[25]

In June 1858 Montalembert went to England and during his visit listened to a debate in the House of Commons. He thereupon published an article in *Le Correspondant*[26] in which he praised the British Parliamentary system, criticized the French press for sympathizing with the mutinous sepoys in India, and stated that he went to London 'to breathe an air more pure, and to take a life-bath in free England'. When he returned to France he was prosecuted for insulting the Emperor and the Constitution of the Empire, because by praising the freedom that prevailed in England he had implied that a similar freedom did not exist in France.

The prosecution of Montalembert was of course fiercely denounced in Britain, where it was feared that if he were convicted by Louis Napoleon's docile judges, he would be sentenced to a short term of imprisonment, after which the Minister of the Interior would be able at any time in the future to send him to Cayenne. His conviction would also entail a loss of his political rights, which would prohibit him from sitting in the Chamber or publishing articles in the press. After a trial which was widely reported in the foreign press – the French newspapers were forbidden to report it by a decree of the Minister of the Interior – Montalembert was found guilty and sentenced to six months' imprisonment and a fine of 3000 francs. He gave notice of appeal, but to his indignation the Emperor pardoned him and remitted the sentence before his appeal could be heard, and in view of this, the Court of Appeal declared itself incompetent to hear the appeal.[27]

Louis Napoleon and Eugénie went as usual to Compiègne for their autumn visit in 1858. Palmerston was one of the guests that year, though he had hesitated before accepting the hospitality of Napoleon III, fearing that it would be politically compromising in Britain.[28] After he had left Compiègne, a select group of guests remained for the final week. There were outings to Pierrefonds and amateur dramatics, in which the Comtesse de Walewska was cast in the role of a pretty peasant girl. Walewski was not very pleased to see his wife dressed up as a peasant, but Marianne herself did not mind, though she objected to having to refer to another actor as her 'lover'; she wished to change 'lover' to 'a man who is in love with me'. Mérimée opposed the alteration, and quoted the authority of the Académie to show that 'amant' did not necessarily imply any more than 'a man who is in love' with a woman; but Marianne got her way, and the script was changed.[29] The other actors could understand her reluctance, in all the circumstances, to refer to her 'lover', especially in view of the gossip that was going on about the Emperor's recent gift of a country mansion and park to Walewski. No one believed that it was given in appreciation of Walewski's services at the Foreign Office.

On the day before the guests were due to leave Compiègne, Eugénie asked Mérimée to draft a petition to the Emperor, worded in the proper form, which they would all sign, humbly beseeching the Emperor to allow them to remain at Compiègne for a few more days, even if they were fed on nothing but bread and water. Eugénie signed first, signing 'Wife Bonaparte', and insisted that all the other guests should sign. She then gave the petition to the two-and-a-half-year-old Prince Imperial to present to the Emperor. Louis Napoleon informed them most solemnly that their petition had been granted; but next day, when they sat down to dinner with the usual formality, the servants entered and served them all with dry bread and water. After eating his bread and drinking his water, the Emperor rose from the table and prepared to leave the dining room, and the guests had of course to rise and follow him, along with Eugénie, who was as surprised as the rest of them at the dinner that had been served. As the Emperor rose from the table, the servants entered with the first course of an excellent meal, and the Emperor invited them to start dinner again.[30]

The Emperor and Empress returned to the Tuileries in time for Christmas and the receptions on 1 January 1859. The diplomats' New Year's greetings were as usual conveyed by the Papal Nuncio as the doyen of the diplomatic corps, and the Emperor said a few words of greetings to the individual ambassadors. When he came to Hübner, he said: 'I regret that our relations are not as friendly as I would wish, but please write to Vienna and say that my personal feelings towards the Emperor are still unchanged.'[31] Hübner did not immediately see any sinister significance in these words. All the diplomats knew that Franco-Austrian relations had been strained, and Hübner found that while some of those who had heard Louis Napoleon's words to him thought that they were spoken in a spirit of hostility, others believed that he had meant them as a gesture of reconciliation. But Lord Chelsea, the First Secretary at the British embassy, went straight from the Tuileries to the fashionable Union Club in Paris and reported that Louis Napoleon had addressed words to the Austrian Ambassador which meant war. The news spread through Paris, and then abroad, and share values crashed on every Stock Exchange in Europe.[32] The panic grew worse when Victor Emanuel, opening the Piedmontese Parliament on 18 January, declared that he could not close his ears to the 'cry of anguish' which had reached him from the oppressed people in other parts of Italy.

For the next four months the diplomats and journalists waited to see if France and Piedmont would go to war with Austria. In Piedmont there was a passionate desire for war, but in France, although the Radicals and Socialists and many of the working classes supported war, the Church and the middle classes were against it.[33] At first, Hübner found Eugénie very anti-Austrian, as she had been for the past two years; but as the danger grew, and aristocratic and middle-class opinion became increasingly anti-war, Eugénie changed her tone and also became anti-war.[34] As for Louis Napoleon, his attitude was as usual the great enigma for the diplomats. Mérimée thought that he would prefer a war, but that he would not go to war if he could reach a favourable settlement by peaceful means.[35]

Malmesbury worked hard for peace; there was nothing that the British Conservative government wanted less than a war waged by France to liberate Italy. He proposed a Congress of the Great Powers to settle the problems of Italy, and supported the Austrian demand that Piedmont should disarm. Louis Napoleon had always made it clear to Cavour that he would only go to war if the Great Powers remained neutral; and in view of their attitude he agreed to the proposal that Piedmont should disarm along the frontier of Lombardy, and that a Congress to settle the affairs of Italy be held in Paris, at which France, Britain, Austria, Prussia, Russia and Piedmont should be represented. In April 1859 Cavour came to Paris to stiffen Louis Napoleon, but could not persuade him to change his position.

Hübner, in Paris, was impressed by the anti-war feeling and was convinced that Napoleon III would not go to war with Austria; but he feared that, by threatening war as a bluff, Napoleon III would force Austria to agree to a Congress at which France and Piedmont would achieve their ends without war and would irrevocably weaken Austrian influence in Italy. At Hübner's suggestion, the Austrian government refused to attend a Congress at which Piedmont was represented, but agreed to a Congress of the five Great Powers to which Piedmont, like the other Italian states, could send observers. On 16 April, at the British embassy, Lord Cowley said thoughtlessly and half-seriously to Hübner that the sensible thing for Austria would be to invade Piedmont, crush the Piedmontese army in a nine-day war as she had done in 1849, and then accept the invitation to a Congress. Hübner thought that this was an excellent suggestion, and passed it on to Vienna.[36]

On 22 April the Austrian Ambassador in Turin presented an ultimatum to the delighted Cavour: unless Piedmont agreed within five days to disarm and withdraw her troops from the Austrian frontier in Lombardy, Austria would declare war. On 25 April the French Ambassador in Vienna told the Austrian government that if Austrian troops crossed the Ticino and invaded Piedmont, France would consider it as a declaration of war on France. The Austrians crossed the Ticino two days later.[37]

CHAPTER 34

THE WAR IN ITALY

ON 3 May, Louis Napoleon issued a proclamation informing his subjects that Austria, by invading Piedmont, had declared war on France. He stated that the French would be fighting for the liberation of mankind, because though 'France has shown her hatred of anarchy ... she has not thereby abandoned her civilizing role'. He was careful to state that he was not going to Italy 'to foment disorder or to shake the power of the Holy Father whom we have replaced on his throne', and gave no hint that he had made a secret treaty with the excommunicates Victor Emanuel and Cavour by which the Holy Father was to be deprived of three-quarters of his territory.[1]

On 10 May he left Paris to take command of his army in Italy, having appointed Eugénie as Regent in his absence. As he rode at the head of the Imperial Guard from the Tuileries along the Rue de Rivoli to the Gare de Lyon he was greeted with tremendous enthusiasm by the people; but this time it was the workmen in *blouses*, not the well-dressed bourgeois, who cheered the loudest, and his greatest reception came as he passed through that old revolutionary quarter, the Faubourg Saint-Antoine. They shouted 'Vive la guerre!' and sang the forbidden 'Marseillaise' without being arrested by the police. Many of the Emperor's Conservative supporters were disquieted.[2]

Eugénie went with Louis Napoleon in the train as far as Montereau, and after a tearful and well-publicized farewell returned to Saint-Cloud to take over the government of France.[3] Prince Napoleon went with the Emperor to Italy, having been appointed to command an army corps. His newly-married wife, Princess Marie Clotilde, Victor Emanuel's daughter, stayed in Paris with Eugénie. They became close friends, for Eugénie never allowed her dislike for Marie Clotilde's husband and father, or her political opinions about Italy, to embitter her against Marie Clotilde, who was as devout a Catholic as herself. The Empress always treated Marie Clotilde with special kindness, and sympathized with her as the wife of a militant atheist who hated and mocked her religion.

Louis Napoleon sailed from Marseilles on the imperial yacht *La*

Reine Hortense, and landed at Genoa on the morning of 12 May. The quay was filled with cheering crowds acclaiming him as the liberator of Italy. Victor Emanuel was not there to greet him, as he had taken command of the Piedmontese army at Alessandria, where he was anxiously awaiting an Austrian drive to capture Turin before the French arrived; but Cavour was at the dockside. When Cavour bowed and attempted to kiss the Emperor's hand, Louis Napoleon would not let him, and instead kissed him on both cheeks, greeting him as 'my dear Cavour'. Louis Napoleon went to the town hall and repeatedly showed himself on the balcony to the cheering crowds. He received another great ovation in the evening at the opera, when he went with Cavour to see *Ione*, which was based on his friend Bulwer Lytton's *Last Days of Pompeii*.[4]

Arese was in Genoa, and he visited Louis Napoleon and thanked him for coming with an army to liberate Italy. Louis Napoleon told him to thank God for having made Franz Joseph send his troops across the Ticino.[5]

The Emperor left for Alessandria next morning, and established his headquarters there. The French succeeded in rushing 200,000 soldiers to Piedmont in twenty-five days, some going by sea to Genoa and others to Turin by railway, which for the first time in history was used as a vital means of communication in wartime. The Austrians, who had a far less well-developed railway system in their rear in Lombardy, moved much more slowly. Their expected attack did not develop, partly because of the rainy weather, but chiefly thanks to the dilatoriness of their Commander-in-Chief, General Gyulai.

The combined French and Piedmontese armies of 270,000 men were placed under the supreme command of Napoleon III. Cavour persuaded the Emperor to agree, somewhat reluctantly, to employ Garibaldi and his little force of volunteers to harass the Austrian right flank by partisan warfare in the mountainous district around Lake Como. The employment of Garibaldi as an auxiliary to the Allied armies alarmed the Conservatives and Catholics in France, though the French press stressed that he was now a reformed character who was no longer dressed in his famous red shirt but in the blue uniform of a Piedmontese Major-General. Prince Napoleon was sent with his army corps to occupy Tuscany. This did his reputation no good, for as no fighting took place in Tuscany throughout the campaign, his presence there did nothing to remove the smear of cowardice which he had acquired, rightly or wrongly, in the Crimea.

By the end of May the bad weather had given way to an exceptionally hot summer in Northern Italy and throughout Europe, and Louis Napoleon advanced his armies across the Ticino. On 4 June they made contact with Gyulai's main army at Magenta. Thanks to faulty intelligence, neither Louis Napoleon nor Gyulai realized at first that a major battle was about to take place; but within an hour or so 54,000 French troops were in action against 58,000 Austrians. Louis Napoleon sat on his horse throughout the battle a little way behind the front line, chain-smoking cigarettes.[6] He was in the line of the Austrian fire – a fact which the press in Paris did not fail to mention. At Magenta, and throughout the campaign, the French suffered a very high casualty rate among their general officers, for the Austrian snipers, recognizing them by their splendid epaulettes, tried to pick them off with considerable success.[7]

Magenta was finally decided by fierce bayonet fighting along the railway line, the bloodiest action being around the local railway station and a farmhouse on the Turbigo road which the Austrians tried to hold at all costs. At nightfall the Austrians withdrew, leaving the French victorious.[8] The French lost 4600 killed, wounded and missing, and the Austrians 10,200. The ground, according to the *Times* correspondent with the French army, was 'like the remains of a great rag fair; shakoes, knapsacks, muskets, shoes, cloaks, tunics, linen all stained with blood'.[9]

At Magenta, the Piedmontese army, which was stationed a few miles away, did not march towards the sound of the gunfire, and took no part at all in the battle. The Piedmontese press nevertheless claimed it as a great Franco-Italian victory, which angered the French soldiers, for the only Italians who fought at Magenta were some conscripts from Lombardy who were serving in the Austrian army. Victor Emanuel, who in minor engagements a few days earlier had shown great personal courage, visited Louis Napoleon's headquarters that evening to apologize for the Piedmontese inaction; but Louis Napoleon was exasperated, and said to Victor Emanuel: 'Sire, when one is in duty bound to join forces in the face of the enemy, a scrupulous adherence to one's obligations and instructions is to be expected. I regret that Your Majesty has not done this.'[10]

As a result of Magenta, the Austrians retreated right across Lombardy to their next line of defence on the River Mincio, and the French and Piedmontese troops entered Milan. For the last eleven years, the capital of Lombardy had been the centre of the active and passive resistance to the Austrians, and had borne the brunt of the reprisals. The people gave an enthusiastic welcome to their liberators. Early on the morning of 8 June, Louis Napoleon and Victor Emanuel, after travelling by train to within fifteen miles of Milan, got out at the little station of Bobbiette and rode into Milan on horseback at the head of their bodyguards. They entered the city at 8 a.m., riding side by side;

the Emperor had the place of honour on the right, but he moved over to the side of the road to allow Victor Emanuel, on his left, to occupy the crown of the road. Next day they both attended the *Te Deum* in the cathedral and a gala performance of the opera at La Scala.[11]

For the Commander-in-Chief and for the civilian population the war had a good deal of glitter; but the *Times* correspondent described what he called the 'darker side', when the hundreds of wounded French soldiers and Austrian prisoners-of-war arrived in Milan after an agonizing journey in the jolting trains, the slightly wounded men sitting with their crutches in third-class compartments, and the seriously wounded lying on straw in the goods carriages. The French wounded were lovingly nursed by the women of Milan; the wounded Austrian prisoners-of-war were less well treated by their Italian nurses, though the French soldiers bore their prisoners no ill-will and often showed them special consideration.[12] At the start of the campaign Louis Napoleon had announced that, for the sake of humanity, he would release all wounded prisoners-of-war without requiring any French prisoners-of-war to be returned in exchange, and the Austrians reciprocated. Louis Napoleon also ordered the French Post Office to make special arrangements to forward letters to and from the prisoners-of-war and their families in Austria.[13]

The French army advanced to the River Adda, moving, in the words of the *Times* correspondent, like a boa-constrictor which moves forward, then coils up, and then uncoils and advances again.[14] The French soldiers marched in the intense heat, not in close formation, like the British army, but as the French army always marched on campaign, each soldier walking at his own pace in groups, in pairs, or singly, like ramblers on a walk. Every man carried in his knapsack his equipment, a large loaf of bread, the hard unsalted biscuit which he ate in his soup, and his piece of the tent in which he and his comrades would sleep at night. They were accompanied by the famous *cantinières* of the French army – the women who cooked their meals, served their drinks, kept up their spirits, and in many cases, as the moralists rightly feared, satisfied their other fundamental desires. On the battlefields the *cantinières* brought water and comfort under fire to wounded soldiers, and several of them were awarded military decorations for their valour.[15]

On 17 June, Louis Napoleon established his headquarters at Brescia, which was decorated and illuminated in his honour and was crowded with French soldiers who filled the cafés and queued up at the tobacconists to buy cigars and tobacco for their pipes.[16] No one knew where the army would be going, because their Commander-in-Chief, Napoleon III, who took all the decisions himself after consulting his staff, was as secretive about his military operations as he always was in his diplomacy; the soldiers said that he 'waged war like a conspirator'.[17] But on 23 June he heard that the Austrians had crossed the Mincio to engage his army. They were commanded by their Emperor, Franz Joseph, himself, who had dismissed Gyulai for incompetence after Magenta and had taken personal command of the army with his headquarters at Verona. Many of his advisers thought that this was an unwise decision; who would be the scapegoat if there was another defeat?

For fifteen hours on 24 June, 107,000 French and 44,000 Piedmontese troops fought a battle against 151,000 Austrians along a twelve-mile front stretching in a semicircle around a number of villages from Pozzolengo in the north, past Castiglione, Solferino, Cavriana and Medole in the centre to Castel Grinaldo in the south.[18] Not since the battle of Leipzig in 1813 had so many men taken part in a battle. The Austrians held all the heights, and at 4 a.m. the French and Piedmontese began the attack to dislodge them. Louis Napoleon, stationing himself first at Castiglione, directed the battle all day under fire, throwing the army corps of Forey, Trochu, Ladmirault and Regnault de St Jean d'Angely into the battle in the morning, and holding those of Canrobert, MacMahon and Niel in reserve until the final stages in the afternoon. Franz Joseph commanded the Austrians from the village of Volta.

Louis Napoleon's enemies in Paris denied that he had shown courage or had been under fire at Solferino. Changarnier, who returned from exile in October 1859 to live quietly in France, told dinner-table stories of Louis Napoleon's cowardice at Solferino, where he had always been at least two miles behind the lines. Changarnier, who knew the man who prepared the Emperor's cigar boxes with twenty-five cigars in each box, told everybody that Louis Napoleon had done nothing during the battle except smoke fifty-three cigars; but officers who were present at Solferino praised Louis Napoleon's courage. One member of the Emperor's staff was killed at his side.[19]

As usual in nineteenth-century battles, a number of civilians wandered on to the battlefield to watch, among them a young Swiss, Henri Dunant, who was on holiday in Italy. He was appalled at the savagery of the fighting, which he vividly described four years later in his book *Un Souvenir de Solferino*:

They disembowel each other with sabre or bayonet; there is no more quarter given, it is a butchery, a combat of wild beasts, mad and drunk with blood; even the wounded defend themselves to the last gasp; he who has no longer any weapons seizes his adversary by the throat, tearing it with his teeth . . . the horses crush the dead and dying under their iron hooves.[20]

On the Austrian side the Croats, and on the French the Zouaves, were particularly ferocious; they beat in the skulls of the wounded with their rifle butts.

After fierce fighting and heavy losses, the French finally stormed the key point, the Cypress Hill. By 2 p.m. a French regiment had captured the heights of Solferino, with the regimental goat leading the way and reaching the summit quite unscathed amid the shambles. Louis Napoleon then turned his attention to the last Austrian stronghold at Cavriana. Franz Joseph was at Cavriana, surrounded and impeded by his generals and staff officers whose sole concern was to ensure his personal safety; Louis Napoleon was less than half a mile away, directing the attack from the foot of the hill. At 3 p.m. the Austrian centre broke, and Franz Joseph ordered a general retreat. As he rode off towards Goito the hot weather, which had lasted for several weeks, ended in a tremendous thunderstorm with heavy rain, which put a stop to all operations on the battlefield, as it was too dark for the troops to see anything. When the sky cleared an hour later, the French found that the Austrians had gone.

The losses on both sides were very heavy – the French, 11,670 killed, wounded and missing; the Piedmontese, 5521; the Austrians, 22,537. The medical services were quite unable to cope with the situation, and the devotion of the French *cantinières* to the wounded of both armies on the battlefield did little to relieve their sufferings and their agonizing thirst, especially as the dry weather of the previous weeks had caused a water shortage in the district. As the wounded lay helpless on the battlefield, local peasants came and robbed them of their boots. The corpses lay unburied for two days, after which they were thrown so hastily into large communal graves that Dunant believed that in some cases the living had been buried with the dead.[21] The Zouaves, burying their comrades, said cheerfully: 'Your turn today, ours tomorrow.'[22]

Dunant rounded up some English tourists whom he found near by, and persuaded them – some eagerly, some reluctantly – to help him care for the wounded. Several aristocratic French ladies, hearing rumours about the situation at Solferino, went at once from their châteaux in France to the headquarters of the French army corps in the battle area, and asked the Corps Commanders – whom in most cases they had met at balls – for permission to help nurse the wounded. Italian women of all classes did the same.[23] But Dunant believed that such devotion and improvisation was not enough, and in his book he appealed for the setting-up in advance of an organization to help the wounded in wartime.[24] Louis Napoleon, like many other sovereigns, responded to his appeal and gave his support to the decision to establish the International Red Cross which was taken at a Conference which met in 1864 under the chairmanship of General Dufour at Geneva.

On the evening of the battle, Louis Napoleon sent a cable to Eugénie: 'Great battle. Great victory'.[25] He slept that night in a house at Cavriana, and next day sent another cable to the Empress: 'I have spent the night in the room occupied on the morning of the battle by the Emperor of Austria'.[26] This delighted the French public, and has been accepted by later historians; but it was ridiculed by the Austrian staff officers, and was in fact untrue. Franz Joseph slept on the night of 23 June at Valleggio; he spent several hours in Cavriana during the battle, but did not alight from his horse.[27]

In Paris the Empress-Regent was unhappy about the war, and shocked at the news that she heard of the horrors of Solferino. She now received the reports from the secret police which were normally sent to the Emperor, from which she learned not only the extent of police surveillance of men who had had even the remotest links in the past with any of the Republican refugees in England,[28] but also the secret police's assessment of the reaction of various political groups in different parts of France to the war in Italy. 'The Socialists are calm, very satisfied with the war; they applaud the success of Garibaldi. No cause for anxiety. The Orleanists continue their criticism; no cause for anxiety. The fanatical section of the Legitimists do not cease to condemn the war.'[29] More worrying was the attitude of the clergy, who feared that the war was threatening the position of the Holy Father; 'this is noticeable in Seine-et-Marne, Pyrénées-O[les], Bouches-du-Rhône, and above all in Alsace.'[30] Someone had overheard the Bishop of Nancy criticizing the war. The Bishop of Montauban showed great lack of patriotism, and several parish priests had preached against the war; it was even being reported in Franche-Comté that some priests had sent money to Austria. In many parishes – the Empress-Regent was given a list of them – the parish priests had refused to hold a *Te Deum* on 12 June for the victory at Magenta, though the Socialists took part in the public rejoicing on 12 June everywhere except in the Loiret. At Montmorillon in Vienne the Imperial Prosecutor had suppressed a rowdy demonstration by some youths who were celebrating too noisily the victory of Magenta; the secret police had investigated, and had discovered that the Imperial Prosecutor was a secret Legitimist sympathizer.[31]

In Paris the police were even more overbearing than usual. Two aristocratic gentlemen who were looking at the same newspaper in front of the Palais Royal were threatened with arrest for holding a meeting, and were told that they must each read their newspapers separately. Nassau Senior saw two working-class men and a woman in the same street ordered to move on by the police when they stood talking together about horses.[32]

After the victory of 24 June, Louis Napoleon moved his head-quarters forward to Valleggio on the Mincio, where he was joined by Prince Napoleon and 35,000 men who had come from Tuscany. The Austrians had withdrawn into 'the Quadrilateral' – the formidable defensive works based on Mantua, Peschiera, Verona and Legnano in which Radetzky had successfully held out during the most critical period of the war of 1848. As the Piedmontese army began to invest Peschiera, the world waited for a third and even bloodier battle than Magenta and Solferino. Then, to the surprise of his generals, soldiers, allies and enemies, Louis Napoleon offered the Austrians an armistice till 15 August, and proposed that he and Franz Joseph should meet to discuss peace terms. The Austrians agreed, and the armistice was signed on 8 July.[33]

There was much speculation at the time – and it has continued ever since – about the reason which induced Napoleon III to make peace with Austria after Solferino. He seems to have been influenced by four factors. In the first place, he was shocked by the butchery of Solferino, and realized that he would suffer even greater casualties if he tried to storm the defences of the Quadrilateral. Secondly, he resented the attitude of the Piedmontese. They had done better at Solferino than at Magenta; but though he told his soldiers, in his order of the day after Solferino, that the Piedmontese army had fought as bravely as the French and was 'truly worthy to march at your side',[34] he felt that Cavour's plan was for the French to do most of the fighting and for Piedmont to reap most of the advantages. Thirdly, he was worried at the possibility that a prolongation of the war would lead to it developing into the general European war which he had always been determined to avoid. There was no sign of Britain or Russia abandoning their policy of neutrality;[35] but Prussia was becoming alarmed at the French successes. 'The Franco-Sardinian army is moving nearer to the frontiers of Germany', wrote the official *Preussische Zeitung* of Berlin on 22 June – before Solferino.[36] On the day after the battle, the Prussian delegate at the meeting of the Diet of the German Confederation proposed that an army corps should be sent to the Upper Rhine; and it was rumoured that the Diet was about to call up 350,000 soldiers. 'Prussia is one vast camp', wrote the *Times* correspondent in Berlin on 1 July.[37] Eugénie, alarmed at the prospect of a Prussian attack on the Rhine, wrote to Louis Napoleon and urged him to make peace as soon as possible.[38]

Fourthly, Louis Napoleon was alarmed at the spread of revolution in Italy – particularly in the Papal States – and conscious of the difficulties in which this would involve him with the clergy in France. The outbreak of the war had been followed by popular risings in Tuscany, Parma, Modena and Lucca, and in the Papal province of the Romagna;

in all these territories, revolutionary provisional governments had been established which were demanding union with Piedmont. The arrival of Kossuth in Genoa was also disturbing, for Kossuth was obviously trying to incite a revolution in Hungary which might lead to the disintegration of the Austrian Empire and Red revolution in Central Europe.[39]

Two months later, Louis Napoleon told the new Austrian Ambassador to France, Prince Richard von Metternich, the reasons why he had offered Franz Joseph an armistice:

I stopped the war because I was afraid of the sacrifices in blood which it would continue to demand; because I was disgusted to have the Revolution following my heels, and Kossuth and Klapka as allies; I would be seen as the leader of all the scum of Europe; and lastly, I foresaw sooner or later a general war, and I proposed to the Emperor of Austria that we should come to an agreement and make peace.[40]

At 7 a.m. on the morning of 11 July, Louis Napoleon rode on horseback from Valleggio, with Marshal Vaillant, General Fleury and his staff and a small escort of cavalry, to the town of Villafranca, about five miles away, where he was to meet Franz Joseph. Villafranca had been Franz Joseph's headquarters for a few days after Solferino, but he had returned to Verona after Villafranca had been bombarded by the French. Louis Napoleon arrived at Villafranca before Franz Joseph, so he rode out along the Verona road to meet him. They met a mile or so outside Villafranca, and after saluting and shaking hands, and presenting their staffs to each other, the two Emperors – one of them aged fifty-one and the other twenty-nine – rode back to Villafranca side by side. Louis Napoleon offered Franz Joseph the place of honour on the right, but Franz Joseph insisted that Louis Napoleon should ride on the right. As they entered Villafranca they left the road and took a short cut across the rubble of the houses destroyed by the recent French bombardment, and went to the house that had been Franz Joseph's headquarters and which was still standing.

Franz Joseph and Louis Napoleon went into the conference room by themselves without anyone accompanying them and were quite alone together during their interview; no interpreter was necessary, as both men spoke perfect French and German. The journalists peering in through the window could see them sitting at a table, both of them smoking cigarettes and occasionally making a note on the writing paper which had been provided for them. Outside, the French and Austrian officers did not talk to each other, but stood in their two separate groups, while the French painter Adolphe Yvon, who had come in Louis Napoleon's party, sketched the Austrian soldiers in their picturesque uniforms.

The two Emperors talked for just under an hour, during which time they agreed on peace terms and the future of Italy. Austria was to cede all Lombardy to Piedmont except for the fortresses of Mantua, Peschiera and Borgoforte, thus retaining the Quadrilateral intact. An Italian Confederation was to be established, on the pattern of the German Confederation, consisting of all the Italian states, with the Pope as president. Austria was to retain her sovereignty over the province of Venetia, but it would be granted home rule under an Austrian Prince, who would be Governor for Franz Joseph, and it would be a member of the Italian Confederation. The Habsburg rulers of Tuscany, Parma, Modena and Lucca would return as sovereigns to their territories, but no French, Austrian or other foreign troops would be employed to compel their subjects to accept them. The Papal States, including the Romagna, would remain under the Pope's sovereignty. These terms were to be embodied in a formal peace treaty which was to be drawn up at a meeting of French, Austrian and Piedmontese plenipotentiaries at Zürich.

The meeting was over by 11 a.m. Franz Joseph rode a little way with Louis Napoleon along the road to Valleggio, and then the two Emperors said good-bye.[41] As soon as he reached Valleggio, Louis Napoleon was visited by Victor Emanuel, whom he had not consulted about the peace terms. He informed Victor Emanuel of what he had agreed with Franz Joseph. Victor Emanuel reluctantly accepted the position; but Cavour was furious and resigned as Prime Minister, and throughout Italy there was great indignation at the French 'betrayal' of their Piedmontese allies and their failure to liberate Venetia.

On 14 July, Louis Napoleon left Valleggio for Milan. His arrival in Milan did not arouse the enthusiasm with which he had been greeted there on 8 June, but there were no hostile demonstrations against him.[42] Next day he reached Turin, and left by train for Paris. On 17 July he was reunited with Eugénie at Saint-Cloud.

CHAPTER 35

1860

O N 14 August 1859, Louis Napoleon led his victorious army through the streets of Paris from the Place de la Bastille to the Place Vendôme as he had done after the Crimean War. Next day he celebrated the *Fête Nationale* by granting an amnesty to all political prisoners and detainees in Algeria and Cayenne, thus releasing all those who had been detained after the June Days of 1848, after the *coup d'état*, and after the round-up that followed Orsini's bombs, though most of them had already been freed. The last detainees sailed from Cayenne in October.[1]

But the peace of Villafranca was not popular in France – least of all in the army, who had been eager to advance to new triumphs – and it intensified the feelings in the European Foreign Offices that Napoleon III was not to be trusted. The French government was sensitive to the criticism, and seized the issues of *The Times* that reported it.[2] Louis Napoleon told a deputation from the Chambers who welcomed him on his return from Italy that he had reluctantly abandoned his aim of freeing Venetia because he was confronted with the prospect of a long siege of the Quadrilateral and of a war on the Rhine as well as on the Adige. 'I made war against the wishes of Europe in order to serve the cause of Italian independence; as soon as the destinies of my country were in peril, I made peace.' But he pointed out that much had been achieved; Lombardy had been liberated, and the proposed Italian Confederation meant that there was now a new Italian nation.[3]

This thought did not evoke much enthusiasm in France, for if the Radicals and Socialists welcomed the liberation of Italy, the French soldiers had returned from Lombardy disgusted with their Piedmontese allies. They felt that French blood had been shed to liberate Lombardy and that they had received no reward except Italian ingratitude.[4] Eugénie shared the general feeling. On 26 August she wrote to Arese:

I am working *as hard as I can* to become Italian. . . . But are you not afraid of proving to Europe that the job of a Redeemer is a job for

456

fools?. . . The Emperor even went for a while *against the feelings of his own country* and had to revive the feelings of generosity and glory to make the country accept . . . a struggle from which it could derive no good except *gratitude* and in which a reverse could have struck it cruelly.[5]

Louis Napoleon's Italian policy had led him into difficulties which became increasingly frustrating during the next few years. It is not uncommon for elderly men to live politically in the past and to wish to fight again the battles of their youth; but few of them have the opportunity to do so as effectively and as disastrously as Napoleon III. In 1831 he and his brother had fought with the revolutionaries of the Romagna to establish a Confederation of Liberal Italian states under the presidency of the Pope; but in 1859 the Mazzinians and Radicals wished to establish one Italian republic, the Piedmontese government and the Liberals of Europe wished to see Italy united under King Victor Emanuel, and the Conservatives wished to maintain the *status quo*. No one except Napoleon III wished to create an Italian Confederation, least of all the Pope, who under Louis Napoleon's scheme was to be its president. Yet Louis Napoleon clung to his idea, and for seven years committed French foreign policy to working for it. In addition to the political weakness of his position, Louis Napoleon's generous temperament, which so often affected his political decisions, had led him to feel a personal sympathy for Franz Joseph when he met him at Villafranca. He frankly told the Austrian Ambassador, Metternich: 'When I saw your young Emperor, I was unable to refuse what he asked. I agreed to everything without thinking of the difficulties which I should encounter.'[6]

Despite his pledge to Franz Joseph, he did not succeed in persuading the revolutionary provisional governments in Tuscany, the Duchies and the Romagna – and the Piedmontese agents who controlled them – to allow the Grand Duke, the Dukes, and the Papal Governors to return; and as the use of force to restore them had been ruled out at Villafranca, he gave way and allowed first the Duchies and then Tuscany to be annexed by Piedmont. Franz Joseph, who felt that Napoleon III had betrayed him by not restoring the Habsburg rulers of Tuscany and the Duchies, refused to perform his part of the Villafranca agreement with regard to Venetia, which was not granted home rule as a member of the Italian Confederation; and the Confederation, which nobody wanted except Louis Napoleon, never came into existence.

Louis Napoleon was contemplating convening a Congress of the Great Powers, at which he hoped that the Pope would be represented, which would sanction the new territorial arrangements in Italy, including the cession of the Romagna to Piedmont. In preparation for this, he resorted to a procedure which he adopted on several other occasions: he arranged for the eminent journalist, M. de La Guéronnière, to publish an anonymous pamphlet advocating a new line of policy, and started a rumour that he himself had either written or inspired the pamphlet. This enabled him to test the public reaction to the policy that he wished to adopt. On 22 December 1859 the pamphlet, *The Pope and the Congress*, was published, after a great deal of advance publicity and rumours about the Emperor's authorship, and 43,000 copies were sold in the first four days.[7] The pamphlet suggested that none of the arguments in favour of the temporal power of the Pope required him to rule over a larger, rather than a smaller, expanse of territory, and that in view of the disturbances which had troubled the Papal government in the Romagna during the previous thirty years, it might be to the Pope's advantage to relinquish his sovereignty over the Romagna and to concentrate on consolidating his government in the city of Rome and the remaining provinces of his States.[8]

Le Pape et le Congrès produced a violent reaction from the Catholic Church. The Papal Nuncio protested to Walewski, who denied that the pamphlet expressed the opinions of the French government. It was attacked by Veuillot in *L'Univers* and by the Bishop of Orleans, Dupanloup.[9] The Pope, replying to the New Year greetings of General Goyon, the commander of the French troops in Rome, said that he prayed to God to allow His light to fall on the august leader of the French nation, 'so that, illuminated by this light ... he will recognize the falsity of certain principles which were put forward a few days ago in a pamphlet which is an insidious monument of hypocrisy and an ignoble tissue of contradictions'.[10]

The pamphlet caused alarm in Madrid, and Paca wrote to Eugénie about it. Despite the rumours to the contrary, Eugénie stoutly defended the Emperor's policy. Cowley told Queen Victoria that 'the Empress, who is much devoted to the Pope, is in despair about the pamphlet, but will not believe that the Emperor had written it';[11] but Cowley was misinformed, as he often was. Eugénie, in her reply to Paca, wrote that *Le Pape et le Congrès*, which had been written by M. de La Guéronnière, did represent Louis Napoleon's policy, but that Paca could not have read it, or she would have realized that it upheld the principle of the temporal sovereignty of the Pope.[12]

The official French press hastened to explain that the views expressed in *Le Pape et le Congrès* had been misunderstood;[13] but Louis Napoleon cheerfully went off to Fontainebleau for two days' shooting, and while there wrote a letter to the Pope on 31 December. Writing as 'Your Holiness's devoted son', he said that if the Pope had followed his earlier advice and granted reforms in his government, revolution might not have spread to the Romagna; but in the existing circumstances, 'I say with sincere regret, and painful though the solution may be, that it seems to me that the best way of complying with the true interests of the Holy See would be to sacrifice the revolted provinces'.[14]

The Pope replied with an encyclical stating that his conscience would not permit him to follow the advice of the Emperor of the French and relinquish his sovereignty over the Romagna. When Veuillot published the text of the encyclical in *L'Univers*, Louis Napoleon suppressed *L'Univers*, on the grounds that it had 'made itself the organ of a religious party whose pretensions become daily in more direct opposition to the rights of the State'.[15] He also suppressed the leading Catholic newspaper in Brittany, *La Bretagne*, which had published a letter to the Emperor from three deputies of Brittany protesting against the Piedmontese seizure of the Romagna. The bishops were not so easily dealt with as the press. The Bishop of Poitiers ordered his clergy to read out in the pulpit his statement condemning *Le Pape et le Congrès*; and the Archbishop of Paris ordered the Pope's encyclical to be read out in the churches in his diocese.[16] The Bishop of Autun, less specifically, condemned 'sacrilegious pamphleteers'.[17]

When Louis Napoleon opened the new Parliamentary session on 1 March 1860, he criticized the 'unthinking impressions' which had made part of the Catholic world forget that for the past eleven years 'I alone maintain in Rome the power of the Holy Father, without having ceased for a single day to venerate in him the sacred character of the chief of our religion'.[18] But for the first time since he came to power, he was in conflict with the Church. The Minister of the Interior ordered the Prefects to report any cases of abuse of the freedom of the pulpit for seditious purposes. At the end of March, the Pope issued a bull excommunicating everyone who had played a part in depriving the Holy See of the Romagna. *Le Moniteur*, without mentioning the bull, published an official government statement drawing attention to an old law which made it a criminal offence to publish any Papal bull in France without the consent of the government.[19]

After the suppression of his newspaper, Veuillot went off on a six weeks' visit to Rome. On the journey he got into conversation with another traveller on the train, with whom he became so friendly that they met each other often in Rome; and when the time came for him to return to France, Veuillot postponed his journey for a few days so that he could travel with his friend. They reached Paris late in the evening and went together to a hotel, where they shared a room for the night. Next morning Veuillot went to have a bath, and returned to find that his friend and his dispatch-case had disappeared; but his friend had left a note, telling Veuillot to collect his dispatch-case from police head-quarters in the Rue Jérusalem. There Veuillot found his friend, who identified himself as a member of the secret police who had been sent to spy on Veuillot in Rome. He handed Veuillot his dispatch-case, but retained all the contents, which included letters which Veuillot was carrying from the government in Rome to the Papal Nuncio in Paris, as well as notes for articles by Veuillot and letters written to Veuillot in Rome by his children.

Veuillot went at once to the Nuncio, who protested to the new Foreign Minister, Thouvenel, at the seizure of diplomatic correspon-dence by the police. Thouvenel told the Nuncio that he had no grounds for complaint, as Veuillot had not been registered as a carrier of the diplomatic bag; but the letters addressed to the Nuncio were handed over to him, and the letters of Veuillot's children were returned to Veuillot, though the police kept Veuillot's notes. Veuillot was sure that the police had been searching to see whether he was carrying copies of the bull of excommunication.[20]

In return for the acquisition of Tuscany, the Duchies and the Romagna, Louis Napoleon persuaded Cavour, who returned as Prime Minister of Piedmont in January 1860, to adhere to the promise which he had made at Plombières to cede Savoy and Nice to France.[21] The cessions were to be subject to the approval of the population in plebis-cites in all these territories; the great new democratic principle of the referendum under universal suffrage would thus justify what might otherwise be seen as a sordid diplomatic deal. When the treaty ceding Savoy and Nice to France was published in March 1860, it caused great resentment in Switzerland, for the Swiss feared that Louis Napoleon's next step would be to annex Geneva, and it was sharply denounced in Germany and Britain. In Italy, there was strong opposition to the cession of Savoy and Nice, despite all Cavour's efforts to persuade the Italians that Piedmont, by acquiring Lombardy, Tuscany, the Duchies and the Romagna in exchange for Savoy and Nice, had had much the best of its bargain with Napoleon III.

Palmerston, who had returned to power with the pro-Italian enthusiast, Lord John Russell, as his Foreign Secretary, was incensed that Napoleon III and Cavour had succeeded in deceiving the British government for eighteen months about the secret agreement at Plom-bières, and that France should upset the territorial frontiers laid down in 1815 without consulting the other signatories of the Treaty of Vienna. Louis Napoleon was annoyed at the British attitude. He could not understand how any British statesman could believe that the annexa-tion of Savoy and Nice was a threat to British interests.[22]

The disclosure of the secret negotiations about Savoy and Nice, coming after Louis Napoleon's shifty Italian policy in the summer and autumn of 1859, caused a general feeling of distrust of the Emperor to take firm root throughout Europe.[23] Drouyn de Lhuys, who since his resignation as Foreign Minister had been vilifying and slandering the Emperor in secret, told Nassau Senior that Louis Napoleon 'trusts to stratagem and fraud. The Uncle was a lion, this man is a bear. He does not bound. He does not go straight. He crawls on slowly and tortuously, draws back if he is opposed, and returns.'[24]

The French government sent agents to Savoy and Nice who pointed out to the local inhabitants the economic advantages of union with France, and urged them to vote for cession in the referendum. The annexation by France was approved in Nice by a majority of 25,943 to 260 with 4743 abstentions, and in Savoy by 130,533 to 235 with 4610 abstentions. Despite all the criticisms of the conduct of the election campaign and the voting procedure, there is no doubt that a large majority in both Nice and Savoy were in favour of being incorporated into the French Empire. In Parma, Modena and the Romagna there was a vote of over 99 per cent in the referendum in favour of annexation by Piedmont, though in Tuscany nearly 30 per cent of the electorate abstained.

Almost immediately, Louis Napoleon's Italian policy ran into new difficulties. On 5 May 1860, Garibaldi sailed from Quarto with 1089 volunteers to liberate Sicily from the King of Naples' government, and before the end of the month he had defeated 20,000 Neapolitan troops and captured Palermo. His success aroused the wildest enthusiasm in Britain, and this convinced every European Conservative that Garibaldi had been secretly assisted by the British government. In France, the Catholic press immediately sounded the alarm; Veuillot's new paper, *Le Monde*, which he had started after the suppression of *L'Univers*, wrote on 18 May that 'the Revolution is on the eve of a new triumph' and would not cease until the Sovereign Pontiff had been overthrown. *La Gazette de France* stated that 'since the time when Luther burned the Pope's bull in the market place at Wittenberg . . . calling all Germany to sedition, the Revolution has not given a more audacious defiance to Europe'.[25] But the comment of the official government press, though mildly censuring Garibaldi's expedition as an act of piracy against the kingdom of Naples, was much more restrained; and the government did not prevent Prince Napoleon's newspaper, *L'Opinion Nationale*, from praising Garibaldi and opening subscriptions for funds to be sent to him.[26] There was a good deal of enthusiasm for Garibaldi in France, and not only in Radical and Socialist circles. Admiral Bouet told Senior that, at an ordinary 'bourgeois' wedding in the middle of May, 'nothing but Garibaldi was talked about. Even the Bride and Bridegroom seemed to think of nothing else.'[27]

Louis Napoleon was not unsympathetic to Garibaldi. Thouvenel's first reaction to the news that the Thousand had sailed for Sicily was to make a protest to the Piedmontese Ambassador, Nigra; but Nigra had the impression that Thouvenel did not really mind, and during the following days he thought that French official reaction was becoming more favourable to Garibaldi.[28] 'At the Tuileries', he reported, 'they are obviously not displeased at what is happening, and go so far as to say that the King of Naples has only got his deserts and that France is not paid to act as policeman for the Bourbons.'[29] Only Eugénie adopted a violently hostile attitude to Garibaldi. 'The Empress is furious against Garibaldi', wrote Nigra on 22 May. 'The Emperor is forced to undertake his defence against the violent interjections of his august spouse.'[30]

By July, Garibaldi was master of all Sicily and was preparing to cross the Straits of Messina and invade the mainland. Louis Napoleon did not wish to see Garibaldi conquer the whole of the kingdom of Naples; he probably hoped that the position would develop into a stalemate between the King of Naples and Garibaldi, and that he would then be able to obtain the throne of Naples for his Murat cousin.[31] He proposed to the British government that a joint British and French naval force should be sent to the Straits to prevent Garibaldi from crossing. Eugénie, who did not yet realize that Victor Emanuel and Cavour were at least half-encouraging Garibaldi, told Nigra about the French proposal to London. This time her diplomatic indiscretion had more serious results than usual. Nigra immediately informed his government, who sent their agent in England, Lacaita, to persuade Lord John Russell to reject the proposal;* and though Russell told the French government that Britain would have no objection if the French acted alone against Garibaldi, Louis Napoleon hesitated to do this. Garibaldi crossed the straits on 18 August. On the same day, Nigra wrote to Cavour that 'the Emperor expresses himself in an almost favourable manner about Garibaldi'.[32]

Garibaldi swept through Calabria and entered the city of Naples on 7 September. On the last stages of his journey he was accompanied by a number of English tourists, one of whom, as the French press did

*The well-known story of Eugénie's intervention, of Lacaita's visit to Russell's house while Russell was talking to Persigny and Lady John Russell was ill in bed, and the trick by which Lacaita gained access to Russell by pretending that Lady John wished to see him, has been doubted; but it is supported by the evidence of Lady John herself. As to this, see Trevelyan, *Garibaldi and the Making of Italy*, pp. 104–7 and n.

not fail to mention, was Bernard's defence counsel, Edwin James. General Goyon's French troops were still in Rome; but the Pope no longer trusted Napoleon III to defend him, and appealed for Catholic volunteers to join his tiny Papal army. While Radicals and Liberals from all over the world, and especially from Britain, joined Garibaldi's forces, the Catholics from France, Belgium and Ireland enrolled under General Lamoricière in the Pope's army. By far the largest contingent came from France, especially from Brittany and the other Catholic and Legitimist strongholds; they were commanded in many cases by officers from the families of the old nobility. Before marching off from their parishes, they were usually blessed by their parish priest, and often by their bishop, at public ceremonies.

The government press tried to divert attention from the plight of the Pope by acclaiming the acquisition of Savoy and Nice. In August, Louis Napoleon and Eugénie set out on a tour of the newly acquired territory. After stopping at Lyons, where Eugénie charmed the women-workers in the silk factories by trying her hand at operating the loom with considerable success, they entered Savoy. They were received with great enthusiasm at Chambéry, Chamonix, Bonneville and Annecy and in the villages, with banners of welcome, illuminations at night, and the constant playing of 'Partant pour la Syrie'. The smiling Empress accepted bouquets from the children, and the Emperor spoke to workmen and old soldiers wearing the St Helena medal, gave gifts of money to charities, and promised the mayors financial assistance from the government to build new roads, start new industries, and extend the railway line. At Aix-les-Bains he promised a grant of 500,000 francs to transform the town into a famous spa.[33]

At Chambéry he was visited by the Piedmontese Minister of the Interior, Farini, and the Commander-in-Chief of the Piedmontese army, General Cialdini. They had officially come to convey Victor Emanuel's good wishes on the occasion of the transfer of the territory to France; but the real purpose of their mission was to sound Louis Napoleon on Cavour's plan to invade the Papal States and the kingdom of Naples. After discussing with Conneau how best to present their case to Louis Napoleon, they told him that Garibaldi's volunteers, who consisted largely of Mazzinians and Radicals, would soon enter Naples and pass on from there to invade and conquer the Papal States, including the city of Rome; only the intervention of the Piedmontese army could stop Garibaldi and 'the Revolution'. As the Piedmontese army could not reach Neapolitan territory without going through the Papal States, they would have to invade the Marches and Umbria, but would keep well clear of Rome and the Patrimony of St Peter.

This placed Louis Napoleon in a dilemma. He knew that the

invasion and annexation of the Marches and Umbria by Piedmont would arouse the indignation of the French Catholics, who would put him under strong pressure to declare war on Piedmont; but if Victor Emanuel and Cavour did not stop Garibaldi, he would have to do it himself by sending large reinforcements to Rome, and making an enemy of all Liberals, of most Italians, and of the Piedmontese government, as well as further damaging his relations with Britain. He therefore allowed Farini and Cialdini to believe that he would acquiesce in the invasion of the Papal States by Piedmont, and apparently encouraged them to act as quickly as possible, so that he could confront the Catholic pressure in France for intervention by the argument of the *fait accompli*.[34]

Cavour was delighted when he heard about the interview. 'The Emperor has been perfect', he wrote. 'The Emperor has approved of everything. . . . He said that the diplomats would utter loud cries, but they would let us get away with it; that he himself would be placed in a difficult position, but that he would put forward the idea of a Congress.'[35] Cavour gave instructions that the result of the interview should be kept absolutely secret. A few days later, Louis Napoleon met Arese, and gave him just the same impression that he had given Farini and Cialdini as to his attitude to an invasion of the Papal States by the Piedmontese.[36]

From Savoy Louis Napoleon and Eugénie went to Marseilles, where the Emperor announced plans to demolish and rebuild the Old Port district, and then to Toulon. A lunatic fired a pistol at him in Toulon, but he was unhurt. After visiting Nice, he and Eugénie sailed to Ajaccio, saw the house in which Napoleon I and Louis Bonaparte were born, and left on 15 September for Algiers.[37] Many people had expected the Emperor to cancel his visit to Algiers, because four days earlier the Piedmontese troops had invaded the Papal States; but it was announced in the press that the Emperor would be in touch from Algiers with the government in Paris by means of the underwater cable line from Toulon to Algiers which was being laid by a French frigate and an English merchant vessel. In fact, the cable broke forty miles out from Toulon, and during this period of international crisis it took more than forty-eight hours for news from Paris to reach Algiers.[38]

For personal as well as political reasons it was an unfortunate time to be away from Paris, because Paca was lying dangerously ill at the Hôtel d'Albe in Paris with a mysterious spinal ailment which no doctor had been able to diagnose. Eugénie, who had written constantly to Paca throughout the tour of Savoy and the south of France, was very anxious about her sister's health; but she had no idea, when she and

Louis Napoleon landed at Algiers on the morning of 17 September, that Paca had died a few hours earlier during the night of the 16th.[39]

The Emperor and Empress stayed in Algiers in the beautiful Moorish palace built by Hasan Pasha in the sixteenth century.[40] Eugénie had heard before they left Corsica that Paca's condition had taken a turn for the worse, and on the day they landed in Algiers wrote to Maria Manuela that she was 'driven mad' by the news.[41] Next day she laid the foundation stone of the new Boulevard de l'Impératrice, which was to run along the sea-front, and went with Louis Napoleon to a gathering of Arab tribesmen on the great Metija Plain. Ten thousand Arab horsemen and twelve squadrons of Spahis galloped across the plain firing their rifles, after which there was a hunt of gazelles, ostriches and falcons, and a ceremony at which a long line of Goums from the desert rode up to the Emperor's tent, and, dismounting, made their obeisance to him and to the Empress. According to General Fleury, the tribesmen did not disguise their admiration for her beauty, and she enjoyed this. In the evening, Louis Napoleon attended a great ball given by the city authorities. Eugénie did not go, because of her anxiety about her sister's health; but next day, on 19 September, she attended a military review of French troops at which the Bey of Tunis was present.[42]

In the evening of 19 September, Louis Napoleon heard from the Duke of Alba that Paca had died, the news having been delayed because of the rupture of the cable. At 8.15 p.m. he cabled to Alba: 'I have received the fatal news. I have not yet dared to tell the Empress.'[43] He then attended a banquet without Eugénie, and they sailed at midnight for Marseilles. They had intended to leave Algiers next day, but Louis Napoleon cut the visit short by some hours because of Paca's death. He had not yet broken the news to Eugénie; and on the ship Fleury, in view of her anxiety about Paca, encouraged her to think that Paca might be better by the time they reached Paris, although he knew that she was dead.

There is no doubt that Louis Napoleon delayed in telling Eugénie of Paca's death, and that Eugénie afterwards resented this; but the story told by Fleury in his memoirs twenty-four years later, which is the chief source of information on the subject, has made Louis Napoleon's conduct appear far worse than it really was. According to Fleury, Louis Napoleon was informed of Paca's death when they landed at Algiers on the morning of 17 September, but at Fleury's suggestion withheld the news from Eugénie in case it should prevent her from carrying out her official duties in Algeria, and did not tell her until four days later, shortly before they landed at Marseilles on the morning of 21 September.[44] This is not true. Owing to the break in the cable,

Louis Napoleon only heard of Paca's death in the evening of 19 September; during nearly the whole of their sixty hours' stay in Algiers, both Louis Napoleon and Eugénie knew that Paca was dangerously ill, but neither of them knew that she was dead.

We have no information, apart from Fleury's inaccurate story, of the precise moment during the sea-voyage to Marseilles at which Louis Napoleon told Eugénie; but the delay was long enough to anger her, and perhaps to lower her opinion of her husband's strength of character, for Paca's grandson, the seventeenth Duke of Alba, was conscious many years later that she still resented it. Napoleon I would have told her, a little brusquely, and prescribed the precise extent and length of her mourning for Paca; Napoleon III postponed the painful interview for as long as possible. This reluctance to face unpleasant interviews, and to tell people unpleasant facts, may have been one of the reasons why Louis Napoleon so often misled foreign ambassadors into thinking that he was more sympathetic to their government's policy than he really was.

He had done so in his conversations with Farini, Cialdini and Arese. He had led them to believe that he would acquiesce in the Piedmontese invasion of the Papal States; but he now sent a strong protest to the government of Piedmont and withdrew his ambassador from Turin. This was not, as many people believed, part of a cunning plan that had been agreed at Chambéry, for Cavour was taken aback at Louis Napoleon's attitude. 'The Emperor had approved our plan without reserve', he told Nigra; 'I do not know in what way our execution of the plan can have displeased the French government.'[45] Louis Napoleon, in his farewell talk with Nigra before the ambassador left Paris, told him that Cavour had badly bungled the business; he should have waited until Garibaldi had actually invaded the Papal States before sending in the Piedmontese army. He told Nigra that the important thing now was that the Piedmontese should fight Garibaldi to a finish, and that clashes between Piedmontese and French troops in the Papal States should be avoided at all costs, because otherwise France and Piedmont would find themselves at war. Nigra left Paris on 1 October. He reported to Cavour that, on a personal basis, the Emperor and Empress had been 'exquisitely kind' about it, and that the Emperor had said that he hoped to see him again soon.[46]

The French Catholics demanded action against the Piedmontese.[47] The Bishop of Poitiers stated in a pastoral letter to his clergy that the fighting between the Catholic volunteers and the Piedmontese invaders was a repetition of 'the battle of Michael and his hosts against Lucifer and his rebellious legions', and that the volunteers were fighting 'for truth, for justice, for the Church, for Jesus Christ . . . against the cohorts of the Revolution and of Hell'.[48] But the Paris working class were more angry about the increase in the price of tobacco. They held a protest demonstration, throwing their cigar stubs, their chewed tobacco and the dregs in their pipes into the Emperor's private garden at the Tuileries.[49]

Louis Napoleon sent reinforcements to the French forces in Rome, where General Goyon now had 20,000 men under his command; but they took no part in the action of the volunteers against the Piedmontese army. By the beginning of October the story was circulating in Paris that one of the French volunteer officers taken prisoner by the Piedmontese in the battle of Castelfidardo had said to Cialdini: 'Well, General, you have beaten us, but we shall soon have our turn, for General Goyon and our countrymen under his command are not far off.' Cialdini replied: 'You must think me very simple to have come here without your Emperor's permission. It was I who planned the campaign with him at Chambéry, and his last advice was that if the thing was to be done it should be done quickly.'[50]

The Piedmontese did not do it quite quickly enough. By the beginning of November they had occupied the Marches and Umbria and the whole of the kingdom of Naples except for the port of Gaeta; but here the King of Naples' forces held out for three-and-a-half months against the besieging Piedmontese army and navy. Louis Napoleon sent a French squadron to Gaeta to support the King of Naples and break the Piedmontese blockade; but the squadron took no action against the Piedmontese, who were careful not to fire on it. Louis Napoleon withdrew the squadron in January 1861, and was undoubtedly relieved when Gaeta surrendered on 13 February. The whole of the Italian peninsula was now incorporated into Victor Emanuel's kingdom except Austrian Venetia and the remnants of the Papal States in the Patrimony of St Peter, which included Rome, Civitavecchia and Viterbo, but only about a quarter of the territories which the Pope had ruled in the spring of 1859.

In the middle of November 1860, Eugénie left Paris on a visit to England and Scotland. Her journey gave rise to considerable speculation in France and abroad. Le Moniteur reported that she had been greatly afflicted by her sister's death and was taking a holiday on her doctor's orders; but people wondered why, if she was travelling for health reasons, she should go to England and Scotland in the November fogs and not to Nice or the Riviera, or to Spain. It was rumoured that she had had a terrible quarrel with the Emperor and had violently reproached him for betraying the Pope; others said that she was still resentful because he had not immediately informed her of Paca's death; and others that she had gone to see the eminent Scottish specialist, Dr Simpson, because Paca's death had aroused her anxieties about the pains which she sometimes felt in her own spine.[51]

She crossed the Channel on 14 November, travelling incognito as the Comtesse de Pierrefonds with two of her ladies, two gentlemen and ten servants, and taking ordinary cabs from London Bridge Station to Claridge's Hotel.[52] After a day's shopping in London she travelled by train in an ordinary first-class reserved compartment to York, where she stayed the night and visited the minster before going on to Edinburgh. By now her presence was being widely reported in the British press, and in Edinburgh the Provost and city council called on her at the Douglas Hotel, and a band played 'Partant pour la Syrie' beneath her bedroom window. She visited Holyrood Palace, the castle, and John Knox's house in Edinburgh, attended a *Te Deum* for the Prince of Wales's safe return from the United States, and climbed half-way up Arthur's Seat, but could go no further because of the heavy frost. She went to Perth, Dunkeld, Blair Atholl and Stirling, and then to Glasgow and the Duke of Hamilton's house at Hamilton. On the way to Blair she met the Duke of Atholl by chance on the road, and he took her to the house and showed her over it by the light of a tallow candle before she returned by moonlight to Birnam.

Her hope of travelling incognito had to be abandoned. In Glasgow she drove from the Queen's Hotel through the streets in a carriage with the Provost and the Duke of Hamilton amid cheering crowds and took the train to Manchester. When her train stopped at Preston, she was troubled by a crowd of well-dressed ladies and gentlemen who tried to peer in through the windows of her carriage and who had to be chased away by her attendants and the police; at Bolton she was loudly cheered at the station; and when she left the train in Manchester the police had great difficulty in clearing a path through the crowds to enable her to reach the Queen's Hotel. After the strain of the crowds in Glasgow and Manchester, she decided not to visit Liverpool, where thousands of people were awaiting her, and travelled straight from Manchester to Leamington. She spent a few more days at Claridge's in London, and visited Queen Victoria at Windsor. The Queen was shocked at her appearance and mood of depression; but Eugénie told her that since she had been in Britain she had been able to eat properly for the first time since Paca's death.[53] The Empress sailed from Folkestone to Boulogne on 13 December. The Emperor travelled to Amiens to meet her and brought her to the Tuileries.

The cheers which had greeted Eugénie in Scotland and Lancashire were remarkable, because Napoleon III had never been more unpopular in Britain; and the British press, while paying tribute to the Empress's charm and popularity, indignantly repudiated the suggestions in the French press that her welcome proved that the people of Britain were in sympathy with the Emperor's policy.[54] The secret agreement with Cavour, the French naval building programme – especially of steamships – and the fortifications at Cherbourg produced what was almost a war-scare in Britain. Palmerston used the public mood to press forward with his scheme for building forts along the south coast and volunteers enlisted to defend the country against the threat of French invasion. 'Form, Form, Riflemen Form!', wrote Tennyson,

> Be not deaf to the sound that warns,
> Be not gull'd by a despot's plea!
> Are figs of thistles? or grapes of thorns?
> How can a despot feel with the Free?
> Form, Form, Riflemen Form! . . .
> Form, be ready to do or die!
> Form in Freedom's name and the Queen's!
> True we have got – *such* a faithful ally
> That only the Devil can tell what he means.[55]

A great military camp was established on Chobham Heath in Surrey to defend the realm against an invasion by this new Napoleon Bonaparte.

> Britannia's deeds proud France may read,
> Victory all times did crown her;
> If Boney comes to Chobham Camp
> We'll show him English power![56]

The French press occasionally made a sour reference to the Volunteers in Britain who were so openly preparing to fight the French, but continued to talk of Franco-British friendship. In November 1860 an officer in the Volunteers wrote to Napoleon III and suggested that, as a gesture of good will, a group of Volunteers should visit Paris in uniform as guests of the French government. Mocquard wrote back warmly welcoming the suggestion, which was approved by the Duke of Cambridge, the Commander-in-Chief, and Sidney Herbert, the Secretary of State for War; but a flood of indignant letters in the British press caused the visit to be cancelled.[57]

More friction arose between Britain and France when, in July 1860, the Muslims in Damascus massacred the Christian and Jewish populations of the city and burned six thousand of their houses and the French Consulate.[58] There was great indignation in Europe, especially in

France, and Louis Napoleon proposed to the Great Powers that an international expeditionary force, composed largely of French troops, should be sent to Syria to protect the Christians and punish the ringleaders of the riot. Russia, Austria and Prussia agreed; but there was strong opposition in Britain, because it was thought that Napoleon III was using the massacres as an excuse to occupy Syria and in due course to annex it to France. Kinglake hinted in a debate in the House of Commons that the massacres had been incited by French agents in order to provide an excuse for French intervention; and Palmerston feared that if French troops were established in Syria, they would never leave.[59] But the Cabinet overruled Palmerston, and agreed to the intervention on the understanding that the troops would be withdrawn within six months.

The Turkish government also agreed, and 10,000 French troops under General Beaufort sailed for Syria. Louis Napoleon told them that they were the worthy children of the heroes who had borne the Cross of Christ to Syria at the time of the Crusades; and the French bishops praised him for rescuing the Christians in Syria at the same time as they condemned him for betraying the Pope.[60]

At the end of six months, Louis Napoleon asked the consent of the Great Powers to keep the troops there for a little longer, because there would be fresh massacres of Christians if they were withdrawn. Britain reluctantly agreed that they should stay for another six months but no longer. They left in July 1861. A Conference of ambassadors had meanwhile assembled in Constantinople to discuss how to protect the Christians in Syria, and it was agreed to establish a separate Christian administration in the Lebanon under the nominal sovereignty of the Sultan and under French protection. The Christian government was set up in 1864 and lasted until the dissolution of the Turkish Empire in 1918.

Only in the Far East were Britain and France able to collaborate, and at the very time when Anglo-French relations were at their worst, French and British soldiers were fighting side by side as allies in a minor war in China. In 1858 the murder of a French priest in Kwangsi province in China gave Louis Napoleon the opportunity to appear as the champion of the Catholic faith in yet another part of the world, at a time when Britain was engaged in hostilities with China as a result of the continued friction at Canton which had followed the Opium War. The French press contrasted the position of Britain – fighting to force opium on the Chinese – and of France, who wished only to defend the freedom of Christian worship there;[61] but Louis Napoleon, persevering as always in his policy of friendship with Britain, proposed that a combined French and British military expedition should compel the

Emperor of China to grant British and French diplomatic representatives, missionaries and traders access to Peking and other Chinese cities.

In May 1858 an Anglo-French force sailed up the Peiho River to Tientsin and forced the Chinese envoys to sign a treaty granting these demands and agreeing to pay compensation to Britain and France for murdered Englishmen and Frenchmen and for the insults to the French and British flags. But when an Anglo-French naval squadron sailed up the Peiho in June 1859, on its way to Peking, with the diplomatic representatives on board, it was attacked without warning at the Taku forts at Tientsin and forced to turn back, leaving several prisoners, including some of the diplomats, in the hands of the Chinese. When the news reached Paris and London, Napoleon III and Palmerston declared that French and British honour must be avenged, and in the late summer of 1860, 4000 French and 6000 British troops set out to march on Peking under the joint command of General Montauban and General Sir James Hope Grant. Palmerston had given orders that Grant's force was not to be equipped with the new British rifle, as he did not wish the French to know about it;[62] and Lord John Russell sent secret orders to Lord Elgin, the High Commissioner in China, as to what to do in the 'unfortunate, though improbable, contingency' of the outbreak of war between Britain and France while they were still fighting as allies against China. As it would be 'discreditable to European civilization' if the two allies should begin fighting against each other on Chinese soil, Elgin was to propose to the French that they should conclude an armistice which was to last until they had defeated the Chinese and had returned to Europe.[63]

The Anglo-French army entered Peking on 6 October 1860, though it was not until 9 December that the news reached Paris and London. While the British troops forced the Great Gate of Peking, the French occupied the Emperor's Summer Palace of Yuen-ming-Yuen, some twenty miles north of the city. The grounds surrounding the palace stretched for many miles, and contained beautiful gardens, canals crossed by willow bridges, pagodas, and forty-two smaller palaces apart from the Emperor's main residence. 'It is impossible, Monsieur le Maréchal,' wrote Montauban to Vaillant, the Minister of War, 'for me to describe to you the wonders of this imperial dwelling. Nothing in Europe can convey any idea of such luxury.'[64]

The French and British soldiers were burning with a desire for revenge, for several of the captured British and French diplomats and missionaries had been tortured in the grounds of the Summer Palace, and some of them had died of their treatment. Montauban therefore allowed the French troops to loot the Summer Palace. The soldiers filled their pockets with silver objects, then threw them away to refill the pockets with gold, and finally threw away the gold to take priceless jewelled ornaments, especially watches and clocks; the *Times* correspondent found one soldier with ninety-two watches. Most of the soldiers resold the loot to their comrades for a small fraction of the value. They then went through the rooms of the palace with sticks, breaking all the valuables which were too big to carry away. 'The destruction of furniture, mirrors, clocks and articles of *vertu* by the French soldiery was something almost painful to behold', wrote the *Times* correspondent amid 'the crash and din' of the destruction.[65]

After two days the British liaison officers and Montauban stopped the private looting and divided out what remained of the spoil between the British and the French to be sold by auction to the soldiers for the benefit of the British and French tax-payers. The sale raised £8000, but the *Times* correspondent estimated that the true value of the property looted and destroyed exceeded £6 million.

Lord Elgin and Sir James Hope Grant, like so many of the British commanders in India and China, were Scottish Calvinists who believed that it was more virtuous to destroy than to loot. They disapproved privately of the looting by the French, but insisted that the Summer Palace should be destroyed in order to punish the Emperor of China for the ill-treatment of the British and French prisoners. Montauban opposed the idea, but a British regiment burned all the palaces, pagodas and temples, felled the trees, drained the lakes and tore up the lawns and flower-beds.[66]

The destruction of the Summer Palace was applauded by public opinion in Britain, and the French were happy about the loot.[67] Victor Hugo in Guernsey wrote bitterly that the Summer Palace, like the Parthenon, the Pyramids, the Coliseum and Notre-Dame, was one of the Wonders of the World:

> One day two bandits entered the Summer Palace. One of them looted, the other burned. . . . We Europeans are civilized, and for us the Chinese are barbarians. This is what civilization has done to barbarism. In the eyes of history, one of these two bandits will be named France, the other will be named England.[68]

But Louis Napoleon told the Chambers, when he opened the new session in February 1861, that 'the Cross, the emblem of Christian civilization, once again surmounts, in the capital of China, the temples of our religion which have been closed for more than a century'.[69]

After four weeks' occupation, the British and French forces withdrew from Peking; but the French stayed much longer in Indo-China.[70] At the far south of the Chinese Empire, the Emperor of Annam reigned over the four provinces of Tongking, Laos, Cambodia and Cochin-China. Here too there were French Catholic missionaries who were periodically murdered, and in 1858 Napoleon III and the Spanish government sent a joint expeditionary force from Manila in the Spanish colony of the Philippines. The French Radicals thought that Eugénie was responsible for the decision to send the troops, having been incited to do so by the bishops.[71]

The French and Spanish forces landed in Cochin-China and captured Saigon, and when the Spaniards withdrew, the French remained. The King of Cambodia, who was usually at war with the Emperor of Annam, asked the French for help, and as the Emperor of Annam refused to receive a French diplomatic mission, the French made this an excuse to annex Cochin-China to the French Empire. Louis Napoleon kept an army of 2000 men in Cochin-China under Admiral Bonnard, who built towns, established industries, improved agriculture, and from time to time suppressed revolts of the native population and sent punitive expeditions against the Emperor of Annam. The French stayed in Cochin-China for ninety-six years; but it was not until after the fall of the Second Empire that the Third Republic annexed Tongking, Laos and Cambodia and established the colony of French Indo-China which lasted until 1954.

Louis Napoleon also pressed forward with the colonization of West Africa. When he became Emperor, France held only the bridgehead in Senegal which had been acquired by Louis XIV in the seventeenth century; but in 1854 the French Governor of Senegal, General Faidherbe, began to move inland, and within a few years French explorers, followed in many cases by French troops, had advanced 700 miles to the east as far as Segu on the Niger. Faidherbe engaged successfully in constant military operations against local Arab tribes and established a colony which lasted for a few years longer than French rule in Indo-China.[72]

It was again the murder of French Catholic missionaries which gave Louis Napoleon the opportunity to send a naval expedition to the South Pacific to seize the islands of New Caledonia, about a thousand miles off the east coast of Australia. After a few months of tension with England, the British government waived its claims to the territory, and allowed Louis Napoleon to annex the islands to the French Empire. In 1864 he established a penal settlement there. He claimed that he did so for humanitarian reasons, as the climate in New Caledonia was better for Europeans than in Cayenne.[73]

With an expanding empire in Asia, Africa and Australasia, Napoleon III in 1861 turned his attention to another continent, North America. The results were to be disastrous.

CHAPTER 36

RE-DRAWING THE MAP OF EUROPE

O N 24 November 1860 the Emperor surprised France and the world by issuing a decree allowing free parliamentary discussion in the Senate and the Legislative Body. There was to be a debate on the Emperor's speech at the opening of each Parliamentary session; certain ministers were to be appointed to reply to the criticisms on behalf of the government; and the press were to be free to publish a report of the debates which was to be sent to them each day by the Presidents of the two Chambers.[1] The measure was welcomed by the Liberals in France and abroad. Some of them thought that it was significant that Eugénie was away in Scotland when the decision was taken, but her absence was almost certainly a coincidence.

The grant of free parliamentary discussion was a big step towards the liberalization of the régime. The five Opposition deputies – Favre, Ollivier and their three colleagues – took advantage of it to attack the Emperor's policy, and their speeches were fully reported in the press, though any newspaper or other publisher who published any account of the proceedings in the Chambers, other than the official verbatim report, was guilty of an offence, and journalists and publishers were occasionally sent to prison for this. There was little progress towards freedom of the press; and all meetings of more than twenty persons were still illegal unless the permission of the government had been obtained.[2]

At times the government allowed a little more freedom to the press than it had done during the first eight years of the Empire; but this was always followed by the suppression of a newspaper, or by an official warning, when this was least expected.[3] *La Jeune France* received a warning for publishing extracts from a report of a completely non-political speech by Louis Philippe's son, the Duc d'Aumale, at a dinner of the Royal Literary Fund in London;[4] and the *Revue des Deux Mondes* was warned because of a contribution by the famous historian, Edgar Quinet, in which he stated that Napoleon, and not Grouchy or any other general, had been to blame for the defeat at Waterloo.[5]

Apart from the official warnings, there were unofficial ones delivered by an official of the Ministry of the Interior, who was known as 'the black man' because of the conventional dark suit that he always wore. He went on his rounds every morning, visiting the newspaper offices, and telling the editors that some article, or some passage in an article, in the newspaper had displeased the government, and that the editor would be well advised to be more careful in future.[6]

Important changes were taking place in the position of the working classes and of trade unions. Wages were rising, and by 1861 the employers were complaining that though strikes were illegal and punishable by long terms of imprisonment, it was in practice impossible to persuade the police to take action against strikers because the government was terrified of the working classes and the Emperor was a Socialist. Workmen who were formerly satisfied with 35 sous (7p) a day now asked 3 francs (12½p) a day, and got it; and landowners could not find girls who would work on their farms for 200 francs a year, though a few years ago they paid the girls 80 francs a year.[7] In August 1861, Madame de Tocqueville told Senior that 'the workpeople believe that the rich are their enemies, and that the Emperor is their friend, and that he would join them in an attempt to get their fair share, that is an equal share of the property of the country'; and she added: 'I am not sure that they are mistaken.' Ampère said that Pereire, the President of the Crédit Mobilier, was so afraid of his workmen that he sent carriages to bring them from their homes to their place of work.[8]

Law followed practice, and in 1864 the government introduced a bill in the Chambers legalizing trade unions and strikes. Immediately a wave of strikes broke out in all the industrial centres of France – among the cab drivers, the shop assistants in the department stores, and the tailors in Paris; among the miners in the North; and among the metalworkers at Le Creusot, in the factory owned by Schneider, who had formerly been a minister in Louis Napoleon's government and was now the President of the Legislative Body[9] The law legalizing strikes coincided with the formation in London of the International Working Men's Association[10] – which in later years was known retrospectively as the First International – whose guiding spirit was Karl Marx and his friend Friedrich Engels. The French section of the International was particularly active, and gave a political content to many of the strikes. The government often used the police and the law courts against the strikers, but only to the extent of preventing violence against blacklegs, attacks on the mines and factories, or unlawful picketing or obstruction of the public highway. In many cases the strikes were wholly or partly successful.

Eugénie was opposed to the Emperor's policy of liberalization. In 1903 she told Filon that she had urged Louis Napoleon to maintain his dictatorial régime in full rigour during his lifetime, and to allow a new and liberal régime to be introduced after his death on the accession of the Prince Imperial.[11] There was a logic in her scheme, because Louis Napoleon had made himself so hated by the Reds and other opposition elements during his years of absolute dictatorship that they were certain to use any freedom which he gave them to attack and weaken him, whereas the Prince Imperial, starting with a clean sheet, could have won all the credit for the liberalization policy. But she supported Louis Napoleon's policy of wooing the Opposition deputies, and was particularly charming and attentive to Ollivier and his colleagues when they came to parties at the Tuileries. Ollivier thought that her opposition to liberalization was due to her dislike and distrust of the press. He believed that she was much less opposed to freedom of public meeting than to freedom of the press; and when the middle classes, after the wave of strikes that followed the legalization of trade unions, demanded that the unions should again be suppressed, Eugénie assured Ollivier that both she and the Emperor would never agree to this, as it would provoke a revolution.[12]

Her opposition to the reforms brought her into conflict with Prince Napoleon, who always urged the Emperor to go farther and faster along the road to freedom. Prince Napoleon founded a newspaper, *L'Opinion Nationale*, which advocated the liberalization policy; and he also made use of his position in the Senate, of which he was a life member by virtue of his rank as an Imperial Prince. In February 1861 he caused a great sensation by making a speech in the Senate urging the withdrawal of the French troops from Rome. He was strongly attacked by the Ultramontane Senators and by the bishops in their pastoral letters; but the Emperor wrote him a letter, which he disclosed to the press, congratulating him on his speech, which Louis Napoleon said that he approved of in general, though he disagreed with some parts of it.[13]

In February 1862, Prince Napoleon caused an even greater outcry by another speech in the Senate in which he stressed the revolutionary traditions of Bonapartism. He said that when Napoleon returned from Elba, he issued a proclamation denouncing the nobles and the traitors – 'les nobles et les traîtres'. The Senators misheard him, and thought that he had said 'les nobles et les prêtres', and, enraged at this attack on the clergy, they shouted him down, a proceeding which was unheard of in the Senate debates.[14]

The conflict between Eugénie and Prince Napoleon led to a painful incident at the annual banquet at Compiègne on 15 November in honour of Eugénie's saint's day in 1863. Prince Napoleon sat on Eugénie's right during the dinner, and the Emperor invited him to make a speech proposing the Empress's health. 'I am a little afraid of your speeches,' said Eugénie gaily, 'although you are such a brilliant orator.' Prince Napoleon did not appreciate the joke, and asked to be excused from proposing the Empress's health, as he was not used to public speaking. 'So you will not propose the Empress's health?' said the Emperor. 'Not if Your Majesty will relieve me of the duty', replied Prince Napoleon. Prince Joachim Murat then proposed Eugénie's health in a voice choking with anger, and the indignant guests cut Prince Napoleon for the rest of the evening; but both Louis Napoleon and Eugénie appeared to be quite unruffled, and when they all rose from the dinner table, Eugénie took Prince Napoleon's arm as they walked into the drawing-room.[15]

Filon, despite what Eugénie had told him about her opposition to the Emperor's liberalization policy, wrote that there was no truth in the popular belief that she was the leader of a reactionary party at court. He stated that this idea had been deliberately fostered by the Emperor, who wished to create artificially two parties in the government – the one Liberal, urging him forward, and the other Conservative and Catholic, holding him back; and he wished Eugénie to take the credit and the blame whenever he pursued a reactionary Catholic policy. Filon says that Louis Napoleon's tactic was helped by one of his former mistresses – he means Marianne de Walewska – who had fallen from the Emperor's favour, and hoped by discrediting the Empress to regain her influence at court; so, while pretending to be Eugénie's friend, she secretly plotted to discredit her by furthering Louis Napoleon's scheme. It is quite impossible to accept Filon's story. Walewski was a well-known supporter of the Conservative and Catholic party, and a campaign by his wife to discredit Eugénie as an Ultramontane could not have benefited him, but only Prince Napoleon and the Liberal faction in the Cabinet.[16]

When diplomatic relations with Austria were resumed after the war of 1859, Franz Joseph sent Prince Richard von Metternich, the son of the great statesman, as Ambassador to Paris. Eugénie became a close personal friend of Metternich and his wife. Princess Pauline Metternich, the daughter of the aristocratic Hungarian family of Sandor, became famous and notorious in Vienna through her splendid horsemanship, her daring habits and her striking personality; the Viennese said of her that just as there was only one imperial capital and one Vienna, there was only one non-royal princess, Pauline Metternich.* Only her most spiteful enemies realized that she was an ugly woman.

*Es giebt nur a Kaiserstadt,
 Es giebt nur a Wien,
 Es giebt nur a Fürstin,
 Es ist die Metternich Paulin.[17]

When she came to Paris as ambassadress, she made an equal sensation there. Mérimée described her as 'half *grande dame* and half *lorette*'[18] – a mixture of a great aristocratic lady and a semi-prostitute of the Notre-Dame-de-Lorette district. She dressed unconventionally and smoked cigars in public, and when in England bought shrimps from a stall in the street and ate them in her carriage out of her handkerchief. She was a gifted amateur musician and actress. Once, when Waldteufel failed to arrive to conduct the orchestra at a ball at Princess Mathilde's – he had made a mistake about the date – Princess Metternich played dance tunes on the piano for the dancers. She excelled in the amateur theatricals at Compiègne, and during the Paris cab strike in the autumn of 1865 she gave a wonderful performance as a cab driver on strike in her best Parisian accent and slang. It is not surprising that she became a great favourite with the Empress.[19]

Eugénie's friendship with the Metternichs facilitated her attempts to help Louis Napoleon's foreign policy by her personal, informal diplomacy. It has often been suggested that this friendship was the cause of her sympathy with Austria and her anti-Italian and anti-Prussian policy; but this is to do Eugénie an injustice. As Metternich knew, her liking for him would never make her forget that her duty was to further the policy of her husband and of France. She was almost as friendly with the Italian Ambassador, Count Nigra, as she was with Metternich; and the Prussian Ambassador, Baron von der Goltz, was in love with her. She enjoyed his admiration, referring to him as 'poor Goltz'.[20]

In June 1861, Cavour died suddenly at the age of fifty. Louis Napoleon took the opportunity, while sending his condolences to Victor Emanuel, to re-establish the diplomatic links which he had broken off after the invasion of the Papal States and to recognize the title of King of Italy, which Victor Emanuel had assumed four months before. The declared aim of Victor Emanuel and his ministers was now to obtain both Rome and Venetia. The Mazzinians and Radicals, including Garibaldi, wished to liberate both territories immediately by revolutionary action; the Italian government knew that this was impossible, but hoped by diplomacy to persuade Napoleon III to assist them to obtain the two provinces. The French Catholics, having seen the Pope deprived of three-quarters of his territories in 1859 and 1860, were determined to ensure that the French troops remained in Rome to prevent Victor Emanuel from stealing the last remaining territory from the Pope.

If Louis Napoleon had unequivocally supported the *status quo* in Italy, the Italian government would probably have reluctantly accepted the position and compelled Garibaldi to do likewise. In October 1862

General La Marmora told Arese that they could have created the kingdom of Italy without Rome if Louis Napoleon had clearly told them in 1860 that they could never have the city.[21] But Louis Napoleon continued to encourage the Italian government to believe that he personally wished them to have Rome, and would arrange for this as soon as French public opinion would permit. 'The Roman question is always the stumbling-block', he wrote to Arese on 2 January 1863. 'This question is treated too lightly in Italy; in France and Europe it is very serious, and independent of my personal undertakings. Public opinion in France will not be at all favourable to the abandonment of Rome. We must therefore resign ourselves to wait for events to bring a favourable solution.'[22]

Louis Napoleon was still obsessed with his scheme for an Italian Confederation which no one else wanted. Eugénie told Metternich that the Emperor thought, as she did, that a united Italy was a potential threat to French security; and he repeatedly suggested breaking up Victor Emanuel's kingdom into four independent states of an Italian Confederation.[23] He proposed that Austria should cede Venetia to Victor Emanuel and receive Turkish territory in the Balkans as compensation; in return for Venetia, Victor Emanuel would relinquish Tuscany, Umbria and the Marches, which should form the kingdom of Central Italy, and the South, which should once again become the kingdom of Naples, with Rome and the Patrimony of St Peter remaining under the Pope. But neither Austria nor Italy would agree to this.

Eugénie's Italian policy did not differ from Louis Napoleon's except on the one point that she was resolutely determined that Victor Emanuel should not have Rome and that French troops must stay in Rome to stop him from taking it. The Liberals and Radicals in France and Europe thought that she was responsible for keeping the troops there, and the most far-fetched stories were told about her attitude. She was said to be utterly dominated by her confessor, Monsignor Bauer, a converted Jew who had become a fanatical Catholic Ultramontane; she was terrified that not only the Emperor but she herself and the Prince Imperial would be excommunicated by the Pope if France abandoned Rome; worse, that the Prince Imperial would be struck dead by divine vengeance.[24] In November 1862, Lord John Russell, now Earl Russell, stung by the suggestion that the French had remained in occupation of Rome because of Britain's pro-Italian policy, wrote to Cowley: 'It is the Empress & not the British Government who retains the French troops in Rome.'[25] This was a grotesque oversimplification, in view of the violent feelings of millions of French Catholics on this issue.

She approved of Louis Napoleon's stand against the more obnoxious forms of Catholic extremism. When a play was performed at the Porte Saint-Martin Theatre denouncing the kidnapping of the Jewish Mortara boy by the Catholics in Rome – 'Victor Séjour', the author of the play, was in fact the Emperor's secretary, Mocquard – Eugénie went to see it with Louis Napoleon, and joined with him in demonstrative applause which distressed Viel Castel and the Ultramontanes. Nor did she object when Louis Napoleon banned the Jubilee which the Archbishop of Toulouse had proclaimed to celebrate the tercentenary of the massacre of 4000 Huguenots by the Catholics in Toulouse during the Wars of Religion in 1562. The Archbishop protested that he had merely wished to celebrate the fact that on that occasion the Catholics had forestalled a plan by the Huguenots to massacre *them*.[26]

Eugénie supported Louis Napoleon's policy of creating a Confederation of the four Italian states; at least, she acted as his agent in pressing this policy on the Austrian Ambassador. She repeatedly pestered Metternich to cede Venetia to Italy, until in the end he lost his temper, and she apologized and promised not to mention the subject again.[27] But she favoured a hard line on Rome. According to Viel Castel, who, as an intimate friend of Princess Mathilde, was in a position to know, the Cabinet was divided. Eugénie and Walewski thought that the troops should be kept in Rome at all costs; but Thouvenel, the Foreign Minister, and Fould and Persigny wished to withdraw them and leave the Pope to his fate. Eugénie was particularly opposed to Persigny, and resented his official warnings, as Minister of the Interior, to the French Catholic newspapers which criticized the Emperor's Italian policy.[28]

Louis Napoleon hoped to withdraw the troops from Rome as soon as he could persuade the Italian government to give an undertaking not to invade the Papal States; but after the events of 1860 Eugénie did not think that the word of the Italian government could be trusted.[29] When she talked for over an hour to Malmesbury about Rome at the Tuileries in October 1862 he found that she was not the '*dévote*' that he had expected; but she said that it would be a scandal if the Pope were forced to flee from Rome and become a refugee.[30]

As usual, she did not allow political differences to interfere with personal friendships. In March 1863, Conneau warned Arese that the Italian cause was very unpopular in France, and that the Emperor, Mocquard, Fleury and Conneau himself were the only people in France who were sympathetic to Italy; but he added that the Empress shared the Emperor's strong personal liking for Arese: 'You are probably the only Italian whom she likes.'[31] This was not accurate, as she was also very friendly with Nigra.

In the summer of 1862 Garibaldi went to Sicily, and in a speech at

Marsala strongly attacked Napoleon III as the man who was preventing the unification of Italy. He launched the slogan 'Rome or death!', and prepared once again to cross the Straits and march north to liberate Rome. Louis Napoleon called on Victor Emanuel to stop him.[32] The Pope was convinced that there was a conspiracy between Garibaldi, Victor Emanuel and Napoleon III to deprive him of Rome; he thought that the fraud of 1860 would be repeated – that as Garibaldi marched on Rome, Victor Emanuel would send his army into the Papal States, ostensibly to save them from 'the Revolution', but really to seize them for himself, while Napoleon III again pretended to protest but secretly encouraged Victor Emanuel in his wicked plan.[33] The result was that, while Thouvenel, and Louis Napoleon himself, strongly urged the Italian government to send their troops against Garibaldi, the Ultramontanes, the Austrian government, the French Ambassador in Rome – Gramont – and Eugénie were earnestly hoping that Victor Emanuel would not act against Garibaldi, so that Louis Napoleon would be forced to send a French army into Italy to crush Garibaldi, which would cause a final breach between France and Victor Emanuel's government.[34]

On 29 August the royal Italian army attacked Garibaldi's men at Aspromonte in Calabria, where Garibaldi was wounded and taken prisoner. Eugénie was sorry, for she had hoped, as she told Metternich, that the unity of Italy would be destroyed by Garibaldi's sword.[35]

Garibaldi's Aspromonte venture ended all hopes of negotiating an immediate withdrawal of French troops from Rome, and Thouvenel resigned.[36] He was succeeded as Foreign Minister by Drouyn de Lhuys, whose policy was more hostile to Italy and who won the support of Eugénie. But two years later Louis Napoleon reached an agreement with Italy which he hoped would solve the Roman problem. By the Convention of 15 September 1864, he agreed that French troops should be withdrawn from Rome and that the last would leave by 31 December 1866; and the Italian government gave an undertaking not to violate the frontiers of the Papal States or to allow any bands of irregulars to do so.[37] The Convention was strongly attacked both by the Radicals – because the Italian claim to Rome had been abandoned – and by the Pope and the French Catholics, who thought that Victor Emanuel's troops would march in as soon as the French left.

After the war crisis of June 1859, Louis Napoleon tried to improve his relations with Prussia. In June 1860 he invited Prince William, the Regent of Prussia, to meet him at Baden, with the Grand Duke of Baden and Lady Douglas, now the Duchess of Hamilton, acting as their hosts. Prince William, whom he had last met at Malmaison in 1814, was determined not to allow him to drive a wedge between Prussia and the other German states, and he therefore replied to Louis Napoleon's invitation by suggesting that all the other German sovereigns should also come to the meeting at Baden. This was not what Louis Napoleon had intended, but he had no choice except to agree to meet them all.[38]

He arrived at Baden on the evening of Saturday 16 June and spent the Sunday there. Apart from the Grand Duke of Baden and the Prince Regent of Prussia, there were eight other sovereigns in Baden – the King of Württemberg, the King of Bavaria, the King of Saxony, the old blind King of Hanover, the Grand Duke of Hesse-Darmstadt, the Grand Duke of Saxe-Weimar, the Duke of Nassau and the Duke of Saxe-Coburg-Gotha. The Prince and Princess of Hohenzollern, the Prince and Princess of Fürstenberg, Princess Augusta of Prussia, and the Duchess of Hamilton were also at the meeting.

Louis Napoleon strolled around the town, accompanied only by one A.D.C., and talked to the passers-by. He did not have even the A.D.C. with him when he drove himself in a phaeton and pair to the King of Hanover's hotel and walked in unexpectedly and asked to see the King. A waiter took him up to the King's suite. The blind King was furious when he heard them walk in, and asked who dared enter his apartments uninvited. The waiter replied curtly 'The Emperor of the French', and left Louis Napoleon alone with his irate fellow-monarch. He soon appeased the angry King of Hanover, and the King was delighted when the Emperor took the Grand Cross of the Legion of Honour out of his pocket and conferred it on the King. Louis Napoleon then walked across to an annexe of the Hôtel d'Angleterre to visit the Duke of Nassau before attending a state banquet given by the Grand Duke of Baden in the Old Castle, at which the King of Hanover appeared wearing his Legion of Honour. After taking tea with the other sovereigns at the Duchess of Hamilton's in the evening, Louis Napoleon left at 10 p.m. on the night train to Paris, having accomplished nothing during his twenty-four hours in Baden except an exercise in public relations which was less successful than the one at Stuttgart in 1857. Princess Frederick William of Prussia told her mother, Queen Victoria, that he was hissed in the streets of Baden, and that hardly anyone took off their hats to him.[39]

Sixteen months later, he had the opportunity for longer talks with the Prince Regent of Prussia, who ascended the throne as King William I when his brother died on the night of New Year's Day 1861. King William agreed to be the guest of Louis Napoleon and Eugénie at Compiègne in October 1861; but though he delighted his host and hostess by his elderly courtesy,[40] and assured Louis Napoleon of his friendship for France, he refused to enter into any commitment independently of Austria and the other states of the German Confederation. 'I have preserved my independence entirely', wrote King William to Prince Albert in England, 'and represented the interests of Germany, as I had done at Baden.'[41]

In June 1862 the Prussian Ambassador in St Petersburg, Count Otto von Bismarck, was transferred to the Paris embassy. He had already been presented to Napoleon III, having been in Paris at the time of Queen Victoria's visit there in 1855, and again two years later for the Conference on Neuchâtel. As Ambassador he was on excellent terms with Louis Napoleon, and greatly admired Eugénie's political intelligence; he thought that she was the only *man* in the Emperor's entourage. He was already planning to make Prussia the greatest power in Central Europe, but thought that, in the early stages at least, this could best be achieved by maintaining friendly relations with France. He had been Ambassador in Paris for only three-and-a-half months when King William recalled him to Berlin and appointed him prime minister, giving him a free hand to crush the Liberal Parliamentary Opposition and establish the dictatorship of the Crown. Louis Napoleon awarded Bismarck the Legion of Honour as a mark of his appreciation on his appointment as Chancellor of Prussia.[42]

But Louis Napoleon soon came into conflict with Bismarck over the Polish insurrection which broke out against the Russian government in January 1863. The cause of Polish freedom aroused the passionate sympathy of the French people, as it had done in 1830, when Louis Napoleon had been among the first to criticize the failure of Louis Philippe's government to help the Poles. It was the only issue which united the Catholics and the Reds, both of whom supported the Polish revolutionaries, claimed them as their own, and accused each other of hypocrisy for doing likewise. Walewski for once championed the cause of national independence, as did Eugénie. But the position was awkward for Louis Napoleon, who did not wish to injure his relations with Russia; and when his government spokesmen in the Chambers, and the official press, declared that it was no kindness to the Poles to lead them to believe that France could give them any effective help, it was obvious that Louis Napoleon was not prepared to go to war with Russia, or even to damage his friendly relations with the Tsar, for the sake of Poland.[43]

At the outbreak of the insurrection, Bismarck saw an opportunity of preventing it from spreading into Prussian Poland, and also of winning Russian friendship, by collaborating with Russia against the Polish revolutionaries. He stationed troops on the border with Russian Poland, who prevented the escape of the defeated revolutionaries across the Prussian frontier and handed over those whom they captured to the Russians for punishment. Bismarck's action shocked Liberal opinion throughout Europe, and was strongly condemned in France and Britain; and it gave Louis Napoleon an excuse to intervene by claiming that Bismarck's action had made Poland an international question and no longer an internal Russian one.[44] Louis Napoleon, who could do nothing against Russia, could threaten Prussia along the Rhine. He sent notes to both Russia and Prussia protesting against their actions in Poland, but the language of the note to Prussia was much more threatening than the tone employed to Russia. Palmerston and Russell, who were even less inclined than Napoleon III to do anything effective to help the Poles, joined Louis Napoleon in the protests to Russia and Prussia; but Louis Napoleon's strong attitude towards Prussia made the British statesmen fear that his object was not to help the Poles but to regain the Rhine as the frontier of France.

On 21 February 1863, Eugénie had a three-hour talk with Metternich. She said that though he would doubtless think that she was insane, she would 'overtake the Emperor and immediately go much further than he'. She then opened Le Sage's atlas at the map of Europe and suggested to Metternich how it could be altered. The kingdom of Poland should be reconstituted by Russia, Prussia and Austria relinquishing their Polish provinces. If Austria wished, an Austrian Archduke could become King of Poland, but Eugénie would prefer to give Poland to the King of Saxony, whose ancestors had reigned in Poland in the eighteenth century. In return, the King of Saxony would cede Saxony to Prussia, who would also be given all the territories of the German sovereigns north of the Main and up to the borders of Bohemia, but would cede Silesia to Austria and the left bank of the Rhine to France. '*France* would cede *nothing*!', noted Metternich. Austria would cede Venetia to Victor Emanuel, who would relinquish Central and Southern Italy to a kingdom of Central Italy and a resurrected kingdom of Naples. Austria would be compensated for the cession of Venetia and her Polish provinces by being given, in addition to Silesia, the Turkish provinces on the east coast of the Adriatic; and Russia, in return for ceding Russian Poland, would recover the left bank of the Danube in Bessarabia and would be granted the Turkish possessions in Asia Minor. The rest of Turkey in Europe, including Constantinople, would be given to Greece. The Turkish Empire would thus be dissolved, to the benefit of Christianity and morality. There would remain a number of dispossessed German sovereigns to whom no new territories had been awarded; they could be made Emperors of some South American republics, to carry European civilization to the American hemisphere, like Archduke Maximilian in Mexico.[45]

Metternich immediately wrote to Rechberg, the Austrian Foreign

Minister, about the flight over Europe that he had taken with the Empress – 'what a *flight* and with what a bird!'[46] However fanciful these proposals might be, he had no doubt that Napoleon III was thinking along these lines and had put up Eugénie to discover Austrian reaction to the proposals. Rechberg replied in sarcastic vein. 'It would be ungallant to remain silent about the confidential things that the Empress was good enough to say to you', he wrote on 27 February; 'I am far from treating as a joke the journey which you made through three-quarters of the world in such august company.' Rechberg was disturbed by the glimpse which it gave him of Napoleon III's intentions, and particularly resented the proposals for strengthening Prussia in North Germany. 'If the imperial couple wish to seduce us, they should present us with a more appetizing dish', he wrote; 'if we indulge in fantasy, let it be at least frankly favourable to us. Otherwise we prefer to remain on a realistic level.' Rechberg therefore instructed Metternich to let Louis Napoleon and Eugénie know of Austria's 'absolute repugnance' to their proposals as far as Germany was concerned.[47]

The Polish revolutionaries were still holding out when the Schleswig-Holstein problem, which had been lying dormant since 1852, was reopened by the action of the Danish government in enforcing a new constitution on the people of Holstein which violated the status of the Duchy and tightened the King of Denmark's control. The German Federal Diet, with the support of the German Liberals, threatened to go to war with Denmark to liberate Holstein and Schleswig; and Bismarck, skilfully posing to the Great Powers as the opponent of the German national movement and at the same time overbidding the Liberals for nationalist support in Germany, joined with Austria in a military alliance and proposed to send troops into Holstein.

In November 1863, Louis Napoleon proposed that a Congress of sovereigns should be held in Paris to settle both the Polish and the Schleswig-Holstein questions. He favoured such a Congress both because of his visionary idea that questions of peace or war should be settled by common action between the Great Powers and because he hoped to use his diplomatic finesse to fix things behind the scenes in secret negotiations during the Congress. Rechberg, bearing in mind Eugénie's proposals to Metternich, was suspicious of Louis Napoleon's motive in calling for a Congress. Palmerston strongly opposed the plan for the Congress, and Britain's refusal to take part scuppered the whole project. Russia refused to discuss with any foreign government their handling of an internal rebellion in their Polish provinces, though Tsar Alexander promised Louis Napoleon to deal as mercifully as possible with the rebels after he had defeated them. Bismarck accepted the French invitation to the Congress in order to curry favour with

Louis Napoleon, knowing that the British refusal had made it impossible for the Congress to be held.[48]

Louis Napoleon was angry at the British refusal to attend a Congress, which prevented him from doing anything to help the Poles. Eugénie was even more angry, and scolded Metternich at Compiègne, accusing Austria of having prompted the British rejection. Louis Napoleon therefore refused to collaborate with Britain in the Schleswig-Holstein dispute, in which Palmerston and Russell had rashly made public statements giving the impression that they would defend the Danes against an attack by Prussia and Austria. In November 1863 Louis Napoleon secretly offered Prussia an anti-British and anti-Austrian alliance. Bismarck gave a friendly and guarded reply, but informed the Austrian government of Louis Napoleon's proposal. Unlike Louis Napoleon, Bismarck was shrewd enough to realize that it does not pay to double-cross an ally.[49]

On 24 December 1863 the Prussian and Austrian troops invaded Holstein. On 1 February 1864 they entered Schleswig, and by 18 February they were in Jutland. It seemed as if Denmark would be overrun, and the French became alarmed. Drouyn de Lhuys told Goltz that if the Prussian and Austrian advance continued, France might have to abandon her policy of neutrality, and the Ambassador reported to Bismarck that the French attitude was hardening. But when Britain, on 20 February, proposed to France that they should take joint action to help Denmark, the French government rejected the proposal. Cowley believed that Eugénie was chiefly responsible for this decision. He reported that her friendship with Metternich made her pro-Austrian, and therefore sympathetic to the Prusso-Austrian action against Denmark; and he also mentioned that she was very anti-English.[50]

In April, having captured the important Danish defence position at Düppel, Bismarck accepted the British proposal to attend a conference in London; then in June, Prussia and Austria resumed hostilities, and in another short campaign forced Denmark to accept their terms. Austria took Holstein and Prussia took Schleswig. The British government, unable to fulfil their unofficial pledge to help Denmark, was humiliated; Louis Napoleon looked on unconcernedly.

CHAPTER 37

PROBLEMS OF A BIOGRAPHER

MANY people in France felt that Schleswig-Holstein, like Poland, had been a setback for Louis Napoleon. Even zealous Bonapartists, who until the war in Italy had regarded the Emperor as being almost infallible, now thought that he was losing his touch, and criticized him beneath their breath. Some of them attributed it to the fact that he was too engrossed in writing his biography of Julius Caesar to be able to concentrate on state affairs. He originally intended writing a short book; but he became more and more interested in the subject as his research carried him deeper into the history of the first century B.C. He asked Mérimée and other historians to help him with the research, and spent many hours tramping round the sites of ancient Roman and Gallic camps and theatres; when he went with Mérimée in June 1861 to Alise to see the excavations of Alesia, where Vercingetorix had fought his last battle against Caesar, he walked on the hillside for three-and-a-half hours in the hot sun, looking at the terrain with the greatest interest.[1]

His opponents ridiculed the idea that he was writing the book himself, and believed that he was plagiarizing the work of paid hackwriters; but his secretaries knew that this was untrue, and were struck by how much harder he worked on Julius Caesar than he had ever done on the state papers. He had lost all interest in social life and wished only to retire to his study in his slippers and dressing-gown and dictate his book.[2]

The fact that he was once more researching for a book gave him an excuse to make an approach, after a ten-year breach, to Hortense Cornu. He wrote to her asking her to help him with the research, as she had done when he was writing his books at Ham. She responded to his appeal and did some work for him; but they did not meet, and their letters had none of their old warmth.[3]

One day he sent his old servant Charles Thélin, who had been at his side in the escape from Ham, to Hortense with a jade vase which had been taken from the Summer Palace in Peking; but he then found that the lid of the vase had been misplaced. He spent the whole day looking for the lid, and did not transact any public business. His courtiers were amazed that he should waste his time in this way, when some servants could have looked for the lid; but Hortense was not in the least surprised. It was just what she would have expected of him.[4]

In March 1863 he wrote to her, saying that he would risk a rebuff and invite her to come to the Tuileries to see him again after twelve years, as he was so eager for her to see his son. On the Prince Imperial's seventh birthday, he sent Madame de Walewska to fetch Hortense Cornu, who felt unable to refuse. At the Tuileries the Emperor embraced her, and all etiquette was dispensed with as she talked with him, the Empress and the Prince Imperial; and after this she visited him regularly in his study before dinner on Sunday evenings to help him with Julius Caesar and to talk about old times. She also met the Empress frequently, and found that she was charming, and not the Catholic bigot that she was supposed to be. Madame Cornu thought that Eugénie was a less emotional person than Louis Napoleon, and less in love with him than he was with her. She also thought that Eugénie was much firmer with the Prince Imperial, who was unashamedly spoilt by his father.

As for the Emperor, he had grown fatter and was in worse health than when she had last seen him. He took much less exercise than formerly, rarely riding and walking even less. He was still as reluctant as ever to take decisions, whether it was about Poland, or the inclusion of some doubtful anecdote about Caesar in his biography, or the fixing of the date of the general election; and when she found him particularly happy, she knew that it was because he had at last made up his mind on some point and the painful decision-making process was over.[5] She did not disguise the fact that she was still a Republican, but usually avoided politics and talked about his book, which she thought was very good. 'I sometimes forget', she told Senior,

all that has passed since we saw one another for the last time before December 1851, when he was still an innocent man. But from time to time the destruction of our liberties, the massacres of 1851, the deportations of 1852, and the cruelties which revenged the *attentat* rise to my mind, and I shrink from the embrace of a man stained with the blood of so many of my friends.[6]

He began writing the book in 1860, and the first volume was published nearly five years later on 1 March 1865, the second volume following in December 1866. The Emperor's name did not appear on the title page, but the preface, which was dated 'The Tuileries Palace, 20 March 1862', was signed 'Napoleon'. The first volume, which opened with a long introductory section on the history of Rome from its foundation, went up to Caesar's appointment as Proconsul in Gaul; the second volume, dealing with the campaigns in Gaul, ended with the crossing of the Rubicon, when Caesar, 'having begun the conquest of Gaul with four legions, will begin the conquest of the universe with only one'.[7] He never wrote the third volume which would have completed the work.

His *Histoire de Jules César* is a magnificent biography. If Napoleon III had never been an Emperor, and was not remembered in history for all his achievements and blunders, he would surely be thought of today as a great historical biographer. The book has all the ingredients of a good biography – strong sympathy with his hero, but never hagiographical in approach and never suppressing unpalatable facts; meticulously researched, and with a careful weighing of the conflicting theories of earlier biographers in passages relegated to the footnotes so as not to interfere with the flow of the narrative; the expression of broad historical principles as well as countless points of detail; and a clear and forceful style of writing.

The book was of course widely reviewed, and for the most part sycophantically, in the French press, though the Emperor had given instructions to the newspapers that the reviewers should write freely and honestly about the book without any fear or favour.[8] Charles Longuet, who later married Karl Marx's daughter Jenny, was the editor of *La Rive Gauche*, a left-wing journal with a very small circulation among Socialist students. He asked his colleague Rogeard to review Louis Napoleon's book, knowing that Rogeard had a knowledge of Roman history. Rogeard said that he hated Louis Napoleon too much to be able 'to write seriously, like so many others, about the illustrious author, the august personage, the crowned historian', but that he was willing to write an article for the newspaper which would use the publication of the book as an excuse to attack the Emperor. Longuet agreed, and the result was Rogeard's *Les Propos de Labienus*, which appeared in two instalments of *La Rive Gauche*. It was a discussion between Labienus the younger and another Roman on the occasion of the publication of the memoirs of Augustus in A.D. 7. Labienus laments the old days of the Roman republic, and condemns the crimes of Augustus, referring only to actual events in which the real Augustus took part in the first century B.C.[9] But the hidden meaning was obvious to everyone, especially as the official government press often compared Louis Napoleon to Augustus, the nephew of the great Julius Caesar who became as great as his uncle.[10]

The first part of *Les Propos de Labienus* appeared on 4 March 1865. Next week the printer became frightened and refused to print the second part; but Longuet found another printer, and when the second part appeared on 18 March the whole edition of 5000 copies was sold out within two hours. Another 5000 copies were reprinted next day and sold out at once; and two days later, a second reprint of another 5000 copies were seized at the printer's by the police. Rogeard fled to Brussels, but was tried in his absence and sentenced to five years' imprisonment and a fine of 500 francs, the printer receiving one month's imprisonment and a fine of 500 francs. The court ruled that 'the pamphlet, under the guise of portraying the Roman Empire at the time of Augustus ... deals in fact with France and the sovereign who governs her', and 'under this veil the author of the book engages incessantly in the most outrageous imputations and slanders against the Emperor's person'. *Les Propos de Labienus* was published in the Belgian press and in an English translation in the *Daily News*, and sold 30,000 copies abroad; but it was banned and seized by the police in Austria, Prussia, Spain and Italy.[11]

La Rive Gauche was one of several manifestations of the new resistance that was rising among the students on the left bank. The old Opposition had to some extent reconciled itself to the régime, though a few zealots like Blanqui and Miot were again arrested and sentenced to new terms of imprisonment for forming a 'secret society'.[12] Louis Napoleon had always been eager to offer the hand of friendship to old opponents who were prepared to make their peace and accept the régime. The *Times* correspondent noted that many of the most obnoxious government officials who showed the greatest vigour in suppressing the freedom of the press were former Reds who had been ardent revolutionaries in 1848. Viel Castel was alarmed at the extent to which Reds had infiltrated the government service.[13]

Louis Napoleon himself went out of his way to show his friendship to his former enemies. When he visited Boulogne soon after he became Emperor, he gave the Legion of Honour to a soldier who had arrested him after the defeat of his *coup* in 1840. He told another soldier, who had received the Legion of Honour for his loyalty on that occasion, that he regretted that he could not give him the Legion of Honour as Louis Philippe had already done so, but would award him the Military Medal instead.[14] When Thiers slipped on the ice and broke his nose during the bitter weather of February 1855, the Emperor sent a message of sympathy.[15]

He preserved his friendship with Vieillard, who, unlike Hortense Cornu, never broke off personal relations with him, though he usually opposed government policy in the Senate, being almost the only Senator to do so in the early years of the Empire. Louis Napoleon was at Fontainebleau in May 1857 when he heard that Vieillard was dying at his house in the Rue Saint-Lazare in Paris. He went at once to

Vieillard for a last farewell. A few days later he sent his Chamberlain, Chaumont-Quitry, to represent him at Vieillard's funeral. As the cortège was about to leave the house, they were informed that Vieillard had stipulated in his will that there was to be no religious ceremony at the funeral. Chaumont-Quitry insisted on delaying the departure to the cemetery until he had cabled to the Emperor asking for instructions. He was right; Louis Napoleon cabled back that he was not to attend the funeral. If he had, the repercussions in Catholic circles might have been serious.[16]

The great Hebrew scholar, Ernest Renan, had left his seminary and renounced the priesthood as a young man in the days of Louis Philippe, and his books on Biblical history aroused the opposition of the Catholic Church. This made it very difficult for the government to give him a Chair at any university. But Louis Napoleon cultivated his friendship, sent him on an archaeological expedition to Phoenicia at government expense, and eventually in 1862 appointed him to the Chair of Hebrew Studies at the University of Paris against the wishes of the Catholic party, and, if rumour was correct, despite the opposition of the Empress.

In his first lecture, Renan said that Jesus Christ was 'an incomparable man'. There was a storm of protest from the Church, and demands for his resignation, for his words were held to deny the divinity of Christ. This divinity was explicitly denied by Renan next year in his *Life of Jesus*. The Bishop of Arras published a reply to Renan, in which he asserted that Christ was the second person of the Trinity. The Emperor sent a letter to the Bishop, which was published in the newspapers, congratulating him on his defence of the faith against Renan; but Louis Napoleon also sent a private letter to Renan assuring him of his personal esteem. The Catholics got to know about the letter to Renan, and murmured their disapproval. Renan could not survive the storm, and was dismissed from his Chair in June 1864. Louis Napoleon appointed him to the position of Deputy Curator, under Mérimée, of the Bibliothèque Impériale; but Renan and his friends saw this appointment as a bribe to keep him quiet, and he refused it.[17]

Antonio Panizzi of Modena had been a member of the Carbonari in the 1820s before he became the principal librarian of the British Museum and Sir Anthony Panizzi. When Eugénie was in London in 1860 she visited the British Museum and was shown round by Panizzi. She liked him, and told Mérimée that she hoped that Panizzi would come as her guest to Biarritz, though she realized that, as an ardent supporter of Victor Emanuel and the cause of Italian liberation, he might be unwilling to accept the invitation.[18] Mérimée promised to sound Panizzi about this, and in September 1862 Panizzi and Mérimée were both guests at the Villa Eugénie.

Panizzi's visit was a great success, except that his enormous bulk – he ate a great deal and took very little exercise[19] – made it difficult for him to keep up with the Emperor and Empress and their party in the walks in the mountains near Biarritz. One day they climbed Mont Larune on the Franco-Spanish frontier, riding on horseback to the 3000-foot summit. After admiring the magnificent view over Spain, they began the descent down the very steep and rugged path. All the others dismounted and walked down on foot, but Panizzi would not do this and managed at considerable risk to descend on horseback. Half-way down, they stopped for supper at a well-known country inn. Panizzi would not dismount, because he thought that if he did he would not be able to mount again; so he remained outside while the others dined in the inn. Louis Napoleon and Eugénie came to his assistance, one of them bringing him a glass of wine and the other a sandwich. It was dark before they reached the foot of the mountain, where the servants met them with carriages and torches. Panizzi drove back to the Villa Eugénie with the Emperor and Empress in the imperial carriage. They congratulated him on his feat in remaining for five hours in the saddle, but he said that it was the horse that deserved to be congratulated.[20]

These excursions, like Louis Napoleon's prowess on the ice in the Bois de Boulogne in the winter, took place during the intervals between other periods when he was prostrated by increasing ill-health. In addition to the rheumatism from which he had suffered since his days in the damp prison at Ham, he first showed symptoms in 1861 of stone in the bladder, for which he underwent treatment by taking the waters at Vichy. He spent an increasing amount of time playing patience and lying on the sofa chain-smoking cigarettes in the overheated rooms which he liked and which Eugénie detested.

Eugénie too sometimes complained of ill-health, and did not find it easy to throw off the depression caused by Paca's death. In the summer of 1861, when Berlioz came to the palace, she asked him to play Chopin's Funeral March, and, after hearing it, withdrew to another room to hide her tears.[21] She found solace in reading. In the spring of 1863, when she was not yet thirty-seven, she wrote to her mother that she had gone out very little during the previous winter, although the weather had been very mild, because she wished to retire like a bear alone to her corner and read books. 'Everything goes, youth, beauty, gaiety, but fortunately intellectual life remains, and this provides a refuge.'[22] She was still very beautiful, and she herself was the only person who thought that she was no longer young.[23]

In October 1863 she went to Spain, sailing from Biarritz to Cadiz when the Emperor and the Prince Imperial returned to Paris. She visited Seville, and sailed on to Alicante and Valencia. Although her visit was unofficial, she was invited to Madrid by Queen Isabel, and there were banquets at the royal palace and the French embassy. She went to Aranjuez and Toldeo before returning to Valencia and sailing to Toulon and returning to Paris.[24] There was great speculation in the press as to why she went to Spain. The *Times* correspondent thought that it was to compel Queen Isabel to receive her, because there had been comments on the Queen's failure to visit the Emperor and Empress at Biarritz when she was on holiday near Santander, as she usually was every September, and there were rumours that she was reluctant to greet the daughter of her former lady-in-waiting as her royal equal.[25] In fact, Eugénie went to Spain, against the advice of Mérimée and other friends, simply because she wished to see her native land again.

There was another spate of rumours in September 1864, when, on the advice of her doctors, she went without the Emperor for a holiday to Schwalbach in Hesse.[26] Some said that she had gone off in a huff because she was annoyed that the Emperor was negotiating the Convention of 15 September with Italy about the withdrawal of the French troops from Rome; others believed that she was upset because of his love affair with Justine Marie Lebœuf, a twenty-five-year-old housemaid in a Boulogne hotel who had come to Paris, changed her name to Marguerite Bellanger, and become an actress in light comedies at the Folies Impériales. Various romantic stories have been written about the circumstances in which Marguerite Bellanger first met Louis Napoleon; but the prosaic truth appears to be that she had set her heart on becoming the Emperor's mistress, and that Mocquard, who as a playwright knew many actresses, thought that the Emperor would like her and arranged a meeting.

There is no doubt that Louis Napoleon fell passionately in love with her, and despite his failing health began a tempestuous affair – his first with a working-class French girl since Alexandrine Veugeot at Ham. He usually fell in love with foreign women – with the Swiss peasant girls at Arenenberg; with the German Frau von Zeppelin; with Madame Saunier from Mauritius; with the half-Corsican, half-German Princess Mathilde; with the English girls, Georgiana Damer, Mrs Edwards and Miss Howard; with the itinerant Jewess, Rachel; with the Italian Virginia de Castiglione; with the half-Italian, half-Polish Marianne de Walewska; and with the Spanish-Scottish-Belgian Eugenia del Montijo.

Eugénie was alarmed when she heard of Louis Napoleon's infatuation for Marguerite Bellanger. She feared for the effect on his health, and the possibilities of public scandal and blackmail which might result from an affair with an actress. She therefore called on Marguerite and offered her money to break off the affair; but Marguerite refused, and in the course of their talk Eugénie got to like her, and raised no further obstacle to her relationship with the Emperor. As usual, he treated his mistress very generously, both during and after the affair. Marguerite eventually married a Prussian business man, and died at an advanced age.[27]

Eugénie's tolerance towards Marguerite Bellanger, like her tolerance to Marianne de Walewska, caused adverse comment in the more rigid Catholic circles. Viel Castel thought that, like Madame Dubarry with Louis XV, she was trying to ingratiate herself with the Emperor by providing him with nice mistresses;[28] but it was really Eugénie's strong sense of loyalty and duty which prompted her. She showed the same qualities when she visited the cholera hospitals in Paris and Amiens during the epidemics of 1865 and 1866. The visits were widely publicized, and won the admiration, not only of the officials who made the fulsome speeches of congratulation, but of everyone in France except the Radicals and the other opposition elements.[29] She also showed interest in prison reform, particularly with regard to juvenile offenders.[30]

In May 1865 she was again called upon to perform the duties of Regent when the Emperor paid a second visit to Algeria. This time he stayed there for nearly a month.[31] His object was to appease the passions which had been stirred by the Arab revolt the year before. He promised to pay compensation to the French colonists who had lost their property in the revolt, and he assured the Arabs that those who submitted to French authority had nothing to fear. He emphasized that they would be free to practise their religion, and that there would be no attempt to compel them to become Christians; there had been some anxiety about this, for the zeal of the French Catholic missionaries for converting heathens and infidels was well known. He visited a mosque in Algiers where prayers were said for him and for Eugénie and the Prince Imperial. 'I have Christian children and I have Mussulman children', he said,

and I am responsible for both before God, the common Father of all men. My justice shall be equal for all. Tell your fellow-worshippers that I hold power for the good of all who walk in the right path, and that I shall find means to punish with rigour all those who will not remain on the true road of obedience and good conduct.[32]

He travelled a little way inland, going by railway as far as Blida and then by road across the Metija plain and along the cliffs to Medea, and stopping for breakfast at Paul Perrage's famous inn; and he visited

Oran, Mostaganem and Philippeville. He was entertained by leading Muslims in Algiers at a great banquet in the Mustapha Palace, where the food was African – soup of the tortoise of the Boudouca, porcupine garnished with antelope kidneys, quarters of the Quergian gazelle, the loins of young wild boars from the Oued-Hullouf, salmis of Carthaginian hens, antelope cutlets, ostrich from the Oglat-Nadja and ostrich eggs, and Arabian pastries – ouidax, macroudes, scerakboracs and oribians.

While the Emperor went to Algeria, Prince Napoleon went to Corsica to unveil a statue of Napoleon I at Ajaccio. In his speech he stressed the revolutionary nature of Napoleon I's dictatorship, referred to the overthrow of the aristocracy and to Napoleon's clash with the Papacy, praised the victory of the cause of freedom in the American Civil War, declared that 'an Austrian alliance shall never be the policy of France', and said that the time had now come to capture Rome, 'this last fortress of the Middle Ages. . . . They are strange Catholics who would make the future of religion depend on a temporal power maintained in Rome by force.'[33]

The Catholics in France were furious. In the Senate, the Marquis de Boissy asked if this represented government policy; if so, it was 'nothing less than the banner of insurrection and civil war unfurled by a Prince of the imperial family'.[34] Eugénie was of course indignant with Prince Napoleon. As soon as she received the report of the speech, she ordered Le Moniteur not to print it; and it was printed in Le Constitutionnel in a censored form, the references to the American Civil War, to the Austrian alliance and to Rome having been deleted. But Eugénie refused the demand of the majority of the ministers that she instruct Le Moniteur to publish a government statement repudiating the speech; nor would she permit an official warning to be sent to Prince Napoleon's L'Opinion Nationale, which had published the speech in full. She refused to take any action against Prince Napoleon during the Emperor's absence. At a dinner party at the Tuileries, the guests began to criticize the speech; but Eugénie cut them short, and suggested that, like Le Moniteur, they keep silent about the speech. The secret police reports, which in the Emperor's absence were again sent to her, informed her that all over France the people were condemning Prince Napoleon's speech. There were complaints, too, that the Emperor had taken no action about it in Algiers.[35]

After a week, the Emperor did react. On 23 May he wrote from Algiers to Prince Napoleon, and ordered Le Moniteur to publish the letter. 'Sir and very dear cousin, I feel bound to inform you of the painful impression which I have experienced in reading your speech at Ajaccio.' He stated that he could not accept Prince Napoleon's interpretation of Napoleon I's policy; Prince Napoleon had expressed 'feelings of hatred and malice which no longer apply in our epoch. . . . And besides, can we really, pigmies that we are, appreciate at its true value the great historic figure of Napoleon? It is like standing before a colossal statue, incapable of understanding it.'[36]

When the Emperor's letter was published, two hundred Senators and Deputies called at the Tuileries to sign the visitors' book as a gesture of their approval; and the Empress-Regent was cheered at the Odéon Theatre.[37] Prince Napoleon replied to the Emperor in a short letter stating that in view of the Emperor's letter and its publication in *Le Moniteur*, he resigned as a member of the Privy Council and as chairman of the committee which had been appointed to organize the International Exhibition in Paris in 1867.[38]

The Emperor returned to Paris on 10 June. On his journey to Paris, he sent a message to Prince Napoleon, who had retired to his country estate at Meudon, inviting him to come at once to the Tuileries to discuss the position; but on the day that the Emperor reached Paris, Prince Napoleon was injured in a road accident, being trampled on by the horses of his carriage, and he was confined to his bed. When the Emperor heard this, he wrote to Prince Napoleon expressing his sorrow at the accident, and telling him that although he had felt compelled to repudiate his Ajaccio speech, his personal friendship for him was unimpaired.[39]

In August, Louis Napoleon had a short but happy holiday with Eugénie. She had bought back Arenenberg, which Louis Napoleon had sold when he was a prisoner at Ham; she paid for it out of her personal allowance, keeping it a secret from him until the transaction was completed. Louis Napoleon had in fact been told about it by the officials who were handling the transaction, but he pretended not to know until Eugénie revealed the secret.[40]

After spending a few days at Châlons Camp, Louis Napoleon and Eugénie took the train to Arenenberg, where they arrived on the evening of 18 August. It was twenty-seven years since Louis Napoleon had last seen the château, when he had been forced to leave Switzerland in October 1838. The Duc de Montebello, who as Louis Philippe's Ambassador in Lucerne had demanded his expulsion, was now Louis Napoleon's Ambassador in St Petersburg, and his wife, the Duchesse de Montebello, was one of Eugénie's ladies-in-waiting and was with them at Arenenberg. Louis Napoleon found several of his old acquaintances at Ermatingen and elsewhere in the neighbourhood, and he and Eugénie spent two days at Arenenberg, visiting the district and going in a steamer along Lake Constance, before leaving on the morning of 21 August for France. On their way home they stayed the night at Neuchâtel, where the Empress's ladies, following the Emperor and Empress in a carriage on the way from the station to the hotel, had an accident and were thrown out of the carriage. They suffered injuries and had to go to hospital. Eugénie was very distressed, and though the Emperor went on to Paris as planned, to deal with urgent state affairs, Eugénie stayed in Neuchâtel until her injured ladies were sufficiently recovered to travel with her.[41]

Soon after she reached Paris, she left with the Emperor for Biarritz. The guests at the Villa Eugénie in September 1865 included Bismarck. He made a very favourable impression on his hosts and the other guests, as he usually did; they found him less stiff and more amusing than most Germans. One of the guests, Madame de La Bédoyère, who was German by birth, was so impressed by Bismarck that Eugénie and the others pretended to believe that she had fallen in love with him, and Eugénie coaxed Mérimée into making a stuffed figure resembling Bismarck and putting it into Madame de La Bédoyère's bed as a practical joke.[42]

The Emperor and Bismarck had political talks at Biarritz, but Mérimée noticed that neither of them dropped the slightest hint about what they had discussed.[43] This is not surprising, because Louis Napoleon had offered Bismarck a free hand in South Germany and neutrality in an Austro-Prussian war in return for the cession of the Rhineland to France. As usual, he had used Eugénie to make the first advances. In August, before Bismarck left Berlin, she had a talk with Goltz, and tentatively suggested the bargain. Goltz sent a coded telegram to Bismarck giving details of the conversation; it was intercepted and decoded by the Austrian Foreign Office, who informed Metternich.[44] It did not, of course, spoil his personal relations with the Empress.

CHAPTER 38

MEXICO AND THE
AMERICAN CIVIL WAR

SEVERAL of Louis Napoleon's advisers have been blamed for his disastrous involvement in Mexico – Morny, who was connected with a group of international financiers who made a surreptitious profit from the venture; a number of Mexican right-wing clericals who instigated the intervention; and above all Eugénie, who is said to have inspired the decision to send troops to instal a Catholic and Conservative régime in Mexico.[1] In fact the Mexican policy, which was originally thought out and put into operation by Louis Napoleon himself without consulting his ministers, bears all the hallmarks of his general political conduct and objectives – to crush Red Republicanism by force; to instal a Liberal Catholic ruler with the consent of the silent majority of the electorate; to oppose the Ultramontane policy of the Papacy and the native bishops; to act in the belief, which he stated in Algiers in 1860, that 'Providence has called upon us to spread across this earth the benefits of civilization';[2] to further the financial interests of French investors;[3] to maintain French honour by revenging, at whatever cost, a minor military setback at the opening of the campaign; to avoid a prolonged war against a Great Power; and to use deceit as a method of achieving these objectives. Metternich told Cowley that Louis Napoleon's handling of the early stages of the Mexican affair had given him a greater insight into the Emperor's character than years of common intercourse would have done.[4]

Louis Napoleon's Mexican policy failed because it was based on two miscalculations – that the Mexican Radicals had no support in the country and that the South would win the American Civil War.

During the years before 1861, Mexico had undergone a series of civil wars which made many of the older generation of Mexicans, whose memories went back forty years, yearn for the good old days when the country was a peaceful Spanish colony without bandits and revolutionaries. By 1861 power had passed to the Radical leader, Benito Juarez, a lawyer from the province of Oaxaca of pure Indian blood.

The Radicals were violently hostile to the Catholic Church and the landowning aristocracy; they confiscated Church property, expelled monks and nuns from their convents, and outraged the feelings of many Mexican Catholics. Several of the leading Conservative politicians fled to France.

One of them, José Hidalgo, had been a friend of Eugénie when she was a girl in Spain. She happened to see him walking in the streets of Bayonne when she was driving through the town during her stay at Biarritz in 1858. She invited him into her carriage, and they renewed their old friendship. She introduced him to the Emperor, and during the next few years he was a frequent guest at Biarritz, the Tuileries, Saint-Cloud and Compiègne.[5]

Hidalgo was associated with two prominent Mexican Conservatives, General Almonte and José Gutierrez de Estrada, who were refugees in Paris. The three men had their rivalries and disagreements, but were united in believing that Mexico could only be saved from the Radical Juarists by European military intervention and the establishment of a European Prince as Emperor of Mexico.[6] Hidalgo put forward this idea to Eugénie. She naturally listened sympathetically to his stories about the summary executions of Conservatives, the expropriation of Church property, the sufferings of the monks and nuns expelled from their convents, and the burnings and desecrations of churches by the Juarists, and of how the Catholic Conservatives in Mexico hung portraits of Napoleon III in their houses, looking to him to save the Church in Mexico as he had saved the Holy Father in Rome.[7] She thought that the civil war in Mexico was a struggle between the Church and the Revolution, like the struggle between the Pope and Garibaldi in Italy, between the Emperor and the Reds in France, and like the struggle which took place, not long after her death, in Spain in 1936-9, when her nephews and relations played such a prominent part on General Franco's side.[8]

But on the Mexican question, as in most other political matters, Eugénie followed, and did not lead, Louis Napoleon. When she and Hidalgo appealed to Louis Napoleon to save Mexico, he sympathized but refused to intervene. He knew that a policy of intervention would bring him into conflict with the United States, who had annexed a large part of Mexican territory after their victory in the war of 1846-8 and considered that Mexico was within their sphere of influence. For forty years the U.S. government and public had vigorously asserted the doctrine laid down by President Monroe in 1823 – that the United States would not permit any European power to acquire new colonies or to extend its influence on the American Continent. The Monroe Doctrine had never been accepted by the European Powers, who feared

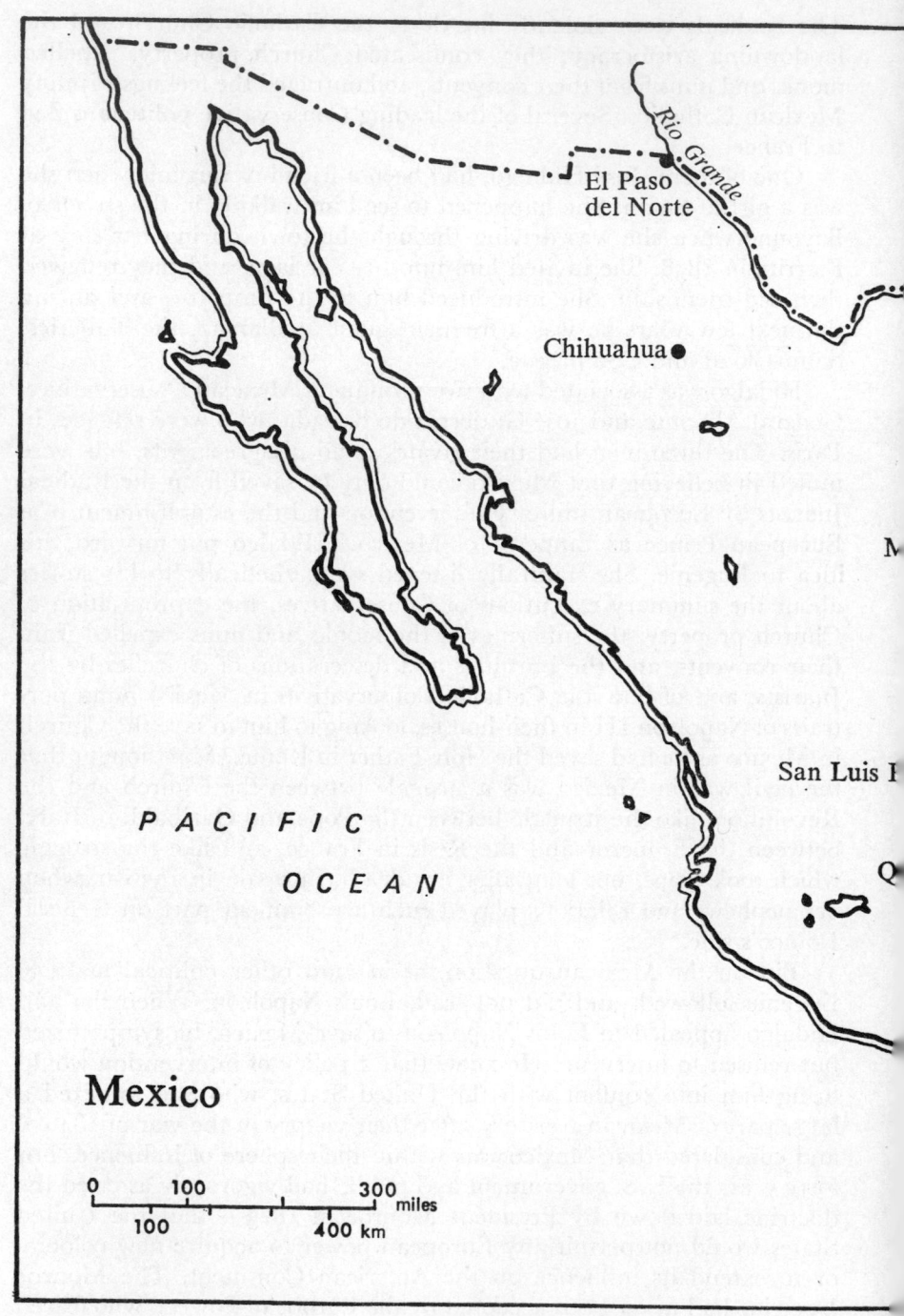

Rio Grande

El Paso
del Norte

Chihuahua ●

PACIFIC

OCEAN

San Luis

Q

Mexico

0	100		300 miles
	100		400 km

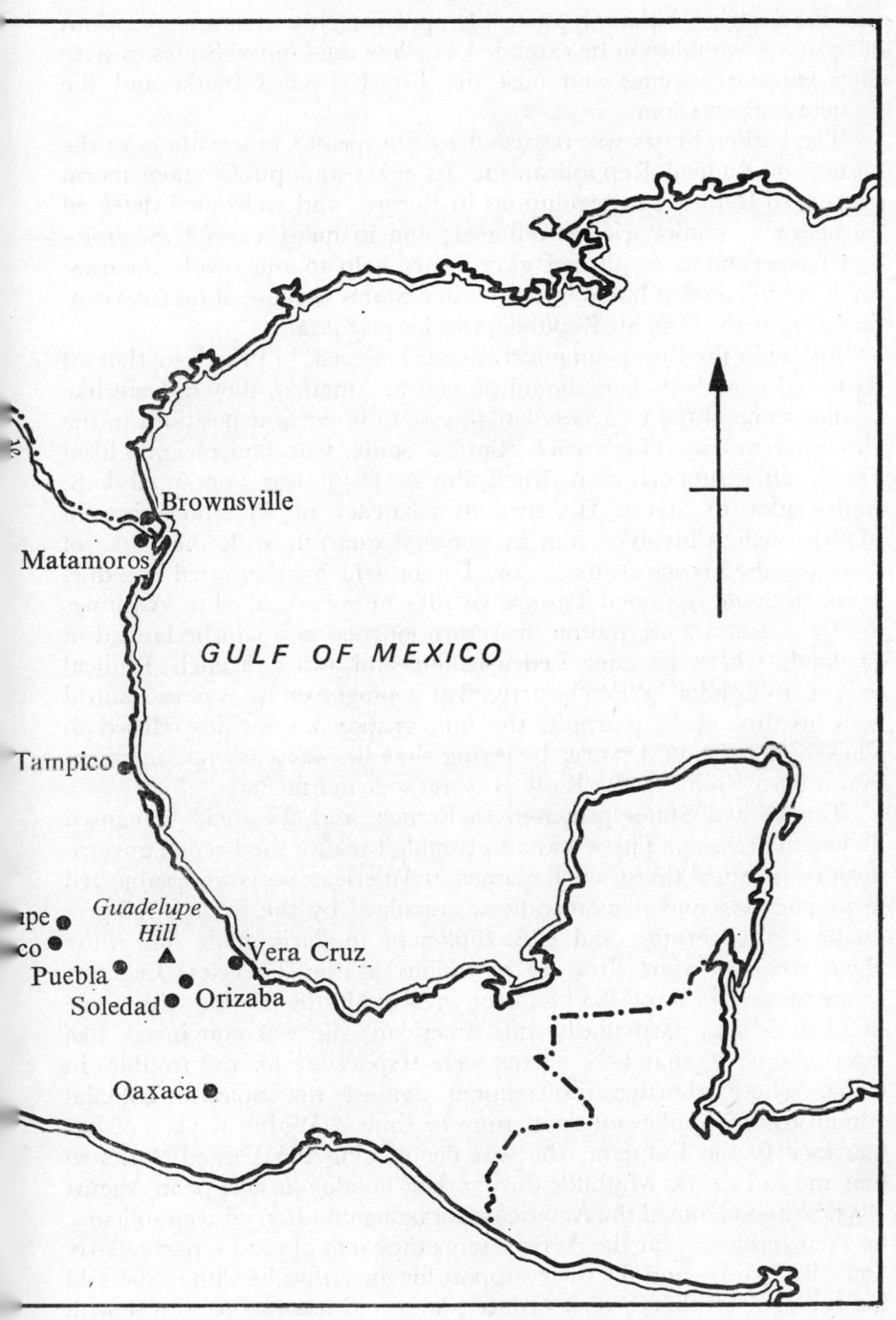

Brownsville

Matamoros

GULF OF MEXICO

Tampico

Guadelupe
Hill ▲

ape
co

Puebla   Vera Cruz

Soledad   Orizaba

Oaxaca

that the doctrine, although ostensibly applying only to new acquisitions of territory, would soon be extended to allow the United States to seize their existing colonies and oust the British from Canada and the Spaniards from Cuba.

The United States was regarded by European Conservatives as the bastion of Radical Republicanism. Its press and public gave moral support to Republican revolutions in Europe, and welcomed defeated European revolutionaries as refugees; and in many cases U.S. diplomatic representatives abroad gave secret help to the revolutionaries. Louis Napoleon was hated in the United States because of his intervention against the Roman Republic and his *coup d'état*.

Although the European governments believed, in principle, that all Reds and trouble-makers should be sent to America, they did not like it when some of the refugees of 1848 rose to important positions in the U.S. government. The French Radical Soulé, who had escaped from France after supporting Ledru-Rollin in 1849, was appointed U.S. Ambassador to Spain. His strident advocacy of Republicanism in Madrid society involved him in personal quarrels with the Duke of Alba and the French Ambassador, Turgot, which culminated in a duel in which Soulé wounded Turgot. In 1854 he was recalled to Washington for consultations, and on his return journey to Spain he landed in England, where he met Ledru-Rollin and other French Radical refugees in London. When he arrived at Boulogne on his way to Madrid with his diplomatic passport, the immigration authorities refused to allow him to enter France, believing that he was carrying messages from Ledru-Rollin to the Radical secret societies in Paris.[9]

The United States protested to France, and the incident caused diplomatic tension. There was also trouble because the French government complained that French seamen in American ports were subjected to propaganda and demonstrations organized by the French refugees in the United States; and U.S. diplomats in Paris made difficulties about wearing court dress at receptions at the Tuileries. Eugénie, whose brother-in-law Alba had been involved in the friction with Soulé in Madrid, was particularly anti-American; she was convinced, like most Spaniards, that U.S. agents were responsible for the troubles in Cuba, where abortive insurrections against the Spanish colonial administration broke out from time to time.[10] Within a year of her marriage to the Emperor, she was denouncing the United States to him and to Princess Mathilde during their holiday at Dieppe in August 1853. She condemned the Americans for being unashamed Republicans, for their insolence, for the Ambassadors they sent abroad – particularly Soulé in Spain – and for their support for guerrillas in Cuba. She told Louis Napoleon that, sooner or later, he would have to go to war with the United States. Louis Napoleon tried to calm her, and said that war was out of the question.[11]

When the American Civil War broke out in April 1861, the first reaction of the governments of both Britain and France was delight at at the prospect of U.S. power being weakened, temporarily by the war, and permanently, if the South won, by the dissolution of the Union. Their joy soon turned into acute anxiety when they discovered that, contrary to their expectations, the North succeeded in enforcing an effective blockade of the Southern ports which prevented Southern cotton from reaching the mills of Lancashire and the silk factories of Lyons, Saint-Étienne and Tarare. The American Civil War caused widespread unemployment and distress among the working class in both Britain and France, which in France was not relieved by the discovery that in the near future Indo-China would be able to produce an abundant cotton crop.[12]

At the outbreak of the Civil War, Louis Napoleon proclaimed French neutrality, forbade French subjects to enlist in the fighting forces of either side, and announced that no Federal or Confederate warship would be allowed to stay for more than twenty-four hours in a French port. In France, as in Britain, sympathy was divided on broadly political lines, though there was not, in France, such an active campaign in Parliament and in the press in favour of both North and South as there was in the freer political atmosphere of Britain. The Socialists, Radicals and Liberals strongly supported the North because of its sympathy with the anti-slavery cause. The Conservatives and Catholics usually supported the South.[13] The Abolitionist movement in the United States, as in Britain, was strongly supported by Protestant Nonconformist preachers and sects; but the Catholic Church, though it urged slave-owners to treat their slaves with paternal kindness and to emancipate them in appropriate cases, had always refused to condemn the institution of slavery, which had been found to be compatible with Christianity in Constantine's Rome and in the French and Spanish empires in the sixteenth and seventeenth centuries. Many Southern slave-owners in the Confederate States were Catholics; and the Pope and the Catholic bishops in the United States adopted an attitude of strict neutrality in the American Civil War.

Eugénie and the Conservatives in the French government sympathized with the South; but Prince Napoleon supported the North, and paid a visit to Washington and the Northern states in the first months of the Civil War. As for the Emperor, he as usual did not commit himself and kept everyone guessing. He encouraged the supporters of the South to hope that he would apply his principle of nationalities to the South's struggle to win their national independence from the

North; but though the political forecasters were always expecting him to give diplomatic recognition to the South, he never did so.[14]

In November 1861 the South sent two prominent politicians, James Murray Mason and John Slidell, to be their unofficial representatives in London and Paris. The two envoys succeeded in running the Northern blockade and reaching Cuba, and set out from Havana to Southampton on the British merchant ship, the *Trent*; but the *Trent* was stopped on the high seas by a Northern warship, and Mason and Slidell were removed and taken as prisoners to Washington. The British government demanded that they be released and allowed to sail to England, and when the demand was rejected, threatened to go to war with the North.

France was indirectly concerned with the case, because Slidell was on his way to take up his duties as the Confederate representative in Paris; but French public opinion was divided on the usual political lines, and Louis Napoleon adopted an equivocal attitude. As on other occasions, he ordered *Le Moniteur*, the official government organ, to make no comment, and instructed *Le Constitutionnel*, which was everywhere regarded as a 'semi-official' newspaper, to advocate government policy. But *Le Constitutionnel* changed its line three times in a week about the *Trent*. At first it stated that as Britain was France's ally and the United States had been her friend since the time of La Fayette, France could only maintain strict neutrality in the dispute, and in any case she was not involved, as the *Trent* was a British ship. Then *Le Constitutionnel* asserted that Britain was in the right and the United States in the wrong, and that if the United States got away with this violation of international law in the case of the *Trent*, they would tomorrow be doing the same to a French ship. Finally it reverted to its former line of strict neutrality. The Catholic press, which was usually anti-British, strongly supported Britain over the *Trent*; but Prince Napoleon's *L'Opinion Nationale*, which usually supported Liberal Britain, now argued that France must not quarrel with her friend the United States for the sake of the nation which had allowed Napoleon to die on St Helena and was drilling her Volunteers with the avowed purpose of fighting against the French.[15]

On 3 December, Thouvenel sent a note to Washington stating that though the matter did not involve France, the French government believed that in international law Britain was right, and the United States wrong, about the *Trent*, and hoped that France's friend, the United States, would not be so foolish as to become involved in war with Britain on the issue, as this would have very serious consequences for the United States in its war against the South. It still took about three weeks for letters from Paris to reach Washington, and it was not until 27 December that the U.S. Secretary of State, Seward, replied to Thouvenel, informing him that as the United States had already decided to release Mason and Slidell before Thouvenel's note arrived, there was no point in his replying to Thouvenel's arguments.[16] Mason and Slidell were released, and Mason arrived in London and Slidell in Paris in January 1862. Slidell, who remained in Paris until the end of the Civil War, established a very friendly relationship with Louis Napoleon; and Eugénie singled him out for special attention when he was her guest at Biarritz in 1863.[17]

It was the American Civil War which decided Louis Napoleon to intervene in Mexico. He was immediately provided with an excuse for intervention. When Juarez entered Mexico City and established his government there in April 1861 the state was bankrupt, and he was confronted with demands from the governments of Britain, France and Spain for payment of the debts owed to their nationals by the previous Mexican governments against whom he had been fighting. As he refused to pay, the governments of Britain, France and Spain decided to intervene by force, in the accepted manner of European Powers dealing with backward debtor nations in the nineteenth century. They would send a joint naval force to seize the port of Vera Cruz and pay the creditors out of the customs duties collected at the port. When they had raised enough money to pay the debts due to their nationals and the costs of the expedition and occupation, they would evacuate Vera Cruz and return home.

In July 1861, Louis Napoleon was visited at Vichy by his old friend General Prim, the Spanish Prime Minister.[18] They discussed the possibility of joint intervention, together with Britain, at Vera Cruz, and Louis Napoleon suggested that instead of merely collecting the debts due from Mexico, they should establish a European Prince as Emperor of Mexico, maintain him there with French and Spanish troops, and nullify the Monroe Doctrine at a time when neither the United States nor the Southern Confederacy would be able to do anything about it owing to their involvement in the Civil War. Prim turned down the suggestion; he realized that Spain, as the former colonial power, would encounter more opposition than anyone else in Mexico, where it was a common saying that, in order to end the anarchy in the country, most Mexicans would welcome the rule of any foreign Prince, provided only that he was not a Spaniard.[19]

In September, Hidalgo stayed at the Villa Eugénie in Biarritz, and one evening after dinner discussed Mexico with Louis Napoleon and Eugénie. To his delight, Louis Napoleon said that he was now willing to use the opportunity provided by the three-power intervention at Vera Cruz to place a European Prince on the Mexican throne. Various

Princes were considered, including the Archduke Maximilian of Austria, Franz Joseph's brother, who had married Princess Charlotte* of Belgium, King Leopold's daughter. Louis Napoleon and Hidalgo agreed that Maximilian would be unwilling to accept an offer of Mexico; but Eugénie, who in her animation remained standing though the Emperor and Hidalgo were sitting down, suddenly tapped herself on the breast with her fan and said that her intuition told her that the Archduke Maximilian would be prepared to accept.[20] Maximilian had gained a reputation as a Liberal when he was Governor of Venetia, and had made a favourable impression on Louis Napoleon and Eugénie when he visited Paris in May 1856. They did not know that he was anti-French in sentiment, and had formed an unfavourable opinion of Eugénie during his Paris visit, disapproving of her informal relationship with her ladies and her lack of imperial dignity.[21] At this very time, in August and September 1861, Maximilian was unsuccessfully trying to persuade Palmerston to make a secret military alliance with Austria against France in the Adriatic.[22]

At Louis Napoleon's suggestion, Almonte and the Mexican exiles in Paris offered Maximilian the Mexican throne. Maximilian accepted the offer with great enthusiasm, but Franz Joseph and the Austrian government were much more hesitant. They immediately suspected that Louis Napoleon's motive in proposing Maximilian was to be able afterwards to ask Franz Joseph to show his gratitude by ceding Venetia to Italy. Metternich was particularly critical of the idea; but Franz Joseph did not wish to disappoint his brother or annoy Napoleon III by vetoing it, and he agreed on the express understanding that Louis Napoleon must not expect Austria to cede Venetia or do anything else in return.[23]

In October 1861, Louis Napoleon wrote to Flahault, who fifty years before had been his mother's lover and was now Ambassador in London, and instructed him to tell Palmerston that the French government was in favour of placing Archduke Maximilian on the throne of Mexico. If Mexico, which had attracted a great deal of French capital, were saved from anarchy by being placed under Maximilian's rule, 'it would form an impassable barrier to the encroachments of North America, it would form an important opening for English, Spanish and French trade', and 'would render great services to our manufactures by extending its cultivation of cotton'. He explained that Mexican refugees had been urging him for some time to give them a monarch. 'At that time I could only indulge in fruitless wishes', but now 'the American

*She was known by the Spanish name 'Carlota' to the Mexicans, and, strangely enough, to many twentieth-century writers; but she always called herself 'Charlotte' in her native French.

war has made it impossible for the United States to interfere in the matter, and, what is more, the outrages committed by the Mexican government have provided England, Spain and France with a legitimate motive for interference in Mexico'.[24]

Palmerston was personally sympathetic to the proposal, but his Foreign Secretary, Earl Russell, and most of his Cabinet were opposed to it. The Prince Consort, who had known Princess Charlotte of Belgium ever since she had stayed at Windsor as a child, believed that Louis Napoleon's object in Mexico was to regain the support of the French Catholics that he had lost by his Italian policy; and the Prince was surprised that Maximilian and Charlotte were prepared to collaborate in this project. On 5 November, less than six weeks before his death, he wrote to Charlotte's father, King Leopold, and authorized him to show the letter to 'Max and Charlotte'. He warned them of the dangers involved in playing the role of Philip II's Duke of Alba on the American continent, and of the predicament in which they would find themselves if Louis Napoleon one day decided to withdraw his troops and leave them in the lurch.[25]

On 31 October 1861 the governments of Britain, France and Spain signed a Convention in London agreeing to take joint action at Vera Cruz to recover the debts due to their nationals. By Article 2 of the Convention they agreed not to acquire any territory in Mexico 'and not to exercise in the internal affairs of Mexico any influence of a nature to prejudice the right of the Mexican nation to choose and to constitute freely the form of its government'.[26] But rumours were circulating in Paris that Louis Napoleon intended to instal Maximilian as Emperor of Mexico. When Favre raised the matter in the Legislative Boby, Billault stated that French objectives did not go beyond the terms of the Convention of 31 October, and *Le Moniteur* published a note from Thouvenel to the British government stating that the French government knew nothing about any offer to Maximilian; but Thouvenel privately told Cowley that though the French government knew nothing about it, the French Emperor did.[27]

Juarez, hearing of the preparations by Britain, France and Spain to seize Vera Cruz, asked the United States for financial help. The U.S. government offered to pay the British, French and Spanish creditors in full if the three powers took no action against Mexico; but Palmerston and Louis Napoleon did not wish to see the United States strengthen its influence in Mexico by replacing them as Mexico's creditor, and rejected the offer. A Spanish advance-guard captured Vera Cruz on 17 December 1861, and the Allied forces – 6300 Spanish under General Prim, 2800 French and 800 British – arrived during the next few weeks.[28]

Juarez's troops did not resist the invaders, but Juarez called on the inhabitants of Vera Cruz to boycott the Allied occupation forces. Nearly the whole population left the town, and the peasants in the near-by countryside refused to sell food to the Allies. The French and Spanish troops then advanced to Orizaba in order to commandeer the food supplies.[29] The British thought the reaction of the inhabitants at Vera Cruz was ominous, for they had encountered nothing like this in China, and they decided to leave Vera Cruz as soon as possible.

In February 1862, Juarez sent representatives to negotiate a settlement with the three Allied powers at Soledad, near Orizaba. He offered to pay the creditors by instalments. The British and Spanish envoys wished to accept the offer; but the French representative, Saligny, made it clear to them that the French had come to Mexico to overthrow Juarez's government and to collaborate with the Conservative Catholic Mexican forces. When the British and Spanish envoys protested, Saligny told them that he was acting on orders that he had received from Louis Napoleon himself. Meanwhile General Almonte had arrived at Vera Cruz in a French warship and installed himself there at the head of a Mexican administration under the protection of the French forces.[30]

Eugénie was indignant at the timid attitude of the British and Spanish governments, and was especially incensed against Prim; but though she was an enthusiastic supporter of intervention in Mexico, the responsibility for the decision was Louis Napoleon's, not hers. When she passionately advocated the policy to Metternich, he knew that this meant that Louis Napoleon favoured it. Louis Napoleon, Eugénie, Maximilian, Charlotte and King Leopold were all equally optimistic.[31] 'Never, in my opinion, will any task produce greater results', wrote Louis Napoleon to Maximilian on 14 January 1862,

for it is a question of rescuing a whole continent from anarchy and misery; of setting an example of good government to the whole of America; and lastly of raising the monarchist flag, based upon a wise liberty and a sincere love of progress, in the face of dangerous Utopias and bloody disorders.[32]

Eight days later, Charlotte wrote to Eugénie: 'Your Majesty . . . seemed obviously marked out by Providence to initiate a work which one might call a holy one' because it would further the cause of the Catholic religion in Mexico.[33]

Louis Napoleon and Eugénie afterwards said that they had been misled by Almonte and the Mexican refugees about the strength of the Conservatives and the weakness of the Liberals in Mexico; but they were repeatedly warned of the true position by their allies in the spring of 1862. The British Ambassador in Mexico City, Sir Charles Wyke, wrote to Russell on 22 February that most of 'the Old & wealthy families' in Mexico supported the French intervention, but that their plans should not be confounded with the feelings of the Mexican people.[34] Russell passed on this warning to the French government on more than one occasion.[35]

On 17 March, Prim wrote to Napoleon III from Orizaba, and warned him that if he intended to give the throne of Mexico to the Archduke Maximilian, he would encounter strong opposition from the Mexican people:

It will be easy for Your Majesty to lead Prince Maximilian to the capital and to crown him as King; but this King will have no support in this country except that of the Conservative leaders. . . . Some wealthy men will likewise support a foreign monarch who will arrive supported by the soldiers of Your Majesty; but that monarch will have nothing to uphold him on the day when that support shall be withdrawn, and he will fall from the throne raised by Your Majesty, as other powers of the earth will fall on the day when Your Majesty's imperial mantle shall cease to cover and defend them.[36]

Louis Napoleon and Eugénie were well aware of the risks that they were running in Mexico; but they were both of them gamblers by instinct, and they gambled and lost. Forty years later, Eugénie admitted to Paléologue that the Mexican Conservatives had misled her about the strength of the Juarist movement in Mexico; but her only regret in 1904 for her Mexican policy was that it had failed, and she still felt that she and Louis Napoleon had been justified in gambling on its success.[37]

On 16 April, Saligny announced that France was at war with the government of Juarez. The British and Spanish forces sailed for home, leaving 3000 French soldiers in occupation of Vera Cruz, Orizaba and the surrounding countryside, which they handed over to the administration of General Almonte.[38]

The French Commander-in-Chief in Mexico, General de Lorencez, announced that the French army would advance to Mexico City, two hundred miles from Vera Cruz, and overthrow the anarchical government of Juarez which was oppressing the Mexican people and had affronted France. The French army of occupation would then enable the Mexicans to choose the government of their preference, after which they would leave Mexico. The French forces set out for Puebla, sixty-five miles from Mexico City. They found leaflets in French strewn along the road, appealing to them to go home and not to allow themselves to be used to suppress the liberty of a foreign people 3000 miles from the shores of France, who would fight for their freedom with the same devotion as the French had shown in 1792. Lorencez ordered a small body of men to go ahead to seize and destroy the leaflets before the main body of the troops arrived; but many soldiers saw them, and some sent them to their families in France.[39]

On 5 May the French encountered a Mexican force on Guadelupe Hill a few miles east of Puebla; it was commanded by General Zarogoza and his deputy commander, the thirty-two-year-old Juarist, Porfirio Diaz. Three times the French tried to storm the hill, and three times they were repulsed. Then, as they were regrouping for a fourth assault, Zarogoza's cavalry charged down the hill and routed them. The French lost 500 killed and wounded, and withdrew towards Orizaba.[40]

In France, the government press had reported that the army in Mexico had captured Puebla.[41] Even Russell believed it, and assured Queen Victoria that the French would soon enter Mexico City, though he was sceptical of their long-term success in Mexico.[42] On 7 June – letters from Mexico took more than a month to reach Paris – Eugénie wrote to Charlotte: 'General Lorencez considers that he is now master of the country'; and on the same day Louis Napoleon wrote to Maximilian that Lorencez expected to enter Mexico City at the latest on 25 May.[43] *1862*

When the news of the battle of 5 May reached Paris, the government announced that the troops had encountered a much stiffer opposition than they had expected, and that French honour would be avenged.[44] Lorencez had reported that he would need 30,000 troops to conquer the Juarists, so 30,000 men would be sent as soon as possible to Vera Cruz. But it took nearly a year before the reinforcements reached Vera Cruz, and during this year dissatisfaction grew in France. Even zealous Bonapartists were saying that the Emperor had bungled things, and that even if their troops eventually captured Puebla and Mexico City it would be at a great cost in French lives and money, and would bring no material advantage to France.[45]

The censored French press did not publish much news from Mexico, but when it did, people read between the lines of the encouraging reports. When *Le Moniteur* described the bravery of the French troops who pressed forward to Orizaba in the face of superior numbers of Mexicans to rescue four hundred of their comrades in the hospital there who were threatened by the Juarist guerrillas, the Parisians asked how it came about that four hundred French soldiers were in hospital. It confirmed the rumours that yellow fever was raging among the forces at Vera Cruz. The troops wrote home describing the raids of the Juarists and the surprise of the French to find that the despised Mexicans, who fifteen years before had been quickly beaten by a greatly inferior U.S. force, were now fighting with a passionate determination at the call of their supposed oppressor, Juarez.[46]

By the beginning of 1863, 20,000 soldiers had sailed for Vera Cruz from Brest and Cherbourg, and another 9000 had gone straight from Algeria.[47] On 19 February, General Forey, who had replaced Lorencez, began the advance on Puebla[48] for which Eugénie had been impatiently waiting; she had complained that Forey had been proceeding 'so gently' in Mexico.[49] By 10 March the French, dragging their heavy guns, had climbed 7500 feet to the plateau on which Puebla stands and had begun the siege of the city. Puebla was defended by General Ortega and nearly 20,000 men, who repulsed several French attacks.[50] The defenders threw newspapers, printed in French and Spanish, over the walls to the French soldiers; they contained quotations from Victor Hugo's *Napoléon le Petit*. 'You are soldiers of a tyrant', the newspaper stated; 'the best France is on our side. You have Napoleon, we have Victor Hugo.' When Victor Hugo heard of this, he published a message to the people of Puebla: 'Men of Puebla . . . it is not France that makes war on you, it is the Empire. . . . Valiant men of Mexico, resist. . . . The Empire, I hope, will fail in its infamous attempt, and you will conquer.'[51] It was reported in France that European Reds were fighting for the Juarists at Puebla, and the battle was seen as a struggle between Napoleon III and the international Revolution.[52]

In Paris the Empress was closer than ever to Hidalgo. On Maundy Thursday she asked him to come with her when she went, incognito and veiled, to make the round of seven churches. She stood with him in her place in the queue, and obeyed the vergers' instructions. At Saint-Sulpice, when it was her turn, after waiting for a quarter of an hour, to kiss the crucifix, Hidalgo was surprised that she unhesitatingly pressed it to her lips, although it had just been kissed by a Negro in a lackey's livery.[53]

On 29 March, at Puebla, General Bazaine's corps stormed the key defence point of Fort San Xavier, a former convent, and captured it room by room after savage fighting with the bayonet.[54] Forey's communiqué announcing this reached Paris in the middle of May during the general election campaign. As usual, the government and the Prefects used all their influence to secure the return of the official candidates, and the Opposition campaigned under great difficulties; when some eminent Liberal deputies met to draft their election manifesto, they were prosecuted and convicted of holding an illegal meeting under the law banning secret societies.[55] Louis Napoleon was confident that news of the capture of Puebla would arrive before polling day on 31 May, and would have a decisive influence on the election;[56] but Forey's dispatches, while stating that the final capture of Puebla was only a matter of days, asked for reinforcements to be sent from France. No further news had come from Puebla by 31 May, when 152,643 electors in Paris voted for the Opposition candidates and only 82,607 for the government. In all France, the government obtained its usual large majority, but the Opposition had 33 deputies instead of their former five.

Juarez sent all his available men to relieve Puebla, and himself accompanied the army. The French defeated him at San Lorenzo. The position of the defenders of Puebla was now hopeless, and the city and 12,000 soldiers surrendered unconditionally on 7 May.[57] The news reached Paris on 11 June. The guns of the Invalides fired a salute to inform the people of this great triumph for French arms, and the government ordered a *Te Deum* to be held for the victory of 'the cause of civilization, the interests of the Catholic religion, and the honour of the French flag';[58] but the official press announced that another 10,000 men would be sent to Mexico.

After the fall of Puebla and the defeat of the relieving army, Juarez could not hold Mexico City. Forey entered the capital on 10 June, and Juarez retreated to San Luis Potosí, two hundred miles to the north. The news of Puebla and Mexico City had all the effect in France which Louis Napoleon had hoped. All criticism ceased; the people acclaimed the great triumph of their army and their Emperor, and believed that the war was over.

The French launched a drive against the Juarists in the north. On Christmas Eve they captured San Luis Potosí, and Juarez retreated to Chihuahua, six hundred miles to the north-west. Until the fall of Mexico City, the French had granted Juarez's men all the rights of prisoners-of-war; but in the autumn of 1863, Forey sent flying columns to mop up Juarist guerrillas and hang them without trial as irregulars. Colonel Dupin, who had served in China and made a small fortune by selling his loot from the Summer Palace, was placed in command of a counter-guerrilla unit of Mexican collaborators and African Spahis.[59] On 21 August 1863, Mérimée wrote to Panizzi that Dupin

has started as one ought to begin with this scum, by hanging and shooting all whom he captures. The local people thought this was very good, and eagerly act as our spies. It is thought that a few months' hunting will be enough to make the country quite safe. I wonder![60]

In the towns, Juarist supporters were seized as hostages, to be executed if the Juarists murdered French soldiers or Mexican collaborators.

By the summer of 1863 the American Civil War had lasted longer than any war in which a great power had been involved since 1815. After the defeat of the Northern offensive against Richmond in the summer of 1862, the diplomats, politicians and journalists in Europe were certain that the North would never succeed in conquering the South, and that the war would eventually end in a negotiated peace in which the North recognized the Confederacy as an independent state.[61] The continuation of the war by the North was therefore seen as senseless slaughter. Louis Napoleon, in his speeches to the Chambers and his New Year messages, expressed the hope that the tragic strife in America would soon come to an end;[62] but while he officially adopted an attitude of neutrality, he became increasingly sympathetic to the South.

The pro-Confederate lobby in the British House of Commons thought that Louis Napoleon was more favourable to their cause than were the British government, and on several occasions they tried to use him to exert pressure on Palmerston and Russell. In April 1862 William Lindsay, the M.P. for Sunderland, went to Paris and to the annoyance of Thouvenel had a private talk with the Emperor. Lindsay urged the Emperor to counter the effect of the blockade of the Southern ports, which was beginning to hurt in France and England, by recognizing the South; but Louis Napoleon took no action beyond informing the British government of his talk with Lindsay, and he readily accepted Russell's argument that though the blockade did great harm to Britain and France, it was not easy to see how recognition of the South could remedy this evil.[63]

Six months later, after the fluctuating military campaign in Virginia and Maryland in the summer of 1862, Louis Napoleon at last made a definite move in favour of the South. He proposed to Britain that their two governments should offer to mediate between the belligerents in America.[64] As Lincoln could not accept the mediation of a foreign power between the U.S. government and its rebels, he would refuse the Anglo-French offer; and Britain and France would then grant diplomatic recognition to the Southern Confederacy. An influential section in Palmerston's government favoured the immediate recognition of the South; but other ministers opposed it, and Britain rejected Louis Napoleon's proposal as premature. Louis Napoleon received information that the British Ambassador in Washington had told Seward about his *démarche* and had claimed the credit with Seward for rejecting it; and though Louis Napoleon professed to accept the British denial of this report, it made him chary of taking any further steps in favour of the South.

In May 1863 another Northern offensive against the South was defeated at Chancellorsville, and a few weeks later Lee invaded the Northern state of Pennsylvania. When the news of his success reached Europe, the Confederate agents redoubled their efforts to obtain recognition from Britain and France. Lindsay went to Paris with his Parliamentary colleague, Roebuck, and had an interview with Louis Napoleon while the Foreign Minister, Drouyn de Lhuys, was away on holiday in the country.

The Emperor and the M.P.s afterwards gave conflicting accounts of what was said at their talk, which Louis Napoleon tactfully attributed to the fact that their conversation had taken place in English. The M.P.s returned to London and stated in the House of Commons that Louis Napoleon had told them that he wished to recognize the South, but was prevented from doing so by the British government. Louis Napoleon denied this, and authorized Drouyn de Lhuys to give Cowley a copy of the letter that he had written to Drouyn de Lhuys immediately after his talk with Roebuck and Lindsay. He said that when the M.P.s urged him to take the lead in recognizing the South, he had replied that though he favoured the Southern cause, he would not venture to propose recognition to the British government in view of the British reaction to his proposal of October 1862, and that any new initiative must come from Britain.[65]

On 30 June 1863, Roebuck moved a motion in the House of Commons in favour of recognition of the South, and claimed that he had the support of Louis Napoleon. But it did the Southern cause no good in Britain that Napoleon III was thought to be in favour of it; and though Roebuck was supported by an influential minority in Parliament, there was a general feeling in Britain that Louis Napoleon was meddling in British politics on the recognition issue. Palmerston and Russell decided to postpone recognition; and soon afterwards the news arrived of Lee's defeat at Gettysburg and of Grant's capture of Vicksburg on the Mississippi. After this, nearly everyone in Europe except Louis Napoleon realized that the North would eventually win. In the summer of 1864, when a Southern army reached the outskirts of Washington, Louis Napoleon said to Ancel, the deputy for Le Havre: 'Lee will take Washington, and then I shall recognize the Confederates. . . . he is probably in possession of the Capitol now.'[66] But it was only a diversionary raid. The French and British governments took no further action as regards either mediation or recognition of the South, and resigned themselves to seeing the United States emerge from the Civil War victorious, united, and one of the strongest military powers in the world.

In the summer of 1863, Louis Napoleon still had some time to spare before the North conquered the South. It was at this time that the Confederate government made secret peace proposals to the United States, suggesting that the North and the South should sign an armistice and unite to expel the French from Mexico; but Lincoln turned them down, and stated that he would think about Mexico after the South had capitulated.[67] The Mexican Conservatives now decided to offer the crown to Maximilian. Louis Napoleon would have liked to have held a referendum in Mexico so as to be able to claim that Maximilian had been chosen Emperor by universal suffrage; but Forey persuaded him that it was impossible to hold a referendum while Juarez's guerrillas were still active in many parts of the country, and he agreed that in the circumstances the will of the Mexican people could be expressed through the Council of Notables that Forey had installed in Mexico City and through the local authorities in those parts of Mexico which the French controlled.[68]

In September 1863 some Conservative Mexican delegates sailed for Europe, and after seeing Louis Napoleon and Eugénie at Biarritz went on to Maximilian's mansion of Miramar near Trieste. They offered Maximilian the imperial crown of Mexico. He replied that he must first obtain the consent of his brother, the Emperor Franz Joseph, the head of the Habsburg family. His initial enthusiasm had waned as he observed the extent of the Mexican resistance to the French army and the delay by Britain and France in recognizing the Southern Confederacy, on which he relied as a buffer between Mexico and the United States; but his chief reason for hesitating to accept the crown was his reluctance to agree to Franz Joseph's condition that he should waive his right of succession to the imperial throne of Austria.[69]

Louis Napoleon was very eager that Maximilian should accept Mexico, and reassured him about the United States. 'Once the country is pacified, both physically and morally, Your Imperial Highness's government will be recognized by everybody', he wrote to Maximilian on 19 September 1863. 'The United States are well aware that, since the new régime in Mexico is the work of France, they cannot attack it without at once making enemies of us.' But Louis Napoleon was afraid that Maximilian's well-known Liberalism would go too far, and wrote again to Maximilian on 2 October:

Allow me to lay great stress on one point: a country torn by anarchy cannot be regenerated by *parliamentary* liberty. What is needed in Mexico is a *liberal* dictatorship; that is to say, a strong power which shall proclaim the great principles of modern civilization, such as equality before the law, civil and religious liberty, an upright administration, an equitable judicial procedure, etc[70].

515

In private, Louis Napoleon himself now had serious misgivings about Mexico. In October 1863, within a few days of the visit of the Mexican representatives to Miramar, he had a talk with the former British Ambassador in Mexico, Sir Charles Wyke, who was spending a few days in Paris. He agreed with Wyke that it had been a great mistake to allow Almonte to go to Vera Cruz in February 1862, and that he had been misled by Almonte and the other Mexican Conservatives in Paris into underestimating the resistance of the Mexicans. He also admitted that Saligny and Forey had blundered in supporting the extreme reactionaries in Mexico, and said that for this reason he was replacing them by Monsieur de Montholon and General Bazaine. But he believed that it was too late for him to withdraw from Mexico without loss of face; he could now only hope that his new civil and military chiefs, and Maximilian when he arrived, would bring about a better situation.[71]

At the end of March 1864, Louis Napoleon and Eugénie heard that, in view of Franz Joseph's attitude about the right of succession to the Austrian throne, Maximilian had decided to refuse the crown of Mexico. They were shocked by the news. On 27 March, Eugénie wrote to Metternich, asking him to do all he could to persuade Maximilian to accept, because his refusal would place Louis Napoleon in an acutely embarrassing position; and next day Louis Napoleon wrote to Maximilian:

Your Imperial Highness has entered into engagements which you are no longer free to break. What, indeed, would you think of me if, once Your Imperial Majesty had arrived in Mexico, I were to say that I can no longer fulfil the conditions to which I have set my signature?

Two months earlier, on 30 January, he had reminded Maximilian what these conditions were, and had repeated his guarantee that he would never abandon Maximilian: 'The French army will leave Mexico only gradually, and when it can do so without compromising the existence of the new government'; and when the army was withdrawn, a Foreign Legion of 8000 men would remain in Mexico for another six to eight years.[72]

On 10 April 1864, Maximilian accepted the crown, and four days later left Miramar with Charlotte. The Mexican delegates to Miramar thought that their new Empress's beauty would be worth more to Maximilian in Mexico than 40,000 soldiers.[73] Maximilian and Charlotte reached Vera Cruz on 31 May, nearly a year after the French had captured Mexico City.

On 11 June, 150 carriages filled with ladies of the Mexican aristocracy, and 500 of the highest-ranking gentlemen on horseback, went out of Mexico City along the road to the village of Gualupe, where their new Emperor and Empress had slept on their last night before entering their capital. Next day they entered the city in great pomp amid the cheers of at least some of the population.[74] Charlotte was happy. On 13 June she wrote to her father, King Leopold: 'Things are much less bad here than I expected; the population is enthusiastic and sincerely loves us. . . . When one says that France represents civilization, people think that one is being too flattering, but in Mexico it is literally true, and my enthusiasm for the French army is unbounded.' She added that 'the French army is full of enthusiasm for Max'.[75]

Maximilian was recognized as Emperor of Mexico by nearly every government in Europe. To finance the new Emperor's régime, a Mexican loan was floated in Paris and other European capitals. The historians afterwards dismissed the loan as a failure; but at the time the response was thought to be excellent, and many of the French working class subscribed. The price of the stock rose to 340 francs. It was an impressive testimony of public confidence in Maximilian and Napoleon III. 'What has become of Juarez, nobody seems to know or care', wrote the *Times* correspondent in Mexico City on 29 October. 'Like all Mexican celebrities he has run his little course, and probably will never more be heard of.'[76]

In April 1864, Garibaldi visited England and received a triumphal welcome in London, to the annoyance of Louis Napoleon and the French Catholics and to the great indignation of Eugénie.[77] One evening during his visit he dined at Lord Clanricarde's, and after dinner sat in the smoking-room with Malmesbury and other guests. Someone said that the career of Napoleon III had been even more successful than that of Napoleon I. 'We must wait for the end of the story', said Garibaldi.[78]

CHAPTER 39

SADOWA, QUERÉTARO,
AND THE EXHIBITION

IN the spring of 1865 the Opposition deputies in the Chamber launched an attack on the government's policy in Mexico, deploring 'the blood shed in Mexico for a foreign Prince'.[1] On 18 March, the Minister of State, Rouher, intervened in the debate to announce another glorious triumph for French arms; he had just heard that Marshal Bazaine had captured Oaxaca, the capital of Juarez's native state, along with the Juarist leader, Porfirio Diaz, 4000 rebel prisoners, and between 50 and 60 guns. Marshal Forey spoke in the debate, and said that he hoped that Diaz, who had committed unspeakable atrocities against Mexican collaborators, would be shot out of hand;[2] but Diaz was held as a prisoner-of-war until he escaped.[3]

The Opposition motion was defeated by 225 votes to 16;[4] but the news of the victory at Oaxaca had a double effect on the French public. Until Rouher's announcement they had heard nothing about Diaz at Oaxaca, and had believed that all resistance had ended in Mexico; now it appeared that 4000 rebels with 60 guns had been holding Oaxaca. What else was being suppressed in the Paris newspapers?

In America the military position of the South was desperate; but Louis Napoleon was strangely optimistic about the future. 'We have been rather uneasy at the news from America', he wrote to Maximilian on 1 March 1865. 'However, it looks as if the war will still last a long time, and when peace comes, the United States will think twice before declaring war on France and England.'[5] In fact, the American Civil War lasted only another forty days.

Louis Napoleon was on the point of leaving for Algeria when the news arrived, on 23 April, that Lee had surrendered to Grant at Appomattox on 9 April and that the North had won the Civil War. The news of Lincoln's assassination, five days after Appomattox, took a little less time to arrive, and was known in Europe on 26 April. Eugénie wrote a personal letter of sympathy to Mrs Lincoln, and wrote to the Empress Charlotte that she thought that the assassin was not a supporter of the South but a Northern Radical who had killed Lincoln because he was too moderate. The European press praised the murdered President in a way that they had never done during his lifetime. Apart from taking the opportunity to condemn international terrorism and regicide, the government press in France praised Lincoln for his wisdom in not intervening against the French in Mexico, and confidently predicted that his successor, President Andrew Johnson, would likewise realize that the Emperor Maximilian and his French allies constituted no threat to the United States.[6]

In the Chamber, Rouher, urging the public to subscribe to the Mexican loan, declared that France had 'succeeded in introducing order, civilization and liberty' into Mexico, and that 'in a few years hence that country, completely pacified, will bless France and will contribute to the spread of her commerce and her grandeur'.[7] A few days later he assured the deputies: 'I declare, in the name of the Emperor, and in the name of France, that the French army will not return home until its object is completely attained.'[8]

But in the United States public opinion was indignant about Mexico, and a great pro-Juarez press campaign was launched during the summer of 1865. Johnson and his Secretary of State, Seward, were under strong pressure from the Radicals in Congress to pursue a tougher policy towards the defeated slave-owners of the South, and the Radicals also demanded action against the French in Mexico, who had violated the Monroe Doctrine and had established an imperial despotism on the free soil of the American continent. Johnson and Seward, on their part, tried to appease the anger of the Radicals on the Reconstruction issue by an anti-French posture about Mexico. The U.S. government recognized Juarez as President of Mexico, and rejected Drouyn de Lhuys's suggestion that they should recognize Maximilian. U.S. citizens subscribed freely to funds to provide arms for Juarez. The French Ambassador had frequently to complain of breaches of the U.S. Neutrality Act as volunteers sailed from New York in the east and San Francisco in the west to the little harbours in northern Mexico to enlist in Juarez's forces.[9]

The French press published articles praising the United States and Franco-American friendship; but privately Louis Napoleon and his ministers were worried. When Lee surrendered at Appomattox, Grant had 950,000 men under his command. The total number of the French armed forces was 420,000; there were 16,000 in Rome, 2000 in Indo-China, 34,000 in Mexico, 57,000 in Algeria, Senegal and elsewhere overseas, and 310,000 in France.[10] Louis Napoleon was sure that the United States could not afford to keep 950,000 men under arms, and that public opinion in the United States would insist that the troops be allowed to go home. During the summer of 1865 the U.S. government sent 700,000 of them home, but retained 250,000 in the army – more than eight times the French forces in Mexico – and sent 25,000 men to Texas to man the frontier along the Rio Grande, under the command of the war hero, the dashing General Sheridan.[11] At a dinner in New York on 3 August in honour of Ortega, Juarez's Ambassador in Washington, a message from Sheridan was read out to the guests:

> It is of no use to beat around the bush in this Mexican matter; we should give a permanent government to that republic. Our work in crushing the rebellion will not be done until this takes place. . . . Most of the Mexican soldiers of Maximilian's army would throw down their arms the moment we crossed the Rio Grande.[12]

General Grant and General Sherman also made public statements in favour of intervention in Mexico.[13] By October the *Times* correspondent in New York was reporting that the man in the street there was confident that the United States could win a war against France. 'The most moderate men reply to all questions about Mexico, "The French will have to go." But the large majority say plainly, "We mean to drive the French out." '[14]

But Johnson and Seward did not want to start another major war,[15] especially as Britain might support her French ally in a war against the United States on the issue of the Monroe Doctrine and against Radical Republicanism. So with both governments eager to avoid war, and knowing that the other was equally eager, there was scope for negotiation and bluff. During the summer of 1865, the French army in Mexico made a drive to destroy the Juarists as soon as possible. In May, General Aymond captured Chihuahua, and Juarez fled two hundred miles to the north to the little village of El Paso del Norte – today Ciudad Juarez – on the southern bank of the Rio Grande, and consequently just on Mexican soil. As El Paso del Norte was nearly a thousand miles upstream from the mouth of the Rio Grande, it was almost inaccessible to French attack; and if the worst came to the worst, Juarez could cross the river and take refuge in the United States. The French navy patrolled both the Atlantic and the Pacific coasts of Mexico; on the east coast they sailed up to the mouth of the Rio Grande and captured the port of Matamoros. Across the river was the U.S. naval base at Brownsville and Sheridan's army.

There were incidents along the Rio Grande. Sheridan's subordinate officers opened fire with their batteries on Maximilian's gunboats in the river, and the French and Mexican forces fired back. Small units of U.S. soldiers crossed the river and helped the Juarists in raids on forts held by the French army.[16]

Drouyn de Lhuys urged the United States to discontinue their support for Juarez – 'an ex-President flying from village to village is no more the head of a government than a few bands of guerrillas, pillaging and infesting the high roads, are armies'[17] – and reminded the United States that France, unlike the United States in 1848, had not annexed large tracts of Mexican territory. Again the French press proclaimed that the Juarist resistance was over; but shrewd readers noticed that *Le Moniteur* kept reporting the recapture of towns which had never been reported as having been lost.

As a move in the game of bluff with the United States, Bazaine persuaded the reluctant Maximilian to issue his notorious proclamation of 3 October 1865: 'Mexicans! the cause which Don Benito Juarez upheld with so much valour and constancy collapsed some time ago'; and Juarez's term as President of Mexico, under his own Republican Constitution, had expired.* 'Henceforth the contest will be solely between the respectable men of the nation and bands of criminals and highwaymen ... who burn villages and rob and murder peaceful citizens, decrepit old men and defenceless women.' Consequently all rebels captured would in future be shot within twenty-four hours in accordance with the accepted laws of war.[18]

When the United States protested to France against this order, Drouyn de Lhuys replied that it had nothing to do with France, and that the United States should raise the matter with the government of the Emperor of Mexico, with whom, as he well knew, the United States had refused to have diplomatic relations; but he added that the French government believed that the order was justified, as the Juarists were now only a band of marauders. He did not mention that Maximilian had issued the order at the insistence of Bazaine, who had received a letter from Louis Napoleon, written from Châlons Camp on 17 August, instructing him to urge Maximilian to be less weak and tolerant towards the rebels.[19] The French generals were much more to blame than Maximilian for the execution of Juarists. When the Juarist leader Romero was captured, Maximilian gave orders that he was not to be shot, since, unlike other guerrilla leaders, he had never committed atrocities against French soldiers or Mexican collaborators. Bazaine told the Empress Charlotte that Romero would be shot either with or without Maximilian's consent; and the execution took place.[20]

But Maximilian knew that the Juarists were far more than a defeated guerrilla remnant. On 29 June 1865 he wrote to Charlotte:

*Juarez extended his term as President by his own decree, on the grounds that it was impossible to hold elections while the country was under French occupation.

'It must be said, openly, our military situation is the worst possible . . . much worse than last autumn.'[21] He needed more troops and more financial aid from France.

Louis Napoleon, as usual, hoped to get out of his very difficult position by a clever sleight of hand, by an apparent concession which would in fact turn out to his advantage and enable him to gain by indirect means what he had failed to get by direct methods. This had worked in the case of Romania and Neuchâtel; why not in Mexico? In the autumn of 1865 he decided to withdraw his troops from Mexico in stages in return for an undertaking by the U.S. government to enforce the Neutrality Act and prevent U.S. citizens from sending aid to Juarez. He would replace the French troops with Belgian and Austrian volunteers who would rush to the rescue of their compatriots, Maximilian and Charlotte, and Dupin's counter-guerrilla corps would also remain.[22] This, he believed – or at least pretended to believe – would enable Maximilian and his loyal subjects to extirpate the Juarist bandits quite easily. In November 1865 the U.S. government announced that they would enforce the Neutrality Act, and stopped several groups of volunteers from going to Mexico to help Juarez.[23] 'This virtually ends the Mexican contest', wrote the *Times* correspondent in Philadelphia on 14 November. 'Juarez depends entirely upon aid from the United States, and the enforcement of the neutrality laws ends even his hopes of success.'[24]

When Louis Napoleon opened the new session of the Chambers in January 1866 he announced that he was about to withdraw his troops from Mexico because Maximilian's régime was now secure; the 'dissidents', who no longer had a leader, had been dispersed, and Mexico's trade with France had increased from 21 million francs to 77 million francs.[25] But three weeks later, Marshal Forey opened a debate in the Senate on the situation in Mexico. As he began to speak, a freak thunderstorm burst over Paris, and the rain fell so heavily that the life of the city was brought to a standstill for twenty-four hours; but those Senators who had reached the shelter of the Luxembourg Palace had other things to worry about. Forey said that people in France had a totally false impression about the situation in Mexico. The military position there was very serious; if the French troops were withdrawn, the Juarists would quickly overrun the country. The troops in Mexico should be kept there for the time being, even if it was impossible to send out more reinforcements.[26]

In April 1866, Drouyn de Lhuys informed Seward that one-third of the French forces in Mexico – 10,000 men – would embark for home in November; another 10,000 would leave in March 1867; and the final contingent would be withdrawn in November 1867.[27] Thus encouraged, Juarez in the spring of 1866 began to move back along the road that he had travelled during the previous three years. In March he captured Chihuahua; in June, Matamoros; in July, Monterey; by August he was advancing on San Luis Potosí.

Louis Napoleon's plan to send Austrian and Belgian volunteers to help Maximilian did not materialize. A small number of Belgians served in Mexico, but most of them were killed when their unit was trapped by Juarist guerrillas in the summer of 1865. The Austrian government allowed an Austrian Legion to be recruited in Austria, and by May 1866 4000 volunteers were on the point of sailing for Mexico when the U.S. Ambassador in Vienna – he was the historian, John Motley – informed the Austrian government that if the volunteers were allowed to sail, the United States would consider that Austria was at war with the Republic of Mexico and could not guarantee that the United States would remain neutral in this war. The Austrian government thereupon prevented the volunteers from leaving Austria, and the Legion was dissolved.[28]

Austria had no wish to be embroiled with the United States in May 1866, for she was on the point of going to war with Prussia to decide which of them was to dominate Germany; and Italy was preparing to join in on Prussia's side in return for a Prussian promise of Venetia. Louis Napoleon gave no clear indication of what policy he would pursue in the event of war. He put forward his usual proposal for an international Congress, hoping that the Congress would not only find a peaceful solution of the Austro-Prussian conflict but also adopt his plans for redrawing the map of Europe by cessions and compensations. He half-promised diplomatic support to both Prussia and Austria, and even hinted at a military alliance with Austria in certain circumstances, in order to induce Austria to attend the proposed Congress. If war broke out, he intended to remain neutral, hoping by hints of help to persuade both belligerents to agree to his proposals for the revision of frontiers; but if Prussia won and threatened to become too powerful in Germany and Central Europe, he would intervene, either diplomatically or militarily, to prevent this. He told Metternich that he would not enter the war on Austria's side because he could do more to help Austria diplomatically by remaining neutral, but that if Austria would cede Venetia to Italy he would put pressure on Italy not to declare war on Austria.[29]

Eugénie wished to make an alliance with Austria,[30] and for the first time – much more clearly than in the case of Italy and Rome – she opposed Louis Napoleon's policy. She shared the fears which many Frenchmen felt about Prussian expansionism, and felt that in the conflict of 1866 Protestant Prussia and Liberal Italy represented a disturbing, aggressive and revolutionary force against Catholic and imperial Austria, which stood for stability and legitimacy. On 5 May, Metternich wrote to Rechberg that 'the Empress would quite like to have a go together with us'*; she had got out the map in the presence of the Emperor and Metternich and had suggested frontier rectifications in Austria's favour. On 23 May, Metternich reported that she was longing to hear the news of the outbreak of war and that she thought that everything would then take a turn for the better.[31] Prince Napoleon's Radical and pro-Italian sympathies made him as usual take the opposite position to Eugénie.

On 11 June, Austria declared war on Prussia, and next day a secret treaty between France and Austria was signed in Vienna. As late as March 1866, Metternich was refusing even to discuss with Louis Napoleon and Eugénie the possibility of Austria ceding Venetia; but by the treaty of 12 June Austria agreed to cede Venetia to France if Austria won the war, in return for a promise by France to remain neutral in the war, to put diplomatic pressure on Italy to remain neutral, and only to cede Venetia to Italy if Italy promised not to invade the Papal States. Italy nevertheless declared war on Austria on 20 June; and though the Austrians defeated the Italians at Custoza four days later, they were themselves defeated by the Prussians on 3 July at Sadowa in Bohemia. Everyone expected the Prussians to march on Vienna; but next day Austria signed a treaty with France by which she promised to cede Venetia to Louis Napoleon on the understanding that he would give it to Italy. Louis Napoleon thereupon informed Prussia that if the Prussian armies marched further south into Austria, the French troops would cross the Rhine.[32]

Bismarck, who had decided to win Austrian good will by a soft peace, did not wish to march on Vienna, and used the risk of French intervention to persuade his King, his generals and the Italians, to agree to generous peace terms; but Austria lost Venetia. On the morning of 19 October 1866, Austria ceded Venetia to France, and for five minutes it was part of Louis Napoleon's empire before it was ceded by France to Italy.[33]

Louis Napoleon was suffering acutely from stone in the bladder, which had been occasionally troubling him since 1861 and took a sharp turn for the worse in the summer of 1866. Metternich, who was as exasperated with Louis Napoleon's policy as he was pleased with Eugénie's, was exaggerating when he wrote on 26 July that Eugénie 'will do all she can to galvanize the corpse that she has at her side';[34] but on 28 July the Emperor's doctors sent him to take the waters at

* 'Die Kaiserin möchte ganz gerne mit uns losschlagen.'

Vichy. Louis Napoleon took Drouyn de Lhuys with him to Vichy, and kept in touch with the international situation; but Eugénie, at Saint-Cloud, presided at the Cabinet meetings and was in communication with the Foreign Office officials in Paris. 'The Empress seems to me', wrote Metternich on 6 August,

> to have gone over completely to the Opposition political camp. She allows anti-Italian and anti-Prussian articles to be written, carries on a secret correspondence with certain people in Vichy and Châlons, and makes war to the death against Prince Napoleon. . . . All the important officials who remain here are so influenced by the Empress that I am now surrounded only by Prussian-eaters and enemies of Italy. Unfortunately Drouyn de Lhuys is with the Emperor . . . at Vichy. Tomorrow we shall find out what is happening there. The Empress fears the worst.[35]

He enclosed with his letter to Rechberg the reports of the French secret police which Eugénie had given him.

Eugénie was justified in fearing the worst. On 3 August the French Ambassador in Berlin, Benedetti, made a secret proposal to Bismarck: France would agree to Prussia seizing territory in South Germany if Prussia allowed France to annex Belgium and Luxemburg. Benedetti was acting on secret instructions from Louis Napoleon, who had not informed his ministers. Bismarck persuaded Benedetti to put this proposal into writing, and filed away the document for future use.[36]

Louis Napoleon's doctors knew that they were taking a risk in sending him to Vichy, because though some patients benefited by the waters there, others became worse. The waters did the Emperor no good, and after a week at Vichy the doctors advised him to return to Saint-Cloud and rest.[37] Two days after he returned from Vichy, the Empress Charlotte of Mexico arrived at the Grand Hotel in Paris. She had come to ask Louis Napoleon not to abandon Maximilian. He told her that he was too ill to see her, which was certainly true, and sent Eugénie to call on her at the Grand Hotel; but Charlotte insisted on seeing him, and threatened to force her way into his presence, so he reluctantly agreed to receive her at Saint-Cloud.[38]

During Charlotte's thirteen days in Paris, she saw Louis Napoleon five times and Eugénie six times, and also spoke with several members of the government; but despite their embarrassment in the face of her rising indignation, they made it plain to her that they could not supply any more military or financial aid to Maximilian because of the opposition of the French Chambers, though Charlotte suggested that Louis

Napoleon should confront the Chambers with another *coup d'état*. On 29 August, Louis Napoleon for once made his attitude unequivocally clear in a letter to Maximilian: 'I begin by stating to Your Majesty that it is henceforth *impossible* for me to give Mexico another *écu* or another man.'[39] He advised Maximilian to abdicate and sail for Europe with the departing French army; but Maximilian declared that he would never leave his loyal subjects, and would fight with them to the death against the Juarist bandits.[40]

Charlotte went on from Paris to Rome to appeal to the Pope, but he could not help her. Her mind then gave way, and she retired, insane, to Miramar. She held Louis Napoleon responsible for everything, denouncing him as a Mephistopheles, and believed that he was trying to poison her.[41] 'No power can help us,' she wrote to Maximilian, 'for he has Hell on his side, and I have not. . . . *He means to commit a long premeditated evil deed, not out of cowardice or discouragement, or for any reason whatsoever, but because he is the evil principle on earth, and wants to get rid of the good.*'[42] She was taken from Miramar to Belgium, where she lived for another sixty years without recovering her sanity till she died in 1927.

The tragic story of the Empress Charlotte, and her account of her visit to Paris, have been repeatedly used to discredit Napoleon III; but whatever other criticism may be made of Louis Napoleon's actions in Mexico, he cannot be reproached for his behaviour to Charlotte in August 1866. The Juarists, the U.S. government, the French troops stationed in Mexico, and the European subscribers to the Mexican loan, all had reasons to complain of Louis Napoleon's policy in Mexico; but Maximilian and Charlotte, his partners in his unscrupulous, unwise and unsuccessful gamble, had none.

Although Louis Napoleon had decided to withdraw from Mexico, his officials did not take the necessary measures in time, and by the autumn he realized that there would not be enough ships available to evacuate 10,000 troops from Vera Cruz by the given date of November 1866. The French government therefore announced that the departure of the first 10,000 would be postponed to the spring of 1867.[43] On 23 November 1866, Seward cabled a strong but tactfully worded note to Paris; it was the longest diplomatic note that had ever been sent by cable, and the use of the cable – which had finally been laid across the Atlantic on 8 September 1866 – in itself gave a sense of urgency and excitement to the note. Seward stated that the French decision to leave the whole French army in Mexico until the spring, which had been taken without consultation with the United States, was 'found in every way inconvenient and exceptionable' by the U.S. government; that U.S. troops had been ordered to cross the Rio Grande to replace the departing French troops and preserve order in Mexico until 'President Juarez' was in effective control of the country; but that in order to avoid the risk of a clash between the U.S. and French forces, the advance across the Rio Grande would be postponed to enable the French government to give a satisfactory reply to the note.[44]

The French government declared that they would never submit to threats from a foreign power, but would withdraw the troops from Mexico at the time of their own choosing. They then informed the United States that they had decided to change the evacuation plans: instead of withdrawing in three stages, the whole army in Mexico would be evacuated in March 1867.[45] When this was known, the Juarist forces quickly advanced, harassing the French as they moved along the roads to Vera Cruz, cutting off isolated units and exterminating many of them. Maximilian decided to stay and fight the rebels with 10,000 of his native Mexican soldiers; but the last French soldier sailed from Vera Cruz on 16 March 1867. On 2 April, Porfirio Diaz captured Puebla, and executed all Maximilian's officers above the rank of lieutenant. On 15 May, Maximilian and his army, who had been besieged in Querétaro, surrendered to the Juarists, and Napoleon III was reduced to asking the U.S. government to use its influence to persuade Juarez to spare Maximilian's life. The Juarists entered Mexico City on 21 June and Vera Cruz on the 27th.[46]

Louis Napoleon at last decided to admit that he had suffered a defeat in Mexico; in the Chamber, Rouher called it the single failure to set against the Emperor's long row of successes.[47] Louis Napoleon planned two more successes which should make the people forget Mexico: another Great Universal Exhibition was due to open in Paris on 1 April 1867, and he hoped to persuade the King of Holland to cede Luxemburg to him. The Treaty of Vienna in 1815 had given Luxemburg to the King of Holland to rule as hereditary Grand Duke; but Luxemburg was also to be a member of the German Confederation, and Prussia occupied the fortresses in the Grand Duchy as a bulwark of the Allied defences against France. The government of Louis Philippe had failed to upset the Luxemburg settlement when Belgium won its independence from Holland after 1830.

There was some support in Luxemburg for union with France, and French agents encouraged the agitation. Louis Napoleon made secret proposals to the King of Holland that he should cede Luxemburg to France in return for a Franco-Dutch military alliance against Prussia. At the same time, he suggested, equally secretly, to Bismarck that Prussia should consent to the cession, and agree to give up the Prussian fortresses in Luxemburg, in return for a free hand against Austria in South Germany. Bismarck gave no definite reply to Louis Napoleon, but leaked the news of the negotiations, with the result that there was a storm of protest and anti-French feeling in Germany.

At the end of March 1867 there was a danger of war between France and Prussia over Luxemburg. But Bismarck, though he was beginning to think that war with France would one day become inevitable, had no wish to hasten it. He was determined that, if war came, France should fight alone; and the best way to achieve this was to build up in the remaining years of peace an international image of France as the aggressor and Prussia as the peace-loving victim of aggression. He therefore reached a compromise with Louis Napoleon about Luxemburg. France agreed to abandon her claim to Luxemburg and to recognize its independence and neutrality; Luxemburg withdrew from the German Confederation; and Prussia evacuated the fortresses in Luxemburg, which were dismantled.

The Luxemburg crisis did not wreck the Great Universal Exhibition. Exhibitions were getting bigger and better. The Paris Exhibition of 1855 had eclipsed the London Exhibition of 1851; the London Exhibition of 1862 had eclipsed the Paris Exhibition of 1855. Now the Paris Exhibition of 1867 was to outdistance completely all previous exhibitions, as the Imperial Commissioners whom Louis Napoleon had appointed to run the Exhibition made plain in their advance publicity. London in 1851 had covered 70,000 square yards and cost $7\frac{1}{2}$ million francs; Paris in 1855, 115,000 square yards and 11 million francs; London in 1862, 120,000 square yards and 15 million francs; but Paris in 1867 would cover 146,588 square yards and would probably cost 20 million francs. Since Christmas, the public had been admitted to the site to see the preparations in progress at an admission charge of 1 franc; nearly 5000 people went every day during the week, and nearly 9000 every Sunday.[48] Apart from the usual industrial and cultural exhibitions, there was a very popular innovation: for the first time at an international exhibition, there was a restaurant and a café at which dishes of the various countries were served by waiters of the different nationalities. The only drawbacks at the Exhibition were a shortage of chairs, owing to a dispute about a company's monopoly, and the fact that the ladies' lavatory could only be reached by going through the public bar of the restaurant, so that no respectable woman would use it.[49]

As 1 April approached, it was obvious that most of the national pavilions would not be ready in time, and many requests were made to postpone the opening; but the Imperial Commissioners insisted that it should open on time, and Louis Napoleon opened it on 1 April, though only four of the thirty pavilions – the British, Russian, Swedish and Danish – were ready.[50] The Emperor and Empress walked around for three-quarters of an hour among the packing cases and the un-packed 'exhibits'.* As they entered the British pavilion, Eugénie smiled at two English sailors who were standing there. 'Ah, Bill', said one delighted sailor to the other, 'she *guv* me such a look!'[52]

Outside the Exhibition, Paris provided its best selection of operas, operettas and *cafés chantants*. Offenbach, who had come to Paris from the Rhineland as a child, had given the Parisians a series of successful operettas and had scored a sensational triumph in 1864 with *La Belle Hélène*. There was no overt immorality in his plots or songs, and the very popular duet from his *Geneviève de Brabant*, the 'Couplet des hommes d'armes', had none of the seditious implications of the English 'Gen-darmes' Song' into which H. B. Fernie afterwards translated it; but the spirit of Offenbach, the *cancan* which was first danced in his *Orphée aux enfers* in 1858, and the atmosphere and activities in the auditorium and backstage, helped to convey to the world an impression of Paris under the Second Empire which was very different from the Paris of the pulpits and the law courts where the Ultramontane clergy denounced immorality and prosecuted Baudelaire and Flaubert. 'Paris!', wrote Wilfrid Scawen Blunt. 'What magic lived for us in those two syllables! what a picture they evolved of vanity and profane delights, of triumph in the world and the romance of pleasure! How great, how terrible a name hers was, hers the fair imperial harlot of civilised humanity.'[53]

For foreign, especially British, visitors Paris meant the smell of roasting coffee and bad tobacco,[54] and freedom from restraint. Respect-able English girls, who would never go out in London without being escorted by a servant, were prepared to do so in Paris. During the Exhibition of 1867 Blunt took one of them, a cousin of his, to a café in the Rue de Beaujolais, bought her strawberries, kneeled and kissed her feet, and declared his love for her. She responded by laughing and mocking a little; but on the day before she returned to England he found her reading her Bible. 'I have been too long away from respect-able life', she said.[55]

For the Exhibition, the Théâtre des Variétés in the Boulevard Montmartre put on a new Offenbach operetta, *La Grande-Duchesse de Gérolstein*, which was as great a success as *La Belle Hélène*. Everyone in society had to see it; even Eugénie went with Louis Napoleon, although she did not like operetta. So many foreign Princes went to see *La Grande-Duchesse* and to visit the leading lady, Hortense Schneider, after the performance, that the passage from the stage door to her dressing-room became known as the 'Passage des Princes'.[56]

In the Tuileries Gardens an Austrian band entertained the

---

*This word was first introduced into the English language during the London Exhibition of 1862, but only came into general use in 1867.[51]

well-dressed ladies and gentlemen strolling in the gardens. They played the Overture to Wagner's *Rienzi*, Johann Strauss's 'Morgenblätter', and Zimmermann's 'Annette Polka', but broke into their programme to play 'Partant pour la Syrie' whenever the Emperor or Empress drove past in their carriage. Johann Strauss himself came to Paris, and conducted at a ball at the Austrian embassy which Princess Metternich gave for Louis Napoleon and Eugénie and the Crown Prince and Crown Princess of Prussia. Strauss impressed the dancers by the virtuosity of his performance, but exasperated them by taking the quadrilles much too slowly.[57]

As soon as the Luxemburg crisis was safely settled, the foreign royalties made arrangements to visit Paris, and they began to arrive at the beginning of June. The Polish refugees and their French Radical sympathizers protested against the visit of Tsar Alexander II, and this worried the French government and the police. On 1 June the Tsar arrived at the Gare du Nord. Louis Napoleon went to meet him at the station, with a full escort of cavalry, and the two Emperors drove together along the boulevards to the Tuileries, from where the Tsar went to the Élysée which had been placed at his disposal during his stay in Paris. All along the route from the Gare du Nord the shouts of 'Long live the Emperor!' were drowned in the louder shouts of 'Long live Poland!' The Parisians laughed next day when they read in *Le Moniteur*: 'Along the whole route Their Majesties received from the population the most enthusiastic ovations.'[58]

Some of the respectable members of the Establishment, who strongly disapproved of the demonstrations against the Tsar, were a little shocked when they heard that when the Tsar's train stopped at Creil on its way to Paris, the Tsar had sent a cable to the Russian embassy ordering them to reserve a seat for him at the Théâtre des Variétés for that evening's performance of *La Grande-Duchesse de Gérolstein*. As no one expected him to go to the Théâtre des Variétés, there were no demonstrators awaiting him there. His visit to the Cluny Museum in the Latin Quarter was kept secret to avoid demonstrations; but while he was in the museum a student who tried to get in was told that it was closed to the public because the Tsar was there. The student ran off to tell his comrades, and by the time the Tsar came out there was a crowd of students in the street crying 'Vive la Pologne!' There were some arrests, as there were when the Tsar encountered another demonstration during his visit to the Palais de Justice.[59]

Great precautions were taken when the Tsar went with Louis Napoleon and Eugénie to a gala performance at the Opera; but there were shouts of 'Vive la Pologne!', and about thirty arrests, in the street, and some boos inside the theatre.[60]

On 5 June the King of Prussia and Bismarck arrived, and next day the King and the two Emperors attended a great military review in the Bois de Boulogne. After the review, Louis Napoleon drove home in a carriage with the Tsar and the Tsar's two sons. As they were driving out of the Bois de Boulogne and passing the rocks of the cascade, a man fired a pistol at the Tsar. The bullet went through the nostril of one of the horses, passed between the Emperor and the Tsar, and wounded a lady on the other side of the road who had come to Paris from the provinces for the Exhibition. Louis Napoleon said to Alexander: 'Sire, we have been under fire together.'[61]

The shot had been fired by a twenty-year-old Pole named Beregowski, who as a boy of sixteen had fought in the Polish insurrection of 1863 and had recently come to Paris from Brussels. He cried 'Vive la Pologne!' as the police arrested him. There was so much sympathy for the Poles that the Paris jury found him guilty with extenuating circumstances. He was sentenced to life imprisonment with hard labour.[62]

There were balls every night during that second week of June – at the Russian embassy and the Tuileries, and a great ball and reception at the expense of the Paris ratepayers at the Hôtel de Ville, with Haussmann acting as host to the Emperor, the Empress, the Tsar, the King of Prussia, and the Princes and the lesser German sovereigns; but it was Bismarck who attracted most attention from the crowds in the street who watched the guests arrive.[63] On the last day of the Tsar's visit, he was taken for a day's shooting at Fontainebleau. Just before the shoot was due to start, the police received a report of a plot to assassinate the Tsar in the forest. They decided to cancel the shoot. They did not wish to alarm the Tsar by telling him about this new attempt to kill him, so Eugénie kept the Tsar and her other guests talking in the drawing room until she pretended to notice that there was no time to go shooting as the Tsar's train was shortly due to leave.[64]

The Exhibition did not close until November, but the last great event was the prizegiving ceremony on 1 July, in the presence of the Emperor and Empress and the eleven-year-old Prince Imperial and a new selection of foreign royalties who had arrived in Paris – the Sultan of Turkey, the Viceroy of Egypt, the Prince of Wales, the Duke of Cambridge, Prince Umberto of Italy and the son of the Tycoon of Japan – and of 20,000 other invited guests. A choir of twelve bass voices sang a hymn which had been specially composed by Rossini for the occasion. Rossini himself did not think very highly of his composition; he said that it was neither Bach nor Offenbach.[65]

While the Empress smiled graciously, and the Prince Imperial sat as still as he could – but sometimes jumping up from his chair in his excitement – the Emperor stood relaxed in his general's uniform, betraying no emotion as he listened to the closing lines of Rossini's hymn:

> Pour nos amis bat notre cœur!
> Aide au vaincu, gloire au vainqueur![66]

But just before he left Saint-Cloud for the prizegiving ceremony, he had received news that the Emperor Maximilian had been executed by a Juarist firing squad at Querétaro on 19 June.[67] Maximilian had been convicted by a military court of officers – the eldest was aged twenty-three – of the murder of Mexican patriots who had been executed under the provisions of his proclamation of 3 October 1865. The U.S. government's envoy asking for clemency had not reached Juarez at San Luis Potosí until it was too late; some people said that the envoy had not hurried on his journey.[68] 'Napoleon III ought to be satisfied with his handiwork', wrote the Juarist newspaper, the *Boletín Republicano*:

> the victims of the massacre of 2 December are being incessantly multiplied, and the flag of France continues to cover itself with filth and blood wherever it waves. The death of the Archduke and of those who adhered to his cause ought to weigh heavily on the humbug who from the imperial throne of France seeks to govern the world.[69]

Appeals for clemency for Maximilian had been sent by Queen Victoria, the King of Prussia, the Tsar, and many other sovereigns and governments, and when the news of the execution reached Europe, the courts went into mourning and the press denounced the murder.[70] Two Radical voices which might have been expected to influence Juarez – those of Garibaldi and Victor Hugo – asked him to show mercy to Maximilian; but other Radicals adopted a harsher attitude. In Congress in Washington, old Thaddeus Stevens and other Congressmen praised the execution;[71] Senator Howard of Illinois said that 'the most arrant felon of the age' had received 'just punishment'.[72] In New York, Clemenceau, who was living in the United States as foreign correspondent of *Le Temps*, wrote to a friend that he hated all these Emperors, Kings, Archdukes and Princes with the same merciless hatred that was felt in 1793 for Louis XVI. 'Between us and these people there is a war to the death. They have tortured to death millions of us, and I bet we have not killed two dozen of them.'[73]

Franz Joseph had been one of the few sovereigns who had not visited Paris during the Exhibition, and at the end of August Louis Napoleon and Eugénie went on a state visit to Austria, meeting Franz Joseph at Salzburg. The official reason for their visit was to express their condolences on Maximilian's death;[74] but many journalists and diplomats believed that the real business at Salzburg was the negotiation of a Franco-Austrian alliance against Prussia. On their way to Salzburg they passed through four German states. The Grand Duke of Baden and the King of Württemberg, who were on friendly terms with Prussia, were a little cool in their reception, merely exchanging a few words with Louis Napoleon in his carriage at the railway stations; the Grand Duke of Hesse-Darmstadt and the King of Bavaria, who supported Austria, gave them a warmer welcome, travelling with them in the train to the boundaries of their states.[75]

The people reacted differently from their sovereigns. At Stuttgart, Louis Napoleon and Eugénie were cheered by the people at the station; but the local Radicals organized a hostile demonstration at Augsburg, where Louis Napoleon stopped to show Eugénie the house in which he had lived and the school which he had attended forty-five years before. When they arrived at the station there were a few cheers which were drowned in hisses and shouts of 'Be quiet! There goes a tyrant! Are you Germans?'[76] Louis Napoleon and Eugénie drove from the station to the Three Moors Hotel by the side streets in order to avoid another hostile demonstration.

Next morning they had a pleasanter time, attending Mass at the hotel, which was celebrated by a priest who had been at school in the city with Louis Napoleon. They were then received at the *Gymnasium*. Louis Napoleon showed Eugénie the date '1823' that he had carved on a window sill in one of the classrooms, and he broke off a twig from a tree in the garden to retain as a souvenir of his schooldays. They went to the house where he had lived with Queen Hortense, and he spoke in German to the occupiers of the house.

The King of Bavaria met them at the station and travelled with them to the Austrian frontier. The train stopped for a few minutes at Munich, but the police had taken steps to prevent a repetition of the Augsburg demonstration, and no one was allowed to enter the station except four gentlemen of the French embassy and their wives.[77]

Franz Joseph and the Empress Elizabeth received them at Salzburg. The city was decorated and illuminated, and fires were lit on the summit of all the mountains around. There was a banquet at Heilbronn Castle, a gala performance at the Court theatre by actors of the Burgtheater of Vienna of Baron Münch-Bellinghausen's dramatic poem *Wildfeuer*, a visit to the ex-King Ludwig I of Bavaria, and a reception at the City Hall, where Louis Napoleon spoke in German to the Mayor and officials; and Eugénie visited the Grand Duchess Sophie, Maximilian's mother, at Ischl. There were only tentative political discussions between the two Emperors at Salzburg, but they agreed that their Foreign

Ministers should remain in Salzburg for further talks after the sovereigns had left.[78]

During their stay at Salzburg, Eugénie visited the local beauty spots with Count Wilczek, who had been appointed by Franz Joseph to act as her escort. At the Kugelmühle on the Untersberg she dared Wilczek to climb with her up the very steep and dangerous rocky path beside the waterfall to the spring 150 feet above. At first he refused to risk the Empress's safety on such a climb; but after she had taunted him with cowardice, he agreed, and they reached the summit, though they got soaked to the skin and he had to carry her in his arms for a short part of the way. His exploit earned him a rebuke from Franz Joseph but a gift from Eugénie of the gloves that she had been wearing on their expedition, which was the traditional way in which a Spanish lady rewarded a gentleman who has risked his life for her sake.[79]

While Louis Napoleon and Eugénie were in Salzburg, a new crisis was coming to a head in Italy. The last French troops left Rome in December 1866, just in time to comply with the terms of the Franco-Italian Convention of 15 September 1864; but during the summer of 1867 Garibaldi travelled through Italy addressing enormous crowds and again raising the slogan 'Rome or death!' A garrison of French volunteers remained in Rome under General Dumont as part of the Pope's forces. The Italians accused France of violating the Convention of 15 September by keeping them in Rome; the French government denied this, and said that they were volunteers who had no connection with the French army – a claim difficult to uphold after General Dumont had warned his men that any deserters from his force would be court-martialled when they returned to France.[80]

As Garibaldi's movement became increasingly threatening, the French government urged the Italian government to take action against Garibaldi and his volunteers; but Victor Emanuel and his ministers would not commit themselves.

The French Catholic hierarchy and their press went into action again on behalf of the Pope, with Dupanloup, the Bishop of Orleans, in the van. At the Belgian Catholic Congress at Malines he warned of the menace that was threatening France and Christendom – the menace of Liberalism. Juarez and Garibaldi were Liberals; young Liberals in Portugal threw stones at nuns in the street; there was a shameful proposal by Liberals to erect a statue in France to Voltaire, who had called the Catholic Church 'l'infâme'; and he himself had seen, on a visit to Brussels, that the local Liberal Association had premises next to an inn called 'Hell'.[81] The Catholic press and the bishops and priests in the churches organized collections for funds to buy arms for the volunteers in the Pope's army, and Catholics all over France signed petitions to the Emperor reminding him that France was the eldest daughter of the Church, and calling on him to raise the standard of France against the standard of Revolution. Prince Napoleon's *L'Opinion Nationale* went against the Catholic tide, saying that France must not play in 1867 the role of Philip II of Spain. Some Radicals organized collections for Garibaldi, but these were suppressed.[82]

On 24 September the Italian government arrested Garibaldi and sent him to his home on the island of Caprera, which they surrounded with warships to prevent him from leaving; but his son Menotti led his volunteers into the Papal States, and on 13 October Garibaldi escaped from Caprera and put himself at the head of the invaders. The Italian government, which had not dared to arrest him as he passed through Florence after his escape, was obviously either unable or un-willing to stop his invasion of the Papal States. They offered to send the Italian army into the Papal States to destroy Garibaldi and the Revolution; but this would have been a repetition of the events of 1860, and the Italian proposal was vigorously rejected by the Pope and the French Catholics.[83]

At a Cabinet meeting at Saint-Cloud on 25 October, it was decided to send 8000 French troops to Rome immediately to protect the Pope against the invaders, as the Italian government had broken the Convention of 15 September 1864 by allowing Garibaldi and his volunteers to launch their invasion from Italian soil.[84] The Radicals accused Eugénie of being responsible for the decision to send the troops; they said that when she heard about Garibaldi's slogan 'Rome or death!', she commented: 'Death if they like, but Rome never'.[85] Eugénie strongly supported the decision to send the troops against Garibaldi;[86] but it is absurd to hold her primarily responsible for the intervention, in view of the irresistible pressure on the government from the Catholics throughout France. The decision of the Cabinet on 25 October was virtually unanimous; and Rouher, whom Eugénie and Drouyn de Lhuys had regarded a few years before as one of the pro-Italian faction in the government, was the chief spokesman in the Chamber for the policy of intervention in 1867.

The troops landed at Civitavecchia on 28 October, and on 3 November marched to Mentana, thirteen miles north-east of Rome, where Garibaldi was attacking the Papal army and their French volunteers. The French troops arrived at 3 p.m., just when Garibaldi was on the point of winning the battle, and opened fire with their new rifle, the *chassepot*, which had never been tried out in action. Its range was longer and its effect much more deadly than the muskets of the Garibaldini, who fell back in complete disorder while the French infantrymen just stood and shot them down; in the words of one of

Garibaldi's men, it was a battle between those who fled and those who stood still.[87]

The Garibaldini retreated across the Italian frontier, and were interned by the Italian authorities. Rome and the Pope were saved; the Revolution was defeated. Rouher stated in the Legislative Body that 'Italy shall never gain possession of Rome';[88] and to the indignation of the Liberals and of many moderate Catholics, the French commander at Mentana, General Failly, declared that 'our *chassepots* have done wonders'.[89]

CHAPTER 40

ROCHEFORT AND SUEZ

AT the end of October 1867, in the last days before Mentana, Franz Joseph came on a state visit to Paris. His programme included the inevitable banquet given by Haussmann at the Hôtel de Ville. As Franz Joseph, Louis Napoleon and Eugénie descended from their carriages at the Hôtel de Ville, they were greeted with shouts of 'Vive Garibaldi! No intervention!' from a section of the crowd in the street. The police arrested the demonstrators, who were sentenced, some to three months' imprisonment, others to shorter terms, for shouting seditious slogans and resisting the police. Their counsel claimed that it was not seditious to cry 'Vive Garibaldi!'; but the court ruled that it was, at a time when the French army was fighting against Garibaldi.[1]

The demonstration outside the Hôtel de Ville was the start of a political campaign of a kind which had not been seen in Paris since the *coup d'état* of 1851. During the remaining years of the Second Empire, open demonstrations against the régime continued and became increasingly violent. The Socialists played the leading part in these demonstrations, taking over the leadership of the Republican opposition from the older Radical leaders. In December 1867 the leaders in Paris of the French section of Marx's International were put on trial and sentenced to three years and lesser terms of imprisonment for organizing a secret society. There were riots at Toulouse against the call-up of young conscripts for the army; and at Bordeaux men were arrested and imprisoned for marching through the streets singing the 'Marseillaise'. The wave of strikes continued; the miners' strike in the North against a 10 per cent wage cut led to violence and clashes with the troops.[2]

Suddenly in the summer of 1868 an aristocratic writer of musical comedies appeared on the political scene and became the most formidable opponent that Louis Napoleon had ever encountered. He was the Marquis Henri de Rochefort, the son of a Legitimist nobleman. He had abandoned the use of his title and become a journalist on the staff of *Le Figaro*, as well as writing *Le Monsieur bien mis* and a row of other successful vaudeville shows for the Folies Dramatiques. In June 1868 he published the first number of *La Lanterne*, a tiny pocket-size fifty-page magazine in a striking red cover; its title had associations with the cry 'A la lanterne!' of the revolutionaries of 1792.

Rochefort's weapon was irony. He stated that he was a Bonapartist because his favourite sovereign was the Bonapartist Emperor Napoleon II, who had reigned for only a few days. He ridiculed the Emperor's love for his dog Nero, which had been written up in the government press;[3] and he wrote about Eugénie: 'Her Majesty the Empress of the French presided yesterday at the Council of Ministers. How surprised I would be if I learned that Madame Pereire [the chairman's wife] had presided at the administrative council of the Crédit Mobilier.'[4] But Rochefort only referred very occasionally to the Emperor and Empress. He usually sniped at ministers and government officials, which was doubtless why he was so unpopular with the authorities.

La Lanterne was a tremendous success. After the sensation caused by the first issue, the second number sold 68,000 copies. The Minister of the Interior then used his power to ban, without giving any reason, the sale of a newspaper in the newsvendors' kiosks and elsewhere in the streets; this power was often exercised against Radical and Socialist newspapers. But the circulation of *La Lanterne*, which could now be obtained only by subscription, rose to 90,000 copies. The red cover of *La Lanterne* was seen everywhere in the streets and on the buses, and the jokes were retold all over Paris. In August, after ten issues had appeared, the government banned *La Lanterne*. The police seized the eleventh issue from the printers; not content with this, they went through the streets, snatching copies out of the hands of readers whom they saw carrying it. Rochefort fled to Brussels, and in his absence was sentenced to three years' imprisonment.[5]

A few days after the suppression of *La Lanterne*, the Prince Imperial, who was aged twelve, was sent to perform one of his first public duties in presenting the prizes to the successful pupils at the Charlemagne College in Paris. A prize for Greek composition had been won by the fifteen-year-old son of General Cavaignac. The Prince Imperial stood on the platform, with the Minister of Education and other officials, and the prizewinners walked up to receive their prizes as their names were called out; but when young Cavaignac's name was called, he remained seated in his chair. His name was called again. This time he half rose, but his mother, in the visitors' seats, made a gesture to him to remain seated, to show that he would not accept a prize from the hands of the son of the man who had arrested his father in the middle of the night on 2 December 1851. A friend of young Cavaignac, who was standing beside him, applauded, and the other students, both inside and outside the hall, joined in the applause. The Prince Imperial was upset and puzzled by the incident, and returned to Fontainebleau to tell his father about it and to be comforted by the loving Emperor. No action was taken against young Cavaignac, but his friend who led the applause was expelled from the College. *Le Constitutionnel* deplored the incident, and reminded young Cavaignac that the Reds had hated his father as much as they hated the Emperor.[6]

In September 1868, while the Emperor, the Empress and the Prince Imperial were at Biarritz, a Liberal revolution broke out in Spain, and within a week the rebels were in control of the whole country. Queen Isabel, who was on holiday near San Sebastian when the revolution broke out, fled across the frontier into France and was met by a solemn-looking Emperor and Empress at the railway station at La Négresse near Biarritz.[7] Personal relations between Isabel and Eugénie had not been too friendly since Eugénie became Empress of the French;[8] but Eugénie now went out of her way to show sympathy and offer hospitality to her former sovereign, who settled in Paris in a mansion in the Champs-Élysées.[9]

Louis Napoleon and Eugénie followed Queen Isabel to Paris, leaving Biarritz on 17 October. Neither of them ever again saw the Villa Eugénie.

Eugénie was even more distressed than Louis Napoleon at the events in Spain, for power in Madrid passed into the hands of Marshal Prim;[10] apart from the fact that Prim was mildly Liberal and anti-clerical, they both felt that he had let them down in Mexico in 1862. To their relief, Prim did not proclaim a republic, but announced that the Spanish parliament would adopt the conventional course of looking for a King among the royal houses of Europe. The months passed by, and Prim did not find a King. The Radicals spread the rumour that Eugénie was intriguing to obtain the crown of Spain for the younger Don Carlos, the extreme right-wing Ultramontane Carlist leader. In October 1868 *Le Constitutionnel* denied the rumour, and stated that the Empress fully supported the Emperor's policy of allowing the Spaniards to choose their King without any outside pressure.[11] The rumour was in fact untrue, for Eugénie, despite all her Conservative and Catholic sympathies, was never a Carlist.

The question of the Spanish Succession had not yet led to any difficulties with Prussia; but ever since Sadowa, fear of Prussia had been increasing in France. Anti-Prussian articles appeared in the French press. Eugénie and the Catholics, who favoured an alliance with Austria, sympathized with the anti-Prussian feeling; but the Liberals were in the forefront of the anti-Prussian campaign, though Prince Napoleon and his *Opinion Nationale* were pro-Prussian. Émile de Girardin led the way in *La Liberté*, and ceaselessly attacked Prussia.[12]

539

In September 1866, *Le Charivari* published the provocative poem which Alfred de Musset had written during the Mehemet Ali crisis in 1840 in reply to Becker's patriotic German song, 'Sie sollen ihn nicht haben, den freien deutschen Rhein'. Musset's poem, 'Nous l'avons eu, votre Rhin allemand', boasted that once again, as in Napoleon I's time, the French soldiers would have the Rhine and the German girls too. Above the poem, *Le Charivari* printed an even more provocative cartoon of a leering, lascivious French soldier holding out his wine-glass to be filled by an aloof but fascinated young German girl.[13] In May 1868 an anonymous pamphlet was published in Paris, by the official publisher Dentu, advocating a preventive war – 'sharp, short, but decisive' – to crush Prussia before her growing strength made her as powerful as France.[14] The Prussian press responded comparatively mildly to the French attacks, which helped Bismarck to pose before international opinion as the injured party and the patient advocate of peace.

Bismarck had not revealed the secret offers made to him by Louis Napoleon about Belgium; but after the Luxemburg incident in the spring of 1867, there was anxiety in many quarters about Louis Napoleon's designs on Belgium. In February 1869 the French government negotiated an agreement with the Belgian railway company by which a majority shareholding in the company was sold to the French government. There was an outcry in the Belgian Chamber; many deputies feared that the agreement would give Napoleon III a stranglehold over the Belgian economy and national defence. Under pressure from the deputies, the Belgian government banned the agreement. France then protested, and the French press adopted a threatening attitude. The Belgian Minister of Communications visited Paris and spent several weeks in critical negotiations before a satisfactory compromise was arranged; but Franco-Belgian relations worsened as a result.[15]

The Empire was becoming more liberal, despite periodical acts of repression which came suddenly without any particular reason. Delescluze, who since his release from Cayenne had lived quietly in France, founded a new Radical newspaper, *Le Réveil*. In the first number, which appeared in July 1868, *Le Réveil* stated that it would advocate Liberty, Equality and Fraternity and the principles of the Revolution of 1789, because if 'France has always risen again after so many torments . . . she owes this only to the Revolution'.[16] Delescluze was prosecuted for this article, the court ruling that by saying that France owed her salvation to the Revolution, he was advocating revolution against the Emperor Napoleon III. He was sentenced to three months' imprisonment and a fine of 5000 francs. People were still prosecuted for reading the old illegal books – Victor Hugo's *Napoléon le Petit*, Schoelcher's *Le Gouvernement du Deux Décembre, Les Nuits de St-Cloud* and the *Mariage de César*; but Rochefort's *La Lanterne*, which was now published in Brussels and smuggled into France, was more popular. An English traveller who was reading *La Lanterne* in the train from Brussels to Paris had it confiscated at the French frontier; but the official who took it from him looked at it and chuckled with delight as he read Rochefort's jibes at the Emperor.[17]

Side by side with the semi-freedom of the press was the semi-freedom of public meeting. During the winter of 1868–9 the government allowed the Socialist groups to hire three dance-halls in working-class districts in Paris for public lectures; but a policeman was present at every meeting, with power to close the meeting at his discretion. These meetings at the Folies-Belleville, the Pré-aux-Clercs and the Redoute were attended by three or four hundred people, most of them working men, with a few middle-class men and a few women among them. The speeches from the platform were very violent, and the cheering and heckling from the floor very noisy. When reports of the proceedings appeared in the press, the Conservatives became alarmed, and the Conservative deputies and newspapers suggested that the government ought not to allow the meetings to take place.[18]

The *Times* correspondent, hearing that many of the speakers were uneducated working men, and that some women also spoke, went to see and hear these strange phenomena. He was surprised to find that though the speakers occasionally attacked the government and the right-wing parties, they spent most of the time denouncing the left-wing Opposition deputies, the Radicals, the old exiled leadership in London, and the other Socialist groups whom they accused of being traitors to the revolution and agents of the bourgeoisie. The policeman sat bored and half-asleep amid the commotion, but when a speaker said that 'the French people sentence Charles Louis Napoleon Bonaparte, known as Napoleon III, to forced labour for life',[19] the policeman woke up and closed the meeting. Sometimes the audience refused to leave the hall when the policeman ordered them to go; he then went for reinforcements, and there was violence, arrests and sentences of imprisonment.[20]

The feast of All Souls on 2 November was traditionally the occasion for honouring the dead. On 2 November 1867 a group of Radicals and Socialists went to Montmartre cemetery and made speeches at the grave of Godefroy Cavaignac, the general's brother, who had been a leading Republican in the reign of Louis Philippe.[21] The police broke up the meeting and made some arrests. By the time that All Souls' Day came round again, the Radicals had discovered in the same cemetery the obscure and unkept grave of Baudin, the deputy who had been killed on the barricade in the Faubourg Saint-Antoine on 3 December

1851. Delescluze, in *Le Réveil* of 29 October 1868, called on the people to assemble on All Souls' Day at the graves of Godefroy Cavaignac and Baudin, and described Baudin and his fellow-victims as 'martyrs who fell defending the law'.[22] There had been rumours that the police would close the cemetery, but, unlike in the previous year, they allowed the crowds to assemble and speeches to be made at Godefroy Cavaignac's graveside. The Radical demonstrators wanted a confrontation with the police, and provoked one at Baudin's grave.[23]

Delescluze, in *Le Réveil*, opened a subscription to erect a memorial to Baudin in the cemetery, and was prosecuted. His supporters called a protest demonstration at Baudin's graveside for 3 December, the anniversary of his death. The police closed the cemetery and sealed off the whole district of Notre-Dame-de-Lorette. The demonstrators tried to break through the police cordon, and there were sixty-two arrests, though the press gave the figure as three hundred.[24]

At Delescluze's trial the Imperial Prosecutor, Grandperret, stated that the Emperor did not ordinarily object to the erection of memorials to his political opponents, but would not tolerate a public subscription which was an excuse for revolutionary preparations. Delescluze, as a recidivist with his years in Cayenne on the record, was sentenced to six months' imprisonment and a fine of 2000 francs. The Court of Appeal remitted the prison sentence and upheld only the fine, on the grounds that his years in Cayenne should not have been taken into consideration, as their effect had been nullified by the Emperor's amnesty of 1859.[25]

Apart from the left-wing political activists, there was a general mood of discontent, especially in Paris, at the arbitrariness of the press censorship, at the real or alleged financial scandals and the immorality and corruption of officials and big business men, and above all at Haussmann's continual building projects and his extravagance with the ratepayers' money. Great new boulevards had been cut through the old streets during the unceasing building activity of the last fifteen years, culminating in the ceremonial opening of the new boulevard by the Emperor. The procedure had become standardized: at the end of the boulevard furthest from the Tuileries a covered stand was erected and was occupied by influential people who had wangled, intrigued and paid to get an admission ticket. When everyone was in his place the Empress would drive up in her carriage with the Prince Imperial and take the seat of honour in the stand. Then the Emperor entered the boulevard at the other end, riding alone some twenty yards ahead of his escort of cavalry and taking off his hat to acknowledge the cheers of the people lining the route. He rode the whole length of the boulevard to the grandstand, where Haussmann received him and made a speech in honour of the new Augustus, the nephew of a greater Julius Caesar, who had built a Paris which eclipsed Augustus's Rome. The Emperor, in his speech of reply, praised all who had played their part in building the boulevard, regretted that individual interests must sometimes suffer in the achievement of great projects, and spoke encouragingly about the state of the Empire at home and abroad.[26] Then he entered the Empress's carriage and drove back with her and the Prince Imperial along the boulevard to the Tuileries.

After the Boulevard de Strasbourg, leading south from the terminus of the Strasburg Railway, was opened in December 1853, Louis Napoleon opened the Boulevard de Sébastopol, which extended the Boulevard de Strasbourg to the river, in April 1858; the Boulevard Malesherbes, running north-west from the Madeleine, in August 1861; and the Boulevard du Prince Eugène, named in honour of his uncle Eugène de Beauharnais, in December 1862.[27] The Boulevard du Prince Eugène ran from the Place du Prince Eugène – today the Place de la République – with its military barracks on the north side of the square, absolutely straight for 3200 metres to the great square on the south-east edge of Paris where the city corporation had welcomed the young King Louis XIV when he returned from the Pyrenees with his Spanish bride in 1659. In honour of the occasion, the square was named the Place du Trône. The revolutionaries in 1793 renamed it the Place du Trône Renversé, but now it was again the Place du Trône. In the middle of the Place du Trône a triumphal arch was erected with twelve Corinthian columns, on the summit of which was a winged chariot carrying the two figures of 'War Victorious' and 'Peace Laborious'. On the arch the words were inscribed: 'To the Emperor Napoleon III, To the Armies of the Crimea, of Italy, of China, Cochin-China, Algeria, 1852–1862'. They left a space between 'Cochin-China' and 'Algeria' large enough to take the word 'Mexico'.[28] The arch was demolished after 1870 and the Place du Trône renamed the Place de la Nation.

As the building process continued year after year, the criticism did not die down, though many people admitted, rather grudgingly, that the new Paris was impressive. People said that Haussmann was going to pull down Notre-Dame in order to have the pleasure of rebuilding it.[29] They said that when Morny cheated his discarded mistress out of money to which she was entitled, the Emperor made it up to her by ordering that a new square should be built around her house, so that the house could be demolished and she could be awarded as compensation a sum greatly in excess of its value.[30]

The plan to build a new boulevard through the Luxembourg Gardens aroused the strongest opposition, which culminated in a noisy demonstration at the Odéon Theatre in the Quartier Latin in March 1866 when the Emperor and Empress went there to a gala performance of Émile Augier's play *Contagion*. Louis Napoleon and Eugénie took in good part the cries of 'Vive le Luxembourg!', and a few days later, after he had visited the Luxembourg Gardens, Louis Napoleon ordered the plan to be drastically reduced in scale and only a small part of the gardens was destroyed.[31]

As well as choosing suitable names for the new boulevards – Sébastopol, Magenta, Prince Eugène – Louis Napoleon and Haussmann renamed many of the existing streets, changing the absurd and quaint old names which some of the streets had borne for centuries, and renaming them Avenue de l'Impératrice, Avenue Joséphine, Rue de la Reine Hortense, Rue Morny, and even, amid the mockery of the Parisians, Boulevard Haussmann.[32] But in the salons and the cafés they remarked with a snigger that no boulevard or street had been named after King Louis Bonaparte, the Emperor's father.[33]

By 1868 the city of Paris was on the verge of bankruptcy, and when this was announced there was a new outcry against Haussmann. The Opposition attacked him in the Chambers and demanded an inquiry into his financial administration; and Jules Ferry wrote a best-selling pamphlet with the punning title *Les Comptes fantastiques d'Haussmann*.[34]

It was against this background of violent political demonstrations, industrial unrest and general discontent that the general election was held in May 1869. The Minister of the Interior and the Prefects as usual tried to influence the election, calling on the voters to elect the Emperor's candidates, and throwing out hints of financial discrimination against districts which returned an Opposition deputy. A number of deputies who had formerly supported the government now formed an independent group between the government and the Left Opposition. It became known as the Third Party. The Left Opposition, the Third Party, the Legitimists and the Orleanists all put up candidates in the elections. In Paris and other left-wing districts, the Socialists, to the delight of the government, put up candidates against the Left Opposition and against Delescluze's Radicals.[35]

There was a good deal of violence during the election campaign, with clashes between the police and working men and students taking place in nearly every part of Paris, not only in the working-class districts but also in the fashionable areas in the city centre, leaving a great deal of broken glass. Students threw missiles at the police, and the mounted police and army cavalry units charged the crowds and injured many of the demonstrators and several peaceful onlookers. In Paris, 132 persons were arrested; 67 of them were under twenty years of age. There were also clashes in the provinces. In Amiens the army sent 3000 cavalrymen to disperse a procession of demonstrators singing the 'Marseillaise' and shouting 'Vive la République!'[36]

The election results were a defeat for Louis Napoleon. With nearly 80 per cent of the electorate voting, the government candidates received 4,445,287 votes against a total of 5,579,885 for all the Opposition parties, though these were divided between 2,446,931 for the Left Opposition, 1,124,648 for the Third Party, 786,020 for the Legitimists and Orleanists, and 1,221,886 for other parties. In Paris the Radicals in most cases beat the Socialists; but Rochefort, who was a refugee abroad, was elected later in the year at a by-election. He thereupon returned to Paris to take his seat in the Chamber, expecting to be arrested and sent to serve the prison term to which he had been sentenced in his absence; but the Emperor pardoned him.[37]

In view of the election results, it was obvious that unless Louis Napoleon was prepared to disregard the Chamber completely and in effect carry out a new *coup d'état*, he would have to allow a coalition of the Left Opposition and the Third Party to take office in place of Rouher and his supporters in the government party. But the Socialists and Radicals were not prepared to wait for this. The results of the final ballot in the election were announced on 7 June. On that evening, a Socialist demonstration in the Boulevard Montmartre and another in the Boulevard Saint-Michel led to violence, and a policeman was severely injured when hit on the head by a bottle. The next evening the demonstrations were even more violent, and fighting between police and demonstrators went on till 2 a.m. in Belleville. The riots continued on the evenings of 9 and 10 June, starting at about half-past 9 and continuing till 1 or 2 a.m., in the Boulevard Montmartre and other central parts of Paris, with shouts of 'Vive Rochefort!' and 'Down with the police!', and the singing of the 'Marseillaise'. The police announced that when a demonstration became threatening or illegal, they would call on all those present to disperse, and after that anyone who remained, whether a demonstrator or an onlooker, would be fair game for their sabres and batons. One thousand and thirty-three persons were arrested. Three-quarters of them were under thirty years of age and more than a third were under twenty.[38]

Foreign tourists left Paris. The international press reported that France was on the verge of another revolution. Then, after four nights of rioting, in the early afternoon of 11 June, Louis Napoleon and Eugénie drove out from Saint-Cloud along the Rue de Rivoli, the Grands Boulevards, and back by the Rue de la Paix. They sat in an open carriage without any escort, and the horses moved forward at a walking pace. As news of their coming spread through Paris, thousands of people came out into the streets from the houses, offices and shops, and gave them a tremendous ovation. At times the crowds were so dense that the carriage was brought to a halt, and Louis Napoleon and Eugénie spoke a few words to the people around the carriage. The people cried 'Vive l'Empereur!', 'Vive l'Impératrice!', and 'Down with the rioters!' There was another riot that night, but the police had less difficulty in clearing the Boulevard Montmartre, and the whole city was quiet on the night of 12 June.[39]

Next day the cavalry patrols were withdrawn, and there were no more disturbances for the time being; but the Paris bourgeois and small tradesmen, with their broken windows and shattered nerves, wondered when the trouble would start again. Many of them had voted against the government in the general election; but as they cursed the Socialists and the students, and thanked God for the army and the police, they remembered that the Emperor had saved them from Red revolution in 1851, and prayed that he would save them again in 1869.[40] 'The fear and horror of Socialism', wrote the *Times* correspondent, 'is still the protecting god of the Empire.'[41]

But the Emperor's stone had become much worse, and at the end of August he was very ill. The public first became alarmed when it was announced that he would not be going to Châlons Camp this year. The court officials refused to admit that he was suffering from anything worse than his usual rheumatism; they leaked the rumour that he did not go to Châlons because it would have been pointless to do so, as his rheumatism prevented him from riding a horse, but that he was going for walks every day in the park at Saint-Cloud. This was untrue; he was in fact confined to his bed in the palace, and so ill that his doctors ordered that none of his ministers should have access to him. Because of his illness, Eugénie and the Prince Imperial went without him to Corsica for the celebrations in Ajaccio on the centenary of the birth of Napoleon I. On 26 August the rumour spread in Paris that the Emperor was dying, and the Bourse panicked. They believed that his death would be the signal for Red revolution.[42]

The official bulletins said that he was getting better, and government circles pointed out that Eugénie would not have gone to Corsica with the Prince Imperial if the Emperor were dying; but the rumours persisted. As usual, the government's lies made matters worse; the bulletins now said that he was better and had got up for breakfast, but the previous bulletins had said that he was walking in the park.

It was semi-officially stated that the Emperor was well enough to go out in his carriage, and that he would drive through the streets of Paris on 5 September. He did not come. The officials said that a change in the weather had had a slightly adverse effect on his rheumatism, and had necessitated a change of plan; but the rumour spread that he had died, and the Bourse fell again. On 10 September he was well enough to come to Paris, and although it was a rainy day he drove with Eugénie in a closed carriage along the Champs-Élysées and the boulevards and returned to Saint-Cloud. At once prices rose on the Bourse.

He made a good recovery, and before long was riding in the Bois de Boulogne. The government persisted in saying that he was suffering from nothing worse than a severe attack of rheumatism, and kept his stone a strict secret.[43]

Public confidence in his health increased when, despite earlier rumours to the contrary, Eugénie did not cancel her visit to the East for the official opening of the Suez Canal. The canal had at last been completed, thanks to the persistence for more than ten years of Eugénie's cousin Ferdinand de Lesseps, and thanks to French capital and to Napoleon III's diplomatic support in the face of the initial opposition of the British and Turkish governments. Eugénie left Paris on 30 September 1869 with a suite of thirty-seven ladies, gentlemen and servants, including her Alba and other Spanish nieces. She travelled overland to Venice, where she embarked on the imperial yacht *L'Aigle* for Constantinople. There was a hitch in the welcoming arrangements in Turkey; when the Empress's yacht arrived at Besika Bay in the middle of the night, she sailed past the ship containing the Grand Vizier and the French Ambassador who were waiting to receive Eugénie in the Dardanelles, as the ships missed each other in the dark.[44]

But a far more serious incident was not reported in any newspaper or mentioned in any diplomatic dispatch. We know about it today only from Eugénie herself. When she visited the Sultan, he took her to his harem. As they were walking arm in arm to the harem, they met the Sultan's mother in a long dark corridor. The Sultana-Valide was so outraged to see an unveiled European woman on her son's arm that she assaulted Eugénie. In view of Eugénie's tendency to improve a good story at her own expense, we should perhaps accept this one with a grain of salt, especially as Eugénie told two slightly different versions to Queen Victoria at Windsor in 1876 and to her friend Isabel Vesey when she revisited Constantinople with Miss Vesey in 1910.*

She told Queen Victoria that the Sultana-Valide gave her a violent punch in the stomach which nearly knocked her over, that a violent argument then broke out between the Sultan and his mother – she could not understand it, as it was in Turkish – and that the incident

*The discrepancies between the two stories may be partly accounted for by the fact that this part of Queen Victoria's Journal survives only in the form in which it was transcribed by Princess Beatrice, who sometimes slightly altered and shortened the Queen's original manuscript.

ended with everyone laughing. She told Miss Vesey that the Sultana-Valide slapped her face very hard.[45] Perhaps really she only tried to push her out of the way. But whatever the Sultana-Valide may have done, there was obviously an unpleasant incident which could have had serious diplomatic repercussions if it had become known to the foreign journalists in Constantinople, and if the touchy French newspaper editors had heard about this insult to French honour in the person of their beautiful Empress. But Eugénie's discretion and sense of humour saved the situation.

After a week of festivities and military reviews in Constantinople, where she awarded the Legion of Honour to several Turkish statesmen, she sailed out of the Bosporus escorted by a great flotilla of ships and landed at Alexandria. She stayed in Egypt for a month, sailing up the Nile and attending receptions as the guest of the Khedive. The Emperor Franz Joseph, the Crown Prince of Prussia, Prince William of Orange and Prince William of Hesse had also come to Egypt for the opening of the canal; the other powers were represented by their ambassadors and consuls. On 15 November *L'Aigle* sailed from Alexandria and anchored five miles out at sea off Port Said, where the opening ceremony was to take place next day.[46] During the night Eugénie was delighted by an incident which had not been planned in the official celebrations; some sailors from a Spanish ship, which had come to Port Said for the inauguration ceremony, rowed alongside *L'Aigle* and serenaded the Empress with an Andalusian love song.[47]

The ceremony next morning took place on the shore at Port Said, where a row of chalets and a platform had been erected for the occasion. Eugénie, wearing a lavender silk dress, cut low and trimmed with very big flounces of white, and a hat with a large black feather, sat facing the Mediterranean between the Khedive, in his blue and gold-laced uniform with jewelled scimitar, on her right, and Franz Joseph, in his white Field-Marshal's uniform, on her left, while a joint Christian and Muslim religious service took place.[48]

At 8.30 next morning a flotilla of forty ships set out on their journey through the canal. It was headed by *L'Aigle*, with Eugénie standing on the bridge with her nieces and ladies. A quarter of an hour behind came the second ship, with Franz Joseph on deck, followed at fifteen-minute intervals by the Crown Prince of Prussia's yacht, the Prince of the Netherlands', the Prince of Hesse's, the Russian Ambassador's, and the *Psyche* with the British Ambassador and Admiral Milne on board. The ships' captains had all been instructed not to exceed a speed of five maritime miles, or nine kilometres, an hour, in passing through the canal, and to reduce this speed at the bends to four maritime miles, or seven kilometres, an hour. It took eight hours to complete the journey to the half-way stage at Ismailia, where Eugénie and her fellow travellers stayed the night. Eugénie was fresh enough to ride on a dromedary through Ismailia to the cheers of the Egyptian people. Next day she led the flotilla on the second lap of the journey from Ismailia to Suez.

Her visit to Egypt culminated in a great state ball given by the Khedive at Ismailia to six thousand guests. They packed the ballroom so tightly that there was no room to dance; but though the dancing had to be abandoned, everyone enjoyed the lavish refreshments provided and admired the beauty of the Empress of the French.[49]

While Eugénie was in the East she was the centre of a political storm in Paris. After the general election the Left Opposition and the Third Party joined forces and constituted a majority in the Legislative Body. They refused to support any government except a coalition government of their two parties with Émile Ollivier as Prime Minister. Louis Napoleon was very reluctant to get rid of Rouher and appoint a government under a Premier who for years had been the leading critic of his régime in the Chamber; and he held out for several months, trying to avert an Ollivier government by eventually accepting Rouher's resignation and appointing a government without a Prime Minister and composed of comparatively unknown political figures. After Eugénie left Paris for Constantinople, Louis Napoleon went to Compiègne for his autumn visit with the Prince Imperial and with Princess Mathilde acting as hostess to a much smaller number of guests than usual. He invited the political leaders to Compiègne, and tried to arrange a political combination which would be a workable alternative to Ollivier.[50]

The Emperor had complete discretion as to the date on which the new Legislative Body should meet, and after other general elections in earlier years he had often waited for six months before summoning the Chambers; but in the new political climate the Left demanded that the Chambers be convened as soon as possible so that a left-wing government could be constituted. They insisted that the Chambers should meet on 26 October 1869; but Louis Napoleon, hoping to gain time for his attempt to form a new government, summoned the Chambers for 29 November. There were strong protests from the Radicals and Socialists, who declared that the date was being postponed until after Eugénie had returned to Paris so that she could be there to prevent the formation of a Liberal government and perhaps to carry through a *coup d'état*.[51]

But in fact Eugénie, though she had always had doubts about the Emperor's liberalizing policy, had reluctantly come to accept it as inevitable; she thought that it was too late to turn back now. 'My very dear Louis', she wrote to the Emperor on 27 October on her journey down the Nile,

I am perhaps too far away and out of touch with events to speak in this way, but I feel thoroughly convinced that continuity of policy is the only real strength. I dislike violent changes, and I do not believe that it is possible to bring off a *coup d'état* twice in one reign. I am really talking at random, for I am preaching to the converted.[52]

As Louis Napoleon refused to summon the Chambers for 26 October, the Socialists and Radicals announced that they would march on the Chamber on the 26th, force their way in, and begin Parliamentary business without waiting for the Emperor to open the session. Everyone expected revolution to break out on 26 October, and fear spread and the Bourse slumped as the dreaded date approached.[53] The British Chargé d'Affaires in Paris, Lionel Sackville-West, reported to the Foreign Office that even the Bonapartists believed that 'the Second Empire has gone off the rails. It is no longer being guided. It is hurling itself at an accelerating speed towards the abyss.'[54]

The government announced that it had taken all necessary measures to maintain order, and to strengthen public confidence Marshal Bazaine was appointed Commander of the Imperial Guard in Paris; but as usual the hopes of the supporters of order rested on the Emperor. He returned to Paris from Compiègne for the occasion. Arriving at the Tuileries in the afternoon of 25 October, he went to the Opera in the evening and was loudly cheered by the crowds in the street. Next morning the troops and police were stationed at key points in Paris; but no demonstrators were to be seen. The Radical leader Pyat, and Raspail and Victor Hugo, had called on their followers not to take part in any illegal action on 26 October; and the government was helped by the fact that it rained most of the day, and there was also a fall of snow. During the afternoon the Emperor walked under a covered roof in the gardens of the Tuileries, from where he could be seen by people in the street, who cheered him; and in the evening, after a day free from all disturbances, he received another ovation when he went to the Théâtre Français.[55]

He opened the Chambers on the day that he had fixed, 29 November, with the Prince Imperial and Prince Napoleon standing at his side; but the Empress's seat was vacant, for contrary to all the Socialist and Radical rumours she did not return to Paris from the East till 5 December. The Emperor had never received a warmer welcome from the deputies than on this occasion; they cheered most loudly when he

declared that he would be personally responsible for preserving order –
'L'ordre, j'en réponds'.[56]

At the close of the speech, the deputies were called by name to
come forward to swear the oath of allegiance to the Emperor. Rochefort had boycotted the opening ceremony, refusing to be present to
hear the Emperor's speech, though he had decided to take the oath on a
later occasion so as to be able to take his seat. When his name was
called, there was silence, and one of the deputies laughed. The Emperor
also laughed, and then most of the other deputies joined in.[57]

Rochefort came to the Chamber a few days later, and said that the
Emperor, by laughing at him, had insulted a deputy and had committed a breach of the privileges of the Chamber. A government
deputy said that if the Emperor and the deputies had laughed at Rochefort, it was because Rochefort was a ridiculous figure. 'I may be
ridiculous,' said Rochefort, 'but not as ridiculous as the gentleman who
walked on the sands at Boulogne with an eagle on his shoulder and a
bit of fat in his hat.'[58] When Louis Napoleon heard of Rochefort's
inaccurate account of his exploits at Boulogne in 1840, he laughed
heartily.[59]

Louis Napoleon at last accepted the inevitable, and on 2 January
1870 Ollivier became Prime Minister. At the New Year's Day reception,
the Emperor told the deputies that while he had hitherto been entrusted
by the nation with the whole power of the government, he would
henceforth share it with the Chambers. He had, in fact, resigned
himself, half-willingly and half-reluctantly, to becoming a constitutional sovereign with a Prime Minister who had the support of the
majority of the deputies of the Legislative Body. The new régime became known as the 'Liberal Empire' – a phrase adopted by Ollivier
himself – but as far as political freedom and liberty of the press was
concerned, at least for the Socialist and Radical extremists, the only
liberal thing about it was that Ollivier was Prime Minister instead of
being an Opposition deputy.[60]

Ollivier began by dismissing Haussmann from his position as
Prefect of the Seine. He also insisted that Eugénie should no longer
attend Cabinet meetings, and she and the Emperor accepted this.[61]

Ollivier's government immediately ran into a political storm.
Rochefort's paper, *La Marseillaise*, published an article attacking the
Bonaparte family, including Louis Napoleon's cousin, Prince Pierre
Bonaparte, the son of Lucien, Prince of Canino. Pierre was a turbulent
character. As a youth he had been a member of the Carbonari; he had
been accused – falsely, he said – of murdering a policeman in Rome, a
gamekeeper in Belgium, and another man in Albania. He had been a
Radical deputy in France in 1848 and had opposed the *coup d'état* of

2 December. He married a working-class Parisian girl, by whom he had had two illegitimate children, and lived with her in a large mansion at Auteuil; but he and his wife were never invited to court, and never met the Emperor.[62]

In reply to the article in *La Marseillaise*, Pierre Bonaparte challenged Rochefort to a duel. On 10 January two of the journalists on the staff of *La Marseillaise* called on Pierre Bonaparte at his house at Auteuil; they were Ulric de Fonvielle and a twenty-year-old son of a Jewish cobbler named Salmon, who wrote under the pseudonym Victor Noir. They went up to Prince Pierre's study, and he asked them if they came as Rochefort's seconds. According to Prince Pierre, Victor Noir struck him in the face, and Fonvielle drew a revolver from his pocket. Prince Pierre immediately drew his own revolver and shot Victor Noir, firing a second shot at Noir as he staggered down the stairs. As Noir reached the street, he collapsed and died. As soon as Ollivier heard the news, he asked the Emperor's permission to arrest Prince Pierre; but the Prince had already surrendered to the police at Auteuil and had been taken to the Conciergerie.[63]

On the evening of 11 January, Socialist and Radical demonstrators rioted in Paris, and next day a crowd estimated by some at 50,000 and by others at 300,000 left their places of work and marched to Neuilly to attend Victor Noir's funeral.[64] 'I was weak-minded enough to believe', wrote Rochefort in *La Marseillaise*,

that a Bonaparte could be something other than a murderer.... Today we mourn the loss of our poor dear friend Victor Noir, murdered by the bandit Prince Pierre Napoleon Bonaparte. For eighteen years France has now been in the bloody hands of these ruffians, who, not satisfied with cannonading the Republicans in the streets, entice them into foul snares and massacre them in their houses. People of France, do you not think that we have had enough of this?[65]

Ollivier sent the army to patrol the streets of Paris, and prosecuted Rochefort for insulting the Emperor and the imperial family. Rochefort was sentenced to six months' imprisonment and a fine of 3000 francs. There were protest demonstrations against his arrest and sentence, with violent clashes between the demonstrators and the army. In the Tuileries, they heard the cries of the demonstrators and the noise of the clashes during the balls, but everyone pretended not to notice.*[66]

*Filon (*Recollections of the Empress Eugénie*, p. 74) states that this was during the riots of June 1869; but he must be mistaken, because in June 1869 the court was at Saint-Cloud and the demonstrations were in the Boulevard Montmartre. The demonstrations of January 1870 were in the Champs-Élysées and the court was at the Tuileries.

Under the Constitution, Pierre Bonaparte, as a Prince of the Imperial Family, could not be tried before the ordinary criminal courts, but only by a special procedure in the High Court with a jury selected by lot from the members of the General Councils of the Departments. As the members of the General Councils were elected in the local government elections under the usual pressure from the Prefects, and tended to be men of position, the Conservative bias of the jury was inevitable.

Prince Pierre's trial opened at Tours on 21 March, and was conducted in a way which shocked not only the left-wing press but also the correspondents of *The Times* and even of *Le Constitutionnel*. The prosecution was conducted very fairly by the Imperial Prosecutor, Grandperret; but the *Times* correspondent complained that the Judges, Grandperret, and above all the police and ushers, treated Prince Pierre with the greatest respect, which contrasted sharply with their behaviour to Rochefort, who was still serving his prison sentence and was brought to Tours to give evidence for the prosecution. Prince Pierre adopted an arrogant attitude in the dock; he showed no sign of regret for the death of Victor Noir, whom he always referred to as 'Salmon', nor any consideration for the feelings of Noir's mother, who sat in court throughout the trial with Noir's thirteen-year-old brother and other members of the family. When Prince Pierre interrupted the witnesses for the prosecution, he was mildly reprimanded by the court; but when Fonvielle, who was the key witness for the prosecution, shouted at Prince Pierre 'You foully murdered Victor Noir!', he was sentenced to ten days' imprisonment and a fine for contempt of court.

On the seventh day of the trial, the jury gave a verdict of Not Guilty. Counsel for Victor Noir's family asked the court for 4000 francs damages for the family as compensation for Noir's death. The court awarded them 25,000 francs. This surprising award, which may have been an attempt to rectify to some extent the miscarriage of justice of the jury's verdict, was interpreted by the critics of the Bonapartes as a proof that a Bonaparte Prince could buy the right to murder his enemies. As Prince Pierre left the court he was surrounded by many society people, who shook him warmly by the hand.[67]

Louis Napoleon had been deeply distressed by the whole proceedings. When he first heard of Victor Noir's death the tears came to his eyes at this new unexpected source of trouble which had arisen to inaugurate the new Liberal Empire. After the verdict, he wrote a courteous letter to Prince Pierre asking him to leave France; but Prince Pierre indignantly refused. When the war broke out a few months later, Prince Pierre wrote to the Emperor offering to serve in the army, and he also wrote to Eugénie asking for an interview. Louis Napoleon answered with an evasive letter. Eugénie did not reply, and when she and Prince Pierre were refugees in England, she refused to receive him and his family at Chislehurst or to have any contact with him.[68]

La Marseillaise gave the news of the verdict: 'Pierre Bonaparte is acquitted. Victor Noir is in his grave. Ulric de Fonvielle is in prison. Paschal Grousset is in prison. Henri Rochefort is in prison. Millière, Rigault, Bazire, Dereure* are in prison. Pierre Bonaparte is acquitted.'[69] *Le Constitutionnel* deplored the verdict, but said that Rochefort and the Socialists were largely to blame for it, because they had converted the case into a political issue. *The Times*, after saying that the Emperor could not be blamed for the disgraceful sycophancy which government officials and the middle classes showed to an Imperial Prince, expressed the opinion that the jury would have convicted even an Imperial Prince, on the evidence in the case, if the man whom he had killed had been anyone except a journalist on the staff of *La Marseillaise*.[70] Many of them undoubtedly took the point of view of Mérimée, who as soon as he heard about Victor Noir's death wrote: 'Served him right'.†[71]

While Parisian intellectuals and society were raging or exulting over Victor Noir and Prince Pierre, they were chuckling over George Sand's latest novel *Malgrétout*, which was being serialized in the *Revue des Deux Mondes*. In the third instalment, which was published on 1 March 1870, the English heroine of the novel, the sincere and puritanical Miss Sarah Owen, meets the wicked Spanish beauty, Mademoiselle d'Ortosa, who is the illegitimate daughter of a notoriously immoral Spanish Countess. Mademoiselle d'Ortosa, who was educated in Paris, London and other European cities, is a splendid horsewoman who excels in the hunting field, thoroughly enjoys her food, and smokes cigars. She is surrounded by aristocratic male admirers, whom she treats as her slaves, leading them on only to have the pleasure of repulsing them; for Mademoiselle d'Ortosa, as she tells Miss Owen, has one great ambition: she is determined to marry 'a King, an Emperor, or at least an heir presumptive or Prince Regent'. She does not wish to be forgotten overnight when her beauty fades, like a vulgar actress; she will win immortal fame by playing an important and reactionary part in politics; she will force the democratic lion to lie in chains at her feet.[72]

The readers of the *Revue des Deux Mondes* had no doubt about the identity of Mademoiselle d'Ortosa. None of the reviewers named her,

---

*Grousset, Millière, Rigault, Bazire and Dereure were prominent followers of Rochefort who had been imprisoned for their part in the riots which followed Victor Noir's death.
†'Served him right' is in English in Mérimée's original French.

but *L'Indépendance Belge* commented that 'without knowing the model, I would say that it is an accurate picture'. Eugénie was hurt and surprised that George Sand should wish to portray her in this guise, because she had always befriended George Sand, and had unsuccessfully tried to persuade the Académie Française to admit her as their first woman member. Eugénie wondered what she had done to offend George Sand. She asked Mérimée to ask George Sand to issue a statement denying that she had intended to draw a picture of her in *Malgrétout*.[73] Mérimée not only hated George Sand as a Socialist and a Radical, but had also had a night of sex with her nearly forty years before which had been an unpleasant experience for both of them.[74] He advised Eugénie not to approach her and thus 'put your white hands in the mud'.[75]

But Eugénie had a higher opinion of George Sand than Mérimée had, and asked Flaubert to raise the matter with her.[76] George Sand ingenuously, though perhaps sincerely, expressed surprise that anyone could have thought that Mademoiselle d'Ortosa was Eugénie. 'I know, my friend,' she wrote to Flaubert,

> that you are devoted to her. I know that she is very good to those unfortunate ones who are recommended to her; that is all I know of her private life. I have never had any disclosure or document about her, not one word, not one fact, which would have authorized me to portray her. So I drew a figure of the imagination, I swear it. . . . I do not make portraits; it is not my line. I invent.[77]

In April 1870 Louis Napoleon, for the first time since 1852, exercised his powers under the Constitution to ask the people to vote in a referendum. He asked them whether they approved of 'the liberal reforms in the Constitution carried out since 1860 by the Emperor with the co-operation of the great bodies of the State' and of the new Constitution of the Liberal Empire. Voting was to take place within a fortnight, on 8 May.[78] The Socialists and Radicals called on their followers to boycott the referendum, and abstain. Victor Hugo, from Guernsey, wrote that the only referendum in which he and the Republicans should take part would be one in which the author of the *coup d'état* of 2 December put the question to the people: 'Shall I leave the Tuileries for the Conciergerie and offer to stand trial?' To this question, Victor Hugo would vote Yes.[79]

Unlike in all previous elections, the government exercised very little pressure during the referendum campaign, and the Opposition were allowed almost equal freedom of propaganda with the government. But on 30 April the government announced that they had discovered a plot by the Socialist International to assassinate the Emperor and blow up the Tuileries with a bomb. Ollivier took the opportunity to arrest over four hundred Socialists, including the leaders of the French section of the International, and to suppress three left-wing newspapers on the day before polling day.

The Socialists claimed that the plot story had been fabricated by the police and the government in order to scare the electors into voting for the Emperor in the referendum. After the voting was over, the authorities released all except eighty of the arrested Socialists, and in the trials of the others it transpired that only a handful of men on the fringe of the Socialist movement – the International claimed that they were police spies – were connected with the assassination plot. Thirty-eight of the most active members of the French section of the International were put on trial at the end of June for organizing the strikes at Schneider's works at Le Creusot, for smuggling in money from the International in London to *La Marseillaise*, and for planning a subversive campaign for the overthrow of the government and the Empire. Seven were sentenced to one year's imprisonment, and twenty-seven to lesser terms; four of them, including the most prominent strike-leader, Assi, were acquitted.[80]

The assassination plot had probably much less effect on the referendum results than the Socialists and Radicals made out. The Yes vote was 7,257,379; the No vote 1,530,909; about one-and-a-half million voters abstained. In Paris, the Emperor was defeated, 111,363 voting Yes and 156,377 No. The referendum of 8 May 1870 almost certainly represents the true degree of support for Louis Napoleon and his régime, both in Paris and in France as a whole, and is perhaps the result that would have been obtained at a free election at most times during the eighteen years of the Second Empire. Louis Napoleon was entitled to regard it as a great vote of confidence in himself and the new constitutional Liberal Empire which was beginning.

The Radicals and Socialists in Paris rioted again. The demonstrators sang the 'Marseillaise', broke shop windows, and built barricades with overturned buses; the police charged and injured the demonstrators; and Louis Napoleon and Eugénie again drove slowly through the streets of Paris on the afternoon after the riots amid the cheers of the people.[81] The Socialist painter, Courbet, delighted the opposition intellectuals by refusing the Legion of Honour that Louis Napoleon surprisingly offered him;*[82] but the anti-Socialist measures

*The well-known story that at a private view of the rejected pictures at the exhibition in 1853 Louis Napoleon struck Courbet's picture *Les Baigneuses* with a whip is almost certainly untrue, though Courbet himself believed it. It is quite out of keeping with Louis Napoleon's character. If the incident had occurred, it would almost certainly have been mentioned by Viel Castel, who hated Courbet and claimed the credit for excluding his pictures from the exhibition that year.[83]

of Ollivier, and the personal popularity of the Emperor had once again defeated the Red peril; and the government press assured the people that the Emperor was once again in excellent health.[84]

On 30 June 1870 Ollivier addressed the Chamber. He declared that the Emperor's victory in the referendum was a 'French Sadowa'. He was equally happy about foreign affairs. 'The government has no uneasiness whatever', he said; 'at no epoch was the peace of Europe more assured.'[85]

CHAPTER 41

SEDAN

Two days after Ollivier's speech, Marshal Prim announced in Madrid that the Spanish government had offered the crown of Spain to Prince Leopold of Hohenzollern, a distant cousin of King William of Prussia; the offer was subject to the Prince's acceptance and to ratification by the Spanish Cortes. By established custom, the Prince could not accept the crown without the consent of the King of Prussia as the head of the Hohenzollern family. The German press stated that King William did not know in advance of the offer to Prince Leopold, and had not yet been asked for his consent. In fact, Bismarck had been secretly negotiating with Prim for a year about the possibility of Prince Leopold's accession to the throne of Spain.

The French press immediately protested at the prospect of a Hohenzollern on the Spanish throne, and on 6 July the new Foreign Minister, the Duc de Gramont, who like Eugénie favoured an alliance with Austria against Prussia, told the Chamber that France would not permit Prince Leopold to become King of Spain. Ollivier added that he had no doubt that Prussia would yield in the face of French firmness, but that 'if a war be necessary, the government will not enter upon it without the consent of the Legislative Body'. Gramont's statement and Ollivier's mention of war were greeted with great enthusiasm by the deputies, and in the public galleries the ladies rose to their feet and waved their handkerchiefs as they joined in the wild applause. Next day the Paris press called for war with Prussia, and on 8 July their language was even more violent.[1] The government instructed the Ambassador to Prussia, Benedetti, to demand that King William should publicly refuse his consent to Prince Leopold's acceptance of the throne of Spain.

Unknown to anyone outside his very intimate circle, the Emperor was very ill. He had a very painful recurrence of the stone. On 1 July he was examined by five doctors – his old friend Conneau, who had been with him at Arenenberg and Ham and had delivered Eugénie of the Prince Imperial; Baron Corvisart, his official chief physician; Nélaton, the most famous French surgeon of the day, who had operated on Garibaldi's foot wound after Aspromonte and on many other

The Emperor Maximilian of
Mexico

The Empress Charlotte

The Prince Imperial on his eighteenth birthday, 16 March 1874

famous patients all over Europe; Dr Sée, a specialist in bladder diseases; and Dr Ricard. They diagnosed the presence of stone, but did not think that it was sufficiently serious to require an immediate operation which would put the Emperor out of action at such a time. In 1873 Dr Constantin James, in his book on the causes of Napoleon III's death, alleged that the doctors on 1 July 1870 advised an immediate operation, but sent their report to Eugénie, who decided, in view of the serious international situation, to conceal the report from Louis Napoleon and to override the doctors' decision to operate; but in fact Eugénie was never shown the report, and did not discover that Louis Napoleon was suffering from stone until two-and-a-half years later.[2]

While the world waited for the Prussian answer to the French note, the Paris press kept up their violent attacks on Prussia, with Girardin, as always, leading the demand for a preventive war. He wrote in *La Liberté* that sooner or later France and Prussia must fight it out, and the sooner the better; and the public took up the slogan 'Finissons-en!' – 'Let's get it over!' The *Times* correspondent thought that the calm tone of the German press infuriated the French all the more, like the man who is enraged when his opponent will not lose his temper.[3] Neutral sympathy was being alienated from France to a greater degree than Bismarck could have dared to hope.

Only *Le Siècle, Le Journal des Débats* and Delescluze in *Le Réveil* opposed the call for war. Delescluze demanded that a referendum should be held before war was declared; but all the other newspapers, including the Radical and Opposition press, called for a war which would revenge the humiliation of Sadowa. Paradoxically, while on the one hand they talked of the necessity of a preventive war to destroy the Prussian menace, they were all convinced that the invincible French army could defeat the Prussians with the greatest ease. Army officers sent challenges to any deputy or journalist who expressed the slightest doubt of their ability to thrash the Prussians; and Favre was shouted down in the Chamber when he expressed some mild reservation about the inevitability of war.[4] *Le Gaulois* wrote that if France did not force Prussia to yield to her demands, 'no woman in Europe would consent to take a Frenchman's arm'.[5]

At the Opera, Girardin, in the stalls, called on the orchestra to play Alfred de Musset's 'Le Rhin allemand'. They told him that they did not know it. 'Il est plus difficile à apprendre qu'à prendre!', he shouted back amid the applause of the audience.[6]

For once, the French Cabinet was unanimous about foreign policy; convinced – quite rightly – that Bismarck had plotted for Prince Leopold of Hohenzollern to obtain the throne of Spain, they were determined not to allow Prussia either to gain its objective or to withdraw gracefully.

Prussia must be either humiliated or destroyed in war. Gramont and Ollivier made this very clear in their discussions with the British and Austrian Ambassadors, though both Lord Lyons and Metternich thought that it would be wiser to leave Prussia a bridge over which to retreat.

The Emperor and Empress were less bellicose than most of their subjects. Many people afterwards held Eugénie responsible for the war. 'All has been caused by *Her*, they tell me', wrote Princess Mathilde;[7] and in 1874 Prince Napoleon's newspaper *La Volonté Nationale* wrote that Eugénie had said: 'It is my war, at last!'[8] She strongly denied this, and so did the man to whom she was alleged to have said it.[9] On several occasions she declared that she was in favour of peace, but not a peace with dishonour. This meant that, like the Cabinet and the great majority of the nation, she was in favour of peace only if it involved a Prussian humiliation. When Marshal Vaillant went to Saint-Cloud on 7 July he found the courtiers chauvinistic, the Emperor worried, and the Empress depressed;[10] but if Eugénie seemed to the bellicose Vaillant to be depressed at the prospect of war, by next day she had thrown off her depression, at least for the benefit of the neutral foreign diplomats, for on 8 July Metternich wrote that the prospect of 'a political triumph or war has made her look ten years younger'.[11] As usual, as she herself admitted to Paléologue in 1906, she had allowed herself to be influenced by the pressure of public opinion in her circle,[12] and became nearly as enthusiastic for war as the ladies who waved their handkerchiefs delightedly at Gramont's declaration in the Chamber; but she had not much more responsibility than they for the course of events.

The Emperor's attitude was of course much less straightforward than hers. On 6 July, Metternich was surprised to find him very happy about the situation; he was sure that there would be no war, but he chuckled at the thought that there was no way in which Bismarck could extract himself from the situation with honour.[13] He knew that his subjects felt that he had been humiliated by Bismarck at Sadowa, and now it was his turn to humiliate Bismarck. At the same time, he was playing his old game of conducting secret diplomatic negotiations behind his ministers' backs, and in concert with the Spanish Ambassador in Paris he made approaches to Prince Leopold of Hohenzollern's father to urge him to persuade Prince Leopold to refuse the crown of Spain; but he instructed Gramont to insist that Prince Leopold's renunciation must be publicly stated to have been made at the order of the King of Prussia, as France would not be satisfied if the Prince renounced merely at his father's direction.[14] He also favoured his usual idea of settling everything at an international Congress; but Eugénie was sure that the French nation would not stand for the idea of a Congress. 'I doubt whether this does justice to the feelings in the Chamber and the country', she said.[15]

On 11 July, Benedetti spoke to King William at the watering spa at Ems, and asked him to refuse his consent to Prince Leopold's candidature; Bismarck was on holiday at his estates in East Prussia. King William agreed to order Prince Leopold to withdraw. Ollivier announced the Prussian surrender in the Chamber on 12 July and hailed it as a French triumph and a Prussian humiliation. Bismarck thought the same, and considered resigning as Chancellor. But Gramont and Ollivier did not conceal their regret that the Prussians had given in; and the deputies and most of the press were disappointed that there was to be no war.[16] Girardin wrote in *La Liberté* that if a shepherd finds a wolf attacking one of his lambs, he does not refrain from shooting the wolf because the wolf drops the lamb and runs away when it sees the shepherd with his gun: if France let the Prussian wolf retreat, the wolf would be back soon to seize not only a lamb but a sheep as well.[17] Louis Napoleon sensed the public regret that there would be no war. 'The country will be disappointed', he cabled to Ollivier on 12 July; 'but what can we do?'[18]

He was in complete agreement with the decision which was taken at the Cabinet meeting on the same day to instruct Benedetti to ask for further guarantees from Prussia and to require King William to give an undertaking that he would never in the future allow Prince Leopold to accept the crown of Spain. When Benedetti confronted King William on the promenade at Ems on the afternoon of 13 July and asked him to give this undertaking, the King was annoyed, refused to do so, and walked away a little abruptly. He told Bismarck what had happened in the famous 'Ems telegram' which he sent to his Chancellor in Berlin with authority to publish it in the press; and Bismarck, eagerly seizing the opportunity to have war instead of humiliation, published the telegram with a minor deletion which made it marginally more defiant towards France than the King's original text. It is preposterous to suggest, as the French spokesmen afterwards did, that Bismarck's version of the Ems telegram amounted to a forgery and that he was as much responsible for the war as the French government and nation. Nor can Napoleon III escape a major share of the responsibility for the war, for he still had some personal power, even in the Liberal Empire, and made no real attempt on 14 July to prevent the declaration of war.[19]

The Ems telegram aroused the fury of the French press, for the statement that King William had refused to meet the French Ambassador was regarded as an insult to France. 'Prussia insults us!', wrote

Le Constitutionnel; 'let us cross the Rhine! the soldiers of Jena are ready!'[20] A Cabinet meeting was held on 14 July, and a decision was taken to order immediate general mobilization and to declare war next day. The Emperor raised the possible alternative of calling a Congress, but agreed with Ollivier that public opinion would never tolerate it. According to Gramont, Eugénie attended the Cabinet meeting, spoke very excitedly and strongly in favour of war, and swung over the ministers who were hesitating, giving a majority of four in favour of declaring war; and Ollivier stated that she mocked his efforts to avoid war, refused to speak to him at dinner, and turned her back on him.[21]

Great crowds filled the streets of Paris on the evening of 14 July. The students who a year before had demonstrated and rioted in support of Rochefort now demonstrated in favour of war. Now, as in 1869, they sang the 'Marseillaise'; but they cried 'Down with Prussia! Down with Bismarck! Long live war! To Berlin!' There were a few shouts of 'Vive l'Empereur!', and a few shouts for peace from the supporters of the International; but they were drowned in the cries of 'Vive la guerre!' For the first time for years, the police made no attempt to stop the singing of the 'Marseillaise'. Next day the Emperor issued an order to the police to permit the 'Marseillaise', and it was repeatedly sung in the streets and cafés of Paris during the next few days, sometimes together with 'Partant pour la Syrie', and with Hortense Schneider's hit song from *La Grande-Duchesse de Gérolstein*, 'Ah! que j'aime les militaires'. No well-known professional singer could walk through the streets without being stopped by the passers-by and asked to sing the 'Marseillaise'.[22]

At 10 a.m. on 15 July, Baron Vitzthum, who had been sent by Franz Joseph on a special mission to Paris, saw Louis Napoleon at Saint-Cloud. He urged on him the advisability of a Congress. The Emperor said that he favoured the idea of a Congress, 'but it must not stop us from fighting'. He then told Vitzthum that he did not expect any assistance from Austria in the war, but asked only that an Austrian army corps should be sent to Bohemia to tie down some Prussian forces on the Austrian frontier. Vitzthum reacted very coldly to this suggestion, and said that a lightning conductor in the wrong place could attract the lightning.[23]

In the afternoon of 15 July, Ollivier informed the Chambers that France had declared war on Prussia. He told them that he accepted the situation 'with a light heart'.[24] Only a small minority of Frenchmen were shocked by his words. *The Times* gave one of them the opportunity of expressing his opposition to the war anonymously in the paper. 'Military triumphs we may obtain', he wrote on 16 July, ' – in that respect France has no reason to feel distrust – but what political success can possibly wait on victory?' A week later he wrote deprecatingly of the over-confidence of the public. 'Our people have not yet realized . . . that we are invading a country where we shall be received with execration, and which will be united to a man against us.'[25] It never occurred, even to him, that the invasion would be the other way round.

The French government and press stressed that they were fighting against Prussia, not Germany, hoping to arouse the Catholic sympathies of the South German states;[26] but they completely failed to weaken German unity and enthusiasm for the war. France fought without allies, for neither Britain, Russia, Austria nor Italy liked or trusted Louis Napoleon; and at the end of July Bismarck published the secret memorandum which he had extracted from Benedetti in August 1866 containing Louis Napoleon's offer of a free hand for Prussia in South Germany in return for Prussian acquiescence in the annexation of Belgium by France.[27] Louis Napoleon hoped in vain for Italian support. He always expected the Italians to feel grateful for what he had done for them in 1859; but they also remembered 1849 and 1867. As soon as the war began, he decided to withdraw the greater part of his troops from Rome and bring them to fight in France; but he refused to respond to tentative offers from the Italian government to enter the war on the side of France if he allowed them to seize Rome.[28]

Louis Napoleon appointed Eugénie as Regent and took the supreme command of the army himself. Princess Mathilde was shocked at his decision, and pointed out to him that he was too ill even to ride a horse; but he laughed off her objection with a joke.[29] He announced that the fourteen-year-old Prince Imperial would be going with him to the army: 'He is proud to bear his share of the dangers of those who fight for their country.'[30] The press duly reported the Prince Imperial's preparations for his departure – how his locks were cut to comply with the prescribed army haircut, how the Empress was the first to insist that he should become a soldier, how she herself packed his bags. Meanwhile on 26 July the press reported that France had won the first engagement of the war – a cavalry skirmish near Niederbronn in which the French wounded five Germans and captured eight horses without suffering any casualties.[31]

Everyone expected the Emperor to ride through Paris at the head of his bodyguard when he left to join the army, as he had done in 1859; but he was too ill to ride, and to the great disappointment of the people – who were not told the reason for it – he left on 28 July by train from his private railway station in the park at Saint-Cloud, going by the *ceinture* and the Strasburg Railway to Metz, where he established his headquarters. When he reached Metz, he drove in a carriage from the railway station to his headquarters to the surprise of the troops, who had expected him to ride on horseback.[32]

In his proclamation to his soldiers at Metz on the evening of his arrival, he displayed the only trace of realism which was to be found in the utterances of the politicians and journalists of France in July 1870. He told them that they would be fighting against 'one of the best armies in Europe', adding that 'nothing is too difficult for the soldiers of Africa, the Crimea, China, Italy and Mexico'.[33] But the people were surprised that at the end of July, after seventeen days at war, the French armies were not yet fighting on German soil; so was Moltke, who had assumed that the French would immediately invade Germany and could not understand why they had declared war a fortnight before they were ready to take the offensive.[34]

By the beginning of August the Prussians, astounded at their luck in not having been attacked and invaded first, had crossed the frontier into France. On 2 August there was a minor engagement at Saarbrücken, where Bazaine's cavalry attacked a German force. The press reported that the Emperor and Prince Imperial had been under fire at Saarbrücken, and that the Prince Imperial had seen two dead bodies and had picked up a bullet and carved his initials on it.[35]

On 6 August the news reached Paris that the first major battle of the war had been fought and that the French had won a great victory: 70,000 French had defeated 120,000 Prussians, capturing 25,000 prisoners, including Prince Frederick Charles. The people celebrated and sang the 'Marseillaise' in the streets until news arrived that it was a false report which had been deliberately spread in order to manipulate the Bourse, and that in fact the Prussians had won the battle of Woerth. The Prussians captured 4000 French prisoners and 30 cannon at Woerth. When the truth was known in Paris, a mob attacked the Bourse, and demonstrators in the streets called for the resignation of the government.[36]

Eugénie issued a proclamation: 'Frenchmen! The opening of the war has not been in our favour. Our arms have suffered a check. Let us be firm under this reverse and let us hasten to repair it.'[37] Against the advice of Ollivier, she summoned a meeting of the Chambers. The left-wing deputies, who four weeks earlier had been shouted down when they expressed doubts about the war, now took the lead in criticizing the government and the High Command. Ollivier resigned, and was replaced as Prime Minister by the Comte de Palikao, who as General Montauban had led the army to Peking in 1860.

All over Paris people were criticizing the régime, but hardly anyone spoke about the Emperor.[38] It seemed as if the Second Empire was melting away by common consent.

After the defeat at Woerth Louis Napoleon's advisers on 6 August urged him to launch a counter-attack on the Germans at Saint-Avold. Moltke thought that this would be the best tactic for the enemy to adopt, but wrote to General Blumenthal: 'Such a vigorous decision is hardly in keeping with the attitude they have shown up till now.'[39] Louis Napoleon decided to go to Saint-Avold to discuss the plan of attack with Bazaine, and early on the morning of 7 August ordered his train at Metz; but before he had left the station he received news that the Germans had captured Forbach and were threatening Saint-Avold. He seemed stunned by this news. He immediately sent an order from the train for the whole of Bazaine's army in the Metz district to retreat to Châlons, where they could join the reserves in Châlons Camp and prepare for further action.[40]

The news of the proposed retreat shocked Ollivier and the government in Paris, who sent a telegram to the Emperor warning him of the effect which a retreat to Châlons would have on public morale. Louis Napoleon thereupon rescinded the order and instead ordered the army to fall back towards Metz.[41] He was in such pain from the stone that he could not think clearly, and decided to entrust the command of the army at Metz to Bazaine and return to Paris. When he told Eugénie of his intention, she sent him a telegram strongly advising against this course. 'Have you considered all the consequences which would follow from your return to Paris under the shadow of two reverses?', she cabled on 9 August,[42] when the demonstrations in Paris against the government were becoming menacing.

Louis Napoleon accepted her advice, but as he was convinced of the necessity of handing over the command of the army to Bazaine, he decided to go to Châlons Camp. On 14 August he left Metz with the Prince Imperial in a third-class railway carriage after appointing Bazaine as Commander-in-Chief.[43] On the 18th, Bazaine was decisively defeated by the Germans at Gravelotte-Saint-Privat, and a few days later the Germans invested Metz and Bazaine's army.

At Châlons Camp, the Emperor had a meeting on 17 August with MacMahon, Prince Napoleon and General Trochu, who was a friend of Prince Napoleon and was thought to have mildly Liberal sympathies. Prince Napoleon urged the Emperor to appoint Trochu as Military Governor of Paris with emergency powers and to return himself to Paris, leaving MacMahon in command of the army at Châlons. When Louis Napoleon hesitated, and said that he must first consult the Empress, Prince Napoleon asked him whether he or Eugénie was the sovereign of France. Louis Napoleon sat utterly downcast, in pain and despair. 'I seem to have abdicated', he said.[44] He accepted Prince Napoleon's advice, and Trochu left at once for Paris, arriving in the middle of the night to confront an indignant Eugénie, who had been awakened from her sleep to be told of his arrival.[45] He showed her the Emperor's order. She reluctantly accepted his appointment as Governor of Paris, but cabled to Châlons, again urging Louis Napoleon most strongly not to return to Paris; apart from the disastrous effect on morale, she feared that he would be assassinated in Paris.[46] Louis Napoleon changed his mind again about returning to Paris, and stayed at Châlons Camp. He sent Prince Napoleon to Florence to urge his father-in-law, Victor Emanuel, to enter the war on France's side.[47]

The mood of the French people had changed almost overnight after the first defeat at Woerth, and after Gravelotte-Saint-Privat they were in a state of great alarm. A month ago they were sure that their soldiers would soon be in Berlin; now they were equally sure that the Germans would soon be in Paris. Refugees from the countryside were pouring into Paris, and at the same time the Parisians were moving out; by the end of August, the families could be seen entering the city every evening in their carts piled high with bedding, furniture, food and valuables, and containing the grandparents, the mother dressed in black, and the children – all the family except the men who were in the army.[48] Some of the children made the same journey again as grandparents in 1940.

The government urged the Empress to leave Paris, but she firmly refused to go. She talked to her friends, and wrote to her mother in Madrid, in a state almost of exhilaration about the impending battle for Paris.[49] Her relations with Trochu were very bad. Knowing his intimacy with Prince Napoleon and the Liberals, she did not trust him to defend her and the régime; but she knew that his appointment was very popular with the Parisians, and as always her sense of duty and honour caused her to accept his appointment and collaborate with him to the full. He on his part promised to defend her with his life. 'I am a Catholic, I am a Breton, I am a soldier', he told her; 'before they reach you, Madame, they will pass over my dead body.'[50] She did not believe him at the time, and afterwards was convinced that he had always intended to betray her.

On 26 August, MacMahon and his army marched forward, hoping to link up with Bazaine, who according to the plan of campaign was to break out of the German ring around Metz with his army and join MacMahon's forces at Montmédy. The Emperor accompanied MacMahon's headquarters, but left the command to MacMahon; he could only travel by carriage, and was in such pain from the stone that he was once seen throwing his arms around a tree and hugging it in a desperate effort to endure his agony.[51] The soldiers were beginning to grumble against him, especially at the luxury in which he and his entourage lived, which contrasted so strongly with the conditions of the common soldiers. He was accompanied by a large number of useless court officials and servants.[52] This was particularly inexcusable, for during the war of 1859 he had been very conscious of how greatly an army is impeded by baggage wagons, and had told the British Field-Marshal Lord Clyde (Sir Colin Campbell) that it was essential to get rid of them as far as possible.[53] But he would always have found it difficult to dismiss his household servants, and was certainly incapable of doing so in his present state of health.

Before accompanying MacMahon's advancing army, the Emperor sent the Prince Imperial to comparative safety at Avesnes under the escort of some officers and servants.[54] The Prince's grandmother suggested that he should be sent to Spain, but Eugénie would not hear of it. 'Thank you for your offers, but I cannot accept them', she wrote to Maria Manuela on 31 August.

Of all my trials, the hardest for my heart is to see Louis [the Prince Imperial] threatened by all sorts of dangers. But I can change nothing; it is his destiny. . . . He must stay in his country, as long as his country will have us. It is impossible to run away in the hour of danger and return when times are good. Believe me, it is not the throne that I am defending, but honour, and if after the war, when there is no longer a single Prussian on French soil, the country does not want us any more, believe me, I will be happy, and then, far from the noise and the world, I can perhaps forget what I have suffered.[55]

On 29 August the vanguard of MacMahon's army, under the command of General Failly, the victor of Mentana, met the Germans at Beaumont. On this occasion Failly's *chassepots* did not work wonders, but were outmatched by the Prussian needle-gun. Failly was defeated, losing 7500 men – more than twice the German losses. There was an outburst of popular indignation in Paris against Failly, and Eugénie reluctantly advised Louis Napoleon to dismiss him,[56] and Louis Napoleon did so. As a result of Failly's defeat, MacMahon fell back on Sedan, eight miles from the Belgian frontier. Here he and his 110,000 men, with the Emperor among them, were surrounded by 250,000 Germans, who attacked them on the morning of 31 August.

The battle was broken off at nightfall, but was resumed next morning on a glorious summer day.[57] Louis Napoleon managed to mount a horse and rode out to the battlefield, exposing himself to the enemy fire as he chain-smoked cigarettes; his officers thought that he was deliberately seeking death. By the afternoon he was convinced that the position was lost, and, like at Magenta and Solferino, he was appalled at the slaughter and sufferings of his men. He decided to spare them further losses, and at 3.15 p.m. on 1 September, against the protests of his generals, he ordered the white flag to be raised over Sedan, and wrote his famous letter to the King of Prussia: '*Monsieur mon Frère*, Having been unable to die in the midst of my troops, it only remains for me to place my sword in Your Majesty's hands. I am Your Majesty's good brother, Napoleon.'[58]

A messenger passed through the German lines under a flag of truce and took the letter to King William, who was watching the battle with Bismarck from a hilltop near the village of Frénois, two miles south-west of Sedan. Bismarck immediately dictated the King's reply to the Emperor:

Monsieur mon Frère, Regretting the circumstances in which we meet, I accept Your Majesty's sword, and I beg you to name one of your officers, furnished with full powers from you, to negotiate the capitulation of the army which has fought so bravely under your command. I on my side have chosen General Moltke for this purpose. I am Your Majesty's good brother, William.[59]

On the morning of 2 September, Louis Napoleon drove out of Sedan towards King William's headquarters at the château of Bellevue, two miles west of Sedan on the road to Domchéry. Bismarck met him on the road, and, riding bareheaded beside his carriage as a sign of respect, took him to a weaver's cottage, where they sat in the garden in the morning sun. Louis Napoleon explained that he and his army had surrendered as prisoners-of-war, but that he had not capitulated as Emperor on behalf of the French nation. To Bismarck's annoyance, he insisted that as a prisoner-of-war he was no longer head of the French government and could not negotiate about peace terms or on any other subject; all negotiations would have to be conducted with the Empress in Paris.[60]

He went on to the Villa Bellevue and waited till King William arrived. The two sovereigns met on the front steps of the château. They had had several previous meetings – at Josephine's dinner table at Malmaison in 1814; at the Sunday get-together of the German Princes at Baden in 1860; at Compiègne in the following year; and amid the festivities of the Paris Exhibition. They talked for about half an hour at the Villa Bellevue. King William was very courteous. He asked Louis Napoleon if he had any preference as to where he should be imprisoned, and suggested the palace of Wilhelmshöhe near Kassel, where Louis Napoleon's uncle Jerome had lived when he was King of

Westphalia in Napoleon I's time. Louis Napoleon said that he had no request to make except that he should be taken to Germany by a route which would avoid as far as possible having to travel through the French countryside. King William suggested that he should go through neutral Belgium. Bismarck had no objection; he was sure that Louis Napoleon would not try to escape, and told his secretary that he did not mind in the least if he did.[61]

It was raining heavily on the morning of 3 September when Louis Napoleon set off from the Villa Bellevue to the Belgian frontier. He wore his general's uniform with the Legion of Honour, and drove in a carriage with two German generals, accompanied by a retinue of his gentlemen and servants and a small escort of German cavalry. They had all been granted permission by the Belgian government to travel through Belgium. The rest of his numerous servants, and his equipment, followed him to Wilhelmshöhe by a different route. On his way to the Belgian frontier he met columns of French prisoners-of-war; they received him in complete silence. Because of his illness and the pain which a jolting carriage caused him, he could only travel in slow stages, and he spent the first night at Bouillon in the Hôtel des Deux Postes. He was in such pain that he could not sleep at all, and paced around his bedroom all night. From Bouillon he sent a cable to the officers escorting the Prince Imperial ordering them to take the boy across the frontier into Belgium; and though they received contradictory orders from Eugénie, who insisted that her son must not run away, they took him to Belgium and from there to England.[62]

Next day, on that fatal 4 September 1870, Louis Napoleon went on to Verviers, and on the following day took the train from Verviers across the German frontier to Kassel. He was received at the station at Kassel by a guard of honour, who played the traditional *Zapfenstreich* tune with which visiting sovereigns were greeted in Germany, and as night fell he drove out to the palace of Wilhelmshöhe.[63]

Eugénie at first refused to believe the rumours that the Emperor had surrendered at Sedan; when she received his cable on 2 September she was shocked at the news, but quickly recovered her composure.[64] The government kept the news secret for eighteen hours; then, on the afternoon of 3 September, Palikao informed the Chamber that Mac-Mahon and his army had been defeated and had surrendered at Sedan, but he made no mention of the Emperor. Favre rose to ask 'Where is the Emperor? Is he in communication with his ministers?' 'No', said Palikao, and said no more. Favre then demanded the resignation of the government and the appointment of Trochu with supreme powers.[65]

The crowds began to gather on the boulevards between 8 and 9 o'clock on the evening of 3 September. They converged on the Place Vendôme, singing the 'Marseillaise' and shouting 'Resign!' – 'la déchéance!' The cry had never been used as a slogan by the Emperor's opponents. The Socialists and Radicals in the crowd raised their usual shout of 'Vive la République!' A handful of loyalists ventured to shout 'Vive l'Empereur!', and many more cried 'Vive la France!' But the cry of the evening was 'La déchéance!' From the Place Vendôme they went to the Place de la Concorde and swarmed around the Tuileries.[66] At 1.30 a.m. a government proclamation was posted to the walls of Paris. After stating that 40,000 men – less than half the true figure – had been captured by the Germans after a heroic three-day battle against overwhelming odds, it called on the people to rally to support the new army which was being formed to defend Paris, and added, as if by an afterthought: 'Your patriotism, your union, your energy will save France. The Emperor has been taken prisoner in the struggle.'[67]

When the Chambers met at midday on 4 September,[68] the crowds streamed in and demanded that the deputies should proclaim the downfall of the Empire and the establishment of the Republic. Favre led them to the Hôtel de Ville, where he proclaimed the Republic and the establishment of a Provisional Government with Trochu – whom Eugénie had never trusted – as President, Favre as Vice-President and Foreign Minister, Gambetta as Minister of the Interior, Jules Simon as Minister of Education, and Rochefort, just released from prison, as Minister without Portfolio and President of the Committee for the Supervision of Barricades. During the afternoon the crowds assembled around the Tuileries, where the flag flying at the masthead showed that the Empress was in residence; during the morning, she had inspected a new window in her bedroom which the builders had finished inserting that very day.[69] Two hundred thousand people surrounded the palace, singing the 'Marseillaise' and shouting 'La déchéance!'

The ministers and officers of the household came to the Tuileries early in the afternoon, told the Empress that the Republic had been proclaimed at the Hôtel de Ville, and urged her to escape at once, as her life was in danger from the mob. She refused to leave; but soon afterwards Metternich and Nigra – acting as her personal friends, not as ambassadors – arrived at the Tuileries and strongly urged her to go. At last she agreed. As the mob was all around the palace, they could not leave by the Place du Carrousel; but Eugénie led them along a private passage through the Prince Imperial's quarters, which were being repaired and redecorated during his absence with the army, through the museum of the palace to the Louvre, and out into the street of Saint-Germain-l'Auxerrois. As they passed through her son's apartments and the museum, Eugénie looked for the last time at the loved mementoes and artistic treasures, and wondered sadly what would become of them.

There were crowds in the Rue Saint-Germain-l'Auxerrois, but they did not notice the little group of men and women – Eugénie, Metternich, Nigra, and the Empress's lady-in-waiting Madame Lebreton – who slipped out of a doorway of the house. Metternich hailed a cab. They were just about to get into it when a street urchin cried out 'There is the Empress!'; but Nigra seized him roughly by the collar and told him to be quiet, as the ladies were friends of his, and they went off in the cab to the house of Dr Evans, the American dentist of Louis Napoleon and Eugénie in the Avenue de l'Impératrice. Next day the crowds tore down the street name-plate and removed all signs at street corners, shops and buildings which bore the name of the Emperor or Empress.

Dr Evans was not at home, so Eugénie sat in his waiting room till he arrived.[70] He gave her shelter for the night while he arranged for her escape to England. She left early next morning with Evans, his nephew Dr Crane, and Madame Lebreton in Evans's carriage, heading for Deauville on the Channel coast, where Mrs Evans was on holiday. As they drove to the north-west along Route Impériale Number 13, Eugénie was in good spirits, and had not lost her sense of humour; she told Evans that she had often said that if ever there was a revolution, she would not escape to England in a carriage like Louis Philippe had done in 1848; yet here she was, doing precisely this.[71]

When they reached Pacy-sur-Eure, some fifty miles from Paris, their horses were too tired to proceed, but they managed with considerable difficulty to hire horses and carriages to take them on to La Rivière, thirty miles from the coast, where they had to stay the night in a small inn. Next day, on 6 September, they went on to Deauville by railway. At the station, Eugénie experienced for the first time the rudeness of a railway official, which so many of her husband's subjects had encountered under the Second Empire. It sharply brought home to her the change in her position; then, as the train moved off, he touched his cap, and she consoled herself by thinking that he had recognized her, and that his rudeness was a ruse to keep her identity secret and to help her to escape.[72]

At Deauville, Evans left Eugénie with Mrs Evans at the Hôtel du Casino and went across by the ferry to Trouville to look for a ship to take them to England. At 2 p.m. he found the *Gazelle*, the yacht of the English gentleman Sir John Burgoyne, who was on holiday at Trouville with his wife. According to Evans, Burgoyne at first refused to take Eugénie to England, but eventually agreed under strong pressure from Evans and Crane to refer the matter to his wife, who decided that they must agree to take Eugénie. Burgoyne gave a very different account in his letter ten days afterwards to Queen Victoria's secretary, General Ponsonby; he told Ponsonby that after consulting Lady Burgoyne about the adequacy of the accommodation which they could provide for the Empress, he 'at once agreed' to take her.[73] At midnight Eugénie walked through the rain and the puddles with Evans and Crane and went on board only a few minutes after Burgoyne had got rid of two Prussians who had asked to look over his yacht and whom he suspected, probably wrongly, of being spies.

They sailed at 7 a.m. on 7 September. They had a rough crossing; another yacht, whose master was Burgoyne's cousin, was lost at sea that day. Eugénie told Evans many years later that she had thought they would go down, but that she had always loved the sea and felt that if she were drowned on this crossing it would be the best death for her. Ollivier afterwards commented that if the yacht had gone down with all hands, no one would ever have known what had happened to Eugénie;[74] but Mrs Evans, who remained at Deauville, knew where she was. The press on 5 September had reported that she had escaped to Belgium.[75]

It took them nearly twenty-four hours to reach the Isle of Wight, but they landed at Ryde at 7 a.m. on 8 September. Here they learned that the Prince Imperial, of whom Eugénie had heard nothing since Sedan, had reached Dover from Ostend on 6 September and was now staying at the Marine Hotel in Hastings. Eugénie joined him there on the evening of 8 September.[76] Three days later, she wrote from Hastings to Maria Manuela: 'I want you to know that I only left after the proclamation of the Republic and when I was invaded at the Tuileries. So I did not desert my post.'[77]

The British public had always loved Eugénie, even when they had most hated Napoleon III, and she was now welcomed with great sympathy in England. Many people wrote to her at Hastings offering to place their houses at her disposal.[78] She rejected a suggestion that she should take a house near Windsor, because then Queen Victoria would have no excuse for not visiting her, and if the Queen did not come, the public would interpret it as a snub.[79] She accepted an offer from Mr Strode of a lease of his house, Camden Place, at Chislehurst. Strode had known Louis Napoleon in England thirty years before; he was a friend of Miss Howard, who appointed him as her executor. When she died in France in 1865 he found Louis Napoleon's letters to her, and wrote to the Emperor telling him that he had burned them all.[80]

Eugénie and the Prince Imperial moved into Camden Place on 24 September.[81] Four days earlier, Victor Emanuel's soldiers had entered Rome after a few days' siege and bombardment. The liberation of Italy was complete; Eugénie was in exile; Louis Napoleon was a prisoner-of-war.

In the opening chapters of his biography of Julius Caesar, Louis Napoleon had discussed the reasons why the Kings of Rome fell from power and were replaced by the Republic.

They disappeared because their mission was accomplished. There seems to be a supreme law which fixes a useful term of life for institutions as well as for human beings. Until this term has expired, nothing can resist them; plots and revolts all fail against the unassailable strength of the thing that they are trying to remove. But when an apparently unshakeable institution ceases to be useful to the progress of humanity, then neither traditions, nor courage, nor the memories of a glorious past can delay by a single day the downfall that destiny has decreed.[82]

This 'useful term of life' expired for the Second Empire in 1870.

PART VI

THE EMPRESS EUGÉNIE

CHAPTER 42

CHISLEHURST

Louis Napoleon stayed at Wilhelmshöhe as a prisoner-of-war for six-and-a-half months. Most of his retinue followed him there – four generals, his A.D.C.s and equerries, his coachmen, his hairdresser Monsieur Caumont, who told everyone he met that 'Communism is at the bottom of it all',[1] and forty gentlemen as well as the servants and eighty-five of his horses. They all lived in the palace and stables at Wilhelmshöhe at the expense of the Prussian government, who added the cost to the bill for reparations which they would present to the French Republican government in the peace treaty. After a few days nearly fifty of the servants and sixty-three horses were sent away as being redundant, but the rest remained.[2]

Louis Napoleon received many visitors at Wilhelmshöhe.[3] The first to come was his cousin the Duchess of Hamilton, who had been criticized in the French press at the beginning of the war because her son was fighting in the German army.[4] Afterwards many of his relations and several of his English friends came; the hotels in Kassel did good business by providing accommodation for Napoleon III's visitors. At the end of October, Bazaine, after being besieged in Metz for nearly three months, surrendered the city without orders from the French Republican government, and was denounced in Paris as a traitor. He was sent as a prisoner-of-war to a mansion a few miles from Wilhelmshöhe. Like Louis Napoleon, he was on parole, and they often visited each other. High-ranking German generals and officials of the district were frequently Louis Napoleon's guests at dinner. He discussed military strategy with them, particularly his favourite topic, artillery. They were surprised and impressed by the excellence of his German vocabulary and accent.

His stone improved a little while he was at Wilhelmshöhe. He wrote to the Duc de Mouchy that he did not suffer from it continually, but had only an occasional attack.[5] He took a good deal of exercise, walking every day in the extensive grounds of the palace. He kept up his daily walk right through the winter, though it was a very severe winter all over Europe and at Wilhelmshöhe the temperature for several weeks

577

stood at 10°C. below freezing. When he first arrived at Wilhelmshöhe he stayed in the left wing of the palace, with its splendid view over the park, but when the cold weather came he moved to the right wing, where there were stoves, not open fireplaces as in the left wing. He sometimes went for drives in the surrounding countryside in a carriage, and after the snow fell, in a sleigh.

He wrote two short books on the war and French military preparedness in 1870,[6] but unfortunately did not write the third volume of his biography of Julius Caesar. He read Alexandre Dumas père's *Three Musketeers* for the first time; he had never heard of it, although it had been published nearly thirty years before.[7]

He readily acknowledged that King William was treating him with great kindness. People regarded this in two different ways, depending on their political viewpoint and to some extent on their generation. Some saw it as a praiseworthy example of the civilized courtesy of a gentlemanly war; but the democrats and Radicals considered it to be a violation of the principles of equality and justice that Napoleon III, whom they regarded as being responsible for the war and the defeat, should live in comfort and luxury at Wilhelmshöhe while the captured French rank-and-file, who were innocent victims of his wickedness and incompetence, were penned up in harsh conditions in the prisoner-of-war camps. Already during the campaign in France there had been complaints among Louis Napoleon's soldiers of the luxury in which the Emperor lived when on campaign. The complaints grew stronger among the 82,000 captured prisoners-of-war at Sedan, who after the battle lay in the streets of the little town, trying to find shelter in doorways and under arches, while the famished horses, many of whom had received no food for two days, ran wildly through the streets.[8]

Conditions were not much better in the prisoner-of-war camps near Stettin, at Glogau, and on the Wahnerheide near Siegburg, though the Germans denied the allegations of ill-treatment which were published in the French and foreign press, and claimed that the conditions of the French prisoners-of-war were no worse than those of the privates in the German army. At the height of the bitter weather in December 1870 some French prisoners-of-war were moved from Frankfort to Stettin in open cattle trucks without overcoats or any covering; when the train reached Kassel, one man was found to have died of exposure and several others had frozen limbs. This was very different from the conditions in which their former Emperor lived at near-by Wilhelmshöhe. Louis Napoleon was distressed by the stories that he heard about the conditions of the French prisoners-of-war in Germany, and on several occasions he contributed money to buy them warm clothing and other comforts.[9]

The difference between the Germans' attitude to Louis Napoleon and to the ordinary French soldier and civilian was emphasized by the nature of the war after Sedan. Favre immediately opened peace talks with Bismarck, but broke them off when Bismarck demanded the cession of Alsace and Lorraine. Favre protested that, as the war had been started by Napoleon III and not by the French people, Prussia should grant generous terms to the Republic. Bismarck, remembering the cries of 'A Berlin! Vive la guerre!' in Paris in July, insisted that Prussia needed Alsace and Lorraine as security against any French government that might come to power in future. When Favre would not accept this, Bismarck threatened to negotiate with Napoleon III and replace him in power in Paris. The French Provisional Government then called on the nation to wage a people's war. Everyone was to fight the invader, civilians as well as soldiers, even prisoners-of-war in the prison camps in Germany. King William and Bismarck, while treating Louis Napoleon with the greatest consideration, executed *francs-tireurs* by firing squad, bombarded and starved the civilian population of Paris, and instituted a harsher régime in the prisoner-of-war camps after prisoners had tried to organize a resistance movement in the camps.[10]

As the German army encircled Paris, they captured Saint-Cloud, and occupied the palace, which in its elevated position was a good observation post. The Crown Prince, who had been one of the most successful of the Prussian commanders, found a decorative screen in Eugénie's boudoir in the palace, and sent it to his wife in Berlin. The Crown Princess – Queen Victoria's daughter 'Vicky' – had adored Eugénie when she first met her, at the age of fourteen at Windsor in 1855;[11] and though her Liberal sympathies had led her to condemn Louis Napoleon's policies, she had not forgotten the great kindness which Eugénie had always shown her.[12] She sent the screen to Queen Victoria and asked her to pass it on to Eugénie. The Queen's first reaction was to do so; but Lord Granville then pointed out that as the screen was the property of the French government, it had been taken as loot by the Crown Prince, and Queen Victoria might be placed in an embarrassing position if it were known that she had handled looted property. He therefore advised her not to unpack the screen and to place it in store until after the war, when the Crown Princess could give it to Eugénie if she wished.[13]

As Louis Napoleon firmly refused to negotiate with the Prussian government as long as he was a prisoner-of-war, Bismarck in September and October 1870 made secret and tentative approaches to Eugénie at Chislehurst in the hopes that, as Regent, she would order Bazaine to surrender at Metz and would agree to cede Alsace and Lorraine to

Prussia if Prussian troops replaced Louis Napoleon on the throne of France. Eugénie refused to negotiate with the Prussians, though an unauthorized intermediary tried to do so on her behalf. She did, however, write a personal letter to King William asking him not to annex Alsace and Lorraine. In a very courteous reply, the King regretted having to cause her distress, but stated that, as King of Prussia, he must first consider the interests of his country, and Prussian security required the possession of Alsace-Lorraine.[14]

She also tried to win the support of the neutral powers, appealing for help to both the Tsar and Franz Joseph.[15] In the middle of October, Queen Victoria's son, Prince Arthur, visited her at Camden Place. He wrote to Queen Victoria that 'several times the Empress broached the subject of the Neutrals interfering to stop the war, but of course I was careful in my answers'.[16]

At the end of October, Eugénie travelled through Belgium to Wilhelmshöhe and spent four days with Louis Napoleon before returning to Chislehurst. Apart from wishing to see him again, she wished to consult with him about Bismarck's overtures. Louis Napoleon told her that she had done right in refusing to negotiate with Prussia.[17]

In France, Napoleon III was being denounced in the most violent and scurrilous language; but he issued no statement from Wilhelmshöhe in reply to the slanders. Then, on 29 January 1871, the French Provisional Government capitulated and signed the armistice with the Germans; eleven days before, King William of Prussia had been proclaimed German Emperor at Versailles. On 8 February, Louis Napoleon for the first time issued a political statement from Wilhelmshöhe. He declared that he had remained silent as long as French troops were fighting the enemy, but now that the armistice had been signed he felt entitled to point out that the Provisional Government was illegal and did not derive its authority from universal suffrage.[18] After the Provisional Government had ordered that a general election be held for a new National Assembly, Louis Napoleon issued another statement in March, stating that on four occasions in twenty years he had received the support of the overwhelming majority of the electorate, and that only a government which had been supported by the nation in a referendum conducted under universal suffrage had any lawful authority in France.[19]

On 1 March the Assembly met at Bordeaux, and a resolution was moved for the deposition of Napoleon III, who was declared 'to be responsible for all our misfortunes and the ruin, the invasion and the dismemberment of France'. The former Chief of the Emperor's Cabinet Secretariat, the Corsican Conti, was the only deputy in the Assembly who spoke against the motion; he reminded the deputies that many of them had taken the oath of loyalty to the Emperor. The deputies roared at him 'Thief! Murderer! To the galleys with him!', and some of them rushed to the rostrum and assaulted him. The President of the Assembly had to suspend the session. When it was resumed, the deposition of Napoleon III was carried with only six deputies voting against the motion.[20]

Under the peace treaty the prisoners-of-war were to be released at once, and Louis Napoleon made arrangements to go to England. Before leaving Wilhelmshöhe he wrote to Queen Augusta, the new German Empress, 'to thank Your Imperial Majesty for the care with which I have been surrounded, by your order, during my stay in this château'.[21] He left on the morning of 19 March, being seen off with due solemnity by a guard of honour, and in the early afternoon of 20 March reached Dover from Ostend. Eugénie and the Prince Imperial were waiting to meet him on the waterfront, along with all the local officials and a large crowd of onlookers, and it was with great difficulty that the police managed to force a way for him through the crowd to reach the Lord Warden Hotel and the railway station. He travelled with the directors of the South-Eastern Railway Company on a special train to Chislehurst, surprised and moved at the warmth of the welcome which he had received from the people of Dover.[22]

Chislehurst, fifteen miles from central London, was still right out in the Kent countryside in 1871. Camden Place was on the edge of the common. It was said to have been the house of the antiquary William Camden in the sixteenth century, and was certainly the home in the middle of the eighteenth century of Lord Camden, the Lord Chancellor, who took his title from the name of the house; but it was completely rebuilt during the nineteenth century. In 1813 a notorious murder was committed in the house, the master and mistress being battered to death by a manservant whom they had caught trying to rob them.[23] Queen Victoria, who visited Eugénie at Camden Place soon after she arrived there,[24] described it as 'that small house', and referred to 'the poor Emperor's humble little rooms';[25] but the house had twenty rooms, apart from the kitchens,[26] and stood in pleasant grounds with lawns hidden by trees from the public view. Louis Napoleon lived there with Eugénie and the Prince Imperial, Prince Joachim Murat, Conneau, Corvisart, his secretaries Filon and Franceschini Piétri, and a household of thirty-two other ladies and gentlemen and twenty-three servants. The total inmates of the house, including Louis Napoleon and his family, were entered as sixty-two in the census return of 1871.[27]

Most of the servants at Camden Place were French, but seven of them were British. One of these was a girl of twenty named Hannah

Wilton,* who in the summer of 1872 stole seven £20 notes from Louis Napoleon's cash box and gave them to her boy friend. Hannah and her friend were arrested when they bought a coat priced at twenty-four shillings from a tailor in Cheapside and offered one of the stolen £20 notes in payment. Louis Napoleon wrote to the magistrate at Sidcup who tried the case and asked him to deal leniently with the girl. Her friend was acquitted, but Hannah was found guilty of larceny. The magistrate said that in view of the Emperor's plea on her behalf he would deal with her as leniently as possible, and sentenced her to three months' imprisonment instead of the six months which he would otherwise have given her.[28]

For the third time Louis Napoleon was an exile in England, but his life was very different now from what it had been in 1839 and 1846, when he had gone to the opera and the theatres and the town and country houses of the aristocracy, and had lived a gay social life. Now he was in poor health and saddened in spirit; but he was still reasonably active during his first year in England. In April 1871, Eugénie wrote to Queen Victoria that 'the Emperor still suffers, but his condition is not alarming'.[29]

Five days after he arrived at Camden Place, the Prince of Wales called on him, and on 27 March he was taken by special train to Windsor to meet Queen Victoria. He met her again in July in the house of Prince and Princess Christian of Schleswig-Holstein, her son-in-law and daughter, at Frogmore near Windsor, and she visited him at Camden Place on 20 April 1872, which was his sixty-fourth birthday.[30] She would have come more often had it not been for one great difficulty; the Emperor liked very hot rooms, and the Queen liked very cold rooms. Their mutual friend, Lady Sydney, mentioned the matter to the Duc de Bassano, who assured her that the Empress disliked the Emperor's overheated rooms as much as the Queen did.[31]

Apart from his visits to Windsor and Frogmore, Louis Napoleon took the Prince Imperial to visit his old acquaintance Angela Burdett-Coutts at Holly Lodge, her house in Highgate,[32] and occasionally visited high-ranking officers at Woolwich. He was once taken by the Prince of Wales to the Marlborough Club, and in August 1871 went with Eugénie and the Prince Imperial to visit the famous steamship, the *Great Eastern*, at Sheerness.[33] He and Eugénie spent a few days that month at Cowes with Eugénie's Spanish nieces. They went yachting with an American girl, Jennie Jerome, who was soon to become Lady Randolph Churchill and the mother of Sir Winston Churchill. She had been presented to Louis Napoleon at the Tuileries, and was shocked

*Her name is given both as Hannah Wilton and Hannah Whifton in the press reports of the case.

to see how 'old, ill and sad' he looked as he leaned against the mast on the yacht. 'Even in my young eyes', she wrote in later years, 'he seemed to have nothing to live for.'[34]

During the summer of 1871, Arese visited him at Camden Place. This touched him, as their relations had become strained after Mentana; yet Arese was now a more loyal friend in adversity than were many of the fawning courtiers of the Second Empire.[35]

Louis Napoleon was not often seen at Chislehurst, except sometimes when he walked across the common to the little Roman Catholic church of St Mary to attend Mass, though normally he went to Mass in his private chapel at Camden Place, where the Catholic parish priest, Father Goddard, officiated. On two occasions he watched a local cricket match. When he went with Eugénie and the Prince Imperial to see the Bickley Park Club play Beckenham, he sent a note of congratulation to a fielder in the deep who had brought off a catch on the boundary close to where Louis Napoleon and his party were sitting. On another occasion, at Chislehurst, he was introduced to the captain of the local team. He asked him whether the game was played for money, and was duly impressed when the cricketer replied: 'No, Sire, for honour.'[36]

In his misfortune, the people of England forgot their detestation of his despotism, and their fears of his fleet at Cherbourg, and remembered only that he had always sought British friendship in his foreign policy. Two days before he arrived from Wilhelmshöhe, the Socialists and extreme Radicals seized power in Paris and proclaimed the rule of the Commune, with his old opponents Delescluze, Miot, Pyat and Rochefort playing a leading part in the revolution. His other opponents, Thiers and Favre, sent his former A.D.C. General Gallifet to crush the rebellion in Paris, and in the course of two months of civil war the Communards shot the Archbishop of Paris, demolished the Colonne Vendôme and burned the Tuileries, while Gallifet, at the orders of Thiers, shot 30,000 Communards in summary executions, and sent thousands more to suffer in the prison camps at Satory and in the penal settlements of New Caledonia. Louis Napoleon was shocked by the events in Paris and the burning of the Tuileries.[37] Many people in England were conscious that the horrors perpetrated on both sides during the Commune had not occurred when the Emperor ruled in France. At the height of the Commune a number of Anglican clergymen wrote to 'His Imperial Majesty the Emperor of the French, K.G.' to tell him that they hoped that he would soon return to France 'to restore once again social order and religious liberty' and to save the country 'from the inroads of a barbarous Socialism and the curse and despotism of an anti-Christian Republic'.[38]

He was equally popular with the ordinary non-political British working man. In June 1871 the workmen employed by the contractor of the sewage works for the Greenwich District Board stopped outside the gates of Camden Place on their annual excursion to Sidcup and serenaded the Emperor with 'God Save the Queen' and 'Auld Lang Syne'. Louis Napoleon walked down to the gate with Eugénie and the Prince Imperial and was welcomed by the firm's solicitor, who stated in a prepared little speech that they knew that the Emperor was a friend of England and that they hoped that he would soon be restored to the throne of France.[39]

The French Republican government was a little alarmed at these pro-Bonapartist manifestations in Britain. The inhabitants of Chislehurst believed that a number of secret agents of the French government were operating in their midst; according to local tradition, these agents sometimes perched themselves in the trees on the common overlooking the grounds of Camden Place in order to observe what was going on there.[40] The French government was displeased at the number of visitors from France who went to Chislehurst to attend the celebrations at Camden Place on the Bonapartist National Day on 15 August 1871 and on the Prince Imperial's sixteenth birthday on 16 March 1872; and they banned an attempt by many society ladies in Paris, and by Bonapartists in Marseilles, to hold special Masses on Eugénie's saint's day on 15 November 1871.[41]

In September 1871, Eugénie went on a three-month visit to Spain to see her mother and her relations and friends. She could not travel through France, but sailed from Southampton to Lisbon and went on to Madrid, Seville and Cadiz, while Louis Napoleon and the Prince Imperial went to Torquay, where they stayed for five weeks with Angela Burdett-Coutts. They returned to London by way of Bath, staying at the York Hotel.[42] On his return to Camden Place, Louis Napoleon for the first time since reaching England gave an interview to a journalist, which was published in the world press. He denied that he was conspiring to regain the throne of France; he said that after being a head of State for twenty-two years, a man does not conspire, but preserves his dignity.[43]

The stone continued to trouble him. In addition to Conneau and Corvisart at Camden Place, he consulted the eminent physician, Sir William Gull, and in July 1872 called in Sir Henry Thompson, the famous surgeon who had cured King Leopold I of the Belgians of stone in 1863. Thompson had used the crushing operation on King Leopold, which had first been used in 1822 by the French surgeon Civiale, under whom Thompson had studied in Paris. Unlike the older cutting operation, it was bloodless, which was a real advantage before modern developments in medicine reduced the risks of septicaemia. Civiale himself had not ventured to use his crushing operation on King Leopold, but Thompson had done so with complete success and achieved a great international reputation as a result.

Thompson examined Louis Napoleon on a day when the irritation was less than usual, and found no grounds for undue anxiety; but he was sufficiently worried to suggest that he should conduct a sound on Louis Napoleon under chloroform.[44] Louis Napoleon refused to agree to this, and went off with his doctors' approval for a holiday at Bognor with Conneau in attendance, while Eugénie took the Prince Imperial to Scotland. They visited Edinburgh, Melrose Abbey and Sir Walter Scott's house at Abbotsford, and went north to Inverary, Oban, Fort William and Inverness, staying at the houses of the local nobility. They climbed Ben Nevis on a sunny and cloudless day, going up as far as the lake on ponies but climbing the last 3000 feet on foot. Eugénie, at the age of forty-six, had lost none of her youthful vigour.[45]

When they returned to Chislehurst in the middle of August, Louis Napoleon took the Prince Imperial to Brighton. They stayed at the recently opened Grand Hotel and visited the Aquarium.[46] Louis Napoleon had last been in Brighton in 1848, when he sat on the pier and told a friend that he had bet Princess Mathilde that he would be Emperor of the French within four years. Now he was no longer looking four years ahead, but only at the glories and mistakes of the past.

From Brighton he went with Eugénie and the Prince Imperial to Cowes, where they stayed first at the Marine Hotel and then rented Beaulieu House. Louis Napoleon's health took a turn for the worse in the Isle of Wight, and he was badly troubled by the stone when they returned to Chislehurst on 30 September.[47] During the next three months the disease got worse, and he was rarely able to go driving in that depressing autumn. The Prince Imperial began a three-year course at Woolwich Military Academy, and though he soon became very popular there and greatly enjoyed the life, he was unhappy and homesick during his first term.[48] Eugénie at Camden House watched the rain day after day, as England and all Western Europe suffered from floods. 'The rain has been falling incessantly for the last two months', she wrote to her niece the Duchess of Montoro in Spain on 10 December. 'We shall become aquatic animals if this goes on.'[49]

At the end of October, Louis Napoleon was examined by another very eminent surgeon, Sir James Paget, who was worried about his condition, and the doctors at last persuaded him to call in Sir Henry Thompson for another examination. On Christmas Eve he was examined by Thompson, who decided that he must carry out a sound as soon as possible, and did so under chloroform on Christmas Day in the presence of Conneau, Corvisart, Gull, and a local practitioner, Dr Foster, as well as the anaesthetist, Dr Clover. Thompson discovered that the stone was very large, but thought that it was just sufficiently friable for the crushing operation to be possible, though he realized that this would not be easy. Eugénie was then told for the first time that Louis Napoleon was suffering from stone.[50]

On 2 January all the doctors were in attendance again, and in the morning Thompson carried out another sound under chloroform. In the afternoon chloroform was given again, and Thompson performed the crushing operation. He moved into residence at Camden Place so as to be able to deal exclusively with the Emperor's case, and next day wrote to the Prince of Wales, who had asked to be kept informed. He told the Prince that although 'H.M. suffered a good deal' after the operation he had slept quite well during the last part of the night, and 'altogether he is in *quite* as good a condition as I could have expected'.[51] But Thompson was anxious, and on the afternoon of 4 January wrote to the Prince of Wales's secretary, Francis Knollys:

The Emperor goes on fairly well, not quite so flourishing perhaps now as yesterday; on the whole about the same – I regard the case as a very grave one. In the *strictest confidence* I tell you this. The stone is so large. The Emperor is *very sensitive*, and is difficult to manage. I shall want all my force, all my resources to get him through, and I may fail. I am very anxious.[52]

During 4 and 5 January Louis Napoleon was in considerable pain, which was relieved by doses of opium. As the débris of the crushed stone was causing great irritation, Thompson decided on a second operation on the morning of 6 January, when much broken gravel was removed. A third operation was performed on 7 January, but was soon abandoned because the parts were so irritated, although it was clear that a fourth operation would be necessary as soon as the Emperor was strong enough to stand it. He slept better on the night of 8 January. He was seen at 11 p.m. by all his doctors; at 2 a.m. by Conneau, at 4 a.m. by Corvisart, and at 6 a.m. by Thompson. All three of them, and Clover, examined him at 9.45 a.m. on 9 January, and decided that he was fit enough to stand the fourth operation at noon.[53]

Fifty minutes later, Thompson came into Louis Napoleon's room and was alarmed to see that his condition had greatly deteriorated. Eugénie was about to leave for Woolwich to visit the Prince Imperial, but was advised to stay, as the Emperor had had a slight relapse. She afterwards described the events to Queen Victoria, who recorded them in her diary. She took off her hat & went towards his room, which was close by. As she came to the door, Dr Corvisart opened it, calling out 'Father Goddard, Father Goddard', & she at once saw that there was danger. When she came into the room & kissed the Emperor's hand, they said to him 'Voilà l'Imperatrice' but he no longer was able to see her, though he still moved his lips to kiss her. In 5 or 10 minutes afterwards all was over![54]

He died at 10.45 a.m.

The doctors realized that in view of the suddenness of the death and the status of the patient there were likely to be repercussions in both medical and political circles. They therefore asked Eugénie's permission to perform a post-mortem examination, which was carried out at Camden Place on 10 January by Dr Burdon Sanderson in the presence of Conneau, Corvisart, Thompson, Gull, Clover and Foster. It revealed that Louis Napoleon was suffering from kidney disease. The report stated that 'death took place by failure of the circulation and was attributable to the general constitutional state of the patient', and added that he would in any case soon have died from the kidney disease. The report was signed by six of the seven doctors, but not by Sir William Gull, who left Camden Place immediately after the examination and before the report had been drafted. That evening he issued a separate report from his house in Brook Street in which he stated that he agreed with the opinion of his colleagues except that he thought that the stone was of longer duration than they suggested.[55]

Gull's disagreement with the other doctors had no bearing whatever on the cause of the Emperor's death; but his action in leaving Camden Place and issuing a separate report increased the public feeling that Louis Napoleon had been killed by someone's negligence. At the bottom of it lay the deep-rooted ill-feeling between Britain and France. Britain had scored off France when Thompson cured King Leopold after Civiale had failed to do so; now France could score off Britain by making out that Thompson had bungled the operation on Napoleon III.

The matter was argued in articles in medical journals, and afterwards in books. *The Lancet* hinted that the doctors ought to have discovered the extent of the Emperor's kidney disease, and that in view of this they should not have subjected him to the long strain of the crushing operations, but should have proceeded by cutting, or not have operated at all. Dr Sée disclosed that he and one of his colleagues had advised an immediate operation in July 1870 which would have saved the Emperor's life. Dr Debout d'Estrées revealed that, three months after Napoleon III's death, Gull had told him in confidence that in

587

January 1873 he had advised against the operation because the state of the Emperor's kidney disease made it too risky. The French doctor, Constantin James, used the case to further his campaign against chloroform. He believed that, apart from the fact that all anaesthetics were undesirable – it was better that the patient should remain conscious to guide the surgeon's hand and sustain himself by his will-power – chloroform was a dangerous poison, and the cumulative effect of small doses would eventually be fatal. He had known several cases where this had happened, and was not surprised that the Emperor had died after being given chloroform twice in four days.[56]

Queen Victoria was most displeased with the articles in *The Lancet* and the *British Medical Journal* and at the disclosure of intimate clinical details about the Emperor's last illness. On 10 January she wrote to her own doctor, Sir William Jenner:

The reputation of the Medical Profession suffers by the disgusting publicity given to the poor Emperor's illness & sufferings. . . . You may use my name & say how horrified I am. Surely the agonies of a sick room ought to be sacred to the Medical Attendants. How did it all come out?[57]

She was never able to discover how it all came out; all the doctors and the members of the household at Camden Place denied that they had been responsible for the leak.[58]

Princess Caroline Murat told another story in the memoirs which she wrote a few years before her death in 1902 and gave to her friend Robert Leighton to publish posthumously. When they appeared in 1910, in Eugénie's lifetime, Leighton stated that he had made no alterations in Princess Murat's manuscript; and it is more than likely that the embittered old Princess, who during her last years could eat nothing except dry toast because of her digestive troubles,[59] was personally responsible for her interesting but quite unreliable memoirs. Caroline's sister, Princess Anna Murat, was a great favourite of Eugénie during the Second Empire; the Empress pushed her into the social limelight at the Tuileries and Compiègne, and gave her a wedding dress costing 80,000 francs when she chose the Duc de Mouchy from among her many suitors and married him in 1865.[60] But Eugénie and Caroline did not get on well. Caroline's memoirs reek with hatred of Eugénie.[61] She held Eugénie responsible for every political and private disaster suffered by Napoleon III and the dynasty; accused her of favouring only Spaniards, of hating all the Emperor's relations, and of ill-treating the Prince Imperial when he was a child; and never forgave her for one occasion when Caroline arrived late for dinner at Chislehurst, after losing her way in a London fog, and Eugénie scolded her mercilessly without allowing her to say one word of excuse.[62]

Caroline Murat states that she was at her London home at 11 a.m. on 9 January 1873 when she heard the newsvendors crying out that Napoleon III had died. Shocked and incredulous, she drove through the melting snow to Chislehurst. On arriving at Camden Place she met Eugénie, who told her that Louis Napoleon had died from an overdose of chloral which had been given him the night before to alleviate the pain and make him sleep. His four doctors had decided that he should have the chloral, and the dose was measured out by Corvisart. The Emperor was very reluctant to take it – Caroline Murat believed that some instinct warned him that it would be fatal to him – but Eugénie insisted that the doctors had prescribed it, and he reluctantly accepted it under her pressure. So, according to Caroline Murat, Eugénie was the unwitting cause of Louis Napoleon's death.

The Murats wrote to Sir William Gull, and asked him if this story was true; but Gull gave a non-committal answer. Eleven years later, Caroline Murat called in Gull when her little daughter was seriously ill with peritonitis, and she took the opportunity to ask him about the Emperor's death. He told her that the Emperor died from an overdose of chloral, which had been negligently measured out by Corvisart; and Gull said that this was the reason why he had refused to sign the post-mortem report. Caroline Murat also wrote that Madame Rouher refused to believe the chloral story, and to prove it false she herself took the same dose of chloral that Corvisart had given to Louis Napoleon; as a result, she nearly died, and was saved only by her youth and good health.[63]

Unreliable though Princess Murat may be, an overdose of chloral is a possible explanation of Louis Napoleon's death, and more plausible than Dr James's theory about chloroform or the suggestion that Sir Henry Thompson could not perform a competent crushing operation. It would not necessarily involve any negligence on Corvisart's part in measuring the dose, because as Louis Napoleon was suffering from kidney disease to a far greater extent than his doctors realized – this could not be ascertained with certainty in the state of medical knowledge in 1873 – a dose of chloral which would normally be harmless might have been fatal in his case. But whatever the cause of death, it did not make much difference to Napoleon III. He would in any case have died within a few years from the kidney disease; and in a historical sense, he died at Sedan, or earlier at Metz.

CHAPTER 43

ZULULAND

ON 14 January the body of Napoleon III lay in state in the hall of Camden Place. Over 17,000 people walked past the body; many of them had come from France. Next day it was taken to St Mary's Catholic church at Chislehurst and buried there. The Prince Imperial and Prince Napoleon were the chief mourners and walked behind the coffin; Eugénie, as was considered appropriate, did not attend the funeral, but received the members of the family in Camden Place and accepted their condolences.

Queen Victoria and the Prince of Wales were represented at the funeral, and the French Bonapartists came in great strength. They included all the Bonapartes and the Murats; Fleury, Canrobert and Palikao; the Duchesse de Malakoff and Madame de Saint-Arnaud, the widows of the two Marshals; Rouher, Haussmann, Gramont, Benedetti and Schneider; the Empress's former ladies, the Marquise de Gallifet and Madame de Pourtalès, and Marianne de Walewska; and Lord Cowley and the Lord Mayor. Thirty-one deputies of the National Assembly and forty Prefects attended. There were two notable absentees – Ollivier and MacMahon, who no longer used his title of Duc de Magenta and a few months later became President of the French Republic. There was room for only 184 people in the church, but it was announced that every Frenchman who wished to do so could assemble in the grounds of Camden Place and follow the coffin to the church. A crowd of about 20,000 assembled outside the church, including at least 1000 Frenchmen. Many of them cried 'Vive l'Empereur! Vive Napoléon IV!'[1]

Eugénie received messages of sympathy from Franz Joseph, Alexander II, and other European sovereigns, including the German Emperor and Empress; but in France the Republican press did not spare the memory of Napoleon III. The *Charente-Inférieure* was more restrained than many: '*Requiescat in pace* in the oblivion of history for our benefit and yours.' Others were harsher. 'Napoleon III did evil', wrote *Le Républicain* of the Dordogne, and added that he was 'the man of the repression ... the adventurer, the vulgar conspirator'. *L'Avenir* of

Eugénie, about 1880

(Left to right) Piétri, Antonia d'Attainville, Eugénie and Primoli
at Farnborough Hill, about 1912

Eugénie and her relatives at the Liria Palace in Madrid
a few days before her death in July 1920

Rennes commented that 200,000 Frenchmen would still be alive, two provinces would not have been lost to France, and 5 million francs would have been saved if he had died three years earlier. The *Courrier* of Saumur wished that he had died twenty-five years earlier, and spoke of the contempt felt for 'that sinister and cursed race', the Bonapartes. *L'Avenir National* regretted his death because it would not now be possible to bring him to justice for the crime of December 1851.[2]

His Will was found among his papers; he had made it in 1865. Apart from a few legacies to servants, he left his whole private fortune to Eugénie, being satisfied that she would recompense any deserving person whom he had overlooked in the Will. Prince Napoleon and his supporters were dissatisfied, and alleged that Louis Napoleon had made a second Will which Eugénie had destroyed.[3]

If Napoleon III had been reigning in France at the time of his death in January 1873, he would have been succeeded by the Prince Imperial as Napoleon IV, with Eugénie acting as Regent until the new Emperor reached the age of eighteen. This would take place in just over a year's time, on 16 March 1874. What kind of a young man was Napoleon IV? What were his political views? and what chance had he of returning to reign in France? He had been brought up as a child by an English nanny, Miss Shaw; he had been much in the public eye, with his intelligence and other virtues being repeatedly stressed in the press. At an early age he was accused by the Radicals of being an incipient reactionary and Ultramontane who was completely under his mother's influence;[4] and after Napoleon III's death it was assumed that Eugénie would be the Catholic and Conservative power behind the throne if the Prince Imperial ever reigned in France.

Prince Napoleon tried to wean him away from her. He was very friendly to the Prince Imperial when he came to Chislehurst for the Emperor's funeral, and soon afterwards invited him to come for a prolonged stay with him in Switzerland. Eugénie was very reluctant to let him go, and confided her fears to Queen Victoria, who disapproved of Prince Napoleon as a dangerous Radical. Apart from the fact that Eugénie did not wish to be separated from her son, she feared that both politically and morally he would be corrupted by Prince Napoleon, and she told Queen Victoria that the Prince Imperial had absolutely refused to go.[5] This confirmed the opinion, held by Prince Napoleon and many other Radicals, that the Prince Imperial was a pawn in his mother's hands.

Despite all the stories to the contrary, Eugénie was not an inveterate personal enemy of Prince Napoleon. She strongly disapproved of his politics, but never showed personal vindictiveness towards him. She was perhaps affected by the stories that he was secretly in love with her, and was indulgent to him because of this; at any rate, she was always ready to offer him an olive branch. When he publicly insulted her at Compiègne in 1863 by refusing to propose her health, she immediately offered him her arm as they left the dining room; after his speech at Ajaccio in 1865, she refused to condemn him publicly and waited for the Emperor to take action from Algiers; and after Louis Napoleon's death she tried hard to effect a reconciliation and avoid an irrevocable split in the Bonapartist movement.[6]

But the Prince Imperial had not only Eugénie in the house at Camden Place; he also had Rouher in a cottage at the end of the garden, for Rouher divided his time between Paris and Chislehurst. Rouher, who had been one of the six men who had plotted the *coup d'état* of 1851 and who had sent the troops against Garibaldi in 1867, was still a great adversary of Radicalism and of Prince Napoleon's left-wing Bonapartism. He inspired the propaganda of *Le Pays* and *L'Ordre*, the two Bonapartist newspapers in Paris, and set out to groom the Prince Imperial as a Catholic and Conservative Bonapartist.[7]

Eugénie did not approve of Rouher's schemes and of the attempts of the Bonapartists to involve her son in French politics. Her shrewd, straightforward realism, which had made her oppose the attempts of Louis Napoleon to weaken his dictatorship by introducing the hazards of the Liberal Empire, now led her to see that the Bonapartists had no chance at all of overthrowing the Third Republic. She disagreed on this point with her mother. Maria Manuela, who was over eighty and blind,[8] but as ambitious as ever, wrote to Eugénie from Madrid urging her to work for a Bonapartist restoration in France; but Eugénie told her that the crown of France was a crown of thorns, and believed that 'the era of men sent by Providence is passed'.[9] When Maria Manuela told her that Louis Napoleon had once said to her 'that when he found an obstacle he surmounted it', Eugénie replied that probably when he said this, it

was because he felt that he was sitting on an excellent horse and that *nearly all the probabilities were in favour of his surmounting it*, because with all the courage, the resolution and the energy in the world, if the horse is fagged out it is more than likely that you will break your head without succeeding.[10]

She was conscious that times were changing. The great railway strike in the United States in 1877 alarmed, but did not surprise, her, and she was sure that similar strikes would soon take place in Europe, because 'the questions that confront us today are more social than political. It is madness not to bother about them and to think that it suffices to be strong to scatter them. Bayonets have never stopped an idea from taking root in a nation.'[11] She told Maria Manuela that

> a skilful person must try to have on his side what you call the Popular Hydra and there is no longer any force which can go against it. The Kings, the Princes and the nobility have weakened each other for centuries so that they can now achieve nothing if they unite. We must reckon with new forces.[12]

The Bonapartists organized a great rally at Camden Place on the Prince Imperial's eighteenth birthday on 16 March 1874. Advertisements were placed in the Bonapartist newspapers in France and preparations were made to run excursion boats and trains to bring thousands of Bonapartists from France. The French government was alarmed. They announced that they had taken no steps to prevent military and civil officers from going to Chislehurst for Napoleon III's funeral, because he had once been the head of state in France; but the eighteenth birthday of the Prince Imperial was another matter, and any army officer or civilian official who attended would be dismissed from the service. They announced that no civil servants would be granted permission to go on holiday to England until after 16 March had passed, and any of them who were already in England must return to France before 16 March.[13]

Three weeks before his birthday, the Prince Imperial gave an interview to a French journalist. He said that he would take the opportunity of declaring his programme: 'I know very well that it will be attributed to Monsieur Rouher, but I care little for that.' He said that he was busy pursuing his military studies at Woolwich, and had no immediate plans to return to France as Emperor; but when only two flags remained flying in France '– the flag of anarchy and the standard of the Empire – France will not hesitate in her choice'. He said that he would never come to power by a *coup d'état*, because his father had told him that the *coup d'état* had always been a cannon-ball dragging around his feet.[14]

Nearly 6000 people came from France to Chislehurst on 16 March; they crowded into the grounds of Camden Place, and cried 'Vive l'Empereur! Vive Napoléon IV! Vive l'Impératrice!' The Bonapartes and the Murats came, with the Duchesse de Malakoff, the former Imperial Prosecutor Grandperret, 65 of the 87 Prefects who had held office under the Second Empire, and 14 sitting deputies in the National Assembly of the Third Republic. But Prince Napoleon did not come, and this was widely reported, and was seen as a sign of a definite split in the Bonapartist movement between the Prince Imperial, Eugénie and Rouher on the one side, and Prince Napoleon on the other.[15]

In February 1876 a general election for the Chamber of Deputies was held throughout France. Rouher stood as the Bonapartist candidate in Ajaccio; but Prince Napoleon, who had always cultivated a personal following in Corsica, also stood as a candidate in opposition to him. On 31 January the Prince Imperial wrote from Camden Place to the Corsican Bonapartists and told them to vote for Rouher and not for Prince Napoleon:

Prince Napoleon Jerome offers himself as a candidate to the people of Ajaccio . . . against my will; he relies on our enemies. I am forced to treat him as such. . . . When the Emperor was alive, his authority was not questioned in the bosom of his family. As for me, I have the duty of establishing mine.[16]

Many Bonapartists who were opposed to Prince Napoleon regretted that the tone of the Prince Imperial's letter was quite so harsh. Rouher was elected, but Prince Napoleon's supporters succeeded in getting the election annulled for irregularities, and in the new election Prince Napoleon was successful. The Bonapartist movement was irrevocably split.

The Prince Imperial had now finished his military studies at Woolwich. The Radicals spread the rumour that he was a dunce who had only gained entry to Woolwich through royal influence; but the Bonapartists published his examination results, which showed that he came eleventh out of thirty-two cadets in his class, which was a creditable result, as he studied and took the examinations in English, a foreign language.[17] He spent his holidays with his mother at Chislehurst, and went with her to visit Queen Victoria, and other members of the royal family. In April 1876, when he went without Eugénie to stay with the Queen's daughter Princess Louise, Marchioness of Lorne, at Tunbridge Wells, Eugénie was filled with a desire to go to Clifton to see the place where she had been to school in 1837; but something prevented her from going, and she never went there.[18]

Soon after she came to England, Eugénie began a close friendship by correspondence with a new young friend, her niece Luisa, Duchess of Montoro, Paca's daughter, in Madrid. For the first time since Paca's death she had a relative to whom she could write confidentially, free from the political and other tensions which to some extent marked her correspondence with her mother. 'Louisette' was eighteen, men were falling in love with her, and she was worrying as to whom she should marry. Eugénie told her that she knew how difficult and unpleasant it was to refuse offers of marriage, but that she must not marry any man with whom she was not in love. She married the Duke of

Medinaceli in October 1875; four months later she died of a miscarriage. Another of Eugénie's close friendships had ended in tragedy.[19]

Travel was Eugénie's great solace. In the summer after Louis Napoleon died, she took the Prince Imperial to Arenenberg, where she had spent two days with Louis Napoleon in 1865. She and her son loved the charming little château above the lake where Louis Napoleon had lived for twenty years nearly half a century before, and they went there for six successive summers from 1873 to 1878. Eugénie spent the whole summer there, and the Prince Imperial joined her at the end of July after the end of term at Woolwich. They could not travel through France, but the Emperor William I and Bismarck had no objection to their going through Germany.[20]

While Eugénie was at Arenenberg in September 1876, the Paris Socialist paper *Les Droits de l'Homme* published what they claimed was an extract from the official French law reports, the *Gazette des Tribunaux*, of 28 September 1831. The document stated that a death certificate at the Royal Chancellery at Valladolid recorded that Don Joaquin de Montijo, husband of the Countess Maria Manuela de Montijo, had died on 30 October 1823, leaving two children, a girl who died at the age of nine months in 1823 and a son who died in 1827 aged fifteen years. *Les Droits de l'Homme* commented:

> But the person who in Paris, in the elegant world where Napoleon III noticed her, bore the name of Mademoiselle de Montijo, was born on 5 May 1826! She therefore came into the world *three years after the death of her father*. So it was thanks to a daring forgery of official government documents that the French were made to believe that their Sovereign Lady was the legitimate daughter of a great Spanish nobleman.

It added that the late Duchess of Alba had also been illegitimate.[21]

The story was thereupon reprinted in the *Journal du Havre*, the *Courrier de l'Aisne*, and in *Le Siècle*. The article in *Le Siècle* stated that the page of the *Gazette des Tribunaux* of 28 September 1831 was torn out of the records by government order during the Second Empire, but that the journalists of the *Journal du Havre* had found an unmutilated copy of the original *Gazette des Tribunaux* in the Bibliothèque Nationale.

Eugénie saw *Le Siècle* at Arenenberg, and was quite nonplussed. On 6 October she wrote to Maria Manuela asking her if she had any idea who this Joaquin de Montijo might be. Maria Manuela had already written to Rouher stating that the newspapers must have become confused by the Spanish names, and she brought an action for libel in the French courts against all the newspapers who had published the story. Grandperret, who had returned to private practice at the Paris bar after the fall of the Empire, was Maria Manuela's counsel, and he won the case; but though the jury gave a verdict for Maria Manuela, the sum awarded to her as damages was so small as to be almost contemptuous.[22]

Eugénie went on from Arenenberg to Italy, and spent the winter of 1876–7 in Florence and Rome. While she was in Rome she called on King Victor Emanuel. He received her in a room in the palace which was hung with pictures of the German Emperor William and other members of the Hohenzollern family; but there was no picture of Napoleon III. Victor Emanuel saw her look of displeasure as she looked at the pictures, and asked her if she was displeased with what she saw. She replied that on the contrary she was displeased with what she did not see. He began to make excuses, but she left without offering him her hand.[23] She was expressing the indignation which so many Frenchmen felt at Italian ingratitude to the liberator of Lombardy, and refused to understand that after Villafranca and Mentana the Italians had forgotten Magenta and Solferino.

In the summer of 1877 she spent three months in Spain.[24] Next year she decided to go to a watering spa, and ironically chose Ems, where she rented a villa for a few weeks in July 1878, and went on in August to Vienna. Her reception in Vienna, which was widely reported in the world press, surprised many people and caused some irritation in France. The Emperor Franz Joseph visited her at her hotel, and gave a great banquet in her honour at Schönbrunn Palace; and she was also visited by several leading Austrian statesmen, including her old friend Prince Metternich, and by the German Ambassador, Prince Reuss, who had been a guest at Compiègne in past days.[25]

The visit to Ems had caused rumours about the state of her health. When she returned to England from Arenenberg with the Prince Imperial in October 1878 she fell on the quayside at Dover and cut her cheek. The Prince Imperial picked her up in his arms and carried her to the Lord Warden Hotel, where she was revived. She was able to continue the journey to Chislehurst,[26] but it was rumoured that her griefs had made her grow prematurely old at fifty-two, and that she might not long survive.

The Prince Imperial was twenty-two, and had finished his course at Woolwich, He had nothing to do, and was bored by society life. There were rumours that he was going to marry Princess Thyra of Denmark or Queen Victoria's daughter, Princess Beatrice, as well as the usual unfounded gossip about secret marriages and love affairs with girls in London and Chislehurst; but there is no reliable evidence of any emotional entanglement.[27] He was on very intimate terms with his mother, though he seems to have resented the fact that she kept him short of money, and to have had at least one quarrel with her about this.[28]

He longed to win military renown on some battlefield. He had an additional incentive to do so because the Radicals in France had accused him of cowardice and desertion for leaving the army before Sedan and crossing into Belgium. It was a harsh judgement to pass on a fourteen-year-old boy who had been sent to safety by his father, though the criticism was provoked by the propaganda which had been previously put out by the official newspapers of the Second Empire, praising him lavishly for doing his duty in the ranks of the defenders of his country. The Republicans had mercilessly ridiculed him on account of the press reports in August 1870 of his picking up the bullet on the battlefield at Saarbrücken; he felt so sensitive about it that he kept a newspaper cutting on the subject in his wallet.[29] He contemplated volunteering for the Austrian army. Eugénie was opposed to this idea; she thought that if Austria remained at peace, he would spend all his time playing billiards and making love to some Italian singer, whereas if war broke out he would have to fight against Tsar Alexander II, who had shown him kindness when he visited Woolwich in 1874.[30]

In January 1879 the British government sent an army to conquer the troublesome African tribes in Zululand. The Prince Imperial asked to be allowed to serve in the British army. There was almost universal opposition to his plan. The French Bonapartists not only feared that he might be killed there, but knew that he would be quite out of touch in Zululand, unable to seize any unexpected opportunity which might suddenly arise for action in France, and unable to issue proclamations and statements to the press along the lines suggested to him by Rouher. The British War Office opposed it, because they thought that they would be held responsible if he were killed, and foresaw many other possible difficulties if he went. But he was determined to go, and threatened to volunteer as a private under a false name if he could go in no other way. Eugénie was very alarmed when the recruiting sergeants went round Chislehurst, and decided that it would be better to arrange for him to go as a staff officer than as a private. As usual, she was careful not to involve her friend Queen Victoria by attempting to use her personal influence with the Queen; but the Prince Imperial approached the Duke of Cambridge, the Commander-in-Chief of the British Army, who told the Queen of his great disappointment at being refused.[31] 'I never saw a young man more intent for going', the Duke of Cambridge wrote to the Queen, 'and the Empress his Mother I hear quite takes his view of the case.'[32]

The Queen and the Duke agreed to allow him to go, not as an

officer of the British army but as a distinguished visitor attached to the general staff. The Prime Minister, Disraeli, learned to his surprise and dismay that the Prince Imperial was sailing for Zululand next day, although the Cabinet had decided that he was not to go. 'I did all I could to stop his going,' he said afterwards, 'but what can you do when you have to deal with two obstinate women?'[33]

Eugénie went to Southampton to see him sail on 27 February in the *Danube*. He had hoped the ship would call at St Helena, but she sailed straight from Madeira to Cape Town. After staying for a few days at Government House, the Prince Imperial proceeded to Durban and joined the British forces invading Zululand.[34] At first he was attached to the headquarters of Lord Chelmsford, the Commander-in-Chief; but later, in order to give him wider experience, Chelmsford sent him to the headquarters of the Quartermaster-General, Lieutenant-Colonel Harrison. Chelmsford gave Harrison precise instructions about the Prince Imperial. He was to be treated exactly like any other junior staff officer, except that he was not to be allowed to go on any distant reconnaissance without Chelmsford's special permission; and if he went on any surveying operation near the camp, he was always to be provided with a sufficient escort and accompanied by an officer.[35]

Colonel Harrison established his headquarters at Itelezi Ridge, and from here, on 1 June 1879, he sent out a reconnaissance party of six cavalrymen under Lieutenant (Acting Captain) Carey into Zulu territory. Without referring to Lord Chelmsford, he allowed the Prince Imperial to accompany the party. He said nothing to Carey about who was in command of the party, assuming that Carey knew that by the Queen's Regulations Carey himself, as the senior officer present, would be in command; and he gave no clear instructions to Carey about his relationship or duty towards the Prince Imperial, beyond saying to him 'You can now look after the Prince.' Throughout their expedition, Carey behaved as if the Prince Imperial was in command, deferring to his wishes in all matters. Afterwards the four surviving soldiers in the unit were asked who they thought was in command. 'The Prince', replied Trooper Le Tocq. 'I do not know who was in command of the escort', said Corporal Grubb. 'I do not know who was in command', said Trooper Cochrane. 'I could not say who was in command, the Prince or Lieutenant Carey', said Sergeant Willis, though he added that they had reported to Lieutenant Carey before starting out. Asked who gave the word of command, he replied: 'I would not be sure. I do not recollect, but I think it was the Prince.'[36]

At midday the Prince suggested that they should off-saddle at a place beside a river at the edge of the long grass. No soldier with experience of Zulu warfare would have off-saddled here, because he would have known that Zulus might creep unobserved through the long grass until they were within a few yards of their unsuspecting enemies. Carey was worried about off-saddling so near the grass, and suggested that they off-saddle up on the bridge; but the Prince Imperial said that he preferred to go nearer to the river, and they did as he wished. They rested here until 3.35 p.m., when Carey, who was worrying about a possible attack, urged that they should leave at once. The Prince Imperial said that they could wait for another ten minutes before leaving, but five minutes later he gave the order to mount. Carey said and did nothing. 'I never heard anybody give orders except the Prince to saddle-up and mount', said Trooper Cochrane at the court martial.

They were on the point of mounting and departing when a band of Zulus, perhaps as many as forty or fifty, emerged from the long grass a few yards away; about a dozen of them were armed with rifles, and the rest with the Zulus' missile javelin, the assegai. Seeing themselves outnumbered, Carey and the other members of the party mounted and galloped off in all directions. Two of them were shot and killed by the Zulus' rifle-fire. A third, Trooper Le Tocq, reached the shelter of a *donga* (a gully) about 500 yards away, and waited there, thinking that the party would regroup. The others galloped away without pausing, with Carey leading the way.

But when the Prince Imperial tried to mount, he seized the wallet strap, which broke, and he fell back on the ground, dropping his sword as he tried to draw it from the scabbard, and being almost trampled on by his horse, who galloped away after the other fleeing horses. He tried to run for the cover of the *donga*, but after he had covered 250 yards he realized that it was hopeless, and turned to face the Zulus as they hurled their assegais at him. He picked up one of the assegais and prepared to use it as a weapon, and faced them with his revolver in his left hand and the assegai in his right, but went down under the assegais which were thrown at him. Le Tocq then joined the flight.[37]

Next day Colonel Harrison sent out a unit under the command of Surgeon-Major Scott to recover the bodies. Scott found the corpse of the Prince Imperial where he had fallen; the Zulus had not mutilated it, as they had mutilated the corpses of the two troopers who were killed, out of respect for the courage with which he had fought. He had eighteen assegai wounds, all of them in front; five of the wounds might each have been fatal in itself.[38]

When Carey reached the camp on the evening of the Prince Imperial's death, he wrote an emotional letter to his wife.[39] The letter is not nearly as incriminating as it has been made out to be, but it contains some damaging admissions.*

*For the text of the letter, see Appendix.

Eugénie's secretary, Mademoiselle Thérèse Gaubert, said in later years that she was with Eugénie at the hour on 1 June when the Prince Imperial was killed, and that Eugénie suddenly seemed to smell violets – the favourite Bonaparte flower – and had an intuition that this meant that her son was thinking of her at that moment.[40] Every day she waited both eagerly and anxiously for the postman to come. She read reports in the press that the Prince Imperial was ill and even that he had died, but also other reports of how he had distinguished himself on reconnaissance parties in Zululand.[41]

The news of the Prince's death reached England on 19 June. Queen Victoria was the first to be informed, and next morning sent Lord Sydney to tell the Empress before it was published in the press.[42] But once again, as in the case of Paca's death, misguided men tried to withhold the truth from Eugénie for as long as possible. The officers of her household had already heard the news, but did not tell her. A letter written by Lord Dorchester to her secretary, Piétri, who was on holiday in Corsica, was placed by mistake among her letters; it referred to the 'terrible news'. She was gravely alarmed, and, summoning Corvisart, asked him whether the news referred to the Prince Imperial. Although Corvisart knew the truth, he told her that it could not refer to the Prince, for if it did she would already have been informed about it by Lord Sydney.

Immediately afterwards, Sydney arrived, and saw the Duc de Bassano. The Duke insisted that, as the Empress's Chamberlain, he must tell her the news himself; but at the last moment he could not bring himself to do so, and merely told her that the Prince was wounded. She said that she must go at once to South Africa to see him, and Bassano said that if she did, she might perhaps arrive too late. She was now convinced that they were keeping the full facts from her, and protested angrily. A moment later, Sydney and Corvisart came into the room together, and Sydney told her that he had bad news for her – the worst possible news. He then said that the Prince had been killed. She collapsed into a chair, and sat staring into space.[43]

She was utterly prostrated by the blow. In 1865, when she heard that a French colonel had been killed in Mexico, she wrote cheerfully enough to the Empress Charlotte that though his death 'has grieved us very much, unfortunately nothing can be achieved without causing some suffering to poor mothers' hearts'.[44] But it was different now. She did not leave the house for thirty-two days, and it was not until 23 July that she went out into the garden for the first time. At night she prayed in the chapel; during the day she sat alone in a darkened room, only reluctantly accepting a little food, because a nervous contraction of the throat made it almost impossible for her to swallow.[45]

On 25 June she managed for the first time to write a short letter to Maria Manuela in Madrid: 'Dear Mother, Today I have the courage to tell you that I am still alive, because pain does not kill. Your very devoted daughter, Eugénie'.[46]

The bodies of the two troopers who had been killed with the Prince Imperial were buried on the spot; but the Prince's body was taken back to England. Lord Chelmsford ordered the troops to pay proper respect to the body at every stage on the journey, bearing in mind the glorious military name which the Prince bore and the fact that his father had been Britain's loyal ally.[47] The body reached Chislehurst on 11 July, and lay in state in Camden Place until next day. The funeral on 12 July was attended by the British royal family, with the Prince of Wales and the Duke of Cambridge acting as pall-bearers, and Queen Victoria herself watched from her carriage. Many leading generals and statesmen of the Second Empire came from France; so did nearly ninety deputies of the Chamber of Deputies. The 1400 policemen on duty at the funeral estimated the crowds at between thirty-five and forty thousand.[48]

The press in Britain and throughout Europe expressed great regret at the Prince Imperial's death; but in France it aroused strong anti-English feelings. *Le Figaro* had sent a correspondent to Zululand who had had several interviews with the Prince shortly before his death, and he immediately accused Carey and the British army of betraying the Prince and of being responsible for his death. The French press in general took up this theme. The less responsible commentators suggested that he had been assassinated in Zululand by the British, by the Communists, or by the Freemasons; but even more sober observers suggested that the British army would have taken better care of one of Queen Victoria's sons than they had of the Prince Imperial.[49]

Caroline Murat had married an Englishman, Mr Garden, but she voiced a feeling which was prevalent among many French Bonapartists when she blamed England for all the misfortunes of the Bonapartes. It was excessive affection for England which had caused Napoleon III to compromise French interests by seeking British friendship; the Empire had fallen because of the policy of Ollivier, the product of constitutional government, which Napoleon III had adopted in France in imitation of England; Napoleon III had died at the hands of an English surgeon; and now a cowardly English officer had left the Prince Imperial to die fighting in England's war.[50]

Princess Murat had her own spiteful dig at Eugénie. The officers in Zululand reported that the wallet strap on the Prince Imperial's saddle, which had torn when the Prince tried to mount at the moment of the attack, was of very poor quality. According to Princess Murat, when the

Prince Imperial's equipment was being prepared before he left for Zululand, Fleury suggested that his saddlery should be specially made by the best saddlers in London; but Eugénie, who despite her great wealth was miserly and always stinted the Prince Imperial of money, said that this would be an extravagance, as excellent ready-made saddlery could be bought much more cheaply in the shops. So Eugénie, by her meanness, had been responsible for her son's death, just as she had been responsible for her husband's death by pressing him to take the chloral.[51]

On 12 June, at Camp Upoka River in Zululand, Lieutenant Carey appeared before a court martial, charged with misbehaviour before the enemy on 1 June 'when in command of an escort in attendance on His Imperial Highness Prince Napoleon . . . in having, when the said Prince and escort were attacked by the enemy, galloped away and in not having attempted to rally the escort or otherwise defend the said Prince'. Carey, who conducted his own defence, pleaded Not Guilty and based his case on two arguments: that the Prince, and not he, was in command of the unit and responsible for the decision as to where to off-saddle; and that, faced with a greatly superior enemy force, there was nothing to be done except *sauve qui peut*, every man for himself. All the four surviving members of the escort were called as witnesses for the prosecution, but when cross-examined by Carey agreed with him that the Prince Imperial, and not he, had been in command; and three of them said that if they had been in the Prince's position they would not have expected the others to risk their lives in a hopeless attempt to rescue them. Only Le Tocq said 'If I had been in the Prince's place, I should have expected someone to come and help me.'

The prosecuting officer summed up the case against Carey in a nutshell: the Prince Imperial had been abandoned.

> Think of the distance he was able to run after the vanishing horsemen – 250 yards according to Le Tocq, and about 225 yards by the map; yet the Prince is left to his death by a party of mounted men, armed with breach-loading rifles, who had gained the comparative safety of the *donga*, in full view of which this brave young man was simply hunted down without a hand being raised in his defence.[52]

The court returned a verdict of Guilty, and sentenced Carey to be cashiered; but they forwarded to the confirming officer a recommendation for mercy, on the grounds 'that the Prisoner was evidently under the impression that the Prince Imperial held some military status and was the senior officer',[53] and because of Carey's previous good record. Lord Chelmsford added his own recommendation to mercy when he forwarded the report of the court martial to the Duke of Cambridge in London. He said that he did not think that Carey was a coward, but that the suddenness of the attack had made him lose his head and forget that it was his duty, as commander of the escort, to try to rally the men.[54]

Eugénie had no vindictive feelings towards Carey.[55] When Queen Victoria visited her at Camden Place on 17 July for the third time since the Prince Imperial's death, she found that the little ante-room in which Eugénie sat was no longer in complete darkness, although the blinds were drawn. Eugénie suddenly 'with the greatest fervour' asked that no action should be taken against Carey, as 'he may have a mother'.[56] The Queen said that it was of course not entirely in her hands, but she would see what could be done. She summarized her own view of the case ten days later: 'Poor Lieut. Carey lost his head but all were wanting in what wd obtain a V.C.'[57]

Her attitude was to change during the next few weeks. It has often been said that the wishes of the Queen and of the Empress for leniency were communicated to the Duke of Cambridge, and were decisive in influencing his decision in Carey's favour; but in fact Eugénie was careful to make no attempt at all to influence the Duke's decision, and the Queen's inclination was against leniency. At no period of English history had the independence of the administration of justice from royal authority been so zealously guarded as at the end of the nineteenth century, and the Queen's wishes had no effect on the decision in Carey's case.

The papers of the Carey court martial were sent in the ordinary way to the Judge Advocate-General, Mr Cavendish Bentinck, who immediately decided that it would be quite impossible to uphold Carey's conviction. In the first place, the members of the court martial had forgotten to take the oath before the start of the proceedings, which in Bentinck's opinion automatically invalidated the trial. Apart from this, he did not see how Carey could be charged with having failed to 'defend' the Prince Imperial when he had never been expressly entrusted with the duty to do so, as he had no more obligation to defend the Prince than to defend the two troopers who had been killed on the same occasion.[58]

The usual procedure in such cases was for the Judge Advocate-General to send his recommendation to the Queen, who automatically approved it and returned it to him within forty-eight hours for him to forward to the Adjutant-General who laid it before the Duke of Cambridge as Commander-in-Chief. In view of the political implications and the royal involvement in Carey's case, Bentinck did not do this, but went to Windsor to discuss the matter with the Queen, and the case was also considered by the Cabinet. This departure from the usual procedure caused the Adjutant-General to make a formal protest to the Queen; but Bentinck's visit to Windsor and the Cabinet's interference made no difference to Carey's fate. The Lord Chancellor, Lord Cairns, took exactly the same view of the case as Bentinck did.[59]

The Queen accepted their advice with great reluctance. If the Judge Advocate-General and the Lord Chancellor said that the sentence of cashiering could not be upheld, she 'of course' would not confirm the sentence;[60] but she felt strongly that Carey should not remain in the army.

> I dare say that *legally* Lieut. Carey has *not* committed a fault *capable* of being punished *as an act of cowardice, but* I *do* think that *no* Prince, or far less than a Prince that no friend, no Superior – no fellow-creature should be left in great danger, without those with him or one of them being prepared to lay down his *life for him.* I am sure *thousands* would do it.[61]

As the days passed, and all her advisers one after the other insisted that the verdict and sentence against Carey be set aside, the Queen's opinion hardened against Carey. By 7 August she was writing in cipher to Colonel Stanley, the Secretary of State for War: 'But he *is* guilty.... the C. Martial sh^d not be quashed.'[62]

The Duke of Cambridge, though advised by all the lawyers that he must find in Carey's favour, was under pressure from the army as well as from the Queen not to do so. On 16 August the Adjutant-General issued a memorandum on the Duke's behalf which the Queen thought was excellent.[63] It quashed the sentence of the court martial, but blamed Carey for abandoning the Prince Imperial. It stated that although at the moment of the attack 'defence was impossible and retreat imperative', the Duke would say – 'and he feels that he speaks with the voice of the army' – that it was very regrettable that the survivors departed without first making sure that there was nothing that they could do to help their comrades who were left behind.[64]

On 22 August, Carey arrived at Plymouth, in his native county of Devon, and was presented with a message signed by three thousand people in Plymouth expressing their 'entire confidence' in 'your valour as a British officer and your honor as a gentleman'.[65] He duly received the congratulations of the Leicester Liberal Club and other organizations who felt that he was the innocent victim of the malice of the Queen, the Bonapartists and the Establishment. He gave interviews to the press, and repeated his story that the Prince Imperial had been in command of the reconnaissance on 1 June and had therefore been to blame for the decision to off-saddle at the edge of the long grass.[66] Eugénie was disgusted. 'If I wanted him pardoned,' she wrote to Maria Manuela, 'I was far from thinking that they would *glorify* a man whose only claim to posthumous fame is that he saved himself as fast as his horse could carry him, leaving behind him a comrade and two men.'[67]

She knew about the speed of his horse because she had read the letter that he wrote to his wife on the evening of 1 June. How she obtained it is perhaps the biggest mystery in the story of the Prince Imperial's death. About a week after the Prince Imperial's funeral, Mrs Carey was visited by a lady, Miss Octavia Scotchburn, who told her that she was a friend of the Empress and wished to do all she could to help Carey. She persuaded Mrs Carey that Eugénie would be moved to sympathy if she read Carey's letter, and Mrs Carey entrusted it to her. Carey afterwards protested that she had done so without his consent.[68] On 23 July, Miss Scotchburn sent it to Eugénie 'with the permission of his almost broken hearted young wife' and asked Eugénie to read the letter and return it.[69] She received a reply from Eugénie's lady-in-waiting, Mademoiselle de Larminat, stating that 'we' have decided that Eugénie was not at present in a fit state to receive the letter, and that as Miss Scotchburn had asked Eugénie to return the letter, they were returning it at once after making a copy to show to the Empress at a later date.[70]

Neither Eugénie nor any member of her household took any further action about the letter for a month; but on 31 August, at the height of the controversy in the press about Carey's conduct, Eugénie sent the letter to Queen Victoria. She explained that Mrs Carey had arranged for it to be sent to her, hoping no doubt that she would send it to the confirming authorities and that it would influence them in Carey's favour and cause them to quash the sentence of the court martial; but Eugénie had thought that it was more likely to influence them against Carey, and therefore did not think it right to show it to the Queen until after the confirming authorities had taken their decision.[71]

The Queen was interested to know who Miss Scotchburn was, but had difficulty in finding out. Eugénie at first said that she had never met Miss Scotchburn, but afterwards thought that she might perhaps be the English maid of one of her former ladies-in-waiting. Other reports which reached the Queen stated that Miss Scotchburn lived in Dartmouth, that she was aged between thirty-five and fifty, that she was a teacher of foreign languages and music, that she had been in Princess Murat's household in Paris under the Second Empire, and that she had been arrested as a Bonapartist spy in Paris soon after 4 September 1870.[72] She was probably merely a well-intentioned busybody; but her mysterious antecedents, her connection with the bitterly anti-English Caroline Murat, her past activities as a Bonapartist spy in Paris, and certain apparent contradictions in the statements made by the officers of Eugénie's household,* raise the possibility that she may have been less well-intentioned than she made out when she visited Mrs Carey and obtained the incriminating letter from her. If so, we can be sure that Eugénie herself would not have been aware of this.

That letter of 1 June ruined Carey. Queen Victoria became more and more indignant about 'that miserable despicable man *Carey*',[74] and was determined to force him, by social pressure, to leave the army. She sent copies of the letter that he had written to his wife to a large number of people in political life and in the army, as well as to all the members of her family;[75] and when officers who had distinguished themselves in Zululand were invited to Balmoral, she showed them Carey's letter. Nearly all of them made the comments about Carey that she wished to hear; even the Lord Chancellor, who thought it unfortunate that a man's private letter to his wife should be used to ruin him, had no excuses to make for Carey.[76] But Carey stayed on in the army, although his brother officers turned their backs on him in the mess, until he died, a broken man, four years later.

---

*The Duc de Bassano wrote to Carey that he had not shown the incriminating letter to Eugénie until after Carey had made his statements to the press on 22 August; but Eugénie told Queen Victoria that she decided not to make the contents of the letter known as long as the authorities were still considering whether or not to confirm the verdict of the court martial, i.e. before 16 August. It is also strange that Miss Scotchburn should have sent Eugénie (who forwarded it to Queen Victoria) a copy of Miss Scotchburn's letter to Mrs Carey telling her that she had sent Eugénie the incriminating letter 'which you so kindly entrusted to me'. Did Miss Scotchburn wish to provide Eugénie with proof that she had obtained the letter with Mrs Carey's consent?[73]

CHAPTER 44

FARNBOROUGH HILL

THE death of the Prince Imperial ended all possibility of a Bona-partist restoration in France. A few days after the news of his death reached England, Piétri unlocked a drawer in the Prince Imperial's desk at Camden Place and produced the Prince's Will, which the Prince had made in February, just before he sailed for Zululand.[1] In the Will, he appointed Rouher and Piétri as his executors, and Prince Napoleon's son, Prince Victor, to be his successor as head of the Bonaparte family and Emperor, thus by-passing Prince Napoleon, who was next in line of hereditary succession. He inserted a special appeal to Eugénie to support his action.

> With me dead, the duty of continuing the work of Napoleon I and Napoleon III falls on the eldest son of Prince Napoleon, and I hope that my dearly beloved mother, in supporting him to the limit of her power, will give to those of us who are no longer alive this last and supreme proof of her affection.[2]

On 30 June, the Bonapartist Senators and deputies met at Rouher's house in Paris to discuss the Prince Imperial's Will. During their meet-ing they received a cable from Eugénie strongly urging them not to publish the Will; though almost knocked out by her son's death, she had the presence of mind to act in an attempt to prevent the final split with Prince Napoleon which would follow from the announcement of his disinheritance by the Prince Imperial. But Rouher and his colleagues did not heed her request, and published the Will.[3]

Prince Napoleon came to the Prince Imperial's funeral. Eugénie, who remained in seclusion in her room at Camden Place throughout the funeral, sent word to Prince Napoleon and Princess Mathilde asking them to have tea with her afterwards; but though Mathilde accepted the invitation, Prince Napoleon did not. He left Chislehurst im-mediately after the funeral without communicating with Eugénie.[4]

Eugénie was fifty-three when the Prince Imperial died. In the first weeks after she heard of his death, she seemed a broken woman. It was reported that she would enter a convent, and many of her acquaintances thought that she would not long survive. She herself thought so too. Her mother wrote to her from Madrid offering to come to Chislehurst, though she was now aged eighty-five. Eugénie asked her not to come, as she wished to be alone; but she wrote frequently to Maria Manuela, telling her that she wished for death, as all her dear ones were dead; every day that passed was blessed, as it brought her one day nearer death. Her gloom was deepened by the Chislehurst climate that had always depressed her, and by the dreadful weather during the freak summer of 1879, which was one of the coldest ever known in the south of England. She told Maria Manuela that it was colder in Chislehurst in July than in Spain in the winter; but she refused to leave England.[5]

After three months, her grief was as great as ever. 'My dear Mother, I am really *crushed*', she wrote on 5 September;

> I am now alone, a foreigner in the country where I must live and die. At present there still remains a reflection of the sympathy to which great disasters give birth, but soon this will disappear like the furrows that a ship leaves in the sea. One day *The Times* will say that I have snuffed out. Here they will remember my life, the brilliant hours, my griefs, and all will be over. Not one friend will pray at my tomb. Alone in life, alone in death.[6]

But she had another forty-one years of life ahead of her – a new life in new surroundings, where her physical and moral vitality in the end enabled her very largely to throw off her grief and depression. Her first step to recovery was taken at the beginning of October 1879, when she accepted Queen Victoria's invitation to stay for a month at Abergeldie near Balmoral in the Scottish Highlands. She went for walks and excursions, met the Queen several times, and was touched by the kindness and sympathy of the Queen's Highland servant, John Brown.[7]

Her friendship with Queen Victoria was one of the great solaces of her life. When the Queen and the Empress first met at Windsor in 1855 they formed an instant friendship which developed into a much more intimate relationship after 1870. It has often been said that Eugénie was afraid of Queen Victoria and ill at ease with her; but this idea, which emanates from a few remarks by the Queen's private secretary, General Ponsonby,[8] is not borne out by their correspondence, though Eugénie was naturally conscious after 1870 of the differences in their two positions – the one a ruling sovereign, the other a deposed refugee. She was not sure whether she ought to continue treating the Queen as an equal; and when the Queen dropped the formal style in which both of them had written to each other during the Second Empire, Eugénie continued to address the Queen as 'Your Majesty'. After 1870 Queen Victoria wrote to Eugénie 'Ma bien chère Soeur', and ended 'Votre bien affectionnée Soeur et amie'; Eugénie wrote to her 'Madame', ending 'De Votre Majesté la toute dévouée sœur et amie'. This continued until the end of February 1881, when the Queen asked Eugénie to write in the same informal style which she herself used; and on 2 March, Eugénie for the first time began 'Ma bien chère Sœur, Puisque vous voulez que je ne vous écris plus Madame ni Majesté . . .'[9]

In November 1879, Eugénie heard that her mother was dying in Madrid. In view of the urgency, she applied to the French government for permission to travel through France. Her application was granted, but her ship was delayed in the Channel by bad weather, and after a dreadful crossing she missed the train connection and had to stay the night and all next day in Paris before catching the train to Madrid. In Spain, all the railway stations were gaily decorated in honour of the arrival of the King's bride, Princess Maria Cristina of Austria; and Eugénie travelled through the incongruous gaiety only to find that again, as in the case of the deaths of her father and her sister, she was to arrive too late. Again she felt that the news of a bereavement was being kept from her, though this time there was more excuse. King Alfonso came to the station in Madrid to meet her, and no one felt able to tell her that her mother had died until the ceremonies of the meeting with the King had been completed, and she was told the news by the King himself in the carriage after leaving the station. In Madrid she met her old English governess, Miss Flower, who had remained in Maria Manuela's service until her death.[10]

Eugénie was back in Chislehurst before Christmas,[11] making preparations for a visit to Zululand to see the place where the Prince Imperial had been killed. The British government was glad to be able to provide every facility for her journey as a small atonement for the national sense of guilt about the Prince Imperial's death. She was accompanied by General Sir Evelyn Wood, who had served in the Zulu War, by Lady Wood, by the Marquis de Bassano – the son of her Chamberlain the Duc de Bassano – by Dr Scott, who had found the Prince Imperial's body on the day after he was killed, by Lieutenant Slade, who had been a friend of the Prince Imperial at Woolwich, by Captain Bigge – afterwards Lord Stamfordham and private secretary to Queen Victoria and to George V – and by several other officers and ladies, some of whom had been given the duty of writing regular reports to Queen Victoria about the Empress's journey.[12]

They embarked at Southampton on 25 March 1880 on the Union Steamship Company's ship the *German*, which three years before had been the first ship to achieve the target of making the journey from England to Cape Town in under twenty days, taking nineteen days eight-and-a-half hours over the journey. On this occasion the *German* was only a day slower, for she sailed from Plymouth on 26 March and reached Cape Town on 16 April, doing an average of 300 miles a day. Eugénie enjoyed the voyage, though she suffered from the great heat on the Equator. She spent most of her time on deck, knitting, and established a very friendly relationship with Captain Coxwell, the Union Steamship Company's most experienced ship's master who had been specially chosen to command the *German* on this voyage.[13] She talked cheerfully with the officers in her party, correcting their mistakes in French; and she was amused when Lieutenant Slade said to the Marquis de Bassano, who had been slightly indisposed: 'J'espère, Marquis, que vous ne sentez pas mauvais', and Bassano replied: 'J'espère que non.'[14]

After staying for a few days at Government House in Cape Town, Eugénie sailed on to Durban in the *German*. As they sailed out of the harbour at Cape Town, the officers of a French ship, the *D'Estrées*, stood on deck and saluted their former Empress, which greatly pleased her, because she had inspected the *D'Estrées* when she was being built. Enormous crowds turned out to see her arrive in Durban. She and her party went from Durban to Pietermaritzburg, going as far as they could by railway along the newly constructed line which only extended thirty-five miles from Durban. The stations had not yet been built, and the party had to alight at the end of the line at Bolton's Creek on a makeshift platform which had been hastily erected in forty-eight hours for the Empress's arrival; but Eugénie told William Ridley, the resident engineer (my grandfather), that it was the most 'wonderful' railway she had ever travelled on.[15]

The party, which with its escort of mounted police and guides consisted of 86 people and 200 animals, had to go on from Bolton's Creek to Pietermaritzburg, and from there to their destination at Ityotyosi, by horse and spider wagon, travelling the 317 miles from Pietermaritzburg to Ityotyosi in twenty-six days. Eugénie sat in a spider carriage with Lady Wood or with Mrs Campbell, whose husband had been killed in the Zulu War.[16] 'The ladies look very neat in their white Helmets and dust coats', wrote Lieutenant Slade, '& the Empress is quite a picture.'[17]

Eugénie's mood varied greatly from day to day. She had been more cheerful on the ship than at any time since the Prince Imperial's death. She was utterly depressed at Cape Town, weeping bitterly and being unable to speak to the Governor, Sir Bartle Frere, and she was equally depressed on arriving at Durban. On the horse and wagon journey to

Ityotyosi, she was changeable.[18] 'At times she is bright & cheerful, but oftentimes sorely depressed', wrote Captain Bigge to Queen Victoria from Londmann's Drift on 9 May.[19] She sometimes sat sadly in her tent, reading letters written to her by the Prince Imperial five years before; at other times she walked energetically in the evenings after they had bivouacked for the night, on one occasion walking seven miles. She was happier once she got away from the staring crowds at Cape Town and Durban, though she was greatly irritated by an over-zealous authoress, the notorious 'Lady Avonmore', who was writing a popular biography of the Prince Imperial. She pestered Eugénie for an interview, and pursued her the whole way to Ityotyosi; but Wood and Bigge prevented her, almost forcibly, from seeing Eugénie.[20]

Before leaving England, Eugénie had received a letter from a woman whom she did not know, asking her to place some flowers on the grave of her husband who had been killed in Zululand. She insisted on going to the place to perform the mission on her journey to Ityotyosi.[21]

They reached their destination on 25 May and stayed for a week at Ityotyosi, so as to be there on the anniversary of the Prince Imperial's death on 1 June. Eugénie was grief-stricken during the days at Ityotyosi, sleeping badly at nights, eating almost nothing and sustaining herself with beef tea, praying on the spot where her son fell, and planting violets and shrubs around it. But her companions were struck by her kindness and consideration for others, even in the midst of her own grief. One evening at Ityotyosi, Slade, Bigge and Mrs Campbell went out for a long walk and lost their way. When it was already dark they saw a light in the distance, and, making for it, found that it was Eugénie who had come out herself, alone, beyond the edge of the camp, as she was anxious about them and hoped to guide them in with her lamp.[22]

While Eugénie was praying on the fatal spot, Sir Evelyn Wood and Colonel Scott interviewed a number of Zulus who had been members of the band who killed the Prince Imperial. At first the Zulus were afraid to talk, because they feared that they would be punished for having killed the Prince; but after they had been persuaded that no reprisals would be taken against them, they told Wood and Scott that the Prince Imperial had fought more bravely than any enemy they had ever encountered. They added a few details which had not been observed by Trooper Le Tocq or known in Europe, telling how the Prince Imperial had dropped his sword and died fighting with revolver and assegai.[23] Eugénie was taken aback when Wood and Scott told her this; she had formed such a vivid picture in her mind of her son lying dead on the field still grasping his sword in his hand.[24] 'I tried to persuade the Empress', wrote Slade, 'that it was much braver even to turn and defend oneself with one of the enemy's arms than with one's own sword.'[25]

Once 1 June was passed, Eugénie was eager to get back to Chislehurst as soon as possible, and they set off on the return journey, though she was suffering from a sudden attack of sciatica. On 7 June they crossed the battlefield of Isandhlwana, and saw many skulls and bones of dead soldiers. Eugénie insisted that they stop and spend a day covering them over with earth, and herself took part in the work.[26]

She sailed for home from Durban, and landed at St Helena, conscious that 'I am the only person named Bonaparte who will have visited the place where the founder of our race died'.[27] The ship also called at Ascension Island, where a ship's officer stationed on the island who had to return urgently to England, came on board with his five young children, although there was not really room for them in the ship. When Eugénie heard about this, she gave up one of her party's rooms to the family, and with her usual love of children spoke to them often on the voyage and gave each of them a golden sovereign.[28]

While Eugénie was in Africa, a political controversy of which she knew nothing had been raging in England about the Prince Imperial. Soon after the Prince's death, a committee was formed, with the Prince of Wales and two of his brothers as Presidents and Lord Sydney as Chairman, to arrange for the erection of a monument to him by public subscription; and the Dean of Westminster agreed that the monument should be placed in Westminster Abbey. A storm of protest arose from the Radicals in Britain and from the Republican government in France, who had heard an untrue rumour that the Prince would be referred to on the monument as 'Napoleon IV'. The Dean refused to give way to pressure, and the Queen, though she would personally have preferred to have had the monument at Windsor, was determined that there should be no retreat in the face of the Radical clamour and that the scheme to erect it in the Abbey must go ahead.[29]

One of the leaders of the opposition to the monument was the Radical freethinker, Frederic Harrison. 'The Abbey is the resting place of great Englishmen, not of foreign conspirators', he declared. 'To carve on it a name which stands for treachery and bloodshed, and so to make it serve the plot against a friendly people, is an outrage. . . . The French people tell us this is being done at Royal suggestion. I can only say that if the English Monarchy ever sinks so low as to make common cause with the dregs of the Corsican banditti, it will perish as they have done.'[30]

Fourteen Liberal M.P.s formed a committee to oppose the erection of the monument. On 15 July 1880 a packed public meeting was held in St James's Hall in Westminster to protest against it, and three eminent Liberal historians – John Morley, R. A. Freeman and J. A. Froude – supported the opposition movement. Next day a resolution protesting against the proposed monument was carried in the House of Commons by a majority of 15 votes.[31]

The Queen was 'shocked and disgusted' at the action of the House and at the opposition to the erection of a monument to 'a Young Prince who *fell because* of the *cowardly Desertion* of a *British* officer',[32] and asked 'What is to be done? to this disgracefully illbehaved H. of Cs.'[33] But in view of the opposition and the vote of the House Lord Sydney announced that the Memorial Committee had decided to abandon the scheme to erect the monument in the Abbey.[34] 'It is disgraceful', wrote Queen Victoria. 'The Queen will for the future do all she can to prevent any P^{rce} British or foreign from being *buried there* again!'[35]

She had always preferred St George's Chapel at Windsor to the Abbey as the site for the monument, and announced that it would be erected there.[36] There were new protests. A petition was sent to the Dean of Windsor protesting against the plan to erect a monument to 'the reckless as most unfortunate adventurer, the late Louis, reputed son of the Ex-Emperor Napoleon the Corsican' in 'St George's hallowed Shrine commemorating British valour and deeds of glory won on the fields of Cressy, Poictiers, and Agincourt, in the Middle Ages, down to that of Waterloo in the present century'; it was a '*Jesuitical* attempt of the French Imperialists connived at by the late Jewish alien administration, guided by the Brompton Oratorians, Cardinal Manning and their Cobourg-Belgic affiliations'.[37] But the Queen had one conclusive answer to the protests: 'It is *my* Royal Chapel.'[38]

Eugénie landed at Southampton on 27 July. The Queen and her other friends hoped that no one would tell her about the resolution of the House of Commons against the Prince Imperial monument; but she heard about it from an indignant Frenchwoman who wrote to her from France. She then demanded to see a full report of the debate in the House, and after reading it, wrote to Queen Victoria to ask her not to erect the monument at Windsor, for if she did, the Radicals would launch an attack on the Queen and the monarchy. She also decided to leave England and live at Arenenberg in protest against the attitude of the House of Commons. Eventually she was persuaded to stay in England, and to withdraw her objection to the monument at Windsor, by General Sir Lintorn Simmons, who had been Governor of the Military Academy at Woolwich when the Prince Imperial was there, by Sir Evelyn Wood and Lord Sydney, and by Algernon Borthwick, the editor of *The Morning Post*.[39] When she saw the monument by J. E. Boehm in St George's Chapel, she liked it.[40] As for Queen

Victoria, she declared enthusiastically that the monument was 'one of the finest productions of modern Art'.[41]

But though Eugénie ultimately decided not to leave England, she was determined to leave Chislehurst. The late nineteenth century was not a period when simple little churches like St Mary's at Chislehurst were appreciated; Eugénie wished to build an enormous mausoleum for Napoleon III and the Prince Imperial, like the mausoleum that Queen Victoria had built for Prince Albert at Frogmore. Her neighbour at Chislehurst, who hated Roman Catholics, was unwilling to sell her the land for this purpose; and in any case, she was determined to leave Camden Place, which held so many unhappy memories for her.[42] When she first went there in 1870 she was lamenting everything that she had lost in France; afterwards she lamented the loss of Napoleon III, and, as she wrote later, failed to appreciate her good fortune in having a son who was still living.[43] Now it held the most tragic memories of all – of those days in June and July 1879 when she had sat, day after day, alone in the dark room brooding over the Prince Imperial's death.

On the advice of Sir Lintorn Simmons,[44] she bought Farnborough Hill, the house at Farnborough in Hampshire belonging to Thomas Longman the publisher. It stood on elevated ground to the north of the town of Farnborough, with a fine view over its fields to the east as far as the railway line. Eugénie also bought a large tract of park and woodland, including a lake, to the west on the other side of the road from Farnborough to Camberley. The road was a quiet country lane in Eugénie's time, though her friends lived to see it develop into a dual carriageway with an almost continuous stream of traffic.[45]

The house, which had been built in 1860, was a striking example of mid-Victorian gothic style. It had twenty-three rooms, but Eugénie thought that this would be too small for her, so she decided to add a new wing with another eighteen rooms. She also began to build the great mausoleum, about half a mile to the south of the house. When completed, its dome rose high into the sky and could be seen for several miles around, and Eugénie could see it from the window of her drawing-room. She would bring the bodies of Napoleon III and the Prince Imperial here, and when she herself died her body was also to be laid to rest there.[46] She built an abbey beside the mausoleum, and arranged for some Premonstratensian monks to come from France, where things were not so agreeable now for monks as in the days of the Second Empire; their duties were to say masses for the dead three times a year – on 9 January, 5 May and 1 June, the anniversaries of the deaths of Napoleon III, Napoleon I and the Prince Imperial. Later the Premonstratensians were replaced by Benedictines from a monastery at Storrington in Sussex.

She did not move into Farnborough Hill until the work of enlargement had been carried out, but she would not stay any longer at Camden Place. She left Chislehurst on 23 March 1881, 'saying farewell for ever to that house where I have lived and suffered',[47] and moved to Coombe Cottage, a house near Kingston upon Thames that she rented from the Baring family; it had fine views across the country as far as Wimbledon.[48] She only returned to Chislehurst for the Mass in St Mary's church for her husband and son on 9 January and 1 June in every year; and after their bodies were moved to Farnborough Abbey in January 1888, she only once returned to Chislehurst. On 20 February 1890, along with the Prince of Wales and many other distinguished personages, she went to Chislehurst to attend Lord Sydney's funeral; but she never again set foot in Chislehurst during the remaining thirty years of her life, though she was living only forty miles away at Farnborough. When Father Goddard, the Roman Catholic priest at Chislehurst who had been at Napoleon III's deathbed, asked her to visit Chislehurst, she sent him, through her secretary, an abrupt refusal.[49]

When she returned to places of happier memories, the result could also be painful. Although she had always reproached the Italians for their ingratitude to Napoleon III, in 1881 a monument to him was erected by public subscription in Milan. Eugénie attended the unveiling ceremony, and she was again given permission to travel through France.[50] The animosities of the past were beginning to disappear; even the Communard prisoners in New Caledonia were amnestied in 1880. On her return journey from Milan in October, Eugénie stayed with the Duchesse de Mouchy in the Boulevard de Courcelles in Paris. She visited Notre-Dame, where she had been married and her son had been christened, and Fontainebleau, which was quite unchanged. At Fontainebleau she was recognized by the Keeper, who was most surprised to see her, as her visit to Paris had not been reported in the press, and he and all the staff of the palace welcomed her warmly. When she entered the Prince Imperial's apartments she burst into tears, and the palace officials and the ladies and gentlemen of her retinue withdrew and closed the door behind them, leaving her alone with her memories. She wandered among the ruins of Saint-Cloud and the weeds of the abandoned gardens. An old servant had remained there as a caretaker, and he recognized her, burst into tears, and knelt and repeatedly kissed her hand. She felt like someone who had been dead for centuries and had come to life again, only to find that all the people she knew had long since died.[51]

When she returned to England she rented a house in Princes Gate in London, but spent a great deal of time at Farnborough Hill, for she found that the builders, who were getting on with the work very slowly, worked a little faster when she was there to hurry them up. In the spring of 1882 she finally moved to Farnborough Hill, which was her principal place of residence during the remaining thirty-eight years of her life.[52]

The house was only a few miles from the military centre of Aldershot. Both Eugénie's Conservative politics and her romantic nature attracted her to the British army. She never failed to send a telegram of congratulation to Queen Victoria when news arrived of some British victory in the colonial wars of the 1880s and 1890s, though it was as a mother, not as an Anglophil, that she sent a telegram of sympathy to Lady Randolph Churchill when her son Winston was taken prisoner by the Boers during the Boer War.[53] Eugénie became friends with many of the high-ranking army officers stationed at Aldershot, especially with those who had known the Prince Imperial at Woolwich or in Zululand. When Queen Victoria's son, the Duke of Connaught, who was the general in command of the garrison at Aldershot, drove past the gates of Farnborough Hill in November 1894, he saw Eugénie standing at the roadside in front of the lodge with her former lady-in-waiting, Madame de Gallifet, and Gordon Barnet, the proprietor of the *New York Herald Tribune*, to watch the Rifle Brigade march past. The Duke, noticing that Madame de Gallifet was 'still very good looking' and 'had a wonderful skirt on', got out of his carriage to greet the Empress.[54]

One of the military residents of Farnborough seemed likely to be a less congenial neighbour. Part of the wood on the other side of the road belonged to Captain Greene, a retired army officer who remembered Waterloo and had always hated the French and the Bonapartes. When Eugénie came to Farnborough Hill she wished to buy part of his land, but he firmly refused to sell, and made it known that he would not permit the Empress to trespass in his woods. He did not, however, erect any impassable barrier between their two properties, and one day when Eugénie and a lady-in-waiting were strolling in the wood, she realized that she had ventured on to Captain Greene's property. She was about to beat a hasty retreat and escape before she was caught there, when she ran straight into him round a bend in the path. She apologized for trespassing so charmingly that she completely appeased his anger, and they became friends. She invited him to dine at Farnborough Hill and he sometimes sent her pheasants as a gift for her table, though she could never persuade him to sell his part of the wood to her.[55]

Eugénie soon found that leaving Chislehurst was not enough to make her forget her griefs. It took twenty years before she recovered from the blow of the Prince Imperial's death. Her moments of cheerfulness and her delight in her new surroundings soon gave way to utter depression. 'Poor Empress Eugenia!', wrote the German Empress Augusta, 'she is one of the most unhappy women I know.'[56] She seemed to meet death everywhere. She was deeply affected when the ladies and servants of her household died,[57] and felt that 'Death has come so often to strike down our little colony that we seem every year to pay a higher tribute than our neighbours'.[58] Even her religious faith was shaken. 'I prayed so much for my son when he left', she wrote to the Duchesse de Mouchy in 1899, 'that I no longer trust in prayer, as he was not returned to me, and I can no longer pray. It is wrong to say "Pray and it will be granted to you", for then what mother would lose her son?'[59]

Anniversaries always reduced her to despair – not only the tragic dates of 9 January and 1 June, but also New Year's Day, with its memories of the receptions at the Tuileries, the Bonapartist *Fête Nationale* of 15 August, and her saint's day on 15 November. She dreaded their approach, and was always relieved when they had passed.[60]

Her visit to Fontainebleau and the ruins of Saint-Cloud in 1881 had been a painful experience, and after this she tried as far as possible to avoid the places which she associated with the past. She never again went to Arenenberg after the Prince Imperial's death, and presented it as a gift to the canton of Thurgau.[61] She was in Paris in December 1888 and planned to spend Christmas there with the Duchesse de Mouchy; but she suddenly shrank from the prospect of a Christmas in Paris for the first time without Napoleon III and the Prince Imperial, and on Christmas Eve she left Paris for London,[62] and spent Christmas in Brown's Hotel in Dover Street. She wrote to Queen Victoria:

I preferred the cold which grips the heart in a banal hotel bedroom to the feeling of isolation in the midst of the noise of a great city where one has lived for so many happy years. I have revisited the places where I lived, of which not a trace remains; the ruins themselves have been destroyed; nothing remains, absolutely nothing.[63]

Her depression affected her health, and her poor health intensified her depression. She suffered from rheumatism, gout, neuralgia and headaches, and often from coughs, colds and 'flu. She underwent a course of massage from the famous Dutch specialist, Dr Metzger, who had developed massage as a new and fashionable remedy, and she spent several weeks in Amsterdam being treated by him in the summer and autumn of 1887 and again in the autumn of 1888; but she was in no mood to appreciate the beauties of Amsterdam, and on her autumn visits complained of the cold and the fogs of Holland in November. In her state of ill-health and gloom, she found it hard to find a climate which suited her. She had so often complained of the rain at Chislehurst and the necessity for fires in July, but the hot weather and drought of August 1893, combined with the anniversary date of 15 August, distressed her. She had never known it so hot in England; the heat was suffocating even at night; at the seaside there was always a little breeze, but not at Farnborough.[64]

The death of the Prince Imperial had made her lose all interest in French politics. 'If you knew how much what is called politics disgusts and wounds me',[65] she wrote in one of her last letters to her mother. But a sense of duty to the Bonaparte family, if not to the Bonapartist cause, always roused her to action in a crisis. In January 1883, Prince Napoleon went to Paris and placarded the streets with an appeal for a referendum to be held to decide whether the people wished for a continuation of the Republic or a return to the Empire. He was arrested and charged with sedition. The Conservative Bonapartists in Paris promptly repudiated him. Eugénie again leapt to his defence, and risked seriously compromising her position in England, as well as arrest in France, in a desperate attempt to preserve Bonapartist unity.

On 22 January she arrived in Paris, and summoned a meeting of the Bonapartist leaders in the Hôtel du Rhin in the Place Vendôme, choosing the hotel which Louis Napoleon had used as his headquarters during his presidential election campaign in 1848. She pleaded with them not to issue a statement denouncing Prince Napoleon; but they refused to follow her advice, as they had done about the Prince Imperial's Will, and she returned to Farnborough on 24 January.[66] Queen Victoria had been very worried about her safety while she was in Paris, as she had no idea that she was going there.[67] Eugénie had been careful not to tell her in advance so as not to compromise her in French politics; but when she returned to Farnborough Hill, she explained to the Queen why she had gone to Paris:

If my relations with Prince Napoleon had been everything that they ought to be, there would have been no need for me to act as I did, having no need either to approve or criticize his actions; but everybody knew what our relations were, and they were being used against him like a weapon. I thought it my duty to bring back unity into the family by giving the Prince my moral support on this occasion.[68]

She afterwards told the Queen that Prince Napoleon 'had behaved very well'.[69]

Prince Napoleon was brought before the court on 9 February and acquitted on the grounds that he had not incited violence or committed any criminal offence in issuing his proclamation. He was released from prison and expelled from France by order of the government. He came to London, and in May went to Farnborough to thank Eugénie for her exertions on his behalf; and on 1 June he attended the memorial Mass for the Prince Imperial at Chislehurst. He came for a more prolonged visit five years later, when he and his wife and daughter stayed with Eugénie at Farnborough Hill in June 1888. He was there for a week, and Marie Clotilde, with whom Eugénie had always been friendly, stayed on with her daughter after he had left.[70]

In March 1891 Prince Napoleon died in Rome. His family hastened to his bedside, but he refused to see his eldest son, Prince Victor, whom he had disowned after the Prince Imperial had appointed Victor as his successor. Prince Napoleon disinherited Victor, his daughter and his wife Princess Clotilde, and left all his property to his second son, Prince Louis, who lived in Russia and was serving as an officer in the Russian army; and he appointed Prince Louis to succeed him as Emperor and head of the family. Eugénie was particularly disgusted with Prince Napoleon's action in disinheriting Marie Clotilde, who had nursed him devotedly throughout his last illness, although he had not spoken one word to her; but though Eugénie confided her feelings, in the strictest confidence, to Queen Victoria, she did not utter a word of criticism in public of Prince Napoleon's conduct and did nothing to encourage the rumours in the press.[71]

Prince Napoleon's Will was void under French law, which required a father to leave part of his property to his eldest son; but the family did not contest the Will, and Prince Louis, who was on excellent terms with his mother, brother and sister, made the necessary provisions for them.[72] The family met at Moncalieri on 31 March, and decided to recognize Prince Victor as Emperor. Next day they visited Eugénie, who was on holiday at San Remo. It was the last occasion on which a reunion of the Bonaparte family aroused interest, speculation and anxiety in the world press. Large crowds assembled to see Eugénie drive to the station at San Remo to meet them. She took them to the Hotel Victoria, where they stayed for two days holding banquets and discussions. They informed the press that the talks were concerned only with family matters, and were entirely non-political.[73]

CHAPTER 45

A NEW LIFE

FROM San Remo Eugénie crossed the frontier into France and spent several weeks in the spring and summer of 1891 at the Cap Martin Hotel at Cap Martin near Monte Carlo. The hotel had been built by an English company, and though at the moment it stood alone among the pinewoods on the deserted promontory, the company hoped to develop the area by building villas for wealthy visitors. Eugénie went there again next year, when Queen Victoria's grandson, Prince George – afterwards King George V – also stayed in the hotel. 'She likes Cap Martin so much', wrote Prince George, 'that she has just bought some land on it, where she is going to build herself a villa.'[1] She was sure that it would be a good investment, and that the land would soon be worth double what she was paying for it.[2]

At Cap Martin, as at Farnborough Hill, she had trouble with the builders, and here too she found that she could only get them to work properly by staying in the half-finished house.[3] She therefore stayed in the villa during the phenomenally cold winter of 1894–5, and became depressed, because 'the Midi without its blue sky and the light is more gloomy than the North'.[4] It was no longer 1854, when she was young and beautiful and the wife of a dictator, and could inspire the Paris builders to repair the Élysée in seventy-two hours for the reception for the Duke of Cambridge and Lord Raglan.

She named the villa the Villa Cyrnos – the Greek word for Corsica – and some years later built another almost identical villa near by for her guests, which she named the Villa Teba.[5] After 1893 she stayed at the Villa Cyrnos nearly every year during the late winter and early spring.[6] It had the advantage of being an area with no earlier associations for her. The Riviera had been a fashionable holiday resort for wealthy foreigners, especially the English, since the 1850s, but it was a part of France which Eugénie had not known when she was Empress; apart from the state visit to Nice in 1860 after the annexation, the frequent press reports of her impending visits to the Riviera during the Second Empire had always proved to be unfounded. Cap Martin, like Farnborough Hill, was a new district where she could lead a new life.

She never went across to the west coast of France to see Biarritz, where in due course the Villa Eugénie vanished, like the Tuileries and Saint-Cloud; it was accidentally burned down in 1903.[7]

The French were beginning to forget the Bonapartes. In 1892 Pope Leo XIII issued an encyclical instructing the French Catholics to accept the Republic as their lawful government; and a few years later the Dreyfus affair gave the traditional right-wing forces in France a new cause to which to rally. The army, the Church and the peasantry, who forty years earlier had looked to Louis Napoleon to save them from the Reds, formed the mainstay of the anti-Dreyfusard cause. The new violent wave of anti-semitism was led by Drumont in *La Libre Parole*. He claimed that Eugénie, as a pious Catholic, must be one of his supporters and a good anti-semite, conveniently forgetting her friendship with the Rothschilds and the other Jews at court under the Second Empire; but Eugénie refused to permit him to name her as one of his supporters.[8] Most of her Bonapartist friends were anti-Dreyfusards, but she herself was convinced of Dreyfus's innocence, perhaps because she lived in England, where Queen Victoria and nearly all the British Establishment were pro-Dreyfus.[9]

The Dreyfus affair aroused the most bitter passions in France, and led to a breach of personal relations between Dreyfusards and anti-Dreyfusards; but Eugénie maintained her friendship with her acquaintances in both camps, though on one occasion the learned Byzantine scholar, Professor Schlumberger, refused to shake hands with the Prince of Monaco at the Villa Cyrnos because the Prince had written a letter to the press inviting Madame Dreyfus to be his guest in Monaco.[10] Schlumberger had first met Eugénie on a mountain path near Les Eaux-Bonnes when he was aged nine and the Empress was on holiday there in the summer of 1854. When their mutual acquaintance, Dr Darralde, presented him to her, the little boy forgot to remove his hat, and she lifted it from his head 'with a charming gesture', telling him that a man must always take off his hat to a woman.[11] This began a friendship which not even *l'Affaire Dreyfus* could disrupt.

Eugénie's connections with England and France had not lessened her love of Spain, and her patriotic fervour was stirred by the Cuban revolt against Spain and the war between Spain and the United States in 1898. The Spaniards hoped that the European powers would intervene on their side, but they all remained neutral and left Spain to her fate. Eugénie's Spanish relatives asked her to use her influence on behalf of Spain; but she had been too near the centre of power in the old days to have any illusions that she could still influence the course of events.[12] 'What am I except only Eugenia Guzman, and no longer young?'[13]

She tried as tactfully as possible to use her friendship with Queen Victoria when the Queen, who was staying at Nice, visited her at Cap Martin in the spring of 1898; but she knew that it was useless. She told Paca's daughter-in-law, Rosario, Duchess of Alba, that she had tried to win Queen Victoria's sympathy by talking more about the Queen Regent and the little King Alfonso XIII than about Spain,

> because impressions are so lasting in her country that they are still in the time of the Spanish Armada; she listened to me, her eyes full of sympathy, but did not say a word: she had again become the con- stitutional Queen with her ministers as the only political organ of her country; it drove me to despair![14]

Eugénie shared the indignation of the Spaniards when the British Prime Minister, Lord Salisbury, in a speech that was everywhere interpreted as referring to the Spanish-American War, declared that there were 'living' and 'dying' nations in the world, and that the living nations would inevitably replace the dying nations as the leaders of world power.[15] She was not impressed by the admiration which her English friends expressed for the courage of the Spanish soldiers and sailors; she thought that English policy was: 'If you are weak we admire you, if you are strong we will help you.'[16] She decided to stay in Paris until the war was over, as she was so irritated by the British attitude.[17]

She gave her friends in Spain the benefit of her political experience, urging them to grant independence to Cuba at once; if they did not sacrifice Cuba, they would lose the Philippines as well. It would be easier to hold the Philippines than Cuba, because there the American navy would be fighting further from its bases, and the European powers, who cared nothing for Spain or Cuba, might act to keep the United States out of Asia; and Spain should try to win the friendship of Japan, which was a rising power in the Far East. She even urged her Spanish relatives to seek the support of the German Emperor William II, whose proposal for international mediation had been turned down by the British government, and she encouraged her friend Mr Barnet of the *New York Herald Tribune* to publish articles supporting the war against Spain, as this would enable him to retain political influence in the United States which might be useful during the peace negotiations.[18]

Meanwhile, if the Spanish government were to salvage the Philip- pines by a compromise peace, it was essential to start a movement in Spain in favour of peace, and she offered to subsidize a press campaign for peace.[19] 'Talking like an Englishwoman, do you think it would be possible – it would be easy in London – to form a Ladies League which in the name of humanity would call for peace?'[20] But her advice was not adopted, and in the peace treaty Spain was forced to grant independence to Cuba and to cede the Philippines and Puerto Rico to the United States.

She had thought and acted purely as a patriotic Spaniard during the Spanish-American war; but she expected her Spanish relations to pander to her personal and Bonapartist prejudices, even when this interfered with their public duties in Spain. On two occasions, this led to a quarrel with her nephew Carlos, sixteenth Duke of Alba, and his wife Rosario. After Maria Manuela's death, Rosario, along with Queen Victoria, became the chief correspondent to whom Eugénie confided her innermost feelings; but in 1893 Alba was sent by the Queen Regent of Spain to congratulate King Umberto of Italy on his silver wedding. Eugénie was furious, and thought that in view of her well-known opposition to the royal house of Savoy and to Italian unification in the past, it was an affront to her that her nephew Alba should have been sent on this mission. Her attitude seems particularly unreasonable, as she had not only frequently visited Italy but had been very favourably impressed by King Umberto's tactful handling of the situation when Prince Napoleon was dying two years before.[21] 'Please let your husband know', she wrote to Rosario – ordinarily she always referred to Alba as 'Carlos' – 'that if he is intending to go home by way of here, he should not do so . . . because it will be impossible for me to receive him.'[22] Rosario wrote to say that she could not understand why Eugénie objected to Alba's performing the duty which the Queen Regent had assigned to him. 'My dear niece,' replied Eugénie, 'you are much too intelligent not to understand why I am hurt.'[23]

She was pleased when Alba was sent to Buenos Aires in April 1901, hoping that it would renew the links between Spain and her lost colonies;[24] but there was a second quarrel in July, when Alba invited the Duke of Orleans, Louis Philippe's great-grandson, to meet members of the Spanish government at the Liria Palace. Eugénie was so angry that she cancelled her plans to visit Spain and asked Rosario how people in Madrid would feel if she invited the Carlist pretender to meet Lord Lansdowne, the British Foreign Secretary, at Farnborough Hill.[25]

Earlier in the year she had lost her friend Queen Victoria, whom she had seen for the last time at Cowes in August 1900, when she had with difficulty persuaded the Queen not to risk crossing from her yacht to Eugénie's in the open sea, but to wait until the two yachts were alongside in the harbour.[26] 'The Queen is dying,' she wrote to Rosario on 22 January 1901, 'she will not last out the day. . . . For me it is an immense loss. . . . I shall feel more than ever a foreigner and alone in this country; I am profoundly sad and discouraged.'[27]

She was losing the friends, not only of her own generation, but of the younger generation as well. In October 1901, Alba died. She was profoundly affected, despite their recent quarrel. 'All my dear ones have been taken from me one after the other', she wrote to Rosario. 'What a sad end to my life!'[28]

Then, at the age of seventy-five and the beginning of the twentieth century, Eugénie began a new life. It was as if, with all her old friends dead and no one to whom she could confide her past sorrows, she became a different person, infected by the youthful spirit of the great-nephews and great-nieces and the other young people who surrounded her in the optimism of Edwardian England at the dawn of the golden new century. For twenty years after the Prince Imperial's death, she had constantly stated that she longed for death; during the next twenty years she often said cheerfully that she had died in 1870.[29]

Her young Spanish relatives came to England every year for the polo season, and stayed at Farnborough Hill. There was Paca's grandson, the seventeenth Duke of Alba, 'Jimmy Alba', who later became Alfonso XIII's Foreign Minister and General Franco's Ambassador in London; his brother Hernando, Duke of Peñaranda, who was killed by a revolutionary mob as a Franco supporter during the Spanish Civil War; and Fernando, Count of Mora, who married Eugénie's cousin Solange, Ferdinand de Lesseps's daughter, and carried out experiments with electrical apparatus at Farnborough Hill.[30] The Peñaranda title was one of the three that Eugénie held which carried with it the rank of Grandee, and she assigned it and the Grandeeship to Hernando.[31] Eugénie's niece Antonia de Nava de Tajo married a Frenchman, Pierre d'Attainville, and later, after his death, took Eugénie's secretary Bacciochi as her second husband. Antonia lived with Eugénie at Farnborough Hill as her most intimate lady-in-waiting.

The young people enjoyed themselves at Farnborough Hill. They played hockey, and took part in cycle races on a cycle track – *la piste* – which Eugénie had constructed for them in her park. The tennis was less satisfactory, because Eugénie, despite the protests of the young people, gave in to her gardener's demand that the smallest possible area should be taken from the garden when the court was being built, with the result that the run-back behind the base lines was quite insufficient to enable them to play a serious game.[32] They smoked cigarettes, and sat up late at night, after Eugénie had gone to bed, telling each other stories about her love affairs and attempted suicides as a young girl in Spain which they had read about in the popular biographies of Eugénie which frequently appeared after Clara Tschudi set the fashion in 1899.

They treated the Empress with all the proper etiquette. Her nieces curtsied to her every morning when they greeted her and when they wished her good-night, and she was still able to delight them with her famous *révérence de l'Impératrice*[33] – her graceful acknowledging curtsy which had been famous under the Second Empire. The entry to dinner was a formal and picturesque ritual. The guests lined up in the hall and walked in order of precedence behind the Empress, whose long train of her evening dress trailed on the ground behind her.[34] Once seated at table, Eugénie could relax to the extent of taking off her shoes, as she had always done at dinner, even at the Tuileries, knowing that no one would notice, as she would be the first to rise from the table; but the secret became known one evening when someone lost a ring, and it was found inside one of Eugénie's shoes when she slipped her feet into them again at the end of the meal.[35]

They all addressed her in the third person as 'Sa Majesté' and 'Elle'; but she was often referred to in the press and elsewhere as 'the ex-Empress Eugénie'. This greatly annoyed her, not so much because of injured pride as because it was inaccurate. 'I may be the ex-Empress of the French,' she said, 'but I am still the Empress Eugénie.'[36]

She maintained her friendship with the British royal family after Queen Victoria's death.[37] She visited King Edward VII on his yacht at Cowes during his convalescence in August 1902 and heard from him all the details of his operation for perityphlitis which had caused the postponement of his coronation;[38] and several members of the royal family visited her at Farnborough Hill. She had always felt great affection for Princess Beatrice, who had so often accompanied Queen Victoria on her visits; and after Princess Beatrice's daughter, Princess Ena, married King Alfonso XIII of Spain, the King and Queen of Spain were guests at Farnborough Hill.[39] Her Bonaparte and Murat relations by marriage often came, including the head of the family, Prince Victor Bonaparte, with his wife Princess Clémentine, the daughter of King Leopold II of the Belgians.

She was perturbed by the frequency with which the sovereigns whom she knew were assassinated at the turn of the century. She had liked the Empress Elizabeth of Austria ever since their first meeting at Salzburg in 1867, when they had admired each other's legs and measured the thickness of their calves;[40] and she warmly praised Elizabeth's beauty to Queen Victoria. Afterwards, the Empress was her guest at Cap Martin.[41] In 1898, the Empress Elizabeth was assassinated by an Anarchist in Geneva. Eugénie did not like the Italian royal family, but she was shocked at the assassination of King Umberto in 1900, and of the King of Portugal and his son in 1908. She was particularly disgusted at the unsuccessful attempt on the lives of King Alfonso and Queen Ena on their wedding day in Madrid in 1906:[42] 'I cannot believe that in the classical land of Don Quixote, a young and pretty woman should be subjected to such an attempt on her wedding day.'[43] She was always sensitive where Spain was concerned. She was indignant at the anti-Spanish propaganda in the world press which followed the summary execution of the Anarchist leader, Ferrer, in Barcelona in 1909, and saw in it the dangerous hand of 'the International'.[44]

Eugénie maintained her friendship with Sir Lintorn and Lady Simmons, with General Sir William Butler and his artist wife, and with Sir Evelyn Wood.[45] When Sir Evelyn came to play tennis at Farnborough Hill, he wore a frock-coat and top hat with his white flannels and tennis shoes, and knelt on the gravel path near the tennis court to kiss the Empress's hand.[46] Eugénie got to know Ethel Smyth soon after she moved to Farnborough Hill.[47] Ethel Smyth was a keen cyclist, and would ride her bicycle up the drive of Farnborough Hill wearing the fashionable cycling bloomers; but thinking that Eugénie would object to her wearing trousers, she would nip into the bushes beside the drive and change into a skirt before arriving at the house, not knowing that Eugénie knew what she was doing and was laughing about it.[48]

On one occasion – unless this was another of Eugénie's good stories – Ethel Smyth came to blows with Eugénie's young cousin Solange de Lesseps in the passage at Farnborough Hill, as a result of a quarrel between Ethel Smyth and Solange's exuberant fiancé Fernando, Count of Mora. Eugénie told Isabel Vesey that she was in the little drawing-room with Antonia d'Attainville, when Antonia, 'hearing a commotion, hurried out and found Miss Smyth and Solange exchanging resounding blows'. Antonia 'hustled Ethel out of the house' before Fernando appeared on the scene.[49]

Ethel Smyth was a keen suffragette, and composed a march for the women's suffrage movement, though she never took part in any violent action for the cause. She introduced Mrs Pankhurst to Eugénie, who was very favourably impressed by the suffragette leader. Ethel Smyth states that Eugénie was 'an ardent suffragist'.[50] Eugénie had always been in favour of increasing the opportunities open to women. She had astounded her hearers in 1853 by suggesting that an Order, like the Legion of Honour, should be created for women. When she was Regent in 1865 she had awarded the Legion of Honour to Rosa Bonheur, the painter, the first woman to receive it. She had tried unsuccessfully to persuade the Académie Française to admit George Sand as its first woman member, but had succeeded in her attempts to allow women to work in the Post Office.[51] But if Ethel Smyth persuaded her to support the women's suffrage movement, Eugénie had changed her mind since she had ridiculed a demand for women's suffrage in Spain in 1876.[52] In any case, she took care not to express an opinion in public about issues of British politics. For this reason, she firmly resisted the repeated efforts of a lady who lived near by to persuade her to join the local branch of the Primrose League, and was very amused at the lady's persistence.[53]

The household at Farnborough Hill was a very happy one, united by its devotion to the Empress; but there were a few unhappy dissentients there. Ethel Smyth states that, though ordinarily very kindhearted, Eugénie 'was capable, even in the case of old friends and old servants, of a curious harshness that would amaze and puzzle'.[54] She inspired the deepest love and devotion in so many, and yet a small minority of individuals, like Prince Napoleon and Princess Caroline Murat, hated her with great intensity. Her housemaid at Farnborough Hill, Adela Cox – today Mrs Mason – resented the discipline in the household and did not like the foreigners there. One of her duties was to go into the Empress's bedroom every morning and draw back the curtains; but during her two years in her service Eugénie never once spoke to her, as Napoleon III would almost certainly have done. She remembers how, if the bolster was badly placed in the Empress's bed, Eugénie would wake the housemaids at eleven o'clock at night and make them come and arrange it properly;[55] but other servants spoke of her kindness to them and her interest in their well-being and comforts.

At eighty-three, she still had a touch of her old instinct to tease. When she travelled from London to Paris in February 1909 she amused herself on the train journey in France by preventing her old secretary, Piétri, from falling asleep, gently kicking him and chiding him: 'Piétri, are you asleep? What an idea! You are not tired!'[56]

An even more unhappy member of the household than Adela Cox was Eugénie's lady-in-waiting, Mademoiselle d'Allonville, who was the great-niece of Barras and afterwards married the Marchese de Smours. She wrote bitterly about Eugénie in her unpublished memoirs. She was unhappy at Farnborough Hill from the day of her arrival on 3 February 1890, when she was shown into the room which Eugénie herself had prepared for her – 'that room in which I was destined to suffer so much'[57] – until her departure eighteen years later after the last of a series of quarrels with Eugénie. She did everything wrong, was unpopular with everyone, and was constantly scolded by Eugénie. Despite all Mademoiselle d'Allonville's efforts, Eugénie refused to allow her to present her relations to her; and when, in an attempt to show her sense of humour, Mademoiselle d'Allonville rode her bicycle straight into a group of Eugénie's young relatives and friends who were taking part in cycle races on *la piste*, she was roundly abused by Eugénie in front of everybody and forbidden to ride a bicycle again.[58] Her resentment was all the greater because she rigidly refrained from making any criticism of the Empress to her friends or to the newspapers; and ten years after she left Eugénie's service, she was writing bitterly that Eugénie would probably live to be a hundred and would continue 'to let slip the years of grace which God in His inexhaustible mercy grants to her without any effort to do good, or even to try to make amends for the ill she has done'.[59]

Everyone was amazed by Eugénie's physical vitality. In the 1880s most of her friends, like Queen Victoria, had thought of her as 'the poor Empress' who had suffered so much and looked old, ill and haggard, and so different from the beautiful, carefree young Empress of the Tuileries and Saint-Cloud;[60] to her young companions of the 1900s, she was the wonderfully active and high-spirited old lady whose youth was for them a legend, not a memory. When she was over seventy she learned to ride a bicycle, and though she did not take part in the races on *la piste*, she wobbled along slowly, with a servant walking alongside ready to catch her if she fell off.[61] She walked briskly in her garden and her park, and sometimes in the town of Farnborough, and to the east side of her estate to the house where her land agent, Thomas Lancaster, lived.[62] It was many years since she had mounted a horse, but she could indulge both her love of horses and her love of children in talking to Lancaster's little daughter and her Welsh cob. Lancaster strongly objected when Prince Victor and Princess Clémentine strolled all over his garden without asking his permission; but Eugénie never did, and if she wished to see him she walked up to the front door and knocked.[63]

She spent much of her time reading, until her eyes began to fail at the very end of her life. She read *The Times* every day and the latest books on politics, history and literature.[64] She also knitted and played patience, and took a special delight in doing jigsaw puzzles. When she was in Paris, she would often encourage her nieces and companions to go out to the theatre, while she happily remained at the Hôtel Continental playing patience.[65] Sometimes she stayed up late at night playing patience in her bedroom at Farnborough Hill, and occasionally she roamed round the house and asked Jones, her private detective, to play cards with her or to fry her an omelette in the middle of the night.[66] Unlike Napoleon III, she had always had a hearty appetite, and particularly liked indigestible Spanish dishes served with a great deal of oil.[67] Edward Blount, who married the third Duc de Bassano's daughter, was a little taken aback, when he dined with her and fish was served, by her habit of plunging her fork into the fish's eye and depositing it as a tit-bit on his plate, urging him to eat it, as it was the best part of the fish.[68]

She loved children. At Cap Martin she became very friendly with

Kenneth Clark, the seven-year-old son of the owner of a neighbouring villa. The first time they met she invited him to kiss her, but he was frightened of her aged face and refused the kiss for the lack of which, if the rumour be true, Camerata had shot himself. She was not offended with Kenneth Clark, and it was the start of a friendship which grew on their frequent walks in the olive groves near the Villa Cyrnos. Today Lord Clark still speaks of her kindness, charm and courtesy to him, and pays a tribute to her extraordinary vitality by stating that she was 'still quite young' when he knew her; in fact she was eighty-four.[69]

In 1889 a school for girls was opened by nuns at Hillside in Farnborough, less than a mile to the south of Farnborough Hill; after Eugénie's death, the school was transferred to the house at Farnborough Hill where she had lived. Eugénie allowed the children to use her park for their summer outing and sometimes on other days of the year, and usually had a cheerful word for them when she met them; but if she caught them slouching along in a slovenly manner she would give them a sharp reprimand, tapping the ground impatiently with her stick as she did so. She gave a cup as a prize for good conduct at Hillside, and was usually present on speech day to see it presented to the best pupil; and she also sometimes visited the village school,* where the children's compulsory education ended at the age of eleven when Eugénie first came to Farnborough.[70]

She would sit and talk for many hours to the children of her friends and neighbours – to Anne Pollen, today Mrs Chamberlin, who remembers the beautiful smell of the violets on the Empress's dress, how she gave her *bonbons* as she sat on the little stool beside her, and how she was never angry when the child, in her joy at seeing the Empress, ran excitedly up to her and forgot to curtsy as she had been taught to do. Once the little girl provoked general laughter by saying that when she grew up she wanted to be a policeman. Eugénie quelled the laughter and said that to be a policeman was to be a very good person, and added that her husband the Emperor had once been a London policeman, when 'a lot of wicked men were going to hurt other people and fight and make trouble and the policemen had to be ready to fight them'.†[71] By this time, nearly all the Chartists' demands had been granted; but Eugénie still regarded them with the eyes of the aristocracy of 1848.

But Eugénie showed great interest in the modern inventions which had caused such a change in social life. Napoleon III did not live to

*Mrs Florence Barber, the daughter of Eugénie's carpenter Dumpor, who was a pupil at the school, told me in 1976 that she remembers seeing Eugénie's first arrival at Farnborough in 1882.
†These words are Mrs Chamberlin's in 1976, but they undoubtedly represent the gist of what Eugénie said and the impression that they conveyed to the child.

see the introduction of the telephone, the motor car, the cinema, the wireless and the aeroplane. Eugénie installed the telephone at Farnborough Hill, and had an internal telephone system with telephones all over the house.[72] She was very interested in Marconi's successful experiments with transatlantic wireless communication, and had wireless installed on her yacht.[73] She bought a motor car, and like other employers at the time transformed her coachman into her chauffeur. She was always a little nervous in a car, because she was afraid that they would have an accident or run over a hen. In travelling, she showed the cautious side of her dare-devil temperament, and when catching a train insisted on arriving at the station long before the departure time.[74]

When she was in Venice in July 1906, she decided that she must go, for the first time in her life, to see a film in a cinema. She persuaded her secretary, Piétri, and her companion, Miss Vesey, to take her to a small hall in a working-class district, where they sat on a hard wooden bench and watched a film about a comic thief and two clever dogs which must have been one of the early silent Hollywood farces.[75]

Within a few miles of Farnborough Hill, Colonel Cody was carrying out experiments in aviation at the Balloon House in Aldershot. The Empress and her household visited him on several occasions, and saw his aeroplane; and when Cody and Colonel Capper made their experimental flight in an airship over Farnborough in 1907, Eugénie, with the Scotts, the Veseys, and the Marquis of Santa Cruz's daughter, the young Princess Metternich, went up to the tower at Farnborough Hill to watch the flight. They saw, through the September mist, the airship rise from Cove Common and pass over the house with Cody and Capper saluting the Empress as they passed, while she and her party waved their handkerchiefs at the airmen. The airship was in the air for a quarter of an hour, and after making a semicircle over Frimley landed safely again at Cove Common.[76] By 1914, Cody and his fellow-aeronauts were reaching a speed of 70 m.p.h. in the air.[77]

Eugénie was nearly eighty when she made the acquaintance of the Vesey family who lived at Frimley and, like many of the Empress's neighbours, were a military family. Miss Isabel Vesey became one of the Empress's closest friends during the last fifteen years of her life. She was originally asked to dinner at Farnborough Hill because of Eugénie's dread of the number thirteen. Eugénie half-believed the superstition that if thirteen people sat down to dinner, the first to rise from the table would die within the year; this disconcerted her, since etiquette prescribed that she herself should always rise first. She invited Isabel Vesey to be the fourteenth person at dinner, and the friendship grew.[78] Miss Vesey became utterly devoted to her, and

Eugénie performed many acts of kindness to her and to her relatives. She knitted a jersey for Miss Vesey's baby niece, Veronica Fowke – today Mrs Burnett – who was a great favourite of hers, and once gave Miss Vesey's sister Rosie a pair of her boots. But though Rosie took only size 3 in shoes, Eugénie's boots were much too small for her.[79] The Countess of Teba's tiny feet had not grown larger since the 1840s.

Eugénie took Miss Vesey with her, not only to Cap Martin, but on the journeys further afield that she made on her yacht the *Thistle*, which she first hired and afterwards bought from the Duke of Hamilton.[80] She usually invited a number of young men and women from the French and Spanish aristocracy to join the party on the *Thistle*. The young people flirted with each other, enjoyed the trip, and adored the Empress. She allowed them a free rein, but insisted on propriety in dress. Eugénie, who had once shocked her elders by wearing the provocative Andalusian Maja dress, now insisted that her nieces should wear stockings under their long bathing dresses when they bathed in the sea.[81]

In the summer of 1906, starting from Cap Martin, Eugénie and her party sailed to Elba to see Napoleon's house, and to Civitavecchia, Montenegro and Venice. They had tea in Venice with Eugénie's old friend Nigra, whom she had not seen since they parted in the street outside the Tuileries on 4 September 1870. From Venice, Eugénie and Miss Vesey travelled overland to Ischl in Austria, where the Emperor Franz Joseph entertained them with great hospitality and renewed his old acquaintance with Eugénie.[82] They arrived at Ischl on 11 July; but neither Eugénie nor Franz Joseph seems to have mentioned that it was the forty-seventh anniversary of his meeting with her husband at Villafranca.

In the following summer Eugénie went with Miss Vesey and other friends on the *Thistle* to the fiords of Norway. Eugénie was in fine form, signing the autograph books for the German and American tourists who clustered around her at the hotels, and climbing the mountains, leaving the paths to take short-cuts up the steepest gradients and scrambling over high walls.[83] The German Emperor William II was at Bergen on his yacht, and he visited Eugénie on the *Thistle*. Their meeting was afterwards described by Paléologue in his book *Les Entretiens de l'Impératrice Eugénie*, and by Isabel Vesey in her articles in *The Times* after Eugénie's death. In Paléologue's account, Eugénie, as a patriotic Frenchwoman, only agreed very reluctantly to meet the Kaiser; but Miss Vesey, though she describes the great animosity of Eugénie's French entourage to the Kaiser, and makes fun of his pomposity, wrote at the time that Eugénie 'rather likes him'.[84] Neither account quite reveals the close links which existed between Eugénie and the Prussian royal family after 1870 – the affection felt for Eugénie by the old Empress Augusta and by the Empress Victoria, whom Eugénie had visited in Germany in 1890,[85] and the fact that William II had called on Eugénie at Farnborough Hill in 1894.[86] Nor did they refer to the screen of Saint-Cloud.

Eugénie caught cold in Norway, and as she could not shake it off, her doctor advised her to winter in a warm climate. She therefore decided to spend the first three months of 1908 in Ceylon, and fulfil her lifelong ambition of visiting India. In 1837 she had run away from school at Clifton and stowed away on a ship in order to get to India, but had been caught before the ship sailed; in 1869, she had asked the British Ambassador to make arrangements for her to go on to India after the opening of the Suez Canal,[87] but had decided to return to Paris to face Rochefort's revolutionaries. Now, at eighty-two, she sailed to Colombo in the S.S. *Mooltan*, travelling incognito as an ordinary passenger.[88] When she and her party entered the dining-room of her hotel in Cairo she was not recognized, and she heard one of the other diners say sniffily that she and her party were obviously Thomas Cook tourists. This amused the Empress, because she always asked Cook's to arrange her accommodation when she travelled.[89]

At Colombo she was a guest at Government House. A young government official, Leonard Woolf, met her there, and fifty years later wrote unrepentantly that 'her face to me seemed positively ugly'.[90] She fell ill at Colombo, and on medical advice agreed to return to England without going to India, convinced that she was fated never to reach the land of her childhood dreams.[91]

In 1909 she visited Constantinople and Madrid,[92] and then went with Isabel Vesey in the *Thistle* to Ireland, where they were the guests of the Viceroy, Lord Aberdeen, in Dublin and of Lady Ormonde at Kilkenny Castle. They sailed home through a tempest between Waterford and Plymouth which left Eugénie badly bruised when she was flung across her cabin, but she was undaunted in spirit.[93] They went further afield in 1910, going to Naples, Sicily, Greece and Turkey. Eugénie showed her usual energy at Naples, where she visited Pompeii. They arrived in Palermo at the end of May, during the celebrations to mark the fiftieth anniversary of the liberation of the city by Garibaldi.[94] They set out to see the famous Museum in Palermo, with its prehistoric relics, but by mistake walked into the new Garibaldi Museum. Miss Vesey noted that this 'rather disgusted' the Empress, 'as she heartily disliked Garibaldi', and they glanced at his red shirt, and left.[95]

In Constantinople, Eugénie showed Miss Vesey the places that she had seen in 1869, and went to tea with the Sultan.[96] He watched her closely as she drank her tea, and snatched the cup from her almost before she had finished drinking. He explained that this was because King Leopold II of the Belgians, during a recent visit, had made off with a valuable pipe after he had finished smoking it. After Eugénie's death, Miss Vesey published this story in *The Times*, but stated merely that the pipe had been taken by an unnamed sovereign, being too tactful to reveal that it was Prince Victor Napoleon Bonaparte's father-in-law.[97] The readers of *The Times* assumed that the delinquent monarch must have been the wicked Kaiser, and several subsequent writers have told the story naming William II as the culprit.

Eugénie was now willing once again to go back to Paris, and often stayed at the Hôtel Continental on her way from Farnborough Hill to Cap Martin. From the windows of the hotel she could see the Tuileries Gardens; but when her friends asked her how she could bear to see the grounds in which she had once walked as Empress, she replied that she felt that she was an entirely different person from the woman of the past: 'I died in 1870.'[98] In February 1909 she went with Miss Vesey to see the Musée des Arts Décoratifs which was in the small remaining part of the Tuileries which had not been destroyed during the Commune; it was the first time that Eugénie had set foot in the Tuileries since the revolution of 4 September.[99] Forty years had passed since that 'année terrible', and thirty years since her painful return visit to Fontainebleau and Saint-Cloud in 1881. When she went to Versailles with Miss Vesey in 1906, the guide who showed her her wedding coach and the Prince Imperial's cradle did not recognize her. When she corrected an inaccurate statement that he had made, he asked her how she came to be so well-informed; then he recognized this old lady as the historical character about whom he had so often lectured to the tourists.[100]

Politicians and men of letters, as well as people in society, were eager to obtain an introduction to the Empress Eugénie and call on her at the Hôtel Continental. Maurice Paléologue first met her there in 1901, after Princess Mathilde had arranged it, and began a friendship which continued for many years in Paris and at Farnborough Hill. She talked to him about current politics and the prospects of a European war as well as about the past and the days of the Second Empire.[101] His account of their talks in his book is interesting and revealing, although it is coloured and occasionally distorted by his own political prejudices and by the outlook of a younger generation.

Her relationship with Lucien Daudet was different from that with Paléologue. She had patronized Lucien's father Alphonse Daudet when she was Empress, and when Lucien was twenty-one he called on her at the Villa Cyrnos in 1899.[102] He approached her in a spirit of adoration, and at Cap Martin, in Paris and at Farnborough Hill he continued to regard her in this light. 'I had the great honour of knowing her well,' he said after her death, 'and the joy of admiring her without any qualification, the pride of having experienced since my adolescence a benevolence which was infinitely greater than I deserved.'[103] He asked her permission to write a book about her. She agreed on condition that he painted her with her faults as well as with her virtues, and his book *L'Impératrice Eugénie* was published in 1911. She appeared in it as utterly faultless, but though she gently chided him for his uncritical admiration, she was human enough to enjoy it and kind enough to permit it.[104]

It was Daudet who introduced Jean Cocteau to the Empress. Cocteau first came across her when she appeared around the corner in a winding alley in her garden at Cap Martin, striding along much too fast for her attendants – she was nearly eighty – and striking off the heads of the flowers with her stick, for she hated flowers, though she had so often accepted bouquets with a gracious smile in the old days. There was nothing unkind in Cocteau's description of her as 'leaning on a stick like some goat fairy', and as being 'a blot of ink in bright sunshine' in the black dress that she always wore in her widowhood; for it was his visual, not a metaphorical, picture of her. Like others who knew her, he was struck by her sudden loud laughter, 'which broke in two and threw her backwards',[105] and by her heavy but skilful eye make-up, which also impressed Dorothy Mostyn and the other school-girls at the convent school at Farnborough.[106]

Eugénie liked Cocteau, and asked him to come again. He visited her at the Hôtel Continental, and heard her arguing with her lady-in-waiting during the Second Empire, the Comtesse de Pourtalès, about modern fashions. The Comtesse disliked the habit of the young girls who wore coloured wigs, but the Empress maintained that she and her lady-in-waiting had indulged in equal excesses in their youth, with their crinolines, their tasselled boots, and their linen pantalettes which could be seen underneath their skirts. Cocteau sat very still, fearing that if he moved he might 'make the cock crow and send the ghosts away'.[107]

CHAPTER 46

THE END OF AN ERA

EUGÉNIE was eighty-eight at the outbreak of the Great War in August 1914. Once again France was engaged in a desperate struggle with Prussia, and once again, as in 1859, her friend Franz Joseph was an enemy sovereign. On the day after Britain declared war, sentries with fixed bayonets were on duty at many key points in Farnborough while troops were rushed by railway to Portsmouth for embarkation for France. Eugénie was told that it might be necessary to place anti-aircraft guns on her terrace, but she was perfectly happy about this, as she thought that the war would give France the opportunity to revenge 1870.[1]

Her great-nephew Hernando, Duke of Peñaranda, who was coming to Farnborough Hill for the polo season, succeeded in crossing the Channel before civilian transport was stopped, but his five polo ponies and his new Rolls-Royce car were commandeered by the French authorities at Boulogne. Before the end of August, Prince Victor and Princess Clémentine arrived from Belgium, having been persuaded, much against their will, to leave the country with the other Belgian refugees. Eugénie motored to Folkestone to meet them, and brought them to Farnborough Hill, where they stayed for the duration of the war.[2]

Eugénie immediately offered the *Thistle* to the British Admiralty, and was delighted when the yacht was rigged out as a minesweeper, with guns fore and aft.[3] She also offered the War Office the use of the new wing of Farnborough Hill as a convalescent home for wounded officers. She was told that if it was to be used at all it must be as a properly equipped hospital for wounded officers with a doctor and a staff of nurses. Eugénie agreed; her own doctor, Dr Attenborough of Farnborough, acted as doctor at the hospital, and Lady Haig, who had been a lady-in-waiting to Queen Alexandra before marrying General Sir Douglas Haig, was Commandant of the Hospital. Eugénie had become friendly with the Haigs when Sir Douglas was in command of the garrison at Aldershot in the last years before the war; and when he left for France in August 1914, Lady Haig took up her duties at the hospital and lived with Eugénie in the other wing of Farnborough Hill. Two nurses and other staff were engaged, and Isabel

Vesey took over unofficially and saw that the necessary things were done.[4]

Eugénie showed great interest in the hospital. She visited the patients every day and spoke to each of them, and arranged the tables and other furniture in their rooms; but Miss Vesey, who thought that the Empress's furniture arrangements were quite impracticable, usually moved the chairs and tables back again after Eugénie had gone. Eugénie sometimes asked those patients who were not bedridden to have tea with her in her part of the house, and occasionally entertained their wives to tea when they visited their husbands.[5]

The hospital was one of the most comfortable and friendly in the country, and the patients found it delightful; but the relations between the staff were not so happy. There was a conflict from the start between Lady Haig and Miss Vesey. Lady Haig was a famous society lady and a well-known public figure; Miss Vesey was very efficient and afraid of nobody. At first Lady Haig was on excellent terms with Dr Attenborough. 'Lady H. likes a *man*', wrote Isabel Vesey; 'as Dr A. said, she will do anything for a man & worries the women.'[6] Miss Vesey complained that 'Lady Haig won't bother herself with domestic details she likes to put on her white cap & trot round with the doctor'.[7] But Lady Haig claimed that she worked so hard at the hospital that she risked endangering her health.[8]

The friction between Lady Haig and Miss Vesey was painful for the Empress, because she liked them both very much. She was very reluctant to get involved in the quarrel, and she was worried that reports of the bickerings at Farnborough Hill would reach Sir Douglas Haig at the front and distract his attention from his military duties. She therefore tried to smooth things over, and did not give Miss Vesey the backing to which Miss Vesey thought she was entitled.[9]

On 29 September 1914, King George V, who had come to Aldershot to review Kitchener's army before their departure for France, came with Queen Mary, the Prince of Wales, and Princess Mary, to tea at Farnborough Hill. They were received by the Empress, with Princess Clémentine and Miss Vesey in attendance, and, as Miss Vesey put it, 'Lady Haig becomingly attired in her nurse's costume presided at the hospital with Dr Attenborough'.[10] The King talked to all the officers in the hospital. The Prince of Wales was not at all shy and spoke excellent French, but Princess Mary was very shy, and sat with her parasol clasped tightly in front of her during tea. Queen Mary smoked a cigarette, but Princess Mary firmly refused to smoke, although everyone tried to persuade her to do so. The King and Queen came again at the end of May 1915, with Queen Alexandra, Princess Mary and Princess Victoria. 'They all tripped about,' wrote Isabel

Vesey, 'talking & laughing & introducing themselves. . . . At one moment our one bedridden patient, a Major, had 1 King 2 Queens & 2 princesses hovering over his bed.'[11]

By this time relations between the staff were worse than ever, and Dr Attenborough too had turned against Lady Haig. As a conscientious and security-conscious patriot, he was alarmed at Lady Haig's habit of reading aloud to the patients extracts from the letters that Sir Douglas wrote to her from France in which he gave away what Attenborough thought were military secrets, but which Lady Haig doubtless believed were matters of common knowledge; and Lady Haig would loudly voice her complaint, to patients and staff alike, that Sir Douglas was unable to launch an offensive on the Western Front because he had no ammunition. Eugénie would not reprove Lady Haig, being still concerned above all about not worrying Haig at the front. By the summer of 1915, Lady Haig was insisting that the Empress dismiss some of the nurses, and Dr Attenborough was threatening to resign unless Lady Haig left. Whatever the rights and wrongs of the dispute, it is to the credit of both parties that they never allowed any hint of their feud to reach the patients, who were quite unaware of it, and thought of Farnborough Hill, both then and in retrospect, as a happy haven of contentment amid the strains of war.[12]

Soon afterwards, Haig told Lady Haig that he was worried that she might injure her health by overworking at the hospital, and he was also concerned about the special problems raised by her presence at the hospital in view of his official position. In the summer of 1915, Lady Haig left, and Isabel Vesey was appointed Commandant in her place. Eugénie had succeeded in her object of avoiding a quarrel with either of her two friends; for while Isabel Vesey believed that the Empress had skilfully utilized Sir Douglas Haig's feelings in order to get rid of Lady Haig, Lady Haig herself was convinced that Eugénie was very put out that she was leaving.[13] 'I was very touched', wrote Lady Haig, 'by a charming letter she wrote me afterwards in which she said she looked at my empty place at table and greatly regretted my absence.'[14]

Eugénie adapted herself well to wartime conditions, though for the first time in her life she had difficulty in keeping and finding servants.[15] She was irritated to discover that, after all her years in England, and despite her position and her hospital, she was still an alien in Britain and subject to the legal restrictions imposed on alien residents. Her Spanish relatives, as neutral aliens, were unable to serve in the British army or take part in other activities; and a German monk at Farnborough Abbey was nearly the victim of a spy-scare.[16] In October 1915 there was an air raid on Farnborough by German zeppelins, and there were several other air raids during the next three years, because

Farnborough and the Aldershot district, with their military establishment and the aircraft factory at Farnborough, were a target for the German Air Force. Eugénie was excited and stimulated by the air raids. Whenever the police came round, calling out 'All lights out! Zeppelins in the vicinity!', she would make sure that all the curtains were well drawn, and then went up to the tower at the top of the house to watch.[17] But at the insistence of the military authorities, she had to fill in the lake in her park, which was a landmark for the enemy aircraft on moonlit nights.[18]

In September 1915, Eugénie heard that Piétri was dying of cancer in Paris after nearly fifty years in her service. She was determined to visit him before he died, and although she was eighty-nine, and cross-Channel travel was dangerous in wartime, she obtained, through her influence, the necessary permission to make the journey by Folkestone and Boulogne. This time she did not arrive too late at a deathbed. Piétri recovered sufficiently to travel back to Farnborough Hill, but died there in December. He was buried on the stairs leading down to the vault where the bodies of Napoleon III and the Prince Imperial lay awaiting Eugénie's.[19]

Piétri had been the pivot of the household at Farnborough Hill; but Eugénie appointed a young man, Count Bacciochi, to replace him, and carried on despite deaths, war and mishaps. In May 1918 Eugénie was walking up the great staircase at Farnborough Hill with her hands full, and therefore not holding on to the banisters, when she lost her balance and fell down the whole flight of stairs. She cut her forehead and was severely bruised, but no bones were broken; and as the nurses from the hospital hurried to her and carried her slowly up the stairs, she commented that she was taking longer to go up than to come down. It was a dangerous fall for a woman of ninety-two; but after ten days in bed she had completely recovered.[20] By 1 July she was well enough to watch a play performed by the members of her household for the officers in the hospital; she said that she thought it was very well acted, though she 'talked loudly most of the time' throughout the performance.[21] Within a few months she was playing hide-and-seek with Miss Vesey's little niece Veronica Fowke in the downstairs passage at Farnborough Hill.[22]

Armistice Day, 11 November 1918, was a moment of triumph for Eugénie; she had lived to see the revenge for 1870. She had all her life been influenced politically by the prevalent opinion among her friends, her class and her compatriots, and in England during the Great War she identified herself completely with the cause of Republican France. She shared the admiration of the other readers of *The Times* for the war leadership of the dauntless Clemenceau,[23] now 'Père la Victoire' but once the young student demonstrator who had been thrown into the Mazas prison by her husband's police. Her friend Dr Hugenschmidt, who was said to be the illegitimate son of Napoleon III and the Countess of Castiglione, was a frequent visitor at Farnborough Hill. He was Clemenceau's doctor in Paris.

One day in 1918, when the Allies were discussing the future of Alsace-Lorraine after their victory, Eugénie mentioned to Hugenschmidt that in October 1870 King William of Prussia had written to her regretting that he could not forgo the annexation of Alsace-Lorraine because its possession was a vital strategic necessity for Germany. Hugenschmidt was very interested, because some of the Allied statesmen were opposing the French demand for Alsace-Lorraine on the grounds that the population of the provinces was German, and that its transfer to France would violate the principle of self-determination advocated by President Wilson in his Fourteen Points. King William's letter would prove that Germany had seized Alsace-Lorraine, not because its inhabitants were German, but for purely strategic reasons. Hugenschmidt asked her to send the letter to Clemenceau. In 1870, in the days when Louis Napoleon was being treated as an honoured guest while a prisoner-of-war at Wilhelmshöhe, she would never have sent a private letter from a fellow-sovereign to the Radical leader of a Republican government; but Eugénie had changed with the times. She sent the letter, not to Clemenceau, but to his Foreign Minister, Pichon, explaining to Alba that she preferred sending it to Pichon rather than to that 'Communard' Clemenceau.[24]

She did not go with public opinion to the extent of abandoning her old ideas about war and foreign policy. In 1914 she checked the outbursts of anti-German hatred expressed by some of the officers in her hospital, and disapproved of calling the Germans 'les boches'.[25] She still took the attitude of her class in the Crimean War and the War of 1859, that an enemy soldier should be respected for doing his duty to his sovereign. By 1918 she had been sufficiently outraged by what she had heard of the conduct of the German army in France and Belgium – particularly the bombardment of Rheims cathedral and other churches – to give up her plan to return to Aachen cathedral the Charlemagne relic, the piece of the True Cross which Napoleon I had taken from Aachen; instead, she presented it to Rheims cathedral.[26] With her old ruthlessness, she thought that the Allies should overcome the German reluctance to sign the peace treaty in June 1919 by re-imposing the blockade; but she knew that it would be impossible to hold down 70 million Germans for ever, because she remembered Napoleon I's failure in Spain, and she condemned the reparations clauses of the Treaty of Versailles.

639

She regretted the break-up of the Austrian Empire, and the creation of independent states in Hungary and Czechoslovakia. She ridiculed the League of Nations and President Wilson's Fourteen Points. After the Russian Revolution of March 1917 she hoped that the 'Girondins' in the new Russian government would remember the fate of Louis XVI and Marie Antoinette and would send the Tsar and his family to safety abroad before they themselves were overthrown and replaced by extremists. When the Bolsheviks came to power, she thought that they were even worse than the French Jacobins of 1793, but did not, like so many of her contemporaries, believe that they were on the verge of collapse; on the contrary, she feared that they would one day dominate Europe.[27]

She strongly disapproved of the demand that Kaiser William II should be extradited from Holland and put on trial before an Allied court as a war criminal. This would have been too glaring a contrast to the treatment accorded by the Germans to Napoleon III at Wilhelms-höhe. But the 1914–18 war was the revolutionary war that Kossuth and Mazzini had demanded and Louis Napoleon and Palmerston had feared – a war led by the political descendants of Kossuth and Mazzini, by Lloyd George, Clemenceau, Wilson, Masaryk, Pilsudski and Veni-zelos; and this was none the less true because Lenin and Trotsky and a new generation of more extreme revolutionaries were denouncing it as an imperialist war. On 10 November 1918, the last evening of the war, the poet Alfred Noyes told his audience at the Carnegie Hall in New York that the reactionaries who opposed the trial of the Kaiser 'would permit the Emperor to return to his yacht and his champagne dinners while 20 million men he has murdered lie rotting in the ground'.[28] He echoed the feelings of the common soldiers in the prisoner-of-war camps in 1870 who had resented the luxurious captivity of Napoleon III; but Eugénie was still one of Noyes's 'reactionaries' who believed in the old courtesies. When she heard of the revolution in Germany in November 1918 and of the Kaiser's flight to Holland, she sympathized with him, remembering her own escape from the Tuileries. She hoped that he was not short of handkerchiefs on the journey, as she had been in 1870.[29]

She expressed her opposition to a vindictive peace and her anxieties for the future in her talks in 1918 and 1919 with Wickham Steed, the brilliant and famous foreign correspondent of *The Times*. When Steed came to Farnborough Hill a few days after the Armistice, she told him that she would be prepared to embrace Clemenceau for his services to France in the war, but regretted that he had refused to attend the *Te Deum* in Notre-Dame for the victory; if he had done so, she said, he could have become First Consul. 'I fancy M. Clemenceau cherishes no such ambition', said Steed. 'No matter', said Eugénie. 'He can make good his mistake. A fortnight hence he will go to Strasburg. He must visit the cathedral. He may still unite France and give the lesson of unity and moderation.' 'May I give M. Clemenceau this advice from Your Majesty?' asked Steed. 'No', said Eugénie. 'I told you I died in 1870.'

A week later, Clemenceau came to London with Marshal Foch, and Steed told him what Eugénie had said. 'Is that old woman still alive?' said Clemenceau. But when he went to Strasburg he visited the cathedral, and in his speech referred to the fact that he had seen an old nun singing the 'Marseillaise', which he called 'a great lesson of unity and moderation'. These were the words that Eugénie had used to Steed and that Steed had repeated to Clemenceau.[30]

Eugénie was losing her sight because of a cataract in her eye, and she was very old. She had outlived her only son, all Paca's children, and most of the younger generation of her relations. Franz Joseph, four years younger than she, had died at the age of eighty-six after a reign of sixty-eight years. Rochefort, born in the same year as Franz Joseph, had escaped from the penal settlement of New Caledonia to which he had been sentenced as a Communard, had returned to France under the amnesty, had become a prominent right-wing anti-semite and anti-Dreyfusard, and had eventually died at the age of eighty-three. The young Mexican revolutionary, Porfirio Diaz, had ruled Mexico for thirty-three years as a right-wing dictator, had been overthrown by a new generation of revolutionaries who had forgotten that he was ever a Radical, and had died in exile in Paris at the age of eighty-five. But Eugénie lived on, along with the Empress Charlotte in Belgium, who, after more than fifty years of insanity, still believed that she was living in her palace in Mexico.

At the beginning of December 1919, Eugénie left Farnborough Hill to spend the winter at Cap Martin for the first time for six years. In Paris she consulted an eye specialist, who advised against an operation for the cataract, because he doubted whether she could stand the anaesthetic at her age. She reached Cap Martin in time for Christmas, and stayed for four months at the Villa Cyrnos. In February she sent a cable to the Duke of Alba in Spain asking him to come to Cap Martin. When he arrived, she told him that she knew that she would die soon, and was glad of it, as she was losing her sight and could not bear to live without being able to read a newspaper; but she wished to visit Spain once more before she died, and once again see Seville during the Easter Fair. Alba told her that Dr Barraquer of Barcelona might be able to operate on the cataract and restore her sight; but she said that all the specialists whom she had seen had declared that this was impossible.[31]

In the middle of April she sailed from Marseilles to Gibraltar, and landed on 24 April at Algeciras, where the Spanish and British ships in the harbour greeted her with a gun salute. A special train had been ordered to take her to Seville, but she preferred to travel in Alba's open car.[32] As they walked along the pier to the car, he suggested that she should obtain some sun glasses to protect her eyes from the glare of the sun during their motor journey; but she told him that the sun of Spain had never harmed her eyes. They reached Alba's palace in Seville after a seven-hour motor journey, and next morning King Alfonso called on her. She was in splendid spirits during her stay in Seville. She visited many friends and attended an evening of Andalusian folk-songs, but was saddened when she heard of the death of a young conjuror in Seville. 'Has he a mother?' she asked.[33]

She went on with Alba to the Liria Palace in Madrid, where she arrived on 2 May 1920,[34] three days before her ninety-fourth birthday. It was not the same Madrid that she had known eighty years before. Ariza House had been demolished, though Carabanchel, like the Liria Palace, was unchanged.* Fancy-dress balls, attended by the royal family, were still being held at the Teatro Real, where Eugénie had gone to fancy-dress balls in the 1840s; but now the guests were told to come in costumes of the time of Goya, who had been living when Eugénie first knew Madrid.[35]

All her relatives brought their children to see her, and many other people called, including the French Ambassador.[36] She seemed to take on a new lease of life. She expressed a wish to fly in an aeroplane, and then thought better of it, because she was afraid that if she did, people would say that she was 'a crazy old woman'.[37] She suddenly asked Alba about the doctor in Barcelona who could perform the operation for her cataract, and Alba brought Dr Barraquer to Madrid. Barraquer examined her eyes in the garden of the Liria Palace. He told her that they were beautiful eyes. 'Still?' she said.[38] Soon afterwards he carried out the operation there, in a few seconds without an anaesthetic. When the bandages were removed, she could see clearly once again.[39]

Alba was about to be married, and Eugénie suggested that the wedding reception should take place at Farnborough Hill. On 9 July he left for London to make the arrangements for the wedding and to open an exhibition of Spanish art at Burlington House. Eugénie was to follow him three days later.[40]

On Saturday 10 July she sat down to an excellent lunch, and with her usual healthy appetite ate an exceptionally large meal. Later in the

*Both Carabanchel and the Liria Palace were completely destroyed during the Civil War of 1936–9, but the Liria Palace, unlike Carabanchel, was rebuilt on almost exactly the same model by Alba after the war.

day she felt a sharp pain, and thought that it was because she had overeaten. The pain grew worse, and she was carried to her bedroom, and placed fully dressed on the bed, and they never undressed her. She felt cold, even in the Spanish summer, and they brought her hot-water bottles; she remained conscious and composed, and told them where to place the bottles.[41] Next morning she lost consciousness, but became conscious again a few minutes before she died, saying to Alba's sister, 'I am tired; it is time for me to go away.'[42] She died at 8 a.m. on Sunday 11 July. For many years she had thought that Sunday was her unlucky day, for both Paca and the Prince Imperial had died on a Sunday, and it was on a Sunday that she had fled from the Tuileries in September 1870.[43]

She had made her Will in September 1916. She left legacies to the members of her household and to charities in Biarritz and elsewhere, and a painting by Greuze to Sir John Burgoyne in gratitude for his help in September 1870. The bulk of her property was divided between the Bonapartes and her Spanish nephews and nieces. She declared that she died a Roman Catholic, and directed that there should be no flowers at her funeral.[44] She had no wish to have flowers around her when she could no longer strike off their heads.

They dressed her corpse in a nun's habit,[45] and it lay in state in the chapel at the Liria Palace for four days. Many mourners, including the King and Queen of Spain, came to pay their tribute. On 16 July it was taken through the streets of Madrid on the funeral coach of the Spanish royal family, with the Infante Fernando and the Duke of Alba walking behind the coach, to the Northern Station and placed on the train to Paris, escorted by Alba and Peñaranda. It reached Farnborough on 18 July.[46]

General Lord Rawlinson, the general commanding the garrison at Aldershot, was on the station platform with his staff to receive the body, which was taken on a gun carriage to the abbey church. As the coffin, covered with a Union Jack, was lifted off the gun carriage, the band played the 'Marseillaise'[47] – the song that had been banned in France throughout all except the last seven weeks of the Second Empire; the song that had been sung by the followers of Mazzini and Garibaldi as they fought the armies of Louis Napoleon at Rome in 1849, by the defiant Reds in the prisons of France and the penal settlements of Algeria, by Rochefort's demonstrators during the nights of rioting in Paris in 1869, by the crowds before the Tuileries on 4 September 1870. But for General Lord Rawlinson and the population of Farnborough in 1920 the 'Marseillaise' was the national anthem of their French ally, not the song of the international Revolution. Sixty-five years and an era had passed since the state visit of 1855, and the regimental bands of the British army had forgotten how to play 'Partant pour la Syrie'.

The Kings and Queens of England, Spain and Portugal attended the funeral in the abbey church on 20 July, along with Princes and Princesses, Ambassadors, relatives and privileged friends. Dom Cabrol, the French Abbot of Farnborough, who preached the sermon, said that the congregation was

> an assembly of Kings and Queens, a Cardinal Archbishop of West-minster, a Bishop of Portsmouth, a Prince of the family of the Napoleons, a Princess Clémentine of Belgium; the families of Alba, Murat, Tamames, Santana, Peñaranda; the Villabars, the Moras, the Albuheras, the Locingas, the Priolis, the Bassanos, the d'Attainvilles, the Bassompières, the Walewskis, the Clarys, the Bacciochis, the Marquis de Girardin, Comte Fleury, Colonel Nitot, Colonel Sau-tereau, Dr Hugenschmidt, Lucien Daudet and so many others.[48]

Outside the church, the guns and the gunners were stationed ready to fire the twenty-one-gun salute in honour of the deceased Empress; but at the last moment the War Office gave orders that the salute was not to be fired after a protest had been received from the French government.[49]

The three tombs now lie in the crypt together – Napoleon III and the Prince Imperial on the ground, and Eugénie on a higher level, in accordance with the wish that she had expressed during her lifetime, because she shrank from the idea of being placed far below the ground.[50] She never lost the morbid fears associated with corpses and death that she had felt ever since she had been forced to watch by the corpse in Ariza House in the early 1830s.

The sovereigns, the princes, the ambassadors, the troops and the journalists had assembled for the funeral for one reason only – because the Prince-President had fallen in love with Eugenia del Montijo sixty-eight years before at Fontainebleau. To most of the people in the abbey church at Farnborough, he was a historical character of another epoch. As Eugénie said, it was time for her to go away.

APPENDIX

Letter from Lieutenant J. B. Carey to his wife from Zululand on 1 June 1879, as copied by Miss Octavia Scotchburn and sent by Eugénie to Queen Victoria (see above, p. 559) From the copy in the Royal Archives at Windsor (RA R5/15).

Itelezi Ridge Camp
12 Midnight 1 June

My own one, you know the dreadful news ere you receive this by telegram. I am a ruined man I fear, though from my letter which will be in the papers you will see I could do nothing else. Still the loss of a Prince is a fearful thing. To me, the whole thing is a dream; It is but 8 hours since it happened (3.55 P.M. 1 June).*

Our camp *was* bad, but then I have been so laughed at for taking a squadron with me that I have grown reckless and would have gone with two men.

To-morrow we go with the 17th Lancers to find his body. Poor fellow! But it might have been my fate! The bullets tore around us, and with only my revolver what could I do? The men all bolted and I now fear the Prince was shot on the spot as his saddle is torn as if he tried to get up. No doubt they will say I should have remained by him, but I had no idea he was wounded, and thought he was after me.

My horse was nearly done but carried me beautifully. My own darling! I prayed as I rode away that I should not be hit and my prayer was heard. Annie! what will you think of me! I was such a fool to stop in that camp! I feel it now though at the time I did not see it. As regards leaving the Prince I am innocent, as I did not know he was wounded, and thought our best plan was to make an offing.

Everyone is very kind about it all here, but I feel a brokendown man. Never can I forget this nights adventure.

My own, own sweet darling, my own little, my darling child, my own little Eddie and Pelham! Mama darling, do write and cheer me up! What will the Empress say! Only a few minutes before our surprise, he was discussing politics with me and the campaigns of 1800 and 1796, criticising (sic)* Napoleon's strategy and then talked of Republics and Monarchies! Poor boy! I liked him so very much! He was always so warm and good natured. Still I have been surprised, but not that I am not careful, but only because they laughed at all my care and foresight, I should have done very differently a week ago but now had ceased to care. Oh! Annie! How near I have been to death. I have looked it in the face, and have been spared. I have been a very, very wicked man, and may God forgive me! I frequently have to go out without saying my prayers and have had to be out on duty every Sunday. Oh! for some Christian sympathy. I do feel so miserable and dejected! I know not what to do; of course all sorts of yarns will get into the papers and without hearing my tale I shall be blamed; but honestly Pet (?)* between you and I, I can only be blamed for the camp. I tried to rally the men, in the retreat, and had no idea the poor Prince was behind. Even now I don't know it but fear so from the evidence of the men. The fire on us was very hot, perfect volleys; I believe thirty men or more were on us. Both my poor despised horses have now been under fire. The one I rode to-day could scarcely carry me, but did very well coming back. Oh! I do feel so ill and tired! I long for rest of any kind. This daily work on the saddle all day is very trying and this excitement has broken me down. If the body is found at any distance from the Kraal tomorrow, my statement will appear correct. If he is in the Kraal why then he must have been shot dead, as I heard no cry. Enfin! nous verrons. Time alone will solve the mystery.

Poor Lord Chelmsford is awfully cut up about it, as he will be blamed for letting him go with so small an escort.

The Times and Standard correspondents have been at me for news, also the Figaro, but the Daily News will give a garbled (?)* version as he is away from here at present.

Pet! My own treasure, I cannot write more! Good night my own one, I will try & let you know a few words tomorrow. I now try to sleep till réveille at 5 A.M. and it is now nearly one and so very cold. God bless you, my own one! J.B.

---

*The passages in parentheses were obviously added by one of the copyists, probably by Queen Victoria's private secretary.

BIBLIOGRAPHY

ABBREVIATIONS

A.A.   Alba Archives, Liria Palace, Madrid.
B.L.Add.   British Library, Additional Manuscripts.
C.G.   *Correspondance Générale de Prosper Mérimée* (Paris, 1941–64).
F.M.   Fitzwilliam Museum, Cambridge.
L.F.   *Lettres Familières de l'Impératrice Eugénie* (Paris, 1935).
Orig. Dip. *Les Origines Diplomatiques de la Guerre de 1870–1871* (Paris, 1910–32).
P.R.O.   Public Record Office, Kew.
Prob. Ven. *Il Problemo veneto e l'Europa* (Venice, 1966–7).
RA   Royal Archives, Windsor Castle.
R.D.M.   *Revue des Deux Mondes* (Paris, 1845–1932).

MANUSCRIPT, TYPESCRIPT AND UNPUBLISHED SOURCES

'Army Book 27: Admission and Discharge Book, Empress Eugenie Hospital from Sept. 14th 1914. Closed Sept. 4th 1919' (Dr Attenborough's MSS.).
Beinecke Library MSS. (Collection of American Literature) (Yale University Library).
Wilfrid Scawen Blunt – 'Alms to Oblivion' (the 'Secret Memoirs') (Fitzwilliam Museum, Cambridge).
Bromley Central Library, Miscellaneous MSS.
General Sir William Butler's Papers (Mrs R. L. Butler's MSS., Chelsea).
Camden Place MSS., Chislehurst.
Catalogue of Sale of Contents of Camden Place by Christie, Manson and Woods at Camden Place on 12, 13 and 14 June 1889.
Clutton, Margaret M. – 'Memories of my Childhood' (Bromley Public Library).
Father Conway's Diary (Farnborough Abbey MSS.).
Corvisart Papers (Farnborough Abbey MSS.).
Mr B. Coxwell's MSS., Uckfield.
Farnborough Abbey Miscellaneous MSS.
Mr Ivor Guest's MSS., Bromley Central Library.
Kirkpatrick, General C. – 'Records of the Closeburn Kirkpatricks' (Mrs M. Butler's MSS., Whiteparish, Wiltshire).

Count Malvezzi's MS. (Mrs P. Ovenden's MSS., Georgenympton, Devon).
Montijo Papers (Alba Archives, Liria Palace, Madrid).
National Library of Scotland MSS.
Palmerston Papers (British Library MSS.).
Register of Births, Marriages and Deaths (St Catherine's House, London).
Royal Archives, Windsor Castle.
Russell Papers (Public Record Office, Kew).
Nassau Senior's Journal (Royal Archives, Windsor Castle).
Lady Simmons's Papers (Miss A. Oreman's MSS., Hythe.).
Miss Charlotte Slade's Papers (Farnborough Abbey MSS.).
'Diary of the Marchesa Emilia Dusmet de Smours' (née Mademoiselle d'Allonville) (Farnborough Abbey MSS.).
Vesey, Isabel – 'A Collection of Happy Memories 1906–20' (cited as 'Isabel Vesey's MS.') (Mrs Veronica Burnett's MSS., Bethesden, Kent).
Miss Isabel Vesey's Diary (Mrs Veronica Burnett's MSS., Bethesden).
General Sir Ivo Vesey's tape-recorded talk, 11 August 1966 (Burnett MSS., Bethesden).
Vesey Papers (Burnett MSS., Bethesden).
Queen Victoria's Journal (Royal Archives, Windsor Castle).

NEWSPAPERS AND JOURNALS

L'Assemblée Nationale (Paris, 1850–1).
Birmingham Gazette (Birmingham, 1839).
Birmingham Journal (Birmingham, 1839).
Boletín Republicano (Mexico City, 1867).
British Medical Journal (London, 1873).
Le Charivari (Paris, 1851–66).
El Clamor Publico (Madrid, 1844–8).
Le Constitutionnel (Paris, 1848–70).
Le Corsaire (Paris, 1849–51).
Courrier de Marseille (Marseilles, 1850).
Court Journal (London, 1838–9).
Daily News (London, 1851).
The Daily Telegraph (London, 1858–70).
Démocratie Pacifique (Paris, 1849).
Le Dix Décembre (Paris, 1849).
Les Droits de l'Homme (Paris, 1876).
L'Echo Rochelais (La Rochelle, 1848).
La Época (Madrid, 1849–1920).
L'Estafette (Paris, 1849–51).
L'Événement (Paris, 1850–1).
El Heraldo (Madrid, 1842–53).
The Hillside Magazine (Farnborough, Hants, 1924–44).
Illustrated London News (London, 1851–73).
L'Indépendance Belge (Brussels, 1851–70).

Journal de Paris (Paris, 1815).
Journal des Débats (Paris, 1838–70).
Journal Officiel de l'Empire Français (Paris, 1869–70).
Journal Officiel de la République Française (Paris, 1870–1).
The Lancet (London, 1873).
La Lanterne (Paris and Brussels, 1868).
The London Magazine (London, 1908).
Manchester Guardian (Manchester, 1839–58).
La Marseillaise (Paris, 1870).
Moniteur: *Gazette Nationale ou Le Moniteur Universel* (Paris, 1804–68).
The Morning Advertiser (London, 1851).
The Morning Post (London, 1846–70).
Le Napoléon (Paris, 1850).
Le Napoléon Républicain (Paris, 1848).
The Natal Mercantile Advertiser (Durban, 1880).
Le National (Paris, 1838–51).
La Patrie (Paris, 1851).
Le Patriote de la Meuse (Bar-sur-Ornain, 1851).
Le Pays (Paris, 1851).
Le Petit Caporal (Paris, 1848).
Le Peuple (Paris, 1849).
Le Rappel (Paris, 1869).
La Rédingote Grise (Paris, 1848).
Le Réveil (Paris, 1868–70).
Revue de l'Empire (Paris, 1842–5).
Revue des Deux Mondes (Paris, 1845–1932).
Saturday Review (London, 1874).
Le Siècle (Paris, 1848–51).
Sussex Daily News (Brighton, 1872).
The Times (London, 1831–1920).
L'Univers (Paris, 1849–51).
La Voix du Peuple (Paris, 1850).

PRINTED BOOKS AND ARTICLES

ABERDEEN, 4TH EARL OF, and PRINCESS LIEVEN. *Correspondence of Lord Aberdeen and Princess Lieven* (Camden Society, 3rd Series, Nos. 60, 62) (London, 1938–9).
ACTON, LORD. *Historical Essays and Studies* (London, 1907).
ADKINS, N. F. *Fitz-Greene Halleck* (New Haven, 1930).
ALBA, 17TH DUKE OF. 'La Emperatriz Eugenia' (lecture at Barcelona University), in *Boletín de la Real Academia de Historia*, CXX, 71–101 (Madrid, 1947).
— *The Empress Eugenie* (lecture delivered at The Ark, Oxford, 5 June 1941) (Oxford, 1941).

AMBÈS, BARON D'. *Mémoires inédites sur Napoléon III: Le Mémorial de Chislehurst* (ed. C. Simond and M. C. Poinsot) (Paris, 1909–11).

ANSTRUTHER, I. *The Knight and the Umbrella* (London, 1963).

APPONYI, COUNT R. 'La ville et la cour sous le règne de Louis-Philippe: Extraits du journal du comte Rodolphe Apponyi' (*Revue des Deux Mondes*, VI(xxi). 105–40, 390–41) (Paris, May 1914).

ARBELEY, P. 'Un dernier amour de Stendhal: Eugénie de Montijo' (*La Revue Hebdomadaire*, 31 Dec. 1932, pp. 580–610).

ARESE, F. 'Notes d'un voyage dans les Prairies' See Bonfadini.

ARMANDI, GENERAL. *Ma Part aux événements importants de l'Italie Centrale en 1831* (Paris, 1831).

AVENEL, G. D'. 'Le Port des Lettres depuis sept siècles' (*Revue des Deux Mondes*, VI(xxii). 138–64) (Paris, July 1914).

BAC, F. *Napoléon III inconnu* (Paris, 1932).

BAINVILLE, J. *Napoléon* (Paris, 1931).

BALLANTINE, SERJEANT W. *Some Experiences of a Barrister's Life* (London, 1882).

BALLEYDIER, A. *Histoire de la Révolution de Rome* (Paris, 1851).

BARKER, NANCY NICHOLS. *Distaff Diplomacy: The Empress Eugénie and the Foreign Policy of the Second Empire* (Austin, Texas, 1967).

BARRAS, P. DE. *Mémoires de Barras* (ed. G. Duruy) (Paris, 1895).

BARROT, O. *Mémoires posthumes de Odilon Barrot* (Paris, 1875–6).

BARTHEZ, E. *The Empress Eugénie and her Circle* (London, 1912).

BAUDELAIRE, C. *Œuvres Complètes de Charles Baudelaire* (Paris, 1930).

BEAUMONT-VASSY, VICOMTE E. DE. *Histoire Intime du Second Empire* (Paris, 1874).

BEUST, COUNT F. E. *Memoirs of Friedrich Ferdinand Count von Beust* (London, 1887).

BEYLE, H. See Stendhal.

BIGELOW, J. *Retrospections of an Active Life* (New York, N.Y., 1909).

Biographie de Louis-Napoléon Bonaparte, représentant du peuple (Paris, 1848).

BITTARD DES PORTES, R. *1849: L'expédition française de Rome sous la Deuxième République* (2nd edn., Paris, 1905).

BLAKISTON, N. See *Problemo veneto e l'Europa*; Russell, Odo.

BLOUNT, SIR E. *Memoirs of Sir Edward Blount* (London, 1902).

BONDE, BARONESS (née ROBINSON). *Paris in '48: Letters from a Resident describing the events of the Revolution* (ed. C. E. Warr) (London, 1903).

BONFADINI, R. *Vita di Francesco Arese* (Terni and Rome, 1894).

BONNET, J. *Mes Souvenirs du Barreau depuis 1804* (Paris, 1864).

BORREL, M. 'Le divorce de Mme. Patterson Bonaparte' (*Revue des Deux Mondes*, VI(xxii). 138–64 (Paris, July 1914).

BRIFFAULT, F. T. *The Prisoner of Ham* (London, 1846).

BUDÉ, E. DE. *Les Bonaparte en Suisse* (Geneva and Paris, 1905).

BUSCH, M. *Bismarck: some secret pages of his history* (London, 1898).

BUSHELL, T. A. *Centenary Programme* (Chislehurst, 1970).

— *Imperial Chislehurst* (Chesham, 1974).

CABROL, DOM F. *L'Impératrice Eugénie: Discours prononcé à ses funérailles le 20 Juillet 1920* (London, 1920).

CARDIGAN, COUNTESS OF (COUNTESS OF LANCASTRE SALDANHA). *My Recollections* (London, 1909).

CARETTE, MADAME (née BOUVET). *My Mistress, the Empress Eugenie* (London, 1889).

CASSAGNAC, G. DE. *Souvenirs du Second Empire* (Paris, 1879–82).

CASTELLANE, COMTE V. DE. *Journal du Maréchal de Castellane 1804–1862* (Paris, 1895–7).

CASTELOT, A. *Napoléon Trois* (Paris, 1973–4).

CAVELLOTTI, F. *Storia del Insurrezione di Roma nel 1867* (Milan, 1869).

CAVOUR, COUNT C. *Lettere edite ed inedite di Camillo Cavour* (ed. L. Chiala) (Turin, 1883–7).

CAVOUR, C. and NIGRA, C. *Il Carteggio Cavour-Nigra del 1858 al 1861* (Bologna, 1926–9).

CESENA, A. DE. *L'Angleterre et la Russie* (Paris, 1859).

CHATEAUBRIAND, VICOMTE F. R. DE. *Mémoires d'Outre-Tombe* (ed. E. Biré) (Paris, 1880).

CHEVALIER, M. 'Journal de Michel Chevalier' (ed. M. Blanchard) (*Revue des Deux Mondes*, VIII(xii). 170–89) (Paris, Nov. 1932).

CHIALA. See Cavour.

CHURCHILL, LADY R. See Cornwallis-West.

CLARK, KENNETH. *Another Part of the Wood* (London, 1974).

COCHELET, LOUISE (MADAME PARQUIN). *Mémoires sur le reine Hortense et la famille impériale* (Brussels, 1837–8).

COCTEAU, J. *Paris Album 1900–1914* (trans. Margaret Crosland) (London, 1956).

CORLEY, T. A. B. *Democratic Despot: a Life of Napoleon III* (London, 1961).

CORNWALLIS-WEST, MRS GEORGE (LADY RANDOLPH CHURCHILL). *The Reminiscences of Lady Randolph Churchill* (London, 1905).

Correspondence respecting affairs in China 1859–60 (Parliamentary Papers) (London, 1861).

CORTI, EGON CAESAR, COUNT. *Maximilian and Charlotte of Mexico* (trans. by Catherine Alison Phillips) (New York, N.Y., 1968 edn.) (first published 1923).

La Cour de Rome et l'Empereur Maximilien (Paris, 1867).

CUVELLIER, BEATRICE. 'The Empress Eugenie today' (*The London Magazine*, Jan. 1908) (London, 1908).

DALLING, LORD and ASHLEY, EVELYN. *The Life of Henry John Temple, Viscount Palmerston* (London, 1870–6).

DANSETTE, A. *Histoire du Second Empire* (Paris, 1961–76).

DAUDET, L. *Le centenaire de l'Impératrice Eugénie* (lecture in Brussels, 11 Mar. 1926) (Amboise, 1926).

— *Dans l'Ombre de l'Impératrice Eugénie: lettres intimes adressées à Madame Alphonse Daudet* (3rd edn., Paris, 1935).

— *L'Impératrice Eugénie* (Paris, 1911) (reprinted as '*L'Inconnue*').

DECAUX, A. *La Castiglione* (Paris, 1953).

DELESCLUZE, C. *De Paris à Cayenne: Journal d'un transporté* (Paris, 1869).

DE PUY, H. W. *Louis Napoleon and His Times* (Buffalo, N.Y., 1852).

DES GARETS, COMTESSE (née MARIE DE LARMINAT). *Auprès de l'Impératrice Eugénie* (Paris, 1928).

DESJARDINS, A. *P.-J. Proudhon* (Paris, 1896).

DESTERNES, SUZANNE and CHANDET, HENRIETTE. *L'Impératrice Eugénie intime* (Paris, 1964).

Les Deux Cours et les nuits de St-Cloud (London and Brussels, 1852).

Diplomatic Study on the Crimean War – Russian Official Publication (London, 1882).

DOLLÉANS, E. *Proudhon* (Paris, 1948).

DUBOSCQ, A. *Louis Bonaparte en Hollande* (Paris, 1911).

DU CASSE, BARON A. *Les dessous du coup d'état, 1851* (Paris, 1891).

DUMAS, ALEXANDRE (père). *Mémoires d'Alex. Dumas* (Brussels, 1852–6).

DUNANT, J. H. *Un Souvenir de Solferino* (3rd edn., Geneva, 1863).

DUNCOMBE, T. H. *The Life and Correspondence of Thomas Slingsby Duncombe* (London, 1868).

EMERIT, M. 'Histoire et légende: la naissance de Napoléon III' (*Revue de la Méditerranée*, XII. 172–85) (Algiers, Jan.–Feb. 1952).

— See Napoleon III.

The Emperor and Empress's Visit to London! (London, 1855).

Enciclopedia Universal Ilustrada (Barcelona, Madrid and Bilbao, 1909–75).

Encyclopaedia Britannica (11th edn., London, 1910).

England's Disgrace (leaflet) (London, 1855).

EUGÉNIE, EMPRESS. *Lettres Familières de l'Impératrice Eugénie* (ed. 17th Duke of Alba and G. Hanotaux) (Paris, 1935).

EUGÉNIE DE GRÈCE, PRINCESS. *Pierre Napoléon Bonaparte* (Paris, 1963).

EVANS, T. W. *The Memoirs of Dr Thomas W. Evans* (ed. E. A. Crane) (London, 1905).

FALK, BERNARD. *Rachel the Immortal* (London, 1935).

FAZY, H. *James Fazy* (Geneva and Basle, 1887).

Les Femmes Galantes des Napoléons by H. Magen [?] (Berlin and Geneva, 1862).

FERRY, JULES. *Comptes fantastiques d'Haussmann* (Paris, 1868).

FILON, A. *Memoirs of the Prince Imperial* (London, 1913).

— *Recollections of the Empress Eugénie* (London, 1920) (cited as 'Filon').

FLAUBERT, G. *Madame Bovary* (Paris, 1930 edn.).

FLEISCHMANN, H. *Napoléon III et les Femmes* (Paris, 1913).

FLEURY, GENERAL COUNT E. F. *Souvenirs du Général Cte Fleury* (Paris, 1897–8).

FORGES, MARIE-THÉRÈSE. *Gustave Courbet 1819–1877* (Catalogue of Royal Academy of Arts Exhibition) (London, 1978).

FORSTER, J. *Walter Savage Landor* (London, 1869).

FOX, H. E. *The Journal of the Hon. Henry Edward Fox (afterwards fourth and last Lord Holland) 1818–1830* (ed. Earl of Ilchester) (London, 1933).

FRANZ JOSEPH, EMPEROR. *Briefe Kaiser Franz Josephs an Kaiserin Elisabeth 1859–1898* (ed. G. Nostitz-Rieneck) (Vienna and Munich, 1966).

FRASER, SIR W. *Napoleon III* (London, 1895).

GARIBALDI, G. *Autobiography of Giuseppe Garibaldi* (trans. by A. Werner), Vol. III, Supplement by Jessie White Mario.

GAULOT, P. *L'Expédition du Mexique (1861–1867) d'après les documents et souvenirs de Ernest Louet, Payeur en chef du Corps Expéditionnaire* (Paris, 1906).

GIRAUDEAU, F. *Napoléon III intime* (Paris, 1895).

GISQUET, H. J. *Mémoires de M. Gisquet, ancien préfet de police* (Paris, 1840).

GLEICHEN, HELENA. *Contacts and Contrasts* (London, 1940).

GORIAINOV, S. 'Lettres à Alexandre Ier' (*La Revue de Paris*, Sept.–Oct. 1907, pp. 676–80) (Paris, 1907).

GRANVILLE, A. B. *Autobiography of A. B. Granville: Eighty-Eight Years of the Life of a Physician* (ed. Paulina B. Granville) (London, 1874).

GRANVILLE, HARRIET, COUNTESS. *Letters of Harriet Countess Granville 1810–1845* (ed. Hon. F. Leveson Gower) (London, 1894).

Greek Papers: *Further Correspondence respecting the Demands made upon the Greek Government* (Parliamentary Papers, 17 May 1850) (London, 1850) (cited as '*Greek Papers*, III').

— *Further Correspondence respecting the Demands made upon the Greek Government* (Parliamentary Papers, 24 June 1850) (London, 1850) (cited as '*Greek Papers*, VII').

GREVILLE, C. C. F. *The Greville Diary* (ed. P. W. Wilson) (London, 1927) (cited as 'Greville (Wilson ed.)').

— *The Greville Memoirs: a Journal of the reigns of King George IV and King William IV* (ed. H. Reeve) (London, 1875) (cited as 'Greville, I').

— *The Greville Memoirs: a Journal of the Reign of Queen Victoria from 1837 to 1852* (ed. H. Reeve) (London, 1885) (cited as 'Greville, II').

GRONOW, R. H. *The Reminiscences and Recollections of Captain Gronow* (London, 1892 edn.) (first published 1862).

GUEDALLA, P. *Palmerston* (London, 1926).

GUERZONI, G. *Garibaldi* (Florence, 1882).

GUEST, IVOR. *The Ballet of the Second Empire* (London, 1953).

— *Napoleon III in England* (London, 1952).

— *The Romantic Ballet in England* (London, 1964).

GUILLEMIN, H. *Le coup du 2 Décembre* (Paris, 1951).

GUIZOT, F. *Mémoires pour servir à l'histoire de mon temps* (Paris, 1858–67).

HAIG, COUNTESS. *The Man I knew* (Edinburgh and London, 1936).

Hansard (Official Parliamentary Report) (London, 1858–80).

HARRISON, GENERAL SIR R. *Recollections of a Life in the British Army* (London, 1908).

HAUSSMANN, BARON E. *Mémoires du Baron Haussmann* (Paris, 1890–3).

HAUSSONVILLE, COMTE G. O. D'. 'Souvenirs' (*Revue des Deux Mondes*, VII(xvii). 481–509) (Paris, Oct. 1923).

The History of The Times (London, 1935–52).

HOLLAND, SIR H. *Recollections of Past Life* (London, 1872).

HORTENSE, QUEEN. *Mémoires de la Reine Hortense* (ed. J. Hanoteau) (Paris, 1927) (cited as 'Hortense, I, II and III').

— *La Reine Hortense en Italie en France et en Angleterre pendant l'année 1831* (first published Paris, 1834, in Vol. III of *Mémoires de la Reine Hortense* (Paris, 1927)) (cited as 'Hortense, III').

HOWARD, M. *The Franco-Prussian War* (London, 1961).

HÜBNER, COUNT A. *Neuf ans de souvenirs d'un Ambassadeur d'Autriche à Paris* (Paris, 1904).

HUGO, VICTOR. *Choses Vues* (Paris, 1914 edn.).

— 'L'Expiation' (in Hugo, *Poésies*).

— *Histoire d'un Crime* (Paris, 1877–8).

— *Napoléon le Petit* (London, 1852).

— *Œuvres Complètes* (Paris, 1880–90).

HULTMAN, H. *Prinsen av Vasa* (Stockholm, 1974).

HUTCHINS, S. E. *The Chislehurst Chiseller, or How History is Carved* (Chislehurst, 1970).

HYSLOP, L. B. and HYSLOP, F. E. *Baudelaire: a self-portrait* (London, 1957).

IRVING, P. *The Life and Letters of Washington Irving* (London, 1862–4).

JAMES, CONSTANTIN. *Des Causes de la Mort de l'Empereur* (Paris, 1873).

JEROME BONAPARTE, KING. *Mémoires et Correspondance du Roi Jérome et de la Reine Catherine* (Paris, 1861–6).

JERROLD, B. *The Life of Napoleon III* (London, 1874–82).

JOHN, KATHERINE. *The Prince Imperial* (London, 1939).

JORDAN, RUTH. *George Sand* (London, 1976).

KARÉNINE, W. *George Sand* (Paris, 1899–1926).

KÉRATRY, COMTE E. DE. *La Contre-Guérilla Française au Mexique* (Paris, 1868) (first published in *Revue des Deux Mondes*, II(lxi). 966–1011 (Paris, Feb. 1866)).

— *L'Empereur Maximilien, son élévation et sa chute* (Leipzig, 1867).

KINGLAKE, A. W. *The Invasion of the Crimea* (London, 1863).

KURTZ, H. *The Empress Eugénie* (London, 1964).

LA CHAPELLE, COMTE A. DE. *Œuvres Posthumes et autographes inédits de Napoléon III en exil* (Paris, 1873)).

LA GORCE, P. DE. *Histoire du Second Empire* (Paris, 1894–1905).

LA GUÉRONNIÈRE, L. E. DE. *Le Pape et le Congrès* (Paris, 1859).

LAITY, A. *Relation historique des Événements du 30 Octobre 1836* (Paris, 1838).

LAMEYRE, G. N. *Haussmann, Préfet de Paris* (Paris, 1958).

LAPLACE, MADAME DE. *Lettres de Madame de Laplace à Elisa Napoléon* (ed. P. Marmottan) (Paris, 1897).

LAROUSSE, P. *Grand Dictionnaire Universel du XIXᵉ siècle* (Paris, 1866–76).

LASSERRE, H. *Notre Dame de Lourdes* (Paris and Limoges, 125th edn., 1892) (first published 1869).

LAVISSE, E. *Histoire de France contemporaine depuis la révolution jusqu'à la paix de 1919* – Vol. VI, SEIGNOBOS, C. *La révolution de 1848 – Le second empire (1848–1859)* (Paris, 1921).

LEBEY, A. *Louis-Napoléon Bonaparte et la Révolution de 1848* (Paris, 1907–8).

— *Louis-Napoléon Bonaparte et le Ministère Odilon Barrot 1849* (Paris, 1912).

LECOMTE, G. *Napoléon III: Sa Maladie, Son Déclin* (Lyons, 1937).

LEGGE, E. *The Empress Eugénie 1870–1910* (London and New York, 1910).

— *The Empress Eugénie and her Son* (London, 1916).

LESSEPS, F. DE. *Mémoire présenté au Conseil d'État: Exposé des faits relatifs à la mission de M. Ferdinand de Lesseps à Rome, Mai 1849* (Paris, 1849).

LEVEY, G. C. 'Exhibitions' (*Encyclopaedia Britannica*, 11th edn., London, 1910).

LINDSAY, J. *Gustave Courbet, his life and art* (Bath, 1973).

LLANOS Y TORRIGLIA, F. DE. *Maria Manuela Kirkpatrick Condesa del Montijo* (Madrid, 1932).

LOLIÉE, F. *La Fête Impériale: les femmes du Second Empire* (Paris, 1907).

— *La vie d'une Impératrice: Eugénie de Montijo* (Paris, 1907).

LOUIS BONAPARTE, KING. *Historical Documents and Reflections on the Government of Holland by Louis Bonaparte, ex-King of Holland* (London, 1820).

LUMLEY, B. *Reminiscences of the Opera* (London, 1864).

LUZIO, A. *Felice Orsini* (Milan, 1914).

MACARTNEY, C. E. and DOREANCE, G. *The Bonapartes in America* (Philadelphia, Pa., 1939).

MACK SMITH, D. *The Making of Italy* (London, 1968).

— *Victor Emanuel, Cavour, and the Risorgimento* (London, 1971).

MADDEN, R. R. *The Literary Life and Correspondence of the Countess of Blessington* (London, 1855).

MAGEN, HIPPOLYTE [?]. *Histoire Satyrique & Véritable du Mariage de César avec la Belle Eugénie de Gusman ou la femme de César, 1853* (London, 1871 edn., in which Magen is named as the author; but this is doubtful, as he was imprisoned in Cayenne when it was first published in 1853).

— See *Les Femmes Galantes des Napoléons*.

MALMESBURY, 3RD EARL OF. *Memoirs of an ex-Minister* (London, 1884).

Mariage de César. See Magen.

MARIO, JESSIE WHITE. *The Birth of Modern Italy: posthumous papers of Jessie White Mario* (ed. Duke of Litta-Visconti-Arese) (London and Leipzig, 1909).

— *Life of Garibaldi.* See Garibaldi.

— See Orsini, *Austrian Dungeons in Italy*.

MARTET, J. *M. Clemenceau point par lui-même* (Paris, 1929).

MARTIN, KINGSLEY. *The Triumph of Lord Palmerston* (London, 1924).

MARTIN, SIR THEODORE. *The Life of His Royal Highness The Prince Consort* (London, 1875–80).

MARX, KARL. *The Class Struggles in France* (London, 1934).

— *The Eastern Question* (London, 1897).

— *The Eighteenth Brumaire of Louis Bonaparte* (trans. Eden and Cedar Paul) (London, 1926 edn.).

MASSON, F. 'L'Impératrice Joséphine et le Prince Eugène (1804–1814) d'après leur correspondance inédite' (*Revue des Deux Mondes*, VI(xxxv). 721–51; (xxxvi). 295–329, 788–822) (Paris, Oct.–Dec. 1916).

— *Napoléon et sa famille* (Paris, 1897–1919).

MASUYER, VALÉRIE. 'Extraits du Journal de Mademoiselle Valérie Masuyer' (*Revue des Deux Mondes*, VI(xxii). 574–620, 829–74; (xxiii). 295–325; (xxiv). 229–69; (xxvi). 92–120; (xxvii). 848–73; (xxviii). 607–45; (xxx). 366–404) (Paris, Aug. 1914–Nov. 1915).

— *Mémoires Lettres et Papiers de Valérie Masuyer* (ed. J. Bourguignon) (Paris, 1937).

MAUPAS, C. E. DE. *Mémoires sur le Second Empire* (Paris, 1884–5).

MAXWELL, SIR H. *The Life and Letters of George William, Fourth Earl of Clarendon* (London, 1913).

MAZZATINTI, G. 'I Moti del 1831 a Forli' (*Revista Storica del Risorgimento Italiano*, II. 237–50) (Turin, 1897).

MAZZIOTTI, M. *Napoleone III e l'Italia* (Milan, 1925).

Mémoires sur Madame la Duchesse de St-Leu ex-reine de Hollande suivis des romances composées et mises en musique par elle-même (London, 1832).

MÉRIMÉE, P. *Correspondance Générale de Prosper Mérimée* (ed. M. Parturier, P. Jusserand and J. Mallon) (Paris, 1941–64).

— *Mosaïque* (Paris, 1888).

METTERNICH, PRINCESS PAULINE. *The days that are no more: some reminiscences* (ed. E. Legge) (London, 1921).

— *Souvenirs de la Princesse Pauline de Metternich* (Paris, 1922).

MOLTKE, COUNT H. VON. *Militärische Korrespondenz* (Berlin, 1892–7).

MONNERVILLE, G. *Clemenceau* (Paris, 1968).

MONTHOLON, GENERAL COUNT. *History of the Captivity of Napoleon at St Helena* (London, 1846–7).

MONYPENNY, W. F. and BUCKLE, G. E. *Life of Benjamin Disraeli, Earl of Beaconsfield* (London, 1910–20).

MOSTYN, DOROTHY. *The Story of a House: Farnborough Hill* (Farnborough, 1974).

MURAT, PRINCESS CAROLINE. *My Memoirs* (ed. R. Leighton) (London, 1910).

NAPOLEON I. *Correspondance de Napoléon Ier* (Paris, 1859–70).

NAPOLEON III. *Analyse de la question des sucres*. See Napoleon III – *Œuvres*.

— *Le Canal de Nicaragua*. See Napoleon III – *Œuvres*.

— *Considérations politiques et militaires sur la Suisse* (Paris, 1833).

— *Du passé et de l'avenir de l'Artillerie*. See Napoleon III – *Œuvres*.

— *Extinction du paupérisme*. See Napoleon III – *Œuvres*.

— *Histoire de Jules César* (Paris, 1865–6).

— *Lettres de Napoléon III à Madame Cornu* (ed. M. Emerit) (Paris, 1937).

— *Manuel d'artillerie à l'usage des officiers d'artillerie de la République helvétique* (Zürich, 1836).

— *Napoléon III et le Prince Napoléon: Correspondance inédite* (ed. E. d'Hauterive) (Paris, 1925).

— *Œuvres de Napoléon III* (Paris, 1856–69) (cited as '*Œuvres*').

— *Œuvres Complètes du Prince Napoléon-Louis Bonaparte* (Paris, 1845).

— *Rêveries Politiques*. See *Œuvres Complètes du Prince Napoléon-Louis Bonaparte*.

NELSON, HORATIO, VISCOUNT. *The Dispatches and Letters of Vice Admiral Lord Viscount Nelson* (ed. Sir N. H. Nicolas) (London, 1845–6).

NICHOLS, T. L. *Forty Years of American Life* (London, 1864).

NORMAN, P. *Scores and Annals of the West Kent Cricket Club with some account of the neighbourhoods of Chislehurst and Bromley and of the families residing there* (London, 1897).

NORRIS-NEWMAN, C. L. *In Zululand with the British throughout the War of 1879* (London, 1880).

Notes and Queries, 3rd Series, vol. I (London, 1862).

OLLIVIER, E. *L'Empire Libéral* (Paris, 1897–1909).

— 'La fin de l'Empire' (*Revue des Deux Mondes*, VI(xxi). 773–801; (xxii). 5–50, 241–74) (Paris, June–July 1914).

— *Journal 1846–1869* (ed. T. Zeldin) (Paris, 1961).

— 'Napoléon III, Général en chef' (*Revue des Deux Mondes*, IV(cliii). 5–37, 326–58) (Paris, May 1899).

Les Origines Diplomatiques de la Guerre de 1870–1871 (Paris, 1910–32).

ORSI, COUNT. *Recollections of the last Half-Century* (London, 1881).

ORSINI, F. *The Austrian Dungeons in Italy* (trans. by Jessie White) (London, 1856).

— *Memoirs and Adventures of Felice Orsini* (Edinburgh, 1857).

PAILLERON, MARIE-LOUISE. 'Une ennemie de l'Autriche: la princesse Christine Trivulce de Belgiojoso' (*Revue des Deux Mondes*, VI(xxvi). 805–39) (Paris, Apr. 1915).

PAINTER, G. D. *Marcel Proust* (London, 1959–65).

La Paix par la Guerre (Paris, 1868).

PALÉOLOGUE, M. *The Tragic Empress: Intimate Conversations with the Empress Eugénie* (trans. by H. Miles from *Les Entretiens de l'Impératrice Eugénie*) (London, 1928).

Le Pape et le Congrès. See La Guéronnière.

Papiers et Correspondance de la Famille Impériale (Paris, 1871).

Les Papiers Secrets du Second Empire (Brussels, 1870).

PEREY, L. 'La Reine Hortense d'après des documents inédits' (*La Vie Contemporaine*, VII(i). 334–62) (Paris, Jan.–Mar. 1894).

PERSIGNY, F. DE. *Lettres de Londres* (Paris, 1840).

— *Relation de l'entreprise du Prince Napoléon-Louis* (London, 1837) (3rd edn., New York, 1837).

PLANCHÉ, J. R. *The Recollections and Reflections of J. R. Planché (Somerset Herald)* (London, 1872).

PONSONBY, ARTHUR (LORD PONSONBY OF SHULBREDE). *Henry Ponsonby* (London, 1943).

PRICE, R. *The French Second Republic* (London, 1972).

PRIMOLI, COUNT J. A. 'L'enfance d'une souveraine' (*Revue des Deux Mondes*, VII(xvii). 752–88) (Paris, Oct. 1923).

Il Problemo veneto e l'Europa 1859–1866 (ed. R. Blaas, N. Blakiston, G. Dethan) (Venice, 1966–7).

Procès de Armand Laity Ex-Lieut. d'Artillerie (ed. R. Saint-Edme) (Paris, 1838).

PROUDHON, P. J. *Carnets de P.-J. Proudhon* (ed. P. Haubtmann) (Paris, 1960–74).

QUINET, E. 'La Campagne de 1815' (*Revue des Deux Mondes*, II(xxxiv). 334–69; (xxxv). 5–61, 521–65) (Paris, Aug.–Oct. 1861).

RAYLEIGH, P. *History of Ye Antient Society of Cogers 1755–1903* (London, 1904).

RÉCAMIER, JEANNE. *Souvenirs et Correspondance tirés des papiers de Madame Récamier* (Paris, 1859).

REINACH, J. *Histoire de l'Affaire Dreyfus* (Paris, 1901–11).

RÉMUSAT, CLAIRE DE. *Mémoires de Madame de Rémusat* (Paris, 1883).

RICHARDSON, JOANNA. *The Courtisans* (London, 1967).

— *Princess Mathilde* (London, 1969).

— *Rachel* (London, 1956).

RIDLEY, JASPER. *Lord Palmerston* (London, 1970).

ROCQUAIN, F. *Napoléon Ier et le Roi Louis* (Paris, 1875).

ROGEARD, A. *Les Propos de Labienus* (8th edn., Brussels, 1865).
— *Les Propos de Labienus: Histoire d'une Brochure* (Brussels, 1866).
ROMIEU, F. A. *L'Ère de César* (Paris, 1850).
— *Le Spectre Rouge de 1852* (Paris, 1851).
RUSSELL, ODO. *The Roman Question: Extracts from the despatches of Odo Russell from Rome 1858–1870* (ed. N. Blakiston) (London, 1962).
SAINT-ARNAUD, MARSHAL A. L. *Lettres du Maréchal de Saint-Arnaud* (Paris, 1855).
SAND, GEORGE. *Correspondance 1812–1876* (Paris, 1882–4).
— *Letters of George Sand* (ed. R. L. de Beaufort) (London, 1886).
— 'Lettres inédites de George Sand et du Prince Napoléon' (*Revue des Deux Mondes*, VII(xvii). 303–40) (Paris, Sept. 1923).
— 'Malgrétout' (*Revue des Deux Mondes*, II(lxxxv). 545–85, 801–44; (lxxxvi). 5–48, 257–95) (Paris, Feb.–Mar. 1870).
— *Souvenirs et Idées* (Paris, 1904 edn.).
SCHLUMBERGER, G. *Mes Souvenirs 1844–1928* (Paris, 1934).
SCHNEIDAWIND, K. *Aus dem Hauptquartiere und Feldleben des Vater Radetzky* (Stuttgart, 1856).
SCHOELCHER, V. *Le Gouvernement du Deux Décembre* (London, 1853).
SCHRAMM, E. 'Donoso Cortés und Napoleon III' (*Ibero-Amerikanisches Archiv*, XI(i). 14–38) (Berlin and Bonn, Apr. 1937).
SCRIBE, E. *Théâtre Complet de M. Eugène Scribe* (Paris, 1838–42).
SEIGNOBOS. See Lavisse.
SENCOURT, R. *The Life of the Empress Eugénie* (London, 1931).
— See Wellesley, Sir V.
SENIOR, NASSAU. *Conversations with distinguished persons during the Second Empire from 1860 to 1863* (ed. by his daughter M. C. M. Simpson) (London, 1880).
— *Conversations with M. Thiers, M. Guizot, and other distinguished persons during the Second Empire* (ed. by his daughter M. C. M. Simpson) (London, 1878).
(These published works contain part of Senior's Journal. All my references are to the MS. in the Royal Archives.)
SERMONETA, VITTORIA COLONNA, DUCHESS OF. *Things Past* (London, 1929).
SIMPSON, F. A. *Louis Napoleon and the Recovery of France* (London, 1923).
— *The Rise of Louis Napoleon* (London, 1925 edn.) (cited as 'Simpson, I').
SMITH, W. H. C. *Napoleon III* (London, 1972).
SMYTH, ETHEL. *As Time went on* (London, 1936).
— *Impressions that remained* (London, 1919).
— *Streaks of Life* (London, 1921).
— *What happened next* (London, 1940).
SÖDERGÅRD, Ö. *Les lettres de George Sand à Sainte-Beuve* (Geneva and Paris, 1964).
SOUTHEY, ROBERT. *The Life of Nelson* (London, 1813).
STANLEY, LORD. *Disraeli, Derby and the Conservative Party: Journals and Memoirs of Edward Henry Lord Stanley 1849–69* (ed. J. R. Vincent) (Hassocks, 1978).

STANMORE, LORD (HON. SIR ARTHUR GORDON). *The Earl of Aberdeen* (London, 1893).

— *Sidney Herbert, Lord Herbert of Lea: a Memoir* (London, 1906).

STARKEY, ENID. *Baudelaire* (London, 1933).

STEEFEL, L. *The Schleswig-Holstein Question* (Harvard, Mass., 1932).

STÉFANE-POL. *La Jeunesse de Napoléon III: Correspondance inédite de son Précepteur Philippe Le Bas* (Paris, 1902).

STENDHAL (H. BEYLE). *La Chartreuse de Parme* (Paris, 1922 edn.).

STODDART, JANE. *The Life of the Empress Eugénie* (London, 1906).

TCHERNOFF, J. *Associations et Sociétés Secrètes sous la deuxième république 1848–1851* (Paris, 1905).

TEMPERLEY, HAROLD. 'Three Dispatches of Prince Metternich on the origins of the War of 1870' (*English Historical Review*, XXXVIII. 90–94) (London, Jan. 1923).

TENNYSON, ALFRED, LORD. *The Works of Alfred Lord Tennyson* (London, 1897).

TEW, E. L. H. *Old Times and Friends* (London and Winchester, 1908).

THAYER, W. R. *The Life and Times of Cavour* (London and New York, 1911).

THIRRIA, H. *Napoléon III avant l'Empire* (Paris, 1895–6).

THOUVENEL, L. *Pages de l'Histoire du Second Empire* (Paris, 1903).

— *Le secret de l'Empereur* (Paris, 1889).

TICKNOR, G. *Life, Letters and Journals of George Ticknor* (ed. G. S. Hillard) (Boston, Mass., 1876).

Times. See *History of The Times*.

TSCHUDI, CLARA. *Eugénie Empress of the French* (trans. E. M. Cope from Norwegian) (London and New York, 1900 edn.).

TURQUAN, J. *La reine Hortense d'après les témoignages des contemporains* (Paris, 1927).

VALERA, JUAN. *Correspondencia* (Madrid, 1913).

VEGA, VENTURA DE LA. *El Hombre de Mundo: Comedia original en Cuatro Actos y en Verso* (Madrid, 1845).

Verhuell-Bonaparte, ex-empereur (London, 1870).

VERNER, WILLOUGHBY. 'The Empress Eugénie' (*The Nineteenth Century and After*, LXXXVIII. 296–306) (London, Aug. 1920).

VÉRON, L. *Mémoires d'un Bourgeois de Paris* (Paris, 1853–5).

VESI, A. *Rivoluzione di Romagna nel 1831* (Florence, 1851).

VICCHI, L. *Il generale Armandi* (Imola, 1893).

VICINI, G. *La Rivoluzione dell'anno 1831 nello stato Romano* (Imola, 1889).

VICTORIA, QUEEN. *Letters of Queen Victoria* (ed. A. C. Benson, Lord Esher, G. E. Buckle) (London, 1907–32).

VIEL CASTEL, COMTE H. DE. *Mémoires du Comte Horace de Viel Castel sur le règne de Napoléon III* (Paris, 1883–4).

VILLAVIEJA, MARQUÉS DE. *Life has been good* (London, 1938).

VILLIERS, G. *A Vanished Victorian: being the Life of George Villiers Fourth Earl of Clarendon* (London, 1938).

VINCENT, J. R. See Stanley.

VIZETELLY, E. A. ('LE PETIT HOMME ROUGE'). *The Court of the Tuileries 1852–1870* (London, 1907).

WAP, J. J. F. *Mijne Reis naar Rome in het voorjaar van 1837* (Breda, 1838).

WELLESLEY, F. A. *The Paris Embassy during the Second Empire* (London, 1928).

WELLESLEY, SIR V. and SENCOURT, R. *Conversations with Napoleon III* (London, 1934).

WELSCHINGER, E. 'La neutralité belge' (*Revue des Deux Mondes*, VI(xxiii). 6–17) (Paris, Sept. 1914).

WIKOFF, H. *Biographical Sketches of Louis Napoleon Bonaparte, First President of France* (Dublin, 1850).

WILCZEK, COUNT H. *Happy Retrospect* (London, 1934).

WILLIAMS, R. L. *The Mortal Napoleon III* (Princeton, N.J., 1971).

WILLIAMS, S. T. *The Life of Washington Irving* (New York, N.Y. 1935).

WITTE, BARON J. DE. 'Carol Ier Roi de Roumanie' (*Revue des Deux Mondes*, VI(xxiv). 81–93) (Paris, Nov. 1914).

WOOLF, LEONARD. *Growing* (London, 1961).

WOUTERS, F. *Les Bonaparte depuis 1815 jusqu'à ce jour* (Brussels, 1847).

WURZBURG, C. VON. *Biographisches Lexikon des Kaiserthums Oesterreich* (Vienna, 1856–91).

ZANOLINO, A. *La Rivoluzione avvenuta nello Stato Romano l'Anno 1831* (Bologna, 1878).

NOTES

At the time of the Second Empire, news items and reports of foreign correspondents in *The Times* were often published only in the later editions of that paper on the day they were received in London, and then reprinted in the earlier, but not the later, editions on the following day. The edition is not named in the paper. Readers, therefore, who consult my sources may sometimes find them in *The Times* of the day before, or the day after, the date given in my reference, according to whether they read the earlier or the later editions of the newspaper.

Foreword

1. Larousse, *Grand Dictionnaire Universel du XIXe Siècle*, II. 920–46; XI. 804–15, 819–33. In addition to the 15 columns covering the years 1805–21, there are further passages dealing with the bibliography of Napoleon I and other matters.
2. Jerrold, *Life of Napoleon III*, II. 84–85.
3. *Times Literary Supplement*, 25 Jan. 1923.
4. Alba, 'La Emperatriz Eugenia' (*Boletín de la Real Academia de Historia*, CXX. 71–101). Alba gave very similar lectures to The Ark in Oxford in 1941 and to the Institut Français in Madrid in 1952, which have both been published.

PART I

Chapter 1 – King Louis and Queen Hortense

1. Briffault, *The Prisoner of Ham*, p. 346.
2. Bainville, *Napoléon*, p. 13.
3. Painter, *Marcel Proust*, I. 96.
4. Hanoteau's Notes to *Mémoires de la Reine Hortense*, I. 2–3n.; and see *The Journal of the Hon. Henry Edward Fox*, p. 278, for Fox's talk with Hortense on this subject.
5. See the story as told by Letizia to Valérie Masuyer in Rome in 1830, in Valérie Masuyer's Diary (*Revue des Deux Mondes*, VI(xxii). 850–2).
6. Louis Bonaparte, *Historical Documents and Reflections on the Government of Holland*, I. 45–49.

7. Hortense, *Mémoires*, I. 9–10.
8. Hanoteau's Notes in Hortense, I. 18n.
9. Hortense, I. 19, 25.
10. Hortense, I. 21–23.
11. Alexandre de Beauharnais to Josephine, 4 Thermidor, An II (22 July, 1794) (Hortense, I. 33–34n.).
12. Barras, *Mémoires*, II. 52–70.
13. Louis Bonaparte, I. 54–81, 87–111, especially pp. 66–67.
14. Hortense, I. 37, 54, 58, 66, 93–94, 104–9, 105–6n.; II. 114; Louis Bonaparte, I. 119–21, 125–7; Fox, p. 352.
15. Hortense, I. 1.
16. Hortense, III. 119.
17. For Hortense, see Fox, pp. 237, 249, 251–2, 261–5, 267, 269, 271–3, 278.
18. Hortense. III. 191n., 274, 317n.
19. For the rumours, and Hortense's attitude towards them, see her conversations with Fox, in Fox, pp. 263–4, 266.
20. Dr Bouvier's report, 28 May 1812 (Duboscq, *Louis Bonaparte en Hollande*, pp. 52–58); Hortense, I. 127, 127–8n.; Louis Bonaparte, I. 83, 124–5, 131. See also Duboscq, pp. 59–61, 62–63n., 64.
21. Hortense, I. 135, 173–4, 220; Fox, pp. 271, 323.
22. Hortense, I. 136.
23. Senatusconsulte of 28 Floréal, An XII (in *Le Moniteur Universel*, 30 Floréal, An XII (20 May 1804)); Hortense, I. 201.
24. Hortense, I. 219–28.
25. Decree of 16 Frimaire, An XIV (*Le Moniteur*, 29 Frimaire, An XIV (20 Dec. 1805)); Hortense, II. 121.
26. Louis Bonaparte, I. 141–55; Hortense, I. 241–2; *Le Moniteur*, 6 June 1806.
27. Louis Bonaparte, I. 163; II. 32; Hortense, I. 254, 270–1; Madame Rémusat, *Mémoires*, III. 34; Fox, p. 251; *Moniteur*, 7 July, 27 Aug., 22, 24, 26, 27 Sept., 2, 4, 5, 14, 18 Oct., 24 Nov. 1806; 4, 11, 23, 28, 31 Jan., 3, 5 Feb. 1807.
28. Hortense, I. 282–6.
29. Hortense, I. 287–93, 300, 303–6, 318, 320; Josephine to Eugène de Beauharnais, 11 June 1807 (*R.D.M.*, VI(xxxvi). 314–15); Napoleon I to Hortense, 20 May, 2 June 1807 (*Correspondance de Napoléon Ier*, XV. 310, 380); Louis Bonaparte, II. 108–9; Madame Rémusat, III. 138–42; *Moniteur*, 10, 19, 24 May, 13, 31 July, 22 Aug. 1807; Masuyer (*R.D.M.*, VI(xxii). 849); Jerrold, I. 433.
30. Hortense, I. 299; Louis Bonaparte, II. 109–10; Louis Bonaparte to Napoleon I, 5 June 1807 (Rocquain, *Napoléon Ier et le Roi Louis*, pp. 121–2); Louis Bonaparte to Hortense, 14 Sept. 1816 (Turquan, *La reine Hortense d'après les témoignages des contemporains*, II. 128–33); *Moniteur*, 13, 31 July 1807.
31. Hortense, I. 301–15; Madame Rémusat, III. 142–3; *Moniteur* 22 Aug. 1807.

32. Hortense, II. 15–16; Madame Rémusat, III. 143–5, 209; Bac, *Napoléon III inconnu*, pp. 1–33; Duboscq, pp. 66–67.
33. Castelnau to his son (the future Marshal), 19 July 1807 (Perey, 'La Reine Hortense d'après des documents inédits', in *La Vie Contemporaine*, Jan.–Mar. 1894, p. 350). For the best study of the question of Napoleon III's paternity, see Emerit, 'Histoire et légende: la naissance de Napoléon III' (*Revue de la Méditerranée*, III. 172–85); see also Dansette, *Histoire du Second Empire*, I. 21–32. For Hortense Cornu's opinion, see Nassau Senior's Journal, 21 May 1860 (RA K45, pp. 11–12).
34. Hortense, I. 315–18, 324; Louis Bonaparte to Napoleon I, 9 Aug. 1807 (Rocquain, pp. 123–4); Louis Bonaparte to Hortense, 23 Nov. 1809 (Duboscq, p. 229); *Moniteur*, 22 Aug., 30 Sept. 1807.
35. Louis Bonaparte to Hortense, 14 Sept. 1816 (Turquan, II. 128–33); Louis Bonaparte, I. 127; III. 199.

Chapter 2 – The Prince of Holland

1. Hortense, I. 324, 330; Madame Rémusat, III. 145–6.
2. Louis Bonaparte, II. 37–40.
3. Hortense, II. 1–3; *Moniteur*, 21 Apr. 1808.
4. Napoleon I to Hortense, 23 Apr. 1808; Napoleon I to Cambacérès, 23, 25 Apr. 1808; Napoleon I to Fouché, 23 Apr. 1808 (Hortense, III. 367–8); Hortense, II. 3.
5. Louis Bonaparte, II. 277–87; Hortense, II. 3; *Moniteur*, 28 Apr., 1, 4 May 1808.
6. Hortense, II. 3 5; Madame de Laplace to Elisa Bacciochi, 16 July 1808 (*Lettres de Madame de Laplace à Elisa Napoléon*, p. 133); *Moniteur*, 6 Sept. 1808.
7. *Moniteur*, 3 June 1808.
8. Napoleon I to Joseph Bonaparte, 6 Sept. 1795; Napoleon I to Louis Bonaparte, two letters of 21 July, two letters of 29 July, 30 July, 21 Aug., 15 Sept., 25 Oct., 5 Nov., two letters of 6 Nov., 16 Nov., 15 Dec. 1806; 23, 30 Mar., 4, 19, 30 Apr., 18, 22 July, 20, 23 Oct., 13 Nov., 16 Dec. 1807; 26 Feb., 3 Apr., 6 May, 19 June, 17 Aug. 1808; 21 Mar., 17 July, 13 Aug. 1809; 6 Jan. 1810; Napoleon I to Clarke, 4 Sept., 1809; 8 Mar. 1810; Napoleon I to Champagny, 19 Aug. 1807, 11 Oct. 1809 (Jerrold, I. 14n.; Rocquain, pp. 13, 15–16, 23, 30–31, 56–57, 65–68, 76, 86–88, 98–104, 111–12, 115, 115–17n., 123, 133, 136, 143–4, 146–7, 159, 166–70, 172, 176–7, 179–80, 196–7, 204, 210, 212, 218, 234, 259; *Correspondance de Napoléon I*er, XV. 509–10).
9. Louis Bonaparte, I. 179.
10. Napoleon I to Louis Bonaparte, 30 June, 3 July 1806; 30 Mar., 4, 30 Apr. 1807; 20 May 1810 (Rocquain, pp. 4–6, 99–104, 115, 115–17n., 273–6; Louis Bonaparte, III. 282–9).
11. *Moniteur*, 23 Dec. 1806, 5 Sept., 30 Oct. 1807, 31 Jan. 1808; Louis Bonaparte to Michaud, 4 Aug. 1806; Louis Bonaparte to Dejean, 9 Aug.

1806; Louis Bonaparte to Champagny, 22 Sept. 1807; Louis Bonaparte to Roëll, 23 Jan. 1808; Louis Bonaparte to Napoleon I, 22 Sept. 1807; 16 Mar. 1809; Louis Bonaparte to Oudinot, 12 May 1810 (Duboscq, pp. 83–90, 172, 192–3, 292n., 391–2; Rocquain, pp. 126–7); Napoleon I to Louis Bonaparte, 15 Dec. 1806; 13 Jan., 25 Feb., 29 Sept. 1807; 21 Sept., 12 Oct. 1808; 17 July 1809; Napoleon I to Champagny, 6 Mar. 1810 (Rocquain, pp. 86–88, 91, 93–94, 128, 184, 189, 204, 258); Hortense, II. 13; Louis Bonaparte, I. 226–7, 297–304, 309–18; II. 31, 118–20, 137–42, 170–1, 179, 183–4, 206; III. 122–6, 132, 165, 191.

12. Napoleon I to Louis Bonaparte, 27 Mar. 1808; Louis Bonaparte to Napoleon I, 4 Sept. 1808 (Rocquain, pp. 165–6, 182–3); Louis Bonaparte to Joseph Bonaparte, 9 Aug., 1 Oct. 1808 (Duboscq, pp. 253, 266–9); Louis Bonaparte, II. 307–10.

13. Louis Bonaparte to Madame de Boubers, 17 May, 2, 8 June 1808; 2 Jan., 28 June 1809; Louis Bonaparte to Letizia Bonaparte, 20 May, 8 June 1808; 28 Mar., 1809; Louis Bonaparte to Madame de Broc, 12 Aug. 1808; Louis Bonaparte to Lucien Bonaparte, 14 Aug. 1808; Louis Bonaparte to Hortense, 23, 29 Aug., 23 Nov. 1809; Louis Bonaparte to Napoleon Louis, 28 Aug. 1808; Louis Bonaparte to Napoleon I, 4 Sept. 1808; Louis Bonaparte to Jerome Bonaparte, 15 Oct. 1808; Louis Bonaparte to Verhuell, 29 Oct. 1808 (Duboscq, pp. 209–22, 226–30, 239–40, 254–5, 277); Napoleon I to Hortense, 17 July 1808 (Hortense, II. 369); Hortense, I. 331, 333, 341n.; II. 1, 5.

14. Louis Bonaparte to Hortense, 23 Aug. 1808 (Duboscq, pp. 214–15).

15. Louis Bonaparte, II. 328–30, 436–40; III. 44–49; Napoleon I to Louis Bonaparte, 6 Mar. 1809 (Rocquain, p. 195).

16. Louis Bonaparte, III. 196, 200; Hortense, II. 50n., 51, 52n.

17. Napoleon I to Louis Bonaparte, 21 Dec. 1809 (Rocquain, pp. 228–32; Louis Bonaparte, III. 228–37).

18. Louis Bonaparte, III. 196–266, 271; Hortense, II. 65–67, 70; *Moniteur*, 17, 21, 30 Apr., 16 May 1810.

19. Hortense, II. 73–81; Louis Bonaparte, III. 291–5, 298–307; Napoleon I to Champagny, 23 May 1810; Napoleon I to Louis Bonaparte, 23 May 1810; Napoleon I to Clarke, 24 June 1810 (Rocquain, pp. 276–8, 281–2); *Moniteur*, 7, 22 June 1810; Fox, p. 251.

20. Louis Bonaparte, III. 319–23, 326–9; Louis Bonaparte to Napoleon I, 1 July 1810; Louis Bonaparte to Hortense, 1 July 1810 (Rocquain, pp. 282–3); *Moniteur*, 10 July 1810.

21. *Moniteur*, 22 July 1810.

22. Louis Bonaparte, III. 336–41, 392–4; Hortense, II. 103n., 105–6n., 123.

23. *Moniteur*, 6 Nov. 1810.

24. Louise Cochelet, *Mémoires sur la reine Hortense et la famille impériale*, I. 44–46.

25. Cochelet, I. 44–46, 54, 64, 76, 171, 212; Hortense, I. 189n.; II. 105–6n.

26. Jerrold, I. 69–72, 72–73n.

27. Cochelet, III. 128.

28. Cochelet, III. 19–21.

29. Hortense, III. 174, 191n., 274, 317n.
30. Cochelet, I. 286–7; II. 105.
31. Cochelet, I. 212, 287–9.
32. Cochelet, I. 172–3.
33. Hortense, I. 178, 186, 190, 248–9; II. 38, 40; *Moniteur*, 22 June 1809.
34. Guedalla, *Palmerston*, p.88.
35. Hortense, III. 151.
36. Cochelet, I. 17–18.
37. Cochelet, I. 19–21.
38. Cochelet, I. 74.
39. Hortense, II. 164, 167–8; Cochelet, I. 77, 82–84, 117, 119; *Moniteur*, 19 June 1813.
40. Cochelet, I. 119–24.
41. Louis Bonaparte, III. 356–62; Louis Bonaparte to Napoleon I, 4 Aug. 1813, 1 Jan. 1814; Napoleon I to Louis Bonaparte, 16 Jan. 1814 (Louis Bonaparte, III. 396–403); Hortense, II. 171.
42. Cochelet, I. 134–5.

Chapter 3 – The Restoration and the Hundred Days

1. Hortense, II. 200; Cochelet, I. 288–9.
2. Hortense, II. 190.
3. For the flight from Paris to Navarre, see Hortense, II. 183–98; Cochelet, I. 183–204; Louis Bonaparte, III. 363, 365.
4. Hortense to Louise Cochelet, 9 Apr. 1814 (Cochelet, I. 222–3); Hortense, II. 194n., 200; Cochelet, I. 207.
5. Leopold of Saxe-Coburg to Hortense, 14 Apr. 1814 (Hortense, II. 203–5).
6. Hortense, II. 205–6; Hortense to Louise Cochelet, 12 Apr. 1814 (Cochelet, I. 234–5).
7. Hortense, II. 211–12.
8. Hortense, II. 216, 221–2, 231, 235–7; Cochelet, I. 278. *Le Moniteur* of 15 May 1814 wrongly reported that the Tsar was present at the memorial mass.
9. Hortense, II. 242; Cochelet, I. 285–7, 293.
10. Hortense, II. 231, 246–50; Cochelet, I. 300–8.
11. Hortense, II. 251–3, 263; Cochelet, I. 318–21; Masson, *Napoléon et sa famille*, X. 187–9.
12. Hortense, II. 214–15, 254–7 and n., 301, 301–2n.; Cochelet, II. 198.
13. Jerrold, I. 80–81; Cochelet, II. 202–5.
14. Decazes to Louis Bonaparte (June 1814); Louis Bonaparte to Hortense, 28 Aug. 1814; Hortense to Louis Bonaparte (Sept. 1814) (Masson, X. 168, 173–6); Hortense, II. 230, 262–3, 277–8, 284–5; Louis Bonaparte, III. 367, 369–70; Masson, X. 177–8.
15. Hortense to Alexander I, 4 Oct. 1814 (*La Revue de Paris*, Sept.–Oct. 1907, pp. 680–3); Hortense, II. 277–81, 284; Cochelet, II. 240–4.

16. *Journal de Paris*, 23, 29 Jan., 1, 4, 5 and 11 Feb. 1815; Hortense, II. 285–7, 308–9; Louis Bonaparte, III. 370; Bonnet, *Mes souvenirs du barreau*, pp. 22–30, 430–5; Masson, X. 194–204; *Moniteur*, 8 Mar. 1815.
17. Hortense, II. 310–11; Cochelet, II. 267–72; Jerrold, I. 72, 73n.
18. Hortense, II. 313, 317–18, 326; Cochelet, II. 291.
19. Hortense, II. 325, 329–33; Hortense to Eugène de Beauharnais, 20 Mar. 1815 (Jerrold, I. 92 and n.); Cochelet, II. 320–1.
20. Hortense, II. 334; *Journal de Paris*, 22 Mar. 1815; Cochelet, III. 6; Madame Récamier, *Souvenirs et Correspondance*, II. 76–80.
21. Hortense, III. 337–9.
22. *Moniteur*, 15 Apr., 7, 8, 14, 15, 16 and 20 May 1815; Hortense, II. 358; Cochelet, III. 22–23, 30–35, 63–68.
23. Hortense to Alexander I, 25 Mar. 1815 (*Revue de Paris*, Sept.–Oct. 1907, pp. 698–701); Hortense to Eugène de Beauharnais (21 Mar. 1815) (Cochelet, II. 322–3); Hortense, II. 342–7; III. 8; Cochelet, III. 68, 80.
24. Cochelet, III. 51–53; French Government's statement of 29 Mar. 1815 (in *Moniteur*, 15 Apr. 1815).
25. Cochelet, III. 70–80; *Moniteur*, 2 June 1815; *Journal de Paris*, 2 June 1815; Hortense, III. 2–3, 11–13.
26. Hortense, III. 14; Cochelet, III. 92–93; Jerrold, I. 94–95; Persigny, *Lettres de Londres*, pp. 41–46; Briffault, pp. 6–9.
27. *Moniteur*, 18 June 1815.

Chapter 4 – The Road to Exile

1. Hortense, III. 17–18; Cochelet, III. 105–7; *Moniteur*, 19 and 20 June 1815; *Journal de Paris*, 19 June 1815.
2. Hortense, III. 24–25, 27, 37–38, 40, 46; Cochelet. III. 122, 127, 135–9; *Moniteur*, 21, 23 and 24 June 1815; *Journal de Paris*, 22 June 1815.
3. *Journal de Paris*, 26, 27 and 29 June 1815; Hortense, III. 50, 52, 58–59; Cochelet, III. 164–6.
4. Hortense, II. 345; III. 61.
5. Hortense, III. 60, 64; Cochelet, III. 188–90, 192; *Moniteur*, 21 July 1815; *Journal de Paris*, 22 and 23 July 1815; Masuyer (*R.D.M.*, VI (xxii). 584).
6. Hortense, III. 61–62, 94; Cochelet, I. 300; III. 219–22, 225n.
7. For the last days in Paris, see Hortense, III. 65–67; Cochelet, III. 193–4, 207–9, 212.
8. For the journey from Paris to Geneva, see Hortense, III. 68–71, 75; Cochelet, III. 236–43; *Journal de Paris*, 25 July 1815.
9. Hortense, III. 66–67, 69, 73–74; Cochelet, II. 9.
10. Hortense, III. 76n.
11. *Journal de Paris*, 19 July 1815.
12. *Moniteur*, 26 July 1815; Hortense, III. 125n.; Jerrold, I. 58n.
13. For the stay at Aix-les Bains, see Hortense, III. 76, 79–89, 92, 94;

Cochelet, III. 259–63, 273–6; IV. 11–12; *Journal de Paris*, 27 Aug., 26 Sept. 1815; *Moniteur*, 28 Aug. 1815; Louis Bonaparte, III. 370.

14. Minutes of meeting of Allied ministers, 27 Aug. 1815 (in Cochelet, III. 308).

15. Finot to Hortense, 6 Sept. 1815; Minutes of meeting of Allied ministers, 21 Oct. 1815; Ivernois to Louise Cochelet, 26 Oct. 1815; Wyss to Hortense, 17 Nov. 1815; Martroy to Fabre, 19 Nov. 1815; Woyna to Hortense, 25 Nov. 1815 (Cochelet, III. 310–11; IV. 33–35, 42–46); Hortense, III. 92, 95; Cochelet, IV. 21, 54–55; *Journal de Paris*, 19 Nov. 1815.

16. Hortense, III. 95–102; Cochelet, IV. 55–85; *Journal de Paris*, 9 Dec. 1815; Budé, *Les Bonaparte en Suisse*, pp. 128–43.

Chapter 5 – Monsieur Le Bas

1. Hortense, III. 125–7.

2. Hortense to Capo d'Istria, 1 Sept. 1916; Hortense to Alexander I, 1 Sept. 1816; Capo d'Istria to Hortense, 27 Sept. 9 Oct. 1816 (*Revue de Paris*, Sept.–Oct. 1907, pp. 705–8).

3. For the stay at Constance and the move to Arenenberg and Augsburg, see Hortense, III. 103, 104n., 107, 114, 120–5, 137, 139–41; Cochelet, IV. 86, 88–90, 99–100, 133, 140–4, 181–206, 249–50, 253–4, 271–3, 276–7, 284, 288; *Journal de Paris*, 29 Dec. 1815; Jerrold, I. 125; Lavalette to Louise Cochelet, 30 Sept. 1816 (Cochelet, IV. 230–3); Masuyer (*R.D.M.*, VI(xxii). 585).

4. Stratford Canning to Castlereagh, 21 Feb. 1817 (Simpson, I. 38–39).

5. Hortense, III. 142, 144–5.

6. For Bertrand, see Duchesse de Bassano to Louise Cochelet, 4 May (1817) (Cochelet, IV. 296); Bertrand to Flament, 4 June 1823 (Stéfane-Pol, *La jeunesse de Napoléon III*, pp. 32–35).

7. Cochelet, IV. 248–9; Jerrold, I. 76.

8. Cochelet, IV. 249 and n.; Stéfane-Pol, pp. 35–36.

9. Le Bas to his stepfather, 5 Aug. 1821 (Stéfane-Pol, pp. 94–95).

10. Le Bas to Lembert, 4 Dec. 1820 (Stéfane-Pol, p. 73).

11. Stéfane-Pol, pp. 39–41.

12. Stéfane-Pol, pp. 40–41, 45–46; Le Bas to his stepfather, 28 Oct. and 13 Nov. 1820; 17 Dec. 1821 (Stéfane-Pol, pp. 58–64, 104).

13. Le Bas to his stepfather, 14 (24?) July, 10 Aug. 1820; 15 June, 5 Aug., 17 Dec. 1821; Le Bas to Devaux, 17 Sept. 1820; Devaux to Le Bas, 18 Oct. 1820; Le Bas to Lavalette, 10 Nov. 1820; Le Bas to his mother (Nov. 1820); Le Bas to Lembert, 4 Dec. 1820; Le Bas to his family, 15 May 1821; Le Bas to Mocquard, 15 July 1821 (Stéfane-Pol, pp. 41–44, 49–55, 60–61, 65–73, 82–83, 89, 95–96, 105–6).

14. Bertrand to Le Bas, 1 July 1821; and see also Bertrand to Le Bas, 1 Nov. 1821 (Stéfane-Pol, pp. 84, 101).

15. Bertrand to Le Bas, 14 July 1821 (Stéfane-Pol, p. 87).

16. Louis Napoleon to Hortense, 24 July 1821 (Jerrold, I. 99–100).
17. Le Bas to his mother, 15 Oct. and (Nov.) 1820; Le Bas to his stepfather, 7 Feb., 25 June, 12 Nov., 30 Dec. 1822; 4 June, 13 July, 12 Aug., 15 Sept. 1823; 23 May 1827; Le Bas to Boissonade, 30 Dec. 1822; Le Bas to his wife, 21, 31 Aug.; 7 Sept. 1823; 23 May 1827 (Stéfane-Pol, pp. 56–58, 66, 110, 130–1, 159–61, 177, 181–2, 184–91, 352–4); see also for the visit to Marienbad, Louis Bonaparte to Armandi, 2 Aug. 1823; Armandi to Louis Bonaparte, 12 Aug. 1823 (Vicchi, *Il generale Armandi*, pp. 64–65).
18. Le Bas to his stepfather, 13 Nov. 1820; 12 Aug., 22 Dec. 1823; 17 Apr., 2 Sept. 1824; Le Bas's Diary, 16, 21, 22 Nov. 1823; Le Bas to his wife, 6 Nov. 1823; 8 Jan. 1824; 2 Mar. 1827 (Stéfane-Pol, pp. 61–62, 182, 205, 219, 222, 225–7, 241–2, 261, 343); Jerrold, I. 126 (from Fritz Rickenbach).
19. Le Bas to his stepfather, 9 Mar. 1826 (Stéfane-Pol, p. 323).
20. Le Bas to his wife, 14 May 1824 (Stéfane-Pol, pp. 244, 246).
21. Le Bas to his stepfather, 14 (24?) July 1820; 17 Dec. 1821; 12 Nov. 1822; 22 Feb. 1823; 19 Feb. 1826; 14 Aug. 1827; Le Bas to his mother, 21 Aug. 1820; Grand Duchess Stéphanie of Baden to Le Bas, 20 Nov. 1824; Armandi to Le Bas, 26 Jan. 1827 (Stéfane-Pol, pp. 43, 54, 105, 160, 165, 280–2, 321, 341–2, 356).
22. Le Bas to his stepfather, 7 July 1827 (Stéfane-Pol, p. 356).
23. Masuyer (*R.D.M.*, VI(xxvii). 857); Bac, *Napoléon III inconnu*, p. 73.
24. Le Bas to his stepfather, 7 Sept., 4 Oct. 1827; Le Bas's draft letter to Hortense (Sept. 1827) (Stéfane-Pol, pp. 358–60, 363–4).
25. Le Bas to Falloux, 6 Feb. 1849 (Stéfane-Pol, p. 366).
26. Stéfane-Pol, p. 368; Bac, pp. 146–7.
27. Stéfane-Pol, p. 366.

Chapter 6 – Revolution in the Romagna

1. Borrel, 'Le divorce de Mme Patterson Bonaparte' (*R.D.M.*, VI(xxii). 165–71); Fox, pp. 315, 317, 319.
2. Masuyer (*R.D.M.*, VI (xxii). 850–3); Fox, pp. 198, 299–300.
3. Masuyer (*R.D.M.*, VI (xxii). 606–7); Orsi, *Recollections of the Last Half Century*, pp. 56–57, 168–70; Hortense, III. 172n.
4. Hudson Lowe to Montholon (Oct. 1816?) (Montholon, *History of the Captivity of Napoleon at St Helena*, I. 219–21). See also Masuyer (*R.D.M.*, VI (xxii). 617–18).
5. Malmesbury, *Memoirs of an Ex-Minister*, I. 33; Blount, *Memoirs*, pp. 34–35; Fox, p. 277; Masuyer (*R.D.M.*, VI(xxii). 830); Jerrold, I. 107 (from Hortense Cornu); Wikoff, pp. 174, 177.
6. Orsi, p. 5.
7. Granville to Palmerston, 24 Jan. 1831 (B.L.Add. 48455).
8. Malmesbury, I. 23; Orsi, pp. 5, 79; Eugénie to —, (1908) (Luzio, *Felice Orsini*, p. 315); Masuyer (*R.D.M.*, VI(xxiii). 296).

9. Louis Napoleon to Louis Bonaparte, 19 Jan. 1829; Louis Bonaparte to Louis Napoleon (Jan. 1829) (Giraudeau, *Napoléon III intime*, pp. 23–24).

10. Louis Napoleon to Hortense, 21 July 1830; Hortense to —, (autumn 1830) (Jerrold, I. 138–9, 137n.); Hortense, III. 179–80; Briffault, p. 11.

11. Louis Napoleon to Hortense, Aug. 1830 (Jerrold, I. 137n.); Hortense, III. 172–3; and see Louis Napoleon's notes on the Revolution of 1830, in Bac, pp. 187–9.

12. Hortense, III. 199; Orsi, pp. 37–38; Armandi, *Ma Part aux événements importants de l'Italie Centrale en 1831*, p. 5.

13. Masuyer (*R.D.M.*, VI(xxii). 588–98); Hortense, III. 183.

14. Masuyer (*R.D.M.*, VI(xxii). 604).

15. Masuyer (*R.D.M.*, VI(xxii). 604–6).

16. Masuyer (*R.D.M.*, VI(xxii). 600, 606).

17. Hortense, III. 172–3, 184–6, 200–2; Masuyer (*R.D.M.*, VI(xxii). 607, 857).

18. Masuyer (*R.D.M.*, VI(xxii). 613–16).

19. Hortense, III. 186, 188; Masuyer (*R.D.M.*, VI(xxii). 831, 833).

20. Masuyer (*R.D.M.*, VI(xxii). 855).

21. Hortense, III. 193–8; Masuyer (*R.D.M.*, VI(xxii). 857–60).

22. Hortense, III. 199, 213, 279.

23. Orsi, pp. 66–79; Hortense, III. 202–3; Masuyer (*R.D.M.*, VI(xxiii). 301); Vicini, *La Rivoluzione dell'anno 1831 nelle stato Romano*, p. 7. Orsi wrongly gives the date of the meeting as 26 February. Dansette (I. 61) dates it 28 Dec. 1830.

24. Hortense, III. 214–16, 218.

25. For Louis Napoleon's part in the revolution in the Romagna, see Armandi, pp. 12–13, 26–32, 168–9; Vicini, pp. 165, 169, 172, 174, 331; Masuyer (*R.D.M.*, VI(xxiii). 298, 301–3, 305, 308, 312, 323); Hortense, III. 221–2, 239–40, 247; Napoleon Louis to Jerome Bonaparte (Feb. 1831); Napoleon Louis to Gregory XVI (Feb. 1831) (Jerome Bonaparte, *Mémoires du Roi Jérome*, VII. 463–6); Berneti to St-Aulaire, 28 Mar. 1831; Pralormo to Della Torre, 13 Mar. 1831 (Zanolino, *La Rivoluzione avvenuta Nello Stato Romano l'Anno 1831*, pp. 14n., 72); Stölting to Hortense, 25 Feb. 1831; Armandi to Hortense, 3 Mar. 1831 (Hortense, III. 221–6); Jerrold, I. 168; Zanolino, p. 13; Vesi, *Rivoluzione di Romagna del 1831*, pp. 20–22; Jerome Bonaparte, VII. 459–67; Wouters, *Les Bonaparte depuis 1815 jusqu'à ce jour*, p. 196; Giraudeau, pp. 44–45.

26. For the conflicting versions of Napoleon Louis's death, see Masuyer (*R.D.M.*, VI(xxiii). 317, 319–21); Masuyer, *Mémoires*, pp. xxviii–xxix n.; Orsi, p. 83; Armandi, p. 33; Turquan, II. 173–4n.; Wikoff, p. 56n.; D'Ambès, *Le Mémorial de Chislehurst*, pp. 69–70; Mazzatinti, 'I Moti del 1831 a Forli' (in *Rivista Storica del Risorgimento*, II. 237–50).

27. Senior's Journal, 7 Apr. 1862 (RA K51, pp. 359–60, 365–6) (from Hortense Cornu).

Chapter 7 – From Ancona to Tunbridge Wells

1. Hortense, III. 226, 230, 257; Masuyer (*R.D.M.*, VI(xxiii). 312).
2. Hortense, III. 229–30.
3. Hortense, III. 231–3, 234–5n., 243–6; Masuyer (*R.D.M.*, VI(xxiii). 314, 317, 321).
4. Hortense, III. 228, 246–8, 251–4; Masuyer (*R.D.M.*, VI(xxiii). 310; (xxiv). 233).
5. Hortense, III. 249, 257, 271; Masuyer (*R.D.M.*, VI(xxiv). 229, 247, 271).
6. For the events at Ancona, see Hortense, III. 247–8, 255–6, 258–9; Masuyer (*R.D.M.*, VI(xxiv). 233, 235–7).
7. Hortense, III. 129–33, 259.
8. Hortense, III. 270–1.
9. Masuyer (*R.D.M.*, VI(xxiv). 246).
10. For the journey from Ancona, see Hortense, III. 260–71; Masuyer (*R.D.M.*, VI(xxiv). 237–47); Jerrold, I. 176–81.
11. Louis Napoleon to Louis Philippe (Apr. 1831) (Jerrold, I. 183–4).
12. Hortense, III. 278; Masuyer, *Mémoires*, p. xxviii–xxix n.
13. Hortense, III. 281, 283; Masuyer (*R.D.M.*, VI(xxiv). 250, 254).
14. For the events during the stay in Paris, see Hortense, III. 283, 285–91, 297, 303, 306–10; Masuyer (*R.D.M.*, VI(xxiv). 256–61, 263–4, 268–9; (xxvi). 93, 102); Guizot, *Mémoires pour servir à l'histoire de mon temps*, II. 218–19.
15. Masuyer (*R.D.M.*, VI(xxvii). 861).
16. Hortense, III. 323.
17. ibid.
18 Louis Napoleon to *Le Temps*, 17 June 1831 (Masuyer, in *R.D.M.*, VI(xxvii). 852–3).
19. *Moniteur*, 22 Sept. 1831.
20. Masuyer (*R.D.M.*, VI(xxvii). 869).
21. For the stay in England, see Hortense, III. 310–16, 319, 322–6; Masuyer (*R.D.M.*, VI(xxvi). 93–96, 100–1, 105, 107–11, 113, 116; (xxvii). 849–50, 852–4, 856, 861–72); Sir Henry Holland, *Recollections of Past Life*, p. 183; *The Times*, 20 June 1831.
22. For the journey through France, see Hortense, III. 327, 329, 331, 335–6, 339–40; Masuyer (*R.D.M.*, VI(xxvii). 873).

Chapter 8 – Princess Mathilde

1. See Louis Napoleon to Henry Fox, 19 Sept. 1831 (Ivor Guest MSS.); Gisquet, *Mémoires*, I. 350.
2. Gisquet, I. 292, 351–3; II. 176–83; IV. 366–70.
3. Henri Fazy, *James Fazy*, p. 92.

4. *Rêveries politiques*, especially pp. 7–10 (in *Œuvres Complètes du Prince Napoléon-Louis Bonaparte*.

5. Louis Napoleon to Anderveert (May 1832) (Budé, p. 213).

6. *Considérations politiques et militaires sur la Suisse*, pp. 12–13, 76–77.

7. ibid., p. 7; Louis Bonaparte to Louis Napoleon, 12 Sept. 1833 (Giraudeau, p. 31); Rocquain, pp. i–ii.

8. Bac, p. 174; Masuyer (*R.D.M.*, VI(xxx). 388).

9. Bac, pp. 96 97, 169–70, 176, 179; Masuyer (*R.D.M.*, VI(xxvi). 110; (xxvii). 865; *Mémoires*, p. 418); Jerrold, I. 119; Ollivier, *Journal*, I. 178.

10. *Papiers et correspondance de la famille impériale*, II. 142.

11. Masuyer, *Mémoires*, pp. 419–20.

12. Hortense to Countess Arese, 18 Mar. 1832 (Bonfadini, *Vita di Francesco Arese*, pp. 35–36); Bac, pp. 171–2, 176.

13. Dumas, *Mémoires*, II(x). 131.

14. Jerrold, I. 234.

15. Laity, *Relation historique des Événements du 30 Octobre 1836*, p. 21; Jerrold, I. 313n. Dansette (I. 93) has no doubt that the meeting with La Fayette took place.

16. Joseph Bonaparte to his wife, 13 July 1838 (Ivor Guest MSS.); Louis Napoleon, 'Quelques mots sur Joseph Napoléon Bonaparte' (*Œuvres de Napoléon III*, II. 413–59); Giraudeau, p. 48.

17. Louis Napoleon to Vieillard (Mar. 1833); Louis Napoleon to Hortense (Mar. 1833) (Dansette, I. 94).

18. Le Bas to his stepfather, 10 Mar. 1827 (Stéfane-Pol, p. 344); Masuyer (*R.D.M.*, VI(xxvii). 852).

19. Jerrold, I. 234.

20. Louis Napoleon to Hortense, 19 July 1834 (Jerrold, I. 242n.).

21. Louis Napoleon's letter to the press, 14 Dec. 1835 (Briffault, pp. 359–60; Jerrold, I. 243–4). Jerrold wrongly dates it August 1834.

22. Dansette, I. 101–2; Castelot, *Napoléon Trois*, I. 208–13.

23. Castelot, I. 207; Bourguignon's notes to Masuyer's *Mémoires*, p. 299n.

24. Louis Napoleon to Hortense Cornu, 29 Aug. 1842 (Castelot, I. 403).

25. Bac, pp. 75, 82; Masuyer, *Mémoires*, pp. 443–4.

26. Bac, p. 170n.

27. Bac, pp. 73–77, 162, 240; Chateaubriand, *Mémoires d'Outre-Tombe*, V. 587.

28. Louis Napoleon to Chateaubriand, 4 May 1832 (Jerrold, I. 263, 435); Valérie Masuyer to —, 16 and 29 Aug. 1832 (Bac, pp. 164–6); Chateaubriand, V. 582, 585–8.

29. Fox, pp. 237, 347, 351; Greville, I(i). 303; Bac, pp. 78, 184.

30. Bourguignon's notes to Masuyer's *Mémoires*, p. 290n.

31. Masuyer (*R.D.M.*, VI(xxx). 367).

32. Masuyer (*R.D.M.*, VI(xxx). 368).

33. For Mathilde's stay at Arenenberg, see Masuyer (*R.D.M.*, VI(xxx). 367–87).

34. Masuyer (*R.D.M.*, VI(xxx). 380–1, 392–3).

Chapter 9 – From Strasburg to New York

1. Hortense to Parquin (Nov. 1836) (*R.D.M.*, VI(xxviii). 638).
2. Dansette, I. 109.
3. Masuyer (*R.D.M.*, VI(xxx). 402).
4. Jerrold, I. 342–3, 452.
5. Persigny, *Relation de l'entreprise du Prince Napoléon-Louis*, p. 37; Masuyer (*R.D.M.*, VI(xxviii). 607–8).
6. Persigny, *Relation de l'entreprise du Prince Napoléon-Louis*, p. 42.
7. Laity, pp. 43–48; Persigny, *Relation de l'entreprise*, pp. 27–30.
8. For the events at Strasburg on 30 October, see *Moniteur*, 2, 3 Nov. 1836; 10, 12, 14 Jan. 1837; Laity, pp. 50–64; Persigny, *Relation de l'entreprise*, pp. 38–52; Guizot, *Mémoires*, IV. 199–202; Louis Napoleon to Hortense (Nov. 1836) (*Œuvres*, II. 65–87); Laure de Franqueville to her sister Fanny, 30 Oct. 1836 (*R.D.M.*, VI(xxviii). 611–14); Jerrold, I. 336–59, 451–7; Wikoff, pp. 78–87; Thirria, I. 51–103; Simpson, I. 107–21.
9. D'Avenel, 'Le port des lettres depuis sept siècles' (*R.D.M.*, VI(xxii). 162).
10. *Moniteur*, 2 Nov. 1836.
11. Laure de Franqueville to her sister Fanny, 30 Oct., 6 Nov. 1836; Valérie Masuyer to Hortense, 4 Nov. 1836 (*R.D.M.*, VI(xxviii). 612, 614–16, 628); Guizot, *Mémoires*, VI. 198–9.
12. *Moniteur*, 2 Nov. 1836.
13. Laure de Franqueville to Valérie Masuyer, 6 Nov. 1836; Masuyer (*R.D.M.*, VI(xxviii). 630); *Moniteur*, 11 Nov. 1836.
14. *Moniteur*, 3 Nov. 1836; *The Times*, 3, 4 and 12 Nov. 1836.
15. Castelot, I. 259.
16. Louis Napoleon to Hortense (Nov. 1836) (Simpson, I. 339–40).
17. *Moniteur*, 13, 14, 16 Nov. 1836; 16 Jan., 7 Mar. 1837 (speech of counsel for the prosecution at the trial and debate in the Chamber of Deputies).
18. Laity, pp. 68–70; Laure de Franqueville to Valérie Masuyer, 10 Nov. 1836; Hortense to Parquin (Nov. 1836); Masuyer (*R.D.M.*, VI(xxviii). 632, 635–6, 639); *Moniteur*, 20 Nov. 1836.
19. Laity, p. 71.
20. Laity, p. 70; Masuyer (*R.D.M.*, VI(xxviii). 633, 637); Guizot, IV. 202–3.
21. Valérie Masuyer to Laure de Franqueville, 31 Jan. 1837; Hortense to Persigny, 5 Feb. 1837 (*R.D.M.*, VI(xxviii). 643, 645).
22. For Louis Napoleon's journey to America, see Louis Napoleon to Hortense, 12, 14 and 29 Dec. 1836; 1, 5, 10 Jan. 1837; Louis Napoleon to Vaudrey, 15 Apr. 1837 (*Œuvres*, II. 88–96; Jerrold, I. 417, 421, 463, 467); Persigny, *Relation de l'entreprise*, p. 48; Jerrold, I. 420.
23. *Moniteur*, 20 Jan. 1837.
24. ibid., 17 Jan. 1837.
25. ibid., 20 Jan. 1837.
26. For the trial, see *Moniteur*, 10, 12, 13, 15, 16, 17, 18, 19, 20, 21, 23 Jan. 1837; Jerrold, I. 381–412.

27. *The Times*, 4 Nov. 1836.
28. Louis Napoleon to Hortense, 14 Dec. 1836 (Jerrold, I. 464–5).
29. Louis Napoleon to Louis Bonaparte, 10 Apr. 1837; Louis Napoleon to Hortense, 17 Apr. 1837 (Jerrold, II. 4–5, 5–6n., 10–11, 11n.); and see Jerrold, I. 420. For Point Breeze, see Caroline Murat, *My Memoirs*, pp. 30–32.
30. Monnerville, *Clemenceau*, p. 47.
31. Louis Napoleon to Louis Bonaparte, 10 Apr. 1837 (Jerrold, II. 10–11, 11n.).
32. Masuyer, (*R.D.M.*, VI(xxx). 403–4); *Life, Letters and Journals of George Ticknor*, I. 88.
33. Louis Napoleon to Joseph Bonaparte, 22 Apr. 1837; and see also Louis Napoleon to Hortense, 17 Apr. 1837 (Jerrold, I. 424, 468–9; II. 5, 6n.). See also Giraudeau, p. 71.
34. Wap, *Mijne Reis naar Rome in het voorjaar van 1837*, pp. 228–9.
35. Masuyer, *Mémoires*, p. 416.
36. Arese to Valérie Masuyer, 16 Apr. 1837 (Masuyer, *Mémoires*, p. 405); Nichols, *Forty Years of American Life*, I. 352; Adkins, *Fitz-Greene Halleck*, pp. 278–9; Williams, *The Life of Washington Irving*, II. 46, 381; Pierre Irving, *The Life and Letters of Washington Irving*, III. 88.
37. Jerrold, II. 17.
38. For Louis Napoleon in the United States, see General Webb to Jerrold, 28 Apr. 1874; General Wilson to Jerrold, 28 Apr., 9 June 1874 (Jerrold, II. 12–13, 17–19, 18–19n., 21n.); Masuyer, *Mémoires*, pp. 416–17; Wikoff, pp. 88–97, 381–91.
39. Arese to Valérie Masuyer, 6 June 1837 (Masuyer, *Mémoires*, p. 411); Arese, 'Notes d'un voyage dans les Prairies' (Bonfadini, pp. 456–541).
40. Hortense to Louis Napoleon, 3 Apr. 1837 (Jerrold, II. 33–34, 34n.).
41. Louis Napoleon to Van Buren, 6 June 1837 (Jerrold, II. 22–23).
42. Arese to Valérie Masuyer, 6 June 1837 (Masuyer, *Mémoires*, pp. 410–11).
43. Louis Napoleon to Hortense, 9 July 1837 (Jerrold, II. 23–25, 25n.).
44. Information from the late Miss Mildred Stock.
45. Louis Napoleon to Hortense, 9 July 1837; Louis Napoleon to Louis Bonaparte, 12, 15 July 1837 (Jerrold, II. 23–25, 25n., 27–28, 28–29n.); Persigny to Valérie Masuyer, 24 July 1837; Louis Napoleon to Valérie Masuyer, 30 July 1837 (Masuyer, *Mémoires*, pp. 413–15); Bourqueney to Molé, 31 July 1837; Sébastiani to Molé, 21 July 1837 (Ivor Guest MSS.).
46. Masuyer, *Mémoires*, pp. 399–401, 415, 427–8, 430–4.

Chapter 10 – From Switzerland to London

1. Masuyer, *Mémoires*, pp. 434–54; Briffault, p. 354.
2. Louis Napoleon to Louis Bonaparte, 10 May 1838 (Jerrold, II. 54n.); Bac, pp. 262–3.

3. Louis Napoleon to Capefigue, 10 Nov. 1846 (Briffault, pp. 335–8; Jerrold, II. 380n.); Louis Napoleon to Mme L—, 18 Apr. 1843 (Bac, p. 274); *The Times*, 23 Apr. 1847; Jerrold, II. 30–31; Briffault, pp. 27–30; Wikoff, pp. 105–6.

4. Jerrold, II. 50–51.

5. *Procès de Armand Laity*, p. 10; Thirria, I. 104–13.

6. Montebello to Government of Lucerne, 1 Aug. 1838 (Jerrold, II. 488–9); *The Times*, 13 Aug. 1838.

7. Molé to Montebello (14 Aug. 1838) (*Journal des Débats*, 6 Sept. 1838; *The Times*, 7 Sept. 1838).

8. *The Times*, 27 Aug. 1838; *Moniteur*, 24 Sept. 1838.

9. Louis Napoleon to Anderveert, 20 Aug. 1838; Louis Napoleon to Vieillard, 10 June 1842 (Jerrold, II. 68–70, 466); *The Times*, 1 Sept. 1838.

10. *Moniteur*, 5 Sept. 1838; *The Times*, 6 Sept. 1838; Simpson, I. 149–50; Palmerston to Granville, 29 Sept. 1838 (B.L.Add. 48507).

11. Louis Napoleon to Anderveert, 22 Sept. 1838 (Jerrold, II. 75–76, 76–77n.).

12. *The Times*, 2 Oct. 1838.

13. Government of Lucerne to Montebello, 6 Oct. 1838; Molé to Montebello, 12 Oct. 1838 (Jerrold, II. 489–91).

14. *The Times*, 20 Sept., 2, 9 Oct. 1838; *Le National*, 26 Sept. 1838; Jerrold, II. 83.

15. *The Times*, 23, 24, 25, 26 Oct. 1838.

16. For Louis Napoleon's expulsion from Switzerland, see Jerrold, II. 62–80; Thirria, I. 114–38; Simpson, I. 146–56.

17. Jerrold, II. 85; *Morning Post*, 23 Apr. 1839; Sir William Fraser, *Napoleon III*, pp. 17–18.

18. Disraeli's note (undated) (Monypenny and Buckle, *Life of Benjamin Disraeli, Earl of Beaconsfield*, II. 491–2).

19. Jerrold, II. 83; *The Times*, 29 Oct. 1838.

20. Fraser, p. 18; Jerrold, II. 85.

21. Fraser, p. 7; Planché, *Recollections and Reflections*, II. 45.

22. Greville, II(i). 167.

23. Jerrold, II. 84, 86.

24. Fraser, p. 15.

25. Jerrold, II. 87, 120.

26. Persigny, *Lettres de Londres*, p. 73; Jerrold, II. 87.

27. *Morning Post*, 8 June 1839; Fleischmann, *Napoléon III et les femmes*, pp. 124–5 (citing *La Presse*, 18 Aug. 1839, and *Journal du Havre*).

28. *The Times*, 26 Nov. 1838; *Court Journal*, 15, 29 Dec. 1838; 12, 26 Jan., 2 Feb. 1839; *Birmingham Journal*, 26 Jan., 2 Feb. 1839; *Birmingham Gazette*, 28 Jan. 1839; *Manchester Guardian*, 30 Jan. 1839; Ivor Guest MSS.

29. Miss Eva Billington's statement (Guest MSS., 'App.B. Emily Rowles', pp. 4–7); Norman, *Scores and Annals of the West Kent Cricket Club*, p. 236n.; Fraser, pp. 1–3, 216–17.

NOTES

30. *The Times*, 10 July 1839; Anstruther, *The Knight and the Umbrella*, pp. 153, 161, 165–6.
31. Anstruther, pp. 182, 209–23; Malmesbury, I. 105–6.
32. Anstruther, p. 171; *see Le National*, 14 Nov., 5 Dec. 1848.
33. *The Times*, 4 Mar. 1840; *Morning Post*, 4 Mar. 1840; Jerrold, II. 116–17; Malmesbury, I. 112.
34. *Œuvres*, I. 15–233.
35. Jerrold, II. 112.
36. *Œuvres*, I. 1–13.
37. For passages cited and summarized, see ibid., I. 5, 7–9, 13, 22, 25, 28, 112, 126, 138–40.
38. *The Times*, 18 May 1839.
39. For Louis Napoleon in England in 1838–40, see Jerrold, II. 83–92; Guest, *Napoleon III in England*, pp. 31–53.

Chapter 11 – Boulogne

1. *The Times*, 25 Nov. 1840; Guest MSS.
2. Malmesbury, I. 120; Planché, II. 46; Orsi, pp. 128–9; *Moniteur*, 8 Aug., 1840; Dansette, I. 151, 153, 170–4.
3. Capt. Hay's statement to Lord Stanley (1856) (Vincent, *Disraeli, Derby and the Conservative Party*, pp. 160–2).
4. For the preparations for Boulogne, see Orsi, pp. 129–50.
5. Louis Napoleon's proclamations to the Army, to the inhabitants of the Pas-de-Calais, and to the French people (*Moniteur*, 16 Sept. 1840; Jerrold, II. 137–40, 482–5).
6. For the events at Boulogne, see the reports of the local officials, and the preliminary depositions and the evidence at the trial, in *Moniteur*, 7, 8, 9, 10, 11, 14 Aug., 16, 17, 29 Sept., 1 Oct. 1840; Orsi, pp. 151–9; Wikoff, pp. 106–14; Thirria, I. 155–87; Jerrold, II. 127–31.
7. *Moniteur*, 9, 10, 11 Aug. 1840; Mérimée to Lavergne, 8 Aug. 1840 (Mérimée, *Correspondance Générale*, II. 422–3); *The Times*, 8 Aug. 1840.
8. *Moniteur*, 29 Sept. 1840.
9. For the trial, see ibid., 29, 30 Sept., 1, 2, 3, 7 Oct. 1840; Jerrold, II. 151–81, 486–8; Thirria, I. 187–206.
10. *Moniteur*, 9 Oct., 2, 16 Dec. 1840; Briffault, p. 69.
11. Louis Napoleon, 'Au mânes de l'empereur' (*Œuvres*, I. 435–7).

PART II

Chapter 12 – Childhood in Spain and Paris

1. Isabel Vesey's MS., p. 8; Kurtz, *The Empress Eugénie*, p. 10.
2. Eugénie to Rosario, Duchess of Alba, 27 Jan. 1901 (*Lettres Familières de l'Impératrice Eugénie*, II. 177).

675

3. Southey, *Life of Nelson*, II. 264. See also letter from Cadiz, 29 Oct. 1805 (*Nelson's Letters*, VII. 291).

4. For Cipriano's youth, see Kurtz, pp. 5–9; Primoli, 'L'enfance d'une Souveraine' (*R.D.M.*, VII(xvii). 754–5); Filon, *Recollections of the Empress Eugénie*, p. 9.

5. General Kirkpatrick, 'Records of the Closeburn Kirkpatricks', App.II (unpag.); App. VI, pp. 4, 8–9; Kurtz, p. 5.

6. Certificate of Lyon King-of-Arms, 16 May 1791; Escott Kirkpatrick to his cousin, 28 Jan. 1853; Countess Montijo to Miss Jane Kirkpatrick of Nithbrook, Dumfries, 8 July 1854; Campbell Gracie to *The Dumfries and Galloway Standard*, 15 Dec. 1860 (General Kirkpatrick, App. II (unpag.); App. VI, pp. 3, 10, 16); *The Times*, 22 Jan. 1853; Llanos y Torriglia, *Maria Manuela Kirkpatrick Condesa del Montijo*, p. 19.

7. Countess Montijo to Rouher, 5 Oct. 1876 (Alba Archives, Montijo c 43–3); Kurtz, pp. 9–10; Llanos y Torriglia, pp. 27–28.

8. Mérimée to Stendhal, 5 July 1836 (*C.G.*, II. 60); Viel Castel, *Mémoires*, II. 122, 130; Villiers, *A Vanished Victorian*, p. 262; *Les Femmes galantes des Napoléons*, p. 148; *Mariage de César*, p. 16.

9. Mérimée to Lavergne, 29 July 1835 (*C.G.*, I. 450).

10. Eugénie to Rosario, 11 Mar. 1902 (*L.F.*, II. 183–4). For the other version of the story, see Primoli (*R.D.M.*, VII(xvii). 757–60); Kurtz, p. 12.

11. Vesey MS., p. 15; Ethel Smyth, *Streaks of Life*, p. 8; Kurtz, p. 13.

12. Information from the Princess of Bavaria.

13. Filon, p. 13; *Life, Letters and Journals of George Ticknor*, I. 233; Mérimée to Lavergne, 23 Jan. 1835 (*C.G.*, I. 385).

14. Williams, *Life of Washington Irving*, I. 360–78; II. 381.

15. Mérimée to Sophie Duvancel, 8 Oct. 1830; Mérimée to Countess Montijo, 16 May 1845 (*C.G.*, I. 77; IV. 294).

16. Llanos y Torriglia, p. 37; Primoli (*R.D.M.*, VII(xvii). 769); Vesey MS., p. 9.

17. Primoli (*R.D.M.*, VII(xvii). 760–1); Alba, 'La Emperatriz Eugenia' (*Boletín de la Real Academia de la Historia*, CXX. 77).

18. Primoli (*R.D.M.*, VII(xvii). 761–2); Mérimée, *Mosaïque*, pp. 282–4.

19. Mérimée to Roger-Collard, 12 Nov. 1834 (*C.G.*, I. 355); Castellane, *Journal*, III. 104; *L.F.*, I. 4; Vesey MS., p. 10.

20. Mérimée to d'Aragon, 11 July 1835; Mérimée to Cavé, 6 Nov. 1834 (*C.G.*, I. 349, 444); Vesey MS., pp. 8–9.

21. Mérimée to Lavergne, 29 July 1835; Mérimée to Gasparin (1836) (*C.G.*, I. 450; II. 9).

22. Paca del Montijo to Count Montijo, 8 July 1836 (*L.F.*, I. 233); and see *L.F.*, I. 4.

23. Isabel Vesey's MS., p. 10; Ethel Smyth, *Streaks of Life*, p. 8.

24. Primoli, (*R.D.M.*, VII(xvii). 768); Isabel Vesey's MS., p. 25.

25. See Eugénie's letters to her father in A.A., Montijo c 8–9.

26. Eugénie to Montijo, 2 Jan. 1837 (*L.F.*, I. 8).

27. Eugénie to Montijo (Apr. 1837) (*L.F.*, I. 9).

28. Mérimée to Sharpe, 18 May 1837 (*C.G.*, II. 102); Smyth, *Streaks of Life*, pp. 7–8.
29. Primoli (*R.D.M.*, VII(xvii). 765–7); Vesey MS., pp. 10–11.
30. Mérimée to Sharpe, (Aug. 1837), 17 Sept. 1837 (*C.G.*, II. 127, 131).
31. Mérimée to Countess Montijo, 16 Mar. 1839 (*C.G*, II. 206).
32. Filon, p. 15.
33. Information from Brigadier Jervois; Vesey MS., p. 33.
34. Primoli (*R.D.M.*, VII(xvii). 767–8).
35. Mérimée to Colonel Brack (Dec. 1837); see *C.G.*, II. 139.
36. Filon, pp. 13–14.
37. *L.F.*, I. 235.
38. Arbeley, 'Un dernier amour de Stendhal: Eugénie de Montijo' (*Revue Hebdomadaire*, Nov.–Dec. 1932, pp. 581, 593); Stendhal, *La Chartreuse de Parme* (1922 edn.), I. 76n.
39. Certificate of the Gymnase, 19 Oct. 1838 (*L.F.*, I. 235).
40. Filon, p. 15.
41. Mérimée to Countess Montijo, 16, 30 Mar. 1839 (*C.G.*, II. 206, 212).
42. Mérimée to Countess Montijo, 23, 26 Mar., 6 Apr. 1839 (*C.G.*, II. 208, 210, 214); Arbeley (*Rev.Heb.*, Nov.–Dec. 1932, p. 593); Stendhal, *La Chartreuse de Parme* (1922 edn.), II. 366n.

Chapter 13 – 'An Infuriating Girl'

1. Eugénie to Stendhal, Dec. 1839 (Filon, pp. 16–17).
2. Paléologue, *The Tragic Empress*, p. 73.
3. Mérimée to Jenny Dacquin (12 Mar. 1842) (*C.G.*, III. 154).
4. Mérimée to Countess Montijo, 13, 16 Oct. 1840; 19, 20 Feb. 1841; 29 May 1846; Mérimée to Jurnieu, 9 Jan. 1841; 18 Sept. 1843 (*C.G.*, II. 448–9; III. 2, 20, 27, 427–8; IV. 455); *El Heraldo*, 7 Mar. 1846; 20 June 1847; 25 July 1848; *El Clamor Publico*, 24 July, 1 Sept. 1848; *La Época*, 29 Apr., 31 July 1851; Llanos y Torriglia, pp. 106–8.
5. Countess Montijo to Lavergne, 10 Sept. 1842 (*C.G.*, III. 255n.).
6. Mérimée to Jenny Dacquin, 2 Dec. 1842 (*C.G.*, III. 254–5).
7. *El Heraldo*, 1 Mar. 1843; Mérimée to Jenny Dacquin, 7 Feb. 1843; Mérimée to Countess Montijo, 18 Mar. 1843 (*C.G.*, III. 307, 337–8); Llanos y Torriglia, pp. 81–83.
8. Mérimée to Countess Montijo, 24 Feb., 11 Mar. 1843 (*C.G.*, III. 319, 333); *El Heraldo*, 14 Feb., 1, 4, 13, 17 Mar. 1843.
9. Paléologue, p. 62; Filon, p. 38.
10. Eugénie to (Alba), 16 (17) May, 1843 (*L.F.*, I. 21–22).
11. Mérimée to Jenny Dacquin (24 June 1843); Mérimée to Countess Montijo, 20 Oct. 1843 (*C.G.*, III. 388, 442).
12. Mérimée to Countess Montijo, 4, 11, 18, 25 Nov., 2 Dec. 1843; 3 Feb. 1844 (*C.G.*, III. 450, 455, 457, 462, 466; IV. 21).
13. Alba (op. cit., CXX. 78).
14. Irving to Mrs Storrow, 29 Feb. 1844 (Beinecke Library MSS.); Irving

to Mary Irving, 15 Mar. 1844 (P. M. Irving, *Life and Letters of Washington Irving*, III. 264); *El Heraldo*, 15, 16 Feb. 1844.

15. *El Heraldo*, 1 Mar. 1843; 12 Feb. 1845; 31 Jan., 10, 27 Feb., 3 Mar., 18 Apr., 17 Nov. 1846; 31 Jan., 17 Nov. 1847; 14 Jan., 18 Feb., 14 Mar., 9 Dec. 1848; 7, 31 Jan., 27 Feb., 11 Dec. 1849; 31 Jan., 3, 13, 19 Feb. 1850; 4 Feb., 12 Mar., 17, 30 Dec. 1851; *El Clamor Publico*, 15 Mar., 19 Nov., 6 Dec. 1848; *La Época*, 10, 13, 17, 18 Feb., 2 Mar., 16 Nov. 1850; 16, 30 Dec. 1851; Llanos y Torriglia, p. 129.

16. Lord Canning to Malmesbury, 21 Oct. 1847 (Malmesbury, I. 203).

17. Mérimée to Countess Montijo (Sept. 1840) (*C.G.*, II. 445); Llanos y Torriglia, p. 83.

18. Dalling and Ashley, *Life of Palmerston*, III. 247.

19. *The Times*, 8 Jan. 1845; *El Clamor Publico*, 13, 27 Feb., 30 Apr., 24 Nov., 1 Dec. 1848; Mérimée to Delessert, 26 July 1847; Mérimée to Madame de Valon, 30 Oct. 1849 (*C.G.*, V. 128, 530); *La Época*, 8 Oct. 1849.

20. *El Heraldo*, 22 Jan., 20, 21, 25 Feb., 8 Mar. 1846; 19, 22, 29 Feb., 14 Mar. 1848; 16 Feb. 1849; *El Clamor Publico*, 13, 27, 29 Feb., 15 Mar. 1848; *La Época*, 6 Oct. 1850; Llanos y Torriglia, p. 130.

21. *El Heraldo*, 24 June, 16 Aug., 26 Oct. 1843; 11 Jan., 27 Apr., 21 June, 12 July, 27 Nov. 1844; 28 Jan., 18 Feb., 4 Apr., 3 Aug., 15, 20 Nov., 10 Dec. 1845; 28 May 1846; 30 Apr., 17 Oct. 1847; 22 Jan., 22 Feb., 13, 28 Apr. 1848.

22. Smyth, *Streaks of Life*, pp. 23–25; Filon, p. 12; Vesey MS., unpag. p. opp. p. 24, pp. 30–31.

23. Filon, p. 19; Primoli (*R.D.M.*, VII(xvii). 775–6).

24. *El Heraldo*, 17 Sept. 1844; *El Clamor Publico*, 19 Sept. 1844.

25. *El Heraldo*, 8, 18 May, 28, 30 Sept., 3 Oct., 4 Nov. 1845; Llanos y Torriglia, pp. 111–13; Ventura de la Vega, *El Hombre de Mundo*, passim. See also *La Época*, 13 Aug. 1850.

26. Mérimée to Countess Montijo (31 Aug. 1840); Mérimée to Delessert, 26 July 1847 (*C.G.*, II. 441; V. 128); Primoli (*R.D.M.*, VII(xvii). 768–9).

27. Beijens to Materne, 27 Jan. 1853 (RA J76/55); Clara Tschudi, *Eugénie Empress of the French*, p. 28; Isabel Vesey's Diary, 29 June 1910; Vesey MS., p. 92; Malmesbury, II. 282; Daudet, *L'Impératrice Eugénie*, p. 175; Mérimée to Sharpe, 5 May 1837 (*C.G.*, II. 99).

28. Mérimée to Stapper, 4 Sept. 1830; Mérimée to Jenny Dacquin 2 Dec. 1842 (*C.G.*, I. 72; III. 255); Mérimée, *Mosaïque*, pp. 239–82; *El Heraldo*, 10 Oct. 1846; 18 May, 1 Aug. 1847; 26, 27 Mar., 16 Apr., 10 May, 20 June 1850; 14 Apr., 30 June 1852; *La Época*, 1 May, 25 June 1850; 6 Sept. 1851; Lord Canning to Malmesbury, 21 Oct. 1847 (Malmesbury, I. 202).

29. Tschudi, pp. 29–30. Clara Tschudi is very unreliable, but states that this information is quoted from someone who was present with Eugénie at a bullfight.

30. *El Heraldo*, 28 June 1848.

31. Primoli (*R.D.M.*, VII(xvii). 779–80).

32. Valera to his mother (Jan. 1847) (Valera, *Correspondencia*, I. 10).

33. Mérimée to Countess Montijo, 1 Feb., 9 May 1845 (*C.G.*, IV. 233, 292–3); *El Heraldo*, 1 May 1845.

34. *El Heraldo*, 18, 20, 25 Oct. 1846; Primoli (*R.D.M.*, VII(xvii). 780); Dumas to Primoli, 8 Apr. 1877 (ibid., pp. 781–2); Llanos y Torriglia, p. 104.

35. Kurtz, p. 24.

36. Mérimée to Countess Montijo, 27 Dec. 1845, 17 Jan. 1846 (*C.G.*, IV. 405, 415).

37. Mérimée to Countess Montijo, 26 Feb., 11 May, 30 Nov. 1844; 14 Feb. 1846 (*C.G.*, IV. 37, 103, 215, 421).

38. Mérimée to Countess Montijo, 19 June, 11 Sept. 1847 (*C.G.*, V. 108, 160).

39. Eugénie to Mérimée (undated) (*C.G.*, II. 479–80n.); Filon, pp. 20–21.

40. Ollivier, *Journal*, II. 193 (from Eugénie).

41. Kurtz, p. 23.

42. Primoli (*R.D.M.*, VII(xvii). 777); Dandet, *L'Impératrice Eugénie*, pp. 127–8.

43. Llanos y Torriglia, p. 134.

44. Primoli (*R.D.M.*, VII(xvii). 773–4, 778).

45. Primoli, ibid., pp. 776–7, 779; Beijens to Materne, 27 Jan. 1853 (RA J76/55); *Mariage de César*, p. 11.

46. *The Times*, 22 Oct. 1847.

47. A.A., Montijo c 51–21; see also c 49–16; *El Heraldo*, 9, 17 Nov. 1847.

48. For Countess Montijo's appointment and dismissal as Camerara Mayor, see *The Times*, 12, 14 Apr., 9 Nov., 28 Dec. 1847; Llanos y Torriglia, pp. 121, 124–6.

49. Countess Montijo to Isabel II, 16 Dec. 1847 (A.A., Montijo c 51–22).

50. *The Times*, 10, 29 Nov. 1847; Lord Canning to Malmesbury, 21 Oct. 1847 (Malmesbury, I. 201).

51. Mérimée to Delessert, 11 Aug. 1847; Mérimée to Countess Montijo, 14 Aug. 1847 (*C.G.*, V. 135, 137); Beijens to Materne, 27 Jan. 1853 (RA J76/55).

52. Primoli (*R.D.M.*, VII(xvii). 783–8).

53. Alba, op. cit., CXX. 79, 81; Llanos y Torriglia, p. 111.

54. Caroline Murat, p. 115; Tschudi, pp. 25–26; Jane Stoddart, *The Life of the Empress Eugénie*, p. 29; Kurtz, pp. 21–22, 26–27.

55. Ethel Smyth, *Streaks of Life*, pp. 31–32.

56. *Les femmes galantes des Napoléons*, I. 164–5. For other versions of the story, see Caroline Murat, p. 115; Senior's Journal, 24 May 1853 (RA K18, pp. 255–6).

57. Ethel Smyth, op. cit., p. 31; Kurtz, p. 27; Alba, op. cit., CXX. 78.

58. Alba, ibid., p. 78.

59. Villavieja, *Life has been good*, pp. 161–3.

PART III

Chapter 14 – The 'University' of Ham

1. Briffault, pp. 69, 100, 123–4.
2. Orsi, pp. 164–5.
3. Jerrold, II. 192.
4. Briffault, pp. 75, 119–20; Wikoff, pp. 26, 38–39, 67, 70; Orsi, p. 185. For Malmesbury's visit, see Malmesbury, I. 157–9.
5. Senior's Journal, 21 May 1860 (RA K45, p. 13) (from Hortense Cornu); Castelot, I. 396–8; Emerit, *Lettres de Napoléon III à Madame Cornu*, I. 153–60.
6. Wikoff, pp. 70, 72.
7. Briffault, p. 125.
8. ibid., p. 128.
9. Louis Napoleon's protest, 22 May 1841 (Briffault, pp. 83–89).
10. Briffault, pp. 73, 119–21, 123–4; Wikoff, p. 115.
11. Briffault, p. 74.
12. Louis Napoleon to Vieillard, 17 Dec. 1841 (Jerrold, II. 463–4); Briffault, pp. 137–8.
13. Louis Napoleon to Hortense Cornu, 8 June, 30 July, 8 Aug., 3 Oct. 1841 (*Lettres de Napoléon III à Hortense Cornu*, II. 8–9, 11–13, 17–18); Sismondi to Louis Napoleon, 22 June 1841 (Briffault, pp. 146–51); Briffault, p. 145.
14. Briffault, pp. 138–9; Dansette, I. 186, 193. For the history of artillery, see *Du Passé et de l'Avenir de l'Artillerie* (in *Œuvres*, IV. 1–424); for Louis Napoleon's articles in the *Progrès du Pas-de-Calais* at various dates between 14 June 1841 and 23 Dec. 1844, see *Œuvres*, I. 451–77; II. 3–64, 299–323.
15. *Œuvres*, I. 235–342; see especially pp. 241, 243. See also Louis Napoleon's interesting article on James II, 'L'Union fait la Force' (*Œuvres*, I. 439–49).
16. 'Analyse de la question des sucres' (*Œuvres*, I. 163–295); Jerrold, II, 233–47; Louis Napoleon to Hortense Cornu, 17 (?), 29 July, 3, 9, 10, 29 Aug. 1842 (*Lettres de Napoléon III à Madame Cornu*, II. 25–32).
17. *Œuvres*, II. 288.
18. 'Le traite des nègres' (*Œuvres*, I. 461–6, especially pp. 461–2).
19. 'Extinction du paupérisme' (*Œuvres*, II. 107–61, especially pp. 120–1); Jerrold, II. 279–84.
20. George Sand to Louis Napoleon (26 Nov. 1844); Louis Blanc to Louis Napoleon, 12 Feb. 1846 (Briffault, pp. 376–81); George Sand in *The Times*, 5 Feb. 1873; Jerrold, II. 285–8, 294–301.
21. 'Réponse à Monsieur de Lamartine' (*Œuvres*, I. 351–70, especially pp. 357, 370).
22. Castellon to Louis Napoleon, 6 Dec. 1845 (Jerrold, II. 318–19).
23. 'Le canal de Nicaragua' (*Œuvres*, II. 461–543, especially pp. 480, 482–3);

Jerrold, II. 312–29; Orsi, pp. 191–6; Briffault, pp. 185–96; but see Malmesbury, I. 158–60, for a different version of the negotiations with Nicaragua.

Chapter 15 – Escape

1. Louis Napoleon to the Minister of the Interior, 25 Dec. 1845; Louis Napoleon to Louis Philippe, 14 Jan. 1846 (Jerrold, II. 319–20, 320n., 335–6); Odilon Barrot to Louis Napoleon (undated); Ferdinand Barrot to Louis Napoleon, 17 Feb. 1846; Marie to Louis Napoleon (undated) (Briffault ,pp. 256–7, 382–5); Orsi, pp. 197–9, 201; Briffault, pp. 205–61.
2. Dansette, I. 208.
3. Wikoff, p. 166n.
4. For Conneau's part in the escape, see Conneau's statement (Briffault, pp. 301–5); Louis Napoleon to Degeorge (May 1846) (Jerrold, II. 348–50); Orsi, pp. 217–19; Briffault, p. 307; Hortense Cornu's statement, in Senior's Journal, 17 Feb. 1854 (RA K19, pp. 98–99).
5. For the escape, see Briffault, pp. 263–92; Louis Napoleon to Degeorge (May 1846) (Jerrold, II. 348–50); The Times, 3 June 1846; Orsi, pp. 206–16; Jerrold, II. 344–54. For a slightly different and rather less probable account, see Hortense Cornu's statement, in Senior's Journal, 17 Feb. 1854 (RA K19, pp. 95–100).
6. Malmesbury, I. 173.

Chapter 16 – London Again

1. Louis Napoleon to St-Aulaire, 28 May 1846 (Briffault, pp. 293–4); Orsi, pp. 216–17, 219–20; Briffault, p. 311.
2. Bac, pp. 275–6; Dansette, I. 181–2; Treaty between Louis Napoleon and the Duke of Brunswick (Dec. 1845); Louis Napoleon to Orsi, 9 Dec. 1845, 2 Mar. 1846 (Orsi, pp. 183–4n., 199–201, 247). For the conflicting versions of Orsi and Duncombe about the negotiations with Brunswick, see Orsi, pp. 173–89, 246–7; T. H. Duncombe, Life of T. S. Duncombe, II. 10–11; Jerrold, II. 385–7.
3. The Times, 5 June 1846; Louis Napoleon to Vieillard, 1 June 1846 (Jerrold, II. 357n.); Malmesbury, I. 19.
4. Foster, Walter Savage Landor, II. 466.
5. Morning Post, 18 Aug., 21 Sept. 1846; Senior's Journal, 21 May 1860 (RA K45, p. 12) Guest, Napoleon III in England, pp. 69–70.
6. Guest, pp. 71–2; Morning Post, 14, 29 Oct. 1846.
7. Jerrold, II. 89–91, 382–3; Wikoff, pp. 248–9; Morning Post, 7 Dec. 1846; 8, 19 Jan., 1 Feb., 20 Oct., 20 Nov. 1847; 21 Jan. 1848.
8. Louis Napoleon to Vicomte de C—— (undated) (Wikoff, pp. 292–8).
9. Ivor Guest MSS. For Kirkland, see Tew, Old Times and Friends, pp. 16–17, 23–24.

10. Fraser, pp. 3–5; Countess of Cardigan, *My Recollections*, p. 17; Gronow, *Reminiscences and Recollections*, I. 253–4; *Morning Post*, 9 Mar. 1847.
11. *Notes and Queries*, III(i). 334–5.
12. *The Times*, 6, 21 Apr., 19 July 1847.
13. *Morning Post*, 14 May 1847.
14. *The Times*, 7 May 1847.
15. ibid., 5, 7, 10, 12, 14, 17, 19, 21, 26, 28, 31 May; 2, 7, 9, 11, 14, 16, 18, 19, 21, 23, 25, 28 June; 2, 5, 7, 9, 10, 12, 14, 16, 23, 26, 28 July; 3, 4, 5, 11, 13, 18, 20, 21, 23 Aug. 1847; *Morning Post*, 5 May 1847.
16. *The Times*, 19 July 1847.
17. ibid., 5, 6, 8, 12, 15, 19, 22 July; 5, 9 Aug. 1847; *Morning Post*, 2, 15, 20 June, 14 Nov., 5, 15 Dec. 1846; 13 Apr., 14 May, 10 July 1847; 8 Feb. 1848.
18. Lumley, *Reminiscences of the Opera*, pp. 198, 265.
19. Legge, *The Empress Eugénie and her Son*, pp. 241–2.
20. Falk, *Rachel the Immortal*, p. 202; Louis Napoleon to Hortense Cornu, 26 July 1846 (Jerrold, II. 460); *The Times*, 4, 9 July 1846; Castelot, I. 442.
21. *Morning Post*, 16, 21 Sept. 1846.
22. Wikoff, pp. 169–73.
23. *Morning Post*, 7 Aug. 1847.
24. Filon, p. 14n.
25. For Miss Howard, see Guest, *Napoleon III in England*, pp. 78–79; Fleischmann, *Napoléon III et les femmes*, pp. 133–81. For scandalous contemporary accounts, see *The Eventful History of Lizzie Howard*, and *The Life and Career of Lizzie Howard*.
26. For Pollard's case, see Ballantine, *Some Experiences of a Barrister's Life*, I. 293–7; *The Times*, 3, 5, 7, 10 July 1847.
27. Lady Cardigan, p. 56; *Morning Post*, 25 Dec. 1847.

Chapter 17 – 1848

1. *El Clamor Publico*, 25, 29 Feb. 1848; *El Heraldo*, 29 Feb. 1848.
2. Louis Napoleon to the Provisional Government, 28 Feb. 1848 (*Œuvres*, III. 5–6).
3. Louis Napoleon to the Provisional Government, 29 Feb. 1848 (*Œuvres*, III. 6–7).
4. For Louis Napoleon's visit to Paris, see Orsi, pp. 226–45; *Le National*, 29 Feb. 1848; and see Malmesbury, I. 217.
5. *The Times*, 10 Apr. 1848.
6. Malmesbury, I. 225; Simpson, I. 278n.
7. Florence Robinson to Mrs Ashburnham, 28 Feb.; 6, 10, 14, 18, 31 Mar.; 3, 21, 26 Apr.; 1, 4, 8, 15, 18, 25, 29 May; 1, 5, 8, 22 June 1848 (Baroness Bonde, *Paris in '48*, pp. 20, 35–36, 40–41, 45–49, 55, 58, 70, 76, 101–2, 107, 119–23, 138, 148, 153–8, 161–2, 166, 170, 177–8, 182–3, 197–8); Senior's Journal, 25 May 1848 (RA K1, p. 57)
8. Seignobos (Lavisse, *Histoire de France Contemporaine*, VI. 79).

9. Castelot, I. 494.

10. Thirria, I. 275–7; *Biographie de Louis-Napoléon Bonaparte*, p. 8.

11. *The Times*, 10 June, 4 July 1848. For the Charente, see Mérimée to Mme de Boigne, 18 June 1848 (*C.G.*, V. 333).

12. *The Times*, 13 June 1848; Thirria, I. 279, 281–2.

13. *The Times*, 20 June 1848; Florence Robinson to Mrs Ashburnham, 11, 15, 19, 22 June 1848 (Bonde, pp. 183–5, 188–90, 192–4, 197); Dansette, I. 223; Seignobos (Lavisse, VI. 95).

14. Louis Napoleon to Sénard, 14 June 1848 (*Œuvres*, III. 13–14).

15. Louis Napoleon to Sénard, 15 June 1848 (*Œuvres*, III. 14–15).

16. Lebey, *Louis-Napoléon Bonaparte et la Révolution de 1848*, I. 262–3; *The Times*, 15 June 1848.

17. For the debates in the National Assembly, see *Le National*, 13, 14, 15, 16, 17 June 1848; *The Times*, 15, 17, 19 June 1848; Véron, *Mémoires d'un Bourgeois de Paris*, VI. 82; Thirria, I. 283–8, 291–301.

18. Marquise de Boissy to Lady Blessington, 20 June 1848 (Madden, *Life of Lady Blessington*, II. 255).

19. Mérimée to Mme de Boigne, 18 June 1848 (*C.G.*, V. 335).

20. Seignobos (Lavisse, VI. 103); *The Times*, 28 June 1848. See also *Le National*, 29 June 1848.

21. For the June Days, see Florence Robinson to Mrs Ashburnham, 25, 26, 29 June 1848 (Bonde, pp. 199–220); Hugo, *Choses Vues*, pp. 459–65; *The Times*, 26, 27, 28, 29, 30 June 1848; Seignobos (Lavisse, VI. 100–3).

22. *The Times*, 26 June 1848.

23. *Morning Post*, 23 June 1848.

24. Vallon to Mérimée, 24 June 1848 (*C.G.*, V. 332–3n.). Vallon is wrong in stating that Lady Ailesbury's party took place 'avant hier'.

25. For the atrocities, real or alleged, on both sides, see Florence Robinson to Mrs Ashburnham, 25, 26, 29 June, 3, 13 July 1848 (Bonde, pp. 206–8, 210–13, 218–21, 224–30); Mérimée to Mme de Boigne, 27 June 1848; Mérimée to Jenny Dacquin, 27 June 1848; Mérimée to Countess Montijo, 28 June 1848 (*C.G.*, V. 336, 339–40); Véron, VI. 60–62.

26. Mérimée to Mme de Boigne, 27 June 1848; Mérimée to Langrené, 28 June 1848 (*C.G.*, V. 336–7, 342); *The Times*, 28 June, 3 July 1848; Seignobos (Lavisse, VI. 104–6).

27. Seignobos (Lavisse, VI. 108–10).

28. ibid., VI. 105; *The Times*, 28, 29, 30 Aug. 1848; Proudhon to Girardin (Sept. 1848) (*The Times*, 16 July 1849).

29. *The Times*, 5 May 1848; *Morning Post*, 8, 17 May; 11, 21, 25 Aug. 1848.

30. Guest, *Napoleon III in England*, p 90; see Guest MSS. for the source of the story.

31. Lumley, *Reminiscences of the Opera*, p. 266.

32. *The Times*, 23 Sept. 1848.

33. Jerrold, II. 388.

Chapter 18 – The Tenth of December

1. *Le National*, 25, 27 Sept. 1848; *The Times*, 26, 28 Sept. 1848; Hugo, *Choses Vues*, pp. 503–4.
2. Proudhon to Girardin (Sept. 1848); Proudhon's diary, 26 Sept. 1848 (*The Times*, 16 July 1849).
3. For the debates about the Constitution, see Seignobos (Lavisse, VI. 115–24).
4. *The Times*, 9, 10 Oct. 1848; Thirria, I. 358–66. For the change in public opinion about Lamartine, see Florence Robinson to Mrs Ashburnham, 11, 15, 28, 29 May; 11, 25, 26 June; 3 July 1848 (Bonde, pp. 125–6, 139, 154, 160, 186, 202, 212, 220–1).
5. Thirria, I. 366–9; Senior's Journal, 29 Mar. 1852 (RA K13, pp. 56–58).
6. *Le National*, 10 Oct. 1848; see also Malmesbury, I. 259.
7. *The Times*, 12, 31 Oct. 1848.
8. *Œuvres*, III. 21–23; *The Times*, 27, 28 Oct. 1848; Thirria, I. 375–6, 378–9.
9. *The Times*, 6, 7 Nov. 1848.
10. Seignobos (Lavisse, VI. 113–14, 125).
11. Senior's Journal, 25 Mar. 1852 (RA K13, pp. 58–59, 62); Seignobos (Lavisse, VI. 125); Dansette, I. 245–6.
12. *The Times*, 8, 9, 11, 20, 23, 25 Nov. 1848.
13. Dansette, I. 242.
14. *The Times*, 22, 25, 30 Nov.; 2, 6 Dec. 1848.
15. Mérimée to Francisque-Michel, 20 Jan. 1849 (*C.G.*, V. 434); Hugo, *Choses Vues*, p. 506.
16. Dansette, I. 249.
17. *Le National*, 20 Nov. 1848.
18. *The Times*, 25 Nov.; 2, 6, 7 Dec. 1848; Dansette, I. 224, 251.
19. *The Times*, 14, 15, 17, 18 Nov. 1848.
20. *Le National*, 17, 21, 26 Nov. 1848; *The Times*, 16 Nov. 1848; Dansette, I. 249–50.
21. *Le National*, 12, 14, 16 Nov.; 5 Dec. 1848; see also Dansette, I. 250.
22. Senior's Journal, 25 Mar. 1852 (RA K13, pp. 60–61); Seignobos (Lavisse, VI. 126).
23. Senior's Journal, 29 Mar. 1852 (RA K13, p. 81); Fleury, *Souvenirs*, I. 70–71; Dansette, I. 246.
24. *Œuvres*, III. 24–28; *Le National*, 1 Dec. 1848; *The Times*, 1 Dec. 1848; Jerrold, III. 36–39.
25. *Le National*, 1 Dec. 1848.
26. *Le Constitutionnel*, 4 Dec. 1848; *The Times*, 5, 11 Dec. 1848.
27. Thiers to Boitel, 3 Dec. 1848 (Senior's Journal, 25 Mar. 1852 (RA K13, p. 63n.)); *The Times*, 6 Dec. 1848; Jerrold, III. 41.
28. *The Times*, 30 Nov., 1, 2, 4, 13 Dec. 1848.
29. *The Times*, 12, 13 Dec. 1848.
30. For the election campaign, see Thirria, I. 380–467; for an analysis of the results, see Dansette, I. 253.

PART IV

Chapter 19 – The Élysée

1. Senior's Journal, 29 Mar. 1852 (RA K13, pp. 80–81).
2. Fleury, I. 76–78; *The Times*, 22 Dec. 1848.
3. Masuyer (*R.D.M.*, VI(xxii). 845; (xxx). 194).
4. Dansette, II. 259.
5. Senior's Journal, 21 Apr. 1854 (RA K21, pp. 70–71); *The Times*, 28 Dec. 1848; 23 Jan. 1849.
6. Senior's Journal, 3 Apr. 1852 (RA K13, p. 129).
7. Louis Napoleon to Malleville, 27 Dec. 1848 (Jerrold, III. 61–62); *The Times*, 9 Jan. 1849.
8. *The Times*, 27 Dec. 1848; Fleury, I. 199–200; Mérimée to Laborde, 25 Dec. 1848, (*C.G.*, V. 420–1).
9. Fleury, I. 82.
10. Senior's Journal, 21 Apr. 1854 (RA K21, p. 72); Louis Napoleon to Miss Howard (c. 1850) (Nat. Lib. of Scotland, MS. 10220, f.21); Dansette, I. 286.
11. *The Times*, 22 Nov.; 6, 19, 27, 28 Dec. 1848; 6, 8, 27 Mar.; 3, 17 Apr.; 30 May; 14 June 1849.
12. Senior's Journal, 3 Apr. 1852 (RA K13, p. 129).
13. Henri Fazy, *James Fazy*, pp. 241–2.
14. *The Times*, 27 Jan. 1849; Senior's Journal, 18 Sept. 1860 (RA: K47) (from Changarnier); Dansette, I. 269.
15. *Le Peuple*, 27 Jan. 1849.
16. Senior's Journal, 29 Mar. 1852 (RA K13, pp. 83–86).
17. *The Times*, 31 Jan. 1849.
18. ibid., 30 Jan. 1849; *Le Corsaire*, 29 Jan. 1849.
19. *The Times*, 31 Jan., 1 Feb. 1849; Fleury, I. 88–90. For the Radicals' view of the events of 29 Jan., see *Démocratie Pacifique*, 31 Jan. 1849.
20. *The Times*, 17 Feb. 1849.
21. ibid., 12, 20 Feb. 1849.
22. ibid., 22 Feb. 1849.
23. ibid., 15 Feb. 1849.
24. *Démocratie Pacifique*, 18 Mar. 1849; *L'Estafette*, 18 Mar. 1849; *The Times*, 23 Feb., 13, 15, 19 Mar. 1849. Cf. Hugo, *Choses Vues*, pp. 482–6, who states that it was Chopart, not Nourry, who was reprieved after the postponement of the execution.
25. *The Times*, 17 Mar. 1849.
26. *Le Peuple*, 19 Mar. 1849.
27. *The Times*, 17 Mar. 1849.
28. ibid., 17 Mar., 24 Apr. 1849; 20 Jan. 1851; Malmesbury, I. 243–4; Thirria, II. 176; Fraser, p. 18.
29. *The Times*, 9 Oct. 1851; Gronow, I. 119; Falk, *Rachel the Immortal*, p. 202.
30. Mérimée to Madame de Langrené (Mar. 1849) (*C.G.*, V. 441); *El*

Clamor Publico, 10 Dec. 1848; *El Heraldo*, 15 Mar. 1849; *The Times*, 24 Apr. 1849.

31. Eugénie to Paca (Mar. 1849) (*L.F.*, I. 23–24).
32. Filon, p. 21.
33. Filon, pp. 21–22 (from Eugénie).

Chapter 20 – Rescuing the Pope

1. *The Times*, 16, 31 Mar. 1849.
2. ibid., 18 Apr. 1849.
3. Balleydier, *Histoire de la Révolution de Rome*, II. 103, 112–13; Bittard des Portes, *L'Expédition française de Rome*, pp. 63–70, 96–98, 114, 153; *The Times*, 17 May 1849; Lesseps to Mazzini, etc. 17 May 1849 (Lesseps, *Mémoire présenté au Conseil d'État*, p. 142); Schneidawind, *Aus dem Hauptquartiere des Vater Radetzky*, p. 124; Marie-Louise Pailleron, 'Une ennemie de l'Autriche: la princesse de Belgiojoso' (*R.D.M.*, VI(xxvi). 829–30).
4. *La Patrie*, 3 May 1849; *L'Estafette*, 7, 8 May 1849; *Le Siècle*, 9 May 1849; *The Times*, 5, 7 May 1849.
5. Louis Napoleon to Oudinot (8 May 1849) (*Œuvres*, III. 41).
6. *Le National*, 9 May 1849; *Démocratie Pacifique*, 10, 11 May 1849; *Le Peuple*, 9 May 1849; *The Times*, 11 May 1849.
7. The number of Radical and Socialist deputies elected is usually given as 180; but see Dansette, I. 276, 400.
8. See Balleydier, passim.
9. Lesseps, *Mémoire présenté au Conseil d'État*, pp. 17–95, 141–65; Balleydier, II. 187–90.
10. Oudinot to Rosselli, 1 June 1849 (Bittard des Portes, p. 200). For a defence of Oudinot's actions, see Balleydier, II. 205.
11. *The Times*, 6, 7, 9 June 1849.
12. *Œuvres*, III. 43–83.
13. *Le National*, 9, 10, 11, 12 June 1849.
14. For the events of 13 June, see *The Times*, 15, 16 June 1849; Senior's Journal, 18 Sept. 1860 (RA K47) (from Changarnier); for the Radical view, see *Le National*, 14 June 1849.
15. *Œuvres*, III. 83–84.
16. *The Times*, 28 Mar.; 20 Apr.; 4, 7, 8, 15, 26 May; 14 June; 5, 6, 26 July; 13, 14 Aug.; 3 Sept.; 9, 16 Oct. 1849; 7, 8, 9, 11, 12 Feb.; 4, 9, 26 Mar. 1850.
17. *The Times*, 19 June 1849.
18. Oudinot to Gorzkowski (May 1849) (Bittard des Portes, p. 159).
19. Armandi to Louis Napoleon, 11 Jan. 1849; Louis Napoleon to Armandi, 9 Feb. 1849 (Vicchi, pp. 81–83).
20. Jerrold, III. 82 and n.
21. *The Times*, 18 June, 10 Sept. 1849.
22. *Œuvres*, III. 86–90, 105–9; *The Times*, 16 July; 3, 4, 11 Sept. 1849.

23. *Œuvres*, III. 90–101; *The Times*, 31 July; 2, 3, 13, 14 Aug. 1849; Thirria, II. 99n.
24. Louis Napoleon to Odilon Barrot (Aug. 1849) (Barrot, *Mémoires*, III. 361–4).
25. Balleydier, II. 266, 308–10, 325, 376–8; Bittard des Portes, p. 413n.
26. Louis Napoleon to Ney, 18 Aug. 1849 (*Œuvres*, III. 102–3); Dansette, I. 281.
27. *The Times*, 8, 10 Sept. 1849; Dansette, I. 281.
28. *L'Univers*, 8 Sept. 1849.
29. *The Times*, 28 Sept. 1849.
30. *The Times*, 11 Oct. 1849; Dansette, I. 282–3; Louis Napoleon to Odilon Barrot, 14 Oct. 1849 (Barrot, *Mémoires*, III. 444–5, where it is wrongly dated 14 Apr.); Senior's Journal, 31 Mar. 1852 (RA K13, pp. 126–32).
31. *The Times*, 18, 25, 30 Oct. 1849; Dansette, I. 282–3.
32. *Œuvres*, III. 110–13.
33. Thirria, II. 162.

Chapter 21 – Crushing the Reds

1. *The Times*, 23 Nov. 1849.
2. ibid., 27 Nov. 1849.
3. Thirria, II. 173n.
4. Seignobos (Lavisse, VI. 141–3, 148); Senior's Journal, 4 Apr. 1852 (RA K13, pp. 141–3).
5. *The Times*, 30 Oct. 1849.
6. ibid., 15, 17 Nov. 1849.
7. ibid., 19, 24 Dec. 1849; 12 Jan. 1850.
8. ibid., 24 Apr. 1850.
9. ibid., 8, 9, 11, 16 Mar. 1850; *L'Événement*, 15 Mar. 1850; Marx, *The Class Struggles in France*, p. 128.
10. *Courrier de Marseille*, 16 Mar. 1850; *The Times*, 21 Mar. 1850.
11. Thirria, II. 187.
12. *Le Napoléon*, 17 Mar. 1850; and see *L'Assemblée Nationale*, 13 Mar. 1850; *Courrier de Marseille*, 14, 15, 16 Mar. 1850.
13. Senior's Journal, 4 Apr. 1852 (RA K13, pp. 145–8) (from Thiers).
14. Seignobos (Lavisse, VI. 141–3, 148).
15. *The Times*, 15 Feb. 1850.
16. *L'Assemblée Nationale*, 15, 18, 19, 20, 25 Apr. 1850; *The Times*, 18 Apr. 1850.
17. *The Times*, 19 Apr. 1850.
18. ibid.
19. *L'Événement*, 22, 23, 24, 26, 27, 28, 29, 30 Apr. 1850; *The Times*, 16, 19, 20, 24 Apr. 1850.
20. *The Times*, 2 May, 1850; *L'Assemblée Nationale*, 30 Apr. 1850.
21. For Thiers's speech, see Thirria, II. 223; and see Thiers's statement to Senior, in Senior's Journal, 4 Apr. 1852 (RA K13, pp. 150–5).

22. See Thiers's speech on 17 Jan. 1851 (Jerrold, III. 125); Senior's Journal, 11 May 1850 (RA K4, p. 11).
23. See *The Times*, 24, 27, 29 May 1850.
24. For the debates, see Thirria, II. 220–4.
25. Seignobos (Lavisse, VI. 154); *The Times*, 19 July 1850.
26. Victor Hugo, *Choses Vues*, p. 523 (from King Jerome).
27. Senior's Journal, 21 May 1860 (RA K45, p. 14) (from Hortense Cornu).
28. *The Times*, 14 May 1850.
29. *Œuvres*, III. 131–4.
30. *The Times*, 12, 13, 14 June 1850.
31. ibid., 18 Aug. 1849; 14 June, 29 July, 31 Aug., 10 Sept. 1850.
32. ibid., 15 Nov., 6, 19 Dec. 1849; 5, 29 Jan.; 5, 12 Apr.; 4, 21, 27 June; 27 Aug.; 7, 26 Sept.; 7, 15, 23, 25 Oct. 1850; 22 Feb., 1 Mar., 19 Aug. 1851.
33. Louis Napoleon's report to the National Assembly, 12 Nov. 1850 (*Œuvres*, III. 158–60); *The Times*, 23 Nov., 31 Dec. 1849; 27 May, 21 June, 14 Nov. 1850; 14, 15, 21 Mar. 1851.
34. For the suppression of 'secret societies' and the Socialists and Radicals, see the reports of the arrest and trial of Gent and his associates in *The Times*, 28, 30 Oct. 1850, 1 Sept. 1851; and see Tchernoff, *Associations et Sociétés Secrètes sous la deuxième république*, passim; Seignobos (Lavisse, VI. 155–7).
35. *The Times*, 9 Jan., 25 Oct., 9 Nov. 1850; 11 Apr., 22 Aug. 1851; Seignobos (Lavisse, VI. 156); and see *La Voix du Peuple*, 13 Apr. 1850.
36. *The Times*, 2, 5 Oct. 1849; 12 Jan.; 19 Apr.; 29 May; 10, 18 June; 5, 8, 13 July; 13 Aug.; 1, 25 Oct. 1850; 28 July 1851; Seignobos (Lavisse, VI. 157).
37. Seignobos (Lavisse, VI. 157, 365–70); *The Times*, 27 June 1850.
38. *The Times*, 8, 29 June; 27 Aug.; 4, 8, 17 Oct. 1850.
39. Seignobos (Lavisse, VI. 154).
40. *La Voix du Peuple*, 19, 20 Apr. 1850; *The Times*, 22 Apr.; 23, 24, 30 May; 26 June; 26 Dec. 1850.
41. *L'Événement*, 16, 18 May; 9–10, 12 June 1851; *Charivari*, 17, 18 Apr. 1851; *The Times*, 15 Oct. 1850; 19, 21 Apr.; 14 June; 23 Aug. 1851.
42. *Patriote de la Meuse*, 21 Mar., 22 June, 13 July 1851; *The Times*, 3 Apr., 12 July 1851.
43. *The Times*, 18, 22 Sept. 1851.
44. Mocquard to Hortense Cornu, 8 Mar., 9 Oct. 1851; Louis Napoleon to Hortense Cornu, 30 Aug. 1851 and undated (*Lettres de Napoléon III à Madame Cornu*, II. 263–5).
45. Louis Napoleon's Message to the National Assembly, 12 Nov. 1850 (*Œuvres*, III. 191–2); see Senior's Journal, 3 Apr. 1852 (RA K13, pp. 132–9).
46. *The Times*, 20 May 1850.
47. For the Don Pacifico crisis, see Palmerston to Wyse, 19 Apr. 1850; Gros to Wyse, three letters of 24 Apr. 1850; Wyse to Gros, 24 Apr. 1850; Normanby to La Hitte, 20 June 1850 (*Greek Papers*, III. 275–6, 355–60;

VII. 1–2); *Hansard*, 17 June 1850 (H.L.), 25 June 1850 (H.C.); Louis Napoleon's Message to the National Assembly, 12 Nov. 1850 (*Œuvres*, III. 192); Ridley, *Lord Palmerston*, pp. 381–7, and the authorities there cited.

48. For the Schleswig-Holstein crisis, see Louis Napoleon's Message to the National Assembly, 12 Nov. 1850 (*Œuvres*, III. 193–4). For the British attitude to Louis Napoleon's policy, see *The Times*, 28 Oct. 1850. For Persigny's visit to Berlin, see Reeve to Heyer, 8 Feb. 1850 (RA I18/33).

Chapter 22 – Chicken and Champagne

1. *The Times*, 22 June 1849.
2. Senior's Journal, 29 Mar. 1852 (RA K13, p. 83).
3. Dansette, I. 301.
4. ibid. See also Mérimée to Countess Montijo, 16 Aug. 1850 (*C.G.*, VI. 190).
5. *The Times*, 17, 19, 20, 21 Aug. 1850.
6. *Œuvres*, III. 140–1, 147.
7. *The Times*, 23, 24 Aug. 1850.
8. ibid., 26, 27 Aug. 1850; *Œuvres*, III. 148–9.
9. *The Times*, 29, 30 Aug. 1850. For the visit to Eastern France, see also Thirria, II. 283–301.
10. *Œuvres*, III. 152.
11. *The Times*, 6, 7, 9, 10, 12, 13, 14, 16 Sept. 1850; Thirria, II. 310.
12. Thirria, II. 304.
13. *The Times*, 10, 12, 14 Oct. 1850.
14. *Le Corsaire*, 28, 29, 30 Sept. 1850; *The Times*, 1 Oct., 25 Nov. 1850.
15. Senior's Journal, 27 Apr. 1854 (RA K21, p. 104); Malmesbury, I. 258.
16. Thirria, II. 346; Seignobos (Lavisse, VI. 191).
17. *Œuvres*, III. 199.
18. Thirria, II. 349; Dansette, I. 303.
19. *The Times*, 6, 7, 8, 12 Nov. 1850.
20. Seignobos (Lavisse, VI. 191–2).
21. Fleury, I. 123–4.
22. Senior's Journal, 25 Apr. 1854 (RA K21, p. 95) (from Montalembert).
23. For the debate on Changarnier's dismissal, see Thirria, II. 391–410; for the political crisis, see *The Times*, 6, 7, 8, 9, 10, 11, 16, 17, 20, 21, 22, 25 Jan. 1851; and see Mérimée to Countess Montijo, 12 Jan. 1851 (*C.G.*, VI. 156).
24. Hübner, *Neuf ans de souvenirs d'un ambassadeur d'Autriche à Paris*, I. 5 (18 Jan. 1851).
25. *L'Événement*, 19 June 1850; *The Times*, 5, 8, 12 Feb., 17 Mar. 1851; Thirria, II. 229, 236–7, 239–41, 427–34; Dansette, I. 294, 309, 311.
26. Mérimée to Countess Montijo, 22 Sept. 1851 (*C.G.*, VI. 250–1); Viel Castel, I. 155–6; *The Times*, 21 May, 24 June, 29 Nov. 1851; Senior's Journal, 15 May 1851 (RA K10, p. 90); Dansette, I. 316–19.
27. Romieu, *Le Spectre rouge de 1852*, pp. 21, 63, 67, 83, 94–95.

28. Fleury, I. 127.
29. Saint-Arnaud to his brother, 15 Mar. 1850 (*Lettres du Maréchal de Saint-Arnaud*, II. 247).
30. Saint-Arnaud to Launaguet, 20 Mar. 1848; Saint-Arnaud to his brother, 14 Dec. 1848; 4 June, 24/29 Oct. 1849; Jan.; 3 Feb.; 30 Mar., 1 June, 5 July, 15 Sept., Nov. 1850; 12/22 Jan. 1851; Saint-Arnaud to Forcade, 15 Dec. 1848; 22 Mar., Apr. 1850 (ibid., II. 169–70, 189–91, 207–8, 224, 237, 240, 250–3, 258–9, 284–5, 299, 304, 309, 312); Dansette, I. 327–8.
31. Saint-Arnaud to Forcade, Apr. 1850 (Saint-Arnaud, *Lettres*, II. 259).
32. Fleury, I. 133, 141; *Le National*, 30 May 1851.
33. Thirria, II. 457 and n.; Seignobos (Lavisse, VI. 195).
34. *The Times*, 2, 4, 5 June 1851; and see *The Times*, 3, 4, 8, 9 July 1851 for Louis Napoleon's visit to Poitiers and Beauvais.
35. *Œuvres*, III. 211.
36. Thirria, II. 465–6.
37. Thirria, II. 510.
38. *Le National*, 20 July 1851; *L'Estafette*, 20 July 1851; *L'Assemblée Nationale*, 20, 21 July 1851; *Patrie*, 20, 22 July 1851; Thirria, II. 492–515, 522.

Chapter 23 – Operation Rubicon

1. Maupas, *Mémoires sur le Second Empire*, I. 214; Fleury, I. 145–52; Dansette I. 329–30.
2. Thirria, II. 527n.
3. *Le Pays*, 12 Sept. 1851.
4. Jerrold, III. 215.
5. Dansette, I. 331.
6. *Le Corsaire*, 17 Oct. 1851; *La Patrie*, 18 Oct. 1851; *L'Assemblée Nationale*, 28 Oct. 1851; Thirria, II. 530–1.
7. Thirria, II. 533.
8. Maupas, I. 191–2.
9. *Le Constitutionnel*, 20 Oct. 1851.
10. *Œuvres*, III. 266.
11. *Œuvres*, III. 267–71; *Le Pays*, 26 Nov. 1851; *Le National*, 26 Nov. 1851; *L'Assemblée Nationale*, 26 Nov. 1851; *The Times*, 27 Nov. 1851.
12. *The Times*, 18 Sept. 1851; Thirria, II. 526.
13. *Œuvres*, III. 222–3, 260–5; *The Times*, 6 Nov. 1851.
14. *Le National*, 18 Nov. 1851; *The Times*, 17 Nov. 1851; Thirria, II. 561–4.
15. Saint-Arnaud's order (*The Times*, 3 Nov. 1851); *L'Assemblée Nationale*, 17 Nov. 1851; *Le Corsaire*, 17 Nov. 1851; *The Times*, 19 Nov. 1851.
16. *L'Assemblée Nationale*, 18, 20 Nov. 1851; *Le Corsaire*, 18 Nov. 1851; *The Times*, 20 Nov. 1851; Thirria, II. 545–57, 557–8n.; Dansette, I. 333–6.
17. Véron, VI. 166.
18. Maupas, I. 272–6; Dansette, I. 339–40.
19. Jerrold, III. 230.
20. Véron, VI. 171–5; Maupas, I. 298–301; Thirria, II. 576–7.

21. *Œuvres*, III. 271–5.
22. Du Casse, *Le dessous du coup d'état*, pp. 130–2; *The Times*, 4 Dec. 1851.
23. *Le National*, 2 Dec. 1851.
24. Senior's Journal, 18 Sept. 1860 (RA K47).
25. *The Times*, 8 Dec. 1851.
26. Dansette, I. 355.
27. *The Times*, 6, 8, 13 Dec. 1851.
28. Gronow, II. 180–2.
29. Hübner, I. 41–42.
30. For the *coup d'état* and the events of 2, 3 and 4 Dec., see Véron, VI. 177–219; Gronow, II. 155–86; *La Patrie*, 3, 4, 5, 6 Dec. 1851; *The Times*, 3, 4, 5, 6, 8, 13 Dec. 1851; *Illustrated London News*, III. 224–95 (13 Dec. 1851); Viel Castel, I. 222–30; Senior's Journal, 21 Dec. 1851; 18 Sept. 1860 (from Changarnier) (RA K12, pp. 6–7; K47); Fleury, I. 162–93; Malmesbury, I. 289–93; Jerrold, III. 224–95; Guillemin, *Le coup du 2 Décembre*, pp. 355–403.
31. *The Times*, 12 Dec. 1851; Malmesbury, I. 298.
32. Viel Castel, I. 235–6; 238. For the 'jacquerie' in the provinces, see *La Patrie*, 9, 10, 11, 15, 26 Dec. 1851; *The Times*, 15, 16, 20 Dec. 1851; Jerrold, III. 296–303; Price, *The French Second Republic*, pp. 290–321; Dansette, I. 358–67; Guillemin, pp. 404–13.
33. Seignobos (Lavisse, VI. 213).
34. Dansette, I. 368.
35. *Le Pays*, 10, 19, 20 Dec. 1851; *La Patrie*, 8 Dec. 1851.
36. *L'Univers*, 14 Dec. 1851; Jerrold, III. 318–23.
37. *L'Univers*, 5 Dec. 1851.
38. *The Times*, 23 Dec. 1851.
39. ibid., 18 Dec. 1851.
40. For the voting results, see Seignobos (Lavisse, VI. 213–16).
41. Price, p. 322.
42. George Sand to Mazzini, 23 May 1852 (George Sand, *Correspondance*, III. 331); and see Senior's Journal, 21 Dec. 1851 (RA K12, p. 1).
43. *The Times*, 1, 3 Jan. 1852; Senior's Journal, 3 Jan. 1852 (RA K12, pp. 162–4).
44. *The Times*, 3 Jan. 1852.

Chapter 24 – 'The Empire means Peace'

1. Decrees of 31 Dec. 1851, 6 Jan. 1852 (*The Times*, 3, 9 Jan. 1852).
2. Seignobos (Lavisse, VI. 225).
3. The Constitution, and Louis Napoleon's Preamble, 14 Jan. 1852 (*Œuvres*, III. 287–315).
4. Seignobos (Lavisse, VI. 219).
5. For the activities of the Mixed Commissions and the statistics of the arrests and deportations, see Price, pp. 291–315; Seignobos (Lavisse, VI. 216–21); Dansette, I. 371–3; *The Times*, 18 May 1852; for George Sand's

intervention on behalf of the deportees, see George Sand to Louis Napoleon, 20 Jan.; 2, 3, 12, 20 Feb.; Mar. 1852 (George Sand, *Correspondance*, III. 262, 279–85, 287–92, 306–11); Karénine, *George Sand*, IV. 174–238.

6. *The Times*, 24, 26, 27 Jan. 1852; Seignobos (Lavisse, VI. 224). For a Bonapartist defence of the expropriation of the Orleans property, see Jerrold, III. 354–63.

7. See Seignobos (Lavisse, VI. 228–30) for the directives of Morny and Persigny about the elections.

8. Persigny's circular, 11 Feb. 1852 (Lavisse, VI. 230).

9. Seignobos (Lavisse, VI. 234).

10. *L'Assemblée Nationale*, 4, 29 Dec. 1851; *Le Pays*, 3–4, 10 Dec. 1851; *L'Estafette*, 3–4, 15 Dec. 1851; *Le Siècle*, 3–4 Dec. 1851; *Le Corsaire*, 12 Dec. 1851; *Le Constitutionnel*, 3, 9, 10–12 Dec. 1851; *The Times*, 4, 12 Dec. 1851.

11. *The Times*, 20 Feb. 1852.

12. *Daily News*, 5 Dec. 1851.

13. For the passages quoted and referred to, see Hugo, *Napoléon le Petit*, pp. 9, 25–26, 34, 36–37, 124–5, 168.

14. Hugo, 'L'expiation', Part VII, lines 14–92.

15. *Les Deux Cours et les Nuits de St-Cloud*, pp. 11, 13, 90, 108–9; *The Times*, 26, 27 Oct. 1852.

16. Hugo, *Histoire d'un crime*, I. 177–9; Dolléans, *Proudhon*, pp. 225–71; Desjardins, *P.-J. Proudhon*, I. 180–210; Dansette, I. 351, 375–6.

17. Marx, *The Eighteenth Brumaire of Louis Bonaparte*, pp. 127–8, 132.

18. Emerit, in *Lettres de Napoléon III à Madame Cornu*, I. 37–38; see also Senior's Journal, 6 May 1857 (RA K38, pp. 177–8).

19. Louis Napoleon's speech to the Chambers, 29 Mar. 1852 (*Œuvres*, III. 324–5).

20. Malmesbury to Seymour, 29 Mar. 1852 (Malmesbury, I. 324).

21. Thirria, II. 173n.

22. Seignobos (Lavisse, VI. 241).

23. *The Times*, 9, 12, 16 Dec. 1851.

24. ibid., 22 Dec. 1851.

25. *El Heraldo*, 19 Dec. 1851; but see *La Época*, 7 Dec. 1851.

26. Nicholas I to Louis Napoleon, 22 Jan. 1852 (RA J73/31).

27. *The Morning Advertiser*, 4, 5, 6, 8, 10, 11, 18 Dec. 1851.

28. *The Times*, 10, 13 Dec. 1851; Hugo, *Histoire d'un crime*, II. 182–8; Senior's Journal, 3, 8 Jan. 1852; 19 Apr. 1861 (RA K12, pp. 203–5, 277; K49, pp. 95–101).

29. *The Times*, 27 Dec. 1851.

30. Derby to Malmesbury, 5 Dec. 1851; 18 Jan. 1852 (Malmesbury, I. 292, 300). For Aberdeen's view, see Aberdeen to Princess Lieven, 19 Dec. 1851; 1 Jan., 4 Feb. 1852 (*Correspondence of Lord Aberdeen and Princess Lieven*, pp. 606, 609, 614).

31. Queen Victoria to Leopold I, 4, 9 Dec. 1851; Leopold I to Queen Victoria, 5, 19 Dec. 1851 (*Letters of Queen Victoria*, I(ii). 404–6, 408–9,

414); *Morning Advertiser*, 11 Dec. 1851; Greville, II(iii). 420–1.

32. Palmerston to Normanby, 3 Dec. 1851 (Dalling and Ashley, *Life of Palmerston*, IV. 291). See also Palmerston's memorandum, ibid., IV. 287–9; Jerrold, III. 221–3, 306–14; Malmesbury, I. 297.

33. *The Times*, 21, 23, 24, 25, 26 Feb. 1852.

34. ibid., 22 Dec. 1851; 11, 28 June, 31 July 1852; *La Patrie*, 7 Dec. 1851.

35. *The Times*, 24 Jan., 3 Feb., 24, 27 Mar. 1852; Haussonville, 'Souvenirs' (*R.D.M.*, VII(xvii). 489); Malmesbury to Cowley, 2, 11, 26 Mar. 1852; Malmesbury to Westmorland, 8 Mar. 1852; Malmesbury's diary, 21 Apr. 1852; Derby to Malmesbury, 3 Oct. 1852 (Malmesbury, I. 310–11, 313–15, 323–4, 331, 352–5).

36. *The Times*, 23 Feb. 1852; and see Persigny to Malmesbury, 26 Dec. 1851 (Malmesbury, I. 294–6).

37. *Hansard* (H.L.), 3 Feb. 1852; Tennyson, 'The Third of February 1852' (*The Works of Alfred Lord Tennyson*, pp. 221–2).

38. *The Times*, 28 Feb. 1852.

39. ibid., 21, 22 Apr. 1852.

40. ibid., 3 Sept. 1852.

41. ibid., 18, 20, 21 Sept. 1852.

42. *Œuvres*, III. 336–7; *The Times*, 23, 24 Sept. 1852. See also *The Times*, 25, 27, 28 Sept. 1852 for Louis Napoleon at Grenoble and Valence.

43. Wellesley, *The Paris Embassy during the Second Empire*, p. 7.

44. *The Times*, 29, 30 Sept.; 1, 4, 5, 6, 7, 8, 9, 11, 12, 13 Oct. 1852.

45. *Œuvres*, III. 341–4; *The Times*, 13 Oct. 1852.

46. *The Times*, 14, 16, 18, 20 Oct. 1852; *Œuvres*, III. 345–6.

47. *The Times*, 25 Oct., 1 Nov. 1852.

48. Louis Napoleon's speeches to the Senators, 4, 7 Nov. 1852 (*Œuvres*, III. 347–50); *The Times*, 9 Nov. 1852; Louis Napoleon to Vieillard, 9 Nov. 1852 (Jerrold, III. 404, 404–5n.).

49. *The Times*, 3 Dec. 1852.

Chapter 25 – Mademoiselle de Montijo

1. Eugénie to Paca (spring 1849), 9 Sept. 1849 (*L.F.*, I. 25–28).

2. Mérimée to Mme de Langrené, 31 Aug. 1849 (*C.G.*, V. 498); *La Época*, 9 June 1849.

3. *La Época*, 27 June 1849.

4. ibid., 6, 7 July 1849.

5. Mérimée to Countess Montijo, 28 June 1849 (*C.G.*, V. 473); see Corneille, *Cinna*, III, III, 905.

6. Leopold I to Queen Victoria, 8 Apr. 1853 (RA Y78/48); *El Heraldo*, 23 Oct., 11 Dec. 1849; 6, 20 Jan.; 16 May 1850; *La Época*, 14, 30 Nov. 1849; 10 Apr. 1850.

7. Eugénie to Paca (May 1850) (*L.F.*, I. 31).

8. *La Época*, 2 Mar.; 9, 31 July; 7, 13, 27 Aug. 1850; 5 Feb. 1851; *El Heraldo*, 9, 30 July, 27 Aug. 1850.

9. *La Época*, 11, 14 Mar. 1851; *El Heraldo*, 12 Mar. 1851.

10. *El Heraldo*, 16 Apr. 1851; *La Época*, 6 Apr. 1851.

11. Kurtz, p. 32; Fraser, p. 14.

12. Malmesbury, I. 285.

13. Kurtz, p. 32; Filon, p. 22; Eugénie to Paca, 26 Oct. 1851 (*L.F.*, I. 37); *La Época*, 2 Dec. 1851 (Supp.); 28 Jan. 1853; *El Heraldo*, 2 Dec. 1851; 29 Jan. 1853.

14. Beijens to Materne, 27 Jan. 1853 (RA J76/55).

15. *El Heraldo*, 15 Apr. 1852; Eugénie to Paca (May 1852) (*L.F.*, I. 40).

16. For Miss Howard and her breach with Louis Napoleon, see Fleury, I. 204–10; see also *Papiers Secrets du Second Empire*, I. 14–16.

17. *The Times*, 22, 23 July 1852.

18. Princess Augusta of Prussia to Queen Victoria, 28 July 1852 (RA Y123/96).

19. Viel Castel, II. 34.

20. Alexandrine, Grand Duchess of Saxe-Coburg-Gotha to Queen Victoria, 10 Sept. 1852 (RA Y26/109).

21. Hultman, *Prinsen av Vasa*, pp. 225–6, 229.

22. Kurtz, pp. 35–36.

23. *The Times*, 16 Nov. 1852.

24. Filon, p. 23; Viel Castel, II. 122; Valdegamas to the Spanish Foreign Office, 25 Jan. 1853 (*Ibero-Amerikanisches Archiv*, XI(i). 32–33).

25. Fleury to Countess Montijo, 20 Nov. 1852; Eugénie to Galve, (Nov.) and 20 Nov. 1852 (*L.F.*, I. 45–46, 241); Hübner, I. 81.

26. *The Times*, 20, 21 Dec. 1852; Filon, p. 23.

27. Viel Castel, II. 130–1, 139, 146–9; Cowley to Russell, 10 Jan. 1853; Macdonald to Phipps, 24 Jan. 1853 (RA J76/8, 38); *Mariage de César*, p. 21.

28. Eugénie to Paca (Jan. 1853) (*L.F.*, I. 53).

29. Alba, op. cit., CXX. 80.

30. Cowley to Russell, 20 Jan. 1853 (PRO/FO 519/210, ff. 46–47); Malmesbury, I. 378.

31. Malmesbury, I. 378.

32. Greville (Wilson ed.), II. 439; Prince Hohenlohe-Langenburg to Walewski (Dec. 1852) (RA Add. A19/35).

33. Caroline Murat, p. 115; Senior's Journal, 24 May 1853 (RA K18, pp. 255–6).

34. Cowley to Russell, 17 Jan. 1853 (RA Add. A19/45).

35. *El Heraldo*, 21 Nov., 26 Dec. 1853.

36. Filon, pp. 23–24.

37. *The Times*, 21 Jan. 1853; Loliée, *La vie d'une impératrice*, p. 40.

38. Viel Castel, II. 146 (17 Jan. 1853).

39. Hübner, I. 101; Hübner to Buol, 26 Jan. 1853 (Wellesley and Sencourt, *Conversations with Napoleon III*, p. 43).

40. Cowley to Russell, 20 Jan. 1853 (PRO/FO 519/210, f. 47). See also Greville (Wilson ed.), II. 439–40, for Cowley's opinion of Eugénie.

41. Hübner, I. 100–1. For the ball, see also *The Times*, 14 Jan. 1853; *El Heraldo*, 18 Jan. 1853.
42. Napoleon III to Countess Montijo, 15 Jan. 1853 (*L.F.*, I. 48).
43. Eugénie to Paca (15 Jan. 1853) (*L.F.*, I. 47).
44. *The Times*, 21, 22, 26 Jan. 1853; *Morning Advertiser*, 21 Jan. 1853; Viel Castel, II. 150.
45. *The Times*, 27 Jan 1853
46. *El Heraldo*, 25 Jan. 1853; but see *La Época*, 24, 25, 26, 27 Jan. 1853.
47. *Morning Advertiser*, 21, 22, 26 Jan. 1853.
48. *The Times*, 14 Sept. 1852, 27 Jan. 1853.
49. Russell to Cowley, 21 Jan. 1853 (PRO/FO 519/197).
50. Cowley to Russell, 17 Jan. 1853 (RA J76/19).
51. Hübner, I. 103.
52. *Œuvres*, III. 357–60.
53. RA, Queen Victoria's Journal, 24 Jan. 1853.
54. Viel Castel, II. 153. See also II. 122, 130–1, 138–9, 146–56, 158, for Viel Castel's comments on Napoleon III's courtship of Eugénie.
55. Valdegamas to the Spanish Foreign Office, 25 Jan. 1853 (*Ibero-Amerikanisches Archiv*, XI(i). 33).
56. *The Times*, 24, 26, 27, 29 Jan.; 3 Feb. 1853; Beaumont-Vassy, *Histoire intime du second empire*, pp. 34–35; *Mariage de César*, p. 26.
57. Eugénie to Paca, 22 Jan. 1853 and last week of Jan. 1853 (*L.F.*, I. 50, 52–53).
58. *La Época*, 31 Jan. 1853; *The Times*, 31 Jan. 1853; *Morning Advertiser*, 31 Jan. 1853; *El Heraldo*, 2 Feb. 1853.
59. Schoelcher, *Le Gouvernement du Deux Décembre*, p. 437n.
60. Emerit's Preface; Napoleon III to Hortense Cornu, 20 Sept. 1853 (*Lettres de Napoléon III à Madame Cornu*, I. 39; II. 267).
61. Eugénie to Paca (last week of Jan. 1853) (*L.F.*, I. 54); *The Times*, 28 Jan. 1853.
62. Hübner, I. 103–5; *Moniteur*, 30 Jan. 1853; *The Times*, 31 Jan. 1853.
63. Eugénie to Paca (30 Jan. 1853) (*L.F.*, I. 55).
64. Eugénie to Paca (last week of Jan. 1853) (*L.F.*, I. 54).
65. *The Times*, 29, 31 Jan. 1853; *Moniteur*, 31 Jan. 1853; Hübner, I. 105; Cowley to Russell, 30 Jan. 1853 (PRO/FO 519/210, p. 50); Lady Augusta Bruce to the Duchess of Kent, 31 Jan. 1853; Lady Augusta Bruce to Baroness Spaeth, 8 Feb. 1853 (RA J76/48a, 58).

PART V

Chapter 26 – Troubles and Scandals

1. *Moniteur*, 7 Feb. 1853; *The Times*, 8 Feb. 1853.
2. *Moniteur*, 4 Feb. 1853; *The Times*, 1 Feb. 1853; Cowley to Russell, 7 Feb. 1853 (RA J76/59); Viel Castel, II. 262–3.

3. *The Times*, 8, 9 Feb.; 13 June; 22 Oct. 1853; Decree of 8 Dec. 1851 (*The Times*, 9 Mar. 1853).

4. For the activities of the 'secret societies' and the proceedings against them, see *The Times*, 11, 14, 22 Nov., 12 Dec. 1853; 17 Jan. 1854; 19 Oct., 22 Nov. 1855; 29 May, 16 Aug., 23, 30 Oct. 1856; 9 Feb., 11 May, 1 June 1857; 3 Mar., 6 Sept. 1858; 12, 21 July 1862; 27 Feb. 1864; 10, 14 Nov. 1866; 9 Mar. 1868; 27 Mar. 1869; 16 Feb. 1870.

5. Victor Hugo, 'Déclaration à propos de l'empire', 31 Oct. 1852 (Hugo, *Œuvres Complètes*, II. 47).

6. Delescluze, *De Paris à Cayenne*, pp. 21, 27; *The Times*, 21 Oct. 1853; Viel Castel, II. 261.

7. Senior's Journal, 18 May 1853 (RA K18, pp. 135–6); *The Times*, 14, 15 Mar. 1853.

8. Schoelcher, *Le Gouvernement du Deux Décembre*, p. 435n.

9. Castelot, I. 419–21, 429–30, 439.

10. *The Times*, 16 Apr. 1853.

11. Beaumont-Vassy, pp. 34–35; *The Times*, 3 Feb. 1853.

12. *Les femmes galantes des Napoléons*, pp. 216–18.

13. *Mariage de César*, p. 22.

14. ibid., p. 21.

15. Mérimée to Francisque-Michel, 28 Jan. 1853 (*C.G.*, VII. 16).

16. Leopold I to Queen Victoria, 2 Feb. 1853 (RA J76/54).

17. Leopold I to Queen Victoria, 28 Jan. 1853 (RA J76/41).

18. Leopold I to Queen Victoria, 8 Apr. 1853 (RA Y78/48).

19. Prince Albert to Marie, Dowager-Duchess of Saxe-Coburg-Gotha, 4 Feb. 1853 (RA M42/72).

20. Prince Albert to Leopold I, 22 Jan. 1853 (RA Add. A19/47).

21. RA, Queen Victoria's Journal, 20 Jan. 1853.

22. Queen Victoria to Leopold I, 1 Feb. 1853 (RA Y98/3).

23. Alba, op. cit., CXX. 85; Senior's Journal, 20 Apr. 1857 (RA K38, p. 81); Queen Victoria to Leopold I, 30 Oct. 1855 (RA Y100/43); Malmesbury, I. 388; Filon, pp. 49–51; Hübner, I. 174, 197–8; II. 107; Viel Castel, II. 199; *The Times*, 11 June 1858, 3 Jan. 1863, 22 Dec. 1864, 2 Feb. 1869.

24. Hübner, I. 173.

25. ibid., I. 347.

26. See thirteen letters from Eugénie to Paca between 22 Feb. 1853 and 22 Feb. 1854, and another letter in the autumn of 1854 (*L.F.*, I. 63–105, 112–13).

27. For the Camerata scandal, see *Les femmes galantes des Napoléons*, pp. 242–6; Beaumont-Vassy, pp. 71–76; Caroline Murat, pp. 157–63; Viel Castel, II. 167, 169, 172–3; Loliée, *La fête impériale*, pp. 33–36; Cowley to Clarendon (Mar. 1853) (RA J76/65).

28. *Les femmes galantes des Napoléons*, p. 246.

29. Loliée, *La vie d'une impératrice*, pp. 125–6.

30. *Moniteur*, 1 May 1853; Hübner, I. 127; *Les femmes galantes des Napoléons*, pp. 243–4.

31. Hübner, I. 127; Wellesley, *The Paris Embassy during the Second Empire*, p. 19.
32. Hübner, I. 135; Mérimée to Countess Montijo, 31 May 1853 (*C.G.*, VII. 65).
33. Hübner, I. 143.
34. Milbanke to Russell, 19 Jan. 1853; Cowley to Russell, 4 Feb., 10 Apr. 1853 (RA J76/50, 51, 72); Senior's Journal, 28, 30 Mar. 1854, 11 Sept. 1860 (RA K20, pp. 125–6, 128, 135; K46, p. 244); Hübner, I. 124; *The Times*, 14, 28 Mar.; 4, 8, 9, 12 Apr. 1853.
35. Haussmann, *Mémoires*, II. 43–56.
36. *The Times*, 1 Nov. 1862.
37. Senior's Journal, 22 Apr. 1858 (RA K41, p. 83).
38. ibid., 8 Feb., 4 May 1854 (RA K19, pp. 29–30; K22, pp. 23–24).
39. ibid., 18, 20 May 1853; 2 Apr. 1862 (RA K18, pp. 140–1, 159; K51, p. 324); *The Times*, 30 Nov. 1864, 26 Dec. 1865.
40. *The Times*, 17 Nov. 1856; 2, 19 Nov. 1860; 15 Aug., 22 Oct. 1861; 19 Sept., 1863; 13 Apr. 1868.
41. ibid., 14 Dec. 1864, 12 Dec. 1866, 15 Oct. 1867, 8 Mar. 1869.
42. Viel Castel, IV. 261; V. 163; Mérimée to Panizzi, 30 June 1867 (*C.G.*, XIII. 534); *The Times*, 12, 13 June; 7 Nov.; 19 Dec. 1867; 7 May 1868; 8 Mar. 1869.
43. *The Times*, 6 June 1867.
44. ibid., 27 July 1867.
45. Senior's Journal, 9 May 1853 (RA K17, pp. 17–18); *The Times*, 20 Mar. 1857, 15 Aug. 1861.
46. *The Times*, 10 Oct. 1865, 12 Dec. 1866.
47. For the progress of the rebuilding programme, see Haussmann, *Mémoires*, vol. III; *The Times*, 27 Aug.; 10, 24 Sept.; 19 Oct.; 21 Dec. 1860; 15, 29 Aug. 1861; 6 Jan., 9 Dec. 1862; 21 June, 24 Aug. 1864; 11 Aug., 27 Sept., 21 Oct. 1865; 6 Jan.; 7, 13, 31 Mar.; 8 May; 12 Dec. 1866; 22 Jan. 1868.
48. *The Times*, 9 June, 7 July, 1 Nov. 1853; Cowley to Clarendon, 6 July 1853 (RA J76/81).
49. Hübner, I. 150.
50. *The Times*, 15, 16, 17 Aug. 1853; Viel Castel, II. 224.
51. Viel Castel, II. 244; *The Times*, 14, 28 June; 30 Aug.; 21, 22 Sept.; 24 Dec. 1853; 10 Jan. 1854.
52. *The Times*, 28, 30 Dec. 1853; 18 Oct. 1855; 20 Aug., 12 Nov. 1857; 4 Mar. 1858; 4 Oct. 1861; 14, 19 Nov. 1867.
53. ibid., 29 Nov. 1864; 15 Mar. 1866; 25 Oct.; 6, 13, 25 Nov. 1867.
54. ibid., 16 May 1853, 3 Nov. 1866.
55. ibid., 16 May 1853.
56. ibid., 10 Nov. 1856; 20 Aug. 1857; 21 Jan. 1861; 4 Jan. 1867; 13, 17, 18, 28 Jan.; 3 Feb.; 4 June 1868; *Journal Officiel*, 21 Jan. 1869.
57. *The Times*, 23 Nov. 1853; 2 May 1865.
58. For the best summary of Napoleon III's social policy, see W. H. C. Smith, *Napoleon III*, pp. 107–21.

59. *The Times*, 23, 25 Aug.; 9 Sept. 1853.

Chapter 27 – The Drift to War

1. Malmesbury, I. 374–5.
2. *Diplomatic Study on the Crimean War* (Russian Foreign Office publication), I. 121–2.
3. ibid., I. 130–45.
4. Senior's Journal, 17 Feb. 1854 (RA K19, p. 102).
5. Cesena, *L'Angleterre et la Russie*, p. 27; *The Times*, 5 Nov. 1858. For Thiers's view, see Senior's Journal, 28 Nov. 1852 (RA K16, p. 26).
6. Senior's Journal, 15, 16 Sept. 1860 (RA K47, pp. 1, 7); *The Times*, 25, 28, 29 July; 6, 7 Aug.; 3, 18 Sept. 1856; 5 Jan. 1869.
7. *Dip. Study on Crimean War*, I. 87–88.
8. ibid., I. 73, 80.
9. Malmesbury to Hamilton, 21 Nov. 1852; Malmesbury to Cowley, 29 Nov., 4 Dec. 1852; Malmesbury's Journal (Malmesbury, I. 361–4, 369–70, 372–3, 379); Cowley to Russell, 25 Jan. 1853 (RA J76/45).
10. Malmesbury, I. 379.
11. Malmesbury to Hamilton, 21 Nov. 1852 (Malmesbury, I. 368); *Dip. Study on Crimean War*, I. 90–93, 101–3.
12. *Dip. Study on Crimean War*, I. 94–96; Seymour to Russell, 7 Jan. 1853 (RA J76/25).
13. Fraser, *Napoleon III*, p. 162.
14. Prince Albert to Marie, Dowager Duchess of Saxe-Coburg-Gotha, 10 Dec. 1852 (RA M42/70).
15. *L'Événement*, 8 Mar. 1850; *Le National*, 5 June 1851.
16. Derby to Malmesbury, 3 Oct. 1852; Malmesbury to Derby, 8 Oct. 1852 (Malmesbury, I. 352–7); Clarendon to Cowley, 13 Sept. 1853 (RA J76/82).
17. Nesselrode to Princess Lieven (?) (Dec. 1852) (Stanmore, *Earl of Aberdeen*, pp. 220–1).
18. Malmesbury, I. 387–8; Greville (Wilson ed.), II. 465–6.
19. Kinglake, *The Invasion of the Crimea*, I. 318, 482–5; Stanmore, pp. 220–1, 227, 243–4.
20. For the text of the Vienna Note and the Russian memorandum, see *Dip. Study on Crimean War*, I. 214–17n.
21. *The Times*, 28 Nov.; 2, 6 Dec. 1853.
22. ibid., 2, 25 Jan. 1854; RA, Queen Victoria's Journal, 21, 23 Jan. 1854; Viel Castel, II. 203–5; III. 14, 151.
23. RA, Queen Victoria's Journal, 28 Jan. 1854.
24. Napoleon III to Nicholas I, 29 Jan. 1854 (*Œuvres*, III. 373–9).
25. *The Times*, 18 Feb. 1854.
26. ibid., 16, 17 Feb. 1854.
27. Nicholas I to Napoleon III, 28 Jan./9 Feb. 1854 (*The Times*, 6 Mar. 1854).

28. *Œuvres*, III. 384–5.
29. Nicholas I's proclamation, 9/21 Feb. 1854 (*The Times*, 6 Mar. 1854).

Chapter 28 – The English Ally

1. See Senior's Journal, 2 Apr. 1862 (RA K51, pp. 328–9); *The Times*, 22 June 1865, 12 Apr. 1866.
2. Cowley to Clarendon, 27 Apr. 1854 (PRO/FO 519/213, f. 10).
3. *The Times*, 15 Apr. 1854; Senior's Journal, 12 Apr. 1854 (RA K21, p. 48).
4. Senior's Journal, 16, 18, 19 Apr. 1854 (RA K21, pp. 54–55, 60–63) (from Hortense Cornu).
5. *The Times*, 25 July, 11 Aug. 1854.
6. ibid., 11, 17, 18, 22, 25, 26, 31 Aug. 1854.
7. ibid., 8, 16, 17, 18, 19 Aug. 1854; *Œuvres*, III. 390–1.
8. *The Times*, 31 Aug.; 4, 30 Sept. 1854; Napoleon III's Order of the Day, 2 Sept. 1854 (*Œuvres*, III. 394).
9. *The Times*, 5, 6, 7, 8, 9, 11, 12 Sept. 1854.
10. Prince Albert's memorandum, 12 and 13 Sept. 1854 (RA J76/84; Sir Theodore Martin, *Life of the Prince Consort*, III. 108–9, 115).
11. *The Times*, 18, 19, 20, 22, 25 Sept. 1854.
12. ibid., 27, 30 Sept.; 2 Oct. 1854.
13. ibid., 12 Sept.; 2, 3, 4, 5 Oct. 1854.
14. ibid., 3 Oct. 1854 (omitted from Napoleon III's speech of 31 (*sic*) Sept. 1854 in *Œuvres*, III. 396–8).
15. *The Times*, 6, 7 Oct. 1854.
16. ibid., 6 Mar. 1854.
17. Jessie White Mario, *The Birth of Modern Italy*, p. 252; Marx, *The Eastern Question*, p. 19.
18. Barbès to Napoleon III, 18 Sept. 1854; Napoleon III to Billault, 3 Oct. 1854 (*Œuvres*, III. 398–9).
19. Barbès's letter, 11 Oct. 1854 (*The Times*, 16 Oct. 1854).
20. *The Times*, 7, 14 Jan. 1854; 20 Sept. 1855; Senior's Journal, 24 Feb. 1854 (RA K19, pp. 175–7).
21. Senior's Journal, 20 May 1855 (RA K26).
22. ibid.

Chapter 29 – Queen Victoria

1. *The Times*, 11 July, 18 Aug., 19 Dec. 1854; 28, 29 Mar. 1855; Mérimée to Mme de Boigne, 26 July 1854 (*C.G.*, VII. 334).
2. *The Times*, 17 Oct. 1855.
3. ibid., 10 Nov. 1854 (letter from Dr Lévy); 15 Nov. 1854 (letter from C. P. Shepherd); 23 Nov. 1854; 26 Jan. 1855.
4. Viel Castel, III. 109; Mérimée to Countess Montijo, 17 Feb. (two letters), 20 Mar. 1855 (*C.G.*, VII. 433–4, 436–7, 452); RA, Queen

Victoria's Journal, 18 Apr. 1855; *The Times*, 17, 19, 21, 22, 23, 27 Feb.; 5 Mar. 1855.

5. *The Times*, 20 Feb. 1855.

6. Napoleon III to Palmerston, 26 Feb. 1855 (RA G25/29).

7. Clarendon's memorandum, 6 Mar. 1855 (RA G26/2); Mérimée to Countess Montijo, 17 Feb. 1855 (*C.G.*, VII. 436–7); RA, Queen Victoria's Journal, 17 Apr. 1855; *The Times*, 12, 13, 15, 23, 27 Mar. 1855.

8. *The Times*, 17 Apr. 1855.

9. T. G. Owen's letter in *The Morning Post*, 19 Apr. 1855.

10. Victor Hugo, 'Lettre à Louis Bonaparte' (Hugo, *Œuvres Complètes*, II. 136).

11. *England's Disgrace* (leaflet).

12. *The Emperor and Empress's Visit to England!* (broadsheet).

13. For the state visit of Napoleon III and Eugénie to England, see *The Times*, 16, 17, 18, 19, 20, 21, 23 Apr. 1855; RA, Queen Victoria's Journal, 16, 17, 18, 19, 20, 21 Apr. 1855; Sir T. Martin, III. 237–58; Malmesbury, II. 18; Greville (Wilson ed.), II. 443.

14. Queen Victoria to Leopold I, 4 Jan. 1853 (*Queen Victoria's Letters*, I(ii). 526).

15. RA, Queen Victoria's Journal, 17, 19 Apr. 1855; Sir T. Martin, III. 240, 256–7.

16. RA, Queen Victoria's Journal, 17 Apr. 1855; Sir T. Martin, III. 245.

17. Prince Albert's memorandum, 19 Apr. 1855; Queen Victoria to Leopold I, 24 Apr. 1855 (RA J76/89; Y100/18); Mérimée to Countess Montijo, 20 Apr. 1855 (*C.G.*, VII. 466).

18. RA, Queen Victoria's Journal, 17 Apr. 1855.

19. *The Times*, 19 Apr. 1855.

20. Disraeli to Mrs Brydges Williams, 1 May 1855 (Monypenny and Buckle, IV. 5).

21. Mérimée to Countess Montijo, 29 Apr. 1855; Mérimée to Mme de Xifre, 8 May 1855 (*C.G.*, VII. 472, 477–8); Hübner, I. 324; *The Times*, 30 Apr.; 1, 4 May 1855; *Œuvres*, III. 419–20; Beaumont-Vassy, pp. 133–5.

22. *The Times*, 30 Apr. 1855; Queen Victoria to Leopold I, 1 May 1855 (*Queen Victoria's Letters*, I(iii). 154).

23. *The Times*, 4, 7, 8, 9, 11, 12, 14, 16, 17 May 1855.

24. ibid., 17, 28 Mar.; 14 Apr. 1855.

25. Mérimée to Countess Montijo, 29 Apr. 1855 (*C.G.*, VII. 473); Greville (Wilson ed.), II. 566–7.

26. *The Times*, 16, 17 May 1855.

27. ibid., 7 Feb. 1867; Levey, 'Exhibitions' (*Encyclopaedia Britannica*, 11th ed., X. 67).

28. Mérimée to Mrs Senior, 8 June 1855; Mérimée to Panizzi, 4 July 1855; Mérimée to Mme de Boigne, 8, 29 July 1855; Mérimée to Langrené, 27 Sept. 1855 (*C.G.*, VII. 488, 500–1, 506, 530); *The Times*, 5 Apr.; 10, 16 Aug.; 13 Sept. 1855.

29. Information from Mrs Yehudi Menuhin; *The Times*, 2 July 1855; Bac, p. 299.
30. *The Times*, 30 July, 6 Aug. 1855.
31. Mérimée to Mme de Boigne, 20 Aug. 1855 (*C.G.*, VII. 518).
32. For Queen Victoria's visit to Paris, see RA, Queen Victoria's Journal, 18, 19, 20, 21, 22, 23, 24, 25, 26, 27 Aug. 1855; Queen Victoria to Leopold I, 23 Aug. 1855 (RA Y100/32); *The Times*, 18, 20, 21, 22, 23, 24, 25, 27, 28 Aug. 1855.
33. *The Times*, 20 Aug. 1855.
34. Greville (Wilson ed.), II. 446–7.
35. RA, Queen Victoria's Journal, 26 Aug. 1855.
36. Mérimée to Mme de Boigne, 26 Aug. 1855 (*C.G.*, VII. 522).
37. Queen Victoria's Journal, in Sir T. Martin, III. 341; see also RA, Queen Victoria's Journal, 25 Aug. 1855, where Princess Beatrice has transcribed the entry with a slightly different wording from Sir Theodore Martin's.
38. Villiers, *A Vanished Victorian*, pp. 261–2.
39. *The Times*, 28 Aug. 1855.
40. RA, Queen Victoria's Journal, 27 Aug. 1855; *The Times*, 28 Aug. 1855.
41. Napoleon III to Queen Victoria, 1 Sept. 1855 (RA M57/14).
42. Pélissier to Napoleon III, 10 Sept. 1855 (*The Times*, 13 Sept. 1855).
43. *The Times*, 10 Sept. 1855.
44. Viel Castel, III. 189–90; Fraser, pp. 126–32; *The Times*, 31 Dec. 1855.
45. For the peace negotiations through Seebach, see *Dip. Study on Crimean War*, II. 350–4; *The Times*, 2 Jan. 1856.
46. *The Times*, 28 Jan. 1856.
47. For the Peace Congress, see *Dip. Study on Crimean War*, II. 352–4, 378–9; L. Thouvenel, *Pages de l'histoire du Second Empire*, pp. 225–45.
48. Lady Ely to Queen Victoria, 26 Feb., 16 Mar. 1856 (RA S8/21; J77/4); Hübner, I. 403; Viel Castel, III. 219; *The Times*, 11, 17, 18 Mar. 1856.
49. *The Times*, 19, 21 Mar. 1856; information from Mrs Yehudi Menuhin.
50. Bordeaux Municipal Council to Napoleon III (*The Times*, 21 Mar. 1856).
51. *The Times*, 20 Mar. 1856.
52. ibid., 17 Mar.; 1, 4 Apr. 1856.
53. ibid., 16, 18, 19 June 1856.
54. ibid., 21 June 1856.

Chapter 30 – The High Noon of the Empire

1. Viel Castel, III. 243; *The Times*, 4, 5, 6, 7, 9, 10, 13, 16, 24 June 1856.
2. Napoleon III's speech opening the Legislative session, 16 Feb. 1857 (*Œuvres*, V. 30).
3. *The Times*, 14 June, 21 Aug., 6 Dec. 1856.
4. Baron de Witte, 'Carol Ier, Roi de Roumanie' (*R.D.M.*, VI(xxiv). 81–93); *The Times*, 17, 19 Apr. 1866; 29, 30 May; 1, 19 June; 10 Aug. 1867; 18 Mar., 8 May 1868; 1 June 1870.
5. For the Neuchâtel crisis, see Napoleon III to Dufour, 24 Oct. 1856

(Budé, *Les Bonaparte en Suisse*, pp. 245–7); *The Times*, 18, 19, 22, 24, 27, 31 Dec. 1856; 1, 14, 15, 19, 20, 21, 24 Jan.; 13 Feb.; 6 Mar.; 29 May 1857.

6. Mérimée to Mme de Boigne, 8 Aug. 1857 (*C.G.*, VIII. 353).
7. Filon, p. 26; Hübner, I. 386; Schoelcher, *Le Gouvernement du Deux Décembre*, p. 539.
8. Hübner, I. 242.
9. Mérimée to Countess Montijo, 1 Jan. 1854 (*C.G.*, VII. 239).
10. Hübner, I. 342–3.
11. ibid., I. 309–10.
12. For Napoleon III's life at Plombières and Vichy, see *The Times*, 11, 19, 23, 26 July; 8 Aug. 1856; 10, 28 July 1858; 22, 27 July 1861; 21, 30 July; 1, 2, 11 Aug. 1862; 22 July 1863; 29 July 1864; 31 July, 9 Aug. 1865; 15, 28, 31 July 1868.
13. *The Times*, 15 Aug. 1857.
14. For Châlons Camp, see *The Times*, 8, 16, 17, 24 Sept.; 7, 12 Oct. 1857; 8, 10, 13, 15, 17 Aug. 1860; 17 July 1861; 15, 26 Aug. 1863; 5 Sept. 1864; 18 Aug. 1869; and see Colonel Claremont to Cowley, 2 Aug. 1864 (RA J81/9).
15. *The Times*, 18, 19 Sept. 1857.
16. ibid., 7, 12 Oct. 1857; 13 Oct. 1858; 16 Aug. 1865; 17 Aug. 1867.
17. ibid., 30 Apr., 10 Dec. 1856.
18. For the life at Biarritz, see *The Times*, 27 Aug.; 5, 8, 12, 15, 26 Sept. 1856; 11, 25 Sept. 1858; 14, 26 Sept.; 4, 10 Oct. 1859; 9, 12, 18, 26, 28 Sept.; 3, 4 Oct. 1861; 9 Sept., 19 Oct. 1863; 12, 13 Sept. 1865; 16, 31 Oct. 1866; 12 Sept., 5, 7, 9 Oct. 1867; 19 Sept., 12 Oct. 1868; Filon, pp. 43–46; Caroline Murat, p. 167; Wilfrid Scawen Blunt, 'Alms to Oblivion', Vol. II (F.M., Blunt Papers, MS. 41-1975, pp. 160, 162); Eugénie to Queen Victoria, 14 Mar. 1889 (RA Z138/43).
19. Eugénie to Queen Victoria, 5 Apr. 1889 (RA Z138/44).
20. Malmesbury, II. 291n.
21. Leopold I to Queen Victoria, 11, 20 June 1864 (RA Y86/40, 43); Mérimée to Panizzi, 13 June 1864 (*C.G.*, XII. 156–7).
22. Viel Castel, IV. 223; *The Times*, 24 Dec. 1855; 14, 21, 23 Jan., 30 Dec. 1861; 6 Jan. 1862; 8 Jan., 30 Dec. 1864; 13 Jan. 1868.
23. Barthez to Octavie, 24 Sept. 1863 (Barthez, *The Empress Eugénie and her Circle*, p. 238).
24. Barthez to Octavie, 5–12, 12–26 Sept. 1856, 24 Sept. 1863, and note (undated) (Barthez, pp. 88, 101n., 112–13, 238).
25. For Compiègne, see *The Times*, 13 Dec. 1855; 24, 30 Oct., 1, 11 Nov. 1856; 19 Nov. 1858; 9 Nov. 1859; 9, 11 Oct., 28 Nov. 1861; 20, 23, 27, 30 Nov. 1863; 25 Nov.; 2, 9 Dec. 1864; Filon, pp. 51–52; Fleury, II. 193–210.
26. Hübner, I. 441; *The Times*, 11, 24 Oct.; 11 Nov. 1856; 15 May 1857.
27. Malmesbury, II. 144.
28. Mérimée to Jenny Dacquin, 24 Nov. 1858; Mérimée to Pasquier, 25 Nov. 1858 (*C.G.*, VIII. 613).

29. Viel Castel, III. 313.
30. *The Times*, 10 Oct.; 1, 6, 11, 15 Nov. 1856.
31. For the election of 1857, see ibid , 8, 17, 18, 19, 20, 22, 23, 24, 25, 26, 27, 29, 30 June; 2, 7, 11 July; 15 Aug. 1857
32. ibid., 19 June 1857.
33. Hübner to Buol, 4 Aug. 1857 (Hübner, II. 39–40).
34. *The Times*, 10 July 1857.
35. ibid.
36. Viel Castel, IV. 43, 49–51, 120–1, 124, 126; Senior's Journal. 10, 23 Apr., 8 May 1857 (RA K38, pp. 6–7, 101–2, 196); *The Times*, 17, 21 Apr.; 4, 13, 23, 24, 28, 30 July; 7, 8, 10 Aug.; 7 Sept. 1857.
37. *Le Constitutionnel*, 19 Oct., 7 Nov. 1857; *The Times*, 22 Oct.; 11, 14 Nov; 7 Dec. 1857.
38. *The Times*, 13 Nov. 1857.

Chapter 31 – Eugénie and 'Plon-Plon'

1. Corley, *Democratic Despot*, p. 137; Kurtz, p. 95.
2. Senior's Journal, 10 Apr. 1857 (RA K38, p. 7).
3. Bac, pp. 301–2.
4. Viel Castel, IV. 337.
5. Barthez to Octavie, 5–12 Sept. 1856 (Barthez, p. 85).
6. Decaux, *La Castiglione*, pp. 84, 86–87.
7. Cavour to Countess Castiglione, 20 Feb. 1856 (Decaux, p. 78).
8. Cavour to Cibrario, 25 Feb. 1856 (Decaux, p. 91).
9. Viel Castel, IV. 65.
10. ibid., IV. 103–5; *The Times*, 11, 13, 16 July 1857.
11. Viel Castel, IV. 336; see also V. 32.
12. Filon, pp. 33–35.
13. Caroline Murat, pp. 152–3.
14. Viel Castel, IV. 335; see also IV. 224.
15. Napoleon III to Arese, 25 June 1855 (Bonfadini, p. 147).
16. Bonfadini, pp. 147–63.
17. Senior's Journal, 28 Apr. 1859 (RA K43, p. 29).
18. *The Times*, 13 Apr., 7 Sept. 1853; 30 Oct. 1855.
19. ibid., 15 Oct. 1855; 29 June, 27 July 1857; 28 Jan. 1859; 6, 9 Aug. 1860; 23 Dec. 1861; 27 Jan. 1866; 26, 30 Jan. 1869.
20. ibid., 22 Sept. 1862.
21. See the verbatim report of the trial, in Flaubert, *Madame Bovary* (Paris, 1930 ed.), pp. 558–630.
22. ibid., p. 629.
23. Enid Starkey, *Baudelaire*, pp. 254–68.
24. Baudelaire to Eugénie, 6 Nov. 1857 (Hyslop and Hyslop, *Baudelaire*, pp. 132–3).

25. *The Times*, 20 Oct. 1855; see also 6 Oct. 1858.
26. ibid., 5, 6, 7, 9, 10, 20, 22, 23, 24, 31 Jan.; 2 Feb. 1857; Viel Castel, IV. 9–10, 15–17.
27. For the Mortara case, see *The Times*, 19, 20, 25 Oct.; 24, 25 Nov.; 27, 28 Dec. 1858; Viel Castel, V. 255–6; VI. 7. For the Coin case, see *The Times*, 22 Aug., 17 Sept. 1864.
28. Viel Castel, III. 186; Malmesbury, II. 37; *The Times*, 24, 26, 27, 29, 30 Nov.; 1, 7, 8, 10 Dec. 1855; and see Isabel Vesey's MS., p. 50.
29. Eugénie to Alba, 24 July 1856; Eugénie to Countess Montijo, 29 Mar., 6 Apr. 1876 (*L.F.*, I. 133–4; II. 56–59); Mérimée to Countess Montijo, 17 Sept. 1859; 23 Mar., 28 June 1869; Mérimée to Eugénie, 18 Mar. 1869; Mérimée to Jenny Dacquin, 12 June 1869; Mérimée to Mme Delessert, 23 June 1869; Mérimée to Turgeniev, 30 June 1869 (*C.G.*, IX. 250; XIV. 428, 432, 515, 519, 525, 533); RA, Queen Victoria's Journal, 27 Oct. 1879; Ethel Smyth, *Streaks of Life*, pp. 11, 35, 50; Ethel Smyth to Lady Ponsonby, 9 Nov. 1893 (Smyth, *As Time went on*, p. 317).
30. Eugénie's statement to Ethel Smyth (Smyth, *Streaks of Life*, p. 33).
31. Mme Carette, *My Mistress, the Empress Eugenie*, pp. 106–7.
32. Eugénie to Paca (Oct. 1853) (*L.F.*, I. 96).
33. Mérimée to Panizzi, 26 Apr. 1864 (*C.G.*, XII. 116).
34. Filon, pp. 36–37, 40–42; and see Mérimée to Countess Montijo, 4 Mar. 1857 (*C.G.*, VIII. 246).
35. Ollivier, *Journal*, II. 279.
36. Smyth, *Streaks of Life*, p. 34.
37. Hübner, I. 149.
38. RA, Queen Victoria's Journal, 17 Apr. 1855.
39. Eugénie to Paca (spring 1854) (*L.F.*, I. 106).
40. Eugénie to Alba, 18 July 1854 (*L.F.*, I. 109).
41. Eugénie to Paca, 31 Dec. 1857 (*L.F.*, I. 143).
42. Viel Castel, II. 165–6; III. 27, 41, 76; V. 35; Hübner, I. 320–1, 441; II. 312; Mérimée to Jenny Dacquin, 17 Nov. 1861, 27 July 1867; Mérimée to Clair, 28 July 1867 (*C.G.*, X. 402; XIII. 562, 565); Filon, p. 75; Smyth, *Streaks of Life*, p. 26.
43. See *The Times*, 7 Oct. 1865.
44. For the bitter criticism of *Les Misérables* by the Establishment in France, see Senior's Journal, 11 Apr. 1862 (RA K51, p. 469); *The Times*, 16 Apr., 8 Oct. 1862; Viel Castel, VI. 163, 165.
45. *The Times*, 20 Apr. 1861.
46. ibid., 19 Sept. 1856; 25 Sept., 1 Oct. 1858; 29 Dec. 1863; 6 Sept. 1865; 28 Aug. 1868; Fraser, pp. 22–28.
47. ibid., 27 Nov. 1863; 24, 30 Nov.; 7 Dec. 1866; 26 Oct. 1868.
48. *Mariage de César*, p. 15.
49. *Les femmes galantes des Napoléons*, pp. 162–3.
50. Isabel Vesey's MS., p. 69; Barthez to Octavie, 22–26 Sept. 1856 (Barthez, pp. 108–9).
51. Barthez to Octavie, 30 Sept. 1856 (Barthez, p. 126).

52. Hübner, I. 173; Viel Castel, II. 189; Eugénie to Paca (Mar. 1857) (*L.F.*, I. 136–8); Senior's Journal, 10 Apr. 1857 (RA K38, p. 3); Mérimée to Countess Montijo, 11 Apr. 1857 (*C.G.*, VIII. 279).

53. Malmesbury, II. 282 (talk with Napoleon III on 27 Oct. 1862); RA, Queen Victoria's Journal, 7 Aug. 1857.

54. Eugénie to Paca, 3 May 1857 (*L.F.*, I. 141–2); Hübner, II. 18; Viel Castel, IV. 30.

55. Senior's Journal, 5 May 1858 (RA K41, p. 169).

56. Filon, pp. 38–39; Paléologue, p. 62.

57. Ollivier, *Journal*, II. 295 (8 July 1867).

58. Senior's Journal, 6 May 1859 (RA K43, pp. 137–8).

59. For Prince Napoleon's career, see anonymous memorandum, 6 Mar. 1862 (RA J79/84).

60. *The Times*, 14 Mar., 19, 22 May 1854.

61. ibid., 2, 21, 24 Nov.; 13, 23 Dec. 1854; Viel Castel, III. 102–4; Lord Howard de Walden to Clarendon, 12 Dec. 1854; Senior's Journal, 2 Mar. 1855 (RA J76/87; K23, pp. 4–5).

62. *The Times*, 21, 25 Nov. 1854.

63. ibid., 21 Dec. 1853; 8, 31 Jan.; 10, 13 Feb.; 16, 22 Mar. 1855.

64. Senior's Journal, 5 May 1858 (RA K41, p. 169); Hübner, II. 203.

65. *The Times*, 15, 20, 24, 27, 30 Apr.; 2, 6, 9, 11 May 1857.

66. Hübner, II. 30; Viel Castel, IV. 52; Mérimée to Countess Montijo, 23 May 1857; Mérimée to Mme de la Rochejaquelin, 1 Aug. 1857 (*C.G.*, VIII. 299, 343); *The Times*, 11, 12, 14, 19 May 1857.

67. Viel Castel, IV. 56, 78; Hübner, II. 24; Senior's Journal, 8 May 1857 (RA K38, p. 194); *The Times*, 14 May 1857.

68. Queen Victoria to Napoleon III, 6 June 1857 (RA M57/62).

69. For the visit to Osborne, see RA, Queen Victoria's Journal, 6, 7, 8, 9, 10 Aug. 1857; *The Times*, 6, 7, 8, 11 Aug. 1857; for the security, see Malmesbury, II. 78; Clarendon to Queen Victoria, 18 July 1857 (RA B16/62).

70. Napoleon III to Queen Victoria, 15 Aug. 1857 (RA J77/52).

71. RA, Queen Victoria's Journal, 10 Aug. 1857.

72. Hübner, II. 42; Viel Castel, IV. 136; Malmesbury, II. 78; Queen Victoria to Leopold I, 12 Aug. 1857 (RA Y102/26); *The Times*, 10, 11, 14, 15 Aug. 1857.

73. For the Stuttgart meeting, see *The Times*, 26, 28, 29, 30 Sept.; 1, 2, 3, 6 Oct. 1857; see also Fleury, I. 397–401.

74. Hübner, II. 163; RA, Queen Victoria's Journal, 30 Apr. 1859.

75. *The Times*, 14 Oct. 1857.

76. For the figures of French and British naval strength, see *The Times*, 10 Aug. 1860.

77. *Le Constitutionnel*, 7 Sept., 17 Nov. 1857; Viel Castel, IV. 132, 135–6, 152–3, 158–64, 168–9, 178, 194–7, 199–200, 206, 209–11, 213–14, 219; Mérimée to Ellice, 31 Aug. 1857 (*C.G.*, VIII. 368).

78. *The Times*, 5 Nov. 1858.

79. Hübner, II. 56.

80. ibid., II. 3; see also I. 386; II. 24.
81. ibid., II. 81.
82. ibid., II. 82.

Chapter 32 – Orsini's Bombs

1. *Moniteur*, 14 Jan. 1858.
2. Hübner, II. 86; *The Times*, 4, 9, 11, 12 Jan. 1858.
3. For the incidents on 14 January, see Eugénie to Countess Montijo, 15, 18 Jan. 1858 (*L.F.*, I. 146–9); *Moniteur*, 15, 16 Jan. 1858; *The Times*, 15, 16, 18, 19 Jan. 1858; Hübner, II. 87–89, 91, 92–93n.; Mérimée to Countess Montijo, 16 Jan. 1858 (*C.G.*, VIII. 434–5); Napoleon III to Queen Victoria, 17 Jan. 1858; Eugénie to Queen Victoria, 17 Jan. 1858 (RA, M57/76, 77); Viel Castel, IV. 225–7.
4. Mérimée to Countess Montijo, 16 Jan. 1858 (*C.G.*, VIII. 435).
5. Hübner, II. 91 (from Eugénie).
6. For the background of the four conspirators, see Beaumont-Vassy, pp. 230–41.
7. Allsop to Bernard, 1 Jan. 1857 (*The Times*, 14 Apr. 1858).
8. *The Times*, 24 Feb.; 13, 14 Apr. 1858.
9. Hübner, II. 90.
10. ibid., II. 111.
11. Senior's Journal, 7 Mar. 1858 (RA K40, p. 59); *The Times*, 28 Jan. 1858.
12. Billault to Napoleon III, Jan. 1858; Napoleon III's decree, 18 Jan. 1858 (*Moniteur*, 20 Jan. 1858); *The Times*, 21 Jan. 1858.
13. Senior's Journal, 7 Mar. 1858 (RA K40, p. 46).
14. ibid., 6 Mar.; 19, 24 Apr.; 3, 5, 31 May 1858 (RA K40, pp. 39–40; K41, pp. 48–49, 92–98, 145–8, 150–1, 166–8).
15. ibid., 3 May 1858 (RA K41, pp. 146–8).
16. ibid., 11 Apr. 1861 (RA, K49, p. 20).
17. ibid., 6 Mar. 1858 (RA K40, p. 40).
18. Martet, *M. Clemenceau peint par lui-même*, p. 183.
19. Delescluze, *De Paris à Cayenne*, pp. 73, 100–2, 107, 196–218, 242–6, 272, 278. For conditions in Cayenne, see Louis Blanc's letter to *The Times*, 25 Aug. 1856, and the ensuing controversy (*The Times*, 29, 30 Aug.; 1, 2 Sept.; 3 Oct. 1856).
20. *Moniteur*, 20, 22, 23, 24, 26, 27, 28, 29, 30, 31 Jan.; 2, 3, 5 Feb. 1858.
21. ibid., 27 Jan. 1858.
22. ibid., 29 Jan. 1858.
23. ibid., 31 Jan. 1858.
24. *The Times*, 16 Jan. 1858.
25. Mérimée to Countess Montijo, 1 Mar. 1858 (*C.G.*, VIII. 483).
26. Hübner, II. 118–19 (from Rouher); Senior's Journal, 9 Mar. 1858 (RA K40, pp. 71–72).
27. Viel Castel, II. 141–2; III. 67.
28. *Moniteur*, 26, 27 Feb. 1858; Hübner, II. 125; *The Times*, 27 Feb., 1 Mar. 1858.

29. Hübner, II. 124, 134, 145. For the text of Orsini's letter to Napoleon III, 11 Feb. 1858, see *The Times*, 3 Mar. 1858.
30. Eugénie to Paca, 21 Jan. 1858 (*L.F.*, I. 150).
31. Hübner, II. 119–20, 285–6; Viel Castel, IV. 253–7; Senior's Journal, 6 Mar. 1858 (RA K40, pp. 33–34); Eugénie to — (1908) (Luzio, *Felice Orsini*, pp. 315–16); Paléologue, pp. 158–60.
32. Hübner, II. 125n.
33. Senior's Journal, 6 Mar. 1858 (RA K40, p. 42).
34. *The Times*, 15 Mar. 1858.
35. Malmesbury to Cowley, 4 Mar. 1858 (Malmesbury, II. 102).
36. *The Times*, 24 Feb. 1858.
37. For Bernard's trial, see *The Times*, 13, 14, 15, 16, 17, 19 Apr. 1858. See also Fraser, pp. 85–93.
38. *The Times*, 20, 21, 22, 23 Apr. 1858; Eugénie to Cowley, 18 Apr. 1858 (Wellesley and Sencourt, pp. 136–8). See also *Le Constitutionnel*, 20 Apr. 1858; Viel Castel, IV. 260.
39. Queen Victoria to Princess Victoria, 28 Apr. 1858 (RA Add. U32, p. 144); RA, Queen Victoria's Journal, 21 Apr. 1858; Malmesbury to Cowley, 15 Apr. 1858 (Malmesbury, II. 115).
40. Mérimée to Jenny Dacquin, 28 Apr. 1858; Mérimée to Countess Montijo, 29 Apr. 1858 (*C.G.*, VIII. 512–14).
41. Mérimée to Vaillant, 8 May 1858; Mérimée to Panizzi, 16 May, 5 June 1858 (*C.G.*, VIII. 515–16, 524–5, 537).
42. Malmesbury to Cowley, 2, 6, 14 Mar. 1858 (Malmesbury, II. 101–3, 105–7).
43. Hübner, II. 142.
44. Mérimée to Countess Montijo, 29 Apr., 8 Dec. 1858 (*C.G.*, VIII. 514, 621–2).
45. Malmesbury, II. 115.
46. Queen Victoria to Leopold I, 20 Apr. 1858 (RA Y103/13).

Chapter 33 – Cavour and Cherbourg

1. Mérimée to Ellice, 31 Jan., 1 Mar. 1858 (*C.G.*, VIII. 464, 481).
2. See Hübner, II. 92–93, 111–12, 285–6, 299; Malmesbury, II. 157, 161; Senior's Journal, 26 Apr. 1859; 17 May; 28, 29 Sept. 1860; 28 Mar.; 2 Apr.; 12, 15 Aug. 1861 (RA K43, pp. 16–17; K44, pp. 145–6; K47; K48; K50).
3. Napoleon III to Victor Emanuel II, 31 Mar. 1858 (*Carteggio Cavour-Nigra*, I. 83).
4. Cavour to Salmour, 8 Aug. 1857 (ibid., I. 58).
5. Nigra to Cavour, 10 May 1858 (ibid., I. 87).
6. Thayer, *Life and Times of Cavour*, I. 527–8, 533.
7. For the talks between Napoleon III and Cavour at Plombières, see

Cavour to Victor Emanuel II, 24 July 1858 (*Cavour-Nigra*, I. 103–14). See also Cavour to La Marmora, 24 July 1860, and Cavour's notes (ibid., I. 98–102, 114–16).

8. Hübner, II. 196; Hübner to Buol, 29 July 1858 (ibid., II. 200–2).
9. *The Times*, 30 July; 2, 18 Aug. 1858.
10. For the Cherbourg fêtes, see *The Times*, 6, 7, 9, 10, 11 Aug. 1858; Fraser, pp. 138–53.
11. Viel Castel, IV. 335–6 (from Chaumont-Quitry).
12. For Napoleon III's speech, see *Œuvres*, V. 64.
13. RA, Queen Victoria's Journal, 5 Aug. 1858.
14. *The Times*, 10 Aug. 1858.
15. Viel Castel, IV. 311, 313; Malmesbury, II. 129.
16. *The Times*, 9 Aug. 1858.
17. Mme Carette, pp. 11–29; Mérimée to Countess Montijo, 24 Aug. 1858 (*C.G.*, VIII. 571); Viel Castel, IV. 320; *The Times*, 12, 14, 16, 18, 19, 20, 21, 23 Aug. 1858.
18. *The Morning Post*, 16, 17, 18, 19, 20, 21, 23, 24 Aug. 1858.
19. ibid., 18 Aug. 1858; *The Times*, 23 Aug.; 21 Oct.; 6, 11, 17 Nov. 1858; Mocquard to MacCabe, 31 Oct. 1858 (*The Times*, 6 Nov. 1858).
20. Lasserre, *Notre Dame de Lourdes*, pp. 193–4, 277–8, 300–1, 349–52, 354.
21. *The Times*, 3, 6, 9, 10, 18 Sept. 1858.
22. *Hansard*, 17, 24 June 1858 (House of Lords).
23. *Le Constitutionnel*, 21 June 1858.
24. *The Times*, 9, 12, 13, 14, 15, 16, 18, 25, 26, 27, 29, 30 Oct.; 4, 15 Nov. 1858.
25. Napoleon III to Prince Napoleon, 30 Oct. 1858; Napoleon III to the Minister of Marine, 1 July 1861 (*The Times*, 9 Nov. 1858; 10 July 1861). See also *The Times*, 3 Nov. 1858.
26. Full text in *The Times*, 13, 17 Nov. 1858.
27. ibid., 1, 8, 10, 15, 16, 19, 22, 25, 26, 27, 29, 30 Nov.; 1, 2, 3, 4, 9, 22, 23, 27, 29 Dec. 1858.
28. Palmerston to Clarendon, 31 Oct., 2 Nov. 1858 (Maxwell, *Life and Letters of fourth Earl of Clarendon*, II. 162–3).
29. Mérimée to Countess Montijo, 8 Dec. 1858 (*C.G.*, VIII. 620).
30. Mérimée to Fanny Lagden, 30 Nov. 1858; Mérimée to Countess Montijo, 8 Dec. 1858 (*C.G.*, VIII. 614, 620–1).
31. Hübner, II. 244.
32. Mérimée to Panizzi, 7 Jan. 1859 (*C.G.*, IX. 14); *The Times*, 3, 4, 5, 6, 7, 8 Jan. 1859.
33. Mérimée to Countess Montijo, 17 Feb., 16 Mar. 1859; Mérimée to Panizzi, 8 Apr. 1859 (*C.G.*, IX. 52, 71–73, 92); Viel Castel, V. 437.
34. Hübner to Buol, 14, 19 Jan. 1859 (Hübner, II. 256, 259, 263); see also II. 284; Leopold I to Queen Victoria, 25 Feb.; 8, 15 Apr. 1859; Queen Victoria to Leopold I, 9 May 1859 (RA Y81/109, 115, 116; Y104/16).
35. Senior's Journal, 5 May 1859 (RA K43, p. 123).
36. Hübner to Buol, 13 May 1857; two letters of 7 Apr. 1859; 15 Apr. 1859; and Hübner's diary (Hübner, II. 25–30, 311, 372–8, 385–95, 404).

37. Buol to Cavour, 19 Apr. 1859 (Hübner, II. 416–18); *The Times*, 23, 25, 26, 27, 28 Apr. 1859.

Chapter 34 – The War in Italy

1. Napoleon III's proclamation, 3 May 1859 (*Œuvres*, V. 78–80).
2. Mérimée to Panizzi, 10 May 1859 (*C.G.*, IX. 115–16); Viel Castel, V. 51; Senior's Journal, 28 Apr., 13 May 1859 (RA K43, pp. 35, 241); *The Times*, 11, 12, 13 May 1859.
3. Viel Castel, V. 52; *The Times*, 12 May 1859; Bigelow, *Retrospections of an Active Life*, I. 211.
4. *The Times*, 12, 14, 18 May 1859.
5. Bonfadini, p. 382.
6. Senior's Journal, 24 Apr. 1861 (RA K49, p. 143) (from Changarnier).
7. *The Times*, 27 June 1859.
8. ibid., 6, 14, 24 June 1859.
9. ibid., 14 June 1859.
10. Ollivier, 'Napoléon III – Général en chef' (*R.D.M.*, IV(cliii). 336).
11. *The Times*, 14, 17 June 1859.
12. ibid., 14 June 1859; Dunant, *Un Souvenir de Solferino*, pp. 63, 88.
13. *The Times*, 30 May, 6 June, 6 July 1859.
14. ibid., 25 June 1859.
15. ibid., 27 June, 12 July 1859.
16. ibid., 25, 27 June 1859.
17. ibid., 25 June 1859.
18. For the battle of Solferino, see Dunant, pp. 8–39; *The Times*, 27, 30 June; 2, 4, 9 July 1859.
19. Senior's Journal, 21 Sept. 1860; 15, 25 Apr. 1861; 25 Apr. 1863 (RA K47; K49, pp. 67–68, 156–7, 160, 163–4; K54, p. 165); Dunant, pp. 41–42; Viel Castel, V. 85; Eugénie to Paca, 28 June 1859 (*L.F.*, I. 166).
20. Dunant, p. 17.
21. ibid., pp. 47–58.
22. *The Times*, 27 June 1859.
23. Dunant, pp. 66–149; *The Times*, 7 July 1859.
24. Dunant, pp. 150–70.
25. *The Times*, 27 June 1859.
26. ibid.
27. ibid., 16 July 1859; Franz Joseph to Empress Elizabeth, 23, 26 June 1859 (*Briefe Kaiser Franz Josephs an Kaiserin Elisabeth*, I. 25–26).
28. 'Service Confidentiel. Pour l'Impératrice. Bulletin politique hebdomadaire' (A.A., Montijo, c 48–10, Week of 19–26 June 1859, p. 1).
29. ibid., Week of 22–29 May 1859, p. 1.
30. ibid., Week of 19–26 June 1859, p. 4.
31. ibid., Week of 15–22 May 1859, p. 3; Week of 22–29 May 1859, pp. 2–3; Week of 12–19 June 1859, pp. 1, 4; Week of 19–26 June, pp. 3–4; Week of 26 June–3 July 1859, p. 6; Week of 3–10 July 1859, pp. 4–5. See also

Mérimée to Panizzi, 30 June 1859 (*C.G.*, IX. 148–9); Viel Castel, V. 63–64.

32. Senior's Journal, 27 Apr. 1859 (RA K43, pp. 27–28).
33. *The Times*, 8, 9, 11, 12 July 1859.
34. Napoleon III's proclamation, 25 June 1859 (*Œuvres*, V. 86–87).
35. For British neutrality, see Malmesbury to the British Ambassadors to all the German states, 2 May 1859 (Malmesbury, II. 205–6).
36. *The Times*, 23 June 1859.
37. ibid., 4 July 1859.
38. Ollivier, *Journal*, II. 270; Ollivier, 'Napoléon III, Général en Chef' (*R.D.M.*, IV(cliii). 350–1); Paléologue, p. 76. Both Ollivier and Paléologue were told about this by Eugénie.
39. Mérimée to Panizzi, 15 July 1859 (*C.G.*, IX. 168); *The Times*, 16 July 1859.
40. Metternich to Rechberg, 5 Sept. 1859 (*Il problemo veneto e l'Europa*, I. 30).
41. For the Villafranca meeting, see *The Times*, 19, 21 July 1859.
42. ibid., 20 July 1859.

Chapter 35 – 1860

1. *The Times*, 15, 16, 17, 18, 26 Aug.; 22 Sept. 1859; *Moniteur*, 14, 17, 18 Aug. 1859; and see Louis Blanc's letter in *The Times*, 24 Aug. 1859.
2. *The Times*, 16, 18, 20, 21 July 1859; Mérimée to Panizzi, 12 July 1859; Mérimée to Ellice, 18 July 1859; Mérimée to Countess Montijo, 24 July 1859 (*C.G.*, IX. 161, 174, 184–5).
3. Napoleon III's speech of 19 July 1859 (*Œuvres*, V. 89–92).
4. Mérimée to Panizzi, 19 July 1859; Mérimée to Jenny Dacquin, 19 July 1859; Mérimée to Ellice, 23 July 1859; Mérimée to Countess Montijo, 24 July 1859; Mérimée to Pasquier, 27 July 1859; Mérimée to Ampère, 2 Aug. 1859 (*C.G.*, IX. 176, 178, 182, 185–6, 193, 204); Viel Castel V. 88.
5. Eugénie to Arese, 26 Aug. 1859 (Bonfadini, pp. 185–6).
6. Metternich to Rechberg, 5 Sept. 1859 (*Prob. Ven.*, I. 30).
7. *The Times*, 23, 26, 28, 29, 30, 31 Dec. 1859; 5, 6, Jan. 1860.
8. *Le Pape et le Congrès*, pp. 6–7, 10–13, 21–23, 36–37.
9. Odo Russell to Russell, 1 Jan. 1860 (Blakiston, *The Roman Question*, p. 74); *The Times*, 30, 31 Dec. 1859; 2, 12, 16 Jan. 1860.
10. ibid., 12 Jan. 1860.
11. RA, Queen Victoria's Journal, 5 Jan. 1860.
12. Eugénie to Paca, 14 Jan. 1860 (*L.F.*, I. 166–7).
13. *The Times*, 26, 29, 30 Dec. 1859.
14. Napoleon III to Pius IX, 31 Dec. 1859 (*Œuvres*, V. 100–3).
15. *The Times*, 30 Jan. 1860; Napoleon III's decree, 29 Jan. 1860 (*The Times*, 31 Jan. 1860).
16. *The Times*, 21 Jan.; 7, 17, 24 Feb. 1860. For the anger of the French Catholics, see Mérimée to Panizzi, 10 Jan. 1860; Mérimée to Countess

Montijo, 24 Mar. 1860 (*C.G.*, IX. 361, 427); Viel Castel, V. 155, 220, 234, 245–52, 258, 260–5; VI. 278.

17. *The Times*, 25 Feb. 1860.
18. *Œuvres*, V. 115–16.
19. *The Times*, 22 Feb.; 2, 3 Apr. 1860; Papal Bull of 29 Mar. 1860 (*The Times*, 6 Apr. 1860).
20. *The Times*, 5 Apr. 1860.
21. See Malmesbury, II. 204–5, for his talk with Napoleon III on 6 Apr. 1861, and II. 240 for his talk with Persigny on 1 Dec. 1860; and see Senior's Journal, 11 May 1860 (RA K44, pp. 102–5); Napoleon III to Persigny, 25 July 1860 (*The Times*, 1 Aug. 1860).
22. *The Times*, 10 Mar. 1860. For the tensions between Palmerston and Persigny, and between Britain and France, see Malmesbury, II. 215–16, 218–26.
23. See Nigra to Cavour, 12 Aug. 1860 (*Cavour-Nigra*, IV. 152).
24. Senior's Journal, 1 June 1860 (RA K45), where 'A.B.' is Drouyn de Lhuys; see Senior to Prince Albert, 12 Oct. 1860 (in RA K46, frontispiece).
25. *The Times*, 21 May 1860.
26. ibid., 8, 18 May 1860.
27. Senior's Journal, 24 May 1860 (RA K45, p. 216).
28. *The Times*, 14 May 1860; Nigra to Cavour, 10, 14, 20 May 1860 (*Cavour-Nigra*, III. 293, 296, 306).
29. Nigra to Cavour, 14 May 1860 (*Cavour-Nigra*, III. 296).
30. Nigra to Cavour, 22 May 1860 (ibid., III. 310).
31. Senior's Journal, 28 Mar. 1861 (RA K48).
32. Nigra to Cavour, 18 Aug. 1860 (*Cavour-Nigra*, IV. 166).
33. Eugénie to Paca, 25 Aug. 1860 (*L.F.*, I. 175–7); Paléologue, pp. 29–31; Mérimée to Mme de Boigne, 9 Sept. 1860 (*C.G.*, X. 7); *The Times*, 24, 29, 30, 31 Aug.; 1, 3, 4, 6, 7, 8 Sept. 1860.
34. Cavour to Nigra, 29 Aug. 1860 (*Cavour-Nigra*, IV. 186–7).
35. ibid.
36. Cavour to Nigra, 2 Sept. 1860 (ibid., IV. 190).
37. *The Times*, 10, 11, 12, 13, 14, 17, 18, 19, 21, 24, 25 Sept. 1860.
38. ibid., 17, 20, 21 Sept. 1860.
39. Eugénie to Paca, 23, 25, 30 Aug.; 4, 6, 9 Sept. 1860 (*L.F.*, I. 175–84); *The Times*, 18, 20, 21 Sept. 1860.
40. *The Times*, 19 Sept. 1860.
41. Eugénie to Countess Montijo, 17 Sept. 1860; Eugénie to Alba, 17 Sept. 1860 (*L.F.*, I. 185).
42. *The Times*, 24, 27 Sept. 1860; Fleury, II. 186.
43. Napoleon III to Alba, 19 Sept. 1860 (*L.F.*, I. 262).
44. Fleury, II. 184–7.
45. Cavour to Nigra, 12 Sept. 1860 (*Cavour-Nigra*, IV. 202–4).
46. Nigra to Cavour, 26 Sept. 1860 (ibid., IV. 230–1, 233–4).
47. *The Times*, 4, 8, 13, 19, 22 Oct.; 24, 26 Nov. 1860.
48. ibid., 3 Oct. 1860.

49. ibid., 1 Nov. 1860.

50. ibid., 8 Oct. 1860.

51. *Moniteur*, 13 Nov. 1860; Mérimée to Countess Montijo, 14 Nov. 1860; Mérimée to Jenny Dacquin, 17 Nov. 1860 (*C.G.*, X. 70, 73–74); *The Times*, 14, 15 Nov. 1860; Leopold I to Queen Victoria, 22 Nov., 14 Dec. 1860; Queen Victoria to Leopold I, 4 Dec. 1860; Eugénie to Queen Victoria, 15 Nov. 1860; Princess Victoria to Queen Victoria, 20 Nov. 1860; Senior's Journal, 13 Aug. 1861 (RA Y82/91; Y105/41; J31/76; Z10/15; K50); Eugénie to Alba, 21 Oct., 13 Nov. 1860 (*L.F.*, I. 194–5, 202); RA, Queen Victoria's Journal, 16, 21 Nov. 1860.

52. For Eugénie's visit to England and Scotland, see *The Times*, 16, 17, 19, 20, 21, 22, 23, 24, 28, 29 Nov.; 1, 3, 4, 5, 13, 14, 15 Dec. 1860; Queen Victoria to Leopold I, 4, 11 Dec. 1860 (RA Y105/41, 42); RA, Queen Victoria's Journal, 28 Nov., 4 Dec. 1860; Malmesbury, II. 239.

53. Eugénie to Alba (end of Nov. 1860) (*L.F.*, I. 203); RA, Queen Victoria's Journal, 4 Dec. 1860.

54. *The Times*, 6 Dec. 1860.

55. 'Riflemen, Form!' (published as 'The War' by 'T.' in *The Times*, 9 May 1859; *Works of Alfred Lord Tennyson*, p. 892).

56. 'Chobham Camp' (Kingsley Martin, *The Triumph of Lord Palmerston*, p. 104n.).

57. *The Times*, 7, 9, 10 Nov. 1860.

58. For the Syrian crisis, see *The Times*, 18, 19, 20, 23, 24, 26, 27, 28, 31 July; 2, 6, 7, 8, 9, 10, 28, 30 Aug.; 15 Nov.; 10 Dec. 1860; 12 Jan; 16, 20 May; 3 June 1861; W.H.B.'s letter (*The Times*, 15 July 1861); Napoleon III to Persigny, 25 July 1860 (*The Times*, 1 Aug. 1860); *Hansard*, 3, 24 Aug. 1860; (H.L.), 3 Aug. 1860.

59. *Hansard*, 24 Aug. 1860; Palmerston to Russell, 19, 20 (two letters), 22, 26, 27, 30 July 1860 (PRO 30/22/21, ff. 177–8, 191–8).

60. Napoleon III's speech, 7 Aug. 1860 (*Œuvres*, V. 122); *The Times*, 25 Aug., 7 Sept. 1860.

61. Viel Castel, IV. 18–19, 265.

62. Palmerston to Herbert, 5 Oct. 1860 (Stanmore, *Sidney Herbert*, II. 299).

63. Russell to Elgin, 10 May 1860 (RA J79/27).

64. Montauban to Vaillant, 8 Oct. 1860 (*The Times*, 22 Dec. 1860).

65. *The Times*, 31 Dec. 1860.

66. For the looting and destruction of the Summer Palace, see *The Times*, 11, 15, 17, 22, 25, 28, 29, 31 Dec. 1860; 14 Jan. 1861; Elgin to Russell, 25 Oct. 1860 (*Correspondence respecting affairs in China 1859–60*, pp. 213–15).

67. Mérimée to Ellice, 12 Dec. 1860; Mérimée to Gobineau, 13 Dec. 1860; Mérimée to Countess Montijo, 18 Dec. 1860 (*C.G.*, X. 127, 133, 144).

68. Victor Hugo to Capt. Butler, 25 Nov. 1860 (Hugo, *Œuvres Complètes*, III. 200–1).

69. Napoleon III's speech of 4 Feb. 1861 (*Œuvres*, V. 136).

70. For French operations in Indo-China, see *The Times*, 30 Dec. 1856; 14, 28 Oct.; 17 Nov., 9 Dec. 1858; 28 Mar., 8 July, 17 Oct., 28 Dec. 1861; 6, 20, 22 Feb.; 4 Apr.; 14 May; 17, 24, 28 July 1862; 6, 9 Feb.; 20, 27

Mar.; 13 Apr., 12 May, 1 June 1863; 13 Jan., 18 May, 12 Aug., 7 Sept. 1864; 9 Aug., 8 Nov. 1865; 11 Jan., 30 July, 13 Sept. 1866; 14 Jan.; 1 Aug. 1867; 11 Aug. 1868.

71. Beaumont-Vassy, p. 307.

72. For French operations in Senegal, see *The Times*, 18 Apr. 1862; 22 Sept. 1863; 27 Dec. 1865; 17 Sept. 1866; 21 Oct. 1869.

73. For Eugénie's interest in the penal colony in New Caledonia, see Baroche's memorandum, 30 Apr. 1867 (A.A., Montijo, c40-42).

Chapter 36 – Re-drawing the Map of Europe

1. *The Times*, 26 Nov. 1860, 24 Jan. 1861.

2. ibid., 20 June 1864.

3. See ibid., 31 Jan.; 22 Feb.; 30 Nov.; 19, 23, 26, 31 Dec. 1861; 21 Jan. 1862; 10 Feb. 1863; 17, 18, 25 Mar.; 25 Apr.; 9, 17 June; 18, 28 July; 6, 8, 9 Aug. 1864; 8 Feb., 14 Mar.; 24, 30 June 1865; 21 Jan. 1867.

4. ibid., 16, 21, 28 May; 31 July 1861; 26 Jan. 1863.

5. Quinet, 'La Campagne de 1815' (*R.D.M.*, II(xxxiv). 834-69; (xxxv). 5-61, 521-65); *The Times*, 21, 24 Oct. 1861.

6. *The Times*, 21, 28 May 1861.

7. Senior's Journal, 4, 6 Apr.; 19 Aug. 1861 (RA K48, pp. 145-7, 169-70; K50); and see *The Times*, 2 Dec. 1862.

8. Senior's Journal, 19 Aug. 1861 (RA K50).

9. For the strikes, see *The Times*, 13, 18 Oct.; 24 Nov.; 8, 22 Dec. 1864; 19, 25 May; 12, 16, 19, 20, 21, 23, 24, 26, 28, 29 June; 11, 27 July; 12 Sept.; 3 Oct.; 7, 21 Nov.; 11, 16, 26 Dec. 1865; 23, 25 Mar.; 4, 22, 23, 24, 25 Apr.; 1 May 1867; 12, 18, 19, 22, 29 Oct. 1869; 20, 21, 22, 24, 25, 27, 29 Jan.; 1 Feb.; 23, 24, 26 Mar.; 2, 4, 5, 9, 11, 13, 20, 22, 23, 27, 28 Apr. 1870; and see Napoleon III to Ducoux, 3 Dec. 1865 (*The Times*, 11 Dec. 1865).

10. *The Times*, 5 Oct. 1864.

11. Filon, p. 81.

12. Ollivier's Journal, 18 May 1864; 7 May, 27 June 1865; 11, 30 Jan. 1867; 5 Feb. 1868; Ollivier to Princess Wittgenstein, 10 Sept. 1865 (*Journal*, II. 125, 191-4, 198).

13. Napoleon III to Prince Napoleon, 2, 7 Mar. 1861 (*Napoléon III et le Prince Napoléon*, pp. 212-13); *The Times*, 2, 4, 12 Mar. 1861.

14. ibid., 24, 26 Feb. 1862.

15. Mérimée to Fanny Lagden, 15 Nov. 1863; Mérimée to Mme de Boigne, 17. Nov. 1863; Mérimée to Panizzi, 18 Nov. 1863; Mérimée to Countess Montijo, 18 Nov. 1863 (*C.G.*, XI. 513-14, 519-20, 522-3, 525); Viel Castel, VI. 283; and see *The Times*, 23 Nov. 1864.

16. Filon, pp. 76-79; Viel Castel, V. 26. See also *The Times*, 24 Jan. 1867.

17. Legge's Preface to Princess Metternich, *The days that are no more*, p. 40.

18. Mérimée to Jenny Dacquin, 13 June 1861 (*C.G.*, X. 305).

19. Caroline Murat, pp. 148, 248; Viel Castel, VI. 81; *The Times*, 16 May

1862; 9 Dec. 1864; 30 Nov. 1865; and see Mérimée to Countess Montijo, 29 June 1861 (*C.G.*, X. 311).

20. Filon, p. 36.

21. La Marmora to Arese, 14 Oct. 1862 (Bonfadini, p. 300).

22. Napoleon III to Arese, 2 Jan. 1863 (Bonfadini, p. 304).

23. Metternich to Rechberg, 9 July 1860, 30 June 1861, 1 Sept. 1862 (*Prob. Ven.*, I. 179, 393, 516).

24. Duke of Saxe-Coburg-Gotha to Prince Consort, 30 Nov. 1859; Anonymous memorandum, 30 Apr. 1862; Queen Victoria to Leopold I, 4 Dec. 1860; Senior's Journal, 21 May, 7 Sept. 1860; 13 Aug. 1861 (RA J79/9, 109; Y105/41; K45, p. 12; K46, pp. 191–2; K50); A. Bixio to Cavour, 24 Oct. 1860 (*Cavour-Nigra*, IV. 264); Caroline Murat, p. 219; *The Times*, 22 Sept. 1866.

25. Russell to Cowley, 13 Nov. 1862 (RA J36/51).

26. Viel Castel, V. 255; VI. 7; *The Times*, 9, 11 Apr. 1862.

27. Metternich to Rechberg, 27 Sept. 1859, 1 Sept. 1862, 5 Mar. 1863; Metternich to Mensdorff, 22 Mar. 1866 (*Prob. Ven.*, I. 39, 515–16, 531–2, 723–5).

28. Viel Castel, VI. 56–57, 185–6, 191.

29. Metternich to Rechberg, 17 June 1861 (*Prob. Ven.*, I. 380–1); Cowley to Russell, 21 Feb. 1862 (RA J79/79); L. Thouvenel, *Le secret de l'Empereur*, II. 302–95.

30. Malmesbury, II. 283.

31. Conneau to Arese, 7 Mar. 1863 (Bonfadini, p. 308).

32. For official French reaction to Garibaldi's Aspromonte campaign, see *Le Constitutionnel*, 23 Aug. 1862; *Moniteur*, 25, 28, 31 Aug. 1862; *The Times*, 23, 26 Aug.; 1 Sept. 1862.

33. Odo Russell to Russell, 26 July 1862 (Blakiston, p. 235).

34. Thouvenel to Gramont, 6 Sept. 1862 (L. Thouvenel, *Le secret de l'Empereur*, II. 384); Metternich to Rechberg, 24 Aug. 1862 (*Prob. Ven.*, I. 509).

35. Metternich to Rechberg, 1 Sept. 1862 (*Prob. Ven.*, I. 514).

36. Napoleon III to Thouvenel, 15 Oct. 1862; Thouvenel to Mercier, 1 Dec. 1862 (L. Thouvenel, *Le secret de l'Empereur*, II. 438–9, 448).

37. For the text of the Convention of 15 Sept. 1864, see L. Thouvenel, *Le secret de l'Empereur*, II. 457–9.

38. *The Times*, 14, 16 June 1860; RA, Queen Victoria's Journal, 13 June 1860.

39. *The Times*, 19, 20, 21 June 1860; Cowley to Russell, two letters of 20 June 1860 enclosing Pourtalès's report; Princess Victoria to Queen Victoria, 22 June 1860 (RA J79/33, 34, 35; Z9/72); RA, Queen Victoria's Journal, 21, 25, 26 June 1860; see also Malmesbury, II. 229.

40. *The Times*, 10 Oct. 1861.

41. William I to Prince Consort, 6 Nov. 1861 (RA J79/72).

42. *The Times*, 5 Nov. 1862.

43. See the controversy between Dupanloup and Quinet (*The Times*, 20 Mar. 1863); Viel Castel, VI. 132, 220; Paléologue, pp. 222–3; Metter-

nich to Rechberg, 29 Mar. 1863 (*Prob. Ven.*, I. 546); Senior's Journal, 21 Apr. 1863 (RA K54, p. 129); *The Times*, 19, 20, 23 Mar.; 20, 23, 24, 25 July 1863.
44. *The Times*, 23 Feb. 1863.
45. Metternich to Rechberg, 22 Feb. 1863 (*Prob. Ven.*, I. 524–8).
46. ibid., p. 525.
47. Rechberg to Metternich, 27 Feb. 1863 (*Prob. Ven.*, I. 528–30).
48. Napoleon III's letter to European sovereigns, 4 Nov. 1863 (*Œuvres*, V. 290–2); Sir George Grey to General Grey, 11 Nov. 1863; Queen Victoria to Napoleon III, 11 Nov. 1863; Franz Joseph to Napoleon III, 17 Nov. 1863 (RA J80/31, 33, 49); Rechberg to Metternich, 17 Nov. 1863 (*Prob. Ven.*, I. 581); *The Times*, 7, 17, 18, 23, 28 Nov. 1863; Steefel, *The Schleswig-Holstein Question*, pp. 114–15, 122, 210–14.
49. *The Times*, 28, 30 Nov. 1863; Metternich to Rechberg, 27 Nov. 1863 (*Prob. Ven.*, I. 595–6); Goltz to Bismarck, 24 Nov. 1863 (Steefel, p. 118).
50. Cowley to Russell, 23 Feb. 1864 (PRO/FO 519/231); Steefel, pp. 185–97.

Chapter 37 – Problems of a Biographer

1. Eugénie to Countess Montijo, 2 Dec. 1861 (*L.F.*, I. 214); Mérimée to Mme de La Rochejaquelin, 21 June 1860; Mérimée to Mme Lenormant, 18 July 1860; Mérimée to Jenny Dacquin, 24 Oct. 1860, 24 June 1861; Mérimée to Panizzi, 8 Apr.; 11, 24 June 1861; Mérimée to Countess Montijo, 29 June 1861, 3 Jan. 1865; Mérimée to A. E. B. Tylor, 2 July 1861 (*C.G.*, IX. 508, 527; X. 46, 268, 302, 309–10, 312–13, 320; XII. 318); Viel Castel, VI. 171, 244, 246, 248; Senior's Journal, 7 Apr. 1861, 15 Mar. 1862 (RA K48, pp. 186–8; K51, p. 120); Malmesbury, II. 279, 281–2 (talk with Napoleon III on 27 Oct. 1862); *The Times*, 14, 25 July 1862.
2. Senior's Journal, 13, 14, 15 May 1860; 7 Apr. 1861; 3 Apr. 1863 (RA K44, pp. 109–14, 124–5; K48, p. 188; K51, p. 35).
3. ibid., 7 Apr. 1861, 7 Apr. 1862 (RA K48, p. 191; K51, pp. 372–3).
4. ibid., 7 Apr. 1861 (RA K48, pp. 190–1).
5. ibid., 15 Mar., 7 Apr. 1862; 3, 20 Apr. 1863 (RA K51, pp. 122, 368; K54, pp. 28–30, 32, 118–19).
6. ibid., 3 Apr. 1863 (RA K54, pp. 30–31).
7. *Histoire de Jules César*, II. 515.
8. *The Times*, 2 Mar. 1865; Senior's Journal, 15 Mar. 1862 (RA K51, p. 120).
9. Rogeard, *Les Propos de Labienus*, pp. 3–19.
10. *The Times*, 12 Apr. 1858, 24 Aug. 1861.
11. Rogeard, *Les Propos de Labienus: histoire d'une brochure*, pp. vi–xxiii, xxv–xxviii, 74–78; *The Times*, 27, 28 Mar.; 20 Sept. 1865.
12. *The Times*, 6 Mar., 21 July 1862.
13. ibid., 25 Dec. 1865; Viel Castel, III. 36; IV. 95; V. 125.
14. Viel Castel, III. 57–59; *The Times*, 6 Oct. 1853.
15. *The Times*, 26 Feb. 1855.

16. ibid., 25 May 1857; Viel Castel, IV. 69, 73–76.
17. *The Times*, 12, 30 Apr.; 3, 4 June 1864; Napoleon III to Bishop Parisis, 14 Nov. 1863 (*The Times*, 23 Nov. 1863); Viel Castel, VI. 162.
18. Mérimée to Panizzi, 31 July 1862 (*C.G.*, XI. 161–2).
19. Mérimée to Fanny Lagden, 6 Sept. 1863 (*C.G.*, XI. 459).
20. Mérimée to Fanny Lagden, 29 Sept. 1862 (*C.G.*, XI. 193–5).
21. Ollivier, *Journal*, II. 22 (from Berlioz).
22. Eugénie to Countess Montijo (1863) (*L.F*, I. 217).
23. Mérimée to Mme de Boigne, 21 Dec. 1864; Mérimée to Countess Montijo, 21 Dec. 1864 (*C.G.*, XII. 302, 306).
24. *The Times*, 5, 9, 12, 19, 20, 21, 23, 24, 26, 28, 30 Oct. 1863.
25. ibid., 19 Oct. 1863; Mérimée to Panizzi, 1 Oct. 1863; Mérimée to Fanny Lagden, 2 Oct. 1863 (*C.G.*, XI. 479–82).
26. Mérimée to Mme de Boigne, 18 Sept. 1864 (*C.G.*, XII. 228–9); Leopold I to Queen Victoria, 13 Sept. 1864; Crampton to Russell, 17 Oct. 1863 (RA Y86/64; J79/128); Cowley to Russell, 6 Dec. 1864 (PRO/FO 519/231); *The Times*, 9, 14, 15, 17, 21 Sept.; 5 Oct. 1864.
27. For Marguerite Bellanger, see Bac, pp. 308–13; Mérimée to Panizzi, 2, 11 Oct. 1864 (*C.G.*, XII. 247, 252); *Papiers secrets du Second Empire*, I. 12–13; Ollivier, *Journal*, II. 195 (10 May 1865); Michel Chevalier's diary, 28 Apr. 1867 (*R.D.M.*, VIII(xii). 180); Fleischmann, *Napoléon III et les femmes*, pp. 257–90; Joanna Richardson, *The Courtisans*, pp. 126–31.
28. Viel Castel, VI. 132–3, 173–4.
29. *The Times*, 25, 27 Oct. 1865; 18 July 1866; 8 Feb. 1867; Mérimée to Panizzi, 5 July 1866 (*C.G.*, XIII. 155–6).
30. Baroche's memorandum, 30 Apr. 1867 (A.A., Montijo, c 40–42); *The Times*, 8 Aug. 1865; see also *The Times*, 11 July 1872; Filon, pp. 249–50.
31. For Napoleon III's visit to Algeria, see *The Times*, 1, 2, 3, 5, 6, 10, 11, 15, 16, 18, 19, 22, 23, 24, 25, 29, 30, 31 May; 2, 7, 8, 9 June 1865; Mérimée to Panizzi, 23 June 1865 (*C.G.*, XII. 462).
32. *The Times*, 18 May 1865.
33. ibid., 18, 20, 22, 23 May 1865.
34. ibid., 27 May 1865.
35. ibid., 23, 24, 27, 29, 30 May; 2, 16 June 1865; 'Service Confidentiel. Pour l'Impératrice. Bulletin politique hebdomadaire' (A.A., Montijo, c 48–10, Report of 19 May 1865, p. 2; Report of 1 June 1865, pp. 1–2).
36. Napoleon III to Prince Napoleon, 23 May 1865 (*Œuvres*, V. 244–5).
37. *The Times*, 31 May 1865.
38. Prince Napoleon to Napoleon III, 27 May 1865 (*The Times*, 29 May 1865).
39. *The Times*, 12, 14, 16, 17, 21 June 1865.
40. Bac, p. 275.
41. *The Times*, 14, 16, 19, 23, 24, 25, 26, 28, 31 Aug.; 2, 7 Sept. 1865; *Moniteur*, 26 Aug. 1865.
42. Mérimée to Fanny Lagden, 9 Oct. 1865 (*C.G.*, XII. 553–4).
43. Mérimée to Panizzi, 13 Oct. 1865 (*C.G.*, XII. 555–6).
44. Mensdorff to Metternich, 11 Aug. 1865 (*Prob. Ven.*, I. 684–6).

Chapter 38 – Mexico and the American Civil War

1. Sir Edward Blount, *Memoirs*, pp. 150–3; *Papiers secrets du Second Empire*, I. 33–36; Senior's Journal, 5 Apr. 1862, 29 Mar. 1863; Cowley to Russell, 10 Mar. 1862 (RA K51, p. 343; K54, p. 3; J101/54); Malmesbury, II. 274; Beaumont-Vassy, pp. 310–15; *The Times*, 7 Feb., 12 Mar., 10 Sept. 1863; 23 May 1865; and see W. H. C. Smith, *Napoleon III*, pp. 164–81.
2. Speech of 19 Sept. 1860 (*Œuvres*, V. 126).
3. *The Times*, 4 Feb. 1862; 28 Jan., 27 Sept. 1864.
4. Cowley to Russell, 6 Mar. 1862 (RA J101/53).
5. Corti, *Maximilian and Charlotte of Mexico*, pp. 74, 77–80 (from Hidalgo's 'Notes Secrètes').
6. Senior's Journal, 14 Mar. 1862 (RA K51, pp. 114–18) (talk with Guttierez).
7. ibid., 30 Apr. 1863 (RA K54, p. 194); *The Times*, 1, 3 Oct. 1861; 1 Apr., 13 May 1862; 18 Dec. 1863.
8. See Antonia d'Attainville to Isabel Vesey, 6 Jan. 1940 (Burnett MSS.).
9. Viel Castel, III. 80–81; *The Times*, 30 Oct.; 3, 6, 8 Nov. 1854.
10. *The Times*, 16 Aug. 1853; 3 Nov. 1854; Viel Castel, III. 250–1; Eugénie to Countess Montijo, 8 Oct. 1868 (*L.F.*, I. 222).
11. Viel Castel, II. 243 (from Princess Mathilde).
12. *The Times*, 18, 23 Jan.; 6 Mar.; 16 Sept.; 18 Nov.; 11, 12 Dec. 1862.
13. ibid., 17, 23 Dec. 1861; 1 Jan., 18 Nov. 1862.
14. Senior's Journal, 21 Apr. 1863 (RA K54, p. 131); *The Times*, 13, 17 May 1862; 25 Feb. 1863; see also Leopold I to Queen Victoria, 6 Dec. 1861 (RA Y83/40).
15. *The Times*, 30 Nov.; 5, 7, 9, 10, 12, 14, 16, 21, 30 Dec. 1861; 11, 13, 14 Jan. 1862.
16. Thouvenel to Mercier, 3 Dec. 1861 (L. Thouvenel, *Le secret de l'Empereur*, II. 197–203); Seward to Mercier, 27 Dec. 1861 (*The Times*, 13 Jan. 1862).
17. Slidell to Benjamin, 25 July 1862; 18 June 1863 (Bigelow, I. 514–20; II. 12–14); *The Times*, 9 Aug., 14 Nov. 1862; 15 Sept. 1863.
18. Napoleon III to Prim, 24 Jan. 1862 (*The Times*, 30 Apr. 1862).
19. Cowley to Russell, 17 Jan. 1862; Senior's Journal, 12 Mar. 1862 (RA J101/16; K51, pp. 115–16); *The Times*, 18 Feb. 1862.
20. Corti, pp. 99–102.
21. Maximilian's report to Franz Joseph (May 1856) (in Corti, p. 52).
22. Palmerston to Queen Victoria, 2 Sept. 1861 (RA J79/70).
23. Bloomfield to Russell, 30 Jan., 8 Feb. 1862; Cowley to Russell, 4, 11 Feb.; 6 Mar. 1862; Senior's Journal, 14 Mar. 1862 (from Drouyn de Lhuys) (RA J101/29, 33, 35, 37, 53; K51, p. 113); Gramont to Thouvenel, 26 Jan. 1862 (L. Thouvenel, *Le secret de l'Empereur*, II. 233); Mensdorff to Metternich, 19 Nov. 1864 (*Prob. Ven.*, I. 657–8); *The Times*, 15 Feb. 1862.

24. Napoleon III to Flahault, Oct. 1861 (Corti, pp. 361–2).
25. Prince Consort to Leopold I, 5 Nov. 1861 (RA J101/1).
26. *The Times*, 18 Nov. 1861.
27. ibid., 14 Mar. 1862; Cowley to Russell, 17 Jan.; 4, 5, 11 Feb. 1862; Russell to Crampton, 2 Feb. 1862 (RA J101/17, 31, 33, 34, 37).
28. *The Times*, 31 Oct. 1861; 4, 27 Jan.; 1, 3, 5, 7, 25 Feb.; 4, 12 Mar. 1862.
29. ibid., 18 Feb., 7 Mar., 1 Apr. 1862.
30. Wyke to Russell, 20 Jan., 27 Mar. 1862; Cowley to Russell, 6, 14 Mar.; 30 Apr. 1862 (RA J101/22, 53, 58, 82, 97); *The Times*, 20, 28, 31 Mar.; 4 Apr.; 6 June 1862.
31. See Leopold I to Eugénie, 19 May 1865; Eugénie to Leopold I (May 1865) (A.A., Montijo, c 33–27).
32. Napoleon III to Maximilian, 14 Jan. 1862 (Corti, p. 365).
33. Archduchess Charlotte to Eugénie, 22 Jan. 1862 (Corti, p. 366).
34. Wyke to Russell, 22 Feb. 1862 (RA J101/41).
35. Russell to Cowley, 18, 20 Jan.; draft of Aug. 1862; Cowley to Russell, 13 May 1862 (RA J101/18, 23, 89, 105).
36. Prim to Napoleon III, 17 Mar. 1862 (*The Times*, 14 June 1862).
37. Paléologue, pp. 97–103.
38. Admiral Jurien's and Saligny's proclamation, 17 Apr. 1862 (*The Times*, 22 May 1862); Russell to Cowley, 13 May 1862 (RA J101/88); *The Times*, 23 May 1862.
39. *The Times*, 18 July 1862.
40. ibid., 9, 16, 17, 18 June 1862; Lorencez's report, 22 May 1862 (ibid., 3 July 1862).
41. ibid., 2, 16 June 1862.
42. Russell to Queen Victoria, 8 June 1862 (RA J101/103).
43. Eugénie to Archduchess Charlotte, 7 June 1862; Napoleon III to Maximilian, 7 June 1862 (Corti, p. 373).
44. *The Times*, 16 June, 11 July 1862.
45. Mérimée to Countess Montijo, 3 June, 9 July, 21 Dec. 1862; 4 June 1863; Mérimée to Panizzi, 2, 18 July; 11 Oct. 1862; 3 Jan., 21 Mar. 1863 (*C.G.*, XI. 115, 134, 139, 151, 200, 264, 285, 367, 393).
46. *The Times*, 7, 10 June; 17, 18, 19 July; 1 Aug.; 22 Sept.; 29 Nov. 1862; Senior's Journal, 29 Mar. 1863 (RA K54, p. 3).
47. *The Times*, 9, 17, 24 Sept.; 17 Dec. 1862; 5 Jan. 1863.
48. ibid., 30 Mar. 1863.
49. Corti, p. 204.
50. For the siege of Puebla, see *The Times*, 4, 11, 12, 14, 16, 30 May; 3, 9, 12, 13, 18 June; 21 July; 7 Aug. 1863.
51. Victor Hugo's message to the people of Puebla (Hugo, *Œuvres Complètes*, II. 253–5).
52. *The Times*, 16 May 1863.
53. Corti, p. 206.
54. Forey to Vaillant, 2 Apr. 1863 (*The Times*, 16 May 1863); *The Times*, 18 June 1863.
55. *The Times*, 15, 18, 25, 29 May; 8 June 1863.

56. Viel Castel, VI. 233.
57. Forey to Vaillant, 18 May 1863; Napoleon III to Forey, 12 June 1863 (*The Times*, 16 June 1863); *The Times*, 12 June 1863.
58. *The Times*, 6 Aug. 1863.
59. For the activities of the 'counter-guerrillas' and the summary executions of Juarists, see Kératry, *La Contre-Guérilla Française au Mexique* (first published in *R.D.M.*, II(lxi). 966–1011 (15 Feb. 1866)); *The Times*, 7, 29 Aug.; 30 Sept.; 26 Oct.; 11 Nov. 1863; 29 Sept. 1864; 18 Mar., 10 Apr., 23 May, 28 Nov., 2 Dec. 1865; 24 Jan., 25 Apr. 1866.
60. Mérimée to Panizzi, 21 Aug. 1863 (*C.G.*, XI. 448).
61. Thouvenel to Mercier, 24 July 1862 (L. Thouvenel, *Le secret de l'Empereur*, II. 348); Senior's Journal, 2 May 1863 (RA K54, p. 235).
62. Speech of 27 Jan. 1862 (*Œuvres*, V. 152); *The Times*, 5 Jan. 1863.
63. Cowley to Russell, 15 Apr. 1862; Napoleon III to Cowley, 20 Apr. 1862 (RA J79/104, 108).
64. Drouyn de Lhuys to Mercier, 30 Oct. 1862; 9 Jan. 1863 (*The Times*, 14 Nov. 1862; 29 Jan. 1863); *The Times*, 10, 14 Nov. 1862; 24 Jan., 26 Feb. 1863.
65. Russell to Cowley, 14 July 1863; Memorandum of correspondence shown by Drouyn de Lhuys to Cowley, 14 July 1863; Napoleon III to Drouyn de Lhuys, 14 July 1863 (RA J79/119, 121, 124); Roebuck to Slidell, 1 July 1863 (Bigelow, II. 29–30); *The Times*, 6 July 1863.
66. Bigelow to Seward, 6 Aug. 1864 (Bigelow, II. 204–5).
67. See *The Times*, 3 Oct. 1863.
68. Walsham to Russell, 27 Sept. 1863 (RA J101/126); Metternich to Rechberg, 12 Aug. 1863 (*Prob. Ven.*, I. 564); *The Times*, 2 Nov. 1863.
69. *The Times*, 5, 6 Oct. 1863; Bloomfield to Russell, 7 Aug. 1864 (RA J102/10).
70. Napoleon III to Maximilian, 19 Sept., 2 Oct. 1863 (Corti, pp. 384–5, 389).
71. Wyke to Russell, 19 Nov. 1863 (RA J101/130).
72. Eugénie to Metternich, 27 Mar. 1864; Napoleon III to Maximilian, 30 Jan., 28 Mar. 1864 (Corti, pp. 338–9, 395, 399).
73. *The Times*, 13 Oct. 1863.
74. ibid., 30 July 1864.
75. Empress Charlotte to Leopold I, 13 June 1864 (RA J102/20).
76. *The Times*, 29 Nov. 1864.
77. Eugénie to Empress Charlotte (Apr. or May 1864) (Corti, p. 834).
78. Malmesbury, II. 321.

Chapter 39 – Sadowa, Querétaro and the Exhibition

1. *The Times*, 12 Apr. 1865.
2. ibid., 22 Mar. 1865.
3. ibid., 28 Oct. 1865.
4. ibid., 12 Apr. 1865.

5. Napoleon III to Maximilian, 1 Mar. 1865 (Corti, p. 887); see also Napoleon III to Bazaine, 1 Mar. 1865 (Gaulot, *L'Expédition du Mexique*, II. 101).

6. *The Times*, 24, 27, 28, 29 Apr.; 1, 4, 25, 27 May; 9, 10, 20 June 1865; *Moniteur*, 27 Apr.; 8, 24 May 1865; Eugénie to Empress Charlotte, 30 Apr. 1865 (Corti, p. 906); Drouyn de Lhuys to Eugénie (Apr. 1865), 25 May 1865 (A.A., Montijo c 6–75, 80); Bigelow to Seward, 28 Apr., 6 June 1865 (Bigelow, II. 511–12; III. 61).

7. *The Times*, 10 Oct. 1867.

8. ibid.

9. ibid., 22, 23, 25 May; 16 June; 15 Aug.; 3, 27 Nov. 1865; 15, 18 Jan. 1866; President Johnson's Message to Congress, 4 Dec. 1865 (*The Times*, 18 Dec. 1865).

10. *Moniteur*, 24 May 1865; *The Times*, 11 Apr. 1863; 24, 25, 27 May; 10 June 1865.

11. *The Times*, 22 Aug. 1865; Grant to Sheridan, 17 May 1865 (Sheridan, *Personal Memoirs*, II. 208–9).

12. *The Times*, 15 Aug. 1865.

13. ibid., 16, 18, 19 Oct.; 28 Nov. 1865; 11 Sept. 1866.

14. ibid., 16 Oct. 1865.

15. ibid., 22 Jan., 6 Feb., 10 May 1866.

16. ibid., 2, 7, 11, 12, 15 Dec. 1865; 30, 31 Jan.; 3, 22, 26 Feb.; 5 Mar. 1866; Sheridan, II. 210–28.

17. Drouyn de Lhuys to Montholon, 17 Aug. 1865 (*The Times*, 1 Feb. 1866).

18. Maximilian's proclamation, 3 Oct. 1865 (*The Times*, 6 Nov. 1865).

19. Drouyn de Lhuys to Montholon, 25 Jan. 1866 (*The Times*, 2 Feb. 1866); Napoleon III to Bazaine, 17 Aug. 1865 (Gaulot, II. 170–1); Bazaine to Napoleon III, 19 Oct. 1865 (Ollivier, *L'Empire libéral*, VII. 530); Corti, pp. 537–9.

20. *The Times*, 13 Mar. 1865; 22 Aug. 1867.

21. Maximilian to Empress Charlotte, 29 June 1865 (*La Cour de Rome et l'Empereur Maximilien*, p. 40).

22. *The Times*, 26, 31 Oct.; 9 Dec. 1865; 25, 31 Jan. 1866; Cowley to Clarendon, 4, 6, 12, 19 Jan.; 13, 23, 28 Feb. 1866 (RA J102/29, 30, 34, 36, 37, 39, 40).

23. *The Times*, 10, 16 June; 27 Nov.; 15, 21 Dec. 1865; 8, 10, 13, 22 Feb. 1866; Drouyn de Lhuys to Eugénie, 25 May 1865 (A.A., Montijo c 6–80).

24. *The Times*, 27 Nov. 1865; and see also 8 Dec. 1865, 22 Feb. 1866.

25. Speech of 22 Jan. 1866 (*Œuvres*, V. 252).

26. *The Times*, 14 Feb. 1866.

27. ibid., 6 Apr. 1866.

28. ibid., 23 May, 2 June 1865; 17 Mar.; 7, 9, 10 May 1866.

29. Metternich to Mensdorff, 7 Apr.; 5, 9, 16, 23, 29 May 1866 (*Prob. Ven.*, I. 728, 758–61, 775, 782, 815, 828).

30. For Eugénie's policy, see Paléologue, pp. 108–19.

31. Metternich to Mensdorff, 5, 23 May 1866 (*Prob. Ven.*, I. 758, 815).

32. Metternich to Mensdorff, 22 Mar. 1866; Treaty of 12 June 1866 (*Prob. Ven.*, I. 723–4, 858–9); Napoleon III to Victor Emanuel II, 11 Aug. 1866 (*The Times*, 1 Sept. 1866); *The Times*, 4, 5 July 1866.
33. Act assigning Venetia to France, 19 Oct. 1866; Pillet to Moustier, 20 Oct. 1866 (*Prob. Ven.*, I. 956–7; III. 791–2).
34. Metternich to Mensdorff, 26 July 1866 (*Prob. Ven.*, I. 903).
35. Metternich to Mensdorff, 6 Aug. 1866 (ibid., I. 907).
36. *The Times*, 25 July 1870.
37. ibid., 11, 22 Aug. 1866.
38. For the Empress Charlotte's visit to Paris, see ibid., 9, 11, 13, 15, 21, 22, 23, 24 Aug. 1866; 20, 21 Sept.; 1 Oct. 1867; Mme Carette, pp. 280–4; Mérimée to Fanny Lagden, 8, 15 Aug. 1866; Mérimée to Panizzi, 12, 19, 28 Aug. 1866; Mérimée to Lisa Przezdziecka, 14 Aug. 1866; Mérimée to Countess Montijo, 16 Aug. 1866 (*C.G.*, XIII. 171–2, 176, 179–80, 183, 195); Kératry, *L'Empereur Maximilien*, pp. 158–9; Corti, pp. 666–89.
39. Napoleon III to Maximilian, 29 Aug. 1866 (Corti, p. 945).
40. Scarlett to Stanley, 8 Oct., 5 Nov. 1866; Fane to Stanley, 21 Dec. 1866 (RA J102/50, 53, 62).
41. Corti, pp. 686, 709–14.
42. Empress Charlotte to Maximilian, 22 Aug. 1866 (Corti, p. 685).
43. *The Times*, 8 Nov., 5 Dec. 1866.
44. Seward to Bigelow, 23 Nov. 1866 (*The Times*, 20 Dec. 1866).
45. Bigelow to Seward, 3 Dec. 1866 (Bigelow, III. 617); *The Times*, 6 Dec. 1866; 16 Feb. 1867.
46. *The Times*, 5, 23, 24 Jan.; 1, 2, 4, 5, 6, 21, 26 Feb.; 14, 15, 20, 22 Mar.; 26 Apr.; 6, 11, 20 May; 10 July 1867; *Moniteur*, 10 July 1867.
47. ibid., 3 July 1867.
48. ibid., 7, 21 Feb. 1867.
49. ibid., 16 Apr.; 24 June; 8, 27, 29 Aug.; 7 Sept. 1867.
50. ibid., 30 Mar., 3 Apr. 1867.
51. ibid., 17 Apr. 1867.
52. ibid., 3 Apr. 1867.
53. Wilfrid Scawen Blunt, 'Alms to Oblivion', Vol. II (F.M., Blunt Papers, MS. 41-1975, p. 186).
54. *The Times*, 22 Sept. 1862.
55. Wilfrid Scawen Blunt, op. cit. (F.M., Blunt Papers, MS. 41-1975, pp. 304, 306).
56. *The Times*, 25 Sept. 1867.
57. ibid., 30 May, 3 Aug. 1867; Princess Metternich, *Souvenirs*, pp. 73–76.
58. *The Times*, 3, 4 June 1867; *Moniteur*, 2 June 1867.
59. *The Times*, 5, 7, 8, 12 June 1867.
60. ibid., 7, 8 June 1867; 27 Jan., 8 Aug. 1868.
61. ibid., 7, 8, 10 June 1867; Cowley to Stanley, 7 June 1867 (RA J82/134).
62. *The Times*, 17, 20, 26 July 1867; Mérimée to Tripet, 16 July 1867 (*C.G.* XIII. 551).
63. *The Times*, 10, 12, 13, 15 June 1867.

64. ibid., 14, 18 June 1867.
65. ibid., 3 July 1867.
66. ibid.
67. ibid., 4 July 1867.
68. Middleton to Stanley, 23 June 1867 (RA J102/90); *The Times*, 4, 10, 19 July 1867.
69. *Boletin Republicano*, 21 June 1867 (enclosed in RA J102/90).
70. Bahneen to Marques, 27 May 1867; Stanley to Bruce, 29 May 1867; Sir G. Grey to Stanley, 30, 31 May 1867; Bloomfield to Stanley, 31 May 1867; Middleton to Stanley, 6 June 1867; Derby to Queen Victoria, 13 June 1867; Stanley to Queen Victoria, 14 June 1867 (RA J102/74, 75, 76, 77, 78, 79, 86, 87); *Moniteur*, 3, 5, 7 July 1867; *The Times*, 4, 5, 6 July 1867.
71. Victor Hugo to Juarez, 20 June 1867 (Hugo, *Œuvres Complètes*, II. 299–303); Garibaldi to Juarez, 5 June 1867 (Jessie White Mario, in *Garibaldi's Memoirs* (Werner ed.), III. 436); *The Times*, 25, 29 July 1867.
72. *The Times*, 22 July 1867.
73. Monnerville, *Clemenceau*, p. 54.
74. *The Times*, 7 Aug. 1867.
75. ibid., 26 Aug. 1867.
76. ibid.
77. ibid.
78. Beust, *Memoirs*, II. 33–37; *The Times*, 19, 20, 21, 22, 23, 24, 27 Aug. 1867.
79. Wilczek, *Happy Retrospect*, pp. 44–47.
80. Cavellotti, *Storia del Insurrezione di Roma nel 1867*, pp. 131–51; *The Times*, 2, 5, 19 Aug. 1867.
81. *The Times*, 12 Sept. 1867.
82. ibid., 17, 21, 22, 25, 26 Oct.; 2 Dec. 1867.
83. Mack Smith, *Victor Emanuel, Cavour, and the Risorgimento*, p. 345; *The Times*, 1 Nov. 1867.
84. *Moniteur*, 26, 27 Oct. 1867; *The Times*, 28 Oct. 1867.
85. Jessie White Mario, *The Birth of Modern Italy*, p. 322.
86. Lyons to Stanley, 11 Nov. 1867 (RA J83/24).
87. Guerzoni, *Garibaldi*, II. 543.
88. *The Times*, 6 Dec. 1867.
89. ibid., 14 Nov. 1867; see also Mérimée to Fanny Lagden, 6 Nov. 1867; Mérimée to Mme de Beaulaincourt, 8 Feb. 1868 (*C.G.*, XIII. 659; XIV. 27); *The Times*, 5 Dec. 1867.

Chapter 40 – Rochefort and Suez

1. *The Times*, 1, 16 Nov. 1867; Princess Metternich, *Souvenirs*, pp. 168–87.
2. *The Times*, 24, 26 Dec. 1867; 14, 25, 27 Mar.; 1, 9, 15 Apr. 1868; 17, 18 June; 11 Oct. 1869.
3. ibid., 16 June 1868.
4. *La Lanterne*, 31 May, 6 June, 8 Aug. 1868 (I. 20, 89–93; II. 34).

5. ibid., 4 July 1868 (I. 359); *The Times*, 18 June; 28 July; 8, 11, 13, 15, 18, 24, 25, 28, 29, 31 Aug. 1868.
6. Duruy to Frossard, 10 Aug. 1868 (*Papiers Secrets du Second Empire*, V. 61–62); Mérimée to Mme de Beaulaincourt, 20 Aug. 1868 (*C.G.*, XIV. 220); *La Lanterne*, 15 Aug. 1868 (II. 19–22); *The Times*, 14 Aug. 1868.
7. *Moniteur*, 1 Oct. 1868; *The Times*, 3, 5 Oct. 1868.
8. *The Times*, 7 Aug. 1861; 19 Oct., 3 Nov. 1863.
9. Eugénie to Isabel II (1868) (Llanos y Torriglia, p. 184); *La Lanterne*, 10 Oct. 1868 (p. 1); *The Times*, 29 Oct., 22 Dec. 1868; 4 Jan. 1869.
10. For Eugénie's opinion of Prim, see Eugénie to Countess Montijo, 24 June 1866 (*L.F.*, I. 219–20).
11. *The Times*, 28 Oct. 1868; 5 Jan.; 23 Aug. 1869.
12. ibid., 5 July 1866; 25 Apr. 1867; 26 Aug. 1868; 18 Feb. 1869; Mérimée to Panizzi, 16 Apr. 1867 (*C.G.*, XIII. 488).
13. *Le Charivari*, 8 Sept. 1866; *The Times*, 10 Sept. 1866.
14. *La paix par la guerre*, pp. 5–30; *The Times*, 28 May 1868; see also Mérimée to Clair, 6 Nov. 1868 (*C.G.*, XIV. 290).
15. *The Times*, 17, 18, 19, 20, 22, 23, 25 Feb.; 18, 19 Mar. 1869.
16. *Le Réveil*, 2 July 1868.
17. ibid., 27 Aug. 1868; *The Times*, 24 Aug., 18 Sept. 1868; 30 Jan. 1869.
18. *The Times*, 19, 28 Nov., 9 Dec. 1868; 4, 29, 30 Jan.; 4, 23 Feb. 1869; Mérimée to Countess Montijo, 11 May 1869 (*C.G.*, XIV. 488).
19. *The Times*, 3 May 1870.
20. For the meetings, see ibid., 28, 29 Jan.; 15 May; 17, 20 Nov. 1869; 30 Apr., 2, 3, 28 May 1870.
21. ibid., 18 Nov., 9 Dec. 1867; 9 Nov. 1868.
22. *Le Réveil*, 29 Oct. 1868.
23. *The Times*, 9, 12 Nov. 1868.
24. *Le Réveil*, 5 Nov. 1868; *The Times*, 11, 13, 14, 18 Nov.; 4, 5, 7 Dec. 1868.
25. *Le Réveil*, 17 Dec. 1868; *The Times*, 17 Nov., 17 Dec. 1868; see also *The Times*, 28, 30 Nov.; 2 Dec. 1868; 22 Jan. 1869.
26. Speeches of 3 Apr. 1858; 13 Aug. 1861; 7 Dec. 1862 (*Œuvres*, V. 61–63, 141–4, 172–5).
27. *The Times*, 13 Dec. 1853; 7 Apr. 1858; 15 Aug. 1861; 8, 9 Dec. 1862; Hübner, II. 133–4; Mérimée to Countess Montijo, 21 Dec. 1862 (*C.G.*, XI. 264).
28. *The Times*, 9 Dec. 1862.
29. ibid., 12 Dec. 1866.
30. Senior's Journal, 9 Apr. 1861 (RA K49, pp. 3–4).
31. *The Times*, 25 Apr. 1862; 16 Dec. 1865; 22, 24 Feb.; 21 Mar. 1866; Leopold II to Queen Victoria, 20 Mar. 1866 (RA Y159/13).
32. *The Times*, 25 Sept. 1863; 18 Nov. 1865; 12 June, 17 Oct. 1868.
33. *La Lanterne*, 6 June 1868 (I. 72–75); *The Times*, 12 June 1868.
34. *The Times*, 20 Sept. 1867; 29 May; 12, 18, 22 June; 22 July 1868; 24, 27 Feb.; 2, 3, 6 Mar. 1869; Ferry, *Comptes fantastiques d'Haussmann*, pp. 5–93.

35. *The Times*, 29 Mar., 26 Apr., 15 May 1869.
36. ibid., 15, 17, 18, 20, 22, 28 May 1869.
37. ibid., 8 June; 4, 8, 15, 16, 20, 23 Nov. 1869.
38. ibid., 9, 10, 12, 14, 16, 19, 22 June 1869; Mérimée to Jenny Dacquin, 12 June 1869 (*C.G.*, XIV. 514).
39. *Journal Officiel*, 12 June 1869; *The Times*, 12, 14, 15 June 1869; Filon, pp. 66–67.
40. Mérimée to Panizzi, 11 July, 7 Nov. 1869; Mérimée to Princess Mathilde, 26 Oct. 1869; Mérimée to Countess Montijo, 28 Oct., 24 Nov. 1869 (*C.G.*, XIV. 541, 642, 647, 655, 667); Lyons to Clarendon, 2 June 1869 (RA J83/81).
41. *The Times*, 16 June 1869.
42. *Journal Officiel*, 31 Aug. 1869; *The Times*, 19, 21, 25, 26, 27, 28, 30, 31 Aug.; 1, 2 Sept. 1869; Clarendon to Queen Victoria, 4 Sept. 1869 (RA B25/77).
43. *Journal Officiel*, 11 Sept. 1869; *Le Réveil*, 10 Sept. 1869; *The Times*, 7, 8, 9, 10, 11, 13, 14, 18 Sept.; 23 Oct.; 16, 20 Nov. 1869; 14 Apr. 1870; Metternich to Beust, 20 Sept. 1869 (Wellesley and Sencourt, pp. 350–3).
44. *The Times*, 9, 25, 27, 28 Sept.; 2, 4, 8, 9, 11, 12, 15, 16 Oct. 1869; Comtesse des Garets, *Auprès de l'Impératrice Eugénie*, pp. 51–80.
45. RA, Queen Victoria's Journal, 6 July 1876; Isabel Vesey to Mrs Vesey, 25–26 June 1910 (Burnett MSS.); Isabel Vesey's MS., pp. 85–86.
46. *The Times*, 15, 16, 18, 21, 23, 25 Oct.; 1, 15, 16, 17 Nov. 1869; Mme des Garets, pp. 81–139.
47. Alba, op. cit., CXX. 84–85.
48. *The Times*, 30 Nov. 1869.
49. ibid., 19, 20 Nov.; 7, 11 Dec. 1869; Mme des Garets, pp. 147–57.
50. *The Times*, 14, 19 Oct.; 13 Nov. 1869.
51. ibid., 1, 7, 14 Oct.; 25 Nov.; 11 Dec. 1869; Lyons to Gladstone, 18 Sept. 1869 (RA J83/92).
52. Eugénie to Napoleon III, 27 Oct. 1869 (Filon, p. 82; *Papiers secrets du Second Empire*, I. 9–10).
53. *The Times*, 9, 13, 18 Oct. 1869.
54. Sackville West to the Foreign Office, 26 Oct. 1869 (RA J83/95).
55. *The Times*, 15, 19, 20, 21, 25, 26, 27, 28 Oct. 1869; *Le Rappel*, 20 Oct. 1869; Victor Hugo to Jourdan, 12 Oct. 1869 (Hugo, *Œuvres Complètes*, II. 377–9).
56. Napoleon III's speech, 29 Nov. 1869 (*The Times*, 30 Nov. 1869); *The Times*, 30 Nov.; 1, 6 Dec. 1869; and see Clarendon to Queen Victoria, 10 Dec. 1869 (RA B25/103).
57. *The Times*, 4, 8 Nov.; 1, 13 Dec. 1869.
58. ibid., 13 Dec. 1869.
59. Legge, *The Empress Eugénie and her Son*, p. 145.
60. Napoleon III to Ollivier, 27 Dec. 1869 (*The Times*, 29 Dec. 1869); Napoleon III to Fourcade, 27 Dec. 1869 (*Journal Officiel*, 29 Dec. 1869; *The Times*, 30 Dec. 1869); *Journal Officiel*, 2/3 Jan. 1870; *The Times*, 3, 4, 8, 11 Jan. 1870; and see 18, 19 May 1870.

61. *The Times*, 7, 8 Jan. 1870; Lyons to Clarendon, 4 Jan. 1870 (RA J83/105); Filon, p. 83.
62. For Pierre Bonaparte, see Viel Castel, VI. 86; Mérimée to Panizzi, 16 Jan. 1870 (*C.G.*, XV. 11); *The Times*, 13, 21 Aug.; 22 Nov. 1849; 22 July 1851; 13, 26 Jan. 1870; Pierre Bonaparte to Napoleon III, 19, 25 Mar.; 25 Apr. 1867; Napoleon III to Pierre Bonaparte (Apr. 1867) (*Papiers secrets du Second Empire*, I. 27–30).
63. For the killing of Victor Noir, see *Le Constitutionnel*, 11 Jan. 1870; *The Times*, 12, 13 Jan. 1870; Eugénie de Grèce, *Pierre Napoléon Bonaparte*, pp. 314–26.
64. *The Times*, 13, 14, 15, 18 Jan. 1870.
65. *La Marseillaise*, 12 Jan. 1870.
66. ibid., 13 Jan. 1870; *The Times*, 13, 14, 15, 18, 19, 24 Jan.; 8, 9, 10, 11, 12 Feb. 1870; Filon, p. 74; Eugénie de Grèce, pp. 326–52.
67. For the trial, see *The Times*, 22, 23, 24, 25, 26, 28, 29, 31 Mar. 1870; Eugénie de Grèce, pp. 353–76.
68. *The Times*, 17 Jan.; 31 Mar.; 2, 5 Apr. 1870; Napoleon III to Pierre Bonaparte, 2 Apr. 1870; Pierre Bonaparte to Napoleon III, 2 Apr. 1870 (Eugénie de Grèce, pp. 378–9); Eugénie de Grèce, pp. 380–1, 391–2; Caroline Murat, pp. 275–7, 279.
69. *La Marseillaise*, 29 Mar. 1870.
70. *Le Constitutionnel*, 29 Mar. 1870; *Le Réveil*, 29 Mar. 1870; *The Times*, 29 Mar. 1870.
71. Mérimée to Panizzi, 16 Jan. 1870 (*C.G.*, XV. 12).
72. George Sand, 'Malgrétout' (*R.D.M.*, II(lxxxvi). 18–29) (1 Mar. 1870).
73. Mérimée to Countess Montijo, 19 Mar. 1870; Mérimée to Panizzi, 20 Mar. 1870; Mérimée to Mme de Beaulaincourt, 26 Mar. 1870 (*C.G.*, XV. 68–70, 77); George Sand to Eugénie, 6 Oct. 1857; 14 May 1861 (A.A., Montijo c 40–77).
74. George Sand to Sainte-Beuve, 22–24 July 1833 (Södergård, *Lettres de George Sand à Sainte-Beuve*, p. 45).
75. Mérimée to Mme de Beaulaincourt, 26 Mar. 1870 (*C.G.*, XV. 77).
76. Flaubert to George Sand, 17 Mar. 1870; Flaubert to Hortense Cornu (Mar. 1870) (Karénine, *George Sand*, IV. 240–3).
77. George Sand to Flaubert, 19 Mar. 1870 (*Correspondance de George Sand*, V. 369–70); see also George Sand to Girardin, 3 July 1870 (ibid., V. 384–5).
78. Napoleon III's decree, 23 Apr. 1870 (*The Times*, 25 Apr. 1870); see also *The Times*, 13, 15, 16, 18 Apr. 1870.
79. Victor Hugo, 'Le Plébiscite' (Hugo, *Œuvres Complètes*, II. 428).
80. *Journal Officiel*, 1, 4 May 1870; *La Marseillaise*, 3 May 1870; *Le Réveil*, 24, 29 June; 1, 2, 4, 7, 10 July 1870; *The Times*, 16, 18, 25 Apr.; 2, 5, 6, 7 May; 22 July 1870.
81. *Journal Officiel*, 13 May 1870; *The Times*, 10, 11, 12, 13, 14, 16, 18 May 1870; see also 4 May 1870.
82. *The Times*, 2 July 1870; Courbet to Richard, 22 June 1870 (Lindsay, *Gustave Courbet*, p. 244).

83. Viel Castel, II. 212.
84. *The Times*, 27 Nov. 1869; 12, 14 Apr.; 16, 20, 22, 24, 27, 28, 30 June; 2 July 1870.
85. ibid., 1 July 1870.

Chapter 41 – Sedan

1. *The Times*, 7, 9, 11 July 1870; Ollivier, *L'Empire libéral*, XIV. 118–20, 146–8.
2. Giraudeau, *Napoléon III intime*, p. 407; Constantin James, *Des causes de la mort de l'Empereur*, pp. 3–4; Lord Acton, *Historical Essays*, pp. 212–13; Paléologue, pp. 142–4.
3. *Le Constitutionnel*, 8, 10 July 1870; *The Times*, 9, 11, 12, 13, 14 July 1870.
4. *Le Réveil*, 11, 14, 16, 18 July 1870; *The Times*, 9, 12, 14, 15 July 1870.
5. Ollivier, XIV. 118; *The Times*, 11, 12 July 1870.
6. ibid., XIV. 147.
7. Princess Mathilde to Caroline Murat, 25 Nov. 1870 (Caroline Murat, p. 227).
8. Caroline Murat, pp. 183–6; Lord Acton, *Historical Essays*, pp. 219–20.
9. Lesourd to Benedetti, 9 Apr. 1874 (Ollivier, XIV. 622–3); Paléologue, p. 127; Filon, pp. 87–88.
10. Ollivier, XIV. 117–18.
11. Metternich to Beust, 8 July 1870 (*English Historical Review*, XXXVIII. 92–93).
12. Paléologue, pp. 129–30, 135–42.
13. Metternich to Beust, 8 July 1870 (Wellesley and Sencourt, pp. 363–4).
14. Ollivier, XIV. 132–3; Napoleon III to Gramont, 12 July 1870 (Ollivier, XIV. 260–1).
15. ibid., XIV. 370.
16. *Le Constitutionnel*, 13 July 1870; *The Times*, 13, 14 July 1870.
17. *The Times*, 12 July 1870.
18. Napoleon III to Ollivier, 12 July 1870 (*Les origines diplomatiques de la guerre de 1870–1871*, XXVIII. 251–2).
19. Napoleon III to Gramont, 12 July 1870; Benedetti to Gramont, 13 July 1870 (telegram and letter) (*Orig. Dip.*, XXVIII. 260–1, 293–4, 315–17). For the Ems telegram and Bismarck's alterations, see Abeken to Bismarck, 13 July 1870, and the text published in the *Norddeutsche Allgemeine Zeitung* of 13 July 1870 (*Orig. Dip.*, XXVIII. 463–4, 497). For Napoleon III's reluctance to go to war, see RA, Queen Victoria's Journal, 27 Oct. 1879.
20. *Le Constitutionnel*, 15 July 1870; *The Times*, 16 July 1870.
21. Malmesbury, II. 416 (from Gramont); Ollivier, XIV. 293; Barker, *The Distaff Side*, pp. 194–200.
22. *The Times*, 15, 16, 18, 20 July; 3 Aug.; 3 Sept.; 3 Dec. 1870; Filon, p. 89.
23. Vitzthum to Andrassy, 16 Jan. 1873 (Wellesley and Sencourt, pp. 365–7).

24. *The Times*, 18 July 1870.
25. ibid., 18, 25 July 1870.
26. *Journal Officiel*, 3 Aug. 1870; *The Times*, 3, 4 Aug. 1870.
27. See text of Benedetti's memorandum, in *The Times*, 25 July 1870; Lyons to Granville, 31 July 1870 (RA J64/20); *The Times*, 28 July, 1 Aug. 1870.
28. Napoleon III to Gramont, 15 July 1870 (*Orig. Dip.*, XXVIII. 383); *The Times*, 3 Aug. 1870.
29. Paléologue, p. 145.
30. Napoleon III's proclamation, 22 July 1870 (*Journal Officiel*, 23 July 1870; *The Times*, 25 July 1870).
31. *The Times*, 20, 23, 28, 30 July; 15, 24 Aug. 1870; Eugénie to Countess Montijo, 17 July 1870 (*Papiers Secrets du Second Empire*, I. 83).
32. *The Times*, 25, 29, 30 July; 1 Aug. 1870; Filon, p. 90.
33. Napoleon III's proclamation, 28 July 1870 (*The Times*, 30 July 1870).
34. Howard, *The Franco-Prussian War*, pp. 77–78.
35. Napoleon III to Eugénie (undated) (Filon, p. 95); Mérimée to Countess Montijo, 6 Aug. 1870 (*C.G.*, XV. 146–7); *The Times*, 4, 6, 8 Aug. 1870; Paléologue, p. 147.
36. *Journal Officiel*, 7 Aug. 1870; *The Times*, 8 Aug. 1870; Mérimée to Jenny Dacquin, 9 Aug. 1870; Mérimée to Panizzi, 16 Aug. 1870 (*C.G.*, XV. 148, 151).
37. Eugénie's proclamation, 7 Aug. 1870 (*The Times*, 8 Aug. 1870); and see Filon, p. 102.
38. *The Times*, 12, 16, 24 Aug.; 5 Sept. 1870.
39. Moltke to Blumenthal, 7 Aug. 1870 (Moltke, *Militärische Korrespondenz*, III. 204).
40. Howard, pp. 122–3.
41. ibid., pp. 124–5.
42. Eugénie to Napoleon III, 9 Aug. 1870 (*Papiers secrets du Second Empire*, I. 79); Howard, pp. 133–4.
43. *The Times*, 20 Aug. 1870.
44. Howard, pp. 185–6.
45. Count Malvezzi's MS., p. 3 (Ovenden MSS.) (from Eugénie).
46. Paléologue, pp. 189–90.
47. *The Times*, 27 Aug. 1870.
48. ibid., 20, 30, 31 Aug.; 1, 6 Sept. 1870; Mérimée to Panizzi, 21, 24, 25, 26, 28 Aug. 1870; Mérimée to Countess Montijo, 24 Aug. 1870; Mérimée to Jenny Dacquin, 29 Aug. 1870 (*C.G.*, XV. 155–62, 164–6).
49. *The Times*, 31 Aug.; 1, 2 Sept. 1870; Mérimée to Mme de Beaulaincourt, 16 Aug. 1870; Mérimée to Panizzi, 16, 22 Aug. 1870; Mérimée to Mme de Rayneval, 17 Aug. 1870; Mérimée to d'Antas, 21 Aug. 1870 (*C.G.*, XV. 151–4, 156, 158).
50. Malvezzi's MS., p. 3 (Ovenden MSS.) (from Eugénie).
51. Lecomte, *Napoléon III, sa maladie, son déclin*, p. 58.
52. *The Times*, 2, 8, 13 Sept. 1870.
53. Senior's Journal, 15 Apr. 1861 (RA K49, pp. 66–67).
54. Filon, p. 129.

55. Eugénie to Countess Montijo, 31 Aug. 1870 (*L.F.*, I. 229–30); see also Mérimée to Countess Montijo, 8 Sept. 1870; Mérimée to Mme de Beaulaincourt, 13 Sept. 1870 (*C.G.*, XV. 167–70).
56. Eugénie to Napoleon III (Aug. 1870) (*Papiers secrets du Second Empire*, I. 79).
57. For the battle of Sedan, see *The Times*, 3, 5, 7, 8, 13, 22, 24 Sept. 1870; William I to Queen Augusta, 2 Sept. 1870 (*The Times*, 5 Sept. 1870); Napoleon III to his generals at Sedan, 12 May 1872 (*The Times*, 25 May 1872); Howard, pp. 205–23.
58. Napoleon III to William I, 1 Sept. 1870 (Howard, p. 219).
59. William I to Napoleon III, 1 Sept. 1870 (ibid.).
60. *The Times*, 19, 22, 24 Sept. 1870.
61. William I to Queen Augusta, 4 Sept. 1870 (*The Times*, 5 Sept. 1870); *The Times*, 5, 13, 19, 24 Sept. 1870; Fraser, p. 239; Busch, *Bismarck: some secret pages of his history*, I. 159.
62. *The Times*, 6, 19, 22 Sept. 1870; Napoleon III to Leopold II, 3 Sept. 1870; Leopold II to Queen Victoria, 4 Sept. 1870 (RA J65/21, 22).
63. *The Times*, 5, 6, 9, 12 Sept. 1870; Fraser, p. 232.
64. Filon, pp. 133–5; Paléologue, pp. 193–4; Eugénie to Duke of Huescar, 2 Sept. 1870 (*L.F.*, I. 230).
65. *The Times*, 5 Sept. 1870.
66. ibid., 5, 6 Sept. 1870.
67. Govt. proclamation, 3 Sept. 1870 (*Journal Officiel*, 4 Sept. 1870; *The Times*, 5 Sept. 1870).
68. For the events of 4 Sept., see *The Times*, 5, 6, 7 Sept. 1870; Ollivier, 'La fin de l'Empire' (*R.D.M.*, VI(xxii). 22–58 (1 July 1914)); Filon, pp. 136–57; see also Mérimée to Panizzi, 4 Sept. 1870; Mérimée to Mme de Beaulaincourt, 13 Sept. 1870 (*C.G.*, XV. 166–7, 169).
69. Malvezzi MS., pp. 1–2 (Ovenden MSS.); Isabel Vesey's MS., p. 86.
70. For Eugénie's escape from Paris, see Dr Evans, *Memoirs*, pp. 359–466; Filon, pp. 158–69; Isabel Vesey's MS., pp. 72–74; Burgoyne to Ponsonby, 15 Sept. 1870 (RA I85/119); *The Times*, 12 Sept. 1870.
71. See also Paléologue, pp. 206–7.
72. Isabel Vesey's MS., p. 73.
73. Burgoyne to Ponsonby, 15 Sept. 1870 (RA I85/119).
74. Ollivier, 'La fin de l'Empire' (*R.D.M.*, VI(xxii). 49).
75. *The Times*, 6 Sept. 1870.
76. Evans, *Memoirs*, pp. 472–6; *The Times*, 7, 12 Sept. 1870. For the Prince Imperial's movements from Avesnes to Hastings, see Filon, *Memoirs of the Prince Imperial*, pp. 74–83.
77. Eugénie to Countess Montijo, 11 Sept. 1870 (*L.F.*, I. 231–2).
78. Isabel Vesey's MS., p. 48; Ponsonby to Granville, 1 Oct. 1870 (RA I66/39).
79. Eugénie to Duchess de Mouchy, 21 Sept. 1870 (Suzanne Desternes and Henriette Chandet, *L'Impératrice Eugénie intime*, p. 247).
80. Lady Ely to Queen Victoria, 3 Dec. 1870 (RA J83/156); Caroline Murat, p. 211.

81. *The Times*, 26 Sept. 1870.
82. Napoleon III, *Histoire de Jules César*, I. 23.

PART VI

Chapter 42 – Chislehurst

1. *The Times*, 13 Sept. 1870.
2. ibid., 12, 16, 27 Sept. 1870.
3. For Napoleon III at Wilhelmshöhe, see ibid., 14, 16, 21, 27 Sept.; 5, 20, 24 Oct.; 2, 3, 7 Nov. 1870; 3, 10 Jan. 1871.
4. ibid., 23 July 1870.
5. W. Falconer to A. Falconer, 18 Sept. 1870 (Guest MSS.).
6. See *The Times*, 31 May 1871.
7. Caroline Murat, p. 214.
8. *The Times*, 8 Sept. 1870.
9. ibid., 12, 29 Sept.; 18 Nov.; 30 Dec. 1870; 3, 5, 10, 11, 13, 17, 28 Jan. 1871.
10. ibid., 26, 29 Dec. 1870; 3, 10 Jan. 1871.
11. Queen Victoria to Duchess of Sutherland, 5 Nov. 1855 (RA Add. A24/332); RA, Queen Victoria's Journal, 17 Apr. 1855.
12. Victoria, Crown Princess of Prussia, to Queen Victoria, 6, 24 Sept. 1870 (RA I65/42, Z25/17); see also Crown Princess of Prussia to Queen Victoria, 10 July 1873 (RA J84/17).
13. Crown Princess of Prussia to Queen Victoria, 4 Jan. 1871; Granville to Queen Victoria, 8 Jan. 1871; Ponsonby to Queen Victoria, 8 Jan. 1871 (RA I68/7, 16, 17).
14. *The Times*, 20 Oct. 1870; 30 Jan. 1871; Isabel Vesey's MS., pp. 88–89; William I to Eugénie, 25 Oct. 1870 (Filon, pp. 228–9); Paléologue, pp. 232–4; Filon, pp. 175–232.
15. Eugénie to Alexander II, 13 Sept. 1870 (*The Times*, 10 Oct. 1871); Franz Joseph to Eugénie, 12 Oct. 1870 (Filon, pp. 173–4); Alexander II to Eugénie, 20 Sept./2 Oct. 1870 (A.A., Montijo, c 33–72; Filon, pp. 171–3).
16. Prince Arthur to Queen Victoria, 19 Oct. 1870 (RA J83/153).
17. Eugénie to Countess Montijo, 16 Nov. 1870 (*L.F.*, II. 7); *The Times*, 2, 3, 5, 7 Nov. 1870; Filon, pp. 175–226.
18. Napoleon III's proclamation, 8 Feb. 1871 (*The Times*, 13 Feb. 1871).
19. Napoleon III to the President of the National Assembly, 6 Mar. 1871 (*The Times*, 10 Mar. 1871).
20. *The Times*, 3, 6 Mar. 1871.
21. Napoleon III to Empress Augusta (Mar. 1871) (RA J68/168).
22. Leopold II to Queen Victoria, 19 Mar. 1871 (RA Y159/50); *The Times*, 20, 21, 23 Mar. 1871; unsigned memorandum, 'Llegada del Emperador Napoleón á Inglaterra' (A.A., Montijo, c 43–7).
23. Bushell, *Imperial Chislehurst*, p. 73.

24. *The Times*, 1 Dec. 1870.
25. RA, Queen Victoria's Journal, 20 Feb. 1873.
26. Catalogue of Sale of contents of Camden Place, 12–14 June 1889 (Bromley Central Library MSS.).
27. Guest MSS.
28. *The Times*, 9, 10 Sept. 1872.
29. Eugénie to Queen Victoria, 21 Apr. 1871 (RA J68/193).
30. *The Times*, 28 Mar.; 10 July 1871; 20, 22 Apr. 1872; Queen Victoria to Sir T. Martin, 31 Mar. 1871 (RA Y168/55); RA, Queen Victoria's Journal, 20 Apr. 1872.
31. Lady Sydney to Lady Ely (May 1872) (RA 84/4).
32. *The Times*, 26 July 1871; Sir A. Bodkin to Ivor Guest, 8 Feb. 1948 (Guest MSS.).
33. *The Times*, 5, 21 July; 26, 30 Aug. 1871; Napoleon III to Edward, Prince of Wales, 4 Mar. 1872 (RA T5/103).
34. Lady Randolph Churchill, *Reminiscences*, pp. 30–31.
35. Eugénie to Arese, 12 Oct. 1871 (Bonfadini, p. 367).
36. Philip Norman, *Scores and Annals of West Kent Cricket Club*, p. 237.
37. Queen Victoria to Princess Louise, Marchioness of Lorne, 3 Apr. 1871 (RA Add. A17/462); RA, Queen Victoria's Journal, 8 July 1871.
38. Dr Lee, etc., to Napoleon III (undated) (*The Times*, 12 May 1871).
39. *The Times*, 19 June 1871.
40. Local tradition.
41. *The Times*, 19 Aug., 17 Nov. 1871; 18 Mar. 1872.
42. ibid., 11 Sept.; 19, 21 Oct.; 4, 15, 18, 23 Dec. 1871.
43. ibid., 23 Oct. 1871.
44. *The Lancet*, 11 Jan. 1873; *British Medical Journal*, 11, 18 Jan. 1873; Jenner's summary of Thompson's letters of 5, 6, 9 Jan. 1873 (RA J84/54a).
45. *The Times*, 30, 31 July; 1, 2, 5, 6, 7 Aug. 1872.
46. *Sussex Daily News*, 19 Aug. 1872; *The Times*, 15, 19 Aug. 1872.
47. *The Times*, 24, 26 Aug., 4 Sept., 1 Oct. 1872.
48. ibid., 22, 24 Feb. 1875; Eugénie to Queen Victoria, 20 Feb. 1875 (RA J92/28).
49. Eugénie to Countess Montijo, 30 Nov. 1872; Eugénie to Duchess of Montoro (Nov.), 10 Dec. 1872 (*L.F.*, II. 12–14).
50. *The Lancet*, 11 Jan. 1873; Jenner's summary of Thompson's letters of 5, 6, 9 Jan. 1873 (RA J84/54a); Eugénie to Countess Montijo, 30 Dec. 1872 (*L.F.*, II. 14–15).
51. Thompson to Prince of Wales, 3 Jan. 1873 (RA J84/9).
52. Thompson to Knollys, 4 Jan. 1873 (RA J84/10).
53. Jenner's summary of Thompson's letters of 5, 6, 9 Jan. 1873 (RA J84/54a); *The Lancet*, 11 Jan. 1873.
54. RA, Queen Victoria's Journal, 20 Feb. 1873.
55. Post-mortem report, 10 Jan. 1873; Sir William Gull's report, 10 Jan. 1873 (*British Medical Journal*, 18 Jan. 1873).
56. *British Medical Journal*, 18 Jan. 1873; *The Lancet*, 18 Jan. 1873; Dr Debout

d'Estrées's statement, 22 Feb. 1910 (Legge, *The Empress Eugénie*, pp. 87–88); James, *Des causes de la mort de l'Empereur*, pp. 4–6.

57. Queen Victoria to Jenner, 10 Jan. 1873 (RA J84/23); see also Queen Victoria to Helps, 10 Jan. 1873; Queen Victoria to Lady Ely, 12 Jan. 1873 (RA J84/22, 30).
58. Jenner to Queen Victoria, 11 Jan. 1873; Lord Sydney to Queen Victoria, 11 Jan. 1873 (RA J84/28).
59. Caroline Murat, p. 280n.
60. *The Times*, 30 Nov. 1865.
61. Caroline Murat, pp. 121, 123, 133–8, 183–6, 195–7, 271–7, 299 and n., 300–1, 311–15, 321–2, 325.
62. ibid., pp. 271–3, 292–3.
63. ibid., pp. 263–6.

Chapter 43 – Zululand

1. *The Times*, 14, 15, 16 Jan. 1873; Filon, pp. 262–71; Princess Helena to Queen Victoria, 12 Jan. 1873; Theodore Martin to Queen Victoria, 15 Jan. 1873 (RA J84/29, 43).
2. *Grand Dictionnaire Larousse*, XI. 829; *The Times*, 11 Jan. 1873.
3. Napoleon III's Will, 24 Apr. 1865; Solicitors' statement (*The Times*, 30 Apr. 1873); Filon, pp. 272–4; *The Times*, 17 Feb. 1873.
4. *The Times*, 7, 8 Sept. 1868.
5. Filon, pp. 276–7; RA, Queen Victoria's Journal, 20 Feb. 1873.
6. See Lyons to Gladstone, 18 Sept. 1869 (RA J83/92).
7. Caroline Murat, p. 265; Filon, pp. 280–1.
8. RA, Queen Victoria's Journal, 3 May 1873.
9. Eugénie to Countess Montijo, 7 Mar. 1876 (*L.F.*, II. 53).
10. Eugénie to Countess Montijo, 4 Feb. 1879 (*L.F.*, II. 74–75).
11. Eugénie to Countess Montijo, 31 July 1877 (*L.F.*, II. 63–64).
12. Eugénie to Countess Montijo, 26 Sept. 1876 (*L.F.*, II. 60).
13. *The Times*, 17, 18, 21 Feb.; 13 Mar. 1874.
14. ibid., 26 Feb. 1874.
15. ibid., 16, 17, 19, 24 Mar. 1874; *Saturday Review*, XXXVII. 352–3 (21 Mar. 1874); Caroline Murat, pp. 283–6.
16. Prince Imperial to Piétri, 31 Jan. 1876 (*The Times*, 12 Feb. 1876).
17. *The Times*, 8 Aug., 1 Oct. 1874.
18. Eugénie to Countess Montijo, 11 Apr. 1876 (A.A., Montijo c 43–4).
19. Eugénie to Duchess of Montoro, 7, 18 Aug. 1870; 1 July, (Nov.), 10 Dec. 1872; (Aug.), 14, 29 Aug.; 21 Sept. 1873; 11, 20 Jan.; 5 Mar.; 5 Apr.; 28 Sept.; 8, 16 Oct. 1874; 1, 21, 29 Jan.; 17, 23 Feb.; 8 Mar.; 11, 20 May 1875; Eugénie to Duke of Huescar, 11 Feb. 1876; Eugénie to Countess Montijo, 17 Feb. 1876 (*L.F.*, I. 225–6; II. 8–9, 11–14, 17–43).
20. *The Times*, 26 June, 18 July 1873; 27 July, 19 Sept. 1874; 14 Aug., 20 Sept. 1875; 27 Mar. 1876; RA, Queen Victoria's Journal, 18 Dec. 1873; 26 June 1875.

21. *Droits de l'Homme,* 29 Sept. 1876.
22. *Le Siècle,* 3 Oct. 1876; Eugénie to Countess Montijo, 6 Oct. 1876; Countess Montijo to Rouher, 5 Oct. 1876; Rouher to Countess Montijo, 30 Nov. 1876; Questionnaire answered by Countess Montijo (Oct. 1876) (A.A., Montijo c 43–3); Eugénie to Countess Montijo, 23 Nov. 1876 (*L.F.,* II. 62).
23. Filon, p. 283; Paléologue, p. 155.
24. *The Times,* 2, 12 Mar.; 9, 30 Apr.; 3, 8 May; 13, 17 July 1877.
25. Eugénie to Countess Montijo, 8 July 1878 (*L.F.,* II. 72); *The Times,* 10 July; 5, 6 Aug. 1878.
26. *The Times,* 17, 19 Oct. 1878.
27. Bigge to Ponsonby, 7 Feb. 1887; Note by Ponsonby (autumn 1893) (RA Add. A34/29; Add. A12/2106A).
28. Col. Torrington to Ponsonby, 8 July 1879 (RA Add. A12/474); Caroline Murat, p. 313.
29. Filon, pp. 288–90; Queen Victoria's memorandum, 17 July 1879 (RA R7/38); Paléologue, p. 147.
30. Filon, pp. 285–6.
31. Eugénie to Countess Montijo, 25 Feb. 1879 (*L.F.,* II. 83); Prince Imperial to Duke of Cambridge, 21 Feb. 1879; Queen Victoria's memorandum, 17 July 1879 (RA R5/1c; R7/38); RA, Queen Victoria's Journal, 17 July 1879.
32. Duke of Cambridge to Queen Victoria, 23 Feb. 1879 (RA R5/1c).
33. Monypenny and Buckle, *Life of Benjamin Disraeli, Earl of Beaconsfield,* VI. 436.
34. Eugénie to Countess Montijo, 26, 28 Feb.; 17, 22 Apr. 1879 (*L.F.,* II. 83–86, 88–90).
35. Carey's court martial, 12 June 1879 (Lt-Col. Harrison's evidence); Ellice's memorandum, 16 Aug. 1879 (RA R5/40a; R8/34); Ellice to Sir Garnet Wolseley, 16 Aug. 1879 (Norris-Newman, *In Zululand with the British,* p. 313).
36. Carey's court martial, 12 June 1879 (RA R5/40a).
37. For the Prince Imperial's death, see Carey to Lt-Col. Harrison, 1 June 1879; Lord Chelmsford to Sir Bartle Frere, 2 June 1879; Carey's court-martial, 12 June 1879; Lady Downe to Queen Victoria, 13 July 1879; Eugénie to Queen Victoria, 7 June 1880 (RA R5/18, 20a, 40a; R6/102; Z169/11); General (formerly Lt-Col.) Harrison, *Recollections of Life in the British Army,* pp. 172–8; but see Gen. Woodhouse's letter, 1 Nov. 1928 (RA Add. J/1562).
38. Eugénie to Countess Montijo, 5 Aug. 1879 (*L.F.,* II. 107); Queen Victoria's notes on Prince Imperial's wounds (undated) (RA Z169/1).
39. Carey to Mrs Carey, 1 June 1879 (RA R5/15).
40. Information from Mrs Anne Chamberlin (from Mlle Gaubert).
41. Eugénie to Countess Montijo, 8, 12, 25 May; 4, 9, 14, 16, 18 June 1879 (*L.F.,* II. 92–101); Eugénie to Lady Sydney, 13 June 1879 (RA R5/30).
42. Lady Frere to Ponsonby, 19 June 1879 (RA R5/39); RA, Queen Victoria's Journal, 19, 20 June 1879; *The Times,* 20 June 1879

43. RA, Queen Victoria's Journal, 21 June 1879 (from Lord Sydney), 30 June 1879 (from Duc de Bassano).
44. Eugénie to Empress Charlotte (June 1865) (Corti, p. 910).
45. Eugénie to Countess Montijo, 23 July 1879 (*L.F.*, II. 103); RA, Queen Victoria's Journal, 23 June, 12 July 1879; Corvisart's bulletins, in *The Times*, 25, 30 June; 3, 4 July 1879.
46. Eugénie to Countess Montijo, 25 June 1879 (*L.F.*, II. 101).
47. Katherine John, *The Prince Imperial*, p. 483.
48. RA, Queen Victoria's Journal, 12 July 1879; *The Times*, 14 July 1879.
49. Caroline Murat, pp. 317–21.
50. ibid., pp. 257–8, 319.
51. ibid., pp. 321–2, 322n., 325.
52. Carey's court martial, 12 June 1879 (RA R5/40a).
53. Glyn to Chelmsford, 17 June 1879 (RA R5/40a).
54. Chelmsford to Duke of Cambridge, 19 June 1879 (RA R5/40a).
55. Eugénie to Countess Montijo, 30 July 1879 (*L.F.*, II. 106–7); Eugénie to Piétri (undated); Queen Victoria to Beaconsfield, 26 June 1879 (RA R7/10; H25/62); RA, Queen Victoria's Journal, 17 July 1879.
56. Queen Victoria's memorandum, 17 July 1879 (RA R7/38); see also Eugénie to Pickard (undated) (RA Add. E1/8797); *The Times*, 13 July 1920.
57. Queen Victoria's note, 27 July 1879 (RA Add. A12/480).
58. Bentinck's memorandum sent to Queen Victoria, 28 July 1879 (RA R7/90).
59. Ponsonby to Queen Victoria, two letters of 26 July, and 27 July 1879; Queen Victoria to Duke of Cambridge, 26 July 1879; Ellice's memorandum, 6 Aug. 1879; Lord Cairns's memorandum, 7 Aug. 1879; Ponsonby's memorandum, 10 Sept. 1879 (RA R7/79, 80, 81, 87; R8/13, 15, 85).
60. Queen Victoria's memorandum, 10 Aug. 1879 (RA R8/20).
61. Queen Victoria to Duke of Cambridge, 26 July 1879 (RA R7/82).
62. Queen Victoria to Stanley, 7 Aug. 1879 (RA R8/14).
63. Queen Victoria's memorandum (Aug. 1879) (RA R8/33).
64. Ellice's memorandum, 16 Aug. 1879 (RA R8/34).
65. *The Times*, 19 Aug. 1879.
66. ibid., 20, 22, 28, 29 Aug. 1879.
67. Eugénie to Countess Montijo, 23 Aug. 1879 (*L.F.*, II. 111).
68. Carey to Mlle de Larminat, 11 Sept. 1879 (RA R8/89).
69. Octavia Scotchburn to Eugénie, 23 July 1879 (RA R7/64).
70. Mlle de Larminat to Octavia Scotchburn, 25 July 1879 (RA R7/66).
71. Eugénie to Queen Victoria, 31 Aug. 1879 (RA R8/65).
72. Mlle de Larminat to Princess Beatrice, 12 Sept. 1879; Ponsonby to Queen Victoria, 19 Sept. 1879; Sydney to Lady Ely, 23 Sept. 1879; Jennings to Sydney, 13 Oct. 1879 (RA R8/91, 101, 107; R9/13).
73. Octavia Scotchburn to Mrs Carey, 24 July 1879; Duc de Bassano to Carey, 29 Aug. 1879; Eugénie to Queen Victoria, 31 Aug. 1879 (RA R7/65; R8/61, 65).

74. Queen Victoria to Beaconsfield, 13 Sept. 1879 (RA B62/11).
75. Beaconsfield to Queen Victoria, 4 Sept., 6 Dec. 1879; Queen Victoria to Gen. Marshall, 7 Sept. 1879; Dr Macleod to Queen Victoria, 7 Sept. 1879; Queen Victoria's memorandum of talk with Chelmsford, 7 Sept. 1879; Queen Victoria's memorandum of talk with Buller and Sir E. Wood, 10 Sept. 1879; Col. Maule to Queen Victoria, 19 Sept. 1879; Pickard to Duke of Cambridge, 22 Sept. 1879; Duchess of Cambridge to Ponsonby, 21 Oct. 1879; Pickard to Prince of Wales, 5, 10, 15 Sept. 1879; Ponsonby to Duke of Cambridge, 20 Sept. 1879; Queen Victoria to Beaconsfield, 13 Sept. 1879; Sir M. Hicks-Beach to Queen Victoria, 10 Jan. 1880 (RA R8/74, 77, 78, 79, 87, 100, 104; R9/21, 52; Add. A5/193, 194, 195; E61/27; B62/11; O37/7); RA, Queen Victoria's Journal, 13 Oct., 15 Dec. 1879.
76. Cairns to Queen Victoria (Sept. 1879) (RA R8/99).

Chapter 44 – Farnborough Hill

1. *The Times,* 28 June 1879.
2. Prince Imperial's Will, 26 Feb. 1879 (RA R5/li) (copy).
3. *The Times,* 1 July 1879; Caroline Murat, pp. 314–15; Filon, pp. 291, 305–7.
4. Eugénie to Countess Montijo, 24 July, 23 Aug. 1879 (*L.F.,* II. 104–5, 111); Sydney to Queen Victoria, 13 July 1879 (RA R6/104); *The Times,* 15, 18 July 1879.
5. Eugénie to Countess Montijo, 8, 18, 21, 24, 25 July; 8 Aug. 1879 (*L.F.,* II. 101–6, 108–9); *The Times,* 14 July 1879.
6. Eugénie to Countess Montijo, 5 Sept. 1879. (*L.F.,* II. 115).
7. Sir L. Simmons to Pickard 20 Aug. 1879; Eugénie to Queen Victoria, 17 July 1883 (RA R8/35; Z137/59); RA, Queen Victoria's Journal, 3, 6, 9, 16, 17, 19, 23, 25, 26, 27, 28, 29, 30 Oct. 1879; *The Times,* 2, 4, 7, 14, 21, 28, 31 Oct. 1879.
8. Ponsonby to Lady Ponsonby, 28 Oct. 1889 (Ponsonby, *Henry Ponsonby,* p. 382).
9. Eugénie to Queen Victoria, 2 Mar. 1881 (RA Z137/24).
10. *The Times,* 22, 24, 26 Nov. 1879; Llanos y Torriglia, pp. 236–7, 240; Empress Augusta to Queen Victoria, 29 Nov. 1879 (RA I52/106); RA, Queen Victoria's Journal, 16 Dec. 1879.
11. *The Times,* 10 Dec. 1879.
12. Bigge to Queen Victoria, 4 Apr. 1880 (RA R9/129).
13. *The Times,* 26, 27 Mar.; 17 Apr. 1880; Slade to Charlotte Slade, 25, 29 Mar.; 9 Apr. 1880; Slade to Corvisart, 30 Mar. 1880; Duc de Bassano to Corvisart, 16 May 1880 (Farnborough Abbey MSS.); Capt. Coxwell to Union Steamship Co., 2 Apr. 1880; Mrs Campbell to Queen Victoria, 19 Apr. 1880 (RA R9/127, 138); Coxwell MSS.
14. Sir E. Woods to Capt. Fleetwood Edwards, 17 May 1880 (RA R9/135).
15. *The Times,* 21 Apr. 1880; Eugénie to Piétri, 18 Apr. 1880 (Filon, p. 296);

Slade to Charlotte Slade, 2 May 1880 (Farnborough Abbey MSS.); *Natal Mercantile Advertiser*, 27, 28 Apr. 1880.

16. Slade to Charlotte Slade, 20 Apr., 2 May 1880 (Farnborough Abbey MSS.); 'Proposed Route' (Apr. 1880); Bigge to Queen Victoria, 16 May 1880 (RA R9/148; R10/13).

17. Slade to Charlotte Slade, 2 May 1880 (Farnborough Abbey MSS.).

18. Slade to Corvisart, 19 Apr. 1880; Slade to Charlotte Slade, 19 Apr. 1880; Duc de Bassano to Corvisart, 16 May 1880 (Farnborough Abbey MSS.); Scott to Edwards, 20 Apr. 1880; Bigge to Queen Victoria, 26 Apr. 1880 (RA R9/144; R10/2).

19. Bigge to Queen Victoria, 9 May 1880 (RA R10/8).

20. Slade to Charlotte Slade, 6 May, 7 June 1880; Marquis de Bassano to Corvisart, 16 May 1880; Scott to Corvisart, 22 May 1880 (Farnborough Abbey MSS.); Bigge to Queen Victoria, 9 May 1880 (RA R10/8); see also Filon, pp. 297–300.

21. Bigge to Queen Victoria, 9 May 1880 (RA R10/8).

22. Slade to Charlotte Slade, 30 May; 1, 7 June 1880 (Farnborough Abbey MSS.); Eugénie to Piétri, 30 May 1880 (Filon, pp. 302–3); Bigge to Queen Victoria, 27 May 1880; Sir E. Wood to Queen Victoria, 10 June 1880 (RA R10/22, 34); Filon, pp. 303–5.

23. Slade to Charlotte Slade, 30 May; 1, 7 June 1880 (Farnborough Abbey MSS.); Eugénie to Huescar, 11 May 1880 (*L.F.*, II. 123); Bigge to Queen Victoria, 27 May 1880 (RA R10/22); Sir E. Wood's letter to *The Times*, 28 July 1880.

24. Eugénie to Countess Montijo, 1 Sept. 1879 (*L.F.*, II. 112).

25. Slade to Charlotte Slade, 30 May 1880 (Farnborough Abbey MSS.).

26. Slade to Charlotte Slade, 7 June 1880; Scott to Corvisart, 8 June 1880 (Farnborough Abbey MSS.).

27. Eugénie to Duchesse de Mouchy, 20 June 1880 (cited by Desternes and Chandet, p. 295); see also Duc de Bassano to Corvisart, 28 June 1880 (Farnborough Abbey MSS.).

28. Information from Mrs Marjorie Cameron Osbourn, whose mother was one of the children.

29. Ponsonby to Beaconsfield, 23 July 1879; Ponsonby to Northcote, 24 July 1879; Sydney to Ponsonby, 29 July 1879 (RA R7/63, 67, 71); *The Times*, 25 Feb., 9 Mar., 9 July 1880; Elizabeth Cuthbert, 'A Monument to the Prince Imperial' (*Report of the Society of the Friends of St George's, 1977–1978*, p. 385).

30. *The Times*, 9 Mar. 1880.

31. ibid., 4 June, 16 July 1880; *Hansard*, 16 July 1880.

32. Queen Victoria to Gladstone, 18 July 1880 (RA B31/91).

33. Queen Victoria's memorandum, 17 July 1880 (RA R10/54).

34. *The Times*, 20, 22 July 1880.

35. Queen Victoria to Ponsonby, 17 July 1880 (RA R10/63).

36. *The Times*, 23 July 1880.

37. Pyecroft to Dean Wellesley, 19 July 1880 (RA R10/71).

38. Queen Victoria to Ponsonby, 21 July 1880 (RA R10/77).

39. Duke of Connaught to Queen Victoria, 18 July 1880; Borthwick to Ponsonby, 29 July 1880; Eugénie to Queen Victoria, 29 July, 1 Aug. 1880; Simmons to Edwards, 31 July 1880; Queen Victoria to Eugénie, 31 July 1880; Sir E. Wood to Eugénie, 1 Aug. 1880; Sir E. Wood to Queen Victoria, 1 Aug. 1880; Sydney to Queen Victoria, 2, 4 Aug. 1880 (RA Add. A15/3349; R10/113, 118, 119, 120, 121, 125; Z136/47, 48, 49); RA, Queen Victoria's Journal, 27 July 1880; *The Times*, 27, 28 July 1880.

40. Bigge to Queen Victoria, 16 June 1881 (RA J86/163); *The Times*, 5 Apr. 1881.

41. Queen Victoria to Gladstone, 18 July 1880 (RA B31/91).

42. Isabel Vesey's MS., p. 5; Legge, *The Empress Eugénie*, pp. 245–6.

43. Eugénie to Queen Victoria (June 1880) (RA Z137/50).

44. Kurtz, p. 321.

45. For Farnborough Hill, see Duke of Connaught to Queen Victoria, 5 Oct. 1880; Princess Beatrice to Duchess of Teck, 26 Nov. 1882 (RA Add. A15/3373; Add. A8/2546); Isabel Vesey's MS., pp. 12–13.

46. Bigge to Queen Victoria, 28 Nov. 1880 (RA R10/156); RA, Queen Victoria's Journal, 4 Apr. 1881; Isabel Vesey's MS., p. 31; Dorothy Mostyn, *The story of a house: Farnborough Hill*, p. 42; personal observation.

47. Eugénie to Queen Victoria, 24 Mar. 1881 (RA Z137/27).

48. RA, Queen Victoria's Journal, 16 May 1881.

49. Eugénie to Queen Victoria, 2 June 1881 (RA Z137/31); *The Times*, 11 Feb. 1882; 10 Jan. 1884; 10 Jan., 1 June 1885; 11 Jan. 1886; 21 Feb. 1890; Monseigneur Goddard to Eugénie, 13 Sept. 1891; Christine de Arcos to Goddard, 24 Sept. 1891 (Legge, *The Empress Eugénie*, pp. 378–9); and see Legge, ibid., pp. 368–82.

50. *The Times*, 26 Apr., 12 Oct., 1 Nov. 1881.

51. Christine de Arcos to Queen Victoria 30 Oct. 1881; Eugénie to Queen Victoria 15 Nov. 1881 (RA Z137/38, 39).

52. RA, Queen Victoria's Journal, 8 Dec. 1881; *The Times*, 9 Dec. 1881; Eugénie to Queen Victoria, 22 Nov. 1881; (June 1882); Princess Beatrice to Princess Mary, 26 Nov. 1882 (RA Z137/40, 50; Add. A8/2546).

53. Queen Victoria to Duke of Cambridge, 26 July 1879; Eugénie to Queen Victoria, 16 Sept 1882 (RA R7/82; O16/38); RA, Queen Victoria's Journal, 16 Sept. 1882, 21 Dec. 1899; Ethel Smyth, *Streaks of Life*, p. 36; Lady Randolph Churchill, *Reminiscences*, p. 317.

54. Duke of Connaught to Duchess of Connaught, 19 Nov. 1894 (RA Add. A15/7522).

55. Isabel Vesey's MS., pp. 13–14.

56. Empress Augusta to Queen Victoria, 29 Nov. 1879 (RA I52/106).

57. Eugénie to Queen Victoria, 17 Nov. 1886; 4 Nov. 1887; 29 Dec. 1893 (RA Z138/26, 32, 70); RA, Queen Victoria's Journal, 15 Aug. 1880; 21 Dec. 1899.

58. Eugénie to Queen Victoria, 14 Mar. 1889 (RA Z138/43).

59. Eugénie to Duchesse de Mouchy, cited by Desternes and Chandet, p. 311.

60. Eugénie to Queen Victoria, 1 June 1885; 2 June 1886; 2, 9 Jan. 1888; 16 Nov. 1889; 16 Aug. 1893 (RA Z138/18, 24, 35, 36, 48, 66).
61. Filon, p. 312.
62. *The Times*, 25 Dec. 1888.
63. Eugénie to Queen Victoria, 27 Dec. 1888 (RA Z138/41).
64. Eugénie to Queen Victoria, 2 June, 13 July, 19 Nov. 1887; 19 Nov. 1888; 25 Dec. 1889; 1 Jan., 4 June, 4 Dec. 1890; 12, 27 Mar. 1891; 2 Jan. 1893; 24 Dec. 1895; 1 Jan. 1896 (RA Z138/29, 30, 33, 40, 49, 50, 51, 53, 56, 57, 65, 73, 74); RA, Queen Victoria's Journal, 25 Feb., 6 Dec. 1880; 8 Dec. 1881; 30 June 1882; 27 Nov. 1886; 19 Oct. 1887; 6 Dec. 1890; 3 Dec. 1896; 26 Mar.; 2, 21 Apr. 1898.
65. Eugénie to Countess Montijo, 24 July 1879 (*L.F.*, II. 105).
66. *The Times*, 23, 24, 25 Jan. 1883; Filon, pp. 306–7.
67. Lyons to Queen Victoria, 23 Jan. 1883; Bigge to Queen Victoria, 28 Jan. 1883; Queen Victoria to Duke of Connaught, 23 Jan. 1883 (RA J87/35, 47; Add. A15/3928); RA, Queen Victoria's Journal, 22, 23, 24, 27, 29 Jan.; 17 Mar. 1883.
68. Eugénie to Lady Ely, 28 Jan. 1883 (in RA, Queen Victoria's Journal, 29 Jan. 1883).
69. RA, Queen Victoria's Journal, 17 Mar. 1883.
70. *The Times*, 10, 14 Feb.; 19, 23 May 1883; Eugénie to Queen Victoria, 18 May 1883 (RA Z138/38).
71. *The Times*, 9, 14, 18 Mar. 1891; Eugénie to Queen Victoria, 8 Apr. 1891 (RA Z138/59).
72. Eugénie to Queen Victoria, 30 Mar., 8 Apr. 1891 (RA Z138/58, 59).
73. *The Times*, 23 Mar., 2 Apr. 1891.

Chapter 45 – A New Life

1. Prince George to Queen Victoria, 8 Apr. 1892 (RA GV AA12/2).
2. Eugénie to Queen Victoria, 30 Mar., 8 Apr. 1891 (RA Z138/58, 59).
3. Eugénie to Queen Victoria, 21 Dec. 1893, 1 Feb. 1895 (RA Z138/69, 72).
4. Eugénie to Queen Victoria, 1 Feb. 1895 (RA Z138/72).
5. Information from the Princess of Bavaria.
6. For a description of the Villa Cyrnos, see RA, Queen Victoria's Journal, 16 Apr. 1895; Isabel Vesey to Mrs Vesey, 9 May (1910 or 1912) (Burnett MSS.); Isabel Vesey's MS., pp. 43–45, where the date of Eugénie's acquisition of the Villa Cyrnos is wrongly typed as 1883.
7. Eugénie to Queen Victoria, 14 Mar. 1889 (RA Z138/43); Paléologue, p. 34n.
8. Kurtz, p. 339n.
9. Reinach, *Histoire de l'Affaire Dreyfus*, III. 53; V. 217; Eugénie to Duchesse de Mouchy, 2 Sept. 1899 (cited by Desternes and Chandet, p. 314).

10. Kurtz, p. 338.
11. Schlumberger, *Mes Souvenirs*, I. 17.
12. Eugénie to Rosario, Duchess of Alba, 12 Apr., 31 May 1898 (*L.F.*, II. 146, 157).
13. Eugénie to Rosario, 26 Apr. 1898 (*L.F.*, II. 148).
14. Eugénie to Rosario, 11 May 1898 (*L.F.*, II. 152).
15. *The Times*, 5 May 1898; Eugénie to Rosario, 20 May 1898 (*L.F.*, II. 155).
16. Eugénie to Rosario, 11 May 1898 (*L.F.*, II. 152).
17. Eugénie to Rosario, 7 June 1898 (*L.F.*, II. 161).
18. Eugénie to Rosario, 22 Oct. 1897; 26 Apr.; 6, 12, 20 May; 4, 7, 17, 19 June 1898 (*L.F.*, II. 144–5, 148, 150, 154–5, 159–60, 162–3).
19. Eugénie to Rosario, 19 June; 5, 6, 8, 10, 15 July; 14 Aug. 1898 (*L.F.*, II. 164–73).
20. Eugénie to Rosario, 19 June 1898 (*L.F.*, II. 164).
21. Eugénie to Queen Victoria, 30 Mar. 1891 (RA Z138/58).
22. Eugénie to Rosario, 18 Apr. 1893 (*L.F.*, II. 139).
23. Eugénie to Rosario, 28 Apr. 1893 (ibid.).
24. Eugénie to Rosario, 27 Jan. 1901 (*L.F.*, II. 176–7).
25. Eugénie to Rosario, 21 July, 1 Aug. 1901 (*L.F.*, II. 177–9).
26. Eugénie to Rosario, 22 Jan. 1901 (*L.F.*, II. 175); RA, Queen Victoria's Journal, 18 Aug. 1900.
27. Eugénie to Rosario, 22 Jan. 1901 (*L.F.*, II. 174–5).
28. Eugénie to Rosario, 17 Oct. 1901 (*L.F.*, II. 181).
29. Isabel Vesey's MS., pp. 14–15.
30. Information from Mrs Paice; Isabel Vesey's Diary, 2 Mar. 1909; Rose Vesey to Mrs Fowke, 16 Apr. 1918 (Burnett MSS.).
31. Eugénie's assignment of the Peñaranda title and grandeeship, 10 May 1902 and draft (1903) (A.A., Montijo c 206–9; 208–29).
32. Isabel Vesey's MS., pp. 17–18; Ethel Smyth, *What happened next*, p. 96; Isabel Vesey to Ivo Vesey, 23 Feb. 1909, and undated (1909) (Burnett MSS.).
33. Filon, p. 251; Princess Metternich, *Souvenirs*, p. 82; Kurtz, p. 355; tape-recording by General Sir Ivo Vesey.
34. Ethel Smyth, *Impressions that remained*, II. 240.
35. Isabel Vesey's MS., pp. 35–36.
36. Verner, 'The Empress Eugénie' (*The Nineteenth Century and After*, LXXXVIII. 297–8); Isabel Vesey's MS., p. 67.
37. Mary, Duchess of York to George, Duke of York, 5 Dec. 1894; George, Duke of York (later Prince of Wales) to Mary, Duchess of York (later Princess of Wales), 2 Aug. 1896; 15 Aug. 1909; Princess of Wales to Augusta, Grand Duchess of Mecklenburg-Strelitz, 15 Aug. 1909 (RA GV CC5/102; GV CC1/154; GV CC4/35; GV CC25/40); Eugénie to Alba, 12 May 1910 (*L.F.*, II. 196).
38. Eugénie to Rosario, 9 Aug. 1902 (*L.F.*, II. 187–8).
39. Isabel Vesey's Diary, 26 Nov. 1907 (Burnett MSS.); Isabel Vesey's MS., pp. 26–29; Legge, *The Empress Eugénie*, pp. 260–7.

40. Wilczek, *Happy Retrospect*, pp. 47–48.
41. Eugénie to Queen Victoria, 2 Sept. 1867; 1 Feb. 1895; 22 Sept. 1898 (RA M57/97; Z138/72; I 88/77); Isabel Vesey's MS., p. 45; Paléologue, p. 151.
42. Eugénie to Rosario, 31 July 1900; Eugénie to Alba, 19 Feb. 1908 (*L.F.*, II. 173, 192); Isabel Vesey to Mrs Vesey, 1 June 1906; Isabel Vesey's Diary, 13, 15 Apr. 1913 (Burnett MSS.).
43. Eugénie to Alba, 3 June 1906 (*L.F.*, II. 189).
44. Eugénie to Alba, 27 Aug. 1909 (*L.F.*, II. 193–4).
45. Eugénie to Sir L. Simmons, 25 Oct. 1884; 11 July 1885; Eugénie to Lady Simmons, 24 Sept. 1897 (Oreman MSS.); Sir William Butler to Eugénie (1899 ?); Eugénie to Butler, 1 Jan. 1900 (Mrs Butler's MSS.).
46. Ethel Smyth, *Streaks of Life*, p. 19.
47. Ethel Smyth, *Impressions that remained*, II. 81.
48. Alba, op. cit., CXX. 75–76; Duchess of Sermoneta, *Things Past*, p. 129.
49. Isabel Vesey to Mrs Fowke, 15 Jan. 1914 (Burnett MSS.).
50. Ethel Smyth, *Streaks of Life*, p. 58.
51. Viel Castel, II. 279; *The Times*, 14 June 1865; Isabel Vesey's MS., p. 37; Harrisse to George Sand, 26 Mar. 1870 (George Sand, *Souvenirs et Idées*, p. 172); Ruth Jordan, *George Sand*, pp. 319–21; Ethel Smyth, *As time went on*, p. 48.
52. Eugénie to Countess Montijo, 29 Mar. 1876 (*L.F.*, II. 56).
53. Isabel Vesey to Mrs Vesey, 9 May (1910 or 1912) (Burnett MSS.).
54. Ethel Smyth, *Streaks of Life*, p. 18.
55. Information from Mrs Mason.
56. Isabel Vesey's MS., p. 68.
57. Mlle d'Allonville's MS., p. 2 (Farnborough Abbey MSS.).
58. Isabel Vesey to Mrs Vesey, 25 June, 20 July 1906; Isabel Vesey to Louisa Vesey, 25 July 1907 (Burnett MSS.); Isabel Vesey's MS., p. 19.
59. Mlle d'Allonville's MS., p. 3 (Farnborough Abbey MSS.).
60. Queen Victoria to Crown Princess of Prussia, 18 Aug. 1880 (RA Add. U32); RA, Queen Victoria's Journal, 25 Feb., 16 Aug., 6 Dec. 1880; 26 Mar. 1898.
61. Isabel Vesey's MS., p. 19.
62. Information from Mrs Florence Barber (née Dumpor), and Mrs Ruby Crotty (née Hammond).
63. Information from Mrs Goode-Crook (née Lancaster).
64. Ethel Smyth, *Streaks of Life*, p. 63.
65. Isabel Vesey's Diary, 11 May 1910; 15 Apr., 5 May 1913 (Burnett MSS.); Isabel Vesey's MS., pp. 48, 71–72, 81.
66. Information from Mrs Jones.
67. Ethel Smyth, *Streaks of Life*, p. 29; Mrs Anne Harris to Isabel Vesey, 15 Oct. 1920 (Burnett MSS.).
68. Information from Miss Claire Blount.
69. Kenneth Clark, *Another Part of the Wood*, p. 25; information from Lord Clark.
70. Dorothy Mostyn, *The Story of a House: Farnborough Hill*, pp. 49, 78, 84;

information from Sister Mostyn; *Hillside Magazine*, 1943–4, p. 13; information from Mrs Barber.

71. Information from Mrs Anne Chamberlin.
72. Information from Sister Mostyn. The original internal telephones are still in the house at Farnborough Hill.
73. Isabel Vesey's MS., p. 46; Ethel Smyth, *Streaks of Life*, p. 68.
74. Isabel Vesey's Diary, 25 May 1910 (Burnett MSS.); Isabel Vesey's MS., p. 103; Ethel Smyth, *Streaks of Life*, p. 57; information from Sister Mostyn.
75. Isabel Vesey's MS., p. 56.
76. Isabel Vesey's Diary, Sept. 1907 (Burnett MSS.).
77. *The Times*, 13 July 1914.
78. Isabel Vesey's MS., p. 29.
79. Information from Mrs Paice and Mrs Veronica Burnett.
80. For the *Thistle*, see Isabel Vesey's MS., pp. 45–47; Duke of York to Duchess of York, 2 Aug. 1896 (RA GV CC1/154).
81. Isabel Vesey's MS., p. 48.
82. Isabel Vesey's Diary, 18 May; 28 June; 10, 12, 14 July 1906; Isabel Vesey to Mrs Vesey (July 1906), 13, 15, 16 July 1906 (Burnett MSS.); Isabel Vesey's MS., pp. 48–63; Isabel Vesey in *The Times*, 9 Oct. 1920; Paléologue, pp. 151–6.
83. Isabel Vesey's Diary, 16, 19 July 1907 (Burnett MSS.); Isabel Vesey's MS., pp. 64–65.
84. Isabel Vesey's Diary, 26, 27 July 1907; Isabel Vesey to Louisa Vesey, 25 July 1907; Isabel Vesey to Dolly Vesey, 28 July 1907 (Burnett MSS.); Isabel Vesey's MS., pp. 65–67; Isabel Vesey in *The Times*, 11 Oct. 1920; William II to Eugénie, 16 July 1907 (A.A., Montijo, c 33–3); Paléologue, pp. 209–11.
85. Eugénie to Queen Victoria, 4 June 1890 (RA Z138/51).
86. Bigge to Queen Victoria, 13, 14 Aug. 1894 (RA I60/85, 86); see also Eugénie to Queen Victoria, 1 Feb. 1895 (RA Z138/72).
87. Clarendon to Queen Victoria, 6, 16 May 1869 (RA B25/37, 42).
88. Isabel Vesey's Diary, 26 Dec. 1907; 7 Jan. 1908 (Burnett MSS.); *The Times*, 27 Dec. 1907; 8, 11, 16, 27 Jan.; 20, 31 Mar. 1908. See also Piétri to Knollys, 12 Dec. 1907; Morley to Knollys, 13, 15 Jan. 1908; Knollys to Morley, 14 Jan. 1908 (RA W66/3; W5/30, 31, 32).
89. Isabel Vesey's Diary (undated, 1908); Isabel Vesey's MS., p. 42.
90. Leonard Woolf, *Growing*, p. 141.
91. Isabel Vesey's MS., pp. 76–77.
92. Duke of Connaught's Diary, 25 May 1909 (RA Add. A15/8445); Legge, *The Empress Eugénie*, pp. 346–50; Isabel Vesey to Mrs Vesey, 25 June 1910 (Burnett MSS.).
93. Isabel Vesey's Diary, 19, 21, 26, 27 July 1909; Isabel Vesey's MS., pp. 77–80; Isabel Vesey in *The Times*, 12 Oct. 1920.
94. Isabel Vesey's Diary, 25, 30 May; 14, 18 June 1910; Isabel Vesey to Mrs Vesey, 11 June 1910 (Burnett MSS.); Isabel Vesey's MS., pp. 81–83.

95. Isabel Vesey's Diary, 2 June 1910.
96. Isabel Vesey's Diary, 27 June 1910; Isabel Vesey to Mrs Vesey, 25, 30 June 1910 (Burnett MSS.); Isabel Vesey's MS., pp. 83–87, 89–93.
97. Isabel Vesey's Diary, 29 June 1910; Isabel Vesey to Mrs Vesey, 30 June 1910 (Burnett MSS.); Isabel Vesey's MS., pp. 91–92; Isabel Vesey in *The Times*, 13 Oct. 1920.
98. Isabel Vesey's Diary, 24 July 1906; 13 Feb. 1909; *The Times*, 16 July 1914 (letter from T.H.W.); 12 July 1920; see also Beatrice Cuvellier, 'The Empress Eugénie' (*The London Magazine*, Jan. 1908); Legge, *The Empress Eugénie*, pp. 313–14, 359–60.
99. Isabel Vesey to Dolly Vesey, 13 Feb. 1909; Isabel Vesey's Diary, 13 Feb. 1909; Isabel Vesey's MS., p. 70 (Burnett MSS.).
100. Isabel Vesey to Dolly Vesey, 24 July 1906; Isabel Vesey's Diary, 24, 29 July 1906; Isabel Vesey's MS., p. 75 (Burnett MSS.).
101. Isabel Vesey to Mrs Vesey, 20 July 1906; Isabel Vesey to Louisa Vesey, 11 Jan. 1914; Isabel Vesey to Dolly Fowke, 15 Jan. 1914 (Burnett MSS.); Paléologue, pp. xiii, xv, 17.
102. Kurtz, p. 342.
103. Lucien Daudet, *Le Centenaire de l'Impératrice Eugénie*, pp. 8–9.
104. Eugénie to Daudet, 3 Mar. 1912 (ibid., p. 12).
105. Cocteau, *Paris Album*, pp. 143–6.
106. Information from Sister Mostyn; see also Duchess of Sermoneta, p. 124.
107. Cocteau, p. 147.

Chapter 46 – The End of an Era

1. Isabel Vesey to Dolly Fowke, 5 Aug. 1914 (Burnett MSS.); Isabel Vesey's MS., p. 96.
2. Rose Vesey to Isabel Vesey, 6 Aug. 1914; Isabel Vesey to Dolly Fowke, 23 Sept. 1914 (Burnett MSS.); Isabel Vesey's MS., p. 103.
3. Isabel Vesey to Dolly Fowke, 1 Oct., 5 Nov. 1914 (Burnett MSS.); Isabel Vesey's MS., pp. 95–96.
4. Isabel Vesey to Dolly Fowke, 3, 23 Sept. 1914 (Burnett MSS.); Lady Haig, *The Man I knew*, p. 116.
5. Isabel Vesey to Dolly Fowke, 9 Apr., 16(15 ?) Sept. 1915 (Burnett MSS.); information from Sister Mostyn, Brigadier Jervois and Mrs K. M. Harris; *The Times*, 10 Oct. 1916. See also Isabel Vesey's MS., pp. 96–100.
6. Isabel Vesey to Dolly Fowke, 23 Sept. 1914 (Burnett MSS.).
7. Isabel Vesey to Dolly Fowke, 5 Nov. 1914 (ibid.).
8. Lady Haig, p. 117.
9. Isabel Vesey to Dolly Fowke, 17 Nov. 1914 (Burnett MSS.).
10. Isabel Vesey to Dolly Fowke, 1 Oct. 1914 (ibid.); see also Isabel Vesey's MS., pp. 104–5.
11. Isabel Vesey to Dolly Fowke, 3 June 1915 (Burnett MSS.).
12. Isabel Vesey to Dolly Fowke, 6 Jan.; 3, 17 June 1915; Rose Vesey to

Dolly Fowke, 10 June, 21 July 1915 (ibid.); information from Brigadier Jervois.

13. Isabel Vesey's MS., p. 99; Lady Haig, pp. 129, 131–2.

14. Lady Haig, p. 132.

15. Isabel Vesey's MS., p. 102; Isabel Vesey to — (1919) (fragment) (Burnett MSS.).

16. Ethel Smyth, *Streaks of Life*, p. 58; Ivo Vesey to Dolly Fowke, 29 June 1915 (Burnett MSS.); Father Conway's Diary, 10 Aug. 1914 (Farnborough Abbey MSS.).

17. Isabel Vesey to Dolly Fowke, 6 Jan., 19 Oct. 1915 (Burnett MSS.); Eugénie to Alba, 20 Jan. 1915 (*L.F.*, II. 198); Father Conway's Diary, 11, 17 Jan.; 6 Mar.; 1, 3 Apr.; 22 Aug.; 26 Sept. 1916; Ethel Smyth, *Streaks of Life*, p. 30.

18. Information from Sister Mostyn.

19. Isabel Vesey to Dolly Fowke, 16 (15 ?) Sept. 1915 (Burnett MSS.); Father Conway's Diary, 14 Dec. 1915 (Farnborough Abbey MSS.); Isabel Vesey's MS., pp. 108–9 (where the date of Piétri's death is wrongly given as 1916, as it is by Daudet and Kurtz. The correct date (14 Dec. 1915) is given in Father Conway's diary, in Isabel Vesey's diary, and in the Register of Births, Deaths and Marriages.)

20. Isabel Vesey to Dolly Fowke, 4 June 1918 (Burnett MSS.); Isabel Vesey's MS., pp. 98–99.

21. Isabel Vesey to Dolly Fowke, 2 July 1918 (Burnett MSS.).

22. Information from Mrs Veronica Burnett (née Fowke).

23. Verner, 'The Empress Eugénie' (*The Nineteenth Century and After*, LXXXVIII. 299); Wickham Steed ('Our Special Correspondent') in *The Times*, 14 July 1920.

24. Alba, op. cit., CXX. 96–97; Ethel Smyth, *Streaks of Life*, pp. 42–43.

25. Information from Brigadier Jervois; Daudet, *Dans l'ombre de l'Impératrice Eugénie*, p. 252.

26. Paléologue, pp. 236–9; Dorothy Mostyn, p. 57; and see Eugénie to Alba, 20 Jan. 1915 (*L.F.*, II. 197–8). For the Charlemagne relic, see *The Times*, 26 Sept. 1866.

27. Verner, op. cit., LXXXVIII. 297–9, 301–3, 305; Isabel Vesey's MS., p. 110; Eugénie to Duchesse de Mouchy, cited by Desternes and Chandet, p. 320.

28. *The Times*, 12 Nov. 1918.

29. Rose Vesey to Dolly Fowke, 12 Nov. 1918 (Burnett MSS.).

30. Wickham Steed ('Our Special Correspondent') in *The Times*, 14 July 1920.

31. Isabel Vesey to Dolly Fowke, 21 Feb. 1920; Isabel Vesey to Mrs Vesey, 24 Feb., 16 Mar. 1920; Note in Isabel Vesey's Diary (1920) (Burnett MSS.); Isabel Vesey's MS., p. 114; Alba, op. cit., CXX. 97–98; information from Mrs Paice; *The Times*, 4 Dec. 1919; *La Época*, 27 Feb. 1920.

32. *La Época*, 24 Apr. 1920; *The Times*, 26, 29 Apr. 1920; Verner, op. cit., LXXXVIII. 306.

33. Alba, op. cit., CXX. 98–99.
34. *La Época*, 3 May 1920.
35. ibid., 4, 10, 12 Feb. 1920.
36. Alba, op. cit., CXX. 99; *La Época*, 7, 22 May 1920; information from the Princess of Bavaria.
37. Alba, op. cit., CXX. 100; see also Isabel Vesey's MS., p. 19; Ethel Smyth, *Streaks of Life*, p. 29.
38. Alba, op. cit., CXX. 100.
39. ibid.; *La Época*, 16 June 1920; *The Times*, 12 June 1920.
40. Alba, op. cit., CXX. 100.
41. Dolly Fowke to Fowke, 18 July 1920 (from Dr Hugenschmidt) (Burnett MSS.); see also Daudet, *Le Centenaire de l'Impératrice Eugénie*, pp. 73–77; *La Época*, 12 July 1920.
42. Alba, op. cit., CXX. 101.
43. Alba, *The Empress Eugénie*, p. 18 (where Alba incorrectly states that Eugénie's father died on a Sunday; Cipriano del Montijo died on Friday 15 Mar. 1839).
44. Eugénie's Will, 30 Sept. 1916 (A.A., Montijo, c 52–6).
45. Father Conway's Diary, 28 July 1920 (Farnborough Abbey MSS.).
46. *La Época*, 13, 14, 15 July 1920; *The Times*, 16, 19 July 1920; for the journey from Madrid to Farnborough, see Daudet, *Le Centenaire de l'Impératrice Eugénie*, pp. 77–80.
47. Father Conway's Diary, 18 July 1920; Isabel Vesey's MS., p. 115; *The Times*, 19 July 1920; Princess Clémentine Bonaparte to Duchesse de Mouchy (cited by Desternes and Chandet, p. 328).
48. Cabrol, *L'Impératrice Eugénie: Discours prononcé à ses funérailles*, p. 3.
49. For the funeral, see Dolly Fowke to Fowke, 20 July 1920 (Burnett MSS.); Father Conway's Diary, 20 July 1920 (Farnborough Abbey MSS.); *The Times*, 21 July 1920.
50. Information from Mrs Paice.

INDEX

In this index E = Eugénie and LN = Louis Napoleon
(as Napoleon III is usually referred to)

745

INDEX